BERTRAND RUSSELL

The Spirit of Solitude
1872–1921

RAY MONK

THE FREE PRESS
NEW YORK   LONDON   TORONTO   SYDNEY   SINGAPORE

THE FREE PRESS
A Division of Simon & Schuster Inc.
1230 Avenue of the Americas
New York, NY 10020

THE FREE PRESS and colophon are trademarks
of Simon & Schuster Inc.

Manufactured in the United States of America

10 9 8 7 6 5 4 3 2 1

Library of Congress Cataloging-in-Publication Data

Monk, Ray.
    Bertrand Russell : the spirit of solitude / Ray Monk
            p.   cm.
    Includes bibliographical references and index.
    ISBN 0–684–82802–2
    1. Russell, Bertrand, 1872–1970.   2. Philosophers—England—
Biography.   I. Title.
B1649.R94M65   1996
192—dc20
    [B]   96–15103
                                                              CIP

ISBN 0–684–82802–2

Previously unpublished letters and manuscripts
by Bertrand Russell © McMaster University 1996

Excerpts from *The Letters of T.S. Eliot* edited by Valerie Eliot, copyright © 1988 by SET Copy-
rights Limited, are reprinted by permission of Harcourt Brace & Company.
Excerpts from "Mr. Apollinax" in *Collected Poems 1909–1962* by T.S. Eliot, copyright 1936 by Harcourt Brace & Company, copyright © 1964, 1963 by T.S. Eliot, are reprinted by permission of
the publisher.
Extracts from *The Letters of D. H. Lawrence* and from 'The Blind Man', in *The Complete Short Stories
of D. H. Lawrence,* are reproduced by kind permission of Lawrence Pollinger Ltd and the Estate of
Frieda Lawrence Ravagli.

First published in the United Kingdom in 1996 by Jonathan Cape,
Random House, 20 Vauxhall Bridge Road, London SW1V 2SA

Dedicated to the memory of my friend

Tony Lambert

How grimly Rogojin had spoken that morning about 'losing his faith'. That man must be suffering terribly . . . Rogojin wasn't just a passionate soul, he was a warrior; he wanted to bring back his lost faith by force. He felt an agonising need for it now . . . Yes! To believe in something! In someone!

Fyodor Dostoyevsky, *The Idiot*

CONTENTS

ILLUSTRATIONS

The author and publishers would like to thank the following for permission to use photographs: McMaster University, Hamilton, Ontario (for 1–5, 9–10, 12, 20, 30, 35–6, 41–2, 54–8, 61–8); the Bertrand Russell Peace Foundation (for 7 and 11); Mrs Barbara Strachey (for 13–19, 23–8, 37–9); Mrs Katharine Tait (for 59–60); Dr David Lewis (for 6 and 8); Trinity College, Cambridge (for 21–2); Dr Michael Nedo (43); the Houghton Library, Harvard University (48–50).

The author would also like to thank Dr Kenneth Blackwell, Sheila Turcon, Dr David Lewis, Katharine Tait and Mr Tony Simpson of the Bertrand Russell Peace Foundation for their kind help with picture research.

ACKNOWLEDGEMENTS

The suggestion to write on Russell came from David Godwin, then Editorial Director of Jonathan Cape, to whom I am grateful, both for the original suggestion and for the enthusiasm with which he encouraged me during the five years it has taken me to carry it out. His successor at Cape, Dan Franklin, has been similarly encouraging and to him also I owe many ideas as to how the book could be improved. The late Erwin Glickes of the Free Press, New York, was extremely kind and helpful to me while I was researching the book, and met me on several occasions to discuss it, both in London and in New York. I much regret that he died before I could show him anything of what I had written. My editor at Vintage for many years, Sarah Westcott, was a great help to me throughout my research, and I am grateful also for the enthusiasm of Frances Coady, previously at both Vintage and Random House, and for the ever-reliable guidance and advice of my agent, Gill Coleridge.

My greatest debt during the writing of the book was to Kenneth Blackwell, the Russell Archivist at McMaster University, editor of the journal *Russell* and co-editor of the extraordinary *Bibliography of Bertrand Russell*. There is probably no book on Russell containing original research and published in the last twenty-five years that does not owe something to Dr Blackwell, but, in my case, the debt is enormous. On my many visits to the Archives I spent my lunchtimes and evenings discussing my work with Dr Blackwell, and, even when he disagreed with the line I was taking, he was unfailingly helpful in suggesting points for me to look at and consider. I would also like to thank his wife, Kadriin, and their family, for putting me up at their house several times during my last visit to Canada, and for tolerating my incessant talk about Russell. For similar hospitality and kindness I would like to thank Nicholas Griffin, his wife Cheryl and their son Richard.

Back in England, I was able to continue my conversations with Dr Blackwell by e-mail, and, for the last few years, have benefited from extending those conversations to the group of Russell experts who belong to 'Russell-l', the Internet listserve that he established. I would like to thank those members of the listserve who have answered my enquiries and exchanged ideas with me, including: Stewart Candlish, Ivor Grattan-Guinness, Anthony Grayling,

Louis Greenspan, Nicholas Griffin, Peter Hylton, Gregory Landini, John Lenz and Charles Pigden.

Sheila Turcon, previously of the Russell Archives, made a number of valuable suggestions to me when I met her in Canada, and, since I returned, has been especially helpful in researching on my behalf the evidence in Russell's surviving correspondence concerning his intriguing and mysterious relationship with Vivien Eliot. I am very grateful to her, both for her diligence and patience and for the interest she showed in my work.

Professor John Slater of the University of Toronto helped me in a number of ways: allowing me access to his enormous private collection of Russelliana; photocopying several documents from that collection; alerting me to sources I would not otherwise have known about; showing me copies of his work for forthcoming volumes of the *Collected Papers*, and discussing my work with me at various stages. For all this, I am greatly indebted to him.

Ending in 1921, with the birth of Russell's first son, this volume does not deal with the tangled relationships that existed within his family, but, for information on those relationships and for their kindness and help generally, I would like to thank Russell's daughter, Katharine Tait, and his grand-daughter, Felicity Russell. What I learned from them will be contained in my second volume.

Many people working on related projects have been very kind in sharing their research with me. Caroline Moorehead generously lent me her extremely useful index card list of people whom she had contacted while researching her own biography of Russell; Francisco Rodríguez-Consuegra made available to me the fruits of his work (soon to be published) on the relationship between Russell and F. H. Bradley; James Connelly kindly photocopied for me the letters he had transcribed at the Bodleian Library between Russell and Harold Joachim; and Miranda Seymour answered many questions relating to her own research on the life of Russell's lover, Ottoline Morrell.

I owe a special debt of gratitude to Nick Griffin and his assistant, Alison Miculan, for making available to me the vast number of transcriptions they had made of Russell's letters in preparation for their work on *The Selected Letters of Bertrand Russell*. These transcriptions saved me many hours of research in the Archives and were exceptionally useful.

For helpful discussions of my work at various stages of its completion, I am grateful to Sir Peter Strawson, Frances Partridge, Anthony Gottlieb, Richard Rempel and my colleagues at Southampton University, David Pugmire, Tony Palmer and Peter Middleton. I would also like to thank, in this regard, my audiences at Swarthmore College, Philadelphia; the University of New Mexico, Albuquerque; the University of Kent; the Thackeray Society at the Reform Club; and the University of Southampton – at each of which I read a paper summarising the theme of my book and discussing the relationship between Russell and Joseph Conrad.

I was able to spend long periods of time in Canada using the Russell Archives owing to the generosity of York University, Toronto, and McMaster University, Hamilton, of which the former employed me for a term as a visiting lecturer and the latter bestowed upon me the honour of a Hooker

Distinguished Research Fellowship. For enabling me to take up these opportunities, I would like to thank the University of Southampton for giving me leave from my duties as a lecturer, and for giving me, in addition, a sabbatical semester in order to concentrate on writing the book. The library at Southampton University has given me great assistance, both in the use of its own stock and through its excellent inter-library loan service.

To my copy-editor, Mandy Greenfield, I am indebted for many useful suggestions as to how the text could be improved, and I am grateful to her for the great care and attention she brought to her immense task. Kenneth Blackwell, Richard Rempel, John Slater, Nick Griffin and Desmond Christy read the book in proof and were able to save me from a number of errors, both major and minor.

In working on this book, I have taken even more leave from my family than I have from my university, and I would like to express my great appreciation and gratitude to Jenny and our children, Zala, Danika and Zeno, for suffering my absences and distractions with such understanding and support.

Southampton
April 1996   RAY MONK

INTRODUCTION

'How on earth does one explain madness and love in sober prose with dates attached?'

So asked Virginia Woolf in exasperation as she struggled to complete her biography of Roger Fry. After a lifetime of enjoying the novelist's luxury of describing fleeting images, thoughts and feelings from the inside, she found it understandably intolerable to be wrestling with the purely external records that constitute the biographer's raw data. How is biography even possible? she asked. How is one to know that the *really* significant events in a person's life have not gone unwritten and unrecorded?

In general, of course, such scepticism about biography is unanswerable. And yet, there are people whose tendency to describe and record everything in their lives, large or small, inner or outer, gives their biographers at least a fighting chance of producing, if not an explanation, then at least a description of the 'madness and love' of their lives. Virginia Woolf was herself one of these people ('The one experience I shall never describe', she once wrote, 'is my death'). Bertrand Russell is another.

The quantity of writing that Russell produced in his lifetime almost defies belief. His published output is extraordinary enough (the recently completed *Bibliography of Bertrand Russell* lists over three thousand publications), but the huge archive of papers and letters he left behind is, if anything, still more remarkable. The Russell Archives estimate that they have over 40,000 of his letters. This is in addition to the vast number of journals, manuscripts and other documents in their collection. Rarely can Russell have passed a day in his long lifetime (he died on 2 February 1970, a few months before his ninety-eighth birthday) without writing, in one form or another, two or three thousand words.

A perhaps surprising amount of this vast output is concerned with himself. Aside from the dozens of autobiographical writings that Russell produced for publication, his letters, particularly the two thousand or so he wrote to Ottoline Morrell, contain a record of his life, opinions and feelings that is matched in its detailed self-absorption perhaps only by Virginia Woolf herself. An opportunity exists, then, for a biography of Russell to be written that shows, in all (or, anyway, in much of) its complexity, his own particular forms of love and madness.

The biographies of him published so far fall some way short of fully exploiting this opportunity. Indeed, the first biography of him, Alan Wood's *Bertrand Russell: The Passionate Sceptic* (published in 1957, while Russell was still alive), was written before the opportunity really existed. Though he had the advantage – and, to some extent, the disadvantage – of the co-operation and help of Russell himself, Wood had no access to Russell's unpublished manuscripts and correspondence. Lacking, therefore, the means (and, as far as one can judge, the inclination) to probe beneath the surface, what Wood presents is a rather anodyne version of Russell's life and career, of the sort that Russell himself wished at that time to see in print.

The other two biographies so far published – Ronald Clark's *The Life of Bertrand Russell* (1975) and Caroline Moorehead's *Bertrand Russell* (1992) – are more searching in their exploration of Russell's private life, and their authors less constrained in what they could see and publish. But both suffer from the same fault: namely, a more or less complete lack of interest in Russell's philosophical work.

The issue of the relevance of a writer's life to his or her work has been much debated in recent times, but often, it seems to me, it is approached from the wrong direction. The question for a biographer is not whether a writer's work can be understood in isolation from his or her life (of course it can, as Shakespeare's work amply demonstrates), but rather whether the life can be understood in ignorance of the work. Biography is not a service industry; it does not receive its purpose from the help it gives to literary criticism, intellectual history or any other 'discipline'. It is an autonomous literary genre. As Richard Holmes has recently said, it is 'an art of human understanding, and a celebration of human nature'. The point of a biography is no more and no less than to understand its subject. It does not need to claim to be a necessary precondition for understanding a body of work; understanding an interesting person is justification enough.

Where that person is a writer, however, the question arises whether he or she can possibly be understood without some attempt to master their work. I think the answer to this is, in general, 'no', and, certainly, in the case of Russell, one cannot hope to understand him without understanding the role played in his life and in his imagination by his hopes for philosophy. And, one cannot begin to understand that without some understanding of the philosophy itself.

Russell himself provided the key to understanding his richly varied and amazingly productive life in the 'Prologue' to his *Autobiography*, in which he described the 'three passions, simple but overwhelmingly strong [which] have governed my life':

> the longing for love, the search for knowledge, and unbearable pity for the suffering of mankind. These passions, like great winds, have blown me hither and thither, in a wayward course, over a deep ocean of anguish, reaching to the very verge of despair.

In focusing on only two of those passions, the biographies by Ronald Clark and Caroline Moorehead have imposed upon themselves an unnecessary restriction, which has prevented them from fully grasping the twists and turns of this 'wayward course' and, therefore, the exact nature of the 'despair' that Russell mentions.

The aim of this book is to chart this course more precisely, by trying to take into account the full force of each of the 'great winds' that Russell describes: his need for love, his yearning for certain knowledge, and his sometimes overpowering impulse to become involved in the great political issues of his day. To understand the course his life took is to understand the power of each of these great passions and the tensions that existed between them, forcing him, on occasion, to abandon, in turn, philosophy for love, politics for philosophy, love for politics, and so on.

To understand why these three great passions were felt by Russell to be in conflict with each other, why the winds they represented blew him in opposing directions, it is necessary, I think, to understand the extent to which they were, for him, alternative answers to a single problem: the problem of his acute sense of isolation and loneliness, a problem that was for him compounded by his extraordinarily deep-seated fear of madness. Something of this is hinted at in the poem 'To Edith', which prefaces his *Autobiography*, and the first stanza of which reads:

> Through the long years
>   I sought peace,
> I found ecstasy, I found anguish,
>   I found madness,
> I found loneliness.
> I found the solitary pain
>   that gnaws the heart,
> But peace I did not find.

In each of their various ways, Russell's three great passions were attempts by him to overcome his solitariness through contact with something outside himself: another individual, humanity at large, or the external world.[1] The first was compromised by his terror of madness, which led him to fear the depths of his own emotions; the second by his discovery that he felt alone even in a crowd; and the third by the progressive scepticism, the increasing loss of faith, that characterised his philosophical development (the 'retreat from Pythagoras', as he called it).

As far as possible I have tried to show, rather than state, the force of these conflicting passions and the fears and anxieties that underlay them. I have, that is, sought to present, in as clear a way as possible, Russell's life and personality as revealed by his own words. Hence there is scarcely a page that does not contain two or three quotations from Russell himself. I am aware

---

[1] Whether this was conceived as the Hegelian Absolute of his first philosophy, the eternal world of Platonic forms that inspired his great work on the philosophy of mathematics, or the more humdrum world of everyday facts with which he ended.

that the personality thus revealed is one that many will find repellent, but it has not been my aim to present him in an unfavourable light. There are many things for which I admire Russell greatly – his enormous intelligence, his commitment to philosophical clarity and rigour, his dedication to the causes of social justice and international peace, and so on. But the challenge to those of us who admire Russell for these qualities is to understand how they can coexist with a sometimes quite chilling coldness to those close to him, and a disturbing capacity for deep and dark hatreds.

When Russell told Ottoline that the character in fiction with whom he felt most 'intimate' was Dostoyevsky's Rogojin – the sinister, embittered murderer of *The Idiot*, consumed by hatred, disappointment and jealousy – he was, I think, revealing something crucially important in understanding his own character, something that, like his philosophical preoccupations, has not received due emphasis in the biographies of him published so far. What I hope to have shown, chiefly through quotation, is how the author of *The Principles of Mathematics* and the co-author of *Principia Mathematica* could possibly have seen himself in this light. If the portrait that results is less attractive than those previously drawn, it is also, I hope, more complex and interesting, and, I believe, more accurate.

Part I
1872–1914

I

GHOSTS

'**I** shall never lose the sense of being a ghost,' Russell once wrote to his lover, Ottoline Morrell. He felt it particularly, he told her, in 'moods of misery'. He remembered, for example, the moment when he first became aware of how unhappy he was in his first marriage. He was sitting outside, with his wife and her family, when he was suddenly overcome by a sense of not really being there, of having, so to speak, lost contact with the people around him. He was 'with them, but suddenly not of them'. In his old age, he told his daughter Kate about a recurring dream he used to have, which expressed the same feeling of isolation and separation:

I imagine myself behind plate glass, like a fish in an aquarium, or turned into a ghost whom no one sees; agonizingly I try to make some sort of human contact but it is impossible & I know myself doomed forever to lonely impotence. I used to have this feeling often before I had children; since then it has been rare.

Russell was nearly fifty when he had his first child. Until then, his feeling of being a ghost, of being cut off from the people around him, was central to his personality and the determinate characteristic of much of his life. It was the origin of that chilling detachment of which he was capable in his relations with people close to him, and also of his tendency to form intense and stormy relationships, in which his hopes of overcoming his detachment and of finally making human contact fought a losing battle with his fears that he would once again fail. To a large extent, the story of the first half, at least, of his life is the story of those battles to overcome the distance he felt between himself and the rest of the world.

As he told Ottoline Morrell, this sense of ghostly withdrawal was a symptom of, and a reaction to, unhappiness, of which, in the first few years of his life, he experienced a good deal – more, perhaps, than could be borne without withdrawal. When he was two years old, his mother died of diphtheria; a few days later, his sister died of the same illness, leaving his father devastated and without much of a will to live himself. His father died eighteen months later, when Russell was still only three. He was then placed in the care of his grandparents, and, when he was six, his grandfather too died, after which he would lie awake at night wondering when his grand-mother in turn was going to die and leave him. It was indeed a ghostly world in which to grow up; a world in which the dead were as present as the living, in which the objects of one's emotional attachments proved time and again to be transitory and unreliable, and in which, therefore, detachment may have seemed the only possible response.

At the time of his birth, however, there was no hint whatsoever of the darkness that was to follow. He was born – Bertrand Arthur William Russell – on 18 May 1872 in a pleasant and comfortable family home called Ravenscroft (now Cleddan Hall), Monmouthshire, the third child of Viscount Amberley, heir to the Russell earldom, and his wife, Kate.

The Russells were among the greatest of the great Whig families, and the unusual name 'Bertrand' was chosen in deference to a piece of family mythology that was characteristic of the type. Like most of the Whig dynasties, the Russells owed their position and their wealth to the creation by Henry VIII of a new aristocracy out of the spoils of his attacks on the monasteries and the old Catholic nobility. The Russells' share of this enormous booty included Woburn Abbey, Tavistock Abbey, large parts of Devon, Cornwall and Dorset, and several hereditary titles, most notably that of Earl of Bedford (later raised to a dukedom after the Glorious Revolution of 1688). However, in common with many such families, they hankered after an older, prouder, more glorious past, one that linked them to the Norman Conquest and the old French baronial families. And so, in the early nineteenth century, under the sixth Duke of Bedford (Bertrand Russell's great-grandfather), a family history was produced by the historian and family librarian J. H. Wiffen that showed them to be the descendants of William, Baron of Briquebec, whose son, Hugh Bertrand, had crossed the channel with William the Conqueror in 1066.

This story was demolished when a later duke employed a more scrupulous historian, who poured cold water on Wiffen's fanciful genealogy and traced the Russells back instead to a family of wine-merchants in Dorset, who, in the fourteenth century – when Bordeaux was still under British rule – made a decent living by importing claret to Britain and exporting wool to France. The discovery of these more humble origins was no great blow to Bertrand Russell, who probably never really believed in the Baron of Briquebec anyway, and did not much care whether his family had come over with the Conqueror or not. Neither did he show much pride or even interest in the enormous wealth and political influence of some of his ancestors. By the time of Henry VIII's death, John Russell, who had risen from obscurity in Dorset to become the first Earl of Bedford, was one of the richest and most powerful men in the country. During the reign of Henry's successor, the boy king Edward VI, the already vast amounts of land that the Earl of Bedford owned were increased still further when he acquired no fewer than fifteen more manors, including, most notably, Covent Garden. A few generations later, yet more land was acquired when Lord William Russell, the son of the fifth Earl of Bedford, married the daughter of the Earl of Southampton and received through inheritance an estate that included the manor of Bloomsbury, then a rather insignificant piece of grazing land but now a prestigious part of London, still owned by the family and, for many generations, their chief source of income.

With land and wealth went power, and during the eighteenth century, when British politics were dominated by the great Whig oligarchs, the fourth Duke of Bedford, widely regarded as the richest peer in England, was the head of one of the leading political factions and, in an age famously unsqueamish about such things, was severely criticised for his unscrupulous machinations. According to 'Junius', a scathing observer of the political scene at that time, the fourth Duke 'bought and sold more than half the representative integrity of the nation'. Even to less jaundiced eyes, the duke was regarded as manipulative and self-seeking, but his colossal wealth made him impossible to ignore. Throughout the middle decades of the eighteenth century there was not an administration that could afford to neglect altogether his influence, and he was, at various times, appointed Secretary of State, Lord Lieutenant of Ireland, Lord President of the Council and special ambassador to France. His greatest power, however, lay not in these high offices, but in the system of patronage he exploited to ensure that many Members of the House of Commons were in Parliament to represent, not a party as we now know it, but the interests of the Duke of Bedford and the faction he led.

Russell took a special interest in the history of his family, but of these two ancestors – the first Earl and the fourth Duke of Bedford – who had played such a large part in the political life of England, he said very little. The version of family history that he grew up believing, and which he held dear, was one handed down to him by his grandfather, Lord John Russell, whose concerns were altogether loftier than those of these mere power-brokers. Lord John was a younger son of the sixth Duke of Bedford, and, as such, thanks to the system of primogeniture, inherited very little, even while seeing his brother become one of the wealthiest men in the country. Thus freed from merely material concerns, Lord John's political career was driven by political principle rather than by the self-serving manoeuvring of his ancestors, and he was responsible for many progressive measures, including, most notably, the Great Reform Act of 1832. He rose to become the acknowledged leader of his party, twice served Queen Victoria as Prime Minister (in reward for which he was made an earl in 1861), and was one of the greatest statesmen of his day, the 'last doge of Whiggism', as he was called by Sir William Harcourt. He was also an indefatigable ideologue. When out of office, he wrote voluminously about the history of Whiggism, the constitutional history of England and the history of his own family, in such a way as to reveal that in his mind all three subjects tended to merge to become one. It was this potent fusion of national history, party politics and family pride that he bequeathed to his grandson.

From this perspective, the history of the Russell family is characterised, not by the ever-greater accumulation of wealth and political influence, but rather by centuries of commitment to 'civil and religious liberty', the power they received from the Crown largely forgotten in favour of an emphasis upon the power they used against the Crown. Thus they are seen, not as the beneficiaries of royal favour on a gargantuan scale, but rather as bulwarks against royal tyranny. For Lord John, and subsequently for Bertrand Russell, the family history begins, not with the huge gifts given by Henry VIII to the first Earl of Bedford, but four generations later with the stand taken by Lord William Russell against the succession to the throne of the Catholic James II.[1] And this stand is interpreted, not as the expression of religious intolerance against Catholicism (still less, of course, as the desire to protect what had been church property), but as a principled defence of constitutional liberties. In Lord John's eyes, Lord William was *the* family hero, for, in opposing James's succession, he – along with Lord Shaftesbury, John Locke and others – founded the Whig tradition. Moreover, he gave his life to the cause. In 1683, he was executed for his part in the Rye House Plot to kill James and his brother Charles II, and became in consequence the first Whig martyr and subsequently a hero of the Glorious Revolution, his death a symbol of the right of parliament to oppose the power of the Crown.

In 1819, at the beginning of his political career, Lord John published a biography of Lord William Russell, which – in the eyes of both the family and the Whig party – fixed the image of him as the embodiment of Whig principle. It was a life with a moral, namely that 'As long as there is a large portion of people who consider monarchy only as the best protection for liberty, the Whig party will flourish.' An even bigger hero of Lord John's, and one who, though not a Russell, was perhaps even more important in shaping the nature of the family mythology and ideology, was Charles James Fox. Several times in his writings Bertrand Russell uses the phrase 'Foxite Whig' to describe his grandfather, and thus, by implication, to describe the political tradition in which he himself grew up, without deeming it necessary to explain who Charles James Fox was and what he stood for. This in itself is revealing, a throwback to the 1830s and 1840s when veneration of Fox was almost universal among the great Whig families, when they all had busts or portraits of Fox in their homes and when they christened at least one of their sons 'Charles' and often added 'Fox' to their surnames. From this background (and, after he went to live with his grandparents, Russell lived in the world of the 1830s and '40s, even during the 1870s and '80s), it probably required an effort of the imagination to realise that there might be people who had never heard of Charles James Fox.

By the time he died in 1806, Fox had achieved mythic status among the Whig families by taking a stand against both the wars with the French and the suppression of civil liberties that were enforced in the course of those wars. The broad ideological division among the Whigs at that time was between those who followed Edmund Burke in his horror at the French Revolution and his distrust of the extension of democracy, and those who followed Fox. The latter were a tiny minority, but in successive generations when policies associated with Fox – peace with France, parliamentary reform and the extension of individual liberties – gained in popularity, it became an

---

[1] To a large extent, the secondary literature on Russell has been strangely content to repeat, uncritically, this version of his family history. The 'Introduction' to *The Selected Letters of Bertrand Russell*, for example, begins: 'The first Russell to make his mark on the political life of his country was Lord William Russell.'

increasingly influential minority. The proud boast of the Russell family was that, among the few Whig peers who counted themselves supporters of Fox at the height of his political opposition and isolation were the fifth and sixth Dukes of Bedford.[2] Fox's nephew, Lord Holland, and his wife were at the centre of this increasingly influential group of Whigs, and chose as their parliamentary champion Lord John Russell. Thus, as well as editing a two-volume edition of Fox's correspondence and writing a three-volume *Life and Times of Charles James Fox*, Lord John paid homage to Fox throughout his political career. With self-conscious regard for himself as the parliamentary inheritor of the Foxite legacy, he pursued Foxite policies – especially peace and parliamentary reform – whenever he could.

This tradition was one to which Bertrand Russell was proud to belong, and one that shaped much of his thinking, both about his place in the world and about politics in general. Though he lived till 1970, Russell never lost the habit of defining himself in terms of disputes that had raged seventy years before he was born: disputes between Burke and Fox, between Pitt and Fox, between Tory and Whig. When, for example, in 1936, he wrote a mock obituary, he said that his life 'had a certain anachronistic consistency, reminiscent of that of the aristocratic rebels of the early nineteenth century'. That is to say, he too, like his grandfather, belonged with the Foxite Whigs.

Russell's father, Lord Amberley, too, was content to place himself in this tradition, and, in line with Lord John's dictum that 'in all times of popular movement the Russells have been on the "forward" side', threw his support behind the more radical wing of the Liberal Party (as the Whigs had become by 1870), represented by the ideas of Jeremy Bentham and John Stuart Mill and, in particular, by the call for an extension to the right to vote to include working people and women. There was nothing iconoclastic about this Radicalism, and it involved no split between father and son. Indeed, Amberley was not the stuff of which iconoclasts are made. Unlike his father, he lacked vitality and robustness, and, consequently, his political career was short-lived. For less than two years he represented Nottingham as a Liberal, but in the election of December 1868 he contested the seat of North Devon and was defeated, largely because of the furore that was created when it emerged that, in principle, he supported birth control. The vitriol heaped upon him over this issue removed altogether what little taste he had for practical politics, and

---

[2] The fifth Duke of Bedford paid for his loyalty to Fox by becoming the target for one of the most famous polemics in the English language: Edmund Burke's splendidly vituperative 'Letter to a Noble Lord'. The duke, perhaps rashly, had objected to Burke's Crown pension on the grounds that it was excessive. In reply, Burke took the opportunity to remind Bedford of where his own – far more excessive – wealth had come from. The duke, he wrote, was 'the leviathan among all the creatures of the crown', who 'tumbles about his unwieldy bulk [and] plays and frolics in the ocean of the royal bounty. Huge as he is, and whilst "he lies floating many a rood", he is still a creature. His ribs, his fins, his whalebone, his blubber, the very spiracles through which he spouts a torrent of brine against his origin, and covers me all over with the spray, everything of him and about him is from the throne. Is it for *him* to question the dispensation of the royal favour?'

he withdrew to Ravenscroft to write a philosophical treatise called *An Analysis of Religious Belief.*

Bertrand's mother, Kate, was made of sterner stuff, and, even after their semi-retirement to Ravenscroft, ventured out to speak publicly in support of the Women's Suffrage Society, rousing the most powerful woman in the country to fury. 'I wish I could whip that Kate Amberley,' Queen Victoria is reported to have said. Generally, though, life at Ravenscroft for the first year of Bertrand Russell's life was quiet and even idyllic. The house was set in forty acres of beautiful countryside overlooking the Wye Valley, and, while Kate nursed the baby Bertrand (a 'very fat & ugly' baby, she reported affectionately, 'I have lots of milk now but if he does not get it at once or has wind or anything he gets into such a rage & screams & kicks & trembles till he is soothed off'), Frank, the eldest boy, a rambunctious and unruly eight-year-old, wandered the grounds barefoot with his younger sister, Rachel (then four, and universally adored), following him, while Amberley sat in the library working on his book. The chief blot on this otherwise serene family life was Frank's wildness, but Lord John advised the Amberleys not to worry: Charles James Fox had been very naughty as a boy, too, but he had turned out all right.

Through correspondence with various members of the family, the Amberleys kept in touch with practical political life, and in letters to their friends John Stuart Mill and Helen Taylor they debated issues of political theory and principle. In May 1871, Amberley published an article called 'Can War be Avoided?' in the *Fortnightly Review*, which, in the wake of the Franco–Prussian War, advocated a process by means of which future disputes between countries should be resolved, not by war, but by appeal to an international authority similar to the present-day United Nations. The article served as a focus for discussion among his friends and family for several months and was a forerunner of Bertrand Russell's own later political campaigns.

Socially, the Amberleys' life was unexciting. They avoided the London season, and their contacts with other people consisted largely of occasional visits to the various country homes – Naworth Castle, Woburn Abbey, Pembroke Lodge – of their relatives. In matters of politics and religion, the Amberleys were radical and unconventional ('I do not remember ever being taken to church or having the name of God inflicted upon me,' Frank recalls of his days at Ravenscroft), but there was nothing bohemian about their style of life, and their place in the upper reaches of Victorian society was confidently assumed. It was a life that combined the benefits of privilege with the satisfaction of being on the side of progress, the freedom from convention with the confidence and assurance of belonging to a long and proud tradition. Unfortunately for Russell, despite being the life he was born into, it was not a life he would ever have the chance to enjoy.

A strange prelude to the series of disasters that befell the family in Russell's second year is recorded in Amberley's journal for 19 January 1873. On that day, he and Kate went to visit a 'remarkable medium' called Mrs Acworth who lived at Haywards Heath, and took part in a seance. Kate, Amberley and

Mr and Mrs Acworth sat round a table until the hand of either Mrs Acworth or her husband began to shake convulsively, indicating that a spirit wished to speak to them. One spirit who did choose to communicate was that of Janet Chambers, a woman with whom Amberley had been in love before he married Kate, and whom he might have married, had she not died suddenly in the autumn of 1863. She did not, however, say anything of consequence beyond reassuring Amberley that she was happy. Then one of the evil spirits that troubled Mr Acworth revealed itself to be that of James II, that figure of contempt for all true Whigs. He said he was very worthless. Kate and Amberley laughingly agreed, upon which, Amberley's report records: 'Dr Acworth very gravely remarked that he did not think we ought to say this of a spirit who announced himself as worthless. These bad spirits intercede with him for his prayers on their behalf, yet do him mischief.' In the end, Amberley concludes: 'We both came home perplexed, but not convinced.' They were, no doubt, right to be sceptical. But, if the spirit of James II *had* set out to avenge himself on the Whigs by putting a curse on the Amberleys, he could hardly have improved upon the extraordinary sequence of disasters and appalling suffering they were about to undergo.

The world of the Amberleys first began to darken the following May, when news came of the death of John Stuart Mill. Mill had been a hero and intellectual mentor to both the Amberleys long before they got to know him in 1865, but in the last few years of his life they had become close friends with both him and Helen Taylor, his step-daughter. Shortly after Bertrand's birth, Kate wrote to Helen Taylor asking her if she would consider being the boy's (secular) godmother. 'We hesitated to ask such a favour of Mr Mill,' she added, 'otherwise he too cd. have been god father – for there is no one in whose steps I would rather see a boy of mine following in ever such a humble way, than in Mr Mill's.' Miss Taylor accepted on behalf of them both, providing Bertrand Russell with the most appropriate godparents imaginable.

On 12 May 1873, Kate wrote to her mother about the effect of Mill's death on Amberley. He was, she told her, 'very unhappy about it'. Mill was 'so particularly kind & affectionate to Amberley approving of him in every way so much that Amberley will miss his strong moral support much & his warmth of interest & tenderness.' Amberley had always been delicate, and suffered any kind of disappointment or upset very badly. A month after Mill's death, he reported what he describes as an 'epileptic seizure' that worried him enough to consult a doctor and to take his advice to cease work on his book. Lady Russell, Amberley's mother, was deeply alarmed at the news and began sending almost daily medical advice gathered from her own family doctor. Epilepsy, in Lady Russell's eyes, being akin to madness, she also tried to reassure the Amberleys that there was no hereditary mental illness in the Russell family. True, Lord John's brother Cosmo was paralysed by strokes, and another brother, Henry, was 'strange & unsteady of brain', but, after all, these were only half-brothers, children of his father's second wife, Lady Georgiana Gordon, and 'I always understood their strangeness of mind & ill health to be inherited from the Gordons.' As reassurance it was unconvincing and it is evident that Lady Russell was very worried indeed for her son's health.

To add to her worries, the Amberleys decided, in July, to have living with them an amateur scientist by the name of Douglas Spalding, whom they had met a few years previously through Mill and who was now dying of tuberculosis. Spalding had trained as a lawyer, but his real interest was the experimental study of instinct in animals, about which he had already published a pioneering article. Presumably as a way of enabling Spalding to continue his researches, Mill had suggested to the Amberleys that they take Spalding on as a tutor for their children. Following hard on the heels of the worrying news about Amberley's health, Lady Russell found the suggestion of hiring Spalding extremely alarming, and pointed out to Kate that 'a consumptive person might not be a right person to be with yr children'. Nevertheless, the Amberleys persisted, and Spalding moved into Ravenscroft in the summer. Their determination to employ him seems odd, especially as Frank – like many of the Amberleys' friends and relations – took a passionate dislike to Spalding the moment he met him. Spalding's position as tutor was, according to Frank, only a 'nominal' one: 'he also became the friend and confidant of the household, and exercised a sinister influence over it . . . He was a consumptive in a rather advanced stage, with hollow sunken cheeks, a sallow complexion and rather long black hair, and I was much intrigued by a little wooden tube which he always kept in his mouth to breathe through – why, I do not know . . . He was not the type to attract children . . . He beat me.' Lady Russell's reservations, it seems, were not entirely unfounded.

Spalding's work on animal instinct became famous after it was cited by William James in his chapter on instinct in *Principles of Psychology*. Particularly well-known is his discovery that chickens at birth will follow the first thing they see, apparently taking it to be their mother. At Ravenscroft, Spalding continued his experiments, much to the disgust of some of the Amberleys' guests, who complained that he made the house disgusting by allowing his chickens to wander about the drawing-room and the library. He also conducted experiments to investigate whether birds learnt to fly or whether it was instinctual, and, to this end, kept fledgling swallows and other birds cooped up in small boxes before letting them out to see if their ability to fly had been impaired. The purpose of these experiments was lost on most of the household, who regarded Spalding, as Frank did, as a nuisance and a rather sinister, grotesque figure. To little Rachel, he was just rather odd. 'Spaldy has got robins and a hive of bees in his room,' she reported incredulously to her grandmother. As for his tutoring, 'I suppose that we did have lessons,' Frank remembered, 'but the only recollections that survive definitely are of his scientific experiments':

One was to cut the heart out of a freshly killed salmon and stand it by itself on a dish, when it continued to beat for an incredible time – my impression is more than twenty-four hours . . . Another experiment was neatly to decapitate a wasp, when it continued with its legs to clean the place where its head ought to be.

Throughout the summer Amberley's health continued to worsen, and in the autumn it was decided to take a few months' holiday on the Continent, in the hope that this would help him recover. The problem was in deciding what to do with the children, or rather, with Frank, for 'sweet little Rachel' and 'dear Bertie' could quite happily be left with Lord and Lady Russell. Frank was too much of a handful. On this subject, Lady Russell offered a piece of emphatic advice: 'Frank *must not* stay at Ravenscroft with Mr Spalding.' Rather than that, she offered to have all three 'pets', though her enthusiasm for having Frank was manifestly less than whole-hearted, and in the end the Amberleys decided to take Frank – together with Spalding – with them. Lady Russell did her best to dissuade them from this, arguing that Spalding's health was 'an insurmountable obstacle to him as travelling companion, poor man', and that she could look after him at Pembroke Lodge, the Russells' home in Richmond, where he would have the best medical advice at hand. Besides, Frank wasn't so bad really, and, if Spalding was going in order to provide congenial conversation and society for the Amberleys themselves, why not choose instead 'some bright, clever, healthy Doctor'.

The Amberleys ignored this advice and, with Frank and Spalding, left for the Continent on 9 December, arriving in Rome a week later. In Rome, Amberley's health got even worse, and he stayed in bed much of the time, leaving Kate and Spalding to visit galleries and museums together and to explore Rome. It is possible to see in Lady Russell's concern about Spalding some sign that she sensed something of the real nature of his relationship with the Amberleys, for the truth was, as Spalding confessed soon after they reached Rome, that he was in love with Kate, a confession to which the Amberleys reacted in the most extraordinary way. As Russell, who learnt the story much later, put it:

> Apparently upon grounds of pure theory, my father and mother decided that although he [Spalding] ought to remain childless on account of his tuberculosis, it was unfair to expect him to be celibate. My mother therefore allowed him to live with her, though I know of no evidence that she derived any pleasure from doing so.

In a spirit of philanthropy, then, Kate – with Amberley's knowledge and consent – became Spalding's lover.

The record of the Amberleys' lives becomes rather sketchy from this point, because, after they died and Lady Russell discovered what had gone on between Kate and Spalding, she was so appalled that she ordered their journals and a good deal of their correspondence to be destroyed. What survives are charming letters to the Amberleys from Pembroke Lodge, reassuring them that everything is fine with the children and commenting on public events, such as the victory of Disraeli over Gladstone in the general election of February 1874. When Lady Russell was ill, the job of looking after Bertie fell to Amberley's sister Agatha, who reported that 'he has quite taken to me – & cries when he goes away', and gave an early anticipation of his future life:

Yesterday he insisted on lifting all alone an *enormous* book out of the shelf to a little stool where he sat down with it open before him – in a fit of laughter at his own wisdom! He will certainly be a book worm!

Rachel wrote, via her nursemaid, accounts of the flowers in the garden, of her education and her little brother's vocabulary, which, by April, included 'cake', 'biscuit', 'spoon', 'please' and 'Amberlie Bamberlie'. In April, Queen Victoria visited the house, and, reported Agatha, disappointed Rachel, who expected her to have a crown on her head and various other magnificences, while 'Bertie made a nice little bow – but was much subdued & did not treat Her Majesty with the utter disrespect I expected.'

At the beginning of May, towards the end of the Amberleys' holiday in Rome, the first of the major tragedies in the family occurred, when Amberley's brother William suffered a nervous breakdown from which he never recovered. In March he had been at home on leave from his cavalry regiment, the Ninth Lancers, which was then stationed at York, and had written the Amberleys a cheerful enough letter about what fun Rachel and Bertie were – 'Bertrand, I think, is his granny's favourite, & has a perpetual smile on his face' – and about how happy he was at York, except that 'politics in Yorkshire are exceedingly Tory'. But, soon after he returned to York, his whole life fell apart. The story that Bertrand Russell heard later in life is that Uncle Willy's fellow-officers teased him 'because he was chaste':

They kept a bear as a regimental pet, and one day, for sport, set the bear at him. He fled, lost his memory, and being found wandering about the country, was put in a workhouse infirmary, his identity being unknown. In the middle of the night, he jumped up shouting 'the bear! – the bear!' and strangled a tramp in the next bed.

The fate of his Uncle Willy haunted Russell for much of his life, offering, as it seemed to, the awful possibility of one day, suddenly, randomly and without warning, losing one's reason and being transformed into a violent, potentially murderous, lunatic. The image of being strangled by a madman, and that of being himself a madman strangling someone else, exercised a terrific hold on his imagination and came to him, in his nightmares and in his waking thoughts, with an almost obsessive repetition.

Until he was twenty-one, however, he knew nothing about his Uncle Willy, other than that he was an invalid. After his breakdown, Willy spent the rest of his life (he died in 1933 at the age of eighty-four) hidden away in an asylum, the true nature of his illness a closely guarded family secret. Bertrand Russell recalls that, as a young boy, he noticed that any allusion to insanity caused his grandmother a spasm of anguish, 'and I speculated much on the reason. It was only many years later that I discovered she had a son in an asylum.'

The records of the asylum in question, Chiswick House, have survived. They show that William Russell was admitted on 12 May 1874 and was diagnosed as suffering from 'advanced dementia'. A few days earlier, they state, he had left York suddenly and was found 'dressed slovenly and apparently unconscious' in the streets of Sandbach in Cheshire. He was taken to the local workhouse by the police, who returned to him a knife they had earlier confiscated from him. With this, he wounded one man in the throat and stabbed another. He was then put under restraint and taken to Chiswick House, where, somehow, they discovered his true identity. He never recovered his sanity. The day after he was admitted he tried to force his way out, and was given bromide to calm him down. After a while, he grew less violent, though he continued to entertain strange suspicions; that his food was being poisoned, and that the people he met were shams. When he was taken to meet Lord John, for example, he insisted that the real Earl Russell was dead and that the person he had been talking to was an impostor. For the first five years that he was hospitalised, he continued to be prone to apparently random attacks of rage and violence, and was, on occasion, inclined to 'shouting and singing and making strange faces'. After that he quietened down, and, for the last thirty or so years of his life, was regarded as 'very amiable and amenable, living almost entirely in a dream world'. The final diagnosis was schizophrenia.

Amberley had little time to grieve for his brother. On the way home from Italy, Frank began to suffer from a pain in his throat so bad that he could not swallow any food. On arrival in London, this was diagnosed as diphtheria, and he was isolated and treated by Mrs Garrett Anderson, who was, according to Frank, the only woman doctor then practising. Staying in London to convalesce, he was nursed back to health by Kate and her Aunt Maude. One 'blessed day', as Frank recalls, some weeks later, he found himself able to swallow some gooseberry fool and was soon declared fit and well again. Upon his recovery, everything he had been in contact with was destroyed or disinfected, and he and Kate went home to Ravenscroft, where Amberley, Rachel and Bertie were waiting for them. Sadly, the precautions they took were insufficient. The diphtheria infection survives longer than they had realised, and Frank was still a carrier of the disease, even though he was no longer ill. On 21 June, Kate wrote to her mother: 'We had just really settled down again and had just begun to enjoy to the full our country home and our children when today we are grievously distressed by our darling Rachel having diphtheria.' At the first sign of Rachel's illness, Bertie was packed off immediately with his nursemaid to her mother's farmhouse on the edge of the Ravenscroft estate.

Rachel, reported Kate, was a good patient and took her medicine, but she slept badly and seemed to be suffering more than Frank had done. On 24 June, Rachel herself wrote to Lady Russell, thanking her for the doll and cradle she had sent: 'I am in bed with diphtheria and my throat hurts very much. Spaldy has two rabbits.' The following day, Kate reported that she, too, was in bed with diphtheria. On 28 June, just three days later, Kate died. In his distress, Amberley could manage only a brief note to Kate's mother: 'You will know from the doctor that all is over. I cannot say more. It ended this morning early. I am too too wretched to write more.' On 3 July, Rachel, too, died, and Amberley, completely heartbroken, wrote to his mother in despair:

My Dear Mama,

. . . The child too had to go, and I have lost for ever the sweet caressing ways and the affectionate heart that might if anything could have been some consolation. And now the desolation is indeed complete . . . I know how I shall feel it hereafter when I miss her. Of all the children she was the dearest to me, and so my two greatest treasures in this world are gone almost at one blow. It is cruel, unspeakably cruel!

After that, Amberley sank into a deep depression, in which, in Frank's words, 'all incentive to life and effort had been removed'. He devoted himself to finishing *An Analysis of Religious Belief*, a task he was now determined to carry through as a way of honouring Kate, and left Frank and Bertie in the care of the servants and of Douglas Spalding, who, Frank says, 'became more than ever an evil influence'. In November 1875, Amberley finally finished the book, and duly dedicated it to Kate's memory. The book shows every sign of the writer's depression: it is flat, lifeless and almost unreadably dull. Its general thesis is that, though no one of the great religions of the world is literally true, and though there is no reason to believe in a personal God, yet there is something true in all religions, a 'universal religion', at the centre of which is an unknowable 'something' that is rightly to be regarded with reverence and veneration. On its last page, Amberley writes of the terrible fate of 'continuing to live when the joys of life are gone, and its purest happiness is turned into the bitterest pain'. Just over a month later, on 9 January 1876, he gave up the struggle and died. Officially the cause of death was bronchitis, but it is clear that he had lost the will and the desire to prolong the pain of living any longer.

Under Amberley's will, which, presumably, he had discussed with Kate before her death, the guardians appointed to look after Frank and Bertie and, in particular, to see to their education, were Douglas Spalding and T. J. Sanderson. The latter was a close friend of Amberley's from Cambridge, who shared the Amberleys' radical views, especially their rejection of traditional Christianity. Lord and Lady Russell might have tolerated Sanderson as a guardian for their grandchildren, but Spalding they regarded as totally unsuitable: he was socially inferior, he was loathed by Frank, and he was, in any case, going to die soon. They determined to oppose the will. Then they looked through the papers left by the Amberleys: the letters, journals and diaries that were later edited by Bertrand Russell and published as *The Amberley Papers*. One must suppose that these were not intended to be seen by Lord and Lady Russell, or else, surely, the Amberleys would have done something to edit them, so as to prevent the Russells from discovering that Kate and Spalding had been lovers. As it was, the Russells did discover, and, as Bertrand Russell later put it, the discovery caused them 'the utmost Victorian horror'. They were now implacable: Spalding could not possibly act as the children's guardian. Sanderson was at first inclined to fight the case, but, after taking legal advice, he was persuaded to give in. The children were made wards of Court and the Amberleys' will amended so that Frank and Bertie were now put under the care of Lady Russell and Amberley's younger brother, Rollo Russell. Thus, in February 1876, Sanderson delivered Frank and Bertie to Pembroke Lodge, which became Bertie's home for the next fourteen years.

Bertie was not yet four years old, and, no doubt utterly bewildered by all that had happened. Frank, however, was ten, and quite old enough to understand and to resent the situation. From the very first, he loathed Pembroke Lodge ('P.L.', as it was invariably called by the family). Not that the house itself was very much worse than Ravenscroft. It was a large enough, two-storey eighteenth-century house at the edge of Richmond Park, surrounded by about fourteen acres of garden and built on a hill that afforded wonderful views over the Epsom downs. It belonged to the Queen, who had given it to Lord John when he was Prime Minister during the 1840s, originally for his lifetime, and then, after his death, for that of his widow, too. For the house itself, and especially the garden, both Bertie and Frank came to have a great affection. What Frank loathed with venom was the atmosphere that prevailed among the household, which, he wrote, 'I may sum up by saying that it was timid, shrinking, that of a snail withdrawing into its shell':

> . . . full of high principle and religious feeling of the same kind that surrounded Queen Victoria . . . At every point it recoiled from the touch of real life and everything so vulgar as facts. Religion might occasionally be spoken of with bated breath and in a hushed curate sort of voice, but sex, birth, swearing, trade, money, passion, were subjects I never heard mentioned . . . To come from the free air of Ravenscroft into this atmosphere of insincerities, conventions, fears, and bated breath, was like a nightmare to me, young as I was, and during all the years I had to endure it the P.L. atmosphere never ceased to be a nightmare.

'The first and immediate effect upon me', Frank recalls, 'was the great circumscription and constriction of my life.' Where before he had been free to wander barefoot around the grounds of Ravenscroft, and to go cantering unsupervised around the Monmouthshire countryside on his pony, now he was never allowed beyond the grounds of the house, even to go into the park, and the idea that he might wander alone into the village of Petersham or the town of Richmond was quite unthinkable: 'there was always the possibility of scarlet fever or of my meeting someone who was not nice.' As Frank remembers it: 'No moment of my day was free from supervision.' And, while under the care of his parents he had never so much as heard the word 'God', still less been subject to the demands of organised religious instruction, at Pembroke Lodge he had imposed upon him a strict and pious training in the virtues of faith:

> I had to attend morning prayers: I was taken to church for the first time in my life. Much of the time I received lectures on morals, ethics and conduct with which I did not agree, and for the first time in my life answers were refused to my searching questions.

Lord John was eighty-three years old when Frank and Bertie came to Pembroke Lodge, and is remembered by both as a genial old man with a nice smile, who was wheeled around in a bath-chair and who devoted himself primarily to his books. Lady Russell was over twenty years younger and was undoubtedly the dominant influence on the whole household, though, somewhat strangely, Frank reserves his bitterest scorn for Rollo, Amberley's youngest brother, who was then only twenty-six and, having abandoned a career at the Foreign Office because of bad eyesight, spent all his time at Pembroke Lodge. Rollo was an extremely retiring man, almost cripplingly reserved, and considered by most who knew him to be harmless, if rather ineffectual. He took a serious interest in science, especially meteorology, which was later to have an important influence on Bertie's life. For Frank, however, he was the embodiment of all that was loathsome about Pembroke Lodge:

> . . . My Uncle Rollo possessed the outward figure of a man, but was a perfect production of the sheltered life, the extreme instance of what a man can become when he spends his whole life surrounded by adoring females. They treated him in the best Jane Austen manner as the male to be looked up to as their natural protector, as the counsellor to be relied upon – I think it probable that in his own eyes he was an Atlas supporting upon his strong shoulders the burden of decisions almost too grievous to be borne. In actual fact he passed his whole life under domination either of people or of phantoms, and never once knew the meaning of freedom . . . In speech he was halting, inconclusive and nervous; in appearance small and shy. It will be gathered that I did not admire him, and this tendency not to admire was increased by the way in which he was looked up to, quoted and deferred to by the rest of the household.

Some light on the apparently inexplicable degree of contempt with which Frank regarded Rollo is shed later on in Frank's memoirs, when he tries to get to the core of why Pembroke Lodge was so very odious:

> There were many things I found irritating in the life at P.L., but most of all the constant questioning 'Where have you been?' 'What have you done? 'Who have you seen?' . . . An additional irritation was the tone of voice in which conversation was generally conducted, a sort of hushed and pained undertone, as if one were in church with a corpse where some vulgar person had just committed the indiscretion of speaking in a natural voice. I do not suppose my Uncle Rollo for one moment realised, or if he had realised, could possibly have understood, how passionately I desired to kick him in the shins when he adopted this voice.

Both Bertie and Frank sensed this 'hushed and pained undertone', and both understood it to be in some way connected with their mother and father, about whom their new guardians at Pembroke Lodge were unnaturally silent. 'Of my parents', Bertrand Russell wrote later in life, 'I was told almost nothing – so little that I vaguely sensed a dark mystery.' The silence was

cruel, and, of course, did not stop the young Bertie from thinking about his
parents. While he played in the garden, he 'wove fantasies about my parents
and my sister . . . I used to wonder what sort of people they had been.'
Cruellest of all, when he once expressed to his grandmother his wish that his
parents had lived, 'she proceeded to tell me that it was very fortunate for me
that they had died.' At the time, Russell says, he attributed this attitude of
his grandmother to jealousy: 'I did not, of course, know that from a Victorian
point of view there was ample ground for [it].'

By various means, the boys were given to understand that their parents had
been very wicked, though it was never said so outright and, of course, the
reasons for thinking so were never given. By looks, sighs and hushed voices,
though, the message was conveyed that they had had a lucky escape in being
saved from their sinful parents by their more virtuous grandparents. 'The
most frequent and maddening P.L. expression', Frank remembers, 'was that
it was "so sad" ':

> My father's later life was 'so sad': any attempt to draw the immaculate
> Bertie into mischief of the most innocent kind was 'so sad': my unkind and
> wicked want of affection was 'so sad': the way in which I failed to
> appreciate the love that surrounded me was 'so sad' . . . I never had a single
> thought or a single purpose which was not sane, reasonable, and even
> meritorious and natural to ebullient youth. But the iron entered into my
> soul, and I never entirely recovered my natural freedom and frankness.

As Frank could remember only too clearly what life at Ravenscroft, and
what his parents and his sister, had been like, he resolutely resisted the
Pembroke Lodge outlook on his parents and on life generally. In consequence,
he was thought to be very wicked. 'The Russells never understood him at all,'
Bertrand Russell said about his brother, 'and regarded him from the first as
a limb of Satan.' It was seen as very important to prevent Frank from
corrupting Bertie's more innocent soul, and, as far as possible, the two were
kept apart. The Russells had originally intended to educate them both at
home, but Frank proved so intractable that they sent him to school:

> It was their intention to save me from the awful contamination of public
> schools and to endeavour to turn me into a perfect replica of Uncle Rollo.
> Bertie, whom they caught younger and who was more amenable, did enjoy
> the full benefits of a home education in the atmosphere of love, with the
> result that till he went to Cambridge he was an unendurable little prig.

The final straw came in the summer of 1877, when, for the sake of Lord
John's health, the family rented a house belonging to the Archbishop of
Canterbury at Broadstairs, on the Kent coast. There, Frank decided that life
with the Russells had become so intolerable that he had to get away, and so,
stealing three pounds from his grandmother's purse, he ran away in the
middle of night. After spending the night sleeping in a haystack, he walked
to Margate, from where he hoped to get a train to London. At Margate,

however, the first policeman who saw him delivered him back to the Russells, and, after he refused to promise not to run away again, the Russells gave him up and sent him to a private school in Cheam. Bertie's recollections of the summer in Broadstairs are much happier. It was the first time he had experienced the delights of the seaside – the limpets, sea-anemones, rocks and sands, fishermen's boats and lighthouses – and possibly the first time he was struck by a philosophical question. 'Aunty, do limpets think?' he asked his Aunt Agatha. 'I don't know,' she replied. 'Then', he said, 'you must learn.'

After he was sent to school, Frank was a good deal happier, the only blight on his happiness being the expectation that every Sunday he would write a letter to his grandmother. He seldom did, feeling 'that I could not say the kind of things she would like me to say'. Before the end of his first year at school, Frank, then twelve years old, was told that he had become the second Earl Russell. Lord John had died at the age of eighty-six on 28 May 1878. 'Heard old Lord Russell was dead,' wrote Queen Victoria in her diary the next day, after reading about it in the newspaper:

> A man of much talent, who leaves a name behind him, kind and good, with a great knowledge of the Constitution, who behaved well on many trying occasions; but he was impulsive, very selfish . . . vain, and often reckless and imprudent.

Writing to Lady Russell the following day, the Queen was less qualified in her praise, describing Lord John as 'one of my first and most distinguished Ministers', and hoping that Lady Russell would be comforted in her bereavement by Agatha ('your dear and devoted daughter') and by the thought that 'your grandsons will grow up to be all that you could wish'.

In the case of Frank, that comfort had long been denied to her, but in Bertie Lady Russell still invested great hopes that he might grow up to be a Russell worthy of the name. He was just six, and, displaying no sign of the rebelliousness of his brother, showed yet every sign of being extremely intelligent and, potentially at least, virtuous. After Lord John's death, Bertie fell more directly under the care of Lady Russell and Agatha. One reason for this was financial: Lady Holland, in recognition of Lord John's contribution to the Foxite cause, had settled £2,000 a year on him for the duration of his life. Now that this was no longer available, economies had to be made, and the number of servants was reduced. Before his grandfather's death, Bertie had spent more time with the servants than with his guardians; now he grew closer than before to all three of his guardians: Lady Russell, Agatha and Rollo. An outsider's impression of the kind of environment these three relations created has been left by Amabel Huth Jackson, who used to visit Pembroke Lodge as a young girl. 'Even as a child', she recalls, 'I realised what an unsuitable place it was for children to be brought up in':

> Lady Russell always spoke in hushed tones and Lady Agatha always wore a white shawl and looked down-trodden. Rollo Russell never spoke at all . . . They all drifted in and out of the rooms like ghosts.

For both Bertie and Frank, Agatha and Rollo – and, come to that, Uncle Willy and Amberley himself – served as dire warnings of the potential effects of striving to live up to Lady Russell's moral expectations. One went mad, or became enfeebled, or withdrew from the world to become a ghost. The source of the problem, Bertrand Russell came to think, lay in his grandmother's abhorrence of natural impulses, particularly sex. 'I do not think that she ever understood the claims of animal spirits and exuberant vitality,' he writes in his *Autobiography*. 'She demanded that everything should be viewed through a mist of Victorian sentiment.' In *The Amberley Papers* he wrote that, though she loved and respected her husband, she 'was never physically in love with him. Indeed Puritan inhibitions probably made her incapable of passionate love . . . in the unconscious part of her character she suffered certain strains and distortions which, as time went on, made her increasingly hostile to the claims of vigorous life, with the unfortunate results for those who came under her influence.'

It is clear that, despite Frank's comments about Bertie being amenable to the influence of the Russells and being, as a result, an 'unendurable little prig', Bertie did not consider himself in the same light. Where Frank's resistance against the Pembroke Lodge regime was overt and outspoken, Bertie's was covert and entirely unspoken. What Frank did not know – what nobody at Pembroke Lodge knew – is that Bertie led a life unfettered by the demands of his grandmother, a life that existed, however, only inside his own mind. While outwardly he was the 'angel child' (as Frank put it), inwardly he was as fierce in his independence as – perhaps fiercer than – Frank. 'Throughout the greater part of my childhood', he recalled, 'the most important hours of my day were those that I spent alone in the garden, and the most vivid part of my existence was solitary. I seldom mentioned my more serious thoughts to others, and when I did I regretted it . . . Throughout my childhood I had an increasing sense of loneliness, and of despair of ever meeting anyone with whom I could talk.'

While Frank ran away physically, Bertie did the same mentally. His real life, the most 'vivid' part of his existence, was lived quite apart from the family, while the part of his life spent in the company of others was a sham, a ghostly other-life:

So many things were forbidden to me that I acquired the habit of deceit, in which I persisted up to the age of twenty-one. It became second nature to me to think that whatever I was doing had better be kept to myself, and I have never quite overcome the impulse to concealment which was thus generated. I still have an impulse to hide what I am reading when anybody comes into the room, and to hold my tongue generally as to where I have been, and what I have done. It is only by a certain effort of will that I can overcome this impulse, which was generated by the years during which I had to find my way among a set of foolish prohibitions.

He, no less than Frank, considered the prohibitions and restrictions to which they were subjected foolish, and he too resented the continual questions about where he had been and what he had done, but where Frank was roused to open fury, Bertie's tactic was to lie, to keep the truth to himself. The advantages of this were enormous: it allowed him to lead a free and vivid mental life, untrammelled by his grandmother's piety. But the disadvantages were possibly even greater: like the snail in Frank's metaphor for Pembroke Lodge, Bertie's life was spent inside a thick shell – or, as he would sometimes dream, behind a sheet of glass – from where he remained untouchable by other people, and also unable to touch them.

Furthermore, while thoughts can happily remain unspoken and hidden, repressed feelings are often dangerous and disruptive and demand some kind of expression, even if only in dreams and nightmares. In old age, Russell took to writing fiction, which, though it went completely unrecognised at the time, was, he says in his *Autobiography*, 'a great release of my hitherto unexpressed feelings'. The truth of this remark can be seen in a short story he wrote called 'Satan in the Suburbs', which – though rightly derided as a work of fiction – is, as a piece of autobiography, possibly the most revealing thing he ever wrote, giving an almost terrifying glimpse of the emotional life he kept hidden from his grandmother. It also reveals the 'hitherto unexpressed feelings' that he harboured for most of his life about the series of bereavements he had suffered by the age of six.

The central figure in the story, the satanic Dr Mallako, lives in Mortlake, where he wreaks havoc on the lives of his respectable, suburban neighbours by encouraging them to develop to the full the less respectable sides of their natures: the destructive jealousies, hatreds and ambitions, which previously they have kept hidden and unexpressed and the existence of which they have denied even to themselves. The nameless narrator of the story is a scientist, who, seeing what has become of his neighbours under the influence of Dr Mallako, tries to resist the strange urge he himself has to become one of the doctor's clients. In an effort to shake off what he feels to be an insane and dangerous obsession with Dr Mallako, he plunges himself feverishly into 'a very abstruse scientific investigation'. But it is no good. Driven underground, the urge yet remains, and the doctor appears to him in his nightmares: 'Each night I would wake in a cold sweat, hearing the ghostly voice saying "COME!"'

From talking to his neighbours, the narrator realises that the doctor's power lies in his ability to read 'secret thoughts' and to bring them out into the open, 'like monsters of the deep emerging from their dark caves to bring horror to the crews of whalers'. The realisation is a challenge to his hitherto optimistic view of human nature, and he begins to despair at the thought that all people, even the most conventional and respectable, have a dark side; that each and every one of them has some nasty secret about themselves that they keep hidden. Reflecting on this, he becomes 'increasingly filled with a general detestation of mankind'. Dr Mallako, he realises, is not a uniquely evil person, but simply the catalyst for the evil that lies within all of us:

. . . in his malignant mind, in his cold destructive intellect, are concentrated in quintessential form all the baseness, all the cruelty, all the helpless rage of feeble men aspiring to be Titans . . . in many who are timidly respectable there lurks the hope of splendid sin, the wish to dominate and the urge to destroy.

Eventually, the narrator becomes completely possessed with the desire to punish the sinful, that is, the entire human race. He thus invents and builds a device designed to boil all the water on the Earth, contemplating with satisfaction as he does so the vision of the world getting hotter and drier and the unbearable thirst of mankind growing until, at last, 'in a universal shriek of madness, they will perish'. After that, he reasons, 'there will be no more Sin', the planet will become dead like the moon, 'and it will then be as beautiful and as innocent'.

When the machine is finished, he sets it to go off at noon and calls on Dr Mallako, hoping to spend the few remaining hours of life's existence on Earth gloating at his triumph over the sin that Mallako represents – 'a triumph', he concedes, 'achieved perhaps by what some might think a wickedness even greater than his own', but, he insists, 'redeemed by the purity of a noble passion'. The narrator's triumph, however, turns out to be a delusion: as he explains his machine in detail to the doctor, Mallako spots a flaw in the design and informs him that it will not work. Humiliated and dejected, the narrator turns to go, but Mallako stops him and suggests that they co-operate on a machine that *will* work, for, as he explains, he too loathes mankind – not, however, self-righteously but in the spirit of revenge, which is far more terrible. 'You imagine in your miserable way that you hate mankind,' Mallako tells the narrator. 'But there is a thousand times more hate in my little finger than in your whole body. The flame of hate that burns within me would shrivel you to ashes in a moment.'

When Mallako explains why he is consumed with such all-consuming hatred, he describes a childhood strikingly similar to Russell's own. At the age of six, he tells the narrator, he lost both his parents,[3] and was put into the care of a philanthropic old lady, towards whom he bore deep feelings of resentment and contempt, which, however, he repressed in order to win her approval and so continue to receive her kindness:

---

[3] An interesting, and, I think, significant detail here is that, in the story, Dr Mallako's parents do not die as innocent victims of disease and illness. Rather, his father – a prince – deserts his working-class wife and sinks to become, first a waiter in a New York restaurant and then a jailbird. Meanwhile, his mother becomes an alcoholic and takes to knocking the young Mallako about when drunk. One day, when Mallako is six years old, as they are walking down the street, she swings a blow at him, he ducks, and she is run over by a passing lorry. In many respects – the fact that the father is of higher social standing than the mother, that the mother is wicked, and that the boy is better off without both – this seems to be an imaginative, fictionalised version of how Lady Russell regarded the Amberleys. Perhaps its origins lie in the 'fantasies about my parents' that Russell used to weave while he was alone in the garden at Pembroke Lodge, for, if we were to imagine a young boy trying to flesh out Lady Russell's evident disapproval of the Amberleys, this is exactly the sort of story we might suppose he would invent.

She was persuaded that I was a good little boy. She adopted me, and educated me. For the sake of these benefits, I put up with the almost intolerable boredom that she inflicted upon me in the shape of prayers and church-goings and moral sentiments, and a twittering sentimental softness to which I longed to retort with something biting and bitter, with which to wither her foolish optimism. All these impulses I restrained. To please her I would go on my knees and flatter my Maker, though I was at a loss to see what He had to be proud of in making me. To please her I would express a gratitude I did not feel. To please her I would seem always what she considered 'good'. At last when I reached the age of twenty-one she made a will leaving me all her property. After this, as you may imagine, she did not live long.[4]

'Since her death my material circumstances have been easy,' Mallako goes on, 'but never for one moment have I been able to forget those early years . . . the friendlessness, the dark despair, the complete absence of hope – all these things, in spite of subsequent good fortune, have remained the very texture of my life.' In consequence: 'There is no human being, no, not one, whom I do not hate. There is no being, no, not one, whom I do not wish to see suffering the absolute extremity of torment':

You have offered me the spectacle of the whole population of the globe maddened with thirst, and dying in agonies of futile frenzy. What a delicious spectacle! Were I capable of gratitude I should feel some to you now, and should be tempted to think of you almost as a friend. But the capacity for such feelings died in me before I reached the age of six.

The narrator, appalled by such depths of hatred (unredeemed even by a 'noble passion'), shoots Mallako and disguises the death as suicide. He later marries and tries to forget all about Mallako. But he cannot. Mallako's presence is even more insinuating after his death than it was before, and the narrator is haunted by his whispered taunts: 'You think I'm defeated, do you? . . . You think you have recovered your sanity, do you? . . . Do you not know that my power is spiritual and rests unshakeably upon the weakness in yourself? If you were half the man that you pretended to be . . . you would confess what you have done. Confess? Nay, boast.' At first, the narrator thinks he is just imagining Mallako's voice, but eventually: 'I came more and more to feel that his terrible ghost was real.' At last, driven to distraction, he rises to the 'ghost's' taunts and shouts to the world that he has killed Mallako and is proud of it. His wife, who has been concerned about his mental state for some time, now becomes seriously alarmed, and the story ends with him

---

[4] When Russell became twenty-one, he inherited enough from his family's estate to live independently from his grandmother, and, indeed, after that, her influence on his life – which before had been considerable – became negligible. She died just five years later. When she died, Russell says in his *Autobiography*, 'I did not mind at all.'

looking out of the window to see two policemen and a psychiatrist arriving to have him committed to a lunatic asylum.

In the hands of someone with a genuine talent for novel-writing, the story of 'Satan in the Suburbs' might have been extremely powerful and rather disturbing. However, the depth of its feeling – and it is in a way Russell's most deeply personal and self-analytical piece of writing – is disguised from the reader by the rather light and arch formality of much of the writing. At a superficial glance – which is all most readers were prepared to give it – the story resembles a piece of stilted satire. To Russell's great disappointment, therefore, when he finally overcame nearly eighty years of emotional repression and tried to give some sort of expression to the feelings about his grandmother that he had never before admitted, and to the fears about himself that he had kept hidden, no one realised he had done so. Plans to film 'Satan in the Suburbs' – of which there were many – all came to nothing, because Russell invariably felt that the treatment that his story received from scriptwriters was too light and frivolous. When he next published a volume of short stories, he added a preface insisting that 'not all the stories in this volume are intended to cause amusement', but by then it was too late.

The advantage of using fiction as 'a great release for hitherto unexpressed feelings' is that one can give freer rein to one's expression; the disadvantage is that people will read it as fiction rather than as self-revelation, or, worse, if it is bad fiction, they will not read it at all. Many years earlier, in his twenties, Russell had tried another strategy to express some of the feelings of which he was not very proud, when he published a 'Self-Appreciation' under cover of the pseudonym 'Orlando'. Like 'Satan in the Suburbs', its tone serves to disguise the intensity of the feelings it expresses, which show a startling similarity to those expressed by both the narrator and Dr Mallako in the short story. 'I am quite indifferent to the mass of human creatures,' 'Orlando' declares. 'I wouldn't sacrifice myself to them, though their unhappiness, at moments, about once in three months, gives me a feeling of discomfort, and an intellectual desire to find a way out.' Later on, the misanthropy is more explicit: 'I believe in several definite measures (e.g. Infanticide) by which society could be improved':

> I live most for myself . . . I care for very few people, and have several enemies – two or three at least whose pain is delightful to me. I often wish to give pain, and when I do, I find it pleasant for the moment . . .

On the subject of sin, he echoes the narrator of 'Satan in the Suburbs' when he writes that, though, logically, he can find no meaning for the word 'sin', yet 'psychologically, sin has a meaning to me, and I love to see sinners punished.' He does not believe in an after-life, neither does he wish to, 'as it would not prove this world to be righteous'.

When he was a child, Russell writes in his *Autobiography*, he was 'unusually prone to a sense of sin'. When he was asked to name his favourite hymn, he chose 'Weary of earth and laden with my sin'. A natural consequence of his secrecy was a troubled conscience, the feeling that his secrets were perpetually liable to be discovered. When, one morning during the family's daily prayer meeting, Lady Russell read the parable of the Prodigal Son, Bertie said to her: 'I know why you did that – because I broke my jug.' When she later repeated the story with great amusement, he felt still more humiliated ('Most of my vivid early memories are of humiliations'). She did not realise, he wrote, 'that she was responsible for a morbidness which had produced tragic results in her own children'.

When Bertie was seven, some relief from the oppressive atmosphere of Pembroke Lodge came when the Russells took a house in London for a few months and Bertie and Frank began for the first time to see something of their other grandmother, Lady Stanley of Alderley, and her remarkable family. Lady Stanley was an aristocrat of a quite different stamp from Lady Russell. A few years older than Lady Russell, she had grown up in the atmosphere of robust rationalism that had prevailed in Britain before the succession of Victoria, and, Russell recalls, was 'contemptuous of Victorian goody-goody priggery'.

As might be expected, she took a great liking to Frank and a corresponding dislike to Bertie, whom she dismissed as 'just like his father'. She had a large family of four sons and four daughters, most of them talented, all of them argumentative, and none of them shy. They terrified Bertie and enchanted Frank. Of the sons, Henry was a Muslim, Lyulph an atheist and Algernon a Roman Catholic priest. On Sunday they would all gather for lunch and engage each other in vigorous and unrestrained debate, each contradicting the other and shouting at the top of their voices. 'I used to go to these luncheons in fear and trembling,' Bertie remembered, 'since I never knew but what the whole pack would turn on me.' Frank, on the other hand, felt perfectly at home: 'It was full of instruction, entertainment and pleasure . . . I heard matters freely discussed; I was allowed to speak for myself . . . I loved it.'

Frank came to love the Stanleys as warmly as he hated the Russells, and Lady Stanley's house at 40 Dover Street became for him a second home, a welcome escape from Pembroke Lodge. Bertie remained – to all outward appearances at least – a loyal and devoted Russell. When he looked back on the two families in his old age, however, he found that his sympathies had changed: 'I owe to the Russells shyness, sensitiveness, and metaphysics; to the Stanleys vigour, good health, and good spirits. On the whole, the latter seems a better inheritance than the former.'

What the Russells did provide for Bertie was a superb education. In 1879, Frank was sent to Winchester, where he spent four of his happiest years and made most of the closest friends of his life. Bertie, however, received what George Santayana has called 'a perfect princely education' at home. It was, Santayana says, 'a little like cultivating tropical flowers under electric light in a steaming greenhouse . . . too good for the outdoor climate', but the hot-house method had its advantages. It was, from the very beginning, the education of a future Prime Minister. By the time he was seven, Bertie had absorbed the Whig version of the constitutional history of England from the time of the Norman Conquest to 1815. After 1815, Russell was assured, there was no history, just gossip, although he was readily furnished with that as well, from his grandmother, who had been at the centre of English political life since her marriage in 1841. The grown-up conversation at Pembroke Lodge was mostly of events that had happened a long time ago: his grandfather's visit to meet Napoleon, how his grandmother's great-uncle had defended Gibraltar during the American War of Independence, and so on. And, in addition, there was Lord John's library, to which Bertie had free access and which contained an abundance of works on history and politics.

Lady Russell, whatever her faults, was eminently cultured. She was well-read in French, German and Italian, and had an extraordinarily detailed knowledge of the works of the great English writers, especially those of Shakespeare, Milton, Wordsworth and Byron. She was herself a gifted poet, if not a very inspired or original one, and on birthdays or other occasions would quite often give a recital of a verse she had composed specially for the event, accompanying herself on the piano. She also had – and imparted to her grandson – a deep-seated aversion to unthinking conformity. When one Christmas she presented Bertie with a Bible, she wrote on the flyleaf one of her favourite texts: 'Thou shalt not follow a multitude to do evil' (Exodus 23:2). At various times in his life, this text proved to be a source of inspiration.

One of the greatest events in Russell's early education – indeed, one of the great events in his life – occurred when he was eleven, when Frank, having finished at Winchester and while waiting to take up his place at Balliol College, Oxford, decided to teach his little brother Euclid's geometry. 'I had not imagined', Russell later wrote, 'that there was anything so delicious in the world . . . [It was] as dazzling as first love.' Some details of the event are preserved in Frank's diary, which records that the book he used to teach from was *An Introduction to the Elements of Euclid* by S. Hawtrey, and that the lessons began on 9 August 1883. At the end of the first day, Frank reported that Bertie 'did very well indeed . . . we got half through the Definitions – he is sure to prove a credit to his teacher.' On 7 September: 'Bertie successfully mastered the Pons Asinorum [Euclid's Fifth Proposition] this evening, and in fact did it very well.' A week later: 'I did the 12th prop. with Bertie to-night and so finished Hawtrey's book: he has gone thro' them all with great success and seems to me to thoro'ly understand them: I am very proud of my pupil.'

'Dazzling' and 'delicious' are not words one would naturally associate with learning geometry, and yet Russell's rapturous reaction has an intriguing precedent. According to John Aubrey's *Brief Lives*, when Thomas Hobbes was forty years old, he happened to glance at a copy of Euclid's *Elements*, which was lying open on a desk in a library he visited. It was open at the proof of the famous Pythagorean Theorem. 'By God, this is impossible!' Hobbes exclaimed:

So he reads the Demonstration of it which referred him back to such a Proposition; which proposition he read. That referred him back to another, which he also read. *Et sic deinceps* [and so on] that at last he was demonstratively convinced of that truth. This made him in love with Geometry.

For both Russell and Hobbes, the fascination lay in being able to demonstrate the truth of a proposition. Previously, alone in the garden at Pembroke Lodge, Russell had speculated a good deal about things he did not know, and could not know: what had his parents been like? was his mother really wicked? why did his grandmother tremble at any mention of insanity? were his grandmother's religious beliefs true? On some of these questions he might have opinions, on others he could only weave fantasies, but to none of them could he know for certain the right answer; he could only choose to accept or reject what he was told, and, in the case of conflicting answers from different people, could only decide on the basis of *who* to support, who to give his loyalty to. The beauty of geometry was that the truth of a proposition was not just asserted, it was *proved*; it did not await any kind of denial or counter-assertion, and who said it or what they felt about it were neither here nor there. The idea that something – anything – could be known with certainty in this way was delightful, intoxicating, especially when, as Russell was quick to realise, it opened up the possibility that other things too might be amenable to strict, mathematical proof. Perhaps even disputes between people might be resolved in this way. 'I hoped', Russell wrote in *Portraits from Memory*, 'that in time there would be a mathematics of human behaviour as precise as the mathematics of machines. I hoped this because I liked demonstrations, and at most times this motive outweighed the desire, which I also felt, to believe in free will.'

There was, however, one blemish to the delight he felt in discovering Euclid; though it was delightful and delicious that the truth of the propositions could be demonstrated from the axioms, the question arose as to what reason we had for believing the axioms themselves. The only reason Frank could offer was the merely pragmatic one that, if Russell did not assume the axioms to be true, they could make no further headway with the lessons. In time, Russell hoped for a more satisfying answer, a hope that was to direct the course of his work in philosophy until he and Alfred North Whitehead finished work on *Principia Mathematica* in 1910. In thus causing him to reflect on the possibility of certain knowledge, in suggesting to him the idea of a truth that was detached from the wishes and passions of people, that was invulnerable to emotions, his introduction to geometry was 'the first thing that led me towards philosophy'.

Between the ages of eleven and sixteen, Russell was educated primarily by a series of private tutors hired by the Russells, some of whom played an important role in encouraging the philosophical direction in which his thoughts were moving. There was a fast turnover of these tutors, but they generally seem to have been men of considerable ability, willing to push Russell – especially in languages, history and mathematics – far beyond the level that would normally be expected of a teenage boy. One of them, for example, told him about non-Euclidean geometry – then a very esoteric subject about which even many professional mathematicians would have known very little. Another presented him with a copy of W. K. Clifford's *Common Sense of the Exact Sciences*, a book that had a great influence on Russell, and one that, he later said, he 'read . . . at once, with passionate interest and with an intoxicating delight in intellectual clarification'.

The importance of Clifford's book for Russell was that it crystallised the attitude he had been developing for years about the superiority of reason over intuition, tradition, authority and emotion as a means of arriving at the truth; the attitude that refuses to believe something unless there is some reason for doing so, not just in mathematics, or in science, but in all areas of life. When Clifford's book was reissued in the 1940s, Russell wrote a preface for it, explaining why it had been so important to him as a teenager. Clifford, he wrote, was 'more than a mathematician: he was a philosopher . . . he saw all knowledge, even the most abstract, as part of the general life of mankind, and as concerned in the endeavour to make human existence less petty, less superstitious, and less miserable.' Clifford's book encouraged in Russell a faith that upheld reason as the foundation of all sound belief, and mathematics as the ideal to which all other knowledge should aspire. In the light of this faith:

It was possible . . . to believe that the human species would become progressively more humane, more tolerant, and more enlightened . . . In this beneficent process rational knowledge was to be the chief agent, and mathematics, as the most completely rational kind of knowledge, was to be in the van. This faith was Clifford's, and it was mine when I first read his book; in turning over its pages again, the ghosts of old hopes rise to mock me.

'It is wrong always, everywhere, and for any one', wrote Clifford, 'to believe anything upon insufficient evidence.' It was a view Russell was quick to adopt, and one that gave to his emotional delight in the possibility of demonstrative truth the force of a moral imperative. Not only was it 'delicious' to be able to prove things, it was morally essential.

Such a view, of course, was bound to lead to a head-on collision with the religious faith in which Bertie had been instructed since he was three, the faith of Lady Russell, which was devoutly non-intellectual. Hers was not primarily a faith based on creeds and arguments for the existence of God and the like, it was one based on revelation, on the individual conscience, and above all on love (a word she used, perhaps, even more than 'sad'). A good illustration of the style of her religious thinking is preserved in a letter she wrote to Bertie's governess, Dora Bühler, who had written to Lady Russell about her religious doubts. It was, Lady Russell replied, a subject upon which 'it sometimes seems that we are doomed to work our minds in vain – to seek, and *not* to find . . . to grope about in darkness and say, "Was it not a beautiful dream, and only a dream?" '

'Is it not too good to be true that we are the children of a loving Father who stretches out His hands to guide us to Himself, who has spoken to us in a thousand ways . . . chiefly by that which we feel to be immortal in us – *love* – the beginning and end of God's own nature, the supreme capability of which He has breathed into our souls?' No, it is *not* too good to be true. Nothing perishes – not the smallest particle of the most worthless material thing. Is immortality denied to the one thing most worthy of it?

This is not the style of someone prepared to examine carefully the question of whether or not there exists scientific evidence for the truth of her religious beliefs; so, in line with his general policy of remaining silent about anything that might hurt her, Bertie said not a word to his grandmother about the direction his thoughts were taking: 'the whole of this mental life was deeply buried; not a sign of it showed in my intercourse with other people . . . Indeed, after the age of fourteen I found living at home only endurable at the cost of complete silence about everything that interested me.'

Bertie's conviction about the wisdom of avoiding conflict and of keeping his thoughts to himself can only have been strengthened by the fate of his brother Frank, whose outspokenness and lack of restraint were leading him from crisis to crisis. Frank was, indeed, becoming something of a hot-head. His time at Balliol studying Classics was cut short at the end of his second year when he was sent down for being rude to the Master, the famously indomitable Benjamin Jowett. Frank had been outraged by the accusation by Jowett that Frank had written an improper letter; an accusation, it seems, for which Jowett had only indirect evidence from some unnamed third person. Frank denied that he had ever done or written anything improper and demanded to see the letter, which Jowett refused, whereupon Frank lost his temper, told Jowett that he was no gentleman, that he would have nothing more to do with him and that he would there and then 'shake the dust of Oxford off my feet'.

Thus was a minor crisis turned into a major threat to Frank's reputation; for, after he had left in such a public blaze of indignation, everybody at Oxford naturally wanted to know what the letter contained and to whom it was addressed, and, while Jowett clearly wanted to hush the matter up, it now became a subject for gossip and speculation surpassed only by the trial of Oscar Wilde ten years later. The only half-way credible version of events to have appeared in print is that of George Santayana, who got to know Frank well the year after he left Oxford. According to Santayana, Jowett suspected that Frank had had 'improper' relations with young boys, on the basis of a report from Frank's scout (as Oxford servants are called) that his friend from Winchester, Lionel Johnson, had stayed the night in Frank's rooms. This, suggests Santayana, led Jowett (wrongly, in Santayana's opinion) to link Frank with a letter that had earlier come to his attention in which reference was made either to Johnson or to homosexuality, or both. Whatever the truth, by his impetuosity Frank had made the situation many times worse for himself. When Rollo came to see him during his last days at Balliol, Frank was so rude to him that Pembroke Lodge finally severed relations altogether. At nineteen years old, he was on his own, with no degree, no career, no home, and every gossip in London and Oxford speculating about his sex life.

Frank devoted much of the rest of his life (and almost the whole of his published memoirs) to the attempt to clear his name in regard to both this and the other scandals in which he was involved later in life. And the more he protested his innocence, the more people thought that there must, after all, be something to the allegations. 'In regard to people's reputations', as Santayana observes, 'the polite world is at once cynical and good-natured. It believes the worst and acts as if nothing were amiss.' But this is exactly what Frank was in rebellion against. He wished the world, like he himself, would say what it thought, openly and frankly – that, indeed, it would be a little *less* 'polite'. Not that he wanted the world's approval – almost everything he did seemed calculated to lose that – but he resented it believing things about him that were not true.

Bertie's attitude was just the opposite: he did not mind the world (Pembroke Lodge, in his case) believing things about him that were not true, just so long as he kept its approval – until such time, that is, as he considered that approval no longer necessary to him, or until the price demanded for it was too high. For him, before one took a stand, there was a calculation to be made of advantages and disadvantages. And for the moment, he, like the young Mallako, thought it prudent for the sake of the education he was receiving (among other benefits) to put up with the 'prayers and church-goings and moral sentiments' and the 'twittering sentimental softness', and to resist for a while longer his urge to 'retort with something biting and bitter'.

And yet he needed to discuss his thoughts and doubts with *someone*. When he was fifteen, John F. Ewen, the tutor in whom he had confided most, and with whom he had discussed his religious doubts, was sacked – presumably (so Russell thought, anyway) because Lady Russell discovered that he was an agnostic and suspected him of undermining Bertie's faith. In March 1888, to compensate for the loss of Ewen, Russell decided to keep a diary, in which he would record his thoughts on religious subjects. In order to keep it secret, he hit upon an ingenious method of disguise. Calling the diary 'Greek Exercises', he wrote it entirely in Greek letters, using a system of phonetic transliteration that he had invented himself.

It began on 3 March with a confession:

> I have in consequence of a variety of circumstances come to look into the very foundations of the religion in which I have been brought up. On some points . . . I have been irresistibly led to such conclusions as would not only shock my people, but have given me much pain . . . I have not had the courage to tell my people that I scarcely believe in immortality. I used to speak freely to Mr Ewen on such matters, but now I cannot let out my thoughts to any one, and this is the only means I have of letting off steam.

Russell had not, at this stage, entirely lost his belief in God, but he wanted reasons to believe, and had made a solemn vow to himself: 'in finding reasons for belief in God I shall only take account of scientific arguments . . . and to reject all sentiment'. This vow, he wrote, 'costs me much to keep', but he was nevertheless determined to keep to it.

The imaginative picture of the world that dominates these early philosophical meditations is that of a great machine running in accordance with perfectly deterministic natural laws, which are, in essence, mathematical formulae, and which it might one day be the good fortune of mankind to discover. God has a place in this world as its 'controlling power'. Russell at this stage thought it likely that, ultimately, there would turn out to be just *one* law of nature, 'which law of nature is really pretty much the same as God'. As he well realised, however, this conception of God was about as far removed from his grandmother's 'religion of infinite love' as it was possible to get.

All that was central to Lady Russell's faith – the worship of a benevolent Father who loves us and cares for us, the experience of conscience as the voice of God, the efficacy of prayer, the immortality of the soul, the gift from God of free will so that we might choose good over evil – all this was dispensed with. Most of it was straightforwardly inconsistent with the rigidly deterministic world-view that the fifteen-year-old Bertie had developed, and much of the 'Greek Exercises' was taken up with arguments against immortality, free will, and even the existence of the soul, which showed them all to be ruled out by the uniformity of nature. Neither could conscience be allowed as the basis for morality, as one could see by reflecting that different people's consciences commanded them to do different things. A more objective basis for morality had to be found, and Bertie found it in the utilitarian principle that one should act in the manner 'likely to produce the greatest happiness, considering both the intensity of the happiness and the number of people made happy'. Finally, belief in the efficacy of prayer had to be abandoned, for this would require the occasional exception to the uniformity of the laws of nature and 'we have no certain evidence that law ever has been broken by God'.

Thus, within a few months, he had satisfied himself that requiring one's beliefs to be supported by scientific evidence demolished every plank of his grandmother's religion, except belief in the barest conception of God as the source of natural law. In terms of guiding how he should live, this left quite a gap. 'My doctrines, such as they are, help my daily life no more than a formula in algebra.' There was, however, one great compensation: 'it does give us a wonderful idea of God's greatness to think that he can in the beginning create laws which, by acting on a mass of nebulous matter . . . will produce creatures like ourselves, conscious not only of our existence but even able to fathom to a certain extent God's mysteries!'

'I should like to believe my people's religion,' he wrote, 'but alas, it is impossible . . . The search for truth has shattered most of my old beliefs . . . and worst of all, it has debarred me from free intercourse with my people, and thus made them strangers to some of my deepest thoughts.' He could open his heart more easily to his governess, Dora Bühler, but on 3 May 1888, she left, 'and I am left again to loneliness and reserve'. He began to think that, in his isolation, his self-absorption and his melancholy, he was in danger of going mad. These fears were fuelled by reading an article in *The Nineteenth Century* about the common characteristics of genius and madness, in which he thought he could see himself described, the characteristics being: melancholy ('which I have often had lately'), a desire to commit suicide (which 'has lately been present more or less with me in particular when up a tree'), and sexual passion, 'which I have lately had great difficulty in restraining'.

In fact, along with mathematics and religion, sex was becoming one of his chief preoccupations, one that he had to be especially secret about. On a rare occasion that he had a friend to stay, on this occasion a boy named Jimmie Baillie, they did little else but talk about sex, not only between themselves but also with a page-boy, who, though the same age, was considerably more worldly-wise. Somehow, it was discovered that they had spent the afternoon in 'doubtful conversation', and they were sent to bed and kept on bread and water. 'Strange to say', Russell wrote, 'this treatment did not destroy my interest in sex.' From the age of fifteen, 'I began to have sexual passions, of almost intolerable intensity', which he dealt with like most boys of that age, by masturbating: 'I was much ashamed of this practice, and endeavoured to discontinue it. I persisted in it, nevertheless, until the age of twenty, when I dropped it suddenly because I was in love.' His sexual attentions became focused on the maids in the house, and he used to try to get glimpses of their naked bodies when they were dressing. Eventually, he succeeded in persuading one of the maids to allow him to kiss and hug her, but when he suggested that she spend the night with him, she was horrified, saying that she would rather die and that she was disappointed in him, she had thought he was 'good'. In the face of this rejection, Russell says, 'I became morbid and regarded myself as very wicked.'

Some hope of relieving his loneliness was aroused just before his six-teenth birthday, when it was decided to send him to a 'crammer' school to help him prepare for the scholarship exam for Trinity, Cambridge, his father's old college, to which he had decided to apply to study mathematics. The crammer chosen was B. A. Green's University and Army Tutors in Southgate, North London. Most of the other students were eighteen-year-olds preparing for the army, with little interest in religion or mathematics, but an interest in sex that far outstripped even Russell's and which was unrestrained by notions of wickedness and repression. For a delicate plant like Russell, fresh out of his 'steamed greenhouse', they were alarming company, and rather disgusting. After he had been there a couple of weeks, he summed up his impressions: 'No mind, no independent thought, no love of good books, nor of the higher refinements of morality, it is really sad that the upper classes of a civilised and (supposed to be) moral country can produce nothing better.'

He took refuge in his mathematical studies and in poetry, and tried to prevent his own character from deteriorating. 'It is very difficult', he wrote on 27 May 1888, 'for anyone to walk aright with no aid from religion, by his own internal guidance merely. I have tried, and I may say, failed. But the sad thing is that I have no other resource. I have no helpful religion':

> . . . the great inducement to a good life with me is Granny's love, and the immense pain I know it gives her when I go wrong. But she must, I suppose, die some day, and where then will be my stay? I have the very greatest fear that my life may hereafter be ruined by my having lost the support of religion.

What was needed, he now thought, was a new religion: 'Christianity has had its day. We want a new form in accordance with science and yet helpful to a good life.'

Being two years younger than the other boys at the school, he was a prime target for being teased, and he suffered minor humiliations almost daily: being made to sing for the others, for example, or being woken up in the middle of the night for 'a sponging'. It was a far cry from the hushed tones of Pembroke Lodge, and for a while he was utterly miserable. The 'Greek Exercises' became a diary of personal feeling more than of philosophical reflection. 'I don't suppose anybody hates disturbance as I do,' he wrote on 15 July, 'or can so ill stand mockery . . . the excitement, which to others might appear small, leaves me trembling.' He kept up his spirits, he said, 'by a feeling of contempt . . . for all who "despitefully use and persecute me" ':

I don't think contempt is misplaced when a chap's habitual language is about something like 'who put me on my cold cold pot, whether I would or not? My mother', sung to the tune of 'thy will be done'.

Religious doubt was one thing, but Russell was still sufficiently an 'unendurable little prig' to be shocked at profanity.

Perhaps as a reaction to the coarseness of his fellow-students, or perhaps, as he himself came to think later, as a sublimation of his intense sexual feelings, Russell developed at this time a hitherto unknown 'poetic' side to his nature. Where before he had embraced an austere and uncompromising materialism, now he began to insist that man *did* have a soul, and, that being so, where previously he had accepted only rigorously scientific arguments, now he began to look more favourably on 'poetic' ones, and to see the question of immortality in a different light:

what is the soul? . . . My own answer is that it is anything distinguishing man utterly from dead matter . . . Accepting that definition, we see that man has a soul, for consciousness is undeniable, whatever else may be attacked. One of the many poetic arguments for immortality is that force and matter is immortal, and the soul is surely greater than these . . . Let us not dogmatically deny man's immortality, for innumerable 'poetic' arguments may be urged in its favour . . . and poetic arguments often have something in them.

It is striking, I think – and no coincidence – that the particular 'poetic' argument he gives here for immortality is the very one urged by his grandmother in her letter to Dora Bühler ('Nothing perishes – not the smallest particle of the most worthless material thing. Is immortality denied to the one thing most worthy of it?'). Russell had been very moved the night before he left for Southgate by his grandmother saying a 'beautiful' prayer for him, 'in which among other things she said: may he especially be taught to know God's infinite love for him':

Well that is a prayer to which I can heartily say amen, and moreover it is
one of which I stand in the greatest need. For according to my ideas of
God we have no particular reason to suppose he loves us. For he only set
the machine in working order to begin with . . . Hence I see no reason to
believe in God's kindness towards me, and even the whole prayer was
more or less a solemn farce to me, though I was truly much affected by
the simple beauty of the prayer and her earnest way of saying it. What a
thing it is to have such people! What might I be, had I been worse brought
up!

It is as if, in the contrast between the beauty and poetry of his grandmother's religion and the spiritual emptiness of the bawdy jokes of his
fellow-students, he had come to believe that there had to be something right
about the poetic, even the religious, point of view. Otherwise, life would not
be worth living. Through poetry, as he put it in a diary entry at the time, he
had 'emerged from the base materialism into which my Theology had sunk
me', while at the same time becoming convinced that 'all young men in
England were steeped in brutish stockish materialism'. He was, then, as alone
as ever.

Related to his growing appreciation of poetry and poetic qualities was a
sudden awakening in him of the love of nature. So taken was he by the beauty
of the spring that year that he asked his grandmother whether it was
unusually pretty that year (she said not). One day, around this time, he was
at his grandmother Stanley's house in Dover Street, when, left alone for a
short while, he took from her shelf a volume of Shelley and opened it at
Alastor. He was completely entranced. It was, he said, 'the most beautiful
poem I had ever read', and he felt an immediate affinity with its author: 'Here,
I felt, was a kindred spirit.'

Subtitled 'The Spirit of Solitude', *Alastor* is a poem that might have been
written specially for the fifteen-year-old Bertrand Russell. It tells the story of
an isolated young poet ('He lived, he died, he sung, in solitude'), who is, in
the words of Shelley's preface to the poem, 'led forth by an imagination
inflamed and purified through familiarity with all that is excellent and
majestic in the contemplation of the universe'. He seeks to know and
understand everything about 'the external world', and is happy so long as his
mind is directed towards infinite things. But, after a while, his mind begins
to hunger for communion with 'an intelligence similar to itself', and conjures
up a vision of someone as wise, as wonderful and as beautiful as his need for
perfection demands. But, seeking someone who matches that ideal, he is
'blasted by disappointment' and 'descends to an untimely grave'. The moral
that Shelley draws from this melancholy tale is that those who 'keep aloof
from sympathies with their kind . . . languish, because none feel with them
their common nature. They are morally dead.'

The story is one calculated to appeal to Russell's imagination, and its moral
one that chimed perfectly with his fears that the 'base materialism' of his
philosophical reflections was making him too unsympathetic with his 'people'.
But, in addition to these very powerful points of affinity, *Alastor* begins with

a kind of hymn to nature that expresses Russell's new-found worship of and delight in natural beauty, in a way that does ample justice to its underlying eroticism ('If spring's voluptuous pantings when she breathes/Her first sweet kisses, have been dear to me'). And, as Russell later put it, his enjoyment of Shelley was not marred by his 'accepting conventional beliefs for which there seemed to be no good evidence'. But it was not just Shelley's work that Russell came to love and admire, it was Shelley himself, in whom he saw a mental and spiritual intimacy of the kind he craved. He felt – just as he would later with Joseph Conrad and D. H. Lawrence – that Shelley would understand him in a way that nobody else seemed to. Russell began to fantasise about 'how wonderful it would have been to know Shelley', and to wonder 'whether I should ever meet any live human being with whom I should feel so much in sympathy'.

After this, Russell read all the Shelley he could find, and, for his next birthday, his grandmother Stanley delighted him by presenting him with the three-volume *Complete Poetical Works of Percy Bysshe Shelley* edited by W. M. Rossetti. Apart from *Alastor*, one poem of Shelley's that had special significance for him at this time was the sonnet 'Lift not the painted veil'. When Russell first read it, he 'shuddered with mingled awe and sympathy'. Like *Alastor*, it concerns the glories and the dangers of searching after the truth, of trying to see beyond the 'painted veil' of appearance, behind which, says Shelley, lurk Fear and Hope: 'twin Destinies; who ever weave/Their shadows, o'er the chasm, sightless and drear'. The sonnet goes on to speak of one who *did* lift the veil, who sought things to love and things in which to believe, 'but found them not'. And so:

> Through the unheeding many he did move,
> A splendour among shadows, a bright blot
> Upon this gloomy scene, a Spirit that strove
> For truth, and like the Preacher found it not.

In imitation of this and of other works of Shelley's, Russell composed a sonnet around this time that shows how, having demolished his religious faith with science, he sought to rebuild it with poetry. Like *Alastor* and 'Lift not the painted veil', its theme is the pursuit of truth and a desire for 'something greater than this earth can give', some unattainable perfection. 'Trust in God', the poem advises:

> Who, as he gave thee thoughts which seek for him,
> Will, when this life's short struggle is no more,
> Fulfil thy noblest hopes and satisfy
> That restless striving after perfect life
> Which while thou liv'st doth ever drive thee on.

In an essay on language for his tutors at Southgate, Russell tried to convey something of what he found in Shelley. He spoke of Shelley's extraordinary ability to 'put into words the deepest emotions of a feeling soul', although, he added, 'it must always be true to some extent that "language is but a broken light on the depths of the unspoken." '[5]

Some hope that he might, after all, find a 'live human being' with whom he felt in sympathy came to him when he returned to Southgate in October 1888 to find a new student who, like himself, was preparing not for the army but for a mathematics scholarship at Cambridge, and who, in the company of the future army officers, looked conspicuously 'civilised'. He was shy, he kept his distance from the others, and he did not swear or talk smut; 'in short [he] appeared generally quiet and respectable'. His name was Edward Fitzgerald. In an effort to get to know him, Russell began to follow him when he walked back to his parents' house at Rutland Gate (a long walk from Southgate) and endeavoured to bump into him 'casually'. As both he and Fitzgerald were extremely shy, however, it took a long time for this to get anywhere, and it was not until they were thrown together by going three times a week to the same private tutor in mathematics – a man called Robson, who lived in Notting Hill – that their friendship began to blossom.

Like Russell, Fitzgerald combined a passionate interest in mathematics with a deep love of poetry, especially Shakespeare and Milton, and Russell began to think that he had at last met his ideal. 'Having been lonely so long', he later said, 'I devoted a somewhat absurd amount of affection to Fitzgerald.' He began, every weekend, to stop off at Fitzgerald's home before returning to Pembroke Lodge. His grandmother made discreet enquiries about the family, and was reassured to discover that they were friends of Robert Browning, and (therefore) all right. Browning was, in fact, an especial friend of Fitzgerald's sister, Caroline, who wrote poetry and whom Russell came to regard as 'the ideal of young womanhood'. In her, he wrote, 'I found liberalism in politics and religion, complete emancipation from vulgar prejudices, great culture and wide reading . . . Moreover I found (or thought I found) high moral aims in her, which I was willing to believe were reflected in him.'

Russell was, in short, in love with her, and his friendship with her brother grew in intensity as a result. In the summer of 1889, to his utter joy, he was invited by the Fitzgerald family to accompany them on a trip to Paris and Switzerland. It was Russell's first trip abroad, and a great delight to him. This being the year of the Paris Exhibition, one of his most lasting memories was of going to the top of the newly built Eiffel Tower. Then, in Switzerland, he and Edward Fitzgerald went mountain climbing together. The holiday should have cemented their friendship, but, in fact, it seemed instead to ruin it. One reason for this was Russell's disappointment at discovering that Caroline was to marry Lord Edmund Fitzmaurice later in the year. The hurt and

---

[5] A misquotation of a line from George Eliot's poem, *The Spanish Gypsy*: 'Speech is but broken light upon the depth/Of the unspoken.' The mistake is, I think, revealing: for Russell, as for Derrida (but for very different reasons), writing is the primordial form of language, especially in the attempt to express one's deepest feelings. Several times in his later career, Russell would emphasise the advantages of writing over speech (see, for example, *The Problem of China*, pp. 34–8, in which he discusses the merits of a non-phonetic writing system), and, of course, at this early stage in his life, he would not have attempted in speech to cast even a broken light on the 'depths of the unspoken'.

disappointment of this are still evident, fifty years later, in his description of her in his *Autobiography* as having turned into 'an unmitigated bore'.

Another reason for Russell's disenchantment with Fitzgerald – one emphasised in his diaries at the time – was his belief that Fitzgerald had misled him: 'He was not that ideal friend I have always looked for and still hope to find.' Russell felt betrayed. He believed that Fitzgerald had 'played upon my gullibility for his amusement by pretending to be very poetic and a great admirer, though not worshipper (as I then was), of nature'. What led Russell to think the sympathy he had felt with Fitzgerald was a pretence he does not say, but, by the time they returned to Southgate, his earlier warm affection had been replaced by a fierce and disillusioned hatred. They shared lodgings together and began to squabble violently. When Russell once scolded Fitzgerald for being rude to his mother, Fitzgerald 'was extremely angry, with a cold anger which lasted for months . . . he devoted himself to saying disagreeable things, in which he displayed great skill.' In a passage that recalls his description of the 'flame of hate' that burned in Dr Mallako, Russell writes: 'I came to hate him [Fitzgerald] with a violence which, in retrospect, I can hardly understand':

> On one occasion, in an access of fury, I got my hands on his throat and started to strangle him. I intended to kill him, but when he began to grow livid, I relented. I do not think he knew that I intended murder.

It was as if all the anger he had accumulated since childhood was suddenly released on to the unfortunate Fitzgerald, as if Fitzgerald were being blamed, not just for failing to live up to Russell's Shelleyesque ideal, for failing to remove his loneliness, but for that very loneliness itself. The incident obviously shook Russell more than it did Fitzgerald – which is why, I think, he adds that otherwise rather odd sentence 'I do not think he knew that I intended murder.' Clearly, Fitzgerald, turning purple with the pressure of Russell's hands around his neck, did not think this was a piece of fun. But what struck Russell – as it presumably did not strike Fitzgerald – was the force of the thought that he had really intended to kill him, that he had been just a hair's breadth away from being (like his Uncle Willy) a murderer. Deeply alarmed, Russell did everything he could after this to prevent Fitzgerald mattering to him any more. Superficially, they remained friends, but the depth of their friendship vanished as a result, one suspects, of Russell's fears at the forces of violence within him that had been released. A few months after the incident, Russell wrote in his diary:

> Poor Fitz! I never think of trying any serious subject with him now; he has been entirely spoilt by the conventional and unintellectual atmosphere of Southgate. I also have been spoilt by the unwholesome atmosphere of my own mind, so that I have helped to shut him up almost as much as he has me.

In the 'unwholesome atmosphere' of his mind lay thoughts that he no longer wished either to share or to preserve, and his diary from this time changes dramatically in character, becoming a more or less 'external' record of the day-to-day events in his life. Indeed, he lost the habit of introspection and self-revelation to such an extent that it began to worry him that his 'real' self was becoming lost from view, even to himself. 'The crust is growing so thick', he wrote, 'that I am almost beginning to doubt which is my real self.'

Some indication of how thick the crust was, and how successful he now was at hiding his deepest emotions, can be seen by the fact that, though he fell in love again in the autumn of 1889, soon after his disappointment with Caroline Fitzgerald, he kept it a secret, even to the woman concerned, until four years later. The woman in question was Alys Pearsall Smith, the daughter of a wealthy Quaker family from Philadelphia, who, in 1889, came to live in a large farmhouse called 'Friday's Hill', near Fernhurst, on the border between Surrey and Sussex. They thus became neighbours of Russell's Uncle Rollo, who, some years earlier, had bought a house at High Pitfold in the Hindhead hills, just north of Fernhurst. Every year, the entire Pembroke Lodge household would move to Rollo's house to spend the summer months in the country. One day in September, not long after his return from Paris, Russell was out walking with Rollo, when Rollo suggested that they call in on the Pearsall Smiths, to whom Lady Russell had already paid a neighbourly visit to introduce herself.

Alys was then twenty-two, five years older than Russell, intelligent, well-read and universally regarded as strikingly beautiful. She was a student at Bryn Mawr College, where she studied English and German literature, and had already published an article (a description of Bryn Mawr) in *The Nineteenth Century*. She was also manifestly a woman of 'high moral aims', interested in social reform and passionately devoted to the cause of temperance. As an 'ideal of young womanhood', she surpassed even Caroline Fitzgerald. Russell had, the morning he first met Alys, just finished a German book called *Ekkehard* and, when Alys, by coincidence, referred to it in their conversation and asked if he had read it, he took it as a good omen. 'I fell in love with her at first sight,' he says, though she neither knew nor suspected anything of the sort. Later in the month, she returned to the United States to finish her studies, and he returned to Southgate, and they did not see each other again for another year.

Having seen Caroline Fitzgerald taken away from him by marriage, Russell's strategy was evidently to keep his interest in Alys undisclosed, until such time as he was in a position to offer marriage himself. Thus, though over the next three summers, whenever he stayed with Rollo, he took every opportunity to accompany his uncle on visits to the Pearsall Smiths, he never gave any hint of his feeling for Alys until the summer of 1893, when he reached the age of twenty-one and became legally and financially independent. Until then, knowing that any interest he took in Alys would be frowned upon by his grandmother, and that he would be in a weak position to resist her pressure, he was content to bide his time.

In December 1889, Russell went to Cambridge to sit his scholarship exam. He stayed in rooms in New Court, Trinity, and was warmly welcomed by the Master of Trinity, H. Montagu Butler, who was rather a snob, and took pride

in having in his College the grandson of Lord John Russell and the son of
Lord Amberley, whom he remembered from having been Master of Harrow
during Amberley's time there. Russell was nervous, both at having to dine
with the Master and at having to sit the exam, but he did well enough to
get a minor scholarship, and returned to Pembroke Lodge relieved and
pleased.

During the nine months that remained before Russell could take up his
place at Trinity, he lived at Pembroke Lodge, and continued his preparations
by working a few hours each day on the kind of mathematics he would be
studying at Cambridge, practising his hand at old examination papers and
keeping up his studies with his private tutor, Robson, in Notting Hill, with
whom he went methodically and diligently – though without any discernible
enthusiasm – through J. E. Routh's *Rigid Dynamics*, a standard textbook at
the time. In later life, writing of this period, Russell claimed that he was
troubled by the fallaciousness of the proofs that he was asked to study. 'Those
who taught me the Infinitesimal Calculus', he writes in *My Philosophical
Development*, 'did not know the valid proofs of its fundamental theorems and
tried to persuade me to accept the official sophistries as an act of faith. I
realised that the calculus works in practice, but I was at a loss to understand
why it should do so. However, I found so much pleasure in the acquisition
of technical skill that at most times I forgot my doubts.' Later, he says that
he 'hoped sooner or later to arrive at a perfected mathematics which should
leave no room for doubts, and bit by bit to extend the sphere of certainty from
mathematics to other sciences'.

In the diary he kept at the time, however, there is no hint of these doubts
and hopes. He just records, in a matter-of-fact way, what parts of the text he
had worked on that day, what test papers he had attempted and whether he
had found the questions difficult or easy. The view of mathematics that
emerges is not the grand key to God's great plan of the 'Greek Exercises', but
a more humdrum affair of problems, exercises and techniques, presented
without either complaint or joy. However, this does not mean that his later
recollections are necessarily unreliable, for the diary as a whole is a pretty
mundane affair, written in a deliberate, self-consciously non-introspective
manner that generally steers well clear of any kind of emotional expression.
The most startling example of this comes on 20 June 1890, when Russell
records his first visit to the opera:

> . . . went up to meet Uncle Rollo at the Bedfords' box at Covent Garden.
> He brought Mr and Miss Pearsall Smith and two lady friends of theirs.
> The opera was Gounod's *Roméo et Juliette*. It was my first Opera, strange
> to say, and of course I enjoyed it immensely.

Leaving aside the less than rapturous response to his first experience of
opera, his reaction – or rather non-reaction – to seeing Alys, the girl with
whom he is in love and whom he has not seen for nearly a year, is downright
peculiar, and suggests (as does the whole diary) an effort to keep his emotions
under control and unexpressed as far as possible.

Another indication of this is that there is no mention at all in the diary (until he goes up to Cambridge) of his love for poetry, still less of his worship of nature, even though he was at this time reading a great deal of poetry – Shelley in particular – and even writing some. He had by now come to think that introspection – by which he meant not just self-analysis but any kind of concern with, or expression of, his own feelings – was somehow morally wrong.

Some relaxation comes on 14 July, when he records that he has been reading 'that wonderful chapter in *The Mill on the Floss* where Maggie finds Thomas à Kempis'. Reading about Maggie Tulliver's self-renunciation led Russell to wish that he himself could take to heart the lesson of *The Imitation of Christ* and achieve, like her, a 'sort of holiness'. But, he had to admit, he was not Maggie Tulliver. He had no faith, and 'though convinced of the truth of the blessedness of self-renunciation, I have not enough self-control nor enough steadiness of purpose to be able to practise it for any length of time. I always hanker after a fuller life, after a satisfaction of my highest wants which I know to be inconsistent with the highest life.' He had, he came to realise, been attempting a self-renunciation – of his religious doubts, of his deepest feelings – of which he was not capable:

I am convinced it is useless to try and crush out all the higher parts of my nature (besides being wicked and impious) as I have been trying to do since Christmas; I cannot permanently occupy my thoughts with work so exclusively as never to feel that there are other things needful; and the longer other thoughts are kept down, the wilder and the more painful they will be when they do arise.

Thus, to some extent released from their self-imposed bondage, his thoughts began once more to go where they would, and, inevitably, focused on the doubts about the existence of God, which, among other things, he had been suppressing. In his next diary entry – the last before he left for Cambridge – he announced with a note of tragedy, but also, one senses, with a sense of relief, that the question has at last been settled, that he has lost his religious faith entirely:

Alas! the only shred of faith I had left in me is, for the time at least, gone. I did believe in a Deity, and . . . derived immense comfort from the belief . . . But now! – I have begun to feel that the reasoning which always convinced me before . . . has lost its cogency.

His earlier view that the laws of nature required God as the law-giver had been demolished, he says, by his reading of John Stuart Mill's *Autobiography*. There, Mill recalls that his father had convinced him that the so-called 'First Cause' argument for the existence of God (which argues that the chain of cause-and-effect cannot go on for ever, and thus must terminate in a 'First Cause', that is, God) was invalid. The question 'Who made me?' cannot be answered, because, if the answer 'God' is given, then the question immediately arises 'Who made God?' Strictly speaking, this is a rather different argument from the one Russell had relied upon (you might, in the spirit of Russell's worship of nature, argue that God *is* the law of nature, without picturing Him as the first step in a causal chain). The fact that Russell was prepared to accept Mill's argument with such alacrity and finality suggests that, even before reading Mill, the conception he had of God as the 'controlling power' of the world had lost its hold on him.

This is not to say that Russell did not feel his loss of faith as a loss. He quite clearly did, for with it went, in some ways, a faith in the world itself. 'I doubt', he writes in the same diary entry, 'whether, if I do not regain my old faith, I shall long be able to hold out against the frightful thoughts that crowd in upon my mind':

> I remember an instant of the same pain at Southgate once in thinking of the sadness which is always suggested by natural beauty, when the idea flashed across my mind that when most in harmony with Nature I felt most sad, and that therefore the spirit of Nature must be sad and the Universe a mistake. Then I could not have borne it another instant, for though it came and went like a flash I felt as though I had been stabbed.

This is an intriguing and rather baffling passage. What it seems to be saying is that, stripped of his belief in God, he would not be able to resist any longer the thought that nature, the world itself, is sad; that, as it were, unhappiness is not just a temporary state of mind, but is, in some sense, the truth. But perhaps the thought he is really trying hard to drive from his mind – and to which he feels vulnerable without a belief in God – is that he himself is, despite the thick crust, fundamentally unhappy.

Before he left for Cambridge, Russell wrote another Shelleyesque sonnet, in which he tried to express some of the loss he felt at having finally given up his belief in God. It begins:

> How hateful is the light of day to me
> And all the weary tasks of daily life
> Without that faith which ever led me on
> And gave me hope through thickest clouds of pain!

Somehow, nature, the world, looked different, bleaker, now that he no longer saw it as divine. Later, in his *Autobiography*, he tried to explain the importance to him of his loss of faith:

> What Spinoza calls the 'intellectual love of God' has seemed to me the best thing to live by, but I have not had even the somewhat abstract God that Spinoza allowed himself to whom to attach my intellectual love. I have loved a ghost, and in loving a ghost my inmost self has itself become spectral . . . my most profound feelings have remained always solitary and I have found in human things no companionship. The sea, the stars, the night wind in waste places, mean more to me than even the human beings

I love best, and I am conscious that human affection is to me at bottom an attempt to escape from the vain search for God.

The love and companionship of human beings, even (perhaps, especially) those he loved best, were insufficient. It was too unreliable; they could leave you, or stop loving you, or die. Love, to mean anything, had to be eternal, infinite, always dependable. It had, that is, to be the love of God. But now this love, too, had deserted him. There, too, he had 'loved a ghost'.

2

CAMBRIDGE

In his famous ode, 'Intimations of Immortality', Wordsworth laments the fact that the 'splendid vision' – the view of the world that lends 'celestial light' to 'every common sight' – becomes increasingly difficult to maintain as we get older, until:

> At length the Man perceives it die away,
> And fade into the light of common day.

After he had been at Cambridge a few months, Russell quoted these lines in his diary to illustrate his own state of mind. 'I find myself daily becoming more vulgar and conventional,' he wrote. 'I read no poetry or literature of any sort, I do no thinking, [and] I can look with comparative indifference on natural beauty.' Indeed, he had degenerated to such an extent that 'even Agnosticism is become not unpleasant to me'.

The cause of this deterioration was a state of mind he had rarely experienced before, and to which he found difficulty in becoming accustomed: he was happy. He was surrounded by highly intelligent, well-educated young people, whose company he enjoyed, who seemed eager to become his friends, and with whom he could indulge to the full one of the greatest pleasures in life, of which he had previously been starved: conversation. He found that he 'could say things that I thought, and be answered with neither horror nor derision, but as if I had said something quite sensible'. It was 'intoxicating'. But, also, rather perplexing. It was too enjoyable. He worried that he was achieving 'happiness by brutification'. True, he felt that, in an ordinary sense, his mind was a 'thousand times healthier' than it had been before, but the nagging feeling persisted that, in its very ordinariness, this mental health signalled the death of something important. There was something rather worrying about becoming so normal, about being able at last to fit in so easily with the people around him. Happiness, he could not help feeling, 'is bad for moral and perhaps for intellectual health, and I have not yet found an antidote to these unwholesome conditions'.

Gradually, however, Russell gave up the search for an 'antidote' to happiness and began simply to enjoy himself, without suspecting that he was thereby, in the words of his grandmother's favourite biblical text, following a multitude to do evil. His diary thus falls silent for nearly two years, while he embraced the opportunities for friendship and society that had fallen into his lap.

The first close friend he made was Charles Sanger, who, like Russell, was at Trinity on a minor scholarship to read mathematics. Sanger's rooms were close to Russell's in Whewell's Court, and, according to Russell, the two became 'lifelong friends' after half an hour's conversation. They talked about mathematics, metaphysics, theology, politics and history. On most things they agreed, but that was far less important to Russell than the mere fact of their talking, of their mutual pleasure in each other's conversation.

Apart from Sanger – whom Russell met when he went to Sanger's rooms to deliver some lecture notes – most of the friends he made during this first year at Cambridge in 1890–1 came to him. They came, because Alfred North White-head, the mathematics don who had examined Russell, had been impressed by his ability and had told people to look out for him. From the moment he arrived, therefore, Russell was someone whom people wanted to get to know.

The closest friends, apart from Sanger, that he made in the first few months were Crompton and Theodore Llewelyn Davies, the two youngest members of a large family noted for its brilliance. There were six Llewelyn Davies brothers – sons of the radical churchman, the Reverend John Llewelyn Davies, who became famous for his outspoken attacks on imperialism – all but one of whom won scholarships to either Oxford or Cambridge. Frank had known one of them, Maurice Llewelyn Davies, at Balliol, and, like everyone, had been impressed by his cleverness, though still more by his steadfast refusal to swear: 'I recollect one occasion when, having spilled a cup of boiling tea over his leg, he got up hastily and merely said: "Dear me, how very unpleasant." ' Another brother, Arthur, became, like several of the family, a distinguished lawyer, but is better remembered as J. M. Barrie's 'Mr Darling' in *Peter Pan*. Their sister, Margaret, was a well-known political campaigner and became a close friend of Bertrand Russell through their joint work for women's suffrage.

Crompton and Theodore were devoted to each other, and shared rooms in college. Both brothers, Russell later recalled, were 'high minded and passion-ate', but it was Crompton with whom he became especially close friends. Crompton was, he said (in a description that echoes many of Russell himself): 'one of the wittiest men that I have ever known, with a great love of mankind combined with a contemptuous hatred for most individual men'. At that time Crompton was a passionate adherent to the economic doctrines of Henry George, who advocated a system in which all land-rent should be paid directly to the government. In his *Autobiography*, Russell mocks Crompton for this adherence, and for believing that this system could secure the benefits of socialism without its disadvantages, a belief he holds up as one of Crompton's endearing eccentricities. But, as he says earlier in the book,[1] he himself at this

---

[1] See p. 46: 'My Aunt Agatha introduced me to the books of Henry George, which she greatly admired. I became convinced that land nationalisation would secure all the benefits that Socialists hoped to obtain from Socialism, and continued to hold this view until the war of 1914–18', a passage Russell had evidently forgotten he had written by the time he came to describe Crompton Llewelyn Davies.

time believed in precisely the same doctrine for precisely the same reason, having been persuaded of it by his Aunt Agatha.

Another caller to his rooms, drawn by Whitehead's recommendation, was John McTaggart Ellis McTaggart, who was then a graduate and soon to become a Fellow of College, having been at Cambridge five years already. He was, when Russell first met him, President of the Union. Though he had not yet published his *Studies in the Hegelian Dialectic*, he was already regarded as one of the most distinguished of the younger generation of philosophers. He was renowned in particular for the subtlety of his metaphysics, in which he rejected the tradition of British empiricism in favour of the Absolute Idealism associated with Hegel and the great Oxford philosopher F. H. Bradley. Russell was at first 'in awe' of McTaggart because of his great reputation, but was nevertheless fascinated by his conversation, from which Russell learnt that the empiricist tradition in which he had grown up was now considered almost laughably old-fashioned. He was also astonished to discover that, though McTaggart did not believe in God, he did believe in immortality and in some kind of harmony between ourselves and the universe. McTaggart also believed in the unreality of space and time, and further claimed that all these beliefs were capable of being demonstrated with the strict rigour of a mathematical proof, though, 'the proof, he admitted, was long and difficult'. To Russell, all of this seemed strange and attractive, and, though he did not immediately become a convert, it remained for him, throughout his years as an undergraduate mathematician, an alluring promise of what philosophy might have to offer.

Another close and lasting friendship formed during this year was that with Robert Trevelyan, the second of three Trevelyan brothers, all of whom studied at Trinity. The eldest, Charles, who was then in his third year at Cambridge, Russell knew only slightly, but well enough for him to be a useful contact later on when he became a Member of Parliament. The youngest, George, is probably the best known of the three, becoming later in life a distinguished historian and Master of Trinity, but he did not come up until 1894. Robert, or 'Bob Trevy' as Russell called him, is scarcely known to the public at all, except as a very minor poet. Russell was enormously fond of him and was a regular guest at his home in Surrey, 'The Shiffolds', which, on several occasions in his later life, provided Russell with a peaceful retreat when he needed one.

Russell was slightly surprised at the love of good company he discovered in himself, and the changes in his character that it brought. 'I am now not perceptibly shy, I am fond of fairly agreeable society,' he wrote, as though he could hardly believe it. But, as he was forced to admit, it was practically perfect: 'my society is exactly what I should wish it; not very large, but almost entirely composed of men of ability.'

Much less to his taste was his academic work. In preparing to come to Cambridge, he had been willing to approach mathematics as the study of problems, puzzles and techniques, but now that he was there, he wanted something more profound. His interest in mathematics had always been motivated by the hope it seemed to offer of certain knowledge, first within mathematics and then, by extension, of the world of nature. His interest was thus in pressing ever more rigorously the question: 'How do we know this to be true?' Then, once one had a cast-iron foundation for mathematics, one might hope to use it as a basis upon which to build natural science and, then, a science of human behaviour. This was Russell's dream, his reason for being interested in mathematics in the first place, and it demanded first and foremost a willingness to submit conventional mathematics itself to sceptical questioning.

In this concern with the logical rigour of mathematics, Russell's thinking was marching with that of the times, which witnessed a burgeoning interest among mathematicians in replacing 'intuitive' proofs with more strictly logical ones, and in thus rebuilding the subject upon more secure foundations. Unfortunately, however, this trend had not yet reached Cambridge. If he had been studying mathematics at Halle, or Jena, or Göttingen, Russell would have had a chance to pursue exactly the questions that interested him, and would have been encouraged to study the work of Cantor, Weierstrass and Dedekind, which addressed itself to those questions. The mathematicians at Cambridge, however, knew little about this work. And, even had they known of it, they would not have offered courses on it. Mathematics at Cambridge in the 1890s was – as many pointed out at the time – something of a backwater. While the discipline at large (that is, in Germany) was becoming ever more analytic, the Mathematics Tripos at Cambridge remained wedded to a conception of the subject left over from the days of Newton, a conception that emphasised its physical applications and saw it less as an autonomous body of irrefutable truths than as a training in a series of useful techniques. Thus, while Russell had dreamed of asking and answering fundamental questions about the validity of mathematical knowledge, he found himself instead being trained in techniques for solving problems in geometrical optics and spherical astronomy, for example, 'two subjects of incredible dullness which I had to get up', as he later called them.

The problems with the syllabus were made far worse by the methods of examination and assessment. It was the custom at Cambridge to give the best students in mathematics a precise position in order of merit. The name 'Wrangler' was given to those who gained a first-class degree, and all Wranglers were ranked, so that one might emerge as 'Fourth Wrangler', or whatever. Anyone who wanted a career in Cambridge as a mathematician knew that they had better be among the top ten Wranglers, and it was thus crucially important to the whole system to have some way of ranking them precisely. The way they did this was to set far more problems on each exam paper than any student could possibly hope to complete, and also to set problems that had many different levels of complexity and sophistication and contained traps for the unwary, and so on. The consequence, Russell later said, was that 'the whole subject of mathematics was presented as a set of clever tricks by which to pile up marks in the Tripos. The effect of all this upon me was to make me think mathematics disgusting.'

What he saw of the mathematicians themselves did little to change this opinion. One of the most brilliant undergraduate mathematicians was a man called Percy Cory Gaul, who later became a mathematics don at Trinity Hall. 'Though a wonderful mathematician', Russell wrote of him, 'he is in every respect vulgar and childish and materialistic and selfish. It is a pity to see such a person brought to the fore by the cram system.' He was inclined to think that mathematicians should be made to sit a General Paper and not allowed to proceed unless they had scored a certain minimum in it: 'This would prevent the ignorant uncultured specialist from succeeding in the way he does now and would also . . . encourage general intelligence, which is to my mind far more useful than great knowledge entirely restricted to one subject.'

In those days, there were few mathematics lectures for undergraduates, and most of the teaching took the form of preparation for the Tripos examinations by a 'coach', whom one hired privately. Russell's coach was Robert Rumsey Webb of St John's, who seems however to have made little impression on him. Though Russell must have spent many hours in Webb's company over the three years he was studying for the Mathematics Tripos, the only time he mentions Webb in his autobiographical writings is in *Portraits from Memory*, when, after describing a don who was obviously insane but whom 'it never occurred to anyone to place . . . under restraint', he remarks laconically: 'My Mathematical Coach was not so fortunate. He went mad, but none of his pupils noticed it. At last he had to be shut up.'

Despite his passionate interest in mathematics, Russell was never entirely at home in the company of professional mathematicians: they were too narrow, too uncultured. Of the mathematics dons at Cambridge, the only one of whom he speaks with respect is Whitehead. He took Whitehead's course on statics, and spoke of him as 'extraordinarily perfect as a teacher', but Russell's admiration had as much, if not more, to do with Whitehead's general learning as with his knowledge of mathematics. Whitehead was, he recalled, 'a man of extraordinarily wide interests, and his knowledge of history used to amaze me.' Eleven years older than Russell, Whitehead was in many ways a thorough-going example of a Victorian scholar and gentleman: devoted to his country, loyal to authority and respectful of conventional pieties. His father had been a schoolmaster and then a clergyman in Kent, and Whitehead had been educated first at home and then at Sherborne, an old and distinguished school in Dorset, where he acquired the love of classical literature and of competitive sport (he was captain of both the cricket and football teams, as well as being Head Boy) that were then characteristic of the Victorian public schoolboy. At Cambridge, he was known to his contemporaries as a 'loner', entirely absorbed in mathematics and somewhat diffident socially, and though he had a lifelong love of Trinity College, it is probably true to say that his love of the Kent coast and of his school were greater. Strikingly, one of the qualities that Russell found most impressive and admirable about him was that: 'He was at all times deeply aware of the importance of religion.'

It was through Whitehead's advocacy that, in their second year, Russell and Sanger were elected to the Apostles, the 'Cambridge Conversazione Society', an élite discussion group that was, for Russell and for most of its members, the most important part of their Cambridge undergraduate lives. At any one time 'The Society' (as it was known to its members), consisted of no more than six or seven active members. It had a glorious past going back to the days of Tennyson and Hallam, and it was considered a great honour to be elected. Russell makes astonishingly large claims for it. 'It has existed since 1820,' he writes, 'and has had as members most of the people of any intellectual eminence who have been at Cambridge since then.' Actually, its membership was always rather narrower than this would suggest, and it is not difficult to think of Cambridge graduates of intellectual eminence who were not members (Charles Darwin and Thomas Macaulay are two examples that come readily to mind), but Russell's remark is revealing, I think, of how they saw themselves.

The circle of friends that Russell had made in his first year was (though he did not know it at the time) largely drawn from the Society: Theodore and Crompton Llewelyn Davies were both members, as was McTaggart, while Bob Trevy was elected the year after Russell. This was no coincidence. The chief reason they had befriended him was to assess his apostolic potential, a process that took some time and was deliberated upon with great intensity, for it was important to the Society that every member should be able to discuss intimate and important subjects with every other, that they should, in other words, all be close personal friends: 'It was a principle in discussion that there were to be no *taboos*, no limitations, nothing considered shocking, no barriers to absolute freedom of speculation.' The meetings were held every Saturday night, and, according to Russell, 'would generally end about one o'clock at night'. Even after that, however, 'I would pace up and down the cloisters of Neville's Court for hours with one or two other members.'

The Society generally elected two second-year students every year, and the election that year of two mathematicians was an exception, due to Whitehead's influence. In the main the members tended to be classicists (like the Llewelyn Davies brothers), historians or philosophers. Its two most influential members in Russell's day were probably McTaggart and Goldsworthy ('Goldie') Lowes Dickinson, a classicist from King's with whom Russell struck up a close friendship, despite being aware that in conversation 'I was liable to hurt him by my brutal statement of unpleasant truths.'

What did they talk about, these 'Apostles'? Virginia Woolf, in her biography of Roger Fry, probably sums it up correctly when she says: 'Politics and philosophy were their chief interests. Art was for them the art of literature; and literature was half-prophecy. Shelley and Walt Whitman were to be read for their message rather than for their music.' Russell's first paper for the Society certainly fits this pattern. Called 'Can We Be Statesmen?', it attempts to find an entirely rational basis for the settlement of political questions and concludes, regretfully, that no such thing is at yet achievable.

In Oxford an equivalently élite group would at this time have been discussing Nietzsche, Oscar Wilde, aestheticism and the 'Higher Sodomy', but Cambridge in the 1890s – if one can judge from the discussions of the Apostles – seems to have remained remarkably free from such *fin de siècle* preoccupations. Ten years later it made up for lost ground when the Apostles became dominated by Lytton Strachey and John Maynard Keynes, but, by then, and for that very reason, Russell had lost respect for it. Talking of the

Society during Strachey's period of domination, he says, 'homosexual relations among the members were for a time common, but in my day they were unknown.' This is an overstatement: Lowes Dickinson, for example, was unrepentantly and undisguisedly homosexual and had a deep, if unrequited, love for Roger Fry, while a few years before Russell's election, McTaggart had presented a paper called 'Violets or Orange Blossom?', in which he defended homosexual love. One historian of the Society, indeed, attributes the 'romantic idea of Apostolic homosexuality' to McTaggart and Lowes Dickinson rather than to Strachey and Keynes. It remains true, however, that the discussions in Russell's day had an earnestness and a public-spirited concern with political improvement that the Apostles later abandoned. 'We were still Victorian,' as Russell later put it, 'they were Edwardian.'

At the end of his second year, Russell spent the summer with his Uncle Rollo, who was now married to Gertrude Joachim, the sister of the Oxford philosopher Harold Joachim. During the summer, Russell got to know the Pearsall Smith family much better, and would walk the four miles to their house every Sunday to join them for lunch and dinner. Still, it seems, nobody suspected that he was in love with Alys. They welcomed him with open arms and were only too pleased to have him sit at their table, for, after all, he was Lord John's grandson, as Alys's father would proudly disclose to their other guests.[2] Russell, meanwhile, revelled in the freedom from restraint that existed at their house. 'To me, as to Goethe,' he wrote, 'America seemed a romantic land of freedom, and I found among them an absence of many prejudices which hampered me at home':

After supper they would make a camp fire in the woods, and sit round singing negro spirituals, which were in those days unknown in England.

It was on these visits to Friday's Hill that Russell first got to know well the Spanish-American philosopher George Santayana, to whom he had earlier been introduced by Frank in London. 'As I got to know him better,' Russell recalled, 'I found some sympathy and much divergence . . . towards me, as towards other northern philosophers, his attitude was one of gentle pity for having attempted something too high for us.' Russell appreciated Santayana's suave and meticulous style, which found expression in the way he dressed and the way he talked, no less than in his writing, but he found it somehow 'not quite what a style should be. Like his patent leather boots, it is too smooth and polished.' Once, when he was about to leave for Spain, Santayana remarked to Russell: 'I wish to be in a place where people do not restrain their passions.' 'I suppose this attitude is not surprising', Russell commented, 'in one who had so few passions to restrain.'

---

[2] One might have expected Russell, on occasion at least, to have expressed some irritation at being regarded wherever he went as 'Lord John's grandson', but, if he did, there is no sign of it either in the surviving correspondence or in any of the vast number of autobiographical writings he produced throughout his life.

Russell had by now decided to drop mathematics after he had taken the Part I exams and to concentrate on philosophy, taking Part II of the Moral Sciences Tripos. With just one more year left of his despised Mathematics Tripos, therefore, he was eager to begin reading philosophy. Towards the end of the summer, he received advice from Rollo's brother-in-law, Harold Joachim, who lived nearby and with whom Russell occasionally played tennis. (It probably requires an effort of the imagination to picture Bertrand Russell playing tennis, but his letters of this period are sprinkled with allusions to his doing so.) Russell had evidently asked Joachim for a few suggestions on what to read. He received in reply a long list that included Plato, Descartes, Leibniz, Spinoza, Hume, Locke, Berkeley and Kant, '& by that time', Joachim added, 'you will know much more about it than I do.' Joachim, like McTaggart, was an adherent of the neo-Hegelian school of philosophers, a partisanship that emerges most strongly in his advice on what to read on logic. J. S. Mill's *Logic*, he begrudgingly admitted, had to be read, though it as 'full of fallacies'. Bradley's *Principles of Logic*, on the other hand, was 'first rate – but very hard', and Bosanquet's *Logic* 'good, but still harder'.

When he returned to Cambridge, Russell made a start on Joachim's list, beginning at the beginning with Plato. Buying a second-hand copy of Jowett's translation of the dialogues, he started with the *Symposium* and *Theaetetus*. 'It is really delightful', he wrote to Rollo, 'to get philosophy presented in an easy amusing conversational form, and yet not feel as one does with most French books that the arguments are superficial – such a contrast to the lumbering Germans.' The next month, he started on Hume's *A Treatise of Human Nature*, and seemed to be showing every intention of working his way through the entire list. The Mathematics Tripos, however, was notorious for the amount of training one had to do for it, and in this last year the pressure of work increased enormously. It was not a good time to attempt to read the entire canon of philosophical classics, and word went round that Russell's work in mathematics was beginning to suffer, that he might not, for all his promise, get a first. He was sent for by the philosophy don James Ward, who told him that 'a Wrangler is a Wrangler':

> From this instance of the law of identity he drew the inference that I had better read no more philosophy till after my mathematical Tripos.

For the moment, Russell followed Ward's advice and gave up his extra-curricular philosophical studies and devoted himself, increasingly against his natural inclination, to mathematics.

Towards the end of the Michaelmas Term, on 5 December 1892, Russell's diary comes to life again with an isolated entry that is the most enigmatic of the whole book: a desperate prayer for forgiveness to the God he no longer believes in:

> 1 a.m. O God forgive me; I have sinned grievously. What the others did, that I did also for fear lest I should seem to set myself up above them, for

fear lest I should seem a prig . . . How weak and foolish seem now the paltry motives, the mean fears which I vainly endeavoured to mistake for a broad-minded freedom from prejudice . . . Ah! My God in Thy mercy . . . grant that I may henceforth have strength to stand out against the insidious advances of folly, to draw the line justly between harmless merriment and vicious jesting. May I no more do that which in my heart I abhor to win the paltry and ephemeral good will of those whose respect I forfeit by the very course which deference to them has led me into . . . Give it to me O Lord, if thou canst, to stand out from the follies of my friends no less than from the vices of my enemies; to resist the intoxication of mirth and preserve a sane mind among pleasures as among sorrows.

It was a Sunday, and presumably Russell had been to College chapel, as was then compulsory, and perhaps there, prompted by the sermon, he had come to some sort of realisation about himself, come to see himself once more through the eyes of a devout and stern morality. But what, exactly, had he done? The prayer offers few clues: something to do with 'the intoxication of mirth', with taking jesting beyond 'harmless merriment' into viciousness, something that his friends did and from which they derived pleasure. What clues there are point to its being a very minor transgression, which somehow Russell's acute sense of sin lighted upon and inflated into a 'grievous sin', though the extraordinary and unprecedented depth of his remorse suggests otherwise.

A happier event – though one whose details are equally lost to history – was his first meeting with G. E. Moore, who that year was a freshman, having come up to Trinity from Dulwich College to begin Part I of the Classics Tripos. Moore came from a large family, which, having lived in Hastings at the time of his birth, had moved to the London suburb of Upper Norwood to be within walking distance of Dulwich. His father, like his grandfather before him, was a doctor, and successful enough to retire soon after he moved to Norwood and yet still provide comfortably for his eight children. Of these, Moore was probably closest to his older brother Tom, later well-known as Thomas Sturge Moore, the poet and wood-engraver. In his youth, Moore was famously beautiful and charismatic. Like Russell, he had been earmarked as a potential Apostle by his scholarship examiner, in this case by the classicist A. W. Verrall, who, as Whitehead had done for Russell, told the younger Apostles to look out for Moore. The first friend Moore made in this way was Bob Trevy, and eventually – though it seemed to take longer in Moore's case than in Russell's – this led to his becoming known to most of the undergraduate members of the Society. Russell almost certainly got to know him through Trevelyan, and was, from the first, attracted to Moore by 'the clarity and passion of his thinking, and by a kind of flame-like sincerity which roused in me deep admiration'. Moore, at this time, had little interest in philosophy, and the admiration he excited in Russell, as in almost everybody who met him, owed its origins primarily to his personality and even, to some extent, to his appearance. Russell describes him as 'beautiful and slim, with a look almost of inspiration' and 'a kind of exquisite purity'.

In May 1893, Russell took his Part 1 exams. He was placed Seventh Wrangler (Sanger beat him, being placed second), which was better than had been feared, and something of a relief to Russell, who was only too pleased to be done with the subject. 'When I had finished my Tripos', he wrote, 'I sold my mathematical books and made a vow that I would never look at a mathematical book again.'

3
THE CORPSE IN THE CARGO

In the summer of 1893, Russell's shedding of his past did not end with the symbolic gesture of selling his mathematics books. On 18 May, in the middle of his mathematics exams, he celebrated his twenty-first birthday. This had for him far more than a merely conventional importance; it put his whole life on a different footing. First of all, it meant that his grandmother and his Uncle Rollo were no longer his legal guardians, and second, he inherited £20,000 from his father's estate, giving him an annual income of around £600 – not a fortune, but quite enough to live on. Both legally and financially, therefore, he was now independent. Emotionally, of course, things were more complicated, but, there too, he was determined to break the hold over him of Pembroke Lodge.

He made a start by staying in Cambridge during the summer vacation rather than returning to Pembroke Lodge. Ostensibly, this was to concentrate on his preliminary reading in philosophy, though, in fact, he did little serious study until term started in October, and he devoted the summer instead to more general reading, to theatre-going, and to a single-minded campaign to persuade Alys Pearsall Smith to marry him.

His coming of age and his completion of the Tripos, he was to say later, combined to give him 'an exhilarating sense of liberation and a readiness for adventure'. It was as if, after having had his head buried in his studies for years, he could now look up and take notice of the world around him. Whereas previously he had been content to find literary and religious inspiration in the poetry of his grandparents' generation, now he began to acquaint himself with the culture of the 1890s. The writers he read that summer were those associated with revolt, those of whom he could comfortably assume the older generation would disapprove. Of these, the most important for him were Ivan Turgenev, Walt Whitman and Henrik Ibsen.

'I felt then', he wrote, speaking of this summer, 'that anything hated by conventional, middle-aged people must be good.' In Turgenev's *Fathers and Sons*, for example, he admired the character of Bazarov, the personification of Nihilist revolt, who fiercely rejects the very basis of conventional morality. 'There are no general principles', Bazarov exclaims:

There are feelings. Everything depends on them. I, for instance, take up a negative attitude by virtue of my sensations: I like to deny – my brain's made on that plan, and that's all about it! Why do I like chemistry? Why do you like apples? – by virtue of our sensations. It's all the same thing. Deeper than that men will never penetrate.

It was not that Russell was persuaded of the truth of this as a theory of ethics, but rather that he admired the 'delightfully horrifying' personality required to utter such a dreadful thing. Still, try as he might, he could not see himself as Bazarov and felt more affinity with the amiable and aristocratic Arkady, to whom Bazarov remarks: 'You're a capital fellow; but you're a sugary, Liberal snob for all that.' When he read that, Russell said, 'I trembled at the thought that Bazarov might consider me a "sugary, Liberal snob", which I thought very probable.'

In Walt Whitman's *Leaves of Grass*, Russell saw sexual desire expressed with a frankness he had scarcely thought possible. Here was a man who did not convey eroticism indirectly, with talk of the voluptuous panting of spring, but who came right out with it; who did not tremble with fear at the prospect of lifting the veil, but who, as it were, pulled the veil right off, as much as to say 'what are you frightened of?':

Through me forbidden voices,
Voices of sexes and lusts, voices veil'd and I remove the veil
Voices indecent by me clarified and transfigur'd

I do not press my fingers across my mouth,
I keep as delicate around the bowels as around the head and heart,
Copulation is no more rank to me than death is.

The effect of lines like these upon Russell – who previously had nearly swooned when his teacher used the word 'breast' – was electrifying, and served to confirm him in his view of America as 'a land of promise for lovers of freedom'. Whitman – or 'Walt', as Russell always called him, conferring upon him the intimacy of a close friend – became one of his idols. The first place he visited when he went to America three years later was the house in which Whitman had lived. It was a gesture of respect and gratitude for Whitman's having brought out into the open, and declared healthy and normal, desires that, by the spring of 1893, had become so strong in Russell that he considered them a threat to his sanity. In his *Autobiography*, he tells how while at Cambridge he used to 'career round the country in a state of temporary lunacy' on moonlit nights, and claims: 'The reason, of course, was sexual desire, though at that time I did not know this.' What he meant, perhaps, was that he did not admit it, even to himself. Reading Whitman gave him courage, allowed him to see sexual desire neither as wickedness nor as lunacy, but simply as sexual desire; or, as Whitman put it, in lines that throughout this period Russell liked to quote in illustration of a 'sane and healthy' attitude:

Without shame the man I like knows and avows the deliciousness of his sex,
Without shame the woman I like knows and avows hers.

After the stuffiness and morbidity of Pembroke Lodge, such forthrightness
came to Russell like the fresh air from an opened window.

Lady Russell, of course, would have been quite scandalised at the thought
of her grandson reading such stuff. Her enjoyment even of Shakespeare was
marred by his 'coarseness' ('I never can understand the objections to
Bowdlerism,' she once wrote. 'It seems to me so right and natural to prune
away what can do nobody any good – what it pains the eyes to look upon and
ears to hear'). Now she quite despaired of what she called 'the modern
attraction of ugly subjects'. In this, she was not alone. In the early 1890s a
fierce controversy raged over the 'candid foulness', the 'loathsome and fetid
offal' that was being inflicted on the public in the name of literature. At the
centre of this controversy, and the target for much of the strongest abuse,
were the plays of Henrik Ibsen (the quotations above come from contemporary reviews of Ibsen's play, *Ghosts*). To admire Ibsen in 1893 was to identify
oneself with a rebellion against conventional standards of propriety, to ally
oneself with a movement that rejected polite squeamishness and insisted on
exposing the dark secrets, and revealing the hidden truth, both about
individuals and about society. It was a movement that was threatening or
exhilarating, depending largely on one's age.

For Russell, it was a trend that perfectly matched his mood of rejoicing in
a sense of liberation from the past, and he took great delight in the affront to
respectable sensibilities that Ibsen represented. He treasured in particular a
remark that Whitehead brought to his attention from a hostile review of an
Ibsen play published in the *Cambridge Review*: 'Life presents no problems
to serious and well-conducted persons.' As a summary of the view with
which he was in rebellion, this was perfect, and Russell never tired of quoting
it.

While the controversy raged over Ibsen's morality, the demand to see
his work increased enormously, and his plays dominated the London
stage throughout the summer of 1893. The productions that Russell
sought out were those starring the great actress, Elizabeth Robins. He saw her
play Helda Wangel in *The Master Builder*, Rebecca West in *Rosmersholm*
and Hedda Gabler, all within a few weeks. He also read during this time
most of Ibsen's major plays. Though, much later, he was rather critical of
Ibsen, calling him a 'preacher of bad morals', at this time -- precisely
because of their 'bad morals' – Ibsen's plays 'excited me in a very high
degree'.

The play that was especially notorious, and the one that did most to offend
the sensibilities of 'serious and well-conducted persons', was *Ghosts*, the
theme of which could hardly have failed to capture the imagination of the
twenty-one-year-old Russell. The play, like much of Ibsen's work, concerns
the ways in which our lives are dominated by the past, by the spectral
influence of dead people, discarded ideas, and repressed and unacknowledged
feelings. Its plot consists of a series of revelations that are, in G. Wilson

Knight's memorable phrase, 'like the unwinding of a corpse's wrappings', an image that recalls Ibsen's own famous remark: 'We sail with a corpse in the cargo.'

The play tells the story of Osvald Alving, an artist who has had to stop working because he has begun to show symptoms of a dreadful illness of the brain. He never knew his father, but, on the basis of a 'beautiful illusion' that his mother worked hard to maintain, has always believed him to have been an entirely admirable man, who achieved much that was 'good and useful' before his untimely death. Actually, as Osvald discovers when his mother decides finally to tell him the truth, his father was completely dissolute, and it is because of his dissolution that Osvald has inherited the disease that is rotting his brain. Before he discovers the truth about his father, but already knowing himself to be dying, Osvald seduces a local girl called Regina, who, he hopes, will help him die by administering morphine to him before his mind deteriorates too far. But, in the final revelation of the play, he discovers that Regina is actually his half-sister, another 'ghost' from his father's past. He is left with his loving mother, who refuses however to allow him to kill himself, and so the play ends with Osvald facing a slow, horrible death.

One aspect of this bleak story that has particular resonance in the context of Russell's life is its emphasis on Osvald's suffering as the result of both conventional piety and (still more deadly) well-intentioned familial love and kindness. In *Rosmersholm* – a play that is, if anything, still more resonant with echoes of Russell's life – this familial love is represented as a force that strips people of their vitality and their passion. The title means 'Rosmer's island', and refers to the ancient home of a family that has been celebrated for its good deeds and its piety for several generations. Into this family comes a strong, passionate woman called Rebecca West, who falls in love with Rosmer himself.

Like *Ghosts*, the plot of *Rosmersholm* centres on the unravelling of a dark secret from the past. It begins after Rosmer's wife has committed suicide, and it is revealed that she did so because Rebecca, in the grip of her 'wild, uncontrollable passion' for Rosmer, deliberately led her into it, by telling her that she and Rosmer were having an affair and that she was pregnant with Rosmer's child. Before he discovers this, Rosmer proposes to Rebecca, but is refused. Why, he asks, after learning her secret, did she turn him down, if that is what she was scheming for? Because, Rebecca answers, since coming to live at Rosmersholm she has become so affected by its atmosphere of 'great selfless love' that she no longer has any desire to pursue her own ends; her 'ugly passion' has, under Rosmer's own influence, been replaced by a quiet, selfless gentleness. 'The Rosmers' view of life', she tells him, 'has infected my will . . . And made it sick. Subjected it to laws that meant nothing to me before. You – the life shared with you – has made my mind nobler.' Rosmer brightens at the word 'noble', but is immediately told: 'The Rosmer view of life does ennoble. But . . . but – but . . . it kills joy.'

In all these plays, it is strong, passionate women that offer escape from the life-denying forces of conventional morality and familial love. In this way, the parts played by Elizabeth Robins were, for Russell, embodiments of his own fantasies of being released from the confines and restrictions of his past by a woman unfettered by conformity to tradition.

Alys Pearsall Smith was no Rebecca West or Hedda Gabler, but, as a middle-class American on friendly terms with Walt Whitman, she was bound to seem to Russell enticingly free from the tradition of aristocratic Whig piety in which he had been brought up. Her family, too, showed promising signs of being 'not quite nice'. Her father, Robert Pearsall Smith, for example, had been involved in a widely publicised sex scandal in the 1870s, which put an end to a hitherto successful career as a charismatic evangelist, which he had built up in Europe, following his nervous breakdown in America in 1872. At the root of the scandal was what his wife, Hannah, called: 'the subtle doctrine concerning the physical manifestation of the Holy Spirit'. Taking the image of Christ as the Bridegroom of his followers to its literal conclusion, Robert preached that religious holiness, the divine inspiration of the Holy Spirit, was a kind of consummation so akin to the sexual kind that it could be brought about by sexual submission to one already inspired. This was bad enough, but when evidence began to accumulate that he practised what he preached, invitations to religious conventions were suddenly withdrawn and he was forced to flee to America from the ensuing scandal. By the time he returned to England a decade later and settled in Friday's Hill, he had lost his faith altogether, and generally kept a low profile for fear of arousing too many memories.

Alys's sister, Mary, had defied conventional morality more openly by choosing to leave her husband, Frank Costelloe, and her two daughters, Ray and Karin, to live with her lover, Bernhard Berenson, in Italy. It was through Mary that the family had got to know Walt Whitman. She was an early admirer of Whitman's poetry, and, spiritedly rejecting her mother's view that Whitman had 'written more grossly indecent things than perhaps any other man', had sought and won his friendship, eventually winning the whole family round to an admiration of the man, if not his poetry. Their brother, Logan, had been at Balliol studying classics, and was something of an aesthete, from whom Russell 'learned the right thing to say about Manet, and Monet, and Degas', and who now divided his time between the 'artists' quarter' of Paris, where he became friends with Roger Fry and James McNeil Whistler, and London, where he mixed with Fabian Socialists.

The mother, Hannah, was less promising. The most devout of the family, she was famous as the author of *The Christian's Secret of a Happy Life*, a best-selling guide to 'holiness'. Even she, however, could hardly be described as conventional. She gloried in the title 'heretic' bestowed on her for her unshakeable belief in the so-called 'Doctrine of Restitution', the view that denies Hell and damnation and insists that every soul is destined for salvation; and, when her letters were published, the title her son chose for them was *A Religious Rebel*. Hers was a 'religion of love' of a more emphatic kind even than Lady Russell's, though Hannah herself was something of a firebrand, devoting herself to the causes of women's suffrage and temperance with a ferocious zeal and moralistic fervour. She espoused a kind of feminism that saw women as virtuous, men as wicked, and male homosexuality as one of the worst sins imaginable. One of her closest friends was Lady Henry Somerset, the President of the British Women's Temperance Association, who caused a public scandal by insisting on a legal separation from her husband after she discovered his homosexuality.

In polite society, Lady Somerset was *persona non grata*, but in Hannah's eyes she was a heroine and her story an illustration of the 'monstrous sins' of which men were capable. When, during Oscar Wilde's first trial, it looked as if the jury might not be able to reach a verdict, Hannah was horrified at the prospect that Wilde's 'indecency' would go unpunished, and felt inclined to think that 'judge and jury are all guilty of the same thing, and dare not convict him'. At the next British Women's Temperance Association, she therefore put forward a resolution 'that all men should be castrated'. It was, she argued, 'the only effectual remedy I know'.

Had Russell known these attitudes of Hannah's in 1893, he might have taken warning from them. As it was, his image of the Pearsall Smiths as champions of tolerance, freedom and independence was untarnished, and he began his campaign to marry Alys just a few days after he had completed his Tripos exams by inviting her to Cambridge. To his delight she accepted, and, on 9 June, he, Alys and a cousin of hers went boating on the Cam. It was the day Russell received his examination results, and Alys asked him, in connection with his news of becoming a Wrangler, whether this was not the happiest day of his life. 'To suppose a miserable Tripos List could make me happy!' he confided in his diary. 'And yet I could not undeceive her.'

He did not see her again for two months, but the seriousness of his intentions – along with much else – is revealed in a dream he recorded on 21 July:

> I dreamt last night that I was engaged to be married to Alys, when I discovered that my people had deceived me, that my mother was not dead but in a madhouse: I therefore had of course to give up the thought of ever marrying. This dream haunts me.

Reading this dream, one sees why Ibsen's plays struck such a deep chord. The sense of sailing with a corpse in the cargo was one Russell had had for a long time, perhaps for as long as he could remember. And his grandmother's sensitivity to any mention of madness, together with her dark hints about his mother, made the 'revelation' in the dream the most natural guess as to what that 'corpse' was. But why does he think that, if his mother was mad, then he would 'of course' have to give up the thought of ever marrying?

An answer is provided in a paper he wrote at this time on marriage. It is called 'Die Ehe', and appears to have been written specially for Alys, who must during their meeting in June have voiced some general objections to the very idea of marriage (without, perhaps, realising the importance that Russell attached to the topic). Russell's strategy seems to have been to convince her, first that marriage is not, in any general or theoretical way, objectionable and then to persuade her, in particular, to marry *him*. It is courtship conceived as philosophical debate, and, surprisingly perhaps, it was entirely successful.

The problem addressed by the essay is that the strong, independent sort of women with advanced, modern views – the women, that is, that were Russell's ideal as potential wives – were, on the whole, precisely those women who objected most to the slavery of marriage. How was one to overcome this problem? Russell's answer is that one should outwardly conform to the expectations of a conventional marriage, but privately subvert them, for 'bad customs are best altered by submitting to them in act, while rebelling against them in speech'. His reasons for this are that men and women, especially progressive men and women, should not have to undergo a 'monkish celibacy', and yet, if such people are not to be paralysed by scandal, it is out of the question for them to indulge in 'extra-connubial sexual intercourse'. They thus need to marry.

But Russell has another argument that makes marriage between intelligent, liberal people not just necessary for their well-being, but a moral duty. And this is that such people have an obligation to bear children, for their children 'are almost certain to be centres of liberalism and to advance the cause of unprejudiced opinion and of toleration'. It follows from this that if, on the contrary, they have reason to think that their children will be lunatics, of no use to society at all and rather a burden upon it, then they have a duty not to get married. The 'ghost' raised by his dream, then – the idea that there might be hereditary madness in his family – was one that cut at the root of this argument, and, more deeply and more importantly, of the hopes he had for marriage to Alys.

Writing about the women he admired in Ibsen's plays, Russell said he had 'read with delight Walt Whitman's praise of "the brawny and arrogant woman I love" ' and that he considered Ibsen's women to 'approximate to this type'. Interestingly, therefore, his paper on marriage for Alys opens with the Whitman poem 'Unfolded Out of the Folds', from which that line comes. In its context here, the poem becomes a plea to Alys to enable Russell to realise his true potential:

> Unfolded out of the strong and arrogant woman I love only thence can appear the strong and arrogant man I love.
> Unfolded by brawny embraces from the well-muscled woman I love, only thence comes the brawny embrace of the man.
> Unfolded out of the folds of the woman's brain come all the folds of the man's brain duly obedient.
> A man is a great thing upon earth and through eternity but every jot of the greatness of man is unfolded out of woman.

'I think of Alys all day long,' Russell wrote on the day he recorded his dream. And yet, up to now, he had still not given her any indication of his feelings towards her. When Alys next visited Cambridge, again with her cousin, on 12 August, Russell moved a step closer to his goal by presenting her with 'Die Ehe' ('my little essay on the immorality of not marrying if in any way above the average', as he described it in his diary), and by persuading her to accompany him on a boat trip without her chaperone. It was, he wrote that night, 'the greatest day of my life hitherto'. They discussed love and marriage, still ostensibly in general terms, but, Russell noted, 'whether she remained blind to my feelings throughout I know not: I fear I hinted them unintentionally once or twice.' On the face of it, they were still exchanging theoretical views; Russell advancing the opinion that love was the only thing ultimately worth having, and Alys arguing for the value of independence:

We agreed to a large extent that marriage gave the best opportunity for . . . spiritual love, and that a pure friendship between man and woman is impossible. But I found, what I had always imagined in women, an aversion to sexual intercourse and a shrinking from it only to be overcome by the desire for children.

This aversion was a severe disappointment, as was the discovery that Alys strongly disapproved of her sister's behaviour in leaving her husband for Berenson. Until now, Russell had pictured Alys as an advocate of free love. He nevertheless saw no reason to abandon his campaign just when it was beginning to bear fruit, and was encouraged by Alys's suggestion that they meet again, and by her consent to his suggestion that they continue their argument about marriage through correspondence.

By now, it was surely clear to Alys (if it had not been all along) that Russell had more than a theoretical interest in debating the nature of love and marriage with her, and he was probably overdoing things a little when he brought neo-Hegelian metaphysics to bear on the issue. McTaggart had recently had privately printed a declaration of his views entitled *The Further Determination of the Absolute*, which was read by all the Apostles and exerted a tremendous influence on that whole generation of Cambridge intellectuals, not least upon Russell himself. Trying to sum up his entire *Weltanschauung*, McTaggart asks: 'What is the concrete and material content of such a life as this? What does it come to?' and answers:

I believe it means one thing, and one thing only – love . . . When I have explained that I do not mean benevolence, even in its most impassioned form, not even the feeling of St Francis, I shall have cut off one probable explanation of my meaning. When I add that I do not mean the love of Truth, or Virtue, or Beauty, or any other word that can be found in the dictionary, I shall have made confusion worse confounded. When I continue by saying that I mean passionate, all-absorbing, all-consuming love, I shall have become scandalous. And when I wind up by saying that I do not mean sexual desire, I shall be condemned as hopelessly morbid.

When Russell and Alys got back from their boating trip, he had intended to show her this passage, but found that he had mislaid the book. When he found it, he sent it to her, telling her that he had 'come to the conclusion that all that is important is straightforward and that is hard . . . is unimportant'. McTaggart's conception of love in this passage had an enormous influence on Russell, but it is one that one sees less in his relationships with others than in his philosophical outlook. If one wanted to preserve Lady's Russell's 'religion of love' in the absence of a personal God – and if one further wanted to combine that 'love of God' with the view Russell had had since a teenager of the world as a law-governed whole, the laws of which might one day be known with absolute certainty – then what one would finish up with would be the view McTaggart outlines in this pamphlet.

For the next four weeks, Russell and Alys exchanged their views, keeping up the pretence that their arguments were purely theoretical and disinterested, with Russell continuing to use McTaggart as an authority, the rigour of whose arguments could not be withstood. 'It is a dangerous fallacy to suppose virtue an end in itself,' Russell wrote on 19 August. 'In McTaggart's pamphlet . . . he says (and proves) that there can be no virtue in heaven.' By 25 August, he felt that he was winning the argument. 'I am confident of converting her in time with patience and conversation,' he wrote in his diary on 25 August, 'but then will be only the time to begin what is important to me':

Ah when shall I be able to speak, and will she be horrified and regard all my present conduct as selfish and me as a fool? For me no happy issue I am sure is possible. But to resist is now become impossible to me. I no longer tear up her letters with a gulp and a jerk as I used to do, but treasure them up, and read them constantly. Fool! Fool! Fool!

Alys could no doubt see where all this was leading as well as – or, quite likely, better than – Russell himself. When he next visited Friday's Hill, on 13 September, she took him up to the tree-house that her father had built in order to meditate (it was called the Bo-Tree House, after the tree under which the Buddha had found enlightenment), where she could talk to him undisturbed, and there she made plain to him her grasp of the situation. 'I think if I were conscientious,' she told him, 'I should put an end to this friendship, for your sake; but I care about it too much myself.'

'You couldn't do that,' Russell replied, 'it's the only thing that makes life valuable to me.'

'Well, fortunately I'm not conscientious.'

It was as much reassurance as he needed, and he immediately confided in her the dream he had had in July. It amounted to a proposal of marriage, and was understood as such by Alys, who told him, 'I wish you would put away the thought of marriage: friendship is so much nicer, I don't want to marry, at least for a long time.' On the other hand, more encouragingly, she said, 'We ought to see each other oftener if we are ever to think of it.' The following morning, they took a walk together in the woods before breakfast, and she began by telling him that she was not yet convinced either by the permanence of his feelings ('people develop so much after your age') or by the strength of her own. 'Yes,' replied Russell, 'I think it would be wrong not to wait years before marriage.' She, however, wanted to be sure that Russell was entering the relationship with his eyes open: 'You see if we were to grow very very intimate and I not to fall in love with you at the end it would give you such intense pain.' They resolved to meet as often as possible and to try and get to know each other as intimately as possible ('as we of course both feel that without great intimacy it is folly to become engaged'), with a view, some time in the future, if all went well, to announcing their engagement. 'All is accomplished,' Russell wrote in his diary, 'my wildest hopes had not imagined such success.'

Russell perhaps exaggerated at this stage how much he *had* achieved, for there are signs that, for a few days at least, he was misled by this talk of 'intimacy' to expect a covert sexual relationship. In his diary he curses 'the conventions necessitated by folly and bestiality', and writes that he and Alys have to disregard such conventions 'if we are to act honestly', and yet 'ought not, however we might desire it, *openly* disregard them, as this would lessen our influence and power of doing good and would besides cause both her relations and mine considerable pain, and be completely misunderstood':

Hence concealment and all its attendant dangers. However I have practised it so long at home that I must by now be inoculated against its bad effects. Oh that there could be one morality for the prudent and one for the fools!

A day or two later, he sent Alys, in illustration of his own feelings, Walt Whitman's poem of sexual anticipation, 'One Hour to Madness and Joy', describing it as 'true but immoral'. The poem expresses the rapture Russell must have felt at the thought that he was on the brink of satisfying his sexual desires:

O to be yielded to you whoever you are, and you to be yielded to me in defiance of the world!
O to return to Paradise! O bashful and feminine!
O to draw you to me, to plant on you for the first time the lips of a determn'd man
. . .
To have the gag remov'd from one's mouth!
. . .
To court destruction with taunts, with invitations!
To ascend, to leap to the heavens of the love indicated to me!
. . .
To feed the remainder of life with one hour of fullness and freedom!
With one brief hour of madness and joy.

Alys's response to this was not what he had hoped. Her friendship with Whitman, Russell now discovered, did not imply approval of his sexual openness. On the contrary, in the edition of *Leaves of Grass* that Whitman had presented to her, Alys had cut out the entire 'Children of Adam' section, the part that contains the most sexually explicit poems in the book, and from which this particular poem was taken.

'I am glad you don't like the Walt,' Russell lied in his next letter, after receiving her disapproving reaction. 'I don't either. It was really rather an excess of honesty to represent it as expressing what my feelings had ever been':

> but in any case I cannot see why one should be ashamed of any feeling which has not got the better of one's reason; it seems to me the stronger it is the more glad one should be to have conquered it.

Where before he had talked about 'concealment and all its dangers', Russell now decided to tell his grandmother about his relationship with Alys, which he characterised as one of 'fondness' rather than love, an 'intimate friendship' rather than an engagement. Lady Russell reacted just as Russell might have predicted, and told him that he and Alys were already intimate enough and that, in her opinion, they ought not to write or to meet regularly and Russell was, of course, much too young to be engaged. She also told him something he had not known before, that she had had the same trouble with his father, when, at a similar age, he became fond of Jessie Chambers, and Lady Russell had tried to dissuade him from making any commitment to a girl of such markedly inferior birth. In that case, the issue was resolved by Jessie Chambers's early death, just before Amberley's twenty-first birthday. This time, from Lady Russell's point of view, the situation looked still more ominous. 'The talk was painful,' Russell admitted, but his grandmother was '*much* less unhappy than she might have been: particularly as I assured her that it was at least as likely as not it would never come to marriage and if it did, at any rate not for many years'.

In his *Autobiography*, Russell provides a rather different account of his grandmother's reaction. When he came home from Friday's Hill, he writes, 'I told my people what had occurred':

> ... they reacted according to the stereotyped convention. They said she was no lady, a baby-snatcher, a low-class adventuress, a designing female taking advantage of my inexperience, a person incapable of all the finer feelings, a woman whose vulgarity would perpetually put me to shame.

'But', he adds tellingly, 'I had a fortune of some £20,000 inherited from my father, and I paid no attention to what my people said.'

At Friday's Hill, Russell's joy at having 'accomplished all' had been marred to some extent when, returning from their morning walk before breakfast, Alys was handed a letter from Lady Henry Somerset, which contained an invitation to accompany her to America to preach temperance at the Chicago World's Fair. Alys, Russell later recalled, was thrilled by the letter: 'She read it out triumphantly, and accepted it enthusiastically, which made me feel rather small, as it meant several months of absence, and possibly the beginning of an interesting career.'

Before Alys left for the States on 6 October, Russell met with her to fulfil what he called 'the last and bitterest duty' to make 'a confession of sins belonging to a self that is dead but which can be dead only to myself: no one has the right to consider it so'. What the confession was is unrecorded, although, in her letter of 5 October written immediately afterwards, Alys sounds relieved that it was not as bad as she had feared. Perhaps related to the confession, Russell and Alys had that day spent some time arguing about sexual relations, Russell arguing for some kind of moderate release of sexual desire and Alys countering that 'self-control of a rigid principle would be far easier than that of moderation', for 'it would be very difficult, indeed impossible, for most people to draw the line between moderation & excess. You see, it is an accumulative habit.' And: 'We cannot compare ourselves to animals, for with them it is an instinctive thing':

> I don't believe either that it is a very wholesome relation between men and women who love each other for spiritual and intellectual reasons. I am afraid it might introduce an element that would lower the others, always excepting, of course, when they mean to have children.

So much for the idea of Alys as a champion of 'free love'.

The next day, Russell left for Cambridge for the start of term and to begin Part II of the Moral Sciences Tripos. The areas of the syllabus in which he had chosen to specialise were metaphysics, ethics and the history of philosophy. The Moral Sciences Tripos was in a further state of reformation than the Mathematics Tripos, and teaching was primarily done, not by 'coaching', but by intercollegiate lectures. The numbers attending these lectures were small – usually, no more than three or four – and the lecturer, acting more like a present-day tutor, would set and mark essays as well as lecture. Russell's lecturers were James Ward for metaphysics, Henry Sidgwick for ethics, and G. F. Stout for the history of philosophy. Of these, Sidgwick was probably the most distinguished, his *Methods of Ethics* having already (it was first published in 1874) attained the status of a standard text. Sidgwick's reputation, however, was a casualty of the fashion for Hegelianism that then prevailed at Cambridge, and his brand of utilitarianism was condemned as a mere remnant of the Benthamite tradition that was being swept aside by philosophers like McTaggart. 'We called him "Old Sidg" and regarded him merely as out of date,' Russell later recalled.

Stout was over twenty years younger than Sidgwick and was quite up-to-date. He had the previous year been appointed editor of *Mind* and was thus, professionally, in a position of some influence. His chief interest was in psychology, but his greatest influence upon Russell came in his teaching on the great seventeenth-century rationalists, Descartes, Spinoza and Leibniz. James Ward had been Stout's teacher and, though more or less Sidgwick's age, commanded considerable respect among the younger generation of philosophers, chiefly by importing to Britain the philosophy of mind of the Austrian and German school associated with Franz Brentano, Alexius von Meinong and Rudolf Lotze. He was steeped in German philosophy and culture (one of his favourite sayings was '*Das Denken ist schwer*' – 'thinking is difficult'), and introduced Russell to many of the philosophers whose thought would later direct the course of his own, including, to begin with, Immanuel Kant.

The emphasis on Kant's work in Ward's course on metaphysics possibly accounts for Russell's later misleading description of Ward as a 'Kantian'. Kant's work dominates almost every essay Russell wrote for Ward, including – most significantly for Russell's later development – an essay he wrote in November 1893, in which he tried to defend Kant's theory of geometry. It is the kind of subject one senses Russell had been craving to address throughout his mathematical studies: can we know that Euclid's geometry is necessarily true? Kant had argued that we could, but serious doubt had been thrown upon Kant's view by the creation since Kant's day of non-Euclidean systems of geometry, which, though adopting a different set of axioms, nevertheless were provably consistent and therefore not in any obvious way necessarily false. These systems, however, define spaces that it is difficult to imagine: for example, spaces in which two parallel lines can meet, or in which the angles of a triangle do not add up to 180 degrees. For Russell in this essay, 'The question turns on the imaginability of other spaces', and, in his view, Kant was right about the kind of space that we can imagine: 'space-intuitions are *for us* necessarily Euclidean; and . . . therefore the speculations of meta-geometry [non-Euclidean geometry] have no epistemological importance.' For the moment, the proofs Russell had fallen in love with at the age of eleven were safe, albeit at some cost of objectivity: they now provided necessary truths, not about the external world, but about our spatial intuitions.

Russell's real philosophical mentor, however, was none of his tutors, but J. M. E. McTaggart, whose views Russell quoted at this time almost as if they were infallible. For example, when Alys wrote from Chicago urging him to consider their religious differences and arguing that he would, eventually, come round to a belief in a personal God, Russell replied:

> It would be no use at all hoping that I shall ever believe that God is a Person: no reader of metaphysics could I think be brought to such a view: it is almost as much discredited in Philosophy as Circle Squaring is in Mathematics . . . I should be very glad if you felt enough interested to read a little Metaphysics as I am confident you would soon be convinced of its superiority in every point of view. McTaggart said once in a letter to me that no religion involving a personal God could be a religion of love: and this view he made clear I think in his pamphlet.

He agreed with Alys that 'human relations and work can neither of them afford satisfaction by themselves without faith', but the faith necessary, he argued, was not belief in this or that dogma, 'but rather in the perfectibility of the world and in the ultimate attainment of such perfection'.

At the beginning of November 1893, immediately after Alys's return to England, Russell stayed as an overnight guest of the Pearsall Smith family in their London home in Grosvenor Road. They had, he wrote on 7 November, a 'glorious two days' together. Alys, it seems, had changed her views on marriage utterly. Perhaps from a surfeit of abstruse metaphysics, she now declared all theories to be irrelevant. 'I care far more about your private feelings than about your theories,' she wrote on 8 November, 'just as I would rather have you have an innate sense of honour than a principle that one shd. not do dishonourable actions.' The question was 'not really . . . an academic one, because I have come to the conclusion that it must always be decided on purely personal grounds by each individual, or at any rate, by each woman'.

As Russell and Alys grew closer, Lady Russell watched with ever greater alarm and tried to extract from Russell promises that he would never get bound to Alys in any way and that he would not see her more often than, say, once a month. When Russell refused, she turned to Alys's mother and arranged a meeting at Grosvenor Road on 19 November, at which it was reaffirmed that Russell and Alys were emphatically not engaged and an agreement was reached that they would see each other no more than once a month. Lady Russell's attitude seems to have persuaded Alys that the relationship was a lost cause and she began to show signs of wanting to break it off. On 15 December, after cancelling a meeting with Russell at the last minute in order to go to stay at Eastnor Castle, Lady Henry Somerset's home, Alys wrote to Russell about her ambivalence. She was, she told him, sorry that they had not lived up their declared intention of meeting only as friends. If she could make up her mind to be engaged, then it could be publicly announced, 'but as long as I cannot decide, we can only be friends, or, at least, *ought* only to be friends'. It was tempting to say affectionate things and to hold Russell's hand, 'but I am afraid they are a mistake. Self-expression is not the least necessary to my nature, as it is to yours.' Nothing was decided, however: 'I have had a hundred different minds about you this week . . . which makes it difficult to write. You will need infinite patience, and then you will see that I am not worth it.'

Alarmed by this note of doubt and wavering, Russell replied with one of his most stirring love letters. The 'divine sympathy' they had reached together, he wrote, 'cannot be wrong: merely to have known it is a religion and redeems the world from its sordidness and misery by opening up infinite possibilities. Do not deprive me of moments which have been to me a revelation of a glory I had never dreamt of as possible even in heaven.' Having known that sympathy, 'I can never again have the crushing sense of solitude and isolation, the feeling that if I were known as I know myself I should be despised as I despised myself perhaps even abhorred as I abhorred myself . . . And I believe if you were ever to grow tired of me (which would not surprise me) I should know it at once without your saying anything either before or after.' The letter did the trick. 'Plague it,' Alys replied, 'I wish you did not care so much. And yet I do value your love more than I can say, & I cannot imagine my life without it now.'

A turning point came a day or two later when Russell got hold of his father's journals, from which he discovered that his father had proposed to his mother at the age of twenty-one, that his grandmother had reacted in exactly the same way as she had to Alys, and that his father had recorded reflections in his diary much like those Russell was now recording. 'This gave me an uncanny feeling', he wrote, 'that I was not living my own life but my father's over again, and tended to produce a superstitious belief in heredity.' He immediately transcribed some of the most important passages from their original shorthand and sent them to Alys, who was quite fascinated. 'I never read anything so interesting as your father's journal,' she wrote, 'it certainly is most uncanny, so like you.' From the journals it emerged that Lady Russell had suggested to Amberley and Kate, just as she now suggested to Russell and Alys, that they undergo a separation for six months to test the strength of their feeling for each other. They had agreed, but, to Lady Russell's evident displeasure, it had not made any difference to their plans. The effect upon Russell and Alys of reading this family history was severely to diminish their respect for Lady Russell's objections to their marriage, which now looked like nothing more than a repetition of an old and unreasoned prejudice. 'I should think your Grandmother would have had enough of separating people for six months!' Alys wrote. She was going the next day to Pembroke Lodge for an interview with Lady Russell, but now the old lady offered far less threat: 'She will try to work on my feelings to give you up, I know, but I shan't.'

Russell then gave Alys his mother's journal, which she read over the Christmas period and found so absorbing that it made her forget a Temperance Meeting she had promised to attend. By New Year's Eve, her doubts were apparently overcome, and she wrote to Russell in a different, more affectionate tone, her new-found sense of intimacy with him expressed by the use of the Quaker 'thee'. 'Every now & then,' she told him, 'when I am busy with something else, the remembrance of thy love comes over me with such a joyous rush that it seems too good to be true . . . It *is* nice to be able to say "thee". Anything else seems most unnatural . . . I do love thee, dear Bertie.' She had been to a children's party, '& the dear little things were so happy & so sweet. It made me long more than ever to have children of my own.'

This was far more than Russell had been expecting. 'What can I say?' he replied. 'My heart is too full for words. I am overcome by joy too wonderful to be expressed. Thy letter is divine . . . I have been living all day in a dream of heavenly joy. Dear Alys, I cannot write any more, only silence is adequate.'

The next time they met, they kissed for the first time. It was indeed the first time Russell had kissed a woman since his teenage exploits with the maid at Pembroke Lodge, and the day became etched on his memory with complete vividness. It was 4 January 1894, and London was buried beneath six inches of snow, which he waded through on foot from Vauxhall to Grosvenor Road. 'The snow brought a strange effect of isolation, making London almost as noiseless as a lonely hill top . . . we spent the whole day, with the exception of meal-times, in kissing, with hardly a word spoken from morning till night, except for an interlude during which I read *Epipsychidion* aloud.' On the way home, he walked from Richmond station to Pembroke Lodge through a blizzard. He arrived home 'tired but exultant'. Over the next year, Russell read *Epipsychidion* eight more times.

After that, though no public announcement had been made, neither Russell nor Alys was in any doubt that they were engaged to be married. Alys, with less reason to maintain complete discretion than Russell, reported that both her friend Lion Fitzpatrick and her sister Mary thought that Russell would make a good husband. On her next trip campaigning for temperance, she also told Lady Henry Somerset. Lying in bed in lodgings in Manchester ('it being so much easier to talk in the dark'), Alys and Lady Somerset discussed the prospects for the marriage, and decided it looked promising. Lady Somerset pronounced herself pleased to hear that Russell was sound on 'the Woman Question', and also admired the photograph of him that Alys now took to carrying around with her. 'I said we wanted to be married at a registry office in pyjamas,' wrote Alys, 'but she says it must be a Quaker wedding.'

Until he returned to Cambridge, and even for some time after that, Russell felt compelled to keep his 'engagement' to himself. 'I too long for somebody to talk to about thee,' he told Alys, 'but I am always withheld by distrust.' At Pembroke Lodge, he followed nearly a lifetime's practice of keeping his emotions hidden, both his happiness about Alys and his irritation with his grandmother and his Aunt Agatha. It was, however, becoming difficult, even to one so practised, to hide his feelings. 'I am beginning to look forward very much to getting away from home again,' he wrote on 9 January, 'things here are becoming so strained that I fear for my self-control':

The other night I had it on the point of my tongue to say in the bitterest of tones: 'It's extremely pleasant when people one is fond of accuse one of deliberately lying for self-indulgent purposes.' Most fortunately I was able to control myself by absolute silence and I believe they didn't know I was annoyed at all.

But though he did not let his family into his confidence, their suspicions about Russell and Alys were confirmed daily. The impossibility of keeping his visits to Friday's Hill secret was made apparent to Russell one day when Harold Joachim expressed surprise to hear that Russell had been in the Haslemere neighbourhood without mentioning it. Joachim's mother began to ask people whether there was anything between Russell and Alys. 'All these absurdities', Russell wrote to Alys, 'make me sometimes wonder if we couldn't let our present arrangement be known to all whom it might concern and let the world wag its silly tongue to its heart's content. But I suppose it would be better not?'

To give the gossips as little to talk about as possible – and to minimise the chance of anything definite reaching the ears of Lady Russell – Russell and Alys decided to meet just once a month. 'I fear no amount of work will make the month seem anything but interminable to me,' Russell wrote on 10 January, but he was, nevertheless, relieved to return to Cambridge and immerse himself in his studies. During their separations, he and Alys exchanged letters three or four times a week, trying to iron out their differences about religion, about what kind of home they wanted, and about how they intended to bring up their children. Alys favoured a Christian upbringing, but Russell insisted: 'I could hardly reconcile it to my conscience to have children of mine brought up as Christians.'

Russell's own religion, the pantheistic mysticism that he had embraced as a teenager, was taking a more definite shape under the influence of his reading of Spinoza's *Ethics*, and, especially, Sir Frederick Pollock's book, *Spinoza: His*

Life and Philosophy. 'Ever since I first read Pollock's book,' Russell later told
Ottoline Morrell, 'Spinoza has been one of the most important people in my
world.' His reaction to Spinoza recalls his response to Shelley: it was a
reaction to the man as much as to the work. For the rest of Russell's life,
Spinoza was an important inspiration to him. As he was to put it many years
later in *History of Western Philosophy*:

> Spinoza is the noblest and most loveable of the great philosophers.
> Intellectually, some others have surpassed him, but ethically he is supreme.
> As a natural consequence, he was considered, during his lifetime and for a
> century after his death, a man of appalling wickedness. He was born a Jew,
> but the Jews excommunicated him. Christians abhorred him equally;
> although his whole philosophy is dominated by the idea of God, the
> orthodox accused him of atheism. Leibniz, who owed much to him,
> concealed his debt, and carefully abstained from saying a word in his praise;
> he even went so far as to lie about the extent of his personal acquaintance
> with the heretic Jew.

Spinoza, Pollock writes, 'considered religion as something very real in a
man's life . . . But this religion, as he understands it, is not the religion of
churches and sects. It is independent of dogmatic theology, independent of
any particular knowledge or belief as to revelation, independent even of the
so-called natural theology which holds to the conception of God as a Person
. . . The essence of religion is in Spinoza's mind a cheerful and willing
cooperation with the order of the world as manifested in the nature of man
and society.' In these words, Pollock crystallised the attitude that had
been forming in Russell's mind since he shook off the faith of his childhood, and articulated the view that Russell was to hold for the rest of his life.
This, together with the idea that Spinoza was persecuted and isolated for
holding such an enlightened view, made him, in Russell's eyes, the perfect
hero.

'I wish I had got hold of Spinoza two years ago instead of Thomas à
Kempis,' Russell wrote to Alys on 28 January, 'he would have suited me far
better: he preaches a rich voluptuous asceticism based on a vast undefined
mysticism, which even now has seized hold of my imagination most powerfully.' The following week, he told her he had been reading Pollock's book,
'which seems to me in every way admirable; besides being very well and
interestingly written it displays an amount and variety of learning before
which my brain reels'. Ever afterwards his advice, to his friends, to his
students and to his readers, was to read Pollock's book before trying to master
Spinoza's own rather impenetrable works. Russell never quite took seriously
Spinoza's arguments for his beliefs, dressed up as they are like formal,
geometrical proofs, but regarded him rather as he did Shelley, as the holder
and communicator of an imaginative, poetic kind of truth that transcended
the mundane and for which no arguments could be given. In this he was, to
some extent, echoing the advice he himself received from James Ward.
'Philosophy near akin to poetry,' Russell wrote in his notes on Ward's

lectures, 'imagination in the abstract has got hold of some philosophers, notably Spinoza and Plato . . . But as philosophy [one] can't disguise from oneself that Spinoza falls to pieces.' Spinoza's concept of God, Ward declared, 'means only what is meant nowadays by Absolute or Unconditioned'. This, at least, held out some hope that the pieces might, one day, be put together again, for had not McTaggart claimed to be able to prove what he believed about the Absolute? And, for the time being at least, Russell was inclined to treat this claim with devout seriousness.

In the spring of 1894, as for much of his life, Russell's longing for belief in a mysticism akin to Spinoza's 'intellectual love of God' fought a running battle with a corrosive scepticism that he could never quite shake off, and in which he often took a certain delight. His early enthusiasm for G. E. Moore seems to have been prompted by a conception of Moore as the personification of philosophical scepticism. Moore's great philosophical gift, perhaps his only philosophical gift, was his refusal to be browbeaten into accepting absurd or extraordinary points of view. In this way, he was Russell's perfect discussion partner. Russell's motivation in philosophical thinking was always to find some doctrine that would make the world more intelligible to him; Moore's was rather to understand the doctrines of philosophers. 'I do not think the world or the sciences would ever have suggested to me any philosophical problems,' Moore once wrote. 'What has suggested philosophical problems to me is things which other philosophers have said about the world or the sciences.' A turning point in Moore's life came when Russell took him to meet McTaggart, who, in the course of conversation, advanced his well-known view that time was unreal. Where most undergraduates at that time would have assumed that, if they did not agree with McTaggart, they must have misunderstood him, Moore – who found McTaggart's views 'perfectly monstrous' – questioned him with the impressive persistence and tenacity for which he was later famous. The incident, and others like it, convinced Russell, first that Moore should drop classics in favour of philosophy, and second, that he should be elected to the Apostles. On both counts he got his way.

On 18 February, Russell wrote Alys a rapturous account of Moore's début at the Apostles. Moore, he said, 'looked like Newton and Satan rolled into one'. He had spoken 'clearly and unhesitatingly, and at first with no sign whatever of nervousness' about scepticism:

> . . . at one point he said: Scepticism cannot destroy enthusiasm, there is one which will always remain, and that is the enthusiasm for scepticism. And to see him say it no one could doubt his utter conviction of the truth of what he was saying. We all felt electrified by him, as if we had slumbered hitherto and never realised what fearless intellect pure and unadulterated really means. If he does not die or go mad I cannot doubt that he will somehow mark himself out as a man of stupendous genius.

Russell was not alone in reacting to Moore in this way. Similar accounts have been given by, among others, Leonard Woolf and Lytton Strachey. But

why Moore aroused such fervid and unrestrained admiration is probably
destined to remain a mystery to all subsequent generations, denied the chance
of experiencing at first hand Moore's famously impressive argumentative
style. His written work certainly demonstrates his tenacity, but it is difficult
to feel 'electrified' by it, and few, I think, would now see 'stupendous genius'
in the plodding, repetitive and laboured prose of, say, *Principia Ethica*.
Wittgenstein's rather unkind remark that Moore shows how far it is possible
to go without any intelligence whatsoever probably strikes a more familiar
note to those who know Moore only from his writing, but in the spring of
1894 it would no doubt have seemed quite inconceivable that anyone could
ever think such a thing.

For Russell, Moore possessed such a pure intellectual passion that there
was something rather alien about him. One could admire him for his natural
qualities, much as one admired a tiger, but one couldn't feel close to him. Of
course, to Alys, it was all utterly unintelligible, and Russell felt called upon
to explain. 'I don't see why thee doesn't believe in Moore's enthusiasm
for scepticism,' he wrote on 21 February. 'Thee would if thee could see his
eyes':

> He has strong passions and emotions, but hardly those of a human being:
> they are all intellectual and critical . . . I find it impossible either to like or
> dislike him, because I have seen no trace of humanity in him yet: but there
> is an odd exhilaration in talking with him: his criticism is like the air of the
> high Alps. But an enthusiasm seems to me the most natural thing in the
> world: if you are of an enthusiastic disposition and believe in nothing, you
> have to be enthusiastic about disbelief, as I know from personal experience.
> Truth and holiness and beauty and such things all give way before a
> thorough going scepticism, so that they do not remain for enthusiasm to
> let itself out on.

The impact of Moore's scepticism is apparent in Russell's account to Alys
of the following meeting of the Apostles on 25 February. The subject under
discussion was whether art or social duty was the higher ideal, with Russell
and Crompton Llewelyn Davies defending social duty against McTaggart,
about whose views Russell now spoke with a new tone of disrespect:

> McTaggart ran his Absolute, as usual, and we protested it was useless, and
> if not, worked the other way: but Marsh, being new and not knowing the
> trick, was frightened at such an imposing machinery and was half converted
> to McTaggart. The odd thing about the Absolute is that it always goes
> against the *Chronicle* whatever that paper may happen to say. Also that
> when anybody else uses it McTaggart says it can't be used.

On this particular issue Moore had sided with McTaggart, because,
reported Russell, 'he is a Stoic and thinks happiness doesn't depend on
externals such as food and clothing. Teach the East-ender to appreciate art
and he will be happy. Moore is colossally ignorant of life.'

For the following week's meeting Russell had agreed to give a paper arguing the case for admitting women into the Society. Seeking Alys's advice on what to say, he discovered to his surprise that she was *against* the idea of admitting women. The Society, she argued, was too intellectual for women, who were by nature too sympathetic to engage in impersonal discussions, especially if they happened to be in love with one of their fellow-Apostles. And besides, 'I do not believe very young people of opposite sexes ought to discuss sexual subjects together'; the complete frankness and openness of their discussions would be compromised. In a later letter, Alys conceded that she had perhaps exaggerated 'the proneness of intellectual women to fall in love', and Russell stuck to his original argument. After the meeting he reported that all had voted in favour of admitting women except Lowes Dickinson, though, in fact, it was not until 1970 that the first woman was elected.

Whatever motivated Alys's objections to the election of women to the Society, they were not part of a more general opposition to feminism. On the contrary, she had just written – and had had accepted by *The Nineteenth Century* – a feminist polemic of her own entitled 'A Reply from the Daughters', which defended the right of unmarried women not to devote themselves to the care of their parents. As Russell's Aunt Agatha had devoted her entire life to looking after Lady Russell, and as Agatha's devotion was Lady Russell's greatest comfort in life, Alys could hardly have chosen a theme more likely to prejudice Pembroke Lodge against her. She realised this, and was quite unrepentant. 'I am afraid all young people have to face & then disregard the problem of the loneliness of their older relations', she wrote to Russell:

Old people are almost always lonely, thy Grandmother is no exception, no doubt her own parents were lonely in their time, but she had to leave them to live her own life. And thee will have to leave her, more or less, if thee is to love me & to work. Even thy Uncle Rollo, whose duty to her is more direct & who has no work, leaves her, with a good conscience no doubt, & thy Aunt Agatha would have done so, had she been able to marry. Thy Grandmother is really very fortunate in having thy Aunt.

When the article was published in March, it became the focus for a renewed campaign against Alys led by Agatha and Lady Russell, which served only to harden Russell's attitude still further towards them. On 6 March he wrote to Alys in a tone of contempt towards his family that had previously been kept in check:

My aunt's remark on thy article was very typical of the rankling insinuating disingenuous remarks my people always favour me with on whatever interests me or has value for me: thee can imagine how exquisitely annoying a long course of such pious reserve becomes . . . if they go on the same way & if I see much of them I shall come to hate them & it is only a question of time how soon I shall explode & give them a piece of my mind, as it will be impossible to stand that sort of thing for ever, tho' I shall do my utmost.

During the Easter vacation he would see very little of them, as he had arranged to spend most of it in Rome with his Aunt Maude Stanley, but he had nevertheless to endure a few nights at Pembroke Lodge before he set off. He was, he told Alys, looking forward to it with dread: 'I see already their sad pained expression, their palpable resignation to the ingratitude of youth, their disappointment in one they had thought better of, all conveyed in sighs, half sentences & hints & innuendoes, never said right out; & yet all genuine, poor people.' However, he added, 'All they do is really irrelevant, & I am only superficially annoyed by them now.'

He was, he thought, within sight of freedom from the past. Before going to Pembroke Lodge, he spent a night at Friday's Hill, and wrote to his grandmother in terms that were intended – and were understood as such – to convey a note of self-assertion and independence.

Dearest Granny,

I have just come back from the Pearsall Smiths, where my short stay was of course very delightful. I am very sorry indeed you do not think my future prospects bright, particularly as it must be painful to you: but I am the more persuaded that your fears are groundless, as I find from my father's journal that you had just as great fears about his marriage, which yet was as perfectly happy as any marriage could be, to judge by his journal and my mother's. So I do wish you could get rid of your fears, as I am sure they make you unnecessarily unhappy.

As Russell had anticipated, his night at Pembroke Lodge was fraught. His family considered him still to be under oath not to become engaged to Alys and to see her no more than once a month. They were alarmed by his talk of 'prospects' with her, and outraged by his plan, while on the Continent, to visit Alys's brother Logan in Paris; and still more outraged at hearing that Alys, too, would be visiting her brother at that time. 'I *hear* Mr Logan does not live in the best society in Paris' were the words that greeted Russell when he arrived home. 'I should think you had much better stay at a hotel in Paris, and not identify yourself too much with his friends.' Later, Russell was pressed for assurances that things between himself and Alys were 'where they were'. 'Well, of course, things drift more or less,' Russell replied. 'There was no question of drifting,' his grandmother retorted. 'I have her mother's promise in writing, and hers in words, that it was to be nothing but simple friendship. I suppose I ought to have got hers in writing too but I never thought of it. She is as much bound in honour as any human being can be not to let anything but simple friendship arise.'

'Poor old woman!' wrote Russell to Alys, reporting this conversation, 'as though such things could be ruled by all the promises in the world!' He realised, of course, that his grandmother would feel betrayed when the engagement was finally made public, but had no intention of allowing that to stand in his way. For the moment, however, he had to endure her 'small nastinesses' towards Alys in silence, including her pointed allusions to 'revolting daughters' accompanied (lest the allusion should go undetected) by an unsmiling 'You see the joke?' But, he told Alys, 'I have not the slightest difficulty in keeping my temper, partly because the time is short and partly because nothing they do matters a jot.'

Lady Russell, however, had by no means admitted defeat. As soon as Russell left for Rome, she summoned Alys to Pembroke Lodge, presumably to try and extract from her a reaffirmation of her promise 'not to let anything but simple friendship arise'. By this time, Alys was quite determined that the wedding should go ahead and began to emerge as something like the Ibsenesque strong, independent woman that Russell had hoped to find in her. She was quite unwilling to be browbeaten by Lady Russell, and, unlike Russell, could match Lady Russell's emotional pressure and guileful methods of persuasion with some of her own. 'I shall only mind the interview because I shall be afraid of hurting their feelings or of telling lies,' she wrote to Russell. 'If it gets very embarrassing, I shall cry (I can cry whenever I like!) & perhaps that will touch their hearts & seem to them a sign of sensibility. Poor dears, I *am* awfully sorry for them . . . [but] I love thee too much now to allow anybody to come between us, or to suggest what our relations should be. Thy six months' work has availed thee very well, dear boy.'

Russell was entirely behind her chosen strategy. 'I shd. have thought it was evident that thee can't get out of such an interview without lies,' he wrote, 'but perhaps thee will find some way: tears, the "female weapon" wd. probably be very affective . . . I think we made a mistake in not telling them we were engaged when I was last at home.' Alys's meeting at Pembroke Lodge took place on 20 March and lasted about an hour. The conversation, Alys wrote in her diary, was 'very painful and very fruitless. They think I am behaving in a very dishonourable and indelicate manner in seeing so much of Bertie and writing twice a week. And they do not understand how I can "pursue" him to Paris. I saw it was hopeless to argue with Lady R. so I only repeated that I could not see the thing as she did . . . I felt very sorry for them both but fortunately my conscience is good and what they said didn't influence me in the least.' 'I am sorry thy interview with my grandmother was not more successful,' Russell wrote on 25 March, 'but I am scarcely surprised.' He was now in favour of announcing the enagagement as soon as he returned from the Continent, '& if she asks I will say we have become engaged during our time together at Paris. Our last & final lie.'

In Rome, Russell's time was spent socialising with various aristocratic relations, on both the Stanley and Russell sides of his family. The experience confirmed him in thinking that, whatever happened, he would *not*, as his grandmother wished, marry into his own class. The 'icy reserve' of the aristocracy, he told Alys, '(though I feebly try to ape it) would kill me to live with'. He stayed as a guest of his Uncle Algernon, the youngest of his mother's brothers, who had been an Anglican clergyman but, having converted to Catholicism, was now a Papal Chamberlain and Bishop of Emmaus. In later life, Russell recalled him as being 'completely delightful: urbane, witty, jovial, fat, fond of good food, and (so far as I ever saw) bubbling with enjoyment of life'. In the spring of 1894, however, Russell was in no mood to appreciate either his uncle the Monsignor or any of the other grand relations he was entertained by, and merely counted the days until he could be with Alys once more. 'I shall indeed enjoy Bohemian Paris more after this blight of aristocrats,' he wrote on 25 March.

When he arrived in Paris on 5 April, the 'life of American art students' that Logan enjoyed seemed to Russell 'very free and delightful' in contrast to the 'stiff inartistic aristocrats' with whom he had lived for the previous three weeks. 'I remember', he recalled, 'a dance at which Alys appeared in a dress designed by Roger Fry. I remember, also, some rather unsuccessful attempts to instil culture into me by taking me to see Impressionist pictures in the Luxembourg. And I remember floating on the Seine at night near Fontaine-bleau with Alys beside me, while Logan filled the night with unbending cleverness.'

A few days later, he was back at Pembroke Lodge to find that his grandmother was very far indeed from conceding defeat, even after he told her that he was already 'technically engaged' to Alys. Until he actually married her, she was evidently quite prepared to keep up her opposition to the match, fighting with whatever resources she had. 'She has completely adopted the lachrymose method,' Russell reported to Alys, 'which shows that she feels it her last resource. If I can hold out against it, all will be well.' This was easier said than done, for few could use lachrymosity with quite such devastating effect as Lady Russell, as she had an opportunity to demonstrate, when Russell made the mistake of accusing her of being 'unkind' towards Alys:

> This word seemed to sting her like an adder, far more than I had anticipated: and so it did when I spoke about difficulty in our relations. To this she said in a voice half choked with tears (as her voice was throughout) that such difficulty was only on my side (which seemed to me natural enough, since she has hitherto been the aggressor), and to the other she replied in an agonised tone (which was perfectly real: if thee says she couldn't or shouldn't have felt so much thee will be falling into the same mistake she falls into) that though she had many times had to speak plainly to people in a similar situation before nobody has *ever* told her she was unkind. The idea of blame from a younger person is so foreign to her mind that my words seemed like a combination of sacrilege and cruelty.

It was an effective display, and very nearly successful. 'She was terribly upset by my accusing her of unkindness,' Russell told Alys, 'and in my grief at her pain I could remember none of the unkind things: I was tempted 1,000 times to crawl down but fortunately just avoided it.'

Russell was wrong, however, to think that the 'lachrymose method' was his grandmother's last resource. She had one trump-card left to play, a card that was hinted at by Russell's dream the previous summer: the fear of hereditary madness. Her playing of this was gradual and insidious. It began with her telling Russell the truth about his Aunt Agatha's engagement. Some ten years previously, Agatha had become engaged to a young curate, but had broken it off in circumstances about which Russell had up to now known very little. All he knew was that it appeared to have left her with a broken spirit. He suspected, however, that his grandmother had had something to do with the break-up of the engagement. His grandmother, he had come to think, 'instinctively hated her children's marriages, both from maternal jealousy and from a horror of sex', and, where she had tried and failed to prevent Amberley from marrying, she had, in Agatha's case, tried and succeeded. Agatha, as he later put it in his *Autobiography*, 'was a victim of my grandmother's virtue. If she had not been taught that sex is wicked, she might have been happy, successful and able.'

Just as Russell had earlier used to great effect comparisons between his case and his father's with respect to his grandmother's opposition to marriage, now he tried comparing Alys's situation with that of Agatha. 'I told her she couldn't see thy point of view,' he wrote to Alys, 'and gave her hints of my analogy about my aunt.' He does not say what this analogy was, but it seems almost certain to have rested on the suggestion that, if she did not marry, then Alys would end up a sad, unfulfilled spinster like Agatha.

In fact, Agatha had broken off her engagement because she became afflicted with insane delusions about her fiancé, imagining him to have murdered Lord Clanricarde. So convinced was she that he was guilty that she had tried to take him to the police station, at which point he broke off the engagement. Russell was not told the whole story immediately, but was given the details of Agatha's plight slowly and in such a way that they could not help but play on his imagination. Without being told, at first, about Agatha's delusions, he was shown Agatha's edition of Shelley's poems, which had been given to her by her fiancé. It was a pathetic and stirring thing to behold. As Russell described it to Alys:

> It is marked in pencil with the dates and places when he read the poems to her (or recited them); and others (such as 'That time is dead for ever child') are marked without any comments. So is 'The unheeded tribute of a broken heart'. She marks only for sentiment, and exactly what I marked at 17; with the difference that she *has* a broken heart while I only played at having one. Poor woman! the whole story of her life is in her marks. There is a grim pathos about seeing 'That time is dead' and 'Love's Philosophy' next to each other both marked by her. What a universe between the two! And the most touching thing of all is that she always denies that she is fond of Shelley – I feel as if I could bear any amount of bitterness from her now that I realise what she has suffered.

Russell had about ten days of his Easter vacation left before he had to return to Cambridge, time that his family used to build up slowly a picture of his family as plagued with inherited insanity. Just like an Ibsen play, dark hints were followed time and again by awful revelations.

On 14 April, the day Russell announced to his family that his mind was made up and that the engagement would be made public and formal, Lady Russell mentioned, as though it were mere coincidence, that she had just been writing to her son Willy, who – and this was the first Russell had heard of it – was in a lunatic asylum. Uncle Rollo contributed to the picture by presenting Russell with a written note – marked 'private' – warning vaguely and obliquely of the hereditary dangers of coming from such an old family as the Russells.

In their determination to prove that Russell and Alys should not get married, the Russells now also turned their attention to Alys's family, trying to find more evidence of inherited mental instability. They seem never to have discovered that Alys's father, Robert, had had a nervous breakdown, but word did reach them that Robert's brother Horace was rather odd. Horace exhibited signs of what would now be diagnosed as manic-depressive illness; his state of mind alternating suddenly and alarmingly between moods of extreme excitability (his 'happies', as the family called them) and deep melancholia. He divided his time between his daughter's house in Birmingham and Friday's Hill, where, during his low periods, he would do little except play chess with his brother Robert. In the spring of 1894, gossip reached Pembroke Lodge that Horace was in an asylum, which they seized upon eagerly as fresh evidence for their purposes and as an excuse to demand from Alys the address of the Pearsall Smiths' family doctor in Philadelphia, so that they could make further inquiries about the health of her family.

The next step was to arrange a meeting between Russell and the family doctor, Dr William Anderson, who was undyingly loyal to Lady Russell and perfectly prepared to put his medical authority at her service. Russell met him at Pembroke Lodge on 29 April, at the end of his first week back at Cambridge. As Russell later recalled the meeting:

> The old family doctor, a serious Scotsman with mutton-chop whiskers, began to tell me all the things that I had dimly suspected about my family history: how my Uncle William was mad, how my Aunt Agatha's engagement had had to be broken off because of her insane delusions, and how my father had suffered from epilepsy.

It was designed to unsettle him and it worked. 'I began to feel', Russell wrote, 'as if I was doomed to a dark destiny.'

His resolve, however, was unweakened. While in London, Russell had been to see a performance of Ibsen's *Wild Duck* with Alys, and, inevitably, had been seen by friends of the family. As a result, he received a letter from his Aunt Maude, hoping that the rumours about him and Alys were not true. 'There is even more truth in the report than you feared,' Russell wrote to her. 'I have been in love with Miss P. S. for years . . . and since my return from abroad have become engaged to her.' He nevertheless asked her, for the time being, to contradict any report to that effect that she might hear, since they were not quite ready yet to announce the engagement publicly (and also, though he did not tell her this, he would rather word of his visit to the theatre with Alys did not reach Pembroke Lodge).

Incredibly, during the time since his return from Paris and Rome, Russell had been managing to work at philosophy harder than ever before. His Moral

Sciences Tripos exams were due to be taken in the third week of May, and James Ward had already admonished him for wasting his time over the Easter vacation on the Continent when he should have been working. Nevertheless, the quality of his essays at this time was such that Stout had told him that he was practically certain to get a good first-class mark in the exams, and was possibly even in line for a distinction (a so-called 'starred first'). 'I am still working hard and have succeeded in keeping most of my thoughts on shop,' he wrote to Alys in the midst of the emotionally fraught negotiations with Pembroke Lodge over the question of hereditary insanity. His absorption in abstract questions of metaphysics was impressively intense, and demonstrates the remarkable ability he had developed in his childhood of closing himself off from emotional tension.

Indeed, one senses in these months that his concentration on remote philosophical issues was a welcome relief from his family problems. In philosophy at this time, to a greater extent than he was to manage ever again, he found the kind of comfort that in his childhood had been provided for him by religious faith. Since discovering Spinoza's pantheistic mysticism at the beginning of the year, and identifying Spinoza's God with the 'Absolute' of McTaggart's neo-Hegelianism, Russell had had reason to think that philosophy – McTaggart's philosophy, in particular – might offer him a kind of faith in which his reason, as well as his emotions, could acquiesce. Interestingly, however, when Russell had first come across Spinoza in January, though attracted by his mysticism, he had spoken with some disrespect about the notion that was to become central to his admiration of Spinoza: the 'intellectual love of God'. Spinoza's ideal, he had then written to Alys, seems to have been 'a heaven without emotion, spent in passionless contemplation of propositions of Euclid . . . (though he calls it intellectual love of God to make it sound better)', of a kind that would 'make any modern shudder'. For to the moderns (as for Russell himself at this time, fresh from having spent all day kissing Alys and reading Shelley): 'a heaven without all-absorbing emotional love seems a far less desirable thing than earth with all its drawbacks'.

After the Easter vacation, however, when he returned to Cambridge from a suffocating dose of his grandmother's love, Spinoza's religion of dispassionate contemplation did not seem too bad, after all, and, in an intriguing essay he wrote for Stout immediately prior to his exams, Russell sought to prove that this religion was demonstrably true. This was in response to an assignment from Stout to: 'Discuss the nature and logical validity of the ontological argument for the existence of God, as stated by Descartes'. The ontological argument seeks to prove that God's existence is logically necessary on the grounds that, as God is by definition the most perfect being, He *has* to exist, since, if He did not, He would lack at least one perfection, namely that of existence. Russell's consideration of this argument provided him with one of the great epiphanic moments of his life, which he told and re-told many times in his autobiographical writings, beginning with this account in a letter to Ottoline Morrell written in September 1911:

One day, a week before my last Tripos, I ran out of tobacco while I was working, so I went out to get some. As I was coming back with a tin, I suddenly seemed to see truth in the ontological argument. I threw the tin in the air and exclaimed out loud 'Great God in boots, the ontological argument is sound.' (I can't imagine the reason for such an oath.) So I became a Hegelian.

The last sentence, which seems an odd *non sequitur*, is explained by Russell's essay for Stout, which survives and which shows that what Russell thought the ontological argument established was not the Christian God, or any kind of personal God, but the neo-Hegelian 'Absolute', or Spinoza's God, the one reality that exists unperceived by the senses but dimly conceived by our intellects behind the multitude of changing appearances. In his version, the ontological argument proceeds to argue that: 'Whatever we think, we cannot get away from reality.' If we say anything, even anything negative ('the Absolute does not exist'), we must 'affirm some predicate of reality'. Therefore, 'if we try to deny reality as a whole, there is no positive ground left as basis of our denial. We *must* think the Absolute, and its essence involves existence; hence the ontological argument.'

As Russell makes clear later in his essay, this argument depends on viewing the world as a single whole, that is, on asserting 'monism' – the view that there is, in reality, despite appearances, only one thing. And it gains its religious significance by identifying this one thing (Reality as a whole) with Spinoza's God:

> In Spinoza there is one substance only, i.e. God. God has two attributes, thought and extension; God is immanent in the world, and is the whole of what is: finite minds and finite portions of matter exist only in so far as they are God . . . Nevertheless Spinoza's monism is not so complete as it might be, since extension, for us, exists only as thought about, and the two attributes of God are therefore unnecessary; thought alone would have been sufficient.

What Russell had earlier slightly mocked as 'a heaven without emotion, spent in passionless contemplation of propositions of Euclid' had thus now become the very basis of his religion, what he would later call the 'religion of contemplation', a religion that sees thought as the only reality and understanding as the highest virtue.

A few days before his first exam, Russell took a break from Cambridge by going on a short walking tour of Norfolk with G. E. Moore, who also had Tripos exams that May. 'We mean to walk 15 miles a day,' Russell told Alys, 'but I dare say we shan't walk quite so far really. I feel sure that our whole talk will consist in my trying to persuade him that the phrase "unconscious will" is meaningless, which doubtless seems to thee a very frivolous topic as indeed it does to me.' The holiday was the occasion of an incident that sheds much light on the subsequent strained relationship between Moore and Russell, and on Moore's evident lifelong dislike and disapproval of Russell's character. When they returned to Cambridge on 20 May, the incident was still fresh in Russell's mind and he described it at length to Alys:

> Moore & I came back yesterday morning, having walked 40 miles in two days without perceptible fatigue, & I am indeed 'disgustingly healthy' by now, but also very sleepy. We made friends with a man we met in the hotel, who was very well informed in various matters & a very good linguist, but whose talk consisted almost wholly of his own & his friends' immoralities. Moore is very ignorant, so I drew this man out for Moore's instruction & my amusement, & he poured forth beastly stories, one more horrible & disgusting than the other, till Moore cd. hardly contain himself. Afterwards Moore was tremendously excited & realised for the first time what men are. He was merely an average specimen, but Moore said he was the most wicked man he had ever met or even read about & couldn't have a spark of good in him, wh. was amusing. Moore said he had never known till this term what it was to hate a man, that he had hated one other for a similar reason, but not nearly so much as this one. I tried to persuade Moore most men were just like that, & to shew him the man had only talked because I encouraged him & pretended to be just as bad myself: & I think Moore has really learnt a useful lesson & will take reformers & such people more seriously in future. I shouldn't wonder if Moore wd. have murdered him if they had been much longer together. What made him particularly mad was that, on discovering he had read some indecent classical authors (for his work) the man persisted in regarding him as a sly dog, a very deep person, who hid all sorts of wickedness under an innocent exterior. The whole thing, when I cd. conquer my disgust, was most amusing, & but for me Moore wd. never have found him out, as they wd. only have talked of architecture & history.

The relish with which Russell describes Moore's discomfort is odd, especially when one considers that Alys would have found the stranger's delight in 'immoralities' and his innuendo about the works of Petronius quite as distasteful as did Moore. Did Russell find the prospect of shocking Alys as delightful and amusing as he evidently found Moore's indignant outrage? In any case, the story, and the manner of Russell's telling of it, helps to explain the extraordinary conversation that is recorded by Alan Wood, Russell's first biographer, who presumably heard it from Russell himself:

> *Russell*: You don't like me, Moore, do you?
> *Moore* (after giving the matter careful thought): No.

After which, according to Wood, 'they went on chatting about other things'.

As Russell and Stout had realised, James Ward's fears about Russell's performance in his exams were entirely misplaced. Ward himself told Russell after the results had been announced that he had never seen a better paper than Russell's. He was awarded a 'starred first' and thus practically guaranteed a College Fellowship, should he wish to pursue an academic career. First, however, he had to submit a Fellowship dissertation. After discussing it with Ward, Russell (who had stayed up in Cambridge after his exams) decided on 'the Epistemological Bearings of Metageometry' as a subject for his dissertation, and immediately collected reading lists from both Ward and, for the mathematical side of the subject, from Whitehead. The subject was one he had already written about in an essay for Ward ('Metageometry' being the word Russell and others used at this time for non-Euclidean geometries), and, in many ways, it was an obvious choice, the truth of Euclid's axioms being the subject of Russell's very earliest philosophical thinking. Besides, as he wrote to Alys, it would enable him to 'utilise both my Triposes, and so, I hope, make my dissertation unintelligible to all my examiners'.

With the issue resolved, Russell returned, on 11 June, to Pembroke Lodge to face his family on the question of his forthcoming marriage to Alys. On 31 May, the engagement had been publicly announced, and Russell no doubt hoped that, by the time he returned home, the matter would have been accepted as a *fait accompli*. If so, he was very mistaken. Instead of accepting the situation, his family repeated with ever greater insistence their fears that his marriage to Alys was a grave mistake on medical grounds, drawing attention again and again to Uncle Willy's insanity, Aunt Agatha's delusions and Amberley's epilepsy, and dwelling with equal insistence on Alys's Uncle Horace's mental instability and on rumours that her father too was 'crazy, or at any rate, queer'. 'By emphasising these facts until they rendered me nearly insane', Russell later wrote, 'my people persuaded us to take the best medical opinion as to whether, if we were married, our children were likely to be mad.'

The 'best medical opinion' was that of Dr Daniel Hack Tuke, a psychiatric specialist, who had treated Uncle Willy. Tuke's opinion – 'primed by the family doctor, who was primed by the family', as Russell put it – was that Russell and Alys ought not to have children. The verdict was received at a meeting with Dr Anderson in his house in Richmond on 21 June. After it, Russell recalled:

> Alys and I walked up and down Richmond Green discussing it. I was for breaking off the engagement, as I believed what the doctors said and greatly desired children. Alys said she had no great wish for children, and would prefer to marry, while avoiding a family. After about half an hour's discussion, I came round to her point of view.

When, however, they announced their decision to Pembroke Lodge, a fresh outburst of horror backed by medical advice was aroused, Dr Anderson assuring them that the use of contraceptives was invariably injurious to one's health, and the family claiming that it was practising birth control that had caused Amberley's epilepsy in the first place. During the following few days Russell experienced – what Frank had grown up with – the stifling treatment accorded by Pembroke Lodge to sinners: 'A thick atmosphere of sighs, tears, groans, and morbid horror was produced, in which it was scarcely possible to breathe.'

On 3 July, Russell was packed off on a walking holiday for two weeks with his Cambridge friend Eddie Marsh, while his family attempted to take control of the situation with the help of Dr Anderson. Their plan was for Dr Anderson and Lady Russell between them to persuade Alys to break off the engagement, and, in Russell's absence, for Dr Anderson to deliver a final, authoritative medical verdict on the dangers of birth control and, therefore, on the folly of going ahead with the marriage. Their plans, however, were defeated by a mixture of Alys's stubbornness and Russell's astuteness. While Alys refused to meet either Lady Russell or Dr Anderson while Russell was away, Russell himself pre-empted the medical question by consulting an independent expert, a Dr Philpot. Though he was even more gloomy than Drs Anderson and Tuke about the hereditary insanity in Russell's family, Philpot was positively upbeat on the question of contraception, assuring Russell that he himself had used contraceptives for many years and that no bad effects were to be feared from them.

Armed with Philpot's advice, Russell was now confident that the ultimate victory would be his, so confident that he could even urge Alys to be a little indulgent towards his grandmother. 'I *know*', he wrote to Alys from Wales on 6 July, 'her conscience will be easier, however foolish such a conscience may seem to thee, if she had been allowed to try *everything* which seems to her a possible means of separating us . . . Since the real victory must be on our side we can surely have patience with them for a short time; and when we are married they will be powerless, particularly as this will separate us from them so completely.' He had reason to feel confident, for he had that day successfully turned the tables on his grandmother and, in so doing, effectively sealed his victory.

Lady Russell's last bolt had been shot the previous day, when Dr Anderson had written to Alys attacking the use of contraceptives and asking to see her, and Lady Russell herself had written to Russell commiserating with him over the break-up of his engagement. 'We think a very great deal of you, my Darling,' she wrote, 'you are going through a great trial, and my heart aches for you – but your natural uprightness will with God's help bring you through it all the better and the nobler man . . . the love of 22 years only strengthens in your day of need . . . Oh my boy! we foresaw the likelihood of this trial to you and did so long to save you from it.' These letters were evidently conceived as a *coup de grâce*, but both missed their target. Anderson's only made Alys more determined to resist the Russell family's wishes and elicited from her a firm and spirited reply, refusing to see Anderson or to call off the engagement; while, in reply to Lady Russell's letter, Russell wrote to his Aunt Agatha, playing his trump-card of Dr Philpot's advice:

Dearest Auntie,
    I gather from Granny's letter which I got this morning that she expects that our engagement will be broken off. As I told you before starting, in view of what the Dr I consulted told me, there is no chance of it being broken off, whatever Dr A may say or write . . . I also told you and Granny

that I am taking this fortnight away solely to please her, and not because I have any thought of breaking off the engagement. I only write this because I am afraid of Granny's telling people or hinting to them, that such an event is likely; if a rumour of that sort gets about, I should insist on marrying at once to stop it – Do whatever you think wisest about reading this letter to Granny.

In addition, Russell wrote to Dr Anderson in the same spirit, telling him that, in the light of Dr Philpot's advice, 'I have now *quite* decided on the marriage, and I must beg of you in conclusion not to tell my grandmother anything which may make her more unhappy than she need be.'

Russell's victory over his family, and his separation from them, was now complete, and, when he returned from Wales on 15 July, he moved his belongings out of Pembroke Lodge into Friday's Hill, where Alys had prepared a study for him to work on his Fellowship dissertation. While he was there, his family wrote almost daily, admonishing him for 'the life you are leading', but he was, by now, out of their reach. 'It was clear to me', he writes in his *Autobiography*, 'that they would drive me into insanity if I let them, and that I was getting mental health from Alys.'

The cost of the victory, however, was very great indeed and its effects were to last for the rest of his life. As his dream of the previous summer had shown, he already had a deep-seated fear that something dreadful about his family was being hidden from him, something to do with inherited madness; now that those fears had been shown to be well-founded, they became even more pronounced and central to Russell's perception of himself. The fears about madness that his grandmother had generated, he writes in his *Autobiography*, 'have never ceased to trouble me sub-consciously. Ever since, but not before, I have been subject to violent nightmares in which I dream that I am being murdered, usually by a lunatic. I scream out loud, and on one occasion, before waking, I nearly strangled my wife, thinking that I was defending myself against a murderous assault':

> The same kind of fear caused me, for many years, to avoid all deep emotion, and live, as nearly as I could, a life of intellect tempered by flippancy.

In the early hours of 21 July, just a few days after he had moved into Friday's Hill, and exactly a year after he had recorded the dream about his mother being hidden in a lunatic asylum (and also, he subsequently discovered, Alys's birthday), Russell took up his diary once more:

> This night is the anniversary of my dream about Alys, and also of her birth. Strange coincidence, which, combined with the fact that most of my dream has come true, very strangely impresses my imagination . . . My dream on her birthday; my subsequent discovery that my people had deceived me as in that dream; their solemn and reiterated warnings; the gradual discovery, one by one, of the tragedies, hopeless and unalleviated, which have made

up the lives of most of my family; above all the perpetual gloom which hangs like a fate over P. L., and which, struggle as I will, invades my inmost soul whenever I go there, taking all joy even out of Alys's love; all these, combined with the fear of heredity, cannot but oppress my mind; they make me feel as though a doom lay on the whole family and I were vainly battling against it, to escape into the freedom which seems the natural birthright of others . . . I feel as though darkness were my native element . . . I am haunted by the fear of the family ghost, which seems to seize on me with clammy hands to avenge my desertion of its tradition of gloom –
. . . Painful as it will necessarily be to them, I must for some time avoid seeing more than a very little of my people, and of P. L., otherwise I really shall begin to fear for my sanity. P. L. is to me like a family vault haunted by the ghosts of maniacs, especially in view of all that I have recently heard from Dr Anderson. – Here, thank heaven, all is bright and healthy, my Alys especially; and as long as I can forget P. L. and the ghastly heritage it bequeaths to me I have no forebodings, but only the pure joy of mutual love.

Around this time, he took to re-reading Ibsen, *Ghosts* and *Hedda Gabler* particularly. During the past year, he had begun by seeing Alys as an Ibsenesque heroine and ended by looking at his whole life as an Ibsen tragedy of ghostly revelations. Despite the great price paid, however, there was enormous consolation that the vision he had entertained of being rescued from his background by Alys had been realised. He was now free from Pembroke Lodge. He says that he will avoid it 'for some time', but, in fact, he never lived there again.

Prompted by his fears of being haunted further – this time by the ghost of his grandmother – Russell made one last concession to Pembroke Lodge, when he agreed in August to live separately from Alys for three months. The suggestion had come from his grandmother, who, it now transpired, was dying of cancer, or so, at least, Dr Anderson and his assistant Dr Gardiner seemed convinced. On 17 August, Russell was called from Friday's Hill to Pembroke Lodge to hear from Dr Gardiner the alarming prognosis that his grandmother had, at most, two years left to live. 'Perfect peace of mind is apparently a preventive,' Russell was told, drawing for himself the implication that, therefore, his disruption of Lady Russell's peace of mind over the last few months had been responsible for the cancer. In the sitting-room of Pembroke Lodge, Russell told Alys in a letter that night, he found his grandmother lying on the sofa: 'We embraced in silence for some time and then I looked at her sadly with tears in my eyes and she said, "Well I'm worse than you thought I was"; not with an air of triumph, but of mild reproof for my heartlessness in having felt so little anxiety.' She urged him to live apart from Alys for a while, which, after discussing it with Dr Gardiner and receiving from him the advice that it would diminish her unhappiness and, thereby, improve her health, he agreed to do.

By this time, nothing Lady Russell could do would have made any difference. Before he left Friday's Hill, Russell had experienced what he described to Alys as 'the happiest morning of my life'. He and Alys had gone up into the Bo-tree, where Alys allowed him to kiss her breasts. After that, nothing could have prevented Russell from going ahead with his intention to marry her. And nothing, either, could dampen his spirit, not even the death-bed entreaties of his grandmother. 'All this misfortune, present and prospective, cannot make me unhappy,' he wrote to Alys from Pembroke Lodge, 'when I have my mind so full of our sudden and wonderful conquest of purity and love . . . I am divinely happy in spite of everything, for I believe nothing now can rob us of our perfect purity and joy in each other.' In a later letter, he wrote: 'Thank God we have that divine morning to unite us always.' The memory of it made the thought of a three-month separation hard to bear, and yet: 'I fear for my Grandmother's ghost when she is dead if we don't do anything for her sake.'

The separation began with a week in Penrhos, North Wales, at the home of Russell's Uncle Lyulph Stanley. 'It is deadly dull here,' he wrote to Alys, 'F[riday]'s Hill has spoilt me, for now I am perpetually annoyed at the bar one has to put on one's tongue for fear of people's silly prejudices – while formerly I accepted these as inevitable, just as one might accept rainy weather – And oh dear, they seem so dry and stupid and lifeless compared to the delicious vitality and freedom of the people I like and have been seeing lately . . . However I sit alone with my Henry James and try to live in the world of Socialists and Italian Princesses, which is more interesting – I dare not let myself live in the interesting part of the real world more than I can help for fear of this awful separation the thought of which makes me sick.'

After a few days, however, Russell conceded that 'the conversation here is great fun', and his letters to Alys became filled with transcriptions of the witty and robust exchanges characteristic of Stanley family dinners. One day at lunch, he was greeted by his Aunt Maude with: 'Well Bertie . . . what do you know of a Miss Bryden?'

> I professed complete ignorance of any young lady of that name, so she said 'We've been looking up yr. descent & we want to know what you can tell us about a certain Mr Bryden. Had he a coat of arms?' So then I brightened up & gave them a biography of my great-great-grandfather of that name, persuading them that he *must* have had a coat of arms. 'Then', said Aunt M., 'I congratulate you! You're the only person at this table who has 16 quarterings.' Imagine my pride & elation! I have looked down on all the rest of the company ever since.

The implication of this letter that Russell knew the biographies of all sixteen of his great-great-grandparents is perhaps surprising, though the interest in heraldry and genealogy revealed by it confirms his later reply to a question about what he loved: 'mathematics and the sea, and theology and heraldry, the two former because they are inhuman, the two latter because they are absurd'. What, in the context of the lunchtime conversation at Penrhos, seems to have escaped him is that the Stanleys may – in the light of his recent announcement that he was to marry an American commoner – have had an ulterior motive in reminding him of the purity of his aristocratic lineage.

Returning to Pembroke Lodge on 27 August, Russell decided that he and Alys had better be married sooner rather than later; indeed, as soon as their three-month separation was over. 'We *must* be married in Nov[ember],' he wrote to Alys. 'In fact I regard that as a condition of the separation.' Marrying soon was now, for him, a necessary step in the final liberation from his family, and thus, so he believed now more than ever, in preserving his sanity. 'I grow more and more thankful everyday that I am in no way dependent on them,' he told Alys, 'as I might have been if I had been penniless or a girl; they would undoubtedly have driven me mad like my father and uncle, and now my aunt . . . The more I hate and dread them the more I love thee; if thee had had no other virtue I would have loved thee for that alone.' To soften the blow to his grandmother of his early wedding, Russell told her a lie which, despite its utter implausibility, seemed to comfort her a great deal, namely that he and Alys had no plans of ever sleeping together even after their wedding, so convinced were they of the medical disadvantages of birth control so vividly conveyed by Dr Anderson. It was a cynical deception, as Russell candidly acknowledged. 'Now that I know she is going to die soon,' he wrote to Alys in justification, 'I mind less giving her hopes not likely to be fulfilled.' Disappointing Agatha and Rollo was of no consequence; it was his grand-mother whose disapproval and distress he feared: 'As soon as she is dead there will be no one whose feeling need be spared: if my aunt is in the least obstructive then I shall be able to give her a piece of my mind.'

After just a night at Pembroke Lodge, Russell left to spend a few days with the Burdett family, who had once been neighbours of the Russells in Richmond, but who were now living in Wiltshire. While there he received news of an offer from Lord Dufferin, the British Ambassador to France, of a temporary post as an honorary attaché at the British Embassy in Paris. His first reaction was to refuse. It would, as he put it to Alys, 'be the first step in a career I wish to avoid'. Unless he proved completely incompetent, the offer would lead to others, such as Private Secretaryships and the like, which would, bit by bit, propel him into precisely the kind of career in politics and diplomacy for which his education and background had so perfectly prepared him, but against which he had resolutely set his face. On the other hand, it would fill his agreed three months apart from Alys in a fairly interesting way, and in a way moreover that would allow him to avoid living at either Pembroke Lodge or Friday's Hill. Seeking advice from Alys, he discovered that she was firmly of the opinion that he should accept, both because it would allow him to escape the influence of Pembroke Lodge, and because it would provide him with a good deal of useful practical experience.

On the second point, Russell was deeply suspicious. The one respect in which Alys resembled his grandmother, and in which her aims coincided with hers, was in her preference for practical politics over metaphysical specula-tions, and her desire to see Russell play some part in public life. From this point of view, she, like Lady Russell, entertained hopes that working at the embassy would prove useful in establishing Russell in 'society' and in bringing him into contact with people of considerable political influence. In a letter of 3 September, Russell did his best to quash these hopes. 'I have a passion for experience,' he told Alys, 'but if I am to make anything of the talents I have, I must eschew a vast deal of possible experience, shut myself in my study, and live a quiet life in which I see only people who approve of such a life (as far as possible)':

> I know my own needs, much better than thee does; and it is *very* important to me that thee should back me up in insisting on them. Casual experience of life is of very little use to a specialist, such as I aspire to be; good manners are *absolutely* useless . . . Both of us, too, are in danger of getting intoxicated by cheap success, which is the most damning thing on earth; if I waste these years, which ought to be given almost *entirely* to theoretic work and the acquisition of ideas by thought (since that is scarcely possible except when one is young), my conscience will reproach me throughout the rest of my life. Once for all. G[od]. A[lmighty] has made me theorist, not a practical man; a knowledge of the world is therefore of very little value to me.

Most twenty-two-year-old young men straight out of Cambridge would have accepted Lord Dufferin's offer, thrilled with the prospects it offered of political and social advancement, Russell – as he made sure both Alys and his grandmother understood – agreed to go to Paris *in spite* of those prospects.

Lady Russell hoped that his time in Paris would make Russell forget Alys, and, to this end, tried several times during the days before he left to get him to promise not to write to her during their separation. Russell, of course, refused, and, as he reported to Alys, 'told her there was absolutely no chance of our not marrying'. He himself, however, was worried about keeping Alys alive in his memory. He had not seen her since 17 August, and already, he told her, 'I have lost the power of visualising thee, which I only keep a few days after parting.' For him, letters were vitally important in maintaining contact.

Russell's sense of himself as a 'verbaliser' rather than a 'visualiser' was sharpened soon after he arrived in Paris by his reading of William James's *Principles of Psychology*, in the 'Stream of Thought' chapter of which James writes:

> An exceptionally intelligent friend informs me that he can frame no image whatever of the appearance of his breakfast-table . . . The 'mind-stuff' of which this 'knowing' is made seems to be verbal images exclusively.

'This is almost my own case,' Russell wrote in the margin of the book opposite this passage. Another passage he marked was on the following page where James, talking of the advantage of verbal rather than visual images, remarks that 'the older men are and the more effective as thinkers, the more, as a rule, they have lost their visualising power and depend on words.'

The extent to which Russell's mind depended upon words was measured to some extent in the 1940s by his friend Rupert Crawshay-Williams, who was then interested in the development of 'IQ' tests. Russell, Crawshay-Williams remarked, 'had *par excellence* a verbal (as opposed to visual) imagination. For him reality was mediated in symbols; in many situations there was no grasp of what was going on except via the medium of words':

> His need for verbal symbolisation was dramatically shown when I gave him an IQ test of the analogies type – the type which shows, at its simplest (say) a single-lined circle next to a single-lined square, and then shows by itself a double-lined circle and expects the testee to pick out from various alternative shapes a double-lined square.
> At first Bertie was much faster than any of my pupils at the school had been . . .
> And then, to our surprise, Bertie gave up before he got to the end.
> 'Please can I stop now?' he said. 'I can't do them.'
> We tried to make him go on, but he obviously hated the idea too much; it would have been boorish to try and force him.
> 'But what went wrong?' we asked. 'You were doing so well up to then; and the people who do well on the early questions invariably do relatively well on the more difficult questions.'
> 'I hadn't got any names for the shapes,' said Bertie.

Unable to maintain an image of Alys, Russell was determined to keep up a constant flow of words between them, and, after he left for Paris on 10 September until 17 November, when their three months apart came to an end, he wrote to her every day, usually twice and sometimes three times.

His letters described his day-to-day life, the people he worked with, his impressions of Paris, his tasks at the embassy and so on. But the subject that predominates, and to which he returns again and again, is sex: his views of it, his anticipation of it and his insistent attempts to overcome Alys's slight horror of it. The one memory he had of Alys that never faded was that of kissing her breasts on their last day together, an event which, he tried repeatedly to explain, was for him a great spiritual as well as physical experience. It was, he told her, 'far and away the most spiritual thing there has yet been in my life':

> But surely it must have been also the highest expression of physical love we have yet had – I was brought to it by physical feeling – and it is the only definite sexual thing we have yet experienced – so it gives me great hopes that the highest spiritual love may find its most perfect expression in physical things, and that the two may run parallel instead of conflicting.

So pivotal was the experience for him that he kept Alys's letters after 17 August separately from the others, 'because I feel that that experience made more of a stage and more of a difference in our love than anything that went before . . . It was divine!'

Between his memories of kissing her breasts and his anticipation of their forthcoming wedding night, sex was never very far from Russell's thoughts, and it acquired in his mind a sacred, almost religious significance. The customary way of looking at sex as something dirty – whether it came from a virginal abhorrence of the subject, as in Alys's case, or a smutty attraction to it, such as he found wherever he turned in Paris – filled him with loathing. It seemed sacrilegious, like the profanity of the boys he had known at Southgate. Sex had to be clean and pure. 'A really happy marriage', he told Alys, 'is seldom possible unless the man is pure-minded, and *that* he can never be as long as the only women with whom he can be intimate before marriage are prostitutes, and as long as everything sexual is to him associated primarily with them':

> I am sure the great thing is co-education, and great freedom of intercourse, with perfect knowledge of sexual matters, throughout the period of puberty – if the mystery were removed, half the morbid lust which belongs to that period would be removed with it.

He was thinking, of course, of his own adolescence, of having 'to learn what I could from the smutty talk of immoral companions'. Knowing, as he now did, 'the beauty of a reverent view of sex', the opposing view 'shocks me more and more every day':

> till the society of all men except my personal friends is become nauseous to me, and even of most women, because they think sex is shocking, which is only the other face of impurity – if their minds were pure, and they could think sanely and holily about it they couldn't imagine it shocking.

This last, he reassured Alys, he thought 'applies to thee as thee *was*, not as thee *is*'.

Russell's tasks at the embassy were light, and, finding them boring, he never described them in detail, telling Alys only that they consisted for the most part in copying the despatches of his superiors and in de-coding telegrams. In later life, he claimed that most of the despatches he had to copy were concerned with trying to persuade the French that a lobster is not a fish, though this is presumably an exaggeration designed to express his irritated boredom with the details of diplomatic negotiations. His leisure time – of which there was a great deal – was expected to be filled with social engagements, at which he would have the opportunity of making the acquaintance of important and influential members of the British Establishment. This, however, was exactly what he was determined not to do. These occasions were, to him, even more boring than his work, the talk being mostly of his aristocratic relatives or of sport (of the 'hunting, shooting, fishing' variety), neither of which subject appealed to him in the slightest.

He took instead to wandering around Paris, where, of course, he found little 'purity' and much that shocked him. 'I hate this place', he wrote to Alys:

> I have been walking about at night, and the endless rows of prostitutes with their painted lips and coarse 'allure' get on my nerves and depress me

terribly. The French man too is an unutterable beast: I suffer a physical pang every time I come across any coarseness even of word or feeling . . . It makes me despair of the world and the sex-question to see people so destitute of the rudiments of right feeling as they are here . . . I get to loathe the pettiness of everything, the pleasure-seeking air of the whole town. I should almost love to plunge into some ancient monastery and take any number of vows, to get away from the oppressive sinning of this place.

Some relief, perfect and glorious, from this French smuttiness was provided on 1 October, when he went to the Paris Opera to see a performance of Wagner's *Die Walküre*, the Germanic magnificence of which left him quite intoxicated. 'It has given me a wonderful exhilaration,' he wrote to Alys that night, 'at every note I felt the massive German and worshipped him – I wish I had been born a German – it was glorious to get something so un-French – they seem mere ingenious pigmies beside anything really big of the Teutonic Titanic sort. Even the absurdities – the thunder and lightning – . . . are big and invigorating after the stifling finniky appropriateness of everything French.' The Valkyrie themselves, of course, were much to Russell's taste, his ideal of womanhood writ large, 'a fine apotheosis of the great primitive woman such as Walt [Whitman] loves to praise and such as drawing-rooms destroy'.

Russell's image of Alys herself as 'the great primitive woman' had not, despite everything, been entirely dislodged from his imagination. She stood for him, he wrote on 12 October, 'as the woman of the future, not the transitional struggling woman . . . but the woman born with the victory already won . . . Hardly any other woman has been independent always without having to struggle.' As a Whitmanesque 'brawny and arrogant woman', Alys was made of unpromising stuff, especially where sex was concerned, but Russell was determined to fit her into the mould, partly by exaggerating the element of 'purity' in his own ideal. 'Thee loves me,' he wrote, 'I am sure, chiefly because I give thee what thee had feared no man had to give – purity . . . I also ask what few women can give – frankness and freedom from prudery, combined with purity, not worldliness as it usually would be – and it makes our tie so much closer to feel how we both make demands which seem almost too great to be satisfied, and which yet are satisfied by each other.'

His problem was one of representing – to himself, as well as to Alys – a woman who had cut from *The Leaves of Grass* the very poems that had inspired his ideal of 'primitive strong womanhood' as being free from prudery. His solution was to pretend that such prudery was in Alys's past, and that she was now, whether she realised it or not, 'a splendid animal' (as he put it in one of his letters), the very epitome of physical and mental health. When, for example, she confessed that she was not greatly looking forward to the sexual act, was convinced that she would not enjoy it and hoped that it would not take place very frequently, Russell attributed such feelings entirely to her previous opinion that sex, except for the purpose of procreation, was wicked and replied: 'I'm sure thy former views came from the notion that there was never any desire on the woman's part, which is utterly untrue; I have never been able to see any harm in moderate intercourse, where it is perfectly mutual and *quite* subordinate.'

Eventually, to Russell's delight, Alys admitted that she, too, had erotic thoughts, though she never quite managed to match his enthusiasm for the subject. 'It *will* be divine!', Russell tried to convince her. 'Far more so than we can imagine.' If the latter was true, it was not, in Russell's case at least, for lack of trying. Scarcely a day went by without his trying to imagine what it would be like, and, even in his determination to emphasise the spiritual and the pure, he had to admit he did not find it so very difficult to conjure up a vision of the physical pleasures of the sexual act. 'For physiological reasons,' as he put it, 'the more sensual pleasures are far easier to imagine, so that long absence makes them apt to come into the mind.' The truth of this was borne out in almost every letter he wrote from Paris. Finally he confessed that his memories of their last meeting were beginning to lose their spiritual dimension altogether, and that he could 'hardly ever recall the mood of our last days now – the thought of thy breasts produces only an intense sexual excitement, and none of the divine calm of that time.'

At other times, he spoke of such sexual anticipation with little regret for the associated lack of purity, and an urgent insistence that such desires demanded satisfaction:

I . . . sometimes dream and often think of the time when we shall be able to sleep together – I still have the thoughts which I called impure, but I'm not much afraid of them. I believe – though it all depends on how thee feels – that it would be a good plan, for me at any rate, to indulge physical feelings a good deal *quite* at first till they no longer have that maddening excitement to the imagination which they now have. I lie in bed and they come before my mind and my heart beats wildly and I begin to breathe heavily and sometimes I tremble with excitement – I feel *almost* sure that when once all the physical feelings have been indulged, this intense and almost painful excitement will subside, and whatever is pure and good and spiritual in them will survive . . . Tell me however if thee thinks this view dangerous or if it is distasteful in *any* way to thee, and I will accustom my mind to different expectations.

Alys's response to this was not encouraging, and she even suggested that they should wait a few weeks until after their wedding to have sex. This was deeply alarming, and Russell did his best to scotch the idea. 'Until we have had one experience of coition,' he argued, 'the thought will be fearfully exciting to me if we sleep together – I feel as if it would keep me from sleeping and keep my mind far more on that one subject than it should be – chiefly out of desire for the knowledge of the ultimate experience . . . during these last months I have felt as if the excitement would be too much for me almost, until it happened once.' He tried, he told her, to distract himself from 'that one subject' by repeating poetry and in other ways, 'but I seldom succeed' and he felt he needed a holiday from self-restraint: 'I should want . . . if only for 24 hours [to] break loose from it and just live.' He had, he admitted, 'got impure things for the moment rather on the brain, as I know for a certainty from dreams', but the best way to remedy the situation was to give way, for once, to his desires. His situation, he explained, was rather like that of the early Christian hermits described by Gibbon, who retired to the desert to devote their whole lives to the killing of lust and yet found that they were 'perpetually haunted by visions of naked harlots dancing before them and tempting them to sin'.

This general theme of the futility – and even wickedness – of trying to overcome strong passions by repressing them was developed by Russell in an interesting and revealing paper he wrote at this time for the Apostles called 'Cleopatra or Maggie Tulliver'. 'What shall we do with our passions?' the paper begins:

> Slay them, say Stoicism and Mediaevalism: fix our minds on the sovereign contemplation of virtue, or the Deity, and live a calm, unchanging unruffled life . . . Mrs Grundy's answer is different: to hold our tongues about them and draw the blinds before we indulge them is her gospel . . . As a reaction against both these, the French, and the English aesthetes of the last generation, admit them and glory in them – to indulge them beautifully is morality . . . passions in this Ethic are judged aesthetically, not by their practical consequences.

Against these extremes, Russell pitted the views of the 'Whitmaniacs' (among which, as the paper makes clear, he includes himself) who prize above all tolerance and sanity, and who thus have 'a derived worship for all those passions which the sane and healthy man or woman feels – these are for great Nature, and to be ashamed of them is to be ashamed of sane and normal humanity':

> Hence they too, like the French, glorify passion; but unlike the French, they glorify it only when it makes for health, when . . . it is 'sane lusty and adequate'. 'Without shame the woman I love avows the deliciousness of sex' says Walt.

The view for which the paper argues is that 'the greater a passion is the more it ought to be followed', for 'nothing can be accomplished without powerful passions' and the attempt to repress a passion is harmful to precisely the same extent to which it is powerful – harmful, that is, primarily to one's mental health. When Russell comes to list the dangers of repression, it becomes clear that his paper might equally have been entitled 'Whitman or Pembroke Lodge':

> . . . in time our desires sicken and die: we become purposeless anaemic beings, saints perhaps, but totally incapable of any achievement . . . a person who has resisted a great passion and prevented it from venting itself in action may come to regard with hatred all those who do not so resist,

even where there are no grounds for resisting – such a person is apt to idolise pain, to regard all enjoyment as wicked, and to become in consequence the most fiendish person imaginable in daily life. The passion remains, and not being allowed to take its natural course, it turns to mute rage against all who are more fortunate, and leads to the most ghastly morbid developments.

A common result of the attempt to repress passion, Russell writes later in the paper in a passage that anticipates by nearly sixty years the view dramatised in *Satan in the Suburbs*, 'is an unreasoning hatred of almost every body, and a joy in giving and watching pain'.

While he was working on this paper, Russell reported to Alys a dream he had in which he and she were married and Alys had a child, almost painlessly: 'my Grandmother was vexed at the way thee got off lightly in all life's troubles – she thinks it shows a shallow nature not to suffer as much as possible . . . All my Grandmother said was: First a sigh, then "*She* always gets off easily in all the troubles of life – (another sigh) *some* fortunate people are made that way" – and I said to myself that I always knew thee was a splendid animal, and I was proud of thy being so efficient . . . I always worship physical health and strength. I suppose because I have seen so much of the bad effects of its opposite in my family.'

Other examples that bore out Russell's theme were his Aunt Agatha and he himself, both in his desire for sexual experience and in the strength of his hatreds, not least for Agatha herself. When Alys mentioned that she was taking Eucalyptus for a cold, Russell protested: 'I hate to think of thy smelling of Eucalyptus, because my aunt spends half her life in an atmosphere of it, and I have such a devouring hatred for her that it makes me detest any association with that smell.' He was, as Beatrice Webb once remarked, 'a good hater', which his theory of repression allowed him to lay at the door of his family and of conventional morality. 'I *hate* Frenchmen with the sort of hatred Hedda had for Tesman,' he wrote to Alys (Tesman being Hedda Gabler's husband, a dry, respectable, middle-class academic whom Hedda despises for his timidity, his dullness and his lack of strong, glorious passions), 'all their ways annoy me, and their mere presence is acute pain. I am full of mad and foolish impulses due to repression.'

What these 'mad and foolish impulses' were he does not say, but it would be entirely in keeping with everything else he wrote on the subject of repressed desires to assume that they were in some way to do with inflicting pain and even murder. 'It will grow better as the time of our meeting draws near,' Russell told Alys, 'which will prevent my going quite mad. If the time had been 6 months I dare say I *should* have done something foolish during some part of it.' In 'Cleopatra or Maggie Tulliver', he described 'various instinctive impulses' that prey on the debilitated mind of a person trying to repress his passions, which the mind of such a person no longer had the energy to resist:

At first they are *mere* ideas – what little vigour remains is spent in keeping them so – but gradually they work like madness in the brain, and it becomes impossible to resist. Where, as in Dostojewski's *Crime and Punishment*, the impulse is not trivial, it produces pronounced mania . . . unless some strong and healthy passion is found to replace the one resisted, these impulses are apt to grow more frequent and more dominant, until, at worst, they develop into insanity.

Evidently, he considered himself to be at the stage of using what vigour he had in keeping these impulses as '*mere* ideas', but, consumed by hatred and preyed upon by 'mad and foolish impulses', the danger, if he continued to lead a repressed life, of committing a serious crime was one he, at least, considered entirely real.

The Apostles' meeting, on Saturday, 3 November 1894, at which Russell read 'Cleopatra or Maggie Tulliver' allowed him a welcome opportunity to disrupt his time in Paris with a weekend in England. He was not, of course, permitted quite yet to visit Alys, though as a substitute he arranged to have dinner with Alys's sister, Mary, in London on the Sunday night before his return to Paris. His reaction to being back in England, and especially Cambridge (and, more especially yet, among the Apostles), was ecstatic.

He took with him a short paper he had written on the Axioms of Geometry to show to Ward and to give to Sanger to read out to the Moral Science Club. The paper itself does not survive, but its central argument is preserved in a letter to Sanger, which shows that, in some respects, the view that Russell would later develop in his Fellowship dissertation was already formulated in his mind. This was the view that the question of whether space is Euclidean or non-Euclidean – whether, that is, space is curved or not – cannot be decided *a priori*, but that what *can* be established *a priori*, on the basis of a Kantian argument about the 'necessary features of any possible existence', is that, if space *is* curved, then its curvature must be constant. Within that constraint, the question of whether Euclid's axioms are true or not can only be decided empirically. As Russell predicted, the paper was too technical for the Moral Science Club, but, he told Alys, 'I shall be wildly eager to hear what [Ward] says about it. Short of love, his praise is about the most delightful thing in the world to me.'

'Cleopatra or Maggie Tulliver' was well-received by the Apostles, who voted afterwards on the question 'duty or passion?', with Moore, Marsh and Dickinson voting for 'duty', Sanger, McTaggart and others for 'passion', and Russell himself voting for both 'according to circumstances'. For Russell, though, it was bliss just to be back among the Apostolic fold. 'It has been *perfectly* delightful,' he wrote to Alys. 'I love them all far more than I supposed before . . . Moore though he didn't say much looked and was as glorious as ever – I almost worship him as if he were a god. I have never felt such an extravagant admiration for anybody.' He was delighted to be among people with respect for theoretical pursuits and gratified to be told again and again that he should concentrate on philosophy and not be diverted by economics (in Paris he had conceived the idea of writing a second Fellowship dissertation on the economics of Socialism). He was further delighted to hear – though he claimed to take it with a pinch of salt – that

Ward had said he was so safe for a Fellowship that it did not matter what he wrote about.

The following day, in a 'very good conceit' with himself over his success at Cambridge, he kept his appointment to dine with Mary ('Mariechen', as she was invariably called by her family), prior to accompanying her back to Paris where she intended to study in the Louvre. Alys, without, it seems, realising the fire she was playing with, had asked her sister to kiss Russell for her. Even before he arrived in England, Russell found this idea *'delightful'* and dwelt much on it in his letters to Alys: 'the thought of it is strangely pleasant . . . I am oddly excited – somehow the queer thought of transmitting a kiss by Mariechen requires analysis, it is so complex and confused.' Alys had not, apparently, given the matter the analysis it demanded and failed to see the potential complexities. Given that she had been receiving two letters a day for the past two months on the subject of Russell's pent-up sexual desires, and given also that Mary had for years espoused exactly the kind of Whitman-esque glorification of the body and of natural desire that Alys herself found shocking (and, also that – to Alys's further disapproval – Mary practised what she preached, leaving her husband for another man and then beginning an affair with yet another); given all this, it is quite extraordinary that it had never crossed her mind to wonder what 'confusions and complexities' might arise from encouraging Russell to look upon Mary as an ersatz version of herself.

Mary, in fact, was much closer than Alys to Russell's ideal of the kind of independent, passionate woman, the espouser of free love and the offender of conventional sensibilities, that he had read about in Whitman and Ibsen, and which he had in vain tried to see in Alys. Several times in the past, he had defended Mary's attitudes against what he regarded as the censorious priggishness of Alys and her mother; even – or perhaps, especially – Mary's promiscuity. 'As to her falling in love with different people,' he had written to Alys, 'that is a matter of temperament, and can't be helped. It is objected to, conventionally, but I never could understand why constancy should be a virtue, because it is simply *impossible* to love people because one ought to.'

Now, meeting Mary in London, and travelling with her to Paris, Russell's sympathies for her – and his attraction towards her – grew more intense. In their struggles with their families, in their determination to reject practical politics in favour of creative and intellectual pursuits, and, most ominously of all perhaps, in their criticisms of Alys, they discovered they had a great deal in common, and Russell now took it upon himself to explain, and to some extent justify, Mary to her sister. They got on so well that when they reached Paris, Mary decided to book into the same hotel as Russell, finding a room so close to his that they were able to share the same sitting-room. 'She is rejoicing at her escape from family life,' Russell wrote to Alys, 'and from an atmosphere where she is disapproved of – they are feelings I can sympathise with . . . She feels I suppose that she has a right to conduct her life her own way and I can well imagine so easy-going a person seeing very little harm in such proceedings. However I am biased by her being so agreeable and such a perfect companion for my present mood – I've no doubt really that all thee says is just, only I don't *feel* it.'

This, from Alys's point of view, was bad enough, but what made it far worse was that Russell's sympathy for Mary went hand-in-hand with a more sharply critical attitude towards Alys herself. The picture that Russell drew of his life in the hotel with Mary emphasised their intellectual enjoyment of each other. 'She has produced her Nietzsche and I have produced my Germans too,' he wrote, going on immediately to remark that he and Mary were agreed in thinking Alys to be 'really quite capable intellectually if thee chose':

> Of course one doesn't imagine thee would do any brilliant original thinking but thee might form part of the indispensable intelligent audience, which involves a lot of exertion and severe thinking, in order to get good taste in thoughts. And then thee will be able to criticise my thoughts, instead of laughing at the good ones and admiring those that are really common-place.

Russell's letters to Alys during this time are so appallingly insensitive that it is hard not to see in them some animus against her, some resentment perhaps that she was not more like her sister. Of the first two letters he received from her when he returned to Paris, the first contained a description of her being reduced to tears at the thought of not being able to see him while he was in England, a thought made worse by his obvious enjoyment of her sister's company, and the second made a valiant, but clearly forced, attempt to put a brave face on the situation: 'It *is* nice for thee to have Mariechen there to breakfast every morning . . . and I hope she will be rewarded by finding thee very stimulating. She's of a peculiar nature that can only be stimulated by young men, and I don't mean that in a mean way.' Russell's response to this was resolutely upbeat and revealed himself to be either quite deaf to the plaintive tone evident even in the second of Alys's letters or else completely indifferent to her feelings:

> Thy letter last night was *very* sad – it was *horrid* to think of thee in floods of tears. But it *was* a trying position to be so near each other – especially for thee who had to sit passive while . . . M'chen came to see me. But I'm immensely glad of thy cheerful letter this morning, and it will allow me to enjoy M'chen's society without drawback. She *is* very charming, all the more so for her complete selfishness, since one of her chief enjoyments is the pleasure of pleasing. I am trying to fall in love with her and make these last days pass, and I think I shall succeed enough to avoid too much impatience – she's a fearful flatterer.
>
> We spent the day walking and talking yesterday and I enjoyed it immensely – she is *so* sympathetic and nice, always saying just the thing which, whether true or not, one wishes to hear at the moment.

He was, he told Alys, slightly doubtful about the propriety of being together with Mary at the hotel and had consulted one of his superiors at the

embassy about it: 'He reflected a moment and then said it was all right –
but I didn't tell him we were sharing a common sitting-room.' Thus reassured, Russell felt quite free to be seen out with Mary, and the two of them
went almost every night to the opera together to hear performances of
Wagner.

Having brought Mary and Russell together in this way, and encouraged
Russell to look upon Mary as a substitute for herself, Alys seemed to feel that
she could do nothing now but respond with approval, or at least forbearance,
to Russell's indelicately expressed enthusiasm for her sister. 'I am *so* glad thee
has got M to make the time pass for thee, Dearest,' she wrote on 7 November.
'Thee may fall in love with her all thee likes, but I *shall* be mad if she converts
thee to Nietzsche.' To her diary, however, she confessed her hurt. 'I have
been perfectly miserable the last few days,' she wrote on 9 November. 'I am
so afraid I shall not be able to make B. happy, I am so dull. Cried.' Two days
later: 'Felt depressed and teary.'

Meanwhile, Russell was relentless in keeping her informed about how close
he and Mary were becoming and how much time they were spending
together:

> . . . we dined near the Rond Point, and came home and smoked and read
> Nietzsche, whose confusions I succeeded in pointing out to Mariechen. She
> seems genuinely interested in Metaphysics and is always getting me to talk
> about it, which I enjoy very much.
> (6 November)

> Mariechen and I went to *Carmen* last night, which was charming . . . We
> are to have a Wagner orgy soon, and Mariechen has been pouring forth her
> soul on the subject in a most delightful way. She is so nice and emotional
> that she fits my present mood to perfection.
> . . . I must stop this letter and begin copying – then I'm going to pick
> up Mariechen at the Louvre and walk to Notre Dame to make use of the
> delicious weather. It is lovely to have the days go by – they go so quickly.
> (8 November)

As Alys was no doubt all too painfully aware, there is a naturalness, a
lightness about Russell's descriptions of the times he spent with Mary that
contrasts vividly with the heavy, deeply earnest and often laboured way in
which he wrote both about and to Alys. His letters dwelt almost obsessively
on Mary, her virtues, her faults and the empathy that was growing between
them, and with every day that went by he sounded more and more like a man
in love. On 10 November, he wrote after midnight to say that Mary 'has only
just gone to bed, after a long and interesting talk':

> M. has been making me talk about sexual morality and my reasoning for
> preferring chastity to vice, which I found rather difficult . . . Then she
> repeated a host of poetry, rather well – and then we discussed the Zeitgeist
> and my people and God knows what – & finally she discovered to her

surprise that it was half-past twelve . . . M. is interesting on all sex questions, and has told me many things which I was glad to know . . . she is really, as she says herself, simply in pursuit of enjoyment – only she pursues it in a very graceful manner.

The following night, after returning again from the opera, they sat up till 1 a.m. talking and smoking 'and when M. went to bed she proposed a "sisterly kiss" on the forehead, which I accepted'.

Still more remorseless was the way Russell kept contrasting the things he and Mary talked about, the intellectual intimacy they were enjoying, with the gulf between himself and Alys on the question of theory versus practice, and his urging of Alys to abandon her political campaigning in favour of devoting herself to helping him in his theoretical work. In this view, as he repeatedly emphasised, he had the support of Mary, whose impatience with her husband's devotion to practical politics had been one of the main reasons she left him for Berenson: 'she says she thinks if thee believed in thyself a little more thee could really get more out of brain work . . . than out of meetings and committees – quite apart from the fact that thee would then be able to cooperate with me.'

The following day, he announced himself firmly on Mary's side in her disputes with her mother over morality. 'I am quite unable to see any harm in her scheme of life,' he told Alys (whom, as he well knew, found Mary's way of life as shocking as did their mother), 'it seems to me just as good as it could be, considering her nature and requirements.' Mary had originally planned to leave Paris that day, but she chose to stay on a day or two longer, apparently in order to spend more time with Russell. 'She seems to be enjoying herself very much here, and I think she grows fonder of me from day to day, as I do of her':

I hope thee doesn't think it shocking that on parting last night we repeated the ceremony of the evening before, only cheeks instead of forehead. I have a very sisterly affection for M. and feel as if I had known her always – we have grown singularly intimate during this week tête-à-tête – and it is nice to give the feeling some expression.

Mary finally left Paris on the night of 14 November, 'which I am very sorry for,' Russell told Alys, who, in a last attempt to keep a brave face, had written to him: 'Why should I mind thy kissing [Mary]? It is a pleasant and interesting experience if the person is pleasant . . . and one might as well do it when it seems *a propos*.' Russell's response to this was, to say the least, ungracious:

I didn't ask seriously whether thee minded my kissing her: the question was purely rhetorical and should have had a note of exclamation after it. It makes a natural and friendly end to an evening of talk, and if there had been the remotest possibility of thy minding, of course I wouldn't have done it.

He and Mary had sat up till 2 a.m. to celebrate their last evening together, 'talking in the firelight and reciting poetry to each other', and had agreed to meet again in Paris when she returned on 29 November (although Russell's three-month separation from Alys came to an end on 17 November, his job at the embassy did not finish until 1 December). When Mary left, Alys felt able, finally, to express her feelings. 'Cried most of the morning,' she wrote in her diary on 15 November, 'but felt better after some sleep. Mariechen left Bertie yesterday.' To Russell she wrote a blistering letter of anger, defiance and hurt, pouring forth all the rage she had hitherto repressed and disguised. His last letter, she began, had made her so miserable 'I tore it right up':

> Thy letters have all been utterly unsympathetic since Mariechen has been there, but I tried not to mind because I knew it only that thee was happy and busy. But this one seems more critical and superior than any, and was just too much for me . . . I never mind *thy* criticisms, Dearest, but I do mind echoes of Mariechen. Thee knows how utterly unsympathetic she has always been to anything I have really cared about, and since her last week at home I have had such a loathing of her morals and conduct that I can hardly think of her without shuddering.
>
> . . . It has made me really unhappy that thee should write so very much about my giving up practical work and how much happier it would make thee, when I find I can't do it and still be myself . . . it is so provoking to have thee reinforce thy arguments by Mariechen's . . . thee doesn't know her very well and I have purposely refrained from writing anything about her to thee this week so that thee might form thy own impression. What I do mind is thy taking her say-so about me.

The letter served its purpose. Russell immediately abandoned any hopes he had entertained that Alys might drop practical work in favour of becoming his research assistant, retracted his earlier defence of Mary's character and way of life, and reconciled himself to sharing his life with a stern and sombre moralist, devoted to the cause of temperance, rather than with a carefree and sensual hedonist to whom the pleasures of stimulating conversation, Wagnerian opera and metaphysical speculations were more important and worthwhile than the pursuit of public duty. With, one suspects, an air of wistful resignation, he did his best to repair the damage he had inflicted on his relations with Alys, with a letter begging her forgiveness with as much abject contrition as he could muster:

> I can't tell thee how ashamed and miserable thy letter has made me – Oh how shall I forgive myself? I can't think how I could have been such a *fool* as to write in an unsympathetic way. It is true Mariechen kept drawing pictures which seized on my imagination and I foolishly gave way to them. Oh forgive me Dearest . . . I *have* been blind and brutal. But oh I *will* make it up when we meet if anything can . . .

And so on, and so on, for several pages. He also sent Alys a 1,400-word document entitled 'A Psychological Explanation', which was every bit as abject and which elaborated on the theme of how, in his lonely and vulnerable state, he had been charmed by Mary, who had been 'brimming over with sympathy & friendly frankness, psychological [and] charming to look at', and who had *'seemed* honestly & genuinely anxious for thy happiness', so that 'I abandoned myself utterly to the pleasure of her company.'

The affair took something of the romantic edge off their longed-for reunion in London on 17 November, although in his *Autobiography* Russell claimed that 'making my peace only took ten minutes'. If this was true, however, it was because his contrite letters of the previous few days had paved the way to his forgiveness, and also because, in his contrition, he had surrendered to Alys on every point with regard to Alys's work, their future together, Mary's character and his own moral standards. The final upshot of the affair was thus that, when they married on 13 December 1894, they did so almost entirely on Alys's terms.

When Russell returned to Paris on 20 November to see his brief diplomatic career through to its inglorious conclusion, Alys and her mother began to make arrangements for the wedding. It was, despite Russell's agnosticism, to be conducted according to the Quaker marriage service and held at a Quaker Meeting Hall. Alys took some pleasure in making these arrangements ('I love that marriage service,' she told Russell, 'and have always longed to be married in that way'), but Russell viewed the whole business with an irritable aloofness. 'Don't imagine I really *seriously* mind a religious ceremony,' he wrote to Alys on 23 November, *'any* ceremony is disgusting and the mere fact of having to advertise the most intimate thing imaginable is loathsome to me.' The comment is revealing, showing that, as far as Russell was concerned, the significance of his wedding day was that he would, finally, experience sexual intercourse, and that he could see little more in the ceremony than a public announcement of the fact. He was, he told Alys, 'frantically impatient – that is why I sit over the fire and smoke – any other occupation takes my thoughts away from the one absorbing topic . . . But I am *very* happy all the same, because the goal of impatience is so near.'

Russell's delighted anticipation of the sexual consummation to come was almost enough to soften his distaste for the wedding arrangements. Soon after his return to England at the beginning of December, he attended an Apostles' meeting at which Moore presented a paper called 'Shall we take delight in crushing our roses?', in which he presented what he himself described as 'a conventional view of sexual morality', condemning copulation as immoral if not done with the intention of producing children. With just a few days to go before Russell's wedding night, Moore could not have chosen a subject closer to Russell's heart, and, so he told Alys, 'I spoke perfectly frankly and said there need be nothing lustful in copulation where a spiritual lobe was the predominant thing, but the spiritual love might seek it as the highest expression of union.' At the end of the evening, a vote was taken on the question 'Must copulation be lustful?', with everybody voting 'No' except Moore and McTaggart, who, however, rather against the spirit of Moore's argument, added to his 'Yes' vote the remark: 'But lust is good in its place.'

Despite the eager anticipation of his wedding night, Russell could summon no enthusiasm at all for the wedding itself, and, whenever he was consulted by Alys for his views on whom to invite, who should be best man, and so on, he responded with blank indifference. It was therefore left to Alys and her mother to negotiate with his family over the date and the wording of the invitations, to ask Frank to act as best man, and to decide which of Russell's family and friends should be invited. No doubt one reason for the horror with which Russell viewed the whole proceedings was the suffering he realised the occasion would cause to his grandmother, who was to the last implacably opposed to the marriage. In the event, neither Lady Russell, nor Aunt Agatha, nor even Uncle Rollo chose to attend the wedding, and, apart from Frank, Russell's relations were represented by various Stanleys, including his Uncle Lyulph, his Aunt Maude, his Grandmother Stanley and the Countess of Airlie.

The service, held at the Quaker Meeting Hall in Westminster on 13 December, was for him, Russell later said, a terrifying experience. Hannah, however, was delighted with it. Writing to Mary, she said that there had been 'lovely little sermonettes . . . two prayers and short intervals of silence', the beauty of the last marred only by Lady Stanley, who employed them 'in dropping her stick and shawl and her various belongings which someone had to rush forward and pick up'.

For Lady Russell the occasion was in the nature of a farewell to her beloved grandson. 'You are leaving us now for a new life, a new home, new ties and new affections,' she wrote to him a few days before the wedding. From her point of view, it was a defeat. But, if from Russell's it was a victory, the weapons that his grandmother had used to fight the battle ensured that it was at best a Pyrrhic one, a victory that left him more fearful than ever of the madness he had discovered in his family and, potentially, in himself. In the short-term, as Russell and Alys left for their honeymoon in Holland, he could feel that he was at last free from Pembroke Lodge. The family vault was, though, still haunted by the ghosts of maniacs, and however far he went from his relatives he would always be travelling with a 'corpse in the cargo'.

4

THE WHOLE AND ITS PARTS

Perhaps inevitably, Russell's wedding night did not live up to the 'divine' experience he had been anticipating for so long. He and Alys being both without any sexual experience, he wrote in his *Autobiography*, 'we found a certain amount of difficulty at the start.' However, 'the difficulties appeared to us merely comic, and were soon overcome.' Their honeymoon was spent at the Hotel Twee Stenden in The Hague, from where Alys wrote to her mother that on their first day together they had taken 'a walk on the sea-shore at Schiveningen in a splendid storm of wind', and that they did 'nothing but laugh all the time'. Russell had chosen Holland in the hope that he and Alys might be able to go ice-skating. There was, however, wrote Alys, 'no immediate prospect of skating . . . but we have enough to amuse ourselves without that!'

News of the married couple's sexual progress was eagerly awaited back home, both by Alys's mother and by Lady Russell. 'Now do write me a few private particulars,' wrote Hannah. 'How do thy nightgowns work; does thee like them as well as pyjamas? Does Bertie like the pyjamas . . . who gets up first . . . I want all the particulars.' Alys complied by sending Hannah as many intimate details as she dared commit to writing, but asked her to burn the letter after she had read it. This Hannah did, but the information it contained apparently enabled her to put Lady Russell's mind at rest. 'I may tell thee in the strictest confidence', Hannah told Alys, 'that her great fear seemed to be that you did not live together as man and wife, but I told her that I was sure you did, and this seemed a *great* relief to her.' More likely, however, it was a great disappointment, Lady Russell's enquiries being prompted, one supposes, by the forlorn hope that her grandson might have kept the promise he had made the previous August not to sleep with his wife. With news of the consummation of the marriage died Lady Russell's last hope of preserving her 'angel child' for a more blessed future.

After three weeks in Holland, Alys and Russell travelled to Berlin. During the journey, Russell recalled, his attitude towards Alys underwent an extraordinary, if momentary, change: 'under the influence of sexual fatigue, I hated her and could not imagine why I had wished to marry her. This state of mind lasted just as long as the journey from Amsterdam to Berlin, after which I never again experienced a similar mood.' What does he mean? That he hated

Alys because her voracious appetite for sex had left him exhausted? This seems rather difficult to believe. Everything Alys said, both before and after her wedding – about men generally, about their sexual appetites in particular, and about her own attitudes to sex – would rather give the impression that she looked upon the sexual act with some distaste, if not with outright repugnance. More credible is the idea that 'sexual fatigue' here is a euphemism for 'impotence', a condition from which Russell was to suffer many times later in life, and that Russell looked upon Alys with hatred because she had failed to provide him with the sexual bliss of his fantasies, because (unlike her sister?) she had failed to stimulate him. The flannel nightgowns about which Hannah had so solicitously enquired were, in fact – though it is doubtful he admitted as much to Alys at this stage – loathed by Russell, who complained many times later of how unalluring they were.

In Berlin the marriage – which never reached the heights of rapturous passion that Russell had sometimes hoped for – was saved from premature collapse by a growing sense of companionship and mutual support. The period of his marriage to Alys, Russell was later to say, 'was intellectually the most fruitful period of my life, and I owe a debt of gratitude to [her] for having made it possible'. This she did by attending to the practical details of life on his behalf, leaving him free to concentrate on intellectual matters. That this would be the pattern of their married life had been established in their correspondence the previous autumn, when Russell had emphasised his utter inability to attend to mundane matters for himself. 'Though I curse the aristocracy,' he had written in September, 'they have saddled me with their bad habits, and I cannot approach happiness without a servant. When I am left to myself I get into the sort of state of dumb dreariness and helplessness of Dickens' childhoods – it is silly, but the fact.' A month later, he told Alys:

> There is one respect in which I *shall* be *utterly* and deliberately selfish in marriage – I shall leave bills and buttons and shopping and all such things to thee, because thee is so made thee can do them within the actual time they take, whereas with me they waste the whole day, owing to the disgusting mood they put me in.

In this way, the practical caste of Alys's mind, upon which he and Mary had poured so much scorn in November, was turned to his advantage.

In Berlin, Russell formulated for himself an ambitious long-term plan of study and writing that sought to synthesise, in classic Hegelian fashion, the demands of theory and practice:

> I remember a spring morning when I walked in the Tiergarten, and planned to write a series of books in the philosophy of the sciences, growing gradually more concrete as I passed from mathematics to biology; I thought I would also write a series of books on social and political questions, growing gradually more abstract. At last I would achieve a Hegelian synthesis in an encyclopaedic work dealing equally with theory and practice . . . The moment had a certain importance: I can still, in my memory, feel

the squelching of melting snow beneath my feet, and smell the damp earth that promised the end of winter.

Though he apparently remained unconscious of the fact, the Hegelian synthesis that Russell describes here might serve as a perfect metaphor for the hope that his marriage to Alys would prosper, that their apparently incompatible commitments to, on the one side theory, and on the other practice, might be fused into a harmonious whole.

Russell and Alys stayed in Berlin throughout the first three months of 1895, with Russell attending lectures in economics at the university and both of them making efforts to become acquainted with members of the Social Democratic Party, then the most influential Socialist movement in Europe. Russell's interest in this movement was led by Alys, who saw in Socialism the best hope for achieving women's suffrage, and the German Social Democratic Party as the party most likely to establish a Socialist government. In thus following Alys, Russell was, publicly and deliberately, distancing himself from his aristocratic background. His family, predictably perhaps, had connections with the British Embassy in Berlin – Lady Ermyntrude Malet, the wife of Sir Edward Malet, the British Ambassador in Berlin, was a cousin – and, had they chosen to, Russell and Alys could have spent their time in Berlin being entertained by various titled members of the British and German social élites. At their first dinner at the embassy, however, Alys mentioned that they had attended a Socialist meeting, and, from that moment, they ceased to be respectable among high society, and their first embassy dinner was also their last. Far from being outraged by this offence to Establishment sensitivities, Lady Russell, on this occasion, threw her support behind Russell and Alys. 'The issue was a public one,' Russell later wrote, 'and on all public political issues, both she and my Aunt Agatha could always be relied upon not to be illiberal.'

Towards the end of March, Russell and Alys left Berlin and went to Florence to stay with Mary. 'Bertie and Alys seem really happy,' Mary wrote to Hannah. 'I notice that she has been very much influenced by his way of thinking, but that is natural as he is really so clever. They are eating their breakfast in the dining room now, and I hear the peals of laughter from moment to moment.' To other correspondents she made less effort to disguise her condescension towards her little sister. 'We call her "Conventionality in Progress",' she wrote to Hermann Obrist, 'but I trust under Bertie's guidance she may grow more of a person. I see some signs already.' In her diary she recorded that in the evenings they all entertained one another with conversation and by reading to each other – Russell reading, for example, from the Book of Job and *Prometheus Unbound* – a form of entertainment, she implied, more suited to herself than to her less intellectual sister:

Poor Alys gets *so* bored and sleepy with all these talks and readings and keeps continually looking at her watch and tries to cheer herself up by thinking of other things.

After Florence, Russell and Alys travelled down the Adriatic coast, staying at Pesaro, Urbino, Ravenna, Rimini and other places. 'This remains in my memory as one of the happiest times of my life,' Russell later recalled:

Italy and the spring and first love all together should suffice to make the gloomiest person happy. We used to bathe naked in the sea, and lie on the sand to dry, but this was a somewhat perilous sport, as sooner or later a policeman would come along to see that no one got salt out of the sea in defiance of the salt tax. Fortunately we were never caught.

Returning to England in the early summer, they moved into Friday's Hill, where Russell settled down to write his Fellowship dissertation, which had to be submitted in August. The dissertation itself has not survived, although part of it is preserved as 'The Logic of Geometry', a paper published in *Mind* in January 1896 – Russell's very first philosophical publication. This shows that the central argument of the thesis follows roughly the line suggested by Russell's letter to Sanger the previous autumn: that the question of whether space is Euclidean or non-Euclidean is an empirical one, but that Kant had been right in thinking that some features of space were *a priori*, one of these features being the one Russell had emphasised to Sanger, namely that if space is curved, its curvature has to be constant.

Russell's argument for this centres on what he calls the 'Axiom of Congruence' or the 'Axiom of Free Mobility': the idea that space must be such that fixed bodies, geometrical shapes, should be able to move around it without having to change their geometrical properties. Thus, for example, if one drew a triangle on the surface of a sphere, one could imagine that triangle moving around the surface quite easily, without having to deform itself into a new shape. This is because the surface of a sphere, though curved, is curved constantly, so that one part of its space is just like another. But now consider the surface of an egg: if one drew a triangle on its fat end and tried to imagine sliding that triangle along the surface of the egg to its thin end, one can see that it would no longer fit the surface, because the space is different at either end – the curvature of the egg's surface, in other words, is not constant.

Russell's central claim in his Fellowship thesis was that physical space cannot be like the space on the surface of an egg, its curvature cannot vary from place to place. This has a certain plausibility, and might even be regarded as a platitude, were it not for the fact that, according to the theory of relativity, physical space *is* like the surface of an egg, its curvature increasing in accordance with the gravitational forces exerted on it by large, dense masses. Russell's early theory of geometry and space, therefore, is now regarded as one of the few philosophical theories capable of complete scientific refutation. In the light of this, Russell was in later years rather hard on his 'somewhat foolish' early theory and refused to allow it to be reprinted, though it is in fact an impressively subtle and interesting (even if incorrect) piece of philosophical argumentation.

Certainly, it was perceived as such by Russell's examiners, Whitehead and Ward. In October, Russell, in the second stage of the election process, had to go up to Cambridge to sit exams for his Fellowship application, which consisted of one general essay paper and two mathematics papers. Writing to Alys on 2 October, after the first of these, he sounded confident of his performance and of his chances of election. A week later, however, he reported a depressing conversation he had had with Whitehead about his dissertation:

> He says he and Ward . . . disagreed with almost every view I advocated; Ward also found my metaphysics and Psychology rather thin – like my chances, I thought when Whitehead told me . . . I suspect I am not much good at Philosophy.

Whitehead – who was evidently enjoying himself – told Russell later in the conversation that Ward and Sidgwick were more dissatisfied with the dissertation than he had been, from which, Russell told Alys, 'I drew the blackest inference.' The next day the announcement was to be made and Alys came up to Cambridge to lend Russell moral support. So convinced was Russell that he would not be elected that he and Alys watched the proceedings from his window. As Alys described the occasion to her friend Mary Gwinn:

> The Master & Examining Fellows wrangled about it for three hours and a quarter – then they marched across the Court in the rain, old Sidgwick running after (he always runs, it's good for his liver) to the Chapel, and went in thro' the old doors. There the Holy Spirits revealed the names of the four Fellows, and these were announced to an expectant crowd waiting in the drizzling mist outside. Of course, we could only see the excitement, not hear anything, but Bertie's friends soon came rushing over to tell him.

There had, of course, never been any doubt about Russell's success, and Whitehead later excused himself for the severity of his criticisms by saying with a smile that it was the last time he would be able to speak to Russell as a pupil.

The importance of the Fellowship was to reassure Russell that, in the minds of the people who most counted, he was good at philosophy and therefore was justified in devoting himself to it. The Fellowship ran for six years and carried with it a small stipend, which Russell gave away to the newly established London School of Economics. As for the obligations that went with it, these were so slight as to be almost unidentifiable. Russell did not have to give lectures or tutorials, and did not have to reside in college or even in Cambridge. It was in no sense a 'job', although, as a recognition of his abilities, it was crucially important to Russell's chosen vocation.

Although impatient to get on with his philosophical work, Russell – in deference both to his Hegelian plan to synthesise theory and practice and to Alys's wishes – devoted the next six months chiefly to political questions.

This was the period during which he was most closely associated with Sidney and Beatrice Webb and the Fabian Society (which, however, he did not formally join until 1897, by which time philosophy had almost entirely replaced politics in his preoccupations). The Fabian Society, which, apart from the Webbs, included among its members George Bernard Shaw, H.G. Wells and Graham Wallas, had been founded the previous decade to propagate Socialism. Its name was taken from the Roman general, Fabius, who, during the second Punic War, had avoided pitched battles with Hannibal's Carthaginians in favour of a campaign of continual harassment. Similarly, the Fabians favoured a gradual approach to the establishment of Socialism, and devoted themselves to the promotion of democratic Socialist measures rather than to incitement to revolution. Accordingly, they produced a series of essays, pamphlets and books containing carefully researched investigations into living conditions among the industrial working-class, and arguing for an extension of the franchise to include working people and for the creation of the Welfare State to secure some measure of economic justice.

In 1894, the Webbs' reputation as the joint-heads of this movement was established by the publication of their *History of Trade Unionism*, a reputation that was strengthened a few years later by the publication of their second collaborative book, *Industrial Democracy*. Among admirers and detractors alike, they were both respected and mocked for their diligence, dedication and rather dour devotion to duty. (When Russell discovered that his mother had known Beatrice Webb and her sisters in their youth and had described them as 'social butterflies', he remarked that he at once 'conceived a considerable respect for my mother's seriousness'.)

Russell first met the Webbs soon after their marriage in 1892 when they came to visit the Pearsall Smiths at Friday's Hill. Mary's estranged husband, Frank Costelloe, was a committed Fabian and a close friend of the Webbs, and through him the whole family, especially Logan, had been drawn into the Webbs' circle. On first meeting them, Russell took a liking to Beatrice, but reacted to Sidney with a rather snobbish disdain. Unlike Beatrice, whose family background was *haute bourgeois*, Sidney's orgins were suburban and lower middle-class, and Russell was quick to notice his 'cockney' accent and the fact that he looked anxiously round the table for guidance on picking up the correct cutlery. When he mentioned to his grandmother that he had met Sidney Webb, she responded with a more emphatic snobbery. She had, she said, heard Webb lecture in Richmond and thought that he was 'not quite . . .'.

'Not quite what?' Russell demanded.

'Not quite a gentleman in mind or manners,' Lady Russell finally said.

During the autumn of 1895, Russell was drawn further into the Webbs' orbit, partly through living in close proximity to them. After their marriage the Webbs moved into 41 Grosvenor Road (the road that runs alongside the river at Pimlico, now called 'Millbank'), next door to Frank Costelloe, who lived at number 40, and a few doors away from the Pearsall Smiths' town house at number 44, where Russell and Alys lived whenever they were in London. At this time, the chief preoccupation of the Webbs was the establishment of the London School of Economics, and Russell was asked by them to give one of its first courses of lectures, a series of six talks on German Social Democracy.

In order to research the course – and to give Alys further opportunity to meet Social Democratic leaders, and to study the role of feminism in German Social Democracy and 'the woman question' in Germany generally – Russell and Alys returned to Berlin for two months at the end of 1895. Shortly before they left, Russell's admiration for the Pearsall Smith family, and especially for Hannah, was diminished considerably by seeing how Hannah dealt with her husband's infidelities and the spite with which she treated him generally. Robert had, by this time, become alienated from his entire family except his brother Horace, and relations between him and Hannah, which had been strained for years, took a final turn for the worse when he acquired a mistress, a 'polished female friend', as Hannah described her, who lived across the Thames in Lambeth. According to Barbara Strachey, a great-granddaughter of Hannah and Robert and the author of a history of the Pearsall Smith family: 'when he was in London, Robert could be seen walking across Vauxhall Bridge every morning to visit her, while Hannah and Alys would lurk behind the curtains and point him out to each other in fine female fury'. Robert supposed that the family knew nothing about his affair, and, somewhat carelessly, used to tear up the letters he received from his mistress and throw them in the waste-paper basket. While he was out, Hannah would fit the pieces together again and read the letters out to Alys and Logan amid fits of laughter.

Russell was disgusted by this crass and humiliating behaviour and came to think of Hannah as 'one of the wickedest people I had ever known'. Alys, however, despised her father almost as much as Hannah did, and, in Russell's words, 'had an unbounded admiration of her mother, whom she regarded as both a saint and a sage'. It was an issue on which, like so many others, Russell's sympathies coincided with those of Mary, who liked and sympathised with her father and was similarly disgusted with the self-righteous vindictiveness shown towards him by Hannah and Alys, from whom she too became increasingly alienated. Once, when she was staying at Friday's Hill, Mary wrote to Berenson in despair at the 'stupidity and boringness' of the people around her: 'The impossibility of talking – the dreariness of the platitudes we all utter – the vanities and weaknesses of us all. It is horrible. Bertie is the only person whom I thoroughly like and get on with.'

It was the year of Oscar Wilde's trial and imprisonment, and, while Hannah worried that Wilde would not be punished enough and argued that Wilde's case showed the wisdom of castrating all men, Mary wrote in her diary about how miserable the treatment of 'poor Oscar' (as she called him, just as she often referred to Robert as 'poor father') had made her: 'It is horrible to think what his feelings must be.' Russell's letters and other writings maintain a curious silence about the Wilde case – which in the summer of 1895 was on everybody's minds and lips – but one can with complete confidence, I think, assume his attitude to have been more like Mary's than like Hannah's. With Alys, one feels less confident.

Russell's disgust at Hannah, and Alys's resolute loyalty towards her and all that she stood for, was, Russell says in his *Autobiography*, one of the reasons why his feelings towards Alys changed: 'Sometimes I tried to discuss her mother with Alys, but this proved impossible. In the end, some of my horror of the old lady spread to all who admired her, not excluding Alys.' The context in which these remarks are placed would lead one to think that this horror of Alys dated from about 1901, but in fact his recollections of Hannah's treatment of Robert's affair with his mistress date from the autumn months of 1895, during the very first year of their marriage.

In November of that year, Russell and Alys left for Berlin, where, over the next two months, they had ample opportunity to see for themselves the nature of the Socialist movement and the repressiveness of the Kaiser's government. They attended many Socialist meetings and were given a warm welcome by the leaders of the Social Democrats, August Bebel and Wilhelm Liebknecht, the latter of whom was imprisoned during their visit when the German police decided on a renewed clamp-down on Socialist agitation. Influenced by his horror at this repression, the lectures that Russell wrote on the basis of this visit – which at the end of 1896 were turned into his first book, *German Social Democracy* – concentrate less on what the British might learn from the German Socialists than on what the Germans, both the Government and the Socialists, might learn from British liberalism. In a paper he presented to the Fabian Society on his return from Berlin, called 'German Social Democracy as a Lesson in Political Tactics', Russell argued that both the 'sectarian intolerance' of the Marxists and the reactionary zeal of the police owed their origin to the fact that 'the advanced Liberal, such as we know him at home, is almost non-existent in Germany.' And this, he argued, showed the wisdom of an alliance between Socialists and liberals dedicated to both democracy and economic justice.

His course of lectures was written in the same spirit. As he put it in the preface to the 2nd edition, published in 1965: 'The point of view from which I wrote the book was that of an orthodox Liberal.' The course begins with a lecture devoted to a theoretical analysis of Marxism, in which Russell rejects almost wholesale Marx's economic theories and the doctrine of historical materialism and emphasises that it is as a (false but inspirational) religion that Marxism is properly to be understood. Subsequent lectures deal with the history of the German Social Democratic movement, emphasising the import-ance of Ferdinand Lassalle, and severely criticising the German authorities, especially the tyrannical methods of the German police. In conclusion Russell writes that, if the Social Democrats gain power 'with all their ideals intact and without a previous and gradual training in affairs', then they would be dangerous, for, they might 'like the Jacobins in France, make all manner of foolish and disastrous experiments'. The lesson thus to be learnt is that democratic Socialists who are not bound by dogmatic Marxist theory should work with progressive liberals, and that governments should pursue liberal policies and demonstrate a 'friendliness to the working classes, or rather common justice and common humanity', so that the detestable notion that class war is inevitable should 'find less acceptance, and less ground in the conduct of rulers'.

As a contribution to political and economic theory, *German Social Democracy* is almost self-consciously the work of a gifted and well-informed

Bertrand's favourite attitude for study - book resting on feet -

1 Sketch of the infant Bertrand Russell by his mother, Kate Amberley, 1873.

2 and 3 Lord and Lady John Russell.

4 and 5 Russell's parents, Kate and John Amberley.

6 Russell's birthplace, Ravenscroft, Monmouthshire.

7 The Amberleys, Frank and Rachel outside Ravenscroft.

8 Kate and John Amberley in the study at Ravenscroft.

9 and 10 Frank and
Rachel Russell.

11 Pembroke Lodge in Richmond Park, Bertrand Russell's home from 1876 to 1893 (from a painting dating from 1883).

12 A Russell family group outside the summer house at Pembroke Lodge, 1863. Sitting down are Lord and Lady John Russell, with Amberley standing behind Lord John and his brother Willy to the left of Lady Russell. On the ground at the front is Rollo, while on the extreme right is Agatha.

13, 14, 15 and 16 Russell as a young boy at Pembroke Lodge,
sitting (top right) on his Aunt Agatha's knee.

17, 18 and 19
Russell aged between
eight and ten.

amateur, and, as the first step along Russell's path of Hegelian synthesis between metaphysical theory and practical politics, it is unconvincing. But its general view of the relative merits of Marxism and Liberalism has stood the test of time remarkably well, and, some might say, has been entirely justified by the political history of the twentieth century. What is most impressive about the book, however, is that it was written when Russell's mind was really on other things. When the book was published, he wrote, 'I took no great interest in it, as I had determined to devote myself to mathematical philosophy.'

Even while he was delivering the lectures, Russell spent the bulk of his time thinking not about politics but about mathematics. He had been asked by Stout to review for *Mind* a book on atomism in science by the French philosopher and historian of science, Arthur Hannequin, entitled *Essai critique sur l'hypothèse des atoms dans la science contemporaine*, a task to which he devoted a great deal of time and effort and which turned out to have an important influence on his philosophical development for the next few years. The theme of the book is that science rests on a fundamental contradiction, needing on the one hand to represent everything atomistically – as a series of discrete, numerically countable 'things' – in order that mathematics might be brought to bear upon it, and, on the other hand, having to admit that there are in nature things that are not made up of discrete, atomistic components, but are rather continuous. Motion, for example, is the continuous path of an object through space and time, but, if we are to measure velocity, we have to break this continuity down into discrete 'infinitesimal' differentials and pretend that nothing is lost thereby.

To some extent, Hannequin's critique here is a restatement of the contradictions in the differential calculus that Bishop Berkeley had exploited in the eighteenth century in his famous polemic against Newton, *The Analyst*, in which he ridiculed Newton's Calculus for its theory of 'infinitesimals', for pretending that a Something could, if it is small enough, be regarded as a Nothing, and yet still be used in calculations. What are these 'infinitesimals'? Berkeley taunted. Can we not call them the 'Ghosts of Departed Qualities'? More generally, Hannequin's book might also be seen as a restatement and confirmation of the old idea that analysis is to some degree always a falsification.

One respect in which Hannequin's book breathed new life into these old ideas, and, in so doing, set the agenda for Russell's philosophical thinking, was in its criticisms of some recent attempts by pure mathematicians to overcome these contradictions, in particular that of Georg Cantor who, by developing a whole new system of 'transfinite numbers', claimed to be able to represent continua numerically. 'This criticism of Cantor seems to me sound and good', Russell noted in the margin of Hannequin's book, but, however convinced he was that Cantor's work was mistaken, he was nevertheless curious to discover – something his mathematical studies at Cambridge had not taught him – that these philosophical problems had been at least addressed by pure mathematicians, and he was sufficiently intrigued to make a close study of Cantor's work. While he was giving the lectures on German

Social Democracy, therefore, he used to spend every day at 44 Grosvenor Road, 'reading Georg Cantor and copying out the gist of him into a notebook'.

When he finished giving the course, he and Alys moved into a small cottage not far from Friday's Hill called The Millhangar, where Russell now retired to concentrate on philosophical work. Shortly before they moved into their new cottage, Mary recorded in her diary an interesting four-way conversation that took place at Friday's Hill:

> We were confessing our ambitions last night. Bertie owned to the modest desire to write 'a dialectic logic of all the sciences; and an ethic that should apply to politics'. Alys followed with the hope that she might bring the Woman's Movement and Socialism into closer rapport. Bernhard seemed to be bent on writing a psychological aesthetic of the Fine Arts. My wishes soared no higher than writing a Classic Guide to the pictures in the Louvre.

The conception of philosophy that guided Russell's ambitions at this time was that provided by McTaggart in his *Studies in the Hegelian Dialectic*, which was published in the spring of 1896. McTaggart's emphasis was on the interconnectedness of everything in the world as perceived by Hegel's philosophy. Separateness, according to this doctrine, is an illusion, and is shown as such by a dialectic that proceeds from the lower categories of the understanding – things like space, time and matter – to the highest, the Absolute. Only this latter is independent and real, and only this is rational; all the lower categories are enmeshed in contradictions that are resolved by successive syntheses until one reaches the Absolute. In this vision, logic and religion meet, for the logic of this dialectic shows us that 'all reality is rational and righteous . . . the highest object of philosophy is to indicate to us the general nature of an ultimate harmony, the full content of which it has not yet entered into our hearts to conceive.' 'All true philosophy must be mystical,' McTaggart declares, 'not indeed in its methods, but in its final conclusions.'

In these words, McTaggart summarises the inspirational hope that fuelled the ambition that Russell confessed to Mary, the hope that something like Spinoza's religion might be demonstrated by hard reasoning. Russell's intention was to put some flesh on to the skeleton of McTaggart's view of the dialectic, actually to show the contradictions by which one might move from mathematics to physics, and from physics to metaphysics, and thence to an understanding of the Absolute. Within this scheme, his work on geometry would be the first step, in showing that geometry was enmeshed in contradictions that it could not solve by itself and which needed a dialectic shift to physics to resolve. Then physics would be shown to be contradictory in a manner similar to that used by Hannequin, and thus in need of a dialectical transition to metaphysics. And so on, until the truth of the Spinozistic, monistic conception of the world is perceived and understood.

It was a conception of philosophy diametrically opposed to the 'analytical philosophy' that Russell was to adopt later, and with which he is more readily

associated. It was a conception according to which logical analysis (as opposed
to synthesis) was looked upon with some distrust, and in which the discovery
of contradictions in mathematics was taken to imply, not that mathematics
needed to build upon more secure foundations but that it was inherently
flawed as a means of understanding reality. At this time, Russell considered
philosophy to be superior to mathematics as a means of understanding the
nature of mathematics, because the contradictions that mathematicians swept
under the carpet, philosophers held up to the light. In the summer of 1896,
these attitudes were expressed in an article called 'On Some Difficulties of
Continuous Quantity', in which he discussed 'the difficulties of continua
[that] have been felt by philosophers, and evaded, with ever subtler analysis,
by mathematicians' with the purpose of demonstrating 'what mathematicians
are in danger of forgetting':

> that philosophical antinomies, in this sphere, find their counterpart in
> mathematical fallacies. These fallacies seem, to me at least, to pervade the
> Calculus, and even the more elaborate machinery of Cantor's collections.

The 'mathematical fallacies' that Russell wished to use as examples were
the well-known contradictions of the notions of continuity, the infinitesimal
and the infinite, as those notions were traditionally understood, notions
which, as he was to learn over the next few years, had all either been
dispensed with or provided with more rigorous definitions in the new
mathematics. Indeed, his conversion from a Hegelian philosopher to an
analytical one was due, more than anything else, to his growing appreciation
of these technical developments, which eventually convinced him that mathematicians had more to contribute to the philosophy of mathematics than
philosophers, and also that analysis, not synthesis, was the best means of
arriving at the truth. For the moment, however, Russell remained convinced
of the superiority of Hegelian metaphysics over mathematics and felt able to
dismiss Cantor's approach to the problem of continuity – which he would
later herald as one of the greatest achievements of modern thought – with the
remark: 'Cantor's transfinite numbers . . . are impossible and self-contradictory.'

In the late summer, Russell devoted himself to re-writing his Fellowship
dissertation into a book entitled *An Essay on the Foundations of Geometry*. In
its new form, the essay now ended with an insistence that the contradictions
inherent in the notion of space required a transition to physics, and thus
paved the way for his projected dialectical treatment of all the sciences.
Russell also added a more detailed historical section on the development of
non-Euclidean geometries, which culminated in a detailed philosophical
exposition of the comparatively new subject of 'projective geometry', a kind
of geometry that studies geometrical figures qualitatively rather than quanti-
tatively; which, in other words, makes no reference to the *size* of the shapes
with which it deals. Indeed, it does not, properly speaking, deal with shapes
at all, but rather with collections of points. It is thus more general and more
abstract than other forms of geometry, and, argues Russell, more fundamental. Indeed, what Kant had argued was true of Euclidean geometry – that it

is necessarily true and that its truth is a condition of all possible experience – is, Russell claims, also true of projective geometry.

Russell handed the book over to his publishers, Cambridge University Press, at the beginning of October 1896, a few days before leaving for a three-month visit to America to meet Alys's family and to deliver a series of lectures based on the book at Bryn Mawr and at Johns Hopkins University. Actually, he would be doing both things at the same time, since both sets of lectures had been arranged through members of Alys's family, her cousin Carey Thomas being President of Bryn Mawr and her uncle (Carey's father), Dr James Thomas, a professor at Johns Hopkins. They set sail on 3 October, and the first place they visited when they arrived in America was the home of Walt Whitman in Camden, New Jersey.

Whitman had always stood in Russell's mind as a symbol of sexual frankness and the pilgrimage was no doubt to some extent a confirmation of his faith. When they arrived in Bryn Mawr, Alys, to the consternation of her cousin – and rather oddly, considering her personal attitudes towards, for instance, her father and her sister – gave talks to the students in favour of free love. She also spoke on temperance and women's suffrage, but it was her endorsement of free love that was remembered best and longest, and which became the cause of Russell never again – at least during Carey Thomas's presidency – being invited back to Bryn Mawr. Russell made rather less of a sensation. As well as his lectures on geometry, he talked on 'Socialism as the Consummation of Individual Liberty', but, as he told his Uncle Rollo, 'I doubt whether I shall convert anybody, as Americans seem very much more opposed to Socialism than English people.'

Despite Alys's willingness to shock conventional sensibilities in public on the issue, neither she nor Russell, of course, practised free love. For Russell, however, the visit to the States was marked by a series of flirtations that lend further credence to the idea that, even at this very early stage, he was dissatisfied with his marraige. At Bryn Mawr, for example, he renewed his acquaintance with Helen Thomas, Carey's younger sister, whom he had met briefly in Paris. In his *Autobiography*, he says only that he was 'very fond' of Helen 'for a number of years' and that 'Once or twice I asked her to kiss me, but she refused.' In an unpublished note, however, he admitted that he 'fell more or less in love with Helen, but she kept our relations rigidly correct'. Years later he told her that she had taught him all he knew of unrequited love. With Helen's best friend, Lucy Donnelly, an English lecturer at Bryn Mawr, Russell struck up a friendship that was entirely non-sexual and which was to last until her death in 1948.

Many years after Lucy's death, in 1965, Russell's fourth and last wife, Edith, who knew Lucy well at Bryn Mawr, wrote a biographical sketch of her in which she claimed that Lucy had fallen in love with Russell. She withdrew the claim, however, after it was challenged by Russell himself. Russell evidently looked upon Lucy as a *confidante* rather than as a potential lover, and – especially after her visit to the Russells in the autumn of 1903 – wrote her some of his most revealing and personal letters. Perhaps the very fact that he was not sexually attracted to her allowed him to achieve in his letters to her a degree of honesty in his self-scrutiny that he could otherwise achieve only in his private journals.

Undeniably sexual in its origins, however, was Russell's attraction to another young woman at Bryn Mawr called Mildred Minturn, with whom he flirted openly, both on this occasion and years later on her frequent visits to England. Still more romantically charged was his interest in a very beautiful young Bostonian aristocrat called Sally Fairchild, whom he met towards the end of this trip to America, when he and Alys visited Boston, and with whom, when she visited England a few years later, Russell enjoyed a flirtation that, he said later, 'made a deep impression on me'.

At Boston, Russell and Alys paid a visit to William James, an occasion marked by a display of gratuitous honesty on the part of James's wife, who, in reply to the Russells' suggestion to come and see her and her husband, wrote, 'We shall be very glad to see you', with, as an afterthought, the word 'very' crossed out.

The most important and lasting intellectual effect of this trip was to bring Russell into contact with mathematicians who knew something about the advances in pure mathematics, especially in analysis, that had been made in the second half of the nineteenth century:

> . . . contact with academic Americans, especially mathematicians, led me to realise the superiority of Germany to England in almost all academic matters. Against my will, in the course of my travels, the belief that everything worth knowing was known at Cambridge gradually wore off.

He later said that it was in America that he first heard of Karl Weierstrass, the German mathematician whose name, more than any other, was associated with the movement for greater rigour in the foundations of mathematics, the movement that Russell would eventually recognise as having solved the problems that he, at this time, regarded as proof of Hegelian metaphysics. The people who informed him about Weierstrass were almost certainly Frank Morley and James Harkness, two mathematicians who, having been initially trained at Cambridge, had acquired for themselves an education in the new mathematics that they were now teaching in America, Morley at Haverford and Harkness at Bryn Mawr.

A few years after Russell's visit to Bryn Mawr, in 1898, Morley and Harkness published their textbook, *An Introduction to the Theory of Analytic Functions*, which, chastising other English textbooks for showing 'little or no trace' of recent discoveries in pure mathematics, sought to introduce students to the theory of functions as it had been rebuilt by Weierstrass. An important feature of this was the so-called 'epsilon-delta' method, which showed how continuity could be treated arithmetically, without recourse to 'infinitesimals', without the need for any appeal to 'intuition' and without logical contradiction. Russell studied Morley and Harkness's book carefully, and, in introducing him to the system of Weierstrass, it had a large impact upon his thinking – as he was to say many times in later life, his introduction to Weierstrass was one of the most important events in his intellectual life.

In the winter of 1896, this impact still lay in the future, but Russell's conversations with Morley, Harkness and others in America was enough to dent severely his Hegelian confidence that mathematics was irremediably enmeshed in contradictions, at least to the extent of resolving to improve his knowledge of modern German mathematics. As soon as he returned home in December, he began by reading Richard Dedekind's classic work, *Continuity and Irrational Numbers*, in which Dedekind provides a logically consistent, arithmetical definition of precisely the notions that Russell had claimed could not be defined consistently. The threat that this posed to his Hegelianism was compounded in the spring of 1897 by his actually reading Hegel – which up to now he had considered unnecessary, taking his view of 'Hegelianism' entirely from McTaggart. He read Hegel's *Logic* and was disgusted with its muddle-headed treatment of mathematics, which, he declared to Alys with great disillusionment, seemed to him to consist 'mainly of puns'.

Russell was fond of saying that there were just two types of philosopher: those that think of the world as a bowl of jelly and those that think of it as a bucket of shot. The 'one major division' in his own philosophical thinking came when he, so to speak, gave up the jelly for the shot. The difference, of course, lay in thinking of the world as an indivisible whole and in thinking of it as consisting of discrete – logical and physical – 'atoms'. In a paper called 'Why I took to Philosophy', Russell elaborated on the jelly metaphor as applied to Hegel's philosophy, in a way that sought to explain the attraction the jelly-like world had for him:

> Hegel thought of the universe as a closely knit unity. His universe was like a jelly in the fact that, if you touched any one part of it, the whole quivered; but it was unlike a jelly in the fact that it could not really be cut up into parts. The appearance of consisting of parts, according to him, was a delusion. The only reality was the Absolute, which was his name for God. In this philosophy I found comfort for a time. As presented to me by its adherents, especially McTaggart, who was then an intimate friend of mine, Hegel's philosophy had seemed both charming and demonstrable . . . In a rash moment, however, I turned from the disciples to the Master and found in Hegel himself a farrago of confusions and what seemed to me little better than puns. I therefore abandoned his philosophy.

In the summer of 1897, in the last throes of his Hegelianism, Russell wrote a short paper that shows him to be making a last-ditch attempt to salvage the jelly-like world of Absolute Idealism. It was written, apparently, for the purpose of discussion with Moore, and entitled: 'Why do we regard time, but not space, as necessarily a plenum?' The short answer to this question, he told Alys, is: 'Because we're fools'. The long answer outlined in the paper is that we are misled into thinking that space is analysable into relations between material objects, while we understand intuitively that time is 'plenal', that is, that there are no gaps in it and that therefore time cannot be understood as a sequence of relations. But, Russell urges, what is true of time is true also of space. Space, too, is a plenum, every bit of it being used up by matter in one form or another. Thus, Russell argues, relations are an illusion, the distinction between a relation and an adjective being impossible to make:

> On a strictly monistic view . . . no such distinction can be maintained. Everything is really an adjective of the One, an intrinsic property of the Universe; the Universe is not validly analysable into simple elements at all.

One thing revealed by this essay, and by almost everything Russell wrote at this time, is what he considered analysis to be. Analysis, on his understanding, consists in the identification of the parts of a whole. If, therefore, reality is indivisible, it follows immediately that analysis is an invalid procedure, that, indeed, analysis is always a falsification.

Russell's adoption of a rigorous philosophical monism that rejects the reality of relations was no doubt influenced by F. H. Bradley's influential book, *Appearance and Reality*, which Russell re-read in the summer of 1897. 'Reality is one,' Bradley writes there. 'It must be single because plurality, taken as real, contradicts itself. Plurality implies relations, and, through its relations it unwillingly asserts always a superior unity.' The bucket of shot is, despite itself, one reality. If one considers that each piece of shot is in a determinate relation with the others, then one can regard the individual pieces, together with their relations to the others, as forming a 'superior unity'. The bucket of shot, then, has only the appearance of consisting of different things: its reality is the same as the bowl of jelly: an indivisible whole.

An important element in Russell's abandonment of this conception of the world was his rejection of the emotional and religious comforts it provided. At the end of the year, he presented to the Apostles a paper called 'Seems, Madam? Nay, it is', in which he insisted that the metaphysics of Bradley and McTaggart could not, even if true, provide any emotional comfort. As he put it in a letter to Moore before the meeting, the gist of his argument was that: 'for all purposes which are not *purely* intellectual, the world of Appearance is the real world'. The argument was simple: if 'Reality, as constructed by metaphysics, bears no sort of relation to the world of experience', then it cannot say anything to make that experience – our lives – more bearable and comforting: 'since all experience equally is in time, and the Deity is timeless, no experience is experience of the Deity'. It follows that Russell's original hopes for philosophy – and, especially for McTaggart's metaphysics – were misplaced, that 'we cannot find in philosophy the consolations of religion.' In any case, there was, he now thought, something weak and ignoble about pursuing philosophy in order to find support for comfortable doctrines; far bolder and more worthy would be an attitude that sought simply to know the truth – whatever it might be:

> Why not admit that metaphysics, like science, is justified by intellectual curiosity, and ought to be guided by intellectual curiosity alone?

Having divested himself of his emotional commitment to the metaphysics of monism, it was only a matter of time before, intellectually, he would find it wanting. This process, however, was a gradual one. In the New Year of 1898, he wrote a note headed 'On the Idea of a Dialectic of the Sciences', in which he tried to salvage what he could from his old ambition of constructing a dialectic of all the sciences in the face of his new, harder attitude to the comforts of Idealism and what he now acknowledged to be the success of mathematics in dealing with many of the old contradictions. His hope now was of finding 'a method of turning Appearance into Reality, instead of first constructing Reality and then being confronted by a hopeless dualism'. And the means by which he hoped to do that was by using a dialectical chain of reasoning that began with the contradictions at the heart of the notion of *quantity*, for: 'I believe the only unavoidable contradiction will be that belonging to quantity.' The contradiction to which Russell is referring is that a collection, a quantity, is necessarily regarded both as one thing (*a* collection) and as many (a collection of, say, *five*, things). And, as quantifying, counting, is the very foundation of mathematics, then this contradiction will remain, however successful mathematics is in treating the others.

Before he had developed this idea very far, however, he became convinced that it was fundamentally mistaken. This was largely because, through reading Whitehead's recently published book, *Universal Algebra*, and Dedekind's *Nature and Meaning of Numbers*, he was persuaded to reject the traditional definition of mathematics as 'the science of quantity' and, thereby became convinced that the contradictions of quantity, upon which he had devoted so much time and energy, were simply irrelevant to mathematics. From Dedekind's book, he learned to regard the notion of order, rather than that of quantity, as the central notion in the definition of number (the origin of numbers lies, on this understanding, not in counting how many things there are in a collection, but in putting things in order: first, second, third, etc.). From Whitehead's book, he received – among much else – a completely fresh conception of mathematics, one that made no mention of quantity at all. Mathematics, in Whitehead's definition, was the study of 'all types of formal, necessary, deductive reasoning'. Thus, in Whitehead's book, Russell saw, for the first time, a *mathematical* treatment of symbolic logic, which, in Whitehead's view, is a sort of algebra.

Inspired by this new conception of mathematics, Russell now began work on a book that broke sharply with the language of 'dialectic' and 'synthesis' that had characterised his previous work and which he called, pointedly, 'An Analysis of Mathematical Reasoning'. Russell's faith in analysis had, by now, been confirmed by the work of mathematicians, but what he still needed was a conception of logic – and in particular a conception of the nature of a proposition – to replace that which he had inherited from Hegelianism. And this is what G. E. Moore, to Russell's everlasting gratitude, provided him with in the summer of 1898.

Moore was at this time finishing his own Fellowship dissertation, which, characteristically, took the form of asking what, precisely, a certain person meant by certain words – in this case, what Kant meant by the words 'freedom' and 'reason'. By way of digression on the second of these, Moore engaged in a sustained polemic against the Idealist theory of truth advocated by F. H. Bradley, and endeavoured to put in its place a stridently 'realist' theory that insisted on a strict separation between *what* we believed (a proposition) and our belief in it (a mental state). In this theory, propositions are 'objective'; they are not 'in our minds' but 'out there' in the world. While Moore was developing this view, he and Russell met frequently, either in Cambridge or at The Millhangar, where Moore was often a guest, and, between the two of them, they arrived during their discussions at the conception of logic and philosophy that gave rise to the entire 'analytical' tradition.

The first published statement of this new logic – and the paper that Russell for ever regarded as Moore's greatest contribution to philosophy – was 'The Nature of Judgment', which appeared in *Mind* in January 1899 and which has a claim to be the founding statement of the analytical tradition in philosophy. Moore had previously read the paper to both the Cambridge Moral Science Club (on 21 October 1898) and the Aristotelian Society (on 9 December), but Russell would have known of its views even earlier, both from his discussions with Moore in the summer and from a letter that he received from Moore in September, summarising his position. 'My chief discovery,' Moore writes in the letter, 'which shocked me a good deal when I made it, is expressed in the form that an existent is a proposition.' What this means is that, for Moore, a proposition is something that actually exists. Moreover, in Moore's view, a proposition is analysable. In the Hegelian view, a proposition is a unity that defies analysis; in Moore's conception, on the other hand, it is a *complex* that positively cries out to be broken up into its constituent parts, which parts Moore calls 'concepts'. 'A proposition', Moore writes in 'The Nature of Judgment', 'is nothing other than a complex concept . . . A proposition is a synthesis of concepts . . . A proposition is constituted by any number of concepts, together with a specific relation between them.'

A 'concept', in Moore's rather odd use of the word, is neither a word, nor a thought, but a 'possible object of thought', something close to what Russell would later call a 'logical atom'. Concepts are the building-blocks of the world. 'The ultimate elements of everything that is are concepts,' Moore wrote to Russell, 'and a part of these, when compounded in a special way, form the existent world.' Thus, for Moore, and, even more crucially, for Russell, analysis is not – as it is commonly understood now – a linguistic activity, but an ontological one. To analyse a proposition is not to investigate a portion of language, it is not to attend to words, it is, so to speak, to carve up the world so that it begins to make some sort of sense. 'A thing becomes intelligible first', writes Moore, 'when it is analysed into its constituent concepts.'

In this view – which Russell eagerly embraced – logic and metaphysics are scarcely distinguishable. 'I agree emphatically with what you say about the several kinds of necessary relations among concepts,' Russell replied to Moore's letter, 'and I think their discovery is the true business of Logic (or Metaphysics if you like).' For Russell, a vitally important aspect of Moore's theory – in which, however, Moore himself took little interest – was that it had the consequence that relations, *contra* Bradley (and Russell himself twelve months previously), were real. In providing him with a view of logic that made sense of this, Moore completed the process by which Russell's world lost its jelly-like homogeneity. A consequence of this was that there was now no reason for Russell to distinguish 'Appearance' from 'Reality' in the way customary to Hegelian metaphysics, no need to consider the everyday world of the senses an illusion. 'It was', he later claimed, 'an intense excitement, after having supposed the sensible world unreal, to be able to believe again that there really were such things as tables and chairs.' He 'rejoiced in the thought that grass is really green, in spite of the adverse opinion of all philosophers from Locke onwards'. But, he emphasises, 'the most interesting aspect of the matter to me was the logical aspect. I was glad to think that relations are real, and I was interested to discover the dire effect upon metaphysics of the belief that all propositions are of the subject-predicate form.'

Russell's thinking about the relation between logic and metaphysics, and his new-found conviction of the reality of relations, received a further boost in the summer of 1898 by his having to make a close study of the work of Leibniz. McTaggart, who usually lectured on Leibniz at Cambridge, wanted to spend the year 1898–9 in New Zealand, where he hoped to persuade a woman called Margaret Bird (whom he had met on a previous visit) to marry him (he was successful and returned to England a married man in October 1899). Russell agreed to lecture in McTaggart's place and so spent much of the second half of 1898 studying Leibniz in preparation for the course of lectures that he delivered in the Lent Term of 1899.

Russell's preparation for this, his first set of Cambridge lectures, was extraordinarily thorough. Within a few months he had become an authority on his subject, with a novel and persuasive view of Leibniz's work. 'I found', he later wrote, 'what books on Leibniz failed to make clear – that his metaphysic was explicitly based upon the doctrine that every proposition attributes a predicate to a subject and (what seemed to him almost the same thing) that every fact consists of a substance having a property.' The reason that books on Leibniz failed to make this clear was that Leibniz himself, in his published work at least, failed to make it clear. Thus Russell's own book takes the form of, as he puts it, 'a reconstruction of the system which Leibniz *should* have written', presenting Leibniz's metaphysics as a quasi-formal system of logic, a set of theorems deduced from just five logical axioms, the first of which is: 'Every proposition has a subject and a predicate.'

Russell's view as to why Leibniz himself did not make the logical basis of his metaphysics clear carries an echo of the choices that Russell had made in his own life. 'At an early age', he writes of Leibniz, 'he refused a professorship at the University of Altdorf, and deliberately preferred a courtly to an academic career', a preference which 'led, in the end, to an undue deference for princes and a lamentable waste of time in the endeavour to please them'. Knowing that princes prefer theology to logic, Leibniz produced for their consumption his *Théodicée* and his *Principles of Nature and of Grace*, while leaving his serious logical work unpublished. This was a view of Leibniz that Russell maintained throughout his life. In the chapter on Leibniz in his *History of Western Philosophy*, he writes:

What he published was designed to win the approbation of princes and princesses. The consequence is that there are two systems of philosophy which may be regarded as representing Leibniz: one, which he proclaimed, was optimistic, orthodox, fantastic, and shallow; the other, which has been slowly unearthed from his manuscripts by fairly recent editors, was profound, coherent, largely Spinozistic, and amazingly logical.

It is this second that Russell attempts to reconstruct in his lectures and in the book based upon them, *The Philosophy of Leibniz*, the moral of his reconstruction being that logic is the basis of philosophy: if one misunderstands the nature of the proposition, one misunderstands everything. Thus, he announces:

> That all sound philosophy should begin with an analysis of propositions is a truth too evident, perhaps, to demand a proof. That Leibniz's philosophy begins with such an analysis, is less evident, but seems to be no less true.

From this starting point, Russell finds that: 'The only ground [Leibniz has] for denying the independent reality of relations is that propositions must have a subject and a predicate.' If Leibniz had begun with Moore's conception of a proposition, Russell implies, his whole philosophy would have been different. In this way, the whole book – though Moore is never once mentioned in it – becomes a sustained argument for the importance of Moore's theory of propositions in 'The Nature of Judgment', and helps to explain why Russell invested that theory with such momentous significance.

Throughout these years of intellectual absorption and progress, it is striking what little impact on Russell's life his marriage to Alys seems to have had. One has the impression that she was merely there in the background, a necessary means for Russell of keeping the wheels of day-to-day life moving, but not otherwise of much interest to him. Alys kept up her work on temperance, feminism and Socialism, and was often away at meetings and campaigns, but Russell seems to have remained entirely aloof from this side of her life; the few references to her work in his letters to her from this time tend to be sardonic and flippant, rather than indicative of any genuine interest, and the vision he had entertained of fusing his intellectual interests with her practical concerns seems to have died along with his religious and emotional investment in Hegelianism. 'To outsiders', Helen Thomas commented to a friend, after seeing Russell and Alys at Bryn Mawr, 'she seems really to be a slave. It's quite tragic, I think. I keep wondering whether Bertie is worth it, and how long it will last.'

The 'Self-Appreciation' that Russell wrote for the *Golden Urn* in the spring of 1897 and published under the pseudonym 'Orlando' demonstrates the same determination to face the truth – however ugly – that was later expressed in 'Seems, Madam? Nay, it is'. It presents a rather unflattering picture of him. 'I wish for fame among the expert few,' he confesses, 'but my chief desire – the desire by which I regulate my life – is a purely self-centred desire for intellectual satisfaction about the things that puzzle me'. The social and political concerns that formed the centre of Alys's life are given short shrift:

> I am quite indifferent to the mass of human creatures; though I wish, as a purely intellectual problem, to discover some way in which they might all be happy. I wouldn't sacrifice myself to them, though their unhappiness, at moments, about once in three months, gives me a feeling of discomfort, and an intellectual desire to find a way out. I believe emotionally in Democracy, though I see no reason to do so.
>
> . . . I live most for myself – everything has for me, a reference to my own education. I care for very few people, and have several enemies – two or three at least whose pain is delightful to me. I often wish to give pain, and when I do, I find it pleasant for the moment. I feel myself superior to most people.
>
> . . . I do change as I grow older. Desires do grow duller; many are satisfied, or in a process of continuous satisfaction; others have died from impassibility.

As a portrait of a person's inner life, it is the picture of a ghost, a quasi-substantial being only partially in contact with the people around him, someone whose 'impassibility' has rendered him almost dead of all warmth and emotion. An indication of this 'impassibility' is the curious silence with which Russell greeted the death of his grandmother on 17 January 1898. Though she had undoubtedly been the most important person in his life up until this point, her death is not mentioned in any of his surviving correspondence, and in his *Autobiography* it is dismissed with the disturbingly laconic observation that, though as a child he had lain awake thinking how dreadful it would be when she died, when she did die 'I did not mind at all.'

As for his desires growing duller, there is some evidence to the contrary – at least outside his marriage. His impassive mask seemed to drop whenever he was with someone who aroused him, most notably and frequently, of course, Mary, for whom his passion was by no means spent. In September 1897, he was delighted to find himself alone with Mary for a few days at her villa in Fiesole. The two of them, he wrote to Alys, 'had a jolly tête-à-tête dinner last night, and revived the pleasant feelings of Paris, without their very serious drawbacks'. She was, he said, in another letter during the same visit, 'more charming than ever, and I enjoyed having her to myself, as well as the opportunity to kiss her "on suitable occasions" '. For her part, Mary sounded rather alarmed. 'Bertie was *very* affectionate,' she wrote to Berenson:

> and I didn't quite know what to do. But I think I managed all right by taking a perfectly natural tone of friendliness. I do not want to put it into his head that I notice anything, because then he would get the idea that I

thought something more intimate *was* possible, however undesirable, and I do not believe he really thought it.

The following year, at Friday's Hill, Mary recorded what she describes as an 'amusing' conversation with Alys and Russell, though her account of it is chilling rather than comical:

Alys says she hates men and despises conversation and thinks smoking 'a filthy habit'. But she adores Bertie and so has fashioned her life to be occupied chiefly in these three things. But it is quite true, and it accounts for the queer icy streaks one comes across in her every now and then . . . I wonder if, *à la longue*, even Love can bridge such fundamental differences as there are between her and Bertie. Bertie says he has resigned himself to being *always bored* after he is thirty. 'At home even?' Alys asked. 'Especially at home,' Bertie answered remorselessly.

If this is love, then the atmosphere in which Russell had grown up at Pembroke Lodge was a loving one, for this description is uncomfortably reminiscent of the aggression disguised as affection that Russell saw and despised in his grandmother and his Aunt Agatha.

Though Alys was apparently entirely satisfied with such an arrangement, Russell was not. All his life he had craved companionship and genuine intimacy, only to find himself (as he hints in his 'Self-Appreciation') in a situation remarkably similar to that of his childhood, in which his real life was conducted alone, with his books and his thoughts, and his relations with those closest to him were characterised by stiffness and pretence. In July 1899, Mary reported life at Friday's Hill as being 'pretty dull':

. . . for, as we get older, we are growing apart. Alys cares for Philanthropy, Bertie for Mathematics – Logan and I more or less hang together – but general conversation can't be much but gossip or facts. And we are in this impasse, that we loathe Alys's friends (who loathe us back) and they don't care for ours, so there is scarcely a soul we want to invite here.

Mary was better placed than Alys to understand this situation and to realise how much Russell desired something else, and she saw the danger signs far earlier than did her sister. A month later, for example, she recorded with a sharp eye for significant detail the signs of Russell's growing affection for Sally Fairchild, who had by then arrived at Friday's Hill and, from Russell's point of view at least, breathed some life into the place:

Poor Mother [Mary wrote to Berenson] is dreadfully worried about Bertie's evident flirtation with Miss Fairchild. They go for long walks every evening, and Bertie has deserted his hitherto invariable habits of study and cards, from which nothing used to be able to tear him. And of course they have nothing in common except flirtation.

A week later, she reported that Russell and Sally Fairchild had 'stayed out walking till midnight last night':

Mother was awfully worried, as they were out till 2 the night before. But Alys seems quite delighted. I suppose her idea is that Bertie tends to be too much of a hermit and that anything that brings him out of his shell is a blessing. But I am afraid if she knew as much about him as I do, she wouldn't be contented that a well-known flirt should be his distraction.

Russell himself later recalled becoming 'very fond' of Sally Fairchild that summer, though 'I did not consider myself in love with her, and I never so much as kissed her hand, but as the years went by I realised that she had made a deep impression on me':

> ... and I remember as if it were yesterday our evening walks in the summer twilight while we were restrained by the strict code of those days from giving any expression whatever to our feelings.

Opportunities even for such chaste flirtations as this were rare, and Russell's life was characterised at the time less by moments like these than by the 'invariable habits of study and cards' noted by Mary – the 'life of flippancy tempered by intellect' that Russell describes in his *Autobiography*. The great passion for Russell, now in his late twenties, was, as it had been when he was eleven, the desire to show mathematics to be a body of certain, demonstrable and objective truths.

His loss of the comforts of Hegelian philosophy was more than compensated for by the abandonment of the Idealist conception that mathematics was true, not about the outside world but only about our perception of it. In Russell's new view: 'Mathematics could be *quite* true, and not merely a stage in dialectic', a belief that was for him every bit as inspiring as the contemplation of McTaggart's 'rational and righteous' Absolute Reality, and one that invested his philosophical thinking with a new vitality and an even greater intensity. The imaginative picture that now governed his philosophical work was not that of the great indivisible Oneness of reality, but that of Plato's World of Forms, a world in which each and every abstract object had its own independent and real existence. It is a picture that Russell, in his more cynical old age, poked gentle fun at in his short story 'The Mathematician's Nightmare', in which Professor Squarepunt imagines himself to be seated next to the number Pi and surrounded by the other numbers, each of which 'had its name clearly marked on its uniform':

> Different kinds of numbers had different uniforms and different shapes: the squares were tiles, the cubes were dice, round numbers balls, prime numbers were indivisible cylinders, perfect numbers had crowns ... The numbers danced round Professor Squarepunt and Pi in a vast and intricate ballet ... and as they danced they sang an ode to their own greatness:

> We are the finite numbers.
> We are the stuff of the world.
>   ...

... honoured by the immortal Plato
We think no later mortal great-o.
We follow the laws
Without a pause,
For we are the finite numbers.

What Russell was mocking in this story was a view that he held in all seriousness in the first flush of his new realism. Not only was grass really green, but two plus two really was four. His philosophical task was now, not to expose the contradictions in mathematics, nor even to analyse mathematical reasoning, but rather to demonstrate the soundness and truth of mathematics, to show the solidity of its logical foundations.

The moment this task crystallised in Russell's mind is recorded in a letter he wrote Alys on 5 July 1898. 'The Holy Ghost inspired my works,' he told her, 'and I discovered what was the question I had been asking myself for the last month – which is next door to finding the answer.' What that question was he did not deign to tell Alys, but in a letter to the French philosopher Louis Couturat two weeks later, he told him that his central aim was 'the discovery of the fundamental ideas of mathematics and the necessary judgments (axioms) which one must accept on the basis of these ideas'. This sounds analogous to his previous study of the 'foundations' of geometry, but, with the abandonment of Idealism, both Hegelian and Kantian, the question takes on a drastically different meaning. For it is no longer a request for the 'necessary features of experience', it is a demand for the most basic and fundamental *objective truths* upon which mathematics might be built.

In the spring of 1899, after he had finished lecturing on Leibniz, Russell abandoned his 'Analysis of Mathematical Reasoning' and began a new and vast book called *The Fundamental Ideas and Axioms of Mathematics*. This was never finished either, but its table of contents and the portions of it that survive show it to be a recognisable precursor to *The Principles of Mathematics*, which Russell eventually published in 1903. The 'fundamental ideas' it posits include 'number', 'order' and 'whole and part', his discussion of the last of which shows Russell to be still unconvinced by Cantor's set theory, and, in particular, by his transfinite numbers built upon sets of infinite members. Infinity, Russell still thinks, is beset by contradictions that mathematics cannot yet solve.

To some extent his doubts about Cantor were overcome the following July when he re-read Cantor's work and found that, this time, he could accept Cantor's proofs. He remained, nevertheless, unpersuaded that *all* philosophical problems about infinity were solved by Cantor's work. During this summer, however, his energies were largely taken up with replies and responses to the various reviews that had begun to appear of *An Essay on the Foundations of Geometry*. Of these, by far the most flattering was a 27-page critical study of the book by the great French mathematician, Henri Poincaré, in the prestigious journal *Revue de métaphysique et de morale*. To be reviewed at such length by a man of such eminence was to have arrived, and Russell, hungry for fame and recognition, felt the honour keenly, dashing off a postcard to Moore to tell him about it and writing to Couturat (who had sent a copy of Poincaré's review to Russell): 'I feel very flattered by the attention of such a great man, and I find in many of his remarks a remarkable luminosity. I will set about to reply as soon as possible.'

In general, of course, Russell was by this time of no mind to defend the theory of geometry he had written while still an Idealist. Poincaré, however, had chosen to attack the book from a general philosophical position completely at odds with the Platonism that Russell now advocated. In Poincaré's view, the question of the truth of Euclid's axioms was not an empirical question as Russell had claimed, but rather a *non*-question. Something in the manner of the later Wittgenstein, Poincaré held that the truth of mathematical propositions – in this case the axioms of Euclid – did not arise. Euclid's axioms were neither true nor false, they were rules or conventions that one could choose either to use or not, the question between rival theories of geometry being only one of which system was the more convenient to use. This, of course, was anathema to Russell – more so now than it would have been when he wrote the book – and in a long reply he sought to establish that Euclid's axioms, if they meant anything at all, had to be either true or false. Poincaré, he told Couturat, 'does not seem to realise that a definition ceases to be arbitrary when one postulates the existence of the object defined'.

A related point was raised by the other review of the book to which Russell paid special attention: that of G. E. Moore in *Mind*. Moore's central criticism is aimed at Russell's Kantian method, the 'Kantian fallacy' – as Moore calls it – of arguing for the necessity of a proposition on the grounds of what is or is not a 'possible experience'. This, writes Moore, can at best establish 'some psychological fact', but nothing can be inferred about the nature of space from that fact. To this criticism Russell made no reply, largely because, as he told Moore in a letter of 18 July, 'on all important points I agreed with it'.

These respectful reviews in distinguished academic journals helped to establish Russell's reputation, and in the summer of 1899 his international standing was confirmed when he received an invitation from Louis Couturat to present a paper at the International Congress of Philosophy to be held in Paris the following summer.

Russell and Couturat had been corresponding for nearly two years. In October 1897, Russell had received, to his great delight, a letter from Couturat thanking him for his review of Couturat's book, *De l'Infini mathématique*, which Russell had published in *Mind* the previous January. Couturat wrote that he was, in turn, reviewing Russell's *Essay on the Foundations of Geometry*, even though, knowing little English, he had to read it 'armé d'un dictionaire'. 'One of my day-dreams', Russell later wrote, 'was of receiving flattering letters from learned foreigners who knew me only through my work.' Couturat's was the first such letter he received, and, as such 'was something of a landmark'.

With every letter they exchanged, Couturat and Russell discovered some new point of similarity in their work and philosophical outlooks. Like Russell,

Couturat was concerned with the apparent contradictions in the notion of the mathematical infinite, and, also like Russell, first resisted and then accepted Cantor's transfinite numbers. Like Russell too, Couturat was being drawn increasingly to a so-called 'logicist' view of mathematics by way of an appreciation of the philosophical importance of the work of pure mathematicians in their attempts to provide calculus with more rigorous foundations. Finally – as they discovered in 1900 – both Couturat and Russell were writing books on Leibniz that emphasised the logical basis of his metaphysics. Not unnaturally, a friendship grew up between them through their correspondence, a friendship that was sealed in November 1898, when Russell visited Couturat for a few days at Caen, where he held a professorship.

Couturat's invitation to Russell to the Paris Congress was to have a dramatic influence on Russell's life and thought. In a letter of 2 July, Russell accepted immediately, though he expressed some misgivings about reading a paper, not because he had nothing to say or because he had any doubts about his French, but rather because he still felt unsure about speaking in public. In a subsequent letter, he overcame his misgivings and agreed to speak, offering Couturat an impressive choice of subjects:

> I could read on the infinite, the antinomies, and arithmetic . . . or else, on the notion of order and series, including continuity, and the works of Cantor. Or else, on the analysis of the notion of quantity. Or again, on the necessity of absolute position in space and time.

Couturat chose the last (on the grounds that the other topics would be well covered by other speakers), and, so, in the spring of 1900, Russell wrote 'The Notion of Order and Absolute Position in Space and Time' to read at the Congress. In this paper, Russell argued, against both Kant and the tradition of British neo-Hegelianism (and against his own earlier view), that temporal and spatial relations were part of Reality, and not merely of 'Appearance'.

Towards the end of 1899, Russell's letters to Couturat began to change, being filled with reflections, not on mathematics or logic or Leibniz, but on the Boer War, which, to the surprise of Couturat – and the dismay of Alys – brought out in Russell an unexpectedly fierce patriotism. The war had begun in October, when the Boers, fearful that Great Britain intended to annex the Transvaal Republic, began attacking British garrisons in South Africa. When it looked as if the British would be overrun, reinforcements were sent, but, in December, the British suffered a series of heavy defeats. These defeats, Russell later wrote, 'caused me much anxiety, and I could think of nothing else but the war news'. Every day, he would walk four miles from The Millhangar to the railway station to pick up a copy of the evening paper. Alys was rather puzzled and alarmed at this show of Imperialist sentiment and was, says Russell, 'rather annoyed' by his absorption in the war.

To Couturat, Russell wrote on 18 December that he could hardly think of anything but the war: 'philosophy seems more like children's games in comparison to current events':

I can't help but hope keenly for the success of our armies, first through stupid and instinctive patriotism, but also for deeper reasons . . . I make fun of it all when things go well, but at present I have found myself, albeit reluctantly, carried away by love of the country.

In his next letter, Russell defended the war as one of self-defence against the militarism of the Boers: 'and if we finish by annexing the Transvaal, it will be solely because it is the only way of protecting ourselves.'

Couturat, naturally, was somewhat bemused by these bellicose remarks and continued to pour scorn on Russell's views, forcing him, in a letter of 5 May 1900, to attempt a general defence of Imperialism *per se*. There are two main aims of statesmanship, Russell began: '(a) to preserve and safeguard the peace, (b) to spread civilised government'. The first of these requires there to be as few states as possible, and, since small states can be conquered much more easily than large empires, it follows that, other things being equal, the conquest of the former by the latter is desirable. With regard to the second aim, the spreading of 'civilised government', Russell appealed to a blatantly racist form of Eurocentrism:

If you had read anthropology books, you would know what a truly savage country is, and what are the benefits which result from civilised government. I wish that every part of the world were governed by a European race – it doesn't matter which, to begin the argument: Now, the stronger a nation, the less fear it has of insurrections by the savages – therefore the strongest, *caeteris paribus*, are the best colonists.

It was thus in the interests of civilisation that Britain defeated the Boers, and Russell's 'deep reasons' for willing the victory were therefore shown (to his satisfaction, at least) to be quite distinct from his patriotic feelings: 'I still hold that patriotism is bad; is it not the patriotism of the Transvaal which has led it to fight, instead of submitting peaceably?'

Towards the end of 1899, the Pearsall Smith family learnt that Mary's husband Frank Costelloe was facing death from cancer of the ear, 'a stroke of great good luck', Russell remarked to Mary, intending to demonstrate his support for her, but rather shocking her with his brutality. Before Frank died, the family discovered that he had appointed in his will five Catholic guardians for Karin and Ray, rather than leaving them in Mary's care. Hannah was outraged, and Mary torn with conflicting emotions. When she saw Frank, she reported to Berenson, 'it is awful – that weary wreck, all his life and his ambitions come to nothing, and the horrible pathos of leaving no one to mourn his going.' However:

When I do not see him I feel such anger and indignation and hatred on account of his Will that I could almost echo Bertie's wish to restore him to life and torture him for ten years. Thee can't conceive how painful it is to be swinging from one feeling to the opposite. But on the whole a sort of sickened pity predominates.

Costelloe died on 22 December, and the family eventually succeeded in overturning his will by convincing the Court of Chancery to accept Hannah as the children's guardian.

The extremity of Russell's reaction to Costelloe, however, is initially rather puzzling. He was not personally involved in the question of the children's upbringing, and knew Costelloe only slightly. Why, then, could the thought of Costelloe arouse such bitterness, even while the poor man lay dying prematurely and painfully? The answer, surely, lies in the parallel between the fate of Karin and Ray and that of Russell himself and Frank twenty-five years earlier, and the horror aroused in him at the thought of Costelloe being able to inflict upon his daughters an upbringing characterised by Christian piety of the sort that would cause them to regard their mother as a sinner and a lost soul.

Russell's identification with Karin and Ray (then ten and twelve years old respectively) led him to attempt to inspire in them the love of Euclid that had been such a delight to him when he was their age. The attempt, however, as Mary described to Berenson, was an embarrassing failure:

> Bertie is teaching them Euclid, but alas my beautiful dream of their coming into contact with a 'first-class mind' is upset by the sordid fact that this first-class mind doesn't know how to impart its knowledge, and the poor things are in a perfect maze of miserable bewilderment. For their first lesson he gave them *fifteen* propositions, and they scarcely understood one, poor things! Mother tried to speak to Alys about it, because of course it is an *awful* way to teach, and it makes the children hate the subject. But Alys wouldn't listen to a word, and it was useless.

In the months immediately prior to his leaving for Paris for the Congress, Russell lived at Friday's Hill and devoted himself to yet another draft of what he was by now referring to as his 'big book' and which he had finally settled on calling *The Principles of Mathematics*. The chief difference between this draft and *The Fundamental Ideas and Axioms of Mathematics* of the previous year was that he now fully accepted Cantor's treatment of the continuum (even to the extent of regarding it as logically prior to the differential calculus). Even so, he was still unpersuaded that Cantor's theory of transfinites 'solves any of the philosophical difficulties of infinity, or renders the antinomy of infinite number one whit less formidable'. At the centre of this draft, and given greater prominence even than before, were Russell's reflections of the relation between a whole and its parts. This relation, Russell said, 'is so important that almost all our philosophy depends upon the theory we adopt in regard to it'. To understand this relation is to understand logic itself, and, in particular, the power and the limitations of logical analysis, the analysis, that is, of propositions in Moore's sense. In connection with this, Russell emphasised what he called 'a very important logical doctrine, which the theory of whole and part brings into prominence – I mean the doctrine that analysis is falsification', and attempted to minimise its dangers:

Whatever can be analysed is a whole, and we have already seen that analysis of wholes is in some measure falsification. But it is important to realise the very narrow limits of this doctrine. We cannot conclude that the parts of a whole are not really its parts, nor that the parts are not presupposed in the whole, in a sense in which the whole is not presupposed in the parts, nor yet that the logically prior is not always simpler than the logically subsequent. In short, though analysis gives us the truth, and nothing but the truth, yet it can never give us the whole truth, except where what is in question is a mere collection not taken as whole. This is the only sense in which the doctrine is to be accepted. In any wider sense, it becomes merely a cloak for laziness, by giving an excuse to those who dislike the labour of analysis.

A mere collection of parts is not the same thing as a unified whole. Nevertheless, to understand something is to break it up into its constituent parts.

By the time Russell left for Paris on 31 July 1900, *The Principles of Mathematics* was already a large and impressive work, and at a fairly advanced stage of completion. Divided into seven parts, it sought to analyse the foundations of mathematics, beginning with the notions of number and of the analysis of wholes into parts, and showing how continuity, infinity, space and time, and matter and motion can be understood arithmetically, as relations between numbers. And yet, Russell was still dissatisfied with it, chiefly because the analysis it offered did nothing to resolve the contradiction of infinity, a contradiction he now expressed in this way:

> The number of finite numbers is infinite. Every number is finite. These two statements seem indubitable, though the first contradicts the second, and the second contradicts Cantor.

Having shaken off all traces of his previous Hegelianism, Russell was not inclined to accept an inherent contradiction in the notion of infinity, and, at this stage wanted to accept Cantor's theory of transfinite numbers, which, he remarked, had at least the merit of dragging into the light the difficulties of infinity. The sticking point in his acceptance of Cantor's theory was his inability at this stage to conceive of the 'infinite wholes' defined by it. Not that Russell rejected altogether the notion of an 'infinite whole'. He accepted the need to admit its bare existence for the simple and compelling reason that the class of all numbers, for example, was such a whole. But Cantor's theory went much further than that, and treated these 'infinite wholes' as a part of arithmetic; adding them to each other, adding finite numbers to them, multiplying them, using them to construct a hierarchy of different infinities, etc. And, as yet, neither Russell's notion of a 'whole' nor his conception of a 'collection' would enable him to see how one could *add* a number to infinity to form a new number, nor how one could make sense of the idea of an infinite collection that had *more* members than the class of all finite numbers.

To his almost unbounded delight, Russell discovered during the Congress at Paris that the mathematical logic of Giuseppe Peano offered him a way out of this *impasse*. Peano was the head of a group of Italian mathematicians whose aim was to further the progress made by the earlier generation of German mathematicians in founding mathematics upon rigorous foundations. In pursuit of that aim, Peano invented a special symbolism, the basic elements of which are still in use today and familiar to all undergraduate students of symbolic logic, which sought to eliminate as far as possible any ambiguities in the expression of mathematical proofs, and also to make the logic of those proofs manifest. The ultimate goal of this Italian school was an axiomatic system of arithmetic that would demonstrate the theorems of the differential calculus with the same – and even greater – certainty that the theorems of geometry are proved in Euclid's *Elements*. Peano and his colleagues had already achieved considerable success in constructing a formal system that used only three basic ideas and five initial axioms, upon which the whole of arithmetic could be based.

Russell already knew something of Peano's work before he went to Paris, chiefly through an article that Couturat had published in 1899 called 'La logique mathématique de M. Peano', which gave a critical synopsis of Peano's whole project. The article had inspired in Russell only a mild interest in Peano's system, but seeing Peano himself in Paris was a revelation. 'I was impressed', Russell later recalled, 'by the fact that, in every discussion, he showed more precision and more logical rigour than was shown by anybody else. I went to him and said, "I wish to read all your works. Have you got copies with you?" He had, and I immediately read them all.'

The word 'immediately' should not be taken entirely at face value. Russell was in Paris with Alys (who also presented a paper at the conference, a discussion of 'L'Éducation des Femmes', which, according to Mary's report to Bernhard, 'received great applause'), and also with Whitehead and his wife, Evelyn, and, before they returned home, the four of them took a week's holiday together travelling around France. It was probably during this holiday that Russell first became attracted to Evelyn Whitehead, for whom for many years he harboured an unspoken affection that he later described (without naming Evelyn) in a poem to Ottoline Morrell as one of the three great loves of his life.

The poem, sent to Ottoline on 4 April 1912, reads in full:

> Thrice have I loved. Once in the morning dew,
> Singing with spring-time birds a careless strain,
> Forgetting earth, I soared to heaven, and knew
> Joys that forget the burden of man's pain.

> Again I loved. Piercing the prison of flame,
> Where one stern soul in lonely anguish burned,
> Forgetting earth once more with love I came
> Into that hell whence no light hopes returned.

> Once more I love, and married in my love,
> Heaven and hell have made this love divine;

> Grief deep as hell, joy vast as heaven above,
> Mingle their fires and through man's labours shine.

Russell's letters to Ottoline, the recollections of people who knew Russell at this time (including, most notably, Lucy Donnelly) and Russell's own remarks leave little doubt that the second stanza refers to his repressed and secret love for Evelyn Whitehead.

Indeed, several times in his letters to Ottoline, Russell mentioned the love he had kept to himself and which 'died a gradual death for want of nourishment', and many times he hinted strongly that the object of that affection was Evelyn Whitehead.

Five years younger than her husband, Evelyn was about the same age as Alys, but with a personality more like that of Alys's sister Mary. She was beautiful, proud and cultivated. 'Her vivid life', Whitehead once wrote, 'has taught me that beauty, moral and aesthetic is the aim of existence; and that kindness, and love, and artistic satisfaction are among its modes of attainment . . . By myself, I am only one more professor, but with Evelyn I am first-rate.' Russell came to see in Evelyn a mirror-image of his own dissatisfactions with married life: just as, in his marriage to Alys, all his real life and energy were either repressed or sublimated into his passion for philosophy, so he came to think of Evelyn as a victim of her marriage to Alfred, which had entrapped her in 'a life of utter loneliness, filled with intense tragedy & pain of which she could never speak'. This unspoken bond between the two was to have a dramatic effect upon Russell's life.

In the immediate aftermath of the Paris conference, however, Russell's thoughts were directed more at the enticing possibilities offered by Peano's mathematical logic. As soon as he got back to Friday's Hill, Russell dashed off a letter to Moore, telling him that, as a result of the Congress, he had become 'persuaded that Peano and his school are the best people of the present time' in the philosophy of mathematics. To Couturat a month later he wrote that the Congress had been 'an enormous success . . . I have begun to study the works of Peano and his disciples: I am considering doing an article for *Mind*, similar to the one you did for the *Revue*. I very much admire what Peano has done for Arithmetic . . . the formulaire also seems to me a great and beautiful enterprise.'

The 'formulaire' was Peano's project of providing proofs for all the known theorems of mathematics using the language and methods of his mathematical logic. In 'Recent Italian Work on the Foundations of Mathematics', the article that Russell wrote for *Mind* (but, for some unknown reason, never published), Russell makes extravagant claims for the importance of this project and the successes it has so far achieved. 'The theory of arithmetic,' he declares, 'which, during the last thirty or forty years, has made vast progress, is the finest product of the human intellect; and Peano's account of this theory is undoubtedly the best':

> . . . although the work itself is almost wholly mathematical, its interest is almost wholly philosophical. Its aim is, to discover the necessary and

sufficient premisses of the various branches of mathematics, and to deduce results (mostly known already) by a rigid formalism which leaves no opening for the sinister influence of obviousness. Thus the interest of the work lies (1) in the discovery of premisses and (2) in the absolute correctness of the deduction. Both these points are (or rather should be) of great interest to the philosopher.

Shortly afterwards, in 'Recent Work on the Principles of Mathematics', a more popular article written for *The International Monthly*, Russell used even bolder language. 'One of the chief triumphs of modern mathematics', he writes, 'consists in having discovered what mathematics really is.' And what they have discovered is that mathematics is really nothing more or less than logic:

> All pure mathematics – Arithmetic, Analysis, and Geometry – is built up by combinations of the primitive ideas of logic, and its propositions are deduced from the general axioms of logic . . . And this is no longer a dream or an aspiration. On the contrary, over the greater and more difficult part of the domain of mathematics, it has been already accomplished . . . Philosophers have disputed for ages whether such a deduction is possible; mathematicians have sat down and made the deduction. For the philosophers there is now nothing left but graceful acknowledgments.

The importance that Peano's logical system had for Russell was that, by providing a rigorous foundation for the work of Weierstrass, Cantor and Dedekind, it allowed him to overcome completely his qualms in accepting their work as a definitive solution to the philosophical problems of continuity, infinity and the infinitesimal. The relief and sense of triumph this inspired are expressed with unrestrained enthusiasm in this popular article. The solution of these philosophical problems by mathematics, Russell claims, is the greatest achievement that our age has to boast: 'I know of no age (except perhaps the golden age of Greece) which has a more convincing proof to offer of the transcendent genius of its great men.'

The work of these pure mathematicians Russell could now see as a kind of fulfilment of his adolescent dream of using mathematics to establish a realm of absolutely certain and demonstrable truths. It also provided him with a vision of what might be possible in philosophy. 'What is now required', the article concludes, 'is to give the greatest possible development to mathematical logic . . . to found upon this secure basis a new philosophical logic, which may hope to borrow some of the exactitude and certainty of its mathematical foundation':

> If this can be successfully accomplished, there is every reason to hope that the near future will be as great an epoch in pure philosophy as the immediate past has been in the principles of mathematics. Great triumphs inspire great hopes; and pure thought may achieve, within our generation,

such results as will place our time, in this respect, on a level with the greatest age of Greece.

The hopes that such reflections aroused for his own work inspired Russell to one of the most astonishing bursts of intense philosophical creativity in the history of the subject. He devoted most of August and September 1900 to reading everything that Peano and his followers had written and to writing an article called 'The Logic of Relations', which he published in Peano's journal, *Revue de mathématiques*, in which he made his own contribution to Peano's project by extending it to include the analysis of relations. Then, between October and December, he worked with a purpose and concentration – and success – that has been matched in this century perhaps only by Wittgenstein during his period in Norway in 1913–14.

During these months Russell completely re-wrote *The Principles of Mathematics* in the light of the triumphalist conviction he expressed in his popular article that mathematics was now known with certainty to be a branch of logic. He wrote at an almost feverish pace: ten pages a day and a total of over 200,000 words in less than three months. By the end of the year he had produced a work of astonishing breadth and equally astonishing confidence, which sought to show that the whole of mathematics could be based upon a mere handful of logical notions and axioms. Peano had provided a system in which the only notions that needed to be assumed were those of 'zero', 'number' and 'successor'. What Russell tried now to show was that these could in turn be dispensed with, and the whole edifice built upon nothing more than the notion of 'class'.

The notion of a class thus assumed enormous importance in Russell's philosophy, replacing his earlier preoccupation with the idea of a whole and its parts. The relationship between a class and its members is importantly similar to that between a whole and its parts, and a class, like a whole, might be analysed into its members (parts). But, unlike the notion of a 'whole', a class can be understood independently from that relationship. We can talk of the 'class of married men', for example, without, so to speak, collecting all the married men together, because we have the *concept* 'married man', and we can just think of the class as the extension of the concept. And, without enumerating all its members or even knowing how many members it has, we can with certainty say something about it: such as, for instance, that it contains no bachelors and that it is equinumerous with the class of married women. In this way, the notion of a class can be regarded as logically prior to the notion of number. More than that, Russell showed how classes could be used to define numbers and thus how the whole of Peano's system might be built upon class theory. In addition, the notion of a 'class' – as opposed to that of a 'whole' – enabled Russell to overcome his doubts about Cantor's theory of the infinite, for he could now think of infinite classes without worrying about the problems of infinite 'wholes'.

Intellectually, Russell later said, this period was 'the highest point of my life', an 'intellectual honeymoon such as I have never experienced before or since':

Every day I found myself understanding something that I had not understood on the previous day. I thought all difficulties were solved and all problems were at an end.

. . . My sensations resembled those one has after climbing a mountain in a mist, when, on reaching the summit, the mist suddenly clears, and the country becomes visible for forty miles in every direction. For years I had been endeavouring to analyse the fundamental notions of mathematics, such as order and cardinal numbers. Suddenly, in the space of a few weeks, I discovered what appeared to be definitive answers to the problems which had baffled me for years . . . I went about saying to myself that now at last I had done something worth doing, and I had the feeling that I must be careful not to be run over in the street before I had written it down.

In an act of self-conscious symbolism, Russell finished his manuscript on the very last day of the year, which, for him, was also the last day of the nineteenth century.[1] 'I have been endeavouring to think of a good resolution to make,' he wrote that night to Helen Thomas, 'but my conscience is in such a thoroughly comfortable state that I have hitherto failed':

In October I invented a new subject, which turned out to be all mathematics, for the first time treated in its essence. Since then I have written 200,000 words, and I think they are all better than any I have written before. So I have no good resolution to make.

As he saw in the New Year, he had plenty to toast: in completing his book on mathematics he had fulfilled, not only his boyhood ambition of showing mathematics to rest on absolutely secure foundations, but also the promise he had seen in the work of the analytical mathematicians of establishing a new golden age in philosophy. If he had achieved what he thought he had achieved, he could, without any exaggeration, look upon himself, at the age of twenty-eight, as the author of the most important contribution to the philosophy of logic and mathematics since Aristotle.

Unfortunately, as he discovered all too soon, he had not quite achieved what he thought he had achieved. 'The honeymoon', as he put it, 'could not last, and early in the following year intellectual sorrow descended upon me in full measure.'

---

[1] As a mathematician, Russell regarded the sequence of numbers between 1 and 100 as beginning with 1, and therefore insisted that the twentieth century began in 1901, and not, as popular opinion would have it, in 1900. He thus regarded 31 December 1900 as the last day of the nineteenth century.

5

THE RELIGION OF SORROW

During the extraordinary burst of intellectual energy that had enabled him to complete *The Principles of Mathematics* in a few months at the end of 1900, Russell had grown increasingly close, both personally and intellectually, to Alfred North Whitehead. By contrast, Moore's influence on Russell was by this time comparatively negligible, Moore having shown himself unable and unwilling to follow Russell in his enthusiasm for Peano's mathematical logic, and, in any case, having developed a personal antipathy towards Russell that made meetings between the two somewhat difficult. With Whitehead, on the other hand, Russell was developing a comradeship that was to become vitally important to them both. Their interests were converging in a way that made co-operation between the two natural and mutually beneficial. Both were planning second volumes – Whitehead to *Universal Algebra* and Russell to *The Principles of Mathematics* – that would use logic as a foundation for mathematics, and both were inspired by the possibilities that Peano's work had opened up in this respect. Intellectually, they were, as Moore and Russell had so briefly been, on the same track.

While he had been busy writing *The Principles of Mathematics*, the isolation of The Millhangar had suited Russell perfectly, but now that he was eager for regular discussion with Whitehead, he wanted to be physically closer to him, preferably in Cambridge itself. By chance, an opportunity for the Russells and the Whiteheads to live together in Cambridge for a few months arose in the New Year of 1901, when the historian F. W. Maitland offered to let West Lodge, his house in Downing College, which was large enough for both the Whiteheads and the Russells, while, for the sake of his health, he spent the winter in Madeira. On 18 January 1901, therefore, Russell and Alys moved to Cambridge to spend the Lent Term living with the Whiteheads.

A few weeks after moving into Maitland's house, on 10 February, Russell underwent what was possibly the single most important experience of his life, an event he later called a 'conversion', which affected both his personality and his attitude to life fundamentally and permanently. His description of this event forms what is surely the most extraordinary piece of writing in his *Autobiography*. He begins by saying that Evelyn Whitehead was at this time 'becoming more and more an invalid, and used to have intense pain owing to heart trouble'. Then, he writes:

One day, Gilbert Murray came to Newnham to read part of his translation of *The Hippolytus*, then unpublished. Alys and I went to hear him, and I was profoundly stirred by the beauty of the poetry. When we came home, we found Mrs Whitehead undergoing an unusually severe bout of pain. She seemed cut off from everyone and everything by walls of agony, and the sense of the solitude of each human soul suddenly overwhelmed me. Ever since my marriage, my emotional life had been content with flippant cleverness. Suddenly the ground seemed to give way beneath me, and I found myself in quite another region. Within five minutes I went through some such reflections as the following: the loneliness of the human soul is unendurable; nothing can penetrate it except the highest intensity of the sort of love that religious teachers have preached; whatever does not spring from this motive is harmful, or at best useless; it follows that war is wrong, that a public school education is abominable, that the use of force is to be deprecated, and that in human relations one should penetrate to the core of loneliness in each person and speak to that. The Whiteheads' youngest boy, aged three, was in the room. I had previously taken no notice of him, nor he of me. He had to be prevented from troubling his mother in the middle of her paroxysms of pain. I took his hand and led him away. He came willingly, and felt at home with me. From that day to his death in the War in 1918, we were close friends.

'At the end of that five minutes,' he goes on, 'I had become a completely different person':

For a time, a sort of mystic illumination possessed me. I felt that I knew the inmost thoughts of everybody that I met in the street, and though this was, no doubt, a delusion, I did in actual fact find myself in far closer touch than previously with all my friends, and many of my acquaintances. Having been an Imperialist, I became during those five minutes a pro-Boer and a Pacifist. Having for years cared only for exactness and analysis, I found myself filled with semi-mystical feelings about beauty, with an intense interest in children, and a desire almost as profound as that of the Buddha to find some philosophy which should make human life endurable. A strange excitement possessed me, containing intense pain but also some element of triumph through the fact that I could dominate pain, and make it, as I thought, a gateway to wisdom.

There are a number of striking features of this experience that Russell, in these remarkable passages, passes over in silence. He never, for example, says what it was about Murray's reading of *The Hippolytus* that had moved him so greatly. Nor does he dwell upon his own personal feelings for Evelyn Whitehead herself. In these descriptions, Evelyn's suffering appears merely as an example of the suffering that is characteristic of the human condition generally. However, when, a mere decade after the event, he described it in a letter to Ottoline Morrell, he put a far more personal gloss on it. 'The moment of my first conversion', he told her, 'was this way':

I came to know (what it was not intended I should know) that a woman whom I liked greatly had a life of utter loneliness, filled with intense tragedy & pain of which she could never speak. I was not free to tell my sympathy, which was so intense as to change my life. I turned to all the ways there might be of alleviating her trouble without seeming to know it & so I went on in thought to loneliness in general, & how only love bridges the chasm – how force is the evil thing, & strife is the root of all evil & gentleness the only balm. I became infinitely gentle for a time . . . I resolved to bring some good & some hope into her life. All this happened in about five minutes . . . But it took me rather more than a year to acquiesce in her pain & to learn to love the cause of it, tho' he deserves much love. It was during that year I learnt whatever wisdom I possessed before meeting you.

Put like this, Russell's reaction to *The Hippolytus* begins to make some sort of sense. For at the centre of the play is an intense love that has both to be kept secret and to remain unconsummated: the love of Phaedra, who is married to Theseus, for Theseus's bastard son, Hippolytus. Denied any form of expression, this secret love consumes Phaedra, depriving her of any interest in anything else and, finally, of the will to live. During the first half of the play (the part that Murray read out to his audience in Newnham), Euripides emphasises again and again the corrosive, disabling effect of a deep but repressed love. 'Cursed be they', laments Phaedra, 'whose lips are clean and wise and seemly, but their hearts within rank with bad daring!' To keep such a passion hidden indefinitely is shown to be impossible: eventually, the true feelings in one's heart will be revealed:

> . . . through all this earth
> To every false man, that hour comes apace
> When Time holds up a mirror to his face,
> And girl-like, marvelling, there he stares to see
> How foul his heart!

Sure enough, Phaedra's secret is eventually revealed, first to her hand-maiden and then to Hippolytus himself. The latter, who worships the virginal goddess Artemis and (disastrously for all concerned) refuses to pay homage to Aphrodite, the goddess of love, is disgusted at Phaedra's betrayal of Theseus and declares his hatred for her, whereupon – and this is where Murray's reading ended – Phaedra commits suicide.

The play, with its emphasis on forbidden love, repressed emotion and the pain of silent suffering, spoke to Russell in a way that nothing had done since his absorption in the work of Ibsen, Turgenev and Whitman eight years earlier. Indeed, his reaction to it recalls the still earlier impact upon him as a teenager of Shelley's poem 'Alastor'. Since the revelations of his grandmother before his marriage, Russell had resolved to live as unemotional a life as he could manage and, having fallen in love with Evelyn Whitehead, was all too aware of the suffering caused by a great affection that has to remain unexpressed because of its impropriety.

Central to the power of the 'conversion' itself, however, was Russell's apparent determination to project at least some of his own feelings on to Evelyn herself, to see her as lonely and suffering, and as hiding her very deepest emotions. The power of the experience – as he described it to Ottoline – was precisely that of feeling that he, and he alone, could see into Evelyn's heart, and that in so doing he could, so to speak, hold up a mirror to his own heart and see what had lain there, unseen and unacknowledged, for many years.

One aspect of the experience that Russell seems to have been almost entirely unaware of is the extent to which it contains very strong and resonant echoes of his own childhood. There is a sense in his descriptions of those extraordinary five minutes of a great unleashing of hitherto repressed feelings, a sense that the lid he had put on his emotional life in the wake of the fears of madness that his grandmother had evoked had come flying off. And, it is natural to assume, some of the most powerful feelings that were thus released were those relating to his early bereavements.

A hint of this is evident in his description of taking the hand of Evelyn's son, Eric, and of the closeness that he felt towards the boy. Eric was, at that time, not three as Russell says, but two years and two months old – almost exactly the age that Russell himself was when his mother died. Russell's deep sense of identification with the boy was surely not unconnected with this, especially when one considers that the loneliness, the solitude that was the subject of Russell's preoccupations during his 'conversion' was, in his case, the direct result of the death of his mother. Russell was evidently mistaken about the state of Evelyn's health: she did not suffer from heart failure as he believed, and in fact had a fairly robust constitution (she lived for another sixty years after this incident). Later in life she was diagnosed as suffering from 'pseudo-angina', a form of hysteria in which symptoms of heart attacks are simulated. But nevertheless, as far as Russell was concerned, what Eric was facing was the possible loss at the age of two of his mother.

Russell was fond – perhaps over-fond – of presenting his life as a series of epiphanies, many of which, one suspects, were overplayed by him in later life for the sake of lending drama to the facts of his life. The fundamental importance of this 'conversion', however, is no later invention but was realised by him at the time. Just two days after the event, he wrote to Alys (who was in Manchester on temperance work): 'The day before yesterday seems to me such a remote epoch that it might be two months ago: I have to assure myself solemnly that it is not. Since the time of our engagement, I have felt nothing so poignantly as the last two days.'

A few days later, he wrote to Gilbert Murray, too, to tell him how much his *Hippolytus* had affected him. It was, Russell wrote, 'almost overwhelming':

Your tragedy fulfils perfectly – so it seems to me – the purpose of bringing out whatever is noble and beautiful in sorrow; and to those of us who are without a religion, this is the only consolation of which the spectacle of the world cannot deprive us.

The lyric he liked best, he told Murray, was that with which he had ended his reading, in which the audience is told of Phaedra's suicide, a suicide brought about by:

> . . . that dark spell that about her clings,
> Sick desires of forbidden things.

This lyric, Russell wrote, he had already learnt by heart, 'and it has been in my head ever since'.

Russell liked to describe his 'conversion' as something that brought him closer to other people, something that enabled him to see and feel other people's suffering, but there was at least one person to whose suffering he became extraordinarily blind and indifferent after this experience, and that was Alys. When Alys returned to Cambridge from Manchester, she found that, in the wake of Evelyn's 'heart attack', she was now expected to take sole responsibility for the running of the household, even for the care of the Whiteheads' children. 'Poor Alys has the whole family on her hands,' Hannah wrote to Mary in March, 'and I fear will have for the rest of her life.'

Alys grew increasingly depressed – not, one suspects, primarily because of the additional burdens placed upon her (though those cannot have helped), but because of the absorption by Russell in Evelyn and her rather melodramatic suffering, and the stark and rather cruel contrast it offered with his corresponding neglect of herself. Nevertheless, Alys, dutiful as ever, seems never to have mentioned to Russell the cause of her depression and met her new responsibilities for the Whitehead household with an uncomplaining stoicism. She, indeed, became almost indispensable to the Whiteheads – despite the fact that neither Alfred nor Evelyn liked her very much – and, when the time came to leave Maitland's house, she agreed to live for a time with them at their house in Grantchester, and it was not until May that the Russells eventually returned to Fernhurst.

A good portrait of their life together during this summer is preserved in the diary of Beatrice Webb, who visited them on 1 July 1901. 'The routine of the daily existence', Webb recorded, 'is . . . carefully planned and exactly executed':

> They breakfast together in their study at 9 o'clock . . . then Bertrand works at mathematics until 12.30, then three-quarters of an hour reading together (Ranke's *History of England* since we have been here), a quarter-hour stroll in the garden together. Lunch with us 1.30, chat in our sitting-room or out-of-doors over cigarettes and coffee: then Bertrand plays croquet with Logan Smith (Alys's brother who lives near here) until tea at 4.30. After that mathematics until 6 o'clock: reading with Alys until 7.30, dine at 8 o'clock, chat and smoke with us until 9.30: another hour's reading aloud with Alys until 10.30.

Alys, Webb records, 'has not the gift of intimacy except with her husband . . . She has no art of flirtation, if anything she prefers women to men, and I think really likes the womanly woman better than the professional. She has no moods or they are controlled . . . If she has a defect it is a certain colourlessness of intellect and a certain lack of "temperament". But in a woman are these defects?'

As for Russell himself:

Bertrand is a slight, dark-haired man, with prominent forehead, bright eyes, strong features except for a retreating chin, nervous hands and alert quick movements. In manner and dress and outward bearing he is most carefully trimmed, conventionally correct and punctiliously polite, and in speech he has an almost affectedly clear enunciation of words and preciseness of expression. In morals he is a puritan; in personal habits almost an ascetic, except that he lives for efficiency and therefore expects to be kept in the best physical condition. But intellectually he is audacious – an iconoclast, detesting religions or social convention, suspecting sentiment, believing only in the 'order of thought' and the order of things, in logic and in science. He indulges in the wildest paradox and in the broadest jokes, the latter always too abstrusely intellectual in their form to be vulgarly coarse. He is a delightful talker, especially in general conversation, when the intervention of other minds prevents him from tearing his subject to pieces with fine chopping logic.

'He looks at the world from a pinnacle of detachment,' Webb added, 'dissects persons and demolishes causes':

What he lacks is sympathy and tolerance for other people's emotions, and, if you regard it as a virtue, Christian humility. The outline of both his intellect and his feelings are sharp, hard and permanent. He is a good hater . . . He is intolerant of blemishes and faults in himself and others, he dreams of Perfection in man. He almost loathes lapses from men's own standards . . . I have no 'sense of sin' and no desire to see it punished. Bertrand, on the other hand, is almost cruel in his desire to see cruelty revenged.

It is a perceptive portrait, but what is most striking about it is that the qualities Webb finds noticeably lacking in him – sympathy, tolerance and kindness in human relations – are the very qualities that Russell himself considered he had acquired as a result of his conversion experience. As far as his relations with Alys were concerned, the experience had not broken the hard veneer he had constructed to hide his emotional life, but rather made it even harder.

During this summer Russell was asked by Trinity College to give a course of lectures on the principles of mathematics, starting in the autumn. He accepted immediately, delighted at the chance it would give him to be in Cambridge on a regular basis and thus able to discuss the philosophy of mathematics with Whitehead, and also to present the ideas of *Principles of Mathematics* to an audience. Soon after accepting the invitation, Russell left

Fernhurst for the Whiteheads' house in Grantchester. There, he told Alys, he had, through discussions with Whitehead, 'got back my usual feeling of the importance of work, which I lost in the winter'.

Russell's letters to Alys from the Whiteheads' house show, however, a far greater absorption in Evelyn and in her problems with her husband than they do in the problems of the foundations of mathematics. Russell never admitted to Alys that he was in love with Evelyn, but it is hard to believe (despite her later denials) that she did not suspect as much. Every now and again in his letters there is a tell-tale remark that unconsciously hints at the truth. On 10 July, for example, he wrote: 'I miss thee too very much, in spite of the pleasure of seeing Evelyn.' In other letters he reported long and frank discussions with Evelyn about Whitehead and her frustrations with him. 'Evelyn is more lovable than ever, and I quite like Alfred again,' he wrote on 13 July, leaving no doubt as to where his sympathies lay in this domestic dispute.

These sympathies are evident, too, in the account that Russell gives of this period in his *Autobiography*. 'My relations with the Whiteheads', he writes there, 'were difficult and complex.' He then goes on to represent Whitehead himself as suffering from 'impulses which were scarcely sane', such as the desire to join the Catholic Church and the urge to spend more money than he possessed. As instances of incipient insanity, neither of these is very persuasive, but Russell, alone among Whitehead's friends, insists upon representing him as one step away from madness:

> He used to frighten Mrs Whitehead and her servants by mutterings in which he addressed injurious abjurations to himself. At times he would be completely silent for some days, saying nothing whatever to anybody in the house. Mrs Whitehead was in perpetual fear that he would go mad. I think, in retrospect, that she exaggerated the danger, for she tended to be melodramatic in her outlook. But the danger was certainly real, even if not as great as she believed. She spoke of him to me with the utmost frankness, and I found myself in an alliance with her to keep him sane.

It is possible – indeed, it becomes practically inescapable – to see in Evelyn's discussions with Russell something more than frankness. For one thing, the so-called 'alliance to keep Whitehead sane' took a form that was hugely to Evelyn's advantage: that of Russell surreptitiously providing the Whiteheads with money to meet their bills and to extend their house. As for the size of the bills, all the evidence suggests that it was Evelyn rather than Alfred who was responsible. Victor Lowe, Whitehead's biographer, represents Evelyn as wanting to buy beautiful things and to live in a way more lavish than Whitehead could afford, and rather resenting him for not allowing her to indulge these wishes. She also, in his account, desired more attention than Whitehead, always completely absorbed in his work, was prepared to give her. From Russell, she took both the money and the attention she desired. What she gave in return was what he craved more than anything else: intimacy, the feeling of sharing a secret and passionate communion. Without becoming Russell's lover, she could fulfil the need he had had all his life for a special friend, a true companion. An important aspect of the financial gifts that Russell made to the Whiteheads, one suspects, was that they were unknown to Whitehead himself: they were Russell and Evelyn's secret, and, as such, a symbol of the nature of their relationship. Evelyn, then, allowed – indeed, encouraged – Russell's love for her to be expressed covertly, without allowing it to be consummated. Once, for example, they took a boat together out on the Granta at moonlight, and she listened while he read Matthew Arnold's 'Sohrab and Rustrum' to her, but, as a precaution, she took her daughter Jessie along as a chaperone.

Presumably at Russell's expense, the Russells and the Whiteheads went together on a six-week Mediterranean cruise in August and September 1901. The holiday, it seems natural to suppose, was a centrally important event in shaping the nature of the relationship between the two couples, and yet, frustratingly, the details of it are more or less lost to history. Russell never mentions it in his *Autobiography*, and any mention of it in his subsequent letters to Evelyn disappeared, along with much else, when Evelyn had those letters destroyed. A few unrevealing letters from Alys to Nathaniel Webb are all that survive from those six weeks, and they throw no light whatever on what happened on the cruise. That something important happened is suggested by the fact that Alys, though she had planned to spend the entire six weeks on the cruise, left for home a week earlier than the others.

The summer was pivotal in another respect, too: when they returned from the cruise, Russell let it be known that he could no longer tolerate living at The Millhangar. The reason he gave was that he could not bear to live in close proximity to Hannah, whom he had come to hate, but one feels that this is not the whole truth. He had detested Hannah for six years, and there seems nothing in his relations with her during the summer of 1901 to have brought matters to a head. On the contrary, she seems by this time to have become more or less an irrelevance in his life. I believe that his now open expressions of detestation for Hannah were a substitute for what he really wanted to express at this time, namely the complete loss of his love for Alys herself.

Something of this almost certainly communicated itself to Alys, which surely accounts for the deepening of her depression throughout the autumn. After the Mediterranean cruise, Russell moved in with the Whiteheads at Grantchester, while he prepared for his lecture course, which started in October. At the beginning of November, he was joined by Alys, who, soon after arriving in Grantchester, told Russell for the first time the extent of her misery. Russell advised her to see a doctor, but she refused, fearing that the doctor would recommend a separation. Still, officially, Russell refused to admit to her – or, it seems, to himself – that his feelings for her had changed, and, after the Cambridge term finished, the two of them went on a holiday together to the South of France.

On 30 December, Russell wrote to Helen Thomas in terms that contrast most vividly with the optimistic boasting of the previous year. Hearing that Helen was in hospital with sciatica, he offered his condolences. 'Since I wrote to you this time last year,' he told her, 'the greatest part of my thoughts has been occupied almost continuously with the subject of illness; Mrs

Whitehead's condition has remained a cause of anxiety . . . Some sorrows can only be met by patience, and the reflection that life is both short and unimportant.' He was writing from Friday's Hill. The wind was howling outside, and the house was empty, Alys having gone up to London, so: 'everything inclines to melancholy. But melancholy is on the whole a pleasant mood: "cheerly, cheerly, she loves me dearly, and ah! she is so constant and so kind".' Melancholy, it emerges from this letter, was from now on to be the very basis of Russell's philosophy of life. The only escape from the sorrow of mortal suffering, he insists, is not 'that love that religious teachers have preached', but rather an absorption in the life of the intellect, in mathematics. Emotional sympathy, indeed, was something he now professed rather to despise. 'I have come to feel', he told Helen, 'a certain shame in thinking of transient things, and to regard a year spent, as this year has been, in human sympathy, as something weak and contemptible.' Through mathematics, we escape transience, suffering, and mortality itself:

> The world of mathematics, which you condemn, is really a beautiful world; it has nothing to do with life and death and human sordidness, but is eternal, cold and passionless. To me, pure mathematics is one of the highest forms of art; it has a sublimity quite special to itself, and an immense dignity derived from the fact that its world is exempt from change and time. I am quite serious about this. The only difficulty is that none but mathematicians can enter this enchanted region, and they hardly ever have a sense of beauty. And mathematics is the only thing we know of that is capable of perfection; in thinking about it we become Gods. This alone is enough to put it on a pinnacle above all other studies. If you will contrast the dignity of (say) *Samson Agonistes* with Shelley's 'I fall upon the grass, I die, I faint, I fail', etc., you can conceive of mathematics as standing to Milton as Milton does to Shelley.

Ironically, however, just as Russell began to look to mathematics to provide the perfection he had failed to find in the transient world of human relations, his work on mathematics started to reveal contradictions and flaws in the theory that he had developed the previous year. This made it look as though mathematics might be a good deal less sublime, perfect and beautiful than he had thought. The draft of *The Principles of Mathematics* that he finished with such triumphant ceremony and pride in December 1900 was, therefore, never published, and Russell spent much of 1901 wondering how the theory it presented might be salvaged from the contradictions that now beset it.

What has become known to all students of logic and mathematics as 'Russell's Paradox' was discovered by him in the spring of 1901. At first, he supposed that the problems it presented to his attempts to found mathematics upon logic might quickly and easily be overcome, but by the end of the year he began to realise that something fundamental was amiss. The seeds of Russell's discovery of the paradox are contained, ironically, in the triumphant popular article, 'Recent Work on the Principles of Mathematics', that he had written in the first flush of his enthusiasm for Peano's logic. There, in the context of extolling the philosophical importance of Cantor's work, and of his hierarchy of different infinite numbers, Russell comments on Cantor's proof that there is no greatest number in this hierarchy. This could not be right, Russell thought, since the class of all classes and of all things (that is, the class of everything there is) must surely have the greatest cardinal number there could possibly be. 'In this one point', he wrote, 'the master has been guilty of a very subtle fallacy, which I hope to explain in some future work.'

At the beginning of 1901, Russell devoted a great deal of attention to the paradoxes engendered by Cantor's proof (which, rather dismayingly, seemed closely analogous to the old 'antinomies of infinity' that he thought he had left behind along with neo-Hegelianism), and by April or May had arrived at a paradox that seemed more fundamental than all the others. It arose from considering the class of all classes that are not members of themselves. Some classes *are* members of themselves: the class of all classes, for example. But most classes are not. We ought, then, to be able to form the class of all those classes that are not members of themselves. But now, if we ask of *this* class whether it is a member of itself or not, we seem to arrive at an unavoidable contradiction: if it *is* a member of itself, then it is not, and if it *is not*, then it is. It is rather like defining the village barber as 'the man who shaves all those who do not shave themselves' and then asking if *he* shaves himself or not.

One can see that this problem at first struck Russell as irritatingly trivial; it looks, at first sight, like nothing more serious than a tiresome word-puzzle. 'It seemed unworthy of a grown man to spend his time in such trivialities,' Russell later wrote, 'but what was I to do?' Whitehead, however, seemed to appreciate immediately that it presented a fundamental and difficult challenge. When told by Russell of the paradox, he responded by quoting Browning's line from 'The Lost Leader': 'never glad confident morning again'. What Whitehead perhaps saw immediately – and Russell was to see only gradually – was that the Paradox showed something to be wrong with the very notion of a 'class' as Russell had hoped to use it in his logical foundations for mathematics.

The implications of the Paradox for Russell's hopes for mathematics grew steadily more serious, like a cancer, throughout 1901 and 1902, until they eventually destroyed almost completely his earlier triumphant hopes. What he felt about the Paradox, he later said, was analogous to what a virtuous Catholic must feel about a wicked Pope. At the end of 1901, however, though he had abandoned the hope that a quick solution might be found, the Paradox had still not eroded his faith altogether in what he had described to Helen Thomas as his 'new subject'. He and Whitehead had by this time agreed to join forces to produce a book together that would, at one and the same time, serve as the second volume to *Universal Algebra* and to *The Principles of Mathematics*. They anticipated that it would take them two years; in fact, it took nine years and grew into the massive, three-volume work that is *Principia Mathematica*. Before they could even begin work on it, however, Russell had, in the light of the Paradox, to re-write much of *The Principles of Mathematics* itself. Exactly how he was to re-write it, he did not know, since he had as yet no solution to the Paradox.

His confidence in the general project of showing mathematics to be essentially logic was, however, undimmed, and was expressed, not only in his joint plans with Whitehead, but also in the series of lectures that he delivered at Cambridge in the academic year 1901–2. 'In my course at Cambridge,' he told Couturat in a letter written on 7 January 1902, in which he returns almost to the triumphant, boastful tone of the previous year, 'I began with 22 P[rimitive] p[ropositions] of general logic (such as the syllogism) and I deduced from them all of pure mathematics, including Cantor and geometry, without any new Pp, or primitive concepts. All of this will appear in the book that I plan to publish with Whitehead.' In March, after he had finished the course, he wrote again to Couturat, giving a slightly different account of what he had achieved, but sounding no less pleased with himself:

Did I tell you that in my course at Cambridge I deduced the whole of pure mathematics, including geometry, from 8 undefined concepts and 20 unproved propositions? I gave purely logical definitions of number, and of various spaces. I believe that this work would have pleased Leibniz.

Privately, however, he was less sanguine, and the feeling of melancholy expressed in his letter to Helen Thomas remained his dominant mood, unrelieved even by the pleasure he took in mathematics, which was becoming increasingly, because of the unresolved questions aroused by the Paradox, yet another source of disillusionment and despair.

Throughout much of 1901, Russell had tried to disguise from both Alys and himself the fact that he was no longer in love with her. In November, he wrote a letter that seems, in retrospect, to be an expression of what he wished he felt for her:

Dearest, thee does give me more happiness than I can say – all the happiness I have, in fact. Thee is the only person I know well and yet really and thoroughly admire. I love the absolute certainty that all thy thoughts will be magnanimous and free from all pettiness. Since last winter I have known that life without thee would not be possible. It is alarming to be so absolutely dependent, but so it is.

By January 1902, however, just two months later, he could keep up the pretence no longer. 'I am haunted', he wrote in his diary some months later, 'by the memory of a day in January of this year':

I walked alone through the woods: a cold frosty sun faintly illumined a wintry landscape. Alys was ill at home; anguish lay behind, sorrow and difficulty ahead. It seemed as though winter would never end, and dimly I felt that the springs of other years were gone for ever. But out of the snow two pale untimely primroses raised their struggling heads, giving an earnest of better days to come, when the sun would be warm, the air mild, and sadness merely a poetic memory. Surely, I thought, with the flowers and the nightingales joy too would return, again love will gladden our hearts, and discord will be forgotten. Joy is not dead, but chilled by wintry blasts into sleep; soon, soon, our sorrows will be over, and she will recover the buoyant happiness that used to brighten every moment. I took the two primroses from their bed of snow, and offered them to her as a little token of love. Both of us were touched, deeply touched, and for a moment hope whispered honeyed words; but in our hearts we knew they were lies, we knew that spring was gone and youth was dead, we knew that never again would the sun shine for us as he had shone, never again would our hearts sing with the chorus of mourning birds. The pathos of her life lived in my imagination in that moment, and I longed, with an infinite tenderness, to revivify my dying love. Almost I succeeded; but it was too late. The spring of which those poor flowers fondly dreamed never came, and never will come; in human lives, there is but one spring, and winter, when it comes, is not thawed by gentle winds from southern seas, but deepens slowly into Arctic night.

This diary entry gives the lie to Russell's oft-quoted account in his *Autobiography* of how he realised his love for Alys was dead:

... when we were living with the Whiteheads at the Mill House in Grantchester, a more serious blow fell than those that had preceded it. I went out bicycling one afternoon, and suddenly, as I was riding along a country road, I realised that I no longer loved Alys. I had had no idea until this moment that my love for her was even lessening. The problems presented by this discovery were very grave ... I knew that she was still devoted to me. I had no wish to be unkind, but I believed in those days (what experience has taught me to think possibly open to doubt) that in intimate relations one should speak the truth. I did not see in any case how I could for any length of time successfully pretend to love her when I did not. I had no longer any instinctive impulse towards sex relations with her, and this alone would have been an insuperable barrier to concealment of my feelings. At this crisis my father's priggery came out in me, and I began to justify myself with moral criticisms of Alys. I did not at once tell her that I no longer loved her, but of course she perceived that something was amiss.

Alys had no doubt 'perceived that something was amiss' a good deal before this famous bicycle ride, as her depressions during the spring and summer of 1901 surely indicate. And, as Russell's diary entry reveals, he too had been struggling for some time against the realisation that his love for Alys was dead (he had, after all, 'longed, with an infinite tenderness, to revivify my dying love' a month before the bicycle ride). Nevertheless, though Russell clearly massively exaggerates – as was his wont – the extent to which it was a sudden and unexpected revelation, there seems no reason to doubt that there was a bicycle ride and that there was a moment when he ceased to struggle against the facts and to admit to himself that he no longer loved Alys. His later comments to Ottoline Morrell suggest that the date of this fateful day was around 8 February, and this fits also with a diary entry of 10 February 1903, in which he says: 'Two years ago today Gilbert read his *Hippolytus* at Cambridge. A year ago yesterday I told Alys not to be indiscreet.'

What, exactly, he meant when he told Alys 'not to be indiscreet' is something of a mystery. Perhaps he was urging her not to enquire too deeply into his feelings for her, or perhaps he even confessed something of the nature of his feelings for Evelyn Whitehead and asked her to remain quiet about it. Whatever it was, it could have served only to confirm what Alys had probably been feeling for a long time: the inexorable withdrawal of his love. The next two months at the Whiteheads' house, during which Russell finished his course on the principles of mathematics at Trinity, must have been a deeply miserable period for Alys, and, by the time they returned to Fernhurst at the beginning of April, she was showing signs of a nervous breakdown.

Russell, for his part, had begun to turn his sorrow into the basis of an entire philosophy of life, even a religion, something he was later to call the 'religion of sorrow'. The seeds of this 'faith' are described in his *Autobiography* thus:

> The most unhappy moments of my life were spent at Grantchester. My bedroom looked out upon the mill, and the noise of the millstream mingled inextricably with my despair. I lay awake through long nights, hearing first the nightingale, and then the chorus of birds at dawn, looking out upon sunrise and trying to find consolation in external beauty. I suffered in a very intense form the loneliness which I had perceived a year before to be the essential lot of man. I walked alone in the fields about Grantchester, feeling dimly that the whitening willows in the wind had some message from a land of peace. I read religious books such as Taylor's *Holy Dying*, in the hope that there might be something independent of dogma in the comfort which their authors derived from their beliefs.

Soon after their return to Fernhurst, Russell gave an early hint of the nature of this 'religion of sorrow' in a long letter to Gilbert Murray. The ostensible subject of the letter was ethical theory, Russell taking issue with what he perceived to be Murray's adherence to some form of utilitarianism. Not far below the surface of this theoretical discussion, however, was Russell's reaction to the melancholy that had become his more or less permanent state. In the past, he told Murray, he had regarded it as self-evident that pleasure is the only good and pain the only evil: 'Now, however, the opposite seems to me self-evident. This change has been brought about by what I may call moral experience.'

Without going into details, but in a way that showed that, in his mind, moral theory and autobiography were closely linked, Russell outlined the stages in his own development that had persuaded him to abandon the utilitarian ethics of his youth: first came his decision to pursue philosophy even though he had no doubt that by pursuing other things, such as economics or politics, he could contribute more to human happiness:

It appeared to me that the dignity of which human existence is capable is not attainable by devotion to the mechanism of life, and that unless the contemplation of eternal things is preserved, mankind will become no better than well-fed pigs. But I do not believe that such contemplation on the whole tends to happiness. It gives moments of delight, but these are outweighed by years of effort and depression.

This feeling was confirmed by his absorption in mathematics, which he had come to believe 'is capable of an artistic excellence as great as that of any music', not because the pleasure it gives is comparable to that of music, 'but because it gives in absolute perfection that combination, characteristic of great art, of godlike freedom, with the sense of inevitable destiny; because, in fact, it constructs an ideal world where everything is perfect and yet true'. And the beauty of this world was precisely that it was not human:

> in regard to human existence, I have found myself giving honour to those who feel its tragedy, who think truly about Death, who are oppressed by ignoble things even when they are inevitable; yet these qualities appear to me to militate against happiness.

Generally, he told Murray, 'the best life seems to me one which thinks truly and greatly about human things, and which, in addition, contemplates the world of beauty and of abstract truths.' The essence of his new philosophy was this:

> I hold all knowledge that is concerned with things that actually exist – all that is commonly called Science – to be of very slight value compared to that knowledge which, like philosophy and mathematics, is concerned with ideal and eternal objects, and is freed from this miserable world which God has made.

It was clear that Russell and Alys could not go on living together in the oppressive gloom that had now descended upon their marriage, and, on 14 April, Alys agreed to take a 'rest cure' in Brighton with a Dr Boyle, who ran a sanatorium specialising in such things. The 'cure' involved spending most of one's time in bed, being denied visits from one's friends and family, and having one's activities restricted to reading and a little letter-writing. In a later description of her time at Brighton, Alys remembered only that she was 'very lonely', but she must also have been extremely bored. The original intention was for her to spend just ten days there, but Russell persuaded her to stay longer, first for four weeks, and then throughout the whole of May and most of June as well.

Russell had two reasons for wanting Alys out of the way: first to recover his own mental equilibrium, and second, to finish the necessary re-writing of *The Principles of Mathematics*. For a few days after she left, Russell took a short cycling holiday around Oxfordshire and Wiltshire. The merit of cycling, he told Alys in a letter of 16 April, was that the physical exertion it required 'absorbs me to the exclusion of other pleasures and pains'. When he arrived back at the Whiteheads' house in Grantchester, he told her that he felt 'terribly exhausted by the strain', and pleased that she was at last receiving some treatment for her depression and that she had agreed to be there for four weeks:

> ... even if thee had been coming out in ten days from now, I do not think I could have come back so soon, and my nerves are for the present completely shattered ... I have only just avoided a complete nervous breakdown, which I should have been as slow to recover from as thee – and then we should have had to be separated till both were well.

Living with the Whiteheads, he told Alys in another letter, 'suits me very well, except when I have to watch its effect on thee' (Alys had earlier told him that living at Grantchester had a bad effect on her, and that she felt a little better simply by leaving there). On his cycling tour, 'it was the utmost I could accomplish not to cry in public', but now, at Grantchester, 'I begin to feel more master of myself.'

The implication of these letters was that Alys, and Alys alone, was responsible for Russell's nervous exhaustion, and that, with her out of the way, and with the Whiteheads to take care of him, unhindered by her, everything would once more be all right with him. It was an implication that Alys, pathetically, seemed only too willing to accept. 'I have been a brute of selfishness to weigh thee down like this and shatter thy poor nerves,' she wrote to him on 20 April, 'but when that blank despair overwhelms me I cannot exercise any unselfishness or self-control or fortitude.' Russell replied, not, as Alys no doubt hoped he would, with denials that she was entirely responsible for his nervous state, but with renewed pleas for her to stay away longer. 'I hope thee will let the Dr persuade thee to stay longer,' he wrote on 24 April. 'Everybody tells me it is ridiculous to go for only three weeks, and the half of them regard thee as unreasonable, while the other half regard me as a Tyrant Man who refuses to spare thee any longer.' Lest there should be any question of Russell needing Alys, he hastened to assure her that he was doing very well where he was:

> The weather is heavenly, and in itself soothing to tired nerves. I spend most of my day in the garden: Evelyn is very busy with the Fräulein and the pony and so on, so she is not out much except for calls or shopping.

After hearing that Dr Boyle had ordered Alys to take three months' rest, Russell announced that he had, for the first time, slept a full seven hours ('the best night I have had for a very long time') and that he now felt ready to begin the arduous task of re-writing *The Principles of Mathematics*. 'I must screw myself up to get it done while we are separated,' he told her. 'I cannot, in the time and in my present condition, finish it in style, but I can patch up something that will do for publication.'

Throughout May, Russell, working at an extraordinary rate (he later said that, during this period, 'my energy was ten times what it usually is'), laboured to re-write Part I of *Principles*, the part dealing with the basic logic of the theory and the part that had been destroyed by the Paradox. Like a house that remains intact even while its foundations have crumbled, the rest of the book, Parts II–VII, remained largely unchanged from the earlier draft. In the face of the Paradox, however, the logic to which Russell intended to show mathematics to be reducible lost the crystalline perfection and beauty that it had had in the earlier version, and became ever more complicated and imperfect. The theory that Russell had wanted to advance was one based on the dual notions of 'propositional function' and 'class'. A propositional function is, so to speak, a proposition with a place left unfilled. 'Socrates is mortal' and 'Plato is mortal' are propositions, but 'x is mortal' is a propositional function. To every propositional function, the theory was supposed to go, went a corresponding class, being the collection of 'x's' that render the propositional function true. Thus, the propositional function 'x is mortal' would define the class of all mortal things.

The Paradox, however, by presenting a propositional function to which – on pain of contradiction – no possible class could correspond ('x is a class that does not belong to itself') blew this simple and beautiful theory apart. Where the earlier draft had been triumphant and confident, therefore, Russell's new draft was uncertain and confused. The contradiction haunts the revised Part I – and therefore the entire book – like the proverbial ghost at the feast. Lacking a satisfactory theory to put in the place of the one the Paradox had destroyed, Russell now presents the old theory, together with the admission that it cannot be *quite* right and a mere sketch of an idea as to how it could be improved. This sketch – introduced in a chapter called 'The Contradiction', which now ends Part I – involves distinguishing different logical *types*: terms (what Moore had called 'concepts'), classes of terms, classes of classes, and so on, and then insisting that a propositional function only has a meaning if its variable, x, refers only to some specified type; 'x is a member of itself' is therefore meaningless, because the 'x' is ambiguous between different types.

The solution, to which Russell gave the name 'theory of types', is not worked out in detail, and in any case was one the correctness of which Russell himself was not entirely convinced. He offered it only as a basis for discussion, a gesture that imparted to the whole book – which in its 1900 manifestation had been quite magnificently certain of the truth of its doctrines – a tentative and unresolved note. 'I am not at all satisfied with it,' Russell told Alys on 13 May, 'but I fear it is the best I can do. I think of publishing as soon as possible, as I cannot rest till it is off my mind. This is not the true artistic conscience, but that is a luxury I can no longer afford for the present.' He who looked to mathematics to provide the perfection that mortal life lacked was now about to present to the world a book about mathematics full of self-confessed flaws and imperfections. It was an irony of which Russell was all too conscious, and his feelings for the book came close at times to a passionate loathing.

When the book was nearly finished, Russell told Alys that its completion 'will not give me any feeling of elation, merely a kind of tired relief as at the end of a very long dusty railway journey'. He at first expected the work to last two months, but on re-reading his earlier draft, he persuaded himself that it needed fewer alterations than he had anticipated, and on 23 May – much earlier than he had expected – the work was finished. He felt exhausted and, as he put it to Alys, *sacrificed*, by the effort it had taken:

> I should like to put as a dedication to my book: 'To Moloch this Altar is dedicated by a Sacred Victim.' But I fear the mathematical public might be puzzled.

What did he mean? – that the book was an altar upon which he had sacrificed his childhood, his innocence (just as children were offered up to Moloch)? In a letter to Lucy Donnelly, Russell was more explicit:

> You will wonder at my writing to you: the fact is, I finished today my magnum opus on the principles of mathematics, on which I have been engaged since 1897. This has left me with leisure and liberty to remember that there are human things in the world, which I have been strenuously striving to forget. I wonder whether you realise the degree of self-sacrifice (and too often sacrifice of others), of sheer effort of will, of stern austerity in repressing even what is intrinsically best, that goes into writing a book of any magnitude. Year after year I found mistakes in what I had done, and had to re-write the whole from beginning to end: for in a logical system, one mistake will usually vitiate everything. The hardest part I left to the end: last summer I undertook it gaily, hoping to finish it soon, when suddenly I came upon a greater difficulty than any I had known before. So difficult it was, that to think of it at all required an all but superhuman effort. And long ago I got sick with nausea of the whole subject, so that I longed to think of anything else under the sun; and sheer fatigue has become almost incapacitating. But now at last all is finished, and as you may imagine, I feel a new man; for I had given up hope of ever coming to an end of the labour. Abstract work, if one wishes to do it well, must be allowed to destroy one's humanity; one raises a monument which is at the same time a tomb, in which, voluntarily, one slowly inters oneself.

At the earliest opportunity Russell delivered the book to Cambridge University Press, and then set about repairing his nerves through rest, spending his days basking in the early summer weather in the Whiteheads' garden.

A few days after Russell finished the final draft of *The Principles of Mathematics* the Treaty of Vereeniging was signed, ending the Boer War. 'We decorated the whole place with bunting, and all was gladness,' Russell later recalled in his diary. 'And I too felt a great joy that the outer world was not such a ruin as the inner; but yet, the contrast was all but unbearable, and in solitude I sobbed uncontrollably.'

Russell had still not told Alys what he had known with certainty since February and what she had probably suspected for much longer: namely, that he no longer loved her. On occasion, he had – for the sake of Alys's health and his peace of mind – been forced to lie directly. On 11 May, for example, in the middle of his prodigious final burst of activity on the book, she had written: 'It is funny how my depression suddenly appears and disappears for no reason at all . . . I was growing very near to developing the ridiculous delusion that thee no longer cared for me.'

'I have been very well aware that thee thought I no longer cared for thee,' Russell replied:

But for that, I should have *insisted* on a separation in January, as it was obvious thee ought not to be here. As it was, I was almost distracted by the conflict between thy morbid feelings and the obvious fact that thee ought to go away.

Towards the end of his work on the book, as Russell later confessed in his diary, 'I was writing cold letters to Alys, in the deliberate hope of destroying her affection; I was cruel still, and ruthless where I saw no self-denial practised.' On one occasion, in what both he and Alys seemed to regard as a harmless, absent-minded mistake, but which might perhaps quite naturally be regarded rather as a prime case of a 'Freudian slip', he signed his letter, not with the usual 'Thine devotedly, Bertie', but with the more formal 'Thine most affectionately, Bertrand Russell'.

At the beginning of June, Russell was told that Dr Boyle would now allow him to visit Alys (whom he had not seen since the middle of April) for a Saturday afternoon. The meeting, which was arranged for 7 June, was short and, far from helping to cheer Alys's spirits, threw her still deeper into depression. Russell, she thought, had changed during their separation, and so distressed was she by the change that she broke down in tears, alarming Russell and distancing him still more from her suffering. Before he went, Russell struck an ominous note when he told her: 'I do not believe the separation has been bad for thee – for me, certainly, it has been beneficial.' After the meeting, his letters became still more cold and detached. 'I was not too tired out by any means,' he told her about the afternoon they had shared together, 'when it is only one day, one can rest after it, so that no harm is done.' Alys, one supposes, had been fishing for a somewhat bigger compliment.

At the beginning of her rest cure, Alys had read the three-volume edition of Jane Carlyle's letters edited by J. A. Froude and had sent them on for Russell to read. The unhappy marriage between the Carlyles bears some striking parallels to that of the Russells: Jane Carlyle was almost continuously in bad health, made worse by the indifference shown towards her by her tyrannical and selfish husband, who starved her of affection while demanding much of her. In giving Russell the letters, Alys was perhaps hoping that he would learn some sympathy by seeing in Carlyle's monstrous behaviour towards his wife a reflection of his own treatment of her. If so, she was disappointed. What impressed Russell about the letters – and what he sought to learn from – was the great stoicism displayed by Mrs Carlyle. 'I am sorry I cannot write about myself,' he told Alys on 11 June. 'When one is requiring a great deal of self control, what Mrs Carlyle calls "the new silent system of the prisons" is better than "all about feeling". The chief points are, that I have grown more self contained and more dependent upon society.'

When he received a letter from Helen Thomas saying that her friend Lucy Donnelly regarded him as a 'great romantic', Russell took the opportunity to deny the charge emphatically and to spell out his attitude to the expression and repression of strong feelings. 'The worship of passion', he told her, 'has, I confess, a great instinctive attraction for me, but to my reason it is utterly abhorrent . . . It is not the quantity but the quality of emotions that is important':

> But the fundamental error of romanticism lies in the fact, which it shares with Christianity, that it places the end of each man's life within himself – personal holiness, or personal excellence of some kind, is what is to be achieved. Leaving quite aside the whole daily mechanism of life, which must absorb most people's activity, this theory misconceives radically the purposes which should be aimed at by those who are free to choose their own ends. And it is here, I think, that classicism is infinitely more in the right. There are great impersonal things – beauty and truth – which quite surpass in grandeur the attainments of those who struggle after fine feelings. Mathematics, as a form of art, is the very quintessential type of the classical spirit, cold, inhuman, and sublime. But the reflection that such beauty is cold and inhuman is already romanticism – it gives a shiver of feeling in which Self has its share. The true classical spirit loses itself in devotion to beauty, and forgets its relation to man.

On 12 June, Russell moved back to Fernhurst. Having rested sufficiently to recover from his exertions in finishing *Principles*, he told Alys he was now 'full of plans to work':

> I shall have to read a lot of casual shop first, then polish up my lectures so as to be ready for publication, and then I mean to undertake a systematic study of the great philosophers preparatory to my logic, which is to begin by an exposition and criticism of all previous logics of any importance.

He began with a study of the works of the German mathematician, Gottlob Frege, who was then unknown among philosophers, despite having already published the works that today are regarded by many as the founding classics of the analytical tradition in philosophy, including the *Begriffschrift* ('Concept-script'), *Die Grundlagen der Arithmetik* (*The Foundations of Arithmetic*), *Die Grundgesetze der Arithmetik* (*The Fundamental Laws of Arithmetic*) and the series of seminal essays that include 'Sense and Reference' and 'Concept and Object'. Now, no course in philosophy is complete without a study of these works, but in 1902 they were largely unread, owing chiefly to their subtlety and to the fact that Frege's logical symbolism was more cumbersome and more difficult to grasp than Peano's.

As Russell now discovered, however, Frege had in these works anticipated the main lines of Russell's own philosophy of mathematics, and had indeed, taken much further than Russell himself the project of demonstrating mathematics to be founded upon nothing more than logic.[1] The 'new subject' he had boasted of creating was, he now discovered, no such thing. To Russell's credit, he was quick to acknowledge Frege's priority. 'Do you know Frege, *Grundgesetze der Arithmetik?*' he wrote to Couturat. 'It's a very difficult book, but I have finally succeeded in understanding it, and I found many things in it which I believed I had invented.' He decided immediately to write an appendix to his book, outlining Frege's doctrines in order to bring his work to the attention of the philosophical public, to acknowledge the priority and importance of Frege's work, and to indicate where he and Frege agreed and disagreed with each other. If Russell was disappointed to discover that his work was not as path-breaking as he had thought, there is no hint of this in any of his surviving papers and letters.

Instead Russell's letters show him to be completely absorbed in the study of Frege and the logical issues raised by his work:

I am working very hard and reading St Augustine's Confessions. Life to me is wholly unemotional and dry at present: formal logic fills the crannies of my brain.
(17 June 1902)

I am dull today, being full of Frege; so goodbye.
(18 June 1902)

In his study of Frege, Russell was, naturally, quick to see that the Paradox that had bedevilled his own theory also threatened Frege's. Indeed, it was an axiom of Frege's system that every propositional function determined a class, or, which amounts to the same thing, that every definable collection forms a totality. On 16 June, Russell wrote to Frege to tell him of the Paradox and to argue that it rendered this axiom of Frege's false. Frege's reply to this letter, remarkable for its candid acceptance of the seriousness of the problem raised by the Paradox, has become one of the most often-quoted documents in the history of analytical philosophy:

Your discovery of the contradiction has surprised me beyond words and, I should like to say, left me thunderstruck, because it has rocked the ground on which I meant to build arithmetic . . . I must give some further thought to the matter. It is all the more serious as the collapse of my law V seems to undermine not only the foundations of my arithmetic but the only

---

[1] Actually, in Frege's case, it was merely arithmetic that he believed to be essentially based on logic: geometry, he held, was essentially *non*-logical, being based, as Kant had argued, on our spatial intuitions.

possible foundations of arithmetic as such . . . Your discovery is at any rate
a very remarkable one, and it may perhaps lead to a great advance in logic,
undesirable as it may seem at first sight.

'As I think about acts of integrity and grace,' Russell later wrote, 'I realise
that there is nothing in my experience to compare with Frege's dedication to
truth. His entire life's work was on the verge of completion . . . his second
volume [of *Die Grundgesetze der Arithmetik*] was about to be published, and
upon finding that his fundamental assumption was in error, he responded
with intellectual pleasure clearly submerging any feelings of personal disappointment.'
    In this celebration of Frege's intellectual integrity, Russell's work on the
philosophy of mathematics and his ethic, his 'religion', come together.
Dishonesty, Russell had come to believe, was the root of all evil, and honesty
the basis of all virtue. 'Cultivate honesty', he wrote to Helen Thomas on 27
June, 'and conscience will grow up to it: no happiness results, but exaltation,
inspiration, the sense of fellowship with the heroic spirits of all ages, and
finally a strange, almost mystical serenity, when desire is dead, and Destiny
can no longer affect us with promises of good or threats of evil'. He also
outlined further the concept of sacrificing oneself that lay at the heart of his
notion of *The Principles of Mathematics* as an altar upon which he had been
offered as a victim:

> Of course, self-sacrifice is difficult and very real; it occurs whenever oneself
> as end has to be sacrificed to oneself as means . . . And it is no use
> pretending that the sacrifice may not be real and ultimate: the best conduct
> is very seldom that which would make one the best person.

To act for the best, then, is not the same thing as being a good person.
Indeed, on the contrary, acting for the best, doing the right thing, can often
involve destroying, sacrificing what is best in one's nature. As Russell had said
before, living up to his highest ideals necessitated killing one's humanity. In
the 'Self Appreciation' that he had written in 1897, he had admitted that he
enjoyed causing suffering to others; now he had developed an ethical theory
according to which causing suffering was not only pleasurable, but also
virtuous. The highest good consisted in contemplating the truth, but this
could not be achieved without a good deal of pain and suffering, therefore
– as he had explained to Gilbert Murray in April – the utilitarian doctrine
that pleasure should be maximised needed to be turned on its head: what
should be promoted is truth, with all the tragedy and melancholy it brings in
its wake.
    How literally Russell took this harsh and bitter doctrine was revealed on 28
June, the day after writing this letter to Helen Thomas, when Alys finally
returned home from her rest cure in Brighton. Soon after she arrived back in
Fernhurst, she – hoping, no doubt, to elicit from him some convincing
reassurance – asked him directly whether he still loved her. Despite the
evasions and untruths with which he had greeted similar questions in the past,

Russell now chose this moment to tell the truth. His love for her, he told her unequivocally, was dead. They could remain married, and they could live together, but in future he no longer wished to share a bedroom with her. 'I justified this attitude to her,' he writes in his *Autobiography*, 'as well as to myself, by criticisms of her character.' In a diary entry written nearly a year after the event, Russell describes Alys's reactions to his announcement, and his reactions to Alys's despair, with a detachment that chills the blood:

> . . . the next day came Alys's return, the direct question, and the answer that love was dead; and then, in the bedroom, her loud, heart-rending sobs, while I worked at my desk next door. In the evening I walked with Berenson: the beauty of the western twilight, in that strange wood, was disquieting, wonderful, inspiring. I came home and wrote 'Monotonous, melancholy, eternal', etc.; a strange, unimaginable, unforgettable day. The early part of it I spent reading Maeterlinck's *Le Trésor des Humbles*, in which he says souls are now in closer contact than formerly; certainly that was a day of close contact. Oh the pity of it! How she was crushed and broken! How nearly I relented and said it had all been lies! And how my soul hardened from moment to moment because I left her to sob! In the middle of the night, she came to my door to say she was calmer now, and would hope – poor, poor woman. And she still hopes, but now it is hardly more than a phrase . . . I do not believe, in my soul, that I was justified; and I don't know whether I am justified now. But I have certainly effected a great moral reformation in her; and that depends upon keeping her hopes alive but unfulfilled. This required vacillation – occasional great friendliness, occasional censure. And this I do. But heaven knows it is difficult; and it absorbs my best energies in an inconceivable degree.

Rarely can self-righteousness have been so misplaced and combined with such a dearth of ordinary human kindness. When he read these passages and others like them in later life, Russell, understandably, found them shocking and loathsome. 'My self-righteousness at that time', he writes in his *Autobiography*, 'seems to me in retrospect repulsive.'

The piece of writing he mentions having written that night survives. Self-consciously 'poetic', it is an attempt by Russell to express the inhuman ethic in which he now gloried and which he used to justify both his self-righteousness and his indifference to Alys's emotional pain:

> Monotonous, melancholy, eternal, the waves break on the beach, travelling from the grey horizon to their destined end. So souls emerge from the mystery of birth, and one by one they reach the moaning shore of Death. Vast and sad is the ocean of life . . . O struggling anxious soul, forget thy fretful desires, forget thy hopes and fears, thy joy and thy pains, and look upon the world with open eyes.

Throughout the summer of 1902, Beatrice Webb had taken an intense and concerned interest in the Russells' married life. The Webbs had spent most of May and part of June living at Friday's Hill. Expecting to see much of both Russell and Alys, they were disappointed to discover that Alys was away on a rest cure and that Russell spent most of his time with the Whiteheads at Grantchester. 'A consciousness that something is wrong between them has to some extent spoilt our sojourn here,' Beatrice Webb wrote in her diary on 7 June, 'both Sidney and I being completely mystified.' So concerned was she that she offered to take Alys off to Switzerland to complete her cure. She was too perceptive an observer, however, to believe that Alys's health was the only thing wrong between them. 'It is quite clear to me', she wrote, 'that Bertrand is going through some kind of tragedy of feeling.' She was also concerned lest Russell's uncompromisingly intellectual approach to problems – his insistence on seeing everything clearly, without any shades of grey – should cause more suffering for both him and Alys:

> Bertrand Russell's nature is pathetic in its subtle absoluteness: faith in an absolute logic, absolute ethic, absolute beauty, and all of the most refined and rarefied type. His abstract and revolutionary methods of thought and the uncompromising way in which he applies these frightens me for his future and the future of those who love him or whom he loves. Compromise, mitigation, mixed motive, phases of health of body and mind, qualified statements, uncertain feelings, all seem unknown to him. A proposition must be true or false; a character good or bad, a person loving or unloving, truth speaking or lying. And this last year he has grown up quite suddenly from an intellectual boy into a masterful man struggling painfully with his own nature and rival notions of duty and obligation.

'The first thing to be done', she decided, 'is to get Alys well. I am myself looking forward to the complete change and rest.'

Perceiving it to be Alys's desire, Beatrice Webb endeavoured to do whatever she could during Alys's last four weeks in the sanatorium to keep Russell in Fernhurst and away from Grantchester, chiefly (as she put it in her diary) by 'companionising' him. In this, she was largely successful, though she risked outstaying her welcome and eventually began to irritate Russell somewhat. 'I am sorry to be seeing no more of Mrs Webb,' Russell wrote to Alys shortly before she returned from Brighton, though, he added: 'her prompt energetic executive ways get on my nerves, and I have to make great efforts not to be aware of her table manners.' He was, however, delighted by Beatrice's offer to take Alys to Switzerland and urged her to accept. Any reservations Alys had on the matter were, one supposes, swept aside by his announcement of the death of his love for her. 'I was not really prepared for his confession on my return to Friday's Hill that he had ceased to love me,' she later wrote:

> The shock of the statement was so terrible that I almost died, but managed to keep up outward appearances, and went off to Switzerland with Beatrice Webb for a three week aftercure. It was simply angelic of her to leave Sidney for so long, but as she was homesick for him all the time and I was

utterly miserable, it was not a happy holiday. I didn't confide my trouble to her or to anyone, as I felt it was too strange and abnormal, and would injure Bertie's reputation, as well as hurt my pride.

She did not need to take Beatrice Webb completely into her confidence, however, for Beatrice to realise something of the problem – enough, anyway, to see that it was caused as much, or more, by Russell's state of mind as by Alys's state of health. 'Altogether,' she wrote to her husband at the start of the holiday, 'I am inclined to think that the *mental* hygiene of the husband is more at fault than that of the wife.' In her diary afterwards she recorded that, for her, the holiday had been a complete rest of body and mind: 'the only occupation being to act as a good companion to Alys Russell and to tide her over a bad time.' Alys, she wrote, had been a 'most restful and pleasant' companion, though she felt that she herself, not Alys, had been enjoying the rest cure: 'All the same, I believe I have done her good. I have given her a sane perspective of her own and Bertrand's life. She is a warm-hearted, intelligent and attractive woman, and deserves to be happy and useful.' In other words, Beatrice had tried to make Alys see that the breakdown of her marriage was not entirely her own fault and to restore to her some measure of self-belief and pride.

Any success Beatrice had in this respect was, however, undermined soon after Alys returned to England on 21 July. Russell now declared that, as he could no longer bear to live in close proximity to Alys's mother, he had rented for them a farmhouse called 'Little Buckland' near Broadway in Worcestershire. There he intended to begin work on the second volume of *Principles*, which he and Whitehead had now agreed to write jointly, and in which, it was hoped, the doctrine that mathematics and logic were one and the same would be definitely proved by formally deducing the whole of mathematics from a few logical axioms, in the way that he had outlined in his Cambridge lectures of the previous academic year. As far as Alys was concerned, Russell had now decided to give up his attempt to kill her love for him, on the grounds that, if she continued to love him, he could continue to work his moral improvement upon her character. He thought her malicious and untruthful (he had almost persuaded himself that it was these moral defects that had lost her his love) and that, if they stayed together, he might make her a little less so. As he put it in his diary: 'I realised that Alys's love must not be killed, and that her virtue must be my care.' Disastrously, however, his weird inverted utilitarian ethic still lay in the background: 'still, often, I said things that stabbed her, and I felt dimly that only what gives pleasure is wrong, but what gives pain is always either right or at least pardonable.'

That he was, in inflicting pain on Alys in this way, acting out of malice himself, seems not to have occurred to him. In his own mind he was acting out of a rather grim sense of duty. By his own later admission, he was, during this time in an 'unreal, insincere, and sentimental frame of mind'. Even his mathematical work suffered. When he sent Whitehead a preliminary draft of the beginning of the book, Whitehead replied: 'Everything, even the object of the book, has been sacrificed to making the proofs look short and neat.' This defect, Russell writes in his *Autobiography*, 'was due to a moral defect in my state of mind'.

In his emotional withdrawal from Alys and his absorption in mathematical logic, Russell's frame of mind and his way of life during this time recall his childhood in Pembroke Lodge: everything vital and important to him was kept hidden behind a polite, stiff and priggish exterior. As he put it in a letter of 1 September to Lucy Donnelly: 'I am constructing a mental cloister, in which my inner soul is to dwell in peace, while an outer simulacrum goes forth to meet the world. In this inner sanctuary I sit and think spectral thoughts.' The letter was written from Friday's Hill, where he and Alys were spending a few days before moving to London for the winter. Surrounded by Alys's family, but feeling himself distant from them, Russell described to Lucy Donnelly an experience strikingly similar to (perhaps the same as) the one he later described to Ottoline Morrell as an example of his 'ghost-like' nature:

> Yesterday, talking on the terrace, the ghosts of all former occasions there rose and walked before me in solemn procession – all dead, with their hopes and fears, their joys and sorrows, their aspirations and their golden youth – gone, gone into the great limbo of human folly. And as I talked, I felt myself and the others already faded into the Past and all seemed very small – struggles, pains, everything, mere fatuity, noise and fury signifying nothing.

A phrase that he wrote at about this time which had special significance for him, seeming to sum up his entire mental outlook, was: 'Our hearts build precious shrines for the ashes of dead hopes.'

In London, the Russells took a house in Cheyne Walk, where Alys, according to Russell's diary, was 'miserable the whole time'. In September she had some kind of (presumably nervous) collapse, which worried Russell sufficiently for him to promise never to leave her, but their marriage continued on its grim and joyless descent into sham and melancholy. Though they now slept in separate bedrooms, Alys would every now and then come to see Russell in her dressing-gown after she had gone to bed and plead with him to spend the night with her. 'Sometimes I did so,' Russell later wrote, 'but the result was utterly unsatisfactory.' Very rarely, 'I would attempt sex relations with her, in the hope of alleviating her misery, but she no longer attracted me, and the effort was futile.'

Apart from his work on mathematics (for which he was now receiving warm encouragement and praise from Whitehead), Russell's chief consolation during this winter was the River Thames, of which, from his study at the top of the Chelsea house, he commanded a good view and along which he took long, solitary walks. Looking out of his study window, he told Helen Thomas, 'I see far below me the busy world hurrying east and west, and I feel infinitely remote from their little hopes and fears. But beyond, borne on the flowing tide of the river, the sea-gulls utter their melancholy cry, full of the infinite sadness of the sea; above, Orion and the Pleiades shine undisturbed. They are my true comrades, they speak a language that I understand, and with them I find a home: rest and peace are with the calm strength of nature.'

In keeping with this mood is a remarkable article that Russell wrote at this time called 'The Study of Mathematics', which managed to combine the intellectual triumphalism of his articles on logic and mathematics in the aftermath of the Paris Congress in the summer of 1900 with the emotional gloom that had overcome him in the wake of his discovery that his love for Alys was dead. The work of Cantor, Weierstrass and Dedekind, he repeats, is 'the greatest achievement of which our own age has to boast', but this time the achievement is presented as having a moral as well as an intellectual significance. It has 'conquered for the intellect a new and vast province which had been given over to Chaos and old Night', and, in doing so, has provided a means by which the 'austerer virtues', such as the love of truth, 'may find encouragement for waning faith'. But, even more than that, the 'vast province' opened up by this work – which is nothing less than the Platonic world of unchanging, eternal 'forms' – provides us with a refuge from the grim, changeable world of lonely suffering that is otherwise characteristic of human existence. Mathematics, then, is seen as offering some temporary but glorious relief from the pain of being human:

> The contemplation of what is non-human, the discovery that our minds are capable of dealing with material not created by them; above all, the realisation that beauty belongs to the outer world as to the inner, are the chief means of overcoming the terrible sense of impotence, of weakness, of exile amid hostile powers, which is too apt to result from acknowledging the all-but omnipotence of alien forces ... mathematics takes us still further from what is human, into the realm of absolute necessity, to which not only the actual world, but every possible world, must conform; and even here it builds a habitation, or rather finds a habitation eternally standing, where our ideals are fully satisfied and our best hopes are not thwarted.

'Mathematics is a haven of peace without which I don't know how I should get on,' as Russell put it later in a letter to Lucy Donnelly.

The article – which showed Russell's writing taking a new, more personal and more literary tone – remained unpublished for five years. T. J. Cobden-Sanderson, Russell's erstwhile guardian and now a publisher, turned it down, which, Russell wrote in his journal, 'hurt me very much, making me feel that the new work I have been trying is futile', and Russell had to wait until 1907 to see it in print, after it had been accepted by Desmond MacCarthy for *The New Quarterly*. Then, Russell was relieved and gratified to receive extravagant praise for its literary qualities from, among others, Lytton Strachey. 'Really it's magnificent,' Strachey wrote to him, 'one's carried away upwards into sublime heights – perhaps the sublimest of all! ... it gives one a new conception of the glories of the human mind.'

What neither Strachey nor Russell's other readers appeared to notice was the deeply pessimistic view of the human condition that underlies his conception of the value of mathematics. In this way, it is of a piece with the note of melancholy solitude that Russell struck in his remarks to Helen

Thomas about his feeling 'infinitely remote' from the 'little hopes and fears' of the people he could see from his Chelsea window busily going about their lives – mathematics, like the River Thames and the stars in the sky, being a 'home' of 'rest and peace' precisely because it is divorced from human concerns.

The same tone – at once lachrymose and distant – permeates most of Russell's correspondence during this period, and dominates both the journal he began to keep in November and a series of semi-religious reflections that he wrote this winter, to which he gave the title 'The Pilgrimage of Life'. The thought that dominates these writings is that truth is not compatible with happiness, and that wisdom therefore requires 'austerity', the abandonment of all desire for personal happiness. The religion thus expressed is one that worships a rather grim and vengeful deity called Truth:

> Truth is a stern and pitiless God; he exacts his hecatombs of human sacrifices, he slays with jealous thunder every love which is unfaithful to him, he drives into madness those who cannot bear the full terror of his majestic frown . . . Why worship such a God? Why not fly to oblivion and ease, to kindness and love? . . . In his service is courage, in his service only can the soul grow great, in his service only the shining lights are kindled on the mountain-tops by which, far off in the plain, humanity is guided in the night of fear and perplexity.

The key to wisdom, according to this bleak religion, is renunciation and fortitude in the face of disillusionment. 'With every accession of wisdom,' Russell writes, 'a world of joys is turned into pale and ghostly spectres.' Why this should be so, Russell is not entirely clear. He seems to have thought that it is necessarily true that all hopes are destined to be frustrated:

> Infinite is the sadness of wisdom. She is old, old with the weight of human suffering . . . She has seen the generations of man come and go, she has known the hopes, the disappointments, the despairing cries to Fate for mercy, the failures and the victories, the rashness, the punishment, and the weary, weary acquiescence, that each in turn must endure.
>
> One by one hopes die, and the kingdom of the Past receives them; but still their spectres inhabit our wintry world. There are words we dare not utter, places we dare not see, books we dare not read, lest we summon the pale army of memories, and they imprison us in the dungeon of despair, lest, for a moment of terror, we live once more the life of pain.

The 'mental cloister' he had mentioned to Lucy Donnelly appears now as a prison, one that is characteristic, not of a single individual in a despairing stage of his life, but of the human condition generally: 'We are all born into the world single, separate, imprisoned as in a dungeon by strong walls of Self.' The goal of wisdom, then, is to escape this prison by escaping the limits of one's ego, first by renouncing one's own personal desires and then through love, not personal love, however, but love of a universal, impersonal kind: 'We must learn to love all men, not because they fulfil our ideals in any way, but because our life is bound up with theirs, because we are comrades in this troubled pilgrimage from darkness to darkness.'

The journal Russell kept at this time provides an interesting and revealing complement to this cosmic despair. There, the prison is identified quite explicitly with his desperately unhappy marriage. 'I returned yesterday from four days at Cambridge,' he wrote on 20 November, 'two of which were spent out of prison':

Evelyn was very kind, Alfred agreeable, and the children adorable. We discussed the place of Art . . . She [Evelyn] had been feeling – as I have – that the world is too serious a place for Art; but she cannot stand having it said by people who don't love beautiful things . . . I talked about the great ends of life; the building of the Temple of Humanity; the edifice of the Past, the edifice of reason, the City of God . . . The talk, the atmosphere of people who care for great things, was balm to me; every moment of the two days I expanded and became a better person . . . on Monday she [Alys] came, and I collapsed like a punctured tyre.

One day, he records, he returned home from visiting other people, sat down with Alys, 'making conversation to the best of my ability':

But she remarked that whenever I return after an absence I am silent, and as though living in another world. I must improve in this respect.

Another time, he got home to find Alys having a crying fit: 'I know it is my fault, and I must manage better, but it is hard. She too is lonely – good God, what a lonely world it is.' Such rare displays of sympathy are heavily outnumbered by occasions on which his dislike of, and resentment towards, Alys are painfully manifest:

On Sunday we went to Hampton Court to the Creightons: Alys was at last informed of her election to the Cambridge Women's Dining Club, which pleased her exceedingly. She said to Mrs Creighton that she would like to stay with Evelyn when the dinners occur, that Evelyn was her dearest friend, to whom she felt as a sister, and so on. It made me so sick that I blushed, and it made me dislike her, though according to her lights she was doing rather a fine thing. If only she were not so crude!

We had a beastly dinner . . . Most of the people jarred me, misanthropy and misogyny settled on me like a cloud. At night, I didn't kiss Alys often enough, and she began to cry when I put out the light; but I did nothing to comfort her. (25 November 1902)

Alys and I discussed the future, and I urged her being mostly in town, and my being mostly in the country, on account of our work. She said she would be willing if I loved her. Odd woman! She won't leave me unless I don't want her to do so – she is determined I should suffer somehow. (17 December)

On 13 December, the night of their eighth wedding anniversary, Russell (who normally showed an interest in, and maintained an observance of, anniversaries of all sorts) recorded:

Last night when I went to bed Alys asked the time, which was 12.40. After the light was out she asked if I remembered the date – I had forgotten it was our wedding day. Then presently her misery became uncontrollable, and I had to comfort her somehow. Poor woman!

Since the early summer Russell had been reading and correcting proofs of *The Principles of Mathematics*. Now he added to it two appendices: one containing an extended summary of 'The Logical and Arithmetical Doctrines of Frege', and the other containing a more elaborate presentation of the 'theory of types', which he had previously merely sketched out, together with an admission that, as it stood, this theory did not provide a solution to the problems caused by the Paradox and its cognates. The book ends on a note of self-confessed defeat:

What the complete solution of the difficulty may be, I have not succeeded in discovering; but as it affects the very foundations of reasoning, I earnestly commend the study of it to the attention of all students of logic.

The Preface, too, written on 2 December, strikes the same note. 'The subjects treated are so difficult', he writes, 'that I feel little confidence in my present opinions, and regard any conclusions which may be advocated as essentially hypotheses . . . For publishing a work containing so many unsolved difficulties, my apology is, that investigation revealed no near prospect of adequately resolving the contradiction discussed in Chapter X., or of acquiring a better insight into the nature of classes.'

At last, the book and all its revisions and additions were finished, though the result was not one that Russell could contemplate with any great satisfaction. 'What general value it may have', he told Gilbert Murray, advising him against making the effort to read it, 'is so buried in technicalities and controversies that it is really only fit for those whose special business it is to go in for such things. The later mathematical volume, which will not be ready for two years or so, will I hope be a work of art; but that will be only for mathematicians . . . this volume disgusts me on the whole. Although I denied it when Leonard Hobhouse said so, philosophy seems to me on the whole a rather hopeless business.'

Dissatisfied with 'The Pilgrimage of Life', Russell still yearned to find some way of expressing his deepest attitudes to life, his 'religion of sorrow'. During the Christmas holiday, which he and Alys spent in Florence with Mary and Bernhard Berenson, he decided to try to put his thoughts into a simpler literary form, and one that came more naturally to him: the essay. The result was 'The Free Man's Worship', his best-known and most anthologised essay. It begins with a re-statement of the cosmic pessimism that pervades 'The Pilgrimage of Life', this time couched in terms of a recognition that the 'world

which Science presents for our belief' is entirely purposeless and indifferent
to the hopes and the sufferings of mankind. Wisdom is then seen, as before,
as a Stoic acceptance of the truth that combines the renunciation of personal
desires with an insistence on the freedom of thought. 'To abandon the
struggle for private happiness,' Russell writes, 'to expel all eagerness of
temporary desire, to burn with passion for eternal things – this is emancipation, and this is the free man's worship.' Sympathy for others is preached on
the grounds that we are all united by 'the strongest of all ties, the tie of a
common doom', and, in a passage that Russell himself described as 'written
as exhortation to myself to treat her [Alys] decently', he urges us to look upon
all our fellow-men as comrades:

> . . . let us think only of their need, of the sorrows, the difficulties, perhaps
> the blindnesses, that make the misery of their lives; let us remember that
> they are fellow-sufferers in the same darkness, actors in the same tragedy
> as ourselves.

When the essay was finished, Russell pronounced it 'all right', but reading
through once more the earlier, more poetic reflections, he admitted 'My more
imaginative attempts are weak and affected, and must be discontinued.'

Russell's self-exhortations to treat Alys decently – although they imposed
upon him an emotional discipline no less severe than the intellectual demands
he frequently made upon himself – were entirely sincere and, in the new year
of 1903, began to effect some change in their married life, which became
slightly less awful, at least on the surface. Alys herself began to regain some
measure of her vitality and self-belief, and was again able to pursue some of
her own projects. In January, for example, she decided to find out for herself
what working conditions were like for factory girls by taking a job for a few
days in a rope factory. Her findings were then written up in an article she
published in the *Contemporary Review*. All this, Russell wrote to Berenson,
with as little condescension as he could muster, 'gave her new interests, and
was altogether most beneficial'.

Russell himself was still desperately unhappy: 'My work is second-rate,' he
wrote in his journal on 27 January, 'and all I cared for is gone or going.' His
love for Alys dead, and his feelings for Evelyn denied any expression, he
turned increasingly to the Thames for consolation. 'The river tonight was
beautiful beyond endurance,' he wrote on 11 February. It was 'becoming to
me a passionate absorbing love; I could drown myself to be one with it.' The
only days he enjoyed were those spent 'out of prison', such as two days with
the Murrays at their home in Churt while Alys was away in Manchester with
her mother. 'I have been realising that I don't do enough for Alys,' he
confessed on 8 March, 'but the thought of doing more is unbearable almost.
There is only one thing more I can do, and that is children; if medically not
inadvisable, that is what I must do.'

By this time Russell was already feeling the pangs of thwarted parental
instincts that would later dominate his life, but, even so, the prospect of
adding to the Pearsall Smith clan was not one that filled him with much

joyous anticipation. Suppose, he wrote, that he had a child full of the characteristics of Carey Thomas and Alys's mother: 'It may drive one or other of us mad; but probably it is worth trying. The thought is hell, but so is the fear of her suicide.' A few days later he arranged to see a Dr Savage, who told him that the fear of inherited insanity was much exaggerated, that madness is more often due to unsuitable environments than genetic traits. Accordingly, when, about a week later, it was calculated that Alys was at the most fertile point of her menstrual cycle, Russell 'made the last possible sacrifice' and had sex with her: 'In return I am to have three weeks' liberty. Perhaps that will give me time to recover myself for the moment: till it all begins again.' The act that had previously filled him with rapture at its mere contemplation, now overwhelmed him with loathing. It was, a later journal entry confesses, 'not adequately carried out and failed totally . . . I shirked my duty on that occasion: I ought to have been more self-forgetful.' A few days after the unproductive sexual sacrifice, Russell's loathing for it was perhaps expressed in a letter to Gilbert Murray, in which his customarily gloomy outlook received its most extreme and misanthropic formulation yet:

I have been merely oppressed by the weariness and tedium and vanity of things lately; nothing stirs in me, nothing seems worth doing or worth having done: the only thing that I strongly *feel* worth while would be to murder as many people as possible so as to diminish the amount of consciousness in the world.

The three weeks' liberty – his leave from prison, so to speak – that Russell extracted from Alys as a reward for the loathsome act did not go according to plan. He had intended to spend a week in Devon with George Trevelyan and then to go on to Cornwall to join the, by now, traditional Easter reading party that Moore arranged at this time every year. When, however, Russell wrote to Moore inviting himself to Cornwall, he received from Moore a curt rebuff. 'About the reading party,' Moore wrote, 'since you ask me to say if your coming would make any difficulty, I think I had better tell you that it would.' The mysterious explanation that Russell gives in his journal for Moore's attitude is that Moore 'has never forgiven my homilies, though they produced the reformation I hoped for' – though what these homilies were and why Moore never forgave them, Russell does not reveal.[2] The true explana-

---

[2] One clue might, however, be contained in a letter from Russell to Desmond MacCarthy dated 24 March 1903, in which he, with as much diplomacy as the occasion would allow, explained why he was not, after all, going to join the Easter reading party, even though he had previously announced that he would. The explanation, he said, was that 'my dates didn't fit, as my tour with George ends too early.' He went on to discuss 'the occasion when I spoke to Moore about not talking', providing an equally implausible explanation of that particular 'homily': Alys, he claimed, 'could never understand why I praised Moore, and when I argued the point, she would reply that she had never heard him speak. After some years of this discussion, wishing that she should have some evidence (as the difference was disagreeable to me), I spoke to him in hopes of altering what never vexed *me* in the least, except on account of the domestic question that it raised. I admit freely that it was a most foolish act,

tion is simpler: Moore by this time could no longer bear to be in the same company as Russell. 'Of course,' Moore wrote to Desmond MacCarthy, 'I can't be sure that [Russell] would spoil it for anyone but me; but I do suppose that the others, too, and you yourself, would rather that he would not be there for nearly so long . . . the effect he would have on me would also indirectly make it much more unpleasant for the rest of you; I can't be at my ease while he is there, and I don't know how miserable I might not get.'

At the beginning of April, after Russell returned from his walking tour with George Trevelyan, he and Alys moved to Churt (where the Murrays lived) for the summer. The 'last sacrifice' he had made in March had, unsurprisingly, failed to make Alys pregnant, and, much to Russell's relief, she confessed that she had hated it and did not want a repetition. Consequently, Russell wrote, he felt better disposed towards her, and had even been able to have some 'pseudo-intimate' talk with her. Meanwhile, Russell's work was not going well. 'The power of writing has for the present deserted me,' he noted on 8 April. 'I began on *Principles of Mathematics*, Vol II, but made no progress; then an imperative need of achievement possessed me, so I am writing an article on Meinong. Some few shreds of self-respect come to me in this way.'

One might think from this self-deprecatory tone that the article in question was slight and insignificant. In fact, 'Meinong's Theory of Complexes and Assumptions' is a detailed, subtle and weighty study, so lengthy that, in order to be published in *Mind*, it had to be cut into three separate articles (published, respectively, in April, July and October of 1904). At its centre was an attempt by Russell to deal with the difficult logical problems that had begun to beset the notion of a proposition that he had inherited from Moore's 1898 paper 'The Nature of Judgment'.

During the previous six months, in his correspondence with Frege, Russell had been defending this Moorean notion against Frege's characteristically penetrating criticisms. On 20 October 1902, Frege, realising that he and Russell had been at cross-purposes on the question of the problems presented by the Paradox, asked directly: 'What is a proposition? German logicians understand by it the expression of a thought, a group of audible or visible signs expressing a thought. But you evidently mean the thought itself.' In Frege's theory a proposition has both a sense and a reference, its sense being the thought it expresses and its reference a 'truth value'. Thus, all true propositions, for Frege, had the same reference, namely 'the True', and, likewise, all false propositions referred to 'the False'. This was a part of Frege's doctrine that Russell was never tempted to adopt. 'I cannot bring myself to believe', he told Frege, 'that the true or the false is the meaning of a proposition in the same sense as, e.g., a certain person is the meaning of the name Julius Caesar . . . I understand by a *proposition* its sense, not its truth value.' In a further letter, written at about the same time that he was working on the Meinong article, Russell spelt out in greater detail his view of a proposition as a 'complex object':

---

as were both the hopes which inspired it. But I should be sorry not to have had hopes until experience killed them.'

In all cases, both imagination and judgment have an object: what I call a 'proposition' can be the object of judgment, and it can be the object of imagination. There are therefore two ways in which we can think of an object . . . yet the object is the same in both cases (e.g., when we say 'the cold wind' and when we say 'The wind is cold') . . . Complexes are true or false: in judging, we aim at a true complex.

When pressed to clarify this notion of a 'complex', Russell, one imagines, completely astonished Frege by cheerfully accepting what Frege had regarded as self-evidently absurd. 'Mont Blanc with its snowfields', Frege wrote, in a tone that suggested he did not expect to be contradicted, 'is not itself a component part of the thought that Mont Blanc is more than 4,000 metres high.' On the contrary, Russell insisted:

I believe that in spite of all its snowfields Mont Blanc itself is a component part of what is actually asserted in the proposition 'Mont Blanc is more than 4,000 metres high.' We do not assert the thought, for this is a private psychological matter: we assert the object of the thought, and this is, to my mind, a certain complex (an objective proposition, one might say) in which Mont Blanc is itself a component part. If we do not admit this, then we get the conclusion that we know nothing at all about Mont Blanc.

What Russell found in Meinong's work was a view of 'complexes' at least partially like the one he was defending against Frege. Meinong was no logician. He belonged rather to the specifically continental school of 'descriptive psychology', an offshoot of which was the tradition of 'phenomenology' associated with Edmund Husserl. But, in his attempts to clarify the nature, contents and objects of psychological states such as belief, assumption and perception, Meinong had arrived at a view strikingly similar to that held by Russell. In particular, he had, like Russell, hit upon the notion of a 'complex', which, for Meinong, was the 'Objective' correlative of the subjective state of belief. Thus, what would normally be regarded as the *fact* that (to use Frege's example) Mont Blanc is more than 4,000 metres high is, for Meinong, the 'Objective' of the *belief*: 'Mont Blanc is more than 4,000 metres high'. Meinong, that is, like Russell (but unlike Frege), regards the object of the belief (its reference) to be a complex of objects that includes Mont Blanc itself (with all its snowfields).

There are, however, two seemingly intractable problems with this view that were to dog Russell's entire philosophical career, and which he raises in his article on Meinong with complete frankness about the difficulties they pose for him. The first concerns what one might call the 'unity' of the complex. This is the old problem that Russell had wrestled with earlier, about wholes and parts, and the value and limitations of analysis: a whole is more than a mere collection of its parts, and thus to analyse it into its parts is, to some extent, a falsification. Similarly, if one analyses a complex into its constituents (a Moorean 'proposition' into its concepts, say), something important – namely the unity of the complex – will inevitably be lost. 'The unity of a complex', Russell writes, 'raises a logical problem, of which Meinong seems to be not fully aware.' In the face of this problem, Russell now reacted with the ploy that he and Moore had used earlier in relation to the notions of truth and falsity, and which Moore had made the very core of his argument in *Principia Ethica* with regard to the notions of 'right' and 'good': namely, he declared the unity of a complex to be an 'unanalysable' and an 'indefinable' quality.

The other problem concerns false propositions. The idea that Mont Blanc itself is a constituent part of any truth concerning it, and the associated idea that the *fact* 'Mont Blanc is more than 4,000 metres high' is the object of the belief 'Mont Blanc is more than 4,000 metres high', seem initially very plausible. One might even think they were platitudes. But when Russell, following Moore, identifies the proposition 'Mont Blanc is more than 4,000 metres high', not with the belief but with its object, namely the fact, it becomes very difficult to say what a *false* proposition is. What is the object of the belief that 'Mont Blanc is less than 4,000 metres high?' According to Meinong, both true and false beliefs alike had Objectives. Where they differed was in whether the Objective subsisted or not. In Meinong's theory, objects had different kinds of being: particular objects which occupied space and time *existed*, abstract objects (like numbers) *subsisted*, but some objects (unreal particulars like the characters of fiction and mythology) neither existed nor subsisted. Meinong used these distinctions to explain the difference between true and false beliefs: true beliefs had Objectives which subsisted, false beliefs had Objectives which neither existed nor subsisted – they were, as Meinong put it, 'beyond being'. Russell, however, was unable to accept Meinong's view that there were objects which lacked being of any kind. For him false beliefs had false propositions as their objects, and false propositions had being just as much as true ones.

There are, then, such 'complex objects' as false propositions. The view that had startled Frege thus becomes, in the light of this modification to Russell's theory of propositions, more astonishing still: for now Mont Blanc itself, with all its snowfields, is a constituent part of any number of false propositions ('Mont Blanc is made of cheese', 'Mont Blanc is in England', and so on). Eventually Russell despaired of these 'shadowy objects' (as he later called them) that were false propositions, and revised his theory to get rid of them, but, for the moment, reluctant to abandon the 'liberating' logic of propositions he had learnt from Moore, he was stuck with them.

The article on Meinong may have provided Russell with 'a few shreds of self-respect', but it did little to lift the gloom that had descended on his emotional life, the only partial relief of which seems to have been its repeated expression in the series of confessional letters he wrote at this time to his friends Lucy Donnelly, Helen Thomas, Goldie Lowes Dickinson and Gilbert Murray. 'There is a comfort in saying out what one feels,' he wrote to Helen Thomas, 'without stopping to ask oneself if this feeling is foolish; and if one only mentions one's very sage and dignified thoughts, the effect is a person quite unlike the real one.' To Lucy Donnelly, Russell wrote that he was thinking of making up a set of aphorisms entitled 'Satan's joys', which would express such 'bitter truths' as: 'the reward of service is unrequited love' and 'passions are smirched by indulgence and killed by restraint; the loss in either case is inevitable'. The first of these, he told her, 'is the biography of all virtuous mothers, and of many wives'.

His thirty-first birthday, on 18 May, set him thinking how, in Matthew Arnold's words (which Russell quotes in his journal): 'the bygone year . . . made my tossed heart its very life-blood spill', and he recounted the sorry events of the past year one by one: his cold letters to Alys the previous May, her unhappy homecoming in June, her collapse in September, the miserable winter they had spent in London, and his writing of 'The Free Man's Worship'. Since coming to Churt, he wrote, 'the last chink of daylight has been shut out from my prison, and I have gone back to the old work; it is difficult, so difficult that from sheer despairing fatigue I feel often ready for suicide; and its value has come to seem to me very small; and I make no progress with the Contradiction.'

The publication of *The Principles of Mathematics* in May brought no relief either. 'It seems to me a foolish book,' he told Helen Thomas, 'and I am ashamed to think that I have spent the best part of six years upon it. Now that it is done, I can allow myself to believe that it was not worth doing – an odd luxury!' It was difficult, he told her, to keep up his belief in anything, 'and though it is painful to think my whole life a mistake, it is less trouble than to think the opposite.' In spite of these reflections, he was at work on the second volume: 'when once that is done, perhaps I may be able to shake off the burden for a while.'

Some relief from the gloom in which he now lived came the day after his birthday, when he thought he had discovered a solution to the Paradox that threatened the theory of *Principles*. As he later described it to Philip Jourdain, this 'solution' took the form of denying the existence of classes and basing the whole theory instead on propositional functions (so, for example, instead of speaking of an empty class, one speaks of a propositional function that is always false). In the brief time before he realised that this did not help, that a paradox of propositional functions can be created that is exactly analogous to the old paradox of classes, Russell received a prematurely jubilant telegram from Whitehead: 'Heartiest congratulations. Aristoteles Secundus. I am delighted.' Russell himself remarked in his journal that the relief of solving the Paradox was 'unspeakable'.

It was, however, very short-lived, the first of many false dawns.

Throughout June and July 1903, he worked without success on his book, trying to find some genuine solution to the Paradox. 'Every morning', he later wrote, 'I would sit down before a blank sheet of paper. Throughout the day, with a brief interval for lunch, I would stare at the blank sheet. Often when evening came it was still empty . . . it seemed quite likely that the whole of the rest of my life might be consumed in looking at that blank sheet of paper.' Several times he thought he had found a solution, only to find that it merely created fresh difficulties. By the end of July, he had become dispirited. 'The last four months', he told Lucy Donnelly, 'I have been working like a horse, and have achieved almost nothing':

I discovered in succession seven brand-new difficulties, of which I solved the first six. When the seventh turned up, I became discouraged, and decided to take a holiday before going on. Each in turn required a reconstruction of my whole edifice.

The effort of living with Alys, while preventing himself from being cruel to her, was a torment. 'She is still miserable,' he wrote in his journal, 'she still says things that make me feel rasped through and through, and still day by day I wonder how another twenty-four hours of such utter misery can be endured. But there is every reason to expect forty years of just such torture':

In some ways, her illness makes things easier; when she is bouncing and metallic, she is much harder to bear. Poor woman! When she is not present, I am sorry for her; but when I see and hear her, I become all nerves, and can think of nothing but the wish to escape. She is always bumping into furniture, treading on one's toes, and upsetting lamps; and mentally she does the same thing. She asked me why I won't undress in her presence. The other day she wept, and said she had gone right out of my life: I tried to say gently that I had had to learn to live alone: 'I know', she replied, 'the ascent to the stars must be made in solitude.'

'It is ghastly to watch,' he wrote a few days later to Lucy Donnelly, 'in most marriages, the competition as to which is to be the torturer, which tortured; a few years, at most, settle it, and after it is settled, one has happiness and the other has virtue. And the torturer smirks and speaks of matrimonial bliss; and the victim, for fear of worse, smiles a ghastly assent. Marriage, and all such close relations, have quite infinite possibilities of pain.'

Trapped in this wretched marriage, and thwarted in his attempts to get on with his work on mathematics, Russell became ever more absorbed in the political upheaval that was caused in the summer of 1903 by the launching of 'Tariff Reform', the campaign led by the Colonial Secretary, Joseph Chamberlain, to abolish the hallowed Liberal doctrine of free trade in favour of a system of protective tariffs designed to help Britain and her colonies in their economic competition with countries from outside the Empire. Broadly speaking, the issue was one that divided Liberals from Imperialists, and, as such, one calculated to arouse in Russell all the passion of his inherited Whiggism. Free trade was a policy especially associated with his grandfather, Lord John Russell, one of whose greatest regrets had been that it fell to Robert Peel and not himself to repeal the Corn Laws in 1846. For Russell, the issue was fundamentally a moral one. 'We are all wildly excited about Free Trade,' he wrote to Lucy Donnelly, 'it is to me the last piece of sane internationalism left, and if it went I should feel inclined to cut my throat. But there seems no chance whatever of Chamberlain's succeeding – all the brains are against him, in every class of society.'

He longed to be actively involved in the counter-campaign against Chamberlain, but felt unable to muster the necessary energy. 'If I could get away from her [Alys],' he wrote in his journal, 'I could work at Free Trade as well as mathematics; but I am spending on not being cruel to her as much energy as would make a whole political campaign.'

In the event, as the controversy over Free Trade grew more bitter and his attempts at solving the Paradox remained futile, Russell began to work at Free Trade instead of mathematics, devoting himself during August to the study of all the arguments advanced in favour of protection. The previous year Russell had met and liked the French historian Élie Halévy, who, after finishing a study of philosophical radicalism, was now at work on a political history of Britain in the nineteenth century. When Halévy wrote to him, expressing some measured sympathy for Chamberlain's campaign, Russell was quick to strike back. 'I don't agree with you that any of the arguments of '46 were unsound,' he wrote, 'or have become inapplicable . . . I have been examining lately the arguments, both a priori and of fact, which can be advanced in favour of Protection, and I confess none of them, neither the purely economic, nor the political and social, seem to me to have any validity at all.'

He was writing to Halévy from Normandy, where he and Alys had decided to take a week's holiday with the Webbs. For some months now Russell had sensed that Beatrice Webb's sympathies were with Alys in their manifestly unhappy marriage, and, on this holiday, so he told Gilbert Murray, he 'minded them [the Webbs] more than usual':

> They have a competent way of sizing up a Cathedral, and pronouncing on it with an air of authority and an evident feeling that the L[ondon] C[ounty] C[ouncil] would have done it better. They take all the colour out of life and make everything one cares for turn to dust and ashes.

When they returned to England Russell and Alys took a brief tour of the Lake District and then moved back to London once more for the winter. A good portrait of the rather dismal life the Russells led during this winter is preserved in the letters of Lucy Donnelly to her friend, Helen Thomas. In September 1903 Helen Thomas had married Simon Flexner, a distinguished bacteriologist who was that year appointed Director of the newly created Rockefeller Institute for Medical Research. For Helen, it was a happy match, but for Lucy it was a disaster, and Russell's letters to her throughout the year were full of advice on how to cope with the loss (as she saw it) of her best friend, chiefly through, as Russell put it, the 'consolations of philosophy'. In October, partly to gain some relief from a situation that, she believed, was driving her towards a breakdown, Lucy came to London and stayed with Russell and Alys.

Soon after she arrived Lucy wrote to Helen of the 'cheerless' and 'uncared for' state of the house at Cheyne Walk, and for the next three months provided Helen with a detailed description of the misery that accounted for it. Her admiration for Russell was undiminished   he was, she wrote, 'the most brilliant living mind' – but she noticed in him a change from his time in America. He was 'desperately unhappy', she reported, and 'felt solitude a very nightmare':

My heart went out to him in sympathy: he is very fine, I think. He struggles hard to do right & sets himself the severest standards, and so far as I can see, lives up to them as far as any mortal cd.

Several times, she commented on the deteriorating relationship between Russell and Alys, and made a shrewd guess as to the cause. Russell, she told Helen, 'is in love or in some way involved with Mrs Whitehead'. On one occasion, Evelyn suddenly put off a proposed visit, driving Russell to despair:

He paced up & down his study murmuring in little bursts 'Out out brief candle' etc . . . Then he sat down by the fire & longed for the Mediterranean & sun & warm breezes & told me of once sailing the bay of Palermo & so on – the summer they were there with the Whiteheads very possibly.

Russell spent hours talking to Lucy, sometimes at home and sometimes while out walking. He talked of his inability to get on with his work and his general unhappiness: 'He said in passing that one of the things he minds most is his academic exterior & manners that prevent his talking with or getting near common & uneducated people.' He told her that he lay awake at night wondering whether to devote himself entirely to politics. His philosophical work 'will not go at the moment so that he wastes his time, & he longs for something more human . . . than his work can give him. It is cold and isolating.' When 'The Free Man's Worship' was published in the December issue of *The Independent Review*, Russell felt unhappy about it, 'feeling that the world is sneering & laughing at his intimate feelings', which, Lucy added, it was, especially Alys's brother Logan, who 'is being vy amusing & naughty & witty abt it'.

In fact, by the time Lucy left at the end of the year, Russell had abandoned both self-introspection and (temporarily) his work on mathematics in favour of a more or less complete absorption in the Free Trade debate, which, he hoped, might bring him into at least some contact with 'common & uneducated people' and salvage some self-respect through public service and by acting on a moral imperative. 'Morally, England is on trial,' as he put it in a letter to Halévy. 'I sympathise fully with all internationalism; and my *enthusiasm* for Free Trade is derived from this, not from economics.' Despite this attitude, he also felt strongly that, even on purely economic grounds, Chamberlain's proposals were disastrous, and he argued so in detail in a lengthy review-article for *The Edinburgh Review* called 'The Tariff Controversy', which surveyed the literature put out by Chamberlain and others in favour of tariffs and attempted to show the invalidity of all their arguments. Even here, however, Russell appeals ultimately to the moral imperative of preserving Free Trade. 'Nothing but a steadfast adherence to the ideal of freedom', the article ends, 'can preserve our Empire; nothing else can make it worth preserving.'

By the time the article was published – in the new year of 1904 – things were looking bad for the Free Traders. At the end of December, three by-elections had been won by supporters of Chamberlain, and it was beginning to look as if the next general election would be won by a government led by Chamberlain and dedicated to the imposition of protective tariffs. From Russell's point of view, this prospect was deeply alarming, and he threw himself into the campaign with all his energy. In the first two months of the new year he fired off a series of letters to the Press, published another article trying to take apart the protectionists' case, and even embarked on an exhausting round of public talks, including a series of six lectures at the New Reform Club, and another series of three given at the Borough Hall, Chelsea and the Town Hall, Paddington.

To see Russell in the role of public speaker and campaigner still seemed to many who knew him somewhat incongruous. Logan Pearsall Smith, after attending Russell's first lecture at the New Reform Club, declared it to be 'very clear and intellectual and even witty, and . . . successful in every way', but, he added, watching Russell engage in practical politics seemed to him 'like using a razor to chop wood'. Russell himself was carried along by the evangelical fervour the cause had aroused in him, and by the hope that his gifts of lucid exposition and persuasive argument (if not yet of oratory) could do something to stem the tide of protectionism. 'My experience', he told Gilbert Murray, 'is that any one who has no economic interest in protection can be converted by having the free trade case properly stated, but that very few free traders know what the case is. I believe if voters could be given elementary instruction in the theory of exports and imports, not 20 per cent would be protectionists. And I find everybody anxious to hear the case and listen to reason.'

His optimism was justified when, in January and February, a fresh round of by-elections was won by Liberal Free Traders, and the Chamberlain campaign looked defeated. By this time Russell was exhausted by his efforts and beginning to feel slightly ridiculous in his new role. 'I feel old and rather weary,' he wrote to Gilbert Murray on 17 February, 'the odd process of becoming (subjectively) a personage is taking place in me: I begin to feel weighty and think pompous and official thoughts on matters which the British public conceives to be important. It is a disgusting transformation, like the Prince who was turned into a frog':

> It makes all the things of real importance seem remote and dries up one's springs of feeling strangely. I feel myself one of those absurd old gentlemen I used to wonder at, who, one knew, had thought and felt in their youth, and had acquired the respect of Society because of what they had been and because they had ceased to be so.

'I am glad to think', he concluded, 'I needn't bother with politics much longer. It is a most deadening occupation.'

6

THE LONG NIGHT

After his foray into political activism during the Free Trade controversy of the winter 1903–4, Russell returned, in the spring of 1904, with renewed vigour to philosophy. For the next six years he devoted himself, with a quite heroic tenacity and single-mindedness, to the completion of the book he had planned to write jointly with Whitehead, a book that grew during these years from the single volume originally envisaged as the second part of *Principles of Mathematics* to the monumental three-volume work that was finally published as *Principia Mathematica*.

Russell's work during this six-year period is one of the wonders of the history of modern philosophy. If he had done nothing but his share of *Principia Mathematica*, that alone would have been a prodigious achievement, but in fact he did far more: many of the philosophical articles that are now considered his greatest contribution to the subject – including 'On Denoting', the most heavily discussed of all his writings – were written during this period, as the problems he faced in the writing of *Principia* drove him to construct ever more elaborate theories of the fundamental notions of his philosophy of logic and mathematics, such as 'class', 'type', 'proposition' and 'judgment'. In addition, he carried on, in reviews, articles and correspondence, intricate and often lengthy polemical debates on these new theories with some of the foremost philosophers of the time, including F. H. Bradley, Harold Joachim, William James and Henri Poincaré.

His achievements during this period are all the more remarkable for not being – as the completion of the first draft of *The Principles of Mathematics* had been – the result of an ecstatic sense of inspiration. They were, rather, driven by a dogged determination to see the task through, even though it was a task in which he no longer took any delight. 'The pleasure to be derived from the writing of *Principia Mathematica*', he later said, 'was all crammed into the latter months of 1900. After that time the difficulty and the labour were too great for any pleasure to be possible.' The stoic 'religion' that he had worked out in 'The Pilgrimage of Life' and advocated in 'The Free Man's Worship' was during these years (a period he would later call 'the long night') applied with an almost incredible fortitude. The result for him personally was a curious kind of half-life, one characterised by self-denial and a rather grey joylessness, but one that was, nevertheless, philosophically quite astonishingly fruitful.

As so often in his life, the break between one kind of activity and another – between, in this case, engagement in the Free Trade issue and his work on *Principia* – was marked by a walking holiday, this time in Cornwall. 'It is most soothing to one's nerves to walk all day,' he wrote to Alys from Bude on 19 March, 'and makes all problems look simpler.' A few days later he reported that he was 'getting very great good from my solitude – it gives time really to think things out, and exercise makes one think things out calmly. When I get home, at first at least, thee will find me much less grumpy and nervy than I was in the winter; but I suppose when I get to work I shall relapse into old ways again.'

He returned from Cornwall determined to be kinder, or at least fairer, to Alys, and determined also, it seems, to extinguish the dying embers of his hopeless infatuation with Evelyn Whitehead. When, on 6 April, he resumed his private journal, he began by remarking: 'This journal gives an unduly bad view of Alys':

> I think she has improved greatly, and that I was for a time very unjust to her. She had most of the faults I attributed to her, but she had many virtues that I forgot all about. She has shown great pluck, and a great desire, mainly successful, to be unselfish towards me. But she is full of jealousy, though she never consciously acts upon it . . . she is the very soul of kindness to people who do not come into competition with her. But she dislikes my helping people. She said the other night that Evelyn had told her my friends felt that I am fickle, and my friendship is not to be counted on. She said Evelyn had instanced herself and Alfred, the Davies's and Sanger; to whom Alys added my people and hers. When I think of the causes of my changes towards all of these, I do not feel blameless, but I wonder that she dares to instance them.

One likely cause of Evelyn's accusations of fickleness – and of Alys's dislike of Russell's 'helping people' – was Russell's great affection for Ivy Pretious, a pretty twenty-four year old who served as Secretary of the Free Trade Union and who was a close friend of George and Janet Trevelyan. Russell, with the self-deception characteristic of him during this period, looked upon his interest in Ivy as an example of his ceaseless desire to be 'useful to people in trouble' (as he put it in his journal), which, 'has become my chief consolation, and which, I am sure, I do well.' Ivy's 'trouble' (as Russell saw it) consisted in the attentions she was receiving from the politician and banker Reginald McKenna, a man whom Russell regarded as a 'blackguard' and from whom he sought to save her. In this he was successful, though at the apparent cost of Ivy falling in love with Russell himself. Or so, at least, it was believed by Evelyn Whitehead and Janet Trevelyan, who together sought to warn Russell from taking things with Ivy any further (in Russell's own later words, they 'combined to scold me as a philanderer'), reminding him that both her reputation and his were at stake.

Affecting, at first, to be surprised that his motives should be so miscon-strued, Russell nevertheless took heed of their advice and kept his relations with Ivy impeccably respectable. Writing obliquely to Lucy Donnelly about the matter, and without mentioning any names, he represented the affair as a warning to him not to relax his moral control over himself and to resist the temptation to give way to his impulses. 'Sometimes', he told her, 'I feel as tho' I ought not to know any women well':

> but the difficulty is that I get intimate very quickly, and that, at least in some cases, I seem able to do good; there is also a purely selfish difficulty, which of course ought not to weigh with one, but I fear it does. And sometimes it makes me behave weakly; above all I shrink from inflicting pain, or from disappointing expectations . . . Of course all such problems can be avoided by not undertaking difficult tasks which are not obviously one's business; but I shrink from that way out, tho' it is perhaps the right one.

Eventually, Russell resolved to 'give up trying to be useful to people in trouble' and the most long-lasting effect of his brief flirtation with Ivy Pretious was possibly that it enabled him to put his love for Evelyn Whitehead out of his mind, while he concentrated on his work.

While Russell had been engaged in other things, Whitehead had been working to great effect on his portion of the book, which consisted largely in the more technical, purely mathematical parts of the enterprise. On 9 April, Russell went to Cambridge to spend a week working with Whitehead. 'Alfred's recent work', he wrote to Alys, 'is very good. He has been active for some time past; I only wish my parts of the book got on equally fast.' At this stage, Russell's own work on the book was dominated by his attempts to resolve the fundamental problems caused by the Paradox. By this time these attempts had come to centre on the clarification of the notion of 'denoting' that he had introduced in *Principles*.

'Denoting' was the word Russell used for the purely logical (rather than linguistic) relation between a concept and that to which it refers. Typically, denoting is achieved by means of a description rather than by a name. Thus, the description 'the next prime after seven' denotes the number eleven; 'the positive square root of four' denotes the number two; and so on. Denoting phrases are central to mathematics, especially in Russell's 'logicist' theory, in which they are crucial in identifying classes ('the class of all mortal beings', 'the class of natural numbers'), and by this time, Russell had come to think that the solution to the logical problems raised by the Paradox had to involve a new understanding of denoting itself. For the heart of the problem seemed to lie in the construction of 'empty' denoting phrases, phrases that seemed to denote something, but did not do so, and could not do so, because they led to a contradiction. The chief example of this, of course, was the dreaded denoting phrase: 'the class of all classes which are not members of themselves'.

Hand-in-hand with Russell's earlier naive view that to every propositional function there corresponds a class of objects went the view that every denoting phrase denoted something, even something that was 'non-existent'.

To make sense of this, he had appealed to Meinong's distinction between existence and 'subsistence': classes and numbers, for example (and false propositions), subsisted but did not exist. He now began to subject this view to critical scrutiny. Something had to be wrong with it, for, though he was prepared to accept non-existent things, he could not accept contradictory ones, which is where the view led. Thus forsaking, for the moment, purely mathematical considerations, Russell began to concentrate, in a quite general way, on denoting phrases themselves, particularly those that did not, in fact, denote anything. The example he focused his attention upon – and a phrase that recurs with almost obsessive repetition in his writings from this period – was 'the present King of France'.

His interest in this phrase arises from the following considerations: the sentence 'Edward VII is bald' expresses, in Russell's analysis, a true proposition that 'contains' (in some odd Russellian sense of the word) both Edward VII himself and the concept of baldness. Likewise 'the present King of England is bald' (when spoken in 1904) is a true proposition that contains baldness and the denoting concept 'the present King of England', which, in this case, denotes Edward VII. But what about 'the present King of France is bald'? Does the phrase 'the present King of France' denote anything? If not, if there is no present King of France (either existing or 'subsisting'), are we to say it is a false proposition? And are we to infer from the falsehood of this proposition that its opposite, 'the present King of France has hair', is true? Surely not. Analogously, Russell came to think, we are not compelled to assert either side of the troublesome Contradiction. 'The class of all classes which do not belong to themselves' neither belongs nor does not belong to itself, no more than 'the present King of France' either does or does not have hair.

Such, for the next year, was the focus of Russell's philosophical work. At Cambridge, he told Alys, he and Whitehead had spent much of the time 'discussing whether the present King of France is bald – it is astonishing what intricate and remote considerations can be brought to bear on this interesting question. We finally decided that he isn't, altho' he has no hair of his own. Experienced people will infer that he wears a wig, but this would be a mistake.' On the day before he left Cambridge, he wrote that he and Whitehead had 'had a happy hour yesterday, when we thought the present King of France had solved the Contradiction; but it turned out finally that the royal intellect was not quite up to that standard. However, we made a distinct advance.'

It was enough, anyway, for Russell to approach the problem with renewed hope, and, over the following twelve months, he wrote paper after paper, in which he tried to work out a theory of denoting that would serve the purposes of *Principia*, while avoiding the Paradox.[1] To concentrate on this work, he and Alys moved to a secluded house called Ivy Lodge at Tilford, near Farnham,

---

[1] These papers, which show Russell trying and discounting a bewildering series of variations on his theories of meaning and denotation, have now been published in Vol. 4 of *The Collected Papers of Bertrand Russell*.

just north of Churt. While his work at Tilford went well, his emotional life went underground, his relations with Alys reduced to a pitiful superficiality evident in a pathetic letter that Alys wrote to him on his birthday in May 1904. 'I try very hard always to keep on the surface, as thee wishes,' she told him, 'but I am sure thee will remember how some feelings long for expression':

> I hope thee will not mind my writing thee a real letter on thy birthday . . . I only want to tell thee again how very much I love thee, and how glad I am of thy existence. When I could share thy life and think myself of use to thee, it was the greatest happiness anyone has ever known. I am thankful for the memory of it and thankful that I can still be near thee and watch thy development. When thee is well and happy and doing good work, I feel quite contented, and only wish that I were a better person and able to do more work and be more worthy of thee. I never wake in the night or think of thee in the daytime without wishing for blessings on my darling, and I shall always love thee, and I hope it will grow more and more unselfish.

It is a letter of abject self-effacement, but perhaps it is also possible to see in it a hint of disguised and covert admonishment, a reproach to Russell for being so neglectful towards her. Frances Partridge, who knew Alys well in later life, described her to me once as 'aggressively dull', and something of what she meant is surely evident in this letter. For if dullness can be used as a weapon, still more can the sort of wistful and sorrowful humility that is expressed here.

If it was meant as a reproach, however, it was entirely ineffective. Russell was, by this time, dead to all feelings towards Alys beyond those dictated by his sense of duty. His absorption in his work now took over his entire being. 'I am working hard at Vol. II,' he wrote to Goldie Lowes Dickinson in July. 'When it goes well, it is an intense delight; when I get stuck, it is equally intense torture.' The delights – and the tortures – of romantic love were now behind him. In a letter to Lucy Donnelly in August, he outlined the philosophy of life he now adopted, the attitude that enabled him to push everything else in his life aside in his effort to complete his work. 'I believe the true solution', he told her, 'lies in thinking very seldom and very little about things in general, about whether good or evil preponderates in the world or in the lives of those one cares for':

> The gospel to me has been a cold one, but yet a very useful one: to think almost wholly of what is to be *done*, and hardly at all of the evils one cannot remedy, or of the goods one cannot create. Take things simply and cope with them, as far as possible, one by one; do not add to the sum, and become oppressed by the mass of horror and pain and degradation. I have suffered in the past, over irredeemable evils in other people's lives, up to the extreme limit of my capacity for suffering; and inability to endure the pain has made me believe in remedies, with the consequence of aggravating the evils merely from a lack of self-control in thought. But now, as a rule,

I succeed in dwelling only upon what can be done, however little that may be ... And when one has admitted all the evil in the world, it remains true that there are great and shining things in it: there are heroisms and loves and devotions which redeem it, and which warm all the recesses of the heart like spring sunshine. Learn to think of them: let your contemplative life be filled with them: let them inspire daily courage, and the faith that, come what may, the good is really good, and makes the long toil worth while. It is perhaps inevitable that most of life should be a weariness; but the passionate inspiration of great things ought not to fade from one's life because of sordid surroundings.

This is all that I know about the way to endure life. It is not much, but I find it as a rule efficient.

'Certainty and system', he told her in a further letter, 'are, in the end, what most of my life is devoted to.' And yet: 'I sometimes feel that I have neglected impulse too much: I become too much of a schoolmaster and a prig, and am incapable of some very good things which more impulsive people have.'

At the end of September, he was ready for another walking tour, this time with Theodore Llewelyn Davies in Brittany. 'It is very agreeable to look forward to,' he told Lucy Donnelly, 'I shall get the refreshment that I got in Cornwall in the spring.' Once there, he wrote again, confirming that 'Brittany is quite wonderful – it has a great deal of purely rural beauty, woods and streams and endless orchards of big red apples, scenting all the air.' They walked chiefly on the coast, where 'the Atlantic rules as God.' For Russell, the sea was always an image of the vastness and cruel indifference of a Godless world, and it surprised him at first to find the sea-faring Bretons among the most God-fearing people he had ever met:

Every tiny village has a huge Gothic church, usually very beautiful; many churches stand quite by themselves, facing the sea as relics of ancient courage. At first I wondered how anyone could believe in God in the presence of something so much greater and more powerful as the sea; but very soon, the inhumanity and cruelty of the sea became so oppressive that I saw how God belongs to the human world, and is, in their minds, the Captain of an army in which they are soldiers: God is the most vigorous assertion that the world is not all omnipotent Matter. And so the fishermen became and have remained the most religious population in the world.

In the winter, Russell took a break from his work, and he and Alys moved back to Chelsea, to a house in Ralston Street, where, so he told Lucy, he spent his time 'merely seeing people and enjoying myself'. Being in Chelsea brought the Russells back into the orbit of the Webbs, and at a dinner party in February 1905, they were invited to meet, among others, the Prime Minister, Arthur Balfour, and a South African millionaire called Werner, 'a fat, good-natured, eupeptic German with an equally fat gold watch-chain, and a strong German accent (characteristic of all the finest types of British Imperialists), bearing very lightly the load of blood, of nations destroyed and hatreds generated, of Chinese slavery and English corruption', as Russell described him to Lucy Donnelly. It was, he added, 'an amusing occasion':

> When everyone had come except Balfour and Werner, Mrs Webb observed that we should see which of them thought himself the bigger swell, by which came last. Sure enough, Werner came last; for though Balfour governs the Empire, Werner governs Balfour.

The party did little to strengthen the links between the Russells and the Webbs, the weakening of which had been remarked upon by Beatrice Webb in her diary the previous summer. 'The Bertrand Russells,' she wrote, 'still affectionate and personally interested, have cooled in comradeship, he becoming every day more decidedly Whig and abstract in his political thought, impatient with our criticism of the Liberal opposition and our constant reiteration of the need for concrete knowledge.' Russell, for his part, took a lofty and condescending tone towards the Webbs, describing Beatrice to Lucy Donnelly as having subjected Balfour to a dinner-table lecture that might have been entitled 'the first principles of Government for beginners'. In truth, Russell's interest in politics, though passionate, was never, at this stage in his life, likely to claim his complete attention, except as a temporary diversion from his work on the philosophy of mathematics. 'In spite of occasional aberrations,' as he put it to Élie Halévy, 'my heart is in philosophy, & I could never have peace of mind if I deserted it.'

Outside the philosophy of mathematics, the issue that dominated Russell's thoughts was not that which excited the Webbs, concerning the survival or otherwise of Balfour's increasingly beleaguered Tory administration and the merits of the Liberal opposition; rather, it was the more personal issue that he discussed in his letters to Lucy Donnelly about whether it was desirable, or even possible, to live the life of self-denial, of repression of his impulses, that he recommended to himself. His affections for Evelyn Whitehead had now been successfully deadened ('I have got over my chief sorrow pretty completely,' as he put it in his journal, 'more completely than is desirable, but that can't be helped'). But there still remained the question of whether it was humanly possible to live with a woman for whom he had grown to feel nothing but contempt, irritation and, occasionally, a cold, smouldering anger. He decided it was, but at a great and almost unbearable cost. 'I have learnt a *modus vivendi* with Alys,' he wrote grimly in his journal on 14 January, 'I never look at her, so that I avoid the pain of her insincere expression and the petty irritation of her awkwardness of movement'.

A telling occasion on which Russell found it impossible to maintain this outwardly calm (if horribly frigid) *modus vivendi* was when Alys gave Russell's most prized possession – a miniature painting of his mother – to a servant named Barrett to clean. Barrett was one of a series of unmarried mothers whom Alys, out of a spirit of philanthropy, employed as servants, and one of the things that most vexed Russell was that Alys 'did not feel the sacrilege of giving such a thing to a common whore'. More than that, the unfortunate Barrett spilled water on the painting and smudged it, thus, in Russell's opinion at least, ruining it for ever. Russell was inconsolable at the loss, and refused to take up Alys's suggestion of taking it to a restorer called Mrs Mason, 'whom I think sentimental and self-absorbed and an intolerably bad miniature-painter'. She in any case 'could not have given me back the thing I had loved, with the more intensity because I had not permitted the same sort of love to grow up towards any other possession'. Though recognising that Alys's blame in this mishap was small, Russell nevertheless declared: 'I don't know how long it will take me really to forgive her.'

A further threat to their 'formal and fixed' relations was Alys's jealousy over Ivy Pretious. On 3 April, Russell recorded that 'out of mere kindness', he had assured Alys that she had no reason for feeling jealous, whereupon Alys denied that she ever had: 'Since then, in all the ways I have been able to discover, she has lavished fulsome praises on the object of her jealousy whenever she has mentioned her or had to do with her.' If Alys intended this to soften Russell's attitude towards her, she had misunderstood her man:

Her lies to me were so bland and so apparently candid that my heart hardened towards her again, and I have let her suffer without making any endeavour to comfort her. She has given up kissing me morning and evening, which is a great gain. In other ways, too, she has realised more than before that our relations must be purely formal. My impression is that, unless I relent, she will get tired of living with me, and will take to paying longer and longer visits to her people. They are her only friends: every one else who knows her well dislikes her.

'I have now definitely given up the hope of any serious improvement in her,' the journal concludes, 'and I look forward to a gradually increasing separation, which will probably make the future much easier for me.'

Buoyed up by these hopes, Russell wrote to Ivy Pretious a few days later, saying: 'I begin to see possibilities of emancipation from my bondage; I have been thinking of the future, and it strikes me as likely that during the next two years or so I shall be able to free myself to a considerable extent. This prospect has rather cheered me up, when otherwise I should be depressed.' Whatever expectations he had of his relationship with Ivy, however, were scotched under further pressure from Janet Trevelyan, and a few months later, Russell wrote again effectively putting an end to the hopes he had raised. 'I do not think I ought to come and see you,' he told her, adding: 'of course, there is no change in spirit; only a realisation of things I was too much inclined to forget.' Chief among these 'things', of course, was Alys's distress over Russell's unfaithfulness, which, he said, now that he did not feel so angry towards her, he felt compelled to consider, despite Alys's denials that she felt any jealousy. For, after all: 'I do not think the duty of common humanity does not cease because the victim protests that it is a base injury to think she finds the torture unpleasant.' That, then, was that. In future, he would meet Ivy only 'under Janet's auspices', a condition that, as Ivy would surely realise, made such meetings more or less pointless.

Russell's feelings for Ivy Pretious aroused in him moral self-doubts that were linked in his mind with his dissatisfaction with his work. 'It is strangely difficult for me to live a good life,' he had written in March. 'I feel temptations that I cannot think decent people feel. As I have lost the fire and inspiration that for a time helped me over all difficulties, I have grown aware of new possibilities of serious wrong-doing.' His *modus vivendi* in his relations with Alys was in danger of making him 'generally secretive':

> But that is not the worst. I foresee that continence will become increasingly difficult, and that I shall be tempted to get into more or less flirtatious relations with women I don't respect . . . The worst of it is that, unless I find some way of dealing with it, it will presumably grow stronger; and some day, in a moment of weakness, I may persuade myself there is no harm in acting upon it. It is rather a mental than a physical feeling; it is a desire for excitement, and for a respite from the incessant checking of every impulse. Another difficulty, connected with this, is the very slight interest I take in my work and in philosophy generally. If this can't be cured, my fertility will cease. A sort of paralysis of impulse has passed from my life into my thinking, and seems to me very serious for my intellectual future. But I don't know at all how to deal with these problems.

Had he stayed in Chelsea, things might have turned out very differently. As it was, in April, he and Alys moved back to the country, to Bagley Wood, just south of Oxford, on a plot of land that they had bought the previous year and upon which they had had a house built for them, designed by the architect H. M. Fletcher, a relative of the Llewelyn Davieses. Russell's hopes for the move, as he explained to Ivy Pretious shortly before moving, were that: 'Going to a new place will for a time diminish the complications of my life as well as the pleasure . . . I shall plunge into work, which is almost as good as drink for producing oblivion, and quite as bad for producing headache. I have had a bad conscience about my work; for several years now I have not been enough interested in it, and I must try seriously to recover some of the zest with which I used to pursue it.' What he did not explain, but what became clear in the ensuing months, was that one of the 'complications' of his life that this plan, if successful, would diminish, was his relationship with Ivy herself.

In the event, the plan was successful, and, after the inevitable walking tour (this time in Somerset and Gloucestershire with Bob Trevelyan), Russell and Alys settled in Bagley Wood on 24 April, after which Russell soon immersed himself in his work with all the impressive concentration of which he was capable.

Russell now resumed his attack on the theory of denoting, this time with the explicit intention of using whatever theory he settled on to eliminate altogether from his theory of logic the notion of a 'class' as an existent (or 'subsistent') entity. His hope was that, if there were no such things as classes in his theory, the paradox of classes that had bedevilled it would be rendered harmless. He thus set out to reconstruct entirely the logical foundations of his enterprise in accordance with what he called the 'no–class theory'. The radical nature of this reconstruction (after all, the reduction of mathematics to class theory was supposedly what their book was all about) slightly alarmed Whitehead, who wrote to Russell on 30 April, pleading:

> Now this extreme rigour must be tempered by practical considerations. *Classes* can be kept in common use by the consideration that our object is to systematise the actual reasoning of mathematics, and this actual reasoning does in fact employ classes habitually when it need not do so. Thus our object is to systematise the reasoning involving classes, even when it is a primitive idea which might be avoided.

In other words, even if they did not assume the existence of classes, they had better construct some (more or less artificial) *analogue* of them, or else their system of mathematics would never get off the ground.

Russell's solution to this dilemma is expressed in his undoubted philosophical masterpiece, 'On Denoting'. The paper itself was written at the end of July 1905, but the theory it embodies was arrived at during the previous month. 'The solution,' Russell announced to Lucy Donnelly in a letter written on 13 June, 'which I have now found, throws a flood of light on the problem of the relation of thought to things.' At the heart of the theory of 'On Denoting' is the idea that denoting phrases (and, therefore, in Russell's mind at least, classes) are mere symbols, linguistic conveniences that had no meaning on their own, but only acquired a meaning in the context of a proposition. The phrase 'the present King of France' neither means nor denotes anything – neither a man (existent or subsistent) nor even a concept – it is merely a phrase. The proposition 'the present King of France is bald' has a meaning, but what it means, according to the 'Theory of Descriptions' announced in 'On Denoting', is a threefold assertion:

1. There is a man who is at present King of France.
2. There is only one such man.
3. He is bald.

It is, in effect, three propositions, all three of which must be true if the whole thing is true. And, as the first is false, the entire proposition is false. Its converse, 'the present King of France has hair' is likewise analysed as three propositions:

1. There is a man who is at present King of France.
2. There is only one such man.
3. He has hair.

This is likewise false, for the same reason. Thus, two contradictory statements can be seen to be both false, *without* any paradox. Analogously (though Russell does not spell this out in 'On Denoting'), the two contradictory statements – 1. 'the class of classes which do not belong to themselves belongs to itself', and 2. 'the class of all classes which do not belong to themselves *does not* belong to itself' – can both be regarded as false without contradiction, because there *is* no 'class of classes which do not belong to themselves'. Such, in essence, was Russell's solution to the Paradox that had troubled him now for over four years.

An interesting sidelight on Russell's discovery of this solution has been pointed out by the Russell scholar and logician, Douglas Lackey, who has drawn attention to a letter that Russell received, dated 16 June 1905, from the American mathematician Maxime Bôcher. Commenting on the distinction that Russell had drawn in *The Principles of Mathematics* between the 'class as many' (the members of a class) and the 'class as one' (the class itself), Bôcher remarked: 'I cannot admit that a class is in itself an entity; it is for me *always* many entities (your "class as many"). When we speak of it as a single entity we are considering a new object which we associate with the class, but not the class itself. That is, the "class as one" is merely a symbol, a *name* which we may choose at pleasure.'

This is basically the view that Russell adopted. Its drawback was that it made mathematics itself largely the science of 'linguistic conveniences', but its huge advantage was that it drew the sting from the dreaded Paradox. Not that Russell had entirely given up, at this stage, the notion of mathematics as the study of Platonic entities, but, by now, neither numbers nor classes were conceived by him to be such things. The *real* Platonic entities that were left standing after the 'Theory of Descriptions' were propositions themselves, which Russell still did not (*à la* Frege) conceive to be mere symbols or expressions of thoughts. Propositions, even false ones, were still, on his account, Platonic 'things' that existed (or, at least, 'subsisted', they had some kind of objective 'being'), only now their constituents included neither 'denoting concepts' nor 'classes', but only 'individuals' (such as Socrates) and 'universals' (such as mortality).

This was a huge advance, but the great delight Russell took in it was severely diminished by the news that he received while writing 'On Denoting' that Theodore Llewelyn Davies had died. On 27 July, he received from Theodore's brother Crompton the following bleak note:

> Theodore is dead, drowned while bathing alone on Tuesday in a pool in the Fells, stunned as I have no doubt by striking his head in taking a header and then drowned.
>
> I shall be back in London on Monday. Let me see you some time soon.

Russell responded by leaving immediately for London, to be with Crompton at the flat in Westminster that he had shared with his beloved brother. 'I am here to do what I can for him,' he wrote to Lucy Donnelly, 'there is little enough except to sit in silence with him and suffer as he suffers. As soon as he can get away, I am going abroad with him . . . Crompton's sorrow is crushing, and I hardly know how to bear it. But it is a comfort to feel able to be of some help to him.' Ever since that day, Russell writes later in his *Autobiography*, 'the sound of Westminster chimes has brought back to me the nights I lay awake in misery at this time.' The funeral service was held in Theodore's father's church of Kirkby Longdale, and, writes Russell, 'I was in church when his father, with determined stoicism, took the service as usual, and just succeeded in not breaking down.'

Russell's sympathy for Crompton in his grief for Theodore was both sincere and heartfelt, and provides moving proof that, despite the years of self-enforced coldness, he had not lost altogether his capacity for feeling for other people. In August, he accompanied Crompton on a holiday in Normandy, where, he reported to Crompton's sister Margaret, Crompton was 'wonderfully better than he was in town . . . He enjoys the sands and playing about with the children, who are friendly and jolly . . . we stroll along the coast, or sit on the sands, sometimes talking, sometimes reading.' After the holiday, Crompton wrote to Russell:

> The loss of Theodore seems still a mere phantasy and the strange mixture of dream and waking thoughts and recollections and fact leave me in bewilderment but slowly the consequences of a maimed existence remaining for me makes itself felt, as of a body that has lost its limbs and strength, and has to go on with made-up supports and medical regimen and resignation to the loss of possibilities of achievement and hopes of sunny days.
>
> I cling to you with all my heart and bless you for loving and helping me.

On his return from France, Russell told Lucy Donnelly that the loss of Theodore was a grief 'which admitted of no philosophy at all – I could not see that there was anything to be said in mitigation of the disaster. But I have got myself in hand now, and tomorrow I go back to work.'

Russell's first task upon returning to work was to respond to the opening salvo of what would turn out to be a protracted debate between those who, like Russell, Whitehead and Couturat, believed that mathematics could be founded upon logic alone, and those who, like the great French mathematician, Henri Poincaré, believed mathematics to be founded ultimately upon the kind of 'intuition' that Immanuel Kant had made the basis of his theory of mathematics in *The Critique of Pure Reason*. The Kantians in this debate believed the logicians to be guilty of making mathematics unduly dependent upon mechanical analysis and of paying insufficient heed to the essentially *creative* nature of mathematical reasoning.

The first volley in this debate, however, was fired not by Poincaré himself, but by his nephew, Pierre Léon Boutroux, who, in the journal *Revue de métaphysique et de morale*, published a polemical attack on Russell's *Principles of Mathematics*, based primarily on Couturat's own renderings of Russell's theories. Encouraged to reply by Couturat, Russell wrote an article called 'On the Relation of Mathematics to Symbolic Logic', in which he accused Boutroux of confusing the psychology of the discovery of mathematical truths with the truths themselves. It might be true, Russell argued, that analytical logical systems did not adequately represent the process by which we arrive at mathematical truths, but, nevertheless, they could give a perfectly sound construction of those truths themselves. Boutroux, he claimed, 'confuses the act of discovery with the proposition discovered'. It was an impressive piece of polemic, and, for the moment, the intuitionists were silenced, Boutroux responding to Russell's article only with a personal letter, in which he confessed that his understanding of Russell's work had been unduly influenced by Couturat's representations of it.

As suggested by his reply to Boutroux, Russell's work now took the form of trying to articulate a theory of logic in which there were no classes, or denoting concepts, or even propositional functions, but only complex entities called 'propositions', which were to be analysed into their constituents: individuals and predicates. 'It seems to me broadly possible', he wrote to G. E. Moore on 25 October, 'to maintain that there is nothing complex except propositions.' On 14 December he read to the London Mathematical Society a paper called 'On Some Difficulties in the Theory of Transfinite Numbers and Order Types', in which he first publicly suggested the 'no classes' approach to the Paradox. Soon afterwards, the idea that 'propositions' rather than 'classes' should be the primitive notion of his theory of logic was developed into what he called the 'substitution theory', which he first outlined in an unpublished paper called 'On Substitution'.

The basis of this latter theory was that, instead of working with propositional functions like 'x is mortal', one works instead with straightforward propositions such as 'Socrates is mortal' and 'Plato is mortal'; and, instead of having the notion of a variable 'x', which can be *determined* by individuals like 'Socrates' and 'Plato', one has merely a technique of *substituting* one individual for another in any given proposition ('Socrates' for 'Plato' in the proposition 'Socrates is mortal', for example). The advantage of this is that it does away with both the notions of propositional functions and classes in favour of simply propositions.

The theory had something of the beautiful simplicity of the first draft of *The Principles of Mathematics*, and Russell was, temporarily, quite delighted by it. On the first day of the new year of 1906, he felt able to declare to Lucy Donnelly that: 'My work during 1905 was certainly better in quality and quantity than any I have done in a year before, unless perhaps in 1900. The difficulty which I came upon in 1901 . . . has come out at last, completely and finally, so far as I can judge . . . The result of this is that Whitehead and I expect to have a comparatively easy time from now to the publication of our book, which we may hope will happen within four or five years. Lately I have been working 10 hours a day, living in a dream, realising the actual world only dimly through a mist.'

Another cause for celebration in the New Year was the final collapse of the Balfour government and its replacement by the Liberals under Sir Henry Campbell-Bannerman, who won a landslide victory in the general election that surprised even their own supporters by its extent (the Tories were reduced from 401 seats to 156). Together, the Liberal victory and the progress made in his work produced in Russell the happiest frame of mind that he had known for years.

A note of dissent, however, came from Whitehead, who was not at all pleased with Russell's 'substitution theory', which he regarded, so he told Russell in a letter of 21 February 1906, as a piece of 'excessive formalism'. In rejecting so wholeheartedly the Platonism of *Principles*, he wrote the following day, Russell's new theory 'founds the whole of mathematics on a typographical device, and thereby directly contradicts the main doctrines of Vol. 1.'

In these remarks, Whitehead possibly shows a misunderstanding of the extent to which Russell had rejected his former Platonism. For, even in his substitution theory, mathematics was not for Russell a mere linguistic or 'typographical' study; it was, rather, the discovery of truths external to ourselves, the arrival at true propositions. In a letter to Margaret Llewelyn Davies of 26 March, this Platonism was explained with perfect lucidity and accessibility. Responding to Margaret's bafflement about the more extravagant Platonism expressed in his 1902 paper, 'The Study of Mathematics', Russell explained:

> I did not mean that the objects of mathematical or other abstract thoughts *exist* outside us, still less that there is any universal or divine mind whose ideas we are reproducing when we think. What I meant to say was that the object of any abstract thought is not a thought, either of the thinker or of any one else, and does not *exist* at all, though it *is* something. Thus in mathematics a new theorem is a *discovery* in the sense that the discoverer for the first time apprehends the fact discovered, which fact has a timeless *being*, not *existence*.

In April, Russell went to Cambridge and persuaded Whitehead that his new theory was not, after all, an abandonment of the spirit of *Principles*, and shortly afterwards retired on his own to Clovelly in Devon to work out the substitution theory in detail.

In a letter to Lucy Donnelly of 22 April, Russell reported himself to be enjoying his 'absolute solitude'. He added: 'My work goes ahead at a tremendous pace and I get intense delight from it . . . after any considerable achievement I look back at it with the sort of placid satisfaction one has after climbing a mountain':

> What is absolutely vital to me is the self-respect I get from work – when (as often) I have done something for which I feel remorse, work restores me to a belief that it is better I should exist than not exist. And another thing I greatly value is the kind of communion with past and future discoverers. I often have imaginary conversations with Leibniz, in which I tell him how fruitful his ideas have proved, and how much more beautiful the result is than he could have foreseen; and in moments of self-confidence, I imagine students hereafter having similar thoughts about me. There is a 'communion of philosophers' as well as a 'communion of saints', and it is largely that that keeps me from feeling lonely.

In a sad and disillusioned note appended to this letter, however, Russell added that the substitution theory, the work that had inspired this self-belief, 'was all rubbish, and had to be scrapped'.

Russell's realisation of the flaws in the substitution theory was stimulated by two separate debates that he conducted at this time: one with Harold Joachim about the general nature of truth, and the other with Henri Poincaré about the relation between mathematics and logic. The high point in his faith in the theory was reached with a paper he wrote in Clovelly entitled 'On the Substitutional Theory of Classes and Relations', which he delivered to the London Mathematical Society on 19 May, but which he refused to have published in the Society's *Proceedings* the following autumn, because he had, by then, become dissatisfied with the theory.

One technical reason for Russell's dissatisfaction was his discovery that a paradox of propositions could be generated within the substitution theory analogous to the old paradox of classes. Related to this technical consideration, and confirming its importance, was Russell's persuasion by Henri Poincaré that the problems presented by such paradoxes were even more general and fundamental than he had thought. In a series of articles published in *Revue de Métaphysique et de Morale* under the general title of 'Les mathématiques et la logique,'[2] Poincaré, sneering at the problems caused to the logicians by the paradoxes ('Logic is no longer barren, it begets contradictions,' he mocked), suggested that at the root of those problems were what he called 'vicious circle' definitions; that is, definitions that allowed something (a propositional function, a class, or a proposition) to include itself. Thus, at root, the paradox about classes was shown by him to be but a variation of a paradox that was well known in ancient times: the 'Cretan liar paradox' that arose from the remark reported by Epimenides the Cretan that: 'All Cretans are liars.' Was Epimenides lying? If he was, then he wasn't, and if he wasn't, then he was. This paradox has nothing to do with classes or propositional functions, but is caused by the ability of straightforward propositions to refer to themselves. Thus, whatever the problem is with these paradoxes, it cannot be solved by a theory that merely replaces talk of classes with talk of propositions.

In his reply to Poincaré, 'Les Paradoxes de la Logique',[3] Russell accepted this analysis and suggested that the 'vicious circle' paradoxes identified by Poincaré could be met by a modified version of the 'theory of types' that he had first proposed in *The Principles of Mathematics*. But types of what? In *Principles*, he had proposed distinguishing types of objects ('individuals', 'classes of individuals', etc.), but this, in the light of his rejection of classes, was no longer open to him. Could there be hierarchies of propositions? In his debate with Harold Joachim on the nature of truth, Russell hit upon the basis of a more radical solution. In November 1906, responding to Joachim's book, *The Nature of Truth*, published earlier in the year, Russell presented to the Moral Science Club at Cambridge a paper with the same title, in which he

---

[2] Available in English as chapters II, IV and V of Part II of *Science and Method* (1914).
[3] Now published as 'On "Insolubilia" and their Solution by Symbolic Logic' in *Essays in Analysis*, edited by Douglas Lackey.

rejected Joachim's arguments for a Bradleian 'monistic' theory of truth, in favour of the view that truth is a relation between a judgment and a fact. From this seed emerged the fully-formed 'theory of types' that was eventually published in *Principia*.

With a characteristic readiness to abandon views that he had previously considered definitively correct, Russell now declared that there were, after all, no such 'things' as propositions. A proposition, like a class and a denoting phrase, was a mere symbol, an 'incomplete symbol' that required a context in order for it to be meaningful. In this case, the context it required was someone's mind: a proposition, that is, required to be *judged* true or false by someone in order for it to have a meaning. Fundamentally, therefore, it is not propositions that are true or false, but judgments. But what is a judgment? Is it the relation of a mind to a proposition? Clearly not, for, if there are no such things as propositions, they cannot stand in any kind of relation with anything. Russell therefore developed his notorious 'multiple relation theory of judgment', in which, for example, the judgment that 'Socrates is mortal' is a series of relations between three things: the individual 'Socrates', the predicate 'mortality' and the mind that joins them together. The beauty of this theory is that, as there are no such things as propositions, the question that had troubled Russell previously about the 'subsistence' of false propositions does not arise: there *are* no false propositions, there are only false judgments, and these are not shadowy, 'subsistent' entities, but real, existent, mental acts.

In what has become known as the 'ramified theory of types', Russell put this theory of judgment to use. For now, the hierarchy of types was not one of objects, but of judgments or, more precisely, 'levels of truth': at the first level are judgments about individuals, at the second judgments about classes of individuals (defined 'contextually' *à la* 'the theory of descriptions'), and so on. Side-by-side with this hierarchy goes another hierarchy of 'orders' of propositional functions (conceived of as 'linguistic conveniences'): to the first level of judgment there correspond ordinary propositions (bearing in mind, as always, that these do not really exist), to the second level there correspond 'first order propositional functions', to the third 'second order functions', and so on. The theory of mathematics to which this leads is one of quite dizzying complexity: mathematical statements about numbers are reduced to statements about classes, which are, in turn, reduced to the theory of propositional functions, which is, in turn, embedded in the theory of 'types' of judgments.

If the theory of *Principles* had had the impressive simplicity of a modernist building, this new theory was more like a baroque cathedral, with one complex structure piled on top of another. The analysis it offers of even the simplest mathematical equation is therefore extraordinarily convoluted: the proposition that '$1 + 1 = 2$', for example, is arrived at only half-way through Volume II of *Principia*, by which time it has been shown to be analysable into, and founded upon, a murky morass of definitions, propositional functions and, ultimately, judgments. One must suppose that the chain of reasoning that leads from the complicated theory of logic outlined in Volume I to the mathematical results reached in the subsequent volumes was clear to Russell and Whitehead themselves, but, if so, they were in a tiny minority.[4]

Despite its grotesque complexity, the final 'ramified' theory of types (outlined publicly for the first time in an article published in the *American Journal of Mathematics* in 1908 called 'Mathematical Logic as based on the Theory of Types') seemed to Russell to represent the final step on the road to building the theory of logic that he had been looking for – one that was capable of analysing mathematics while avoiding the paradoxes – and the stage was now set for him and Whitehead to proceed apace with *Principia Mathematica*. After his discovery of this final version of the theory of types, he writes in his *Autobiography*, 'it only remained to write the book out.'

Before he could begin this gargantuan task, however, Russell was provided with an opportunity for a further diversion into political activism by the burgeoning movement for women's suffrage. The campaign to enfranchise women had been given a boost by the election of the Liberals in 1906, but the hopes thus aroused had been thwarted by the divisions within the Liberal Party on the question and by the subsequent vacillations of the government. Like Free Trade, the question was one for which Russell felt an instinctive and inherited passion. His mother had campaigned for the National Union of Women's Suffrage Societies (NUWSS), and his secular godfather, John Stuart Mill, had written an influential pamphlet on the subject. For Russell himself, the merits of the women's case were unanswerable. 'I think women's suffrage important,' he wrote to Margaret Llewelyn Davies, 'not so much on account of the direct political effect, as because I detest the general assumption of women's inferiority, which seems to me degrading to both men and women.'

In 1906, he joined the NUWSS and the following February was elected to its Executive Committee. In May 1907, a by-election was called in Wimbledon, a safe Tory seat, which the Liberals declined even to contest. For publicity purposes, the NUWSS decided to field a candidate and asked Russell himself to stand, an invitation he felt unable to refuse. 'It is horribly annoying,' he told Margaret Llewelyn Davies, 'but I try to regard it as a joke.' As he was the first person ever to contest an election on the issue of women's

---

[4] Empirical confirmation of the utter unintelligibility of the theory of logic at the heart of *Principia* was provided for me when I sent out to six of the world's most distinguished Russell scholars an apparently simple enquiry: how, I asked, would the statement 'Honesty is the best policy' be analysed by the Ramified Theory of Types. In reply, I received from five of the experts five widely different answers, and a candid confession from the sixth that he had no idea. That Whitehead himself, initially at least, found the theory baffling is indicated by a letter he wrote Russell dated 6 January 1908, in which he told him: 'I have been studying you on Types. As far as I understand, I approve highly. But the points are so subtle that I have grave doubts as to whether all the difficulties that you are dodging are really present to my mind.' The letter ends: 'I am in a fog as to where you are.' In broad terms, however, it is clear how the theory of types was intended to solve 'vicious circle' paradoxes such as the Cretan Liar Paradox. According to this theory, when Epimenides says 'All Cretans are liars', he is making a second-level judgment about all his own (and other Cretans') *first*-level judgments. Therefore the truth of this judgment is perfectly consistent with the falsity of all his first-level judgments (see *My Philosophical Development*, pp. 82–3, for an equivalent explanation).

votes, Russell's candidature generated a large amount of publicity. His campaign meetings were well-attended, not least by crowds of men and (to Russell's bewilderment) women opposed to giving women the vote, who did everything they could to prevent him getting his message across. At his first meeting, rats were let loose to frighten the women suffragists, and at the next, eggs were thrown at the platform, one of them hitting Alys.

Polling day was 14 May. Russell, naturally, was heavily defeated (he would never have agreed to stand if he thought there was any danger of actually being elected), but he succeeded in getting over 3,000 votes, which – though 7,000 fewer than the winner, a Tory squire named Henry Chaplin – was, under the circumstances, surprisingly good. The main objective of attracting publicity for the women's cause had certainly been achieved, and, in addition, Russell had shown a mettle in standing up to the hurly-burly of the campaign that surprised even some of his friends. 'What a sporting cove you are!' George Trevelyan wrote to him. 'I hardly thought you were such an adventurer.'

Soon after the election, however, though Russell's commitment to the cause of women's suffrage remained undimmed, his relations with those in the movement became somewhat strained. He became increasingly disillusioned by the divisions among the suffragists, and frustrated by their reluctance to embrace wider political issues – to link their campaign for the enfranchisement of women to the struggle for universal suffrage, for example. He was especially out of sympathy with the WSPU (the Women's Social and Political Union), the more radical wing of the movement led by the Pankhursts, whose allegiance to the Tory Party he found entirely unacceptable, and whose advocacy of civil disobedience offended him. They, in turn, distrusted Russell for his dyed-in-the-wool Whiggism. ('That Mr Bertrand Russell cared very much more for Liberalism than he did for Women's Votes', Sylvia Pankhurst wrote about Russell's Wimbledon campaign, 'was at once apparent'.) After a while, the NUWSS seemed to him little better, and, eventually declaring the suffragists to be cursed with 'the bigotry of a small religious sect', he left them to join the People's Suffrage Federation, a body committed to campaigning for universal adult suffrage, with which Margaret Llewelyn Davies was closely associated.

'I am back at work, trying to forget public affairs,' he wrote to Helen Flexner a few weeks after the Wimbledon election, now safely back at his home in Bagley Wood. He spent the next few weeks writing the aforementioned article outlining the theory of types for the *American Journal of Mathematics*, after which, with the logic of the theory finally settled in its essentials, he felt able to begin the task of 'writing the book out'. Perhaps because he still had no idea how long the book would turn out to be, he rather exaggerated how quickly this relatively mechanical task could be achieved. By September 1907, writing to Ivy Pretious that he had been 'working like a black' on the book, he declared it to be approaching completion. 'In another year or so it ought to be ready for the Press,' he remarked with undue optimism.

The unenviable task of writing the book out fell to Russell rather than Whitehead, because of Whitehead's lecturing commitments. This, and the fact that the logical theory at the heart of the book was almost entirely Russell's invention, have led many to underestimate the role that Whitehead played in the authorship of *Principia Mathematica*, which is often discussed as though it had been written by Russell alone. Russell himself strived to correct this misapprehension whenever he could, emphasising at every opportunity that it was a *joint* work. 'Hardly a page in the three volumes . . . can be attributed to either of us singly,' he insisted. As Whitehead would comment on and correct Russell's work on the philosophical foundations, Russell would in turn modify and seek to improve Whitehead's more purely mathematical work. Each of them, then, in one way or another, contributed something to each successive draft. What fell to Russell to accomplish in these final stages was the copying out into a tidy manuscript of the final, jointly agreed version of the book.

Over the next few months, as he worked on this huge task from ten to twelve hours a day, the manuscript grew ever more vast. By March of 1908, with the end still a long way off, it had grown to 2,400 pages. 'Every time that I went for a walk', Russell later wrote, 'I used to be afraid that the house would catch fire and the manuscript get burnt up.' Extraordinarily, he also found time during these months to write a long critique of William James's theory of truth as expressed in his book *Pragmatism*. In criticising James, Russell was also defending the view of truth as a correspondence between a belief and a fact, which he had outlined in his debate with Joachim a year earlier, for it is precisely that notion that the pragmatist view threatens. 'Our account of truth', James writes, 'is an account of processes . . . having only this quality in common, that they *pay*.' Such a view was anathema to Russell, the very antithesis of his exalted conception of Truth as a 'stern and pitiless God', and of his Platonic insistence on mathematical 'facts'. Paraphrasing James's view (perhaps unfairly) as 'a truth is anything which it pays us to believe', Russell thus heaped scorn upon it. It might, he argued 'pay' to believe in the Roman Catholic faith, but this would not make, say, the doctrine of papal infallibility *true*. Thus, he writes: 'The attempt to get rid of "fact" turns out to be a failure.' Writing to Helen Flexner, he expressed himself more freely:

> . . . to my way of thinking pragmatism is hopeless stuff. I notice that the consolations of religion, which it is proud of preserving, amount to this: That with its definition of *Truth*, the proposition 'God exists' may be *true* even if God does not exist. I think the pope is very right to condemn this presentation of the Christian Faith, tho' I don't think he is politic. He ought to encourage every form of muddle-headedness, just as his priesthood encourages drink, if he were only thinking of the interests of his church.

'I get a great deal of pleasure out of my work,' he wrote to Ivy Pretious on Christmas Day 1907 (a day on which, he told her, 'in honour of our Saviour', he had devoted only 7½ hours to the book), 'and it is by far the most satisfactory thing in my life, so I can't complain of it. Only tonight I am tired and therefore discouraged, and I wish everything was different, beginning with myself.'

The background to the almost superhuman exertion and concentration required to finish *Principia* was the extreme unhappiness of his married life, which, by this time, was so acute that both he and Alys talked of death as a welcome relief. 'I often wondered', Russell writes of this time in his *Autobiography*, 'whether I should ever come out at the other end of the tunnel in which I seemed to be':

> I used to stand on the footbridge at Kennington, near Oxford, watching the trains go by, and determining that tomorrow I would place myself under one of them. But when the morrow came I always found myself hoping that perhaps *Principia Mathematica* would be finished some day.

Alys had now developed a lump in her breast, which she suspected – hoped even – might be cancer. When it was diagnosed as harmless, she wrote in her diary:

> Now my blissful hope . . . is destroyed – even the chance of death. I do so long to leave Bertie free to live with a woman who . . . does not bore him desperately and get on his nerves as I do . . . Little duties keep me going from day to day. But they don't satisfy the awful craving hunger for Bertie's love. It is always there, the volcano, and at first it used to burst out very often in the most unpleasant scenes – tears, recriminations I fear – I don't know and don't like to remember, only there was always the great love at the bottom. Now I can control its expression and I have only made one scene this winter . . . If I could only die – it's such a simple solution. And yet when I dream of it, the agony of parting from Bertie is too great. He is constantly in my thoughts . . . at first, for several years, waking without him was such torture. Even now I feel frightfully jealous of the servant who sees him and often speaks to him before I do.

In the face of this misery, Russell's absorption in *Principia Mathematica* was something of a relief, an escape. In May, writing again to Ivy, Russell said that he now expected the book to grow to about 6,000 or 8,000 pages. 'I have no time to think about anything,' he told her, 'which is very pleasant. And it is comforting to have a big continuous job on hand.'

Something of his attitude is captured in his response to a letter that he received from William James, in which James reproached him for failing to understand the pragmatist view of truth and counselled him: 'My dying words to you are "Say good-bye to mathematical logic if you wish to preserve your relations with concrete realities." ' Passing the remark on to his friend, the mathematician Philip Jourdain, Russell wrote: 'I would much rather, of the two, preserve my relations with symbolic logic.'

Though he had long since accepted the undesirability of pursuing an affair with Ivy, in his letters to her Russell often hinted, in a wistful, plaintive kind of way, of his desire for her. In August 1908, for example, he wrote in reply to a letter in which she had talked of making her will. 'Your kind letter has touched me so much that I must answer it at once,' he told her:

> It doesn't make me shudder to think of your will – it takes a great deal to make me shudder. Like Macbeth, 'I have supped full with horrors' – the worst of them are horrors of which, as long as I live, I shall never be able to speak . . . I can't tell you how grateful I am for your wish to leave me something . . . There is one thing I should particularly like to have, and that is the miniature of you by your Bideford friend. I wonder if you think that feasible? If you were dead, it would be a comfort to me; and it has associations which I value.

Responding to the interest that Ivy had expressed in the book on which he had been working with such complete absorption, Russell wrote that he had nothing to tell her about it: 'It is almost impossible to explain what my book is about.'

'You have a very special place in my thoughts from which you are seldom absent,' he told her the following October, though, he added, he thought it better if she did not, as she had suggested, send him a photograph of herself, for 'I could not let it be known that I had it.'

Meanwhile, the manuscript of *Principia* continued its inexorable growth towards complete unreadability. On 20 October 1908, Russell wrote to Louis Couturat that he expected it to be ready for publication in another year. 'It will be a very big book,' he told him, and 'no one will read it.'

He was right on all counts: almost exactly a year later, the book was finally finished; it was indeed very big (the final manuscript was 4,500 pages long); and, indeed, almost no one has read it (or, at least, not all the way through). The theory of logic contained in the first volume continues to be dissected and debated by philosophers, but the hundreds of pages of formal proofs that make up the later parts of the book have been largely left unread. 'I used to know of only six people who had read the later parts of the book,' Russell wrote in the 1950s. 'Three of these were Poles, subsequently (I believe) liquidated by Hitler. The other three were Texans, subsequently successfully assimilated.'

It was, nevertheless, a monumental achievement, and Russell was justifiably jubilant, when, on 18 October 1909, he could announce to Lucy Donnelly that he was ready to deliver the colossal manuscript to the Cambridge University Press. He was now thirty-seven but felt much older, having worked for so long at such an arduous and draining task. 'I feel', he told Lucy, 'more or less as people feel at the death of an ill-tempered invalid whom they have nursed and hated for years.' He took a certain delight in the book's very impenetrability: 'It is amusing to think how much time and trouble has been spent on small points in obscure corners of the book, which possibly no human being will ever discover.' One is reminded here of the remark by Bach that Wittgenstein was fond of quoting: that his music had been written 'to the glory of God'. To illustrate the kind of attitude expressed by such a remark, Wittgenstein used to point out the attention to detail that medieval craftsmen had expended on the faces that adorned the roofs of the great cathedrals. Nobody would see their work close up, and so nobody would know the lengths they had gone to make their work perfect. Something of the same attitude is contained in Russell's contemplation of his achievement in finishing *Principia Mathematica*. He had not written it for anyone to actually read, but out of an almost religious sense of its inherent value and of the desirability of its perfection. As he put it to Lucy Donnelly:

> It is odd how much emotion has got connected with this book I have been at so long. I have made a mess of my private life – I have not lived up to my ideals, and I have failed to get or give happiness. And as a natural result, I have tended to grow cynical about private relations and personal happiness – whether my own or other people's. So all my idealism has become concentrated on my work, which is the one thing in which I have not disappointed myself and in which I have made none of the compromises that destroy faith. It is a mark of failure when one's religion becomes concentrated on impersonal things – it is monkish essentially. But so it is; and therefore year by year work has become a more essential outlet to my rage for perfection.

To Helen Flexner, he wrote in similar terms: 'I imagine no human being will ever read it through, & those who read bits will never know the pitfalls we are avoiding, or the trouble we have taken to make it easier to read than to write. If we spent half the time at it, it would have looked as if it has cost twice the labour. I am very weary, but I see no near prospect of rest, or even of a state of mind in which I could rest if outward circumstances permitted. I am possessed of devils who scourge me on to activities, useful, useless, & even pernicious.'

The huge manuscript, with its special logical symbols, many of which had been invented solely for the purpose of the book, presented Cambridge University Press with enormous printing problems, and the task of having it typeset, proofread and published dragged on for another four years, the third volume being published in 1913. Estimating that they would lose £600 on the publication of such a monster, Cambridge University Press refused to go ahead with it until they were assured that at least half that sum would be covered by other sources. The Royal Society put up £200, leaving Russell and Whitehead to pay the rest. 'We thus', Russell writes in his *Autobiography*, 'earned minus £50 each by ten years' work.'

Assessing what was achieved by the Herculean labours involved in writing *Principia Mathematica* is difficult. What it set out to do was to demonstrate conclusively that the whole of mathematics could be derived from logic, but, whereas, in *The Principles of Mathematics*, it was reasonably clear what this meant (it meant, essentially, that all propositions about numbers could be re-cast into propositions about classes), in *Principia*, with the complications to the basic logical theory that Russell had felt compelled to add, it is much less clear. The picture is still further muddied by the fact that, for technical reasons, Russell and Whitehead were impelled to add to their stock of 'logical' axioms some that hardly fitted the notion of trivial truisms with which Russell had begun: the Axiom of Infinity, the Axiom of Reducibility and the so-called 'Multiplicative Axiom', all of which, though necessary for the proofs which followed, rather stretched the notion of a 'self-evident truth'.

Perhaps the cruellest blow of all, however, came in 1931, when the logician Kurt Gödel proved conclusively that what Russell and Whitehead had tried to do could not possibly be done: there can, in principle, be no logical theory within which all truths about numbers can be derived as theorems; all logical theories of mathematics are destined to be 'incomplete'. Indeed, the incompleteness of formal theories of mathematics is itself a demonstrable theorem!

Nevertheless, Russell and Whitehead *had* shown something interesting and important: they had, at least, demonstrated that a great deal of mathematics, if not quite all of it, could be derived from within a formal, axiomatic system (whether one thinks of it as a system of logic or of mathematics). And, in the process (and this is perhaps where the most lastingly important aspect of the work lies), they had given an enormous boost to the development of mathematical logic itself, inventing techniques and suggesting lines of thought that would provide the inspiration for subsequent mathematical logicians, such as Alan Turing and John von Neumann, whose work, in providing the theoretical basis for the theory of computing, has changed all our lives.

With *Principia* finally out of the way, Russell involved himself once more in politics. It was an opportune moment to do so: in November, the House of Lords used their power of veto to block the budget drawn up by Lloyd George, and the Liberal Prime Minister, Herbert Asquith (who had succeeded Campbell-Bannerman in 1908), therefore called a general election. At stake was a fundamental constitutional issue: the relative powers of the non-elected Lords against the elected House of Commons, just the sort of issue to fire Russell's imagination. 'A crisis is upon us such as we have not had since 1832,' he wrote to Helen Flexner, possibly overplaying it a bit: 'I have chucked my work till after the General Election, and am throwing myself into politics, speaking and canvassing.'

The candidate for whom he chose to canvass was Philip Morrell, an old Oxford friend of Alys's brother, Logan, who was standing for re-election in the constituency of South Oxfordshire. This was not Russell's own constituency – the candidate for which Russell says in his *Autobiography* 'had broken some pledges which I considered important' (correspondence of the time suggests that these pledges were to do with supporting women's suffrage) – but it would not be unduly cynical, I think, to believe that Russell had other motives for supporting Philip Morrell. For Russell was, by this time, fascinated by Morrell's wife, Lady Ottoline, a tall and striking aristocratic woman, a year younger than Russell, with an extravagant taste in clothes and finery, and a reputation for independence and unconventionality ('Conventionality is deadness' she once wrote in her diary).

With a keen interest in the arts, a great respect for the intellect, a craving for the company of men sexually attracted to her (she had already had an affair with Augustus John, and was about to begin another with the painter,

Henry Lamb), and a love of stimulating conversation, Ottoline had many of the qualities that had aroused Russell's fascination for Alys's sister, Mary, in Paris in 1894. Coming from similar backgrounds, and having several family acquaintances in common, he and Ottoline had met briefly on previous occasions, but Russell, imprisoned by his self-imposed denial of all things sensual, had adopted a disapproving attitude towards her. 'She offended my Puritan prejudices,' he wrote in his *Autobiography*, 'by what I considered an excessive use of scent and powder.'

However, in September 1909 (some months before he chose to support Philip Morrell in his election campaign), Russell had begun to think differently about Ottoline, when she and Philip came, on Logan's invitation, to Bagley Wood. On a walk along the river, Russell and Ottoline fell into a conversation that left both attracted and intrigued by the other. 'Bertrand Russell is most fascinating,' Ottoline wrote that day in her diary. 'I don't think I have ever met anyone more attractive, but very alarming, so quick and clear-sighted, and supremely intellectual – cutting false and real asunder. Somebody called him "The Day of Judgment" ':

> His notice flattered me very much, and though I trembled at the feeling that in half an hour he would see how silly I was and despise me, his great wit and humour gave me courage to talk.

As for Russell, he told her eighteen months later, when they became lovers: 'I remember a day when you came to Bagley Wood and we had a talk on the way to the river; that for me was the beginning.'

Perhaps by coincidence, but perhaps, equally, inspired by her jealousy at Russell's manifest interest in Ottoline, Alys wrote, about the time of the Morrells' visit to Bagley Wood, another painfully sad entry in her diary, in which she had not written since her heart-wrenching entry in 1907 about her disappointment over her suspected cancer:

> Things are no better since I last wrote, and I wake up every morning wishing I were dead. The lump in my breast grew and began to hurt . . . and I was very happy . . . thinking it was certainly a cancer . . . Then came the crushing disappointment when Dr Brooks told me it was non-malignant . . . Time drags, drags . . . Now I know that [Russell's love] is gone, but the belief that it is there still lingers in my instinctive thoughts and in almost all my dreams – it is equally painful to wake up from a dream in which he is my lover as from a dream in which he is scolding me – more painful, because more difficult to readjust myself to.

The day after their visit to Bagley Wood, the Morrells went to visit Alys's mother at her home at Court Place, Iffley, where Alys told Ottoline that Russell had enjoyed their visit and had expressed an interest in coming to see them in London. 'It would be very delightful,' Ottoline wrote, 'but I really have not the courage for it. In ten minutes he would be disappointed and bored. He makes me feel as if I was as empty as a drum.'

Working alongside Ottoline in her husband's campaign may have seemed to Russell the ideal way to build on this mutual attraction, and, indeed, during the campaign in December 1909 and January 1910, their admiration for each other grew still stronger. Travelling together, they toured the village-halls of Oxfordshire, at each of which Russell would deliver an address, often to rowdy and hostile audiences, in support of Liberal policies. 'At some places', Ottoline wrote, 'we were stoned and booed at':

> Watlington was particularly violent. Bertie Russell had come with us to speak at a large meeting there. There seemed no chance of anyone being listened to, much less anyone so quiet and remote as Bertie Russell, but undaunted he stood up and began to speak. Catcalls, whistles and yells redoubled, but something in his passionate sincerity and intellectual force arrested them, and in a few moments, much to our surprise, he was being listened to with attention. Very seldom have I seen intellectual integrity triumph over democratic disorder.

For his part, in starkest contrast to his previous attitude, Russell now found much in Ottoline of which to approve: 'I discovered that she was extraordinarily kind to all sorts of people, and that she was very much in earnest about public life.' There were, however, few opportunities for the two to be together, and the full flowering of their fascination for each other had to wait a further eighteen months.

The result of the election was that Philip Morrell, like many other Liberals, lost his seat,[5] and Asquith's government was returned with a much reduced majority. It was a victory of sorts, but the constitutional issue over the power of the Lords was still undecided and would continue to rage for another year. For, in order to abolish the Lords' power of veto, Asquith had to pass a reform bill in the Lords itself, and, naturally, they vetoed the very bill designed to restrict their power of veto. Thus Asquith was forced to call another general election at the end of 1910, this time on the understanding that, if he won, and the Lords still blocked the Reform Bill, the King would create enough Liberal peers to see it through.

With his passionate involvement in this issue, and with his mind still exhausted from the effort of finishing *Principia* and his taste for further philosophical work correspondingly blunted, Russell thought seriously of taking up politics permanently. In March 1910, he was asked to stand as the Liberal candidate for Oxford City, but declined when he was advised not to emphasise his commitment to women's suffrage. The following month, he was approached by the Liberals in the constituency of Bedford and asked to consider becoming their candidate. On 26 April, Russell addressed the Bedford Liberal Association, outlining the issues he would emphasise in any future election: reform of the Lords, Free Trade and the taxation of land. There was nothing in his speech that any Liberal could take much exception

---

[5] In the following election of December 1910, however, he became MP for Burnley in Lancashire.

to, but, shortly before he delivered it, he was taken aside and asked privately about his attitude to religion. Would he be prepared to attend church occasionally? No, he replied, he would not. As a consequence he was not elected, and the Bedford Liberals chose instead a man with more orthodox opinions and habits called Frederick Kellaway. This, Russell later remarked, was a lucky escape for both the Bedford constituency and himself.

For, by May, Russell had changed his mind about wanting to become an MP, regardless of whether he was selected as a candidate for Bedford or not. After Bedford rejected him, he received offers from other constituencies such as Hastings and St Leonards and South Pancras, but he turned them down, deciding instead to accept the offer he had received from Trinity College, Cambridge, of a five-year lectureship in Logic and the Principles of Mathematics. The prime mover in persuading the college to make this offer was, of course, Whitehead who, on 27 May, wrote to Russell expressing his delight at having got it through the College Council.

Russell accepted immediately, his thoughts by this time having swung back to philosophy, partly under the influence of a debate in which he had become engaged with the great Oxford philosopher, F. H. Bradley. In February, Bradley had written to Russell to tell him of a paper he had just written for *Mind* called 'On Appearance, Error and Contradiction', at the end of which he had included a few pages of criticism of Russell's *Principles of Mathematics*. Essentially, Bradley's criticisms centred on Russell's perennial difficulties about 'unities' and the value of analysis; on, for example, the problems Russell himself had been wrestling with about the 'class as many' and the 'class as one'. On 9 April, Russell wrote Bradley a long reply, conceding the point about classes, drawing Bradley's attention to his new theory of types, and refusing to draw the conclusion that Bradley wished him to draw, namely that the analysis of a 'whole' was impossible.

'There is some prospect of my getting drawn into politics,' Russell ended his letter, 'but if that fails, I shall endeavour to write something for *Mind* on the points you raise.' In reply, Bradley wrote:

> I feel, I must confess, some alarm at the prospect of you being occupied with politics, if that means that you will have no time for philosophy. Will it not be possible to combine them? If not, it is not for me to venture to judge in what direction you feel the greater 'call'. The only thing I feel clear about is this, that no one else will do your work in philosophy so far as human probability goes. And more than this I don't feel I have any right to say.

Such encouragement from the man widely considered to be the greatest living English philosopher would, one suspects, have done much to confirm Russell's decision to return to philosophy, and he hastily wrote to reassure Bradley that there was no chance of his entering politics, after all. 'I am really glad,' Bradley replied. 'I feel no doubt whatever that philosophy would lose greatly by your permanent withdrawal. I don't see who else is going to do the work there, which you would, &, I hope, will do.'

These pleasantries out of the way, Russell and Bradley resumed their philosophical skirmishing, both in print (through the pages of *Mind*) and in correspondence, throughout the following year. In July, Russell published a paper called 'Some Explanations in Reply to Mr Bradley', in which he defended his view that, though a complex has a unity that a mere enumeration of its constituents lacks, it can yet be analysed as being *composed* of its constituents. This prompted from Bradley (in 'Reply to Mr Russell's Explanations', published in *Mind* in January 1911) the predictable accusation that such a view was manifestly inconsistent:

> . . . my difficulty as to 'unities' remains. Is there anything, I ask, in a unity beside its 'constituents' . . . and, if there is anything more, in what does this 'more' consist?

This brought from Russell, in a letter dated 2 March, an acknowledgment of at least temporary defeat:

> With regard to unities, I have nothing short to say. The subject is difficult (in any philosophy, I should add) and I do not pretend to have solved all its problems.

By this time, Russell had taken up his post as a lecturer at Trinity. Having established himself in the pleasant rooms he had been given in Nevile's Court, and with Alys at a safe distance away in a rented cottage called Van Bridge in Fernhurst (the Bagley Wood home having been given up), everything seemed set for a new, quieter, less demanding life as a Cambridge don. Though still only thirty-eight, he was already speaking of himself as 'middle-aged', and wrote to his friends about how much he was enjoying the restful academic life. Free from the strain of his dreadful, hollow shell of a marriage, surrounded by people who valued his work, and having emerged from the tunnel of *Principia Mathematica*, he was in a mellow frame of mind. 'I enjoy living in College very much,' he wrote to Helen Flexner. 'Now I intend to take life easily for some time.'

After a long night, however, one does not fall back to sleep, one wakes up, and what Russell needed more than rest was stimulation, not of the intellect, but of the senses, the emotions and the imagination. As his 'conversion' experience in 1901 might have told him, the extraordinarily strong passions he was capable of controlling temporarily could not be imprisoned for ever. Eventually, a moment would come when they would demand release and turn his world around once more. In the event, all it took to unleash them was a few hours alone with Ottoline Morrell.

7
REAWAKENED VISIONS

In the Easter vacation of 1911, Russell gave a series of three lectures in Paris which, though almost entirely neglected by subsequent commentators, provide an important and compressed statement of his philosophical views, a kind of personal manifesto. The first, given at the Sorbonne on 22 March, was 'The Philosophical Importance of Mathematical Logic', in which he made a number of extravagant claims for mathematical logic: that it 'has resolved the problems of infinity and continuity'; that it 'has made possible a solid philosophy of space, time, and motion'; and also that, in providing the foundation for certain and objective mathematical knowledge, it 'refutes both empiricism and idealism, since it shows that human knowledge is not wholly deduced from facts of sense, but that a priori knowledge can by no means be explained in a subjective or psychological manner.'

The second lecture, delivered on the same day to the French Mathematical Society, was a more cautious and technical discussion of the problems of the Axiom of Infinity and the Multiplicative Axiom, pointing out that, while both axioms were needed to prove many long-established theorems of pure mathematics, neither was itself provable. Since it was possible that either might be false, Russell suggested that they both be regarded as explicit hypotheses.

The third – which is at one and the same time the most interesting and the most little known of the three – was given to the French Philosophical Society the following day. It was called 'Analytic Realism' and was an attempt by Russell to characterise his entire philosophical perspective. The philosophy he espouses, he announces, is *realist* because it upholds the objective reality of abstract, 'Platonic' ideas (such as, he believes, form the subject-matter of mathematics), and *analytic* 'because it claims that the existence of the complex depends on the existence of the simple'. Though no one noticed it at the time, and few have noticed it since, the lecture was the first occasion on which Russell used the term 'logical atomism' to describe his philosophy:

> You will note that this philosophy is the philosophy of logical atomism. Every simple entity is an atom. One must not suppose that atoms need persist in time, or that they need occupy space: these atoms are purely logical.

Why have these lectures remained so obscure? The only one that is at all well known, even among professional philosophers, and the only one that appeared in English during Russell's lifetime, is the first. The other two were published in French soon after they were delivered and since then have been largely forgotten and ignored. In histories of philosophy, in Russell's *Autobiography* and in later biographies, they are scarcely mentioned.

The reason for this strange neglect, for the virtual disappearance of these lectures from history, is that, among the significant events in Russell's life, they became completely overshadowed, even before they were delivered, by what happened on the night before Russell sailed to France to deliver them. For, on 19 March 1911, on his way to Paris, Russell spent the night in London at the home in Bedford Square of Philip and Ottoline Morrell. Philip was away at his constituency in Burnley, so, at the end of the evening, after Ottoline's dinner guests had gone, Russell and Ottoline were left, as Russell put it, '*tête-à-tête*'.

As the conversation moved from politics to more personal subjects, Russell felt emboldened to make hesitant sexual advances towards Ottoline and discovered to his amazement that they were not repulsed. After nine years of emotional and sexual self-denial, the experience of sharing physical and spiritual intimacy with an attractive woman was all but overwhelming, and Russell at once fell in love with Ottoline with a passion whose force changed his entire life. His desire for her was so all-consuming, he later said, that if he had known that Philip Morrell would have murdered them both, he would have been willing to pay the price for just one night with her. As it was, they did not make love that night,[1] but nevertheless stayed up, talking and kissing, until four in the morning.

Russell spent the next few days in Paris 'living in a dream'. His surroundings seemed to him unreal and he had difficulty concentrating on the lectures he had to deliver. When, a few months later, he had to check publisher's proofs of one of them, he wrote to Ottoline: 'it *was* hard to think of the stuff instead of thinking of you.'

Indeed, Russell could not get Ottoline out of his mind. His love for her, he knew immediately, was one of the greatest events in his life. In the train on the way to Paris, instead of preparing himself for the lectures he was to deliver, he wrote to her in unrestrainedly rapturous terms:

> My heart is so full that I hardly know where to begin. The world is so changed these last 48 hours that I am still bewildered. My thoughts won't come away from you – I don't hear what people say . . . I see your face always, though as a rule I can't imagine anybody's face. I love you very dearly now and I know that every time I see you I shall love you more. I long to be with you in beautiful places, where your own beauty and the beauty you create everywhere will be in harmony with other things.

---

[1] In his *Autobiography*, Russell attributes this to 'external and accidental reasons', though what he means by this is rather obscure. The two things that come most readily to mind are: 1. that he failed to maintain an erection, or 2. that Ottoline was having her period at the time, but a fertile imagination could no doubt add to these possibilities indefinitely.

In her journal, Ottoline wrote that, after that first night with Russell, she was 'utterly unprepared for the flood of passion which he now poured out on me . . . It was as if he had suddenly risen from the grave and had broken the bonds that held him.' The image is entirely appropriate. In his love for Ottoline, Russell – who for years had lived a desiccated, deadened kind of existence – suddenly came fully to life. Aspects of his personality that had long been buried now re-surfaced with renewed vigour and vitality. It was not just that years of emotional and sexual repression were lifted, it was that the whole sensual side of his nature was reawakened, as if, all at once, he had regained his sight, his hearing, his sense of touch, and he could now once again take pleasure in seeing, touching, smelling the things in the world. It was a wonderful and overwhelming experience, which left him both ecstatic and somewhat bewildered (the fact that he could see Ottoline's face even when she was not there, for example, clearly took him by surprise), as though, through some miracle, he had regained, along with the use of his senses, his imagination, his sense of beauty and his capacity to love.

Such a fundamental and powerful transformation would, he knew, have a profound effect on all aspects of his life, not least on his intellectual life, which for years had been motivated by precisely the desire to escape from the world of the senses to another, purer, more 'eternal' world of mathematical forms. 'Say good-bye to mathematical logic if you wish to preserve your relations with concrete realities!' William James had once advised him. The question now was whether, in his rediscovered delight in concrete realities, he could preserve his relations with mathematical logic. For what from one perspective looks beautifully eternal, from the other looks coldly inhuman, and the question arises whether a delight in sensual beauty is even compatible with an absorption in mathematical logic. Would Russell have produced such important and original work in logic and philosophy if he had *not* been dead to the world of the senses?

As he travelled in the train towards Paris on his way to deliver his 'manifesto' on the importance of mathematical logic, Russell felt as never before the *unimportance* of it. What struck him now most powerfully were the limitations and inadequacies of a merely logical point of view. 'I feel myself so rugged and ruthless,' he told Ottoline, 'so removed from the whole aesthetic side of life – a sort of logic machine.' In Paris, he knew, he would have to pull himself together and collect his wits. It would not do to be thinking of Ottoline while trying to engage in rigorous philosophical debate. And yet, he also knew it would be difficult, if not impossible: 'I fear the whole thing will seem less important than it did before.'

After his first night in Paris, Russell wrote Alys a letter, the contrast of which with the one he had written to Ottoline could not have been greater:

Dearest Alys,
    I got here without misadventure, after a warm & sunny crossing. Sheffer met me at the Station & dined with me; I bought Bergson [*L'Évolution*

creatrice] at last as I am to meet him at lunch today, & I have been hastily reading him. I probably shan't write again.

Thine aff.

Bertie

By now Alys was used to receiving such notes, and probably at this stage suspected nothing. Russell, however, was already planning a life without her. On the same day that he wrote this brief and curt message to Alys, he was writing to Ottoline about how, if she had a mind to, she could change the whole nature of his existence. 'All my life,' he told her, 'except for a short time after my marriage, I have been driven on by restless inward furies, flogging me to activity & never letting me rest, till I feel often so weary that it seems as if no more could be borne. You would change all that if you were willing. You could give me inward joy and expel the demons.'

The following day, he received a letter from Ottoline, urging the import- ance of keeping the details of their *tête-à-tête* evening a secret from Philip. From Russell's point of view, this struck quite the wrong note. His love for Ottoline was the most wonderful thing that had ever happened to him, he was not going to hide it away like a guilty secret. He replied immediately, arguing that he and Ottoline should not degrade their love in this way. There should be no 'sordid atmosphere of intrigue – prying servants, tattling friends & gradually increasing suspicion'. Instead, Ottoline should tell Philip and he should tell Alys. 'I can acquiesce in your staying with him,' Russell told her (Ottoline had also explained to him that she had no intention of leaving her husband), so long as 'deceit and sordidness is avoided.'

For Ottoline, this was all moving much too quickly. In her marriage to Philip, it is true, she was far from fulfilled, and she had had passionate affairs before, with Augustus John, Henry Lamb and Roger Fry, the last two of which were by no means finished when Russell came into her life. But she was not so dissatisfied with her life that she was prepared to put it on an entirely different footing. She was, despite everything, devoted to both Philip and her daughter Julian, and did not want to leave them. Nor did she want a scandal, which for herself would be bad enough, but for Philip would be absolutely ruinous. Besides, her feelings for Russell were in no way equal to his for her. Far from being consumed with desire, she found him physically rather unattractive. She had, however, an immense respect for his intellect and a deep fascination for his personality, for its intriguing mixture of the romantic and the sceptical; she was also greatly flattered by his attentions, by his confidences and by how enormously important she had suddenly become in his life.

Over the next few years the two sides of her reaction to Russell are recorded separately. In her letters to him, she dwells on her sense of spiritual companionship with him and her admiration of him, and openly encourages his love for her. In her journal, on the other hand – which she allowed Philip to read and which, it appears, was often written *for* Philip to read – she dwells on her ambivalent feelings about Russell and lack of physical attraction towards him. At first glance, the two look incompatible, and the question arises as to where – in her letters or in her journal – she was telling the truth. I am inclined, however, to think that both reactions were sincere and that both her journal and her letters tell a partial truth, each confessing what the other leaves unsaid and each concealing what the other expresses. Her feelings were complex, and – much to Russell's subsequent confusion and despair – difficult, if not impossible, to put in a coherent and consistent way. Compounding this confusion, it is true, was her willingness every now and again to tell 'white lies' rather than confront or hurt either Russell or Philip.

Whatever her true feelings may have been, Ottoline did little to discourage the extraordinary torrent of passionate love that she had inspired in Russell, expressions of which she now began to receive with every post. 'How could I allow him to return to the dreary life that he had risen from?' she asks herself in her journal. 'It seemed that I could not refuse to take upon me the burden of this fine and valuable life.' As for herself, she was, she says, 'partly overcome, carried away and elated by this new experience', but 'underneath there lay a cold, horrible feeling of discomfort that I was not being true':

> . . . the intoxication of his own feelings blinded him from seeing that I was not equally in love with him; to tell him this was more than I had courage to do.

And yet, her letters to Russell show that it was not just his intoxicated state that led him to think that she was equally in love with him. When, on 25 March, he stopped by at Bedford Square on his way back from France, she handed him a note she had written that morning, in which she declared: 'Nothing can stop the force of my love coming to you and yours to me . . . My spirit *is* with you this moment and every moment. I understand you as I understand myself.'

Russell's delight at receiving this note was rather tempered by Ottoline's revelation at the same meeting that, contrary to the impression she had given Russell earlier, she and Philip still had sexual relations. Horrified by the disclosure, Russell now tried to lay down the law, to insist that Ottoline and Philip sleep in separate beds, but Ottoline would have none of it and they parted with the matter still, as far as Russell was concerned, unresolved. In his mind, Ottoline had to choose: if she insisted on continuing to sleep with Philip, he would have nothing more to do with her; if, on the other hand, she valued his love, she had to stop sharing Philip's bed. 'I don't know quite why I have to ask for all or nothing,' he wrote when he was back at Fernhurst, 'but I know that I am right. I feel that if you refuse all, I shall be terribly tempted to accept less, but it would be wrong – I should be somehow degraded by it, and that would degrade our love.'

He honoured and respected Ottoline's 'self-sacrifice', as he saw it, in giving herself to Philip, 'and formerly I should have been more ready to think it right', but 'there is a sort of courage which consists in choosing one's own happiness on those rare occasions when it is right to do so.' He had come to this view, he implies rather mysteriously, on the basis of personal experience – one can only assume he was alluding to his secret love for Evelyn Whitehead:

> There have been many things in my life which I should have wished to tell you, but that I am not at liberty to do so; they would have illustrated why I am so certain of what I think right.

Certainly, Evelyn was much on Russell's mind. He would, he told Ottoline, be very glad if she would visit Evelyn to discuss the situation during what he called this 'time of waiting'. He had, he said, already written to the Whiteheads to tell them about his love for her: 'They are my best friends – they have known all my intimate concerns, or all that could be told, and they have helped me in all difficulties.' This is all the more remarkable because he had not yet told Alys. It was a Saturday night when he returned to Fernhurst, and he and Alys had as weekend guests Alys's nieces, Karin and Ray Costelloe. 'I shall tell Alys on Monday,' Russell promised. 'I can't tell her while she has our visitors on her hands.' Alys was still entirely unsuspecting. Even at a time like this, Russell's ability to disguise his true feelings was as effective as ever:

> It is horrible here – poor Alys gets on my nerves to such an extent that I don't know how to bear it another moment. I always find her very trying after an absence, but this time naturally it is particularly bad. However, I have talked and laughed the whole time, so that unobservant people would have supposed I had not an anxiety or a trouble in the world.

On the same Saturday night that he wrote this letter, Ottoline was sitting opposite Philip in their drawing-room in Bedford Square, writing to Russell to explain how utterly unimportant it was to her that she continued to allow Philip to make love to her:

> . . . what you object to is in *reality* no different from sitting in the same room with him as I am doing now, writing to you. I am as much my own free self as I always am, and I certainly feel farther from him then than I do often when he and I are talking together.

The following day, having received Russell's letter, she wrote: 'You make me nearly obey you, but not quite.' She was not prepared to give way to Russell's demands, even though 'nothing keeps me here except my own will and conviction of what is right.' She would, however, go and see Evelyn Whitehead, if that is what Russell wanted, though she had a feeling that Evelyn did not altogether like her. She asked in return only that Russell should promise to see her again, just once: 'I long for you to take me completely once and let me pour myself into you.'

It was a promise Russell was only too willing to make. 'I feel', he replied, 'that *not* to possess you wholly once is beyond my strength – so the occasion should be made. And I feel that after that we could think more calmly.' It was now Tuesday and he had, as he had promised, told Alys about Ottoline. Alys, he claimed, 'took it very well'. In fact, as Ottoline discovered when she met Evelyn Whitehead the next day, Alys had reacted to the news with misery and rage. Evelyn described to Ottoline how Alys had watched through the window as Russell, in his impatient eagerness to read the latest letter from Ottoline, intercepted the postman and snatched the letter from his hand. She also told Ottoline that Alys had come to Russell in tears every night since the disclosure, begging him to change his mind.

Evelyn's aim, whether motivated by jealousy (as Ottoline thought), or by a selfless desire to prevent unhappiness (as both Alys and Russell seemed to think), was clearly to put an end to the affair between Russell and Ottoline as soon as possible. After Ottoline, in conformity with Russell's request, had paid her a visit on 28 March, Evelyn then, the following day, visited Ottoline at Bedford Square, to urge her to consider her duties as a wife and mother. Throughout the crisis, Evelyn took pains to maintain the confidence of both Alys and Russell and to play a central part in their discussions, acting as intermediary and offering advice to all the people concerned, including Ottoline. And if, in the end, the outcome was influenced little by her machinations, it was through no lack of trying on her part.

As soon as she received Russell's letter telling her about Ottoline, Evelyn sent him a telegram summoning him to London. For the rest of that week, Russell stayed with the Whiteheads at their home in Carlyle Square, which now became the focus of events, the place where the discussions and meetings were held that would decide the future of Russell, Ottoline, Alys and Philip. With regard to Evelyn, Russell was – or perhaps pretended to be – naive to the point of blindness. 'How could you suppose Mrs Whitehead could put me against you?' he asked Ottoline. 'In the first place no human being could and in the second place she would not wish to.' Ottoline was not taken in. 'I have always felt', she wrote in her journal, 'that she was a previous object of his love':

She obviously knew him very well, and both she and her husband had been his greatest friends. I do not think Mrs Whitehead liked me, as was perhaps natural; but I have not much recollection of what she said, except that she told me that he was not faithful or constant. I only remember the discomfort of sitting in a strange, elaborate little drawing-room, talking to a strange elaborate lady, who looked on me with suppressed mistrust and jealousy.

By the middle of the week, Evelyn's conversations with both Ottoline and Russell seemed to be having their intended effect. After her second meeting with Evelyn (at which Evelyn had told her that Russell could not bring himself to see her), Ottoline wrote to Russell to say that she now saw that they must break it off. But she begged for one last meeting to say goodbye. From the Whiteheads' home in Carlyle Square, Russell replied:

You are right, my heart, we must end everything but what we can treasure in our own thoughts. I shall be glad to see you once more, tomorrow morning, here, as soon after breakfast as you can.

At what was intended to be their last meeting the next morning, however, everything changed, and Evelyn's plans became unstuck. In her journal, Ottoline describes what happened in these terms:

I had another interview with Bertie at the Whiteheads' house, to say good-bye and to tell him that it was impossible for me to leave Philip, but he begged me to see him again. His despair weighed on me, and filled me with gloom. I felt it was impossible to cast him off. He was like a Savanarola, exacting from me my life, my time, and my whole devotion, and I cried out, 'Oh, to be free!' . . . If only this awful responsibility had not been laid upon me.

It is a heavily edited, if not entirely fictitious account. One crucially important fact that it fails to mention is that Ottoline arrived at the meeting with a note for Russell, encouraging further meetings. Ottoline's biographer, Miranda Seymour, claims – to my mind quite plausibly – that: 'even before she came to meet him at Carlyle Square . . . Ottoline had made up her mind to end nothing, neither her marriage, nor the burgeoning relationship with Bertie, nor the old, unfinished love-affair with Henry Lamb.' She further claims that, that night, Ottoline went to a party with Roger Fry and returned with him to Bedford Square, where he declared his love for her and she 'allowed him to make love to her and to believe that she loved him'. Evidently, her efforts to be free from Russell's demands on her life, her time and her devotion were a good deal more successful than she implies.

Indeed, perhaps unexpectedly, Ottoline emerges as the undoubted victor of the manoeuvres of a week that she herself described as 'like a nightmare'. By the end of that week, she had successfully fought off both Evelyn Whitehead's attempts to end her affair with Russell and Russell's demands that the affair should occupy the whole, or at least the centre, of her life. After the meeting at Carlyle Square, her relationship with Russell would continue, not on his terms, but on hers. What is more, she had accomplished this without Russell feeling in the slightest bit resentful. Instead, after being convinced that the affair had to end, he now felt rapturous that it was to continue on any terms. 'Dearest,' he wrote, just hours after the meeting, 'I will accept whatever of your time you feel you can rightly give, and I will not ask for more.' And yet, just two days earlier, he had written: 'if you continue to sleep with Philip and I don't break with you, I shall hate him, and probably more and more as time goes on, till it becomes almost madness. I don't demand that you should not stay in the same house.' After the narrow escape of their 'final' meeting, Russell was disinclined to demand anything.

'Our love shall always be sacred,' Russell now promised her, 'and I will give you devotion worthy even of you.' He had, he told her, gone back to reading poetry, 'which I had not read for many years':

You have released in me imprisoned voices that sing the beauty of the world – all the poetry that grew dumb in the years of sorrow has begun to speak to me again.

The image of being released from prison is one that recurs many times in Russell's letters at this period. Two days later, he wrote to Ottoline that he longed to be with her in wild, open places, with the freedom of the wind and the sky and the sea: 'life is so full of prisons, and I love the free spaces of the world.' The extraordinarily powerful feeling of release that he now felt was, of course, due in large part to the happy realisation that he was, at last, free from the prison of his marriage. When he returned for a few nights to Fernhurst, he told Ottoline that 'Alys has agreed not to come to Cambridge again, so we shall cease to have a common life at the end of the Vacation . . . I shall tell people that her rheumatism doesn't allow her to live in Cambridge. She seems to prefer to give the reason that we can't get on together, but except to intimate friends I don't feel I can say that.' Alys was, he said, 'behaving very well', adding rather unconvincingly:

I do not think she is suffering much. All the real pain was nine years ago, when I told her I no longer loved her. Since then life together has been very difficult, and I am quite certain she will be happier when she has abandoned the struggle, and I think she really knows she will. It will be a great boon to me, not only because I hardly know how to endure her, but more because she has a subtle bad influence.

The next day, he gave a more realistic picture of Alys's state:

Alys has been speaking in a most harrowing way, and has made me for a moment full of the thought of her pain. But I am sure, really, that she will be happier when she has given up the struggle to make some sort of life with me – otherwise I could not ask her to give it up. I mind her pain more than the pain of people I like better – it is like the pain of a wounded animal. At times I have thought I ought never to have told her I no longer cared for her, yet I feel that a life of active and constant hypocrisy would have been impossible and wrong. But giving pain deliberately is very terrible.

That he himself saw a connection between the sense of imprisonment he had felt in his marriage to Alys and his yearning for refuge in the eternal world of mathematics is revealed by Russell in his letter to Ottoline the following day (from now on, not a day went by without Russell writing at least once, and often two or three times, to her). Her love, he said, 'revives the worship of beauty that I set out to kill in order to endure my life':

I wonder if you ever read the thing I wrote about why I love Mathematics[2]

---

[2] 'The Study of Mathematics', one of the essays in his *Philosophical Essays*, published the previous year. A few days after this letter, Russell arranged for a copy of the book to be sent to Ottoline, so that she could read this essay and 'The Free Man's Worship'.

– you would be able to understand all but a few sentences of it, and it would tell you how I tried to live. But mathematics is a cold and unresponsive love in the end; and it is hard to generate all one's force from within.

His worship of beauty having been revived, poetry had, for the moment at least, replaced mathematics in his affections, and the letter provides a long description of the complicated train of thought he had undergone in deciding which poet's works would be most fitting as a gift for Ottoline. After rejecting Shakespeare for being 'too finite', and Matthew Arnold for being too schoolmasterly, he had finally settled on Shelley and Blake. It was important to him that they had the same taste in poetry, for it would confirm his view that 'we do seem strangely near in thought and feeling – more so than I could have believed we could be. I have the sense that you will always understand me, though I know I am difficult, because things affect me in strange ways. I believe and hope that I shall always understand you.'

The sense of loss he had experienced in giving up his religious beliefs had never quite deserted him, but now he began to feel that, in his love for Ottoline, he had something that preserved whatever was valuable and beautiful in religious faith without committing him – as religious dogmas inevitably would – to any false beliefs. It was as if, he wrote on 4 April, life were a mountain top in a mist, mostly cold and blank, which now had opened out to offer 'visions of unbelievable beauty'. These visions were the closest one could come to religious revelation, providing the highest, most exalted state it was possible for mortal man to experience. It was an experience that Russell now wanted to share: 'I want to give the visions to others.'

Two days later, he returned to the theme. 'I know you don't feel quite as I do about religion,' he wrote, 'because you believe more than I do.' Such a difference on this – of all topics – was clearly intolerable, and he now sought to minimise it:

I think the difference is not important, because I want to preserve much that belongs with religion, and I care deeply about religion. I lost my belief gradually, between the ages of 14 and 18. I had no friends at all at that time, and no one I could talk to. I minded very much when I came to disbelieve first in immortality and then in God – I was profoundly miserable, supposed that I should never meet any one who would be congenial and whom I could freely talk to. I read Shelley, and wondered whether anybody like him still existed. Then I read Carlyle, hoping to find religion in *Sartor Resartus*, but I saw that he was a rhetorician with no care for truth.

Russell's work on mathematics had, in an indirect way, provided an alternative to religious faith. Now he wanted to address this fundamentally important issue directly, to write something on a subject that affected everyone in a way that everybody could understand. 'I wish very much my work was less technical,' he told Ottoline:

I should like to be able to write things that would say more of what I feel – but hitherto I have found it very difficult. I am full of vague plans, but I don't know what would come of them, I feel that you will help me. So much that goes into religion seems to me important, and I want somehow to make people feel what survives dogmas. Most of the people who think as I do about the dogmas seem to be able to live in the everyday world without windows into a greater world beyond. But to me that would be a prison. Much of what I feel is in Spinoza, but he is difficult, and very few people can get what he has to give. I do not know how to express myself so as to appeal to people, and yet I am certain there is a way, if it could be found. I tried in Free Man's Worship, but that is only for people in great unhappiness. One wants also something for people whose vision is fading because their daily life is all prose.

'And besides all this,' he added, 'it would be such a joy if I could do work that could interest you – it is trying to have to give my best time and thought to things wholly remote.' In a previous letter he had said: 'My whole being is one song to you of love and reverence.' It was not the conventionally extravagant expression that it sounds of a man in love, but a perfectly sincere declaration of intent: he wanted to offer everything in his life to Ottoline. He wanted to tell her all his thoughts, to describe to her the events of his day-to-day life, to share with her all his twists and turns of his moods, and to relate to her in detail his entire life up until he met her. The idea that at the centre of his world was a concern with abstract and difficult problems, about which Ottoline neither knew nor cared anything, was quite unbearable. There were two ways round the problem: he could either educate Ottoline in philosophy so that she could understand something of his work, or he could change the nature of his work so that it dealt with themes of interest to her. Over the next few years, he tried both many times and in different ways. To admit defeat, as, in the end, he was forced to, was to admit that, after all, there were things about Russell that Ottoline was incapable of understanding, and – though this he probably never did quite admit – vice versa.

On 8 April, Ottoline and Philip set off to Studland in Dorset for a month's holiday, in the middle of which Philip would have to return to London on his own for a few days. To both Ottoline and Russell, this seemed a golden opportunity, at last, to consummate their relationship, and they made arrangements for Russell to join Ottoline on 18 April, the day Philip left. It was a rather risky plan. Studland had become a fashionable resort for exactly the kind of people who would know and recognise Ottoline and Russell, and Ottoline could never be sure that she was not going to receive a sudden visit from a Bell or a Strachey, or some other notorious gossip.

They had reason to be cautious. Evelyn Whitehead had expressed to Russell the fear that Philip, in a fit of impassioned jealousy, might become completely unhinged and murder both him and Ottoline. 'I think the things she fears are *possible*,' Russell wrote to Ottoline, 'but highly improbable – so improbable that they are better ignored ... Mrs Whitehead's heart makes her nervous: also she has had more experience of horrors of one sort or

another than most people, so her mind is stocked by such things.' Russell's
reassurance on this point was misplaced. Ottoline did not for a moment fear
that Philip would act as Evelyn had imagined; her anxieties about Philip
sprang from a quite different source. Despite what she had led Russell to
believe, she had not yet told Philip about her affair with Russell. She had so
far told him only that Russell was unhappy with Alys and had asked her for
sympathy and support, which she felt obliged to give him. In Studland she
now told Philip that Russell was in love with her and pressing her to leave
him. Philip's response, far from being murderous, was coldly indifferent. 'Do
you want to go?' he asked her. 'You must if you want to.' Ottoline, so she
claimed in her journal anyway, 'felt hurt that he could ever imagine such a
thing':

> How could he suppose that I should wish to part from him with whom my
> life is entwined, to whom my love and confidence had been given? The
> thought made me utterly miserable.

The upshot was, again, exactly what Ottoline had wanted: Philip and she
remained together and married, but she and Russell remained free to continue
their affair. Philip was devoted to Ottoline, but remarkably free from sexual
jealousy, perhaps because he himself had several lovers other than Ottoline.
Promising to support his wife in whatever she did, he decided to keep his
appointment in London and to give his full consent to Russell's visit.

Alys was another matter. On the day that the Morrells left for Studland,
Alys went up to London to stay with the Whiteheads and to discuss her
marital problems with Evelyn, whose interest in the subject was apparently
indefatigable. In a letter to Ottoline early that morning, Russell said that he
had not had a chance to talk to Alys, but: 'I shall see the Whiteheads Monday
and find out what she has said to them.' No doubt Alys discovered Russell's
latest opinions and thoughts from the same source. 'I *feel*', Russell wrote,
'that she is becoming resigned, and will behave well in return for very small
amounts of my society.' In any case, whatever Alys thought and whatever her
intentions, Russell pleaded with Ottoline not to give up their idea of meeting
in Studland: 'And the plan of putting me in lodgings seems to me worse than
useless . . . You had better keep me in the house. It makes no difference to
Alys's behaviour what you and I do with each other – it is only what I do to
her that matters. And I am *certain* I can keep her in hand, only it means
enduring a certain amount of her.' In any case, he argued, 'unless from
detectives she will know nothing'.

Later the same day, he wrote that he had, after all, had a chance to speak
to Alys before she left for London, and the conversation had confirmed what
he had thought. If he was prepared to keep up the appearance that he and
Alys had not finally separated, by coming to her for the occasional weekend,
she in return would put aside the idea of suing for divorce and thus involving
Ottoline and Russell in a public scandal. For the time being, at least, Russell
was still tied to some extent to Alys, and the only common life he could share
with Ottoline was that conducted through their correspondence. 'Tell me

everything you can in your letters,' he urged, 'hopes and fears and memories and about books and everything':

> We depend terribly on letters for knowing each other . . . *everything* interests me . . . I don't want only to know but to have as much of life in common as possible.

As he and Ottoline could live together only in thought, rather than in body, the clash between their beliefs assumed an even greater importance to Russell than it ordinarily would, and he continued to worry away at the apparent conflict between the dispassionate and critical nature of his philosophical work and the expansive, ecstatic visionary he had become in his love for Ottoline. 'I shall publicly attack things which you believe,' he told her on 10 April, 'but you will know the spirit in which I do it, & you will not mind, will you, Dearest?'

A few days later, Russell came up with a rather startling proposal that would allow Ottoline and him to share a common life in another sense. 'In moments of depression,' he wrote, 'it happens to me to think that nothing in life is as long as life':

> I long for the continuity that comes with children – but that is a useless thought. Would it matter if you had a child? Although I should loathe its not being ostensibly mine, still it would be on the whole a joy.

The suggestion, no matter how tentatively it was made, was outrageous and Ottoline, for the moment, did not respond to it. She considered herself rather a bad mother to Julian, and had no wish for further children. In any case, she had long ago had an operation that made further childbirth impossible.

The thought of children was, for Russell, naturally bound up with his contemplation of the ecstatic thought that in Studland he would, at last, succeed in making love to Ottoline. As the day drew nearer, both of them repeated to each other their growing impatience. 'I do long for you to come now,' Ottoline wrote soon after she arrived in Dorset, 'but I won't think of it . . . we will wait patiently for the 18th.' In their efforts to prevent the world from knowing about their love affair, a narrow escape was made when, shortly before Russell's visit, Lytton Strachey (who was staying with Henry Lamb at Corfe, not far from Studland) wrote to invite himself to stay with Ottoline. He was politely and successfully put off, but a further and perhaps even greater threat presented itself when Alys's brother, Logan Pearsall Smith, who by coincidence was an old friend of Philip's from Oxford, insisted on visiting the Morrells. Russell was quite naturally alarmed. 'You must manage to get him away before I come,' he wrote. Ottoline did manage to get him away, but some damage had been done during Logan's visit by the mention (presumably by Philip) of Russell's impending visit. At this stage, however, Logan had no reason to suspect that Russell was visiting Studland as Ottoline's lover.

On Easter Saturday, just three days before he was due to leave for

Studland, Russell visited his dentist in London and received some rather dreadful news: his dentist suspected him of having cancer. Not being an expert in the field, the dentist could not be sure of his diagnosis and recommended Russell to a specialist, who, however, was away on holiday and would not be available for a few weeks. Russell therefore had to go to Studland with the threat of cancer hanging over him. 'When the dentist told me,' he later wrote, 'my first reaction was to congratulate the Deity on having got me after all just as happiness seemed in sight. I suppose that in some underground part of me I believed in a Deity whose pleasure consists of ingenious torture.' He told neither Alys nor Ottoline, but the thought was never far from his mind and heightened, he said, his happiness during the time he spent in Studland 'by giving it greater intensity, and by the sense that it had been wrenched from the jaws of destruction'.

The three days he stayed with Ottoline, from 18 to 21 April, were remembered by him as being 'among the few moments when life seemed all that it might be, but hardly ever is . . . [the] malignant Deity had after all been not wholly successful'. He had not, of course, told Alys where he was going (she presumably believed that he was leaving for Cambridge, in good time for the start of term on 21 April), but just before he set off he and she had a fierce argument in which she threatened again to name Ottoline in filing for divorce, and he in turn threatened that if she took steps to procure a divorce on those terms he would kill himself. 'I then rode away on my bicycle, and with that my first marriage came to an end,' Russell claims in his *Autobiography*, adding, 'I did not see Alys again till 1950.' He may have ridden away on his bicycle, but the ending of his marriage was a good deal less clean and quick than this statement implies. It was to take a few more months of messy and ill-tempered negotiations before he and Alys agreed on terms of separation, during which he did occasionally see her to discuss the situation.[3]

'There is nothing left but longing for the moment,' Russell wrote to Ottoline, before he set off for Studland, 'it is too near now for philosophy or patience.' He took the train as far as Swanage, and then got a horse-drawn cab the rest of the way. He had arranged with Ottoline that she would stand at the roadside to wait for him, and as the horse made its way up and down the Dorset hills, the journey seemed to him almost unbelievably slow. At last he caught sight of her and immediately jumped out of the cab, letting it go ahead with his luggage.

From Ottoline's point of view, his almost feverish eagerness was a little too over-powering and, to begin with at least, not entirely welcome. 'He assumed at once that I was his possession,' she wrote in her journal, 'and started to investigate, to explore, to probe':

I shrank back, for it was intolerable to me to have the hands of this psychological surgeon investigating the tangle of thoughts, feelings and

---

[3] Another false impression created by this rather odd and misleading account of his separation from Alys is the claim that it took place just days after his return from Paris at the end of March. In fact, it was nearly three weeks later.

emotions which I never yet allowed anyone to see. I felt like a sea-anemone that shrinks at the slightest touch. I forced myself, however, to be brave and to expose myself as much as I could bear; but held the door shut on some things, especially my friendship with Henry Lamb, for I knew by instinct that Bertie would be harsh and critical of him.

Gradually, however, her feeling of 'shyness and strangeness' with Russell began to wear off, 'and I was able to be more natural and easy':

I felt uplifted and flattered that this remarkable man should carry me up with him into worlds of thought that I had not dreamt of; he talked of his life and work and thoughts, and if only he had been just different in his person, should probably have been entirely carried off my feet, and have flown with him through worlds of thought and sense. But, to my shame, however much I was thrilled with the beauty and transcendence of his thoughts, I could hardly bear the lack of physical attraction, the lack of charm and gentleness and sympathy, that are so essential to me, and yet so rare.

Assuming these misgivings to be genuine, and not invented for Philip's sake, Ottoline was entirely successful in disguising them from Russell, whose delight at spending three days and nights alone with her was unalloyed. On his way back to London, he began a letter to her as soon as he got on the train. It was absurd to be writing so soon, he wrote, 'but I can't do anything else':

You fill my heart and mind so completely that I can't take my thoughts off you for one moment. Our three days were an absolute revelation to me of the possibilities of happiness and of love. Each moment, our union seemed to grow more complete and perfect.

The glow remained with him after he returned to Cambridge the next day. 'I go about with such a sense of happiness that I can hardly contain it,' he wrote. In order to be able to come to London as often as he liked, he had 'been cunning' and arranged to give only two lectures a week. During his marriage to Alys, Cambridge had been a welcome and necessary refuge, but now he felt somewhat at odds with its quiet and still atmosphere. 'This place is very much where the civilised half of me belongs,' he told Ottoline. 'I love the courts and the willows, and my own rooms, and the feeling that the things of the intellect are respected here. But the other half of me is restive under the restraint and the artificiality and the absence of anything like real life; and the timidity of mind and body that dons suffer from always seems to me pitiful – they never view life as an adventure except when they are really immoral. The quiet courts, shut in and allowing no horizon, really suit them. It is a pity – a little adventurousness would improve their work enormously.'

It was like being shut indoors after enjoying the freedom of wild, open spaces. 'I rather resent the hold this place and work (which belongs with this place) have on me,' he wrote. More in keeping with his mood than the civilised restraint of college life was the simple beauty of the natural world, his appreciation of which was now immeasurably sharpened:

> All the world is filled with splendour by the thought of you. After I had stopped writing to you this afternoon, I went out to see the sunset and hear the birds – everything seemed a thousand times more beautiful than other springs – the daffodils and young lime leaves and thrushes, and the sky and the meadows – it all seemed transfigured.

This state of heightened sensibilities inevitably brought to mind his 'conversion' experience of 1901, and he now wanted to show Ottoline the unsatisfactory attempt he had made in the light of that experience to express his 'religion' in words. 'The Pilgrimage of Life', which he described to Ottoline as 'various unsuccessful attempts at writing, mixed up with private reflections', still lay unfinished and abandoned, but he evidently thought there was something to be learnt from it, perhaps from understanding why it had not come off. 'You will see just how they fail,' he told Ottoline, 'and why I had to give it up. The only point of your reading them would be to see how they fail.' A few days later, sending the twenty-one fragments that made up 'The Pilgrimage of Life', he described them as 'a set of disjointed reflections . . . with which I tried to solace myself when I needed solace.'

In fact, though the dominant mood of the fragments – one of stoicism in the face of misery and tragedy – hardly chimed with his current ecstasy, there was much in this unfinished work, as Russell surely realised, which still expressed his feelings on issues that were important to him. Nowhere is this more true than in the section on 'Religion', a section one can be sure would be of especial interest now to both Russell and Ottoline. 'What is the true essence of religion,' Russell asks there, 'when all unnecessary dogma, all mere shell and clothing, has been stripped from it?' His answer is that religion is essentially 'a way of feeling, an emotional tone, rather than any specific belief':

> Religion is the passionate determination that human life is to be capable of importance . . . To assert religion is to believe that virtue is momentous, that human greatness is truly great, and that it is possible for man to achieve an existence which shall have significance.

Despite the fact that Ottoline was a believer and Russell was not, there was much in this view of the nature of religion with which she would be able to agree, and no doubt part of Russell's motive in sending it to her was to reveal this area of common ground. It was also to prepare the way for the suggestion that was building in his mind of writing a work on religion that would express more successfully the thoughts he had tried to express in this earlier work. In doing so, it would also enable him to combine in some way his philosophical work with the state of visionary ecstasy inspired by his love for Ottoline.

After Russell had been back at Cambridge just a few days he went to London to be examined by the cancer specialist recommended by his dentist, and discovered to his delight that his dentist's suspicions had been ill-founded: there was nothing much the matter with him. 'This is a relief from what should have been a grave anxiety,' he wrote to Ottoline, 'tho' I can't say it was, because I forgot about it except at moments.' He justified not having mentioned it on the grounds that 'If it had been true, it wd. have destroyed our one chance of real complete happiness to have told you. Being false, it wd. have been a sheer waste.'

With that anxiety out of the way, Russell now sought to prepare both himself and Ottoline for a deep and lasting union. He probably still hoped and half-expected that, ultimately, Ottoline would leave Philip for him. 'Parting grows harder each time,' he wrote to her after a meeting in London. 'I feel it won't be possible soon.' But 'I should like whatever we ultimately do to be done deliberately, and I should like to be sure that you faced all there is to say against me.' He began with Evelyn Whitehead's view that he was not constant in his affections:

An affection which is unsatisfied and doesn't take up my time is not, with me, evidence of a minor interest in other women . . . an affection which finds no expression will in time die. But those are all the reasons for thinking me unconstant. I don't think they come to much. I loved Alys and that came to an end because we were fundamentally uncongenial and I found it out . . . Then, as I told you, I loved once again, 9 years ago; but that was unhappy and died a gradual death for want of nourishment.

The clumsy, indirect nature of this attempted reassurance appears to be due to the fact that Russell felt forbidden from spelling out the situation as clearly as he would have liked. Evelyn Whitehead's view that he was not faithful in his affections, he seems to be trying to say, was based on just one instance of his inconstancy, an instance to which Evelyn quite naturally attached great importance because the subject of that unhappy affection was herself.

The other thing Russell could say against himself was that he had 'a perfectly cold intellect, which insists upon its rights and respects nothing'. This was potentially a far greater threat to his relationship with Ottoline:

It will sometimes hurt you, sometimes seem cynical, sometimes heartless. It is very much more dominant at certain times than at others. You won't much like it. But it belongs with my work – I have deliberately cultivated it, and it is really the main thing that I have put discipline into. In time I believe you will not mind it, but the sudden absolute cessation of feeling when I think must be trying at first. And nothing is sacred to it – it looks at everything quite impartially, as if it were someone else.

'I have preserved my faiths in a very difficult atmosphere,' he told Ottoline, 'the intellect fights every inch of the ground.' And, though he insisted that 'I have its approval in all I feel to you', it must surely have occurred to Ottoline that it was a only a matter of time before his faith in her succumbed to the same force that had defeated all his previous faiths.

For the moment, though, Russell's intellect, rather than laying down the law, was having to submit to a power that was, temporarily at least, still greater. 'I have tried to live on the intellect alone,' he wrote a few days later, 'and, by a natural reaction I am now undervaluing the intellect.' His love for her was so all-absorbing that 'I grudge every thought I cannot share with you . . . I could almost wish I were not a mathematician because you are not . . . I want to give myself utterly and wholly to you.' On 1 May, Russell met Ottoline for a walk around Richmond Park, where, as he put it, 'I belong.' They went to Pembroke Lodge and to the other places of Russell's childhood. Russell spent the day in a rather solemn mood, which in a letter the following day he attributed to a mixture of tiredness and the effects of visiting the Whiteheads. Later in the same letter, however, he dwelt on the subject of his grandmother in a way that suggests another explanation:

> It was rather queer yesterday going with you to places where I had been in childhood, places where I remembered going on sunny days with my grandmother. She would have liked you very much, as soon as she had got over thinking you too smart – she had a passion for dowdiness. You would have liked her, I think, because she was deeply religious and utterly unworldly. She was very full of anxious morality, and you might have felt her stuffy. Like all virtuous people of her time, she was insincere in thought when sincerity would have been shocking – she never, for instance, knew that she hated my brother. My attempts at truth always distressed her, and I soon learnt to keep them to myself.

In his relations with his grandmother, Russell had faced the choice between being true to himself and offending his grandmother's religious sensibility, or pleasing his grandmother by insincerity. He had chosen the latter, with the consequence that he felt towards his grandmother a resentment far deeper and more fierce than he would have done otherwise and adopted a lifelong ability – or perhaps compulsion – to bury his deepest feelings. The awful possibility now beckoned that a similar choice faced him with regard to Ottoline.

During these months Russell did very little work in philosophy. He had agreed to write for the Home University Library – a distinguished series of introductory books on various subjects, edited by Gilbert Murray – a short introduction to philosophy. This should have been a relatively undemanding task, but, though he was contractually obliged to deliver the book in July 1911, by May he had still not started it. He was unconcerned. 'Darling, don't worry about my work,' he wrote to Ottoline. 'I have very little creative work that I ought to do for years to come, in fact I had been wondering how I should keep myself off writing till I had lain fallow for a bit.' As for the book for the series, he added, he had arranged to go away for a fortnight in July with Whitehead, and, if he did not finish it then, he would finish it in August when Ottoline was likely to be away: 'So that is all right.'

In his daily letters to Ottoline, Russell kept very little, if anything, back about himself, his past and his opinions. He quite sincerely wanted Ottoline

to know and understand everything about him. Ottoline, however, had
reasons for keeping some parts of her life to herself – in particular, her
ongoing affair with Henry Lamb. In May, Lamb was in Paris, staying with
his close friends Boris and Julia Anrep, and from there he wrote Ottoline
passionate love letters ('I feel possessed with an immense adoring submitting
love for you, my holy heavenly one!'), urging her to join him. For a week she
prevaricated, and then on 11 May she wrote to Russell with the rather sudden
news that she was going the next day to Paris to visit the Anreps. Once there,
she wrote that she had, by coincidence, happened to meet Lamb. She stayed
in Paris a week, visiting the new exhibitions and enjoying Lamb's company.
She had earlier told Lamb that she was transferring her affections to Russell,
but he had refused to believe it, finding it incredible that any woman would
prefer the stiff, desiccated Russell to a man like himself whose beauty, grace
and talent were universally admired. Throughout her week in Paris, Ottoline
insisted to Lamb that she wanted nothing more than a platonic friendship
with him, but this too he found hard to believe and, in this, he was confirmed
when, on the last night of her stay, Ottoline agreed to sleep with him. When
she returned to London, Lamb wrote to remind her of 'that incredible little
room where you, holy woman, lay . . . and received me'.

In complete ignorance of the true nature of Ottoline's visit to Paris, Russell
continued to write to her every day about his life, his past and their love. 'I
have the most absolute restful confidence in the permanence of our love,' he
told her, 'you are what I have sought through the world, and I do believe I
am what you need.' In her absence, though, his thoughts about their religious
differences were taking on a somewhat harder edge. There was, he wrote,
'something important, which must be approached some day, and which I
rather shrink from approaching'. It had to do with approaching religious
questions with a determination to separate thought from feeling, what one
wanted to believe from what one had a reason to believe. The question
whether God exists should, Russell thought, be approached in the same spirit
as one might approach a purely scientific question like 'Is there a luminiferous
aether?' In Ottoline's belief in God, he thought, her vision was clouded by
desire. He was nervous about engaging in a dispute with her on the question,
however, lest in doing so he spoil the very quality in her with which he had
fallen in love: 'a sort of large-heartedness, and universal love, and power of
reconciling opposites in practice':

I doubt if this quality is compatible with a very sharp clear-cut view of
things; but I should never forgive myself if I took it away from you. And
apart from the harm I should do you, I should do myself harm too, because
this quality in you is infinitely valuable to me – it is . . . what has been
taking all the ruthlessness and harshness out of me.

Ottoline's insistence in reply to this letter that her faith was necessary to
her, and that its loss would cause her to suffer, seemed to harden still further
Russell's attitude. 'I don't want to take away your belief,' he began, 'the
pleasure-loving person in me wd. like to let the whole subject alone':

Still: here is the matter briefly and crudely: I feel no doubt in my mind that yr. beliefs are unfounded, and I have always felt that unfounded beliefs are a misfortune – that in the long run it is best they should always disappear. As regards you, I do not *feel* this, I only abstractly *think* it – I *feel* that yr. beliefs are no barrier between us, and that I don't care to attack them. Yet again I feel I must not be untrue to my faith . . . Of course you wd. suffer if you lost yr. belief – but for my part I wd. rather suffer anything – even morally – than believe what is false or rather what I might find to be false if I looked into it – and I cannot have a different standard for you . . . If once I know yr. belief involves no shadow of disloyalty to truth, I shall be quite easy in my mind and not wish to alter it in any way. But if not, I should not be deterred (I hope) by the knowledge that you would suffer . . . I love you absolutely and with an utter devotion, but for that very reason I cannot, must not shrink from giving you pain any more than I should, if I did right, from giving pain to myself . . . I want to feel absolutely at one with you in what is most serious and important. We must not acquiesce in any more or less superficial harmony. But I am not really troubled, because I know in my depths that it is all right – it is only a mist of words, and our hearts are united. But we must clear away the mist of words.

A few days after Ottoline's return from Paris, Russell told her of what he called his 'dream': 'I want to get free from business, and away from purely technical jobs, and really try to write out something of what I live by in the way of faith . . . I should write everything for you in the first instance, and then prune it to do for others. I see a wonderful future for us stretching through the years, in which we shall help each other to bring good things to the world, and have the bond of mutual strength and a great work in common.' Over the last two weeks of May, their joint commitment to this dream was put to a severe test, when their relationship came under a renewed threat, from which it emerged not only unscathed but very much stronger.

The crisis began with a visit to Ottoline from Roger Fry on 20 May. He had recently returned from Turkey where he had been with Vanessa Bell, with whom he had fallen in love. He was angry at reports he had heard that he was in love with Ottoline, and now demanded to know from Ottoline why she had spread this pernicious rumour. Ottoline denied that she had, but Fry was implacable, and, as Ottoline remembered it: 'After nearly two hours of expostulation on my part and insistence on his, I felt shattered and hopeless and was reduced to tears . . . one of my most intimate and delightful friendships crumbled to dust that Saturday.' From that day on, Fry was unwavering in his hostility to Ottoline. A close friend of some of the most notorious gossips in London literary and artistic circles (including Lytton Strachey and the Bells), Fry was potentially a great nuisance, especially as Ottoline had earlier entrusted him with the secret of her affair with Russell. By the end of the summer, largely through Fry, the secret was out. By then, however, it had largely ceased to matter, because Russell and Alys had, as a result of the next stage of the crisis, come to some sort of permanent agreement.

On the same day that Ottoline was faced with Fry's accusations, Russell went to Fernhurst to spend a night at Van Bridge as part of his agreement with Alys to keep up appearances. He found Alys in what he described to Ottoline as a 'wild and miserable' state. Logan, in discussing with his sister his recent visit to the Morrells at Studland, had casually mentioned Russell's visit there and had gone on to praise Ottoline for her kindness and pleasantness. Alys was furious at what she saw as a betrayal and deceit. 'She began in great anger, threatening divorce,' Russell reported. 'She is very anxious to tell Logan – evidently his friendship for you galled her beyond endurance. Would you mind Logan being told? . . . perhaps he had better be':

> She says, what I find hard to believe, that she had not understood I was going to Studland, and heard it first from Logan. She is very full of anger against us both. I shall have to see more of her than I intended, I think, at any rate for a while. I cannot endure her misery.

'She asked whether if she had a child I would acknowledge it!' Russell added incredulously. It was a possibility he could scarcely take seriously: 'I can't imagine who the father would be. Besides it is a thousand to one against it occurring even if that difficulty had been overcome.' It therefore cost Russell little to say that, of course, he would acknowledge it.

When, a day or two later, Logan was told by Alys of Russell's affair with Ottoline, he reacted with a fury still greater than Alys's and immediately went to Bedford Square to remonstrate with Ottoline. 'Please forgive me,' he wrote the following day, 'and put it down to the feelings of a brother who has been the helpless witness for years of his sister's misery.' In fact, it was the beginning of a life-long obsessional hatred for Ottoline that puzzled and embarrassed even Logan's closest friends. One of them, Robert Gathorne-Hardy, has attributed it to Logan's love for Philip and his consequent jealousy of Ottoline, which 'though violent and vindictive at first, became quiet for a while', but which, with the excuse of the separation of Russell and Alys, 'grew into a monstrous, undiminishing monomaniac obsession, which was very close to madness'. Of all the enemies Ottoline made – and for a kind, generous person she made an astonishing number – Logan Pearsall Smith was undoubtedly the most vehement.

Fortunately for Russell and Ottoline, Philip's resolve to support Ottoline remained unweakened by his old friend's outburst, and equally undiminished was Logan's affection for Philip. The result was that Philip was now able to intervene on Ottoline's behalf and prevent Logan from insisting upon a divorce, which, as Logan knew, would hurt Philip more than anyone else. The Morrells had arranged to spend the weekend at the luxurious country home in Newington, Oxfordshire, of Ethel Sands, the American painter and patron of the arts, and Philip now invited Logan to join them there on the Sunday afternoon to discuss the situation.

Russell, meanwhile, was taking rather a lofty view of the proceedings. 'I feel quite sure Logan and Alys will do nothing irrevocable,' he told Ottoline. 'But I hate to think of such matters and talk of them . . . I find it hard to forgive people who compel one to think of small things in a small way.' Perhaps in an attempt to find refuge from an unbearable situation, Russell's thoughts turned away from the immediate crisis and towards the ethical teachings of Spinoza, who, he told Ottoline, 'is the man to teach love of mankind to people like me'. He offered Ottoline a summary of Spinoza's *Ethics*, emphasising that the effect of Spinoza's teaching is to understand people, instead of feeling indignant towards them when they behave badly. In Spinoza's work, he suggested, may be found a key to the avoidance of strife:

> He takes self-preservation as the root of the passions, and shows how it leads to strife. Then he goes on at last to point out how strife would cease if people put their half into things which all may enjoy together – things in which one person's enjoyment does not prevent another's. The ultimate good which he holds before people is what he calls the 'intellectual love of God' – commentators quarrel as to what he means by it, but I feel I know. He thinks men as individuals are not immortal, but in so far as they love God, their love of God is something deathless, but impersonal. He is filled full with an emotion towards the universe which is at once mystical and intellectual – it must have grown up in him through the feeling of god-like calm that comes when one passes from passionate strife to an impersonal reasoned view of the matter of strife. He thinks strife the fundamental evil, and reason informed by love the cure.

Spinoza, he told Ottoline, pointing out the relevance of this to the matter in hand, had a mind and a heart that were always great, never petty, and 'His life was of a piece with his teaching. If one is in danger of indignation, or of letting desire destroy one's poise, he is just the man to think of':

> There is a very great deal – perhaps the most important part – of what our love gives us, that is quite independent of what others can do. I feel that if we had to part, I should retain all my life the knowledge of what you are, and the knowledge that I have had the perfect and satisfying love which one dreamt of but never hoped to find. That would permanently enrich the world for me, like great poetry or the beauty of nature.

The final moral was: 'they cannot touch our love – they can at worst touch the personal happiness of being together – they cannot touch anything else.'

In subsequent letters, Russell approached the matter from a more prosaic perspective. Among his fears was that the scandal that Logan and Alys threatened would force him to resign his Cambridge lectureship: 'I find I should be rather sorry to be hounded out of this place. It is more nearly a home to me than any other place – I have been here a great deal for the last 20 years, and many important things have happened to me here.' Of the two, he (probably mistakenly) regarded Alys as the greater threat. His view of Logan was that he wanted to hurt Russell but to protect Ottoline, and that once he realised that was impossible, he would drop the idea of divorce. As for Alys, Russell believed, she wanted only to ruin Ottoline. He had, he said, offered to give Alys a divorce on the basis of sham evidence involving another woman, 'but that had no attractions; if you were not brought in, she saw no point in a divorce'.

At the weekend, while he stayed with the Whiteheads anxiously anticipating the negotiations in Newington, Russell tried to imagine life without Ottoline, and found that when he did so, his feelings were far removed indeed from those recommended by Spinoza's ethics: 'I fear I should come to hate Alys with a hatred which would poison everything. I have tried to tell myself that I should stand it well, but I don't believe that is really the truth.' In 'Free Man's Worship' he had recommended that one should try to live with no thought for private happiness but only for a greater good, and for a while he had believed he could do it. 'But I was wrong; and the fire gradually died down, and the inspiration left me, and life grew cold and bare – until you came into my life, and with your love all other good things came back too, and the long night was like an evil dream – scarcely remembered and fading quickly into nothingness. But the thought of going back into the night is almost beyond what I can bear.'

On 28 May, Logan kept his appointment to meet the Morrells at Ethel Sands' house, and, though he was as vehement in his denunciation of Ottoline and Russell as ever, it was clear that he had no intention of insisting on a divorce. Instead, the threat he came armed with was that, if the Morrells continued to see Russell, he would break with them. This was a price Ottoline was only too glad to pay, and so, with considerably more sacrifice, was Philip. 'We decided', as Ottoline put it, 'that Logan's friendship, on the conditions he had laid down, must be given up.' The effect, she wrote, 'was to make me appreciate and love Philip more than ever. I felt now that I had chosen the path, and must gather myself together, and devote whatever time and energy I could spare to Bertie.'

After leaving Newington, Logan travelled with Alys to Cambridge to spell out to Russell their conditions for a separation. They would not go to court, they promised, and they would tell all their friends that Russell and Alys had agreed to live apart, not because another woman was involved, but because they were incompatible: but in return Russell was to promise never to spend another night together with Ottoline. The implied threat was that Russell would never know when he was being watched and that, if, through any source, Alys or Logan heard that he had been observed sleeping under the same roof as Ottoline, legal proceedings would begin immediately.

If Alys thought this condition would hurt Ottoline, she was much mistaken, but, for Russell, it was a very onerous one indeed, and one that he was inclined to hold responsible for the long-term failure of his relationship with Ottoline. In the short term, though, considering what might have been the outcome, his reaction to the weekend's negotiations was one of enormous relief. 'I gather it is quite all right,' he wrote that Sunday night:

Logan and Alys have been here and have agreed to everything. She now agrees to a complete parting, and nothing legal. So all is well. There need be no further agitations. She has a good side which has come uppermost.

For the moment I am too tired to feel much except the stretched cord relaxing.

The following day, the prospect of having his every move with Ottoline watched by private detectives, and of never being free to spend a night with her again, seemed to offer little to celebrate and he found his hatred for Alys returning with renewed intensity: 'whenever I am not on the watch, my imagination is busy concocting letters to her, which would be calculated to make her life unbearable, and would probably succeed. They flash before me in a moment before I know what I am doing. I thoroughly realise this is base, and I am trying to cope with it.'

Alys kept to her side of the bargain, and wrote to her family and friends about their separation without mentioning – indeed, explicitly denying – that Russell had fallen in love with someone else. 'We are telling our friends and begging them not to blame either of us,' she told her sister. 'This is just utter incompatibility – Bertie cannot force his love, and I cannot live with him while he feels as he does. But he easily changes, and I do not give up all hope for the future, as I still love him very very much.' The implication that their separation might be temporary was repeated in other letters she wrote at the time, including one to Russell himself, who became so alarmed by the suggestion that he asked Evelyn Whitehead to make it clear to Alys that their separation was permanent. Evelyn reported back that Russell and Ottoline had more to fear from Logan than from Alys, and that Alys was 'in a very good mood, and determined to put it through in the best way'.

Nevertheless, in her subsequent letters to relations, friends and colleagues, such as the one to G. E. Moore on 18 June, explaining why Russell was staying on in college during the summer vacation, Alys continued to say that she and Russell had agreed to separate 'for a time'. 'I shall always love him,' she told her sister Mary, 'and shall be glad if he wants to come back.' It was a hope she never abandoned throughout the next forty years of her life. As Robert Gathorne-Hardy has remarked: 'There was something like mania in her unperishing love for Russell.' From the summer of 1911 on, she devoted herself to looking after Logan and to working for various good causes. But she always kept an eye on Russell's career, and would sometimes even take a walk in the area where Russell happened to be living and would peer unobtrusively through his windows. There was never in her mind any question of marrying anybody else, or any doubt that she still belonged with Russell.

For Russell, the break had come not a moment too soon and, the more final and complete it turned out to be, the better. He was delighted to be rid once and for all of a woman who had got on his nerves for the last nine years. What slightly irked him was that at Cambridge he was obliged to hide his delight. His separation from Alys was now common knowledge, and if he looked too pleased about it, it was bound to fuel the rumours that were already rife that he had found happiness with someone else. The indomitable Jane Harrison at Newnham, for one, was convinced that Russell had left Alys for another woman. Fortunately for Russell, however, she had been informed by what she considered to be a 'reliable authority' that the woman in question was married and living in Cambridge.

On 12 June Russell met Jane Harrison and tried to convince her that there was no such woman, giving her, he told Ottoline, 'a false impression favourable to myself'. The impression he was aiming to create was that of an 'injured martyr'. 'It is funny that the welfare of Philip and Julian should depend upon my assuming virtues I don't possess,' he wrote on 14 June, 'but since it is so, may God give me strength to play the hypocrite – to manage the half-repressed sigh, the sad smile, the praise of Alys which only exhibits my own nobility of soul & all the rest of the apparatus. When I am bankrupt I can hire myself to a troop of nigger minstrels as the melancholy man who is the foil for the clown.'

'Pretending to be heart-broken when one is filled with happiness is rather a dirty business,' he admitted, but 'as it has to be done I get my fun out of it'. His performance, however, was not quite as good as he considered it, and a week later he learned from Evelyn Whitehead that Jane Harrison, far from being as Russell had reported 'obviously quite reassured', was now more than ever convinced that Russell had a mistress and was beginning to name possible suspects. This was no longer fun, but a serious nuisance. Evelyn even believed that Alys and Logan might have to let out the truth in order to protect the innocent: 'Apparently Mrs Cornford has been mentioned.'

Russell did not have to put up with this atmosphere for long. At the beginning of July 1911 he set off for a fortnight's holiday in the country with North Whitehead. They stayed at Wyche, a small village in the Malvern Hills, in Worcestershire. It was exactly the kind of setting in which Russell usually worked best, and he had reason to hope that a good proportion of *The Problems of Philosophy* might get written during the two weeks. For one reason or another, however, he found that he made little progress with it. The walks and discussions with Whitehead were no doubt a distraction, as was the seemingly endless quantity of proofreading (of *Principia Mathematica* and of one of his Paris lectures) that he had to get through. But these distractions were not by themselves an insuperable barrier to work.

A deeper reason for his inability to get on with his writing was the feeling that turning his mind to philosophical work – or, anyway, to this particular kind of philosophical work – meant turning his attention away from Ottoline. 'I am feeling again what I have almost not felt these four months,' he wrote to Ottoline at the end of his two weeks in Worcestershire, 'the infinite unendurable weariness of inward mental strife.' This was, he thought, 'largely the result of having been working again: I find myself tired out, and on the physical side quite dead; but thinking goes on and on, all the more':

I feel my task of thought just as if it were an order from a superior power – something which *must* be done, without reasoning about it or caring to know why; and I know that it involves the utmost of my powers, a stretching and goading of my intellect which is curiously painful . . . I wonder whether you know and understand the odd sense of dedication that I have towards Philosophy. It has nothing to do with reason, or with any deliberate judgment that Philosophy is important. It is merely what I *have* to do. I often hate the task, but I cannot escape it – and of course at bottom I don't wish to.

His introduction to philosophy was to deal only with metaphysics and the theory of knowledge. 'As I have to keep off religion and morals,' he told Ottoline, 'I can't write anything that wd. interest you very much and this worries me.' He felt, he wrote in an earlier letter, that 'so long as we both have our work utterly separate it makes a separation in what is important':

> I *will* associate you with my work, somehow, in time, even if it means altering the nature of my work. I have done all I ever intended to do in the way of mathematics – when the publication of this big book is finished, I should in any case do no more in that line . . . Most of what I want to write in philosophy will be more or less popular, & I can work in the sort of things we have talked about. I have never before felt anything in my life as important as my work – now I feel our love is more important than anything.

Ottoline and Philip were spending the summer at their country house, Peppard Cottage, in Henley, Oxfordshire, and whenever he had an opportunity, Russell would come to Peppard for the day – taking care, naturally, to stay overnight at a nearby hotel. During these visits he became quite close to Ottoline's daughter Julian, whom he encouraged to come and chatter to him while Ottoline, whose health was becoming increasingly fragile, went to lie down and rest. These moments of quasi-fatherhood served to increase still further Russell's own desperate need for a child, and he began once more to press Ottoline on the subject. He told her that when he made love to her he could not keep the thought of producing a child out of his mind and was convinced that Ottoline, too, had the same secret thoughts. Rather than destroy this cherished illusion, Ottoline chose to lie: 'Yes my darling, it was in my thoughts too all the time you were here, and I was too shy to say anything':

> Darling I *do long* for it too but I would rather it did not come *yet*. I think the strain would be very great. I know you understand but . . . I don't know if it ever would be possible for me on account of the operation.

'I want you to *know*,' she added – rather ominously from Russell's point of view – 'that I shall absolutely understand if in the future the longing for a child is too great and you make other ties.'

This was bad enough, but a few days later Ottoline went further and suggested that, as the love she and Russell had for each other was not selfish, it would not exclude 'affection and love' for other people. It was a tentative step, on her part, towards coming clean about the nature of her friendship with Henry Lamb, with whom, while Russell was in Worcestershire, she had spent a good deal of time, doing the things she liked doing best: going to art

exhibitions, watching ballet and discussing art and literature. Lamb's studio
was in Henley, a short walk away from Peppard Cottage, and Russell had seen
him once or twice on his visits to Ottoline, but it never occurred to him that
Ottoline and Lamb were lovers. Ottoline's talk of affection and love for other
people, however, worried him. On the day he received her letter, he had
suffered, he told her, all day 'by a hypothetical jealousy'. He thought she must
be thinking primarily of *his* affection and love for other people, and he assured
her that this was not what he wanted:

> But I can't help feeling that you also think that *I* ought not to stand in *your*
> way in some hypothetical future. I hope I shouldn't. But my nature is not
> large enough to avoid jealousy . . . If you gave love to anyone else, though
> I could acquiesce and remain a devoted friend, and not in any way alter my
> *opinion* of you, I should not continue to give love. Altogether, you would
> have a first-class tragedy on your hands. If I gave love myself to someone
> else, it would be deeply unfortunate for me – morally I should suffer, and
> there would be a profound inward damage which would lead to spiritual
> ruin . . . It is immeasurably more important to my welfare that I should
> maintain my exclusive love for you than that I should have a child by
> someone else.

Partly because of this 'hypothetical jealousy', and partly because of his
work, Russell had spent the day in a black depression. He was staying the
night at the home of Lucy 'Lion' Phillimore, an old friend of Alys's, and
being with Lion had, he said, 'vividly recalled to me the early days of my love
for Alys, when she was young and happy and blooming, and full of simple
un-self-distrustful kindness':

> Now she is broken, tortured, twisted, with no self-confidence, no hope, no
> purpose. It is all my doing.

'I have written myself out of the blue devils now,' Russell claimed at the
end of the letter, 'and I hardly know what it was all about.' The root of it, he
was inclined to think, was his conviction that Ottoline would grow tired of
him: 'And the moment anything troubles me about you, it opens the
floodgates to all the sorrows of mankind':

> Living without any religious beliefs in not easy. Darling my love to you is
> rather terrible really – it is so absorbing and so necessary to my life. And
> I dread your feeling oppressed by it, and feeling that it is a prison. It shan't
> be a prison to you my Dearest if I can help it.

After returning from his holiday in Worcestershire, Russell decided to
spend the rest of the summer, not in Cambridge, but in lodgings in Ipsden,
a village just a few miles away from Peppard. Every day Russell would bicycle
over to Peppard, arriving at noon and staying until midnight. It was an
unusually hot summer and he and Ottoline spent a good deal of time outside

in the surrounding woods, where they ate picnic lunches, read to each other from Plato, Spinoza and Shelley, and (according to Ottoline's recollections) 'talked of life, politics and things to come'. In a rather over-worked metaphor, Ottoline describes these discussions in the woods as 'a journey through tangled and perplexing forest in search of light and truth, tearing down old dusty growths in my mind, and opening dark windows that had been blocked up in the lower depths of my being'. She would often want to hide 'under shady, sentimental willow trees', but Russell, either gently taking her by the hand, or roughly shaking her and telling her she was not being honest, would insist on her facing the truth. 'It was exhausting but delightful for me to have my mind kept in strict order,' Ottoline writes:

> The beauty of his mind, the pure fire of his soul began to affect me and attract me, and magnetise me with an attraction almost physical, carrying me up into ecstasies such as Donne expresses; his unattractive body seemed to disappear, while our spirits united in a single flame, as if his soul penetrated mine.

The implication here that Russell was at his most physically attractive when seen as a disembodied spirit confirms a view that Russell himself expressed late in life when he wrote about Ottoline: 'Her feelings were romantic and sentimental rather than passionate, and my feelings seemed to her quite unreasonable. I think she thought of me in terms of troubadours and courtly love, not in terms of everyday earthly passion.'

In the summer of 1911, however, Ottoline was supported in this view of Russell by his own intense preoccupation with spiritual and religious matters, and by his determination to see his love for her in the light of that preoccupation. The Spinozistic ideal of overcoming strife by transcending one's own finite ego and taking an 'eternal' view of the world, and his experience of having been spiritually *released* by his love for Ottoline, had somehow become identified with the image of having been released from prison. It was as if Russell's love for Ottoline had become for him a living revelation of the religion that he had earlier outlined in 'The Pilgrimage of Life': the religion of contemplation. The prison now was one's finite self, with all its petty strife and turbulence, from which release could come either through Spinoza's 'intellectual love of God' or through something like his love for Ottoline. That, in elaborating this view, Russell was providing a philosophical foundation for Ottoline's refusal to acknowledge his 'earthly passions' did not, apparently, occur to him.

There had been a time, he told Ottoline, when Hamlet's line, 'The world's a prison and Denmark one of its worst wards' had been constantly on his mind, but 'now there is no prison for me. I reach out to the stars, & through the ages, & everywhere the radiance of your love lights the world for me.' The thought of conveying this experience in a way that might bring enlightenment to others was one that inspired him far more than the relatively mundane task of writing *The Problems of Philosophy*, and, while he was still struggling to finish the latter, he was conceiving in his mind a book – to be called, naturally, 'Prisons' – that would attempt the former. When he moved into his lodgings at Ipsden he hoped, he told Ottoline, that they would give him his own key so that, at night, he could be free to take walks while he thought about this new book. If it turned out as he hoped it would, 'it might be to our time what "Sartor Resartus" was to an earlier generation.'

Ottoline was delighted with the idea, and began to refer to the project as 'our child', hoping, no doubt, that for Russell it would be an adequate substitute for the more earthly kind of offspring. 'Our child is a great joy,' she wrote on 28 July. 'I believe it has come out of our *complete* union just as much as an ordinary child would have.' It was a notion that Russell was, for the moment, only too pleased to adopt. 'You liberate my best,' he wrote to her on the same day:

> and make me know a wisdom to which my whole being responds; I feel that at last I see the world as it is natural to my best to see it. I have been slow to achieve inward harmony, and but for you I might never have achieved it. But now I possess it . . . And out of this inner harmony I feel the power to give a great gift to the world – our child.

The thought seemed to give Russell a new lease of life and he returned to his work with fresh inspiration and a burst of energy. He felt, he told Ottoline, 'like Napoleon playing 6 games of chess and dictating to 7 secretaries all at the same time'. He was working at both 'Prisons' and *The Problems of Philosophy*, and checking more proofs of *Principia Mathematica*. 'It is the force of your belief in the spiritual things that is such a strength to me,' he wrote to Ottoline on 6 August. The intellectual and the spiritual had, at last, been united: 'Often I hardly know whether it is your thoughts or mine that I am expressing, they seem so much the same.'

Though *The Problems of Philosophy* concentrates for the most part on comparatively dry aspects of the subject, Russell found a way of incorporating into it something of his 'vision' by ending the book with a chapter on 'The Value of Philosophy', which, in presenting philosophy as a means by which one could transcend the limits of the immediate and the purely personal, allowed him to use whole paragraphs that he had written for 'Prisons'. 'The man who has no tincture of philosophy', he writes, 'goes through life imprisoned in the prejudices derived from common sense, from the habitual beliefs of his age or his nation, and from convictions which have grown up in his mind without the cooperation or consent of his deliberate reason.' Philosophical thinking frees us from the 'private world of instinctive interests':

> Unless we can so enlarge our interests as to include the whole outer world, we remain like a garrison in a beleaguered fortress . . . if our life is to be great and free, we must escape this prison and this strife.

'Personal and private things', he says, 'become a prison to the intellect.' Philosophy frees the intellect so that it sees as a God might see: 'without a *here* and *now*, without hopes and fears, without the trammels of customary beliefs and traditional prejudices, calmly, dispassionately, in the sole and exclusive desire of knowledge – knowledge as impersonal, as purely contemplative, as it is possible for man to attain.' The book ends with the thought that in philosophical contemplation, 'the mind . . . is rendered great, and becomes capable of that union with the universe which constitutes its highest good.'

'How anxious I shall be to know how that final chapter fares,' Ottoline wrote on 11 August. 'I feel awfully anxious about our child.' She was convinced, she wrote the following day, that Russell's vision would have a transforming effect on his readers and 'lift them out into life and freedom and love and union with others and service'. In this she was simply reflecting back to him Russell's own sentiments. 'To give religion to those who cannot believe in God & immortality has been for years my deepest hope,' he wrote on the same day, 'but the fire left me, & I lost faith. Now I have a deeper, wider, calmer vision than ever before, & your faith makes mine easy.' He was aware, however, that, in time, 'the vision will sleep and be replaced by an icy intellect', but, he added: 'you will know it is only an interval.'

By 18 August the last chapter of *The Problems of Philosophy* was finished, and Russell began to devote himself to putting 'Prisons' into some kind of order. He had, he told Ottoline, at last got 'a really clear vision' of the book, and he provided her with a detailed abstract, chapter by chapter. There were to be seven chapters in all, beginning with an analysis of the 'nature and value of religion', which, like the earlier 'Pilgrimage of Life', saw its essence as lying in the contemplation of eternal truths, and ending with three chapters on contemplation that would 'merely expand what I wrote before'. In between were to be three chapters on, respectively: the world of mathematics, dealing with the platonic existence of universals; the physical world, emphasising the beauty of nature; and the past world, emphasising the importance of history. Ottoline might have been forgiven for thinking that the book as outlined failed to live up to its promise. Despite Russell's claim that 'The Vision is very strong in me tonight – the night is unbelievably beautiful and the wind is full of mystic wonder', the abstract made the book look disappointingly humdrum.

A few days later Russell moved out of Ipsden into a new set of lodgings in the neighbouring village of Checkendon, where he stayed for a fortnight. He devoted this time to working on 'Prisons', without either the distractions or the inspiration of Ottoline's company. Ottoline's health had been getting steadily worse throughout the summer. Her doctor diagnosed neuritis and suggested that she spend some time in a spa resort on the Continent. She chose Marienbad and, having persuaded Philip to agree to Russell's joining her there for a few days in September, set off on 27 August.

On the day she left, Russell reported that he had written seventeen pages of 'Prisons', and no doubt most of the first draft of the book was written before he left for Marienbad on 9 September. Neither this first draft nor any of its revisions have survived. Soon after he finished the book, Russell became extremely dissatisfied with it and presumably destroyed it. What survive are some fragments, from which he took sentences or whole paragraphs to use in other pieces of writing, most notably the last chapter of *The Problems of Philosophy* and the article written in 1912 on 'The Essence of Religion'. 'In the summer I thought Prisons was great,' he wrote the following winter, 'now I see that it was only great in idea, not in achievement.' The reason it failed, he seemed to think, was that it was expository: 'One must have a more artistic form.' Ottoline's own view of its stylistic failings was that it was 'rather too kept down for the subject' and 'too much like a lecture'.

The criticism that hit Russell hardest, however, was that of Evelyn Whitehead, who was blunt enough to point out – as both Russell's abstract and the surviving fragments reveal – that it was just plain boring. It had, she told Russell, 'the dullness that comes to middle-aged men when they marry'. She also said that 'the emotions spoken of are not spoken of so as to be felt' and that 'the intellectual and emotional parts don't belong together.' That Evelyn's criticisms concerned only the style of the book and not its ideas seems to have given Russell the hope that, if only he could find a more appropriate literary form, he might still produce the 'great gift' of which he had dreamed.

In fact, though Russell took no notice of it, Ottoline herself had made a much more penetrating criticism of the book, and had put her finger on why it *had* to fail, when she complained about its excessive emphasis on the impersonal. Russell himself described it as 'a kind of homage to the unimportance of the individual', but this was not something Ottoline, at least, wished to pay homage to. On the contrary, she insisted, '*Individuality is so precious.*' Hers was a personal religion, the essence of which was in no way captured by Russell's Spinozistic vision of impartiality and the disappearance of the self. Throughout the surviving fragments runs a repetition of the thought that 'Self in all its forms – in thought, in feeling, in action – is a prison' and that 'The essence of religion is union with the universe achieved by subordination of the demands of the Self.' The divine part of man, Russell writes, 'feeling the individual to be but of small account, thinks little of death, and finds its hopes independent of personal continuance'. This doctrine provides a basis for dismissing 'earthly love' in favour of the heavenly kind, in a way far more radical than anything Ottoline might ever have wished:

> besides the earthly love, which demands that the object shall be useful, beautiful or good, there is a heavenly love, which loves all indifferently.

The paradox at the heart of 'Prisons' – a paradox hinted at in Ottoline's criticism – is that, though it was inspired by the tremendous passion aroused in Russell by Ottoline, by identifying his love for her with an exalted view of 'impartial worship', of the 'intellectual love of God', it dismisses passion itself as of no account. It thus could not possibly have done justice to the emotions that inspired it. Nor could it have given expression to Russell's enormous sense of release from his dreary life with Alys, for that was not a release *from* the self, it was a release *of* the self, a release that left him finally able to be himself again. Ottoline saw something of this when she asked him whether he could not give more thought to the great diversity among individuals, to the belief that each person could only hope to become a complete whole by trying to 'learn what is best for *him*'.

Increasingly frustrated by Ottoline's denial of his 'earthly love', Russell had yet provided her with a doctrine that showed why one ought to deny such love. The final irony was that this doctrine was not one she found attractive. What Russell had not yet sufficiently realised was that her denial of his earthly passion was the outcome, not of a universally held belief, a general theory, but of an individual reaction. It was not that she sought to rise above such passion altogether, simply that she did not find *him* sexually attractive.

8

HARD DRY REASONING

On 9 September 1911, Russell travelled to Marienbad to join Ottoline. They had planned to spend a week together, with Russell staying in a hotel close to Ottoline's and coming every day to Ottoline's hotel to spend the day with her. These plans were spoilt, however, by the manager of Ottoline's hotel, who did not want his establishment used to pursue what was clearly an extra-marital affair and consequently banned Russell from the hotel. After just a few days Russell was forced to cut his visit short and, somewhat to Ottoline's relief, he returned to England, leaving her to try and repair her reputation in the eyes of the hotel manager. When Philip arrived to join Ottoline, the manager took pleasure in telling him that another gentleman had been to visit her in her room every day before he arrived. To the manager's disappointment but to Ottoline's great relief, Philip remained as imperturbably loyal as ever, and said only that he was glad to hear of it.

After a long return journey to England and an overnight stop in London, it was not until 16 September that Russell arrived back in Ipsden. He returned in a mood for hard work – 'I have the energy of 20 steam-engines, just now,' he told Ottoline – and found that he had plenty to do. Waiting for him were a large pile of proofs, a Fellowship dissertation to examine and 'endless letters', among which was one from H. Wildon Carr, the secretary of the Aristotelian Society. Russell had that summer been elected the Society's President, a post that imposed upon him the duty of giving the opening address at its annual meeting, which was normally held on the first Monday of November. Carr, however, was writing to say that the French philosopher Henri Bergson would be in London in the last week of October and had expressed an interest in attending the meeting. Would Russell mind, therefore, if it was brought forward one week to enable Bergson to come?

Bergson's reputation has declined considerably in recent decades, but in the autumn of 1911 his fame, in both France and England, eclipsed that of any other philosopher. His most celebrated work, *Creative Evolution*, published in France in 1907, had appeared in English that year and was read by all who considered themselves abreast of the times. Whenever Bergson appeared in London, he was fêted by such writers as George Bernard Shaw and Israel Zangwill, and, in literary and artistic circles at least, he was established as the pre-eminently fashionable philosopher of his day. By suggesting that the

Aristotelian Society should re-schedule its annual meeting at late notice to accommodate him, Carr was therefore probably acting as most of his members would have wished. That did not, however, prevent Russell from feeling rather irritated by it. 'Owing to Bergson I shall have to begin my Aristotelian paper while I am here,' he wrote grumpily to Ottoline.

He felt obliged, nevertheless, not only to agree to the request but also to read up on Bergson's work, about which he knew little more than what everyone, in 1911, would have known, whether or not they had read it: namely, that it was a celebration of the *élan vital*, the mysterious life force, which Bergson sought to protect from the clutches of the life-denying counter-force of abstract reasoning. It was not a doctrine that recommended itself to someone of Russell's cast of mind, but in Paris at Easter he had bought Bergson's *L'Évolution créatrice* and had made at least a half-hearted attempt to master it. Under the intoxication of his first night with Ottoline, however, he had been unable to get very far with it. 'I remember sitting in my hotel bedroom struggling to concentrate my mind on him,' he told Ottoline, 'but it would wander off to a wholly irrelevant topic. The élan vital had hold on me too much for me to wish to read about it.'

Now, in Ipsden in September, Russell was in a quite different, more sober frame of mind. 'My imagination is empty for the moment,' he wrote to Ottoline, 'because I put it all into "Prisons", and I feel the need for hard dry reasoning – it has a kind of tonic bracing effect.' The thought of Bergson coming to engage him in philosophical debate, too, concentrated his mind, and, alongside his work on his Presidential Address for the Aristotelian Society, he made a close and critical study of Bergson's work. Having just completed what he had reason to believe would be a best-selling introduction to philosophy and a book on religion that he hoped would rival Carlyle's *Sartor Resartus* in its influence, Russell was beginning to see himself as a popular philosopher whose fame would in time rival Bergson's own, and his preparations for meeting Bergson have about them something of the quality of a boxer's preparations for a title fight against the reigning champion.

He had about a month before the start of term at Cambridge and he was determined to use it well. The pattern of his day, he told Ottoline, was as follows: 'I work in the morning and between tea and dinner. Sometimes a bit after dinner too. In the afternoon I write to you and go out on my bicycle to post my letter somewhere not here. The rest of the day I read Karamozov or go little walks for meditation.' His reading of Dostoyevsky had been influenced by Ottoline and, on the whole, he was enjoying him: 'But I feel the madness of his people, and they make more impression than I quite like. I find Rogojin in the other book [*The Idiot*] dwells in my mind.'

Russell was determined to get himself back into the frame of mind required for rigorous philosophical work. He had, he told Ottoline, 'been very full these days of the sense that I must not grow soft and self-indulgent':

What this means is that I must keep up my interest in abstract and remote things that can't directly interest you. I long so much to share every thought with you that I find it hard to absorb myself in matters in which you can't join – it was so heavenly doing writing that really concerned you ... I used to come back here late, so full of you, and of life and vision – like one inspired.

Now, however, 'my work has no connection with you except that I must do it to live worthily', and he found that, when he did succeed in absorbing himself in things unrelated to her, 'my brain works very well'. He already had some new ideas for his Aristotelian paper, which he 'discussed' with Spinoza and Leibniz, busts of whom he kept on his mantelpiece: 'I do feel myself in a way at home among the great philosophers ... I have conversations with them in which I explain how I am carrying on their work, and I can hardly resist the feeling that they hear and approve – sometimes it is all but a delusion, it grows so strong.'

A few days later, his paper 'On the Relations of Universal and Particulars' was finished. Though convinced it would puzzle its audience, Russell declared himself pleased with it. Its theme was one he had touched upon in a more accessible way in *The Problems of Philosophy*, particularly in the chapter 'The World of Universals', where his concern was to insist that, in addition to the world of ordinary, everyday experience – of 'particulars' – there was another world, that of abstract ideas or 'universals', Plato's 'World of Ideas', a world that he described in evocative, almost poetic terms, as 'unchangeable, rigid, exact, delightful to the mathematician, the logician, the builder of metaphysical systems, and all who love perfection more than life'. The world of particulars contains 'all thoughts and feelings, all the data of sense, and all physical objects' and is, in contrast to the world of universals, 'fleeting, vague, without sharp boundaries'.

In this new paper, Russell sought to define more rigorously these basic metaphysical categories, and to defend the reality of both universals and particulars against those philosophers (like Hume and Berkeley) who insisted that only particulars are real, and those (like, in some interpretations, Bradley and Plato) who insisted that only universals are real. Russell's novel approach to this ancient issue was to give quasi-physical, spatio-temporal definitions of the categories involved. Thus, particulars, the ordinary objects of experience, are defined by the fact that they cannot be in two places at the same time. Universals, in his account, are of two kinds: relations (such as 'to the left of'), which are never in *any* place at any time, and qualities (such as whiteness) which can be in *more* than one place at the same time.

Whatever merits the theory might have – and Russell was soon to be convinced that it introduced as many problems as it solved – it was undeniably ingenious and showed at least that Russell was still capable of producing original philosophical ideas. One slight problem with it as a theme for the occasion was that it did not have any obvious bearing on Bergson's work. When he returned to Cambridge on 30 September, Russell found waiting for him a letter from Bergson, saying that he was looking forward to hearing Russell but did not expect to agree with him. 'I think I must add some paragraphs for him,' Russell told Ottoline:

His view is that the raw material is a continuous flux to which no concepts are exactly applicable. I might suggest that the continuous flux is a philosophic construction, not 'raw' at all.

Before making such an addition, Russell devoted himself anew to the study of Bergson's work, a study that was to dominate his thoughts, not just for the month prior to the Aristotelian Society meeting, but for several months after that. Underlying the intensity of his preoccupation with Bergson, and to a large extent motivating it, was his sense that in combating Bergson he was defending the intellect in what he saw as a titanic struggle against the forces of unreason. As he later put it: 'if he [Bergson] fails in his condemnation of the intellect, the intellect will succeed in its condemnation of him, for between the two it is war to the knife.'

This is an attitude that sits uneasily with Russell's concern throughout the summer to preserve the essence of religion, and one that seems to reflect a growing tension between his sense of vocation as a philosopher and his love for Ottoline, who, in a 'war to the knife' between the intellect and intuition, would be more likely to take the side of the latter. Indeed, in Russell's disparaging descriptions of Bergson's views, Ottoline would, one suspects, have recognised many of her own opinions:

He is the antithesis to me; he universalises the particular soul under the name of élan vital and loves instinct. Ugh!
(2 October)

He thinks the intellect a wicked imp whose practice is to show us everything as space and matter; what reveals the real truth is activity, especially artistic creation.
(9 October)

One of his chapters ends with a wonderful peroration in which he compares human life to a cavalry charge – he describes the whole human race careering so madly that they pass all obstacles, 'perhaps even Death' . . . It is characteristic of him to choose for his ideal a state of things in which reason is entirely dormant . . . He has a very strong imagination, and has conceived the world through and through according to his scheme. For those who like Life and Action and Movement, he is admirable. He hates Plato, because the Ideas are static, and he wants everything to be dynamic, like the cavalry charge. When he is better, he conceives life to be essentially like artistic creation, in which a more or less blind impulse urges one towards something, without one's knowing what beforehand; then, what is created, it is seen to be what was wanted.
(12 October)

To Russell, talk of instinct, action, movement and blind impulses may have sounded repugnantly 'finite', but to Ottoline, these things (especially when allied to the process of artistic creation), far from being antithetical to her

religion, were all part of it. She may have used the word 'eternal' a good deal
when discussing her religion, but Russell was misled if he thought this had
much to do with his own understanding of 'the infinite'. As became
increasingly clear to Ottoline, if not to Russell, her sense of the eternal was
emphatically not that which lay at the centre of his 'religion of contemplation'
– the unchanging, static, Platonic forms exemplified by mathematics. It was
a more dynamic view, one that revered the eternal as manifest precisely *in* the
blind impulse to create.

In his almost desperate desire to believe that his thoughts and Ottoline's
were the same, Russell was often wilfully blind to the evidence that they were
not. While he was working on 'Prisons', he had gone so far as to claim: 'Often,
I can hardly know whether it is your thoughts or mine that I am expressing,
they seem so much the same.' But, now that he was possessed less by 'the
vision' and more by 'hard dry reasoning', it became increasingly clear to him
that this was not so.

Once he realised that Ottoline's faith was not, after all, identical to his own
'religion of contemplation', Russell began to attack it as if engaged in yet
another 'fight to the knife'. The first salvo in this battle was launched just a
few days after returning from Marienbad:

> You with your God and your immortality escape the hardest things, the
> eternal partings, the waste, the sense of injuries which can never be
> repaired. How anyone can believe that a good God devised such a hell is
> astonishing to me.

On 11 October, the day after term began, he told Ottoline that what he
considered the most wonderful thing about her was 'the sense of infinity' she
gave him. 'Do you think it comes from love of God and would be impossible
without belief in Him?' he asked. 'I wonder.' Ottoline, of course, insisted that
it did, prompting him a few days later to renew the attack in stronger terms
and in a way that made it clear that, in this dispute, no less than in that with
Bergson, he saw himself as the defender, not just of his opinions but of reason
itself:

> I am very very much interested in what you write about God. I think, like
> most believers, you greatly overestimate what your belief in God does for
> you – I know I did when I believed. You would find quite as much infinity
> in the world without him. I have realised that hitherto you are quite
> unshaken, because your belief is not based on reason and therefore can't be
> attacked by reason. If I could make you feel that unbelief is nobler I should
> begin to have hope.

In his campaign against Bergson, Russell was given the opportunity to
launch a direct and public attack when, at the start of term, he was asked by
C. K. Ogden, the undergraduate secretary of a discussion group called 'The
Heretics', to give a paper. Offering to give one on Bergson, he promptly
dropped the idea of adding something to his Aristotelian paper and instead

20 Russell, aged nineteen, at
Trinity College, Cambridge.

21 G. E. Moore.

22 A group of Russell's friends at Trinity, showing Charles Trevelyan
(far right, centre row) and (left and centre, top row) Crompton
and Theodore Llewelyn Davies.

23 Friday's Hill House, 1894, with (from left to right) Hannah,
Robert, Alys and Logan Pearsall Smith.

24 Hannah in 1893 (aged
sixty-one), by Sir William
Rothenstein.

25 Hannah and Robert.

26 Alys, 1894.

27 and 28 Alys and her sister, Mary, 1894.

29 Alys and Bertrand Russell, around the time of their wedding in 1894.

31 Lucy Donnelly.

30 Helen Thomas.

32 Walt Whitman.

33 and 34 Evelyn and Alfred North Whitehead.

35 The Millhangar, with Alys sitting in the porch.

36 The Mill House, Grantchester.

37 Alys, 1905 ('Little duties keep me going from day to day. But they don't satisfy the awful craving for Bertie's love').

38 Alys by the sundial at Friday's Hill, 1905.

39 Russell at the time of the Wimbledon by-election, 1907.

set about writing an extended critique of Bergson, which, when it was delivered in the spring of 1912, became one of his most widely celebrated papers.

About a week later, Ogden was visiting Russell again on business connected with 'The Heretics' when, as Russell put it to Ottoline, 'an unknown German appeared, speaking very little English but refusing to speak German. He turned out to be a man who had learned engineering at Charlottenburg, but during his course had acquired, by himself, a passion for the philosophy of mathematics, and had now come to Cambridge on purpose to hear me.' When, later that day, Russell went to give his lecture, he was pleased to find 'my German duly established'. The following day, Russell reported that 'My German friend threatens to be an infliction, he came back with me after my lecture & argued till dinner time – obstinate & perverse, but I think not stupid.' As Russell eventually discovered, this 'German' was actually an Austrian, and his name was Ludwig Wittgenstein. He would, in time, exert a decisive influence on Russell's life, but for the moment he remained only a figure of curiosity, fun and slight condescension, referred to, not by his name, but only as 'my German', 'my German engineer', and even, on occasion, 'my ferocious German'.

On Saturday, 21 October, Ottoline finally returned to London. She had been away five weeks. 'Anybody else that I had seen 5 weeks ago I should feel I had seen quite lately,' Russell wrote after he had seen her briefly, 'but with you it seemed an age.' After leaving Marienbad, she and Philip had travelled widely, visiting Prague, Milan, Pavia and finally Lausanne, where Ottoline had become a patient of Dr Combe, an expert in neuralgia recommended by Ethel Sands. Much had happened to both her and Russell during the separation. 'I felt quite shy at first,' Russell told her, 'feeling I must find where you were again':

Also I thought you wouldn't like me in the mood I get into at Cambridge, I don't like the mood – it is hard, and rather indifferent to real things. That is what makes me sometimes rebel against purely intellectual work.

They were able to spend a few days together in London before Russell had to return to Cambridge to give his Wednesday lecture. They read poetry together and, Russell wrote on his return, 'every moment was heavenly . . . Oh how wonderful it is to have you back, and recover all the joy and feel really alive again.'

To enable him to spend as much time as possible with Ottoline in London, Russell took a small flat in Bloomsbury, in Russell Chambers, Bury Street, opposite the British Museum and just two minutes' walk from Bedford Square, which Ottoline helped him furnish. 'I enjoyed making it pretty and nice for him,' she recalled, 'and it made him happy to have these rooms with a few of his old family possessions in them, such as his mother's portrait and his grandfather's desk. I went round to see him very often.' These visits were remembered by her with something like dread:

How much emotion those little rooms in Bury Street held – intense and burning and very tragic! Bertie demanded so much, and all I could give him was so inadequate to his desires. He would stand at his window looking for my coming, his face growing tenser and tenser, counting the minutes if I was late. As I hurried along the street I dreaded looking up, seeing his face pressed against the panes looking for me. And then it was dreadful leaving him in those rooms, unsatisfied and tragically lonely. How could I satisfy him? The very intensity of his demands seemed to crush me. In my Journal I find: 'Poor Bertie! I feel sometimes when I am with him as if I were in prison – his passion is so possessive and oppressive. When I come home I skip for joy, and often I dance round my bedroom and fling out my arms and sing "Free, free". I feel I should like to dance to a hurdy-gurdy in the street.'

A week after Ottoline's return, Russell came up to London to attend a dinner in honour of Bergson that had been arranged by H. Wildon Carr. Bergson, he wrote to Lucy Donnelly that night, 'is giving lectures in London which are reported in the daily newspapers – all England has gone mad about him for some reason'. The dinner he described as 'amusing'. He was seated next to Bergson on one side and, on the other, Sir Francis Younghusband, the soldier-explorer well known for his adventures in Tibet, who, it seems, had an interest in philosophy. As a philosopher, Russell wrote, Bergson 'never thinks about fundamentals, but just invents pretty fairy-tales', but as a man he was urbane and gentle. George Bernard Shaw made a witty speech and 'Everybody congratulated themselves and each other on their possession of freedom and on their escape from the barren scientific dogmas of the sixties' – everybody, that is, except Russell: 'I still believe in those dogmas, so I felt out of it.' To Ottoline, Russell gave a very similar account, but added an interesting observation on Bergson himself: 'I didn't find out anything except, even more strongly, what one gathers from his books, that he is a very vivid visualiser, but has little auditory or tactile imagination – his whole philosophy is dominated by the sense of sight.'

Two days later, Russell gave his Presidential Address to the Aristotelian Society, and Bergson duly attended to criticise it. Unfortunately, the minutes of the meeting do not record what Bergson actually said, though from a private conversation recorded in *Entretiens avec Bergson* by Jacques Chevalier we learn that Bergson considered himself to have entirely refuted Russell's 'completely materialistic presentation of Platonic forms', and that he attributed Russell's subsequent attack on him as revenge for that refutation. When Russell sent copies of the paper to Ralph Perry in Harvard, he told him:

Bergson, who was present when I read my paper, evidently thought it antiquated nonsense. He said it reminded him of the Greeks, and that in the modern world particulars might be taken for granted but universals could only be accepted after careful proof.

Returning to Cambridge to give his lecture, Russell was in no mood for

Wittgenstein, whom he now found 'very argumentative and tiresome' and even something of 'a fool':

> He thinks nothing empirical is knowable – I asked him to admit that there was not a rhinoceros in the room, but he wouldn't.

After this bizarre exchange, Russell retired to his room to continue the seemingly interminable task of proofreading *Principia Mathematica*, rejoicing in the very tedium of the work, which he declared was 'so much pleasanter than reading Bergson'. To add to his enormous stock of proofreading, the proofs of *The Problems of Philosophy* had arrived. 'It seems to me to read well,' he told Ottoline, whereas the proofs of *Principia* 'have a sort of ghostly feeling. I wrote the stuff such ages ago and have quite forgotten it. I dare say it is the most important work I shall ever have done, but it is hard to judge.' Reading the two works together, the one austerely unreadable, the other deliberately popular, led him to reflect on the contrast, and on his future as a philosopher and writer:

> It is very unlikely that I shall ever do any more math'cal work. I feel it would only be more of the same kind which could just as well be done by some one else. I am surprised to find how much of my philosophy comes into the S.S. ['Shilling Shocker' – his name for *The Problems of Philosophy*] . . . It is odd. I have no doubt that philosophy is worth teaching, but I have grave doubt as to how far it is worth giving one's life to original work in it.

'I long to have long talks with you about my life and how to make the best use of it,' he wrote to Ottoline the next day. His sense of communion with her, he told her, was as strong as ever 'but it depends upon feeling that I am living in the main as well as I can . . . I suppose whatever I did I should feel dissatisfied with myself . . . possibilities are infinite and achievement is finite.'

Whitehead's son, North, was at this time studying economics, but in conversation with Russell had expressed a desire to change to philosophy, 'but from the point of view of his future livelihood it seems undesirable':

> I expressed to him some of my doubts as to the value of philosophy; it surprised him greatly that I felt that. I expect some day I shall have to write out what I think about it; till I do that, I shan't be clear as to what I think.

Whatever doubts about philosophy Russell may have had, he had no doubts whatever about his value to the 'young men' he taught: 'Young men do seem to me so interesting and so important . . . What I try to do here is give people the best conception I can of the intellectual life.' His aim as a teacher, he told Ottoline, 'is to be known as a person whom anybody may interrupt at any moment.'

One young man who took full advantage of this open-door policy was Wittgenstein, who came regularly to Russell's rooms to argue about philosophy. On 7 November, Russell reported Wittgenstein as 'refusing to admit the existence of anything except asserted propositions', a view he maintained with such tenacity a week later that Russell had to put an end to the discussion by declaring that 'it was too large a theme'. Wittgenstein, however, was unstoppable. On 16 November: 'My ferocious German (who is an Austrian I find) came and argued at me after my lecture. He is armour-plated against all assaults of reasoning. It is really rather a waste of time talking with him.'

From these hints, some idea can be derived as to how Wittgenstein's thoughts were developing in reaction to Russell's. His view that nothing exists except asserted propositions, for example, might be seen as a reaction against Russell's Aristotelian paper on universals and particulars, which, even if Wittgenstein did not hear it in London on 30 October, he almost certainly heard in Cambridge when Russell delivered it to the Moral Science Club on 4 November. The problem facing anyone who insists on the discrete reality of both particulars and universals is to explain how they ever come together; how, for example, any particular thing, a snowman, say, can be white (partake of the universal 'whiteness'). Russell's answer to this in his Aristotelian paper was to appeal to an 'ultimate simple relation' of predication that brings the two together as subject and predicate in a fact, or 'asserted proposition' ('The Snowman is white', in which the snowman is the subject and whiteness the predicate).

The problem with this was that, according to Russell, relations are themselves universals, so the question arises as to how *this* universal, the 'relation of predication', is itself related to the other particulars and universals that make up the fact. It looks as though *another* relation is needed to bring them together. And then this other relation will itself be a universal, and so on *ad infinitum* to an infinite regress. Wittgenstein's claim that all that exists are asserted propositions suggests a way out of this mess by imposing a limit as to how far the world can be analysed. The world, he is suggesting, does not break up into particulars and universals, it breaks up into *facts*, in which particulars and universals are already linked together. The problem as to how they are linked does not therefore arise. Or, as he would later put it in *Tractatus Logico-Philosophicus*: 'The world is made up of facts, not of things.'[1]

About a week before the end of term, Wittgenstein came to Russell's room to seek his advice on whether he should continue with philosophy or return to his engineering studies:

---

[1] I am inclined to think that there is a connection between this view and Wittgenstein's earlier, apparently bizarre refusal to admit that we can know empirically that a rhinoceros is not in the room. The world – in this case, the room – is made up of facts, of *positive* facts. Once we have provided a complete description of everything that *is* in the room, we do not need to add a list of the possibly infinite number of things that are *not* in the room in order to make sure that we have not missed something. That there is not a rhinoceros in the room is thus not one of the facts that make up that room, it is something that emerges from there being no such thing in our complete list. Our knowledge that the room contains no hidden rhino, therefore, like our knowledge of all negative facts, is not empirical, but inferential.

. . . he asked me today whether I thought he was utterly hopeless at philosophy, and I told him I didn't know but I thought not. I asked him to bring me something written to help me judge. He has money, and is quite passionately interested in philosophy, but he feels he ought not to give his life to it unless he is some good. I feel the responsibility rather as I really don't know what to think.

A few days later, he and Wittgenstein, for once, talked of other things than philosophy and Russell discovered that he was 'literary, very musical, pleasant-mannered (being an Austrian) & I *think* really intelligent . . . I am getting to like him.' On 7 December, they met for one last arguing session before Wittgenstein returned to Vienna for Christmas, and to write something that would establish once and for all whether he was 'utterly hopeless'.

A few days after the end of term, Russell took the opportunity to write out his thoughts about philosophy, in order, as he told Ottoline, to 'clear up my own ideas'. Almost the only use of philosophy, he had decided, 'is to combat errors induced by science and religion', and what is important in it could be done at a popular level; 'the technical refinements add very little except controversy and long words', a view in which he had been reinforced by seeing how much he could say in *The Problems of Philosophy*.

In emphasising the value of popular philosophy, Russell was no doubt influenced by his desire to write things that would interest Ottoline. The other side of that coin was that among the errors of religion, which it was philosophy's task to combat, were her own beliefs. Over the Christmas vacation he pursued this struggle with such intensity that it threatened to put an end to his relationship with her. The obsessional passion with which he returned again and again to this subject was explained by him in a remarkable letter of 28 November. 'You stir in me strange yearnings,' he wrote, 'partly for the joy of belief, which I must not hope for, partly (what is connected) for a more complete union with you – I don't mean outwardly, tho' that at times I feel over-poweringly, but inwardly – I wish we were united over religion, not only in feeling but in belief':

. . . in imagination I beat myself against your inner Sanctuary, and I see that I can never enter there . . . You know the passion of my love, and the passion of my feelings about religion – where they meet, it is rather terrific.

In his efforts to understand Ottoline's religious faith, Russell probably dwelt too much on its intellectual aspects, the rational grounds she may or may not have had for it, and too little on the role it had played in her life. Ottoline had been brought up in a religious atmosphere, which she had never seen the need to challenge. Her mother, Lady Bolsover, to whom she was devoted, was very devout, and Ottoline's inherited Christian faith had been strengthened when, during her mother's last illness, she had found comfort and inspiration in Thomas à Kempis's *The Imitation of Christ*. Her real religious mentor, however, was a nun called Mother Julian, the head of a sisterhood in Truro, whom Ottoline had met at the age of twenty-one shortly after her mother's death. In her memoirs, Ottoline describes the impression Mother Julian made on her in terms that suggest the intensity of first love, dwelling on the nun's 'amazing eyes', which were 'rather pale and unlike any other eyes I have ever seen':

> They had seen the full pain and light of life, still saw the light and still felt love and reverence. Her presence seemed to radiate some lovely and loving spiritual power. She seemed to me like Saint Stephen, with heavenly lights in her face, and she gave me, above all, such a feeling of reverence that I never lost the desire, when I entered her room, to kneel to her . . . She was absolutely true and perfectly gentle, full of humour and quick to laugh and to sympathise in fun or in grief, reverent above all towards life and towards even the meanest individual. I remember catching sight of her sometimes as I went into the Chapel – she was of course quite unaware of being seen – and the look that was on her face, which was the combination of reverence and worship and light, still seems always in my mind to testify to a divine spirit. If all other beliefs failed, Mother Julian's attitude and face would still remain to me an unanswerable and convincing testimony to an infinite presence in life.

During Ottoline's tour of European cities in September, she had learnt that Mother Julian had died, and, rather than answer Russell's insistent challenge to say what reason she had to believe in God, she wanted, in her grief, to explain to him what Mother Julian had meant to her. Something, at least, of what she felt must have communicated itself to Russell, but it only aroused in him yet more jealousy. 'I know that since Mother Julian's death there is no one to give you all you want in religion,' he wrote to her. 'I long to give you more in that way – it is partly the longing that makes me so rough.'

The thought that Ottoline's religious faith, whether personified by Mother Julian or God Himself, occupied a vitally important and cherished place in her heart that he could never enter, still less fill, drove Russell to fury. On 27 December, after he had spent Christmas with the Whiteheads and she with Philip's family, his feelings got the better of him when they spent a day together in his flat at Bury Street and he launched his most ferocious assault yet on her 'inner Sanctuary'. Almost as soon as they met he subjected her to a fierce and hostile interrogation. Would she admit that, in basing her faith on feeling rather than reason, she was guilty of intellectual dishonesty? Would she agree that faith without proof was unworthy of his respect? To Ottoline it seemed like an attack on her very being, and the ferocity of it persuaded her that she had already lost Russell's respect. She returned to her mother-in-law's house in Oxford in an almost suicidal state, her belief in herself damaged far more severely than her religious faith, which, in fact, remained entirely unaffected by Russell's onslaught. On the train back to Oxford she wrote a bitter but defiant letter to Russell, trying to explain to him how humiliating it was for her to be treated like a confused, mistaken fanatic and how utterly hopeless she thought it was trying to make him see what her faith meant to her. 'I don't know that I should ever be able to make you see what I felt any more than I could not see your adored mathematics,' she wrote, and then crossed it out. By the time she reached Oxford, her mood had changed and she thought only of how sad she would be to lose him. She immediately went to a post office and sent him a telegram reading simply: 'Bless you.'

Back with the Whiteheads at their country home in Lockeridge, Russell felt remorseful and afraid at what he had done and wrote to Ottoline begging forgiveness. 'I have upon me now the horror of a cruel action,' he told her, 'of wanton destruction and ruthlessness':

> I have been too fierce, too violent, too destructive – something of the cruelty of the ascetic has been with me – but Dearest these things will melt away – and they have to do with what prevents me from writing as I wish to write – it is all part of a sort of mental asceticism, which is bad like all asceticism.

He had been picturing her in Oxford 'proud, miserable, ill', imagining her to be feeling 'utterly alone in the world, feeling useless and a mere cumberer of the earth, considering suicide, longing for the rest which only death can bring', and the picture 'wrings my heart – it is terrible'. Thinking of Ottoline's loneliness, he said (but one cannot help feeling that he had also his own loneliness in mind), he was reminded of his conversion of 1901, 'when I first saw that love and tenderness are alone of real value'. He worshipped Ottoline's love, tenderness and devotion and hated 'the furious persecutor in me':

> I long to have the inward poise that you have. But that is not for me. I shall never have it while I am alive. Turbulent, restless, inwardly raging – I shall always be – hungry for your God and blaspheming him. I could pour forth a flood of worship – the longing for religion is at times almost unbearably strong.

Despite all this remorse, however, Russell's analysis of the causes of their disagreement was still somewhat insulting. 'It is difficult to me to understand a mind so genuinely unaffected by argument as yours,' he told her, adding that he had to 'contend against years of habit and the whole tendency of my work to understand your way of reaching your beliefs . . . You do not believe that reasoning is a method of arriving at truth; I do. That is the root of the matter.'

With regard to his desire to strike out at Ottoline, one suspects he got a little closer to the real 'root of the matter', when later in the same letter he remarked, 'I am not nearly as much to you as I wish to be, and the pain of realising it sometimes gives me a kind of frenzy.' Even now, in his remorse, he could not stop himself from reflecting that, though it made him miserable to think of her being unhappy, he could never give her real, inward peace, 'such as Mother Julian gave you'.

The next day, feeling that 'it is far better to find our agreements than our disagreements', Russell sought compromise in the idea that 'what you call

God is very much what I call infinity' and argued that, once this was understood, their beliefs were not as incompatible as they seemed. It was desperately unconvincing, and, as a piece of reassurance, did not address what was – from Ottoline's point of view – the most important question. She cared far less than Russell whether their beliefs were identical or even compatible; what she wanted from him now was reassurance that he did not despise her, that he respected her spiritually and intellectually, and that he loved her as much as ever. In letter after letter over the next few days, Russell was forced to back-pedal furiously in his efforts to provide reassurance on all these fronts. 'I see that we can share intellectual things perfectly,' he promised, and went so far as to assure her that, 'You don't know how *profoundly* you help me when you speak of your religion. It is really all very sacred to me.'

There were limits, however, to how far he *could* back-pedal. 'There is of course one *great* difference between your beliefs and mine', he was forced to admit:

I do not think any spiritual force outside human beings actually helps us . . . Therefore I cannot pray or lean on God. What strength I need I must get from myself or those whom I admire. And this view does seem to me nobler, sterner, braver, than the view which looks for help from without, besides seeming to me truer.

He had to go on putting this view, he insisted, 'and I should like you to conceive it *possible* that some day you *might* think it more true than your present view'; but he would never again, he promised, make the mistake of accusing Ottoline of dishonesty.

In the New Year, stirred by this fierce dispute with Ottoline, Russell conceived the idea of writing what he called a 'spiritual autobiography', the purpose of which would be to show the centrality in his life of his quest for religious faith and its culmination in the 'vision' he had tried to express in 'Prisons'. The idea was partly inspired by trying to explain to Ottoline that his hostile scepticism was not directed at religion *per se*, but only at the type of religion that required adherence to groundless beliefs. 'All that religion has done for you', he told Ottoline, 'can be done by the religion which I believe in.' Though it has not survived, something of the flavour of this spiritual autobiography is no doubt preserved in the letters that Russell wrote in the first few weeks of January 1912:

I do think the spiritual things – the things that make religion – are the great things; they are what make life infinite and not petty.
(1 January)

What we *know* is that things come into our lives sometimes which are so immeasurably better than the things of every day, that it *seems* as though they were sent from another world, and could not come out of ourselves. But our selves have strange hidden powers of good and evil – madness too will come as if from without, and make it seem as though we were possessed. Religion, it seems to me, ought to make us know and remember these immeasurably better things, and live habitually in the thought of them . . . I have hitherto only seen the greatest things at rare times of stress or exultation. In the summer I lived with the vision – when I got back to Ipsden it faded because of my work. When it is strong, the kind of philosophical work I do seems not worth doing; and so when I have to do this work, the vision fades. That was why I hated going back to work so much – it was like going back to prison. What the vision seems to show me is that we can live in a deeper region than the region of little every-day cares and desires – where beauty is a revelation of something beyond, where it becomes possible to love all men . . .

Yet I have another vision . . . in this vision, sorrow is the ultimate truth of life, everything else is oblivion or delusion. Then even love seems to me merely an opiate – it makes us forget for a moment that we draw our breath in pain and that thought is the gateway to despair.
(3 January)

Many of the weaknesses of 'Prisons' Russell thought could be avoided in an autobiographical narrative: he could express in a dramatic and vivid way views with which he no longer agreed and moods he had outgrown: 'And one can make the final outcome more complex and many-sided than in direct exposition . . . Then there is more room for humour and irony and development; and one can be more tentative and undogmatic.' Above all, perhaps, writing in an autobiographical framework would enable him to bring passion to the subject: 'I believe any passion may be infinite if it has its root in something universal – Swift's rage, for instance, is God-like, because it springs from the vision of what mankind might be . . . I think one wants intense passion, intensely insistent, conquered sometimes by still more intense religion.'

Russell returned to Cambridge for the start of term at the height of his enthusiasm for this project and, consequently, in little mood to give his attention to technical philosophy. 'Oddly enough,' he wrote to Lucy Donnelly on 21 January, 'I have developed a certain nausea for the subtleties & distinctions that make up good philosophy; I should like to write things of human interest, like bad philosophers, only without being bad. But perhaps it is the badness that is interesting.' To Ottoline, he declared: 'This year I should have no technical work to do, and I should have the added freedom these months have brought – it ought to lead to wonderful things.' True to his word, during this term he did no technical work, concentrating instead on his spiritual autobiography and on his paper on Bergson for 'The Heretics'.

That Russell's spiritual autobiography remained unfinished is probably largely to do with the fact that, at the end of February, Ottoline left England for Lausanne to be treated once more by Dr Combe for her neuralgia. She did not return until April, by which time Russell's mood was quite different and no longer conducive to expressing 'the vision' in an autobiography or in any other way.

Even before Ottoline left, Russell reported himself to be losing his inspiration and confidence. On 10 February, he told Ottoline that he had been gloomy that morning because of 'dissatisfaction with myself':

I feel at all times instinctively that I ought be either doing creative work or doing what will help it – and when I am uninspired I feel life is slipping away and I am not achieving anything . . . I always feel I am reaching out towards better things than I have ever achieved . . . In the summer I thought Prisons was great – now I see it was only great in idea, not in achievement. This is a severe disappointment . . . I suppose you can imagine the pain of reaching out and stretching and straining to achieve the utmost, and feeling the inspiration leaving one.

He began to feel that his whole life had been set on a wrong course. He felt, he told Ottoline, 'fettered' by the technical work he had done in the past: 'people expect that sort of thing from me and more and more of it turns up, and it is hard to break loose from it.' He felt sure that Trinity would ask him to stay on when his five-year lectureship came to an end, 'and goodness knows what I ought to do then':

I feel the courageous course would be not to stay, but it wd. also be the self-indulgent course, and if no good wd. come of it I should eat my heart out.

He had, he said, been thinking of the 'awful waste' it was that he and Ottoline were not married, and of the fact that Philip and Ottoline were married within days of his discovery that he was no longer in love with Alys: 'It seems strange.' Implied by all this seems to be the view that if, instead of marrying Philip, Ottoline had married Russell, he would now be more sure of his inspiration and would have the courage to break with Cambridge and with technical philosophy. As it was, though 'I feel less interest in my technical work and in things here . . . and only spiritual things matter', and though he felt the writing of his spiritual autobiography to be more important than philosophy, 'I should be afraid to make that sort of writing my only work – inspiration dries up, and it is fatal to try to go on without inspiration.'

He had some idea of what was wrong with his 'spiritual' writing – 'I have always tended to extract the essence and state it baldly and briefly; it wants other things to create an atmosphere' – but as yet little idea of how to correct the fault. He turned from his autobiography to the less demanding task of adapting parts of 'Prisons' for an article on 'The Essence of Religion' for *The Hibbert Journal*. This he showed to Goldie Lowes Dickinson, who was not as enthusiastic about it as Russell had hoped. 'It has a kind of stoic nobility about it,' Dickinson commented. 'And I sympathise with it, but I don't believe I share it . . . At bottom, of course, I don't accept your philosophy. But I think it very important that those who do shall acquire your religion.'

It was not a greatly encouraging response, and Russell temporarily aban-

doned spiritual writing and turned instead to the task he had been putting off
– that of finishing his paper on Bergson. As soon as he did so, he slipped into
'a dry intellectual mood . . . very useful for getting on with my work', a mood
that intensified after Ottoline left for Switzerland on 27 February: 'When you
are gone the light fades out of my soul. I become strangely dead and cold.'
When, after just a few days, he had finished the preliminary work for the
paper and was ready to begin writing, he summarised Bergson's career in a
way that projects on to it Russell's own preoccupation with the tension
between the mystic vision and the hard, dry intellect:

> I think his philosophy is the outcome of some mystic illumination which I
> don't quite understand – I haven't got inside his temperament. I think
> many years ago he must have fallen in love and come to the conclusion the
> intellect was a poor thing: probably nothing has happened to him since, but
> he still looks back to his one moment of life, and his thought is still in the
> grip of instinct.

Almost everything Russell said about Bergson seemed so calculated to
arouse Ottoline's sympathy for him that it is hard to believe that he was
unconscious either of that or of the corresponding fact that he was putting
himself in a very unsympathetic light. On 5 March, he told Ottoline that he
looked upon his work on Bergson as an exercise in 'moral discipline', and
joked somewhat chillingly: 'He describes certain wasps who lay their eggs in
other insects, whom they sting very scientifically so as to paralyse them; he
says they do it by "sympathy"; that is the kind I have!' The paper was
finished on 8 March, three days before it was due to be delivered. 'How easy
critical work is,' Russell commented on completing it, 'one only has to go
through a mechanical process and the result emerges.'
The meeting of 'The Heretics' at which Russell gave the paper was a
memorable event. 'The whole world seems to be coming tonight,' he wrote
that morning, and the day afterwards reported it to be 'a great success . . .
the place was packed and they seemed to enjoy it . . . Not a soul rose to
defend Bergson at the end, so there was no discussion. McTaggart spoke a
few graceful words and we all went away.' When, in the 1950s, Alan Wood
came to write the first biography of Russell, he included the following account
of 'Russell's celebrated lecture on Bergson', which, as Wood could not
possibly have been there, was surely based on an account supplied by Russell
himself:

> Bergson's mystical philosophy of evolution was then enjoying a tremendous
> vogue, which Russell set out to demolish; there was an eager audience to
> hear him, and everyone had a sense of great occasion . . . to enjoy [the
> lecture's] savour, the reader must imagine it delivered in Russell's dry,
> precise and ironic voice, and punctuated by the laughter and applause
> which greeted his sallies. It was an event of some importance in Russell's
> life, helping to re-establish him as one of the leading figures in Cambridge;
> and especially because it was his first big success as a public speaker.

By now Bergson had become almost a symbolic figure for Russell, standing for precisely the kind of philosophy, and the attitude to philosophy, that he sought to combat. 'Writing on Bergson has filled me with ideas about philosophy in general,' he told Ottoline. After finishing his paper he had gone for a twilight walk with Geach, one of his students:

I began to talk about how philosophy should be studied – how people ought to have more of the scientific impulse for collecting queer facts, less fear of spending their time on matters not dignified in themselves but important for their consequences, as the man of science does with his test-tubes; how the love of system, since new facts are the enemies of systems, has to be kept rigidly in check, in spite of being a thing every philosopher ought to have; how vital it is to avoid emotion and edification and the wish to be literary . . . There is so much to be found out by patience and a scientific spirit.

The following day, Russell described to Ottoline a tea party to which Ogden had brought 'an old gentleman named Wolstenholme, with a flowing white beard – an amateur philosopher, a very lovable old man I think', who 'talked and talked about what philosophy could do and couldn't do, not very sensible, but very nice':

You would have laughed at the conversation with Wolstenholme. He said philosophy ought to be concerned with life, at which I burst out against life and the paltriness of an outlook that never got away from Man – a first-rate avalanche. He mildly hinted that one ought not to think there was *nothing* but logic in the world – but I wouldn't hear of there being anything else. After a while I began to see I was absurd, and stopped.

But I simply can't *stand* a view limited to this earth. I feel life so small unless it has windows into other worlds. I feel it vehemently and instinctively and with my whole being. It is what has become of my desire for worship. But I despair of making people see what I mean. I like mathematics largely because it is *not* human and has nothing particular to do with this planet or with the whole accidental universe – because, like Spinoza's God, it won't love us in return. I wish I could get it all said so as to seem convincing.

In Lausanne, Ottoline, glorying in being alone for once, was also reflecting on the relationship between philosophy and life, in a way that showed her to be defiantly determined not to be browbeaten into accepting Russell's view on the matter. 'I am so glad, oh so glad, to get away alone,' she wrote in her journal, 'and to have time to think and read, to store my mind with thoughts and to rest my emotions and nerves and to get away and stand off and view the past year.' She had taken with her Russell's gift of an abridged version of Spinoza's *Ethics* and this, together with Russell's essay on 'The Essence of Religion', had helped her to get clear in her mind the differences between her own views and Russell's.

Spinoza's emphasis on 'the abstract intellectual life', she could now admit, she found alienating because 'I feel I personally learn and take in so much by my *senses* – by sight, by feelings which are not purely intellectual but are of the human and imaginative quality.' And Russell's paper on the essence of religion left her dissatisfied because 'it does not include and draw into itself the ordinary life of men which after all cannot be left outside religion.' Indeed, her view – now that she had, in Virginia Woolf's sense, a 'room of her own' in which to formulate it for herself – was, she realised, the precise opposite of Russell's: where Russell looked to philosophy to provide a perspective removed and remote from mere human life, she longed to bring philosophy down to earth and put it among the ordinary lives of ordinary people:

> Why do they all elaborate philosophies and religions outside the real life we live. Why not fuse them with our life on earth. Life, life is what we are here for and to live it well, not to go into a room and think about it all.

While sitting out on a terrace, thinking of philosophy and of Russell's letters, she watched ordinary people going about their business – reading the newspapers, eating lunch, a young man carrying his child while his wife alongside him pushed their baby in its pram – and: 'I found myself swept with indignation at the intellectuals who elaborate such aloof theories about life and religion and who seem to ignore the everyday lives and needs of such people, who surely need a religion or philosophy that can be inter-penetrated and fused with their ordinary lives.'

Some of this attitude she tried to convey to Russell, who, however, showed no sign in his replies of realising the extent to which it was a rejection of his point of view and treated it as a series of more or less minor misunderstandings of himself and Spinoza. 'I am so glad you like the Spinoza so much,' he wrote on 10 March, explaining: 'I think when he speaks of "intellect" he doesn't mean what one usually means. I don't quite know what he does mean, but the essence of it is to be universal, not particular . . . I don't believe he means to shut out what you want to keep in.' The next day: 'What you say about passion and philosophy is not *at all* rubbish – it is only frightfully hard to bring it in . . . It is not exactly whether one is more or less passionate that makes the difference, but whether one's passions are more or less harmonious. I don't think you would inflict great pain – I would and did.'

'About life and philosophy,' Russell wrote a few days later, 'I don't believe I disagree even by a nuance.' But then, spelling out his attitude to life, he outlined a view completely antithetical to Ottoline's. '*Aloofness* is utterly bad,' he began. 'I never *mean* aloofness, whatever I say.' What he meant was best illustrated by supposing a terrible misfortune had befallen one. How was one to bear it?

> So long as one doesn't travel beyond *life* . . . all the pain of the world will come before one, and it will seem all not worth while. There is nothing there to keep one from suicide. However far you travel from your own

private sorrow, human life in general, if you take it as all in all, is terrible, and would seem better extinct . . . Life grows great by some stoic power of rising above life.

'I know you agree *wholly* with all this,' he said with extraordinary and misplaced confidence, 'there isn't really a shade of difference.'

Ottoline remained unpersuaded. While she was in Lausanne, she was, as Russell came eventually to realise, intellectually and spiritually pulling away from him. She was at this time engaged in a lively and confessional correspondence with Lytton Strachey, and took far more pleasure from Strachey's amusing and gossipy letters – his descriptions of the agonies of his love for Henry Lamb, his pride in the reception of *Landmarks in French Literature* and his frankly egotistical sense of spiritual achievement[2] – than she did in Russell's rather dry and hectoring defence of 'the intellect'. 'Oh,' she exclaimed to Strachey in a letter written at the end of her stay, 'if you only knew the happiness your letters bring!'

Russell, meanwhile, had discovered in Wittgenstein someone with whom he felt 'the most perfect intellectual sympathy'. They had, he said, 'the same passion and vehemence, the same feeling that one must understand or die, the sudden jokes breaking down the frightful tension of thought'. Their friendship, which had developed quickly over the spring term, particularly during the time that Ottoline was away, had begun at the start of term, when Wittgenstein showed Russell what he had written over the Christmas vacation. It was, Russell declared, 'very good, much better than my English pupils do. I shall certainly encourage him. Perhaps he will do great things. On the other hand I think it very likely he will get tired of philosophy.'

Over the next two months, Wittgenstein's interest in philosophy was shown to be as unflagging as it was intense. While Russell worked on his spiritual autobiography and his paper on Bergson, and wondered whether he ought to abandon technical work altogether, Wittgenstein spent the term wrestling with the most abstruse issues of philosophical logic, trying to find a solution to the fundamental unsolved problem that lay like an unlanced boil at the centre of all Russell's technical work, the deceptively simple question: 'What is logic?' His absorption in this question and his passionate commitment to finding some sort of solution made him the kind of student for whom niceties like a basic education in philosophy and logic could be dispensed with.

As Russell was quick to see, Wittgenstein knew only 'a small proportion of what he ought to know', but, as he was also quick to appreciate, it did not much matter. Russell had always felt that the kind of classical education that

---

[2] Strachey was at this time developing what he regarded as his new creed, which he described in a paper to the Apostles in May. What guided his every action, he declared, was ambition; not, however, a vulgar ambition, but rather a spiritual one: 'What I want is the attainment of a true excellence, the development of noble qualities, and the full expression of them – the splendour of a spiritual success. It is true that this is an egotistical conception of life; but I see no harm in such an egotism.'

most philosophers received was a hindrance rather than a help to their understanding of philosophical issues, and he did not mind at all that Wittgenstein knew no Greek, that he had not read a word of Aristotle, or even that he knew practically nothing about the British empiricist tradition. Russell did feel, however, that Wittgenstein ought to have a smattering of logic if he was going to succeed in providing a philosophical foundation for the subject, and so arranged for him to be 'coached' in the subject by the distinguished logician W. E. Johnson. After just a few meetings, however, Johnson refused to teach the student any more because he argued too much, and Russell – after delicately suggesting to Wittgenstein that he was 'terribly persistent, hardly lets one get a word in, and is generally considered a bore' – recognised the wisdom of letting Wittgenstein go on in his own inexorable way unimpeded by the teaching of others. Thereafter, Russell's role in Wittgenstein's philosophical development was that of a sounding-board for Wittgenstein's ideas. Several times in the last few weeks of term, Russell mentions that Wittgenstein had arrived with an original idea on logic (without, unfortunately, saying what these ideas were).

'I like Wittgenstein more and more,' Russell wrote on 8 March. 'He has the theoretical passion *very* strongly – it is a very rare passion and one is glad to find it.' Wittgenstein, he felt, was utterly sincere and quite devoid of 'the false politeness that interferes with truth . . . he lets his feelings and affections appear and it warms one's heart.' What Wittgenstein seemed to demonstrate – and for Russell, the point had tremendous importance – was the possibility of combining an interest in technical philosophy with an intensely passionate nature. Wittgenstein's disposition, he told Ottoline, 'is that of an artist, intuitive and moody. He says every morning he begins his work with hope, and every evening he ends in despair – he has just the sort of rage when he can't understand things that I have.'

This was Russell's dream: an intuitive and moody artist with whom he could have, as he reported having with Wittgenstein, 'a close equal passionate discussion of the most difficult point in mathematical philosophy'. The reassurance that this combination was possible revived in Russell the passion he himself had felt in the early days of his own absorption in mathematical logic. On 12 March, Volume II of *Principia Mathematica* was published. 'It was a mild event getting it,' he told Ottoline, perhaps even a melancholy event: 'Odd how much passion goes into doing a thing and how cold it is when it is done. A vast amount of various people's solid misery is crystallised in the book, and I wd. have done almost anything to bring about the finishing of it, and now it is a mere moment's interest.'

When he saw Wittgenstein later that day, Russell gave him a copy of the volume and a few days later reported that Wittgenstein 'spoke with intense feeling about the *beauty* of the big book, said he found it like music. That is how I feel it, but few others seem to.' What had been 'cold' had now, it seems, come to life, revitalised by the interest that Wittgenstein took in it.

By the time Wittgenstein left for Vienna for the Easter vacation, Russell had come to see him, not just as an exceptionally able student, but, he told Ottoline, someone with genius:

In discussion with him I put out *all* my force and only just equal his. With all my other pupils I should squash them flat if I did so. He has suggested several new ideas which I think valuable. He is the ideal pupil – he gives passionate admiration with vehement and very intelligent dissent . . . Our parting was very affectionate on both sides. He said the happiest hours of his life had been passed in my room. He is not a flatterer, but a man of transparent and absolute sincerity.

. . . When he left me I was strangely excited by him. I love him and feel he will solve the problems that I am too old to solve – all kinds of vital problems that are raised by my work, but want a fresh mind and the vigour of youth.[3] He is *the* young man one hopes for. But as is usual with such men, he is unstable, and may go to pieces. His vigour and life is such a comfort after the washed-out Cambridge type. His attitude justifies all I have hoped about my work. He will be up again next term.

In these early enthusiastic remarks about Wittgenstein, it is possible to see the seeds of a misunderstanding curiously similar to, and indeed running parallel with, his misapprehension about Ottoline's religious faith. Russell was increasingly inclined to see Ottoline and Wittgenstein as personifications of the two warring sides of himself: the mystic visionary on the one hand, and the intellectually austere mathematical logician on the other. But, just as he was inclined to exaggerate the similarities between Ottoline's faith and his own 'vision', so he was equally inclined to over-state the similarities between Wittgenstein's 'theoretical passion' and his own.

Wittgenstein told Russell that he disliked both 'The Free Man's Worship' and the last chapter (taken from 'Prisons') of *The Problems of Philosophy*, but that he liked the ending of the paper on Bergson because, although it expressed similar sentiments, there was 'something solid at the back of it'. These judgments no doubt seemed to support Russell in looking upon Wittgenstein as a fierce opponent of the more religious side of his nature and a defender of 'hard dry reasoning'. But, in the dichotomy that dominated Russell's mind between rigorous logic and visionary religion, there were too few alternatives to accommodate Wittgenstein's point of view, which was captured by neither side of the dilemma.

Some inkling of Wittgenstein's fundamental attitudes can be gleaned from the reasons he gave Russell for disliking *The Problems of Philosophy*, particularly its last chapter. As reported by Russell, his view was that 'people who like philosophy will pursue it, and others won't, and there is an end of it.' '*His* strongest impulse,' Russell added, 'is philosophy.' In his insistence on regarding philosophy as an 'impulse' with no more value than any other impulse, Wittgenstein was rejecting at its very root the conception of the subject that provided Russell's motivation: the idea that philosophy receives its value from providing us with a glimpse of an eternal, immutable world *beyond* impulses, passions and ordinary life. To that extent, in the great war

---

[3] Russell, it is sometimes hard to remember, was at this time still in his thirties (though about to turn forty in May).

between the finite and the infinite, the dynamic and the static, the human and the transcendent, the particular and the universal, Wittgenstein, like Bergson and Ottoline, was on the other side to Russell. What Wittgenstein stood for – as Russell, in his repeated admiring references to his 'passion' might have realised – was a conception of 'hard reasoning' that was anything but 'dry'.

9
PERPLEXITIES

To Russell's great disappointment, on 19 March 1912, the anniversary of
his momentous first evening with Ottoline, Ottoline was still in Lausanne. More disappointingly still, she seemed in no hurry to come back.
When term finished on 15 March, Russell was at something of a loose end
and on tenterhooks to know when Ottoline would return. 'I won't *count* on
you before Friday [i.e. 22 March],' he wrote, 'but I shall *hope*.' In the
meantime, he moved restlessly between friends, staying with Lion Phillimore
on the Monday and dining with the Whiteheads the following night. When
it began to look certain that Ottoline would not, after all, get back by the end
of the week, Russell set off on his own to Dorset for a few days to work off
his impatience by walking along the coast, and also to mark the occasion of
the anniversary himself by revisiting Lulworth, the scene of his happiest times
with Ottoline.

Arriving by train in Wool, six miles inland from Lulworth, Russell decided
to spend the night there. Still anxious to know when Ottoline would get back,
he telegraphed his charlady at Bury Street and gave her the address of his
hotel, so that she could forward any letters that might arrive from Lausanne.
For the next few days, wherever he went, he diligently and promptly kept his
charlady informed of his latest address. After a night in Wool, with pocket
volumes of Shakespeare, Blake and Keats in his pack, he set off for Lulworth.
'I never saw anything more beautiful than the western sea when I got here,'
he wrote to Ottoline. 'There was a black downpour of rain, with a break on
the horizon, so that the distant sea was as white as a mist.' From Lulworth
he walked on to Weymouth, a strenuous and hilly twelve-mile hike. The
weather was foul, but invigorating: 'There were several bouts of violent rain
& hail & the whole way I had to fight against a hurricane . . . I enjoyed
battling with the elements & it did me a lot of good.'

'I love being alone these days,' Russell told Ottoline. 'All the spectres used
to come out & gibber when I was alone. Now I think about you & about plans
of work, & I have no spectres.' He spoke too soon. At Weymouth, finally, he
received a letter from Ottoline, written on 19 March, the very day of their
anniversary. She wrote that she was not, after all, coming straight home from
Lausanne. Instead, she had decided, before returning to England, to spend a
few days in Paris, where she would have a new dress made and, perhaps, meet

up with Lytton Strachey and Henry Lamb. But, she insisted, Russell was not even to think of coming to Paris to join her. What with her maid in the next room, there would be no opportunities for any intimate or romantic encounters.

The letter, forcing upon Russell the belated realisation that Ottoline, far from longing to see him again, was rather enjoying the freedom of her separation from him, plunged him into a wild, almost insane mood of anguish. 'Ever since the letter you wrote on the anniversary of our meeting,' he later told her, 'I have longed for death . . . It is your gradual inexorable withdrawal – like the ebbing tide – that keeps me over and over again at the very last point of agony.'

The day he received the letter he tried to calm himself by finding a remote, sheltered spot at the extreme end of Portland Bill, a peninsula just below Weymouth, where there was 'nothing but rocks and a wild sea and strange melancholy sea birds'. Here, gazing out to sea, he tried to achieve that state of impartial contemplation in which the pain and strife of being human, of living, was of no concern. As he sat there, protected from the rain by the stones around him, he wrote to Ottoline in a tone that did its best to sound elevated rather than hurt. 'How hard it is to get at what one cares for,' he wrote:

> I love everything inhuman. I think passionless strength is what I worship, it seems so remote and wonderful. I believe all my religion starts from the profound conviction that I am a miserable sinner, and most of the rest of the human race too.
>
> Passionate disgust is not a praiseworthy emotion, but it infects me through and through.

'This place does speak to my soul,' he told her; it 'gives me a sense of life which is not the life of man or of anything sentient, and which must be strong because it is unfeeling':

> The endless battle within me makes me like what acts without inward battling: That is why I like necessity and the laws of motion and the doings of dead matter generally. I can't imagine a God not full of conflict; my God, like the one in Genesis, would have repented and sent the flood. So I prefer no God. Life seems to me essentially passion, conflict, rage; moments of peace are brief and destroy themselves. A calm God must be like Spinoza's, merely the course of nature. All this is autobiography, not philosophy.

Characteristically, the letter is not an expression of his despair and rage but of his desire not to be subject to such disruptive and turbulent emotions, of his yearning to be like the sea and the rocks – 'strong because unfeeling'. To a large extent, the depth of Russell's feelings could often be gauged by the coldness of his response. Many of his strongest feelings frightened him, urging him to distance himself from them. If he could rise above his desire for happiness, he wrote later that day, he could live more freely 'but as it is I must always be holding myself in check':

> I think sometimes you think it is only peccadilloes I am afraid of, but it isn't, it is big violent crimes – murder and suicide and such things. I don't know what is the right way to deal with this violence in me.

The way he had dealt with it was to control it with cold reason. 'I doubt if even you know how nearly I am to a raving madman,' he told Ottoline. 'It is only intellect that keeps me sane; perhaps this makes me overvalue intellect as against feeling.' To prove the point, he produced a rather disturbing example:

> I remember when I wanted to commit murder, the beginning was a sudden picture (I hardly have pictures at ordinary times) of a certain way of doing it, quite vivid, with the act visible before my eyes. It lived with me then for ever so long, always haunting me; I took to reading about murders and thinking about them, and always with that picture before me. It was only hard thinking that kept me straight at the time – the impulse was not amenable to morals, but it was amenable to reasoning that this was madness.

This chilling reminiscence is all the more disturbing, because the occasion it describes is not an isolated example: one thinks of Russell's account in the first volume of his *Autobiography* of wanting to kill his best friend, Edward FitzGerald ('in an access of fury, I got my hands on his throat and started to strangle him'), and, later in life, of his reaction to Paul Gillard ('a drunken homosexual spy . . . whom I found sinister and repellent to a degree that roused murderous impulses in me'), and of his third wife Patricia ('Peter') Spence waking up one night to find that Russell was trying to suffocate her with a pillow, and one begins to suspect that Russell had good reason to fear his strongest emotions. It becomes clear, too, why Dostoyevsky's characters made more impression on him than he would have liked, and why Rogojin, particularly, dwelled in his mind. In *The Idiot*, Rogojin, overcome by jealousy and 'brain fever', murders Nastasya, the woman he loves, on the day she had intended to marry his rival, Prince Myshkin (the 'Idiot' of the title). 'Of all the characters I ever read about in fiction', Russell told Ottoline in one of his letters from Dorset, 'none was so intimate to me as Rogojin.' In another, he told her that: 'The side of you that likes Dostoyevsky is very useful to me – most people would despise my inward turmoil.'

For the last few days of his brief walking holiday in Dorset, this turmoil remained unabated, as Russell hurried from town to town like a man possessed. From Weymouth, he walked twenty miles east through the rain to reach Wareham: 'But I was in a fit of madness & did not enjoy anything. About the 18th mile I began to laugh at myself & became sane.' The next day, he woke up feeling 'dry & hard' and 'prepared to demonstrate the idiocy of everybody & everything but otherwise sane', and walked 'faster and further than yesterday', this time twenty-two miles to Christchurch:

I did manage to exorcise my devil a bit by hurrying, and he was expelled altogether (for the moment) by the beauty of the Abbey here . . . So now I am quite tame, but don't go praising Desire again, for indeed you don't know what you are talking about, or you wd. know it is the Devil incarnate, a fierce fiend which wd. overturn empires and lead nations to their ruin if thereby its ends could be compassed. It makes me wish to destroy what I have, because it is not all I want. And it is very near to cruelty.

Ottoline, meanwhile, arrived in Paris on 24 March to find a pile of these disconcerting and unbalanced letters waiting for her. Her reaction was to make light of them – 'I think it was the toothache that made you write so' – and to insist, unconvincingly, *of course* I am longing to get back'. She described to Russell something of her own suffering in Lausanne at the hands of Dr Combe's rather gruesome methods of treating nervous disorders. Dr Combe, it seems, was convinced that the key to a stable nervous condition was a nose stripped of its mucous lining. Accordingly, he first snipped pieces of bone from Ottoline's nose and then inserted electrodes into her nostrils to cauterise the flesh inside. The effects were that her nose streamed continuously, that she was in pain all day long and that all she could smell was burnt flesh. Strangely, however, her faith in Dr Combe was entirely unaffected by this ordeal, and she planned within a few months to return to Lausanne for yet more treatment, this time for her liver (Dr Combe's liver cure was equally novel: a thirty-day course of milk dosed with radium).

As if he had forgotten that there was physical pain in the world as well as emotional torment, Russell seemed almost delighted to be reminded of the fact and reacted to Ottoline's harrowing account with something approaching relish for the proof it offered of a malevolent Deity:

When physical pain flares up beyond a point it is utterly *ghastly*, the most ghastly thing on earth. God made it for his pleasure, having full power to make a world without it. King Leopold, Caligula & the rest were all gentle lambs compared to their Creator. But hush. I must & will be good.

When Ottoline and Russell met again in London at the beginning of April, their conversation inevitably turned to the subject of passion and the 'mad letters' that Russell had written from Dorset. 'Indeed passion is of God,' Russell wrote to her afterwards, 'the unquenchable thirst for heaven – it is the power that drives us on to seek out good. We are all exiles in this nether world, and all passion has something of homesickness.' And yet:

It doesn't do for me to relax too much – the forces inside are too wild – some of them must be kept chained up . . . I had thought possibly now I might let all the dogs have an outing, but some of them are mad dogs and are not safe to leave at large.

At Easter, which that year fell on 7 April, Russell was taken by his brother Frank on a motoring holiday through Cornwall. Passing through Truro, he searched in vain for Mother Julian's sisterhood, telling Ottoline, 'I thought a great deal about your times there.' In St Ives, seeking escape from the people he was with ('for my brother and his wife are very uncongenial, in spite of my affection for him'), he sat outside overlooking the sea and a wide stretch of the coast and reflected on the time he had spent in St Ives three years earlier, 'just after the most miserable time of my life':

> I lodged in a cottage which has now been pulled down to make room for a tourists' lodging house. It seems much more than 3 years ago. That was the only time when I completely lost faith in myself, and thought of myself as a mere cumberer of the earth. I resolved to commit suicide as soon as I could get rid of certain definite obligations which for the moment made it impossible; but I had not yet got rid of them a year ago.

Notwithstanding these sombre reflections and the irritations of being with Frank and Molly, the holiday did Russell good and he returned in much better spirits. On 14 April, he wrote that he had developed a 'morality of passion':

> It is to behave as one might in grand opera or in epic poetry. That is why my violence does not offend me. I could behave like Hamlet or Othello or even Macbeth without feeling degraded, but if I behaved like Richard Feverel I should not think myself fit to live. It came to me through thinking of Tristan and Isolde, and of how rapturous it would be to die together like the people in Rosmersholm.

In addition, he had an 'ascetic morality of religion' and an 'intellectual morality of thought'. 'You will see from all this,' he told Ottoline, 'that I am out of the wood, and enjoying life again.'

Russell was not entirely joking about having a 'morality of passion'. In an unpublished manuscript called 'Dramatic and Utilitarian Ethics' written about this time, he asked why Shakespeare was universally admired, even though, in his depictions of Hamlet, Othello and Macbeth, he might be regarded as 'the champion of murderers'. The answer he gave was that 'the average man cares about drama much more than about happiness.' The dramatic instinct, which finds its greatest expression in love and war, causes us to judge actions in a way quite at odds with the utilitarian calculation of what would best promote happiness. The editors of Russell's *Collected Papers*, in publishing this paper, insist that it is a mere *jeu d'esprit* 'having little to do with Russell's serious ethical thought', but it seems to me to be an entirely earnest attempt to express a conflict within Russell that mirrored that between his 'vision' and his 'hard dry reasoning'. In the cold light of day, Russell adhered to utilitarianism, but there was a side of him that despised the dry, mechanical approach of the 'felicific calculus' and which yearned for the grandeur of a more heroic, more dramatic attitude to life, in which violent emotions, once stirred, were not immediately repressed – the attitude, for example, expressed by Hamlet when he exclaims:

> O! from this time forth,
> My thoughts be bloody, or be nothing worth!

Now this, as Russell points out, 'is not a kindly sentiment', and the paper ends with Russell's re-affirmation of the good, utilitarian reasons why the dramatic ethic, however stirring and seductive, should be balanced by a more calculating attitude. Russell was not, in the end, prepared to adopt his 'morality of passion' in the face of all other moral considerations (he did not really, for example, think he would have been justified in killing either Edward FitzGerald or Alys), but, in the wake of his recent experience in Dorset, the idea that there was something rather splendid and glorious about violent passions – despite the fact that this was completely at variance with his Spinozistic religion – was one in which he now began to take great pleasure.

It was the perfect mood in which to meet Wittgenstein, who returned to Cambridge for the summer term on 23 April. 'He is quite as good as I thought,' Russell reported. 'He lives in the same kind of tense excitement as I do, hardly able to sit still or read a book.' As if to support Russell in his 'morality of passion', Wittgenstein began talking about Beethoven:

> ... how a friend describes going to Beethoven's door and hearing him 'cursing, howling and singing' over his new fugue; after a whole hour Beethoven at last came to the door, looking as if he had been fighting the devil, and having eaten nothing for 36 hours because his cook and parlour-maid had run away from his rage. That's the sort of man to be.

'Wittgenstein brought me the most lovely roses today,' Russell told Ottoline. 'He is a treasure.' He also brought 'some new technical ideas ... which I think are quite sound and important'. If Russell did, as he was tempted to do, give up philosophy to concentrate on creative writing, he would not feel the subject neglected, 'as long as he [Wittgenstein] takes it up':

> I thought he would have smashed all the furniture in my room today, he got so excited. He asked me how Whitehead and I were going to end our big book, and I said we should have no concluding remarks, but just stop with whatever formula happened to come last. He seemed surprised at first, and then saw that was right. It seems to me the beauty of the book would be spoilt if it contained a single word that could possibly be spared.

Earlier in the year, Russell had committed himself to giving a paper to the Philosophical Society of University College, Cardiff, in May, and, after his original suggestion of speaking on 'the philosophical implications of symbolic logic' had been turned down, he had settled on the subject of the analysis of matter. His idea had been to emphasise how little reason we have for believing that there *is* any matter, indeed for believing that there is anything at all 'out there' beyond ourselves. Russell thought this would be a difficult and challenging theme, but when he discussed it with Wittgenstein, his student dismissed it as a 'trivial problem': 'He admits that if there is no Matter then no one exists but himself, but he says that doesn't hurt, since physics and astronomy, and all the other sciences could still be interpreted so as to be true.'

Russell nevertheless stuck to his theme. For him, the paper was an opportunity to see whether he could return to technical work, if his inspiration for other writing deserted him. His spiritual autobiography had for the moment been put to one side, but he had not yet abandoned it altogether. If he ever published it, he told Ottoline, he might do so anonymously under the name of Simon Styles: 'I might invent an author of that name and publish lots of things as his. No one would guess it was me. That's not at all the sort of person I am supposed to be.' His recent fit of passion, he thought, 'has burnt away the last remnants of sentimentality and made me much stronger in the way of writing . . . I might any moment be inspired with a perfect torrent of writing now, if only I could hit on a central idea.' A week or two later, however, he had resolved to 'go back to making technical work my purpose, and trust the other to luck'.

The chief reason for this resolution, he told Ottoline, was that the inequality in their affections made it necessary for him 'to keep passion in check', which, in turn, required him to turn his thoughts away from personal concerns and towards the comfortingly remote and abstract issues of philosophy. 'Dearest, don't think I am unhappy, I really am not at all,' he wrote, protesting, one feels, rather too much. 'I have been two months awaking from a dream; the waking was painful; but now I am awake, and the day is still full of joy.' In an earlier letter he had told her that he could no longer go back to the 'quietism' that had produced 'Prisons'. It was, he said, 'a religion only for the victims and passive sufferers of the world'. The happiness he had felt then was based on an illusion, and now that he had woken up and seen the illusoriness of it, he no longer wanted happiness, he wanted only courage and 'to think about big things rather than small ones'.

What he seemed to be recommending to himself was something akin to the austerity of 'the long night', a rejection of all passion, particularly sexual passion, all beauty and all pleasures except those of the intellect. 'Sometimes', he wrote on 30 April, 'I think *all* beauty, even the most divine, is a devil's draft to make men mad':

I never think that, tho', about the beauty of thought. The same mood that makes you rebel against sex exists in me, but much fiercer and more devastating; it includes along with all sex all beauty, except what has nothing to do with the senses, all emotion except the intellectual love of God, and almost all that you would call religion . . .

'There are two worlds', he told her, 'the world of illusion and the world of fact':

Everything mystical, all beauty that is intoxicating, almost all happiness, belongs to the world of illusion. The problem is to find a beauty and a

happiness that can live in the world of fact. Math'cs is for me one part of
the answer. Love of everybody gives great beauty, but not happiness unless
it is mystical, in which case it is mixed with illusion. There is some
legitimate happiness, tho' very much more pain, in the exercise of one's
faculties. The summit of legitimate joys is the joy of battle, of stripping
away illusions and standing forth naked to meet the storm.

At the root of this defeated and disillusioned return to the stoicism of 'Free
Man's Worship' was the increasingly unbearable sexual frustration that
Russell felt in his relations with Ottoline. Since returning from Lausanne,
Ottoline had made it clearer than ever that it was Russell's mind that
interested her, not his body. 'In the spiritual region you do most fully satisfy
me,' Russell wrote plaintively on 29 April. 'But my lower nature sometimes
yearns after the simple happiness I used to have at first . . . one can't live
always at the highest spiritual level.' Of all the different approaches to this
problem that Russell tried, the least successful was probably the attempt to
argue Ottoline out of her attitude. 'Quite impersonally and impartially,' he
wrote to her, 'I feel your judgment about sex is morbid and maladif. Your
feeling you cannot help, but you can help your opinion. I am much more
anxious you should think truly than feel in the way that wd. suit me.'
 'Sometimes I think we ought to give up everything sexual altogether,'
Russell told her, shifting from arguments to threats. 'It may be we should get
more of the best of each other that way. Only I doubt if I could stand it; I
might find it necessary to break altogether.' In the face of this threat, Ottoline
capitulated to some extent, though Russell now found that her period, her
'lady' as she rather coyly called it, had a frustrating tendency to arrive on just
the days that he and Ottoline had arranged to meet. 'Your lady has certainly
chosen a very inconvenient moment for her visit,' Russell wrote on 11 May,
adding: 'Dearest, don't feel obliged to come to tea tomorrow – I expect it
would be much better for you to rest, wouldn't it?'
 Ottoline had earlier repeated her suggestion that their love should not be
'selfish', hinting that Russell should find sexual relief elsewhere, but Russell
had been quick to reject the idea, arguing that jealousy would make any
relationship that was not exclusive impossible. As his frustration increased,
however, Russell warmed to the idea, only to find that Ottoline – realising,
no doubt, that if she lost Russell's sexual affections she risked losing all his
affections – had meanwhile changed her mind and now insisted on Russell's
exclusive love. The logical inconsistency of her new attitude was pointed out
to her by Russell with mathematical precision: 'Seeing that you, who have the
whole of two men, would suffer greatly if you only had one and a half, you
can perhaps imagine that it is hard to be content with a half, which is three
times less than what would *not* content you.'
 An opportunity seemed to present itself when Russell began to receive
affectionate letters from Mildred Minturn, whom he had met at Bryn Mawr
in 1896 and who had visited him and flirted with him in Oxford in 1904. She
was now married, but that did not appear to Russell at least to be an
insurmountable barrier. After discussing it with Ottoline, however, and with

some regrets, he abandoned the idea of pursuing her and tried to adopt instead the stoic indifference to matters of the flesh expressed in the letters already quoted. A turning point came in May 1912 when, instead of going to bed, he maintained what he called a 'night vigil', during which he exhorted himself to, as he put it, 'remember simple moral truths: not to make demands, nor deliberately to injure others whatever good may come of it.' It was partly as a result of that vigil that he could announce himself to have woken up from the 'dream' of his love for Ottoline.

Instead of seeking complete happiness with Ottoline, or simple sexual relief with someone else, Russell now decided to redirect his passion into his philosophical work. Largely under Wittgenstein's influence, Russell now looked upon *Principia Mathematica*, not as a cold repudiation of passion but as a beautifully austere expression of passion, albeit one of a particularly pure and rarefied nature. 'I have put into the world a great body of abstract thought,' he told Ottoline, 'which is moving those whom one might hope to move by it, and will ultimately, probably, move many people who will have never heard of philosophy':

> What makes it vital, what makes it fruitful, is the absolute unbridled Titanic passion that I have put into it. It is passion that has made my intellect clear, passion that has made me never stop to ask myself if the work was worth doing, passion that has made me not care if no human being ever read a word of it; it is passion that enabled me to sit for years before a blank page, thinking the whole time about one probably trivial point which I could not get right.

It was that passion, the 'theoretical passion' he had identified in Wittgenstein, that Russell sought now to recapture. In this rarefied sense of the word, 'passion' was not the opposite of 'coldness'; rather the two were almost synonymous. 'There is nothing to compare with passion for giving one cold insight,' he declared. He wanted his paper on matter to be 'a model of cold passionless analysis, setting forth the most painful conclusions with utter disregard of human feelings. I haven't had enough courage hitherto about matter, I haven't been sceptical enough . . . Most of my best work has been done in the inspiration of remorse, but any passion will do if it is strong enough. Philosophy is a reluctant mistress – one can only reach her heart with cold steel in the hand of passion.'

The image of reaching a mistress's heart with cold steel is odd and disturbing, suggesting as it does an act of murder rather than of seduction.[1] It was as if in his passion for philosophy, Russell had sublimated the mad, murderous fantasies to which he had been prone. And, indeed, when he began to write 'On Matter', he did so with something of the state of mind of an

---

[1] One is reminded that Rogojin, the fictional character with whom Russell felt most 'intimate', kills his beloved Nastasya with a knife-blow that (as Dostoyevsky takes pains to emphasise) went 'straight to the heart', a murder that the novel presents as the culmination of Rogojin's forlorn attempt to 'reach her heart' in the more usual sense.

assassin, determined to kill off comfortable illusions without mercy. 'It will shock people,' he told Ottoline, 'especially those who would like to agree with me – it is altogether too sceptical.' Its beginning, too, suggests a series of fatal stabbings:

In what follows, I shall endeavour to maintain three theses:
(1) That all the arguments hitherto alleged by philosophers against matter are fallacious;
(2) That all the arguments hitherto alleged in favour of matter are fallacious;
(3) That, although there may perhaps be reason to suppose that there is matter, yet we can have no means of finding out anything whatever as to its intrinsic nature.

In the sparsity of its language and the brisk, ruthless way it deals with the ideas that it rejects, there is something in this opening passage that suggests the work that Wittgenstein would later produce. When Russell showed the passage to Wittgenstein, he was delighted with it, declaring it to be the best thing Russell had done. As Russell continued to work on the paper, however, his tone and his attitude to the problem changed, so that, instead of upholding the radical scepticism that it appears to announce at the beginning, the paper becomes more constructive and goes on to suggest a positive proposal for avoiding scepticism. From the empiricist starting point that the foundation of all our knowledge is our immediate acquaintance with sense-data, Russell suggests that we regard material objects as 'collections of . . . actual and possible sense-data . . . bound together in ways that enable us to regard them as one "thing" '. From Wittgenstein's point of view, this was rather a disappointing turn of argument and in his opinion the paper failed to live up to its opening paragraph. With characteristic directness he told Russell that, having read the whole paper, he did not, after all, think much of it, 'but only', stressed Russell to Ottoline, 'because of disagreement, not because of its being badly done'. Before he received Wittgenstein's final verdict, Russell had, in any case, lost faith in both the paper and his attempt to return to technical work. The day after he finished it, he wrote to Ottoline entirely repudiating the sentiments he had expressed at the end of April. He now insisted that 'it is quite useless talking of parting' and that he could never stop loving Ottoline, or love another woman, and: 'On thinking it over, I find my instinct won't let me go back to technical work at present. I don't feel there is real importance in what I might do':

Ever since your day I have felt technical philosophy unimportant (not math'cs). The paper I am going to read at Cardiff seems to me quite useless, except as an exhibition of candour. I can't go on grinding out that sort of stuff when Life and Death and Love and Fate and Hell and Heaven call to me all day long – it seems trivial. I grow more and more of a sceptic in philosophy, and therefore I feel less and less that there is much to do.

On his way to Cardiff to read the paper, he wrote to Ottoline reaffirming the role she had played in his life in restoring to him 'all spiritual things and the world of beauty', and while he insisted that he still needed some moral effort to control his turbulent passions ('my nature is too full of evil'), the degree of control needed now 'is not so much as to freeze me up again'.

After giving the paper, Russell's mind turned back to creative and spiritual writing. He considered turning the autobiography into a dialogue between an old man and a young man, in which the old one was Russell himself. This way, he thought, 'one could put in all sorts of stuff that otherwise would be out of place'. He longed to get on with it, he told Ottoline, 'but just now the spirit has deserted me'. So, too, had his appetite for philosophy:

It worries me rather having discovered that I have so little belief in philosophy. I did seriously mean to go back to it, but I found I really couldn't think it very valuable. This is *partly* due to Wittgenstein, who has made me more of a sceptic; partly it is the result of a process which has been going on ever since I found you.

Wittgenstein, he felt, could do the work in philosophy that he himself had intended to do, 'and do it better'. After all: 'He starts fresh at a point which I only reached when my intellectual spring was nearly exhausted.' Russell felt that for most of the spring term he had rather neglected his 'young men', including Wittgenstein, because of his absorption with Ottoline, and, partly to compensate, he spent much time during the last week of term meeting and encouraging them. Wittgenstein, he was delighted to learn, was 'thinking of doing philosophy in the regular way here, and perhaps ultimately teaching. It will be a great joy to me if he stays on here':

I told him he ought not simply to *state* what he thinks true, but to give arguments for it, but he said arguments spoil its beauty, and that he would feel as if he was dirtying a flower with muddy hands. He *does* appeal to me – the artist in intellect is so very rare. I told him I hadn't the heart to say anything against that, and that he had better acquire a slave to state the arguments. I am seriously afraid that no one will see the point of anything he writes, because he won't recommend it by arguments addressed to a different point of view.

He and Wittgenstein began to speak of more intimate, even spiritual things, Wittgenstein surprising Russell by saying suddenly how much he admired the text 'What shall it profit a man if he gain the whole world and lose his own soul', and how few there were who did not lose their soul: 'I said it depended on having a large purpose that one is true to. He said he thought it depended more on suffering and the power to endure it.' The difference is revealing: Russell's way of preserving the soul by replacing personal concerns with impersonal ones rests ultimately on the desire to protect it from pain; Wittgenstein's is the more thoroughly stoical, rejecting even the comfort of Russell's 'infinite'.

The deep difference in their outlooks was again revealed in a conversation a few days later about *David Copperfield*:

Yesterday Wittgenstein began on Dickens, saying David Copperfield ought not to have quarrelled with Steerforth for running away with little Emily. I said I should have done so; he was much pained, and refused to believe it; thought one could and should always be loyal to friends and go on loving them. We got onto Julie de Lespinasse, and I asked him how he would feel if he were married to a woman he loved and she ran away with another man. He said (and I believe him), that he would feel no rage or hate, only utter misery. His nature is good through and through; that is why he doesn't see the need for morals. I was utterly wrong at first; he might do all kinds of things in passion, but he would not practise any cold-blooded immorality. His outlook is very free; principles and such things seem to him nonsense, because his impulses are strong and never shameful. I think he is passionately devoted to me. Any difference of feeling causes him great pain. My feeling towards him is passionate, but of course my absorption in you makes it less important to me than his feeling is to him.

Russell's perception of Wittgenstein – particularly his view that Wittgenstein's rejection of a morality based on principles was the consequence of a thoroughly good nature – seems naive and superficial, but one should perhaps regard it as an expression of his ongoing and intense preoccupation with his own nature, of his feeling that he was *not* 'good through and through', and that unless kept in check with principles, morality and reason, he was capable of 'cold-blooded immorality'.

The day after this conversation with Wittgenstein, Russell left Cambridge to spend a month in Lausanne with Ottoline. As Ottoline remembered it, Russell, who 'for some time past . . . [had] been very overwrought and unhappy because I was cold to him', insisted on joining her, and, as a consequence: 'I wasn't allowed to enjoy my loved, solitary peace.' Something of her attitude communicated itself to Russell, whose mood in the days before he left swung wildly from one extreme to the other. 'Oh how heavenly it will be,' he wrote on 27 May. 'I will be *very* good and never never never cut short your rests and be altogether the humble poodle.' Three days later, after a meeting with Ottoline made painful and unsatisfying by her unwillingness to make love to him, Russell was in the depths of a suicidal depression, telling her that he had lost the spring of life and was weary of the world: 'I want to lay down my head and sleep – to be done with strife and the terrible hope of happiness.' He was convinced (with some reason) that Ottoline no longer loved him, and that the last two months, since his walking holiday in Dorset, had inflicted upon their love a 'mortal wound':

If I could face life without you, I would break; I shall try to live without you, since if you go on in the same course it will soon be necessary . . . I feel that if we parted, little as I should intend it, the moment would come when in a sudden impulse I should put myself under a motor for the pleasure of feeling my backbone break.

And, if he avoided suicide, he told her, 'I should not avoid sexual crime, from mere desperation.' The horrible but unavoidable implication was that if Ottoline did not submit to his demands for sex, he would either kill himself or commit rape.

Ottoline responded to this anguished letter by assuring Russell that she did know what he felt and suffered. 'Oh Bertie,' she wrote, 'don't despair. Take at least what I give you', adding, perhaps hopefully, 'I feel you would rather not come to Lausanne.' Russell replied that, whatever happened, he would come: 'This is not a decision of my will; I should come even if I decided not to.' It was simply not in his power to stay away. In the way of love and sex, he would try to be content with what she gave him, and 'at Lausanne the outward circumstances may make it easy to put up with its being so little.' The outward circumstances in question were that Russell and Ottoline were staying in separate hotels at opposite ends of the town, that Ottoline would be spending a good deal of time resting, and that there would therefore be few opportunities for sexual encounters, whatever their inclinations.

Perhaps surprisingly, their time in Lausanne was remembered by both Ottoline and Russell as a happy one, though with the emphasis emphatically on the spiritual rather than the physical side of their love. Russell stayed in the Old Hotel in which Edward Gibbon had finished *The Decline and Fall of the Roman Empire*, and soon settled into a routine of working in the hotel's garden during the morning and then spending the afternoons with Ottoline, reading poetry or walking together. After a short while, Ottoline recorded, he 'soon grew gentler and more tender, more open to spiritual ideas.' The day that was particularly remembered by both of them as an especially happy one was 16 June, Ottoline's birthday, which they spent first in Geneva, where Russell bought her a beautiful, blue enamel watch, and then in Ferney, where they walked through the park and peered in through the gates of Voltaire's house. It was, wrote Ottoline, 'an enchanting day . . . Bertie loved to think he was treading in the paths Voltaire trod.' Russell later remembered their arrival in Ferney as 'one of those moments of inward & outward peace, when time stands still for an instant'.

On the morning of her birthday, Russell sent Ottoline a note 'to say I love you':

If I could give you what you ought to have, union in a great work, the worthy expression of the faith that makes what is good in our lives, I should ask nothing further of Fate. I fear my powers are too feeble for that; but I will still hope and struggle.

Having abandoned the idea of turning his autobiography into a conversation between an old man and a young one, Russell had decided instead to transform it into a novel, the writing of which would be to some extent a joint effort with Ottoline. The result of this collaboration, *The Perplexities of John*

Forstice – completed during the month they spent in Lausanne – conspicuously fails to live up to Russell's dream of a 'great work'. Almost entirely without dramatic incident, memorable characterisation or vivid writing of any kind, it completely justifies Russell's doubts about his powers as a novelist and consists mostly of rather stilted and artificial dialogue. Indeed, it is scarcely a novel at all, its origins as a spiritual autobiography appearing all too visibly beneath the flimsy veneer of fictional situations and characters. Despite its many artistic failings, however, as a record of how Russell saw the progression of his life it is both revealing and fascinating.

John Forstice (a name chosen to evoke the name of Faustus) is a very thinly disguised Russell, who begins the story as 'a single-minded enthusiast, innocent as a child in worldly matters' and 'known to physicists as a brilliant investigator of the constitution of matter'. Having just finished a vast piece of work, Forstice feels a sense of 'escape from the narrow concentration of a great task', and, breaking with habit, attends a garden party. There, in a way that recalls the novels of Thomas Love Peacock, he meets representatives of various world-views, including an Empire-builder, a Socialist and a clever but decadent financier, who take turns to describe to Forstice their outlook on life.

The purpose of these minor characters is really to establish which outlooks on life Russell had rejected at an early stage in his own life. Little time is spent on the narrow selfishness of the Empire-builder or on the spiritual poverty and misguided optimism of the Socialist, but Forstice returns from the garden party genuinely troubled (indeed, perplexed) by the pessimism of the financier. Is everything in life really worthless? he asks himself. 'I must think of this question reasonably, as I should think of a question in physics.' (The limitations of Russell's novelistic powers are, perhaps, already manifest in this soliloquy, which, I am sure, was written without a trace of irony.)

When he gets home, Forstice asks his wife the same question. She reacts by bursting into tears. 'Do you know,' she says, 'that in all the years of our marriage, this is the first time you have shown any real interest in me? We have lived side by side, yet utterly separate; you were so absorbed in your projects and your calculations that often you did not hear what I said.'

Changing, so to speak, from Alys to Evelyn Whitehead, Mrs Forstice now tells her husband what she has kept secret from him for a year, namely that she is dying from an incurable cancer. Overwhelmed by the news, Forstice undergoes a conversion like that Russell had undergone at the sight of Evelyn suffering an angina attack: 'all his abstract interests were thrust out utterly, leaving only a great elemental human devotion ... With a sympathy he had never known before, he saw the thoughts and feelings of others; the force of one great devotion set free the pent-up waters of love towards all the world.'

After his wife dies, Forstice, finding that 'he could not attach the same importance as in former times to abstract work and the things of the intellect', takes leave from his post as a physicist to travel the world in an effort to enlarge his knowledge of mankind and to remove his perplexities about the value of life. On his way home, he attends a meeting in Florence of a group of intellectuals called the 'Amanti del Pensiero' ('Lovers of Thought').

Superficially, this part of the story, too, is like one of Thomas Love Peacock's novels, as Forstice hears at the meeting a succession of speeches on what makes life worth living. On closer inspection, however, it is clear that what we are offered is not a clash of opinions, but a dialectical development of a single view. In particular, each of the speakers represents a stage in Russell's own intellectual development.

The first to speak is the mathematician, Forano (a portmanteau of Frege and Peano), who represents the initial stage in Russell's spiritual growth, his desire to find happiness and value in the eternal world of mathematical forms:

> Mathematics gives most joy when life gives most disgust. Remote from the passion and sordidness, the weakness and failure of our human world, the mathematician enters upon a calm world of ordered classic beauty, where human will, with its violence and uncertainty, counts for nothing; with joyful resignation he contemplates the unchanging hierarchy of exact, certain, shining truths, subsisting in lofty independence of Man, of time and place, of the whole universe of shifting accidental particular things.

Next comes the philosopher, Nasispo (a near-anagram of 'Spinoza'), who presents the familiar thought that the best in human life is to be achieved by rising above ordinary hopes and fears 'into the region of untroubled contemplation'. After him, the poet, Pardicreti (a mixture of Lucretius and Leopardi, whose poems Russell and Ottoline read together in Lausanne), who stresses the need to be creative and not just receptive, active as well as contemplative, to accept the material world analysed by science but to bring to that world the 'central fire', the 'glory' of our own imagination.

The final speech of this series is that of the Russian novelist, Chenskoff, who represents the Dostoyevkian Russell of the spring of 1912, tramping through Dorset as he reflected on his loss of Ottoline's love. 'The artists and madmen and creators', Chenskoff argues, 'are those who have seen heaven for a moment and then they wander through the earth trying to see it again, feeling nothing else counts, all else is exile.' Human life, for him, is always struggling and passionate, and so to begin with he, like Russell on Portland Bill, 'sought relief in whatever was least struggling and least passionate – calm, unfeeling Power. Necessity marching to its conclusions over the recurring generations of crushed lives and bleeding souls':

> I loved waste solitary places, rocky headlands where sea and land contended for mastery in a solemn recurring rhythm, where man and every living thing could be forgotten, where the outward tumult of the waves soothed my inward restlessness, and made me receptive of the unbending calm that lay beneath the noise and foam. Feeling, I thought, turns men from their purposes, makes them weak, irregular, and despicable; to have no feeling is to be strong. I longed to march through a pre-determined development with the ruthless consistency of the material world, to be as regular as necessary, as cruel, as though I were a mere embodiment of lifeless force. Contempt for myself and all mankind, a proud passion to transcend the

vanity of human existence, upheld me in this worship of the eternal sublimity of fate.

But, though he longed for such detachment, Chenskoff found it impossible in the face of 'the infinite pain which I felt to be the ultimate truth of life'. Most of the things that fill people's lives, 'all the energy and idealism, all the frenzy, madness, and wickedness of the world', as well as 'intoxication, cruelty, lust, [and] restless activity' are all inspired by the fear of that pain. But (in an attitude that recalls that expressed by Wittgenstein in his conversation with Russell about how to preserve one's soul) Chenskoff finally saw that the way really to deal with the pain is to turn and face it, 'to take it into the soul and endure while it stabbed and stabbed again.' Thus what is valuable in life is not, after all, to be gained by rising above passion, for 'all real life is passion', but by the forging of one's soul through the 'unimaginable anguish' of accepting life's infinite pain.

Though Russell later expressed most pride in the poet's speech, it is the Russian novelist's speech that seems to be the most obviously heartfelt and is certainly the most vividly written, perhaps because it expresses the feelings and experiences that were most fresh in Russell's mind. The most dreary is the speech of the 'ordinary man', who speaks after the Russian novelist and whose purpose is to express Ottoline's misgivings about philosophers speaking only to the educated élite. In his portrayal of this ordinary civil servant, Giuseppe Alegno, Russell comes closest to irony, though, even here, what looks like satire is perhaps only the result of Russell having no idea at all how an ordinary man would express his misgivings about the views of intellectuals. 'We common people,' Alegno says, 'who are, after all, the great majority of mankind, are too limited, too full of daily cares, to appreciate the refined delights of your various heavens':

We cannot understand mathematics and philosophy, we are indifferent to poetry, and music only pleases us when we can dance to it. We like novels well enough, but they must be about lost wills or amazing murders, not about the mystic marriage of pain . . . Either you must make your gospel as accessible to the poor and needy as Christianity has been, or you must find some other gospel which does not demand exceptional powers in the disciple.

This demand is met by the religious vision of a nun called Mother Catherine,[2] the description of whom was contributed by Ottoline, based on her recollections of Mother Julian. To introduce Mother Catherine, in a device clearly designed to allow him to describe his own love for Ottoline, Russell has Forstice discover that his dying uncle, Tristram Forstice (based on Russell's Uncle Rollo), once had a love affair with Catherine that is recorded in letters and a journal. As he reads through the journal, Forstice

---

[2] It is surely not by coincidence that the nun was given the name of Russell's own mother.

learns of a love that is a 'spiritual meeting in the silent ecstasy of union', and which, to those who have the power of such a love:

> There is . . . some disquieting hint, some wistful suggestion, of a mystical world where solitude is overcome, where the walls that divide each separate soul from its comrades are broken down.

Carrying out his uncle's last wishes, Forstice visits Catherine, who, in a speech added by Russell to Ottoline's description, preaches the gospel of 'Prisons' that 'in every human spirit there is something that is infinite and divine'. And the story ends with Forstice recognising this wisdom as providing the answer to his original question about the value of life, once, of course, it was 'disentangled from the God, the life of prayer, the belief in the power of the spirit, with which in her it was entwined'. Having learnt this lesson, 'with a pang that seemed like a second death', Forstice returned to physics.

On 2 July, while still in Lausanne, Russell wrote to Ottoline to tell her that he had finished *Forstice*. 'It wants changes,' he admitted, 'but it really is good':

> the best part of it is your part, *really*; I am sure anybody would say so. I have much less doubt about it than I had about *Prisons* even at the time; it really is worth something, I feel sure. And I think it is only the beginning of many things. It is all due to you, my Dearest. Don't forget that, if times of discouragement come later.

'Darling, Darling, it would have been *madness* to part,' he told her. 'Don't be too ready to let me go – our love is really sacred and not a thing to kill lightly . . . This month has been very wonderful . . . I do now feel very great confidence for the future.' And yet, in *Forstice* itself, there are signs precisely of a lack of confidence in the future. When the dying Tristram tells Forstice of his past love, he asks him to go to her and tell Catherine 'I loved her to the last', adding, 'There was a time – a very brief time – when she returned my love.' He and Catherine were to have been married after the death of her first husband, who had long been insane, but then her son, who had always been delicate, died and Catherine, full of remorse and blaming her affair with Tristram, joined the sisterhood. 'I wish you to tell her that I have long since understood, long since ceased to feel bitterness,' Tristram tells Forstice, 'that our little moment of happiness has lived in my memory; that my heart has built a precious shrine for the ashes of dead hopes.' The journal that he leaves with Tristram tells the whole story, how: 'The final parting, though he knows it to be inevitable, fills him with impotent rebellion; its very inevitability makes it the more cruel; and increases the anger which he directs by turns against fate and against Catherine . . . Slowly a calmer mood returns . . . Slowly he learns to turn his love to other uses, to universalise it and make it minister to sympathy and wisdom.'

In *Forstice*, then, Russell had not only sought to convey the spiritual importance of his love affair with Ottoline, but had also written a valediction to it. The sense that their affair could not possibly last, and indeed that it was already over, pervades the whole story, from Tristram Forstice's acceptance, despite his rebellion and anger, of the inevitability of his affair with Catherine coming to an end, to John Forstice's return – with a sense of 'second death' – to his study of physics. But perhaps its most poignant expression, emphasising the melancholic sense of what might have been, comes in Russell's description of John Forstice's last sight of Mother Catherine:

As he walked away, some instinct made him look up at the house, and rather to his surprise, he saw her standing at a window with a sad look; he felt she was looking at him as the last link with that past now outwardly and visibly for ever at an end. As he looked up, the second Vesper Bell rang; she turned slowly away and disappeared.

10

THE SHATTERED WAVE

'Coming back to business is horrible,' Russell wrote to Ottoline on 9 July 1912 after arriving back in Cambridge from Lausanne. Waiting for him was a large pile of things to attend to, including:

. . . a letter from a Russian logician complaining that he has not had a notice of the Math'al Congress (my fault!); a complicated set of notes by a schoolmaster on how to teach geometry, with a letter asking my opinion; a new posthumous book of W. James; a very fat book on math'al philosophy by a Frenchman whom I know, full of criticisms of me which I ought to answer; a book on non-Euclidean Geometry by an Italian; various invitations which all raise complicated problems; etc. etc. etc.

Turning his mind to such matters was almost more than he could bear: 'it is so intolerable after thinking of real eternal things.' But, he felt, the good that had been done in Lausanne would not, could not, now be undone: 'I believe we have got *permanently* onto the right basis; I don't think I shall ever rage again; and I feel the whole world incredibly *real* to me and alive, so that I am sure I can go on writing whenever I have enough complete leisure. I now feel no doubt that *Forstice* is very good indeed – and that helps me to feel peaceful.'

He had, he wrote the next day, '*entirely* ceased to feel what troubled me in the letter I got at Weymouth . . . So all the old ghosts are exorcised.' He felt a new sense of harmony between the various sides of his nature, and believed that now 'the main thing I ought to do in the world [is] to make a harmony of intellect and mysticism – not to put them side by side, but to make one fused whole of them.' This 'fused whole' would, presumably, be expressed in works like *Forstice*. For the moment, at least, Russell considered himself to have done with technical philosophy, the advancement of which, in an almost ceremonious gesture, he now made Wittgenstein's responsibility. The occasion for this came a few days after his return from Lausanne, and a few days before Wittgenstein's return to Vienna for the summer, when Wittgenstein brought his eldest sister, Hermine, to tea with Russell. As they sat together in Russell's rooms in Trinity, Hermine was amazed to hear Russell announce: 'We expect the next big step in philosophy to be taken by your brother.'

In the summer of 1912, Russell was not alone in seeking a fusion of intellect and mysticism. The notion was 'in the air', part indeed of the *Zeitgeist* that had created the fashion for Bergson. In July, the Indian poet Rabindranath Tagore arrived in England, and, chiefly through the enthusiastic advocacy of the painter William Rothenstein, was befriended and lionised by many of the same people who had earlier in the year paid tribute to Bergson, including George Bernard Shaw. Among Tagore's admirers was Goldie Lowes Dickinson, who, one evening in July, brought Tagore to Trinity to meet Russell. Years later, Dickinson recounted the meeting in an article for *The New Leader*:

In a Cambridge garden. Mr Bertrand Russell and myself sit there alone with Tagore. He sings to us some of his poems, the beautiful voice and the strange mode floating away on the gathering darkness. Then Russell begins to talk, coruscating like lightning in the dusk. Tagore falls into silence. But afterwards he said, it had been wonderful to hear Russell talk. He had passed into a 'higher state of consciousness' and heard it, as it were, from a distance. What, I wonder, had he heard?

Though Dickinson describes Russell's remarks as 'coruscating', there is no doubt that this meeting, coming as it did at the very moment Russell declared his aim to fuse mysticism and the intellect, is the closest Russell ever came to what D. H. Lawrence would later denounce to Ottoline as 'this wretched worship-of-Tagore attitude' that prevailed in England that summer.

When *Forstice* returned from being typed, Russell was a little more critical of it than he had been hitherto. It was, he recognised, a little short on atmosphere: 'the mood must be more created, less taken for granted – the whole thing wants to be fuller, less bold, less clipped.' But his faith in it was by no means altogether destroyed. 'I used to be unable to feel the importance of imaginary things when I wrote them myself,' he told Ottoline, 'but I don't in this.' The rather curious reason he gave for this was that 'I have a real affection for the man Forstice, as if I were a friend, & I feel it important to make people see what a lovable person he is.' From this one must conclude, either that he considered Forstice to be a genuinely fictional creation and not just a representation of himself, or that he considered the point of *Forstice* to be to convey his own lovableness.

Whatever doubts Russell was beginning to entertain about the literary value of *Forstice* were (temporarily, at least) removed a few days later when he received Goldie Dickinson's reaction to it. Though earlier in the year he had been rather unenthusiastic about 'The Essence of Religion', Dickinson now praised *Forstice* in the most extravagant terms imaginable. 'It seems to me a great piece of writing,' he wrote. 'I do really think it has the quality of the best seventeenth-century prose, which is the highest praise one can give.' He went on to say that, of the various speeches, the two he liked most were those of the mathematician and the philosopher (which is somewhat odd, seeing that the views they express are so close to 'The Essence of Religion'). The poet's speech had confused him, while the Russian novelist's view was 'the one to which I respond least from my own experience' (Dickinson was not the sort of man to liken himself to a crazed murderer like Rogojin, and no doubt would have been shocked had he known that Russell had done so). Alegno, Russell's ordinary man, Dickinson thought 'makes a good diversion ... We must admit, I think, that we have nothing to say in reply', and, finally, the nun was done 'with extraordinary beauty and sympathy':

> Your conclusion is perhaps as far as one can go in words. What can be done in life, only life can show. But the thing you really have to say, and have said, is diffused throughout the whole and lies just beyond the said, as in all art.

'You are the only man I know well who seems like myself to be aware of being on a pilgrimage,' Dickinson wrote, adding that he hoped Russell would publish *Forstice*: 'You will find an audience few but fit.'

Perhaps paying undue attention to the warning at the beginning of Dickinson's letter that 'it is possible I think better of your MS than anyone else would', Russell saw in Dickinson's remarks exactly the encouragement he had been looking for to justify his inclination to concentrate on creative writing. 'The impulse to technical work is spent,' he announced to Ottoline. 'All through last year, it has been fading away: now Dickinson's letter seems to have given it a death-blow.' Now that he had outgrown it, he could look upon his drive to write technical work as morbid and unhealthy: 'In an odd way it belonged with the sense of sin and disgust of human life. It could be revived now by shame and remorse, but not, I think, by anything else':

> I have changed quite enormously since your reign began – you bring out the artist and diminish the nonconformist . . . I don't know at all where it will end . . . I think there is something at bottom that will keep me always as Goldie says, on a pilgrimage. Just now, all my instinctive effort is to get imagination free, as strongly as it used to be to get thought clear . . . It is really amazing how the world of learning has grown unreal to me. Mathematics has quite faded out of my thoughts . . . Philosophy doesn't often come into my mind, and I have no impulse to work at it. My whole impulse, in mental things, is towards imaginative writing – I long to have leisure of mind for it, and to live the sort of life that would suit it.

If he went on being able to write imaginatively, he told her, he would give up academic work altogether at the end of his five-year lectureship, by which time Wittgenstein would be ready to take his place.

This was to be the high point in Russell's self-confidence as an imaginative writer, which over the next two months was steadily and continuously eroded, until by the end of September 1912 it had all but disappeared. It was up against a formidable combination of forces, which included: the discouraging criticisms of *Forstice* that were made by almost everybody who read it, except Dickinson; the influence of Wittgenstein's increasingly intense absorption in philosophical logic and his fierce criticisms of Russell's less technical work;

and (most powerfully of all) the gradual worsening of Russell's relationship with Ottoline. Each one of these would probably have been sufficient by itself to undo the work of Dickinson's encouragement, but together they proved devastating.

Evelyn Whitehead's criticisms of *Forstice* were surprisingly mild. The only part to which she took exception was the speech added by Russell to Ottoline's description of Mother Catherine, which, she thought, was quite unreal and 'obviously an intellectual man's conception of a nun'. This prompted Russell to think about the deficiencies in his characterisation of some of the other people in the story, particularly the other female character, Mrs Forstice. She 'ought to be less shadowy, oughtn't she?' he wrote to Ottoline. 'At present she is not alive at all on her own account.' And the reader, he thought, ought really to know more about Forstice himself, about his past life, for example, and the later parts needed filling out and the beginning lengthened. In fact, all in all, Russell came to feel that it needed to be completely rewritten:

> I believe I ought to work at it for years and years, gradually inventing new incidents. I wish I knew more of the world – it is a dreadful thing to have been a student up to the age of forty!

The most damaging and most straightforward criticism came from Lucy Silcox, to whom it fell to point out to Russell that there was 'quite enough mere discussion' in the story, and that what it needed was some action, some dramatic tension. That this is so, and that it is the chief failing of the book, is so obvious that one must suppose that only politeness prevented others from making the same point. The highest wisdom may or may not consist in the avoidance of strife, but, as Russell came to realise, the best novel-writing emphatically does not. 'What I should like to do', he told Ottoline, in the light of Lucy Silcox's remarks, 'would be to exhibit some kind of strife resulting from too finite an outlook in the people concerned.' But, he acknowledged, 'That wants so much Art.'

In his efforts to improve *Forstice*, Russell became increasingly aware that his limitations as a writer had much to do with the narrowness of his life. 'Wars and pestilences and so on', he was forced to acknowledge, 'are not the things I can do'; he had neither the experience nor the imagination required. His strongest suit as a writer lay in the expression of opinions, and therefore, in place of war, he would have to settle for 'men who believe in war', instead of strife, 'people whose ideal contains strife in some form – imperialists, plutocrats, futurists, Bergson, etc. etc. Strindberg could come in . . . I will try to do them all with love, not with contempt.'

To these unpromising suggestions, he later added the idea of 'an Ecclesiastes pessimist', who 'will be very literary, & will begin on the text "there is no new thing under the sun" ', and whose pessimism would be answered by the philosopher. Apart from increasing the number and variety of opinions expressed, the only other improvement Russell could think of to make the story come alive was to shift its scene from Florence to America, 'perhaps at the opening of the Panama Canal?' There would be 'a collection of men assembled to witness this landmark of human progress', while the pessimist read from an ancient papyrus that he had found about the Pharoahs' building of a Suez Canal. Even as he was suggesting these things, however, Russell could see that it was a lost cause – 'No, this is all too farcical. I must have a simple setting' – and that a solution to the problem of turning *Forstice* into a decent novel was receding further and further.

Final defeat was acknowledged in a letter of 25 September, in which Russell said he had grown quite depressed about 'the failure to get on with *Forstice*'. After that, the story was put aside and Russell, once again, turned back to technical philosophy.

In what is by now discernible as a recurring pattern, Russell's decision to turn away from creative writing and towards philosophy came partly as a reaction to problems in his relationship with Ottoline. In a letter to her in October 1912, Russell described the pattern in this way: 'When I am unhappy I want you so much that I daren't think of it. I want just affection, not wisdom, because that is really no help in those moods. And then I can't reach you and if I can there are endless impalpable barriers – and then I feel life is passing and we are losing touch with each other – and at last I feel to hell with all emotions, and then I settle down to work.'

In accordance with this pattern, the decision to abandon *Forstice* came immediately after a meeting between Russell and Ottoline, during which a crisis in their relationship – which had been building up for months – came to a head. On 24 September, Ottoline records in her journal a visit from Russell to the farmhouse in Churn on the Berkshire Downs, at which she and Philip were staying:

> Bertie came down on Sunday, and spent the afternoon with me, and all yesterday too. He was depressed and self-absorbed, in a fit of darkness and depression.
> ... I could not help feeling intolerant of so much self-absorption and self-pity ... but with genius I suppose it is impossible not to feel so, and I, as a woman, ought to have been tender and sympathetic and cushioning. Poor thing! While we were sitting out on the downs he sobbed and sobbed, and this of course melted me, and I felt how cruel and unsympathetic I had been.

As this passage reveals, Ottoline's attitude to Russell had hardened in the months since their return from Lausanne, and, though insisting to both him and her own journal that she still loved him, she added to her account of this occasion an analysis of his character that shows a keen eye for his faults:

> He is so lonely and tortured by his brain incessantly working, and he cannot be sympathetic in the things that so much affect me. His body and mind seem to have a huge gap between them. His hands are like the paws of a bear: no feeling in them, only force. His intellect is so immense, but *en l'air*: not *en rapport* with the things of this sensual life. No visionary

power or imagination in that direction, or what there is is very arctic and bare. No fancy. He is not narrow, only shorn.

He seems like a delicate, fine, electric instrument, but not fed by ordinary life, only by theories and instincts. And yet at times he has visionary power, but that mood is rare; usually the vision is abstract and mathematical or, if gazing upon humanity, passionate, tragic and pessimistic.

But I have been dwelling too much on his failings. His intellect is supreme, but he lives up there so much that all the rest of him seems to have lost motion. I feel it exhausting, as I have to keep in step with his intellect all the time, and also satisfy his heart.

As well as being exhausted by his intensity, Ottoline had also been hurt and angered by his insensitive egotism. He had, she records, been annoyed with her for wanting quiet times by herself in the day for reading: 'He expects me to be entirely at his disposal, morning, noon, night, and becomes very angry if I am not. He told me that I could never accomplish anything important in life by *my* reading, while I could help him by being with him. This wounded me acutely at the time, and I have never forgotten it.'

In a section that was deleted from the published version of her journals, Ottoline adds to this already damning analysis the wish that Russell would be a little less earnest, and the view that there was a side to her nature which Russell, in his deep, dark earnestness, was utterly unable to understand: the 'wild bohemian artistic side which never gets a look in except in my extravagance about colour and dress and pictures'. It was the side of her that had been drawn to people like Augustus John and Henry Lamb, and which Russell had never satisfied. Augustus John had long gone out of her life, and Lamb finally broke with her soon after her return from Lausanne in July (though, even then, she wrote that she would never stop loving him, 'whatever happens'), but in Lytton Strachey Ottoline had found someone with whom she could indulge this bohemian, artistic side of her nature to the full. And Strachey's homosexuality made it perfect: no matter how much they gossiped or flirted or fooled around together, they would always remain free from the ugly complications that sexual desire seemed inevitably to introduce (as Strachey was finding in his love for Lamb no less certainly than Ottoline in hers for Russell).

In the weeks immediately prior to Russell's emotionally wrought visit to Churn, Ottoline had been spending a great deal of time with Strachey, who, having recently returned from a holiday in Ireland with Lamb 'an emotional, nervous and physical wreck', stayed with Ottoline to recover. Comforting each other, Ottoline and Strachey discovered that they had the same love of high-spirited absurdity, and, to Ottoline's delight, Strachey was prepared to camp it up for her benefit to the very hilt:

At night Lytton would become gay and we would laugh and giggle and be foolish; sometimes he would put on a pair of my smart high-heeled shoes, which made him look like an Aubrey Beardsley drawing, very wicked. I love to see him in my memory tottering and pirouetting round the room with feet looking so absurdly small, peeping in and out of his trousers, both of us so excited and happy, getting more fantastic and gay.

As if to underline the contrast, and to illustrate what was missing in her relations with Russell, immediately following this passage in her published memoirs is the curt sentence: 'Bertie also came to see me here, but I remember little of his visit except a melancholy walk ending in the church-yard.'

Strachey had been staying with the Morrells during the visit that had ended with Russell bursting into tears, though he had been informed in advance that, for the few days that Russell was there, Ottoline's attention would be taken up with 'that wretch Bertie'. No doubt his presence heightened what Russell, before he came, had described as 'a terrible dread of your fading away'. After the visit, Russell returned to Cambridge a changed man. He later described it as 'the time at Churn when I turned my thoughts back to work'. On 27 September, the day after his return, he wrote that he was 'full of thoughts about work'. He had decided to write 'what ought to be an important paper called "What is Logic?"'

Russell's decision to write on this topic was no doubt influenced by Wittgenstein, who, while he was in Vienna during the summer, kept up a correspondence with Russell that was full of tantalising hints of a new theory of logic that was taking shape in his mind. 'Logic is still in the melting pot,' he wrote on 22 June, 'but one thing gets more and more obvious to me':

The prop[osition]s of Logic contain ONLY APPARENT variables and what-ever may turn out to be the proper explanation of apparent variables, its consequence *must* be that there are NO *logical* constants.
Logic must turn out to be of a TOTALLY different kind than any other science.

Though as yet in an undeveloped and embryonic form, there is already implicit in these remarks a conception of logic that completely undermines the view that lay at the foundation both of Russell's philosophy of mathematics and of his 'religion of contemplation'. For, in insisting that logic has neither real (as opposed to apparent) variables nor constants, Wittgenstein seems to be rejecting the idea that there are any logical objects at all. Logic is therefore 'totally different from any other science' in not having a subject matter! This cuts at the very root of Russell's understanding of both logic and philosophy, for he conceived both to be the analysis of logical *forms*. In Wittgenstein's view there are no forms to analyse, and, therefore, *contra* Russell's Spinozistic religion, no forms to contemplate, either.

Among his reports of the latest twists and turns of his thinking on logic, there are remarks in Wittgenstein's letters to Russell that reveal a different side of his nature. For example, in a letter of 22 June, he tells Russell that whenever he has time he reads William James's *Varieties of Religious Experience*. 'This book does me a *lot* of good,' he tells Russell:

I don't mean to say that I will be a saint soon, but I am not sure that it
does not improve me a little in a way in which I would like to improve *very
much*: namely I think that it helps me to get rid of the *Sorge* (in the sense
in which Goethe used the word in the 2nd part of Faust).

Coming at precisely the moment when Russell had expressed his desire to
establish a harmony between the intellect and mysticism, these comments
seemed to Russell to secure a special intimate bond between himself and
Wittgenstein. During August, while he struggled to improve *Forstice*, Russell
sought inspiration in a biography of Mozart and the published letters of
Beethoven. Wittgenstein was delighted to hear it. 'These are the actual sons
of God,' he told Russell, a remark that again struck exactly the right note.
Writing to Ottoline on the day he received Wittgenstein's letter, Russell
commented on 'how glorious it would be to be like Mozart' and then
immediately added: 'I had a letter from Wittgenstein, a dear letter which I
will show you. I love him as if he were my son.'
At the time of these letters Russell was presiding over the philosophical
section of the Fifth Annual International Congress of Mathematicians, which
was being held in Cambridge from 22 to 28 August. 'I find it excites me and
gets hold of me to think of seeing so many people interested in mathematical
philosophy,' he wrote to Ottoline, 'my interest revives and the scent of battle
stirs my blood. The love of power is terribly strong in me. I can't help
reflecting that all these mathematical philosophers have different thoughts
from what they would have had if I had not existed.' The bulk of his time
that particular day had been taken up with the Italian mathematician
Giuseppe Peano, who, though 'now getting old', looked 'the ideal picture of
a logician – he has quite extraordinary nobility from single-mindedness'.
Russell's remarks about Mozart and Wittgenstein were made in the context
of confessing that, in the company of people like Peano, he felt 'an odd sense
of treachery . . . because learning does not absorb me as it does them. I envy
many people their simplicity – they seem so much less torn by conflicting
passions than I have always been, and they seem to work without the agony
and bloody sweat.'
Wittgenstein, of course, was quite different. In the first week of September
1912, Wittgenstein stayed with Russell for a few days at Bury Street, in
between arriving from Vienna and leaving again for Iceland, where he was to
spend a month's holiday with David Pinsent, a Cambridge undergraduate of
whom he had become very fond. 'We talk about music, morals and a host of
things besides logic,' Russell wrote. He was, Russell remarked pointedly, 'a
very great contrast to the Stephens and Stracheys and such would-be
geniuses':

We very soon plunged into logic and have had great arguments. He has a
very great power of seeing what are really important problems.
He gives me such a delightful lazy feeling that I can leave a whole
department of difficult thought to him, which used to depend on me alone.
It makes it easier for me to give up technical work.

The idea that Russell repeats again and again of handing over the subject of mathematical logic to Wittgenstein was taken perfectly seriously by both of them, and, if it was felt as a relief by Russell it was, correspondingly, felt as a great burden of responsibility by Wittgenstein. He *had* to solve the problems he was working on, he felt, because nobody else either could or would deal with them. It was as if he had been given an important and difficult task by God Himself, and he refused to take it lightly. No doubt sensing this attitude and fearful of the potentially inhibiting effect it might have, Russell gave Wittgenstein some 'sage advice' not to put off writing until he had solved all the problems 'because that day will never come':

> This produced a wild outburst – he has the artist's feeling that he will produce the perfect thing or nothing – I explained how he wouldn't get a degree or be able to teach unless he learnt to write imperfect things – this all made him more and more furious – at last he solemnly begged me not to give him up even if he disappointed me.

The following day, Wittgenstein set off for Iceland and did not return to Cambridge until the start of term on 11 October.

While Wittgenstein was in Iceland, Russell's hopes for both his own imaginative writing and his relationship with Ottoline were dashed and, after his emotionally fraught few days in Churn at the end of September, he decided that he was not, after all, going to give up technical work, and that, far from leaving the analysis of logic entirely in Wittgenstein's hands, he was himself going to write a paper on the subject. By an ironic coincidence, and unfortunately for his relations with Wittgenstein, just as he reached this decision, the *Hibbert Journal* chose to publish 'The Essence of Religion', the manuscript of which it had had for months.

On the first day of the new term, therefore, Wittgenstein, having seen the article, burst into Russell's rooms to protest. Russell was in the middle of a letter to Ottoline: 'Here is Wittgenstein just arrived, frightfully pained by my *Hibbert* article which he evidently *detests*.' Later that day, Russell gave Wittgenstein's reasons for hating it: 'He felt I had been a traitor to the gospel of exactness, and wantonly used words vaguely; also that such things are too intimate for print. I minded very much, because I half agree with him.' Two days later, he said that Wittgenstein's criticisms had disturbed him greatly: 'He was so unhappy, so gentle, so wounded in his wish to think well of me.'

Wittgenstein's criticisms of 'The Essence of Religion' came at a moment when Russell was only too willing to accept them, and, in the face of them, he lost faith entirely in the article. He never let it be reprinted and demurred whenever he heard any praise of it, even though its admirers included many distinguished writers. Rabindranath Tagore, for example, wrote to Russell just a few days after it had been published to express his approval and agreement. One cannot apprehend the Infinite through knowledge, Tagore wrote, 'yet when you live the life of the Infinite and are not bound within the limits of the finite self you realise that great joy which is above all the pleasures and pains of our selfish life.' Despite the fact that this is little more than a paraphrase of Russell's own opinions as set forth in the paper, when, many years later, Russell was asked about this letter, he replied harshly: 'I regret I cannot agree with Tagore. His talk about the infinite is vague nonsense. The sort of language that is admired by many Indians unfortunately does not, in fact, mean anything at all.'

Under Wittgenstein's influence, Russell had given up using such language and he now redoubled his efforts to do some decent technical work. On the day that he described Wittgenstein's distress at 'The Essence of Religion', he wrote that his mind was full of the paper on 'What is Logic?' that he had decided to write, and 'which I think may be really important with luck'. He had, he said, been 'arguing logic' with Wittgenstein: 'it is difficult but I feel I must have another go at it.' His determination was short-lived. On the very next day, he confessed that he could not get on with the paper: 'the subject is hopelessly difficult, and for the present I am stuck.' He felt, after all, 'very much inclined to leave it to Wittgenstein'.

What survives of this two-day struggle is a five-page manuscript containing a series of halting, confused and inconclusive reflections, which centre on the definition of logic as 'the study of the forms of complexes'. A complex is Russell's name for the collection of objects – mental or physical, universal or particular – that correspond to a proposition if it is true. For example, to the proposition 'Plato precedes Socrates' corresponds the complex consisting of three objects: Plato, Socrates, and the universal which is the relation 'precedes'. But what is the *form* of a complex? It is, Russell says, 'the way the constituents are put together'. But is the form itself an object? On this point, the paper founders, with Russell being pulled in two opposite directions. On the one hand, forms cannot be objects because, if they were, the question would arise as to how they were related to the other constituents of the complex, and this would lead to an infinite regress. On the other hand, they have to be objects, for otherwise there is nothing for logic to study. 'A *form* is something,' Russell insists, but, as yet, he has little idea what kind of 'something' it is, leaving his definition of logic as 'the study of the forms of complexes' looking rather empty, amounting to little more than the unhelpful statement: 'Logic is the study of something.'

The day after he had abandoned the paper, Russell showed himself to be in a similar position regarding the nature of his own work. 'I don't know yet quite what I want to do,' he wrote to Ottoline, 'but I know I must get going on something important.' His feelings for her were at a low ebb 'because instinct is driving me back to technical thought'. Not that he loved her 'one atom' less than he ever did, it was just that his love was 'imprisoned . . . by difficulties and self-control', and 'I dare not let myself loose because it becomes a madness.' In order to keep himself sane, he had, so to speak, to lock himself up, and the best way he knew of doing that was to immerse himself in philosophy. That he did not, at that moment, have any philosophical questions to think about (other than the ones he had abandoned because they were too difficult) was not an insurmountable barrier, for something would be found to fit the bill. The main thing was to concentrate his mind on something dry and technical, something that saved him from the debilitating effect of dwelling on his emotional life. Though he felt a 'sense of failure and isolation from having to go back to technical work', Russell told Ottoline, and though he minded 'the effort of screwing my mind up to the point where it wd. work on difficult things', he needed to make the effort in order to find some sort of rest. The time had come to say 'to hell with all emotions' and to settle down to work.

Leaving 'What is Logic?' to one side, Russell turned his attention to the paper 'On Matter', which he had written earlier in the year and which he had now arranged to read to the Moral Science Club on 25 October. This he tinkered with for about a week, and got, he claimed, 'the problem *very* much clearer than it has ever been got before'. The problem, perhaps, was clearer, but evidently not its solution. On the morning of the meeting he wrote: 'I don't know yet whether to say there is matter or there isn't!'

In the event he argued, as he had in Cardiff, that matter could be, as it were, 'constructed' from sense-data, 'not only of those which one observer perceives, [but] of all the sense-data which all possible observers would perceive in perceiving the same thing'.[1] After he had given the paper, he told Ottoline that it had not been a success because it was too difficult – 'No one except Wittgenstein understood it at all' – but he himself was quite pleased with it. He began to see it as the beginning of some large philosophical project: 'I see vast problems growing out of it – it seems a central point from which to start one's journey':

I see the materials in it for something very important . . . [It] opens out a host of interesting problems. It is such a comfort to feel keen and have the zest for work, instead of having to force it out by continual efforts.

One of the central ideas for this new piece of work, he said, he had tried out on Wittgenstein, who, instead of destroying it, as he had done Russell's fledgeling work on the nature of logic, had encouraged it.

Within a few days, Russell's philosophical ambitions were completely revived. He wanted, he told Ottoline, to 'start philosophers on a different track, and bring back the union of philosophy and science that existed in the 17th century, as well as in Plato and Aristotle'. The education of philosophers was all wrong: instead of learning the classics, they should, like Wittgenstein, be given a thorough grounding in science and technology. Russell aspired to nothing less than a revolution in the aims and methods of philosophy, a transformation of the whole discipline. 'I feel that I really have got a method that gives more precision than there has ever been,' he wrote, but: 'It is difficult to get people to see it, because philosophers are not trained to precision.' He would change that, both in his teaching and in his writing. He now thought he was capable of another large and important book on technical philosophy:

---

[1] A material object can be perceived from a myriad of different perspectives. Russell's idea was that if we take *what* is perceived from every possible perspective, then that collection of what he calls possible sense-data (or what he would later call sensibilia) *is* the material object.

The work I have done since the big book was finished has some unity that I can't get hold of, if I could, I should probably see how to write a big book. But as yet I don't know what the central theme is. It is an odd blind impulse – I dread the slavery of another big book – it is really frightful – yet I would do anything to get hold of the central idea that wd. make a big book.

The idea for the 'big book' that gradually took shape in his mind was that of using the techniques of mathematical logic to provide a clear and precise philosophical foundation for physical science. *Principia Mathematica* had done it for mathematics and for the mathematical element in science: 'But there are a number of other more elusive a priori elements in knowledge – such problems as causality and matter involve them. It is these I want to get hold of now.' It was, he wrote a few days later, 'a vast & very difficult subject' that 'may easily grow into years of work & a big book'. By 9 November, he was talking in even grander terms of 'a whole new science to be created':

I am sure I have hit upon a real thing, which is very likely to occupy me for years to come. The problem requires a combination of physics, psychology, & mathematical logic . . . It is not really only matter that I am concerned with, but the basis & extent of our knowledge of things & people other than ourselves; matter is merely the technical form that the question takes.

It was, he wrote, in a later letter, 'a fine big canvas that may easily take me 10 years to fill in. The mere thought of it makes my blood tingle. It suddenly makes a whole lot of things interesting that wouldn't otherwise interest me. I only hope I can manage the imaginative effort.' Among the things it made suddenly interesting were the latest developments in physics, with which Russell now endeavoured to acquaint himself, first by reading popularisations and then: 'When I have read enough of them to know my way about, I will start on things that are not popular.'

On 8 December, Russell apologised to Ottoline for 'what I said about murdering love'. It was, apparently, a remark linked to his growing self-belief in his philosophical work, which, upon reflection, he withdrew. What is best in his love, he now insisted, would be strengthened rather than murdered by his technical work. 'The irridescent magical transfiguring quality', however, 'must grow less.' But was it not precisely that quality that *was* the best in his love? Perhaps once, but no longer. Now, the most he could say of his love was that it was a 'help and strength and inspiration', a 'refuge from the loneliness of long tasks unshared'. Now what he prayed for was 'an unconquerable spirit . . . and loyalty to one's task':

I love to think of the bright shining passionless creation, showing no faintest trace of the agony and bloody sweat out of which it grows. That is partly why logic and math'cs inspire me more than religious writing, because they disdain even to notice suffering.

And yet, at the beginning of term, he had said that his impulse to write technical philosophy 'belonged with the sense of sin and disgust of human life' and could be revived only 'by shame and remorse'. Had he been entirely wrong about his own impulses or had he been overcome by shame and remorse? Or had he rediscovered his sense of sin and disgust of human life?

At the end of term Russell took another walking tour on his own, this time in the West Country, in which he again went for long solitary walks in the rain. It was, he told Ottoline, nasty but effective medicine: 'One has time to fetch all the spectres out and have a good look at them. I have been fighting for sanity all this time, keeping sane by a concentrated effort of will, which left me no thoughts for anything else.' In another letter he spoke of his 'extraordinarily strong' impulse to work on 'Matter': 'it quite possesses me and drives me on like the lash of a slave-driver.' Part of his concentrated effort to stay sane, then, was the voluntary submission to the lash of the whip, the tyranny of an impulse, which, though demanding a great deal of his intellect and his energy, yet gave him some release. Perhaps, after all, there remained something penitential about his commitment to technical philosophy, some sense in which it still 'belonged with the sense of sin and disgust of human life'.

In Wittgenstein's case, the connection between the two was quite explicit. He had, that term, been even more turbulent than ever, and, in Russell's opinion at least, close to a nervous breakdown, 'feeling himself a miserable creature, full of sin'. He would come to Russell's rooms for hours, sometimes arguing logic, sometimes remaining silent, often in an almost suicidal despair. Once, when he was pacing up and down, Russell asked him, 'Are you thinking of logic or of your sins?' 'Both,' replied Wittgenstein.

It seems unlikely that Russell confided in Wittgenstein to the extent of revealing that he, too, was at times inclined to draw a connection between thinking about logic and thinking about one's sins. Instead, he acted as the embodiment of British stolidity and common sense, advising Wittgenstein to take more exercise and to eat more sensibly, and passing on Ottoline's advice to drink cocoa at night. But, he had no doubt that such advice would remain unheeded. And he knew, too, what intellectual strain Wittgenstein was under, concentrating his whole being on the very problems that Russell himself had abandoned after two days' struggle. 'He strains his mind to the utmost,' he told Ottoline, 'at things which are discouraging by their difficulty, and nervous fatigue tells on him sooner or later. I think physical remedies can mitigate his bad times, but he will always have them as long as he goes on thinking, I expect.'

Wittgenstein's intense single-mindedness made Russell feel like a compromiser, and the force of his passion like 'a bleating lambkin'. Compared with Wittgenstein, he said, 'you wd. think I had never felt the slightest excitement over anything, but was a mere bundle of common sense'. Midway through the term, they spent the afternoon by the river watching North Whitehead compete in a rowing race. Russell himself found the 'excitement and conventional importance' of the event 'painful', but Wittgenstein found it quite disgusting. At one point Wittgenstein 'suddenly stood still and explained that the way we had spent the afternoon was so vile that we ought not to live, or at least that he ought not; that nothing is tolerable except producing great works or enjoying those of others, that he has accomplished nothing and never will, etc. – all this with a force that nearly knocks one down.'

Knowing Wittgenstein's uncompromising way with frivolousness, Russell felt convinced that he would not fit in with the Apostles, a society that had lost none of its élite nature but had, since it became dominated by Lytton Strachey and John Maynard Keynes, abandoned its high-minded Victorian seriousness in favour of an altogether more modern and lighter atmosphere, in which intellectual conversation went hand-in-hand with homosexual 'intrigues'. Strachey and Keynes, however, were determined to enlist Wittgenstein, convinced that Russell was merely trying to keep this 'genius' to himself. Wittgenstein himself was prepared to give it a few weeks to see whether anything worth while could come of it, and so, on 16 November, he duly attended his first meeting as a member. Russell, too, attended, and reported that 'Wittgenstein livened things up and seemed not too unhappy':

Moore read an old paper of his about Conversion – not very good. Wittgenstein's remarks were interesting as autobiography – he said as far as he knew it, it consisted in getting rid of worry, having the courage that made one not really care what might happen.

After the meeting, Strachey gloated about its success in a letter to his friend and fellow-Apostle Sydney Saxon Turner, sounding triumphant over Russell. 'The poor man', he wrote, 'is in a sad state. He looks about 96 – with long snow-white hair and an infinitely haggard countenance. The election of Wittgenstein has been a great blow to him . . . Of course he could produce no reason against the election – except the remarkable one that the Society was so degraded that his Austrian would certainly refuse to belong to it . . . Wittgenstein shows no signs of objecting to the Society . . . Bertie is really a tragic figure, and I am sorry for him; but he is most deluded too.' In fact, Russell was entirely correct, and within a few weeks of his election Wittgenstein resigned. 'I think he is right,' Russell wrote on 6 December, 'tho' loyalty to the Society wd. not have led me to say so beforehand.'

More to Wittgenstein's taste was the Moral Science Club, which he addressed on 29 November on the subject 'What is philosophy?' His paper – which set a record for brevity by lasting only four minutes – startled his audience by defining philosophy as 'all those primitive propositions which are assumed as true without proof by the various sciences'. The minutes of the Club record, perhaps unsurprisingly, that, although the definition was much discussed, 'there was no general disposition to adopt it'. It is one of the very few hints of the work that Wittgenstein did this term (no written record of which survives) and what is intriguing about it is its relation to the 'new science' that Russell had announced himself as inaugurating, which would use the techniques of mathematical logic to articulate the a priori foundations of the physical sciences. From this, one would gather that, at this stage, Russell and Wittgenstein regarded themselves as collaborators on the same project, with Wittgenstein working on one part of the issue – the construction of a workable theory of the nature of logic – and Russell working on another, the application of logic to the basic concepts of science.

Another indication of their sense of collaboration comes in the letter Wittgenstein wrote Russell from Vienna at the end of the year. He had, he reported, been to Jena to see Gottlob Frege, with whom he had had a long discussion 'about *our* Theory of Symbolism' (italics added), of which he thought Frege 'understood the general outline'. Frege, in any case, promised to think it over. Wittgenstein also reported himself to be making progress with what he called 'the complex problem', presumably the problem that Russell had wrestled with at the beginning of term of explaining what the form of a complex could be. In an important letter written in January 1913, Wittgenstein announced the results of his work. The problems of analysing the forms of complexes, he had decided, were to be solved, not ontologically (by specifying what kind of *thing* a form is), but linguistically (by constructing a symbolism that revealed the logical form of a complex more perspicuously than does ordinary language).

This was a radically new approach to the problem, involving the jettisoning of large parts of the logic that Russell had devised for *Principia Mathematica*, in particular the Theory of Types. 'Every theory of types', Wittgenstein now insisted, 'must be rendered superfluous by a proper theory of the symbolism . . . showing that what seem to be *different kinds of things* are symbolised by different kinds of symbols which *cannot* possibly be substituted in one another's places.' The reason for this, Wittgenstein said, 'is a very fundamental one: I think that there cannot be different Types of things!' There are not particulars and universals, relations and qualities, individuals and forms, there are just *things*, objects, and everything else is to be understood in terms of how it is possible to say anything about those things.

It seems doubtful whether Russell understood at this stage how radical a departure this approach was from his own work on logic, or how widely divergent were the paths down which he and Wittgenstein were now travelling, with Wittgenstein reducing logic to language and Russell himself still wrestling with the problems of 'matter'. Some hint of this divergence, however, is contained at the end of this letter in January, when Wittgenstein remarks that, though he is very interested in Russell's views about matter, 'I cannot imagine your way of working from sense-data forward.' This remark, in its faintly condescending dismissal of Russell's whole approach, perhaps shows that Wittgenstein was never very interested in what Russell himself conceived to be one of his central ideas: the notion that matter could be constructed from sense-data.

Despite this dismissive remark, Russell continued to believe that he and Wittgenstein were partners in the same philosophical movement. Shortly before he received this letter, he wrote to Ottoline of the 'greater school of mathematically-trained philosophers' that he dreamt of establishing, which would seek to produce people just like Wittgenstein. He also complained that he could find few who understood what he was trying to accomplish in his work on matter, 'except Whitehead and Wittgenstein, who feel its importance as much as I do'.

In fact, Russell's work on matter was very much closer to Whitehead's concerns than Wittgenstein's. In the fourth volume of *Principia Mathematica*, which Whitehead was writing on his own, he sought to apply the mathematical logic of the other three volumes to the area of geometry. Though the volume was never finished, one can see the drift of Whitehead's thinking from the paper he published in 1905 called 'On Mathematical Concepts of the Material World' and from the two books he published immediately after the First World War: *An Enquiry Concerning the Principles of Natural Knowledge* and *The Concept of Nature*. Together these show that Whitehead's idea was to define the 'points' of space, the 'instants' of time and the 'objects' of matter using set theory. In particular, a material object was to be defined as a class of sense-data. To a very large extent, then, the ideas and themes that Russell was now working on were borrowed from Whitehead. When he told Ottoline that Whitehead was 'partly the cause of my interest' in the problem of defined matter, he was, if anything, understating the case.

Russell spent the Christmas of 1912 with the Whiteheads at their home in Lockeridge, no doubt devoting much of his time there to 'shop talk' with Whitehead. On 30 December, he left Lockeridge and moved into an inn called 'The Beetle and Wedge' at Moulsford, not far from Cholsey, where Ottoline and Philip were now living. He stayed there for the two weeks that remained before the start of term, trying to make some progress on 'Matter'. When he returned to Cambridge on 14 January, he wrote to Ottoline that he had '*loved* having so much part in your ordinary life . . . I feel we have more than ever before shared mental things – poetry, history, work, etc. You can't imagine how much I love talking to you about work – it seems in a way the crown of life, where all that I care for profoundly meets and mingles.' Ottoline's recollections were, by contrast, rather bleak. In her published memoirs she writes that when she thinks of Breach House in Cholsey, one of her abiding memories is of the room upstairs where she used to meet Russell when he came 'and where I tried to read history and philosophy. To that room I do not desire to return. It is dark and melancholy in my memory.'

In his absorption in his work, Russell evidently did not notice the extent of Ottoline's melancholy, but what he did not fail to notice was that, however much they may have 'shared mental things', physically they did not share much at all. 'It is rather appalling,' Russell wrote, 'to think that you wd. be dead or mad if you let me have my way with you':

> It is a pity our needs are so different, but I suppose there is nothing for it but compromise and a middle course. We must find out how to tire each other as little as possible, and accept the rest as inevitable. I was quite serious in proposing not to see you without making emotional demands, and I do realise how bad they are for you. But I am sure I can learn by sympathy to make fewer demands.

Ottoline was only too willing to accept that they should meet each other less frequently, and, though Russell still wrote to her daily, they agreed to see each other just three times a term. Even so, it was almost more than Ottoline could bear. 'I would give my right hand to be free from Bertie,' she wrote after one of his visits, 'but how can I, now that he depends on me? I cannot write to him what I know would darken his life, perhaps for ever. I sometimes feel quite warmly towards him; I feel how wonderful his intellect is, and then this awful shrinking comes over me.' It was, she wrote, 'pure madness' to have become sexually intimate with Russell:

Anyone who reads this warning – be *careful* to be sure if you can find lasting delight in the body or soul of anyone before being intimate with them. It leads you to give them such pain, if too late you may find things that disgust you.

Again and again one finds dark hints in Ottoline's journals that Russell *disgusted* her, without it being spelled out quite why. Russell himself was inclined to believe that it had much to do with his bad breath,[2] though it seems likely that this was something Ottoline offered as a comfortingly innocuous reason for her lack of physical attraction. The signs in her journal are that her lack of attraction was far more fundamental. Half-way through this winter term she told Russell that she found him 'unsympathetic' and could not live with him even if she were free from Philip (which, in any case, she had no wish to be). The main reason for this lack of sympathy seems to be that she found him unappealingly intellectual. 'Bertie says', she wrote, 'he knows people and their concerns by his intellect, but seldom *feels* them. Now I don't see them intellectually, but feel them *demi physiquement* – really *feel* them and that is the only gift I have.' Because he lacked that gift, she thought, Russell was just not capable of the kind of sympathy that she – and everybody else – really needed:

He is, I am sure, *incapable* of giving. He is too much of an important brain, and he must receive. All his actions are done as if he were asleep, clumsily, and without any spirit or grace in them. This worries me dreadfully: also his bitter criticism, a want of blindness to faults. He has only *intellectual* understanding. It chills me.

I had so hoped to find him really understanding and tender and gay; but that is a myth, and he simply sits waiting for me to give to him . . . In this adventure I have learnt that I must be the giver. Bertie thinks he loves me, but what he really loves is a woman to listen to him and to rely on him; but he does not love enough to forget himself ever. I must love him and give to him, it is my work; and not expect anything back, for he cannot

---

[2] See his *Autobiography*, Vol. I, p. 206: 'I was suffering from pyorrhoea although I did not know it, and this caused my breath to be offensive, which also I did not know. She could not bring herself to mention it, and it was only after I had discovered the trouble and had it cured, that she let me know how much it had affected her.'

deviate a hair's breadth from what he is, or from his self-absorption. I don't believe he is much aware of me, nor does he ever want to follow me in my thoughts and wanderings. He says he does, but I find I cannot talk to him.

For the moment, at least, Russell's philosophical work pushed his thoughts and feelings about Ottoline to the back of his mind. 'I am nervous like a Prima Donna or an orator,' he wrote on 21 January 1913, 'for fear Matter may prove too much for me – It is a difficult task, and my physical energy is not what it was -- the doubt has a constant more or less depressing effect . . . [It] is really a new problem and a new method, and I have always a lurking fear it may be moonshine, tho' at bottom I *know* it is a genuine problem and a genuine method, but perhaps for younger people.'

Wittgenstein was late arriving back from Vienna because of his father's long-expected death from cancer, which, when it finally came, on 20 January, Wittgenstein reported as something of a relief and 'the most beautiful death that I can imagine'. When, about a week after the start of term, he returned to Cambridge, he seemed to some extent to have shaken off the acute depression to which he had been subject before Christmas and to be full of confidence in the progress that he was making in his work on logic. On 4 February, Pinsent records in his diary an occasion when he and Wittgenstein were together in his rooms and Russell happened to appear:

> . . . he and Wittgenstein got talking – the latter explaining one of his latest discoveries in the Fundamentals of Logic – a discovery which, I gather, only occurred to him this morning, and which appears to be quite important and was very interesting. Russell acquiesced in what he said without a murmur.

Two weeks later, Russell wrote to Ottoline detailing a daunting list of tough philosophical assignments that he had given himself:

> I want very much to found a school of mathematical philosophy, because I believe the method is capable of bearing much fruit, beyond what I can ever accomplish. Then I want to get on with Matter – that wants first and foremost a fundamental novelty as to the nature of sensation, which I think I am on the track of – that will be the most important single idea involved. Then I must discover the truth about Causality . . . Then I must reduce both ordinary dynamics and electro-dynamics to neat sets of axioms.

When he thought of it all, he told her 'and all the labour and fatigue and discouragement and wrong ideas that have to be abandoned', his courage quailed, 'and I wish some one else would do it'. But the only person he knew capable of doing it was Wittgenstein, 'and he is embarked on a more difficult piece of work':

> Ten years ago I could have written a book with the stock of ideas I have already, but now I have a higher standard of exactness. Wittgenstein has

persuaded me that the early parts of *Principia Mathematica* are very inexact, but fortunately it is his business to put them right, not mine.

These remarks are revealing. They show how Russell was still inclined to look upon Wittgenstein's work as a kind of 'fine tuning' of his own. He talks as if the inexactitude of the early parts of *Principia* is a mere detail, but those early parts contain the very foundation upon which the whole of the rest was built. And Wittgenstein was not repairing it, as Russell continued to think, but was demolishing it altogether.

Russell's position *vis-à-vis* his philosophical work was, at this time, odd and curiously vulnerable. Believing that logic was the foundation upon which the rest of philosophy was built, he had yet abandoned logic as 'Wittgenstein's business' and turned instead to epistemology (the theory of knowledge) and the philosophy of physics. But how could he carry on building his own structures in ignorance of the foundations upon which they would rest? How could he be so sure that the theory of logic that Wittgenstein would eventually develop would provide a suitable foundation either for his past work on mathematics or for his proposed work on 'matter'?

In November he had accepted an invitation to spend a term at Harvard in the spring of 1914, teaching courses on logic and the theory of knowledge. In response to a request to specify which textbook he would be using on logic, he replied that he was at a loss: 'So far as I know, no book on logic exists.' To know what logic was, the world – and he himself – would have to await the outcome of Wittgenstein's work. In the meantime, Russell would carry on, assuming that whatever Wittgenstein came up with, it would fit without too much disturbance into his own grand design. Thus it was that, while Wittgenstein attacked the foundations upon which Russell and Whitehead had built mathematics, Russell continued to add more floors to the building.

His work on the nature of matter had long focused on the notion of sense-data. Now he became increasingly preoccupied by the idea that, though sense-data were premises as far as epistemology was concerned, as far as the science of physics was concerned they were 'logically late'. That is to say, as far as physics is concerned, sensations are effects, not causes; they are 'functions of physical objects'. Russell's aim (and this is what struck Wittgenstein as perverse) was to reverse this process, and, as Wittgenstein put it, to 'work from sense-data forward' – or, as Russell put it in one of his preliminary attempts to write on matter, his problem was to make the notion of sense-data logically as well as epistemologically basic. For this, as he said, to Ottoline, he needed a new theory of the notion of 'sensation', and thus a whole new epistemology.

Just after his return from Lausanne the previous summer, Russell had reviewed William James's posthumously published collection, *Essays in Radical Empiricism*, and had been especially taken with the first essay in the book called 'Does Consciousness Exist?' In this James argued that there is no such thing as 'consciousness', no such 'stuff' as the mind. Contrary to the tradition of philosophical dualism that goes back to René Descartes, and which envisages the existence of both mind and matter and a fundamental difference between the two, James advanced the view known as 'neutral monism' that denies the difference and the duality and asserts that there is only *one* kind of 'stuff', and that is neither mind nor matter but something 'neutral' between the two.

Russell was reluctant to accept this view, but he became fascinated by it, and accepted at least one of its consequences: namely, that traditional empiricism of the sort advanced by, for example, John Locke and David Hume, has a mistaken view about the nature of sense-data. For Locke and the whole tradition of British empiricism, the data of the senses were themselves mental; they conceived all our knowledge as coming from our senses in the form of 'ideas', which were, so to speak, the 'appearances' of material objects. Thus, sensation was regarded by them as a relation between a mind and a mental 'content', an 'idea', which was in turn related to the outside world. This view notoriously leads to Berkeley's famous denial of material objects, for it seems to entrap us in a purely mental sphere in which the material world is, at best, an inference, not something of which we are directly acquainted (from which it is but a small step to denying that the material world exists). For Russell, as for James, there was nothing essentially mental about the objects of our direct acquaintance; the data of the senses were themselves physical. Thus, when he argued that material objects were 'constructed' out of sense-data, he was not suggesting that, somehow, matter was created by the mind, but that a material object was a set of (physical) sense-data.

The 'fundamental novelty as to the nature of sensation' that Russell was working towards, then, was a view of sensation as a direct relation between a mind and something non-mental, whether it be a physical object or a platonic, abstract idea. This relation he called 'acquaintance'. Over the course of the term, this notion of acquaintance loomed larger and larger in Russell's thoughts, until by March it had entirely replaced 'matter' in his preoccupations and he decided that, before he could begin work on his proposed book on matter, he would have to write a preliminary work on epistemology. This was to be called *The Theory of Knowledge*. When term finished on 7 March, he moved again into 'The Beetle and Wedge' to concentrate on this new work.

Something of the gap that was now opening up between Russell and Wittgenstein is apparent in the report Russell gave Ottoline of a 'terrific contest' that they had had at the end of term. It started when Russell told Wittgenstein that he was in danger of becoming narrow and uncivilised, and that it would be good for him to read some French prose:

He raged and stormed & I irritated him more & more by merely smiling . . . I feel his lack of civilisation & suffer from it – it is odd how little music does to civilise people – it is too apart, too passionate, & too remote from words. He has not a sufficiently wide curiosity or a sufficient wish for a broad survey of the world. It won't spoil his work on logic, but it will make him always a very narrow specialist.

The image of Russell smiling in the face of Wittgenstein's distress is unpleasant and somewhat disturbing, for though Wittgenstein's raging was undoubtedly genuine, Russell's smile could hardly have been so. One almost feels the warmth of their friendship disappearing in the coldness of that smile, indifferent to the irritation it is causing. Two weeks earlier, the hard and disillusioned mood that had descended on Russell received its definitive statement in a powerfully worded letter to Goldie Lowes Dickinson. Responding to Dickinson's continued interest in *The Perplexities of John Forstice*, Russell wrote that during the late summer of 1912 he had 'tried in vain to recapture the mood in which I had written it', but, when the winter came, had given it up to concentrate on the philosophy of matter. He then relayed to Dickinson as much Cambridge gossip as he could think of, though when he had finished he had to confess: 'it all looks curiously trivial', especially when contrasted with the story of the deaths of Captain Scott and his men in the Antarctic, which had occurred the previous year and about which almost everybody in England was reading in the spring of 1913:

> We here in Cambridge all keep each other going by the unquestioned assumption that what we do is important, but I often wonder if it really is. What is important I wonder? Scott and his companions dying in the blizzard seem to me impervious to doubt – and his record of it has a really great simplicity. But intellect, except at white heat, is very apt to be trivial.

That Wittgenstein's intellect was 'at white heat' was beyond doubt, but about his own Russell could not be so sure, nor could he shake off the doubts he had expressed to Ottoline that his work on matter was really all 'moonshine'. Wittgenstein might have had doubts about whether he was capable of answering the questions he had set himself, but about the importance of the work he was as unquestioning as Russell had been when he worked on *Principia Mathematica*.[3] Russell, though, even at the height of his absorption in his work on matter and the theory of knowledge could never be quite free from the thought that his time might really be better spent:

> I feel as if one would only discover on one's death-bed what one ought to have lived for, and realise too late that one's life had been wasted. Any passionate and courageous life seems good in itself, yet one feels that some element of delusion is involved in giving so much passion to any humanly attainable object. And so irony creeps into the very springs of one's being.

In Russell's case, the irony had bitten deep, far more deeply than one might have thought possible for the man who, less than a year earlier, had written *Perplexities*. 'Are you finding the Great Secret in the East?' he asked Dickinson:

---

[3] Though, of course, when Wittgenstein, in 1921, finally published his theory of logic in *Tractatus Logico-Philosophicus*, he insisted that one of the things shown by his work was 'how little has been done when these problems have been solved'.

I doubt it. There is none – there is not even an enigma. There is science and sober daylight and the business of the day – the rest is mere phantoms of the dusk.

Over the Easter vacation, a more prosaic expression of this attitude was presented in an article Russell wrote for *The New Statesman* called 'Science as an Element in Culture', in which talk of a 'fused whole' of science and mysticism was abandoned in favour of outright advocacy of the superiority of the scientific outlook. 'Science', Russell wrote, 'comes nearer to objectivity than any other human pursuit, and gives us, therefore, the closest contact and the most intimate relation with the outer world that it is possible to achieve.' It represents 'a higher stage of evolution than any pre-scientific thought or imagination'. The article ends with some lessons for philosophy:

> The kernel of the scientific outlook is the refusal to regard our own desires tastes, and interests as affording a key to the understanding of the world . . . The scientific attitude of mind involves a sweeping away of all other desires in the interests of the desire to know . . . in philosophy this attitude of mind has not as yet been achieved . . . Until we have learnt to think of [the universe] in ethically neutral terms, we have not arrived at a scientific attitude in philosophy; and until we have arrived at such an attitude, it is hardly to be hoped that philosophy will achieve any solid results.

By the end of the vacation Russell was able to write out a sketch of his proposed book on the Theory of Knowledge that was, he told Ottoline 'much better than anything I had done before in that line'. That he was not entirely confident about the direction his work had taken, however, seems to be indicated by his apparent determination to protect his new project from the withering criticism of Wittgenstein. He was determined that *The Theory of Knowledge* should not, like 'What is Logic?', be throttled at birth. A few days into term, he told Ottoline that he no longer discussed his work with Wittgenstein:

> When there are no clear arguments, but only inconclusive considerations to be balanced, and unsatisfactory points of view to be set against each other, he is no good; and he treats infant theories with a ferocity which they can only endure when they are grown up. The result is that I become completely reserved, even about work.

The Theory of Knowledge was to be treated as a delicate plant, nurtured and protected indoors, before being exposed to the harsher conditions that prevailed outside.

Ottoline was at this time preparing to leave for Switzerland again. Her daughter Julian's health was delicate and Ottoline wanted her to be treated by Dr Combe, in whom she had an apparently indestructible faith. Together with Philip and Julian, she planned to leave for Lausanne on 5 May and to be away for a total of about six weeks. Russell's intention was to write *The Theory of*

Knowledge while she was away. Though, naturally, extremely anxious about Ottoline's departure ('Dearest I do hope I shall be able to keep your love alive now'), Russell rather relished the task he had set himself in her absence. 'The excitement of philosophical construction is coming over me', he wrote, 'more than I have had it for a long time. When it comes, the whole great structure shoots up before one's vision with the swiftness of an Aurora Borealis, and rather like it – great shafts of sudden light piercing the darkness.' On the day before she left, he had 'been bubbling over with delight all day . . . sketching out my book on Theory of Knowledge – I have got the early part quite elaborately sketched, and the whole pretty full in my head.'

Wittgenstein, meanwhile, was feeling paralysed by his work. He told Russell 'with all solemnity' that logic was driving him insane: 'I think there is a danger of it, so I urged him to let it alone for a bit and do other work – I think he will. He is in a shocking state – always gloomy, pacing up and down, waking out of a dream when one speaks to him.' Wittgenstein's 'shocking state', it is now possible with hindsight to see, was in part due to his growing sense of estrangement from Russell himself. Whereas in the spring of 1912, Russell spoke of Wittgenstein with great warmth and feeling, of how he loved him and regarded him as a son, he now seemed, a mere year later, somewhat intimidated by him and kept him at arm's length, both personally and philosophically. Wittgenstein could not have failed to notice that Russell was no longer in any sense his collaborator in logic, and a growing sense of distance was being felt by both of them with regard to personal feelings and morality. In any case, Russell seemed only too pleased to encourage Wittgenstein to turn his mind to other things beside philosophy, as if realising that Wittgenstein's absence could only be beneficial to his own work.

With both Wittgenstein and Ottoline out of the way, Russell set to with quite extraordinary energy. On 8 May, just a few days after Ottoline's departure, he wrote that he could confidently expect to write ten pages a day for the next fifty days and, therefore, might have the book – 500 pages of it – nearly finished by the time she returned. 'It is all in my head, ready to be written as fast as my pen will go,' he declared. 'I feel as happy as a king.' Perhaps 'a God' might have been a better analogy, for what Russell had in his head, in all its detail, was no less than the construction of the world. First, he would describe the nature of experience, then he would demolish both the 'neutral monist' view that there is no such thing as the mind, and the idealist view that there is nothing else; then, having established the existence of a genuine relation between the mind and non-mental objects, he would classify those objects, starting with particulars and going on to relations, predicates and logical forms: 'Then I shall come on to belief, error, etc., then to inference, then finally to "construction of the physical world" – time, space, cause, matter.' Thus would the world be constructed in fifty days.

For the next few days everything went even better than planned, with Russell averaging rather more than ten pages a day, which at any time is a remarkable feat, but in term-time, with a full load of lectures, a busy round of meetings with students and an active social life, is quite awe-inspiring. On

13 May, Russell felt emboldened to tell Wittgenstein about the book. The response confirmed his fears about Wittgenstein's way with defenceless infants – 'He thinks it will be like the shilling shocker, which he hates. *He* is a tyrant, if you like' – and Russell refrained from showing any of the work to Wittgenstein or from discussing it further with him. Three days later, he reported that he had written 110 pages, 'and I really think it is good stuff . . . It fascinates and absorbs me – I have such a power acquired in all the years during which I have learnt to analyse . . . I don't think my mind has ever been better than it is just now. I am *amazed* how much more I know than I did in the winter when I ate my heart out at the Beetle and Wedge.'

'Probably by the time I really finish it, it will be a great big book,' he wrote on 18 May. 'I feel so bursting with work that I hardly know how to wait for the days to roll themselves out – I want to write faster than is physically possible. I haven't had such a fit for ages.' The following day, after staying up late into the night writing up a new theory of time in which, after Whitehead's fashion, Russell defined instants of time as classes of simultaneous events, he decided to take two days off. He had by now written six chapters in less than two weeks. On the second of his days off, Russell had the misfortune to be visited by Wittgenstein, who came 'with a refutation of the theory of judgment which I used to hold. He was right, but I think the correction required is not very serious. I shall have to make up my mind within a week, as I shall soon reach judgment.'

As envisaged by Russell, *The Theory of Knowledge* would have a three-part structure. The first part ('On the Nature of Acquaintance') would present a theory of acquaintance, defining it as a relation between a mind and various types of non-mental objects – particulars, relations, predicates and logical forms – to each of which Russell would devote a chapter. The second part ('Atomic Propositional Thought') would present a theory of judgment, which, in essence, would be the same theory as that contained in earlier works like *The Problems of Philosophy* and *Principia Mathematica*. This is the so-called 'multiple-relation' theory, according to which the traditional view of a judgment as the assertion by a mind of a proposition is abandoned in favour of a much more complicated analysis, in which the proposition is broken down into its constituents ('Socrates loves Alcibiades' into Socrates, love and Alcibiades); the judgment is then understood as a series of relations, 'acquaintances', between a mind and those constituents (to judge that Socrates loves Alcibiades therefore requires acquaintance with Socrates, love and Alcibiades, but not with the proposition 'Socrates loves Alcibiades'). What Russell liked about this analysis was that it dispensed with the need for 'propositions', those curious, shadowy objects he had wrestled with before he discovered his theory of 'incomplete symbols'. The third part of the book ('Molecular Propositional Thought') would deal with the nature of inference.

By the time of Wittgenstein's visit on 20 May, Russell had nearly finished Part I. He had three short chapters to write on, respectively, relations, predicates and logical forms, which, writing at the rate he had set himself, was but a few days' work. After that, he would have to begin Part II on judgment. The fact that Wittgenstein came with a refutation of the 'multiple relation' theory, therefore, ought to have worried Russell rather more than it appeared to do, and it seems likely that he was not quite so insouciant in the face of Wittgenstein's refutation as he appeared in his letter to Ottoline. After all, he had for some time been prepared to acquiesce in almost anything Wittgenstein said with regard to logic, even if it overturned views he had long held.

The extent of this willingness to accept whatever Wittgenstein said, no matter what the consequences, is revealed in the three short chapters that Russell wrote in the days following Wittgenstein's visit, especially in the last on 'Logical Data'. In this, Russell adopts Wittgenstein's view that there are no such things as logical objects, despite the fact that, within his theory, he needs logical forms to be the objects of a special kind of 'acquaintance'. The result is that, though he acknowledges that 'logical objects cannot be regarded as "entities" ' and that therefore 'what we call "acquaintance" with them cannot really be a dual relation', he nevertheless insists that, as there is such a thing as the understanding of such terms as particulars, universals, predicates, etc., there is, after all, 'something which seems fitly described as "acquaintance with logical objects" '. Aware that this hardly makes any sense at all, he offloads the problem on to the analysis of logic: 'In the present chaotic state of our knowledge concerning the primitive ideas of logic, it is impossible to pursue this topic further.' That is, it is Wittgenstein's job to sort it out, and Russell has no idea what the solution might be. Nevertheless, he continues to insist: 'it is clear that we have acquaintance (possibly in an extended sense of the word "acquaintance") with something as abstract as the pure form [of a complex].'

The awkwardness of this view, which appears to both deny and to assert that logical forms are objects, recalls the problems Russell had in 'What is Logic?', and reveals the danger of his decision to plough on with a large work on the theory of knowledge prior to thinking through the more fundamental problems of logic. For it clearly would not do to insist that the clarification of such-and-such a point belonged to logic rather than to epistemology. As Russell himself says in Chapter 4 of *The Theory of Knowledge*: 'it is impossible to assign to the theory of knowledge a province distinct from that of logic.' In effect, he was appealing to the results of a theory of logic in absence of the theory, assuming that, whatever Wittgenstein came up with, it would fit into his own plan.

Hints that it would not do so are contained in Wittgenstein's letter of January 1913, in which he argued for the abandonment of any theory of types. Part of Wittgenstein's argument in that letter indicates the lines on which he may have 'refuted' Russell's theory of judgment. For there he argues against Russell's way of analysing propositions into their constituents ('Socrates is mortal' into Socrates and mortality). If we break the proposition 'Socrates is mortal' up into its constituents, Wittgenstein argues, then we are left with 'Socrates' and 'mortality' (and even the 'form' of the proposition on Russell's later analysis) as, in some sense, objects. And if, as he now believes, there are not different types of object, then 'mortality' and 'Socrates' have to be the same type of thing, in which case there is nothing to prevent us putting them together to form the proposition 'Mortality is Socrates'. But this is not a proposition at all; it is not something that is either true or false, it is just a piece of nonsense. Two things follow from this, in Wittgenstein's view: first, that 'mortality' is not an object in any sense, and second (and therefore) that Russell's theory of judgment, which requires it to be in some sense an object, is wrong. A proposition has a unity that cannot be captured by Russell's theory of judgment.

Thus, when Russell wrote of Wittgenstein's objection that 'the correction required is not very great', he was emphatically wrong: the correction required is the abandonment of the whole scheme of his book *The Theory of Knowledge*, the scheme that starts with our acquaintance with 'objects' and then builds judgments up from a collection of such acquaintances. If Wittgenstein is right, no such scheme could possibly work, and one must – as he had insisted back in November 1911 – begin with the whole proposition.

After Wittgenstein's visit of 20 May, Russell continued writing at the same extraordinary pace, but with markedly less enthusiasm and self-confidence. He finished Part I on 23 May, and the next day began Part II, which opens with a slightly modified version of the 'multiple relation' theory of judgment that Wittgenstein considered himself to have refuted.[4]

On 26 May, Russell reported that, for the first time, he had had 'great difficulty' in getting through his ten pages. The weather was 'oppressively hot, airless and thundery without any actual thunder' and had given him a headache. The next day, he was visited again by Wittgenstein, still bent on showing Russell the error of his ways:

> ... we were both cross from the heat – I showed him a crucial part of what I have been writing. He said it was all wrong, not realising the difficulties – that he had tried my view and knew it wouldn't work. I couldn't understand his objection – in fact he was very inarticulate – but I feel in my bones that he must be right, and that he has seen something I have missed. If I could see it too I shouldn't mind, but as it is, it is worrying, and has rather destroyed the pleasure in my writing – I can only go on with what I see and yet I feel it is probably all wrong, and that Wittgenstein will think me a dishonest scoundrel for going on with it. Well, well – it is the younger generation knocking at the door – I must make room for him when I can, or I shall become an incubus. But at the moment I was rather cross.

Later in the same letter he confessed that he was now 'a little depressed about work'. Still, he carried on writing, and ten days later had finished Part

---

[4] Actually, in this new version, it is first and foremost a multiple relation theory of understanding a proposition, since Russell now takes understanding to be prior to judgment. However, this is a fairly minor change (it may even be the one he mentions to Ottoline as being required by Wittgenstein's attack on his theory of judgment), since almost everything else in the theory remains unchanged: propositions are still 'incomplete symbols' requiring the context of a mind to render them meaningful, and understanding is analysed – as judgment was before – as a series of multiple relations of acquaintance between a mind and the constituents of the proposition. Once a proposition is understood in this sense, it can then be judged true or false, and then the judgment is analysed much as it was before.

II, all seven chapters of it. Even as he continued to write, however, the doubts about the value of the work sown by Wittgenstein's inarticulate criticism grew ever more insistent and he was increasingly convinced that what he was writing – for a reason he did not yet understand – could not be correct. His state of mind as he completed Part II contrasted markedly with that in which, 'happy as a king', he had raced through Part I. Day by day, one can sense his confidence in both himself and the project draining away:

> [I have] recovered from the effect of Wittgenstein's criticisms, though I think in all likelihood they are just. But even if they are they won't destroy the value of the book. His criticisms have to do with the problems I want to leave to him – which makes a complication.
> (28 May)

> My writing goes on steadily – I have reached p. 273 – by Sunday night I suppose I shall reach 300. I am anxious to get on to the constructive part, where I shall deal with our knowledge of the external world – the fundamental part of 'Matter'. I begin to feel the strain a good deal, and it seems to shut out all the rest of the world. I have been feeling as if you were in another universe.
> (30 May)

> . . . I have grown terribly nervous and irritable, and the feeling of work that must be done has grown oppressive. A sort of inner voice keeps on, as persistently as the rumble of a train, saying 'Get on with your work – get on with your work', leaving me no peace when I am doing anything else. And then people who come and talk seem annoying, and I want to be rude to them and make them go . . . And of course I have only superficially and by an act of will got over Wittgenstein's attack – it has made the work a task rather than a joy. It is all tangled up with the difficulty of not stealing his ideas – there is really more merit in raising a good problem than in solving it.
>   Wittgenstein affects me just as I affect you – I get to know every turn and twist of the ways in which I irritate and depress you from watching how he irritates and depresses me; and at the same time I love and admire him. Also I affect him just as you affect me when you are cold. The parallelism is curiously close altogether. He differs from me just as I differ from you. He is clearer, more creative, more passionate; I am broader, more sympathetic, more sane.
>   . . . In spite of Wittgenstein, and even if every particular statement in it is false, I am *sure* the book I am writing is a good book, because it gives an example of scientific method where previous writing has been unscientific. That will certainly be the main thing I shall have achieved – making certain parts of philosophy scientific . . . It is what Galileo did in physics – its value is independent of the truth or falsehood of the particular results one arrives at. It satisfies me as a way of spending one's life. Though it is rather a lonely business, and demands a terrible expenditure of energy.
> (1 June)

I am very sorry my letters have been so wretched – First it needed a great effort to get over Wittgenstein's criticism, and then in the middle came your letter saying you couldn't have me at Lausanne even if J. went home and I felt the only thing was to thrust out thoughts of you for the moment. I wanted to keep clear of emotions that wd. upset my work.
(2 June)

My work-fit is coming to an end. I shall finish the analytic half of the book before you get home, if all goes well. It no longer absorbs my thoughts, and other interests are reviving. What I am writing is not so good as what I wrote at first. I have all but finished 'Self-evidence' – then I go on to 'Degrees of Certainty' and that ends Part II of Book I. I shall have to do Part III in a very sketchy way, because I haven't yet thought much about the questions involved . . . my time for work will be rather interrupted till your return [on 20 June]. But I don't think I will go on at such a high pressure as this last month.
(5 June)

The following day, as he had intended, he finished Part II and then took a break, laying the book to one side, temporarily, he thought, although in fact he never went back to it and neither Part III of Book I nor the second 'constructive' book was ever written.

After a month of extraordinary effort, Russell was exhausted, not just intellectually but also emotionally. This was partly owing to his disappointment in not being able to visit Ottoline in Lausanne, but much more to do with the deterioration of his relationship with Wittgenstein. On 5 June, the day before he finished his writing on the book, some kind of turning point was reached:

I had an awful time with Wittgenstein yesterday between tea and dinner. He came analysing all that goes wrong between him and me, and I told him I thought it was only nerves on both sides and everything was all right at bottom. Then he said he never knew whether I was speaking the truth or being polite, so I got vexed and refused to say another word. He went on and on. I sat down at my table and took up my pen and began to look through a book, but still he went on. At last I said sharply 'All you want is a little self-control.' Then at last he went away with an air of high tragedy. He had asked me to a concert in the evening, but he didn't come, so I began to fear suicide. However, I found him in his room late (I left the concert, but didn't find him at first), told him I was sorry I had been cross and then talked quietly about how he could improve. His faults are exactly mine – always analysing, pulling feelings up by the roots, trying to get the exact truth of what one feels towards him. I see it is very tiring and deadening to one's affections. I think it must be characteristic of logicians – he is the only other one I have ever known intimately.

After he put *The Theory of Knowledge* aside on 6 June, Russell tried to rest his nerves with a series of visits to friends, staying first with Lion Phillimore and then with the Whiteheads. On 13 June, term finished, but before Wittgenstein returned to Vienna, he had arranged for his mother to meet Russell for lunch and tea on Wednesday 18 June. Writing to confirm the arrangement (Russell was to come to the Savoy Hotel in London, where Fanny Wittgenstein was staying), Wittgenstein took the opportunity to articulate precisely the objection to Russell's work which, even in an inarticulate form, had already wreaked so much havoc:

> I can now express my objection to your theory of judgment exactly: I believe it is obvious that, from the prop[osition] 'A judges that (say) a is in the Rel[ation] R to b', if correctly analysed, the prop[osition] 'aRb. v. ~aRb' must follow directly *without the use of any other premiss*. This condition is not fulfilled by your theory.

Or, as he later put it, less technically and even more succinctly: 'The proper theory of judgment must make it impossible to judge nonsense . . . Russell's theory does not satisfy this requirement.'

With this – now deadly precise – parting shot, Wittgenstein left Cambridge, first for Manchester to see an old friend, and then for Vienna. He was not to return until October, and then only for a few days before leaving again for Norway. As far as Wittgenstein was concerned, Russell was now no longer either his teacher or his collaborator, and from this moment on, his work on logic was done in almost complete isolation. Writing to Moore after the summer, Wittgenstein remarked that there was now nobody in Cambridge with whom it was worth discussing philosophy, nobody 'who is not yet stale and is *really* interested in the subject . . . Even Russell – who is of course most extraordinarily fresh for his age – is no more pliable for *this* purpose.' By the summer of 1913, Russell was of no further use to Wittgenstein in his single-minded quest to shed light on the nature of logic.

For Russell's part, Wittgenstein's criticisms – now that he understood how far-reaching they were – left him feeling utterly desolate. 'All that has gone wrong with me lately came from Wittgenstein's attack on my work,' he wrote to Ottoline on 19 June, the day after his meeting with Wittgenstein and his mother:

> I have only just realised this. It was very difficult to be honest about it, as it makes a large part of the book I meant to write impossible for years to come probably. I tried to believe it wasn't so bad as that – then I felt I hadn't made enough effort over my work and must concentrate more severely – some instinct associated this with a withdrawal from you. And the failure of honesty over my work – which was very slight and subtle, more an attitude than anything definite – spread like poison in every direction . . . I must be much sunk – it is the first time in my life that I have failed in honesty over work . . . yesterday I felt ready for suicide . . . The disgust of human life that I have been feeling lately is generally a sign of unrecognised sin.

Ottoline was in no position to comfort Russell. She arrived back in London from Lausanne in the middle of Russell's crisis over Wittgenstein's criticisms, her mind filled with the wonderful achievements of Dr Roger Vittoz, a specialist in the treatment of neurasthenia from whom she had been receiving treatment. Vittoz has a rather special place in the history of literature, for among his patients were, at various times, William James, Joseph Conrad and T. S. Eliot, all of whom spoke warmly about the effectiveness of his methods and the beneficial effects that he had generally upon their lives. The focus of his technique is suggested by the title of the book he published in 1911, *Treatment of Neurasthenia by Teaching of Brain Control*. As Ottoline describes them, the techniques that he taught were what would today probably be called 'positive thinking':

> He taught his patients a system of mental control and concentration, and a kind of organisation of the mind, which had a great effect on steadying and developing me. I found it an enormous help then and always. The man himself impressed me by his extraordinary poise and goodness. Part of the treatment was the formation of the habit of eliminating unnecessary thoughts and worries from one's mind, and to do this one had to practise eliminating letters from words, or one number from a set of numbers. Julian would laugh at me when, perhaps in the tram, she would see me gazing into space – 'There is Mummy eliminating.' I stayed on alone at a little *pension* to finish my course with Dr Vittoz, and this was a very happy time for me.

As a result partly of this technique and partly of being able to spend some time alone (which she often craved when she did not have it and cherished when she did), Ottoline arrived back from Lausanne in precisely the opposite frame of mind to that of Russell: rested, brimming with self-confidence and determined to focus her mind only on the cheerful and positive aspects of her life. She wanted to tell Russell about Vittoz, and about Lausanne and what a marvellous time she had been having. She did not want to listen to lots of gloomy talk about the effects on him of Wittgenstein's criticism. Russell therefore found that among the 'unnecessary thoughts and worries' that Ottoline successfully 'eliminated' from her mind were those connected with himself. Their moods were completely incompatible.

When they met, Russell and Ottoline seemed to talk past each other, neither being really interested in what the other had to say. In his letter of 19 June, Russell apologised for not listening to Ottoline and begged her: 'please do not feel snubbed . . . My mind is so slow in passing to a new topic.' In return, he promised 'not to notice your unintentional snubs'. Two years later, Russell tried to explain to Ottoline what he felt she had not understood during these days after her return from Lausanne:

> Do you remember that at the time when you were seeing Vittoz I wrote a lot of stuff about Theory of Knowledge, which Wittgenstein criticised with the greatest severity? His criticism, tho' I don't think you realised it at the time, was an event of first-rate importance in my life, and affected everything I have done since. I saw he was right, and I saw that I could not hope ever again to do fundamental work in philosophy. My impulse

was shattered, like a wave dashed to pieces against a breakwater. I became filled with utter despair, and tried to turn to you for consolation. But you were occupied with Vittoz and could not give me time.

Nothing could be more calculated to confirm Russell's fears about his place in Ottoline's affections than the technique she had learnt from Vittoz of eliminating worries and unwanted thoughts. His very deepest fear was of being eliminated in such a way. 'I have a rooted feeling,' he wrote on 20 June, '*not* a belief – that you want to shut me out from your life . . . always I have the sense of being unimportant to you . . . When it seems as if you really did love me, there is always a whisper of doubt in my mind.' In his despair, he needed her more than ever, but precisely because he needed her affection, and because this urgent need made him so demanding, he felt – probably with some justification – that he himself was unattractive to her: 'I feel you find me selfish, tyrannical, exhausting, irritating to your nerves, that my impulses constantly hurt you – and so I get a feeling of humiliation.'

In the past he had protected himself against such humiliation by concentrating on philosophy, but now that his impulse to philosophise had been shattered by Wittgenstein, that particular defence – the strongest he had – was no longer available to him and he felt vulnerable as never before. No longer able to say 'to hell with emotion' and get on with work, he was forced to face head-on the terrific power of his fears and longings. As he put it to Ottoline, he had towards her 'two opposite sub-conscious feelings – a longing for your help to get me straight, and a dread of the pain it would involve – like the circulation coming back into frozen limbs'. In his demoralised state, Russell fell prey to his recurring sense of isolation and the accompanying terror of loneliness. 'Without you', he told Ottoline, 'the ghosts come gibbering, the loneliness of Man takes shape and sighs beside me – the world crumbles – and then when I am with you again it is all so different – but I trouble you with the old mad ghosts, instead of forgetting them in the morning sun – I wish it were not so.'

Russell's need for Ottoline was just too great for either of them to bear, and often when they met he felt he had to write immediately afterwards to apologise for his insistent demands. Matters came to a head on 27 June 1913, when, in his frustration and despair, Russell did something – what it was is not mentioned in the surviving letters – for which he felt so ashamed that it brought a temporary halt to their relationship. His sense of humiliation and distress were so acute that immediately afterwards he took the exceptional step of burning the letter that Ottoline had left in his flat. Whether the letter contained details of the action that had so shamed him, or whether he burned it for some other reason (that it contained a painful rebuke, say, or even a farewell) is obviously impossible to say, but the letters he wrote during the following days show that whatever it was consumed him with remorse. 'This can only be one line in haste to say I am sorry,' he wrote soon after Ottoline had left, 'but I will try again':

I mind the way I behave quite terribly . . . I think we ought not to meet while my nerves are so overwrought. It is a great nervous strain, and it leads to my breaking down, which is bad for both. A few more scenes like today wd. put an end of things. I think I had better go back to Cambridge and not see you till I have myself more under control. It wears you out and makes me feel almost too ashamed to go on living . . . I can't tell you how despicable I feel. But I have had much to try me lately. Wittgenstein's attack – the difficulty of getting my lectures done . . . doing my work and not committing suicide seemed as much moral effort as I could make. But I *must* get myself in hand, and I will. Till then I am not fit to associate with . . . really I am not quite and altogether a beast, tho' my behaviour to you looks like it . . . I love you out of hell.

More terrible even than the fear of loneliness was the fear of madness, which now began to overcome Russell so powerfully that he came increasingly to think that he had to part, at least temporarily, from Ottoline. 'The whole thing was a trick of nerves,' he wrote later the same day. 'I feel sure now that I ought not to see you at present, until I am calmer. As soon as I thought of not seeing you just now, my nerves relaxed – now I feel absolutely nothing, not even sorrow for the pain I have given you.' Old fears about hereditary madness were revived and he began dwelling on the fate of his unfortunate Aunt Agatha:

My Aunt Agatha was once engaged to a curate, but – so I understand – she got a notion that he had murdered Lord Clanricarde, and tried to take him to the police-station, so the engagement had to be broken off . . . I seem to attribute equally imaginary crimes to you . . . I must live quietly for a bit and avoid excitements. I have been very nearly out of my mind, but am now quite sane again. Please think of me as kindly as you can.

The next day, he left London for Hindhead, hoping that a walk in the Surrey countryside would rest his nerves. Continuing to brood on the events of the previous day, however, he became more fearful than ever for his mental state and his thoughts of parting from Ottoline became a more or less firm resolution:

It seems to me that we ought to part for good, because continuing leads straight to the madhouse. Besides, a scene of such degradation as yesterday's makes it impossible to stand spiritually upright in a person's presence again. Would you mind if I talked about it to Mrs Whitehead? I want an understanding outside point of view. I wonder whether some day you wd. talk with her. I shd. like you to know that I am not *all* bad – that I *can* be unselfish, and understanding, and sympathetic, where my madness doesn't come in . . . Yesterday you thought I should make a mistake in parting from you, and you thought I was only hurt when I said the opposite. I am not hurt today, but full of clear vision. It seems to me all but certain that to save my reason I must part from you. Don't imagine I say this in anger, or that I shall plunge into reckless immorality. I only want to live quietly and work . . . I really don't underestimate your love. We love each other, but neither gives the sort of love the other wants . . . instinct is too strong for me. However I behave, nothing but insanity lies ahead of me if we go on . . . If you permit my talking to Mrs W. I will try to see her Monday or Tuesday. Forgive this dreadful letter. Nothing lives in me today except the fear of madness.

Ottoline replied that it was '*absurd*' to talk about insanity ('It is simply nerves like I have had myself often') and reassuring Russell: 'I love you, love you my darling and only feel *intense* love and sympathy.' But Russell's mind was made up. As he explained in a letter written on 30 June: 'What has turned the scale has been the realisation that you would *never* give *anyone* the sort of love that would make me happy, and that it is not *only* my bad behaviour that prevents me from getting more.' He nevertheless thought they ought to meet just once more. He would not, he said, want the end to be 'that flaming horror' that had occurred between them on 27 June. Then, he had failed – 'as I constantly do' – in reverence towards her, but if she came to see him one last time in his London flat, he would not do so. 'I can't make any final decision while my nerves are so queer,' he wrote, but one thing was clear: 'the physical relation ought to cease'.

Ottoline did as she was asked and paid Russell 'one last visit' at Bury Street on 30 June, and he kept both his resolutions: to behave well and to insist that they should part. The following day, he left for Cornwall for a walking holiday with the Whitehead boys, Eric and North. Ottoline wrote to him every day, but for the first time since they began their affair he let several days at a time pass without writing to her. He needed, he told her, not to think about her too much. What previously he had done through absorption in philosophy, he now sought to do by physical and mental separation. He had somehow to be cold and unemotional, or else he would succumb to the terrifying, mad impulses that had got the better of him on 27 June. Several times in these letters ending, temporarily, their affair, he insists on his lack of emotional response to what was clearly a very painful situation:

> I am utterly incapable of any feeling of any sort or kind today. Please don't think I am hurt or angry or anything like that – I am only dead.
> (28 June)

> Do *exactly* what you think best about coming this afternoon. It won't upset me if you come, nor yet if you don't. I should like to say I mind the pain I am causing you, but I can't truthfully – I don't mind anything at all as yet. I suppose you are very ill and tired. But it all seems to me as if it were happening to people in a book. Goodbye.
> (30 June)

The professed deadness expressed in these letters is, one cannot help feeling, the wishful thinking of a man who, feeling himself to be a shattered wave, casts envious glances at the invulnerable and impenetrable rocks around him.

II

THE EXTERNAL WORLD AND
THE CENTRAL FIRE

The idea that deep emotion and madness are somehow linked, and that, therefore, one can defeat the threat of insanity by, as it were, retreating to the surface, is one that exerted a powerful influence on Russell's imagination. For many of us, superficiality is something that has to be fought against, a natural inclination, which, like the tendency to rise to the surface in water, requires an effort to resist. For Russell, however, superficiality was something he had to fight for. At various key moments in his life, he strove hard to achieve a certain emotional shallowness in order to fight off what he considered to be impending insanity. Such a moment came in the summer of 1913, when, demoralised by Wittgenstein's attack on his philosophical work and driven to distraction by the frustrations of his relationship with Ottoline, the fear of madness – which never entirely left him – came to dominate his thoughts as completely as it had done in 1894, when his grandmother first told him about his Uncle Willy's incarceration in an asylum, his Aunt Agatha's insane delusions and his father's epilepsy. And, just as he had then, so he now tried desperately 'to avoid all deep emotion' and to live once more on the surface.[1]

Considering himself close to a nervous breakdown, he felt he had to retreat from both Ottoline and the feelings that she aroused in him. He therefore spent most of the months of July and August on holiday, trying to put her out of his mind and thereby regain his mental stability. 'I don't think I shall write much from Cornwall,' he wrote to her on 3 July before setting off. 'I want to sleep mentally.' He kept his word. In the two weeks he spent in Cornwall and the Scilly Isles with Whitehead's two sons, Eric and North, he wrote just a handful of short notes, commenting on the beauty of the sea and the coast, but keeping his innermost thoughts and feelings to himself. When he returned to London on 20 July, he wrote that the strategy had been successful, that he had now got himself in hand and had 'quite banished tragic feeling for the moment'. Evelyn and Alfred Whitehead helped by emphatically insisting that his last two years (the time since he fell in love with Ottoline) had not been unproductive.

---

[1] Cf. p. 86 of Russell's *Autobiography*, Vol. I, where, writing of the fears induced in him by his grandmother's revelations about the mental instability in his family, Russell says that those fears 'caused me, for many years, to avoid all deep emotion, and live, as nearly as I could, a life of intellect tempered by flippancy'.

While he was away he decided on a new theme for the series of eight Lowell Lectures that he was to give in Harvard in the spring of 1914. As these were public lectures and therefore could not be too technical, Russell had at first suggested 'The Place of Good and Evil in the Universe', and had, so he told Ottoline, envisaged the lectures to be 'what Prisons failed to be'. In June, however, he learned that this proposal was considered unacceptable; religious topics were, it seems, vetoed by the terms of the behest that funded the lectures. The topic he now chose was 'On Scientific Method in Philosophy'.

The change from one topic to the other seems somehow symptomatic of Russell's general state at this time, of his preference for the external over the internal (the lectures were later retitled 'Our Knowledge of the External World'). During the two weeks in between his return from Cornwall and his departure for Italy in early August, whenever he met Ottoline (for, inevitably, their 'one last meeting' at the end of June turned out to be no such thing), he discussed poetry with her (concentrating, in particular, on Wordsworth and Dante, especially *La Vita Nuova*), and he listened to her on the subject of Vittoz, but there was little discussion of his inner life and he was careful to keep his own emotions, particularly his sexual passions, at bay. It was as if he had finally accepted that all she could offer him were 'romantic and sentimental rather than passionate' feelings, 'troubadours and courtly love' rather than earthly passion. He had come to feel, he wrote on 23 July, that it was 'not the actual human beings you love, but the God in them':

And when the God abandons them, if they care for your love, they feel lost . . . it is what prevents me from feeling you a comrade – I think of you as my Star, or as the moon sometimes descending from heaven to bring moments of unearthly unquiet joy to Endymion on the cold hill side.

'I don't believe we shall part,' he wrote the next day, 'because the tie is too strong. But I don't feel at all sure that it is not *right* to part. But I don't think it can be settled till after I have gone to America.'

At the beginning of August, he set off on holiday once more, this time for a month's walking tour of the Italian Alps with Charles Sanger. The holiday began with a strenuous trek over the pass from Mont Cenis to Susa, and from there to Turin, where Sanger – not such a good walker as Russell – needed two days of rest to recover. At Turin, Russell was disappointed in his efforts to contact Peano, but – despite his intention to direct his thoughts away from her – was pleased to receive a letter from Ottoline. She wrote that she was depressed, and that she missed both him and his hitherto daily letters. In reply, Russell, scarcely concealing his satisfaction at her unhappy state, did little to cheer her up, reminding her that he too had been unhappy. In her letter, Ottoline had expressed the feeling that she was not as useful as she might be. If she hoped for reassurance on this point, Russell's response must have disappointed her. Her feeling of being useless to others was, he implied, quite justified. What prevented her from being useful, he went on, twisting the knife, was 'a kind of selfishness', the kind that refused to surrender liberty to the accomplishment of a task:

Certain ways of helping people are a pleasure to you, but often the ways in which I want help are not a pleasure to you. It seems to me that you expect an almost superhuman degree of self-repression in me, but that you resent the need of self-repression on your side.

This he offered not as an expression of his own anger towards her, but as a disinterested and perhaps even helpful observation. His opinion of her was, he claimed, quite without 'animus or self-feeling', and motivated simply by a desire to get at the truth. In his very next paragraph, however, the animus and self-feeling are all too apparent:

I am very sorry you miss my letters so much. I have felt the need of not thinking too constantly about you. If I understood you better I dare say I should be happier. When I care for people, I like to be with them; yet you wd. rather ruin my life and work than be very much with me, even if you are quite free. I don't understand this, or how it is that you don't understand my minding it.

Fortunately for her, Ottoline's happiness was no longer in Russell's hands and these remarks did not wound her as much as one might expect – or, perhaps, as much as Russell intended them to. Her remarks about feeling unhappy and dissatisfied, if not entirely false, were exaggerated for Russell's sake. In her memoirs, she writes that the summer of 1913 'was a very lovely one':

I was feeling better in health and not so tired, and so more able to enjoy seeing people, and looking on at the gay and rather sympathetic artistic and intellectual life that existed then in London.

Indeed, she adds, 'Perhaps Bertie's absence helped to make this summer, as it remains in my memory, gay and delightful.'

Among the delights of the cultural life in London at that time was the visit of the Russian Ballet, and one of the highlights of Ottoline's summer was a lunch party at Lady Ripon's house attended by, among others, Stravinsky, Diaghilev and Nijinsky. Ottoline sat next to Nijinsky and was quite fascinated by him: 'he was such a pure artist, a drop of the essence of art . . . [He] talked a good deal about his new ballet *Le Sacre du Printemps* in which he expressed the idea of pagan worship, the religious instinct in primitive nature, fear, ecstasy, developing into frenzy and utter self-oblation. It was too intense and terrible, too much an expression of ideas to please the public who are accustomed to graceful toe-dancing or voluptuous eastern scenes.' It was a far cry from hearing Russell explaining his latest thoughts on the analysis of matter, and, as far as Ottoline was concerned, a more than adequate replacement.

Russell expressed a merely polite interest in what Ottoline told him about Nijinsky, but in the other highlight of Ottoline's social life that summer – her visit to see Joseph Conrad – he had a very genuine and intense interest.

According to Ottoline's memoirs, when she first mentioned to her friend Henry James that she would like to meet Conrad, he did his best to dissuade her, pacing up and down her drawing-room in Bedford Square, his hands held high in horror, saying: 'But, dear lady . . . but dear lady . . . He has lived his life at sea – dear lady, he has never met "civilised" women . . . No, dear lady, he has lived a rough life.' If Ottoline has reported these remarks accurately, one can only think that James was pulling her leg. A long-standing friend and near-neighbour of Conrad's, he could not possibly have thought that Conrad – a Polish aristocrat and an immensely 'civilised' man – was unused to refined company. In any case, if his scruples were genuine, they were quickly and easily overcome, for shortly after this conversation Ottoline received a letter from Conrad inviting her to pay him a visit.

On 10 August, therefore, Ottoline set off from London to Capel House, Conrad's home in Ashford, Kent. She travelled by train, and took Conrad's *A Personal Record*, 'that wonderful book of his reminiscences', to read on the journey, finding, however, that she was too nervous and excited to read it. At Ashford station she was met by Conrad's son, Borys, who drove her to the house. She stayed until five o'clock, and the meeting was enough of a success for her to write enthusiastic accounts of it both in her letters to Russell and in her memoirs. The success was qualified however, to some extent by the fact that, though Conrad extended to her the gracious hospitality of the impeccably mannered Polish nobleman that he was (Ottoline discovered within seconds of meeting him how distorted Henry James's picture had been), it was evident to Ottoline that he was not really greatly interested in her. 'I found I couldn't help desiring that he should like me,' she wrote in her journal, 'and believing also that he was quite indifferent.'

No hint of this indifference, however, is apparent in the account she gave Russell, which emphasised instead how easy Conrad had been to talk to and the apparently intimate nature of their conversation: 'He said his writing was a terrble effort to him . . . that his health never recovered from the Congo. It was such a terrible moral shock to him . . . I felt underneath sadness that he was not more appreciated and a fear that he wrote on too much the same as before.' She also emphasised the potential for a great meeting of minds between Conrad and Russell himself: 'I told him that it was you who had given me his books and I described you a little and he said, "Oh, I like mathematicians" . . . I know you would *love* him . . . Do go and see him when you get back.'

As Ottoline knew, Russell revered Conrad more than any other living writer and would be fascinated to meet him. And, as she also knew, Russell was not the sort of man who would make the first approach in establishing contact with someone, no matter how much he admired them. In her visit to Conrad, then, Ottoline was paving the way for a meeting with Russell that she knew he would cherish and which, as far as he was concerned, could come about only through Ottoline. Coming at a time when Russell was trying to shake off his feelings for her, and when Ottoline was concerned lest he break with her for good, it is hard to resist the suspicion that her meeting with Conrad was, to some extent at least, motivated by a desire to maintain Russell's interest in her.

If this is so, then the plan worked perfectly, for Russell's next few letters are full of gratitude for her having laid the foundation for his own meeting with Conrad:

> It was good of you to tell Conrad about me. What he said about the Congo is *most* interesting – the *Heart of Darkness* is good enough to be worth it, but one couldn't have known that he had been permanently upset by it.
> (12 August)

> I do so feel *all* you tell me about Conrad. Certainly I will go and see him. He must be *wonderful.* I am *sure* you didn't stay too long or talk too much. It must have been an event in his life. I can't say how much I should love to go there with you some day.
> (14 August)

When Ottoline began to fret that she had not heard from Conrad in reply to her letter, Russell reassured her: 'I am *quite quite* sure your visit to Conrad did not bore him. Writing to you would be very difficult to a man like him – it would require much thought, and would involve a great nervous expenditure; so it is not surprising that he has not yet answered. I will try to see him, and I agree that the first time would be better without you.'

When *A Personal Record* was first published in 1911, some critics complained about its lack of intimacy and self-revelation, and in the account of her meeting with Conrad in her memoirs, Ottoline stresses his emotional reticence: 'In his talk he led me along many paths of his life, but I felt that he did not wish to explore the jungle of emotions that lay dense on either side, and that his apparent frankness had a great reserve.' To Russell, though, this very reticence was confirmation of the depth, richness and delicacy of Conrad's inner life. In the preface to *A Personal Record*, Conrad discussed the need to maintain his integrity and his 'horror of losing even for one moving moment that full possession of myself which is the first condition of good service'. He emphasised the lawlessness and danger of 'that interior world where [a writer's] thought and his emotions go seeking for the experience of imagined adventures', while at the same time insisting that 'All intellectual and artistic ambitions are permissible, up to and even beyond the limit of prudent sanity.' Such remarks would have had Russell's entire approval and confirmed him in his belief that he and Conrad were kindred spirits.

Ottoline was at first surprised that Conrad's wife Jessie was so ordinary and unintellectual, but upon reflection decided that this was entirely appropriate: 'She seemed a nice and good-looking fat creature, an excellent cook, as Henry James said, and was indeed a good and reposeful mattress for this hypersensitive, nerve-wrecked man, who did not ask from his wife high intelligence, only an assuagement of life's vibrations.' 'I wonder if a nice fat wife who cooks the meals would suit me!' Russell wrote to her. 'I believe nervous people ought not to live with people who enter into their inner life. Perhaps that is what you feel against me partly.'

Russell felt that he needed to know exactly what Ottoline did feel against him. In an earlier letter, he had asked her to treat him as 'an utterly stupid person, to whom even the simplest things have to be explained.' On 14 August, he wrote that what was necessary to prevent her giving him 'nervous shocks' and tiring him out was that he should understand her, so as to know what to expect: 'Understanding is the solution of all difficulties.' He was feeling cut off, both from Ottoline and from the sense of beauty she aroused in him. That day he and Sanger were in Brescia and had gone to admire the splendid ancient Roman remains for which the town is famous, particularly the celebrated statue of Victory, which, wrote Russell:

> has that strange sense of peace that very great things have . . . It belongs to a world which I feel to be above anything I can ever hope to reach – I always have a sense of being left outside the gates of Paradise when I see such things.

Anxious not to miss an opportunity for a letter from Ottoline and, perhaps, an explanation of what she felt against him, Russell gave detailed instructions as to which poste restante addresses she should write to for the rest of his holiday: on 18 and 19 August they would be in Verona, on 20 August in the town of Garda, and after that at Albergo San Vigilio, on the shores of Lake Garda.

In accordance with these instructions, when Russell arrived at Verona, he found waiting for him a sixteen-page letter from Ottoline, trying to explain to him – as if he were indeed an utterly stupid person to whom everything needed to be explained – what, from her point of view, had gone wrong between them. Though it was just what Russell had asked for, it made extremely unpleasant reading. Among the accusations Ottoline made were that he was too critical, too 'donnish' and too full of grievances; that, in his excessive and intense scrutiny, he robbed her of her spontaneity; that in demanding her complete devotion, he was demanding the impossible; and that, in his emphasis upon his frustrated sexual instincts, he spent too much time analysing their problems and feelings. Having compiled such a list, Ottoline seemed to think (though she insisted that this was not what she wanted) that they should perhaps finally break with each other. In any case, it was clear to her that their relationship should continue only on a platonic basis.

Russell replied to the letter immediately after reading it. 'It is what I asked for,' he told Ottoline, and yet it had made him 'utterly and absolutely miserable – I find I cannot face life without you – it seems so bleak and dark and terrible.' He pleaded with her to give him a chance to try again. He recognised that he had been too critical, but insisted, 'My criticisms of you are hardly ever genuine – they are the result of thwarted instinct.' There was only one criticism that was genuine, which was that at the beginning Ottoline had told him that she and Philip were only friends, a lie that had troubled him for the last year and a half. Now, he had to accept that 'there is no hope of anything approaching happiness for me for the rest of my life':

> I cannot face losing you and I cannot be content with what you give without a greater moral effort than seems possible to me. I have been going down hill for many years past and lately terribly fast. I think it ought to be possible to pull myself together.

The letter ended with Russell figuratively on his knees in supplication: 'I know there is a great calm place where we could live together in peace and perfect spiritual union – but the flesh is weak – O Dearest help me help me . . . Life is hard for me – but I must try to live in the spirit and not in this wretched turmoil of self seeking. I have reached the nethermost pit of pain – Dear dear love don't let me destroy our love. Oh I love you I love you I love you – O help me Dearest have mercy on a struggling Sinner.'

That afternoon, Russell went to the San Zeno Maggiore, a twelfth-century church in Verona, where, while Sanger waited outside, he went inside and found himself on his knees praying: 'I can't justify it, but it was a deep and sincere prayer – a prayer for strength to subdue my instincts.' If he and Ottoline were to go on, he had decided, he had to give up his wish for companionship and for children, 'or for any escape from loneliness':

> If I can conquer these desires (which unfortunately I let loose at the beginning of our relations) I should be then able to get great religious happiness from being with you. But I should have to become a saint to do that. Can I? I don't know.

He and Sanger then ate dinner in the piazza, looking out over the crowds of apparently happy people, gathered to listen to the music. As so often when he was emotionally stirred, being in a crowd made Russell feel unbearably isolated and alienated: 'many of them I loved from their faces, but they seemed separated from me by a vast gulf – I felt so utterly alone that I hardly could keep from calling to them that I too was a human being, and really one of them.'

Sometimes, he confessed, 'the vision of a peaceful family life with a home and children comes before me and maddens me', but the hopes that such a vision inspired were really quite dead. Ottoline was his hope, and thus: 'What I wish at bottom is to become a saint.' He apologised for being dry and donnish, a trait which, he repeated, 'comes out because of checked impulses':

> Of course my constant criticism has chilled you; I quite see that it must cease if we are to go on. – Now, my dear dear Love, I am in your hands. If you think me capable of doing better, after all these many many failures, I will try to conquer those instincts and put them away, and make the most of what you can give. I am *quite sure* that is the right course if I can do it; and that any other course means absolute irretrievable ruin.

As he finished this letter, late at night, he remarked that, if he had the right, he wanted to say to Ottoline: 'God bless you.'

The religiose tone of this letter, of course, was one calculated to win Ottoline's approval, though there is no reason to think that it was disingenuous or affected. Russell no doubt really did kneel in church to pray that his sexual impulses might be subdued, and the penitential style of his remarks was no doubt an accurate reflection of his state of mind. And yet, how difficult it would be for him to conquer his instincts, and how unlikely the idea of him as self-denying saint, was illustrated just a week later on the last day of his Italian holiday in San Vigilio, when he became attracted to a German woman called Liese von Hattingberg, who was on holiday with her two children but without her husband. 'At the end of the evening,' Russell told Ottoline, 'I had an hour's tête-à-tête with her and liked her enormously':

> She is well-educated (has been at three universities!), very nice-looking, gentle and strong-willed . . . In saying goodnight I kissed her hand, and she appeared on the Veranda at 7.30 to wave goodbye [the next morning] . . . I don't suppose I shall ever see her again – the only importance of the incident is that I felt I could now give an affection worth having to someone else. I feel it shameful that it should be so, but so it is. It shows a great poverty of nature in me, and I wish it were otherwise.

'My prayer in Verona was not answered', as he put it earlier in the same letter.

This letter, which was written on his return to England on 29 August, was interpreted by Ottoline as a final farewell. 'Bertie has gone,' she wrote in her journal. 'Such is man. There is nothing for me to say to him, but to open my hands and let the bird fly':

> He is intensely self-centred, poor man, and says I was selfish because I did not sacrifice more to him. I feel his letter tonight was quite final, and that most probably I shall never see him again. Yes: I feel the poorer a great deal. But I don't think he loved me – only desired me. Love could not die like that. Desire could.

In fact, Russell's letter was more ambivalent than this implies. 'I don't know whether my love for you is still alive,' Russell told her, though he seemed certain that 'the sense of a personal relation is snapped'. The reason for this was that 'the passionate side of my love is dead', and, having recognised that he was not, after all, the stuff of which saints are made, this meant that, as far as he was concerned, their relationship ought to finish. Nevertheless, something might endure, for 'if I make up my mind not to look to you for instinctive things, the other things may remain'.

The following day, Russell went to Oxford (where Ottoline and Philip were staying at Black Hall as the guests of Philip's mother) for yet another 'last meeting'. As Ottoline remembered it: 'He was hard and cold and old, as if all his soul had dried up, and kept saying that his love for me was dead. But before he went he quite changed, and all his love came back.' In her journal for that day, she wrote:

> Since this crisis I feel happier and more at ease with him. I suppose what really comes between us is his passion and desire, and that upsets and frightens me, and makes me dislike him.

'I have *really* learnt not to make demands on you, even in my most instinctive thoughts,' Russell wrote to her after this meeting. 'I do think it is permanent this time – it feels quite different. The real love that was obscured by desire is very living in me.' For the next few weeks, the truth of this would remain unchallenged, for, while Russell stayed in Cambridge and tried to write his Lowell lectures on 'Our Knowledge of the External World' before term started on 10 October, Ottoline and her family spent a month in Philip's constituency of Burnley in Lancashire.

Throughout September 1913 without much sense of inspiration or even of effort, Russell kept up a rate of ten pages a day in the writing of his lectures. 'My heart is not in it,' he wrote on 2 September, 'so the stuff is dull'. What bored him, he wrote a few days later, 'is that there is no *new* thought in these lectures, only old ideas that I am trying to make easy to understand'. The lectures presented a popularisation of the main lines of his philosophical work since 1911, beginning with the 'manifesto' he had announced in Paris in the spring of 1911 of the 'philosophy of logical atomism', a philosophy that, basing itself upon the perceived philosophical significance of mathematical logic, sought to bring 'scientific method' to bear on ancient problems. This general approach was then illustrated by its treatment of the traditional problem of our knowledge of the external world, at which point Russell presented a popular version of his views (derived from Whitehead, as he fulsomely acknowledged) that matter can be 'constructed' out of sense-data, and that the fundamental ideas of physics, including space and time, can be given definitions derived from mathematical logic. Finally, Russell outlined, in a *semi*-popular form (for these lectures are markedly more difficult than the others), his view that mathematical logic has solved once and for all the age-old problems of the nature of continuity and infinity, solutions that are 'among the triumphs of scientific method in philosophy'.

It was indeed, for the most part, old ground, and it is little wonder that he could write the lectures so quickly and that he found the work so uninspiring. What is new, and what distinguishes these lectures from, say, *The Problems of Philosophy*, is the disillusioned tone that predominates throughout. There is no talk of the 'value of philosophy' consisting in a contemplation of eternal forms and semi-mystical union with the universe. Instead, there is an insistence (derived from Wittgenstein, as Russell acknowledges in a footnote) that there are no such things as forms, and a robust rejection of mysticism in all its manifestations. In the opening lecture, he deals briskly with the kind of mysticism that, like Bergson's philosophy, rejects the importance of logic in favour of insight and intuition. He begins with a description of the motivation that inspires mysticism, an evocation of the mystical attitude that is, though he does not acknowledge it as such, surely autobiographical. 'In all who seek passionately for the fugitive and difficult goods,' he writes, 'the conviction is almost irresistible that there is in the world something deeper, more significant, than the multiplicity of little facts chronicled and classified by science':

> Behind the veil of these mundane things, they feel, something quite different obscurely shimmers, shining forth clearly in the great moments of illumination, which alone give anything worthy to be called real knowledge of truth. To seek such moments, therefore, is to them the way of wisdom, rather than, like the man of science, to observe coolly, to analyse without emotion, and to accept without question the equal reality of the trivial and the important.[2]

After such purple prose, one expects him to declare that he has known what it is like to experience such 'moments of illumination'. Instead, he insists, 'Of the reality or unreality of the mystic's world I know nothing.' The mystic insight may, he allows, be a genuine one, but it cannot be acknowledged as such without first being tested by reason: 'What I do wish to maintain – and it is here that the scientific attitude becomes imperative – is that insight, untested and unsupported, is an insufficient guarantee of truth.' Intuition is not, as Bergson maintains, infallible, 'like all human faculties, [it] is liable to error'. Russell's illustration of this point is one of the most disillusioned pieces of writing in all his philosophy, and is, despite his reluctance yet again to acknowledge the fact, straightforwardly autobiographical.

Bergson's best example of an infallible intuition, Russell begins, is our acquaintance with ourselves, 'yet self-knowledge is proverbially rare and difficult. Most men, for example, have in their nature meannesses, vanities, and envies of which they are quite unconscious, though even their best friends can perceive them without any difficulty.' Apart from self-knowledge, he continues, 'one of the most notable examples of intuition is the knowledge people believe themselves to possess of those with whom they are in love':

> the wall between different personalities seems to become transparent, and people think they see into another soul as into their own. Yet deception in such cases is constantly practised with success; and even where there is no intentional deception, experience gradually proves, as a rule, that the supposed insight was illusory, and that the slower, more groping methods of the intellect are in the long run more reliable.

---

[2] This Shelleyesque image of the veil was, significantly, used by Russell in a letter to Ottoline of 12 August in an attempt to characterise the nature of his love for her and to convince her it was unchangeable: 'I don't know whether I would change it if I could, but I can't. There is a quality in you that holds me for ever; and makes all other people seem lacking in interest by comparison with you . . . I feel you in contact, more than other people, with the world of wonder, the world behind the veil. I long to seize the wonder and fix it, but I cannot. The struggle wears me out and will perhaps destroy much of my usefulness – but I must keep on.'

This is an extraordinarily sad passage, demolishing, as it does, both the central idea of 'Prisons' – that, in love, people can overcome the walls of their selves – and the conception of his love for Ottoline that he had cherished for the previous two years. The 'visions' of 1911 are now dismissed as illusions: people in love only seem to be transparent to each other, they only think they are seeing into each other's souls. In fact, they are deceived, for, in reality, they are as imprisoned in their own egos as ever. In place of the supposed 'insight', the 'vision', of lovers, the more reliable, more 'groping' methods of reason tell us the truth: that the walls between different personalities never do become transparent.

Despite what he says in this passage, however, Russell had not quite given up the idea that some people could see directly into the souls of others. (Even in this passage, he allows the possibility of such a thing, insisting that the supposed insight proves to be illusory *as a rule*.) To entirely abandon this notion was more than he could bear. It would be to give up all hope of ever overcoming his desperate loneliness, to condemn himself for ever to a life trapped within the prison walls of his self, to the kind of repressed and secretive loneliness that had characterised his life at Pembroke Lodge and much of his marriage. He needed to believe that *someone* could see into his soul, even if he had ceased to believe that Ottoline could do so. Indeed, now that his love affair with Ottoline was all but over, he needed someone more than ever to overcome his agonised sense of separation, someone who, he felt, could really *see* him.

His hopes in this respect became pinned on Joseph Conrad, who, through Ottoline, Russell arranged to visit on 10 September. His extraordinary account of that meeting in his *Autobiography* shows just how unwilling he was to abandon entirely the idea that, at least sometimes, the walls separating him from the rest of humanity became transparent:

> At our very first meeting, we talked with continually increasing intimacy. We seemed to sink through layer after layer of what was superficial, till gradually both reached the central fire. It was an experience unlike any other that I have known. We looked into each other's eyes, half appalled and half intoxicated to find ourselves together in such a region. The emotion was as intense as passionate love, and at the same time all-embracing. I came away bewildered, and hardly able to find my way among ordinary affairs.

In a letter written to Ottoline on the train back to Cambridge, Russell described it slightly differently:

> It was *wonderful*. I *loved* him and I think he liked me. He talked a great deal about his work and life and aims . . . we went for a little walk, and somehow grew very intimate. I plucked up courage to tell him what I find in his work – the boring down into things to get to the very bottom below the apparent facts. He seemed to feel I had understood him; then he stopped and we just looked into each other's eyes for some time, and then he said he had grown to wish he could live on the surface and

write differently, that he had grown frightened. His eyes at the moment expressed the inward pain and terror that one feels him always fighting . . . It is impossible to say how much I loved him.

In Conrad's letters of the period there is little to suggest that either the meeting or the moment when he and Russell looked into each other's eyes had the intense significance for him that they had for Russell. In a letter to Russell a few days after the meeting, he apologised for his 'unusual talkativeness' and commented that, though he did not generally know what to say to people, Russell's personality drew him out and 'instinct told me I would not be misread.' This suggests a certain sense of mutual understanding, but hardly the semi-mystical, 'half appalled, half intoxicated' sense of communion that Russell describes.

Nor did the meeting lead to a close and affectionate friendship, though one might suppose so from some of Russell's later pronouncements. 'I have seen Conrad just twice,' he wrote to Lucy Donnelly in February 1914, 'but he is already one of the people in the world that I am most intimate with – I write to him & he to me on all the inmost things.' In his *Autobiography*, he claims that he and Conrad 'shared a certain outlook on human life and human destiny, which, from the very first, made a bond of extreme strength'. Yet, in the normal sense, there was no such bond. After Conrad had paid Russell a return visit to Cambridge, and Russell had visited Conrad briefly in the summer of 1914, the two did not see each other again until 1921, that is, for another seven years, and then only once or twice before Conrad's death in 1924. And, despite what Russell says to Lucy Donnelly, Conrad's letters to him were not especially intimate, nor were they particularly concerned with 'inmost things'. Conrad presented Russell with a copy of his latest novel, *Chance*, and Russell returned the compliment with *The Problems of Philosophy* and *Philosophical Essays*, and, for the most part, the few letters that Conrad wrote to Russell before their re-acquaintance in 1921 were written as thanks for those books, or else to excuse himself from further meetings on the grounds of pressure of work (he had a deadline of 1 May 1914 to complete *Victory*, the novel on which he was working when Russell met him).

The relationship was, then, somewhat one-sided. But, from Russell's point of view, it was none the less significant for that. For the rest of his life, Conrad had a unique and special importance for Russell that was unmatched by anybody else. He gave the name 'Conrad' to *both* his sons, to the first of whom, John Conrad Russell (born in 1921), he asked Conrad to be a secular godfather. He urged everyone he could to read Conrad's novels; and, to his most intimate friends, he invoked Conrad as the person above all others who understood him in his innermost depths. One of the most striking examples of this comes in a letter he wrote to his then lover Constance Malleson on 23 October 1916, in which he tried to explain the longing that lay at the very heart of his character:

The centre of me is always and eternally a terrible pain . . . a searching for something beyond what the world contains, something transfigured and infinite – the beatific vision – God . . . I can't explain it or make it seem anything but foolishness . . . I have known others who had it – Conrad especially – but it is rare – it sets one oddly apart and gives a great sense of isolation.

This remark gives some hint as to why – even though, in the ordinary sense, Conrad and he scarcely knew each other ('In the out-works of our lives, we were almost strangers,' as Russell says in his *Autobiography*) – he held Conrad up as the one person who saw into his very being. It was not, I think, to do with what they discussed on 10 September; it was rather to do with what Russell saw in Conrad's work, his reading of which led him to visit Conrad with the prior expectation that he would find a deeply kindred spirit. Two of Conrad's novels that stand out as particularly significant in this respect are the two that Russell discusses in his account of meeting Conrad: *The Heart of Darkness* and *Amy Foster*, both of which might be regarded as dramatisations of Russell's deepest fears and anxieties, of his terror of madness and of his acute sense of isolation. The story told in *The Heart of Darkness* is the perfect metaphor for Russell's fear that, if one delves too deeply into one's self, one will find nothing but madness. It concerns a journey along the Congo – undertaken for a reason he does not quite understand – by the narrator, Marlow. Along the way, he sees evidence of the barbarity of Imperialism, but consoles himself with the thought that when he gets to the heart of the jungle he will meet Kurtz, a man whose integrity and abilities are famous. When he finally meets Kurtz, however, he discovers that he is in fact completely insane and even more barbaric than the others. 'His soul was mad,' Marlow says. 'Being alone in the wilderness, it had looked within itself, and, by heavens! I tell you, it had gone mad.' Comparing himself with Kurtz, Marlow says that 'he had made that last stride, he had stepped over the edge, while I had been permitted to draw back my hesitant foot.' And then, in a way that strikingly recalls Russell's description of mystic illumination in *Our Knowledge of the External World*, goes on:

And perhaps in this is the whole difference; perhaps all the wisdom, and all the truth, and all sincerity, are just compressed into that inappreciable moment of time in which we step over the threshold of the invisible.

When, late in life, Russell was asked to explain the bond of sympathy that he felt with Conrad, he did so in a way that, no doubt unconsciously, echoed both this passage and his own earlier characterisation of mysticism in *Our Knowledge of the External World*. It had to do, he explained, with a shared 'Satanic mysticism', the truth of which he had never been convinced about, 'but in moments of intense emotion it overwhelms me'. It consisted in feeling that there were two levels: 'one that of science and common sense, and another, terrifying, subterranean and periodic, which in some sense held more truth than the everyday view'. In Russell's *Autobiography*, the 'shared outlook on human life and human destiny' – to which he attributes his feeling of intimacy with Conrad – is characterised in similar terms, expressed in the image of civilised life as 'a dangerous walk on a thin crust of barely cooled lava which at any moment might break and let the unwary sink into fiery depths'.

It was just such 'fiery depths' ('the central fire'), of course, that he considered himself and Conrad to have fallen into when they looked into each other's eyes. And, in this respect, it is striking that, as Russell recorded in his letter to Ottoline, Conrad's next remark was that he 'had grown to wish he could live on the surface and write differently, that he had grown frightened'. Conrad, more even than Russell, had reason to be frightened: in 1910, immediately after finishing two of his most personal works – the novel *Under Western Eyes* and the short story 'The Secret Sharer' – he had suffered a nervous breakdown that rendered him incapable of work for four months, during which time he feared that his wife Jessie was conspiring with his doctor to put him away in an asylum. Jessie spoke of the breakdown as the 'penalty' that had to be paid for the intensity of the work that preceded it, and, Conrad, too, seems to have thought of it in that way, and to some extent sought protection in a different, less emotionally demanding style of writing. Having, so to speak, peered over the edge into madness, Conrad – like his character Marlow and like Russell himself – pulled back and sought sanity in life at the surface. After 1910, Conrad's work became less intense and more 'external'. According to his biographer, Frederick Karl, 'The completion of *Under Western Eyes* marked the end of an era':

> The year 1909–10 was, in a sense, a watershed for Conrad, manifested psychologically by his nervous collapse for four months and demonstrated literarily by his realisation of an entire phase of personal writings. After *Under Western Eyes*, he would move back to *Chance*, to lighter short fiction, and to *Victory*, little of which was so markedly personal as his fiction from 1899 to 1910.

In *Under Western Eyes*, Conrad, according to Karl, 'reached out for what every artist must do or try to do: to dip so deeply into his psyche for what he fears most that he endangers himself'. Karl then goes on to find interesting and relevant affinities between Conrad and Dostoyevsky in the intensity of this self-exploration. From Russell's point of view, however, there was one crucial respect in which Conrad was precisely not like Dostoyevsky: though both writers were concerned to unearth the subterranean parts of the human psyche, the impulses and desires of which we are most ashamed and afraid, Dostoyevsky's characters seem to illustrate the need for divine redemption, while Conrad's point rather to the necessity and the value of self-control. 'He was very conscious', as Russell puts it (still elaborating on his comment that he and Conrad 'shared a certain outlook on human life and human destiny'), 'of the various forms of passionate madness to which men are prone, and it was this that gave him such a profound belief in the importance of discipline':

> His point of view, one might perhaps say, was the antithesis of Rousseau's: 'Man is born in chains, but he can become free.' He becomes free, so I

believe Conrad would have said, not by letting loose his impulses, not by being casual and uncontrolled, but by subduing wayward impulse to a dominant purpose.

In the modern world, Russell says, there are essentially two philosophies: the one (manifested in various forms of anarchism and romanticism) that is derived from Rousseau and which preaches the abandonment of all forms of discipline, and the other (manifested in various forms of totalitarianism) that seeks to impose discipline from without. Both are to be rejected:

Conrad adhered to the older tradition, that discipline should come from within. He despised indiscipline, and hated discipline that was merely external. In all this I found myself closely in agreement with him.

Perhaps the best illustration of Conrad's attitudes in this respect is the allegorical short story 'The Secret Sharer', in which a young captain of a ship is surprised to discover that he has on board a fugitive from justice, a murderer on the run from another ship. In the ordinary course of events, the captain's duty would be to turn this man in. And yet, he does not do so. Instead, he hides the fugitive in his own cabin, keeping his whereabouts secret, both from his own crew and from the captain of the man's own ship, who comes looking for him. The reason he takes this risk is that he comes to identify strongly with the man. A 'mysterious communication' is established between the two almost as soon as they meet. 'It was', says the captain, 'as though I had been faced by my own reflection in the depths of a sombre and immense mirror.' This murderer, he realises, could easily be himself; he, too, given the appropriate set of circumstances, might be capable of killing someone.

Again and again, the captain returns to this idea of the identification of himself with this fugitive, referring to the 'secret sharer' of his cabin as his 'other self', his 'secret self' or his 'second self' – all three of which Conrad considered as alternative titles for the story. The fugitive, naturally, is grateful to the captain, not only for his practical help, but also for his sympathy. 'It's a great satisfaction', he says, 'to have got somebody to understand.' And yet, as they both know, his presence on the boat *is* a disruption, and while he is in the cabin, the captain makes a number of decisions and gives a number of orders that are inexplicable to his crew in order to help his new friend. Once the fugitive has escaped (the captain steers the boat close enough to an island for the man to jump off and swim to safety), normality is restored and the ship resumes its true course. The story ends with the captain in 'perfect communion' with his ship. He has, as it were, regained control and re-established discipline.

Though Russell does not mention 'The Secret Sharer' in his account of Conrad, it is practically certain that he knew it. After 1906, when he first read *The Heart of Darkness*, he tended to read Conrad's books as soon as they came out. And 'The Secret Sharer' was published (in a collection called '*Twixt Land and Sea* in 1912) at the very height of his interest in Conrad. Ottoline certainly read it, and indeed, in her memoirs, alludes to it in a particularly interesting context: in a discussion of the difference between men and women and the extent to which they are at the mercy of their emotions. 'I find men's opinions – Bertie's and Philip's – are often only the outcome of passing emotions,' she writes, 'and they say and do things in emotion that they don't fundamentally mean.' Women, on the other hand, 'are much more cunning and reserved . . . and control and hide passing emotions.' She goes on:

> I know I do not wish to speak of mine but deal with them in my secret life. I wonder if everyone has a secret companion, a second self, with whom they discuss their thoughts and emotions – a 'secret sharer'. I cannot imagine anyone existing without this secret companion. We wear each other out by our discussions.

Russell's description of meeting Conrad suggests that he looked upon Conrad himself as a 'secret sharer', a 'second self', with whom he shared a 'mysterious communication' and deep understanding. Their shared sense of the ever-imminent danger of sinking into the madness, the 'fiery depths' below the civilised crust, is no doubt part of that empathy. But perhaps even more important is their shared sense of the dreadful loneliness of each individual human being. It is this that dominates Russell's description of Conrad, and in a letter to Ottoline written the day after his meeting, he emphasised: 'One feels his life has been very lonely.' Conrad, like Russell, lost his parents at an early age. His mother died when he was seven, and his father – who, like Russell's father, was utterly broken by the death of his beloved wife – four years later.[3] After that, Conrad was raised by his grandmother and his uncle, and is described in family correspondence of the time as having no childhood companions and of burying himself in books. In other words, his early years are strikingly similar to Russell's, and seem to have had upon him a similar effect. The similarities even extend to their shared love of the sea, which both at various times described as a 'mirror', and which to both seemed symbolic of a vast, natural force that was at the same time reassuringly permanent and reassuringly impersonal.

If Russell had been a great novelist, one might suggest, he would have been Conrad, whose novels seemed to explore his own deepest feelings with greater power and honesty and in more precise language than he had ever managed to do. Whenever he tried, whether in fiction or autobiography or in letters, Russell could not stop himself from describing what he believed rather than what he felt, and it was left to Conrad to articulate the fears and longings that lay at the centre of Russell's being. Perhaps the most powerful example of this

---

[3] In his letter written on the train after his meeting with Conrad, Russell mentioned that Conrad 'talked a lot about Poland, and showed me an album of family photographs of the [18]60s – spoke about how dream-like all that seems, and how he sometimes feels he ought not to have had children, because they have no roots or traditions or relations'. These, presumably, would be photographs of his parents (Conrad's mother died in 1865 and his father in 1869). Evidently Conrad felt that Russell would understand the feelings of loss and displacement that these photographs evoked.

is the short story, *Amy Foster*. If *The Heart of Darkness* provides a perfect metaphor for Russell's fear of madness, then *Amy Foster* – the other story upon which Russell dwells in his description of Conrad – presents an extremely moving dramatisation of his sense of isolation.

In his old age, Russell told his daughter Kate a recurring dream that he used to have before he had children: 'I imagine myself behind plate glass, like a fish in an aquarium, or turned into a ghost whom no one sees; agonisingly I try to make some sort of contact but it is impossible & I know myself doomed forever to lonely impotence.' Such is the situation of Yanko Goorall, the central character in *Amy Foster*, a man from an eastern European country, who on his way to America finds himself the sole survivor when the ship carrying him sinks. He is washed up on the shores of England, but, because he speaks no English, is shunned by the villagers he finds himself among, who misinterpret his gestures of friendliness and his pleas for help, and who see him only as a strange and perhaps insane alien. The one villager who shows him kindness is Amy Foster, who brings him food and teaches him English. He and Amy marry and have a son, in whom he takes great delight and to whom – much to Amy's dislike and suspicion – he teaches the folk songs of his homeland. One day he falls ill and, in his fever, relapses into his native tongue, alarming Amy beyond endurance. Taking their child with her and ignoring his cries for help, Amy abandons him. He dies alone and broken-hearted, unable to understand why he has been deserted by the woman he loves and why he has to lose his beloved son.

If one had set out to write a story calculated to move Russell to tears, one could not have improved upon *Amy Foster*. With its themes of chronic loneliness, of the feeling of being an alien, of thwarted parental affection, and of the fear of the mad and the incomprehensible, it touches many of his very deepest emotions. In his *Autobiography* he describes it as 'extraordinarily moving', and on more than one occasion he unconsciously echoed this description by Conrad of Yanko Goorall:

> He was different; innocent of heart and full of good will, which nobody wanted, this castaway, that, like a man transplanted into another planet, was separated by an immense space from his past.

One of the most striking echoes of this passage comes when Russell is describing himself wandering alone among the joyous crowds celebrating the end of the First World War. 'I felt strangely solitary,' he wrote, 'like a ghost dropped by accident from some other planet.'

At least in Russell's eyes, their meeting on 10 September came as a tremendous reassurance that, even though both were surrounded by aliens, they at least found each other intelligible and familiar. The moment they looked into each other's eyes was one of the most powerful of Russell's life. It even finds its way into Ottoline's memoirs. Conrad and Russell, she writes 'understood each other immediately and even as they walked together in Conrad's garden had a moment of intense intimacy, some spell caught them and made them look deep down into each other's eyes':

Such things happen rarely, it was obviously the recognition that both these souls belonged to the kingdom of the sufferers, and the passionate and the unreconcilable.

For Russell, it was almost as if that one moment was all he wanted from Conrad. 'I shall certainly try to see him again,' he wrote a few days after the meeting, but in fact he made curiously few attempts to do so. Perhaps he respected Conrad's apparent wish to work undisturbed on *Victory*, but perhaps, too, he felt that there was little point in meeting again. The special bond that he felt existed between them was to do with the mutual recognition of the 'central fire', but, after all, neither of them wanted to be consumed by the fire and both had come to the conclusion that they would actually rather live on the surface than be destroyed. In any case, had he not recently written that 'as a rule' the insight of one person into another's soul is shown by experience to be illusory? If he wanted to hold on to the idea that Conrad and he had looked into each other's souls, therefore, perhaps it was only prudent not to subject it to too much experiential testing.

In order to get on with his work and with his life, Russell's descents into the central fire had to be the exception rather than the rule. On 11 September, the day after his visit, he wrote that his meeting with Conrad, 'tho' it is very vivid to me, seems curiously unreal, as if I had dreamed it'. Two days later, talking of Robert Trevelyan and his friend Donald Tovey, the musician, he wrote that they and people like them 'have never come in contact with the fire beneath the crust' and asked 'I wonder if we are right in feeling they ought to?'

It makes life easy to them, and makes them restful to others who have been scorched by the fire. I expect the people who live on the surface have their uses, tho' it is hard to feel any real respect for them.

As if to underline the usefulness of living on the surface, he remarked in the same letter that his work on *Our Knowledge of the External World* was going well, and that his days were 'quiet and peaceful and happy'. He was not going to risk the sort of trouble he had had after the mental exertions of May: 'I am not working at high pressure, and mean to be careful.'

With Ottoline in Burnley, Wittgenstein on holiday in Norway and Cambridge deserted as it always is during the vacations, Russell was enjoying an almost soporific calm. 'My days here', he wrote, 'are so quiet that I have nothing to write about – I go out in the afternoon, I write my ten pages, and most of the rest of the time I play patience. Being free from obsessions is such a delight that I require nothing more to keep me happy.' The following week, he wrote that he was 'in the mood of wanting solitude, which is *very* rare with me'. He was enjoying the rest, especially the inward rest: 'I have fairly vivid intellectual interests, but no wish to read poetry or see friends or do anything involving emotion.' It was the perfect mood in which to write out old thoughts about the external world, and by 25 September the first draft of *Our Knowledge of the External World* was finished.

As he completed each lecture, Russell sent it to Burnley to be read by Ottoline, even while admitting that much of what he had written would be both unintelligible and uninteresting to her. As expected, she found his discussions of the mathematical solutions to the problems of infinity and continuity beyond her. She did, however, show some interest in Russell's quasi-autobiographical discussions of the relation between logic and mysticism. After touching on the subject in the context of a polemic against Bergson in his first lecture, Russell returns to it in his second, 'Logic as the Essence of Philosophy', in which he discusses 'the logic of mysticism' in the work of, for example, Plato, Spinoza and Hegel, as having its origin in an emotionally intense 'mystic mood':

> While the mystic mood is dominant, the need for logic is not felt; as the mood fades, the impulse to logic reasserts itself, but with a desire to retain the vanishing insight, or at least to prove that it *was* insight, and that what seems to contradict it is illusion. The logic which thus arises is not quite disinterested or candid, and is inspired by a certain hatred of the daily world to which it is to be applied. Such an attitude naturally does not tend to the best results.

'All that about the bad logic produced by fading of the mystic vision was good, wasn't it?' Russell boasted to Ottoline. He felt strongly that this lecture (which, despite the fact that it is now Chapter 2 was among the last he wrote) and the others that he wrote towards the end were much better than the others: 'they took much more out of me. It is funny how impossible it is to write even tolerably without lacerating one's spirit.'

While Russell was getting through his ten pages a day of *Our Knowledge of the External World*, Wittgenstein was, he thought, at last making some progress in his work on logic. 'I am sitting here in a little place inside a beautiful fjord and thinking about the beastly theory of types,' he wrote on 5 September. He and Pinsent had hired a little sailing boat, and while Pinsent steered the boat up and down the fjord, Wittgenstein sat thinking about logic: 'Shall I get anything out??! It would be awful if I did not and all my work would be lost. However I am not losing courage and go on thinking. Pray for me!'

Towards the end of his holiday, Wittgenstein wrote that he had 'all sorts of ideas which seem to me very fundamental', and that he was convinced that he would die before being able to publish them: 'my greatest wish would therefore be to communicate *everything* I have done so far to you, *as soon as possible*.' He had a proposal:

> I want to ask you to let me meet you *as soon as possible* and give me time enough to give you a survey of the whole field of what I have done up to now and if possible to let me make some notes for you *in your presence*.

In his diary, Pinsent records that Wittgenstein was quite convinced that he was going to die soon and 'frightfully worried not to let the few remaining moments of his life be wasted'. In Pinsent's opinion, there was no obvious reason to suppose that Wittgenstein would not live a long life: 'But it is no use trying to dispel that conviction, or his worries about it, by reason: the conviction and the worry he can't help – for he is mad.'

At the end of their holiday, Wittgenstein suddenly announced to Pinsent that he wished to live alone in Norway for some years and concentrate on logic. There were too many distractions in Cambridge, and he felt himself on the brink of answering the most fundamental questions concerning the nature of logic. He had to devote himself entirely to the work.

On 2 October, Wittgenstein visited Russell at his flat in Bury Street and stayed late into the night, trying to explain to Russell the work he had been doing and even reading Russell some of the work he had written (which, unfortunately, has not survived). 'I was utterly worn out when he went,' Russell told Ottoline, though he considered the effort worth while; Wittgenstein's work was 'as good as anything that has ever been done in logic'.

Wittgenstein's decision to spend some time alone in Norway was, Russell wrote, 'a blow and an anxiety'. He told Lucy Donnelly that he had tried several ways of talking him out of it:

> I said it would be dark, & he said he hated daylight. I said it would be lonely, & he said he prostituted his mind talking to intelligent people. I said he was mad & he said God preserve him from sanity. (God certainly will.)

All the same, as he admitted to Ottoline, Wittgenstein's decision to leave was in one way 'a godsend': 'he wears me out nervously so that I long for nothing but escape from all serious thought and feeling . . . He was certainly the chief cause of my fatigue before.' It turned out that Wittgenstein could, according to the regulations, come back at any time to finish the residence in Cambridge required to get his degree, 'and he says he means to come back when he has something written.' In the meantime 'He has promised to leave me a written statement of what he has already done before he starts for Norway.' Wittgenstein had already tried to explain it verbally to Russell, but the ideas were too complex: 'I could only just understand by stretching my mind to the utmost.'

On 7 September, while he was in Birmingham saying goodbye to Pinsent, Wittgenstein made a start in dictating his work to a shorthand writer, to be typed out later for Russell. The following day he was in Cambridge, where he visited Russell to dictate further explanations and amplifications of his work. When, however, he sat down to do it, his 'artistic conscience' (as Russell put it) got in the way:

> After much groaning he said he couldn't. I abused him roundly and we had a fine row. Then he said he wd. talk, and write down any of his remarks that I thought worth it, so we did that, and it answered fairly well. But we both got utterly exhausted, and it was slow. Today [9 October] he is coming again, and Jourdain's secretary . . . is coming to take down our conversation in short-hand . . . All this fuss suits me to perfection and

prevents me from feeling impatience, or indeed anything except the wish to drag W's thoughts out of him with pincers, however he may scream with pain . . . Now I must stop. W. and Jourdain's Sce. will be here directly and then I shall have to start a fierce tussle with the combined difficulties of logic and human nerves.

Wittgenstein, Russell said, 'makes me feel it is worth while I shd. exist, because no one else cd. understand him or make the world understand him'. This is no doubt true, though it is open to question how much even Russell understood Wittgenstein's work at this stage. Certainly there is little trace of it in the revisions to *Our Knowledge of the External World*, which he wrote in October and November. At the end of his seventh lecture, 'The Positive Theory of Infinity', he propounds the view that there are no such 'entities' as logical objects, and in a footnote acknowledges that in putting forward this view he is 'making use of unpublished work by my friend Ludwig Wittgenstein'. This, however, is a view that Wittgenstein had persuaded Russell of long before he dictated his work in October 1913.

From the various sessions of dictation with Russell in Cambridge, with the shorthand writer in Birmingham and with Jourdain's secretary, there resulted seven pages of typescript and twenty-three pages of manuscript, which Russell arranged into what is now known as 'Notes on Logic', Wittgenstein's earliest written work. Its central concern is with the nature of a proposition. Having refuted Russell's theory of judgment along the lines that had proved so devastating for Russell in May, Wittgenstein argues that the questions about the nature of judgment and belief 'cannot be solved without a correct apprehension of the form of a proposition'. At the centre of his theory of propositions is the insistence that 'Propositions, which are symbols having reference to facts, are themselves facts . . . Thus facts are symbolised by facts, or more correctly: that a certain thing is the case in the symbol says that a certain thing is the case in the world.'

Thus, the form of a complex, that mysterious pseudo-object that had mystified Russell in his 1912 work 'What is Logic?', cannot be referred to, rather it is mirrored – or, as Wittgenstein would later say, *pictured* – by the form of the proposition. Relations between objects are not 'things' that can be named or spoken of. They are conveyed, rather, by the relations between the symbols that stand for the objects. So, Wittgenstein says, 'that this inkpot is on this table may express that I sit on this chair'. The inkpot on the table is then a proposition that says that Wittgenstein is sitting on the chair. The crucial point is that just two objects (two symbols) – the inkpot and the table – are required to say something about the relation between Wittgenstein and the chair. We do not need another object to correspond to the relation 'sitting on'; rather, we can put the inkpot and the table in some relation between themselves that pictures the fact that Wittgenstein is on the chair. In this way, one fact – that the inkpot is on the table – symbolises another: that Wittgenstein is on the chair. In essence, then – and in a very abbreviated form – the 'Notes on Logic' contain what, in its later manifestation in *Tractatus Logico-Philosophicus*, is called Wittgenstein's 'Picture Theory of Meaning'.

Of this theory there is no trace in *Our Knowledge of the External World*, and, indeed, there is little sign that Russell understood this aspect of Wittgenstein's theory of the proposition until he studied the manuscript that became *Tractatus Logico-Philosophicus* in 1919. The distinction that is required to make sense of the theory, the distinction between saying and showing, is one that Russell was never happy with. The idea that one can show things which one cannot say was always, for him, an unappealingly mystical one. At this stage, in the autumn of 1913, however, he showed no sign of realising that Wittgenstein's analysis of the nature of logic requires such a notion.

Wittgenstein set off for Norway on 11 October. Russell was not to see him again until after the First World War. In Norway, Wittgenstein built himself a hut on the side of the Sogne fjord near a village called Skjolden, where, despite Russell's premonitions that he would commit suicide and his own certainty that he would die before long, he enjoyed the most fruitful period of work he ever experienced in his life. His letters to Russell of October and November show him bursting with new ideas and confidence that he was working towards a complete and definitive solution to the problems Russell had bequeathed him. 'This is an ideal place to work in,' he wrote from Skjolden. 'All sorts of new logical stuff seems to be growing in me, but I can't yet write about it.' He nevertheless tried to outline in broad terms the direction that his work was taking. Having only imperfectly absorbed the 'Notes on Logic', Russell had difficulty following Wittgenstein's latest thoughts and, in his responses and questions, he was often, to Wittgenstein's sometimes impatient chagrin, several steps behind. 'An account of general indefinables?' Wittgenstein groaned, 'Oh Lord! It is *too* boring!!! Some other time!' And a few weeks later:

> I beg you to think about these matters for yourself: it is INTOLERABLE for me to repeat a written explanation which even the first time I gave only with the *utmost repugnance*.

Russell wanted to clarify Wittgenstein's thoughts, because, having translated and arranged the 'Notes on Logic', he wanted to use them in the logic course that he had agreed to give in Harvard in spring 1914.

His own preoccupations were, as they had been for a long time, far removed from Wittgenstein's. In the autumn term of 1913, in furtherance of his dream of establishing a school of scientifically minded philosophers, he began a discussion group, to which he invited those students he considered the best to meet every week to discuss the foundations of physics. He attracted to the group a number of the most promising physics and mathematics students, as well as the best and brightest philosophers, and he had great hopes for it. He had hopes, too, for an American student named Norbert Wiener, who came from Harvard with the reputation of being something of a child prodigy, having gained a Ph.D. at the remarkably young age of eighteen. Though Russell at first found Wiener personally repulsive ('The youth has been flattered,' he wrote to Lucy Donnelly, 'and thinks himself God Almighty'), he came to think well of his intellect and was grateful, in Wittgenstein's absence, to have at least one precociously gifted student. Wiener subsequently studied in Germany and found fame later in life as the founder of cybernetics.

In all this, however – his revisions of *Our Knowledge of the External World*, his preparations for his courses in Harvard, and his dealings with his Cambridge students – one senses in Russell a certain determined lack of passion that was in accordance with his deliberate policy not to over-excite himself after the traumas of the summer. 'I have a civilised side,' as he put it to Ottoline, 'and it is uppermost now.' Rogojin had been banished; fantasies of murder and uncontrollable sexual urges brought under control. 'I will do every thing in my power to make you happy,' he told Ottoline on 14 October, 'and to wipe out the memory of all the torture I have caused you.'

Chiefly, this meant controlling his sexual desire for her. 'Instinctive desires unsatisfied make me unkind and destroy sympathy and tenderness,' he told her, 'so I must keep them under.' Having, however, abandoned the hope that he could become a saint, Russell was not proposing to keep all his sexual feelings under control – simply those directed at Ottoline. The tie between them, he wrote in September, 'wd. not be lessened if I had other ties – perhaps even strengthened, because there wd. no longer be the pain of incompleteness in instinctive ways'. He was thinking of Liese von Hattingberg, with whom he kept up a correspondence throughout the autumn and in whom he evidently vested some hopes of finding an outlet for his 'instincts'.

In the meantime, he concentrated on (as he put it to Ottoline) keeping the 'wild beasts caged'. Ottoline should, perhaps, have been more worried than she seemed to be that his attempts in this area were proving successful. 'My feelings now', wrote Russell in October, 'are of the sort it is easy for you to understand – gentle and patient, not wild-beast feelings':

> That means that the burden and tragedy of life has entered into every corner of my feeling for you, so that I no longer get irridescent joy from you, or the kind of relief which makes the burden drop off for a time. I can't live always seriously and with the deepest things because my most serious feelings are too pessimistic – they wd. drive me mad if I faced them continually; and if they didn't do that, they wd. wear me out and make me useless.

His ambivalent attitude towards the relative value of 'wild-beast feelings' and gentle, patient ones was spelt out further a few days later, in the course of commenting on François Villon, the fifteenth-century French poet, who was notorious for leading a wild and criminal life (among the offences for which he was convicted were burglary, street-fighting and the murder of a priest). Ottoline had evidently been reading Villon's poetry with great enjoyment. 'Yes, Villon is very great,' Russell remarked:

> I don't think tame well-behaved people ever know anything of the mad fire just below the smooth surface of life. But whether it is worth while to know of it, I don't know.

It was a familiar paradox: deep passion, the 'mad fire', was essential to great writing and, in a sense, necessary in order to accomplish anything worth while. And yet it was terrible and destructive, and the 'wild beasts' that it released were a threat to both Russell's relationship with Ottoline and his sanity. For the moment, therefore, despite his admiration for people like Villon and his conviction of their superiority over 'tame well-behaved people', he would do his best to remain on the 'smooth surface' of life.

12

MR APOLLINAX

Despite his claims to the contrary – and despite also his declared intention to approximate as closely as possible to a 'tame well-behaved person' – Russell had not, of course, entirely conquered his 'wild-beast feelings' towards Ottoline, and after her return to London from Burnley in the second week of October 1913 he could not restrain himself, almost whenever they met, from making sexual demands upon her. Ottoline occasionally gave in to these demands, but, whenever she did, she afterwards made it humiliatingly clear that she did so with the very deepest misgivings. 'Yes, my darling, I did love our day together the other day,' she wrote on 22 October, 'but somehow I have an *instinctive* feeling that it is better not to let it happen in the future . . . our relation and intimacy has been so much better since it has stopped.' He was not to think that succumbing to his demands had made her unhappy, she continued, for their relationship was so valuable to her that 'I feel [it] is worthwhile to make any sacrifices to keep it good.'

Russell did not, as he might have done earlier, protest against these humiliations, he merely redoubled his efforts to keep himself as emotionally disengaged from Ottoline as he could. 'There was a long time during which I was often happy with you, but unhappy the moment you were gone,' he told her on 7 November, 'that is not so now. I am not *dependent* on you now – I have a possible life apart from you.'

Ottoline, of course – and this, from Russell's point of view was a large part of the problem – always did have a life apart from their relationship, a life of caring for Julian and Philip and of keeping up a rich variety of friendships and social encounters. In October, she sent Julian to Leysin in Switzerland for a 'sun cure' recommended by Dr Combe, and made arrangements to visit her there in November and to join her there for Christmas. In between, she and Philip would take a holiday in Italy. On 21 November, she left for Rome. Her itinerary was crowded and complicated: after a few days in Rome, she would go first to Leysin to see Julian, then to Lausanne to consult Drs Combe and Vittoz, and finally on a tour of Lombardy, before returning to Rome on 14 December, where after a day or two she would be joined by Russell for a few days before she returned to Leysin for Christmas. For a long time now, she and Russell had got on better when they were apart, and her departure was greeted by both of them almost with relief. 'I feel very happy, and confident in our future,' Russell wrote the day before she left. 'We shall both get *fear* out of our instincts in time, if all goes well, and then things will be quite different.'

Part of the reason that Russell was feeling increasingly independent of Ottoline was that he was, throughout the autumn, making plans to spend more time with Liese von Hattingberg. In what, in retrospect, looks like a piece of spectacularly bad judgment, these plans, too, involved meeting in Rome in December, where, it transpired, she had decided to spend Christmas with her two sons. She was due to arrive in Rome on 21 December, the very day that Ottoline and Philip were to leave for Leysin. Ottoline had no reason to feel threatened by this arrangement, Russell argued, since, with regard to Liese von Hattingberg: 'I find I have lost all interest in her . . . I might see her at Xmas, I suppose, but I have no wish to.' A few days after Ottoline's departure for Rome, however, he sounded a more ominous note, telling her that there were times – such as the previous June – when her aloofness 'chilled' him, and at those times 'I am liable to seek affection elsewhere.' As he found it 'disagreeable' to speak to her about such things, he would now, unless he found himself in a serious relationship with somebody, maintain a policy of silence about his minor *affaires*. To do otherwise would be 'humiliating & cause quite useless pain & strain'.

On 10 December, immediately after term finished and a few days before he left for Rome, Russell paid Joseph Conrad another visit. This is the occasion on which they exchanged books. Two days later, Conrad wrote to say that he had read the first chapter of *The Problems of Philosophy*, but had put it aside to finish a short story (presumably 'The Planter of Malata', which, elsewhere, Conrad records as having been finished on 14 December). 'It was a great pleasure to have a talk with you,' Conrad wrote. 'Under its tonic influence I did quite a lot of work (more or less mercenary) – (but still) after you left us.' He promised again to repay the visit: 'Oh no! You'll not escape my visitation.'

The few days Russell and Ottoline spent together in Rome were, perhaps predictably, spoiled by the tense atmosphere caused by the strange circumstances in which they met. He arrived on 16 December, just five days before Ottoline's departure for Leysin and Liese von Hattingberg's arrival, in a situation calculated to arouse insecurity and jealousy on both sides. To both of them, it felt that, whenever they met, they did so on borrowed time, with Ottoline having to make excuses to Philip for being out for a few hours or even, on one occasion, for the whole day, in order to be with Russell. And, of course, after each snatched moment together – as Russell could not help dwelling on obsessively – Ottoline would return to spend the night with her husband.

Eventually the inevitable happened and Russell's insecurity got the better of him, causing him to make exactly the kind of angry and jealous scene that he spent months trying to avoid. Having arranged to meet Ottoline at the Sistine Chapel, he arrived to find Philip standing next to her. The mere sight of him was enough to strip away the veneer of 'tameness' that he had carefully preserved since the summer, and that evening, after Russell returned to his hotel, he sank – so he told Ottoline in a later letter – into a 'mad' state: 'all alone brooding, with no occupations . . . I lost my balance'. Things were made worse by his nervous anticipation of the imminent arrival of Liese von Hattingberg, an event about which Ottoline, too, was increasingly anxious. 'I hope you won't find her *too* nice,' she wrote on the day she and Philip left Rome. Fearful that this time she might lose Russell for good, she pleaded with him: 'don't be too impatient or too much in a hurry to plunge into things', and tried to reassure him of her devotion:

> My darling darling love – I wish I could satisfy you more. It makes me so unhappy that I don't. I *long* to – and with all my soul . . . My darling darling, I *do* love you.

One senses that, in his jealous anger, Russell would have liked to have responded to this by saying that it was too late, that he had now transferred his affections to Liese von Hattingberg.[1] In the event, he confined himself to pointing out that 'Your letters express so much more of your love than you show when we are together', reassuring Ottoline that she 'need not be afraid of my plunging into things with my German lady. She does not excite me or make me lose my head.'

Nevertheless, one of the first things Russell did after Liese von Hattingberg arrived was to find out the story of her marriage and to establish as precisely as he could the degree to which she was attached to her husband, in both law and in feeling:

> This spring her husband fell in love with another lady, to whom he is now married. My lady loves him still and suffers a good deal, tho' without bitterness, as she says he gets more from his present wife than he ever got from her . . . obviously her husband still holds her heart.

'I like her very much,' he added, 'as much as I did at S. Vigilio. She has a sense of humour, wh. is rare in Germans; and she has a great deal of cheerful courage, and very complete truthfulness.'

On their first day together, he and Frau von Hattingberg (as he almost invariably called her in his letters to Ottoline – it was never 'Liese') walked the hills surrounding Rome, lunched at Nemi, strolled round the lake and exchanged life histories. The next day, they walked round the Borghese gardens and then returned to her lodgings, where they shared what Russell described as a 'very scratch and uncomfortable' lunch, and where he was clearly surprised to discover that 'she has no servant, only a nurse'. In his account of the day to Ottoline there is little indication that he was falling in

---

[1] He got his chance in the 'Personal Memoir' about his love affairs and marriages that he dictated in the 1950s. 'Soon after I had ceased to have relations with her,' he writes about Ottoline, 'she found that her lady's maid and Philip's secretary were both simultaneously pregnant by him. This disillusioned her about Philip and she told me that she felt her life had been a mistake. But so far as I was concerned it was too late.' In this shockingly callous remark, one feels, is the distilled anger of several years of feeling hurt, rejected and frustrated by Ottoline's preference for Philip over him.

love with Liese von Hattingberg, but his letter ends on what was clearly intended to be an ominous note:

> I wish I could be more content with what you give me. But the situation is against nature, and instinct revenges itself in all sorts of ways when one tries to ignore it . . . it grows more and more difficult to me to forget enough to be really happy when I am with you. And thwarted instinct makes me so self-centred and inclined to recklessness. I am sorry it is so – it would not be so in a more generous nature, but I think it would in any one capable of passionate love.

And yet, for the next few days, rather than continuing his pursuit of Liese von Hattingberg, Russell spent his time alone on long walks in the hills. On Christmas Day, he went by himself to Tivoli, where, in the pouring rain, he admired the Villa d'Este and the Temple of Veste. The next day, he walked twenty miles to Hadrian's Villa. 'I don't know whether or when I shall see Frau von Hattingberg again,' he wrote that night. Perhaps his 'German lady' had made it clear that she wanted to spend Christmas alone with her children. Or perhaps Russell had decided that, after all, she could be no replacement for Ottoline, from whom he was now receiving some of the most affectionate letters she had ever written.

In any case, his thoughts now became filled with anticipation of the meeting he had arranged with Ottoline in the New Year in the small Swiss town of Aigle, close – but not too close – to where she and her family were staying. 'I would rather see you at Aigle than at Leysin,' Russell wrote, 'it is very undesirable that I should see P., and even feeling him at hand would worry me.' He felt, he told her, sacrificed to Philip. He was also feeling extremely lonely. There is nothing like spending Christmas on one's own to make one feel utterly bereft of human contact, and, while Liese von Hattingberg celebrated the day with her two sons and Ottoline with her own family, the vision Russell had mentioned of 'a peaceful family life with a home and children' must have tormented him more than ever. Two days after Christmas, at lunch in his hotel, he happened to meet one of his old students, H. T. J. Norton, 'and nearly embraced him, I was so delighted to have some one to talk to'.

By now, he was, it seems, beginning to regret having invested any hopes in an *affaire* with Liese von Hattingberg. On 29 December, his last day in Rome, he had lunch with her, and, while her children took their afternoon nap, she read him poems by Edward Mörike, a poet whom Wittgenstein had long been trying to get Russell to read. Russell enjoyed the occasion, but that afternoon, before meeting her again to take her out to dinner, he found time to write to Ottoline to say that he was emphatically not in love with his German lady '& shall never be, nor she with me . . . she does not touch my imagination . . . I am sorry to have given you so much needless pain – I ought to have waited till all was cleared up. I have a very strong affection for her, & shall try not *to lose sight of her; but things will never go further*.' That night, after he had dined with her, he wrote again to Ottoline to say that he and Liese von Hattingberg had had 'a sort of *éclaircissement*':

I told her that I should certainly never again care for any one as I do for you, and she told me she would certainly *never* give more than friendship in return for anything I had to offer. So that cleared the air, and we had a very happy time, talking of a hundred things.

In other words, perhaps, it had not gone the way Russell had expected and hoped.

A few days later, he arrived in Aigle in what he afterwards described as a 'numb' state. He and Ottoline soon began to argue, and he marshalled all the considerable powers of invective at his disposal to say as many cruel, wounding things as he could think of. He later claimed to Ottoline to have 'felt all your pain and all your love' during their argument and to know 'you were suffering much more than I was'. But, he said, 'it seems as if it were people in a play . . . it seems impersonal and quite outside me'. To Ottoline, it had been all too real, and she decided she could take no more. This time they *had* to part. 'I cannot well put into words all I feel,' she wrote that night, 'all the utter pain of separation to me.' In his 'numb' state, Russell claimed to be able to feel nothing, though he, too, agreed that they should part and the next day he returned home, feeling more utterly alone than ever.

Back in London, he found waiting for him a letter from Conrad, written on 22 December, which was to remain one of his proudest possessions for the rest of his life, and which seemed to acquire an even richer significance due to the circumstances in which he received it. In his *Autobiography*, as well as reproducing the whole letter, Russell quotes the sentences from it that gave him the greatest pleasure. 'I should feel', Russell writes, 'that modesty forbids the quotation except for the fact that it expresses so exactly what I felt about him':

What he expressed and I equally felt was, in his words, 'A deep admiring affection, which, if you were never to see me again and forgot my existence tomorrow, would be unalterably yours *usque ad finem*'.

In their original context, these words were used specifically to express Conrad's appreciation of Russell's *Philosophical Essays*, particularly 'The Free Man's Worship'. In reading *The Problems of Philosophy*, Conrad wrote, he had felt as if he were 'moving step by step, with delight, on the firmest ground' – perhaps an excessively polite way of saying that he found the book rather heavy and laboured – but the *Essays* had given him by contrast 'the sense of an enlarged vision in the clearest, the purest atmosphere':

Your significant words so significantly assembled, seemed to wake a new faculty within me. A wonderful experience for which one cannot express one's thanks – one can only accept it silently like a gift from the Gods. You have reduced to order the inchoate thoughts of a life-time and given a direction to those obscure *mouvements d'ame* which, unguided, bring only trouble to one's weary days on this earth. For the marvellous pages on the Worship of a free man the only return one can make is that of a deep admiring affection, which, if you were never to see me again and forgot my existence tomorrow, will be unalterably yours *usque ad finem*.

As Russell no doubt realised, the phrase *usque ad finem* ('to the very end') was, for Conrad, charged with significance. It was used by him in his novel *Lord Jim* in a scene in which Stein – who in the context represents the scientific point of view – is discussing Jim's romantic inclinations with the more stolid Marlow. Men, says Stein, fall, the moment they are born, into a dream, and, just as when you fall into the sea the best policy is not to fight for air but to submit yourself to the water and let the sea keep you up, so the best policy in life is to 'follow the dream ... *usque ad finem*'. The echo was well chosen: in 'The Free Man's Worship', Russell had argued that the truth about life and about ourselves is almost too horrible to bear and that the wisest course is to pursue our visions, our dreams, 'to the very end', even while recognising them as fictions. Another relevant echo – of which Conrad was certainly, and Russell possibly, aware – is from the Vulgate, the Latin Bible, where, in the Book of Job, God utters the terrible words: *probetur Iob usque ad finem* ('My desire is that Job may be tried unto the end').

Common to all these echoes is the theme of remaining true to one's vision and having the courage to face whatever life throws one's way, a theme which, under the circumstances, Russell felt as a stern and justified rebuke. 'I know I have failed in courage,' he wrote after receiving Conrad's letter. He felt unworthy of Conrad's praise. As he read the letter, he told Ottoline, 'a sense of shame came to me. I felt No, the man who wrote that ['The Free Man's Worship'] is not the man Conrad sees now – the affection he gives is not now deserved – the man who faces a hostile universe rather than lose his vision has become a man who will creep into the first hovel to escape the terror & splendour of the night. The feeling was so strong and swift that I felt for a moment as if I must never see him again.' Having, in parting from Ottoline, turned his back on the most powerful vision he had ever had, how could he face Conrad again?

On the day he received it, Russell sent Conrad's letter on to Ottoline in Switzerland. 'Please read enclosed from Conrad before you read this,' he told her, 'as you won't understand this otherwise. I wish I had got this letter before yesterday [the day he and Ottoline had quarrelled in Aigle]':

His letter has somehow brought me a flash of insight – the insight I have not had all these days. I have had the same insight before, but have lost it. Dearest, we must not break with each other ... It would be spiritual suicide to give you up for the sake of peace. It would not matter to give up physical things, & it would not matter to have other relations if they were compatible with our spiritual union – but that must not be broken. Whatever the pain, love is a sacred thing. And anything else ought to be as serious & deep. I did think this before – I meant to say it yesterday – but I was only half alive – spiritually I was dead ... It is hard for you to bear my pain & not to urge me to seek relief. But the pain is not all you –

it is partly in the essence of living seriously . . . You will think this letter is written in a passing mood. Of course the opposite mood will come back, but this is based on insight. All this time I have been in perplexity, not knowing the right. Now I know it. But if you, for your sake, decide to break, I cannot wonder.

This letter is the utter truth.

The following day, after returning to Cambridge, he wrote that 'The effect of Conrad's letter has lasted.' He was once more spiritually alive, and 'When I am really alive spiritually, I do not feel lonely, but I feel you with me, and the sense of distance diminishes – it is only in fatigue and discouragement and cynicism that I feel remote from you.' Fortified by Conrad's praise, he had returned to the stoicism of the free man's worship, accepting the futility of the search for happiness. Ottoline, he had to accept, could not give him 'ordinary daily happiness', and 'I cannot find it elsewhere without spiritual suicide', therefore he should cease wanting happiness, and Conrad's letter gave him the courage to attempt this.

Linked – in Russell's mind, at any rate – to this moral regeneration was a sudden and astonishing burst of intellectual energy. Within the first few days of returning to Cambridge, in January 1914, he wrote from scratch a long (12,000-word), complicated paper called 'The Relation of Sense-Data to Physics', which, building on the work he had already written about the construction of matter, presented many new and original ideas about the fundamental nature of the physical world and our knowledge of it. The most radical of these new ideas – and the one which, when he looked back on his work as an old man in *My Philosophical Development* (1959), he regarded as the most important – was the thought that space has not three dimensions, but six. Each point in ordinary three-dimensional space he now regarded as a possible 'perspective' on the external world (even when, as in most cases, there is no mind – or mirror, or camera, or whatever – actually looking at the world from that perspective). This 'possible perspective' will itself be a space, a 'private space', having three dimensions. Thus, to properly locate the sense-data (or, more accurately, the 'sensibilia', the possible sense-data) from which the matter in the world is constructed, one would have to give *six* co-ordinates.

Multi-dimensional spaces are now a commonplace in the rarefied world of theoretical physics, but Russell's particular variety – a six-dimensional space made up of three 'private' and three 'public' dimensions – has had very little influence, either in philosophy or physics. Russell himself, however, was in no doubt as to its importance, and continued for the rest of his life to regard his 'discovery' (as he described it to Ottoline) of the six-dimensional nature of space as a major breakthrough. 'The Relation of Sense-Data to Physics' was, he declared soon after he wrote it, 'very good! I don't believe I have ever done anything better.'

In later life, this sense of having made a breakthrough in the first few days of the New Year became the basis for an outrageous piece of mythologised autobiography that Russell first included in a BBC radio talk in 1951 and then repeated in his *Autobiography*. In this account, the three days he spent writing the paper 'The Relation of Sense-Data to Physics' are first of all confused with the three months he spent working on *Our Knowledge of the External World* and then compressed into a single day, producing an utterly fantastic version of events. Having agreed to give the Lowell lectures in Harvard, Russell claimed, he chose as his theme 'Our Knowledge of the External World' and then – try as he might – could not think of what to say on the subject:

> At last, in despair, I went off to Rome for Christmas, hoping that a holiday would revive my flagging energy. I got back to Cambridge on the last day of 1913, and although my difficulties were still completely unresolved I arranged, because the remaining time was short, to dictate as best I could to a stenographer. Next morning, as she came in at the door, I suddenly saw exactly what I had to say, and proceeded to dictate the whole book without a moment's hesitation.

'I do not want to convey an exaggerated impression,' he goes on (presumably without deliberate irony). 'The book is very imperfect . . . But it was the best that I could have done at that time, and a more leisurely method . . . would almost certainly have produced something worse.' In the version published in his *Autobiography*, the story is more or less the same, except that he now sets it on New Year's Day 1914 and is more specific that 'What I dictated to her was subsequently published as a book under the title *Our Knowledge of the External World as a Field for Scientific Method in Philosophy*.'[2]

Assuming that this is really how Russell remembered it, and that he was not consciously deceiving his listeners and readers, his mythologised account offers, perhaps, some revealing indications of what he wished had been the case: first, that *Our Knowledge of the External World*, instead of being for the most part 'dull stuff', a re-working of old ideas that he spent three months working on (one month for the first draft and two months for the revisions) and which bored him even as he was writing it, was actually the product of one extraordinarily prolific day and the outcome of a sudden and fortuitous burst of inspiration, a momentary flash of insight; second, that, after spending Christmas in Rome, he returned straight to Cambridge, and, therefore, the argument he had with Ottoline in Aigle on 2 January never happened.

---

[2] What truth there is in this myth has been extracted by Kenneth Blackwell in his article 'Our Knowledge of "Our Knowledge"' (*Russell*, 12, 1973–4, pp. 11–13), in which he argues that Chapter 3 of *Our Knowledge of the External World* was revised in the light of the ideas Russell had put forward in 'The Relation of Sense-Data to Physics'. Russell's correspondence suggests that this revision – which amounts to the insertion of about five pages into the original – was made on 27 January 1914. Blackwell seems to think that this overlap of material makes it somehow understandable that Russell should have got confused between the paper he wrote in the New Year of 1914 and the series of eight lectures he wrote in the autumn of 1913, and that he should have imagined dictating the whole of *Our Knowledge of the External World* (which runs to 242 pages) in one sitting off the top of his head. I still find it odd that the confusion could have arisen at all, and still odder that it should have persisted, when, one would have thought, the merest glance at the book might have told Russell that his story of its composition was, to say the very least, implausible.

In fact, during the very time that he was writing 'The Relation of Sense-Data to Physics', Russell was writing to Ottoline every day apologising for his behaviour in Aigle and pleading with her not to uphold her resolve to break with him. 'I feel such shame when I think how selfish and wretched I have been,' he wrote on 5 January. 'If your decision is irrevocable, and if you would feel it a needless pain to see me again, don't feel bound to see me. But I should have said we ought at least to try again until I go to America.' The next day: 'I hate the suffering I have caused you. Dearest I love you, and life without you wd. be a blank – I love you Darling, I love you. O forgive me Dearest if you can, and take me back. My whole being yearns for you.'

In the face of such pressure Ottoline relented, first to the extent of saying that her mind was not quite decided, and then, after yet more pleading from Russell ('I cannot bear not to see you again and try to undo some of the dreadful things I said . . . Please let us have a free day together as soon after you come home as possible. I will make you feel you can still give me what is divine'), agreeing not to separate until Russell left for America. Russell even began to feel that Ottoline had adopted a sympathetic understanding of his 'difficulties': 'I used to feel you thought I could overcome them, but they are too deep in my nature and too much bound up with other things – I hate the pain they cause, but they seem ineradicable.'

He now began work on another paper to deliver in America, this time to be read to a more general audience. Entitled 'Mysticism and Logic', it has since become one of Russell's best-known papers, though his own verdict at the time of writing was that 'It is not very good – it is mostly made up of scraps from the other lectures – but it will have to do.' True, large parts of the first two lectures of *Our Knowledge of the External World* are repeated verbatim in the new paper, but, in their new surroundings, they take on a rather different meaning, for the general tone of the paper is less disillusioned and less debunking than that of the earlier lectures. 'The greatest men who have been philosophers', Russell declares at the beginning, 'have felt the need both of science and of mysticism: the attempt to harmonise the two was what made their life.' In the figure of Heraclitus, for example, 'we see the true union of the mystic and the man of science – the highest eminence, as I think, that it is possible to achieve in the world of thought.'

To some extent, then, the paper represents a return to the ideal of 1912 of forging a 'fused whole' of science and mysticism, though the emphasis on the superiority of intellect over intuition remains and the paper ends with the familiar call for a 'truly scientific philosophy', which, 'offering less glitter of outward mirage to flatter fallacious hopes', aims to see the world as much as possible 'without the tyrannous imposition of our human and temporary demands'.

As soon as he finished 'Mysticism and Logic', Russell set to work on a preface that he had been asked to write for the English edition of Henri Poincaré's posthumously published collection of essays, *Science and Method*. It was, he told Ottoline, 'a delicate matter, as the book contains a fierce attack on me, which I thought ignorant and unfair, but which nearly destroyed my reputation in France'. He was, nevertheless, determined to be dignified and complimentary towards Poincaré, who was, after all, 'a wonderful man' and enormously eminent: 'There is no one in science now who is quite as eminent as he was.' It was a difficult piece to write and, though very short, took far longer than 'The Relation of Sense-Data to Physics'. Russell eventually finished it on 19 January, the first Tuesday of term, and 'the *very* last moment before the rush'. The result is a miniature masterpiece of tact and subtlety, paying tribute to Poincaré's achievements and drawing attention to the wit and vividness of his writing, but demurring at his rejection of mathematical logic, and, finally, using the occasion discreetly and unobtrusively as an opportunity for spreading the Russellian gospel. Poincaré's work supplies, Russell concludes his preface by saying, 'the growing need for a generally intelligible account of the philosophic outcome of modern science'.

In everything Russell wrote at this time there is an almost evangelical fervour in his advocation of 'scientific method in philosophy'. For him, it was not just a belief as to the best way to pursue philosophical investigations, it was a cause, a fight to the finish against various forms of philosophical wrong-headedness (of which the three most prevalent and pernicious were F. H. Bradley's idealism, William James's pragmatism and Henri Bergson's evolutionism), a fight in which the forces under Russell's own command were small in number but highly trained and well-armed with mathematical logic. And in Wittgenstein (so he thought) he had a charismatic and able second-in-command, as deeply committed to the cause as he was himself. He was therefore confident of victory and carried the fight to the enemy whenever he could.

This combative spirit is especially evident in the review he wrote in February of A. J. Balfour's Gifford lectures, *Theism and Humanism*, which, as the lectures were not actually published until the following year and Russell was dependent on newspaper reports of them, was something in the nature of a pre-emptive strike. In all sorts of ways, Balfour was the very personification of the views that Russell was at war with. First of all, he spent most of his life as a prominent Conservative politician, rising to become Prime Minister in the despised Tory administration of 1902–5. Second, as the author of 'Creative Evolution and Philosophic Doubt', an article published in *The Hibbert Journal* in 1911, he did much to foster and encourage the enthusiasm for Bergson among British intellectuals. Finally, the tenor of his philosophical thinking, and of these Gifford lectures in particular, was anti-scientific and pro-religion. The point of the lectures was to argue for the existence of God on the basis of the accepted fact of aesthetic and ethical value, which, Balfour argues, would be unintelligible if God did not exist. Along the way, he cast doubt on the certainty of the fundamental beliefs which underlie physical science. It was, Russell wrote to Ottoline, 'rhetorical dishonest sentimental twaddle. The quality of his mind is more disgusting to me than anybody else's in the world.' A few days later: 'It is incredible balderdash. There is something about every word of his writing that fills me with loathing.'

In print (the review was published in *The Cambridge Review* on 4 March), Russell was slightly less scathing, but something of his attitude emerges in his allegation that Balfour 'never aims at promoting thought: he aims rather at showing that it is so painful and laborious as to be better evaded by means of theatrical heroic solutions.' Running throughout the review is the opposition between Balfour's arguments and proper scientific procedure, and it concludes: 'The fundamental defect of Mr Balfour's lectures, it seems to me, is that, in spite of their allusions to science, they are designed to discourage the scientific habit in philosophy.'

In his second set of Gifford lectures, which, because of the First World War, were not given until 1922–3, Balfour returned to the fray and devoted an entire lecture to a criticism of Russell's views. F. H. Bradley, another of Russell's philosophical arch-foes (though one for whom he personally had a great deal of respect) was rather quicker in returning fire. In the New Year of 1914, Bradley published his *Essays on Truth and Reality*, a collection of the papers he had published (mostly in *Mind*) over the previous five years, together with some additional new material, among which was a chapter taking up the argument he had had with Russell in print and responding to the work that Russell had published in the meantime, particularly the 'multiple-relation' theory of judgment that Russell had expounded in his essay 'On the Nature of Truth and Falsehood' in 1910 and again in *The Problems of Philosophy* in 1912.

What is striking about Bradley's criticisms is their similarity to the ones Wittgenstein had put forward so devastatingly in the summer of 1913. Essentially, Bradley's point is that the multiple relations into which Russell analyses a judgment – even if they existed (and Bradley is rather doubtful that they do) – cannot make up a judgment, for a judgment has a unity which is lacking in the series of relations that Russell posits.

Perhaps recognising the affinity between Bradley's point and Wittgenstein's, Russell treated it with great caution and respect. In a letter of 30 January thanking Bradley for a copy of the book, he wrote: 'I fully recognise the vital importance of the questions you raise, particularly as regards "unities"; I recognise that it is my duty to answer if I can, and, if I cannot, to look for an answer as long as I live.' Ironically, however, he went on to suggest that Wittgenstein's work would come to his rescue in this respect. 'Chiefly through the work of an Austrian pupil of mine', he told Bradley, 'I seem now to see answers about unities; but the subject is so difficult and fundamental that I still hesitate.'

It is doubtful whether, at this stage, Wittgenstein still saw himself as a 'pupil' of Russell's. If there was between them the relation of master and pupil, then Russell was by now the pupil, fearful of his master's criticism and almost pathetically eager for Wittgenstein's approval. 'Last June,' he wrote to Ottoline on 18 January, 'I was doing well, and then Wittgenstein reduced me to despair again. But this time I am *sure* I have done well . . . I know Wittgenstein will like the work I have done lately.' Nor, as Russell was about to discover, was Wittgenstein willing to be cast in the role of Russell's lieutenant in the battle for the establishment of a 'scientific method in philosophy'. Indeed, in many ways, Wittgenstein was scarcely on Russell's side at all.

In Vienna over the Christmas period, Wittgenstein had found it impossible to continue his work on logic, and was occupied instead with thoughts about himself. 'Sometimes', he told Russell, 'things inside me are in such a ferment that I think I'm going mad; then the next day I am totally apathetic again':

> But deep inside me there's a perpetual seething, like the bottom of a geyser, and I keep on hoping that things will come to an eruption once and for all, so that I can turn into a different person.

'Perhaps you regard this thinking about myself as a waste of time,' he added, 'but how can I be a logician before I'm a human being! *Far* the most important thing is to settle accounts with myself!'

When Wittgenstein returned to Norway in the middle of January, it was some time before he was able to resume work, and his description of his state of mind could only have confirmed the fears Russell had expressed about him back in October:

> It's VERY sad but I've once again got no logical news for you. The reason is that things have gone terribly badly for me in the last weeks. (A result of my 'holidays' in Vienna.) Every day I was tormented by a frightful *Angst* and by depression in turns and even in the intervals I was so exhausted that I wasn't able to think of doing a bit of work. It's terrifying beyond all description the kinds of mental torment that there can be! It wasn't until two days ago that I could hear the voice of reason over the howls of the damned and I began to work again. And *perhaps* I'll get better now and be able to produce something decent. But I *never* knew what it meant to feel only *one* step away from madness – Let's hope for the best!

In his letter to Wittgenstein (which, like all Russell's letters to Wittgenstein of this period, has not survived), Russell must have said something about his time in Rome with Liese von Hattingberg, at least to the extent of telling Wittgenstein that he had at last read Mörike's work and had enjoyed it. With regard to the latter, Wittgenstein was slightly sceptical; after all, Russell did not enjoy Goethe's work, 'and the beauty of Mörike's work is very closely related to that of Goethe's'. But, he suggested, '*if* you have *really* enjoyed Mörike, then just try Goethe's *Iphigenie*. Then perhaps you'll see the light.'

Wittgenstein's letter ends with some remarks about Russell's forthcoming visit to America, which show, perhaps, how far he was from endorsing Russell's campaign for a scientific philosophy:

> All best wishes for your lecture-course in America! Perhaps it will give you at any rate a more favourable opportunity than usual to tell them your *thoughts* and not *just* cut and dried results. THAT is what would be of the greatest imaginable value for your audience – to get to know the value of *thought* and not that of a cut and dried result. Write to me soon and think of me when you read Mörike.
>
> Yours ever
>
> L. W.

This was the beginning of a quarrel between the two that very nearly resulted in Wittgenstein breaking off all contact with Russell. What, exactly, the quarrel was about is lost to history, since, though Russell seems to have kept all his other letters from Wittgenstein, the one that would shed light on the nature of their disagreement is missing. The next letter in the series from Wittgenstein to Russell that has survived refers to the quarrel in the past tense and gives only vague clues as to its cause. Whatever it was, it was enough to persuade Wittgenstein that 'we really don't suit one another', a thought he had evidently harboured for some time:

> We've often had uncomfortable conversations with one another when certain subjects came up. And the uncomfortableness was not a consequence of ill humour on one side or the other but of enormous differences in our natures . . . Our latest quarrel, too, was certainly not simply a result of your sensitiveness or my inconsiderateness. It came from deeper – from the fact that my letter must have shown you how totally different our ideas are, E.G., of the value of a scientific work. It was, of course, stupid of me to have written to you at length about this matter: I ought to have told myself that such fundamental differences cannot be resolved by a letter. And this is just one instance out of *many*.

Wittgenstein was convinced – and this latest quarrel served simply to confirm him in this – that 'there cannot be any real relation of friendship between us.' He would be grateful to Russell for the rest of his life, he said, but he would not write to him again and did not want Russell to write to him either: 'I want to part from you *in peace* so that we shan't sometime get annoyed with one another again and then perhaps part as enemies . . . Goodbye!'

'It is my fault,' Russell told Ottoline after he had received Wittgenstein's letter. 'I have been too sharp with him.'

From these hints, it is possible to venture a guess as to what had occurred between them: in response to Wittgenstein's remarks about his American lectures, about the value of thought over cut and dried results, Russell – imagining perhaps that he was in agreement with Wittgenstein – replied that, as far as he was concerned, the value of his lectures was primarily that of illustrating the scientific method in philosophy, and that he was not even attempting to offer 'cut and dried results'. He was then (I am speculating) shocked to discover in the letter that has not survived – the one referred to by Wittgenstein in which he wrote 'at length' about how 'totally different our ideas are, E.G., of the value of a scientific work' – that, far from being his closest and most powerful ally in the struggle to establish a scientific philosophy, Wittgenstein did not even believe in such a thing![3] (The

---

[3] Wittgenstein was to be explicit about this later on, but his rejection of the idea of scientific philosophy might be said to be implied in his remark in 'Notes on Logic' that 'The word "philosophy" ought always to designate something over or under, but not beside, the natural sciences.'

disappointment of this, I believe, would alone have been reason enough for Russell to destroy the letter.) Wittgenstein might also in this missing letter have gone on to more personal subjects and tried to explain to Russell the fundamental differences in their outlooks on life, and perhaps even have ventured the kind of brutally frank and devastatingly critical character analysis for which he was later to be feared. In any case (to continue my speculative guess), Russell was appalled by the letter, destroyed it and replied to it in 'too sharp' a manner, perhaps adopting the kind of cold, censorious and bitterly sarcastic tone that he often used in argument with Ottoline. Then, shortly afterwards, regretting his 'sharpness', Russell wrote another, more conciliatory letter (Wittgenstein begins the letter quoted above: 'Thank you for your friendly letter'), hoping to make amends.

If all this is correct – and the evidence surely points to something along those lines, even if the details are wrong – then the attempt at conciliation came too late: Wittgenstein had already made up his mind to end their friendship. Even at this stage, Russell under-estimated the strength of Wittgenstein's feeling. 'I dare say his mood will change after a while,' he told Ottoline, and then, with unconvincing equanimity: 'I find I don't care on his account, but only for the sake of logic.' 'And yet,' he added, finally coming clean, 'I believe I do really care too much to look at it.' He managed to write to Wittgenstein in a way that at least melted his resolve never to write again. 'Your letter was *so* full of kindness and friendship that I don't have the *right* to leave it unanswered,' Wittgenstein replied. But, on the main point, he was resolute: there could be no real friendship between the two. Their differences were, he wrote, 'very deep-rooted':

> You may be right in saying that *we ourselves* are not *so very* different, but *our ideals* could not be more so. And that's why we haven't been able and we shan't *ever* be able to talk about anything involving our value-judgments without either becoming hypocritical or falling out. *I think this is incontestable*; I had noticed it a long time ago; and it was frightful for me, because it tainted our relations with one another.

A relationship, Wittgenstein argued, 'should be confined to areas where both people involved have clean hands, i.e., where each can be completely frank without hurting the other. And that's something *we* can do ONLY by restricting our relationship to the communication of facts capable of being established objectively, with perhaps also some mention of our friendly feelings for one another.' He therefore had a proposal:

> Let's write to each other about our work, our health, and the like, but let's avoid in our communication any kind of value-judgment, on any subject whatsoever, and let's recognise clearly that in such judgments neither of us could be *completely* honest without hurting the other (this is certainly true in *my* case, at any rate).

Russell could write about the technical, the 'objective' aspects of his work, but he was not to talk about the value of it (or of anything else), because, if he did, Wittgenstein would feel he could not be honest without being hurtful. For his part, though he continued to keep Russell informed to some extent about his work, Wittgenstein never again tried to talk to Russell about music, literature and ethics and never again tried to describe or explain his deepest, most intimate attitudes, feelings and states of mind. In the ways that mattered they were not, after all, fighting on the same side.

While Wittgenstein was keeping Russell at a distance, he was courting Moore with ever-increasing insistence. At the end of January 1914, he wrote to Moore asking him when the Easter vacation would begin, and then, on 18 February, wrote again, saying: '*You must come as soon as Term ends.*' Just as, the previous October, he had wanted to explain and dictate his work to Russell, now – having made, at last, some more progress – he wanted to explain and dictate it to Moore. After some understandable hesitation, Moore agreed to the plan, and, after meeting Russell to go through Wittgenstein's 'Notes on Logic', set off to Norway to take down Wittgenstein's latest thoughts. The result was 'Notes Dictated to G. E. Moore', the second piece of Wittgenstein's work to have survived in written form. Wittgenstein regarded it as a substantial advance on his earlier work and wrote to Russell urging him to study it, but, for one reason or another – Moore's reluctance to explain, Russell's reluctance to listen, their mutual reluctance to spend any time with each other – it was not until April 1915 that Russell saw the notes, by which time his mind was almost fully occupied with the war and he was in no state to absorb Wittgenstein's increasingly alien approach to the understanding of logic, language and philosophy.

As Russell was slow to realise (perhaps he never realised it), his relationship with Wittgenstein suffered from the very beginning from his insistence on casting Wittgenstein in a role for which he was unsuited. This, in turn, arose from Russell's determination to see in Wittgenstein and Ottoline symbolic representations of the polarities in his own nature, with Wittgenstein representing the logician, the scientist, and Ottoline the mystic. From this standpoint, Wittgenstein would always remain unintelligible, and it is scarcely any wonder that he felt misunderstood by Russell.

Something similar was at work also in Russell's relationship with Ottoline, and, as it lurched from one crisis to the next, Ottoline, too, felt misunderstood. Unlike Wittgenstein, though, her natural inclination was to cling on to relationships for as long as she could, hoping that they would improve. As illustrated time and again in her life (in, for example, her relationships with Roger Fry, Henry Lamb and Lytton Strachey), she had a quite extraordinarily deep-seated reluctance to part with any of her friends and lovers. Several times she broke with Russell, only to relent, and several times, when Russell looked like breaking with her, she successfully won him back.

Her resolve to break with him after his behaviour at Aigle had already melted by the time she returned to London at the end of January, but within a few weeks they were in the midst of another serious crisis, with both of them talking once more of parting for ever. About a week after she returned, Ottoline – at Russell's insistence – consulted a gynaecologist to determine whether there was any chance at all of her having another baby. While she was waiting to hear the doctor's verdict, Russell wrote to her in what seems a quite shockingly selfish and insensitive manner. 'I have not felt impatient of the Doctor's answer,' Russell told her, 'as I have had difficult work getting my own thoughts and feelings clear':

> I believe and hope that, if the Doctor decides against you, I can still give affection and (I hope) more kindness than hitherto – but it seems as if I could not again give passion. This is not a matter in the control of my will – if it were, I would control it . . . I feel rather weary, and anxious for the future to escape from all deep feeling as much as possible. I am very very sorry, but I really can't help it . . . I *long* to save you pain, but I cannot.

When, a week later, Ottoline received the gynaecologist's opinion that there was no chance of her having a child, Russell wrote to end their relationship with a letter written in that chilling, formal tone that is by now familiar as a sign that he was fighting to prevent being completely overcome by emotion:

> I had thought we should meet again, but from your letter it seems as if it would be useless pain on both sides. I am very sorry indeed that the Doctor's decision is what it is – it makes everything so useless. I should like to hope that after some time has passed we might meet again as friends, and try at least to save something. Would you mind letting me know if you would mind that, or if you would rather not. I should *like* to see you now – my whole impulse is to throw myself at your feet and implore pardon. But I feel we cannot really inwardly pardon each other, in instinct as well as reason – at least not yet. All life looks utterly blank to me.

Ottoline, he seemed to be saying, was not only infertile, but unpardonably so. Later in the same day he wrote a somewhat longer letter, trying to explain his state of mind and why he felt he had to part with Ottoline. 'The longing for children', he told her, 'has grown and grown in me, and the pain of not having a child by you has been terrible. And from the very beginning I have felt pain because you didn't understand the things of instinct . . . You have heart, but not understanding, and so over and over again without meaning it you hurt me':

> I must break with you, or I shall be broken – and I must not be broken yet. Until now I had hoped you would come to understand and not hurt any more, but now I lost that hope . . . I break to save the spring of life and energy that I need.

'You don't know how I have been fighting to keep Hell under,' he wrote, 'it makes me precise and formal and cold but only because Hell is boiling and ready to burst out . . . Goodbye, goodbye.'

In her journal around this time, Ottoline writes of her disappointment with those she has loved – Fry, Lamb, Strachey, as well as Russell – and of feeling 'a dire loneliness that nothing will ever relieve':

I seem to have tried everyone and found them all wanting, and yet I know the fault is my own. It is as if I were condemned to walk through life quite detached; quite apart from others, and not to enter into their lives, never to arouse in others feelings of sympathy or affection, or a desire to give to me . . . So for ever and for ever must I float on with a passionate sense of the tragedy of life inside me. But so it must be.

Did she really think that the selfishness of these people, their seeming inability to give her sympathy and affection, was *her* fault? Apparently, she did. In any case, she did not react to these insensitive letters of Russell's with the outraged anger that one might have expected. On the contrary, she put into action once again the 'last meeting' tactic that had been so successful in the past; first, writing to ask him for one last meeting so that they should at least not part in bitterness, and then, when they met, pleading with him not to leave her. As a result, on 17 February, Russell wrote to say that he had changed his mind, that indeed everything had changed, the whole world was different: 'I have never known such a quick and great change. It was your sudden outburst yesterday morning asking me not to give you up altogether that made the difference. You made me realise that it mattered to you.'

Russell was, however, sufficiently abashed by his meeting with Ottoline to attempt an explanation of his apparent indifference to her feelings:

You feel me terribly selfish – but it is easy for me to be unselfish when reason is on that side – only in what concerns you I often feel reason is on the side of selfishness . . . I get the feeling that I must protect myself or be destroyed . . . the sense of having to fight for my life makes me hard.

Russell's faith in the dictates of his reason was apparently limitless. He had come now to think that, whatever crisis he and Ottoline had, 'we shall always come together again', and that being so, 'I must put out of my head the three things I want and can't have – children, daily companionship and imaginative writing.' Was it possible to put these things out of his head? With the support of reason, Russell seemed to think so: 'I *could* make up my mind never to think of them, if my reason were convinced that I ought to.'

To imagine that he could reason away his longing for children and daily companionship was an extraordinary – and unwarranted – piece of rationalistic optimism, but one can at least see why he should have thought it necessary. But what is imaginative writing doing on the list? Why should he have thought that this need had to remain unsatisfied if he stayed with Ottoline? The answer, I think, lies in his conviction that, whereas good literature required, to some extent, the unleashing of the 'wild beasts', any chance of success in his relationship with Ottoline demanded their complete restraint.

The question of whether he should or should not continue in his efforts at creative writing had been much on his mind in the new year of 1914, the issue having been revived (so he told Lucy Donnelly) by Conrad's letter 'praising "The Free Man's Worship" in about the strongest terms in which writing can

be praised'. In the midst of his crisis with Ottoline over children, Russell had
written to Conrad to propose another meeting and to tell him about *Forstice*.
Conrad put off the suggested meeting on the grounds of pressure of work (he
was coming to the end of writing *Victory*), but he expressed a gratifying
interest in Russell's attempts at imaginative writing. 'I am not surprised at
what you say,' he told Russell. '*Toute haute intelligence a ses moments de rêverie*
['every high intelligence has its moments of reverie']. It was impossible that
yours should not, at one time or another, have known that mood':

> I am supremely interested. Will you send me the fragment before you leave
> for the States? I'll write to you there. The reading may not take more than
> an hour – but what about the impression, mental or emotional, which may
> last for days? And just at present I must guard carefully my own mood,
> which is inferior and fragile, a mere papier-mâché mood, not fit to stand a
> contact with anything genuine and penetrating as anything coming from
> you is bound to be.

Encouraged by this, Russell sent Conrad the typescript of *Forstice*, which
had been lying in a drawer ever since he abandoned it in 1912. Conrad did
not, however, write to Russell in America – perhaps finding it too daunting a
task to express his opinion tactfully in a letter – and Russell had to wait until
July 1914 to hear his verdict.

In the meantime, Russell – always hungry for praise and encouragement –
received from Whitehead the view that his mind, far from deteriorating, had
actually improved over the previous two or three years, 'that in fact it has
risen to an altogether higher class'. 'He says', Russell reported to Ottoline, 'I
used to have great ingenuity in defending rather narrow and limited points of
view, but now I have an altogether broader scope, and that if my present work
develops as it promises, it will put me among the few great philosophers':

> Altho' this is so agreeable, I think it is true, and it really is largely due to
> you. Other things have come in – getting away from Alys, and having the
> stimulus of Wittgenstein – but really you have been the chief cause. I so
> often say horrid things about your interfering with work, that I want you
> *please* to lay to heart the nice things too . . . I feel in myself a freedom from
> prejudice, and an imaginative force, which I did not have till I knew you.

With that said, and with it reaffirmed, in a later letter, that 'whatever
happens we cannot part', Russell prepared to leave for the United States.

His ship, the *Mauretania*, set sail on 7 March 1914 and docked in New
York five days later. From the moment he arrived, Russell was treated as the
great philosopher that Whitehead had encouraged him to believe he was. The
New York Times ran an article describing him as 'one of the foremost lecturers
on philosophy', and, when he arrived in Boston, Russell discovered that
everyone at Harvard – from Lawrence A. Lowell, the President of the
university to all the undergraduates and graduates in the Philosophy Department – wanted to meet him, dine with him, invite him to their club or listen

to him lecture. He was treated, as he had never been treated before, as an international celebrity.

The Harvard Philosophy Department was by this time in something of a decline, having recently lost three of its most distinguished members – William James, who died in 1910; George Santayana, who left for Europe in 1912; and Josiah Royce, who had suffered a stroke and retired – and it was clearly hoping to entice Russell to stay on permanently. Of this, however, no matter how much he was fêted and flattered, there was no chance whatsoever. 'I couldn't *bear* to be here long,' he told Ottoline.

From the very beginning Russell was contemptuous of America in general, and of Boston in particular, and especially so of the pompous Bostonian dignitaries by whom he was fêted. Indeed, the higher their social position, the more scornful he was of them. Thus, President Lowell he found 'an intolerable person – a deadly bore, hard, efficient, a good man of business, fundamentally contemptuous of learned people because they are not business-like'. After attending a dinner with six members of the cream of Boston society, Russell dismissed his fellow-guests as 'the kind of people who are frightfully proud of their ancient lineage because they go back to 1776'. This was not just the smug sneer of a man who could trace his family back to the fourteenth century (though there is, surely, something of that in it), it was also a protest against what he considered the 'musty and atrophied' attitudes of these people. Boston, he told Margaret Llewelyn Davies, 'prides itself on virtue and ancient lineage – it doesn't impress me in either direction . . . I often want to ask them what constitutes the amazing virtue they are so conscious of – they are against Wilson, against Labour, rich, over-eating, selfish, feeble pigs.'

Americans in general he found too conservative and too bland (commenting to Ottoline on 'the American tendency to slow platitude'), and American society alarmed him by being too mechanical, too preoccupied with the material and the mundane aspects of life. 'Nobody here broods or is absent-minded, or has time to hear whispers from another world,' he complained. His own attempts at reflection were too often disturbed by the telephone, an aspect of modern life that he was experiencing for the first time – and loathing. It was, he told Ottoline, 'rapidly driving me mad'. Even among professors there was no atmosphere of meditation, but rather 'a soul-destroying atmosphere' that encouraged merely 'quick results, efficiency, success – none of the lonely hours away from mankind that go to producing anything of value'. As a result, the professors struck him as 'more alert and business-like and punctual than one expects very good people to be'. It was an atmosphere that bred in Russell only melancholy reflections. 'Spiritually we starve and die,' he announced in one of his letters home to Ottoline, 'and pretend to make up for it by duties – it is all folly and self-deception really.'

At first he was put up at the Colonial Club, which he pronounced 'humble and shabby and cheap', a 'regular American place – very dirty, disgusting food, windows *never* opened, spittoons distributed tastefully about the floor, hard efficient un-meditative men coming and going, talking in horrible American voices'. Here he was waited upon by black servants, which, it seems, was another new experience. 'I find the coloured people friendly and nice,' he told Ottoline, 'they seem to have something of a dog's liking for the white man – the same kind of trust and ungrudging sense of inferiority. I don't feel any physical recoil from them.' The odd irrelevance of this last remark suggests perhaps that it was not true. Being away from home seemed to heighten Russell's sensitivity to racial differences. Introduced to the psychologist Hugo Münsterberg, Russell remarked that he was 'not the sort of man I could ever like because of the touch of Jew vulgarity'.

After a week or so, he moved into the flat of H. A. Hollond, a law don at Trinity, who was also visiting Harvard that year and for whose kindness, hospitality and reassuring Englishness Russell was now extremely grateful. At Hollond's flat he had a sitting-room as well as a bedroom to himself, and it was, he wrote, 'a *great* improvement' on the Colonial Club: 'we have breakfast and lunch here, wh. we provide for ourselves (there is only a woman for an hour in the mg.), so it only leaves dinner in the stuffiness among the spittoons.'

As far as Russell was concerned, the one redeeming feature of life at Harvard was the quality of the students, which he considered – in the more technical areas of philosophy, at least – better than that at Cambridge. He took his teaching responsibilities extremely seriously and did not skimp with his time. His scheduled teaching comprised two undergraduate courses, one on logic and one on theory of knowledge, and a graduate class, giving him a total of six hours of lectures a week, held at 9.00 and 11.00 on Tuesday, Thursday and Saturday. But, as well as these scheduled sessions, he held an informal tea for his students once a week and met some of the better ones for regular private tutorials. On top of this, for the first four weeks, he gave his Lowell lectures on 'Our Knowledge of the External World' twice a week, on Monday and Thursday evenings.

'I enjoy my lecturing here,' he wrote to Lucy Donnelly after his first week at Harvard, though 'not the Lowell lectures, wh. I only give for pay and think futile'. Owing to the widespread curiosity created by the great celebrity with which Russell was treated, his first Lowell lecture was attended by around 500 people. It was, however, he told Ottoline, a failure: 'I was seized with shyness. I felt they couldn't like what I had to say and that it was foolish of them to come; so I didn't speak loud enough, and half couldn't hear.' He was certain that there would be far fewer for the second lecture, and he was right; by the third lecture it was down to 250, and no doubt when, in the later lectures, he got on to the mathematical treatment of infinity and continuity, it fell still further. A public lecture is a difficult, if not impossible, setting for serious philosophy – there is little time for questioning, almost no scope for discussion, and many of the audience are drawn by the expectation of entertainment rather than instruction – which is no doubt why Russell considered the Lowell lectures futile. The organisers, he told Ottoline, were 'fussy and old-maidish – fearfully particular about punctuality in starting and stopping, and everything else except the excellence or the reverse of the lecture'.

Far more to his taste were the lectures and seminars that he gave to his students, and the opportunities they presented of spreading his gospel of 'scientific philosophy' and encouraging bright, talented students to study mathematical logic. The first to impress him was Victor Lenzen, who had come to Harvard from the University of California specially to study with Russell ('the chance of a lifetime,' he had been advised by his tutor, the logician, C. I. Lewis). Lenzen signed up for Russell's logic class and remembers Russell as appearing to the students as 'an almost superhuman person. I cannot adequately describe the respect, adoration, and even awe which he inspired.' Some hint of Wittgenstein's influence on the content of Russell's logic course at Harvard – and an intriguing anticipation of the paradox at the heart of Wittgenstein's *Tractatus Logico-Philosophicus* – can be gleaned from a remark that Lenzen recalls Russell making at the very first class: 'A fact is not a thing. When I say that I am talking nonsense. Nevertheless, I want you to take it as a profound truth.'

Lenzen, who had a thorough grounding in mathematics and science and would later become a professor of physics at Berkeley, was the very epitome of the kind of student Russell hoped to draw into philosophy, and he naturally took pains to get to know Lenzen better and to encourage his interest in bringing mathematical techniques to bear on philosophical problems. At the end of his first week's teaching, he invited Lenzen to dine at the Colonial Club to discuss his postgraduate work on the philosophical problems of causality. Lenzen, he told Ottoline afterwards, was 'able and *very* nice – I quite loved him. Obviously my coming is worth while from the point of view of teaching.' Later he wrote with undisguised delight of a piece of gossip he had picked up (presumably through Lucy Donnelly) that Lenzen 'writes long long letters about me to a young lady at Bryn Mawr, full (I am told) of passionate devotion'.

The next week he took to spending the mornings in his office, making himself available to any students who wished to come and discuss philosophy with him. Lenzen, of course, leapt at the opportunity and came frequently, and at the end of the week, on 27 March, Russell reported that two other interesting-looking students had been to see him: 'one, named Eliot, is very well-dressed and polished, with manners of the finest Etonian type; the other is an unshaven Greek, appropriately named Demos, who earns money for his fees by being a waiter in a restaurant. The two were obviously friends, and had on neither side the slightest consciousness of social difference.'

Though he had already written some of the best-known poems ('The Love Song of J. Alfred Prufrock', 'Portrait of a Lady', 'Rhapsody on a Windy Night') that would appear in *Prufrock and Other Observations* in 1917, T. S. Eliot was at this time almost entirely unknown as a poet and seemed destined rather for a career in academic philosophy. He had graduated from Harvard in 1910 with an MA in English literature and had then spent a year in Europe, primarily in Paris, before returning to Harvard as graduate student of philosophy in the autumn of 1911. When Russell met him, he had already completed two years of his graduate studies and was recognised as one of the most promising students in the department. Like many of the best graduate students, he had enrolled in Russell's logic class, even though his philosophical interests and inclinations were really rather at odds with Russell's. In Paris he had attended the lectures of Henri Bergson and was briefly an adherent of Bergson's 'metaphysics of flux' before, in 1913, becoming converted, through reading *Appearance and Reality*, to the Absolute Idealism of F. H. Bradley. His doctoral thesis, begun in 1913 but not finished until three years later (and not published until 1964), was a study of Bradley that sought to defend his metaphysics from the attacks of, among others, Russell and Moore.

When he and Russell met in the spring of 1914, Eliot did not, it seems, see fit to mention either the fact that he wrote poetry or the subject of his doctoral thesis, and the possibilities that existed for intellectual and personal intimacy were not realised until a year later when Eliot came to live in London. In Harvard, he impressed Russell as being extremely civilised in a rather European sort of way, and also as being 'extraordinarily silent', his silence broken only by one memorable and intriguing remark. In response to Russell's praise of Heraclitus, Eliot observed: 'Yes, he always reminds me of Villon.' This remark, Russell later wrote, was 'so good that I always wished he would make another.' Anyone who mentioned François Villon – for Russell, the very personification of the value and danger of submitting to the 'central fire' of the human soul – was bound to attract Russell's attention, and in 1914 (though not later), Heraclitus too held a special place in his imagination; in 'Mysticism and Logic' Heraclitus is exalted as the paradigm of the 'highest eminence' that it is possible to achieve: 'the true union of the mystic and the man of science'. He was also, according to a letter Russell wrote to Lucy Donnelly, the philosopher in history with whom Russell felt most 'intimate'. The idea, then, that there was some affinity between Villon and Heraclitus – even if entirely unsupported by example or argument, as Eliot's remark appears to have been – would have been immediately attractive, and perhaps also a sign to Russell that somewhere beneath Eliot's own civilised crust there was, after all, some fire.

This isolated remark aside, Russell took less interest in Eliot at Harvard than in his friend, Raphael Demos, whose interest in philosophy was passionate and all-consuming. Brought up in Smyrna, Turkey, Demos had acquired a thirst for learning and had emigrated to the United States specifically to improve his education. Having no money at all, he put himself through Harvard by working as a janitor in a student hall of residence (he was later rewarded by becoming himself a professor of philosophy at Harvard). Apparently oblivious to the hardship and poverty of his life, and the special effort required of him – compared to more fortunate students like Eliot – to complete his studies, Demos was completely dedicated to his work, and Russell found it difficult to persuade him to talk of anything else. Primarily because of this dedication, Russell came to like and admire Demos more than anyone else he met during this American visit. One day, after he had felt overcome by fatigue and beset by what he called a 'fit of spleen' against those around him, he went for a walk with Demos and found him 'so full of courage and of passion for philosophy that he really brightened the world for me. The spectacle of courage and high passion is the most consoling that life affords.'

For the first four weeks, Russell was more or less marooned at Harvard, and, apart from a brief visit one Saturday afternoon to Greenwich, Connecticut, to deliver 'Mysticism and Logic' to 'an assembled crowd of neighbours' at a private school, he stayed in Boston the whole time. Once the Lowell lectures were finished, however, he was a little freer, and, immediately after the final lecture, he spent the weekend sightseeing in New York, where he stayed with Helen and Simon Flexner. It was a tremendous relief to get out of Boston. New York was, he wrote to Ottoline, 'far less repulsive than Boston; it has pride of life, exuberant energy, a new form of self-expression – in many ways it is like the Renaissance'. The highlight of his trip was a visit to the Woolworth Building, then the tallest skyscraper in the city, and, Russell reported, 'really *very* beautiful as architecture – like an immensely magnified Gothic spire'. After a month of the stuffy pseudo-European atmosphere of Boston, it was a revelation to encounter something authentically and exhilaratingly American:

> There at last one sees the Americans not imitative, not insincere, achieving the honest temples of Mammon. The building is more than twice the height of St Paul's; from the top one has a view which is really marvellous; the whole town, the sea and islands, the inland country ending in hills as blue as Italy. It was the first moment of that sort of pleasure I had had in America.

Americans, he wrote in the same letter, 'are *terribly* machine-made. They are only really nice when they are quite untouched by culture and retain the roughness of the people – and then they are generally so *terribly* rough that they are like porcupines.'

For the rest of his time as a lecturer at Harvard, Russell took almost any opportunity he was offered to spend time away from Cambridge (the suburb of Boston where Harvard is situated), and submitted himself to an exhausting round of visits to east-coast universities, which he squeezed into the gaps in his teaching schedule. On 14 April, he went to Wellesley College to deliver 'Mysticism and Logic', but found it scarcely an improvement on Harvard. The campus was attractive, he reported, 'but the mental atmosphere struck me as goody-goody'. The following week he arranged to read 'The Relation of Sense-Data to Physics' to no fewer than three universities, all a fair distance from Boston. On Monday, he travelled to Baltimore to present the paper to Johns Hopkins University; on Wednesday to Princeton; and on Saturday afternoon to Smith College, Massachusetts. 'By the time I got back here Sunday night', he wrote to Lucy Donnelly, 'I was exhausted.'

The week started with a visit to Bryn Mawr to stay with Lucy Donnelly and to give an informal talk to some of her students. (As the President of Bryn Mawr was the formidable Carey Thomas, a cousin of Alys's and a fierce opponent of Russell and everything he stood for, a formal invitation was out of the question.) From Bryn Mawr he wrote to Ottoline that he enjoyed 'escaping from New England . . . the most loathsome part of America', and, as an example of what he was fleeing from, gave a description of a Boston dinner he had been at the previous Friday that suggests he had developed an almost physical aversion to the place and its people. His hosts were Hugo

Münsterberg and his wife, who were '*awful* people – and all their guests *horrors*':

> The ugliness of the faces along the table made me almost unable to eat – fat, stupid, complacent, without any redeeming trait of any sort or kind . . . As I think of Cambridge Mass., I find I have an intimate horror of every corner of the place – it all screams at one, like living always with the screech of a railway-engine.

Not that the other places he visited entirely escaped either his scorn or his condescension. Princeton, for example, was 'full of new Gothic, and . . . as like Oxford as monkeys can make it', while his hosts at Smith College, Gerald Stanley Lee and his wife, were 'awful bores – "fancy" bores, with woolly pretentious ideas of their own'. Lee came in for further derision for having written 'a silly book called "Inspired Millionaires" '. At the end of his busy week, Russell wrote to Lucy Donnelly that, now that he could no longer look forward to seeing either her or Helen Flexner again, 'I feel that there is no more enjoyment for me in America, and I merely clench my teeth and count the days. The ugliness and stridency of things and of people's minds are very trying.' What he missed in America was the 'artistic conscience' that had been so perfectly exemplified in Wittgenstein. The work of Americans 'seems done to please men rather than to please God':[4]

> What is lacking is the non-social side of the good life – the blind instinctive devotion to ideals dimly seen, regardless of whether they are useful or appreciated by others. This is what makes me feel lonely here. It is rare enough in Europe, but not so rare as here. There are *two* commandments, to love God and to love your neighbour – and I feel love of God is forgotten here.

A few days later, he was off again, this time to Yale, 'a one-horse place' that he mocked for having compulsory chapel at 8.15 in the morning, and where his host was 'a philosopher named Bakewell, a tiresome fool who hadn't understood a word I said, but insisted that if I understood my own views I should agree with him'. In between, however, his temper had been softened by a walk with Demos, about whom he now spoke just as he had earlier spoken about Wittgenstein: 'I . . . loved him. He has the true passion for philosophy . . . He seems to me already better at philosophy than any of my other pupils . . . I hope someday he may come to Cambridge.'

A recurring theme in these letters from Boston is that culture and learning are not sufficient by themselves to produce anything worth while – they need

---

[4] There is an interesting echo of this remark in a preface that Wittgenstein wrote in 1930 for *Philosophical Remarks*: 'I would like to say "This book is written to the glory of God", but nowadays that would be chicanery, that is, it would not be understood. It means that the book is written in good will, and in so far as it is not so written, but out of vanity, etc., the author would wish to see it condemned.'

to be combined with fire and passion and concentration of purpose. Again and again, Russell criticises the people he is introduced to for their lack of vitality. 'I find the cultured people here feeble,' he pronounced soon after he arrived, a view he adhered to throughout his visit. One of the most perfect examples of this general trait was Benjamin Apthorp Fuller, a historian of philosophy at Harvard, the author of *The Problem of Evil in Plotinus* and a close friend of George Santayana. Towards the end of his visit to Harvard, Russell was invited by Fuller to spend a weekend at his house in the country, where he lived with his mother and his wife. 'It was beautiful there,' Russell wrote to Ottoline, 'the weather like midsummer and the trees like early spring. He has a lake and woods and various agreeable things, and by all the rules he ought to be agreeable himself, being good-natured and cultivated, but for some reason I am always saying to myself "After all, you are an Ass" – tho' I can't make out what makes him one.' To Lucy Donnelly, he was more definite. Fuller, he told her, was full of the classics and talked 'as like an Englishman as he can', but he was 'feeble – quite without the ferocity that is needed to redeem culture'.

On the Sunday, Fuller held a garden party in Russell's honour. Among the guests was T. S. Eliot, who was, Russell remarked in his letter to Lucy Donnelly, 'a similar type' to Fuller: 'proficient in Plato, intimate with French literature from Villon to Vildrach, very capable of a certain exquisiteness of appreciation, but lacking in the crude insistent passion that one must have in order to achieve anything'. In 'Mr Apollinax', the poem that Eliot later wrote describing the occasion, the difference between Russell and the enfeebled, over-cultured Americans he so despised is presented in a way that is strikingly close to that in which Russell describes it in his letters home, with Russell himself being portrayed as the very epitome of 'crude insistent passion'.

The poem centres on the contrasting sensibilities of the hosts, Fuller ('Professor Channing-Cheetah') and his mother ('dowager Mrs Phlaccus'), who are civilised, restrained and forgettable, and their guest, Russell ('Mr Apollinax'), whose 'dry and passionate talk devoured the afternoon' and whose ill-disguised, satyr-like lustfulness recalls:

> . . . Priapus in the shrubbery
> Gaping at the lady in the swing.

It is a picture of staid gentility being disrupted by an indecorous display of exuberance, intelligence and fun, with Eliot repeatedly emphasising the startling impact of Russell's (notoriously loud and raucous) laugh, as if laughing in Boston was somehow considered not quite decent:

> When Mr Apollinax visited the United States
> His laughter tinkled among the teacups
> . . .
> He laughed like an irresponsible foetus.
> His laughter was submarine and profound
> Like the old man of the sea's

. . . .

I looked for the head of Mr Apollinax rolling under a chair

Or grinning over a screen
With seaweed in its hair.

. . .

'He is a charming man' – 'But after all what did he mean?' –
'His pointed ears . . . He must be unbalanced.' –
'There was something he said that I might have challenged.'

Russell later took these last lines as an indication that Eliot had 'noticed the madness' in him, but, surely, the point is rather that Mr Apollinax with his subterranean vitality must have seemed mad to the over-cultivated Bostonians, whose feeble remarks contrast vividly with the elemental power of a figure who rises from the depths of the sea to mock those at the surface, to laugh his head off and to 'devour' the afternoon with dry and passionate talk. If the poem is a satire, its target is not Russell, but his hosts. It ends:

Of dowager Mrs Phlaccus, and Professor and Mrs Cheetah
I remember a slice of lemon, and a bitten macaroon.

'I have thank Heaven only a fortnight more in Harvard,' Russell wrote to Ottoline after he returned from his weekend with Fuller. And yet, he wrote, a few days later, he had not been really unhappy, because he had been so busy with things that 'only require a second-rate effort' and therefore could be accomplished only through an act of will. He had not, he said, tried to do any real work, 'so my thoughts and feelings have been trivial, and when that is the case I am happy . . . Of course I shouldn't be happy long with only that sort of thing, because I should feel I was wasting my life. But anything easy that certainly *has* to be done makes me happy for a time':

However, when I have for a moment come out of my trivial mood, I have felt horribly starved and rasped – I am afraid it made me more affectionate to Helen Flexner than I should have been in Europe. However, she was glad to find me so, and no harm was done.

The happiness of being trivial was under threat from the frustration of a powerful and unsatisfied sexual instinct.

In the same letter – and, surely, in some way connected in Russell's mind with the notion that happiness can sometimes be bought at the expense of being trivial – were some rather cynical and oddly revealing reflections on the supposedly trivial preoccupations of women's minds. That women were, for the most part, preoccupied with trivial things appeared to be common ground between himself and Ottoline. Where they disagreed was on the cause:

I wonder if it is lack of *intellect*, as you say, that makes so many women worry too much over small things. I don't think so; I think it is triviality of soul – they really *care* more about little things than about big ones. A tidy woman, for instance, would rather lose her husband's affection than let him drop envelopes on the floor.[5] I think it is one of the cynical lessons one learns in regard to most women, that they care more (or as much) for small things than for great ones. I don't think it is intellect that is lacking, but proportion in desire.

On his forty-second birthday, 18 May, as was his custom, he took stock of the previous year: 'as far as work goes, this past year has been very satisfactory, but quite the reverse as regards behaviour'. Just lately, he said:

I have been feeling sensible and middle-aged – without faults or virtues, merely an efficient machine. It is comfortable, but death. I shall have to come back to life and pain. (I have not met a single person in this country who would know what that means.)

A week later, to his relief and delight, his time at Harvard came to an end: 'Everybody has been so kind and so generally magnanimous that I feel a brute to be so glad to leave them – but none of them touch one's soul in any way.'

Before leaving America, Russell had arranged a whistle-stop tour of the Midwest, reading either 'Mysticism and Logic' or 'The Relation of Sense-Data to Physics' to three universities – Chicago, Madison and Ann Arbor – before travelling to Montreal (taking in a trip to Niagara Falls *en route*), from where his ship left for Liverpool at dawn on 6 June, giving him just ten days for the entire schedule. At Chicago he would stay as the guest of Dr E. Clark Dudley, an eminent surgeon and professor of gynaecology at Northwestern University, whom he had never met, but, as he told Ottoline, 'whose daughter I used to know at Oxford . . . I am told she writes – when I knew her she tried to, but with quite amazing lack of success.'

Helen Dudley, the daughter in question, had been an undergraduate at Bryn Mawr some ten years previously and had then gone to Oxford to study Greek with Gilbert Murray. At Oxford she had presented herself to Russell and Alys at Bagley Wood, armed with a letter of introduction from Lucy Donnelly. Since then, it seems, she and Russell had had little or no contact and she presumably found out about his trip to the United States through her connections with Bryn Mawr. In any case, Russell, especially now, 'starved and rasped' as he was, was not going to refuse an invitation from an attractive young woman, no matter how little he remembered her. He was, as he had described to Ottoline, hungry not only for sex (though certainly for that as well), but also for real contact with other human souls, and if it had been Helen Dudley's intention to seduce him, she could not have set herself an easier task.

---

[5] This example is so specific (why envelopes, in particular?) that one wonders whether it is not the remembrance of an ancient quarrel he had had with Alys. The suspicion that Alys had been on his mind during this trip, and that his recollections of her were somehow fuelling his antipathy to all things American, is strengthened at the end of this letter, when, in discussing the possibility that Hollond may be in love with an American girl, he says: 'I feel inclined to utter solemn warnings to Englishmen who think of marrying Americans, only I know it would be useless.'

When he arrived in Chicago, Helen was there to meet him, and, Russell writes in his *Autobiography*, 'I at once felt more at home with her than I had with anybody else that I had met in America.' His judgment of her writing abilities suddenly changed: 'I found that she wrote rather good poetry, and that her feeling for literature was remarkable and unusual.' In a letter to Ottoline written on the train to Madison three days later, he was more muted, though evidently still attracted. Helen, he wrote, 'has developed a good deal since I knew her – she has written some poetry which is rather immature but has a poignant quality – I like her very much indeed.' The following night, returning from Madison, Russell stayed again with the Dudleys, before setting off for Ann Arbor, and this time he slept with Helen, and, amazingly, suggested to her that she come to England as soon as possible to live with him, perhaps marrying him later, if he could get a divorce from Alys. Even more extraordinarily, she accepted. On the train to Ann Arbor the next day, Russell wrote to Ottoline, trying – without actually telling her that Helen Dudley now considered herself to be his fiancée – to make some sort of sense of what had happened and what its implications were for his relationship with her.

Despite having assured Ottoline that he would have no adventures in America, he began, he *had* had one, 'a rather important one':

The more I saw of Helen Dudley, and the more I read of her work, the more remarkable she seemed. Yesterday she and I spent a long day in the woods together and I found that I care for her a great deal – not with the same intensity or passion as I feel for you, but still very seriously. I told her I cared for some one else with whom I would not break, but she did not mind that. It ended by our spending the night together – and she will come to England as soon as she can – probably in September or late August . . . The whole family are extraordinarily nice people. The parents have the morals of their generation, and will suffer greatly if it becomes necessary for them to know – but her sisters all sympathised (seeing something was going on), and it was by the active connivance of a married sister that we got time alone yesterday. I am bringing a play of hers with me, which will tell you more about her than my description.

She is 28 – not good looking – her mouth, and still more her nose, very ugly – her eyes an unusual brown, Chinese shaped, very interesting – her figure good. Her face shows great intensity of feeling and a good deal of suffering. She is very passionate, very full of creative impulse, *absolutely* sincere, and without a hint of sentimentalism. I found her withering, like a flower in drought, for want of love and understanding and friends who cared for the sort of thing that makes her work. The impulse to foster creativeness was first aroused, and the rest followed. She cares for me, as far as I can judge, up to the full limit of a generous and lonely spirit . . . The impulse that came over me was like the impulse to rescue a drowning person, and I am *sure* I was right to follow it.

The idea that his motives in sleeping with her were mainly philanthropic was, of course, as Russell later acknowledged, completely untrue. If he had wanted merely to foster her writing career, he could have invited her to London to meet the influential people in the literary world that he and Ottoline knew, without sex ever coming into it. Yet his repeated emphasis of Helen's writing gifts and her creativity does, perhaps, reveal something important about her attraction for him, an attraction that was, for a short time at least, evidently so completely overwhelming that it subdued all thought he might have of the consequences – for his relationship with Ottoline and for his career at Cambridge – of living together openly with her. Her literary ambitions may have been an essential part of that attraction, for they may have suggested to Russell the possibility that, in living with her, he could satisfy all three of his great unfulfilled longings – for companionship, for children and for imaginative writing. Such a promise, it is easy to imagine, would have been so intoxicating, so irresistible as to have made him reckless about all other considerations.

There is something in Russell's description of Helen, too – both in this letter to Ottoline and in his *Autobiography* – that suggests that, philanthropy aside, he was quite genuinely inclined to look upon himself as Helen Dudley's ideal 'secret sharer'. 'Her youth had been lonely and unhappy,' he writes in his *Autobiography*, 'and it seemed that I could give her what she wanted.' She was, he says, 'passionate, poetic, and strange' – the very qualities he had missed in the other Americans he had met and the ones most calculated to encourage the picture he held dear of being, on rare occasions, able to see – where no one else could – into another person's soul. And it was true, he could give her what she wanted and needed; the only question was whether he had been right to think that she, in turn, could give him what he needed and whether, therefore, he really wanted to live with her.

But if Russell was somewhat blind and self-deluded about his own motives in rushing into a serious relationship with Helen Dudley, he was utterly and inexplicably naive about the effect it would have on his relations with Ottoline. 'I do not want you to think that this will make the very *smallest* difference in my feeling towards you,' he told her, 'beyond removing the irritation of unsatisfied instinct':

I suppose it must give you some pain, but I hope not very much if I can make you believe it is all right, and that she is not the usual type of American ... My Darling, please do not think that this means *any* lessening of my love to you, and I do not see why it should affect our relations. I do mind most intensely giving you pain, I do indeed. I long to be with you and to make you *feel* that my love is absolutely undiminished.

When Russell arrived in Liverpool on 14 June, he found waiting for him a letter that Ottoline had written before she received the news about Helen Dudley. In it, she told him that she wanted their relations henceforth to be platonic. Later that day, when he returned to his flat in London, he found another letter from her, giving her response to his extraordinary news: she hoped he and Helen Dudley would be happy together, she wrote, and she thought it best that she and Russell did not see each other again, because she did not want to come between him and Helen.

Ottoline perhaps expected Russell to be devastated by her decision not to see him and to plead with her to change her mind. If so, she was disappointed. In his reply, Russell reaffirmed that, even after having had a week's solitude on the Atlantic crossing coming home, he was still inclined to see his relationship with Helen as 'a very real and serious thing'. He felt some longer trial was necessary before they took the step of living openly together, thus preventing him from carrying on teaching at Cambridge, but 'I should certainly want it to be public as soon as we felt sure.' As for not meeting Ottoline, he seemed almost unconcerned: 'I cannot ask you to see me if you think it better not . . . You must decide everything as you think right . . . For the present, let us at least write – but I believe in the first times with her I might find it hard to write. Afterwards, if any sort of friendship between you and her were possible, it would be good – but those things are difficult':

At present I am harassed by practical problems – when and how to leave Trinity – the necessity of telling the Whiteheads, which I dread doing more than I can say. I don't think you need fear that you would come between us – the impulse is too deep and strong for that.

Faced with this equanimity and with Russell's apparently resolute commitment to Helen, Ottoline changed tack. Almost as if roused by the implied challenge in Russell's suggestion that she could not come between him and Helen even if she wanted to, Ottoline set out to win him back and put into motion once more the unfailingly successful 'last meeting' ruse; only this time, when they met (which they did two days after Russell arrived, when Ottoline – after writing twice to say how much she longed to see him – came to visit him at his flat), she discovered a hitherto unknown sexual passion for him. To Russell, this was as welcome as it was unexpected and his reaction was ecstatic. 'All day I have felt so strangely happy and light-hearted,' he wrote, after Ottoline left, 'it was so *divine* while you were here, my Dearest. I did not in the least foresee that it would be as it was. My Heart, I cannot lose you . . . Don't think I want or intended to go against what you wrote in your letter to Liverpool – at the moment the impulse was overwhelming, but it was quite unforeseen, at least on my side.'

If there had been any doubt that Ottoline could come between Russell and Helen Dudley, that one meeting was sufficient to remove it. Just two days later, after he and Ottoline had met again, this time at Ottoline's house in Bedford Square, cracks in Russell's commitment to his plans with Helen were beginning to appear. 'Our little moment yesterday was *very* happy, wasn't it?' he wrote to Ottoline. 'Your conscience will have nothing to reproach you with if in the end the other [his relationship with Helen] does not develop as I expected, because it could not answer unless it was able to live in spite of not being cut off from you.' He was now more insistent that he would prefer his relations with Helen to remain a secret, 'as I dread giving up teaching'. Already forgetting his promises to Helen, he now presented the matter as a difference of opinion: 'she would very much prefer publicity. This may cause trouble.'

Within days, the cracks had grown to the extent of leaving Russell's commitment to Helen a crumbled ruin. 'I am less fond of H. D. than I have tried to persuade myself that I was,' he told Ottoline on 22 June, 'her affection for me has made me do my utmost to respond. This has brought with it an overestimate of her writing. The truth is that I think well, but not very well, of her capacity for writing, and that I care enough for her to desire a relation which would not deprive me of you or of Cambridge, but that I shrink from anything else. She, however, passionately desires an open relation; I do not at all know in advance what I shall feel . . . But it is not *by any means* decided in my mind.'

What previously had been a 'real and serious thing', too 'deep and strong' for Ottoline to threaten, he now thought of as a momentary weakness, unfit to stand any sort of comparison with his love for Ottoline:

What you give me I shall never get from any one else. The region of deep passion, of mystic sorrow, would never be touched by another . . . I don't think I could feel as I do to you towards any one who gave full instinctive satisfaction. But instinct remains – the actual bottom fact is that the lonely nights grow unendurable and that I haven't enough self-discipline to overcome the desire to share the nights with a woman . . . Only *please* don't think everything is decided, or that the new can give me what you give. That is *absolutely* untrue.

His relationship with Helen, he now thought, rather than being an escape from the triviality of his relations with people in America, was rather just one more example of that very triviality, and, therefore, not worth holding on to if it threatened his much deeper, more spiritual companionship with Ottoline:

Most people, even when I am very fond of them, remain external to me. Alys, even when I was most in love with her, remained outside my inner life. H. D. would never touch it. What I get from most people I like to be with is escape from the inner life, which is too painful to be endured continuously. But what I get from you is an intensification of it, with a transmutation of the pain into beauty and wonder . . . If H. D. finds my keeping up with you intolerable, I shall part from her.

The assassination of the Habsburg Archduke Franz Ferdinand in Sarajevo took place just five days after this letter, on Sunday 28 June 1914, though the event goes completely unrecorded in Russell's correspondence, which continues to dwell on his love for Ottoline and his anxieties about Helen Dudley's impending visit to England. Many in Britain had been expecting war with Germany for some time, but few imagined that it would come about through what was widely regarded as a merely local problem between Austria-Hungary and its neighbour, Serbia, a conflict in which British public opinion was, if anything, on the side of the Habsburgs.

Russell was quicker than most in England to realise the horror of the situation, but even he did not begin to be concerned about the prospect of a

war involving Britain until the end of July. In retrospect, however, the month
between the assassination and the Austrian declaration of war was seen by
both him and Ottoline as a time in which they grew ever closer together as
the impending gloom drew nearer. They took to meeting every Tuesday to
spend the day in Burnham Beeches in the Buckinghamshire countryside,
often returning to Russell's flat in London in the evening, where Ottoline
continued to demonstrate enthusiasm for the physical side of their relationship, which previously she had found fearful and repulsive, and Russell
continued to delight in this novel state of affairs and to push Helen Dudley
ever further from his thoughts and affections. 'It *was* a joy to see you tonight,'
he wrote on 7 July, after one of their Tuesdays together. 'It really *was* a
surprise this time. It was a *heavenly* day – it is such an unspeakable joy to be
easy with each other . . . I don't really think we shall lose what we have now
– it seems to me that, since we know it is possible, we shall always want it.'
'What worries me,' he wrote a few days later, 'is the doubt whether I can
give H. D. enough affection to make her life bearable':

> I certainly cannot if I depend upon her alone, but I think if I still have you
> I can. She loves me very intensely and passionately – I have towards her a
> great tenderness and a great desire to develop her best. But I feel no
> passion, and if she came to care for some one else that seemed capable of
> helping her, I should be glad . . . my soul lives in you.

In his *Autobiography*, Russell claims that it was 'the shock of war' that killed
his passion for Helen Dudley. 'If the war had not intervened,' he writes, 'the
plan which we formed in Chicago might have brought great happiness to us
both.' But, as his letters to Ottoline show, his passion for Helen was dead long
before his thoughts turned to war. Indeed, how far he was from even
considering the possibility of a European war in the middle of July is revealed
by a letter to Ottoline dated 16 July in which he writes that he has received
an invitation from Liese von Hattingberg to join her and her children in Italy
over the summer. 'I think I might go late in August,' Russell writes, with
complete insouciance.
    As late as 21 July, when the Austro-Hungarian Empire was drawing up its
ultimatum to hand to Serbia and was preparing for war, and the diplomats of
the Great European Powers were beginning to talk for the first time of the
possibility that the crisis might lead to a 'general world conflagration',
thoughts of war were far from Russell's mind, which was still preoccupied by
the wonder of the renewal of his relations with Ottoline. 'It seems to me that
you love me as much as you did in early days – is that really true? Do tell me
– I think I had very nearly killed your love.'
    Even more oblivious to the gathering storm was Joseph Conrad, who was,
at this time, preparing to leave for Poland for what he intended to be a short
visit. He left on 25 July, arrived in Cracow on 1 August, just as the
Austro-Hungarian troops were mobilising, and was stranded in Austrian
Poland for the next three months, finally arriving back in England on 9
November, ill and exhausted. On 22 July, just two days before his departure,

he was visited by Russell, who came to hear his verdict of *The Perplexities of John Forstice*. Conrad was, Russell reported on the train back from Kent, 'as delightful as ever, & it was a *great* joy seeing him. The household was rather upset by the prospect of going back to Poland, but it didn't interfere with our talking.' Less delightful was Conrad's verdict – which Russell took to be final and authoritative – on Russell's novella:

> He talked at length about Forstice. His view is that I might leave the 1st and 3rd parts as they are, but that the middle part, in Florence, should be expanded into a long book with conversations of the various characters singly. He says I must not attempt to embody the dialogue – I rebelled, but he was inexorable. I can't bear to sacrifice the poet's speech! He seemed to think by a great deal of work I could make something of it, but not to be sure whether it was worth my while to give so much time to it. He seemed to think very well of the garden party at the beginning. And I am happy to say he liked the nun.

Taking the hint, Russell laid aside *Forstice* and made no more attempts at imaginative writing for nearly forty years.

The death of his literary aspirations weakened still further his enthusiasm for the vision he had entertained in May of leaving Cambridge to share a bohemian writer's existence with Helen Dudley. 'I have grown much more academic in my ambitions,' he wrote to Ottoline on 24 July. 'This is due to middle age and to loss of belief that I can do any other sort of work at all continuously – also to having got over the fatigue of "Principia Math'a" ':

> But partly too Cambridge holds a great part of my affections – I should be homesick for it if I were shut out from it. So much has happened to me here, and the place is so bound up with whatever continuity there has been in my life, that it has a hold on all my habits. This is all a propos of H. D.

But, he added, 'I find I don't want to give her up, if she can acquiesce in keeping it quiet.'

This last comment presumably explains why Russell did not write to Helen to tell her that he had changed his mind about the plans they had made together. In accordance with those plans, and in the absence of any warnings from Russell that things had changed, Helen went ahead and booked her passage and was due to set sail for England with her father on 3 August. Given that it took about a week for mail to travel across the Atlantic, the last date Russell could have written to put her off was 27 July. He did not, because, up to that date, he positively welcomed her coming – so long that is, as she accepted that there was now no chance either of their living openly together or of his leaving Cambridge. He had also decided that he would be her lover only if this did not interfere with his continuing to be Ottoline's lover or with his continuing to regard Ottoline as the chief love of his life; but he did not anticipate Helen's agreement to these conditions and did not feel he would need it, since he was not planning to tell her that he was Ottoline's lover.

To keep this a secret he needed Ottoline's connivance, and on 25 July he wrote, urging her to co-operate. 'I am afraid of troubles as regards H. D.,' he told her:

> I did not represent to her that I wanted her as a means of improving my relations with you, and I did not think so. If that is the truth, it will be a terrible disillusion for her. I find I have no instinct that makes me wish to tell her the whole exact truth, or feel that I ought to – the instinct for telling the truth only comes with great passion . . . I do not want to make her suffer, at any rate not before she has had a time of happiness. Everything *may* turn out very well, but it will be difficult. There are possibilities of extreme tragedy, which must be avoided.

On Tuesday, 28 July, the day it became too late to stop Helen coming, everything changed: Austria declared war on Serbia and the train of events that this might potentially set in motion suddenly became apparent. It was, though neither of them realised it, the last of Russell and Ottoline's Tuesdays together at Burnham Beeches. By now, however, it was almost impossible to ignore the dark clouds completely. 'The war and risk of war is quite awful,' Russell wrote. 'I try not to realise it – the horror of it is too great.' Nevertheless, he was still expecting to meet Ottoline again the following Tuesday, but, as Helen and her father were due to arrive in England on 8 August, he was 'really regretful that H. D. will interfere with our day the week after next'. Matters between Russell and Ottoline were now so harmonious that Russell's previous judgment was turned on its head: now, he saw no possibility that Helen could come between him and Ottoline. Indeed, 'I think her existence is in a way a safeguard for the future. Otherwise I might demand too much.' In any case: 'I think as things will not be open with H. D. it is sure to be temporary. She will dislike the situation, and come to prefer some one else. I hope so.'

Within a few days of Austria's declaration of war against Serbia, diplomacy between the Great European Powers was replaced by military manoeuvres, with the armies on all sides moving into action like great, lumbering, unstoppable machines: Austria against Russia, Russia against Austria and Germany, and Germany against France and Russia. By 31 July, a general European war was unavoidable, but England's involvement in it was not yet quite inevitable. Having by now accepted that his plans to meet Liese von Hattingberg in Italy would come to nothing, Russell was also expecting a cable from Helen Dudley to say that she was not coming, that her father had decided it was unwise. In the meantime, he himself could think of nothing but the prospect of war:

> It looks all but hopeless now. It seems nearly certain that England will be involved. I don't think we ought to be, but I can see a point of view which makes it seem an honourable obligation. It is a ghastly irresistible fate,

driving every one on. I have always hoped that things would keep peaceful long enough for Europe to realise that war is madness – now there will be a new legacy of hatreds and humiliations and brutal triumphs.

At a time when most people in England were looking forward to the war with something approaching relish, these are impressive sentiments – especially when contrasted with his rather brutal and unfeeling remarks about Helen Dudley. It was as if Russell could feel the suffering of a whole nation with more vividness than he could the suffering of an individual. 'I seem to feel all the weight of Europe's passion, as if I were the focus of a burning-glass,' he wrote on 1 August, the day Germany declared war on Russia, making war between Germany and France more or less inevitable – 'all the shouting angry crowds, Emperors at balconies appealing to God, solemn words of duty and sacrifice to cover red murder and rage. It seems as if one must go mad or join the madmen.'

All Russell's thoughts and energies were now directed towards the coming catastrophe, trying to make sense of it and wondering what, if anything, he could do about it. His mind was racing to explain why men would knowingly and calculatingly adopt a course of action that would result in the deaths of countless numbers of their fellows. There had to be some explanation and it had to lie, somehow or other, in a defective understanding. 'The source of all international trouble', he wrote to Ottoline, 'is misdirection and poverty of imagination. We think of others almost exclusively in their relation to us . . . Hatred (and love, except the universal kind) comes from seeing people in relation to ourselves, instead of from their own centre . . . what is wanted is deliberate teaching in schools, by reading foreign novels or poetry (in translation) or whatever else will best make it evident that foreigners have feelings and characters like our own, and are not strange monsters of wickedness.'

Russell's attitude during these days recalls his comment in one of his letters from America about the 'proportion in desire' that was lacking in many women who genuinely care for trivial things more than big ones. His own 'proportion in desire' had now reasserted itself with a vengeance, and, while he was feeling the agonies of all Europe, he seemed callously indifferent to those of the woman whom he had, just a few months earlier, encouraged to come to England to become his lover and possibly his wife. Helen Dudley had not, after all, cabled to put off her visit. Suffering from the 'triviality of the soul' Russell had described as characteristic of her sex, she continued to think that the plans she and Russell had made – and the promise they held for her life's happiness – had some importance, and that they should not be put off unless they absolutely had to be. She and her father were therefore sailing as intended on 3 August. As Russell put it in his letter to Ottoline of 2 August: 'She has argued herself back into happiness and the belief that all will turn out as she wishes':

I feel now an absolute blank indifference to her, except as one little atom of the mass of humanity. I simply *cannot* act as I had intended. I fear I shall break her heart – but the whole affair is trivial on my side, and just now I cannot play at things. If I had even the faintest hope that she could understand, I might come to care for her seriously; but I know she will think it monstrous to forget her because of public things. This day week I must face her.

On the day that Helen set sail, Germany declared war on France, and both Ottoline and Russell came up to London – he from Cambridge and she from Oxford – to do what they could to support Philip's attempts to marshal whatever anti-war feeling there was left among Members of Parliament. 'Do tell P.', Russell wrote before leaving Cambridge, 'that I am *absolutely* with him – it is utter and unspeakable folly for us to join in.' They arrived in London, however, to find, in Ottoline's words: 'excited crowds everywhere; even our own quiet Bedford Square filled with bands of youths marching round singing the "Marseillaise" and waving flags. It went on all night.' With extraordinary fortitude and bravery, Philip got up in the House of Commons that day, after Sir Edward Grey had made his famous speech committing Britain to war if Germany invaded either France or Belgium and the whole House was aflame with war fever, to warn the House against the madness of rushing into the war. He was shouted down and the speech ended his political career, but it was, surely, the finest moment of his life. As Ottoline – with a pride that is manifestly genuine – says: 'If he had not got up in the House there would have been no debate on the question of England joining the war.'

That evening, Russell, as so often in moments of crisis, stirred by the sense of solitariness when amidst crowds of people, wandered the streets around Trafalgar Square, 'noticing cheering crowds, and making myself sensitive to the emotions of passers-by. During this and the following days I discovered to my amazement that average men and women were delighted at the prospect of war.' The following morning, the German army invaded Belgium, and by 10 p.m. that evening, after Germany had ignored Grey's ultimatum, Britain was at war. Ottoline and Russell walked round London together, comforting each other as each step on the way to war was taken. Ottoline writes that, as they walked from the House of Commons in despair after hearing the news of the last irrevocable step: 'I remember a passionate force rose up in me and I felt that by my will-power I could stop it. "It must be stopped, it must be stopped," I kept saying.' That spirit made her indispensable to Russell. 'But for her,' he says in his *Autobiography*, 'I should have been at first completely solitary, but she never wavered either in her hatred of war, or in her refusal to accept the myths and falsehoods with which the world was inundated.'

When Helen Dudley arrived in England on 8 August, she found that there was now no place at all for her in Russell's life and he refused even to see her. The plans they had made together no longer had any vestige of reality for him, they were merely relics from a bygone era, survivals of another place and another time, the time before Britain committed itself to 'the greatest misfortune to mankind since the Napoleonic wars'.

Part II
1914–21

13
AGAINST THE MULTITUDE

'Thou shalt not follow a multitude to do evil.'
(Exodus 23:2)

Russell's acute sense of isolation from the people around him was on the whole a cause of great suffering to him, but the outbreak of war in 1914 revealed it to have one great redeeming feature: it left him immune to the contagious and virulent strain of war-fever that spread throughout the country. As Russell walked through the cheering crowds on 4 August, he felt no desire whatever to be part of them, and, in his isolation, felt that he could still see the simple truths to which they, in their collective fervour, had blinded themselves: that, as he put it in a letter to Lucy Donnelly, 'war is a mad horror, and that deliberately to cause the deaths of thousands of men like ourselves is so ghastly that hardly anything can justify it.'

What particularly pained Russell was the fierce and irrational hatred of Germany that suddenly seemed to overcome almost everyone in Britain, even people whom previously he had considered intelligent and liberal. Fear of German military power and rivalrous concern with Germany's imperialistic ambitions were preoccupations he had hitherto associated only with the Tories, and, over the previous few years, one of the main reasons he had considered it important to Britain that Asquith's Liberal government survived was that he was sure a Conservative government would wage war against Germany. His discovery that enthusiasm to fight Germany was rife among Liberals too was a deep and lasting disillusionment. As soon as war was declared, his faith in the Liberal Party vanished, never to return. 'You were right about the Liberals,' he wrote to his friend, Margaret Llewelyn Davies (a Labour supporter), 'I have done with them. I had never believed anything so frightful could happen. I *feel* as if it meant an end of all happiness for the rest of our lives.'

Immediately after the declaration of war, he expressed his sense of betrayal and disillusionment in a letter to *The Nation*, in which he furiously denounced both Asquith's Ministry and the whole Parliamentary Liberal Party. 'The friends of progress', the letter began, 'have been betrayed by their chosen leaders, who have plunged the country suddenly into a war which must cause untold misery, and which an overwhelming majority of those who voted for the present Government believe to be as unwise as it is wicked . . . no man whose liberalism is genuine can hereafter support the members of the present Cabinet.' He called for a new party to be created from a combination of Labour and the radical wing of the Liberal Party, a party committed to democracy 'not only in legislation, but in administration, in the army, in the Civil Service, and in the conduct of foreign affairs'. If Britain's foreign policy had been subject to democratic pressure, he believed, it would never have led to war, for, as every civilised person surely realised: 'The first necessity for democracy, for civilisation, for any advance in the slow emergence of man from the brute, is Peace':

> Great forces on the side of peace exist in England, France and Germany; but they are not yet in control. In England they could have been, if they had known they were not.

Before the First World War, it was widely accepted by both Liberal and Conservative politicians that open discussion of Britain's foreign policy was not in the national interest. Consequently foreign affairs were rarely debated in the House of Commons, and its approval was not sought for the various alliance treaties and promises by which Britain committed itself to the defence of France and the preservation of Belgian neutrality. In Russell's opinion, this allowed the Government and the civil servants of the Foreign Office to pursue unchecked a policy calculated to lead to war against Germany, despite the fact that most people in the country wanted no such thing. Central to the political programme of the new party he envisaged, therefore, would be its rejection of this 'secret diplomacy' and its willingness for the Government to be led in matters of foreign policy, as it was in domestic matters, by popular opinion.

But had he not seen for himself the cheering crowds in London that gathered to celebrate the announcement of war? Was it not true that war against Germany was endorsed – with great enthusiasm – by popular opinion? For the moment, at least, Russell refused to believe it. How could it be true that the people of a civilised, liberal country like England would knowingly and willingly ally themselves with a barbaric and despotic regime like Tsarist Russia in order to fight their own neighbours and cousins in Germany? No, it was not possible. 'No one whose experience is not confined to London', he argued, 'can doubt that, if public opinion had had time to express itself, our participation on the side of Russia would have been impossible':

> Assuming that the War Fever spreads from Parliament to the average honest man, as it has already spread from the Foreign Office to Parliament, we may yet count, with very great confidence, upon a deep and almost universal revulsion of feeling, as soon as the immediate military peril is at an end.

This optimistic view of public opinion could not last long and Russell was to be haunted by those cheering crowds for a long time to come. More immediately, his confidence that the Government was not supported in its decision to go to war by the majority of Liberal voters received a severe blow when *The Nation*, that house-journal of the liberal intelligentsia, refused to print his letter. Russell was furious. Just a few hours before war was declared, he had attended *The Nation*'s staff lunch and had discussed his views with the editor, H. J. Massingham, who had agreed to print his letter. The next morning, he received a note from Massingham beginning, 'Today is not yesterday . . .' and withdrawing his promise. Under Russell's indignant protests, however, Massingham agreed, a week later, to publish another letter in the same vein. In this, Russell sounded rather less sure that war lacked popular support and used the cheering crowds as an illustration of the dark and terrible forces that the Government had unleashed:

> Those who saw the London crowds, during the nights leading up to the Declaration of War, saw a whole population, hitherto peaceable and humane, precipitated in a few days down the steep slope to primitive barbarism, letting loose, in a moment, the instinct of hatred and blood-lust against which the whole fabric of society has been raised.

The target of his polemic, however, remained the 'secret diplomacy' of the Foreign Office:

> . . . all this madness, all this rage, all this flaming death of our civilisation and our hopes, has been brought about because a set of official gentlemen, living luxurious lives, mostly stupid, and all without imagination or heart, have chosen that it should occur rather than that any one of them should suffer some infinitesimal rebuff to his country's pride.

Though *The Nation* published this letter, it did so with great reservations, and added to it a disclaimer emphasising the journal's disagreement with Russell's views. After publication of the letter, Russell discovered that the Liberal journals in which it would have been natural for him to publish his thoughts about the war, *The New Statesman* and *The Nation* particularly, refused to carry any further articles from him, and he was forced to publish instead in *The Labour Leader*, the weekly journal of the Independent Labour Party.

Further depressing evidence that, among 'genuine liberals', it was he and not the Cabinet that was out of step with majority opinion came in abundance during the first few days of the war. Returning to Cambridge on 5 August, he found waiting for him a letter from Evelyn Whitehead expressing her support for the war, arguing that Germany was a menace to Europe and that 'we cannot sit still and see France smashed'. The following week he received what he described as 'a *very* war-like letter' from her, expressing her satisfaction and pride at her son North's intention to enlist (he was sent to France as a second-lieutenant in the British Expeditionary Force on 22 August). 'I can't tell you how much I mind,' Russell told Ottoline. 'I feel as if my relations with the whole family could never be quite the same. Next to you they are much the most important people in my life.' Alfred Whitehead wrote to Russell expressing himself 'miserable at differing from you on so great a question', and defending Edward Grey's diplomacy. 'You must remember', Whitehead wrote, 'that the Germany which would emerge victorious is not the Germany of Goethe and Helmholtz, but the Germany of the Kaiser, Bernhardt and Treitschke.'

However, the Whiteheads' defence of the war was sober and muted by comparison with that of H. G. Wells, another Liberal from whom Russell expected better. Within days of the declaration of war, Wells announced in print his great enthusiasm for it. In giving Britain the opportunity to crush German militarism, he argued – coining a phrase that would be repeated *ad nauseam* in the coming years – it would be 'The War that will end War'. At Trinity, Russell found that similar views prevailed among nearly all the dons and he felt 'without any ally' in his opposition to the war. The students, meanwhile, were rushing to enlist, adding to Russell's suffering the pain of vicarious parental concern: 'All the young men in uniforms whom I meet here – peaceable civilised young men, risking life for what seems to them duty – I long to shake them by the hand & wish them Godspeed.' Within a few weeks, over a thousand undergraduates had gone off to fight and Cambridge, like every other town in England, was swamped with troops on their way to France. 'It is impossible to convey to you anything of the horror of these past weeks,' Russell wrote to Lucy Donnelly. 'Events of a month ago seem to belong to a previous existence':

> The little sheltered nook in which we tried to live by thought and reason is swept away in a red blast of hate . . . I met an advanced socialist 2 days ago, who told me he was enlisting because he could imagine no greater joy than to see a German fall to his rifle.

After Philip's brave speech in the House of Commons on 3 August, the Morrells' home in Bedford Square became the meeting-place for a group of politicians and writers opposed to the war, including the Labour leader Ramsay MacDonald; the Quaker Joseph Rowntree; the founder of the Neutrality League, Norman Angell; the journalist, E. D. Morel; and Charles Trevelyan, who had recently resigned from the Government because of his opposition to the war. Russell was invited to join the discussions of this group but left feeling unimpressed. 'They talked of starting a party,' he wrote to Ottoline on 11 August, 'it seemed like 8 fleas talking of building a pyramid.' The next day, he joined three of them – MacDonald, Trevelyan and Morel – for dinner, but declared them 'not exciting – political considerations prevent their feeling whole-heartedly all that ought to be felt'.

Nevertheless, when this group evolved into the Union of Democratic Control (UDC), they published a statement of their aims under the heading 'British Foreign Policy, Anti-War Party Manifesto', which expressed many of the views that Russell himself had been urging: that foreign policy should be brought under democratic parliamentary control; that, after the war, no punitive measures, humiliations or annexations should be imposed upon the defeated nation; and that every attempt should be made to re-establish civilised, harmonious relations between the European powers. It was a mild enough programme and one to which Russell could give his full support, even if it did fall a long way short of expressing 'all that ought to be felt'.

One of the assumptions that guided the thinking of Russell, the UDC and almost everybody else in Britain at this time was that, from Britain's point of view at least, the war would be a short and successful one, a question simply of expelling the Germans from France and Belgium and re-establishing the old borders. (What happened on the Eastern Front was another matter, and, many felt, scarcely anything to do with Britain.) So, at this stage, the focus of anti-war feeling lay not in attempting to persuade the British Government to pull out of the war (now that it had entered the conflict, it was felt, there was no going back), but in convincing both the Government and public opinion at large to take a more humane view of the German people, so that, when – as was certain – Britain defeated it, the victory would not be the cause of further ill-feeling between the two countries. In this spirit, Russell wrote to Charles Trevelyan: 'I feel *very* strongly that until the Germans have been expelled from France & Belgium it is better to confine ourselves to terms of peace and other *future* matters, leaving the past to be dealt with when the country is out of danger.'

Thus the emphasis of Russell's earliest writings on the war was not to oppose the war itself but to combat the hysterical anti-German feeling that was being whipped up by the Government and the Press. Nevertheless, his view that the war on the Western Front had been a ghastly mistake, that there was really no reason at all why the nations of Germany, France and England should be fighting each other, required at least some concern with the past, for otherwise it was entirely mysterious why those countries were fighting each other. Despite what he said to Trevelyan, therefore, Russell found himself time and again committing himself to a view of recent history. It was inevitable for, from his point of view, the most pressing question about the war was: why? In 'War: the Cause and the Cure', the first of his articles for *The Labour Leader*, he argued that Britain was at war 'because it has been decreed by a handful of men: the three Emperors, and the Cabinets of London and Paris'. But, by itself, this would not do, for, as he immediately acknowledged, the haunting, nagging question arises:

Why do ordinary citizens obey their insane commands, and even obey them with enthusiasm, and with the utmost degree of devotion and heroism?

On this occasion, the answer he gave was that those ordinary citizens were afraid:

Except in Russia, where loyalty, race and religion are sufficient incentives, the universal motive to obedience is fear – not a craven or personal fear, but fear for home and wife and children, for liberty and the national life.

By playing on such fears, he argued, the Government, through the Press, was able to create enthusiasm for war, even though 'if time for reflection had been allowed it is almost certain that the voice of sanity would have compelled a peaceful adjustment of the rival interests'.

No sooner had he published this view, however, than he became dissatisfied with it. For, though it might explain why people are prepared to go to war, it did little to explain why they did so joyously, why they celebrated the declaration of war. He thus returned to the question again a few weeks later in 'Why Nations Love War', a paper he wrote for Norman Angell's monthly journal *War and Peace*. This time, he sought the answer in basic, primitive instincts: the instinctual dislike of foreigners, the lust for excitement, the desires for triumph, for honour and for power, a passionate devotion to one's own nation, and so on. Not that, he emphasised, he was suggesting that the impulse to war was ineradicable:

> I do not wish . . . to suggest any pessimism as to the possibility of leading civilised nations to abandon the practice of war . . . It may be hoped that Europe as a whole will be in a pacific mood for some time after the end of the present conflict; and if the ultimate permanent good is to result from the hopes of such a period, it is before all things necessary that the cause of war should be thoroughly understood. I do not believe this is to be found merely in the sins of statesmen, but rather in the standards and desires which civilised nations have inherited from a barbarous past. If this is the case, a stable peace can only be attained by a process of popular education and by a gradual change in the standards of value accepted by men who are considered to be civilised.

The answer, then, lay in applying to whole nations the Conradian psychology that Russell had previously applied to individuals, especially himself. One had to recognise that, beneath the thin civilised crust of Western man, there were powerful, dangerous passions that were the residue of his primitive past. If civilisation – of an individual or of a society – were not to be threatened by these passions, they had to be brought under control, through the exercise of self-discipline (in the case of an individual) and through a process of education and international law (in the case of a nation). 'War arouses the wild beast which is latent in most of us,' as he put it in a later article, and, as he had long since realised from first-hand experience, these 'wild-beast feelings' can, if unchecked, overcome even the most civilised of people.

In pursuing this psychological approach to the problem of war, Russell was leaving the concerns of the UDC somewhat behind, which is presumably one reason why he was dissatisfied with their excessively narrow concentration on exclusively political considerations. For Russell, however much he might agree with the UDC's position on the question of democratic control over foreign policy, there was a far more important issue at stake, and that was nothing less than the survival of civilisation itself. This was why it pained him so much to see Britain fight on Russia's side against Germany, for, on his scale of civilised nations, Germany came a good deal higher than Russia (though not, of course, as high as Britain). Before Britain became involved, his moral assessment of the various participants, as explained to Ottoline in a letter of 1 August, was: 'Germany is wholly disinterested and guided by honour against interest [this was before the Germans marched into Belgium], Serbia is very wicked, Austria still more so; Russia bigoted and emotional . . . France terrified.'

Informing these moral judgments (especially that of Russia) – as Russell made almost embarrassingly clear in a UDC pamphlet he wrote called 'War, the Offspring of Fear' – was a tendency to conceive the war in racial terms, together with firm opinions about the degree to which each European race had triumphed over the barbarism in its soul, how civilised they each were. 'Essentially,' he writes, 'this war . . . is a great race-conflict, a conflict of Teuton and Slav, in which certain other nations, England, France and Belgium, have been led into cooperation with the Slav.' Where his own sympathies lay in this racial conflict was left in no doubt: the Austrians were, he wrote, 'a highly civilised race, half surrounded by Slavs in a relatively backward state of culture', while Serbia was 'a country so barbaric that a man can secure the throne by instigating the assassination of his predecessor', and the Russians were a people in whom 'the consciousness of race and religion is still . . . in that primitive condition from which the Western nations have partially emerged'. As for the Germans, they quite naturally, as Teutons, came to Austria's aid against the Slav, fearing, understandably, that 'it would be their turn next to be overrun by the Russian hordes':

It must not be supposed that this conflict is, on the part of the Teuton, aggressive in substance, whatever it may be in form. In substance it is defensive, the attempt to preserve Central Europe for a type of civilisation indubitably higher and of more value to mankind than that of any Slav State. The existence of the Russian menace on the Eastern border is, quite legitimately, a nightmare to Germany.

'The Western war has not the same ethnic inevitability as the war in the East,' Russell went on to claim. It arose, rather, from an entirely preventable series of follies on the part of the Western Governments, and, so long as diplomacy among the Western Governments was conducted sensibly in the future, such a war might, indeed, be prevented from breaking out again.

At the time of its publication, this pamphlet was criticised by supporters of the war for being pro-German, which to some degree it clearly was, but what is most striking about it now is the violence of its anti-Russian feeling. Germany, it comes close to saying, is right to fight Russia, for in doing so it is defending a higher civilisation. Indeed, ironically, Russell's remarks about Russia in this article (and elsewhere) echo the language of anti-German hysteria – 'barbarian hordes' for instance – to which he was so vehemently opposed. It is as if he had taken a stand, not against hatred, but against hatred specifically of the Germans. Hatred of the Russians, he implies, is only to be expected among civilised people.

Behind this animus towards the Russians, and to some extent fuelling it, was Russell's personal concern for two of the people he held most dear: Joseph Conrad and Ludwig Wittgenstein. 'It is partly Conrad who made me hate Russians,' he acknowledged in a letter to Ottoline. 'I used rather to like them, but he obviously loathes them.' In his letters during the first few months of the war, he several times mentions his anxiety about Conrad and his family, who, the last he had heard of them, were heading for Cracow, right in the middle of the area being fought over by the Russian and Austrian armies. As he knew, Conrad's sympathies in that fight would be with the Austrians. Tormented by the thought that Conrad might be killed by the Russians, Russell took to re-reading *Under Western Eyes*, Conrad's most vehemently anti-Russian work, and tried to get a letter through to Conrad, asking if he was all right.

Russell had earlier, on 28 July, the very day that Austria–Hungary declared war on Serbia, written to Wittgenstein, sending him a copy of 'The Relation of Sense-Data to Physics' and wishing him well. In October, he heard (presumably through David Pinsent) that Wittgenstein had joined the Austrian army and that he, too, was in Cracow. 'People are affected by having their friends in it [the war]', Russell wrote to Ottoline:

> It seems strange that of all the people in the war the one I care for much the most should be Wittgenstein who is an 'enemy'. I feel an absolute conviction that he will not survive – he is reckless & blind & ill. I can know nothing till the war is over. If he does survive, I think the war will have done him good.

When it looked as if the German and Austrian armies were making some progress on the Eastern Front, Russell rejoiced: 'I really rather enjoy seeing Russia defeated, because I feel more and more strongly that in the East the interests of mankind are on the side of Germany and Austria.' Though, naturally, 'I don't wish to see the Germans able to bring troops back to the West.'

Mirroring his conception of what was best for the civilisation of mankind generally was his view of what was best for the civilisation of himself, and, in that respect, he felt that his own private and internal war against the Russians had already been fought and won. He could no longer, that is, read *The Idiot* and see himself in the character of Rogojin. 'All the Dostoyevsky devils that used to haunt me are entirely gone,' he wrote to Ottoline, 'melted away, leaving not a trace . . . I am not afraid to face my own soul, as I was – there are no longer spectres in the dark corners.' In this case, the civilising factor had been the revival of his love for Ottoline:

> I don't think it is the war that has got rid of the devils – they were already gone before that – it was the days in Burnham Beeches I think.

What the war had done was to give his love for Ottoline a wider dimension. That her revulsion against the war was as strong as his own was an enormous comfort to him. They were at one in thought and feeling as they had never been since the earliest days of their relationship. 'We are terribly alone in this dreadful world,' Russell told her:

> I cannot tell you all that your love is to me in these days – it is *much* more to me than ever before – today I felt an absolute fullness of union such as I had hardly thought possible in this world – it is quite beyond words, and as the pain of the outward horror increases, I feel your love increasing too,

sustaining courage and keeping faith alive . . . I do not know what I should have done at this time without you, or whether alone I should have had the inward courage to stand out against the world.

'Now my love for you is welded with love of humanity,' he said in a later letter, 'it wouldn't let me do anything that would be against love of humanity, and as soon as that grows dim I feel less fully united with you than when it is strong.'

Of course, there were limits to his love for humanity, the most publicly evident example of which was his apparent detestation of the entire Russian nation ('I wish people could love each other,' he wrote to Ottoline on 23 November, 'but I *cannot* love the Russians, however hard I try'). Another example closer to home was his apparent immunity to any kind of feeling – affection, sympathy, or even ordinary kindness – for the wretched Helen Dudley. 'She is terribly outside my real life just now,' he told Ottoline a few days after Helen's arrival in England. Helen, naturally, was puzzled and hurt by Russell's attitude towards her, and found his absorption in the war an inadequate explanation. She took a long time to accept the situation and kept pressing Russell to explain it to her. He, however, was determined not to tell her the truth about himself and Ottoline, and so could offer her only unsatisfying and implausible reasons for his change of heart. 'It is impossible to be quite truthful,' he told Ottoline, 'but I said I should hate her if I departed in the slightest from mere friendship, and that I felt the same impulse as had made mediaeval people take to celibacy.' Understandably, Helen took a good deal of persuading that Mr Apollinax had become a monk, and she became increasingly bewildered, lonely and, eventually, heartbroken.

The most Russell felt he could do for her was to dissuade her father from taking her straight back to the United States, arguing that, as a promising writer, she ought to meet London's literary society. Her father, however, wanted reassurance that Helen would be taken care of by a responsible household, so Russell, with extraordinarily little regard for the potential consequences, suggested the Morrells' house in Bedford Square. Ottoline, after some hesitation and protest, was persuaded to co-operate with this bizarre idea, about which Russell's only apparent qualm was that Helen might find out the true nature of his relationship with Ottoline. 'I don't think she realises *quite* what you and I are to each other,' he wrote on 12 August, 'and there is no reason why she should':

> It would be very unfortunate if she thought you had anything to do with my change towards her; she certainly doesn't know, and has (so far as I can see) *no* feeling or suspicion towards you. I am sorry you should have this to attend to just now, but I do think it is really important for her to be able to stay.

So, in the middle of August 1914, Helen moved in with Ottoline, whom she henceforth treated with gratitude, admiration and devotion, and whom she took into her confidence about her problems with Russell. For her part, Ottoline's sympathy for Helen was aroused the very day she arrived, when her belongings were unpacked and Ottoline, seeing her cases stuffed full of pretty dresses and underwear (actually, she describes them as 'very over-decorated, cheap and vulgar', but clearly Helen thought they were pretty), realised 'with what hopes and preparations for a honeymoon she had come'. In Ottoline's recollection, Helen was:

> an odd creature of about twenty-seven, rather creeping and sinuous in her movements, with a large head, a fringe cut across her forehead, and thick lips. Her voice was soft, though she spoke with a strong accent, but she did not at all belong to the self-assertive, strident type of American woman: on the contrary, she was languid and adhesive, sympathetic but insensitive and phlegmatic, and entirely without self-assertion.

As Ottoline was the one kind friend in London that Helen had, she told her everything. 'Like a beaten and caged animal', as Ottoline put it, she 'would pace endlessly up and down the room like a panther, pouring out to me all her disappointment, and handing me Bertie's letters to read'. Not realising the trouble that it might make between himself and Ottoline, Russell encouraged this intimacy. 'You were *perfect* with H. D.,' he told her, '& did all that was necessary. She was *very* much touched by your kindness – No, she could not have made me happy; & now she is blotted out.' He was, perhaps, thinking of the role Evelyn Whitehead had played with regard to Alys when he began his affair with Ottoline, listening to Alys's confidences and passing them on to him. However, just as it had then not occurred to Russell that this traffic in confidences might work two ways, and that Evelyn might be passing on to Alys things that he had told her, so now he seemed naively to assume that Ottoline's loyalty and affection for him would remain entirely unaffected by becoming Helen's intimate *confidante*.

In fact, listening to Helen's heart-rending story, and reading Russell's letters to her, had a devastating effect on Ottoline's feelings for Russell, destroying the faith in him that she had re-built since his return from America and severely undermining both her respect for him and her belief in his love. 'He is very odd,' she wrote in her journal:

> for he made great love to her, and told her that he was hers for eternity, and wrote passionate letters to her; and now it is apparently all gone . . . Poor girl, it has been an awful blow to her . . . I feel very keenly the disappointment in Bertie myself. He used all these extravagant terms of devotion to me such a short time ago, and now they are all gone, and he professed to her all the things he professed to me.
>
> Why should one mind? But one does.
>
> After all, why should one wish to curtail love? But one does . . . it makes one grin and mock . . . I feel that this has made me much more detached inside, less believing in love, and more disliking anything that has the tinge of physical love in it.

Over the next few weeks, Ottoline began to reproach both herself and Russell for Helen's misery, while Russell tried in various (entirely unconvincing) ways to insist on Ottoline's irrelevance to his change of attitude towards Helen and on Helen's irrelevance to his feelings for Ottoline. '*Please* don't think anything that has happened is your fault,' he urged her, contradicting what he had said earlier, 'all wd. have gone well but for the war.' As for his own part in Helen's unhappiness, and the fact that he had been less than honest with both of them, he could do little else but admit that he had been in the wrong and hope that it would not matter too much. 'I am profoundly sorry that I have not been straight either with you or with Helen,' he wrote to Ottoline on 21 August. 'I had no idea she had anything to tell you that would surprise you. I told you the truth, and I told her what I *hoped* was the truth, tho' it wasn't. I mind *much more* having robbed you of what you valued – but I *hope* in time that will grow less . . . At present I simply have not room for her in my feelings. And I hope with all my heart that as long as you live I shall not again try any second relation.'

Two days later, having received from Ottoline a letter that made him see that 'the wound is even deeper than I thought', Russell tried a different explanation, so implausible that it smacks of desperation. What had caused the change in his feelings for Helen, he now claimed, was not Ottoline, but 'the realisation that I should lose the power of being of use to people', for he realised that Helen would not understand these philanthropic impulses, 'and so I saw that I could not share the religious side with her':

> *Please* make yourself believe that the things I said to you were not said lightly, or that there has ever been *any* lack of depth in my feeling for you. *It is not true* . . . I have been terribly to blame towards H. D., but you can surely see from the course of events that my feeling for you has been of a different quality. In the first days, while I was travelling home, I did not know this; but I know it now. However, if you think I am still only making phrases, I cannot wonder – only time can really persuade you.

The letter ended with Russell once more on his knees: 'O My Dearest do forgive me.'

Ottoline melted and came, as usual, to Russell's flat the following Tuesday. There she discovered a new aspect to the whole sorry business, a new dimension to Helen's pathetic plight, Russell's coldness in the face of it, and her own part in the duplicity. Helen, it transpired, was in the habit of going to Russell's flat and knocking insistently on the door, knowing, or at least suspecting, that Russell was inside ignoring her. Thus, while Ottoline was there she recalls, 'we heard knock, knock, knock, and hands banging on the door. Bertie refused to open it as he was sure it was she, and I imagined her crying and panting outside. I felt afraid that when I came out I should find a crumpled, collapsed lump of a woman on the stone landing. It was a horrible feeling.' Her feelings of guilt can hardly have been assuaged by Russell's almost jubilant tone in his letter to her that night:

> My Darling Darling – It was *wonderfully* happy today – tho' it was painful when Helen rang at the door – it seemed so intolerably brutal – But it could

not spoil the great great joy of feeling at one with you again. I have had lately such a *much* greater sense of oneness with you in the great things – and I never have the very smallest atom now of the impulses that used to make me say things to you that hurt, or to be rough with you as I used to be . . . Dearest, my heart is so full I can hardly write – I have never felt such a depth of love and reverence for you as now – and without any wish to make selfish demands. I do hope I shall give you less pain henceforth.

Ottoline's reaction to this strange and rather horrible situation was complicated. On the one hand, of course, it was painful for her to listen to Helen's confidences about her suffering at Russell's hands while she knew herself to be (whatever Russell might say) part of the cause of that suffering – especially when Helen told her that she knew Russell was often inside when she knocked on his door, because she could hear his breathing through the door. On the other hand, there seems to have been a part of Ottoline that exulted in her triumph over her rival. During those very days of imagining opening Russell's door and finding Helen a 'crumpled, collapsed lump of a woman' on the doorstep, Ottoline's letters to Russell are charged with the most uncharacteristic sense of sexual excitement and fulfilment. 'Yes, indeed,' she wrote the day after her visit to his flat, 'nothing has ever been so wonderful as these moments. We are absolutely one, all the hindrances and barriers gone and just the absolute union between us. All my being, spiritual and physical, flowed with you.' Two days later, she wrote that Russell was right to be firm with Helen and told him again 'how wonderful every time is to me, my darling . . . I love to feel that you take possession of me more and more.'

But, after all, this rival was also a pathetically unhappy person who treated Ottoline as her best friend, and, in the end, Ottoline's sympathy for Helen and her outrage at Russell overcame her sense of rivalry. 'I am very very sorry that H. D. goes on telling things that bother you,' Russell wrote to her on 29 August, '*do* try to stop her – there is no use in her telling them, and you really know all about it now':

Nothing on earth would induce me ever again to go an inch beyond friendship with her. Her selfishness does not make me *dislike* her, tho' it might make me *hate* her if I were made to suffer by it.

As Helen did not believe that Russell was in earnest about his reasons for not seeing her, he added, 'I must make her realise it by being unyielding. You need not fear that she could make me budge an inch whatever she might do now.'

In fact, to make matters worse, this last statement was not true; Russell was *not* entirely unyielding. In the account of his affair with Helen Dudley that he offers in his *Autobiography*, Russell mentions – with a casualness that in the context is rather disturbing – that, after she came to England, even though he no longer had any passion for her, he 'had relations with her from time to time . . . and I broke her heart'. What he apparently did not bargain for was that, whenever he chose to 'have relations' with her, she would tell Ottoline all about it, leaving him with some explaining to do. 'You *can't* say I have deceived her since she came,' he insisted in a letter to Ottoline:

> I saw her here yesterday (she proposed herself) – at first I was aloof – She begged me not to be – I said we must talk things out first – she said she couldn't talk now, but had made up her mind for more friendship after the next few days, but wanted to wait a few days before coming to that. Then I yielded and became affectionate. She made me promise to give her one night – this morning I have written retracting the promise – I *can't* do it – it would drive me mad – When I am pompous and stiff it is always a cloak for shame.

As evidence that he had not deceived Helen, he wrote out for Ottoline a letter he had received from her rival:

> I feel we must talk things over as soon as possible. Reduced to its lowest form this seems to be what you feel about me. Your feeling for me no longer belongs with the deepest things in your nature, but whenever you have time you would like to embrace me if it wouldn't 'encourage' me.

This, however, may be evidence less for Russell's openness with her than for Helen's insight into his character

By now, Russell realised something of the effect this situation was having on Ottoline's feelings for him, and he became more strident. 'It is a downright falsehood that I asked her to go all lengths,' he began in one of his many letters, trying to dig himself out of the hole that he had landed himself in. 'Don't let us spend all our time talking about her this afternoon . . . I do so want to get away from this horribly personal tangle, which seems so degrading at this time – I am turning to hatred of her, which I don't want to do. But I must let my nerves get a rest from her if I am not to hate her.'

What, from Ottoline's point of view, was particularly undermining of her faith in Russell was the discovery that he had written some of his most passionate letters to Helen at the very time when she and Russell had been meeting every Tuesday for walks around Burnham Beeches; at the time, that is, that he was writing to Ottoline doubting that he had any affection left at all for Helen. Was there any reason to think that he was telling her the truth, while lying to Helen? Even if there were, was there any comfort in that? Russell was caught, as it were, red-handed and could only try to brazen it out:

> Will you try to make up your mind that I have behaved very badly, that I am so full of shame that at moments I can hardly face you, and that I have had a lesson which will keep me from anything of the sort again. And please please don't think you were in a fool's paradise at Burnham Beeches – it is quite untrue . . . What is past is past, and *that* is the truth now. I really don't think it is good for any of us that you should go on letting yourself hear her talk about me. There is nothing new, and it is merely upsetting; and I don't believe it can do her any good after this. There is

not the *faintest chance* of any revival of the feeling I had for her – it is utterly dead, and when a thing is really dead it never revives. If it were not selfish, I should wish most intensely never to see her again. I made an absolute mistake – I never was as fond of her as I thought, and towards the end I forced the note from a hope of being able not to hurt her . . . Dearest, whatever I may have said and done and thought, it has been you *only* that I have truly loved ever since that first Sunday in Bedford Square . . . Just when we have found each other again after years of difficulty, it would be too dreadful if a ghost came between us.

Faced with the possibility of losing Ottoline, Russell's attitude to Helen hardened still further. He would not now open the door of his flat to anyone, in case it might be Helen. 'When you come,' he wrote to Ottoline on 3 September, 'please use your key. Then I need not answer any knocking or ringing.' That day, Helen 'came and knocked ever so long . . . Poor girl, I wish I had not been so headstrong in giving her hopes – but the whole thing is utterly dead – I haven't even the remnant of affection now.'

The next day, he agreed to meet the increasingly desperate Helen, but only out of doors. He told her that he would never again meet her in his flat. Then, he told Ottoline:

she asked if I was in yesterday when she knocked, and I said I was. She said it had been undignified of her to come and you had been shocked; but she kept her tone unemotional. Altogether she made matters easier than I thought she would. Words cannot describe how icy cold I felt towards her – it is really dreadful . . . I can't say how thankful I shall be when she is gone . . . I have such a dread of losing your love that it freezes everything – it has been a paralysing terror all this time.

Ottoline, finding the situation now intolerable, and finding, too, that Helen got on her nerves – she smoked too much, and had a habit of coming to Ottoline in the dead of the night to talk to her about her personal life – decided she could no longer bear to have Helen in her house. She persuaded her friend, the writer Gilbert Cannan, and his wife Mary to take Helen on as a paying guest for a while, after which Helen was packed off to lodgings in Chelsea. To enable her to survive on her own, Ottoline helped to find her a job, and, rather than desert Helen completely, invited her to dinner at Bedford Square once a week to keep an eye on her. Russell professed himself 'amused & pleased' that Ottoline had found work for Helen, and, in response to Ottoline's feelings of guilt at having abandoned a person in need, advised her: 'Never mind if she is hurt.'

After her move to Chelsea, Russell met Helen for what he hoped would be one last time in a restaurant and 'kept things as impersonal as I could'. He now discovered that 'I no longer find it difficult or even very painful to resist' her pleas, and the meeting 'passed off without misadventure'. He was now quite without compunction – 'She is too much of a fighter to appeal to one's sympathy long' – though he admitted the next day that 'I grow hot with shame whenever I think of her.' It was not, however, to be quite the last he saw of her. Before her return to America (a move that Russell now encouraged), she arrived unannounced and evidently very unhappy at his flat on 11 October:

> I wouldn't let her in, & though she asked me for a glass of water I kept her waiting on the stairs while I fetched it. I made her go home & walked as far as the door of her lodgings with her. She says she is terribly lonely. She swore she would not come to my flat again, & said she didn't want to see me again for some weeks. It was painful seeing her.

By these drastic measures Russell successfully fended her off, and Helen went back to Chicago a chastened and broken spirit. Her time in London had not been entirely without compensations, however. Chiefly through Ottoline, she made enough contacts to allow her to think it worth while to make another attempt at entering London's literary society, and towards the end of January 1915 she was back, this time with her sister. 'Fancy Helen being back!' Russell commented, on hearing the news. 'What a bore. I thought she was gone for good.' She eventually did leave for good in 1919, after she and her sister had been for a while Russell's tenants in his Bury Street flat. The last time Russell saw her was in 1924, when he visited her in Chicago during a lecture tour to find that she was suffering from multiple sclerosis and was partly paralysed. Russell found her disturbing. 'When I talked with her, I could feel dark, insane thoughts lurking in the background.' A few years later, on another lecture tour, he visited the Dudleys again, to be told that Helen had suffered a mental collapse and was now completely insane. 'In her insanity,' Russell wrote, 'she told her father all that had happened.' After that, presumably, he was no longer welcome as a guest of the family.

The cost of freeing himself from Helen was that his relations with Ottoline returned to what they had been before he returned from America. Or, rather, they entered a new phase altogether, free from the turmoil of earlier years, but free too from the passion and intimacy of the previous few months. Ottoline was now, for Russell, first and foremost a rock of support for the stand he was taking about the war. This she continued to be, even while her romantic feelings for him were bruised and, for the moment, almost destroyed. 'I quite understand your feeling dead,' Russell wrote to her on 14 October, at the start of the new Cambridge term. 'I do too, except for a deep-down feeling of clinging to you and getting strength from you.'

At Cambridge, Russell had few students and felt disinclined to immerse himself again in academic work. He had arranged to give the prestigious Herbert Spencer Lecture at Oxford in November, but found it enormously difficult to concentrate on it. 'It is terribly hard to think of philosophy,' he wrote to Ottoline. When, a few days later, he received an invitation to give a paper at Manchester University in the New Year, he replied: 'Are there really people in Manchester interested in philosophy still? I am not. I will do my best, but I am afraid I have no *new* ideas.' A week before he was due to give the Oxford lecture, it was still unfinished: 'It worries me, because I can't get interested, or feel that it matters whether I do it well or ill. It will bring me £20, but it will be a miserable pot-boiler.'

Indeed, it was. Called 'On Scientific Method in Philosophy', it consisted almost entirely of thoughts that he had already expressed more vividly in print several times before. The only new element was a piece of vitriol against philosophers, of which Russell was immensely proud, providing as it did some expression of his nauseous reaction against the whole discipline. Arguing against the assumption of progress in the evolutionary philosophy of Bergson, Russell quoted a story from the Chinese sage Chuang Tzu about a Grand Augur debating with himself whether or not to eat a pig. Entertaining first his own and then the pig's point of view, the Grand Augur finally rejects the pig's standpoint and proceeds to eat the meat. 'In what sense, then,' asks Chuang Tzu, 'was he different from the pigs?' Similarly, Russell argues mischievously, the evolutionists who see the progress of life in terms of the development from the protozoon to the philosopher fail to look at the thing from the protozoon's point of view, and, to that extent, 'too often resemble the Grand Augur and the pigs'.

When he sent a copy of the paper to Ralph Perry at Harvard, Russell told him that its real title was 'Philosophers and Pigs', and that it was 'inspired by the bloodthirstyness of professors here and in Germany. I gave it at Oxford, and it produced all the disgust I had hoped.' On 18 November, immediately after giving the paper, he wrote to Ottoline saying that he had not lingered over the event, being in Oxford for a total of three hours. The occasion had done nothing to restore his respect for philosophers. Of the dons who attended, Professor Poulson was 'a stupid old stick-in-the mud', Gilbert Murray 'as squashy as a slug', J. A. Smith a pontificator, and Schiller a 'bounder and cad'. The paper, he said, had been 'designed to infuriate the Oxford pundits', and in this respect it had been a success: 'What I hate is their attempt to make an impressive manner a cloak for complete intellectual atrophy. They were very nice to me personally.'

Russell thought of abandoning the academic life altogether: 'If I could earn an income by journalism or otherwise, I think there would be great deal to be said for leaving Cambridge & throwing myself into work for peace – probably chiefly through the labour people & foreign socialists':

> It is clear the Socialists are the hope of the world; they have gained in importance during this war. I would swallow socialism for the sake of peace. What I can do further in philosophy does not interest me, & seems trivial compared to what might be done elsewhere . . . I can't bear the sheltered calm of university life – I want battle & stress, & the feeling of doing something. I might get a year's leave of absence from here as a time of experiment. What do you think?

As a sort of compromise between academic work and campaigning journalism, Russell agreed to write for *The International Journal of Ethics* an article on 'The Ethics of War'. When he finished it, he sent it to Ottoline, saying that it was 'meant to be very aloof & philosophical, but it is not'. Nor was it the pacifist tract that many might have expected. Russell, indeed, never was a pacifist. As he told Ottoline before he began the paper: 'I don't think war *always* wrong . . . I think our Civil War & the American Civil War were justified on one side. I think it is always wrong when it is for mere national self-interest. But I find I can't take Tolstoy's extreme position.'

In fact, the position he took justifies a surprising amount of bloodshed. Categorising wars into four main types – wars of colonisation, wars of principle, wars of self-defence and wars of prestige – he argued that, when judging the ethics of war, the general principle should be adopted that, if a war furthered civilisation it was justified but otherwise not. This, according to him, justified most wars of colonisation and of principle, some wars of self-defence (those against an inferior civilisation), but no wars of prestige. Thus, 'the conflicts of Europeans with American–Indians, Maoris, and other aborigines in temperate regions' are, for him, the very paradigm of just wars, for, though often ruthless and 'devoid of *technical* justification', they are justified by their consequences: 'if we judge by results, we cannot regret that such wars have taken place . . . [for] it is chiefly through such wars that the civilised portion of the world has been extended from the neighbourhood of the Mediterranean to the greater part of the earth's surface.' Accepting that such wars were for the most part little more than armed theft and that 'many humane people will object in theory to the justification of this form of robbery', Russell nevertheless insisted that, for example, 'the process by which the American continent has been acquired for European civilisation' is entirely justified by the fact that, in this and other cases, there is 'a very great and undeniable difference between the civilisation of the colonisers and that of the dispossessed natives'. Armed theft is virtuous, it seems, so long as the victim is of an 'inferior' civilisation.

The English and American civil wars were, in Russell's view, justified as wars of principle, where 'the progress of mankind depends upon the adoption of certain beliefs or institutions, which, through blindness or natural depravity, the other side will not regard as reasonable'. The idea that the First World War was a war of this type, a war in defence of democracy, he dismissed as absurd on the grounds that, whatever Britain's ally Russia was fighting for, it was not democracy. Indeed, it becomes increasingly clear throughout the article that there can be no possible justification for a war between two civilised nations like Britain and Germany: 'If the facts were understood, wars amongst civilised nations would cease owing to their inherent absurdity.' Self-defence is, in itself, no justification: if attacked by a civilised country, the sensible and wise policy would be to do nothing: 'As between civilised nations, non-resistance would seem not only a distant religious ideal, but the course of practical wisdom. Only pride and fear stand in the way of its adoption.' And, of course, fighting for prestige is not the sort of thing a civilised nation does. Thus, all in all: 'When this great tragedy has worked itself out to its disastrous conclusion . . . the nations will perhaps realise that they have fought in blindness and delusion.'

What shocks the reader now about this article – its view that the forcible seizure of a people's land and property is justifiable when committed by an advanced civilisation upon a primitive one – went unremarked upon at the time of its publication. Russell's comments about non-resistance, however, attracted a good deal of forceful criticism, not least from Ralph Perry in Harvard, who was moved to write a rejoinder, to which Russell in turn replied in a later issue of *The International Journal of Ethics*, removing what he claimed was a misapprehension. He had never intended to imply, he insisted, that Britain should have adopted a policy of non-resistance to German aggression. Britain, he appeared to believe, could have prevented the war on the Western Front by promising to remain neutral in Germany's war with Russia if Germany, in turn, refrained from invading France and Belgium. Now that such a policy had not been adopted and that war had broken out, it was indeed, Russell conceded, in the interests of civilisation that Britain should defeat Germany – though not that it should, in the language popular at the time, 'smash' or 'destroy' it. In other articles he published at about the same time on the same theme, he argued that the best course of action for the population of an invaded country to adopt (and the one the British should adopt in the unlikely event that Germany tried to govern them) was one of passive resistance to the occupying power, of the sort that Gandhi would later use to great effect to make India ungovernable by the British.

In the controversies into which he was drawn by 'The Ethics of War', 'War, the Offspring of Fear' and his other pamphlets and articles, Russell was made increasingly aware that his position relied upon a set of somewhat contentious assumptions about the nature and history of diplomatic relations between Britain, France and Germany. In particular, as he was forced to admit, he assumed too readily that Britain could have remained neutral in a war between France and Germany. Recognising that the Anglo–French *Entente* of 1904 made this impossible, Russell's attentions turned to the history of that agreement, and, when invited to contribute an article to the American liberal magazine *The Atlantic Monthly*, he submitted a 6,000-word analysis of diplomatic relations called 'Is a Permanent Peace Possible?' Ottoline found it dull, and for a while her reaction shook Russell's faith in it. The editor of the magazine, Ellery Sedgwick, however, pronounced it 'admirable in every way', and was only too keen to commission more such articles from Russell. This not only opened up a lucrative market for his journalism, it also gave him the chance to influence liberal public opinion in the United States, a country whose neutrality he considered crucial to the successful resolution of the war.

The article begins with the premise that 'War between civilised States is both wicked and foolish' and asks how, that being so, France, Germany and Britain find themselves at war with one another. The answer, he says, is that 'The present war springs from the rivalry of States. And the rivalry of States springs from certain erroneous beliefs, inspired and encouraged by pride and fear.' Thus 'If wars between civilised States are to cease, these beliefs must be seen to be mistaken, pride must take a different form, fear must become groundless, and the machinery of international relations must no longer be designed solely for rivalry.' In understanding the causes of the war, Russell argues, 'the diplomacy of the last fortnight may be left altogether out of account.' It was not true, as he had apparently believed, that the war could have been averted up to the last minute by Sir Edward Grey. The mad, headlong rush into war during the last weeks of July was but the logical consequence of earlier diplomatic manoeuvres: 'Ever since the conclusion of the Anglo-French *Entente* in 1904 the war had been on the point of breaking out.' What needed to be understood, therefore, were the fears, beliefs and events that produced the *Entente*. As Russell saw it, these were as follows:

> The annexation of Alsace-Lorraine had produced a profound estrangement between France and Germany. Russia and Germany became enemies through the Pan-Slavist agitation, which threatened the Austrian influence in the Balkans and even the very existence of the Austro-Hungarian State. Finally the German determination to build a powerful Navy drove England in to the arms of Russia and France.

So, under the terms of the *Entente*, Britain agreed to support France in acquiring Morocco at Germany's expense, and the French agreed to Britain's occupation of Egypt. Likewise, under the terms of the analogous Anglo-Russian *Entente*, Britain accepted the partition of Persia (giving Russia control of the northern half) in return for control of Afghanistan. The false belief guiding all this dangerous and shameful diplomacy was that the interests of England and Germany were in competition, so that what was bad for Germany was necessarily good for England, whereas the truth was that, from a commercial point of view, they were each other's best customers, that 'when Germany is prosperous England is prosperous'. Yet, stupidly, Britain had been prepared – in 1905 and again in 1911 – to go to war with Germany for the sake of allowing France to call Morocco 'French'. Lacking any possible economic justification, this could only have been for the sake of a childish and foolish pride, for, aside from that, 'what does it matter to either France or Germany which of them owns Morocco?' If this kind of absurdity was to end, if a permanent peace was possible, then genuine self-interest must triumph over foolish notions of 'prestige', and 'men must learn to find their nation's glory in the victory of reason over brute instincts'.

In its attempts to unmask the irrational fears and vainglorious pride that lay behind international politics, Russell's article, perhaps, presented less a history of diplomacy than a psychology of it. The war, he told Ottoline on 20 November, had shattered his illusions about the power of reason in human beings and provided him with a 'pitiless insight into the hidden springs of beliefs and faiths and hopes':

> Underneath I still have faith in human possibilities, but it is slight – I feel very much as if I had been dropped from another planet into an alien race.

This last image, borrowed from *Amy Foster*, shows that during the war Russell pictured himself more than ever as Yanko Goorall, 'full of goodwill which nobody wanted', unable to make contact with the people around him and regarded by them with suspicion and fear.

Conrad himself was now back in England. Russell made urgent attempts to contact him and to see him, but discovered that Conrad was so devastated by his recent experiences that he felt ill and unable to see anybody. He would, in any case, do little to assuage Russell's feelings of alienation, for, as Russell was soon to discover to his great disappointment, Conrad was fiercely patriotic about the war, happy to see his son Borys enlist in the British army and quite determined to do something himself to help the war effort.

At Cambridge, Russell's situation was like Yanko Goorall's, not only in the metaphorical sense that his old friends – the Whiteheads, Gilbert Murray, and so on – were now alien to him, but also in the literal sense that he was surrounded by foreigners. 'The people who come to my lectures', he told Ottoline, 'are two Americans, an Italian, a Jap, & a woman – not a single male Englishman.' As he put it to his old student (now a lecturer at St Andrews), C. D. Broad: 'All the white men are gone or are drilling.' Broad had written Russell a cheering letter congratulating him on his stand and contrasting it with the 'hopeless' attitudes of the philosophy lecturers at his own university, St Andrews. According to Broad one of the most famous of the philosophers there, G. F. Stout: 'goes about talking of the love of freedom which is (under all disguises) the essence of the Slavonic soul':

> As you may know, Stout's foible has always been military tactics, & he now continually discusses them. It would be gratifying to General Joffre to learn how entirely his strategy is approved by the Professor of Logic in St Andrews.

Another member of the philosophy staff, Morrison, 'apparently holds that, while it is always dangerous to use one's reason on political questions, it becomes criminal in time of war'. Meanwhile, the university authorities had put up a notice saying that it thought every able-bodied male student ought to join the Officer's Training Corps. 'The odd thing is', wrote Broad, 'that no one thought it funny or disgusting that a body of fat & stupid old gentlemen should advise young, attractive & promising men to go & get shot in order that nothing might endanger its incomes.' The tone of Broad's letter was a great comfort to Russell, whose attention was immediately drawn to Broad's use of the word 'attractive'. Copying the letter out for Ottoline, he remarked: 'As you might gather, he is homosexual, which makes men much more alive to the dreadfulness of war.'

Despite these glimmers of encouragement, Russell suffered greatly from his isolation. His estrangement from the Whiteheads, particularly, was a source of great remorse. 'I feel the Whiteheads *terribly*,' he told Ottoline. 'I feel the anguish they must be suffering about North – and for the first time since I have known them well I can't give sympathy that will be any good. It is ghastly.' Also: 'The sense of estrangement from one's country is terrible.' The closeness he had shared with Ottoline during the first few days of the war had been an important compensation, but now, since her disillusionment with him over Helen Dudley, there, too, he began to feel the pain of separation. By the middle of December, he felt utterly defeated:

The war has destroyed my ambition. I had put it into philosophy, but that now seems trivial; & I can't compel myself not to feel impotent in the matter of peace and international relations. I could sink into doing nothing for the rest of my days. I seem to have lost all passion, both selfish & unselfish.

While relations between himself and Ottoline were at a low ebb, he needed above all to keep himself occupied, as he tried to explain in a letter of 22 December:

I wish I could make you understand that physical things with you have been quite as sacred and spiritual to me as they have to you. But I suppose it is not a thing any woman could understand. It seems so tragic that this should come just when I had really ceased to feel the grudge I had against you – which I only got rid of when I got back from America – But for this ghost we might now have a real happiness in each other. You would not feel as you do if you *really* understood, but I expect that is physiologically impossible. It was entirely the feeling of failure with you that made me so pessimistic yesterday – it is always that that causes my fits of despair . . . At first what you said brought back my spectres – the vague terror always ready to pounce as soon as my mind is not occupied. But I can avoid that by keeping busy.

He spent Christmas with the Whiteheads, which, he said, 'passed off peacefully'. North was home on leave and had become (according to Russell) 'pro-German'. What lifted Russell's spirits most, however, was the germination in his mind of the idea for a big and important book: a detailed study of international politics. 'I feel *intensely* interested,' he wrote to Ottoline on 26 December, '& I *feel* the book – it is very much alive in me. It will be a merciless savage attack on the whole tradition of diplomacy in all countries . . . The book feels *natural* just as matter did – I believe in it, & feel confident I can make it a really *important* book – it will be a vehicle for an immense volume of pent-up passion.' Buoyed up by the idea of the book, Russell now felt, he told Ottoline, very happy: 'about you, & my work, & my morals – all three hang together'. With regard to the third: 'I have a really firm resolve to avoid philandering in future. I feel inwardly & profoundly that it is unworthy.'

The strength of this resolution was about to be put to the test. For, just as Russell had decided, firmly, inwardly and profoundly, that philandering was unworthy, Ottoline had decided – for reasons that remain obscure – to put temptation his way. In October, Ottoline's old friend, the writer Vernon Lee (they had known each other since before the turn of the century) had arrived back from Italy, accompanied by a young, attractive and intelligent companion called Irene Cooper-Willis. After meeting her at lunch with Vernon, Ottoline came to think that Irene was the perfect person to relieve Russell's loneliness, and several times urged him to take her out for a meal. Finally, in December, she succeeded in getting them both together at a dinner party at

Bedford Square, and, as she had hoped, they took to each other immediately. Irene arranged to meet Russell regularly for private and informal tutorials on Spinoza, and Russell became increasingly charmed by her and convinced of her intellectual abilities.

Irene Cooper-Willis has been described by her friend Enid Bagnold as 'beautiful, severe and Spanish-looking . . . She had dark hair which curled over her ears, held in with a pair of dark green combs . . . Her white collar and cascading linen frill gave her a Portia-like air . . . She looked always as though to answer a Shylock – with beautiful, indignant gravity, shy, but rigid for the right'. Like her friend Vernon Lee, Irene was fervently committed to the pacifist cause, and, when Russell told her of the book he was planning to write on diplomatic history, she at once offered to help as his research assistant. On 29 December, they met to discuss the project. The only barrier in the way of Irene's plan to help Russell was Vernon Lee, to whom Irene felt her first loyalties lay. If Vernon returned to Florence in the New Year, Irene told Russell, she would feel obliged to accompany her, if that is what Vernon wanted. On 2 January 1915, therefore, Russell went to tea with Vernon and the two fought over the right to Irene's assistance. As Russell described it to Ottoline:

> She [Vernon Lee] spoke of Miss C W as if she had been her property – said 'I intend her to work for me' – told me the work she meant to give her was more intelligent than what I planned; then, when I explained how much intelligence I was going to expect of her, she said Miss C W had not enough initiative for that, & could only do mechanical work under direction . . . She said everything she could to discourage me, & was obviously prepared to fight with any weapons, however unscrupulous.

Somehow, Russell won the fight. Vernon did not, in the end, leave for Italy, and perhaps that, for Irene, was the deciding factor. Perhaps she decided that working with Russell would be more interesting than working for Vernon, and that, if Vernon was going to stay in London (which, it seems, she did throughout the war), then she could combine researching Russell's book with seeing Vernon practically every day. In any case, starting on 4 January, Irene went daily to the British Museum to do research for Russell, coming to his flat (practically next door to the museum) in the afternoon for tea and to continue her Spinoza studies.

To guide her research, Russell wrote a twenty-five-page synopsis of the book that he wanted to write. Entitled 'Principles and Practice in Foreign Policy', it was an extension of his very first statement on the war, his view that the war was a betrayal of the 'friends of progress' by the Liberal Government they had elected. It begins in 1906, the year of the election, and contrasts the ostensible issues on which that election had been fought with the policies carried out by the Liberals once in power:

> All friends of progress remember the high hopes inspired by the triumph of 1906 . . . The electors in 1906 imagined that they were voting against

Chinese Labour, Tariff Reform, and wars of aggression. They were mistaken. They were voting to support France in the conquest of Morocco, even at the expense of war with Germany.

Guided by this document, Irene's task was to search back issues of *The Times* looking for material to use to illustrate Russell's basic thesis.

In Russell's mind, the project had now grown into a two-volume work, of which the study of British foreign policy summarised in 'Principles and Practice in Foreign Policy' was to be but the first and smaller volume. The second was to be an ambitious study of European history in general since 1870. Where the first would point to the need for democratic control of British foreign policy, the second would suggest some kind of international reform of diplomatic relations. Russell anticipated that the first volume 'might get done in a year', and presumably imagined himself to be working on the second for many years to come. Not that he was in the slightest bit daunted: 'I love the idea of doing it,' he told Ottoline. In fact, for one reason or another, the project was laid aside after just a few months, and the second book was never even started. Material gathered and written for the first book, however, was eventually used in *The Policy of the Entente, 1904–1914*, which Russell published at the end of 1915 as a reply to Gilbert Murray's defence of British foreign policy, *The Foreign Policy of Sir Edward Grey, 1906–1915*.

Beginning what was intended to be a vast new piece of work had its customary rejuvenating effect on Russell. 'I feel a new man,' he wrote on 3 January, 'full of life & fight, not at all passive or old.' Adding to this sense of new vigour and hope was the pleasure of seeing Irene Cooper-Willis every day. An attractive, intelligent woman, interested in Spinoza, committed to the cause of peace and, evidently, deeply fascinated by Russell himself, Irene was, as Ottoline had foreseen, just the sort of companion Russell craved. On 2 January, before he began to work with Irene, Russell had told Ottoline: 'The world would be a cold & lonely place to me but for you.' Now, inevitably, he began to entertain hopes that Irene too might help to make his world a little less cold and lonely. Ottoline continued to encourage these hopes, presenting Russell with a rather odd situation, and one that he found extremely difficult to come to terms with. Could Ottoline really be encouraging him to take up with someone else? If so, did that mean his relationship with Ottoline was coming to an end, that she wanted to get rid of him? Divided between a strong inclination to pursue Irene and a sense that, somehow, to do so would be to fall into a trap and lose Ottoline for good, Russell spent the following week in a state of bewildered indecision and anxiety.

'It was a queer talk we had about Miss C W,' he wrote to Ottoline on 7 January:

At present I have not the *slightest* impulse towards anything of the sort – but it may grow in time I suppose. But if so it would be not from passion but for the sake of companionship. However I suppose I may be wrong about that. I have made so many mistakes that I incline to rely on your opinion, which seems to be very definite & emphatic on this occasion.

I don't know how much unselfishness there is in your view – I feel it would
be a relief to you not to feel responsible for my happiness.

After Ottoline's reaction to his affair with Helen Dudley, he was extremely
wary. 'My Darling, it is *you* that I love,' he emphasised at the end of the
letter, 'all the passion & yearning, all that is infinite in me, goes out to you.
All that is not easily transferred.'

Later the same day, having received another, even more encouraging letter
from Ottoline, Russell came to indulge his fantasies about Irene more fully,
now confident that he would not, in doing so, risk losing Ottoline. 'I think I
may easily come to have a *very* great affection for Irene,' he admitted, 'not a
very passionate feeling; but one which might give happiness & be free from
the pain of passion':

And I feel pretty sure she would respond, tho' she would be shy & would
need to be led gently. And I think she would interfere as little as any one
could between you & me. She is lacking in your wild side, & in religion;
many things I share with you I could never share with her . . . it is the
something unapproachable & noble in you, that makes you always to me
the incarnation of the wild world's mystery. This is not just a phrase, but
the heart of what I feel. It could live alongside of whatever I might come
to feel for Irene – that would be very good & real, but not mystical or mad.
I think it is true that I run the risk of unbearable loneliness later, which
might drive me into things that would bring shame.

His fear of losing Ottoline, however, remained even stronger than his desire
for Irene, and on 8 January, in response perhaps to some mild expressions of
jealousy on Ottoline's part, he spent the entire day in a kind of agony over
the thought that, in admitting his desire for Irene, he had destroyed Ottoline's
love for him. Late that night, he wrote a fevered, barely sane letter, trying to
explain the 'fearful tangle of feelings' to which he had been subject:

I had a deathbed feeling – not your deathbed, but the deathbed of the glory
& wonder of your love – which I have killed by wanting it . . . A ghost-like
procession of the wonderful times we have had together was passing
through my mind . . . My own judgment, as I told you when we first talked
of it, is against going far with Irene. But I distrust my judgment, & I feel
you want me to go on, & instinct works the same way. Underneath all that
is the terrible sadness of vanished things, the feeling that real life is over,
& the rest is a dull dream . . . [since August] darkness has descended & ice
has come between us . . . I feel all that is important in my personal life is
ended . . . it is a mere pretence that Irene could take your place.

After posting this letter the following morning, he spent another day in
torment, this time about what he had written about his 'deathbed feeling'.
Throughout the day, he wrote no fewer than three letters apologising for what
he called 'a late night letter, which one never ought to post'. He did not really

think all those things about the end of their relationship, he insisted, 'only I wanted them denied'. The root of it was: 'I don't want to drift into anything that wd. make me lose anything of you that I might keep – rather than that I would face *any* loneliness.' Ottoline responded to this tormented outburst with comforting and soothing words, still urging him on but trying to reassure him of the consequences: 'I know she could not fully satisfy you, but I saw, and *you said* she made you happy and kept you from feeling lonely . . . and naturally I wanted [you] to feel that I *understand*.'

In the event, all this agonising turned out to be almost comically misplaced. Irene, it transpired, had no intention whatever of becoming Russell's lover. Russell and Ottoline had misread the signs. Quite what Irene's feelings for Russell were is something of a mystery, and Irene herself seems to have been somewhat confused by them. The only thing she was certain of was that they were not sexual feelings. She had, she claimed, 'an utter, fundamental indifference' to sex and had never in her life had any sexual feelings whatever (she lived to be eighty-eight, and, as far as anyone knows, died celibate). She nevertheless felt some kind of fascination for Russell. 'There were things in him which I positively hated,' she later said, but she also felt 'a violent attraction to him – a longing in a way to get closer and closer even to that which I could not bear but thought perhaps I could only bear if I gave way to him. And sometimes when I was with him I forgot everything and only knew that I was with him and was happy.' She allowed Russell to kiss her, and 'I scarcely troubled at all about my indifference there because I was taken up all the time with trying to understand why in some ways I liked him so much and in other ways hated him. It was that struggle which was in the forefront all the time – & which ended things.'

This, unsurprisingly, is not how it appeared to Russell. During the days that he agonised over the possible effects on his relationship with Ottoline of an affair with Irene, he was in no doubt that any sexual advances he made towards Irene would be welcomed and reciprocated. He, naturally, had not considered the possibility that her fascination for him sprang partly from a determination to understand why he was so loathsome, and he assumed that she was falling in love with him. Thus, once reassured by Ottoline that he would not lose her by pursuing Irene, he made his move, only to meet with a reaction that astonished and bewildered him. Perhaps trying to let him down gently, Irene told him that she was not prepared to be his lover openly, because the scandal would upset her parents. But neither would she be his lover secretly, because she found secrecy intolerable. Thus, she could not be his lover at all. (She was later to become a distinguished barrister, and one almost imagines her presenting this argument as if convincing the jury of a watertight case.)

Russell was not used to having his sexual advances met with logically irrefutable arguments, and he began to cast around for some psychological explanation for Irene's strange attitude, some flaw in her character that would account for her otherwise incomprehensible unwillingness to become his lover. 'She is too law-abiding,' he decided, 'too destitute of recklessness, quite without love of danger.' That being so, he realised, he no longer wanted her to become his lover: 'I feel her too tame – nothing fires my imagination . . . I have a real affection for her, but I do like people to be willing to shoot Niagara.' Carrying this bluff a bit further, Russell seems almost to have persuaded himself that it was he who had decided they should not become lovers and Irene whose advances had been rebuffed. 'Irene's passion develops,' he told Ottoline, 'but I have not enough to give her . . . She is very unhappy in the thought of having to give me up.'

Irene was unhappy at the situation, not because of any thwarted passion for Russell, but rather because, after rejecting Russell's advances, she feared that she would have to give up her work for him. She decided to visit Ottoline to talk it through. 'She will', Russell predicted, 'give the impression that I care greatly for her; the new feeling, that I am telling you, only came up towards the end of the morning, & had not yet pushed its way to the surface.' Ottoline took this with the pinch of salt it deserved, and continued to assume – surely rightly – that, if it were offered him, Russell would not turn down the chance of a sexual relationship with Irene. When Irene came to see her, therefore, she did her best to help Russell in overcoming Irene's resistance to having an affair with him, advising her to go away with Russell from time to time, and urging her to consider his desperate loneliness.

Irene was not to be persuaded, and, shortly after the meeting with Ottoline, wrote Russell a letter in which she spelt out her position and attempted to remove any misconceptions Russell might still have about her purported 'passion' for him:

My dear Bertrand,
    Putting aside all the difficulties of last week, which were, as I have told you, real obstacles to my seeing you, I do realise, I have realised lately, ever since we talked about it on the river, that I do not care for you in the way that makes me come up to your expectations. I am very much to blame, not for feeling as I do, which can't be helped, but for not realising it before. I should have told you before had I known before, on account of the disappointment that [it] has caused you. I have let myself think that it has been only material obstacles which have stood in the way, like having to see after Vernon and things like that, but I see now quite clearly, and I am ashamed for your sake that I have not seen it before, that if I really cared for you fully – even if I cared for you only as much as you cared for me – I should let nothing . . . stand in the way . . . I want to see you but not if you do not want to see me.

In his letters to Ottoline, in the meantime, Russell attempted to keep up the fiction of Irene's desire for him and his own refusal to have an affair with her, although even he had to admit that Irene seemed oddly imperturbable in the face of her alleged disappointment: 'Yes, Irene is strangely unmoved – it seems odd. Perhaps it is that I have been very unmoving – quite without fire and passion.' Irene *was* sexually attracted to him, he continued to insist, only she was frightened by the strength of her own desire: 'It is a pity to be afraid of life as she is, & governed by bogies . . . She would never in any case love very passionately, because she would be afraid of the wildness of passion – if she saw it growing on her, she would discipline it.' This timidity, he repeatedly implied, had put him off her. Elsewhere, he hinted that the reason the affair with Irene came to nothing was that his anxieties about Ottoline prevented it from developing: 'Helen left a mark on me as well as on you – on me a feeling of shame so intense that it makes a constraint & a feeling of hopelessness – which is increased by knowing more of the mark left on you. And I do not believe I should avoid mistakes in future if I attempted still what seems too hard for me.'

Stability was restored when Irene wrote to Russell saying that, despite what had happened, she was still willing to go on as friends and to carry on working for him. Russell gratefully accepted, and, after he returned to Cambridge for the start of the new term on 15 January, she remained in London, working every day at the British Museum. They met to discuss the work every weekend or whenever he was in London, their friendship settling into an almost business-like relationship. Even so, Russell's final and complete acceptance of the fact that, sexually, Irene was a lost cause took a surprisingly long time to develop, perhaps because he continued to be misled by Irene's complicated and ambivalent fascination with him. As late as 26 January, some two weeks after the crisis, Russell was telling Ottoline that, although he did not feel, at the moment, disposed to go 'all lengths' with Irene, he could not say with certainty that it would not happen in the future, 'only I would not *dream* of it if it would repel you or make you retire into yourself'. By 10 February, however, he had accepted that the question of their ever having sexual relations had better be dropped and that 'the best plan is to lapse into merely friendly relations *without any discussion*: I don't believe she will ever raise the question if I don't.'

Indeed, she did not. Instead, she stuck doggedly to her task of collecting newspaper records of the history of British diplomacy from 1906 to 1914, and, in fact, showed a greater commitment to the plan that Russell had drawn up for a book on 'Principles and Practice in Foreign Policy' than he did. Throughout 1915, she continued her researches long after Russell's attention had been diverted to other things, and, even after Russell published *The Policy of the Entente, 1904–1914: A Reply to Professor Gilbert Murray*, she continued to work on the project, feeling perhaps that Russell's rather slight polemical pamphlet did scant justice to the scale of the original conception. In 1919, she put the material she had gathered to use in a book called *How We Got Into the War: A Study of English Liberal Ideals*, which, in some ways, adheres more closely to Russell's initial intention of analysing and charting the way in which traditional liberalism was subverted and betrayed by the Liberal Government that was elected in 1906 amid so much hope and idealism.

By the time she published her own version of their joint project, Irene had drifted apart from Russell. In 1916, Desmond MacCarthy fell in love with her, and, for a year, was tormented by her apparently complete lack of sexual feeling, just as Russell had been. Like Russell, MacCarthy insisted that she had sexual desires but, for some perverse and frustrating reason known, if at all, only to herself, chose to deny them. In August 1917, Irene put an end to her relationship with MacCarthy with a chilly six-page letter, examining, barrister-like, the evidence for and against this theory of denial. She eventually rejected it, telling MacCarthy: 'Because I loved you so in my way I have tried to force myself at times into believing I enjoyed your kisses – but it has been a failure – and there is no-one for whom I would ever again make the experiment.'

She devoted the rest of her life to socialism, feminism, literature, and the law,[1] and spent it defiantly, militantly, free from any further romantic entanglements with men. Her friend Enid Bagnold has said that, though Irene was never really in love with any man, she 'loved and liked women', though, again, without any noticeable signs of sexual desire: 'she had tender warmth for women, but if it led to passion she was unaware of it.' In 1923, something of her feelings of anger and revulsion towards the men with whom she had been involved was expressed in a novel called *The Green-eyed Monster*, which she published pseudonymously as 'Althea Brook'. In this, Russell appears as the predatory Tom Wolfe, while Desmond MacCarthy is the weak and deceitful Edward Russell (giving MacCarthy Russell's name was perhaps a not very subtle hint that she considered them essentially identical, each as bad as the other). By contrast, her devotion to Vernon Lee continued unabated until Lee's death in 1935. After a successful career as a barrister, Irene retired to Kent, where she died in 1970.

Perhaps the oddest aspect of Russell's tepid, abortive affair with Irene Cooper-Willis was the effect it had on his relations with Ottoline, which, in its aftermath, rose to new heights of physical passion. On 15 January, Ottoline wrote to say that she wanted to break their embargo (the one imposed during their negotiations with Alys and Logan back in 1911) and spend a night with him. This they did the following Tuesday, after which they both wrote to each other in terms of unbounded, unparalleled, dionysian ecstasy. 'Last night I could only go on my knees in deep awe and thankfulness that such wonders had been given to one,' Ottoline told him. 'It was simply unearthly, wasn't it? Every *moment* of it up to the last . . . It is worth all the sufferings of hell to love as this.' Russell was still less restrained:

Tuesday night
My Heart, my Life, how can I ever tell you the amazing unspeakable glory of you tonight? You were utterly, absolutely of the stars – & yet of the Eternal Earth too – so that you took me from Earth & in a moment carried me to the highest heights. Your whole being seemed transformed with magic – tonight it was the magic of the Mediterranean, the 'wine-dark sea' – as I have seen it blue & sunny in the foreground, then utter darkness, &,

---

[1] Among her many publications are biographies of Florence Nightingale, Elizabeth Barrett Browning and the Brontës, an anthology of the writings of her friend Vernon Lee and (most intriguingly from the point of view of her connection with Russell) an edited collection of the speeches of Charles James Fox. Her book on Britain's entry into the First World War was followed by two subsequent volumes dealing with the war itself, and, in 1928 the three were published together in a single volume under the title *England's Holy War: A Study in Liberal Idealism during the Great War*.

beyond, strange islands & mountains in a sun-shine that seems eternal. More often you have the magic of the Atlantic – but that is different. I am an instrument passive to your touch – you can bring out of me any music you choose to call forth . . .

Wed. evg

. . . Every moment last night, from the very first to the very last, was a *miracle* – it was beyond & above everything that has ever happened between us – yes, I feel *all* you say about Donne's 'Ecstasy' – it is not *at all* adequate. Last night had *everything* – there was a note of wildness, of 'Hey nonny no, men are fools that wish to die' – it blended in some unimaginable way with religion & the central fires – I had not known before that it could . . . I cannot live in the peaceful plains – I wanted to try, with Irene – but it is dull down there – I want the mountains & the storm & the danger, & the wild sudden beauty, & the free winds of heaven. I have all that with you . . . you have *all*, *all* that my soul craves – I can't tell you the depths & wildness & vastness of my love to you – it gets dammed up & imprisoned when you are cold, but when you want it it comes out in a flood, a torrent, an ocean – more & more, the more you will let me give. You give me what the greatest music yearns for, what made the Sunflower be weary of time, what makes one's life a striving & straining & struggling after Heaven – all that, you gave me last night – it seemed to grow more & more & more – till I felt I must die, then & there, because mortal spirit could bear no more. We have had many many great & wonderful times, but yesterday was more than all of them – more full of flame & fire – with the wildness of our having meant to part – with all the pain of the war – with everything, everything, caught up & transfused in a great world of love, love, love.

'Very very few have ever known what we have,' Russell wrote a few days later, 'very few have the passion, or the power of bearing pain, or the capacity to rise & float in the heights without growing dizzy – And the few that have hardly ever meet any one else who had it. I think of Beethoven – who terrified all who knew him – because the central fire of the world burned in him, & scorched & withered all who were not tempered to live in that white heat.'

In her control, her coolness and her passionlessness, Irene Cooper-Willis had become for Russell a symbol of what he did not want. In the first few days of the war he had written: 'The force that in the long run makes for peace and all other good things is Reason, the power of thinking against instinct.' And in his early article, 'War, the Offspring of Fear', he had likened Europe to 'a house on fire, where the inmates instead of trying to escape and to extinguish the flames are engaged in accusing each other of having caused the conflagration'. In his imagination at that time, the task of bringing sanity, whether to an individual or to a nation, was one of pouring the cold water of reason on the dangerous fires of passion. But in Irene, or so he imagined, he had seen what a person might be like in whom the fire had been extinguished, in whom nothing lived but prudence, sanity, rationality and the desire for peace. And, far from it appearing to him as an ideal of human existence, he loathed it. In the aftermath of his failed attempt to seduce Irene, his letters to Ottoline dwell almost obsessively on Irene's lack of impulsiveness, which, he was now inclined to think, was a denial of life. 'I am really shocked,' he wrote on 21 January, 'at such a fear of life & such a desire to retain the moral vantage-ground . . . The more I think it over the more it repels me.'

When he received a brief letter from Wittgenstein – a late reply to his letter of the previous July, concerned mainly with asking Russell if he had yet read the notes Moore took in Norway – Russell's delight was unfettered, to be once more in contact with someone whose vitality and passion were in the starkest contrast to the bloodlessness of Irene. 'How grateful one is to people who make life splendid,' he wrote to Ottoline. To write only of philosophy while serving on the Western Front was 'so pure & unmoved':

'The free man thinks of nothing less than death' as Spinoza says. It has moved me greatly. It wrings my heart, & yet one feels death hardly matters to such a spirit. I *know* he may survive but I do not *feel* it. His letter is an inspiration & strength.

'The mountains, the storm & the danger' that Russell craved were, of course, not difficult to find for those fighting at the front, and it is striking that, in all his writings against the war, Russell never once criticised those actually doing the fighting and the killing. He had the greatest sympathy for those risking their lives, and a correspondingly heartfelt contempt for what he called the 'bloodthirsty old men' who, in the absence of all the younger dons and most of the students, now dominated Cambridge life, and who took a vicarious delight in the fighting of others. Soon after he returned to Cambridge for the Lent Term, Russell published in *The Cambridge Review* an article calculated to irritate their patriotic pride. Called 'Can England and Germany be Reconciled after the War', it ridiculed the concern with prestige that had led to the naval rivalry between the two countries and proposed as a solution the creation of a neutral international navy that would police the waters, protecting both countries from invasion and rendering their national navies redundant. The only thing standing in the way of the success of this solution, Russell suggested, was national pride and the fear that it would diminish the profits of armament manufacturers.

Though an unremarkable suggestion now, after we have become only too accustomed to the concept of a neutral 'peace-keeping force' protecting hostile forces from one another, at the time Russell's proposal of an international navy seemed outrageous, especially when made with the manifestly disrespectful attitude that Russell displayed towards the British Empire and its Government. A few days after its publication, as Russell was almost delighted to report: 'All the old fogies in the place have been tumbling over each other to attack me about my article.' Leading the old fogies were two distinguished philosophers: W. R. Sorley, the Knightsbridge Professor of Moral Philosophy at Cambridge, and Miss E. E. Constance Jones, a logician and Principal of Girton. Russell replied to their criticisms, prompting a further barrage of letters to which he replied in turn, forcing the editor of *The Cambridge Review* to intervene and declare the debate closed.

∗110·632. $\vdash : \mu \, \epsilon \, \text{NC} . \supset . \mu +_{\text{c}} 1 = \hat{\xi} \{ (\exists y) . y \, \epsilon \, \xi . \xi - \iota'y \, \epsilon \, \text{sm}''\mu \}$

Dem.

$\qquad \vdash . \ast 110·631 . \ast 51·211·22 . \supset$

$\qquad \vdash : \text{Hp} . \supset . \mu +_{\text{c}} 1 = \hat{\xi} \{ (\exists \gamma, y) . \gamma \, \epsilon \, \text{sm}''\mu . y \, \epsilon \, \xi . \gamma = \xi - \iota'y \}$

$\qquad [\ast 13·195] \qquad = \hat{\xi} \{ (\exists y) . y \, \epsilon \, \xi . \xi - \iota'y \, \epsilon \, \text{sm}''\mu \} : \supset \vdash . \text{Prop}$

∗110·64. $\vdash . 0 +_{\text{c}} 0 = 0$ $[\ast 110·62]$

∗110·641. $\vdash . 1 +_{\text{c}} 0 = 0 +_{\text{c}} 1 = 1$ $[\ast 110·51·61 . \ast 101·2]$

∗110·642. $\vdash . 2 +_{\text{c}} 0 = 0 +_{\text{c}} 2 = 2$ $[\ast 110·51·61 . \ast 101·31]$

∗110·643. $\vdash . 1 +_{\text{c}} 1 = 2$

Dem.

$\qquad\qquad \vdash . \ast 110·632 . \ast 101·21·28 . \supset$

$\qquad\qquad \vdash . 1 +_{\text{c}} 1 = \hat{\xi} \{ (\exists y) . y \, \epsilon \, \xi . \xi - \iota'y \, \epsilon \, 1 \}$

$\qquad\qquad [\ast 54·3] \quad = 2 . \supset \vdash . \text{Prop}$

The above proposition is occasionally useful. It is used at least three times, in ∗113·66 and ∗120·123·472.

∗110·7·71 are required for proving ∗110·72, and ∗110·72 is used in ∗117·3, which is a fundamental proposition in the theory of greater and less.

∗110·7. $\vdash : \beta \subset \alpha . \supset . (\exists \mu) . \mu \, \epsilon \, \text{NC} . \text{Nc}'\alpha = \text{Nc}'\beta +_{\text{c}} \mu$

Dem.

$\qquad \vdash . \ast 24·411·21 . \supset \vdash : \text{Hp} . \supset . \alpha = \beta \cup (\alpha - \beta) . \beta \cap (\alpha - \beta) = \Lambda .$

$\qquad [\ast 110·32] \qquad\qquad \supset . \text{Nc}'\alpha = \text{Nc}'\beta +_{\text{c}} \text{Nc}'(\alpha - \beta) : \supset \vdash . \text{Prop}$

∗110·71. $\vdash : (\exists \mu) . \text{Nc}'\alpha = \text{Nc}'\beta +_{\text{c}} \mu . \supset . (\exists \delta) . \delta \, \text{sm} \, \beta . \delta \subset \alpha$

Dem.

$\vdash . \ast 100·3 . \ast 110·4 . \supset$

$\vdash : \text{Nc}'\alpha = \text{Nc}'\beta +_{\text{c}} \mu . \supset . \mu \, \epsilon \, \text{NC} - \iota'\Lambda$ (1)

$\vdash . \ast 110·3 . \supset \vdash : \text{Nc}'\alpha = \text{Nc}'\beta +_{\text{c}} \text{Nc}'\gamma . \equiv . \text{Nc}'\alpha = \text{Nc}'(\beta + \gamma) .$

$[\ast 100·3·31] \qquad \supset . \alpha \, \text{sm} \, (\beta + \gamma) .$

$[\ast 73·1] \qquad \supset . (\exists R) . R \, \epsilon \, 1 \rightarrow 1 . \text{D}'R = \alpha . \text{Œ}'R = \downarrow \Lambda_\gamma ''\iota''\beta \cup \Lambda_\beta \downarrow ''\iota''\gamma .$

$[\ast 37·15] \qquad \supset . (\exists R) . R \, \epsilon \, 1 \rightarrow 1 . \downarrow \Lambda_\gamma ''\iota''\beta \subset \text{Œ}'R . R'' \downarrow \Lambda_\gamma ''\iota''\beta \subset \alpha .$

$[\ast 110·12 . \ast 73·22] \supset . (\exists \delta) . \delta \subset \alpha . \delta \, \text{sm} \, \beta$ (2)

$\vdash . (1) . (2) . \supset \vdash . \text{Prop}$

40 Eighty-six pages into Volume II of *Principia Mathematica*, Whitehead and
Russell establish the 'occasionally useful' proposition that 1 + 1 = 2.

41 Lady Ottoline Morrell.

42 Bertrand Russell by Augustus John, *c*.1913.

43 Ludwig
Wittgenstein.

44 Joseph Conrad.

45 D. H. Lawrence.

46 Garsington Manor.

47 Lytton Strachey, Russell and Philip Morrell at Garsington, *c*. 1915.

48 and 49 Vivien Eliot, 'an incarnate provocation'.

50 T. S. Eliot in his first year at Harvard, 1911-12.

51 The Brotherhood Church, Southgate Road, Hackney, 28 July 1917: 'It was really very horrible... The roughs had horrible degraded faces. The crowd outside as we were leaving was very fierce... I realised vividly how ghastly the spirit of violence is, & how utterly I repudiate it.'

52 Irene Cooper-Willis.

53 Clifford Allen

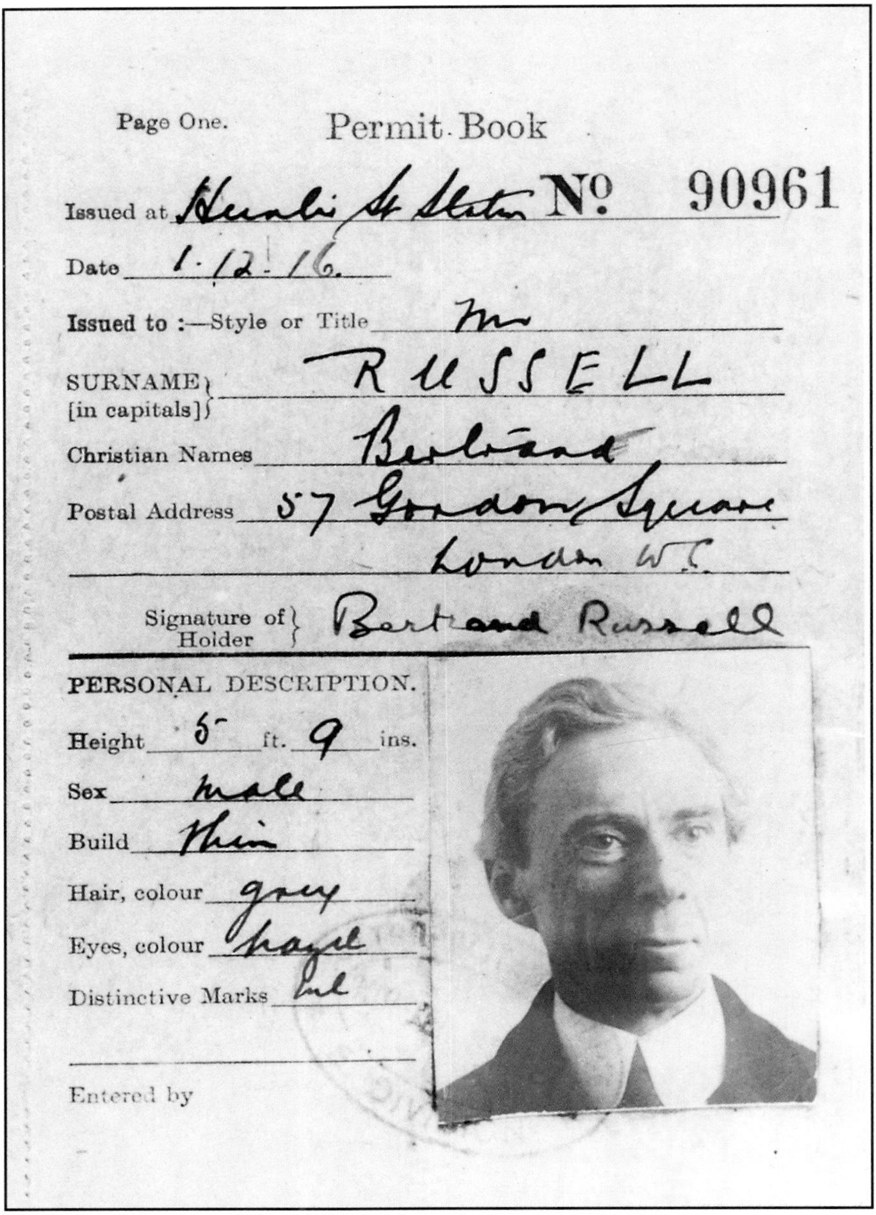

Page One.   **Permit·Book**

Issued at *Hendi & Slater* №   90961

Date *1·12·16.*

Issued to :—Style or Title   *Mr*

SURNAME }
[in capitals] }   *R U S S E L L*

Christian Names   *Bertrand*

Postal Address   *57 Gordon Square*
London W.C.

Signature of }
Holder }   *Bertrand Russell*

PERSONAL DESCRIPTION.

Height   *5* ft.   *9* ins.

Sex   *male*

Build   *thin*

Hair, colour   *grey*

Eyes, colour   *hazel*

Distinctive Marks   *nil*

Entered by

54 Russell's Permit Book, 1916.

For Russell, the furore served only to reinforce his distaste both for the Cambridge establishment and for conventional academic philosophers. His five-year lectureship at Trinity would end in the summer of 1915 and the college was preparing itself to offer him a (more prestigious and more secure) Research Fellowship, which Russell seriously considered rejecting. In the end, he decided to ask instead for a period of leave. There were scarcely any students left to teach anyway. In academic circles, gossip spreads quickly, and, within days of Russell reaching this decision (about how he would respond *if* he were offered a Fellowship), he received a telegram from Harvard, inviting him to visit there again during his period of leave. This he did turn down. 'I have nothing new to say in philosophy,' he told Ottoline, '& I don't want to have to think about it just now.' On 15 February, he kept his appointment in Manchester to read a philosophical paper ('The Ultimate Constituents of Matter', a re-statement of his construction of matter from sense-data, hurriedly written a few days before he delivered it), but, after that, he abandoned philosophy completely for over two years.

One has the feeling during these months that Russell, cut adrift from the people and institutions he had previously been associated with, was looking for something or somebody with whom he could identify and join forces. The Liberal Party had exposed itself as a bunch of duplicitous and idiotically patriotic rogues, Russell's Liberal friends had disappointed him in supporting the Government, Cambridge was in the grip of bloodthirsty old men, and academic philosophers had shown themselves willing to provide pseudo-rigorous justifications for the slaughter of young men. And yet, he could not really identify with those campaigning against the war, either. He never was a pacifist, he rather despised Quakers, he found narrowly political the original founders of the UDC, and, in his reactions to the personality of Irene Cooper-Willis (herself an enthusiastic supporter of the UDC) he had now crystallised in his mind what it was about many peace campaigners that he disliked: it was their lifelessness, their bloodlessness, their dreariness. Attending a UDC meeting on 13 February to hear Goldie Lowes Dickinson speak on 'Europe after the War', he pronounced it 'dreadfully dull'. Venerating the 'fire & flame' in people's souls, the impulse to recklessness and danger, and yet despairing of the bloodthirsty passions that had been unleashed by the war, Russell found himself between two camps, unable to belong to either. Writing to Ralph Perry on 21 February, he told him: 'I cannot escape the feeling of being a stranger to the human race, which is intolerably painful.'

In what would turn out to be a fateful coincidence, on the very day after Russell wrote to Ottoline his ecstatic description of their passionate night together, of the blending of the fire of religion with the wildness of physical passion, Ottoline met for the first time the writer who, more than anyone else, has become associated with such reverence for the sexual act. If anyone could live up to Russell's ideal of someone who combined opposition to the war with a personal and emotional 'fire', if anyone could 'feel wholeheartedly all that ought to be felt', it was D. H. Lawrence, who on 21 January 1915 came to dinner at Bedford Square.

Ottoline and Russell had already formed an impression of Lawrence that, in many ways, matched their earlier veneration of Conrad, as someone with a passionate nature and a deep and rare insight. The two novels that Lawrence had so far published – *The White Peacock* and *Sons and Lovers* – were widely admired among their circle of friends and no doubt helped to foster this impression, but, for Ottoline and Russell, the turning point in their admiration of Lawrence seems to have been their reading of his collection of short stories, *The Prussian Officer*, which Russell read soon after it was published in November 1914. He at once recommended it to Ottoline, who read it the following month and was delighted with it. 'I am amazed how good it is,' she wrote on 31 December. 'He has great passion – and is so alive to things outward and inward . . . It has been a comfort reading anything so real.' The stories she liked best were those, like 'Daughters of the Vicar', which recalled to her the Nottinghamshire of her youth. Feeling strongly that there might be some affinity between herself and Lawrence, she wrote to him at once inviting him to dinner. Lawrence, proud and flattered to be approached by a member of the Bentincks, the grandest family in Nottinghamshire ('One wants the appreciation of the few,' he told Ottoline, 'life itself is an affair of aristocrats'), replied immediately, promising to come at the earliest opportunity.

When he did come, Ottoline found him completely captivating. He was everything she had hoped for. Upon meeting, she writes in her memoirs, 'we at once went back to our memories of Nottinghamshire.' They talked of Sherwood Forest, of the pit villages, of the lives of colliers and their wives, 'and of all those scenes which he has described so vividly in his early books'. He delighted her by talking in the Nottinghamshire dialect and also by speaking with respect of the Bentincks, who, he assured her, were always looked up to by the local people.

'It was impossible not to feel expanded and stimulated by the companionship of anyone so alive,' Ottoline wrote, 'so intensely interested in everyone and everything as he was':

> . . . he seemed to possess a magnetic gift of quickening those he talked to and of making them blossom with new ideas, new enthusiasm, new hopes . . . Indeed, I felt when I was with him as if I had really at last found a friend, that I could express myself without reserve and without fear of being thought silly . . . He seemed to open up the way into a holy land by his gospel of instinctive development.

Ottoline met Lawrence at a time when the spread of his 'gospel' – or, as he more often called it, his 'philosophy' – was of paramount importance to him. He had recently completed a long philosophical essay, which, in a conscious echo of Nietzsche's *The Gay Science*, he called *Le Gai Savaire*. It is now better known as *Study of Thomas Hardy*, the title under which it was eventually published, though the earlier title is less misleading; of its ten chapters, only two or three have anything much to do with Hardy. The rest is taken up with a philosophy of life that owes something to both Nietzsche and Bergson and which, in its preoccupation with the tension between Man and Woman, also recalls the work of Otto Weininger.

Lawrence's philosophical writing may be seen as a kind of mirror-image of Russell's fiction. For just as when Russell wrote fiction, he could not stop himself from writing as a philosopher, from lavishing more attention on abstract ideas than on people and places, so when Lawrence wrote philosophy, he could not stop himself from writing as a novelist, from expressing his thoughts, not through arguments, but through images. In *Study of Thomas Hardy* the central image is that of the poppy, the 'red flame' of nature, which blazes magnificently and triumphantly for the briefest of times before 'Pfff! – and it is gone'. The brief flowering of the poppy symbolises the imper-manence, but also the glory, of life. The flame itself is all that is eternal, it is 'all the story and all the triumph', and to burn briefly but brightly is the only way we or the poppy, or any living thing, have of realising the eternal in us. Life receives its purpose and its meaning through this brief but glorious flowering, this burning, and to live a life of fear, repression and mediocrity, to lack the courage to burst through the bud, so to speak, is to deny life itself. 'The final aim of every living thing, creature or being', according to Lawrence, 'is the full achievement of itself.' Not work, nor children, nor public good deeds will save one from the 'vanity and pathetic transience of mortality'; only the realisation of oneself, 'the real Me', will give one a glimpse of the eternal.

It was a doctrine immediately congenial to Ottoline, and she was, from the first, a ready and fervent convert. After that first meeting of 21 January, she became a regular visitor to Lawrence's house in Sussex, from where she and Lawrence would take walks together through the nearby woods, during which Lawrence took every opportunity to impress his 'gospel' upon her. On one walk, for example, he echoed his own philosophical writing (which, at this stage, he had not yet shown her) when he pointed out to her the little flame-red buds of trees not yet in leaf. 'See,' he said, 'here is the little red flame in Nature.' Ottoline looked at him, she records, and thought, 'In you, too, there certainly dwells that flame.'

Hand-in-hand with Lawrence's 'philosophy' went a denunciation of the war every bit as fierce as Russell's, though importantly different in its motivation. From Russell's point of view, the war was a disaster because it destroyed the old admirable civilisation and replaced it with a new contemp-tible barbarism, and it was a tragedy precisely because it was not inevitable. From Lawrence's point of view, on the other hand, the old order was so rotten and decadent that the war was inevitable, and it at least had the virtue of clarifying the issue, of showing up the need for a radically new kind of life. Western civilisation, he thought, was finished. And it deserved to die, for it had been guilty of the ultimate sin of denying life, of replacing nature with the machine and of repressing the healthy and natural urges of individual people. Better that it should perish quickly and allow a new, more robust society to take its place, one that did not seek to imprison natural impulses within artificial restraints.

At the time of his meeting with Ottoline, the thirty-year-old Lawrence had been seized by a hare-brained scheme to put his ideas about a new life into practice by establishing with his friends a new society. It was to be called Rananim, after a Hebrew song he had heard his friend Samuel Koteliansky sing at Christmas, and its members were to include the Lawrences, Katherine Mansfield, John Middleton Murry and Koteliansky. In order to safeguard it against the corrosive influence of decadent Western civilisation, it was to be established in some faraway place such as a South Pacific island, or possibly, as Lawrence considered at one time, Florida. Lawrence was passionate about this scheme and evidently mistook Ottoline's sympathy for his 'gospel' as an indication that she would be willing to become part of it.

In a letter dated 1 February, just a week or so after they had first met, Lawrence wrote to Ottoline with an alarming proposal. 'You must form the nucleus of a new community which shall start a new life amongst us,' he told her, 'a life in which the only riches is integrity of character':

> So that each may fulfil his own nature and deep desires to the utmost . . . the new community shall be established upon the known, eternal good part in us . . . The ideal, the religion, must now be *lived, practised* . . . After the War, the soul of the people will be so maimed and so injured that it is horrible to think of. And this shall be our hope: that there shall be a life wherein the struggle shall not be for money or for power, but for individual freedom and common effort towards the good.

'It is no good plastering and tinkering with this community,' he told her. 'Every strong soul must put off its connection with this society, its vanity and chiefly its fear, and go naked with its fellows, weaponless, armourless, without shield or spear.'

Ottoline never took Lawrence's fantasies of a new community very seriously, and the nearest she came to realising his suggestion of being the nucleus of such a community was when she invited Lawrence and his wife to come and live in a cottage on her estate. Nevertheless, she seems to have allowed Lawrence to believe that her adoption of his philosophy entailed a commitment to this scheme to establish 'Rananim', and even to think that Russell might be a willing convert to the idea. A few days after this letter to Ottoline, Lawrence wrote to Samuel Koteliansky, announcing proudly that, next time Ottoline visited him, she would bring Bertrand Russell, 'the Philosophic – and Mathematics man – a Fellow of Cambridge University – F. R. S. – Earl Russell's brother'. He also claimed that, when Ottoline and Russell came, they were all 'going to struggle with my Island idea – Rananim – But they say, the Island shall be England, that we shall start our new community in the midst of this old one, as a seed falls among the roots of the parent.'

The idea that Russell, Ottoline and Lawrence would meet to discuss the founding of Rananim in England sounds extremely far-fetched, and one is tempted to think that Lawrence was misled. However, if interpreted in a certain (distinctly non-Lawrentian) way, it does gain plausibility. For, misleading though it may have been to suggest that it had much to do with Lawrence's dream of a new island community, a growing preoccupation of

Russell's as the war dragged on was the idea that, after the war, Britain would have to make a more or less completely new start, both politically and socially. From Russell's point of view, however, one did not have to go to a South Pacific island to escape the old civilisation; the old civilisation had committed suicide, there was nothing to escape from. The point was, rather, to rebuild society on new principles. To that extent, Lawrence's vision of Rananim – despite being clearly an utterly impractical and slightly mad idea – may have seemed to Russell worth discussing, if only because, in thinking about the kind of community one would create – if one *could* create a new society from scratch – one would be forced to think anew the basis of society.

Thus, amid the wreckage of the old world destroyed by the war, such dreams may have seemed, strangely, more to the point than the merely political questions debated by the UDC. A new vision was, Russell thought, precisely what was needed at this time. Moreover, it had to be the vision of someone with deep psychological insight, for Russell was becoming more and more convinced that, fundamentally, the problems of politics and society were psychological in nature. To understand why the war was fought, and, therefore, to have some idea of how to prevent such a thing happening again, one had to understand the impulses, usually unconscious, that directed people's behaviour. As the war, and his experiences with Irene Cooper-Willis had taught Russell, it was no use thinking of the question as a simple struggle between reason and impulse. For not only was it not possible to control one's impulses by the use of reason ('Thought seems a mere bubble – not part of the stream, but a surface thing thrown up by the stream and showing its direction,' he had written on 20 November), it was not desirable either. Without the wildness, the 'flame & fire' of passion, life was drab and scarcely worth living. In a curious kind of way, therefore, Russell had, before he even met Lawrence, arrived at a point of view very like Lawrence's, at the centre of which was the very Lawrentian image of 'the flame'. Nothing, therefore, could have excited Russell's hopes for a person more than Ottoline's description of Lawrence:

> Lawrence is the spirit of the flame. He has indeed a fire within him, a fire which flames into excitement and conviction when a subject or a controversy strikes a light.

Connected with this image of the flame was another hope that Russell had of Lawrence, and possibly the one that loomed largest in his desire to meet him: Russell seemed to sense the possibility of some special intimacy between him and Lawrence, some chance that with Lawrence he could, just as he had with Conrad, experience the peeling away of superficial layers until they reached the 'central fire'. 'One feels from his writing that he must be wonderful,' he wrote to Ottoline, after her first meeting with Lawrence, 'a man with a real fire of imagination – I should like to know him.' He seemed to feel, simply from reading Lawrence's work, that Lawrence would be able to *see* him, to understand him. But, why? What was there in *The Prussian Officer* that might – like Conrad's *Heart of Darkness* and *Amy Foster* – have inspired such a hope?

One story in the collection stands out as being imbued with Russellian themes, namely 'The Shadow in the Rose Garden'. The story concerns a woman who, after being told that her lover, a soldier, has died in Africa, marries someone else with whom she is not in love. Without telling her new husband about her previous love, she takes him to the seaside town where she and her old lover had lived, where, to re-create her old memories, she returns alone to her old lover's house and sits in the rose garden where they used to sit together. While she is sitting there, a shadowy figure approaches her. It is her old lover. He is, she realises, quite mad and fails entirely to recognise her. He sits down beside her and fumbles for his pipe, while she freezes with dread at the realisation that, though it is his face, his body, his hands, 'yet', as Lawrence repeatedly puts it, 'it was not he'. 'He was a handsome, soldierly fellow,' Lawrence writes, 'and a lunatic.' In a way that vividly recalls Russell's own dreams of being strangled by a lunatic, Lawrence dwells on the horror evoked by contact with madness:

> Her eyes searched him, and searched him, to see if he would recognise her, if she could discover him.
> 'You don't know me?' she asked, from the terror of her soul, standing alone.
> He looked back at her quizzically. She had to bear his eyes. They gleamed on her, but with no intelligence. He was drawing near to her.
> 'Yes, I do know you,' he said, fixed, intent, but mad, drawing his face nearer hers. Her horror was too great. The powerful lunatic was coming too near her.

Still he does not recognise her. When the gardener comes to take him back inside, he introduces her with the vague and uncomprehending comment: 'She is a friend of mine.' She walks back to the hotel, where her husband, seeing that she is distraught, forces the truth out of her about her previous love. The story ends with the woman telling her husband: 'I saw him today':

> 'He is not dead, he's mad.'
> Her husband looked at her, startled.
> 'Mad!' he said involuntarily.
> 'A lunatic,' she said. It almost cost her her reason to utter the word.

It is a powerful and memorable scene, and one that carries striking and vivid echoes of Russell's *most* haunting dream: the nightmare he recorded in June 1893 of his mother's secret madness ('I dreamt last night that . . . my people had deceived me, that my mother was not dead but in a madhouse').

For this story alone, Russell would have had reason to think that Lawrence was a man blessed with the kind of insight to understand his secret fears and nightmares; that he, like Conrad, would be able to see straight into his soul. Perhaps this explains why, when he went with Ottoline to meet Lawrence at his home in Greatham, Sussex, on 6 February 1915, he did so with the hope and the expectation that, if he could get to know Lawrence, there would be at least one member of the human race to whom he was not a stranger.

14
BREAKING THE SHELL

'He is amazing,' Russell said of Lawrence a few hours after getting to know him, 'he sees through and through one.'

'But do you think he really sees correctly?' Ottoline asked.

'Absolutely,' Russell replied. 'He is infallible . . . he sees everything and is always right.'

What they talked about at this first meeting is unknown, but, as well as convincing Russell of the infallibility of Lawrence's psychological insight (despite his earlier argument in *Our Knowledge of the External World* and 'Mysticism and Logic' that such 'infallible' insight generally turned out to be illusory), it also seems to have convinced Lawrence that he and Russell were allies in the struggle to create a better life, and, potentially at least, collaborators in the writing of philosophy.

A week after the meeting, Lawrence sent Russell a long letter, giving him a taste of the kind of philosophical writing that makes up *Le Gai Savaire* (or 'Study of Thomas Hardy'). In the letter, the central image is that of 'the shell', which, like Russell's image of 'the prison', is used by Lawrence as a metaphor for repression and confinement. Each human soul is entrapped in a shell that, like the bud of a flower, must be broken in order to let that soul live. For Lawrence, however, it was important that the image is biological rather than institutional, for his concern, in analysing the effects of living within a hard shell, is to understand the ways in which people are deflected from their natural growth. At the root of Lawrence's thinking is a veneration for natural impulses of the sort that Russell would previously have found repugnantly 'finite', but which now chimed perfectly with the quasi-religious reverence for sexual passion that had recently been aroused in him.

The bulk of Lawrence's letter is taken up with a theory of sexual relations, according to which the natural goal of all human life is the love between a man and a woman. Such love is the great adventure of life, the basis of all self-discovery and self-fulfilment. 'Love is,' Lawrence told Russell:

> that I go to a woman to know myself, & knowing myself, to go further, to explore into the unknown, which is the woman, venture in upon the coasts of the unknown, and open my discovery to all humanity.

When an individual is enclosed in its shell, however, such love is not possible. The individual cannot then go out into the unknown, but has to turn in on itself. This can take various forms: first, and probably most commonly, it takes the form of seeking sensation rather than love. Sensationalism, for Lawrence, is the 'repeating of a known reaction upon myself':

This is what nearly *all* English people now do. When a man takes a woman, he is *merely* repeating a known reaction upon himself, not seeking a new reaction, a discovery. And this is like self-abuse or masturbation. The ordinary Englishman of the educated class goes to a woman now to masturbate himself.

Secondly, it can take the form of homosexuality, for sodomy, according to Lawrence, is just another form of masturbation. Yet another form it can take is celibacy. Those souls who are trapped inside their shell, turned in on themselves and unable to enjoy true love, but who are strong enough to resist sensationalism (masturbation), and who have too much honour to use another body as a form of masturbation (homosexuality), remain celibate.

Linked to this theory of individual fulfilment (what Ottoline called Lawrence's 'gospel of instinctive development') is a theory of politics and economics to which Lawrence devoted the rest of this long letter to Russell. His basic thought here is that political and economic questions have to be settled and got out of the way before we can even begin to 'examine marriage and love and all', that is, before we can begin to think about the development of the individual. For, just as an individual can be trapped inside a shell, so, Lawrence argues, can a whole society. In particular, under capitalism the life of the community is trapped 'within the hard, unliving, impervious shell' that is the relentless pursuit of material things. Thus, in politics, just as in psychology, 'we have to break the shell, the form, the whole frame' and render the struggle for basic material necessities obsolete. We have, that is, to overthrow the old order and impose Socialism:

There must be a revolution in the state. It shall begin by the nationalising of all industries and means of communication, & of the land – in one fell blow. Then a man shall have his wages whether he is sick or well or old – if anything prevents his working, he shall have his wages just the same. So we shall not live in fear of the wolf.

This, Lawrence announces, with, as it were, an impatient wave of his hand, 'practically solves the whole economic question for the present'.

Russell was unsure quite how to respond to this extraordinary letter. About its psychology, he said nothing, either because he did not understand it, or because he agreed with it, or perhaps because he was prepared on this subject to bow to Lawrence's superior wisdom. Politically, however, he felt on firmer ground, able to see clearly what Lawrence was saying, and rather discomforted by its unsophisticated, almost juvenile over-simplifications and dogmatism. Lawrence was, he told Ottoline, 'extraordinarily young' in his political opinions, 'thinking (as the young do) that because *he* sees the desirability of Socialism it can be got by a few years' strenuous work. I feel his optimism difficult to cope with – I can't share it & don't want to discourage it.'

Russell's letters to Lawrence have not survived, so we do not know what he said in reply, but the effect it had on Lawrence was to make him feel embarrassed at having got out of his depth. 'I feel quite sad,' he wrote on 26 February, 'as if I talked a little vulgar language of my own which nobody understood . . . You must put off your further knowledge and experience, and talk to me my way, and be with me, or I feel a babbling idiot and an intruder.' Russell's letter, he said, 'was very kind . . . and somehow made me feel as if I were impertinent . . . I feel it impertinent to talk and write so vehemently. I feel you are tolerant when you listen. Which is rather saddening. I wish you'd tell me when I am foolish and overinsistent.'

Not that Lawrence seemed persuaded to alter his views one iota, except possibly to drop the claim that he had a solution to 'the whole economic question'. With regard to the rest, he was quite unrepentant: 'I have only to stick to my vision of a life when men are freer from the immediate material things,' he insisted, for only then can the focus of life's drama return to where it properly belongs 'between individual men and women, not between nations and classes':

And the great living experience for every man is his adventure into the woman . . . The man embraces in the woman all that is not himself, and from that one resultant, from that embrace, comes every new action.

'I wrote a book about these things,' he told Russell. 'I used to call it *Le Gai Savaire*. I want now to re-write this stuff, & make it as good as I can, & publish it in pamphlets, weekly or fortnightly, & so start a campaign for this freer life. I want to talk about it when I come to Cambridge.' But, he added: 'I don't want you to put up with my talk, when it is foolish, because you think perhaps it is passionate.'

The remark shows a perceptive grasp of Russell's attitude towards him. No matter how ill-considered Lawrence's political thought, Russell was prepared to put up with it because of Lawrence's 'fire'. A turning point in their relationship came when Russell invited Lawrence to Cambridge for the weekend of 6–8 March. Quite why he did so is not clear. Did he think it would be good for the dons to come into contact with someone with the revolutionary fire and passion of Lawrence? Or did he think it would be instructive for Lawrence to test his economic theories against Keynes and his philosophy against Moore? He could not in any case, have thought that he was bringing like-minded souls together, and, in the stark contrast between Lawrence and the Cambridge intellectuals, he had probably already decided that his sympathies lay more with Lawrence. Whatever his motives, he was in a much better position to know what to expect than Lawrence, who, in a letter written immediately before his visit, seems somewhat apprehensive, but also rather excited. 'I feel frightfully important coming to Cambridge,' he wrote, 'quite momentous the occasion is for me':

> I don't want to be horribly impressed and intimidated, but am afraid I may be. I only care about the revolution we shall have . . . Don't make me see too many people at once, or I lose my wits. I am afraid of concourses and clans and societies and cliques – not so much of individuals. Truly I am rather afraid.

Lawrence had just finished *The Rainbow* and was excited about that, also: 'I feel like a bird in spring that is amazed at the colours of its own coat':

> Also I feel very profound about my book 'The Signal' – Le Gai Saver – or whatever it is – which I am re-beginning. It is my revolutionary utterance. I take on a very important attitude of profundity to it, & so feel happy.

Lawrence, certainly, did not go to Cambridge thinking that he might learn anything, but rather that he might find converts to his profound and revolutionary gospel, his ambitions for which were growing daily. 'Remember,' he wrote to Ottoline a few days before the visit, 'it is not anything personal we want any more – any of us. It is not honour nor personal satisfaction, it is the incorporation in the great impulse whereby a great people shall come into being, a free race.' Ottoline was to be the Cassandra, the prophetess of this race, a 'great *media* of the truth', a medium through which the truth would come 'as through a fissure from the depths and the burning darkness'. The idea that truth came from darkness, from underground, from a region inaccessible to conscious thought, was becoming increasingly central to Lawrence's philosophy. 'It is not your brain you must trust to,' he told Ottoline, 'nor your will – but to that fundamental pathetic faculty for receiving the hidden waves that come from the depths of life':

> The source of passion is the burning darkness which quickens the whole ball of this earth, from the centre, it is not the bonfire built upon the surface, which is this man or that. But the dark fire, the hidden, invisible passion, that has neither flame nor heat, that is the greatest of all passion.

'Bertrand Russell wrote to me,' Lawrence told Ottoline in the same letter. 'I feel a hastening of love to him.'

Whatever other purpose Lawrence's visit to Cambridge might have had, it served at least to confirm this 'love' that both men felt for each other. 'I love him more & more,' Russell wrote to Ottoline, on 7 March, the Sunday of Lawrence's visit:

> Lawrence has quick sensitive impressions which I don't understand, tho' they would seem quite natural to you. They are marvellous . . . He can't stand the lack of vitality & force of the dons. I hope he won't visit it on me in his thoughts.

The previous evening, Lawrence had dined at high table in Trinity, seated next to Moore, who, however, had found nothing to say to him. The mathematician G. H. Hardy, on the other hand, was, according to Russell, '*immensely* impressed by him – after seeing him, he went round to Winstanley to tell him everybody here was utterly trivial, and at last he had met a real man.'

It was hardly likely that Lawrence – who had earlier analysed both sodomy and celibacy as perversions, symptoms of a life enclosed in a hard shell and denied its natural growth – would find among the dons he met at Trinity many whom he would describe as 'real men'. The strength of his revulsion, however, was extraordinary. Long afterwards, his imagination was haunted by the sight of John Maynard Keynes in his dressing-gown at breakfast in Russell's rooms on the Sunday morning. 'When I saw Keynes that morning in Cambridge,' he later wrote to his friend David Garnett (a junior member of the Bloomsbury group), 'it was one of the crises of my life. It sent me mad with misery and hostility and rage.' For Keynes, too, the breakfast party was a memorable occasion. He begins his essay 'My Early Beliefs' with a vivid evocation of it:

> I can visualise very clearly the scene of my meeting with D. H. Lawrence . . . It was at a breakfast party given by Bertie Russell in his rooms at Nevile's Court. There were only the three of us there . . . My memory is that he [Lawrence] was morose from the outset and said very little, apart from indefinite expressions of irritable dissent, all the morning. Most of the talk was between Bertie and me, and I haven't the faintest recollection of what it was about. But it was not the sort of conversation we should have had if we had been alone. It was *at* Lawrence and with the intention, largely unsuccessful, of getting him to participate. We sat round the fireplace with the sofa drawn across. Lawrence sat on the right-hand side in rather a crouching position with his head down. Bertie stood up by the fireplace, as I think I did, too, from time to time. I came away feeling that the party had been a failure and that we had failed to establish contact.

In his account of the occasion to Ottoline, Russell, like Keynes, was silent on the topic of conversation. He told her simply that, though Lawrence had liked Keynes the night before, 'seeing him this morning at 11, in pyjamas, just awake, he felt him corrupt and unclean'. Russell, however, persevered, and that evening had Keynes to dinner with Lawrence. This time, according to a letter he wrote Ottoline the next day, they 'had an interesting but rather dreadful evening':

> Keynes was hard, intellectual, insincere – using intellect to hide the torment & discord in his soul. We pressed him hard about his purpose in life – he spoke as tho' he only wanted a succession of agreeable moments, which of course is not really true.

This 'hard, intellectual, insincere' attitude was what Keynes was later inclined to think lay at the root of Lawrence's disapproval. The target of

Lawrence's rage, he thought, was 'Cambridge rationalism and cynicism', which were 'then at their height':

> . . . if I imagine us as coming under the observation of Lawrence's ignorant, jealous, irritable, hostile eyes, what a combination of qualities we offered to arouse his passionate distaste: this thin rationalism skipping on the crust of the lava, ignoring both the reality and the value of the vulgar passions.

Keynes's language here strikingly recalls Russell's description of Conrad, of Conrad's belief that civilised life was 'a dangerous walk on a thin crust of barely cooled lava which might at any moment break and let the unwary sink into fiery depths'. This sense of sitting on a volcano of 'vulgar passions', which might erupt at any moment and engulf them in fire, was, it seems, common to members of the Cambridge intellectual élite at the time. Its similarity to Lawrence's favourite image of a flower bursting its bud as the 'flame of nature' is striking; it was as if, in the meeting of the old refined civilisation, represented by Keynes, and the new primitivism, represented by Lawrence, both sides knew that the days of the former were numbered and that, before long, the crust would break.

What Keynes's account of this conflict leaves out, however, is the aspect of Lawrence's rage that Russell was quick to seize upon: his fierce dislike of homosexuality. Lawrence, Russell told Ottoline, with scarcely concealed glee, 'has the same feeling against sodomy as I have; you had nearly made me believe there is no great harm in it, but I have reverted; & all the examples I know inform me in thinking it sterilising'. In the wake of his visit to Cambridge, Lawrence began to describe homosexuals as black beetles, with a loathing that was as fierce as it was obsessive. 'I feel I should go mad when I think of your set,' he wrote to David Garnett:

> Duncan Grant and Keynes and [Francis] Birrell. It makes me dream of beetles. In Cambridge I had a similar dream. I have felt it slightly before in the Stracheys. But it came full upon me in Keynes and in Duncan Grant . . . you must leave these friends, these beetles.

Why beetles? The answer lies in the theory of sexual relations that he had outlined to Russell. The point was, as Lawrence explained to Ottoline, that homosexuals, like beetles, 'are cased each in a hard little shell of his own':

> There is never for one second any outgoing of feeling and no reverence, not a crumb or grain of reverence. I cannot stand it. I will not have people like this – I had rather be alone. They made me dream of a beetle that bites like a scorpion. But I killed it – a very large beetle – I scotched it and it ran off – but I came on it again, and killed it. It is this horror of swarming little selves I can't stand.

Confident in the knowledge that it was not directed at himself, Russell took a delight in the heat of Lawrence's wrath against the sterile atmosphere at

Cambridge, and one begins to suspect that the main reason he invited Lawrence in the first place was to justify and confirm his own distaste. Lawrence, he told Ottoline, 'hates everybody here, as was to be expected', adding the following day, 'His intuitive perceptiveness is *wonderful* – It leaves me gasping in admiration':

> Lawrence is wonderfully lovable. The mainspring of his life is love – the universal mystical love – which inspires even his most vehement & passionate hate.

Lawrence, according to Russell was, in short, 'disgusted with Camb., but not with me', which seemed to be just what Russell would expect from someone blessed with an infallible perceptiveness. From Russell's point of view, the weekend had been a success. 'I felt that we got on *very* well with each other, & made real progress towards intimacy,' he told Ottoline, perhaps revealing what he had most wanted from the visit.

Lawrence, too, wanted intimacy – he was not the sort of person who could get to know anyone without wanting to, so to speak, break their shell – but what in particular he wanted from Russell was encouragement from a distinguished philosopher to continue with his own philosophical writing. As he had intimated in his letter to Ottoline before his trip to Cambridge, his philosophy now took the form of trying to understand the darkness that, he thought, lay at the root of all passion. And, for Lawrence, trying to understand something meant trying to live it. Thus, in his next letter to Russell, written on 15 March, he presented himself as a kind of intrepid voyager, venturing out further into the primeval darkness than anyone had gone before, into a place beyond words and beyond ordinary reality:

> ... sometimes I am afraid of the terrible things that are real, in the darkness, and of the entire unreality of these things I see. It becomes like a madness at last, to know one is all the time walking in a pale assembly of an unreal world – this house, this furniture, the sky & the earth – whilst oneself is all the while a piece of darkness pulsating in shocks, & the shocks & the darkness are real. The whole universe of darkness & dark passions – ... the subterranean black universe of the things which have not yet had being – has conquered for me now, & I can't escape. So I think with fear of having to talk to anybody, because I can't talk.

It is doubtful whether Russell would have made much sense of this, and Lawrence perhaps knew that he would not. He was writing as an explorer to a friend left behind, of things he knew would seem unintelligible. 'I wanted to write this to ask you please to be with me – in the underworld,' he told Russell:

> or at any rate to wait for me. Don't let me go that is all. Keep somewhere, in the darkness of reality, a connection with me. I feel there is something to go through – something very important. It may be it is only in my own

soul – but it seems to grow more and more looming, & this day time reality becomes more & more unreal, as if one wrote from a grave or a womb – they are of the same thing, at opposite extremes. I wish you would swear a sort of allegiance with me.

When Russell hoped that Lawrence would improve his understanding of the darker side of human psychology, he probably did not imagine it would take the form of this sort of report from the underworld, and he seems to have seen in this letter no more than an expression of Lawrence's depressed state of mind. But Lawrence, now a seasoned traveller in subterranean regions, was determined to bring the enquiry closer to home, and in his next letter, written just a few days later, he gave notice that he was determined to include Russell's psyche in these subterranean explorations:

Do you still speak at the U. D. C. of the nations kissing each other, when your soul prowls the frontier all the time most jealously, to defend what it has & to seize what it can. It makes me laugh when you admit it. But we are all like that. Only, let us seize and defend that which is worth having, & which we want.

It was a gentle enough beginning, but it was enough – or should have been – to warn Russell that he could not establish intimacy with someone, could not let them see through the walls that separated him from other people, unless he was prepared for them to see things that he would rather keep hidden. For, with the infallible insight for which Russell revered him, Lawrence had put his finger on the central conflict in Russell's nature: the tension between his feeling of alienation from the rest of humanity and his espousal of a selfless identification with it; and the analogous tension between his fierce, dark hatreds and his ideal of a universal love. When Russell had tried to see Lawrence's own vehement hatreds as springing from a universal mystical love, he was but trying to foist on to Lawrence his own ideal. Lawrence saw this and resisted it.

In a passage added to *Twilight in Italy* in 1915, at the time of their conversations, Lawrence provides – without mentioning Russell by name – a brilliant dissection of the conflict at the heart of Russell's personality, which also implicitly rejects Russell's attempt to foist 'universal mystical love' upon his own passionate hatreds. 'We are trying to become again the tiger, the supreme, imperial, warlike Self,' Lawrence writes. 'At the same time our ideal is the selfless world of equity.' This ideal, he thinks, and therefore the self-conflict it creates, is an aspect of the 'new spirit' which 'developed into the empirical and ideal systems of philosophy'. In describing this 'new spirit', Lawrence characterises it as a combination of a 'Spinozistic' ethic that seeks to overcome the individual ego and a respect for the objectivity of science. What he describes, in other words, is Russell's own 'philosophy of life':

Man is great and illimitable, whilst the individual is small and fragmentary. Therefore the individual must sink himself in the great whole of Mankind.

This is the spirituality of Shelley, the perfectibility of man . . . When a man knows everything and understands everything, then he will be perfect, and life will be blessed . . . When I have submerged or distilled away my concrete body and my limited desires, when I am like the skylark dissolved in the sky yet filling heaven and earth with song, then I am perfect, consummated in the Infinite. When I am all that is not-me, then I have perfect liberty. I know no limitation. Only I must eliminate the Self.

It was this religious belief which expressed itself in science. Science was the analysis of the outer self, the elementary substance of the self, the outer world.

'Our aim', Lawrence writes in a passage in which it is hard not to think that he has Russell directly in mind, 'is a perfect humanity, a perfect and equable human consciousness, selfless. And we obtain it in the subjection, reduction, analysis, and destruction of the Self. So on we go, active in science and mechanics, and social reform.'

'At the same time,' he points out, 'we want to be warlike tigers.' This leads him to an elaboration of a contradiction similar to that which he had smilingly drawn to Russell's attention, between Russell's talk of the nations kissing one another and his prowling, tiger-like, to defend what he had and seize what he could:

That is the horror: the confusing of the two ends. We warlike tigers fit ourselves out with machinery, and our blazing tiger wrath is emitted through a machine. It is a horrible thing to see machines hauled about by tigers . . . It is a still more horrible thing to see tigers caught up and entangled and torn in machinery . . .

We say: 'I will be a tiger because I love mankind; out of love for other people, out of selfless service to that which is not me, I will even become a tiger.' Which is absurd. A tiger devours because it is consummated in devouring, it achieves its absolute self in devouring. It does not devour because its unselfish conscience bids it do so, for the sake of the other deer and doves, or the other tigers . . .

We try to say, 'The tiger is the lamb and the lamb is the tiger.'

In the struggle between the tiger and the machine, Lawrence's sympathies, of course, lay with the tiger. His criticism of Russell was that, like the entire tradition of thought he represented, his sympathies were divided between the tiger and the machine. And, just as Lawrence was not going to allow Russell to transform his tigerish wrath into the love of the lamb, neither was he going to let Russell's own tigerish nature remain invisible behind, so to speak, the machine.

Russell saw the conflict that was looming between himself and Lawrence, in similar terms, as a question of how far one could go in freeing the tiger from the machinery. 'I foresee awful fights with him,' he wrote to Ottoline on 3 April. 'It is odd that Lawrence doesn't understand how Love (the Universal kind) may be just as deep as the tiger.' A few days later, still determined to attribute to Lawrence a 'fund of gentleness & universal love', Russell told Ottoline:

> His view of human nature is very congenial to me, only I don't think *everybody* is a 'Tyger, Tyger', as he does. But I feel he helps one to understand many things.

One can see in Russell's writings on the war around this time a new emphasis on animal instincts in mankind, which, I suspect, owes much to his discussions with Lawrence. In 'On Justice in War-Time', which he was writing at the time of these discussions, he gives special emphasis to something he had previously either resisted or conceded only reluctantly: that men, no less than other animals, have an instinct to fight. Or, as he puts it, with a misanthropy that is only partially ironic, 'Fighting and killing are among the natural activities of males, both of human beings and of the higher animals':

> The spectacle of males killing each other in sexual combat is pleasant presumably to animal females, and certainly to many of those of the species *homo sapiens*. Owing to the activities of the police, opportunities for these pleasures are much curtailed in civilised countries. For this reason, when war is coming there is a liberation of a whole set of instinctive activities normally repressed.

'The war is not being fought for any rational end,' he insists. 'It is being fought because, at first, the nations wished to fight, and now they are angry and determined to win victory. Everything else is idle talk, artificial rationalising of instinctive actions and passions':

> When two dogs fight in the street, no one supposes that anything but instinct prompts them, or that they are inspired by high and noble ends. But if they were capable of what is called thought, if they had been taught that Dog is a rational animal, we may be sure that a superstructure of belief would grow up in them during the combat. They fight really because something angers them in each other's smell. But if their fighting were accompanied by intellectual activity, the one would say he was fighting to promote the right kind of smell (*Kultur*), and the other to uphold the inherent canine right of running on the pavement (democracy).

Whereas Russell writes with evident disgust about the spectacle of dogs driven to fight each other because of their smell, what Lawrence found disgusting about the war (and Russell had still perhaps not understood him properly on this point) was precisely that it was *not* analogous to a dog-fight. The instinctive aggression that animals had for each other was a part of nature that Lawrence had no trouble at all in accepting and even celebrating. That a tiger devours a lamb was entirely in the nature of things. What disgusted him about the war was its impersonal, mechanised nature. It was a long way removed from natural animal passion. And, that, for him, was precisely what was wrong with it.

In his letters to Ottoline of April and May 1915, Russell began to sound a note of scepticism and aloofness about Lawrence. When Lawrence berated Ottoline for dominating people with the strength of her will, Russell commented: 'Lawrence dislikes any will except his own, & he doesn't realise the place of will in the world. He seems to think instinct alone sufficient. I think his meditations on Satan will cure him of this view.' And after he had received a letter from Lawrence full of rage because he had been asked to pay £150 towards the cost of his wife Frieda's divorce from Ernest Weekley ('I cannot tell you how this reinforces in me my utter hatred of the whole establishment,' Lawrence thundered), Russell commented:

It is very unfortunate that he should be driven to hate society more than he already did. It will make it harder to bring him to a less hostile frame of mind. On the other hand, it will distract him from sex. I think political pre-occupations are good for him, tho' not likely to do any political good.

In the first few weeks of May 1915, however, everything changed. The sinking of the *Lusitania* and the introduction of gas warfare by the Germans increased still further the ferocity of public opinion, and that, together with news of the death of Rupert Brooke, brought Russell to new depths of despondency. 'I keep fearing', he wrote to Ottoline on 9 May, 'that something of civilisation will be lost for good, as something was lost when Greece perished in just this way':

Strange how one values civilisation – more than one's friends or anything – the slow achievement of men emerging from the brute – it seems the ultimate thing one lives for – I don't live for human *happiness*, but for some kind of struggling emergence of mind.

On 15 May he wrote in even bleaker terms to his American protégé, Norbert Wiener: 'Feeling here is enormously more fierce than it was. We expect the war to go on for years longer, and only to stop when all the adult males on one side or the other are dead . . . European civilisation, as it existed since the Renaissance is, I think, a thing of the past.'

The destruction of the old order was uppermost in Russell's mind throughout that spring, and a debate raged within him as to what extent he was inseparably a part of that old order, or whether he was to be part of a new society. It was a conflict that was linked in his mind with his friendship for Lawrence, who, with his working-class background and aspirations for a new beginning, seemed to Russell as far removed as one could be from the old order. Towards the end of April, after Ottoline had left her house in Bedford Square but had not yet moved into her recently acquired country house in Garsington, in Oxfordshire, Russell took her on a visit, heavily laden for both of them with a poignant symbolism, to Bolsover Castle, the Elizabethan house in Nottinghamshire that she loved and that was, in some almost spiritual sense, her home. It had been built for her ancestor, William Cavendish, the first Duke of Newcastle, and was now owned by her brother, the Duke of Portland. As they wandered through the various grand rooms, Ottoline took delight in imagining herself back in the world of her seventeenth-century ancestors. 'Do you think one's forefathers affect one, Bertie?', she asked:

> After all, one cannot but be coloured by the sap that flows in the tree, that has given one life. In old days I didn't think about my ancestors, or perhaps I took pride in not feeling proud of them, but now . . . the company of the dead seem to press upon me . . . Just as it is easy to recognise in some old family portrait hanging at Welbeck a nose or a mouth, or the shape of a face, that one has obviously inherited, so do I recognise traits and characteristics that have come down to me.

It was a sentiment that Russell, always keenly aware of the role his family had played in the history of England, could easily understand. And yet, he resisted it. 'Yes,' he replied. 'I suppose coming from a good stock gives one a certain standard and balance, an unconscious assurance and courage, and one isn't so easily tilted awry as those who come out of families who have always had to obey.' But, he insisted, look at the advantages of not coming from a great family, especially the freedom from tradition and 'the primitive free instincts which give vigour and creativeness to such men as D. H. Lawrence for instance'. Above all, 'show me what all these privileged people do now with their inherited sensibility and culture':

> You know they despise art and cultivation as degenerate . . . The only thing they really care for or take seriously is sport or golf, and now the War.

'Why,' he said, 'even this old beautiful place has had its roof removed and panelling taken away, and you say your brother talks of selling the mantelpieces . . . No, no, don't talk to me of their inherited taste and sensibility. I don't believe in it!'

Intermingled with these reflections about the relative merits of the old and new orders was Russell's ambivalence about continuing at Cambridge. When his five-year lectureship came to an end, it had been assumed that Trinity would offer him a Fellowship, but, when Russell applied for two terms' leave of absence, the college asked him to undertake to give the bulk of his time during his leave to philosophy rather than to political agitation. Russell refused and was tempted to leave Trinity altogether. In the end a compromise was reached, whereby Trinity renewed his lectureship rather than making him a Fellow of the college and in turn agreed to Russell taking two terms off to pursue his political work. In the negotiations, Russell told Ottoline, 'I have been made aware of a mass of hostile feeling which I hardly recognised':

> I am only just realising how Camb. oppressed me. I feel far more alive here [in London], & far better able to face whatever horrors the time may bring.

Camb. has ceased to be a home & a refuge to me since the war began. I find it unspeakably painful being thought a traitor. Every casual meeting in the Court makes me quiver with sensitive apprehension.

Lawrence, characteristically, urged Russell to have done with Cambridge. 'If they hound you out of Trinity, so much the better: I am glad . . . Leave your Cambridge then: that is very good.' The old life, with which – in Lawrence's mind – Cambridge was indissolvably attached, had to die to make way for the new spring of life:

Except a seed shall die, it bringeth not forth. Only wait. Our death must be accomplished first, then we will rise up. Only wait, & be ready. We shall have to sound the resurrection soon . . . let us die from this life, from this year of life, & rise up when the winter is drawing over, after the time in the tomb. But we are never dead. When everything else is gone, & there is no touch nor sense of each other left, there is always the sense of God, of the Absolute. Our sense of the Absolute is the only sense left to us.

Leaving Cambridge could only bring him and Russell closer together. 'We are one in allegiance, really, you and I,' he ended the letter. 'We have one faith, we must unite in one fight.'

In his disgust with the elderly dons at Cambridge, Russell was prepared to go along with this talk of allegiance. When in his next letter, Lawrence said how glad he would be when Russell had 'strangled the invincible respectability that dogs your steps', Russell told Ottoline: 'I *feel* he is right, that I should have 10 times the energy if I were done with respectability', and in a strikingly Lawrentian manner he added:

The world grows more and more black and furious. We are nowhere near the worst yet. But a new order *must* emerge from all this.

Freed from academic duties for the next two terms, at least, and increasingly alienated from his old 'home' of Trinity, Russell – though he had not yet burnt any boats – began to entertain thoughts of working outside academia altogether, and was increasingly tempted to throw in his lot with the new order, as represented by Lawrence. Over the summer the two men moved closer and closer to each other. 'Bertie Russell is being separated from the pack,' was how Lawrence put it in a letter to Ottoline. 'I am very glad. Soon he will be an outlaw. I am very glad. Then we are brothers.' As a mark of their allegiance, their brotherhood, Russell agreed to visit Lawrence in Greatham on 19 June to discuss what they might do together. 'I shall be glad to see you again,' wrote Lawrence on 2 June. 'I shall give you my philosophy'.

The first batch of Lawrence's philosophy, called at this time (again in imitation of Nietzsche), *Morgenrot*, was sent by him to Russell on 8 June. 'You mustn't think it bosh,' he instructed Russell, perhaps knowing full well that Russell *would* think it bosh:

I depend on you to help me with it. Don't go against me, & say it doesn't interest you, or that there are beautiful things in it, or something like that. But help me, & tell me where I can say the thing better.

Despite his talk of being united in a brotherhood of outlaws, Lawrence in some ways showed more fear of the authorities, more prudence in the face of danger, than Russell. He had become alarmed at the new daring with which Russell wrote against the Government, which, since the sinking of the *Lusitania*, had taken on a more bellicose character. 'I got the Labour Leader with your article against Lord Northcliffe,' he told Russell

I think Lord Northcliffe wants sinking to the bottom, but you do say rash things, & give yourself away. Let me beg you not to get into trouble now, at this juncture. I do beg you to save yourself for the great attack, later on, when the opportunity comes. We must go deeper & beyond Lord Northcliffe. Let us wait a little while, till we can assemble the nucleus of a new belief, get a new centre of attack, not using Labour Leaders & so on.

The article that bothered Lawrence was 'Lord Northcliffe's Triumph', published in *The Labour Leader* on 27 May 1915. In it, Russell congratulates, with heavy and intemperate irony, the newspaper magnate Lord Northcliffe (owner of *The Times* and the *Daily Mail*) on his success in orchestrating the downfall of Asquith's Liberal government and its replacement by a coalition government, guaranteed to pursue the war with even greater vigour. 'War being good in itself,' Russell writes in one of the passages that Lawrence was probably troubled by, 'it is impossible to have too much of it. Having got war, Lord Northcliffe felt it his duty to try to prolong it.'

The article was indicative of a new tone that entered Russell's polemics against the war at about this time, a reaction to the worsening prospects for those who wanted peace. He was thinking of leaving the UDC and joining the more radical No-Conscription Fellowship. 'The UDC will be all right *after* the war,' he told Ottoline, 'but for the moment they are tumbling over each other in their eagerness to disclaim any lack of patriotism or of determination that the victory must be ours. This puts such a restraint upon what one can say that it half paralyses one.' He was, too, becoming impatient with detailed debates about policy, and more concerned with general and fundamental questions:

I grow less & less interested in the politics of the war, & more & more to feel that the important thing is to denounce *all* war ... I don't like getting involved in irrelevant controversies on questions of fact, which don't really matter one way or another.

Two days later, on 10 June, Russell described to Ottoline a scene he had witnessed on a train in which he had travelled with some wounded soldiers:

One of them described, amid roars of laughter, how a German had knelt before him & besought mercy with tears, but he (the speaker) had put his bayonet through him. Perhaps he was boasting.

It was a side of human nature he was still coming to terms with, and one that he was convinced most pacifists would never understand. 'I wish good people were not so mild,' he wrote the next day. 'The non-resistance people I know here are so Sunday-Schooly – one feels they don't know the volcanic side of human nature':

They would never have denounced the Pharisees or turned out the money-changers. How passionately I long that one could break through the prison walls in one's own nature. I feel now-a-days so much as if some great force for the good were imprisoned within me by scepticism & cynicism & lack of faith. But those who have no such restraints always seem ignorant & a little foolish. It all makes one feel very lonely.

In Lawrence, Russell had met precisely the kind of man who *would* have denounced the Pharisees and turned out the money-changers, and who was not paralysed by scepticism and cynicism. But was he ignorant and foolish? Russell desperately wanted to believe not, but he was forced to admit that he could not take much pleasure in the philosophical writing Lawrence had sent him. 'I can't make head or tail of Lawrence's philosophy,' he confessed to Ottoline. 'I dread talking to him about it. It is not sympathetic to me.' The following day, he described it as 'rather uneducated stuff':

I feel as you would if I wrote about pictures. Yet I believe there is a great deal in it – only the form is bad, & he doesn't know how to say only what is to the purpose. He will be angry, & fight like the devil. I think the imagination out of which it springs is good – rather Blake-ish. But he lacks art, & loses intensity through lengthiness. However, I must read it again before I can feel sure about it.

Despite claiming to dread talking to Lawrence about his philosophy, however, Russell invited himself to Garsington the following week, when he knew Lawrence would be there, presumably with the intention of doing just that.

The few days that Ottoline and Russell spent with the Lawrences at Garsington, 14–16 June 1915, are remembered vividly in Ottoline's memoirs and transformed by Lawrence into the chapter called 'Breadalby' in *Women in Love*. For Ottoline, they were memorable for the sight of Russell, Lawrence and the rest, dressed in white overalls and helping to decorate with gold the panels in one of the rooms, and also for the discordant note struck by Frieda, whom she describes as sitting 'on a table in the middle of the room, swinging her legs and laughing and mocking us':

She had a terrible irritant quality, and enjoys tormenting . . . She was jealous that we all liked and admired Lawrence, or Lorenzo as she calls him, and that we did not consider her as important a person as she is ... I began to fear she would make it difficult to be friends with him, she was already turning him against Bertie because Bertie didn't flatter her.

'In spite of Mrs Lawrence,' Russell wrote to Ottoline, 'it was a *very* happy time to me ... I like the atmosphere of your house & garden *immensely*. It did me all the good in the world being out of doors all day.'

A few days later Russell kept his appointment to visit the Lawrences at Greatham. 'I am glad I went,' he told Ottoline. He and Lawrence had talked, among other things, about Ottoline herself:

He has a very profound and wise admiration for you. He keeps saying you are a priestess, a Cassandra, and that your tragedy is to have never found the God Apollo. He is quite right. He *feels* all your quality as no one else seems to. It makes me love him.

But they had also talked about a joint project. As Lawrence described it to Ottoline, in a letter written while Russell was still there:

We think to have a lecture hall in London in the autumn, and give lectures: he on Ethics, I on Immortality: also to have meetings, to establish a little society or body around a *religious belief, which leads to action*. We must centre in the knowledge of the Infinite, of God.

'You must be president,' he urged Ottoline. 'You must preside over our meetings. You must be the centre-pin that holds us together, and the needle which keeps our direction constant, always towards the Eternal thing. We *mustn't* lapse into temporality':

We must have some meetings at Garsington. Garsington must be the retreat where we come together and knit ourselves together. Garsington is wonderful for that ... That wonderful lawn, under the ilex trees, with the old house and its exquisite old front – it is *so* remote, so perfectly a small world to itself, where one *can* get away from the temporal things to consider the big things. We must draw together.

'Russell and I have really got somewhere,' he announced, 'we are rallying to a point.' As he described it, this 'point' was a movement in which he was to be the prophet, Russell the disciple and the holy script the latest version of his 'philosophy'. In his evangelical fervour, he talked of Russell as if he were a valuable but suspect follower whom one had to watch for signs of backsliding, to make sure he did not lose altogether his always insufficient grip on 'eternal things':

I do want him to work in the knowledge of the Absolute, in the knowledge of eternity. He *will* – apart from philosophical mathematics – be so temporal, so immediate. He won't let go, he won't act in the eternal things, when it comes to men and life. He is coming to have a real, actual, logical belief in Eternity, and upon this he can work: a belief in the absolute, an existence in the Infinite. It is very good and I am very glad.

In his own report of the weekend, Russell struck a similarly upbeat note, sounding almost willing to become the disciple for Lawrence's religion that Lawrence had presented him as being. 'Lawrence is *splendid*,' he wrote. 'I like his philosophy *very much* now that I have read more. It is only the beginning that is poor':

We talked of a plan of lecturing in the autumn on his religion, politics in the light of religion, & so on. I believe something might be made of it. It should make a splendid course on political ideas: morality, the state, property, marriage, war, taking them to their roots in human nature, and showing how each is a prison for the infinite in us. And leading on to the hope of a happier world.

He and Lawrence, Russell now felt, 'are curiously alike in many ways. He is less abstract, & does not feel himself lonely – the simple human feeling he has towards people prevents it – but in many ways we are wonderfully alike. His thoughts about the war are exactly like mine.' Russell had now lost interest in what he thought of as futile peace discussions – 'One might as well send a Quaker deputation to Etna to ask it not to erupt' – in favour of Lawrentian-style thoughts about the infinite. Just as he had needed to believe in Lawrence's 'infallible' insight into people's characters, so now he needed to believe that Lawrence's philosophy was not the 'uneducated stuff' it had at first appeared (though some of his comments give the impression of someone struggling to persuade himself). 'I am *very* glad Lawrence's philosophy seems to you good,' he told Ottoline. 'I think now that it is good. At first, the absence of movement seemed to me a defect, & my intellectual taste was offended now & then. But those are small things.'

He returned to London inspired by his discussions with Lawrence and at once got to work on a synopsis of his lectures. He had finished for the time being with political campaigning, he told Ottoline: 'My impulse is to sit & think . . . It is odd how full of energy & new life I feel – as if I could work all day.'

For the next two weeks Russell worked with the kind of euphoria that he had not known since before the war, and which recalls, ominously, his state of mind in the summer of 1913, when he worked with a comparable industry on *The Theory of Knowledge* manuscript. On 26 June, he remarked: 'My plan of lecturing in the autumn smiles on me more & more. I will certainly do it . . . the thing is *solid* in my mind, not just an airy project. I feel in my finger-tips that I could do it successfully.' Two days later: 'The thought of my lectures pleases me more & more.' Even when he discussed politics, he began to take on a Lawrentian tone, to insist that 'we must' do this, that and the other, without regard to pragmatic considerations:

We must try to found a new school of philosophic radicalism, like the school that grew up during the Napoleonic wars. The problem is to combine the big organisations that are technically unavoidable now-a-days with self-direction in the life of every man & woman. There must, for instance, be railways, but those who work on them need not be their slaves. I believe the State ought to cease altogether, & a man ought to belong to different groups for different purposes, each group chosen by himself, not determined by geography like the state . . . If one could give people hope, they would have the energy to do things.

In awakening in Russell his yearning for 'the infinite', his euphoria during these weeks recalls also the first flush of his love for Ottoline. In fact, Russell was inclined to feel that the inspiration Lawrence had given him was, in some sense, connected with his hopes for his love of Ottoline. 'I feel such a profound sense of union with you these days,' he wrote to her on 28 June, 'when I am most alive I am most one with you':

I feel & hope that at last what I felt I ought to get from you is coming to fruition. I feel free, liberated at last from the old shackles – pedantry & nonconformity – & from respectability & bigwiggery. It is good to throw away one's reputation & start again at the beginning.

The advantage of the work he was now doing over the work he had done in 1913, for example, was that he could share it with Ottoline. 'We always shared spiritual things,' he wrote to Ottoline on 4 July, 'but not mental things fully as long as my work was technical. Now I hope, at least for a time, we can share them altogether – it means a great deal to me.'
One of the 'old shackles' from which he was enjoying his liberty was his academic career, and his dreams of living outside the academic world became more insistent. 'Wouldn't it be delightful', he wrote, 'if I can establish myself in London as an independent teacher like Abelard? I should love the freedom of it.'
There is an air of unreality about Russell's pronouncements during these weeks, and as one reads these letters of late June and early July 1915, one waits with dread anticipation for the impulse to be shattered, as it was in 1913, 'like a wave dashed to pieces against a breakwater'. One reason for this is the utter implausibility of Russell as a disciple of Lawrence's religion. 'Experience gradually proves, as a rule, that the supposed insight was illusory,' he had written in 1913, and so, in this case, one waits for the illusion to be shattered, feeling that one knows with certainty it will be.
Another reason for feeling Russell's euphoria to be founded upon an almost wilful misreading of the situation was the stark contrast between his own political reflections and Lawrence's. He had begun to feel that the State ought to cease to exist altogether, but Lawrence, as he knew, dreamed of establishing a State that would, by nationalising property, land and everything else, ensure that nobody went hungry and that everybody was paid, whether they were fit for work or not. This would, of necessity, have to be a rather powerful State.

It is doubtful whether Lawrence ever imagined that it could be established democratically, but, as his thoughts on politics 'matured' (to the extent that they ever did), the undesirability of democracy loomed larger and larger in his *Weltanschauung*. 'I want the whole form of government changing,' he wrote to Lady Cynthia Asquith (the ex-Prime Minister's daughter-in-law) on 16 June:

> I don't believe in the democratic (republican) form of election. I think the artisan is fit to elect for his immediate surroundings, but for no ultimate government . . . the whole thing should work upwards, every man voting for that which he more or less understands through contact – no canvassing of mass votes.
> . . . women shall not vote equally with men, but for different things. Women *must* govern such things as the feeding and housing of the race. And if a system works up to a Dictator who controls the greater industrial side of the national life, it must work up to a Dictatrix who controls the things relating to private life.
> . . . There will inevitably come a revolution during the next ten years. I only don't want the democratic party to get control. We *must not* have Labour in power, any more than Capital.
> I want you to agree to these things, vitally: because we must prepare the way for this in the autumn.

When Russell agreed to co-operate with Lawrence to produce lectures discussing 'politics in the light of religion', these are the politics and the religion that Lawrence had in mind. One can only imagine that Russell had not understood Lawrence on the subject, for it is certain that he would never have committed his allegiance to anti-democratic politics. Yet it is almost equally unimaginable that they could have got this far without Lawrence expounding to Russell the same views that are contained in his letter to Lady Asquith; during the summer of 1915 he expounded them to all his correspondents. On the other hand, it is true that the first time Lawrence is explicit about it in his letters to Russell is in a letter dated 6 July. 'You must drop all your democracy', Russell was told:

> You must not believe in 'the people'. One class is no better than another. It must be a case of Wisdom, or Truth. Let the working classes *be* working classes. That is the truth. There must be an aristocracy of people who have wisdom, & there must be a Ruler: a Kaiser: no Presidents & democracies.

Perhaps Russell thought that because Lawrence's political opinions were half-baked and unsophisticated, he could easily be talked out of them. If so, he was soon to learn his mistake.

By the time Russell received this letter, he had already completed his synopsis of lectures, which he called 'Philosophy of Social Reconstruction', and had sent it to Lawrence. When it was returned to him on 8 July, it was covered with criticism so severe as to make Wittgenstein's assaults seem tentative by comparison. Lawrence hated what Russell had written. It was, he told Russell, 'all social criticism: it isn't social reconstruction':

> You must take the plunge into another element if it is to be social reconstruction . . . *Do, do* get these essays ready, *for the love of God*. But make them more profound, more philosophical . . . You must go very deep into the State, & its relation to the individual.

Russell, thought Lawrence, had been too concerned to criticise the existing State, instead of providing a blueprint for a new one: 'you must dare to be positive'.

Russell's synopsis, and Lawrence's scribbled comments on it, show that during the entire time the two had thought they were in allegiance, neither had really understood the other's philosophical perspective at all. The points on which they disagreed could hardly be more fundamental.

In his section headed 'The State', for example, Russell had written: 'Only fear now holds State together', against which Lawrence had scrawled: 'There must be a State, & a government.' Where Russell had written, 'Can't *worship* the State', Lawrence had put: 'What can I worship?' And so it continues. Russell: 'I feel more allegiance to mathematics than to the State'; Lawrence: 'Why?' Against Russell's argument that the State (which Lawrence qualified with the word 'existing') 'involves an entirely artificial division of mankind', Lawrence had written: 'You must advance on to the *New State*, where none of our sense of Truth is violated. You must give some conception of it, & your perfect belief in it':

> *Russell*: The State is in its very essence an evil thing, by its exclusions, and by the fact that it is a combination of men for murder and robbery.
> *Lawrence*: The State is the expression of a great metaphysical conception: the conception of God the Creator, who created the earth according to certain Laws, which, if obeyed, would give happiness. We proceed to create our State according to our religious belief, our philosophical conception of life . . . The State *must* represent the deepest philosophical or religious belief.

Clearly, Russell had never realised just how seriously Lawrence took his scheme to build Rananim, nor Lawrence how lightly Russell took it. When Lawrence talked of 'politics in the service of religion', he meant a State founded on (his) religious principles, not a sceptical demonstration that all political ideals are 'a prison for the infinite in us'. Lawrence had expected Russell to show that the *existing* State was a prison, not that all possible States were.

On moral psychology the two were, if anything, even further apart. 'Why should a man be moral?' Russell had asked, and answered: 'Because action against the desires of others makes him disliked, which is disagreeable to him.' Lawrence's comment on this was: 'NO! NO! NO! NO! NO!' Similarly on marriage, which Russell had defined as the result of 'sex instinct plus jealousy' (eliciting another 'No!' from Lawrence):

Russell: Successful monogamy ['now' Lawrence had interposed] depends upon the successful substitution of habit for emotion . . . A character which does not readily form habits, or does not find habits an adequate safeguard against emotion, is not suited to monogamy.

Lawrence: The desire for monogamy is profound in us. But the most difficult thing in the world is to find a mate. It is still true, that a man & wife are one flesh. A man alone is only fragmentary – also a woman. *Completeness is in marriage*. But State-marriage is a *lie*.

On none of these points did Lawrence succeed in persuading Russell to change his mind. However, on one important point, Lawrence's criticisms were accepted by Russell, forcing him to change his text and, so he was to say ever afterwards, considerably improve his lectures. The point at issue comes in the very last section of the synopsis, called 'Life Made Whole'. In this Russell had written, 'No need for hate or conflict: only the failure of inward joy brings them about.' Against this, Lawrence wrote:

There will always be hate & conflict. It is a principle of growth: every bud must burst its cover, & the cover doesn't want to be burst. But let our hatred & conflict be *really* part of our vital growth, the outcome of our growing, not of our desire for sensation.

In the published version of these lectures, *Principles of Social Reconstruction*, Russell adopted Lawrence's view.

On all other points, Russell was persuaded that he was in the right. 'Lawrence is just as furious a critic as Wittgenstein,' he reported to Ottoline, 'but I thought W. right & I think L. wrong.' Nevertheless, Lawrence's criticisms affected him deeply. 'I am depressed,' he told Ottoline, 'partly by Lawrence's criticisms. I feel a worm, a useless creature. Sometimes I enumerate my capacities, & wonder why I am not more use in the world. I suppose scepticism is my real trouble. It is always only by an act of will that I keep it under, & it weakens me.'

The saddest thing for Russell about Lawrence's criticisms was that they left him on his own again. He had longed to find someone who was neither inhibited by scepticism and cynicism nor prey to ignorance and folly, and thought, at last, he had found such a person in Lawrence. And, in finding someone with both wisdom and faith, he believed he might overcome his own paralysing scepticism. Now he was forced to admit defeat and to put Lawrence back into the ignorant and foolish camp, and himself back into the camp of the sceptics and cynics. The alternative was to embrace Lawrence's anti-democratic political philosophy, an alternative that Russell was never in the least tempted to accept.

On 10 July, the two men met in London, ostensibly to thrash out their differences on the lecture syllabus, but really, from Russell's point of view, it was already too late for that. Once he had realised what Lawrence's politics were, he could only be sceptical about them, and he was now inclined to see Lawrence's revolutionary political doctrine as the lunatic fantasy it always was. Acting as a propagandist for Lawrence was now out of the question. 'I told Lawrence that I thought we ought to be independent of each other,' he wrote to Ottoline, 'and not try to start a school':

> When he talks politics he seems so wild that I could not formally work with him . . . He is undisciplined in thought, and mistakes his wishes for facts. He is also muddle-headed . . . His attitude is a little mad and not quite honest . . . He has not learnt the lesson of individual impotence. And he regards all my attempts to make him acknowledge facts as mere timidity, lack of courage to think boldly.

The day with Lawrence was 'horrid'. 'I got filled with despair, and just counting the moments till it was ended.' Russell was, however, still prepared to concede that Lawrence's 'psychology of people is amazingly good up to a point', but presumably he had abandoned his former conviction of its infallibility.

Lawrence seemed slow to realise that Russell had lost all respect for his political views and, in his next two letters, continued to bombard him with anti-democratic tirades and to tell Russell what he *must* say in his lectures:

> In your lecture on the State, you must criticise the extant *democracy*, the young idea. That is our enemy . . . What we must hasten to prevent is this young democratic party from getting into power. The idea of giving power to the hands of the working class is *wrong* . . . The whole must culminate in an absolute *Dictator*, & an equivalent *Dictatrix*. There must be none of your bourgeois presidents of Republics . . . Liberty, Equality & Fraternity is the three-fanged serpent. You must have a government based upon good, better & best. You must get this into your lectures, at once . . . You *must* work out the idea of a new state, not go on criticising this old one.
> (15 July 1915)

> I rather hated your letter, & am terrified of what you are putting in your lectures. I don't want tyrants. But I don't believe in democratic control . . . The thing must culminate in one real head, as every organic thing must . . . something like Julius Caesar . . . It isn't bosh, but rational sense. The whole thing must be living. Above all there must be no democratic control . . . We must have the same general ideas if we are going to be or to do anything . . . This is a united effort, or it is nothing . . . It is no mere personal voice that must be raised: but a sound, living idea round which we all rally.
> (26 July)

But Russell was no longer listening. His conception of the lectures changed as soon as he realised what Lawrence's political views were. He still considered them to say something important about society, politics and psychology, but he no longer thought of them as having anything to do with Lawrence's 'gospel'. They were now for him precisely the kind of 'mere personal voice' that Lawrence decried, and he made steps to organise the lectures himself, quite independently of Lawrence. On 16 July he sent a revised syllabus to C. K. Ogden, then editor of *The Cambridge Magazine*, offering Ogden ten per cent of the gross takings if he would undertake to find a suitable hall and look after publicity and ticket sales. Ogden agreed, and Russell set to work writing the lectures, mostly at Garsington, during the summer and autumn of 1915. They were finished by December and delivered in the New Year, making a moderate profit for both Russell and Ogden. The 'sound, living idea' that Lawrence persisted in urging upon him was, for Russell, quite dead.

By September, Lawrence, too, was making his own plans. Instead of giving his philosophy as a series of lectures, he was now going to publish it in instalments in a journal called *Signature* that he, Middleton Murry and Katherine Mansfield were starting. On 5 September, Lawrence wrote to Russell to tell him about the new venture, with the hope, it seems, of persuading him both to subscribe and to submit a contribution. Russell responded quickly, sending an essay he had just written called 'The Danger to Civilisation', in which he emphasises the catastrophic effect that the war has had on the tradition of European civilisation and argues that: 'If the war does not come to an end soon, it is to be feared that we are at the end of a great epoch.' 'Is our civilisation a thing of no account to all our rulers?' he asks:

> I hope not. I hope that somewhere among the men who hold power in Europe there is at least one who will remember, at this late date, that we are the guardians, not only of the nation, but of that common heritage of thought and art and a humane way of life into which we were born, but which our children may find wasted by our blind violence and hate.

In sending an essay with this theme to Lawrence, Russell was showing once again (for there was no sign that he was being deliberately confrontational) how little understanding he had of Lawrence's thinking about the war and about Western civilisation. The 'effort after mental advancement' that Russell represented as characterising European civilisation since the Renaissance, and which he regarded as 'the most wonderful upward movement known to history', was exactly what Lawrence thought was the problem with Western civilisation! For Lawrence, it was the concern with mental advancement that had led to the disastrous denial of the body and all the unnaturalness of European life that was a consequence of that. Russell's essay was, for Lawrence, just one more manifestation of the malady, and a particularly acute one at that. For Russell seemed to argue precisely *for* the repression that Lawrence took to be the cause of the trouble. 'There is a wild beast slumbering in almost every man,' Russell wrote:

> but civilised men know that it must not be allowed to awake. A civilised man who has once been under the domain of the wild beast has lost his moral self-respect, his integrity and uprightness: a secret shame makes him cynical and despairing . . . it is of the first importance to control hatred.

But, as Lawrence knew from their earlier discussions, this was not actually Russell's view, not all of it, anyway. For Russell, he knew, sometimes at least revered, like himself, the 'beast within' and admired its fire and vitality, even its hatred. Russell, as Lawrence had seen with greater clarity than anyone else, was torn between, so to speak, the tiger and the machine, and yet, here, was denying that truth, that complexity. Knowing that Russell still had respect for his psychological insight, even if he had none for his politics, Lawrence responded to the article on 14 September with a quite extraordinary attack, not on what Russell had said in the essay, but upon Russell himself. 'I'm going to quarrel with you again,' he began. 'You simply don't speak the truth, you simply are not sincere':

The article you sent me is a plausible lie, and I hate it. If it says some true things, that is not the point. The fact is that you, in the Essay, are all the time a lie.

Your basic desire is the maximum of desire of war, you are really the super war-spirit. What you want is to jab and strike, like the soldier with the bayonet, only you are sublimated into words. And you are like a soldier who might jab man after man with his bayonet, saying 'this is for ultimate peace.' The soldier would be a liar. And it isn't in the least true that you, your basic self, want ultimate peace. You are satisfying in an indirect, false way your lust to jab and strike. Either satisfy it in a direct and honourable way, saying 'I hate you all, liars and swine, and am out to set upon you', or stick to mathematics, where you can be true – But to come as the angel of peace – no, I prefer Tirpitz a thousand times in that role.

You are simply *full* of repressed desires, which have become savage and anti-social. And they come out in this sheep's clothing of peace propaganda. As a woman said to me, who had been to one of your meetings: 'It seemed so strange, with his face looking so evil, to be talking about peace and love. He can't have *meant* what he said.'

I believe in your inherent power for realising the truth. But I don't believe in your will, not for a second. Your will is false and cruel. You are too full of devilish repressions to be anything but lustful and cruel. I would rather have the German soldiers with rapine and cruelty, than you with your words of goodness. It is the falsity I can't bear. I wouldn't care if you were six times a murderer, so long as you said to yourself, 'I am this.' The enemy of all mankind, you are, full of the lust of enmity. It is *not* the hatred of falsity which inspires you. It is the hatred of people, of flesh and blood. It is a perverted, mental blood-lust. Why don't you own it.

Let us become strangers again, I think it better.

To receive a letter like this from anyone would be wounding, but to receive it from someone to whom you once attributed an infallible insight, a wonderful intuitive perceptiveness that left you 'gasping in admiration', was quite devastating. Rarely can anger have been so effectively combined with psychological penetration. It was as if Lawrence could see straight into Russell's soul and know what would hurt it most. 'After reading it,' Ottoline says in her memoirs, 'Bertie sat still, quite stunned, for a whole day – he was deeply horrified, for his belief in Lawrence's insight was still unshaken, and he thought it must be true.' Russell himself remembers that the letter almost persuaded him that he should commit suicide, and this is borne out by his letters of the time. In one of them, he says: 'in my despair, I realised that I shall never again be in close touch with anyone':

> That was the substance of my despair. When I got back to my rooms Thursday night, I reached a pitch of despair that I have never reached before. At last I resolved to commit suicide in the spring, after my lectures. That kept me happy till morning.

Lawrence's attack, in forcing him, finally, to retreat behind the prison walls for ever, had persuaded Russell that there was no purpose in living any longer.

Apart from the fact that he believed what he was saying, the motive for Lawrence's attack, I believe, was to show Russell that he could, as it were, penetrate the walls. Lawrence had been slow to realise that Russell no longer identified himself with Lawrence's programme for social renewal, and he felt angry at the way he had been cold-shouldered. On 12 July, a few days after sending Russell his strident reaction to Russell's lecture syllabus, Lawrence had written in warm terms about Russell to Ottoline, telling her that, though he had quarrelled with Russell's lectures, 'I didn't quarrel with him':

> We have almost sworn *Blutbrüderschaft*. We will set out together, he and I. We shall really be doing something, in the autumn. I want you to believe always.

This was two days after the day in London that Russell had found so 'horrid', and at a time when Russell, far from regarding himself as Lawrence's blood brother, was trying to find polite ways of telling Lawrence he wanted to withdraw from their joint scheme. The letters that Lawrence wrote in July were written under the (false) belief that he and Russell were still partners. It was not until August that Lawrence realised that Russell had pulled out of their scheme, and, perhaps more important, that Russell now regarded himself as once more on his own. He reacted with fury. Russell, he came to think, was just like the other people he had met at Cambridge, wanting to stay behind his hard shell. 'What does Russell want?' he wrote to Cynthia Asquith on 16 August:

> He wants to keep his own established ego, his finite and ready-defined self intact, free from contact and connection.

Lawrence began to apply to Russell and Ottoline the views about sensationalism that he had expressed in his very first letter to Russell; that is, that inside their shells, Russell and Ottoline could not make real contact with other people and settled instead for a series of superficial sensations deriving pleasure, not authentically from their own lives, but vicariously through Lawrence himself.

> I've got a real bitterness in my soul, just now, as if Russell and Lady Ottoline were traitors – they are traitors. They betray the real truth. They come to me, and they make me talk, and they enjoy it, it gives them a profoundly gratifying sensation. And that is all. As if what I say were meant only to give them gratification, because of the flavour of personality, as if I were a cake or wine or a pudding. Then they say I, D.H.L., am wonderful, I am an exceedingly valuable personality, and that the things I say are extravaganzas, illusions. They say I cannot think.
>
> All that is dynamic in the world, they convert to a sensation, to the gratification of what is static. They are static, static, static, they come, they say to me, 'You are wonderful, you are dynamic', then they filch my life for a sensation unto themselves, all my effort, which is my life, they betray, they are like Judas: they turn it all to their own static selves, convert it into the static nullity. The result is for them a gratifying sensation, a tickling, and for me a real bleeding. But I know them now, which is enough.

The savage letter to Russell was, I think, designed to show that, indeed, Lawrence did 'know them', that he could break through Russell's shell.

In 'The Blind Man', written in the 1920s, Lawrence turned his friendship with Russell into an extremely powerful short story. The Lawrence character in the story is a man called Maurice Pervin, who was blinded in the war and now lives on a farm. He and his wife had been almost entirely alone since he was wounded, and, writes Lawrence, 'talked and sang and read together in a wonderful and unspeakable intimacy'. The blind man, then, is a personification of Lawrence's conception, spelled out in one of his letters to Russell, of being in touch with the subterranean world beneath and before speech:

> Life was still very full and strangely serene for the blind man, peaceful with the almost incomprehensible peace of immediate contact in darkness.

In other words, it was an advantage being blind. Pervin did not regret the loss of his sight. On the contrary: 'A certain exultance swelled his soul.' Disturbing the peace of this couple, and not entirely welcome, is a visitor, a cousin of Mrs Pervin's called Bertie Reid. Bertie is 'the intellectual type, quick, ironical, sentimental, and on his knees before the women he adored but did not want to marry'. Pervin, by contrast was 'passionate, sensitive . . . a big fellow . . . his mind was slow . . . He was very sensitive to his own mental slowness, his feelings being quick and acute.' So, 'he was just the opposite to Bertie, whose mind was much quicker than his emotions, which were not so very fine.'

Pervin hated Bertie, 'and at the same time he knew the hatred was nonsense, he knew it was the outcome of his own weakness'. Bertie, too, had his weakness, which 'made him unable ever to enter into close contact of any sort. He was ashamed of himself, because he could not marry, could not approach women physically. He wanted to do so. But he could not. At the centre of him he was afraid, helplessly and even brutally afraid.' He was brilliant, successful, a *littérateur* of high repute, rich and a great social success. And yet 'At the centre he felt himself neuter, nothing.' Pervin, on the other hand, *lived* at the centre and 'The rich suffusion of this state generally kept him happy, reaching its culmination in the consuming passion for his wife.'

Bertie finds it hard to understand that Pervin does not mind being blind, that there is 'something' beyond thought and action with which he, in his blindness, is in immediate contact. His wife tries to explain: 'There is something else, something *there*, which you never knew was there, and which you can't express.' Bertie can't get it: 'I'm afraid I don't follow.'

The climax of the story comes when Bertie goes out to the barn to find Pervin. He finds him in the dark and has to hold up his lantern to make him out. They fall into conversation. 'I don't really know you, do I?' says the blind man:

'Probably not,' said Bertie.
'Do you mind if I touch you?'
The lawyer [Bertie] shrank away instinctively. And yet, out of very philanthropy, he said, in a small voice: 'Not at all.'
But he suffered as the blind man stretched out a strong, naked hand to him.

Bertie then has to endure the blind man moving his hand over his head, 'till he had covered the skull and the face of the smaller man, tracing the brows, and touching the full, closed eyes, touching the small nose and the nostrils, the rough, short moustache, the mouth, the rather strong chin':

The hand of the blind man grasped the shoulder, the arm, the hand of the other man . . .
'You seem young,'[1] he said quietly, at last.
The lawyer stood almost annihilated, unable to answer.
'Your head seems tender, as if you were young,' Maurice repeated. 'So do your hands. Touch my eyes, will you? – touch my scar.'
Now Bertie quivered with revulsion.

Bertie lifts his hand to the scar. Maurice suddenly covers it with his own hand and presses Bertie's fingers into the disfigured sockets, 'whilst Bertie stood as if in a swoon, unconscious, imprisoned'. Bertie is mute and terror-struck. He is afraid that the other man will destroy him: 'Whereas Maurice was actually filled with hot, poignant love, the passion of friendship. Perhaps it was this very passion of friendship which Bertie shrank from most.'

---

[1] Compare Lawrence on Russell in his letter to Ottoline of 19 July 1915: 'What ails Russell is, in matters of life and emotion, the inexperience of youth. He is, vitally, emotionally, much too inexperienced in personal contact and conflict, for a man of his age and calibre . . . Really, he is too absurdly young in his pessimism, almost juvenile.'

'We're all right together now, aren't we?' says Maurice. 'It's all right now, as long as we live.' (They have, as it were, sworn *Blutbrüderschaft*, as far as he is concerned.) 'Yes,' says Bertie, trying any means to escape. When they get back to Isabel, Maurice's wife, Maurice is elated, but Bertie is haggard, with sunken eyes. Isabel asks what has happened. 'We've become friends,' says Maurice. But Isabel, seeing Bertie's distraught state, knows better:

> She knew that he had one desire – to escape from this intimacy, this friendship, which had been thrust upon him. He could not bear it that he had been touched by the blind man, his insane reserve broken in. He was like a mollusc whose shell is broken.

Russell rebuilt the shell that Lawrence had broken, and made it stronger than ever. But, as Lawrence clearly realised, the piercing of Russell's protective outer layer was one of the most devastating events in his life. He was never so vulnerable again.

15
MRS E.

The horror with which Russell reacted to Lawrence's devastating letter of 14 September 1915 was to some extent that of seeing his own darkest thoughts about himself expressed by someone else. They were thoughts he preferred to keep in the dark. Every now and then, in his most self-searching and self-critical moods, he might express them privately in letters to Ottoline, but in his published writings he kept them hidden until, in 1953, at the age of eighty-one, he gave expression to them in 'Satan in the Suburbs'. The central character of the story, the satanic Dr Mallako, might be regarded as the very personification of Lawrence's phrase 'devilish repressions', consumed by exactly the kind of all-embracing hatred for the whole of mankind of which Lawrence had accused Russell. Mallako (who, as Russell repeatedly emphasises, represents the secret madness inside all of us)[1] is finally overcome by the narrator of the story, but only at the cost of the narrator being committed to a psychiatric hospital. Implied by the story is thus a terrifyingly bleak view of the relationship between insanity, emotional repression and the expectations of society. The devil, the madness, in us – the story seems to suggest – is the effect of emotional repression, and the only way of overcoming it, of remaining sane, is to express one's feelings openly and to admit one's secrets. And yet, by a terrible irony, the consequence of doing so is to be regarded as mad by the rest of society. The choice facing us then, it appears, is either to be driven genuinely mad by conforming to the expectations of society or to seem mad by confounding those expectations and revealing ourselves as we really are.

In 'Satan in the Suburbs' this moral is illustrated not once, but twice. A character called Mrs Ellerker, who is (apart from the narrator) the only person in the story who confronts, so to speak, the devil within and confesses her guilty secrets, is likewise committed to a psychiatric hospital. As he is waiting to be committed himself, the narrator's thoughts turn to Mrs Ellerker and the connection – one might almost say the bond – between himself and her:

---

[1] In a letter to his publisher, Stanley Unwin, of 24 May 1952, Russell insisted that 'Satan in the Suburbs' was not an ideal title, because 'there is really nothing supernatural about it', and that it 'should really, I think, be called "Horrors Manufactured Here" '. Given the emphasis in the story on Mallako's evil being internal, the word *here*, one imagines, ought really to be accompanied by a hand on the heart or the head.

I see the same fate awaits me as that from which I failed to save Mrs Ellerker. Nothing stretches before me but long dreary years of solitude and misunderstanding. Only one feeble ray of light pierces the gloom of my future. Once a year, the better behaved among the male and female lunatics are allowed to meet at a well-patrolled dance. Once a year I shall meet my dear Mrs Ellerker, whom I ought never to have tried to forget, and when we meet, we will wonder whether there will ever be in the world more than two sane people.

There is a naturalness about this passage that is missing from most of Russell's fictional writing, which is generally marred by a rather arch formality and artificiality. His treatment of the character of Mrs Ellerker contrasts strikingly with that of the other minor characters in the story. While they are merely badly drawn caricatures, she is a real person with real feelings. The reason for this, I feel sure, is that, in his portrayal of Mrs Ellerker, Russell was drawing on real life; in this case, on his affair with T. S. Eliot's wife, Vivien (another 'Mrs E'),[2] which lasted from the summer of 1915, immediately after the collapse of Russell's friendship with Lawrence, to the New Year of 1918.

In the story Mrs Ellerker betrays her rather dull husband to embark on an affair with Mr Quantox, described by Russell as 'sparkling and witty, a man of education and wide culture, a man who could amuse any company by observations which combined wit with penetrating analysis'. After he has got from her what he wants, however, Mr Quantox deserts Mrs Ellerker, leaving her embittered and tormented by her guilty secret. Finally, she tries to confess her misdeeds, but, because of the public esteem in which Mr Quantox is held, she is disbelieved and committed to an asylum.

The story of Mrs Ellerker has obvious parallels with that of Vivien Eliot, who spent the last nine years of her life in a psychiatric hospital (having been committed, it seems, against her will), apparently ignored and forgotten by her husband and her ex-lover, both of whom had deserted her long before her commital – Russell in 1918 and Eliot in 1932 – and both of whom, like Mr Quantox, enjoyed a considerable reputation among the public. Vivien Eliot was committed in 1938 and died in 1947. With her, it is natural to assume, died many secrets that would not have put either Eliot or Russell in a very good light. Was guilt about her one of the 'hitherto unexpressed feelings' to which Russell gave release in 'Satan in the Suburbs'? When he wrote that story, just five years after her death, had he come to think of her fate, as the narrator views that of Mrs Ellerker, as something from which he had failed to save her? And, like the narrator, had he begun to feel that he 'ought never have tried to forget' her?

That Russell had tried to forget her seems undeniable. In his *Autobiography* he gives no hint of the intimacy of his relationship with Vivien. He says

---

[2] In order to give this character a name beginning with 'E', Russell has to interrupt the strict alphabetical order in which he has introduced his other characters. After Mr Abercrombie, Mr Beauchamp and Mr Cartwright, the next character's name should begin with 'D'.

merely that he was fond of both the Eliots and 'endeavoured to help them in their troubles until I discovered that their troubles were what they enjoyed', a remark which, even if one did not know it to be extremely misleading, seems unnecessarily cold and unsympathetic. Later, he says that in the summer of 1915, as Ottoline grew comparatively indifferent to him, he 'sought about for some other woman to relieve my unhappiness' but omits to say that Vivien Eliot was the first 'other woman' in whose company he sought such relief. Even more misleading and, indeed, straightforwardly false, is the disavowal he made to Eliot's friend, Robert Sencourt: 'I never had intimate sexual relations with Vivienne.'[3]

These distortions, evasions and downright lies suggest a man with something to hide, a man with a guilty conscience. Did Russell suspect that he was in some way responsible for Vivien's fate? Certainly others have reached that conclusion. In a conversation with Graham Greene that he recorded in his diary on 21 July 1955, Evelyn Waugh learned, among a great many other pieces of gossip, 'that Mrs T. S. Eliot's insanity sprang from her seduction and desertion by Bertrand Russell'. As Greene knew neither Russell nor the Eliots, one can only assume that this particular piece of gossip had passed between many people before it reached Evelyn Waugh's diary. Perhaps, therefore, little credence should be given to it. T. S. Eliot, though he never accused Russell of causing his wife's mental illness, once told Ottoline that he thought Russell had made Vivien's condition worse.

In Russell's letters to Ottoline and, later, to Constance Malleson, something of his affair with Vivien is recorded – with what degree of frankness it is impossible to say, but sufficient, anyway, to reveal his later comments on the subject as the evasions they are. When, in a letter to Ottoline written in 1917, he tried to summarise what the relationship has meant to him, he did so in a way that makes him sound detached, even callous, towards her. Vivien, he says, turned up at a moment when he needed to regain his independence from Ottoline and he 'used her for the purpose'. Now that this purpose has been served, he implies, he – like Mr Quantox for Mrs Ellerker – has no further use for her.

Russell first met Vivien on 9 July 1915, the day after he received Lawrence's vehement criticisms of his lecture syllabus, and just two weeks after Vivien and T. S. Eliot were married. The marriage, it was already clear, was a disaster. A few days later, Russell recorded his impressions in a letter to Ottoline:

> Friday evg. I dined with my Harvard pupil Eliot & his bride. I expected her to be terrible, from his mysteriousness, but she was not so bad. She is

---

[3] For my reasons for thus categorically dismissing the truth of this claim, see pp. 510–14. Kenneth Blackwell has offered an interpretation of Russell's remark to Sencourt, which clears Russell of uttering a direct falsehood, and which regards him as denying, not that he had sexual relations with Vivien, but only that their relations were truly *intimate*. Whether this sophistry clears Russell of dishonesty is a matter of opinion, but the fact is that he did have sexual relations with Vivien, a fact that, in his correspondence with Sencourt and in his *Autobiography*, he seems extremely – and, to some extent, uncharacteristically – anxious to disguise.

light, a little vulgar, adventurous, full of life – an artist I think he said, but I should have thought her an actress. He is exquisite & listless; she says she married him to stimulate him, but finds she can't do it. Obviously he married in order to be stimulated. I think she will soon be tired of him. She refuses to go to America to see his people, for fear of submarines. He is ashamed of his marriage, & very grateful if one is kind to her.

That Russell should be having this fairly intimate conversation with Eliot and his new wife is in some ways surprising. At Harvard in the spring, he had been impressed by Eliot's intelligence and by the exquisite precision of his language, but there was nothing to indicate that they became particularly close friends. In October 1914, Russell (literally, it seems) bumped into Eliot in New Oxford Street, just outside his flat in Bury Street, and they exchanged a few words on the war, Eliot slightly shocking Russell by declaring that, with regard to the war, he knew only that he was not a pacifist (a position that Russell later caricatured by saying that Eliot did not mind who was being killed or why, just so long as they *were* being killed). But, in this meeting, too, there is nothing to suggest any burgeoning warmth or closeness between the two men.

Between that meeting in October and their dinner the following July, Eliot divided his time between Oxford, where he had a scholarship at Merton College to study the philosophy of F. H. Bradley under Harold Joachim, and London, where he was assiduous in cultivating the friendship of people influential in literary circles, most notably that of Ezra Pound. In the summer of 1915, he decided to move permanently to London to try and make a career for himself as a writer. The letters that he wrote to his family and friends during this summer show that this decision was linked in his mind with his rather sudden – and, as it turned out, reckless – decision to marry Vivien.

Vivienne Hiagh-Wood, as she was when Eliot first met her (she abbreviated her Christian name soon afterwards), came from a wealthy landowning family with a country home in Hampshire. Already, at the age of twenty-six, she was showing signs of the mental instability that would later alarm both Eliot and Russell, though despite this (or perhaps, in some measure, because of it) she exerted a strangely magnetic attraction. Aldous Huxley once called her 'an incarnate provocation'. Her friend Brigit Patmore described her as 'slim and rather small, but by no means insignificant':

> Light brown hair and shining grey eyes. The shape of her face was narrowed to a pointed oval chin and her mouth was good – it did not split up her face when she smiled, but was small and sweet enough to kiss. Added to this, she did not quiver, as so sensitive a person might, but shimmered with intelligence.

Eliot was immediately captivated. He married Vivien after knowing her for only a few months. Just two days after the wedding Ezra Pound wrote (no doubt at Eliot's prompting) to Eliot's father, trying to reassure him that a good living could be made in London as a freelance writer. In the coming months, Russell, too, was to provide further reassurance to Eliot's family on this point, support that Eliot was perhaps trying to enlist when he invited Russell to dinner on 9 July.

Another motive of Eliot's might have been to enlist Russell's help in looking after Vivien during the six weeks that he would be away in the United States. His ship left England on 24 July and he would not be back until the beginning of September. Having made the decision to pursue a career as a freelance writer, Eliot seems to have thought it necessary to brave the potentially perilous journey across the Atlantic to persuade those who might be disappointed by his decision – including his parents and his teachers at Harvard – that he was not acting rashly. Vivien, as Russell reports, refused to go, and no doubt one of the kindnesses towards Vivien for which Russell reports Eliot being grateful was that of promising to see her while Eliot was away.

Given that Russell was evidently quite taken with Vivien and convinced that she would soon grow tired of Eliot, it seems likely that there was something more in that promise than pure philanthropy. Russell was, at this time, desperately lonely. Having been disappointed by Lawrence, and – so he came increasingly to think – abandoned by Ottoline for the circle of friends she had gathered around her at Garsington, he needed, more than anything, the close companionship of someone with whom he could share his inner life and who would allow him (as Ottoline would not) to enter theirs.

A few days after his first meeting with Vivien, Russell left London to move into a flat in the Bailiff's House in Garsington Manor that Ottoline had prepared for him. There, with a well-equipped study overlooking the Berkshire Downs, he had the perfect conditions in which to work undisturbed on his lectures, and, as Ottoline put it, 'Whenever we had visitors that he liked he would come over and have his meals with us.' It should have been ideal, but within a month Russell decided that he could not work at Garsington. His life there lacked the thing he most needed: relief from his oppressive sense of loneliness.

When Russell began work at Garsington, though he had already abandoned any notion of his lectures being tied to Lawrence's 'religion', he had not yet abandoned the notion he had cherished in June of sharing his work with Ottoline, a notion which, as he told her at the time, 'means a great deal to me'. When, however, he tried to talk to Ottoline about his work, he found that a basic lack of sympathy had arisen between them that made such a sharing of ideas impossible. In one conversation recorded by Ottoline, he stressed the differences between his view of truth and Lawrence's, his being scientific and Lawrence's intuitive. As he might have expected, on this divide Ottoline's sympathies lay with Lawrence. 'There really seem to me three worlds,' she wrote, prompted by her conversation with Russell:

> the one which Bertie calls the *real* world, the world of the scientist . . . then the world of the ordinary businessman . . . and then the world of art, poetry and of feeling, of spiritual perceptions and imaginative creation and fantasy . . . This is the world that Shakespeare gave us, human life permeated with

a rich glow and vitality from the affections, the senses, the imagination. This is my world.

Russell, she goes on, though he enjoys this last world – her world – in *literature*, doesn't really live in it. He 'never treats it seriously: he never seems to contemplate the possibility that it could be a Utopia, absorbing into itself the other worlds.'

On one of their walks, Russell startled Ottoline by announcing that he found it difficult to talk to ordinary mortals, 'for the language they use is so inaccurate that to me it seems absurd'. 'When I talk to an ordinary person,' he told her, with a curious mixture of boastfulness and pathos, 'I feel I am talking baby language, and it makes me lonely.' It was as though he expected Ottoline to respond by, on the one hand, trying to relieve his loneliness, while, on the other, admiring the superior rigour of his intellect that made him lonely. In fact, she did neither; she merely found the attitude he expressed rather repellent. 'Oh dear,' she wrote in her journal, 'how terrible to be so removed from human life.'

By the end of his first week at Garsington, when Russell had to return to London to give a talk, it was already clear to him that things would not work out as he had hoped. Though he told Ottoline how touched he had been by all she had done to make him happy and how ideal the conditions there were for work ('I did really get on with the lectures, & I feel happy about them & able to do them now'), the dominant tone of his letter of 17 July was one of sadness. He had been unhappy, he told her, 'because I felt shut out & unable to reach you'. He had to fight against a feeling of defeat: 'I don't want to feel beaten inside, & sometimes the fear of losing heart makes me unkind to you.' He thought he could sense a similar feeling in her, a feeling that, he seemed to think, lay at the root of her changed attitude towards him:

I was *really* not hurt in the very slightest, because I do understand *quite fully* how your feeling has been numbed. It did make me unhappy. But just in the last moments, when we talked about it, I felt I reached you again. If I had been more full of spirits it would have been all right . . . And I feel *quite sure* you will revive as soon as there is anything in the world to give one hope. Don't think you are permanently numbed, I am certain you are not.

When he returned to Garsington, however, it soon became apparent that Ottoline's attitude towards him was not part of a more general 'numbness' caused by the war, but was a reaction against *him*. 'Bertie and I had a walk in the rain yesterday,' Ottoline wrote on 19 July:

He gets dreadfully on my nerves, he is so stiff, so self-absorbed, so harsh and unbending in mind or body, that I can hardly look at him, but have to control myself and look away. And of course he feels this, and it makes him harsher and more snappy and crushing to me. What can I do? I feel I *must* be alone and go my own way to develop my life, my own internal life.

Bertie crushes it out; he would remake me; and the effort of resisting him and of protecting myself makes me desperate. It is far better to be alone than to be false.

Garsington that summer became the haven for disaffected writers, artists and poets for which it is remembered and celebrated in innumerable memoirs and fictional portrayals, including, most famously, Aldous Huxley's *Crome Yellow* and D. H. Lawrence's *Women in Love*. In the company of people like Vanessa and Clive Bell, Duncan Grant, Lytton Strachey, Mark Gertler and Gilbert Cannan, Ottoline was surrounded by others who lived in her world of 'art, poetry and feeling', and Russell was, as he had felt, 'shut out'.

For, though he could more than hold his own in the brilliant and erudite conversation that flowed at Garsington, such company was not what Russell needed. It was not society he craved, but companionship, close, intimate contact with another person. What Ottoline experienced as Russell's crushing out of her internal life, was, from Russell's point of view, simply an attempt to get close to her. Frustrated in this attempt and conscious that, in making it, he was getting on Ottoline's nerves, Russell retreated into his work. But, to his bewilderment, he found that this did not suit Ottoline either. She was, she told him, hurt by his absorption in his work and the rejection of her that it implied. Understandably a little confused, Russell reacted by alternately hitting out at Ottoline and then apologising for his 'cruelty'. 'I am very sorry I hurt you by seeming only to care about my lectures,' he wrote to her from London on 28 July:

I was quite taken aback today when you spoke, because it had dawned upon me that you didn't know I was only protecting myself against your extreme coldness. For months past you have been growing more & more aloof – I was not hurt because I understood it, but I suffered a great deal. You seemed to be finding me a bore . . . With a good deal of effort, I built up my interest in the lectures to help me live through the time till you seemed not to dislike me. When you are cold, I must have other interests, or I shall be simply broken. *Please* don't resent it, or I don't know how I shall get on. For the moment, the lectures have become loathsome to me, but I suppose that will pass off soon.

The work that Russell had hoped he could share with Ottoline was by now proving to be just another barrier between them, leaving him puzzled, resentful and angry. 'I had had you so much in mind in my work,' he tried to explain in a letter of 30 July, '& felt as if it was a bond between us, that I was disappointed.' In this letter, as in so many of this period, he apologises for being cruel:

I am so full of sorrow that I have been so cruel. I do wish I didn't have such an impulse to hurt . . . I am tired and disgusted with myself . . . I long with all my heart to be gentle & kind & loving – I *hate* being cruel, but the Devil seizes hold of me.

'I should be so much happier if I could do things for you,' he told her, 'but the sort of things that it would be good to do are so outside my nature. I sometimes think & think for ever so long to try & think of a present for you, but nothing comes into my head. And I feel so blundering that I give up the attempt.'

As the summer went by, he spent less and less time at Garsington and more in London, until by the autumn he was spending the weekdays in London and coming to Garsington only for the weekends. Having written just three of the projected series of eight, he also temporarily abandoned work on his lectures, which had, as he told Ottoline, become 'loathsome' to him, and began work instead on a very different sort of task: a long polemical reply to Gilbert Murray's pamphlet, *The Foreign Policy of Sir Edward Grey 1906–1915*, which had been published earlier that summer.

Murray's pamphlet was a defence of British foreign policy leading up to the war against the attacks made upon it by anti-war campaigners, most notably Russell (in *War: The Offspring of Fear*) and H. N. Brailsford, best known as the author of *Shelley, Godwin and Their Circle*, who, in a UDC pamphlet called *The Origins of the Great War*, had taken a line similar to Russell's. It sought to label those campaigners as 'pro-German' and to defend in impassioned and patriotic terms both the character and the policies of Edward Grey. It was written, as Russell suspected at the time, 'under the tutelage of the Foreign Office'[4] and might, despite Murray's protestations to the contrary, be regarded as a piece of Government propaganda. Its publication gave Russell the opportunity to complete the critique of British foreign policy that he had begun earlier in the year, material for which (in the form of newspaper cuttings, government documents, and so on) Irene Cooper-Willis had been collecting since January.

But, in returning to this issue, Russell was going back to a way of thinking that he thought he had given up when he became interested in his lectures on social reconstruction. 'I grow less and less interested in the politics of the war,' he had written in June. 'I don't like getting involved in irrelevant controversies on questions of fact, which don't really matter one way or another.' And yet, here he was, engaging in just such controversies and analysing in minute detail the politics of the war.

One immediate cause of this change of direction was no doubt the chance meeting he had with Gilbert Murray's wife Mary at a train station near Oxford on 5 August:

At Calham I heard a voice from the train calling 'Bertie', & there was Mary Murray. She tackled me at once about Gilbert's pamphlet, & I thought it was no use lying. We had a very painful conversation, & at one

---

[4] Under pressure from Gilbert Murray, Russell withdrew this accusation, but recent research has shown that he was quite right: Murray wrote the pamphlet with help and encouragement from the government who provided him with secretarial assistance, offices and research assistance, and also paid for the distribution of 50,000 copies (see *Collected Papers*, Vol. 13, pp. 204–5).

moment I thought we were going to become enemies for life. I have a very strong affection for her, & I should have minded dreadfully. But we smoothed it over & parted friends.

But undoubtedly the main reason for the change was the deterioration in his relationship with Ottoline, which, combined with his break from Lawrence, served to drain him of his previous enthusiasm for the lecture scheme.

In London, so he discovered, he could have the benefit of Vivien Eliot's secretarial skills. Vivien, it turned out, could type to dictation, and throughout the late summer and autumn of 1915 Russell employed her, first on his reply to Murray (which was published in December as *The Policy of the Entente, 1904–1914: A Reply to Professor Gilbert Murray*), and then on *Justice in War Time*, a collection of his articles on the war, which was published in November.

He also came to find Vivien's company a welcome relief after the frustration he felt with Ottoline. In Vivien, he found someone with whom he *could* spend time alone, who was not always surrounded by artists and writers she admired, and who, with her husband away in the United States, actually needed his company. Upon Vivien, too, he could lavish attention and generosity without feeling blundering and inadequate, but simply appreciated. With her, he could be not the stiff, awkward, selfish and repellent creature that Ottoline made him feel, but a wise, successful and urbane man of the world, one who was, moreover, witty, kind and charming.

Exactly how much of Vivien Russell saw while Eliot was away in the States is difficult to establish. For the first few weeks Vivien seems to have spent most of her time living with her family, either in their home in Hampstead, or in their country house in Sussex. But, on 12 August, some two weeks after Eliot's departure, Russell wrote to Ottoline saying that he could not come to Garsington that weekend until late on Sunday afternoon, because he was meeting Vivien for Sunday lunch. The impression he gives in this letter is that this is an isolated occurrence, the first time he has seen her since Eliot left, and possibly the last he would see of her until Eliot got back.

In fact, by the time Eliot returned, around 3 September, Russell and Vivien had become intimate friends, sharing confidences and making joint plans. The Eliots, it had been decided, would move into the spare bedroom in Russell's Bury Street flat. [5] There was little time to discuss this plan with Eliot himself, since almost as soon as he returned to England, he and Vivien went to Eastbourne together on what Russell called 'their sort of pseudo-honeymoon'. Eliot seemed, nevertheless, happy to accept the arrangement. In letters to his family and friends from Eastbourne, from 4 September on, Eliot gave his address until Christmas as c/o Russell at 34 Russell Mansions, Bury Street.

---

[5] Actually, 'spare bedroom' is probably too grand a description for what was little more than a closet. During the time that this arrangement lasted, from September to December 1915, Eliot, when he was not lodging in High Wycombe, slept in the hall or in the sitting-room, which, as his biographer Peter Ackroyd comments, 'suggests a certain lack of married intimacy'.

How close Russell and Vivien had become during Eliot's absence can be seen from a draft letter to Ottoline, written soon after the Eliots left for Eastbourne, in which Russell discussed Vivien at length, showing both a detailed and intimate knowledge of her past and a deep interest in her character. (Eliot, on the other hand, he hardly mentions.) Russell had arrived back in London from Garsington to find what he describes as a 'desperate' letter from Vivien. 'I am worried about these Eliots,' he began:

> It seems their sort of pseudo-honeymoon at Eastbourne is being a ghastly failure. She is quite tired of him, & when I got here I found a desperate letter from her, in the lowest depths of despair & not far removed from suicide. I have written her various letters full of good advice, & she seems to have come to rely on me more or less. I have so much taken them both in hand that I dare not let them be. I think she will fall more or less in love with me, but that can't be helped. I am interested by the attempt to pull her straight. She is half-Irish, & wholly Irish in character − with a great deal of mental passion & *no* physical passion, a universal vanity, that makes her desire every man's devotion, & a fastidiousness that makes any expression of their devotion disgusting to her. She has suffered humiliation in two successive love-affairs, & that has made her vanity morbid. She has boundless ambition (far beyond her powers), but it is diffuse & useless. What she needs is some kind of religion, or at least some discipline, of which she seems never to have had any. At present she is punishing my poor friend for having tricked her imagination − like the heroine of the 'Playboy'. I want to give her some other outlet than destroying him. I shan't fall in love with her, nor give her any more show of affection than seems necessary to rehabilitate her. But she really has *some* value in herself, all twisted and battered by life, lack of discipline, lack of purpose, & lack of religion.

There is a strong element of disingenuousness about this letter, which Ottoline could not fail to have noticed. What Russell evidently wanted her to believe stretches credulity beyond its limits: that, out of a concern for Eliot's welfare, he was willing, in a self-sacrificial spirit as it were, to allow Eliot's wife to fall in love with him, in order to give her some kind of outlet for her anger and her frustration, some satisfaction for her vanity and her need for devotion, and thereby to 'pull her straight', 'rehabilitate' her and thus stop her punishing her husband. Did Russell believe this nonsense himself? In any case, Ottoline did not. What she saw in the letter was primarily that Russell was 'obviously interested' in Vivien. She replied at once, pointing out the obvious weakness in his argument:

> I don't think it would *help her* and help towards making the Eliot life happier to let her fall in love with you. I expect in a way it may have made her already more critical of Eliot . . . I feel *very* strongly that in getting her confidence you are rather separating her from Eliot.

Besides, she said, Russell should think of his reputation: 'I feel you are running a very great risk and I beg and entreat you to be awfully careful – for if you want to do any lecturing or public work any scandal of this kind would entirely damage it and I don't suppose she is worth it.'

Russell made no further attempt to explain how allowing Vivien to fall in love with him would be good for both the Eliots, or to elaborate on the reason he had for thinking that she would fall in love with him (for this is hardly self-evident), but he did try to reassure Ottoline on the subject of his reputation. 'Really there is no occasion for your fears,' he wrote on 10 September. 'Eliot is not that sort of man, & I will be much more careful than you seem to expect':

> And I feel sure I can make things come right . . . I would not for the world have any scandal, & as for the Eliots it is the purest philanthropy – I am sorry you feel worried – there is *really* no need – I am fond of him, & really anxious to be of use to him. The trouble between them was already at its very worst before I came into the matter at all – it is already better, & when I saw him he was very full of gratitude. I must have given you quite a wrong impression when I wrote.

That Eliot was indeed 'full of gratitude' is confirmed by a letter he wrote Russell the next day from Eastbourne. 'Your letter,' Eliot writes, 'coming on top of all your other kindnesses, has quite overwhelmed me. Such generosity and encouragement means a great deal to me at present, above all coming from you.' What he has in mind, however – so at least one might assume – is Russell's kindness in allowing the Eliots to share his flat and perhaps also his encouragement of Eliot's decision to pursue his literary ambitions.

Eliot had, by this time, decided to accept a teaching job that he had been offered at High Wycombe Grammar School, which would mean that during the week he would often be out of town overnight. In his letter to Eliot, Russell evidently mentioned this and asked whether, on those occasions, Eliot would mind if Russell used the flat, even though this would mean that he and Vivien would then be sharing the flat while Eliot himself was away. Eliot seemed entirely unconcerned:

> As to your coming to stay the night at the flat when I am not there it would never have occurred to me to accept it under any other conditions. Such a concession to conventions never entered my head; it seems to me not only totally unnecessary, but also would destroy for me all the pleasure we take in the informality of the arrangement.

What did Eliot think of the intimacy that had developed between Russell and his wife? He seems to have accepted it with equanimity, even to have encouraged it. Could he have been, as Russell implies, grateful for it?

Eliot's biographer, Peter Ackroyd, has speculated that the Eliots' marital problems, which were evident to Russell just two weeks into their marriage, and Vivien's suicidal despair during their 'pseudo-honeymoon' in Eastbourne, both had their origin in what he calls the 'physical failure' of their marriage.

Vivien had a long history of illness: as a child, she had suffered from tuberculosis of the left hand, and, later, from a series of more or less continual headaches, stomach aches and cramps. To relieve the suffering she took a variety of drugs, including morphine-based depressants that were intended to calm down her often violent swings of mood. Her mother considered her always on the verge of 'moral insanity'. No doubt linked to these other symptoms (Ackroyd speculates, plausibly, that the whole set of symptoms add up to what would now be diagnosed as a hormonal imbalance), Vivien also suffered from the age of twelve from an irregular and over-frequent menstrual cycle, which caused her much suffering and embarrassment (she developed, for example, an obsessive habit of washing her own bed linen wherever she slept). This, Ackroyd implies, was the root cause of the sexual failure of the Eliots' marriage. Eliot's 'own fastidiousness and anxiety', he writes, 'must have been greatly compounded by Vivien's menstrual problems'.

One might, of course, question that 'must'; but, if we assume that Ackroyd is right, and imagine Eliot nauseated by his wife's over-frequent menstruation and incapable of sexual relations with her, his attitude to her flirtation with Russell – and Russell's claims that Eliot was 'grateful' to him for flirting with Vivien – begin to make some sort of sense. Everything Eliot did, said and wrote in these years suggests that, even if he was not sexually aroused by her, he was at least very fond of Vivien and felt an acute sense of responsibility for her. Might he not then have been pleased for her sake that Russell was paying so much attention to her? And, of course, pleased for his own sake, too, because it let him off the hook?

But what of Vivien? Was she really falling in love with Russell? The only real evidence for this is in Russell's letters to Ottoline. Everything else that survives suggests that Vivien had an undyingly loyal – though physically frustrated and occasionally sexually unfaithful – love for Eliot. She certainly seems, however, to have enjoyed Russell's attentions and to have taken him into her confidence about her problems and anxieties with Eliot. And, especially, perhaps, she appreciated his generosity, which at this time played a significant part in keeping the Eliots financially afloat. As well as providing them with somewhere to live, Russell gave Eliot £3,000 worth of engineering debentures, helped with their day-to-day expenses, paid for Vivien's dancing lessons and (according to Ottoline) lavished presents on Vivien of 'silk underclothes and all sorts of silly things'.

After the Eliots returned from Eastbourne, on 15 September (the day Russell received Lawrence's splenetic letter), they moved into Russell's flat and, from then on, a pattern of life was established according to which Eliot spent most of his time in High Wycombe (all of his letters from this period give as his address the house in High Wycombe in which he lodged while he was teaching there), leaving Russell and Vivien in the flat, Russell working on his reply to Murray, which he dictated to Vivien at the typewriter.

Eliot had given both his family and his tutors at Harvard the impression that he would return to the United States to finish his Ph.D. It seems doubtful whether he ever had any such intention, but, if he had, he changed his mind as soon as he was back in England, as we find him writing to both his father and to James Woods at Harvard, explaining his decision to stay in England and complete his thesis while teaching at High Wycombe. To overcome the natural scepticism that greeted this plan, Russell was enlisted to write to Eliot's mother, which he duly did on 3 October (on Trinity College headed notepaper, naturally), reassuring her that Eliot's tutors at Oxford thought well of him, that he *could* complete his Ph.D thesis while working as a schoolteacher and that, once he had a Ph.D., Eliot's prospects of a job in a British university were very good. 'I have taken some pains to get to know his wife,' Russell told Charlotte Eliot, 'who seems to me thoroughly nice, really anxious for his welfare, and very desirous of not hampering his liberty or interfering with whatever he feels to be best':

> The chief sign of her influence that I have seen is that he is no longer attracted by the people who call themselves 'vorticists', and in that I think her influence is wholly to be applauded.

With Vivien's help, Russell finished his reply to Murray and sent it off to the publishers, The Labour Press, on 13 October. Writing to Ottoline that day, he admitted, 'I am getting very fond of Mrs Eliot – not in an 'improper' manner – she does not attract me much physically but I find her a real friend, with a really deep humane feeling about the war, & no longer at all unkind to her husband. I feel her a permanent acquisition, not merely an object of kindness, as I thought at first.' A few days later:

> I wondered whether not being any longer sore with you would make me less interested in Mrs E. but I find it doesn't. It is a genuine interest, not an expression of vexation.

Though both Russell and Eliot had worked hard to persuade his family and tutors back home that he would be able to combine his teaching duties with work on his thesis, actually, during this period, Eliot abandoned work on his thesis in favour of the more immediately lucrative business of reviewing books. Russell put him in touch with Sydney Waterlow, the editor of the *International Journal of Ethics*, who commissioned from Eliot two reviews: of Balfour's Gifford lectures, *Theism and Humanism*, and of *The Philosophy of Nietzsche* by A. Wolf.

By the end of October 1915, Russell, having finished work on both the Murray pamphlet and on *Justice in War Time*, was ready to return to work on what he considered a far more important and interesting task: his lectures on social reconstruction. From Garsington he wrote to Lucy Donnelly, telling her that he had 'retired to the country, in rooms near some kind friends, where I can write undisturbed':

> I have finished writing on the war – the sum-total [*Justice in War Time*] is being published by the Open Court Co. in Chicago in a little book. I shall do nothing more about it – but after Xmas I think of giving a set of lectures called 'Principles of Social Reconstruction', in which I shall try to suggest

a philosophy for future radical intellectuals. I wonder whether they will be a success.

Within a month, however, he was drawn by his involvement with the Eliots and by his sense of alienation from Ottoline back to the flat in Bury Street. 'It will be some time', he wrote to her on 10 November, 'before I can make myself believe in my instincts that you do not hate me.' He would be coming 'home' (that is, to Garsington – Russell used the word ambiguously to mean either Garsington or Bury Street) in a few days and was longing to be back, but 'the situation here is anxious & painful, although it is too interesting to be left alone, apart from kindness'. Eliot, he said, he had come to love 'as if he were my son':

He is becoming much more of a man. He has a profound & quite unselfish devotion to his wife, & she is really very fond of him, but has impulses of cruelty to him from time to time. It is a Dostojewsky type of cruelty, not a straightforward every-day kind. I am every day getting things more right between them, but I can't let them alone at present, & of course I myself get very much interested. She is a person who lives on a knife edge, & will end as a criminal or a saint – I don't know which yet. She has a perfect capacity for both.

The problems between himself and Ottoline, Russell attributed largely to a 'lack of physical affectionateness'. The 'flame of passion' that had burnt briefly but brightly between the two in January was now extinguished, and neither expected it to come back to life, but, Russell wrote, 'I do believe all spiritual estrangements are temporary.'

Throughout the autumn of 1915, in the aftermath of Lawrence's devastating criticisms, Russell felt in emotional retreat. Just as he had in the summer of 1913 after Wittgenstein's attack on his work, he felt that, in order to prevent being overcome by the sense of failure, he had to live superficially. 'My inner life must be let alone for a time,' he told Ottoline:

It really is true that I can't get into close contact with the kind of people I can really care for. It was your explanation of Lawrence's feeling that made me see the inevitability of it. But it doesn't really matter – nothing personal really matters.

He would never turn away from Ottoline, he promised, but 'there are times when I must escape from pain & not live much in fundamental things – otherwise I should lose heart':

And it is impossible to be superficial with you. But really there is nothing changed in me underneath, except some loss of personal hope.

'I can't think sanely just now, so I won't think at all' was how he put it a few weeks later, having now realised 'that I am on the way to a nervous breakdown if I don't pull up, & that this whole trouble is within me'. 'You can hardly believe the blackness in which I have been living,' he told her:

I think I ought to get myself in hand before I see you again. I am worse with you than with other people – & it is not good for me to be uncontrolled – & I would rather you didn't see me again till I am in a mood when it might be a pleasure to see me.

The paradox, as Russell put it to Ottoline, was that 'Just because I care for you, you only get the worst of me . . . to other people I am not selfish or self-absorbed.' Nevertheless, he assured her. 'Absolutely nothing personal is *important* to me except you. Apart from you, I want to do my work, & to give any happiness I can, & to find amusements to fill the vacant hours . . . I shall never form any new affection that will be important to me.'

Ottoline might have felt understandably sceptical about this last claim, since, at the same time, Russell was writing to her telling her that he felt 'a very great affection' for Vivien, though, admittedly, he qualified it somewhat by adding that this was 'utterly different from the feeling I have for you':

What makes me care for her is that she affords an opportunity for *giving* a kind of affection that hitherto I have only been able to give in a slight, fragmentary way to pupils – I don't mean that is the whole of it, but it is what is important.

On 24 November, telling Ottoline that he would be seeing a great deal of Vivien, he attempted yet again to define his feelings for her: 'the affection I have for her is what one would have for a daughter, but it is very strong, & my judgment goes with it.'

As the winter approached, Russell began to feel increasingly anxious that he was not getting his lectures written. He felt able to write them neither at Garsington, nor in London. 'I wish you could understand why Garsington makes me unhappy,' he wrote to Ottoline, 'then you would know that I *must not* come there.' His decision not to live at Garsington, he assured her, was not 'a sudden or unreasonable or undisciplined' one. It had, rather, been forced upon him.

I can't do my work or be any use to any one unless I avoid altogether seeing you in the way I have to see you at Garsington. I knew this all along but I didn't want to hurt you, & I thought perhaps I was mistaken, so I tried it. But it is not a thing I would repeat, & if the choice were between that & nothing, I should choose nothing, though that would make the whole future grey.[6]

[6] In his 'Private Memoir' Russell was more direct: 'After she went to live at Garsington in 1915,' he wrote of Ottoline, 'she gave me less and less while at the same time she gave more and more to others.'

And yet, Bury Street was hardly the ideal place to work either. On 8 December, he wrote that he was being turned out of the flat because Vivien was ill, being looked after by her mother. He was in the way and so was going to sleep at the Waverly Hotel round the corner. 'I have been having a horrid higgedly-piggedly pillar-&-post kind of time,' he told Ottoline, and had resolved to spend as little time as possible at Bury Street until he could have the place to himself in peace: 'It is horrid not to be sure of a room to oneself for work & business.' He was now, he said, so worried about his lectures that he would hardly feel human until they were done.

He decided to leave London for the last two weeks of December in order to finish then, spending first a week at Bob Trevelyan's home, The Shiffolds, near Dorking, and then staying over Christmas at his brother's house in Sussex. At both places, in the countryside and away from the emotional complications of life with either Vivien or Ottoline, the conditions for work were perfect and by the end of the year the lectures were practically finished. 'I feel sure now that they will be good,' he wrote triumphantly on 23 December.

His optimism was justified. His series of eight lectures, published as *Principles of Social Reconstruction*, constitute one of Russell's most original and enduring contributions to social and political thought. The theory elaborated in them remained the closest he ever came to fusing his personal vision with his political convictions, and the lectures remained for him, as he put it in 1944, the 'least unsatisfactory' expression of his 'own personal religion'.

The lectures begin with the lesson Russell had learnt from the war and from D. H. Lawrence that people are moved to act as often by blind and unconscious impulses as by conscious and directed desires. Traditional liberalism[7] has assumed too readily that people *know* what motivates them, when much of the time they do not. Furthermore, there has been too much emphasis in traditional liberal thought on the desire for happiness and too little on what Russell calls the 'principle of growth', which he describes as 'an instinctive urgency leading [people] in a certain direction, as trees seek the light':

This intimate centre in each human being is what imagination must apprehend if we are to understand him intuitively. It differs from man to man, and determines for each man the type of excellence of which he is capable.

'The utmost that social institutions can do for a man', Russell argues, 'is to make his own growth free and vigorous: they cannot force him to grow according to the pattern of another man.' It follows that repression, even of destructive impulses, is almost invariably harmful. We should seek, not to

---

[7] Russell was thinking primarily of the utilitarian theories of Bentham and Mill, as he made clear in the opening section of his first lecture, which was, for some reason, omitted from the published version (see *Collected Papers*, Vol. 13, p.296).

repress the impulses that lead to war, far example, but to redirect the energy and the vigour that would otherwise be put into killing people:

> In spite of all the destruction which is wrought by the impulses that lead to war, there is more hope for a nation which has these impulses than for a nation in which all impulse is dead. Impulse is the expression of life, and while it exists there is hope of its turning towards life instead of death; but lack of impulse is death, and out of death no new life will come.

Russell later claimed that he did not discover what *Principles of Social Reconstruction* was all about until he had finished it. This perhaps explains why, though in the preface to the published version of the lectures, he implies that their central idea is the distinction between 'creative' and 'possessive' impulses, together with the conviction that 'liberation of creativeness ought to be the principle of reform both in politics and in economics', in the body of the text this distinction is not mentioned until half-way through the final lecture.

The book, he says, 'has a framework and a formula, but I only discovered both when I had written all except the first and last words'. The lectures discuss, in turn, the state, property, education, marriage and religion, and the belatedly discovered framework is one which organises these in the light of the distinction between possessive and creative impulses. As Russell puts it in the last lecture, 'the State and Property are the great embodiments of possessiveness', while 'education, marriage and religion are essentially creative'. Possessive impulses, he claims, can be redirected so that they become creative. 'The genesis of impulses and the causes which make them change ought to be studied.' We cannot have a satisfactory political theory until we have a deeper understanding of psychology. In the meantime, we can reorganise our institutions of marriage, education and religion, so that, instead of serving to repress our impulses, they serve to release what is best in us: free thought, love and 'the creative vision of the spirit'.

This last notion is what remains in the lectures of the idea he had discussed with Lawrence that they should present 'politics in the service of religion', and, in particular, of the idea debated with Ottoline of showing how each of our political institutions 'is a prison for the infinite in us'. In the lectures as they were finally delivered, this concern for the infinite is expressed as the conviction that 'If life is to be fully human it must serve some end which seems, in some sense, outside human life, some end which is impersonal and above mankind, such as God or truth or beauty':

> Those who best promote life do not have life for their purpose. They aim rather at what seems like a gradual incarnation, a bringing into human existence of something eternal, something that appears to imagination to live in a heaven remote from strife and failure and the devouring jaws of time. Contact with this eternal world − even if it be only a world of our imagining − brings a strength and a fundamental peace which cannot be wholly destroyed by the struggles and apparent failures of our temporal

life. It is this happy contemplation of what is eternal that Spinoza calls the intellectual love of God. To those who have once known it, it is the key to wisdom.

At the end of 1915, Russell returned to his flat in Bury Street, which he now had all to himself once more, the Eliots having moved out on 20 December. He had about two weeks to go before his first lecture on 18 January. The lectures were to be given weekly, on Tuesday afternoons, at Caxton Hall in Westminster. Posters had been printed, leaflets distributed and tickets had gone on sale: three shillings for each lecture, or a guinea for the whole course. Over the next two weeks, Russell kept a watchful eye on how the tickets were selling. For him, much depended upon the success of this venture.

To some extent, however, for the first week of the New Year, his mind was taken off his coming lecture course by the passing of the Military Service Bill, which introduced conscription for all single men aged between eighteen and forty-one, and which received its first reading on 6 January 1916 (it became law on 27 January). It was a large step for the Government to take, one that constituted a massive increase in the powers of the state, but one which, nevertheless, was entirely foreseeable. Russell had seen it coming for months. In his lecture on the state, he had described compulsory military service as 'perhaps the extreme example of the power of the State'. 'It is amazing', he wrote, 'that the vast majority of men should tolerate a system which compels them to submit to all the horrors of the battlefield at any moment when their Government compels them to do so.' Such a system, which, at the time he wrote this lecture, prevailed in France and Germany but not in Britain, was 'a wholly evil thing'.

Now that Britain was about to embrace this evil herself, Russell lost no time in trying to alert people to its pernicious significance. In an article published in *The Labour Leader* as its leading editorial on the day of the bill's first reading, Russell made an impassioned plea for the Labour Party to provide 'an uncompromising opposition' to it. Perhaps thinking that it would sway this particular audience, Russell presented conscription as a conspiracy against organised labour:

> The motive of those who lead the Conscriptionist campaign is clear: it is to obtain a new weapon against organised labour. For the sake of the country, Trade Unionists are exhorted to give new and terrible powers to their future antagonists. The appeal to love of country is a cynical hypocrisy. From the moment when the war broke out certain enemies of Freedom have seen that it gave a rare opportunity for robbing wage-earners of what little liberty they had achieved, and preventing them for many years to come from making any advance on the road to democratic justice. With the enactment of Conscription the cruel plot will have succeeded.

'There is no more horrible crime against liberty', he continued, back on more familiar moral ground, 'than to compel men to kill each other when their conscience tells them to live in peace.'

The day after this was published and the bill had, as anticipated, passed its first reading, Russell went on a short holiday to Torquay with Vivien. This was in fulfilment of a promise he had made her before Christmas. He tried to get out of it, he claimed to Ottoline, 'but I found I should hurt her feelings'. He did not want to go, he insisted (and one cannot help feeling that perhaps he was protesting rather too much), he preferred to be in London during the crisis over the Conscription Bill, and Vivien, he was sure, would rather go with her husband, but Eliot would not go because he had to work on his Ph.D. thesis. And, so, with the utmost regret, Russell was forced to accede to her wishes and go on holiday with her. 'We shall be quite proper,' he added:

There is no tendency to develop beyond friendship, quite the opposite. I have really now done all I meant to do for them, they are perfectly happy in each other, & I shall begin to fade away out of their lives as soon as this week is over.

They stayed at the Torbay Hotel for just five days, from 7 to 12 January 1916. 'I detest it,' Russell wrote to Ottoline, 'but she seems to like it.' He was now inclined to feel that being with Vivien gave him some insight into how it was that he was tiring and oppressive to Ottoline, 'because I see the same thing with Mrs E. in a much more marked degree':

I have been quite fantastically unselfish towards her, & have never dreamt of making any kind of demands, so it has nothing to do with that.

It was, he had now come to see, the clash between the artistic and the inartistic, between those who took pleasure in the things of sight, and those who lived exclusively in thoughts and purposes: 'Having understood this, I see I can't cure it. I am not now in a state of depression at all, but I am trying to see things clearly . . . I simply *must* understand, & avoid getting into such a state again.'

His earlier talk of a nervous breakdown was entirely serious. 'These lectures', he told Ottoline, 'nearly drove me into insanity', and he even began to discuss with Ottoline the idea of going to Switzerland to see Dr Vittoz. But he felt he could see quite clearly what the central problem was: 'Of course the real thing that has troubled me . . . has been my failure with you.' This failure, too, was what accounted for his interest in Vivien:

The reason I am apologetic about Mrs E. is because I can't quite make out why I like her, & feel you wouldn't, & I can't defend her. I believe I like her really because I can be useful to her, so I get over the sense of being a failure & making people unhappy when I want to make them happy. It is a sort of comfort to me to think those two are happier than they would have been if I had not known them.

'Mrs E. does for me what the Germans did last Xmas,' he claimed – that is to say, presumably, that she revitalised him by making him feel useful, by enabling him to perform a public service. And now, since the death, so to speak, of his inner life, public service was all he had to give. His failure with Ottoline was 'a sort of shattering of almost everything . . . an end of personal life, leaving only a kind of public & philanthropic existence'.

While Russell was in Torquay with Vivien, Eliot wrote to him thanking him again for his generosity. 'Vivien says you have been an angel to her,' he wrote:

I am sure you have done *everything* possible and handled her in the very best way – better than I – I often wonder how things would have turned out but for you – I believe we shall owe her life to you, even.

Though Russell reproduces this letter in its entirety in his *Autobiography*, he unfortunately leaves it entirely unexplained how the Eliots could have owed Vivien's life to him.

Russell left Torquay on 12 January, having paid for Eliot to join his wife and spend a few days at the Torbay Hotel himself. Eliot had been intending to come to Russell's first lecture, but because Vivien's condition worsened, he and she had to stay longer than expected in Devon and did not get back to London in time to attend.

Just before his first lecture, Russell received another invitation to go to Harvard as a visiting lecturer, this time encouraging him to give a course on the ethics of contemporary events, as well as on logic. This was the bait needed to hook Russell and on 24 January he cabled his acceptance. The courses would start in February 1917. 'America is important internationally,' Russell told Ottoline, and 'I can have vastly more influence there than here . . . I should be able to go about a good deal, & get to know important men.' On the other hand: 'I *did* want so much not to do any serious work for some time.'

The London lectures on social reconstruction started on 18 January and from the very beginning were a huge success. Immediately before they began, Russell anxiously wrote to friends urging them to come, since, he thought, tickets were selling badly. They did not let him down. Many of his friends, including the Whiteheads, the Bells, the Woolfs, and practically the whole Bloomsbury Group, were regular attenders. In fact, their presence was not needed to make up a decently sized audience. The lectures were well-attended and, indeed, became a fashionable focus for resistance to the war. 'Bertie's lectures help one,' wrote Lytton Strachey:

They are a wonderful solace and refreshment. One hangs upon his words and looks forward to them from week to week, and I can't bear the idea of missing one – I dragged myself to that ghastly Caxton Hall yesterday, though I was rather nearer the grave than usual, and it was well worth it.

Russell was delighted. After the first lecture, he told Ottoline that it had gone off 'better than I expected. There were quite 100 people there, and most of them seemed to like it.' After the second, he reported that 'Owing to my

lectures going so well, I am now rich.' Half-way through the series, he told
Lucy Donnelly that they were a 'great success' and even the start of a new
career. They were, he said, without distorting the facts, 'a rallying-ground for
intellectuals'. He began to think of himself as the centre of a new movement,
the catalyst for a stirring to political protest of intellectuals, 'as they were in
France by the Dreyfus case', and to think of ways in which he could give his
lectures to wider audiences at cheaper rates. 'The chief point of them', he told
Ottoline, 'is to give people hope.' It was also important to him that they
served as a spur to political action. It bothered him that some who came
regularly to the lectures remained uninvolved in the political struggle against
conscription and against the war. Before the last one, he wrote:

> I think of trying to make them less snug in my last lecture, by dotting the
> i's as to what one ought to do – for instance, that if they have agreed with
> any single word I have said, they must give up supporting the war directly
> or indirectly – what do you think? I don't like them just to get a casual
> pleasure & feel broad-minded, & not be *practically* affected.

The last lecture was attended by Ottoline, who has left a rather different
impression of the atmosphere that prevailed at these meetings in Caxton Hall:

> It was rather a comic occasion, for all the cranks who attend lectures on
> any subject were there, and amongst them was a Captain White, who was
> slightly crazy, and would make a long speech about sex and free love,
> pointing out that if children were born from parents who were in love with
> each other they would never want to fight. How would adoring parents ever
> wish for war? Then Vernon Lee got up and made a long speech about a
> cigarette-case, waving her hands about, with her *pince-nez* dangling from
> it; and of course, a representative of Arts and Crafts made an impassioned
> harangue – saying that Arts and Crafts alone would cure any tendency to
> war. Bertie sat looking miserable on the platform. At last he had to ask
> them to sit down.

Russell seemed inclined to take this Captain White rather more seriously
than Ottoline evidently did. A few days before this final lecture, he had
forwarded to Ottoline a letter he had received from White, telling her: 'You
will see that he feels the same sort of hostility or antagonism to me that
Lawrence feels':

> I think it is a feeling that seems to exist in most of the people with whom
> I feel in sympathy on the spiritual side – probably the very same thing
> which has prevented you from caring for me as much as you thought you
> would at first. I wish you could find out and tell me what it is. It makes
> one feel very isolated. People with whom I have intellectual sympathy
> hardly ever have any spiritual life, or at any rate have very little; and the
> others seem to find the intellectual side of me unbearable. You will think I
> am lapsing into morbidness again, but that is not so; I simply want to get

to the bottom of it so as to understand it; if I can't get over it, it makes it difficult to achieve much.

In the same letter, he recalled Wittgenstein's devastating criticisms of 1913, which, he told Ottoline, 'was an event of first-rate importance in my life, and affected everything I have done since'. From that time on, he says, 'philosophy lost its hold on me. This was due to Wittgenstein more than to the war.' The war had given him a new and less difficult ambition, 'which seems to me quite as good as the old one', and 'My lectures have persuaded me that there is a possible life and activity in the new ambition. So I want to work quietly, and I feel more at peace as regards work than I have ever done since Wittgenstein's onslaught . . . I don't know how far you knew all this,' he concluded. 'It has been at the bottom of many things in the last three years.'

Russell did not recover from these onslaughts easily, and it is possible that neither Wittgenstein nor Lawrence – nor even Captain White – realised how deep were the wounds they had inflicted. Lawrence continued to write to Russell for months after his own onslaught in September 1915, apparently oblivious to the irreparable damage he had done to their friendship. Lawrence and Frieda had now moved to Cornwall, from where Lawrence wrote in January 1916 in warm and friendly terms urging Russell to visit them. On 11 February he wrote again, saying that he had been thinking about Russell's lectures: 'Are they really a success, & really vital? Are you really glad? – or only excited? I want to know, truly.' Then, a week later, stung perhaps by the coolness of Russell's responses to his overtures and even perhaps beginning to realise that Russell had long since ceased to be in *Blütbruderschaft* with him, Lawrence fired off another volley of ferocious criticism:

I didn't like your letter. What's the good of living as you do, anyway. I don't believe your lectures *are* good. They are nearly over, aren't they?

What's the good of sticking in the damned ship and haranguing the merchant-pilgrims in their own language. Why don't you drop overboard? Why don't you clear out of the whole show?

One must be an outlaw these days, not a teacher or a preacher. One must retire out of the herd & then fire bombs into it. You said in your lecture on education that you didn't set much count by the unconscious. This is sheer perversity. The whole of consciousness and the conscious content is old hat – the mill-stone round your neck.

Do cut it – cut your will and leave your old self behind. Even your mathematics are only *dead* truth: and no matter how fine you grind the dead meat, you'll not bring it to life again.

Do stop working & writing altogether and become a creature instead of a mechanical instrument. Do clear out of the whole social ship. Do for your very pride's sake become a mere nothing, a mole, a creature that feels its way & doesn't think. Do for heavens sake be a baby, & not a savant any more. Don't *do* anything any more – but for heavens sake begin to *be* – start at the very beginning and be a perfect baby: in the name of courage.

... My love to you. Stop working and being an ego, & have the courage to be a creature.

Where the previous onslaught had thrown Russell into despair, this one simply angered him. In response, so he told Ottoline, he wrote Lawrence 'a nasty letter . . . asking him not to criticise me – I had to stop him, because I find his criticism is paralysing – it is always directed against things one can't change.' What made him angry, he explained in another letter, was Lawrence's 'trying to interfere with the instinctive creative part of me, which he doesn't understand, & can only damage – it was a self-protective anger'. Even so, he said, 'I wish I had written less crossly.' This last qualm was misplaced. For Lawrence, angry exchanges of vitriolic abuse were an accepted part of day-to-day life and certainly no barrier to friendship. Elsewhere in the letter quoted above, he was insisting, for example, with an apparently immovable conviction, that he and Russell were still 'brothers', that Russell should come and live near him and Frieda. To Russell's angry reply, which was clearly intended to mark some sort of breach between them, Lawrence responded in an imperturbably breezy tone ('Are you still cross with me for being a schoolteacher & for not respecting the rights of man? Don't be, it isn't worth it'), still urging Russell to come to Cornwall. Presumably, as the months and years went by without another letter from Russell, Lawrence began to realise that they were no longer friends, still less brothers.[8]

The day after Russell's last lecture, Ottoline met both Eliots for the first time when they all, together with Ottoline's husband Philip, went out to dinner at a restaurant in Soho. According to Ottoline, 'The dinner was not a success.' Eliot himself was very formal and polite, while Vivien struck Ottoline as of the 'spoilt kitten' type: 'very second-rate and ultra feminine, playful and naive, anxious to show she "possessed" Bertie, when we walked away from the restaurant she headed him off and kept him to herself, walking with him arm-in-arm'. Ottoline 'felt rather *froissée* at her bad manners'. The next day Russell and the Eliots joined a rather larger gathering in Bedford Square for what Ottoline remembers as 'a happy gay tea-party', but she was evidently not yet won over. When, a few weeks later, Russell brought Eliot to Garsington for the first time, she found him 'dull, dull, dull':

He never moves his lips but speaks in an even and monotonous voice, and I felt him monotonous without and within. Where does his queer neurasthenic poetry come from, I wonder. From his New England, Puritan inheritance and upbringing? I think he has lost all spontaneity and can only break through his conventionality by stimulants or violent emotions.

---

[8] By December 1916, at least, Lawrence had come to see Russell, not as a blood-brother and potential recruit to 'Rananim', but, along with 'Cambridge, Lowes Dickinson, young reformers, Socialists [and] Fabians' as part of 'that old advanced crowd' that was 'our disease, not our hope' (see letter to Cynthia Asquith, 11 December 1916).

454   BERTRAND RUSSELL: THE SPIRIT OF SOLITUDE

The weekend that Eliot went to Garsington he was supposed to be sailing back to the United States to sit his postgraduate examinations in philosophy at Harvard. It was an obligation that Russell had helped to get him out of by sending a telegram to Eliot's father saying: 'STRONGLY ADVISE CABLING TOM AGAINST SAILING UNDER PRESENT PECULIARLY DANGEROUS CONDITIONS UNLESS IMMEDIATE DEGREE IS WORTH RISKING LIFE'. Eliot's father professed himself 'not greatly pleased with the language of Prof. Russell's cablegram', and his mother wrote to Russell to say she was 'sure your influence in every way will confirm my son in his choice of philosophy as a life work', and confirming that she herself had 'absolute faith in his Philosophy but not in the vers libre'. For the time being, at least, the intervention had achieved its aim of keeping Eliot in London.

Russell was moved to this intervention out of concern for Vivien who was, towards the end of March, becoming ill with worry about Eliot's return to the States, convinced, it seems, that if he went his ship would be sunk by a submarine. Throughout the period of his lectures Russell had settled into a routine of seeing Vivien twice a week for lunch or dinner. Though she continued to fascinate him and he continued to lavish presents on her, there began at this time a slow process of withdrawal that would take nearly two years to complete. Russell's lectures had been successful beyond his dreams, both financially and in terms of how much attention they received and how much influence they had. By the end of the course in March, Russell had recovered much of the confidence that had been stripped from him the previous autumn by Lawrence and Ottoline. Vivien had played a part in that reconstruction, as Russell was to admit. But precisely because it had been successful, he was to have increasingly little need of her.

16

MEPHISTO

The success of the Caxton Hall lectures had a great and lasting influence on Russell's life. It inspired in him vast new ambitions for his political influence and encouraged him to think of himself, not as an isolated campaigner against the war, but as a leader of a whole tide of opinion, a prophet even. It showed, too, that he could survive, even thrive, outside academic life, that he could attract to his lectures a paying audience, one that looked to him, not for help in passing examinations, nor for instruction on some small, technical topic, but for nothing less than a 'philosophy of life'. The sense of purpose, and even of power, that this inspired in him was almost intoxicating. 'I have something important to say on the philosophy of life & politics, something appropriate to the times,' he wrote to Lucy Donnelly in February 1916. The world needed a new doctrine, he told her, the young generation had broken with the old and needed guidance, and, because he was on their side and because there was nothing in his philosophy that 'retains old superstitions & conventions', he was ideally placed to provide it.

His sense of there being, as he put it to Lucy Donnelly, a 'sharp cleavage' between the old life and the new was now sharper than ever. When, in March, after his lectures had finished, he returned to Trinity for an evening, he found it almost intolerably depressing. 'The melancholy of this place now-a-days is beyond endurance,' he wrote to Ottoline:

The Colleges are dead, except for a few Indians & a few pale pacifists & bloodthirsty old men hobbling along victorious in the absence of youth. Soldiers are billeted in the courts & drill on the grass; bellicose parsons preach to them in stentorian tones from the steps of the Hall. The town at night is plunged in a darkness compared to which London is a blaze of light. All that one has cared for is dead, at least for the present; it is hard to believe that it will ever revive. No one thinks about learning or feels it of any importance. And from the outer deadness my thoughts travel to the deadness in myself – I look round my shelves at the books of mathematics & philosophy that used to seem full of hope & interest, & now leave me utterly cold – The work I have done seems so little – so irrelevant to this world in which we are living.

His period of leave was coming to an end; in May he would be required to return to Cambridge to resume lecturing. But the heady state of mind his London lectures had inspired in him would hardly be satisfied with a return to his old way of life. In fulfilling his new, vast ambitions, in delivering his message that was relevant and 'appropriate to the times', he needed a bigger platform than a lectureship at Trinity College could provide.

In later life, emphasising the changes in him brought about by the war, Russell was fond of describing himself as 'a non-supernatural Faust for whom Mephistopheles was represented by the Great War', but, actually, what the war gave him was rather the ambition to *be* Mephistopheles, to possess the power of transforming people's lives by awakening in them new thoughts and desires. As he put it to Lucy Donnelly, 'I want actually to *change* people's thoughts. Power over people's minds is the main personal desire of my life.'

Perhaps in recognition of this – or perhaps for the more mundane reason that he had pointed ears and a devilish grin – his colleagues in the No-Conscription Fellowship, for which he began to work in the spring of 1916, nicknamed him 'Mephisto'. For more than one reason, the nickname could not have been more appropriate.

During the period from January to March in which Russell had been busy with his lectures, the No-Conscription Fellowship had become the centre of a newly invigorated movement against both the Military Service Act in particular and the war in general. It had been founded in November 1914 to campaign against the introduction of conscription, but now, after conscription had become law, it acted as the focus for protest and dissent against the measure, encouraging people to defy the law, and representing the interests of those who did so. The Military Service Act of January 1916 had, at a stroke, made every single man between the ages of eighteen and forty-one liable for military service. It had, as it were, signed up into the army the country's entire population of young, single men. However, in order to overcome liberal misgivings about what was, after all, an extraordinarily illiberal extension of Government power, the Act included a so-called 'conscience clause', by which those with a conscientious objection to killing their fellow men could be exempted from military service. There were three levels of exemption: 1. absolute exemption, which was rarely given on grounds of conscience but was usually reserved for those deemed medically unfit for service; 2. exemption from combatant service, which entailed being conscripted into the Non-Combatant Corps and sent to France to serve behind the lines, digging trenches, and so on; and 3. exemption on condition of taking up work of national importance, such as working on farms or in factories.

In the eyes of many members of the No-Conscription Fellowship, the distinction between the second and third levels was all-important: it was the difference between working for the military and working as a civilian. Many were inclined to accept alternative service so long as it was civilian rather than military work. However, it was not until the summer of 1916 that it was made clear that COs might be granted this third level of exemption. Throughout

April and May it was assumed that the only alternative to absolute exemption was non-combatant military service.

The conscience clause was in some ways an impressive concession to liberal values. As its implementation was in the hands of military tribunals, however, staffed on the whole by people hostile to 'conchies', and who saw it as their job to recruit as many into the army as possible, it was rarely as liberal in practice as in theory, and many who regarded themselves as conscientious objectors were, despite the clause, refused exemption and recruited into the army against their will.

For the No-Conscription Fellowship, the conscience clause presented something of a problem. For most of them, including Fenner Brockway, the original founder of the Fellowship, and Clifford Allen, the chairman and acknowledged leader of the movement, any enforced contribution to the war effort was unacceptable. To them, the only exemption that counted was absolute exemption, and they encouraged their members to refuse not only to fight, but also to take up any form of alternative service. Those who followed this advice were, like Clifford Allen himself, sent to prison, where they were often treated extremely harshly. In time, this treatment weakened the resolve of the Fellowship members, many of whom by the end of the year had compromised their 'absolutist' stand in favour of accepting some form of alternative service. In the early months of 1916, however, the objection to all forms of war service formed the inspirational rallying call for a movement in which Russell saw great hopes, not just for the ending of conscription, nor even just for ending the war, but for putting an end to militarism itself.

For, though he took no active part in the NCF until he had finished his lectures in March, Russell watched closely and almost enviously as its leaders marshalled the widespread and impassioned feeling against conscription into an inspired, effective protest movement, which, in its vigour and moral passion, looked something like the new faith he had told Lucy Donnelly the world needed. 'It is a real ferment,' he wrote to Ottoline in February, 'like the beginning of a new religion.' He longed to be involved: 'I feel the horror of the men on the tribunals, for their persecuting spirit, but I rather envy the men they persecute. It is maddening not to be liable.' (Russell was by now forty-three and just outside the age of conscription.)

In the weeks he had free before the beginning of the new Cambridge term, Russell gave all the time he could spare to supporting the NCF. He joined as an 'associate' member (ordinary membership being restricted to those liable for conscription), and became, with Catherine Marshall (an energetic campaigner whom he already knew from his involvement in the women's suffrage movement), a founder-member of the Associates' Political Committee, whose task was to work towards the repeal of the Military Service Act by propaganda and political pressure. With a number of influential friends (the Prime Minister, Herbert Asquith, was still, even during the conscription crisis, a regular visitor to Garsington), a national reputation as an anti-war agitator and experience of political activism, Russell's value to the NCF was immediately appreciated.

Russell's enthusiasm for the movement was, in these early days at least, almost unbounded. When he attended the large NCF convention held in Devonshire House, London, on 7 and 8 April, he saw in the conviction and the zeal of the 2,000 delegates who attended exactly the kind of passionate, religious opposition to the war that he had been looking for ever since the war began (one is reminded of his earlier complaint that the pacifists he met were not the sort to throw the money-lenders out of the temple). He was delighted. 'Here I am,' he wrote to Ottoline on 9 April, 'back after 2 delirious days & nights of conference of the NCF':

> It has been a *wonderful* 2 days – the most inspiring & happy thing that I have known since the war began – it gives one hope & faith again.
>   . . . The spirit of the young men was magnificent. They would not listen to even the faintest hint of compromise. They were keen, intelligent, eloquent, full of life – vigorous courageous men, full of real religion, not hysterical at all – not seeking martyrdom, but accepting it with great willingness. I am convinced that at least half will not budge an inch for any power on earth . . . I really believe they will defeat the Government & wreck Conscription, when it is found they won't yield. I can't describe to you how happy I am having these men to work with & for – it is a real happiness all day long – & I feel they can't be defeated, whatever may be done to them.

Russell himself had 'said a few words of sympathy' to the meeting and was given a great cheer, but he had missed some of the other speeches because news had come through of a young man who had been arrested and let out on bail, so Russell and some others had rushed off to Lambeth in a taxi, fetched him out of his prison cell and brought him to the meeting, where he received a great ovation. Best of all, from Russell's point of view: 'He said he was reading one of my pamphlets when they arrested him!'

Though Ottoline's sympathies had been firmly behind Russell's anti-war stand from the very beginning, and though she did what she could on behalf of conscientious objectors, Russell's absorption in the politics of the NCF was to become yet one more force pulling him away from her. At first, however, she welcomed his involvement, describing Russell in April as 'working furiously at the No-Conscription Fellowship, very exalted and delirious about them all', and a few weeks later:

> Bertie arrived on Friday, very full of his C.O. work and very happy, quite a changed man, for he is using up all his activities, no surplus left over to go bad. I hope it will last, for it makes him so happy. I think if he can keep up his present enthusiasm he may really lead a movement.

Russell's new colleagues were not really, however, people with whom Ottoline could mix happily and naturally, and there was more than just a hint of condescension in her description of Russell's 'thinking they are really wonderful, as I am sure they are'. When she finally met Clifford Allen, she pronounced him 'rather suburban'. Russell, too, felt the gulf. 'I admire the young men I am working with *very much indeed*,' he wrote to her, 'but of course none of them are comrades to one's inner life. They have *something* that is great & vital & important . . . but not the thirst after perfection – they see the way out of Hell but not the way into Heaven.'

For the time being, though, finding a way out of Hell was the central task in hand, and, in pursuit of this task, Russell was prepared, ultimately, to leave his old friends behind, along with his old ideas. His involvement in the NCF hastened him along the road from liberalism to socialism. Earlier, he had refused to join the Independent Labour Party on the grounds that it was too left-wing. Soon after the NCF convention in London, however, he attended an ILP conference in Newcastle and found, to his dismay and somewhat to his amusement, that to him the party now seemed insufficiently radical. 'I find I now regard the ILP as they regard official Liberals,' he told Ottoline: 'as lukewarm mugwumps, using the phrases of democracy to cover inaction – so one travels!'

In the first flush of enthusiasm after the Devonshire Hall conference, Russell, as part of his role in making propaganda for the movement, made strenuous efforts to convert traditional liberal opinion to the NCF cause. He began with an impassioned letter to *The Nation*, giving the kind of euphoric account of the NCF conference that he had given to Ottoline. Describing the NCF in unrestrainedly sentimental terms as 'a spontaneous association of those who believe in the sacredness of human life and the brotherhood of man, and who are prepared to abide by this faith, even to the death', the letter then went on to characterise the delegates at the conference as having 'all the qualities of the best type of Briton: good humour, capacity for dispatching business, immense determination, and inflexible will':

> But, added to these things, they had something more, something more rare and precious. Like Blake, they had seen a vision; they wished to 'build Jerusalem in England's green and pleasant land'.

If Blake, or Shelley, were alive today, Russell claimed, they would have been there at the conference: 'the Tribunals would have told them to stop talking such sickening rubbish, and they would be at this moment undergoing arrest or solitary confinement in a military prison.' These men, and this movement, would not, Russell claimed, be defeated:

> Let the authorities make no mistake. The men in that Convention were filled with a profound faith, and with a readiness for sacrifice at least as great as that of the soldier who dies for his country. If persecution is to be meted out to them, they will joyfully become martyrs.

The letter went on to defend the NCF's rejection of alternative service on the grounds that 'a stand for peace is the greatest service they can render to the community'.

Russell was forced to spell out what he meant by this in an exchange with his old friend and adversary, Gilbert Murray. Murray was prominent among those Liberals who, though supporting the war, wished to see conscientious objectors treated as humanely as possible. To this end he campaigned for COs to be placed under civil rather than military authority. In other words, he supported the plan to engage them on some form of alternative civil service. From his point of view, therefore, the NCF's rejection of all forms of alternative service rather 'queered the pitch' (as he put it in his letter to Russell). Murray asked Russell whether he had any positive proposal for administering the Military Service Act humanely. 'Or are you out merely to break it by agitation?' If so, 'I see nothing for it but the COs to endure imprisonment and, if necessary, death.'

It was a question to which Russell had no clear answer and on which he was already showing signs of wavering. His interest in the NCF was primarily in its potential as a force against the war and against militarism generally, and, from this perspective, the repeal of the Act was a far greater priority than the amelioration of the suffering of individual conscientious objectors. Indeed, if the Act could be administered humanely, as Murray desired, this would be, from Russell's point of view, rather a setback, since it would diminish the outrage inspired by it. As he had said in his letter to *The Nation*: 'I cannot bring myself wholly to regret the persecution to which the conscientious objectors are being subjected', because their suffering had immense value as propaganda against the war. And, yet, he could hardly welcome the suffering and potentially the death of the 'splendid young men' he had grown to love and admire. In his reply to Murray, he drew back somewhat from his earlier talk of admitting no compromise in the 'stand for peace' and denied that either his or the NCF's primary object was to defeat the Act. 'Our primary object', he told Murray, 'is to take no part ourselves in what we regard as a crime.' All forms of alternative service might be regarded as taking part in the war, and, therefore, the rejection of alternative service by the NCF was 'the unavoidable attitude for those among them who are capable of logical thought'.

Murray, naturally, remained unconvinced and carried on working to find a way of combining conscription with the liberty of individual conscience. Russell had no more success when he tried to explain the NCF position to Alfred North Whitehead. Whitehead responded with a defence of conscription based on traditional liberalism. 'I hold', Whitehead wrote, 'that the State has the right to compulsion both in taxes and in personal service':

> Here I agree with all the great liberal statesmen, e.g., Cromwell, the French Revolutionary Statesmen, Lincoln, J. S. Mill, etc. You used to admire these men; I never suspected your fundamental divergence.

While Whitehead admitted that 'the forcing of conscience is always an evil', and on these grounds would exempt Quakers, for instance, he 'would not exempt men who produce their conscientious objections ad hoc'. On the whole, he considered that 'men who refuse military service are avoiding a plain, though painful duty':

> I am not greatly impressed by men who ask me to be shocked that they are

going to prison, while ten thousand men are daily being carried to field hospitals . . . Frankly, the outcry is contemptible.

Such an attitude, from a man with a son serving in the army, struck Russell – whose frustrated parental feeling grew ever stronger during the war years – as an abomination, and behind many of his pointed remarks about people who wish only to see their sons killed no doubt lies his anguish at the danger facing his beloved North Whitehead, at this time fighting in East Africa, whose father could apparently look on his son's sacrifice with satisfaction.

The full vehemence of Russell's feeling against such a willingness to see young men off to their deaths could not be expressed in his propaganda work. As he put it to Ottoline, he was 'living all against impulse – my impulse is to write biting things about the pleasure men derive from having their sons killed.' On 20 April, however, there appeared in *The Labour Leader* a letter, signed 'FRS', but now known to have been written by Russell, which gave vent to that impulse in the form of a satirical proposal of Swiftian savagery. The plan proposed by 'FRS' was that boys, when they reached the age of eighteen, should be divided into three categories: those in the first category should be painlessly executed in a lethal chamber, those in the second should be deprived of an arm, a leg or an eye, and those in the third should be 'exposed day and night to deafening noises, until they acquire some nervous affliction – madness, speechlessness, mental blindness, or deafness – after which they shall be liberated to form the future manhood of the country'. This plan, he claimed, would be seen at once to be 'enormously more humane and economical than the present mode of conducting the war'.

This change in Russell's mood from euphoric optimism to savage bitterness was largely brought about by his growing realisation of what might happen to the conscientious objectors and how fragile their movement really was. He began to become obsessed with the thought that the military authorities, if they shipped the COs to France, had the legal right to shoot them for disobeying orders. The rumours spreading from the barracks that this is what the Government intended were fuelled when the Chief Recruiting Officer at Guildford, when asked what would happen to a CO who went on refusing to obey orders, replied, 'He may be shot in the end.' It was a possibility that came to haunt Russell. 'Like ordinary deserters,' he wrote to Murray, 'they would merely appear in casualty lists; the public would not know the manner of their death, and you would not believe it.' To Ottoline, he expressed his very worst nightmare: 'If the Govt. chooses to shoot some 5000 people (which it has a perfect legal right to do), it can crush the whole thing. I think Ll. G. would be quite capable of it.'

This was written after Russell had had a chance to meet Lloyd George (then Minister for Munitions, but soon to become Secretary for War) for himself. Lloyd George invited Clifford Allen, Catherine Marshall and Russell to lunch at Walton Heath to discuss the question of alternative service. The meeting gave Russell no grounds for optimism. 'I got the impression', he reported to Ottoline, 'that Ll. George expects the war to go on for a long time yet; also that he thinks the whole situation very black. He seemed quite heartless.' Russell's earlier conviction that the members of the NCF 'will defeat the Government & wreck Conscription' was now replaced with the more sombre reflection that 'the men will have to suffer a good deal before public opinion and Government will cease to wish to persecute them.'

The focus of Russell's work now shifted from trying to persuade liberals of the NCF's case to publicising the suffering of COs. On 15 April he wrote a leaflet, headed 'Two Years' Hard Labour for Refusing to Disobey the Dictates of Conscience', which described the case of Ernest Everett, a teacher from St Helens. Having appealed as a CO before his local tribunal, Everett had been granted exemption only from combatant service. He refused to serve in the Non-Combatant Corps, and was arrested and then court-martialled for refusing to obey orders. His sentence was the unusually harsh one of two years' hard labour. 'He is fighting the old fight for liberty and against religious persecution in the same spirit in which martyrs suffered in the past,' Russell wrote. 'Will you join the persecutors? Or will you stand for those who are defending conscience at the cost of obloquy and pain of mind and body?' It was an effective piece of propaganda. The NCF ran off half a million copies and distributed the leaflet throughout the country.

The battle over conscription intensified still further in May, when the Government introduced a new Conscription Act that made married men liable as well as single men. By then, Russell had returned to Cambridge, for what, though he did not know it, was to be his last term as a Cambridge lecturer for nearly thirty years. He gave his first lecture on 2 May to an audience of six men and two women, but, he told Ottoline, within a couple of weeks he expected five of the six men to be arrested. In such an atmosphere he could hardly return to thinking about abstruse and technical subjects. Even when he attended the Joint Session of the Mind Association and the Aristotelian Society, the most important of the British academic philosophy gatherings, which that summer was held at Manchester College, Oxford, he gave a paper that was as much propaganda as philosophy. Called 'The Nature of the State in View of Its External Relations', it argued for the curtailment of the sovereignty of national states and for the establishment of a world-state 'which shall alone possess armed forces'. Along the way, it contained a barely disguised defence of the right of conscientious objectors to defy an unjust law:

> . . . it must often happen that the purposes of the State are such as cannot commend themselves to men who have more humanity or more insight than most of their contemporaries. Such men, if they have courage, may easily find themselves forced to resist the State. Any theory which would make it their duty to submit, in spite of their adverse individual judgment, would take away something of human dignity and independence.

For Russell at this time, resisting the state was of far greater importance than teaching mathematical logic, and he longed for the end of term on 10 June, when he could devote himself entirely to anti-war agitation. He had become convinced that, as he put it to Ottoline, 'the moment has arrived for a great peace campaign'. A week or so later, he was writing; 'I *long* to stomp the country on a stop-the-war campaign.' Plans were drawn up for a tour of South Wales, sponsored by the NCF, in which Russell would make propaganda speeches urging immediate peace negotiations.

Before these could be implemented, however, Russell was given the opportunity of demonstrating publicly the sincerity of his belief in the right of 'men who have more humanity or more insight than most of their contemporaries' to resist the state.

On 8 May, he wrote to Helen Flexner that he was 'so used to being against the government that I take it as a matter of course . . . If I were a working man I should have been in prison long ago; as it is, I am still at large, & I dare say I shall remain so – but I should not at all object to a term of imprisonment.' A few days later, this view was confirmed when he learnt that someone in Wales had been given a prison sentence for distributing his leaflet about Ernest Everett. 'Why do they let me alone?' he asked Ottoline. On 17 May, he wrote to *The Times* practically begging to be prosecuted: 'I wish it to be known that I am the author of this leaflet, and that if anyone is to be prosecuted I am the person primarily responsible.'

The Director of Public Prosecutions was surprisingly slow to react to this blatant provocation, and it was not until 30 May that Russell's wish to be prosecuted was fulfilled. Two detectives appeared at his rooms at Trinity to serve him with a summons for 'impeding recruiting and discipline'. It was, as he told Ottoline, 'the very thing I wanted . . . The sort of opportunity I have longed for.' The case was scheduled to be heard on 5 June at the Mansion House before the Lord Mayor, giving Russell just a few days to prepare his 'defence' (in effect a propaganda speech that would itself later be turned into an NCF pamphlet). This he wrote on 3 June and sent immediately to the NCF office to be typed up. The argument it presents is that his intention in writing the Everett leaflet was not to impede recruitment or discipline but 'to procure if possible a change in the law, or, failing that, to secure a change in administration'. His speech, as written, ends with a rousing defence of spiritual against militaristic values:

> The noblest thing in a man is the spiritual force which enables him to stand firm against the whole world in obedience to his own sense of right; and I will never acquiesce in silence while the men in whom spiritual force is strong are treated as a danger to the community rather than its most precious heritage. I would say to the persecutors: you cannot defeat such men; you cannot make their testimony of no avail. For every one whom you silence by force, a hundred will be moved to carry on his work; until at last you yourselves will be won over, and will recognise, with a sense of liberation from bondage, that all the material force the world contains is powerless against the spirit of indomitable love.

In court, he got as far as 'you cannot defeat such men' before the Lord Mayor's patience ran out. 'I have allowed you a good deal of latitude because you are not an expert,' he told Russell, but 'Really now you are making a political speech.' He found Russell guilty as charged and fined him £100 plus

£10 costs, with eight days to pay or two months in prison. Russell appealed against the verdict, and his appeal was dismissed on 29 June. This decision, like the original verdict, was entirely foreseeable. Russell had expected nothing else; he was simply, in line with NCF practice, dragging the process out for as long as possible. He duly refused to pay the fine and was perfectly prepared to go to prison. On this occasion, however, he was denied the opportunity. His furniture and books were seized by the police and auctioned. Only if the auction failed to raise enough to pay his fine would he be imprisoned. At the auction, Russell's friends, led by Philip Morrell, bought most of his belongings, ensuring both that his fine was paid and that his possessions were returned to him.

Russell thoroughly enjoyed the trial and the opportunity it gave him to publicise the NCF's case (while he was preparing his defence, he wrote to Ottoline: 'Ever since I got in with the NCF life has been full of happiness'), but its consequences for his own life were to be much more drastic and more far-reaching than he had foreseen. Just two days after the verdict – and several weeks before his appeal was heard – the Foreign Office cabled the British Ambassador in Washington to tell him that Russell, having been convicted under the Defence of the Realm Act, would be refused a passport: 'Please inform the President of Harvard.' The Foreign Office had had its eye on Russell for a long time. After his letter to *The Times*, Lord Newton of the Foreign Office let it be known to his colleagues that he regarded Russell as 'one of the most mischievous cranks in the country', whom it would be 'folly' to allow to go to America, and demanded to know why he was not being prosecuted. Other FO officials took the same view. One wrote: 'I think his effect would be disastrous in the US just now with so much peace talk about.'

Given that Russell's summons to appear in court was issued immediately after these internal FO discussions and given the speed with which the FO acted after the trial, it seems entirely possible that the Home Office acted in prosecuting Russell, not in direct response to his letter to *The Times*, but rather under pressure from the FO; that, in other words, the purpose of taking him to court was precisely to furnish a reason for denying him a passport and thus preventing him from agitating against the war in the United States. As Russell had said to Ottoline when he accepted the Harvard offer, the United States would provide an internationally important platform for his peace propaganda. No one realised that more than the British Government.

Russell was not told of the Foreign Office decision to deny him a passport until 7 July, when he received from James Woods at Harvard a copy of the British Ambassador's letter to Harvard's president informing him that 'Russell has been convicted under "defence of the realm act" for writing an undesirable pamphlet. Under these circumstances it would be impossible to issue a passport to him to leave the country.' Personally, Russell told Ottoline, he was relieved, 'except as regards money':

I *loathed* the thought of the exile. But you cannot imagine how it *infuriates* me as a piece of tyranny. I want a fuss made about it. I want it pointed out that I was going to teach logic & that the Govt. thinks logic wd. put America against us.

His reply to Woods was still more vitriolic. 'The sum-total of my crime', he told him, 'was that I said two years' hard labour in prison was an excessive punishment for the offence of having a conscientious objection to participation in war':

Since then, the same offence has been punished by the death-sentence, commuted to 10 years' penal servitude. Anyone who thinks that I can be made to hold my tongue when such things are being done is grossly mistaken . . . This letter will no doubt never reach you, but it may be found interesting by the Censor.

On this last point, Russell was quite right: his letter never reached Woods but was intercepted by the Home Office. As he said at the end of the letter: 'These are fierce times.'

Just a few days after learning that he was to be prevented from going to Harvard, Russell received the following letter from the chairman of Trinity College Council:

Dear Russell,
    It is my duty to inform you that the following resolution was unanimously passed by the College Council today:
    'That, since Mr Russell has been convicted under the Defence of the Realm Act, and the conviction has been affirmed on appeal, he be removed from his Lectureship in the College.'

The Foreign Office, it seems, had not been the only one lying in wait for him. Russell's relations with the 'bloodthirsty old men' who ran Trinity, while the younger Fellows were at the front, had now reached their logical conclusion.

The decision of Trinity to sack Russell was greeted with outrage within the academic community, even by many of its members who were opposed to Russell's anti-war stance, several of whom wrote to Russell in sympathy and support. Many expressed the view that, as Russell put it to G. H. Hardy: 'There is no hope of any freedom of thought in the British empire if it is to be banished from Trinity. We may as well shut up shop and get ourselves expunged from the list of civilised nations.' Hardy himself immediately began a campaign to get Trinity to invite Russell back and would not let the matter rest until he succeeded, but, as Russell told him: 'I think it unlikely that I can ever again endure the stuffiness of a high table, even if it could endure me.'

For him, he told Ottoline, though he felt 'sad that Trinity should do it', his expulsion was a good thing: 'It decides the issue.' He had, at last, as Lawrence had urged him to do a year earlier, cut himself adrift from established respectability in all its forms and become an 'outlaw'. A year earlier he had written that if he were 'done with respectability' he would have ten times the energy. Now that respectability had done with him, he found that he had been right – he felt positively invigorated. 'I feel I am on the threshold of life,' he told Ottoline. 'Quite lately I have somehow found myself':

> I have poise & sanity – I no longer have the feeling of powers unrealised within me, which used to be a perpetual torture. I don't care what the authorities do to me, they can't stop me long. Before, I have felt either wicked or passively resigned – now I feel fully active & contented with my activity – I have no inward discords any more – & nothing ever really troubles me.

For the time being, he felt that he was where he belonged: outside academic life and in the midst of the struggle against militarism. And, after the war, perhaps he could make a living as an independent teacher, 'like Abelard':

> I will make myself a teacher of all the working-men who are hungry for intellectual food – there are many throughout the country. I am always coming across them. I am amazed at the number of them at my meetings who have read my 'Problems of Philosophy'. I foresee a great & splendid life in that sort of thing – dealing with political ideas, but keeping out of school politics. And I want to enlist all the teachers & men of education who will have been turned out for being COs. There are numbers of them. Think of building up a new free education not under the State! There are infinite possibilities – finance is the only difficulty, but not an insuperable one. I could give heart & brain & life to that.

Far from punishing Russell and damaging his career, the Council of Trinity had simply confirmed him in his choice of career. He was to be a popular lecturer, a shaper of public opinion. Already the NCF had devised a scheme for their 'Mephisto' to give a course of lectures in the autumn, 'like the one I gave in Caxton Hall in the spring, but more popular – to be given in 6 large towns simultaneously, free, but at the expense of local Quakers – each town to pay me £100! I like the plan from every point of view & I expect it will come off.'

In the meantime, however, he had the tour of South Wales to get through, the 'stop-the-war' campaign he had envisaged early in May. The tour took up the first three weeks of July 1916, during which Russell addressed innumerable large meetings, some in the open air and others in large halls, campaigning for immediate peace negotiations. 'An honourable and stable peace can be obtained at once' was his message, 'but the pride of Governments stands in the way. It is time for the people to make themselves heard by demanding negotiations for PEACE NOW.' The publicity surrounding his trial ensured large attendances for all his talks and he found, somewhat to his surprise, a wide degree of support for his campaign. His first talk was at an open-air meeting in Port Talbot, where he addressed a crowd of about 400 and found them to be 'unanimously sympathetic'. That evening he spoke to a packed hall in Briton Ferry: 'they were *all* at the highest point of enthusiasm

– they inspired me, & I spoke as I have never spoken before.' At this meeting a resolution in favour of immediate peace negotiations was 'carried unanimously', though 'presumably the two plain-clothes men who had come to take notes must have abstained'.

The Battle of the Somme had begun just a few days before this meeting, and, before the appalling extent of the casualties on the battle's first day was widely known, many believed that a great breakthrough was imminent. At such a time, it was felt, talk of peace negotiations was particularly foolish. To his delight, Russell discovered that this was not the view of the people of South Wales (not, anyway, those who attended his talks):

> One needs no prudent reticences – no humbug of any sort – one can just speak out one's whole mind. I thought the great offensive would have excited them, but it hasn't.

And speak his mind he did, uninhibited by the fact that everything he said was being recorded in police notebooks. He was, of course, by this time well aware of the dangers. 'I feel little doubt that I shall spend the winter in prison,' he wrote, 'but I don't think I should mind much, because I should not feel it was a waste of time.'

After the meeting in Cardiff on 6 July, he reported, 'The police took down every word I said & I have no doubt whatever that they will get me on what I am saying.' Actually, it was a newspaper reporter who was taking notes, but in the end it amounted to practically the same thing: the notes were, in time, handed over to the Home Office, which, though it seemed initially unwilling to heap further martyrdom on Russell, did eventually use them, as Russell had predicted it would, to 'get him'. In this speech, as in all his other speeches on the tour, Russell called upon Britain to give up the pretence that Germans were uniquely wicked and monstrous, and to abandon the vengeful aim of bringing Germany to its knees in favour of a more humane attitude, one that sought to secure a lasting peace through 'justice and generosity, leading to international cooperation and the comity of nations'.

These harmless, even platitudinous, sentiments might have aroused little ire had not Russell illustrated them with some provocative examples. Most mischievous of all was his comparison of the Allied blockade of German supplies with the German sinking of the *Lusitania*; both, he claimed, might with justice be regarded as the wilful endangering of the lives of innocent women and children. To at least one member of the audience, a Captain Atherley Jones, this was quite outrageous. 'Is it fair', he demanded, 'to make that suggestion when we have millions of men fighting at the front, and people in this country leaving their businesses and suffering sacrifices? I say that, in my opinion, Russell, who has been convicted already for issuing seditious pamphlets, ought to be locked up.' At the time, Russell was inclined to dismiss Atherley Jones as a 'bloodthirsty middle-aged man' who 'spoilt his case by violence'. The enraged captain, however, was determined to make trouble for Russell. Disappointed that Russell was not 'locked up' after his Cardiff speech, he wrote a report of the meeting, emphasising his role in the discussion ('I denounced him as a traitor'), and sent it to the *Daily Express*, which published it on 11 August. It was this press report that eventually prompted the Home Office to acquire the notes from the meeting and add them to the (by now burgeoning) file it kept on Russell. For the moment, however, though they kept a watchful eye on Russell throughout his tour of South Wales, the authorities were in no hurry to act against him, and he was allowed to see the tour through to its conclusion at Brynmawr on 24 July.

After the tour, Russell returned to London to a very changed set of circumstances from those he had left when he set off for Port Talbot on 1 July. Then, he had thought that he would be returning to Cambridge for the Michaelmas Term and leaving for Harvard in the New Year. Now, everything was different; his only source of income for the foreseeable future was the lecture course that Clifford Allen was organising for the autumn, and he was forced to adjust to a life without either respectability or financial security. He began by letting his Bury Street flat and moving into his brother's flat in Gordon Square. As he put it to Ottoline: 'I want to avoid fixed expenses that imply a certain standard of life.' In any case, 'Since you left London there is not much use in my flat. It has changed its character completely, & become a sort of business office.'

Though a perfect *pied-à-terre* from which to conduct NCF business in London, Frank's flat would not be so ideal for writing the lectures that Russell was to give in the autumn. For that, as he put it to Ottoline, he would need 'quiet days'. Writing from Wales on 17 July, he had suggested coming to Garsington to find the peace he needed, but, having returned from Wales, 'terrified at the prospect of plunging into writing again,' memories of the previous autumn seem to have changed his mind. 'I don't yet know where to settle for work,' he told Ottoline. 'I think it would be a mistake to try Garsington again. I should be afraid of all the old troubles coming back.' He clearly already had some alternative to Garsington in mind, however, for in the same letter, he talks of being in London two or three days a week '& in the country the rest of the week, working at my lectures'. In his letters to Ottoline over the next few weeks, it emerged that he had two alternatives in mind: his brother's country home, Telegraph House, and (though this emerged more slowly and insidiously) the seaside town of Bosham in Sussex, where the Eliots were spending the summer, within convenient reach of both London and Telegraph House. In the event, Russell spent August in what he had earlier described as a 'pillar and post' sort of style, travelling between London, where he attended to NCF work, Telegraph House, where he worked on his lectures, Bosham, where he continued his odd affair with Vivien Eliot, and Garsington, where he sought refuge from all the above.

In his letters from Wales, Russell had written to Ottoline about his fears of losing intimacy with her: 'I know extraordinarily little of your inner life now-a-days, & I wish I knew more, but I don't know how to elicit it', and seemed inclined to attribute it to his absorption in political work:

> My own existence has become so objective that I hardly have an inner life any more for the present – but I should have if I had leisure.

'The war keeps one tied to earth,' he wrote later in the same letter. 'And sometimes I wonder if we have both grown so impersonal that it has become difficult to give oneself to personal love.'

Ottoline, however, was only too aware that, where Vivien Eliot was concerned, Russell did not feel the same difficulty in overcoming his 'impersonal' and 'objective' nature, and she could not help feeling somewhat piqued by the contrast. Soon after his return from Wales, she tackled him on the subject:

I had a long talk with Bertie about Mrs Eliot. I don't really understand her influence over him. It seems so odd that such a frivolous, silly, little woman should affect him so much, but I think he likes to feel that she depends upon him, and she looks up to him as a rich god, for he lavishes presents on her of silk underclothes and all sorts of silly things, and pays for her dancing lessons. It takes all his money . . .

The question of how much of his money Russell spent on the Eliots had been raised by him in a letter written a month earlier, soon after his trial. He had dined with Vivien, he told Ottoline, '& discussed money':

The passion of her life is dancing & ever since I have known her I have paid for her to have dancing lessons whenever she has been well enough. I don't suppose she will ever be any good, because of her health, but it is such a passion that I can't bear to baulk it if I can possibly help it.

'Of course,' he added, 'it would save my pocket if her husband got better-paid work. What I have seen of his writing in the way of reviews etc. is really good – it has quality & distinction, although it is done in the evenings after a full day's work at school.' Perhaps, he suggested, Eliot could send some of his work to Ottoline; perhaps she could ask Desmond MacCarthy (a frequent visitor to Garsington, and by now a regular contributor to the *New Statesman* and an influential literary critic) to help in getting Eliot regular work for the *New Statesman* or the *Guardian*? Russell had, he said, been helping the Eliots with ordinary living expenses as well as paying for Vivien's dancing lessons: 'So if you can see any way of helping it will relieve me of a great anxiety.'

Evidently, by the end of July, Ottoline thought the time had come for Russell to relieve himself of this anxiety. His reluctance to do so, in the face of the problems that mounted up for him in the summer of 1916, became increasingly odd and inexplicable. In a letter that must have been written soon after Ottoline's long talk to him on the subject, Russell led her to believe that the conversation had achieved its end:

I am dreadfully worried as a result of our talk about Mrs E. I promised to see her some time this week, & all my thoughts & feelings are in a confusion. I don't know what I want or what I ought to want. I feel sure that the result will be a violent quarrel, whatever I may intend – if not this time, then next. The things you said had a great influence on me. I suppose I must have been already thinking them underneath, though not consciously. But it is difficult to act on them without cruelty. The only part in the matter that I feel on my own account to be wrong is the spending of money. Quite at first, that was justifiable, but it has ceased to be. At the same time, having created the expectation, I can hardly stop suddenly. You may be right that in other ways it is bad, but I don't *feel* that it was. However, since our talk I wish it were done with – that I am clear about. But it can't be yet awhile. The trouble over the money made a great change in my feelings & in my judgment. I struggled against it at first, but in vain. It makes me unhappy & revives the despairs of last autumn. If I were busy with practical things that wouldn't matter, but unluckily it comes just when I have leisure to brood. But I think you were *quite right* to speak.

The only thought that comes to me is that one ought not to spend one's time worrying over private affairs when there is so much to be done. One must try to keep one's thoughts on public matters, & not get absorbed in one's own sins. The thing must be left to time. I am *sure* it will work out as you think right but I ought not to do anything violent or sudden.

Though he recognised that his relationship with Vivien had become a luxury he could no longer afford, he still felt, for some reason, unable to shake himself free from it, at least for the time being. For, indeed, he did not 'do anything violent or sudden', and, throughout the summer, despite claiming to have been convinced by Ottoline's view, spent more of his time at Bosham than at Garsington. 'It will be difficult to do anything sudden,' he wrote on 4 August, '& *really* the whole thing is not so bad as you think.'

Perhaps aware how inexplicable his attitude to Vivien seemed, Russell returned throughout August 1916 to the subject again and again in his letters to Ottoline, either promising that a break with Vivien was imminent, or trying to explain why it was not, without, however, ever sounding entirely convincing on either point:

The problem for me as regards Mrs E. is this: All the faults you suspect exist but they are gradually improving. I have made her trust me & look to me & care for me to a considerable extent. In spite of her faults I have an affection for her, because I feel they spring from a root of despair & that she might become different. And apart from affection, I have incurred responsibility. The affection is not constant, but the sense of responsibility is. I don't want to quarrel – I think with time I can avoid giving her the feeling that I have played her false, without getting into any permanent entanglement. But it will want time. I don't feel secretive about it any longer. (20 August 1916)

I am going . . . to Bosham for a few days. After that I don't expect to see Mrs E. again at any rate till the spring; but I can't be sure. There has been no quarrel of any sort, only a feeling that there is not much good going on. (22 August)

It is not about you that I am unhappy but about Mrs E. I raised hopes in her which I have had to disappoint more or less, & I hate doing that. You know I feel that I make everybody unhappy that I have much to do with: one thing that attracted me to her was that it seemed clear one could make her happy by the very simple method of spending a certain amount of money. If I had succeeded I should have got rid of a morbid oppression. As it is, it has come back. It would have been worth a good deal of money to get rid of it, as it really oppresses me & makes me disagreeable, & exacting from wanting to be reassured. I can afford the money, but it seemed clear that it was wrong to spend so much on a matter of no real importance, & also that I ought not to have to think too much about making money. I said all this to her. She took it very well, but on my side it makes trouble – the pleasure I had was in giving things. It was a revolt against austerity. I get so weary of sacrificing everybody to work. But that is only a weakness.
(undated, but probably 23 August)

You have not done any mischief at all – there had to be a readjustment & I have only been doing what I felt necessary in any case on account of my work. Yesterday I came up by way of Chichester, & had a talk with Eliot there (I didn't see Mrs E. who was ill); it was rather gloomy, but I got quite clear as to what must be done, so I shan't worry any more. It is fixed that I go to Bosham Monday to Friday; then I don't expect to see her during the winter. Seeing her is worrying, & takes up my time & money & her health. I shall go on doing what I have done in the way of money during the winter, but beyond that I have said I can't foresee what will be possible. I can't now decide anything beyond this winter.
     . . . After this next week, I shall like to come to Garsington. Matters with Mrs E. will be decided then. I never contemplated risking my reputation with her, & I never risked it as far as I can judge.
(1 September)

Russell did not, as planned, go to Bosham the following Monday – and the promised 'readjustment' with Vivien was delayed yet again – not, however, because he chose not to go, but because, just hours after this letter was written, he was served with an order from the War Office, banning him from all coastal regions. In a second letter to Ottoline of 1 September, he described this 'queer adventure':

About 12 o'clock, two men in plain clothes appeared on behalf of the War Office, & served a notice on me ordering me not to go into any prohibited area. I was just going to Suffolk, but I had to give it up. I have also had to give up going to Sussex on Monday. I shall also have to give up lecturing at Glasgow, Edinburgh & Newcastle as I had intended to do. I have no notion why they served the notice on me, or whether there is any hope of getting it rescinded . . . I am much more angry over it than anything yet. It is a power conferred on them for dealing with spies, & they choose to suppose that I want to give military information to the Germans. It makes my blood boil.

The 'prohibited areas' covered about one-third of the country, including all of its coastline. The War Office powers invoked against Russell were intended to prevent people whom they suspected of spying for the Germans from signalling to enemy boats. Russell was rightly indignant that such a notice had been served against him. The Government, which never for a moment suspected Russell of wanting to pass on information to the Germans, had evidently panicked. Its real motive in issuing the notice, as emerges from internal government memoranda, was to prevent Russell from keeping an appointment to meet conscientious objectors in Haverhill, Suffolk, on 1 September.

At Haverhill Russell had intended, as a representative of the NCF National Committee, to meet with some COs, who had agreed to take part in a new Government initiative to provide alternative civilian work (in this case, road-digging) to those who had been imprisoned for refusing to accept non-combatant military service. The Haverhill work camp was one of several that had been set up in the summer of 1916 in accordance with this scheme, which was showing signs of being a success in the Government's efforts to defuse the threat to conscription posed by the NCF. The work at these camps was hard and the conditions deliberately harsh (COs, after all, had to be seen to be making some sort of sacrifice – how, otherwise, could one be sure they weren't merely cowards and shirkers?), but at least it was not under any military authority and was a good deal preferable to persecution in prison. For those reasons, many COs – to the delight of the Government and the despair of Russell, Clifford Allen and most of the NCF National Committee – were prepared to co-operate with it.

The effect on the NCF was disastrous. Throughout the summer, its leaders – both those inside and those outside prison – tried without success to think of some way of maintaining the impetus of the movement against conscription in the face of this successful manoeuvre by the Government. They were caught in a dilemma: if they committed the NCF to opposing the scheme, they would risk losing the support of the thousands of its members who had taken advantage of it to escape the hardships of prison; on the other hand, if they advised their members to co-operate with it, what would be left of their resistance to the Military Service Act?

In the face of this dilemma, the NCF was split between 'absolutists' and 'alternativists'. One of the leading alternativists was a man called C. H. Norman, who, in return for his release from prison, had agreed to work at the Haverhill camp. At a committee meeting on 21 August, Norman tried to win the other NCF members round to the scheme, on this occasion without success. 'We thought [it] a mistake,' Russell reported, adding that he considered Norman 'rather the worse morally for his persecution: the fear of going back to it leads him a little to self-deception. But that is not surprising.'

Russell agreed, nevertheless, to visit Haverhill to see what conditions were like there and to chat to the COs. It was a measure both of how important the success of the scheme was to the Government and of how much influence they attributed to Russell, that when the Home Office heard about Russell's proposed visit (presumably it kept some kind of surveillance on NCF committee meetings), it was panicked into seeking any means it could find to prevent him from going.

A few days before Russell's intended visit, a Home Office official called Whiskard, with responsibility for the Government's alternative service scheme, wrote to Sir Ernley Blackwell, his superior at the Home Office, that 'there is no doubt of deliberate intention on the part of the NCF to break down the scheme', and that 'it would be very foolish to allow Russell to go down and harangue them with this object'.

Whiskard's memo happened to catch Blackwell at a time when he was much exercised with the problem of what to do about Russell. After Captain Atherley Jones's report of Russell's Cardiff speech had been published in the *Daily Express*, it attracted the attention of the Home Secretary, Herbert Samuel. Prompted, it seems, by the Home Secretary's concern, Edward Troup, the Permanent Under-Secretary at the Home Office, wrote to the Director of Public Prosecutions, Sir Charles Mathews, asking whether a case against Russell could be made under the Defence of the Realm Act. Russell's remarks in his Cardiff speech, Troup argued, could not be dismissed lightly, presented as they were 'with a good deal of misguided cleverness'. Besides, they knew from Russell's letter to James Woods at Harvard, which had been stopped by the Censor and was now in the possession of the Home Office, how 'deliberately hostile' Russell was and that he was 'anxious to go on an anti-British mission to the USA'. Still, Troup admitted, seeing that last time Russell was taken to court it only served to help his cause, 'it is a difficult question whether we should do more harm than good by prosecuting. He would make a clever defence and publish it as a pamphlet.'

The Public Prosecutor did not think the Cardiff speech provided much of a case against Russell, but he nevertheless agreed that steps should be taken against him and wrote to Sir Ernley Blackwell giving his recommendations. These were: first, that the Press should be told not to report any more of Russell's speeches or to print his letters, and, second, that everything Russell published from now on should be seized by the police. Were such moves to be challenged in the House of Commons, Mathews went on, they could be justified 'by the production to the challenger of the Cardiff speech.'

A few days after receiving this advice, Blackwell received Whiskard's urgent note about the need to prevent Russell from going to Haverhill. With little time to act (this was the day immediately before Russell's proposed visit), Blackwell had to take responsibility for the situation himself and with the Home Secretary away for a few days, the only thing he could think of was to ask the War Office to use its powers to prevent Russell from entering prohibited areas, Haverhill being close enough to the coast to be included in the definition of a 'prohibited area'. This, though it seemed an absurdly large hammer to crack a rather small nut, had the advantage of not requiring any legal proceedings or, indeed, any justification at all, and could therefore be implemented without delay.

It was, however, rather a desperate and ill-considered move, and when news of it reached the Home Secretary, Herbert Samuel, he immediately expressed misgivings. 'I think it would be difficult to defend an order excluding Russell from all prohibited areas,' Samuel wrote. 'There is no question, of course, that he is an enemy agent.' But it was too late, the notice had already been served and the War Office, having been persuaded to issue the ban, would not now consider rescinding it. Russell's view that there was no good reason to continue the war was, in the opinion of Colonel Vernon Kell of the War Office 'very dangerous', and Russell had to be stopped from spreading 'his vicious tenets amongst dockers, miners and transport workers'.

As a defence of the ban, Kell's argument was, as it stood, embarrassingly illogical. For, of course, the ban had *not* prevented Russell from spreading his 'vicious tenets', it had only prevented him from doing so in coastal regions. So long as he chose only to subvert the minds of workers in inland areas, Russell was still at perfect liberty to do so. The same problem bedevilled the idea of producing the text of the Cardiff speech in justification of the ban. For what was its relevance? If it was to show that Russell held subversive opinions, which it was not in Britain's best interests to have expressed publicly, why not silence him altogether? Why, again, pretend that the important thing was to keep him away from the coast? In the face of such questions, Colonel Kell was prepared to adopt the only logical position. 'If Mr Russell should still persist in making speeches similar to his Cardiff one in unprohibited areas,' he remarked, 'then the next step will be to confine his movements to a particular area.'

Unless the Home Office was prepared to advocate this rather draconian measure – and it quite naturally shrank from doing so – it was saddled with a hopelessly inconsistent position. Unable to admit that its immediate purpose was to prevent Russell from keeping his appointment at Haverhill, and unwilling also to admit that it was reluctant to take Russell to court because of his skill in exploiting such occasions, it had to advance in public a defence of the ban that made manifestly little sense. All it could do was keep quiet until it was challenged, and then try to brazen it out.

Russell of course knew nothing of these intrigues against him in the War and Home Offices, and was, quite naturally, baffled by the order. After puzzling it over for a couple of days, he decided that the War Office had simply made a mistake, that it had imposed the ban thinking that, on his South Wales tour, he had tried to incite the miners to strike. Through Sir Francis Younghusband, who managed to combine being a friend of Russell's with having friendly contacts in the War Office, he made efforts to find out exactly what the War Office thought it was up to.

Though extremely angry at the implication that he was a traitor to his country, and annoyed that it forced him to cut short his forthcoming lecture tour, so that it included only Manchester and Birmingham, and no longer Newcastle, Glasgow and Edinburgh, Russell was nevertheless rather enjoying the absurdity of the situation. 'There is a lot of sport to be got out of this matter,' he told Ottoline. 'I am enjoying it . . . The whole thing cheers me up. It is such a comfort to have something immediate & small to fuss about.'

Presumably, he meant 'immediate & small' in comparison to the larger problems of the war, conscription and the internal disputes in the NCF, but his subsequent letters show him dwelling not so much on these as on the wretchedly persistent question of what to do about Vivien, and the perennial puzzle of why Vivien mattered so much to him. It seems that in the days immediately after receiving the order, Russell had seen rather more of Vivien than his letters to Ottoline imply. In his *Autobiography*, he says that when the order was issued: 'I had gone up to London for the day from Bosham in Sussex, where I was staying with the Eliots. I had to get them to bring up my brush and comb and tooth-brush, because the Government objected to my fetching them myself.'[1] On 4 September, while still waiting to hear from the War Office an explanation for the banning order, Russell wrote Ottoline a long letter, showing that, in brooding over his relationship with Vivien, he had come to an important series of self-realisations. After making the, by now routine, promises that 'I shall soon have come to the end of the readjustment with Mrs E.' and that 'As soon as it is settled, I will come to Garsington – I long to come,' he told her:

I have been realising various things during this time. It is odd how one finds out what one really wants, & how very selfish it always is. What I want permanently – not consciously, but deep down – is stimulus, the sort of thing that keeps my brain active & exuberant. I suppose that is what makes me a vampire. I get a stimulus most from the instinctive feeling of success. Failure makes me collapse. Odd things give me a sense of failure – for instance, the way the COs all take alternative service, except a handful. Wittgenstein's criticism gave me a sense of failure. The real trouble between you & me has always been that you gave me a sense of failure – at first, because you were not happy; then in other ways. To be *really* happy with you, not only momentarily, I should have to lose that sense of failure. I had a sense of success with Mrs E. because I achieved what I meant to achieve (which was not so very difficult), but now I have lost that, not by your fault in the least . . . Instinctively, I turn to things in which success is possible, just for the stimulus.

I have always cared for you in yourself, & not as a stimulus or for any self-centred reason: but when I have felt that through caring for you & feeling unsuccessful I have lost energy, it has produced a sort of instinctive resentment. That has been at the bottom of everything – & now that I have at last got to the bottom of it, it won't be a trouble any longer. But unless I can cease to have a sense of failure with you, I am bound to go on looking for stimulus elsewhere from time to time. That would only cease if I ceased to care about work – I am sure all this is the exact truth.

---

[1] The emphasis here (on *staying* with the Eliots and coming up to London 'for the day') is strikingly different from that of his letter to Ottoline of 1 September, in which he had implied that he had been with the Eliots for the day, on his way back to stay in London. Now Bosham was – by order of the Government – a 'prohibited area' and he could not return to the Eliots even if he wanted to.

I would set my will in a different direction as regards you, if I knew of any direction in which I *could* succeed. But I don't think it can be done that way. The rare moments of mystic insight that I have had have been when I was free from the will to succeed. But they have brought a new kind of success, which I have at once noticed & wanted, & so my will has drifted back into the old ways. And I don't believe I should do anything worth doing without that sort of will. It is very tangled.

The series of oppositions that is here being posed is remarkable. On the one hand, we have mystic insight, true love (his love for Ottoline) and inactivity; on the other, the will to succeed, his affair with Vivien and his ability to accomplish anything worth doing. The former belong to his life before the war, the latter to his life as 'Mephisto'. His love for Ottoline, he seems to be saying, had to be withdrawn – for the sake of his work – in favour of the simpler and more superficial affection he has for Vivien. Now that he no longer feels a sense of success with Vivien, he is condemned – again for the sake of his work – to 'go on looking for stimulus', like a vampire looking for its next victim.

It is a remarkable confession, behind which is an implicit, rather chilly, calculation of the relative importance of personal and public virtue. For he could not have thought it admirable to be a vampire, but since he thought it necessary to maintain the prodigious levels of energy he needed for his anti-war work, he was prepared to be one. For the public good, as it were, he was prepared to abandon what was finest in himself. It is a position that carries to its logical conclusion his earlier talk about being so busy with public matters that he hardly had an inner life any more, and, still earlier, his remark about Clifford Allen and the other NCF leaders, that, though they had energy and were doing important work, they were not 'comrades to one's inner life'. Then, however, such a denial of the demands of his inner life was a cause of frustration; now it had become a matter of policy.

The following day, accompanied by Younghusband, Russell went to the War Office for an interview with General George Cockerill. Cockerill had in front of him reports of Russell's speeches in South Wales, and drew attention straight away to Russell's reported opinion that there was no reason for the war to continue another day. This, he told Russell, was a dangerous statement, calculated to undermine the war effort. If Russell would promise to abandon such propaganda and return to mathematics, the War Office would withdraw the ban. Russell, of course, replied that he could not, in all conscience, make such a promise. There then followed a rather odd exchange on the nature of conscience, with Cockerill declaring it to be 'a still small voice', and 'when it becomes blatant and strident I suspect it of no longer being a conscience', and Russell countering that Cockerill did not apply such a principle to those whose consciences impelled them to speak out in favour of the war. This silenced Cockerill for a while, but then he began on an even odder tack. 'Do you not think', he asked Russell, 'there is some lack of humour in going on reiterating the same thing?'

This remark stayed with Russell throughout his life. To be accused of a lack of a sense of humour at such a time seemed so ridiculous that he never tired of repeating the story, saying that 'afterwards I regretted that I had not replied that I held my sides with laughter every morning as I read the casualty figures.' What he did reply was that new issues were constantly arising and that he could not barter away his right to speak on them. He told Cockerill about his forthcoming lecture tour and that he had intended to lecture in Glasgow, Newcastle and Edinburgh, all now in prohibited areas. The lectures would not be propaganda speeches but would rather elaborate on the general principles of politics, 'and no doubt men with sufficient logical acumen would be able to draw inferences'. In that case, Cockerill said, the lectures would not be allowed.

A week later, Russell received in writing the offer that Cockerill had made of withdrawing the order if Russell would agree to abandon anti-war propaganda. He refused: 'I cannot acknowledge the right of the War Office to prevent me from expressing my opinions on political subjects.' Again, in reply to a written request to give his lectures in Glasgow, he was told that permission would be given if he would give 'an honourable undertaking' not 'to use them as a vehicle for propaganda'. This, of course, Russell would not do. As the opening shot in a campaign to exploit the Government's embarrassment over the ban, he wrote up his correspondence with Cockerill and published it in the *Manchester Guardian*, after which he retired to Telegraph House to finish writing his lectures.

The lectures, six in all, were collectively called by Russell 'The World As It Can Be Made', though in 1917 they were published in the United States as *Political Ideals*, the title of the first lecture (they remained unpublished in Britain until 1963). Though the ideas they espouse are broadly the same as those in *Principles of Social Reconstruction*, their expression lacks much of the freshness, life and passion of the earlier lectures, and they seem in comparison rather jaded and uninspired. Where they differ most in their content is in giving rather less emphasis to the 'eternal' and rather more to economic questions. Arguing that 'Capitalism and the wage system must be abolished' as 'twin monsters which are eating up the world', Russell goes on to reject state socialism as an alternative, on the familiar grounds that it would create a too-powerful state, and commits himself to Guild Socialism, an economic system in which 'private capitalistic enterprises should be replaced by self-governing combinations of those who actually do the work'.

On the Saturday after he had finished writing the lectures, 23 September, Russell was given a hero's reception at the NCF London Convention held in the Portman Rooms, Baker Street. Among the audience was a young and strikingly attractive aristocratic actress called Constance Malleson, who was known to most by her stage name 'Colette O'Niel'. Russell had got to know Colette the previous Wednesday at a dinner of left-wingers that included Ramsay MacDonald, Robert Smillie, the miners' leader, and the publisher Francis Meynell. She was a friend of Clifford Allen and had first caught Russell's eye at Allen's trial back in July.

Brought up among the Protestant landed gentry in Ireland, Colette was the youngest child of Lord and Lady Annesley, and had spent her childhood at their country seat at Castlewellan, County Down. As a teenager, however, she rebelled against the expectations of her upbringing and set her heart on a career as an actress. In 1913 she was a rather reluctant débutante, bowing to her mother's insistence that she 'do' the London season, but, after that, she cut herself adrift from her past more or less completely to live a bohemian life in a small flat in London with her husband, the writer and director, Miles Malleson, a member of the NCF and a great admirer of Russell. She and Malleson married only for the sake of her parents, their natural inclination being to live together, unfettered by conventional restraints. The impression she made on a later admirer, the writer Bennitt Gardiner, was of a 'haughty [and] beautiful' theatrical lady, 'obviously a person of consequence . . . imperious, graceful, hypnotic'. When Russell first met her, however, she cut a rather less grand figure: just twenty-one, unknown as an actress (having left the Royal Academy of Dramatic Art in the spring of 1915, she had been offered only one part: as understudy to the leading lady in a wordless play called *L'Enfant Prodigue*) and working at the NCF's offices, performing secretarial tasks. Among NCF members, she was noted more for her youthful vitality and her fierce spirit of independence than for the imperiousness that later impressed Gardiner. What struck everybody who knew her most forcibly was her insistence on freedom. Freedom, as Colette herself often remarked, was her religion, and she insisted on it, whatever relationship she was in. Allen had told Russell that she was 'generous with her time, free in her opinions and whole-hearted in her pacifism', upon which information, Russell says, 'I naturally took steps to know her better.'

After the convention, Russell asked her out to dinner, and, after they had eaten, he walked her back to her flat in Bernard Street. She invited him in and they sat up till the early hours of the morning talking. As Colette remembers it, Russell did most of the talking:

Sitting very upright before a horrible little fire, his body rather stiff, he prodded home his words with those blunt, expressive fingers of his. 'It's not so simple as that –' The phrase cropped up again and again in his talk. Life (he said) was not simple . . . The spirit of socialism was not likeable . . . Freedom should be the basis of everything . . . One wanted to live always open to the world . . .

He went on to speak of how one felt an alien among people with whom one could not communicate in a language they could understand . . . The pain and cruelty and ugliness of the world was as well worth seeing as the joy and beauty of it. One had to look into hell before one had any right to speak of heaven.

After he had gone, I stood a long time staring at a picture of Edward Carpenter which hung on my wall; and I suddenly knew that Carpenter's creed meant nothing to me any more. I had found something stronger. Everything I had believed in had fallen away. Everything I had known and loved. I felt stunted and torn, but I knew I had found myself.

As Russell recalls it, 'We talked half the night, and in the middle of talk became lovers ... in that moment there began for both of us a relation profoundly serious and profoundly important, sometimes happy, sometimes painful, but never trivial.'

Russell's relationship with Colette was to become one of the most important in his life, but in these early days of their affair, it is difficult to know how seriously he took her. In his *Autobiography* he says that, at first, 'I could not believe in my own feelings, and half supposed that I was having a light affair with her':

I had got used to thinking that all my serious feelings were given to Ottoline. Colette was so much younger, so much less of a personage, so much more capable of frivolous pleasures.

But his letters to Colette sound, from the very first, like those of a man in the grip of a deep and serious passion. On the day after their first night together, he wrote that their affair 'can mean a great deal to me', and even sounded a note of warning:

I feel you do not know me and perhaps you will hate me when you do. I feel you are all gentleness, but in me many things are tough and harsh, and there are old scars that are not beautiful.

Is this the confession of a vampire, or are they the words of someone who wanted to regain some spiritual depth? His subsequent letters suggest the latter. 'I *know* that I love you deeply seriously, with all my being,' he wrote, after their next night together, a few days later:

I know I have something to give you that you will feel worth having had whatever the future may be. I know you have everything to give me. I have never before cared for anyone who was happy ... It has given me an untrue view of life much too full of strain and endurance ... I want some much more profound comradeship. I want to take you into the very centre of my being and to reach myself into the centre of yours. I want to know and be known, to share happiness and pain ... I want to fill your life with joy in great things and small, to find out all that gives you delight, to give your mind the freedom of great spaces and your spirit the happiness of growth into the things that reach out into infinity.
(26 September 1916)

Russell's lecture tour was set to start in Manchester on 16 October, and in the intervening weeks most of his time was taken up with NCF business, so that, though he and Colette saw each other whenever they could, it was not as often as Russell would have liked, and their relationship, like that with Ottoline earlier, was conducted largely by letter. The themes of these letters during the first weeks of their love were freedom, expansiveness and eternity. 'Teach me to go out into new and immense worlds: your worlds of thought and infinity,' Colette wrote on 28 September, to which Russell replied: 'You are already where I have struggled to be, and without the weariness of long effort':

> I have hated many people in the past. The language of hate still comes to me easily, but I don't really hate anyone now. It is defeat that makes one hate people – and now I have no sense of defeat anywhere. No one need ever be defeated – it rests with oneself to make oneself invincible. Quite lately I have had a sense of freedom I never had before.
> (29 September 1916)

'I think freedom is the basis of everything,' he wrote, and for that reason 'I don't like the spirit of socialism.'

If Russell still felt himself to be a vampire and his affair with Colette to be just one more instance of his craving for external 'stimulus', then the letters he wrote during these weeks are almost disgustingly cynical, expressing as they do exactly the opposite:

> Do you know how sometimes all the barriers of personality fall away, and one is free for all the world to come in – the stars and the night and the wind, and all the passions and hopes of men, and all the slow centuries of growth – and even the cold abysses of space grow friendly . . . And from that moment some quality of ultimate peace enters into all one feels – even when one feels most passionately. I felt it the other night by the river – I thought you were going to withdraw yourself – I felt that if you did I should lose the most wonderful thing that had ever come to me – and yet an ultimate fundamental peace remained – if it hadn't, I believe I should have lost you then. I cannot bear the littleness and enclosing walls of *purely* personal things – I want to live always open to the world, I want personal love to be like a beacon *fire* lighting up the darkness, not a timid refuge from the cold as it is very often.

Whether cynical or not, this letter is undeniably clever and subtle. While it manages to seem, and even to be, a passionate love letter, it determinedly fixes its sights on the importance of the impersonal and the relative unimportance of the personal. In that way, it is perfectly compatible with the view that sees his love for Colette – even at the height of its passion – as a fairly trivial matter.

By the time he left for his northern lecture tour, Russell and Colette had declared their love for each other and regarded themselves as both lovers and comrades. Before he left for Manchester, Colette wrote to him about the division in the NCF between the 'absolutists' and the 'alternativists', saying how sorry she was that his forthcoming lecture tour would prevent him from doing anything to reconcile the differences. Could he not say something to 'put things right'? In response, he wrote a short declaration of 'What We Stand For' for *The Tribunal*, the NCF journal. Colette was delighted with it, and declared it 'marvellously good' and 'exactly what is needed', though, in fact, it did nothing to resolve the dispute within the NCF except to urge its members to focus on higher things. The aim of the NCF, Russell argued, was nothing less than 'to bring the Kingdom of Heaven to earth'. 'Our minds and thoughts', he wrote, 'must not be filled with the evils of this present moment, but with the vision of the world we hope for.' This vision included 'not only the destruction of militarism (though that might seem a great enough object), but the creation of a free, happier, nobler life for every man and woman in the world'. From such a lofty perspective, the internal dispute of the NCF emerged as an irrelevance: 'If you disbelieve in alternative service, stand out against it, no matter what the Government may do to you; if you believe in it, take it, no matter what the absolutist may say to you.' It seems doubtful whether this adroit piece of side-stepping was appreciated by other NCF members as much as it was by Colette.

On 16 October, Russell began his lecture tour in Manchester. He started in a blaze of publicity. The day after he gave 'Political Ideals', the first of the series of six lectures, in Manchester, Robert Smillie, the President of the Miners' Federation and of the National Council for Civil Liberties, delivered the same lecture in Glasgow, announcing only at the end – to laughter and tumultuous applause – that it was the first of the series of lectures that Russell had been prevented from giving. To coincide with this propaganda coup, the National Council for Civil Liberties rushed out a pamphlet edition of the lecture, which was bought by many in the Glasgow audience. The lecture, then, had been delivered in Manchester by Russell, by Smillie in Glasgow, was available in print, and was about to be given by Russell again in Birmingham. The ban on his being able to give it in Glasgow was beginning to look very silly indeed. G. B. Shaw, for one, was delighted. 'Englishmen were brave enough on the battlefields of France or Mesopotamia,' he remarked, 'but dared not allow Bertrand Russell to speak in Glasgow.'

The Government's discomfort was increased the next day when, in the House of Commons, Charles Trevelyan asked Lloyd George to justify the ban. In reply, Lloyd George, who evidently had been briefed rather badly on the subject, alleged that the Government had information from 'very reliable sources' that Russell 'was about to engage in the delivery of a series of lectures which would interfere very seriously with the manning of the Army'. In a letter to *The Times* the following day, Russell exploited Lloyd George's embarrassment to the full. 'I can only earnestly hope', he wrote, 'that the Secret Service is less inaccurate as regards the Germans than it has proved itself to be where I am concerned.' He went on to explain that, as was evident from the synopsis of the lectures with which he had supplied the War Office, they dealt not with the immediate issues raised by the war, but with more abstract and general themes. If this should be doubted, then 'Political Ideals', 'a perfectly fair sample' of the lectures, was now on sale. Besides, if, as Lloyd George alleged, the lectures would 'undoubtedly interfere with the prosecution of the war', why were they permitted in Manchester?

When Herbert Samuel, the Home Secretary, tried to defend the ban, he only made matters worse when he alleged that Russell had been asked to give an undertaking not to engage in anti-British propaganda, while he was in the

United States, and that a passport had been denied to him only after he had refused to give such an undertaking. It is difficult to know whether Samuel was deliberately lying or had been misinformed, but in any case he afforded both Trevelyan in the House and Russell in *The Times* another opportunity to make the Government look ridiculous.

Russell's two lecture series overlapped with one another, the Manchester series running on Tuesdays, beginning 16 October and ending 20 November, and the Birmingham series on Saturdays, beginning 3 November and ending 8 December. When he was not in either Manchester or Birmingham, he remained in London at Gordon Square. It was a complicated schedule, which involved a good deal of travelling, and many of his letters from this period are headed 'In the train'.

One such letter, written on the way to Manchester on 21 October, marks an important turning point in his relationship with Colette. It was an impressive attempt to come clean about his life. 'I have meant', he began, 'to tell you many things about my life, & every time the moment has conquered me.' Among the things he wanted to tell her were:

I am strangely unhappy, because the pattern of my life is complicated & yours is simple, because I am old & you are young, because with me passion can seldom break through to freedom, out of the net of circumstances in which I am enmeshed; because my nature is hopelessly complicated, a mass of contradictory impulses; & out of all this, to my intense sorrow, pain to you must grow.

In a passage that he omitted when he included this letter in his *Autobiography* (thus making rather a nonsense of the entire letter), he went on to tell her of one important element in the 'net of circumstances' in which he was 'enmeshed': his affair with Vivien. He had, he said, a 'very great affection' for both Eliots, but 'my relation to her especially is very intimate':

If you met her you would be utterly unable to understand what I see in her – you would think her a common little thing, quite insignificant.

He had first met Vivien, he told Colette, fourteen months ago, and he then proceeded to give her the same justification for the affair that he had given Ottoline when it started: that his affection was good for Vivien, and therefore good for Eliot, whom she would punish if Russell stopped giving her affection. He went on to say how much he dreaded spoiling the 'beautiful joy' of Colette, 'which is like a sunny April morning'. This was partly because of the complications of his personality, partly because of the entangled web of relationships he had enmeshed himself in and partly also because of the 'slavery of work': 'I feel that life & the world look much simpler to you than they do to me . . . Can you learn to trust my love when it gives no sign? It is only because my spirit is in prison at times.'

'I cannot give a *simple* happiness,' he concluded. 'I can give you moments of heaven with long intervals of pain between.'

The letter is remarkable for this forthright attempt to spell out what Colette could expect from an involvement with him, as well as for containing one of the most eloquent and penetrating analyses of his inner, spiritual state. 'The centre of me is always and eternally a terrible pain,' he began:

a curious wild pain – a searching beyond what the world contains, something transfigured and infinite – the beatific vision – God – I do not find it, I do not think it is to be found – but the love of it is my life – it's like passionate love for a ghost. At times it fills me with rage, at times with wild despair, it is the source of gentleness and cruelty and work, it fills every passion that I have – it is the actual spring of life within me.

I can't explain it or make it seem anything but foolishness – but whether foolish or not, it is the source of whatever is any good in me. I have known others who had it – Conrad especially – but it is rare – it sets one oddly apart and gives a sense of great isolation – it makes people's gospels often seem thin. At most times, now, I am not conscious of it, only when I am strongly stirred, either happily or unhappily. I seek escape from it, though I don't believe I ought to. In that moment with you by the river I felt it most intensely. 'Windows always open to the world' I told you once, but through one's windows one sees not only the joy and beauty of the world, but also its pain and cruelty and ugliness, and the one is as well worth seeing as the other, and one must look into hell before one has any right to speak of heaven.

By this time, Russell was evidently taking Colette as seriously as he had taken anybody or anything before.

In response, Colette told her husband Miles about the affair. 'He was so gentle,' she told Russell, 'and tucked me up so tenderly.' She and Russell seemed now to feel that some bridge had been crossed. 'I feel utterly one with you now,' she wrote in the same letter, 'not only as lovers but in an almost deeper way.' They decided to go on what Russell calls 'a three days' honeymoon' to a pub called The Cat and Fiddle, high up on the Derbyshire moors above Buxton. The three days were squeezed in between his fifth lecture in Manchester, on 13 November, and his third in Birmingham, on 17 November. 'It was bitterly cold,' Russell recalled, 'and the water in my jug was frozen in the morning. But the bleak moors suited our mood. They were stark, but gave a sense of vast freedom. We spent our days in long walks and our nights in an emotion that held all the pain of the world in solution, but distilled from it an ecstasy that seemed almost more than human.'

The day before he set off on his 'honeymoon' Russell went to see Vivien. She was, he told Ottoline, 'unhappy because she feels I am deserting her. I did my best to make her feel less unhappy but of course there is some truth in her feeling.' He did not, however, tell Ottoline *what* truth there was in Vivien's feelings, or for whom he was deserting Vivien. He had not so far told Ottoline anything about Colette. On his way to The Cat and Fiddle he told Ottoline only that 'I shall be wandering about in the Peak Country for 3 days & I don't know where I shall be.'

That he did not tell Ottoline about Colette is some indication that, even at this stage, on the way to his 'honeymoon', he had still not made up his mind about Colette. One reason for this was that, in October 1916, he became enamoured of yet another married woman. In September, Katherine Mansfield, who in 1909 had entered into a strange and unconsummated marriage with the Cambridge scholar George Bowden (while she was pregnant by another man), had moved, with her lover John Middleton Murry and the painters Dora Carrington and Dorothy Brett, into a house – which they nicknamed 'The Ark' – owned by John Maynard Keynes in Gower Street, just around the corner from Gordon Square. Within weeks Russell became a regular visitor.

In Russell's remarks about Katherine Mansfield, both in his *Autobiography* and in his letters to Ottoline, what is most striking is his emphasis on the sharpness of her mind, an emphasis that contrasts markedly with all Russell's recorded utterances about Colette. Colette was perhaps to surprise Russell by proving herself to be an accomplished writer, but in 1916 this aspect of her was hardly evident. Katherine Mansfield, on the other hand, had had many short stories published, the intelligence of which had impressed all who reviewed them, and her conversation had intrigued and bewitched a wide variety of people in London literary life, not least D. H. Lawrence and Ottoline herself. Immediately prior to coming to London, Mansfield and Murry had made a concerted and successful attempt to ingratiate themselves with Ottoline, and by the autumn of 1916 they were regulars at Garsington parties.

There is another connection that one feels may have intrigued Russell, and that is Mansfield's association with the writer and publisher A. R. Orage. Orage ran the influential literary and political journal *The New Age*, which was one of the first journals to publish Mansfield's stories. He became, indeed, something of a mentor for her during the years 1911–12, when she was starting out on the London literary scene. He was also, together with G. D. H. Cole, one of the founders and leaders of the British Guild Socialism movement, a movement that Russell was beginning in 1916 to feel was the most promising political force in the country and the one with which he could most identify himself. Admittedly, there is little in Mansfield's writing to suggest much of an interest in Guild Socialism, but it would have been impossible to have spent much time with Orage without the subject coming up – and she spent a great deal of time with him at precisely the period when he was helping to develop the theory of Guild Socialism.

Be that as it may, Russell was captivated by Katherine Mansfield in a way in which he never would be by Colette. 'Her talk was marvellous,' he writes in his *Autobiography*. When she spoke about people she was 'full of alarming penetration in discovering what they least wished known and whatever was bad in their characteristics'. Perhaps what he saw in Katherine was some hope that he had found someone who, like Lawrence, could see 'through and through' him, which Colette with her non-intellectual caste of mind and her uncritical adoration of him would never do? With Katherine, perhaps, he would not have to keep explaining and apologising for the contradictory impulses, the web of complications, the old scars that made him the tough and harsh 'vampire' he had become? What he really wanted, one suspects, is someone who had the penetration to see all this, and yet who would love him despite it.

Colette was no doubt sharper than Russell realised. But at this stage, reading her letters to him, one can understand why he might think that, though she was extraordinarily free from the pressures of conventionality and undeniably beautiful, intellectually she lacked depth. Her letters are warm, direct and loving, but they are not the letters of a penetrating intellect. Russell began, perhaps with some justice, to think that he was too complicated, too dark, for her; that, refreshing though her vitality, wildness and innocence were, she was not for him. He would only corrupt her and ruin the very qualities he had fallen in love with. He began to withdraw from her. At the beginning of December, he told her that his work and other engagements would prevent him from seeing her 'for some considerable time'.

Some measure of how sure he was at this time that his affair with Colette was over may be gauged from the fact that he finally admitted its existence to Ottoline. 'In a gay boyish mood I got intimate with Constance Malleson,' he wrote to her on 2 December, 'but she doesn't suit serious moods.' He also told Ottoline that a 'terrible longing' for her had been growing in him for a long time: 'it is not passion any more – the war has all but killed that – it is the hunger for companionship . . . What holds me to you for ever & ever is religion. Everybody else hurts me by lack of reverence.' His last lecture in Birmingham would be given the following Saturday, after which he would like to come to Garsington: 'I should like to stay a longish time – would a fortnight be too long?'

What it amounted to was that Russell was inviting himself to Garsington for Christmas, knowing, no doubt, that Katherine Mansfield would also be there. The day before this letter to Ottoline, Katherine had written to Russell inviting herself to his flat for the following Tuesday. On the day she came, Russell wrote to Ottoline: 'I want to get to know Katherine Mansfield really well. She interests me mentally very much indeed – I think she has a very good mind, & I like her boundless curiosity. I do not feel sure that she has much heart.' He must have written in a similar vein to Katherine herself, for two days later she wrote to him: 'I have just re-read your letter and now my head aches with a kind of sweet excitement':

Do you know what I mean? It is what a little girl feels when she has been put to bed at the end of a long sunny day and still sees upon her closed eyelids the image of dancing boughs and flowering bushes.

To work – to work! It is such infinite delight to know that we still have the best things to do and that we shall be comrades in the doing of them. But on Tuesday night I am going to ask you a great many questions. I want to know more about your life – ever so many things. There is time enough, perhaps, but I feel definitely impatient at this moment.

You have already, in this little time, given me so much – more than I have given you, and that does not satisfy me. But at present my work simply springs from the wonderful fact that you *do* stand for life. And until

Tuesday I shall not read your letter again – It troubles me too greatly, but thank you – Thank you for it.

The 'Tuesday night' in question was 12 December, when both Russell and Katherine would be at Garsington. Her talk about their being 'comrades' in their work ties in with Russell's recollections of their conversations and how much he enjoyed her talk about her writing. He evidently looked to her for similar encouragement. In the letter to Ottoline quoted above, he says that he has been in 'an unusual mood – I suppose from war-depression – not wanting to see people, taking great pleasure in reading, anxious to use my mind in unemotional ways. I think of writing on the philosophy of physics at Garsington . . . I am full of life intellectually – not very full in feeling – I have lots of dim ideas ready to grow as soon as I have leisure. I must have time for writing & reading & just meditating.' Perhaps the perfect mood for spending time with someone whose mind he admired, even though she 'had not much heart'?

Just before Russell gave his last lecture of the northern series and prepared to retire to Garsington for Christmas, a crisis in British politics blew up that made the prospects for peace look even gloomier. On 5 December, the intrigues of Lloyd George were successful in bringing about Asquith's resignation, and two days later it was announced that Lloyd George himself had become the new Prime Minister. This effectively put an end to hopes that the Government would take up the well-publicised suggestion by the Cabinet Minister, Lord Lansdowne, that Britain should negotiate peace with Germany on the basis of a return to the status quo before hostilities, a suggestion in which Russell had seen some grounds for optimism.

Another reason for hoping that a negotiated peace might be obtainable was the victory in the United States presidential election of Woodrow Wilson, re-elected on 11 November after fighting the campaign as the 'peace candidate'. On 4 December, Russell wrote Wilson a long letter, urging him to use the power of the United States 'to compel the European Governments to make peace'. Militarily, Russell argued, neither side had a hope a winning a crushing victory, a fact recognised by the Germans but not by the Allies, who would not sue for peace because they lacked the courage to admit the truth of the situation. The populations on all sides were now sick of the war, which threatened European civilisation itself, and Russell had no doubt that he could speak for all nationalities when he pleaded: 'In the name of Europe I appeal to you to bring us peace.'

The letter – which was exactly the kind of thing the Foreign Office had been worried about from Russell since May – was smuggled out of the country by Helen Dudley's sister, Katherine, who delivered it, amid great publicity, at a dinner in New York held by the American Neutral Conference Committee, a pacifist organisation, on 22 December. After dinner, three members of the committee travelled to Washington to present the letter to the President. The following day, this propaganda coup, as useful to American neutralists as it was to Russell, made the front pages of the New York papers. The *New York Times*, under the headline 'Mysterious Girl

Brings Russell's Peace Plea Here', carried the entire text of the letter. The publicity was a great embarrassment to both the British Ambassador in Washington and the British Government, and the Home Office made it known that Helen Dudley was to be searched thoroughly should she decide to follow her sister back to the United States.

The adventure earned Russell a sharp rebuke from Whitehead, who, like many in Britain, hoped that the Americans would enter the war on Britain's side. Sending Russell a newspaper report about the deportation of French and Belgian people from Germany, he said that such things were happening because of the 'damping down amongst neutrals – America in particular – of the first protests against earlier atrocities'. What, demanded Whitehead, 'are *you* going to do to help these people?' He added to the note an ominous postscript: 'Eric leaves us in April – Flying Corps.'

In preparation, no doubt, for his intended work on the philosophy of physics during his stay at Garsington, Russell had written to Whitehead asking for his preparatory notes on the fourth volume of *Principia*, in which, in extending the 'logicist' analysis of mathematics to geometry, Whitehead had developed a novel theory of space, time and matter. Russell had already made extensive use of Whitehead's ideas on the philosophy of physics in *Our Knowledge of the External World*, and in the preface to that book had made fulsome acknowledgement of the extent of his debt. Whitehead had not complained at the time, but now he wrote saying that he could not let Russell have his notes, because he did not wish to see his ideas published precipitately in a form which 'I should consider a series of half-truths'. He preferred not to send his work until 'I have got it into the form which expresses my ideas'.

The letter marked a turning point in Russell's relationship with Whitehead. In his *Autobiography* Russell says, 'It put an end to our collaboration'. By the time he received Whitehead's letter, however, he had already abandoned his intention of working on the philosophy of physics. 'Philosophy is gone out of my head,' he told Ottoline on 18 December, 'it was only despair that made me turn to philosophy, & now one has no reason for despair.' Germany had, just a few days earlier, issued a Note to the Allies proposing a conference to discuss peace terms, and President Wilson, on the day of Russell's letter to Ottoline, had followed this up by urging the belligerent nations to define their war aims. These proposals, Russell thought, 'bring peace much nearer. I believe that we shall have peace within a year.' These hopes were dashed, however, throwing Russell into his darkest despair of the war, when, on 1 January 1917, the Allies rejected the German proposals.

The year ended on a sombre note, too, for Russell's personal life. At various times in the year he had been involved in no fewer than four relationships with married women. Now, it seemed, they were all coming to an end. Before he arrived at Garsington for Christmas he had distanced himself from Colette; now, he began to discuss his affair with Vivien, too, in the past tense. 'All that you feel against Mrs Eliot as a person is justified,' he told Ottoline on 29 December, 'but she was useful to me, & there was really nothing bad in the whole affair I think. I should have gone all to pieces a year ago without some interest of that kind.'

It was his affair with Colette that had prompted him to 'desert' Vivien, but, it seems, in order to free himself from Ottoline, he needed someone who was 'more of a personage'. This was where Katherine Mansfield came in. While they were at Garsington, Russell and Katherine engaged each other in long conversations late into the night. According to Ottoline, 'The sound of their voices kept me awake most of the night. I made them look uncomfortable next day by telling them that I had heard all their conversation, which of course wasn't true.' According to Russell, Katherine 'hated Ottoline because Murry did not':

> It had become clear to me that I must get over the feeling that I had had for Ottoline, as she no longer returned it sufficiently to give me happiness. I listened to all that Katherine Mansfield had to say against her; in the end I believed very little of it, but I had become able to think of Ottoline as a friend rather than as a lover.

Russell and Katherine Mansfield never did have the passionate love affair that seems hinted at in her letters to him. After Christmas at Garsington, they took the same train to London, and after that saw very little of each other. But she, like Vivien, had served her purpose: by the end of 1916 Russell had finally severed the last remaining emotional ties that bound him to both Ottoline and his pre-war life.

17

THE MISANTHROPE

R ussell returned to London in the New Year of 1917 in a fierce and black depression. All his hopes of December had been quashed: the Allies had rejected the German proposal to discuss peace, the more pacific wing of the Government had been ousted from the Cabinet by Lloyd George, and there were ominous signs that America, far from acting as a peace-broker, would soon become one of the belligerents. Most depressing of all, even after the full horror of the Somme had become public knowledge, enthusiasm for the war still remained undiminished. What Russell had told President Wilson about the universal desire for peace among the ordinary peoples of the belligerent nations was not true. Victory was what people wanted, not peace. Far from opposing this vengeful mood, the Labour Party were as caught up in it as everybody else; at their National Congress in Manchester in the New Year, they passed by an overwhelming majority a resolution to 'fight to the finish'.

In the face of such an ardent and widespread desire to continue the war until victory was won, peace propaganda seemed impotent. Despite knowing full well how many men were dying at the front, how little was being achieved in their doing so, and how long such a slaughter might go on before one side gave in, most people rejected any suggestion of a negotiated peace and seemed only too willing to see their sons, husbands and lovers sent away to fight and be killed. The Whiteheads, for example, even knowing what their eldest son North had been through, were apparently only too happy to see Eric (for whom Russell had a deep, vicarious fatherly affection) enlist.[1] It was more than Russell could bear. Something in him snapped. He was plunged into a dark misanthropic despair that only lifted when spring came. For the first few

---

[1] At the beginning of the war, North had been sent to France as a second lieutenant with the British Expeditionary Force. He fought on the Western Front for a year, before being invalided home in the summer of 1915 suffering from shell-shock. His war might have ended then but for his insistence to be back among the fighting, and in 1916 he was sent to East Africa. On the way to Kenya, he and the troops with him nearly drowned when the ship carrying them ran into a storm in the Bay of Biscay. In Africa he avoided injury but suffered three attacks of malaria and one of dysentery. Eric was less fortunate: he was killed in action in March 1918, when the aeroplane he was piloting crashed over France. 'You loved him and gave him much joy,' Evelyn wrote to Russell when she heard the news.

months of the year, he could hardly bear to see anyone except on official business and spent long periods alone in his Bury Street flat, brooding on the odiousness of the human race and lapsing into a deeply uncharacteristic inertia. Sometimes during this period, he later said, he could rouse himself to do nothing but sit in a chair all day, reading Ecclesiastes.

In letters to Colette and others, he gave vent to what he called his 'utterly hateful mood'. 'I hate the world and almost all the people in it,' runs one such letter:

> I hate the Labour Congress, and the journalists who send men to be slaughtered and the fathers who feel a smug pride when their sons are killed and even the pacifists who keep saying human nature is essentially good, in spite of all the daily proofs to the contrary. I hate the planet and the human race. I am ashamed to belong to such a species. And what is the good of me in that mood? I might as well be dead.

To Catherine Marshall, his colleague on the NCF National Committee, he wrote that he expected peace to come in the autumn, 'after Ll. G. has drunk the blood of half a million young Englishmen in an offensive which he knows will effect nothing'. Not that he thought Lloyd George worse than the rest of mankind, he told her: 'on the contrary I think he belongs to the best 10 per cent':

> . . . it is the human race that is vile. It is a disgrace to belong to it. Being busy is like taking opium, it enables one to live in a land of golden dreams – I must get busy again. The truth is not the sort of thing one can live with.

Such deep pessimism was antithetical to the brisk and businesslike caste of Marshall's mind, and she replied making light of it, advising Russell to get busy 'and get rid of the distorted vision of Truth to which idleness – or plum pudding? – seems to have given rise'.

But Russell was entirely in earnest in his misanthropy. He knew others would find it hard to bear and so, for the most part, he broke off all contact with those who knew him well. On 5 January, he told Colette that he had seen Vivien two days previously and had told her 'I wouldn't see her again for an indefinite time'. Similarly, he told her, he did not want to go to Garsington: 'people with whom I am not intimate don't matter, but I don't want to see people with whom I have to be more or less sincere.' The truth could not be borne and sincerity could not be endured. Unless he could be entirely superficial he preferred to be alone.

'I need a good deal of solitude and leisure to get my mind in order at such times,' he wrote to Colette. He told her that he was 'gradually working through my tangles' by thinking and writing about them. The basis of his depression, he had decided, 'was fury at the allies' refusal of peace, and at the fact that public opinion supported them in that. It brought on a fit of cynical rage – a disposition to wash my hands of the world and retire into the intellectual cloister.'

'Something is gone wrong inside me,' was how he put it to Ottoline. 'I find the human race hateful – affection seems dried up – it makes me very very unhappy':

I should like 6 months solitude in the desert – then perhaps it would come right. I have a despair within me which cannot be cured by affection or by any other human being – till I have mastered it, I seem to have no love left in me.

In another letter he said he had been in a 'very strange frame of mind' for a long time, one in which he had no love for humanity, but only a 'vehement hatred': 'I think I will work at mathematical logic for a time, in hopes of recovering. I have gone on with an act of faith which was simply an effort of will, & now I feel I had grown insincere':

I must build things up again on another level. I feel a shrinking from seeing anybody I know well, because I don't want to talk about things sincerely. Instinct tells me that mathematics is what I need. I have lived too long with temporary things & things full of emotion. I always used to use mathematics as an escape from them, & I must do so again. I need the wide horizons, the cool atmosphere, the feeling of eternity.

The letter then, however, goes on to dwell, not on the external events that were the ostensible cause of his depression, but rather on his relationship with Ottoline. He describes how he had used Vivien for the purpose of withdrawing from Ottoline, and how he had struggled in his relationship with the more 'fastidious' Ottoline to 'keep a certain impulsiveness, a sort of *élan*, a freedom from inhibitions'. He writes of their relationship as something of the past:

No one else will ever take your place in my life. My whole life led up to you, & my capacity for love exhausted itself on you; nothing can ever make up to me for my failure to win you . . . My image of you is all the more wonderful because I could not hold you – but for daily life & practical needs one had to make oneself equally independent.

It was clearly intended to be the final letter of their time as lovers. 'Goodbye my dear,' it ended. 'My heart blesses you, now & always, & my spirit goes out to you in thankfulness & reverence . . . You have given me a store of memories which I shall never lose, & which have made me know the utmost heights to which our life on earth can rise.'

It was as if Russell was in these months undergoing a period of mourning, not only for his hopes for mankind, but also for his more personal hopes for his relationship with Ottoline. He needed his '6 months solitude in the desert', not only to regain his faith in mankind but to readjust to the loss of what had been the greatest love of his life and the mainspring of much that he had said and done for the last six years. He needed to get his life and his relationship with Ottoline on a new footing. 'I don't want to cease to be friends & to see you,' he wrote, 'but it seems as if anything beyond friendship must involve more pain than it is easy to face.'

For her part, Ottoline had probably not been in love with Russell for a long time. She had been very hurt, and – as she now told him – disgusted at discovering that, in his letters to Helen Dudley, he was capable of using the same phrases about 'eternity', and so on, that he had used in his letters to her, and she had long since ceased really to trust him. Since moving to Garsington, she had been surrounded by people with whom she felt more comfortable than she did with Russell, and since about October she had been in love with Siegfried Sassoon. Nevertheless, she felt hurt at Russell's parting and determined to prevent him from hurting her again. 'My rapier is out,' she wrote in her journal. 'I will elude him in future and defend myself from him and be free; free for my own flights, unimpeded by him. Cut all that binds me to him, my soul must be free, and rise above it all.'

In time, they would resume their friendship on a different level, but until March all ties between them were indeed cut, leaving the emotional ground clear, as it were, for Russell to accept his love for Colette as, in some degree, of equivalent seriousness to his love for Ottoline.

Throughout this period of 'mourning', Russell was not entirely paralysed. In January he had been elected 'substitute chairman' of the NCF, a post rendered necessary by the continued imprisonment of the 'real' chairman, Clifford Allen. The job involved much administrative work, of a kind that Russell detested and at which he considered himself to be very bad, and it is unlikely that the job did much to relieve the cloud of gloom that had descended on him, except by keeping him busy and giving him something else to think about. One lasting influence of his time as chairman were the journalistic habits he acquired in producing an editorial for *The Tribune* every week. Whatever other pressures there were on his time, whatever personal or public crisis arose, his editorial was always written on time. It was a discipline that was to stand him in good stead for the rest of his life.

The editorials, however, like the rest of the job, quickly became a grind, and by the early spring of 1917 Russell had become disenchanted with the NCF. 'The NCF no longer interests me,' he wrote to Ottoline in March, 'all the best people are in prison & there seems no way of getting them out. Those who remain are full of petty quarrels & sordidnesses.' He and Catherine Marshall, both severely overworked and fatigued, began to squabble in their letters to each other. 'I like you fleeing to your funk hole!' she wrote on 7 March, accusing him of leaving all the real work to her and others, while he went on a visit to a Home Office work camp. 'I do as much as I can without doing it badly and becoming ill,' Russell replied. Always sensitive to the criticism of friends and colleagues, he found her badgering hard to bear: 'You really must not write me letters such as the one I got from you this morning.'

As he told Ottoline in early March, he went on 'doing things' at the NCF 'in order to be occupied, but not because I think them useful – they seem quite futile'. It was, he said, quite impossible for him to give her any idea how weary and hopeless he felt: 'One just waits for the end of the war – after that I suppose some sort of life may be possible again – if one can live until then.'

55 Russell at Garsington, 1918.

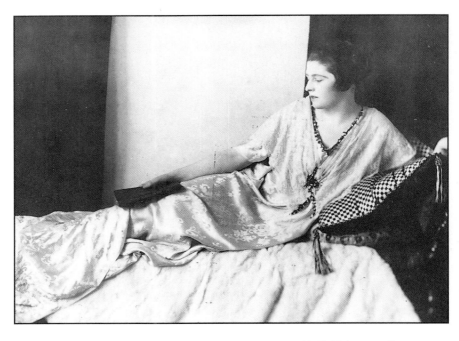

56, 57 and 58 Constance Malleson ('Colette O'Niel') in a studio
pose (top), as Helen in *The Trojan Women* (bottom left) and
in the film *Hindle Wakes* (bottom right).

59 Dora Black at
eighteen.

60 Dora *c*.1920.

61 The British Labour Delegation in Russia, 1920.

62 Russell, Mrs Snowden and L. W. Haden Guest, soon after
their return from Russia in the summer of 1920.

63 Russell and Dora in Peking, 1921.

64 Russell at his desk in Peking, 1921.

65 Russell and Dora in China, 1921.

66 Dora with the baby John Conrad Russell, born in the Russells' Chelsea home, 31 Sydney Street, on 16 November 1921: 'As I lay there on the top floor, the bells of St. Luke's Church at the end of the street were ringing in practice, but to me at that moment they rang for my son.'

67 John Conrad in his bassinet.

68 Russell holds aloft his long-awaited son. 'Yes! Paternity is a great experience... your relation to each other will have its poignant moments arising out of the very love and loyalty binding you to each other' (Joseph Conrad to Russell, 18 November 1921).

Just a few days after this, Russell was shaken out of this torpor by news of what is now known as the 'February Revolution' (because of the difference between the Russian and Western calendar), a combination of industrial strikes and military mutinies that brought the Tsarist regime in Russia to an end. On 15 March, the Tsar abdicated, and two days later a new government was established, led by the Liberal Paul Miliukov, which immediately announced itself committed to the establishment of liberal democracy in Russia. Russell, like most liberals throughout the world, reacted to the news with unfettered delight. 'The Russians have really put a new spirit into the world,' he wrote to Ottoline, '& it is going to be worth while to be alive.'

It was as though he had been woken from a deep sleep. Life, optimism and even his capacity for love suddenly revived in him. He joined forces with the newly established 'Anglo-Russian Democratic Alliance' (made up mainly of NCF members and its supporters), and began writing propaganda with something of the zeal with which he had adopted the NCF cause a year previously. 'The Russian revolution has stirred men's imaginations every-where,' he wrote, 'and has made things possible which would have been quite impossible a week ago. It is vital to seize the moment while the effect is at its height.'

What particularly impressed Russell about the Russian Provisional Govern-ment was its statement of principles issued in March, which promised an immediate amnesty for political prisoners, complete freedom of speech and a free press. To Russell, and to others who had run foul of the British Government in their commitment to peace, the contrast with Britain was striking. A mass meeting was organised in the Albert Hall to celebrate the Russian Revolution and to call upon the British Government 'to follow the Russian example by establishing the same freedoms'. The meeting took place on 31 March and was hugely successful. In a letter whose euphoria recalls his account of the Devonshire House NCF meeting the previous year, Russell told Ottoline: 'I must tell you about the Albert Hall meeting last night':

The Albert Hall was absolutely packed, and 20,000 people had to be refused tickets. Every person there was wanting a real absolute change in everything – not the sort of piecemeal niggling reforms that one is used to, but the sort of thing the Russians have done. There was *no* opposition. The COs came in for their share of applause – that one had expected. But besides that people cheered for a republic, for freedom in India, for all the things one never hears mentioned . . . The whole atmosphere was electric. I longed to shout at them at the end to come with me and pull down Wormwood Scrubs. They would have done it . . . A meeting of the kind would have been utterly impossible a month ago.

Like most people at this time, Russell assumed too readily that the Liberal Provisional Government and the Socialists in the Petrograd Soviet were marching side by side. 'I think the Russian Revolution has brought peace much nearer,' he wrote to Ottoline on 2 April:

It seems clear that the Army is on the side of the extremists, and that therefore they can't be suppressed. The 'Committee of Soldiers and Workmen' seems to be the supreme power . . . It seems that during the war the Revolutionaries have carried out a secret propaganda which has completely altered the views of peasant soldiers, and made them agree with the urban industrial workers. It is all *wonderful*.

He was right about where the real power lay and about what that would mean for Russia's determination to pull out of the war, but his apparent conviction that the Central Soviet and the Provisional Government were at harmony with one another was to prove overly optimistic. But the illusion, while it lasted, was just the tonic he needed. It was the sign he had looked for that the new age would arrive and that it would be glorious, a mixture of all that was best in both liberalism and socialism. He began once more to have faith in both the age and his own role in it. In this optimistic mood, too, he could shake off the past in the form of his relationship with Ottoline and, at last, treat his relationship with Colette, not as a passing flirtation, but as the next great love in his life.

In his mind, his affair with Ottoline had been over since December, but he had still not yet told her anything about Colette apart from his deceptively casual remark at the beginning of December, when he thought that he had finished with Colette. Now, in April, when he was sure his affair with Colette was serious, he came to Garsington and told Ottoline of the seriousness of it. As Ottoline remembers it, Russell spent his time during that visit criticising her for her 'fastidiousness'. She was always looking for the 'transcendental' in everything and was never content with easy, ordinary companionship. Finally, a few days later, he got to the point: Colette had been his mistress for a long time, and the relationship was a good deal more serious than he had at first supposed. As they walked back to Garsington, Russell delivered what Ottoline regarded as his 'parting thrust': 'What a pity your hair is going grey.'

When he got back to London, Russell wrote Ottoline yet another goodbye letter, in which he tried to convince her that the reason he had to break with her was that he had no inner life left. 'Just now,' he told her, '*all* fundamental feelings are rather dead in me, & I have only a lot of surface feelings . . . I can't really ask anybody to enter into my inner life now – it is bad enough having to live it myself – & that isolates me . . . Do be patient & trust me to be all right again when I come to life. But for the moment I am dead – Goodbye.' The language of the letter would have rung true in February, when he was in the midst of his depression, but written as it was in the midst of an exciting rejuvenation inspired by the Russian Revolution, it has rather a hollow ring. Still, it may have been true that he thought his *inner* life was still dead, even if externally he had sprung dramatically to life. Even so, his remarks about Colette in the same letter were unquestionably misleading. 'You mustn't think that I see C.M. constantly,' he wrote, 'only now & then, when I happen to have nothing to do. I haven't seen her now for about a fortnight.'

The very next day, he was writing to Colette, inviting her to share the rest of his life with him. He was, he told her, half-thinking of 'becoming Russian after the war'. Would she join him?

> I long to share a life of adventure with you – high adventure – & great enterprises – I feel together we could do great things – greater & more exciting than anything on the stage. If I could believe you could be fired by the thought! I think you have too modest an ambition . . . You should be an inspirer of *strong* men – . . . you should catch the fire from Tcheidze & Lenin[2] & bear the torch here in years to come . . . I can imagine such a life for you & me – after the war – as shall make every moment glow with the fire of great things nobly done – You could be an orator to move thousands & sway the destinies of the world . . . I love you, & my spirit calls out to you to come & seek the mountain tops.

Disappointingly for Russell, Colette steadfastly refused to 'catch the fire' and saw in the letter chiefly an impassioned plea for her to abandon her career as an actress. 'I know it makes you cross that I stick to the intention of my own job,' she had written to him on 30 April. Now, in reply to this rather desperately 'inspirational' call for her to adopt an alternative career as an 'inspirer of strong men', she responded again with a firm 'no'. 'I feel', she wrote, 'that part of what you say is true of you but not of me; and that what you say about Russia might be true for you but not for me.'

Having decided that his life and Colette's were now entwined, Russell worried about Colette's chosen career. It was not just, as Colette thought, that Russell considered the value of the work disproportionate to the importance she attached to it. It was that it put her in a world of which he knew nothing, a world from which he was excluded, a world, moreover, full of excitement, glamour and sexual temptation. Knowing the importance that Colette attached to her freedom from the restraints of conventional morality, and imagining her surrounded by handsome and glamorous young men, Russell tortured himself, whenever Colette was in work, by dwelling on the opportunities her job provided for sexual adventure.

Besides, he wanted, as he always wanted, his lover to be his comrade and colleague. 'I get so troubled,' he wrote in the same letter of 6 May, 'wondering how your ambitions & mine are ever going to fit in with each other.' Apart from the dream of settling in Russia, he had lately conceived of an exciting new intellectual ambition. 'I am creeping back into life, but not NCF life – scientific rather':

> I am reading Freud on dreams, most exciting – I see in my mind's eye a great work on how people come to have the opinions they have –

---

[2] This was written just a few weeks after Lenin's historic arrival at 'the Finland station', where he was met by the chairman of the Petrograd Soviet, N. S. Chkheidze (Tcheidze, as Russell spells it), and where he made his famous inspirational speech urging the Soviets to seize power from the Provisional Government.

interesting scientifically, & undermining *ferocity* at the base (*unmasking*, I ought to have said) – because it is always hidden behind a veil of morality. The psychology of opinion, especially political opinion, is an almost untouched field – & there is room for really great work in it – I am quite excited about it.

With the competing claims on his attention of this fervent desire to return to intellectual work and the political excitement of the Russian Revolution, Russell's chairmanship of the NCF began to seem less and less interesting, important and attractive. On 3 May he told Catherine Marshall: 'I dislike the work so much that I should be overjoyed if I could have a painful and dangerous illness from now till the end of the war.' His worsening relations with Marshall herself were part of the problem, but a more fundamental cause of Russell's disenchantment was the way the NCF movement had been split apart by the Home Office scheme of alternative work.

Russell's heart was with the 'absolutists' like Clifford Allen who had refused to take part in the scheme and were now enduring severe hardship in prison. But there were only about a thousand of these and their influence was considerably on the wane. Far more numerous were the 'alternativists', or, as they were often called, the 'Home Office men', who had exchanged prison life for work at the camps. These men lacked the heroic qualities that had inspired Russell to throw in his lot with the NCF in the spring of 1916 and their leaders, especially C. H. Norman, the most vociferous of the 'alternativists', were men whose deviousness and readiness to compromise Russell rather despised. And yet, it was his task as chairman to represent these men and resolve their differences. Out of a sense of duty he stuck to the task, but it was not one in which he could take any pleasure at all – the lapses in memory for which he was frequently berated by Marshall were no doubt a symptom of this – and throughout the summer he looked for a way out.

The last straw came when he had to intervene in a dispute that Norman had fermented among the NCF members at a Home Office camp on Dartmoor. In protest against the conditions at the camp and the pointlessness of the 'work' they were asked to do, Norman and others had organised a 'go-slow' policy among the men. When word of this reached the War Office, Catherine Marshall was called in to explain why the NCF were adopting this disruptive and shameful policy of 'slacking'. To Norman's extreme displeasure, she reassured the War Office that the protest did not have the support of the NCF and that she would do everything she could to prevent such behaviour. This, Norman thought, was further evidence that the National Committee, led by Russell and Marshall, did not have the best interests of the Home Office men at heart and he spread word among the camp that Marshall and Russell had conspired with the War Office against them.

Faced with the ensuing uproar against them, the National Committee had to act, and on 9 May Russell travelled down to Dartmoor to put the National Committee's case. He succeeded in calming the waters and in renewing the faith of the men on the National Committee, but the rancour of the dispute only confirmed him in his distaste for what had become of the NCF movement, and soon after he returned to London he drafted a letter of resignation. His reasons for resigning rested on two fundamental convictions: first, that he was not fit for the job ('Writing and speaking are easy to me, but administration is impossible'); second, that working for the NCF was no longer the best way in which he could use his talents to serve the cause of peace. The Russian Revolution had unleashed a more potent force in the struggle both against the war and for a better society, and Russell now felt that he was better employed in doing what he could to secure the triumph of this revolutionary spirit. The NCF's commitment to pacifism and the 'sacredness of life' prevented it from being an appropriate means of marshalling support for revolutionary change, and, to that extent, the Russian Revolution had rendered it obsolete.

Russell had never been a pacifist, but had joined the NCF thinking it the best, most vital force against militarism. Now that a better force had emerged, he felt inclined to identify himself with that and to emphasise, in a way he had not done so before, his ideological differences from the NCF:

A certain amount of bloodshed occurred during the Russian Revolution . . . If it was unnecessary I can of course condemn it; but if the revolution could not be accomplished without it, I cannot condemn it. And I should hold the same opinion as regards this country, if the circumstances were similar. If the 'sacredness of human life' means that force must *never* be used to upset bad systems of government, to put an end to wars and despotisms, and to bring liberty to the oppressed, then I cannot honestly subscribe to it.

The letter was never sent, and Russell continued for a few more months to act as chairman of the NCF, but, in his own mind, he was clear that the spread of revolutionary fervour was of greater importance than the niggling grievances and quarrels of the 'Home Office men'. After May, he had little to do with the men in the camps and concentrated instead on trying to align the NCF with the revolutionary movements inspired by events in Russia and on working for the release of the 'absolutists'.

Russell's faith in the Russian Provisional Government (now dominated by the 'Social Revolutionary' Alexander Kerensky) was increased still further when, on 24 May, they declared their war aims: peace, they said, should be on the basis of 'no indemnities, no annexations' – precisely what Russell had been advocating for years. On 3 June he attended a major conference of revolutionary sympathisers – which included at this time all shades of left-wing opinion – held at the Coliseum Hall in Leeds. Russell, together with Colette and her husband Miles, travelled up to Leeds in a crowded third-class train carriage, a journey they remembered chiefly for the extraordinarily dull stories with which Ramsay MacDonald regaled them. The meeting had been well publicised, and on their way to the hall the delegates were jeered by the crowd and pelted with stones.

Over two thousand people attended, and, according to Russell, all but three voted in favour of all four resolutions. The first of these – 'Hail! The Russian

Revolution' – was moved by MacDonald. The second called on the British Government to accept the policy advocated by the Russians of peace without annexations or indemnities. The third – the one Russell had come to speak in favour of – again called on the British Government to follow Russia's lead, this time in the establishing of civil liberties: freedom of the Press, freedom of speech, a general amnesty for political prisoners. Russell's speech dwelt on the imprisoned absolutists, drawing connections between what they stood for and what the meeting had been called to celebrate. It was, he said, a profound joy to men like Clifford Allen to feel 'that the seed of freedom which they have tried to sow is now bearing fruit . . . they and we must know that they have done much to bring about the new state of opinion in this country and the world.' In the cold light of day this emphasis on the NCF's role in fermenting revolutionary feeling looks overblown and rather unconvincing, but – so, at least, Russell told Ottoline – on the day, his speech received the greatest ovation of the meeting.

The fourth resolution was the most extraordinary of all. It called for the establishment throughout the country of Soviet-style 'Councils of Workmen's and Soldiers' Delegates' to work for peace and 'the complete political and economic emancipation of international labour'. What precisely this meant, no one seemed quite sure, but in the mind of one of its movers, Robert Williams of the Transport Workers' Union, it amounted to a call for the 'dictatorship of the proletariat'. In his account of the meeting to Ottoline, Russell singled out Williams for praise as someone who, unlike Ramsay MacDonald and some of the other leaders, had the appropriate 'sense for swift dramatic action'. Had Russell been caught up in revolutionary fervour even to the extent of abandoning his commitment to parliamentary democracy? I do not think so. In the form of Guild Socialism that he had advocated in *Political Ideals* in 1916 and which he was to elaborate still further in *Roads to Freedom* in 1918, a system of workers' guilds was to coexist with a democratically elected central parliament, and it seems likely that he thought of the councils proposed at Leeds as being in accord with this model. After all, Russia had not yet abandoned its parliament at this time, and, officially at least, power there was shared between the Duma and the Soviet. This is no doubt the kind of thing that Russell wished to see established in Britain.

What especially fired Russell's hopes at this time, and what lay at the heart of his fervent desire for 'swift dramatic action', was the intoxicating thought that the Russian Revolution might inspire a new internationalism that would make war obsolete. 'There seems every hope of a real international spirit throughout Europe,' he wrote to H. Wildon Carr, Secretary of the Aristotelian Society, on 27 June, 'combined with a far more humane economic system.' In *Roads to Freedom*, looking back on the hopes he had entertained, he wrote:

> If the Russian Revolution had been accompanied by a revolution in Germany, the dramatic suddenness of the change might have shaken Europe, for the moment, out of its habits of thought: the idea of fraternity might have seemed, in the twinkling of an eye, to have entered the world

of practical politics . . . Those who (as is common in the English-speaking world) reject revolution as a method . . . overlook the effect of dramatic events in changing the mood and the beliefs of whole populations. A simultaneous revolution in Germany and Russia would no doubt have had such an effect, and would have made the creation of a new world possible here and now.

Throughout the summer, Russell gave a new emphasis in his *Tribunal* editorials to the need for the NCF to identify itself with the revolutionary mood of the times. 'It is impossible to doubt', he wrote on 5 July, 'that the abolition of the capitalist would be a tremendous step towards the abolition of war, and ought therefore to be supported, if it becomes feasible, by those who aim at establishing a secure peace throughout the world.' The NCF had not, however, been formed to oppose capitalism, and many of its leaders, especially the Quakers among them, were reluctant to take Russell's lead in embracing revolutionary socialism. By the slenderest of margins, a decision was made for the NCF to send delegates to the proposed Workers' Councils, but, clearly, this was not an organisation alight with revolutionary fervour and Russell's inclination to withdraw himself from it grew stronger as the summer wore on.

He began to find ways of campaigning against the war and on behalf of the absolutists as an individual, rather than through the NCF. One of the most successful of these was his covert authorship of a small book called '*I Appeal unto Caesar*', which created a good deal of sympathy for the absolutists by highlighting some representative cases, emphasising the decency, respectability and, where appropriate, the piety of the men and also the harshness of the treatment meted out to them in prison. The book was published under the name of Margaret Hobhouse (or 'Mrs Henry Hobhouse', as she insisted on being called), the sister of Beatrice Webb and a veritable pillar of respectable society. Among her friends and acquaintances, Mrs Hobhouse could number Cabinet ministers, peers of the realm and leading Liberal supporters of the war, to all of whom she was known as a woman of moderate and conventional opinions. Her motive in lending her name to this piece of subterfuge was to secure the release from prison of her son, Stephen Hobhouse, who, having become a Quaker, had joined forces with the pacifists and been jailed along with the other absolutists.

The book was published in August 1917 and was an immediate success, going through four editions in its first three months. As hoped, it attracted a wider readership and exerted a stronger influence on public opinion than it would have done had it been published under Russell's name. As Russell rather cheekily pointed out in a *Tribunal* editorial:

As a result largely of Mrs Hobhouse's 'I Appeal Unto Caesar', many influential people who formerly had only contempt and derision for the CO have now come to believe that the policy of indefinitely prolonged imprisonment is not the wisest in the case of men whose sincerity and earnestness are sufficiently patent to arouse public sympathy.

The issue of the treatment of absolutists received a new urgency from the book's popularity and was discussed by the Cabinet on several occasions. The Government could hardly grant them all unconditional release, but it did release those declared to be seriously ill. Among the first to be released were Stephen Hobhouse and Clifford Allen.

Another opportunity to act unilaterally and, potentially, to bring off an even more valuable propaganda coup presented itself to Russell in July when Siegfried Sassoon approached him for advice on how best to protest against the war. Sassoon was then an officer in the Royal Welsh Fusiliers, who had enlisted at the beginning of the war and whose courage had been rewarded with the Military Cross. Though he had been a regular visitor to Garsington for the past year, he was in no way associated with the pacifist cause. Since he had been invalided home in April, however, his disenchantment with the war had grown, through his disgust at the lies told in the Press about the battles he had fought in and his conviction that the war was being needlessly prolonged by politicians. Ottoline, who had been infatuated with Sassoon since September 1916, was, of course, deeply sympathetic with this change in his feelings and arranged for him to discuss the matter with Russell.

With Russell's help, Sassoon drafted a statement saying that as one who had 'seen and endured the sufferings of the troops', he could 'no longer be a party to prolonging those sufferings for ends which I believe to be evil and unjust' and was therefore intending to defy military authority in refusing to fight any longer. The statement was printed as a leaflet and sent to the military authorities. The stage was set for an anti-war gesture guaranteed to attract the widest possible sympathy: Sassoon would be court-martialled and the War Office would be faced with having to punish a man whose courage and sincerity were manifest to all. On this occasion, however, the authorities showed an uncharacteristic subtlety. In a move suggested to them by Robert Graves, Sassoon's friend and fellow-officer, the War Office refused to court-martial Sassoon, but instead had him declared by a medical board to be suffering a nervous breakdown and not responsible for his actions. Instead of being punished, he was sent to a comfortable hospital for mild cases of shell-shock in Midlothian, Scotland. After three months of living in quiet and obscurity, Sassoon began to feel that he had deserted his comrades and asked to rejoin his unit.

Ottoline's account of this episode in her memoirs is rather strange. One might have expected her to express some disappointment at the outcome, and anger with Graves for having (rather cleverly) defused the propaganda value of Sassoon's protest. Instead, she is rather critical of Sassoon himself. 'Siegfried is terribly self-centred,' she writes, 'and, it seems almost as if when he does a valiant action, such as this protest, that he watches himself doing it, as he would look into a mirror.' She had been annoyed with Sassoon for not showing her more attention, and consequently tended to resent it when she saw him lavishing affection on others. When she met Middleton Murry in London during the crisis over Sassoon's protest, for example, she was piqued to be shown by Murry a charming letter from Sassoon 'saying how much he liked him'. 'It shows', she wrote, 'he can be grateful and express himself when he wants to. He has never once said a word of thanks to me, and after all I have done for him.' Perhaps she was jealous, then, of Sassoon's effusive admiration for Russell. After he had issued his statement, Sassoon wrote to Ottoline, perhaps tactlessly, 'I would like above all to know that B. R. is satisfied that I've done something toward destroying the Beast of War.'

Their collaboration in helping Sassoon with his protest did nothing to bring Russell and Ottoline together, but rather seemed to emphasise the distance between them. Throughout the summer Russell grew bolder and more forthright in his acknowledgement of that distance, until on 25 July he felt able to declare, with brutal directness: 'It is true that I am not in love with you now.'

It was not just that he had fallen passionately in love with Colette, but also that, in his revolutionary ardour, he could look upon Colette as a comrade in a way which would have been impossible with Ottoline. Ottoline was far too *ancien régime* for that role. Since the Russian Revolution, Colette had been infused with the same enthusiasm and hope that had inspired Russell; they had worked together in the NCF and attended together the meetings of revolutionary sympathisers. It was probably the peak of their relationship. Russell began to refer to Colette as his 'Heart's Comrade', and they shared a sense of excited optimism in the world which they would help to create.

On 28 July, Russell and Colette's sense of camaraderie was heightened when they attended a riotous meeting at the Brotherhood Church in Southgate Road, Hackney. The purpose of the meeting was to elect a Workers' Council on the lines of those proposed at Leeds, and Russell was hopeful of being elected. But, before proceedings could begin, the doors, which were locked and barred, were smashed in by a fierce mob led by a few soldiers, and the meeting was broken up. As Russell described it later that day:

It was really very horrible. There were two utterly bestial women with knotted clubs, who set to work to thwack all the women of our lot that they could get at – The roughs had horrible degraded faces. The crowd outside as we were leaving was very fierce – several women had almost all their clothes torn off their backs . . . I realised vividly how ghastly the spirit of violence is, & how utterly I repudiate it, on whatever side it may be. The mob is a terrible thing when it wants blood . . . At one moment they all made a rush at me, & I was in considerable danger – but a woman (I don't know who) hurled herself between me & them – they hesitated to attack her – & then the police appeared. She showed wonderful courage.

In his *Autobiography*, Russell provides a slightly lighter account, which makes great play of the fact that the police intervened to save him only when they realised he was the brother of an earl. But it was clear that the occasion had shaken him. He and Colette 'went home together in a mood of deep dejection'.

The meeting marked the end of Russell's involvement in revolutionary politics. Perhaps it caused him to recant his earlier view that revolutionary violence was justified if it could successfully establish socialism. (Something like this might be implied in his remark to Ottoline that it made him realise how utterly he repudiated violence 'on whatever side it may be'.) In any case, after the meeting, Russell's passionate and optimistic fervour was replaced by a more sober assessment of the political scene, and his ardent wish to become involved in the great tide of events was replaced by the desire to retreat to a quieter, more contemplative kind of life.

The day after the meeting, Russell and Colette set off for a three-week holiday in Shropshire. After staying overnight in Knighton, Wales, and then two nights in Ludlow, they settled in a remote farmhouse in Ashford Carbonell, a small village just south of Ludlow, set in the middle of beautiful countryside. There, as Colette remembers it, they 'walked enormously, read Voltaire, bathed in the Teme, and shamelessly enjoyed the good farmhouse cooking'. When Russell threw back his head and roared with laughter, 'the roar of his laughter echoed almost to the distant Clee Hills.' For both of them, it was a blissful interlude. Russell recited to her from memory his favourite poetry, including Shakespeare's Sonnets, and, on one occasion that particularly impressed her, the whole of Shelley's 'Ode to the West Wind'. As he relaxed into the kind of contemplative existence he had not known since the war began, his thoughts increasingly turned back to philosophy. On one walk he became so immersed in a discussion of the rather arcane subject of 'egocentric particulars'[3] that he forgot which way he was going and added eight miles to their route home.

For months Russell had struggled to keep alive his interest in the NCF while the excitement of the Russian Revolution aroused in him more inspiring hopes and plans. Now, he wanted to abandon both in favour of a return to philosophy. 'I wish I could get out of the NCF,' he wrote to Ottoline from Shropshire, 'but I don't see how I can.' As soon as he returned to London, however, he began making plans to devote himself to philosophical work. 'I find myself longing to go back to philosophy,' he wrote to Colette on 19 August, 'feeling I could settle down & do excellent work at it if you were with me enough.' He got in touch with H. Wildon Carr and a few days later was able to announce that, through Carr, he had arranged to give a series of philosophical lectures in the autumn: 'They will start me off on the philosophical road. Perhaps they will grow into a book. I long to be away from bustle – free to love & think.'

---

[3] 'Egocentric particulars' is the rather unusual name Russell gave to what most philosophers now call 'indexicals', those words or expressions of which one has to know who is using them, or when or where, before one can know what they refer to. 'I' and 'you', for example, are 'egocentric particulars', and so are words such as 'here', 'today', 'tomorrow'. Russell's most extensive discussion of the philosophical problems raised by such words is to be found in the chapter called 'Egocentric Particulars' in *An Inquiry into Meaning and Truth*.

18

RETURN TO PHILOSOPHY

Russell returned from his holiday in Shropshire in the late summer of 1917 with, so he told Colette, his head 'full of schemes for philosophical work'. In a letter to Philip Jourdain, now an assistant editor of *The Monist*, he outlined what these schemes were:

> I want to write (1) an Introduction to modern logic, (2) a new edition of 'The Principles of Mathematics', and I want to do a lot of work, applying mathematical logic to the problems of physics along the lines of my book on the 'External World'. If I had done all this, I could die happily.

In another letter to Jourdain a few days later, he spelt out the ways in which he would revise *The Principles of Mathematics*: 'The whole of the first part would need to be entirely and completely re-written; so would the third part; and the second part would need very tremendous alterations.' In other words, the book would need an entirely new analysis of logic. As Jourdain reminded him, Russell had at one time considered writing a series of articles on the question 'What is logic?' 'This sounds exactly the thing for the Monist,' Jourdain wrote. 'Besides I want to know badly what logic is.' Without picking up this very broad hint directly – without, that is, acknowledging that, up to now, he had conspicuously failed to give an adequate answer to this question – Russell did say in his reply what Jourdain no doubt wished to hear, that if and when he managed to write his 'Introduction to Modern Logic', he would like to publish it first as a series of articles in *The Monist*.

What is perhaps most striking about the list of projects Russell gave to Jourdain is that, for the most part, they do not present new thoughts and directions, but rather a reworking of old ground. The plan he had announced earlier to Colette of writing an analysis of the psychology of political opinion – which would indeed have been a bold new departure – is not mentioned. One cannot help feeling that, at this stage, his desire to return to philosophy was motivated, not by a burst of new inspiration, but rather by a wish to retreat from the tedium, strain and, occasionally, the violence of political activism. As he wrote to Ottoline: 'it is an extraordinary rest to turn my thoughts to abstract things.'

Disenchanted by the petty internal quarrels of the NCF and appalled at the violence he had seen at the Brotherhood Church in Southgate, Russell had grown disillusioned with political activity of all sorts. Writing to Colette on 3 September, he told her that he no longer believed in the effectiveness of what he could do for peace, other than writing books. He continued to serve as acting chairman of the NCF, but gave to the job ever-decreasing amounts of time and enthusiasm until, with great relief, he handed the job over to Alfred Salter in the late autumn. Nor was Russell really very keen to write on peace. He kept up his weekly editorial for *The Tribunal* for the last few months of his chairmanship, but otherwise he largely gave up writing propaganda, either in the form of lectures or in the form of articles and books.

Earlier in the year he had agreed to write a book of political theory, a survey of the various kinds of socialism, anarchism and syndicalism, for the American publishers Lippincott, but, whereas previously he might have put all his energies into such a task and relished the opportunity to spread his own political gospel, now he approached it as a piece of hack-work, undertaken, so he told Leonard Woolf in a letter of 6 September, 'solely for the sake of filthy lucre'. He asked Woolf to recommend some literature, especially on anarchism ('I suppose Bakunin must have written something, but to me he is a mere name'), and, throughout the autumn and winter of 1917–18 repeatedly referred to the vast amount of reading he was doing in preparation for the book (which was published in 1918 as *Roads to Freedom*), but his lack of enthusiasm for the project was manifest and it remained unfinished until the following spring.

Even a year earlier, when he had entertained visions of 'endless work on political theory', he had wondered whether 'I shan't some day be suddenly overwhelmed by the passion for the things that are eternal and perfect, like mathematics', for, after all, 'even the most abstract political theory is terribly mundane and temporary.' Now, that day had arrived. 'I *must* get back to working at eternal things,' he wrote to Colette on 27 August. With enthusiasm and relief, he turned his mind to the lectures on mathematical logic that he was to give that autumn, and within just a few days he had made out a syllabus for the course: 'it has quite excited me.'

The two sets of lectures that Russell gave in the autumn and winter of 1917–18, the first on mathematical logic, the second on 'the philosophy of logical atomism', both organised by H. Wildon Carr, were held in a hired room in Dr Williams' Library in Gordon Square, just a few doors away from where Russell was living. They were given on Tuesday evenings, with the first series beginning on 30 October and the second on 22 January. To some extent they were a fulfilment of Russell's dream of earning his living 'like Abelard' in lecturing to a non-university audience, although, unlike the Caxton Hall lectures on social reconstruction and the two sets of lectures organised by the NCF on 'Political Ideals', Russell could not this time count on a large attendance, and most of the money raised by Carr was through sponsorship rather than through ticket sales.

Neither set of lectures seems to have been written down, or, if they were, the manuscripts have not survived. The only hint of what the first set might have contained is the book based upon them, *Introduction to Mathematical Philosophy*, which was written the following year. This is the 'Introduction to Modern Logic' that Russell had mentioned to Jourdain. Essentially, it is a popularised summary of the mathematical logic of *Principia Mathematica*, showing how first ordinary natural numbers, and then rational, real and complex numbers and, finally, Cantor's transfinites, can be defined from the notion of a class. It then discusses the problems with the notion of a class that come in the wake of the paradox and ends with a discussion of all the cumbersome logical apparatus – the Multiplicative Axiom, the Axiom of Infinity, the Theory of Types and the Theory of Descriptions – that was adopted in *Principia* to deal with those problems. It is supposedly intelligible to complete beginners with little or no training in mathematics, though it is in fact rather heavy-going for all but the most determined, and it is hard to believe that, as a course of eight lectures, it attracted very many paying customers.

In the book – and, therefore, one must suppose, in the series of lectures upon which it was based – Russell offers no detailed or extensive discussion of the all-important question Jourdain had put to him: 'What is logic?' But towards the end, he does raise the question and provide an interesting sketch of an answer. Logic, he says, 'is concerned with the real world just as truly as zoology, though with its more abstract and general features'; logic is the study of the formal characteristics of the world. Ordinary language, he emphasises, is inadequate to express logical form and consequently 'logical symbolism is absolutely necessary to any exact or thorough treatment of our subject.' On this point, he ends with something of a rallying-call:

> Those readers, therefore, who wish to acquire a mastery of the principles of mathematics, will, it is to be hoped, not shrink from the labour of mastering the symbols – a labour, which is, in fact, much less than might be thought . . . If any student is led into a serious study of mathematical logic by this little book, it will have served the chief purpose for which it has been written.

Russell had come to believe that one of the main barriers to the acceptance of his general philosophical position was the unwillingness of people without a mathematical training – which includes all but a handful of philosophers – to master logical symbolism. It is a view in which he had been confirmed by reading *A Defence of Idealism* by May Sinclair, a book he reviewed twice: for *The Nation* in August and for *The English Review* the following month. May Sinclair was better known as a novelist than as a philosopher, and it is at first glance difficult to see why Russell took her book and her views so seriously. For not only did he review the book twice, he also sent her a long, typed list of comments too detailed to be included in the reviews.

The explanation, I think, lies in his respect for her amateur status and for her ability to write philosophy in a way that would engage the general public. 'The amateur in philosophy', he writes in his second review of the book, 'has a distinct function':

not as the inventor of new systems or new arguments, but as the interpreter of systems to a public which is not likely to read the technical works of professionals, and also as showing to professionals how their work appears to those whose human interests are not destroyed by familiarity with the controversies of the Schools.

In his earlier review, he complimented Sinclair on her freedom from 'the arrogance which is customary in the writings of almost all professional philosophers' and her success in 'bringing before an untechnical public, the kind of discussions, and the kind of issues with which current philosophy is concerned, in such a manner as to make it clear that these issues have a genuine human interest for people to whom the technical language of philosophy is repellent, if not unintelligible.'

Sinclair's book is a 'Defence of Idealism' in part against Russell's own views, particularly as expressed in *The Principles of Mathematics* (which, much to her subsequent embarrassment, she calls *Principia Mathematica* throughout), but Russell seems to have attributed her rejection of his views almost entirely to her ignorance of mathematical logic, and to have believed that, if only she had mastered the symbolism of *Principia*, she might have brought her gifts to bear on a popular exposition and defence of *his* work rather than that of Hegel. Her book, therefore, was, for him, a perfect illustration of the need for his proposed 'Introduction to Modern Logic'. One might indeed regard *Introduction to Mathematical Philosophy* as having been written with May Sinclair, or people like her, in mind; its purpose being to provide as much understanding of mathematical logic as is needed to philosophise on the subject.

Perhaps in acknowledgement of her status as the paradigm of his intended audience, on the day of his first lecture on mathematical logic Russell invited May Sinclair to lunch. Whether this led to her attending the whole series of lectures is unrecorded, but, to some extent at least, his campaign to introduce her to mathematical logic paid off. Replying to his repeated insistence on her need to master the technicalities involved, she finally promised not to write on philosophy again until she had considered all the points he had raised: 'and to this end I am sending for the 'Principia Mathematica' (not the 'Principles of Mathematics').'

Hand-in-hand with Russell's desire to return to philosophy went his hopes for his relationship with Colette. He felt, he told her, that he could do excellent work if she were with him enough. He no doubt imagined that, after their blissful three weeks away together, she could be persuaded to leave Miles and live with him. Such hopes received a blow, when, on 23 August, Colette wrote to him about her husband. 'The long and the short of it', she told Russell, 'is that he is now *minding* that he's no longer the *central* person in my life.' For Colette, the fundamentally important point, as always, was to assert her own freedom – 'the question of who is to be the central person in my life is one for me alone' – and she was inclined to think that, really, she ought to be living on her own. She doubted, however, whether she could bring herself to leave Miles 'unless he *wanted* it'.

Either Russell did not really believe Colette on this point, or he considered Miles to be an exceptionally tolerant husband, for a couple of weeks later, on a Saturday evening in the middle of September, he proposed to Colette that they should have children together. In the circumstances, it was a quite extraordinary suggestion and one to which Colette, though she did not say so immediately, had no intention of agreeing. Quite apart from the practical difficulties and emotional complications of living with one man while having the children of another, Colette did not actually want children. What she wanted at this time, perhaps more than anything else, was a successful acting career. She had just been offered, and had accepted, the leading part in a film called *Hindle Wakes*, directed by Maurice Elvey, and she was scarcely willing to sacrifice this rare opportunity for the sake of having children.

The very day after this discussion, she travelled to Blackpool for the shooting of the film. She had never made any secret of the fact that she found Maurice Elvey sexually attractive and, from the moment she left for Lancashire, Russell was thrown into an almost frenzied state of jealousy. Miles became worried and wrote to Colette that Russell was 'in a mood verging on a nervous breakdown', that he was unable to sleep and convinced that Colette's time in the north was likely to prove tragic and fatal. Colette had casually mentioned to Russell a rumour that Elvey had contracted syphilis and this served to increase still further Russell's fevered sense of impending disaster.

The letters that Russell and Colette exchanged at this time swing wildly from one extreme emotion to another, especially on Russell's side. From her lodgings in St Agnes on Sea, near Blackpool, Colette wrote that she had been 'thinking quietly to myself about the things we spoke of on Saturday night':

> You know that I want to give you everything that you want. But there'd be a great deal to be thought over and talked about. The situation isn't very simple, as you yourself see. But the thought is never very far from my mind.

While she was writing this, Russell was undergoing agonies of jealousy and anguish. 'I live in hell,' he wrote to Ottoline, 'it comes from within, & I can't escape.' To Colette, he wrote:

> I love you so much . . . You are my window into all the glory of the universe – Through that other window which is my self I look only into horror & black darkness & the red pit of Hell.

Two days later, he could stand it no more. 'The whole region in my mind where you lived seems burnt out,' he wrote to Colette. 'There is nothing for us both but to try and forget each other. Goodbye.' The next day, having perhaps in the meantime received Colette's letter about having children with him, he wrote: 'Thank you, my Beloved, for what you say about the thing we talked of that last night. It would mean so much to me that I hardly dare to think of it in advance. I wonder if that would be cruel to Miles?' He was still, however, tortured with anxiety about the affair he imagined her to be having with Maurice Elvey.

Perhaps in order to bring some stability to his wild turns of mood, Russell wrote a sober assessment of what he thought of Colette's character. It is headed 'WHAT SHE IS AND WHAT SHE MIGHT BECOME 25th Sep. 1917 by BR' and begins: 'The business with Maurice is of a sort that results from a tangle in the soul, causing obscure suffering, wrongly diagnosed, and leading to desires for things that cannot satisfy.' Colette's nature, he went on, is made up of elements that are not easy to harmonise. First, there is the side of her that loves freedom, hates cruelty and wants a simple formula for making the world perfect – 'Morally, this is the best of her.' The trouble is that this side is not 'operative'; she does not act on it, she merely applauds when other people try to make the world perfect: 'Until it becomes operative, the tangle in her soul will remain.' Partly because this side of her make-up lies dormant, 'her soul is filled with a strange ill-understood hunger and despair, of a kind that produces frantic moods and acts of madness in the search for relief. A religion would cure this.'

Second, there is her energy, 'of the kind that makes a dog run while his master walks', which stands in need of a strong belief to give it some purposeful direction. Her happiness 'demands an unusually large amount of sexual adventure', partly because of her capacity for love and partly because of her great vanity: 'Her *energy* makes her enjoy an element of roughness and fierceness in love; this also appeals to her despair.' Her vanity, Russell declares, is 'the worst side of her character'. It is indiscriminate, 'desiring the applause of all and sundry, seeking notoriety, preferring popular success to good work or the esteem of those who care for quality', and, for the moment at least, her dominant trait, directing her to seek to become, not a good actress, but simply a well-known one. This, together with a taste for luxury and comfort, leads her to commercialism, 'with all it attendant evils of competition, envy, shoddy work, and possibly prostitution'. Russell ends with the view that Colette's 'whole moral future depends upon her learning to do work for a public motive rather than a private one'. For this, she needs to acquire a measure of self-control (at present, she 'hardly seems to know that it is possible not to yield to an impulse') and unselfishness: 'But she cannot learn this except by going through hell.'

Whether to give her a chance to reply to it, or to follow its advice, or even perhaps as a way of striking out at her, Russell sent this rather unflattering analysis of her character to Colette herself while she was still in Blackpool. It was received in stony silence. Colette later described it as 'an analysis which very few women would be likely to forgive'. She had not yet admitted to having an affair with Elvey, and now took the opportunity to deny it. Maurice, she told Russell in a letter of 28 September, 'is not my lover in the sense that you are the lover of Ottoline and Mrs E'.

Russell, however, was not to be convinced. To spare himself further bouts of what had been unendurable anguish, he resolved to leave her, and when she returned to London at the beginning of October he delivered by hand a farewell letter. 'If you leave me,' she wrote in reply, 'I'll not kill myself, I'll not give up my work, I'll not give up the NCF; I'll still love you as I'm loving you now; but I shall not tell you what is in my heart. I know that we belong together. If you don't know it, there is nothing I can do.' When Russell failed to reply to this, Colette wrote again: 'I cannot understand. I cannot even attempt to put into words the immense desolation in my heart.' To this, Russell did reply, saying that, though he wished he could still care for her, he could not. In that case, wrote Colette on 11 October, 'I hope to God we never meet again.'

Russell possibly hoped so too. In an effort to put his affair with Colette behind him, he turned once more to Vivien Eliot. Less than a week after the ending (as they both thought) of his relationship with Colette, Russell was making plans to live in the country with Vivien and T. S. Eliot. Like much else in the story of his relations with Vivien, the origins of these plans are lost from recorded history,[1] but it seems a reasonable conjecture that he had discussed the idea with the Eliots before he broke with Colette.

Having spent the summer again in Bosham, the Eliots had returned to London in September, Eliot himself at the beginning of the month and Vivien two weeks later. Vivien found living in London unendurable, and soon after she returned from Bosham, she and Eliot decided to find lodgings in the country. Their initial idea was to give up their London flat and try to find somewhere close enough to London to enable Eliot to commute to his banking job in the City. They had no success in finding anywhere suitable, and, within a few weeks, they were pursuing a rather different plan. Now, they were to keep their flat in London, where Eliot would remain while Vivien moved out to the country to look for a cottage, which Russell and the Eliots would rent together. The timing of this change of plan coincides with the 'ending' of Russell's relationship with Colette.

Under this new plan there was obviously less need for the cottage to be suitable for daily commuting to London, and it seems that the idea was to re-create to some extent the life that Russell and the Eliots had shared in 1915, with Russell and Vivien living together during the week and Eliot joining them for weekends. Eliot was at this time extraordinarily busy in London. As well as his job at the bank, he was giving two evening lecture courses in different parts of London and acting as a contributing editor for *The Egoist*, which required him sometimes to work from its office in Bloomsbury Street. It is hard to see how he could have envisaged spending much time away from London, and he was no doubt only too pleased to fall in with a plan that prevented him having to commute every day and allowed him to keep his flat in London. Indeed, the plan seemed to offer the best of

---

[1] The fact that so few of Vivien's letters to Russell survive is, I can't help feeling, rather suspicious. As the boxes of documentation acquired by the Russell Archives from Russell himself prove, his natural tendency was to keep *everything*. In his correspondence with Colette during this period he mentions several times that he has received letters from Vivien, none of which survive. Neither do her letters from 1915 and 1916, though it is certain there were some. Why he should have thrown away or destroyed his letters from Vivien, I do not know, but that he did so and that, therefore (given his otherwise overriding instinct to horde his letters), he had some powerful reason for doing so, is, I think, almost certain.

all worlds: Eliot could stay in London, Russell could have a quiet place in which to prepare his forthcoming lectures and to work on *Roads to Freedom*, and Vivien could rest her nerves and recover her health in the country. For Russell and Vivien, furthermore, it offered an opportunity to continue discreetly their odd and strangely interminable affair.

Explaining the plan to Eliot's mother in a letter of 22 October, Vivien was rather mysterious about it. She had to be careful what she put in her letters, she told Charlotte Eliot, since 'it is necessary that the censorship about some things must be very strict' and 'one doesn't care to have one's letters destroyed!' But, she went on, 'it is very hard not to be able to explain things in detail to you.' What she found hard to explain, it seemed, was why she and Eliot had both to keep their flat in London and look for something in the country. Why this was something the Censor might be interested in, she does not make clear, but it was actually a very easy thing to explain: they needed the flat in London because of Eliot's commitments, which would necessitate his having to spend, so Vivien estimated, two nights a week at the very least there, and she needed to be in the country for the sake of her health. It was thus no mystery why they would want both a country cottage and a town flat. What Charlotte Eliot might have found a little difficult to understand, however, was how they could afford it, and it was presumably on this point that Vivien felt obliged to censor the truth, for Russell is not mentioned at all in her letter.

While she looked for an appropriate cottage, Vivien was installed as a lodger in a farmhouse – Senhurst Farm, in Abinger Common, Surrey – close to where Robert Trevelyan lived. The farmer had once worked as a gardener for both Russell and Trevelyan, and, though he did not normally take lodgers, was persuaded by Russell to make an exception in this case. Vivien stayed at the farm for a total of about three weeks, from 17 October to about 4 November, for the most part, it seems, on her own. The farm was too remote to be suitable as a base from which to commute, so Eliot stayed in London during these weeks, joining Vivien only at weekends.

Even as he made plans to live with Vivien, however, Russell still hankered after Colette. In a letter to her of 25 October, he struck a note of resignation and defeat. 'I have known real happiness with you,' he told her. 'If I could live by my creed, I should know it still. I feel imprisoned in egotism – weary of effort, too tired to break through into love. How can I bridge the gulf?' How much he saw of Vivien while she lived at Senhurst Farm is impossible to say, but that he spent at least one night with her there emerges from a long letter he wrote Colette on 30 October. The main purpose of the letter was to tell Colette that he still loved her and wanted her back, but, in the course of telling her this, he provided her with an impassioned and anguished account of his brief return to Vivien. 'I told you I was thinking of taking a cottage with the Eliots,' he wrote:

I intended to be (except perhaps on very rare occasions) on merely friendly terms with Mrs Eliot. But she was very glad that I had come back, & very kind, & wanting much more than friendship. I thought I could manage it

– I led her to expect more if we got a cottage – at last I spent a night with her. *It was utter hell*. There was a quality of loathsomeness about it which I can't describe. I concealed from her all I was feeling – had a very happy letter from her afterwards. I tried to conceal it from myself – but it has come out since in horrible nightmares which wake me up in the middle of the night & leave me stripped bare of self-deception. So far I have said not a word to her – when I do, she will be very unhappy. I should like the cottage if we were merely friends, but not on any other footing – indeed I cannot bring myself now to face anything closer.

I want you to understand that the one & only thing that made the night loathsome was that it was not with you. There was nothing else to make me hate it.

. . . The plan of the cottage with the Eliots was an attempt to make myself a life more or less independent of you, but it has failed. If the plan goes through, I shall be more dependent upon you than ever. Apart from you, life has no colour & no joy. A sort of odour of corruption pervades everything, till I am maddened by nausea. I have to break Mrs Eliot's heart & I don't know how to face it. It mustn't be done all of a sudden.

O Colette, I am so tortured & miserable – Should I find rest if I could lie in your arms? Would you let me creep into them, & lie very still? Would you show mercy to a poor wounded suffering thing? I don't want passion – not yet at any rate – I want to come home – You drove me out & put a stranger there, & I felt it was no longer home, but I think you could make me forget, at least for moments.

. . . This is not a courageous letter. Pride has led me a strange dance since you went to Blackpool, but what I am writing now is the real truth.

. . . I need more than one should, certainly more than you have to give. That is why I tried to escape. I thought I had escaped, but I was wrong. Now you will despise me. If so, let me know at once, & I will try again to get free.

Do please write at once – I shall see Mrs Eliot on Thursday evening & I want to have a letter from you first. Tell me all you think – even if it hurts.

One way of interpreting this letter – an interpretation adopted by Peter Ackroyd, for example, in his biography of T. S. Eliot – is to suppose that Russell, having finally succeeded in getting Vivien to bed, was put off by her almost ever-present menstrual discharge and determined never again to sleep with her. This might be so,[2] and, if it is, it would make sense of some of the

---

[2] I am, however, inclined to think that Russell and Vivien had been lovers for a long time before this. My reasons for believing this are: 1. his use of the tell-tale word 'intimate' in his confessional letter to Colette of 21 October 1916, which recalls his confession a few months later to Ottoline of having 'grown intimate' with Colette herself; 2. Colette's description of him as a 'lover' of Vivien's in her letter of 28 September 1917; 3. a letter of Colette's to Kenneth Blackwell of the Russell Archives dated 12 February 1972, in which she writes of the idea that Vivien and Russell had sexual relations: 'I always took it for granted that they had; & when I wrote so to BR he never contradicted me . . . He once appeared in my bedroom wearing black pyjamas, saying that VSE likes them.'

language Russell uses here (it is certainly more convincing than Russell's claim that 'the only thing that made the night loathsome' was that it was not with Colette). But what it would not explain is the letter's most striking feature: its abject tone of *moral* defeat, its confessional talk of self-deception and the nauseating 'odour of corruption' that pervades everything. This does not sound like the expression of a purely physical revulsion; it sounds, rather, like the talk of a man who is nauseated primarily by himself, by the discovery of the moral depths to which he is capable of sinking.

This note of self-censure, even of self-disgust, is echoed in his letters to Ottoline of this time. Russell's long struggle to be free from his feelings for Ottoline reached some kind of completion in the late summer of 1917. Immediately before that, in order perhaps to reassure himself that he was right to leave her, Russell kept up in his letters to her a barrage of criticism of her character and her role in their relationship. Though hurt, Ottoline saw this for what it was. 'He really is tired of me,' she wrote in August, 'and covers up his own change of feeling by putting upon me those imaginary sins.' It was the last gasp of Russell's feeling for her as a lover. When it was finally over – around the time of his long holiday in Shropshire with Colette – Russell's relationship with Ottoline began to take on a more stable quality. He began to see her, not through the eyes of a wronged lover, but as an old and valued friend.

Accordingly, from about the end of summer 1917, Russell's letters to Ottoline took on a new tone; gone was the rancour that had characterised his correspondence with her for so long, and in its place was a tone of candour and authenticity. Now that it was firmly established that they were not lovers, but friends, he seemed to be able to discuss things with her with a depth and a degree of seriousness that he did not even attempt with others. Not that he took her into his confidence about the details of his love life, but, in his attempts to analyse his moral, 'inner' life, he wrote to her in a way that assumed she would understand.

With regard to the sense of moral defeat that is implicit in his letter to Colette, for example, Russell is, in his letters to Ottoline of the same period, quite explicit. 'I have gone downhill morally lately,' he wrote to her on 14 November:

> I want to climb up again. I have let my will get weak, & I am ashamed . . . I hate & loathe my own personal existence – for the moment there is no health for me but in things that are right away from it – I dread having my nose rubbed in the mire. I want wide horizons & fresh breezes.

A little later, on 26 November, he told her that, at last, he had got himself in hand: 'may it last!' One needs self-reliance, he told her, one needs rules and self-control in order to keep desire in harness: 'it is dull, but it seems necessary.' He wanted to work hard and avoid strong emotion of every kind: 'Something has been lost – as always in a difficult struggle – I seem to have lost the capacity for passionate love & for all the ways in which one gets glimpses of heaven.' He was now determined to be – or at least resigned to being – 'sober & drab'. He had grown sane again, he said, partly through having given up his political work, in which the sense of futility 'drives one mad'.

The feeling that pervades these letters of trying to recover from a spell of insanity and of moral descent connects interestingly with a letter Russell had written Ottoline a month earlier, at the height of his crisis over Colette's feelings for Maurice Elvey. 'I cannot hide from you the blackness of my outlook,' he told her, '& yet my whole instinct is that it is best buried deep down, & not brought to the light of day more than I can possibly help':

> I believe there is an issue to be found, & that I shall find it. But I must go down into very deep waters first, & I *know* I must go alone – I must doubt many things which you cannot doubt. I must assimilate & digest the hatred of mankind which came to me last winter, & which I have not yet put in its place. It is a question of slow acquiescence in things that I rebel against.

His sense of the futility of pacifist work, his misanthropy, the emotional turmoil he had experienced over his jealousy for Maurice Elevy (so extreme that it had almost persuaded Miles Malleson that he was having a nervous breakdown), and his sense of having degenerated morally, all seem somehow linked in his mind; all part of the descent into deep waters, the 'slow acquiescence' in unpleasant truths of a kind that Ottoline, with her greater 'fastidiousness' and transcendental purity, would never grasp.

Throughout his letters to both Colette and Ottoline of this period, Russell's metaphors have a striking consistency. Together, they build up a picture of his having made a descent, and, through having his nose rubbed in the mire, so to speak, assimilated some horrible truths, not only about mankind, but also about himself. Now, nauseated by the 'odour of corruption' that surrounded him, he wanted to begin the ascent out of these murky depths. Turning metaphor into literal language, the impression he gives is that, as a result of his break with Colette, he had behaved in a way of which he was deeply ashamed, that what disgusted him about his night with Vivien was not chiefly the fact (if it was a fact) that she was menstruating, but the realisation that he had sunk so low that, despite knowing he was not in love with her and that he would, in the end, have to hurt her – even break her heart – he could not resist the temptation; that, indeed, he was guilty of exactly the kind of lack of self-control of which he had earlier accused Colette, guilty of forgetting that it is, after all, possible *not* to yield to an impulse.

How much of all this Colette saw is open to question. She responded to his long letter of 30 October with sympathy and encouragement, saying that she would come back to him with no regrets. 'Your letter was a *great* happiness,' Russell replied on 1 November. 'I hadn't a thought that my letter would bring you back.' Vivien was still in the country ('so I shan't have to see her tonight') and he was thus free to see Colette rather sooner than he had thought: 'I don't want to argue & reason & explain tonight – I just want the feeling of rest together.' The only thing Colette did not give him, he told her, was 'what I ought not to want – the sense of possession'.

His meeting with Vivien was put off until 6 November. The following day, he reported it as being 'very satisfactory'. He had 'got out of the troublesome part of the entanglement by her initiative – she behaved very generously – it is a *great* relief.' A week later, he had another meeting with Vivien. 'I had a letter from Mrs E. this morning,' he wrote on 13 November. 'I dread seeing her this evening. Nevertheless, the relief of having done something irrevocable persists, though I feel this is shameful.' Extricating himself from his affair with Vivien was proving fairly straightforward; overcoming his jealousy of Elvey would be a different matter. He talks in this letter of subjecting Colette to a 'very painful' time the night before, something that was for him 'a really big step towards getting back to what we both want. It relieved my mind of a lot of tiresome obsessions which I could not have got rid of by silence.' At the root of it, he told Colette, was that:

> I am puzzled by your being capable of falling in love with someone else when you cared so much for me, & by your being able to find happiness in a thing which does so much damage to our relation.

A natural retort might be that there ought to be nothing puzzling about this to a man who had fallen in love with Helen Dudley while he cared for Ottoline, and with Colette while he cared for Vivien. In fact, curious though it may seem, an important element of Russell's complicated romantic life seems to have been his conviction that he could only love one woman at a time, so that when he found himself falling in love with one while still involved with another, he had somehow to convince himself that he had ceased caring for the first.

The meeting with Vivien went much better than he had hoped. 'Mrs E. behaved like a saint from heaven,' he told Colette. 'She put away her own pain & set to work to make me less unhappy – & she succeeded.'

He and Colette decided to find themselves a 'home', a place where they could be together in peace. They found it in a studio flat in Fitzroy Street. Things would be all right when they had a place of their own, Russell assured her. It was what he had wanted back in August. But, as he realised, after all that had happened to weaken both his faith in Colette and his self-respect, they could never expect to look forward to the kind of peaceful and contemplative life that he had envisaged before Colette left for Blackpool. The world for both of them had changed irrevocably. In the event, soon after they spent their first night together in their new 'home' on 29 November, Russell made such an angry 'scene' over Colette's feelings for Maurice Elvey that the place acquired bad associations for both of them and was hardly used again. Colette continued to live at her 'attic' in Mecklenburgh Square and Russell at Frank's house in Gordon Square.

Throughout November and the first two weeks of December 1917, Russell gave his lectures on mathematical logic every Tuesday and divided the rest of his time between reading for *Roads to Freedom* and residual work for the NCF. What he really longed for, though, was time to work on the lecture course that he was to give in the New Year on 'The Philosophy of Logical

Atomism'. For this, he still hankered after a place in the country, and, now that relations with Colette had taken another turn for the worse, he revived the idea of sharing a place with the Eliots. In the first week of December, he and the Eliots took a five-year lease on a house in Marlow in Buckinghamshire, a small town famous for its associations with Shelley, who lived there in 1817–18. 'My head is full of things to work at,' he wrote to Ottoline in December. 'I believe the Marlow plan will give me a quiet peaceful existence in which I can work':

I feel as if I should like never again to feel any strong emotion of any sort or kind. I want a quiet methodical existence, like the end of Candide – emotions are always dreadful in the end. But I don't suppose I shall be able to stick to such a hum-drum programme!

Through emotional exhaustion and a determination to prevent himself from sinking any further morally, Russell adopted at this time a curious kind of quietism. In a letter he wrote to Ottoline on 23 December, just a few days after his last lecture, he told her he was enjoying working on *Roads to Freedom*, but that he would be 'happier still to get back to philosophy in the spring':

Today I went to the Westminster Cathedral & sat there some time – I always think it very beautiful – & listening to the chanting one's mind gets gradually to permanent things, away from exasperation and despair. Mankind are terribly tragic, but there is a splendour through all their blindness.

He spent Christmas with Colette and her mother in London and then went to Garsington to prepare his lectures on logical atomism. From there, he wrote to Colette about the 'Marlow plan'. One of his chief reasons for taking it up, he told her, 'was so as to make myself an existence in which I should not demand of you more than you could give'. On 1 January 1918, he wrote to her about his feelings for Vivien:

I am not in love with her, & I do not care whether I have a physical relation with her or not. But I am happy in talking to her and going about with her. She has a very unselfish affection for me, and but for her I don't know how I should have lived through the unhappiness of these last months. I am intensely grateful to her, and I expect that she will be an essential part of my life for some time to come. But I don't know yet whether that will be so.

Colette replied that she was quite prepared to take his word about Vivien's 'unselfish affection' for him. 'I don't know her and I can't therefore judge in any way':

But what I do know is that you've been, times without number, involved in the most complicated tangles with her (dreading meeting with her and so on), which would seem, perhaps quite as upsetting to your work as the things you hold against me. I also know that you quite frequently find your relations with her oppressive.

But, for Russell, the 'tangles' he had been involved with in connection with Vivien were as nothing compared to the utterly disruptive turmoil he had suffered through his jealous rages against Colette. In his next letter he told her: 'My work-a-day life will be at Marlow, with Mrs E. I shall come up to London one or two nights a week.' The next day, he gave vent to some of his feelings about Elvey: he did not like him, he told Colette, because he was a shirker in the war and because his main object in life was to make money. And because Colette loved him, Russell associated her with those things, rather than with her belief in pacifism and democracy.

In the face of this continued sniping, Colette responded with another angry farewell letter. Russell replied in kind and, on 14 January, wrote to her urging her to forget him and to spare herself the misery that involvement with him would necessarily bring. 'My life is prisoned in pain,' he told her, 'and it is hell for any one to come close to me.' Soon after this, however, he returned to London and once more they were reconciled, establishing a pattern that was to continue for more than a year, of Russell believing and then ceasing to believe that matters between them could be as they were 'before Blackpool'. Throughout this exchange in the New Year of 1918, and for months afterwards, Russell seemed torn between a passionate desire for Colette and an almost equally passionate wish to be rid of desire altogether so as to concentrate better on his work.

During the weeks that he spent at Garsington in the New Year of 1918, Russell prepared what has become one of his best-known philosophical works, his lectures on logical atomism. If his work on mathematical logic showed him yearning once more for the quiet contemplation of 'eternal' things that he had known before the war, the lectures on logical atomism showed him screwing up his courage to face the scenes of past disaster. As he had told Ottoline at the time of his lectures on social reconstruction, he had felt unequal to the demands of original philosophical thinking ever since Wittgenstein's attack on his theory of judgment in 1913. Persuaded that all philosophical problems were fundamentally logical, he yet had chosen a metaphysical subject for his Harvard lectures in 1914, because Wittgenstein had weakened his confidence in his ability to do important work in logic. In despair about this loss of confidence, philosophy had weakened its hold on him and had been replaced by other, less difficult ambitions.

Given this, it was a mark of Russell's renewed confidence in his philosophical abilities that in his lectures in early 1918, he should concentrate on exactly the issues on which he had been criticised so devastatingly by Wittgenstein. In Russell's mind, the lectures were an acknowledgement of how much he had learnt from Wittgenstein, both from Wittgenstein's criticisms of his earlier views and from the 'Notes on Logic' that he had dragged out of Wittgenstein before he left for Norway in the autumn of 1913. 'A very great deal of what I am saying in this course of lectures', he announced in the third lecture, 'consists of ideas which I derived from my friend Wittgenstein.' When the lectures were published as a series of articles in *The Monist*, he repeated the acknowledgement in a short preface, adding: 'I have had no opportunity of knowing his views since August 1914, and I do not even know whether he is alive or dead.'

Though the lectures do indeed show the very great influence that Wittgenstein's 'Notes on Logic' had on Russell, what seems most striking about them now is their very un-Wittgensteinian philosophical perspective. The style of philosophy they present is a peculiarly Russellian one, for which the title 'Philosophy of Logical Atomism' is in some ways rather misleading. A better title would be 'Philosophy of Logical Analysis', for, as Russell says at the beginning of the second lecture: 'the chief thesis I have to maintain is the legitimacy of analysis.' The philosophy he wishes to advance is analytical, and seeks to break down complex things and ideas into simpler ones. Whether this process reaches a terminus in so-called logical atoms is far less important to him than that it should make a start and not be put off by Hegelian talk of the indivisibility, the 'oneness' of reality.

The lectures, then, are a manifesto for the kind of analytical, 'scientific' philosophy for which Russell had sometimes dreamed of founding a school. Russell's conception of analytical philosophy, however, is crucially different from that which has come to dominate academic philosophy in recent times. Today, analytical philosophy is widely held to be characterised by its so-called 'linguistic turn', by its abandonment of traditional philosophical questions about the nature of reality and the mind in favour of the analysis of language. Central to this conception of philosophy is the conviction that logic is essentially linguistic. But, in his 'lectures on logical atomism', just as in his previous lectures on mathematical logic, Russell took the view that logic is the study of the most general features, not of language, but of the world.

Logic, he says in the fourth lecture, is 'concerned with the forms of facts, with getting hold of the different sorts of facts, different *logical* sorts of facts, that there are in the world'. These general features of the world, these forms of facts, are extremely rarefied aspects of reality, so rarefied that it is almost impossibly difficult to think about them at all. In philosophical logic, he says, 'the subject matter that you are supposed to be thinking of is so exceedingly difficult and elusive that any person who has ever tried to think about it knows that you do not think about it except perhaps once in six months for half a minute. The rest of the time you think about the symbols.' The really good philosopher is the one who succeeds in focusing his mind on this exceedingly refined subject-matter once in six months: 'Bad philosophers never do.'

The theory of symbolism is important to philosophy – 'a good deal more than one time I thought' – but its importance is 'entirely negative':

i.e., the importance lies in the fact that unless you are fairly self-conscious about symbols, unless you are fairly aware of the relation of the symbol to what it symbolises, you will find yourself attributing to the thing properties which only belong to the symbol.

For Russell, then, the study of logic and the analysis of language, of meaning, are sharply distinguished; the former is the almost forlorn attempt to focus one's mind on elusive 'forms', the latter, it turns out, is a branch of psychology:

I think that the notion of meaning is always more or less psychological, and that it is not possible to get a pure logical theory of meaning, nor therefore of symbolism . . . the theory of symbolism and the use of symbolism is not a thing that can be explained in pure logic without taking account of the various cognitive relations that you may have to things.

The direction in which Russell was being pulled by this train of thought was diametrically opposed to that which had characterised his earlier work. Earlier, he had been concerned to 'de-psychologise' logic and mathematics, and in the process to turn the attention of philosophers away from psychology and towards logic. Now – though he was probably not fully aware of it at this stage – the natural conclusion to what he was saying was that psychology was actually *more* fundamental to philosophy than logic.

Indeed, in the view that Russell advances in these lectures, psychology implicitly provides the foundations even for logic itself, or at least for a part of it. For, although, in Russell's conception, logic analyses the formal features of the world rather than those of language, nevertheless it is to some degree interested in analysing the structure of propositions, if only to investigate whether or not their form faithfully reflects the form of the facts they describe. Russell's theory of descriptions was an investigation of that sort, leading to the conclusion that the definite descriptions of ordinary language disguise the real logical structure of the facts they describe and ought, if logical veracity is our chief aim, to be replaced by a new, more logically correct, form of symbolism. In theory such a process of replacing misleading linguistic forms by those that, as it were, wear their logical structure on their sleeve, would terminate in the construction of a logically perfect language. The syntax, the grammar, of this language would mirror the logical structure of the world so perfectly that it would be impossible to say anything nonsensical in it: every possible proposition in the language would describe a possible fact in the world.[3]

So logic is, to some extent at least, concerned with propositions. But, Russell says: 'A proposition is just a symbol', and, as the theory of symbolism

---

[3] The vocabulary of such a language, as Russell describes it, would, however, make it completely unusable: each particular in the world would have its own name, which – given that particulars are unique to an individual perspective – means that every word would be private to just one person. See *Lectures*, 59: 'A logically perfect language, if it could be constructed, would not only be intolerably prolix, but, as regards its vocabulary, would be very largely private to one speaker . . . all the names that it would use would be private to that speaker and could not enter into the language of another speaker . . . Altogether you would find that it would be a very inconvenient language indeed. That is one reason why logic is so very backward as a science, because the needs of logic are so extraordinarily different from the needs of daily life.' This conception of a logically perfect, essentially private language forms the target of Wittgenstein's famous 'Private Language Argument' in *Philosophical Investigations*.

is fundamentally psychological, it follows that the nature of logic cannot be fully understood outside a study of psychology. The implications of this 'psychologistic' line of thought were to become increasingly manifest to Russell over the coming months and would loom ever larger in his philosophical work of the next few years, but, in essence, it was already there in 'Lectures on Logical Atomism'.

In some ways, the lectures present an obviously transitional stage in Russell's thought, a stage at which he had abandoned his old views but had nothing yet with which to replace them. Nowhere is this more apparent than in his remarks on the nature of propositions and judgments. A proposition is described as 'just a symbol', but elsewhere he says 'obviously propositions are nothing'. Thus, presumably, they are, like definite descriptions, *incomplete* symbols, in need of a context to make them significant. This is how they were treated in the *Principia*, but, in that theory, the context required was supplied by the mind, by the mental act of forming judgments. But, since 1913, Russell's theory of judgment had lain in ruins, utterly demolished by the criticisms of Wittgenstein. Now, in 'Philosophy of Logical Atomism', Russell devotes an entire lecture to the theory of judgment, in which he acknowledges the power of Wittgenstein's criticisms and accepts the consequence that his old view will have to be abandoned. But, as he frankly confesses, he has as yet no better account to put in its place, and all he can do at this stage is spell out the problems with which a theory of judgment must deal and emphasise their difficulty. At the very centre of his philosophical logic, therefore, he is left with a gaping hole and little idea of how to fill it. He is reduced to apologising for the 'tentative' nature of the lecture and pleading for indulgence on the grounds that 'The subject is not very easy.'

The lectures were published in *The Monist*, spread over four issues from October 1918 to July 1919. Jourdain was delighted with them, though he begged Russell to continue working on the subject, to devote some time to developing a more satisfying theory of propositions: 'I wish you would think out what exactly are the relations between propositions and symbols. I cannot feel at all satisfied with what you say in your lectures on the point.'

Russell would have been only too happy to oblige and probably intended to spend the spring and summer of 1918 in quiet seclusion in his house in Marlow, working on philosophy; not, this time, going over old ground, but trying to develop a new account of philosophical logic, starting perhaps with a new theory of propositions. The appeal of sharing a house with the Eliots may this time have been motivated, not by his attraction to Vivien, but by his hopes that T. S. Eliot would stimulate him philosophically.

Russell had been impressed with Eliot's review of *Mysticism and Logic* that had appeared in *The Nation* in March. It was, he said, the only review 'with distinction' that the book attracted. *Mysticism and Logic*, published in January 1918, is a collection of papers that Russell intended to replace his earlier *Philosophical Essays*, which had been published in 1910. It is a heterogeneous collection, a curious mixture of the popular and the technical, the romantic and the scientific. It includes articles from the early years of the century, like 'A Free Man's Worship', together with articles from the war years, like 'On

Scientific Method in Philosophy'. Altogether, it is a representative selection of his very varied output, reflecting the deep changes – both in his philosophical opinions and in his general outlook – that had taken place through the years. Eliot declared it to be one of the most important books Russell had published. In the more purely philosophical essays in the collection, Eliot writes: 'Mr Russell reaches the level of the very best philosophical prose in the language. The only contemporary writer who can even approach him is Mr Bradley.'

Russell's ambitions of spending time in the country discussing philosophy with Eliot were, however, to come to nothing. In the final twist in his battles with the Government over the war, he was prosecuted under the Defence of the Realm Act and sentenced to six months in Brixton prison at precisely the moment when he had decided to abandon altogether his propaganda work.

The basis for the prosecution was an editorial for *The Tribunal* – one that he hoped would be his last – which he had written at Garsington in the New Year, called 'The German Peace Offer'. It was an uncharacteristically scrappy piece, perhaps reflecting the fact that his mind and heart were elsewhere. In it, he urged the Labour Party to use its influence to compel the Government to accept the offer by the Germans of a general peace, on the lines suggested by the Russians of no annexations and no indemnities. This was a reasonable enough line to take, but in support of it Russell levelled some not very carefully considered abuse at both the British and American Governments. The Western Governments, he argued, were reluctant to respond to the German offer, because to do so would 'afford a triumph to the hated Bolsheviks and an object lesson to democratic revolutionaries everywhere as to the way to treat with capitalists, Imperialists and war-mongers'. They know that they cannot hope for a better peace by continuing the war, he claimed, 'but from the point of view of preventing liberty and universal peace, there is something to be hoped from continuation'. Unless peace came soon, there would be starvation throughout Europe; mothers would be driven mad by the sight of their children starving to death, and men would be reduced to fighting each other for scraps of food. Under such conditions, 'the sane constructive effort required for a successful revolution will be impossible':

> The American Garrison which will by that time be occupying England and France, whether or not they will prove efficient against the Germans, will no doubt be capable of intimidating strikers, an occupation to which the American Army is accustomed when at home.

'I do not say that these thoughts are in the mind of the Government,' Russell remarked and then, with gratuitous abusiveness, added: 'All the evidence tends to show that there are no thoughts whatever in their mind, and that they live from hand to mouth consoling themselves with ignorance and sentimental twaddle.'

It was not one of the most intelligent articles Russell had ever published and ought really to have been allowed to sink into a deserved obscurity. Instead, it became one of his best-known pieces of journalism.

For Russell's ambitions of settling into a quiet, contemplative life, the publication of the article was disastrously ill-timed. In December 1917, his brother Frank had met General Cockerill at the War Office and had persuaded him that Russell was now finished with propaganda and determined to get back to philosophical work. Accordingly, on 17 January 1918, a memo prepared by all three Government departments concerned, the Home Office, the War Office and the Foreign Office, announced their joint agreement that the banning order on Russell ought to be lifted. On the same day, the issue of *The Tribunal* containing 'The German Peace Offer' arrived at the Home Office. As soon as he saw it, General Cockerill wrote to Frank that 'it is more than possible that exception may be taken to this article' and the memo agreeing to lift the ban was put to one side.

What the authorities chiefly objected to were Russell's remarks about the American 'garrison' being used to intimidate strikers. This Russell learned on 1 February, when two police detectives appeared at Gordon Square, asking if he had written the article and, in particular, the sentence containing this accusation. A few days later he received a summons to appear in court charged with making statements 'likely to prejudice His Majesty's relations with the United States of America'. 'It is very annoying,' he wrote to Ottoline, 'particularly as the remarks were rather foolish & not good for propaganda.'

The case was heard at Bow Street Magistrates' Court on 9 February, and, to nobody's surprise, Russell was found guilty. The magistrate, Sir John Dickinson, declared Russell's offence to be 'a very despicable one' and sentenced him to six months' imprisonment in the second division. Russell, who had been expecting a fine, was taken aback both by the severity of the sentence and the hostility of the magistrate, which, he told Ottoline, he felt as an astonishing 'blast of hatred'. He appealed against the verdict, and, as his appeal would not be heard until 12 April, at least he would not be in prison while it was cold. Even so: 'I profoundly dislike the prospect of six months in prison. Besides, I had meant to have done with that sort of work, & to get back to philosophy.'

A few days later, in a letter to Gilbert Murray, he said that he did not, after all, mind the prospect of prison ('the freedom from responsibility will be rather restful'), so long as he had plenty of books to read. At this stage, Russell evidently still had rather a rosy view of what life was like for a second-division prisoner, and imagined himself catching up on a lot of reading and having a great deal of leisure for philosophical reflection. He was shocked out of this comfortable illusion when, on 26 March, he met E. D. Morel, the secretary of the UDC, who had been released in January after serving five months in the second division. Russell was horrified to see the changes that prison life had wrought. The following day, he wrote to Gilbert Murray that, after seeing what had become of Morel, he was now 'impressed by the seriousness of a six months sentence':

> His hair is completely white (there was hardly a tinge of white before) when he first came out, he collapsed completely, physically and mentally, largely as the result of insufficient food. He says one only gets three quarters of an

hour reading in the whole day – the rest of the time is spent on prison work, etc . . . It seems highly probable that if the sentence is not mitigated my mind will not remain as competent as it has been. I should regret this, as I still have a lot of philosophy that I wish to do.

This last sentence was almost ludicrously understated: the deterioration of his mind was not something he would 'regret', it was the one thing he feared more than anything else. Writing to Colette he was more forthright: 'I am dreading prison – ever since I saw Morel . . . Fear is a beastly thing – one feels so ashamed of it . . . What worries me is the thought of having my brain spoilt, just when I am ready to do a lot of really good work.' His worries were increased still further when, on 30 March, he spent a weekend at Marlow with Clifford Allen and was appalled to see the ravages wrought upon Allen's health and personality by prison life.

The day after Russell's meeting with Morel, *The Times* published an editorial discussing the probability that the upper age-limit of conscription would have to be raised from forty-one to fifty-one. Two years earlier, Russell would have welcomed the chance to take his place among the COs in prison, but now the idea deepened still further his gloom about the possible effects of a lengthy incarceration. 'They seem to have decided to raise the military age,' he wrote to Ottoline on 31 March, 'so I suppose I shall remain in prison from April 12 till the end of the war, which may be many years.' He might possibly be granted exemption on the grounds that his philosophical work was of national importance, 'but my duty to the Absolutists seems to make that impossible. It is a pity. My brain is better than it has been for years . . . & I am longing to get on with philosophy.'

A few days later, Russell learned that his appeal would not, after all, be heard until 1 May. This gave him a fighting chance of finishing *Roads to Freedom* before (as was almost certain) he would have to start his prison sentence. In the first two weeks of April, therefore, he was, he told Ottoline, 'working day and night' to finish the book. He was hardly in an ideal mental state to deliver his considered opinion on political theory – in a letter to Gilbert Murray of 9 April, H. Wildon Carr reported Russell as being 'in a very dangerous condition of strain' – and perhaps it is not surprising that the book, being little more than a piece of efficient but fairly uninspired journalism, was something of a disappointment. That it exists at all is impressive enough evidence of his astonishing will-power.

Confirming his allegiance to Guild Socialism that Russell had announced in *Political Ideals, Roads to Freedom* elaborates on and defends that allegiance largely with arguments taken from the work of the founder and acknowledged leader of the British Guild Socialist movement, G. D. H. Cole, particularly *World of Labour* (1913) and *Self-Government in Industry* (1917). Essentially, Guild Socialism is presented as a middle way, a British compromise, between the tyranny of state Socialism and the chaos of anarchism. The bulk of the book is taken up with an explanation of how various political questions, such as work and pay, government and law, international relations, might be approached within the framework provided by Guild Socialism. Though it was originally commissioned as a survey of the various strands of left-wing opinion, neither Marxist Socialism nor anarchism are really presented as serious alternatives to Guild Socialism, and the chapters devoted to them are chiefly historical, concentrating mainly on the biographies of their founders, Marx and Bakunin. In his emphasis on the sacrifices made by these men, and the deprivations they suffered, Russell takes the opportunity to strike a personal note:

> The pioneers of Socialism, Anarchism, and Syndicalism, have, for the most part, experienced prison, exile, and poverty, deliberately incurred because they would not abandon their propaganda; and by this conduct they have shown that the hope which inspired them was not for themselves, but for mankind.

The implied evaluation of Russell's own motives was no doubt conscious – and none the less true for it.

What dominated Russell's thoughts as April drew on, however, were not his hopes for mankind but his hopes for himself, especially his longing to continue working at philosophy. For this, he now realised, he *had* to secure a transfer to the first division. Conditions in the first division were quite different from those which Morel had suffered: prisoners were allowed as many books as they liked, were not expected to do prison work, were given a larger cell and allowed their own clothes and furniture. They were even allowed writing materials. As a first-division prisoner, Russell could live the contemplative life he had imagined before he met Morel. As he knew, however, first-division status was not easy to acquire. Morel had applied for it and been refused; Russell was determined to succeed. In the letter to Murray quoted earlier, he suggested a letter-writing campaign to put pressure on the Home Secretary, Sir George Cave, to have Russell transferred to the first division. 'If private representations fail,' he told Murray, 'letters to the Press will be necessary.'

Soon, thanks mainly to Murray, pressure was coming from all quarters to have Russell put in the first division. Murray had already approached Asquith for help. Now, together with H. W. Carr, he got up a petition of eminent philosophers to present to the Home Secretary, urging that:

> in view of the extraordinary value of his work as a philosopher and mathematician, the danger of his powers being injuriously affected by any extreme strain, and the fact that he had already, before the prosecution, ceased his political activities and returned to philosophy, he be allowed to serve his imprisonment in the First instead of the Second Division.

In addition, Francis Hirst, the editor of the liberal free-trade journal *Common Sense*, approached grandees like Lords Morley, Buckminster, Loreburn and Lansdowne, asking them to write on Russell's behalf to the Home Secretary. Even Alys, whom Russell had not been in touch with for years, joined the campaign, writing to Lord Haldane, the ex-Lord Chancellor, that, though she did not share Russell's views, she knew 'that he is haunted by the fear of his father's malady' and feared that 'what is to anyone a very severe punishment might be fatal to his intellect'. By late April, the signs were good. Ottoline wrote to Russell with inside information that the Foreign Secretary, Arthur Balfour, 'is giving word that you are *not* to go to prison'. This, according to Russell in his *Autobiography*, proved to be the decisive intervention.[4]

When the appeal finally came to court, it was, as everybody expected, rejected, but in his summing up the magistrate, Mr Lawrie, said:

> it would be a great loss to the country if Mr Russell, a man of great distinction, were confined in such a form that his abilities would not have full scope and the sentence [will] be served in the first division.

Immediately afterwards, Russell was put in a taxi and taken to Brixton prison, not to endure the brutal regime of 'hard labour', which had been the lot of many 'absolutist' COs, nor to suffer the ruinous mental deprivation of the second-division prisoner experienced by Morel, but rather to enjoy a kind of life more conducive to serious philosophical work than any he had known since losing his lectureship at Trinity.

---

[4] In his 1959 'Face to Face' BBC television interview with John Freeman, however, Russell told a rather different story, attributing his transfer to his brother's influence over Sir George Cave: 'My brother knew everybody concerned and when the Home Secretary wasn't being very obliging, my brother went to see him: "Oh, you know he was my fag at Winchester. He'll do it." ' It seems likely, however, that Russell was confusing the campaign to have him transferred to the first division with Frank's later (unsuccessful) attempts to get him a remission.

19
PRISON

For the first two or three months of his sentence, life at Brixton prison suited Russell perfectly. Freed from the demands of both political campaigning and romantic attachments, he was able to live precisely the kind of cloistered, contemplative life he had long craved. The conditions, though naturally more austere than he was used to, were not especially harsh. His cell (an extra-large one, for which he paid a rent of two shillings and sixpence a week) was furnished in style by his sister-in-law, Elizabeth,[1] and decorated with flowers from Garsington. He had *The Times* delivered every day, and was, from the great number of books supplied by his friends, able to transform his cell into a reasonably well-equipped study. From Cambridge via his student Dorothy Wrinch[2] came complete sets of the great philosophers and bound volumes of academic journals of philosophy and psychology; from the library at Garsington came works of history, biographies, memoirs and letters; and from a variety of sources came a vast number of novels. He did not even have to eat prison food; as a first-division prisoner he was allowed to order his meals from outside. Nor was he expected to clean his own cell. The first division was designed for those in the habit of employing servants, and, at sixpence a day, Russell could have his cell cleaned for him by another prisoner.

Given these conditions, he was able fairly soon after arriving to establish an extraordinarily fruitful daily routine: four hours of philosophical writing, four hours of philosophical reading and four hours of general reading. Altogether, it was rather like being in a somewhat spartan study centre – or perhaps even

---

[1] In May 1916, Frank Russell married his third wife, Elizabeth von Arnim, known to the public as the author of the best-selling novel *Elizabeth and Her German Garden*. The marriage was a disaster from the start and led to Frank's being viciously caricatured in Elizabeth's 1921 novel, *Vera*.

[2] After his sacking by Trinity College in 1916, Russell, in fulfilment of his dream of being 'like Abelard', continued to teach mathematical logic to a small group of students who came to Gordon Square every week for informal lectures on *Principia Mathematica*. The group included Jean Nicod, a mathematics graduate from Paris, whom Russell described as 'one of the most delightful people that I have ever known'; Victor Lenzen, one of his students at Harvard, who, in 1916, came to Cambridge to study with G. E. Moore and J. J. Thomson; and Dorothy Wrinch, a mathematics graduate at Girton, and subsequently a lecturer in mathematics at Cambridge and, later, at Smith College, Massachusetts.

more like being in a monastery. He was finding it all so agreeable, he wrote to Frank, that he was beginning to think he had missed his vocation by not being a monk in a contemplative order.

The greatest drawback was loneliness. He was allowed just one visit a week of up to three visitors at a time. In order to make the most of these visits, he drew up a list of preferred visitors, marking those he thought compatible with each other. Ottoline generally came with Frank, Colette with Clifford Allen, and Whitehead with H. Wildon Carr. With a warder sitting close enough to hear everything that was said, conversation was stilted and difficult, and real communication was conducted – as so often in Russell's life – by letter. Officially, he was allowed to write no more than one letter a week, which had to be read first by a prison official to see that it contained nothing seditious. Usually this took the form of a sort of circular, addressed to Frank, but containing a series of specific messages for other people: discussions of philosophy for Carr and Whitehead, expressions of devotion to Colette and passages of self-analysis for Ottoline.

For Russell, a limit of one letter a week was obviously intolerable, and he soon invented ways of getting round it. To Colette, he wrote letters in French, disguising them as transcriptions from the correspondence between Madame Roland and François Buzot. By and large, these letters consist chiefly of rather desperate and repetitious declarations of his love, and, as time went by and his frustration at being separated from her increased, strident expressions of fierce jealousy of whoever she was with.

His letters to Ottoline were quite different. They were, Ottoline says in her memoirs, 'a great pleasure, as they expressed his delightful poetic side':

They are indeed, besides being to me very moving, amongst the best interesting and brilliant letters I ever received from him. I was so happy to have established our friendship on a new basis, and he was franker too which was a great comfort.

Most of these letters were smuggled out of prison by hiding them in the uncut pages of books and journals. The first time this ruse was used, Ottoline was puzzled to receive the *Proceedings of the London Mathematical Society*, together with a note from Russell saying that she would 'find it very interesting'. After a good deal of bemused scrutiny, and 'feeling certain that this very unintelligible magazine held some secret communications', she at last turned the volume upside-down and found the letter. She, in turn, sent him several uncut books hiding long letters, and in this way they kept up a flow of affectionate and thoughtful letters that sealed the new basis of their friendship.

In a newspaper article written in the 1930s,[3] Russell provided colourful descriptions of his fellow-prisoners, claiming (perhaps even boasting) that

---

[3] 'Are Criminals Worse than Other People', published in several of the Hearst newspapers in the United States, including the *Washington Herald*, *Los Angeles Examiner* and *San Francisco Examiner*, in October/November 1931.

during the war he had 'associated habitually with criminals'. From the letters he wrote at the time, however, it would appear that he had very little to do with the other prisoners and indeed rather kept his distance from them. 'Life here is just like life on an Ocean Liner,' he wrote in one of his circular letters, 'one is cooped up with a number of average human beings, unable to escape except into one's own state-room.' Given his twelve-hours-a-day reading and writing schedule, it is hard to see how he could have spent much time outside his 'state-room'. Of course, every day he had to take exercise in the yard with the other prisoners, but on those occasions talking was forbidden and his impressions of his fellow-inmates were formed chiefly on the basis of what they looked like. 'I see no sign that they are worse than the average,' he reported to Frank, 'except that they probably have less will-power, if one can judge by their faces, which is all I have to go by.' The closest contact he had with other prisoners was with those he employed to clean his cell, and these prisoners he observed much as an anthropologist might observe the members of a strange and primitive tribe. 'It is queer the different ways there are of living,' he wrote to Ottoline:

> To me pride is essential, but I had a man to clean out my cell who had absolutely none. Fat and elderly, always cheerful and full of fun, he boasted of having spent all his life in prison . . . He knew all the dodges, got plenty to eat when others were near starvation, was a favourite of all the warders, and kept everybody laughing. He had many merits but was utterly and entirely ignoble. A world of people like him would be good-natured, happy, and of no account.

The truth is that Russell did not really want, or need, the companionship of his fellow-prisoners. His prison sentence came just at a time when what he craved most was the solitude and leisure necessary for intense absorption in philosophical questions. In a description that recalls those of Russell when he was writing *Principia*, Ottoline mentions that, when she went to visit him, he at first looked dazed with the change from his solitary existence. She speaks of Russell's 'rather rarefied solitary existence, his mind absorbed by serious problems' and says that she hesitated to intrude on this exalted state with trivia from the outside world. 'Bertie seemed really happy during the first months of his imprisonment,' she writes, and 'enjoyed the seclusion and was able to do a good deal of writing'.

Throughout most of the war, Russell had felt that, in order to concentrate his energies on political work, he had neglected his inner life. Being in prison now freed him from the obligation to put public matters first, and he was able to devote himself to his own thoughts and emotions, without feeling selfish or self-indulgent. 'The holiday from responsibility is really delightful,' he wrote to Frank, 'so delightful that it almost outweighs everything else':

> Here I have not a care in the world: the rest to nerves and will is heavenly. One is free from the torturing question: What more ought I be doing? Is there any effective action that I haven't thought of? Have I a right to let

the whole thing go and return to philosophy? Here, I *have* to let the whole
thing go, which is far more restful than choosing to let it go and doubting
if one's choice is justified. Prison has some of the advantages of the Catholic
Church.

But, allowed to go where they would, his thoughts did not always turn to
philosophy. They also turned inwards, to the kind of reflective scrutiny of his
past and searching analysis of his character to which Russell was always prone
but which overwork had lately made impossible. Several times in his prison
letters he commented on how self-absorbed he had become. Almost anything
he read or thought about might provoke him to reflect upon himself. He read
Lytton Strachey's recently published *Eminent Victorians*, and, though he
enjoyed it and even laughed out loud at its mockery of, for example, General
Gordon, he could not help feeling also a little disquieted by it. It led him to
try and place himself in relation to, on the one hand, Lytton Strachey and
Bloomsbury, and on the other, the despised Victorians. Strachey, he wrote to
Ottoline, 'judges men by an artist's standard, by whether they are delightful
to contemplate':

> this places sincerity high among virtues, and makes the Victorians disgust-
> ing. But they had immense energy, and they had genuinely (in spite of
> cant) a wish to improve the world, and they did improve it. I prefer them
> to Bernardi and Northcliffe, who are sincere but evil; I prefer them even
> to Lytton who is sincere but indifferent to the rest of mankind. He does
> not sufficiently consider men as social forces. At the beginning of the
> Victorian era starvation and ignorance were almost universal, at the end
> there was little starvation and much education. Our age is pursuing the
> opposite, and we shall need a set of Victorians to put us right. The useful
> man is not the same as the delightful man.

Implied here is an expression of how he himself would wish to be judged,
and perhaps also recognition that, when judged by the artist's standard of
being 'delightful to contemplate', he would not measure up as well as, say,
G. E. Moore, the Bloomsbury Group's philosophic hero. The contrast
between being useful and being delightful recalls his letter to Ottoline of the
autumn of 1916, in which he had confessed his vampire-like tendency to feed
off the vitality of others in order to keep up the energy he needed for his
political work. In order to pursue work of public importance, he, like the
Victorians, was prepared to be somewhat less than delightful, was prepared
to sacrifice, to some extent, complete sincerity, and was perhaps even
prepared to be somewhat 'disgusting', if, by so doing, he could be 'useful'.

And yet, on the question of whether one *ought* to be like Strachey or like
the Victorians, Russell was divided within himself. After all, in a different,
less public-spirited, more introspective mood, he, too, placed sincerity high
among the virtues, and, occasionally at least, craved the contemplative
delights, the 'civilised' way of life beloved of Bloomsbury. 'Civilised' was a
word he used repeatedly in this context. Strachey's book, he said, was, despite

its faults, 'exquisitely civilised'. And, in describing his life in prison, Russell wrote to Frank: 'After giving out all these last years, reading almost nothing and writing very little and having no opportunity for anything civilised, it is a real delight to get back to a civilised existence.' Being 'civilised', then, was for Russell something that rather militated against being 'useful', and, to the extent that Russell craved such civilisation, he did so against the pull of an equally strong impulse to be of public service. The unresolved struggle between the two impulses was much to the fore in his prison reflections about himself.

Linked to this struggle was another internal debate that he dwelt upon in the isolation of his prison cell – again centred on the extent to which he felt himself to be a Victorian – between the recognition and the denial of the savage impulses that lay hidden beneath the 'civilised' crust. A week after his letter about Strachey, he wrote that he had been reading two books about journeys along the Amazon. The first, *The Naturalist on the River Amazon* by H. W. Bates, was published in 1864 and is in many ways a thoroughly Victorian book, written with an unreflective confidence in the superiority of European culture over the superstitious and barbaric way of life of the Amazonian tribesmen. The second, *The Sea and the Jungle* by H. M. Tomlinson, published in 1912, is altogether more modern and sceptical, hinting at dark, unseen forces that threaten to penetrate the thin veneer of European civilisation. 'Tomlinson I *loved*,' he told Ottoline:

Bates bores me while I am reading him, but leaves pictures in my mind which I am glad of afterwards. Tomlinson owes much to *Heart of Darkness*. The contrast with Bates is remarkable: one sees how our generation, in comparison, is a little mad, because it has allowed itself glimpses of the truth, and the truth is spectral, insane, ghostly; the more men see of it, the less mental health they retain. The Victorians (dear souls) were sane and successful because they never came anywhere near the truth. But for my part I would rather be mad with truth than sane with lies.

In this contrast, then, Russell – perhaps to some extent regretfully – places himself with the moderns rather than with the Victorians. With the Victorians' energy for public improvement (and perhaps even a necessary precondition for it) went a faith in both man and God that was no longer possible to anyone who had penetrated to the truth, either about the world or about human psychology.

As Russell had told Ottoline the previous autumn, having 'assimilated and digested' the hatred of mankind that came to him in the New Year of 1917, he had reached a 'slow acquiescence' in the dark side of human nature. Now, in his prison letters, he dwelt much on his own dark side, striving to show that here too he had come to accept the truth. In a phrase that carries a familiar echo of the 'hellish repression' of Dr Mallako, he told Ottoline: 'There is a well of fierce hate in me.' This hatred, he wrote, 'is also a well of life and energy – it would not really be good if I ceased to hate'. He reminded Ottoline of 'a certain moment in a churchyard near Broughton':

you told me to make a place for wildness in my morality, and I asked you what you meant, and you explained. It has been very difficult: my instinctive morality was so much that of self-repression. I used to be afraid of myself and the darker side of my instincts; now I am not. You began that, and the war completed it.

The sanity and the success of the Victorians were possible because they never came near the truth about this 'wildness', never realised that, far from being a 'rational animal', man was, when you looked deeply enough, a seething mass of anger, hatred, jealousy and violence. Another truth of which the Victorians were innocent, and one that was much on Russell's mind during his time in Brixton, was the truth about religion. The image he had used in his letters to Colette of his striving after religious truth as a 'passionate love for a ghost' recurs repeatedly in his writing at this time, and it is surely primarily this that he has in mind in the letter quoted above when he talks of the 'spectral, insane, ghostly' truth, the realisation of which is enough to drive one mad. *There is no God.* And yet – and this, perhaps, is what drives one mad – one feels there has to be *something*. In a letter to Ottoline of 11 August, he talked of those (and in this he included both himself and Ottoline) whose lives are spent 'in the quest for something elusive, and yet omnipresent, and at once subtle and infinite':

One seeks it in music, and the sea, and sunsets; at times I have seemed very near it in crowds when I have been feeling strongly what they were feeling;[4] one seeks it in love above all. But if one lets oneself imagine one has found it, some cruel irony is sure to come and show one that it is not really found.
     . . . The outcome is that one is a ghost, floating through the world without any real contact. Even when one feels nearest to other people, something in one seems obstinately to belong to God, and to refuse to enter into any earthly communion – at least that is how I should express it if I thought there was a God. It is odd, isn't it? I care passionately for this world and many things and people in it, and yet . . . what is it all? There *must* be something more important, one feels, though I don't *believe* there is. I am haunted – some ghost, from some extra-mundane region, seems always trying to tell me something that I am to repeat to the world, but I cannot understand the message. But it is from listening to the ghost that one comes to feel oneself a ghost. I feel I shall find the truth on my deathbed and be surrounded by people too stupid to understand – fussing about medicines instead of searching for wisdom.

Russell evidently thought that, in these prison letters, he had come close to expressing the essential truth about himself. 'I dare say', he wrote to Ottoline,

---

4 One thinks here of his ecstatic descriptions of the Devonshire Hall meeting of the NCF in April 1916 and of the meeting in the Albert Hall a year later to celebrate the Russian Revolution.

'you will always think of this time as the time when I wrote the best *letters*.'
The notion of feeling himself to be a ghost, because of the importance he
attached to the ghostly remnants of religious belief, is one he makes much of
in his *Autobiography*. 'Underlying all occupations and all pleasures,' he writes
in a passage that reads like an attempt to get at the very core of his being, 'I
have felt since early youth the pain of solitude':

> I have escaped it most nearly in moments of love, yet even there, on
> reflection, I have found that the escape depended partly upon illusion. I
> have known no woman to whom the claims of the intellect were as absolute
> as they are to me, and wherever intellect intervened, I have found that the
> sympathy I sought in love was apt to fail. What Spinoza calls 'the
> intellectual love of God' has seemed to me the best thing to live by, but I
> have not had even the somewhat abstract God that Spinoza allowed himself
> to whom to attach my intellectual love. I have loved a ghost, and in loving
> a ghost my inmost self has itself become spectral. I have therefore buried
> it deeper and deeper beneath layers of cheerfulness, affection, and joy of
> life. But my most profound feelings have remained always solitary and have
> found in human things no companionship. The sea, the stars, the night
> wind in waste places, mean more to me than even the human beings I love
> best, and I am conscious that human affection is to me at bottom an attempt
> to escape from the vain search for God.

'I shall never lose the sense of being a ghost,' he wrote to Ottoline from
prison. 'It comes less when I am happy, but it comes – and of course here
one has moods of misery . . . That feeling of being a ghost was the very first
sign I had that my marriage was becoming unhappy. I remember the moment
now – a summer evening at Friday's Hill, when the whole P. Smith family
were sitting out, I with them, but suddenly not of them.'

This sense of withdrawal and detachment seems linked to the sense of loss
that is, perhaps, what fundamentally distinguishes Russell's own view of
Victorian certainties from the less reverential view of Strachey and the
Bloomsbury Group. 'I hate all the Bloomsbury crew,' he wrote to Ottoline,
'with all their sneers at anything that has live feeling in it.' When, in a BBC
radio talk he gave in his old age, Russell came to reflect on the differences
between himself and Bloomsbury, he did so on the basis of their respective
attitudes to the Victorian age, this time identifying himself unequivocally with
the Victorians:

> We were still Victorian, they were Edwardian. We believed in ordered
> progress by means of politics and free discussion. The more self-confident
> among us may have hoped to be leaders of the multitude, but none of us
> wished to be divorced from it. The generation of Keynes and Lytton did
> not seek to preserve any kinship with the Philistine. They aimed rather at
> a life of retirement among fine shades and nice feelings, and conceived of
> the good as consisting in the passionate mutual admirations of a clique of
> the élite.

As the months in prison went by, this 'Victorian' side of Russell reasserted itself over his more contemplative, 'civilised' side; his initial enjoyment of the 'life of retirement among fine shades' that had been thrust upon him gave way to a frustrated longing to be *engagé* once more. So long as he was consumed by private thoughts and philosophical ideas, however, he made the most of it. From May until the first few weeks of August 1918, he enjoyed a spell of concentrated absorption in philosophical questions of a kind that he had not enjoyed since finishing *Principia*. 'My only really strong desire', he told Frank in one of his first prison letters, 'is to be able to do some philosophical work while I am here.'

His first philosophical task was to write up the lectures on mathematical logic, which he had delivered the previous autumn, as *Introduction to Mathematical Philosophy*. This he accomplished astonishingly quickly. By 21 May, he had written 20,000 words of the book and just six days later he had 'nearly finished' 70,000 of it. This phenomenal rate (even by Russell's standards) – nearly 10,000 words a day – suggests that much of the writing consisted of little more than transcribing what he had already written for his lectures.

It suggests also a certain impatience to get the task out of the way in order to get on with his other, more original work. Russell arrived at Brixton convinced that he was on the brink of a philosophical breakthrough; that, at last, He could see a way to repair the damage inflicted on both his self-confidence and his philosophical logic by Wittgenstein's demolition of his theory of judgment. 'I had given up logic years ago in despair of finding out anything more about it,' he wrote on 1 July, 'but now I begin to see hope. Approaching the old questions from a radically new point of view, as I have been doing lately, makes new ideas possible.'

At the centre of this new approach was the 'psychologistic turn' first announced in his lectures on logical atomism. During his first three months in prison he read a vast amount of psychological literature,[5] focusing in particular on the work of behaviourists and animal psychologists. His interest in this work lay chiefly in his hope that it might provide the basis for a new theory of judgment. As he wrote in his circular letter of 8 July: 'All the psychology that I have been reading and meaning to read was for the sake of logic':

. . . it was for its sake that I wanted to study behaviourism, because the first problem is to have a tenable theory of judgment. I see my way to a really big piece of work, and incidentally to a definition of 'logic' hitherto lacking . . . I have reached a point in logic where I need theories of (a) judgment and (b) symbolism, both of which are psychological problems.

Immediately after he finished *Introduction to Mathematical Philosophy*, Russell wrote a long review of John Dewey's *Essays in Experimental Logic*,

---

[5] So proud was he of how much he read in prison that Russell kept a detailed list. It includes some fifteen books and over fifty academic articles (all from just three journals: *The American Journal of Psychology*, *The Psychological Review* and the *Archiv für die gesamte Psychologie*), nearly all of them in some way connected with behaviourist psychology.

which gave him the chance to clarify his thoughts on the relation of logic to psychology. What Dewey called 'logic', Russell said – namely, the study of the nature, origin and justification of belief[6] – he would call 'psychology'. But it was no less important for that, and indeed was importantly relevant to what Russell *would* call logic, namely the study of forms of facts. For a crucial question for logic in his sense was: are there facts that are (irreducibly) of the form 'A believes (or judges) p', or can one always reduce beliefs or judgments to some other kind of fact? In this way, a psychological theory that denied that there were such facts, or provided, as behaviourism does, some kind of reductive analysis of them, would have something important to say about logic.

Russell's interest in behaviourism, then, was of a piece with his long-standing interest in 'neutral monism', the theory advanced by William James in his essay 'Does "Consciousness" exist?' that there is no such 'thing' as consciousness or 'the mind', and no fundamental division between the mental and the physical. There is, according to James, but one sort of 'stuff' from which the world is made, and that stuff is neutral between mind and matter. Beliefs, James says, 'are really rules for action; and the whole function of thinking is but one step in the production of habits of action.' In 1913 this aspect of the theory had struck Russell as obviously wrong, and in 'Theory of Knowledge' he rejected neutral monism precisely on the grounds that it was saddled with an untenable theory of belief. Belief, Russell then thought, had to be understood as a relation between a mind and the things in the world.

After Wittgenstein's attack on his theory of judgment, however, Russell rather wished he could accept neutral monism, for then there would be no such thing as 'judgment' in his old sense, and the question of how to analyse it would not arise. In his lectures on logical atomism, therefore, he declared a 'bias in favour of the theory of neutral monism'. But, however much he would like to believe that there were no such facts as 'A believes p', in the end he could not and consequently found 'very great difficulty' in accepting the theory. He therefore, he told his audience at Gordon Square, would continue to assume 'that there are such facts as beliefs and wishes and so forth'.

At the time of his prison sentence, however, the issue was still far from settled, and Russell continued to dwell on the possibility that neutral monism might be not just theoretically convenient but actually true. If it were, he came increasingly to think, much that otherwise remained mysterious about logic, language, psychology and metaphysics would begin to make some kind of sense. Consequently, soon after he arrived in prison determined to pursue work on philosophy, he declared: 'My chief problem is: Can Belief be explained by neutral monism?'

At the back of Russell's mind while he was reading up the recent psychological literature was the project of writing two complementary books:

---

[6] Whether the words 'belief' and 'judgment' mean exactly the same thing is a moot point. Traditionally, a 'judgment' is the assent of mind to a proposition. If one thinks that all beliefs are propositional, then beliefs and judgments are the same thing.

the first, to be called *The Analysis of Mind*, would deal with the theory of judgment, belief and all 'mental' phenomena from a neutral monist perspective; the second, along the lines of the lectures on logical atomism, would draw out the lessons for this analysis for the understanding of logic. It was his boldest philosophical project since *Principia* and he gloried in its ambitiousness. If successful, he wrote, it 'should be another big and important piece of work'. In a later letter, he told Ottoline that it would probably take him about five years: 'It is delicious having a big new problem to play with – and it is heavenly to find I am still capable of new ideas.'

When he tried to put his new ideas down on paper, however, he found it more difficult than he had anticipated. In July, he started writing what he called 'notes on the principles of symbolism', but by the second week of August the work had ground to a halt. In a letter to Frank of 12 August, he said that he had been suffering from bad headaches, which returned whenever he tried to work. He now wanted to get out of prison as quickly as possible. 'I shall not make much further progress with my work until I have had a holiday in country air & a chance to acquire more freshness than is to be found in a prison cell.' In an earlier letter he had said that, though he thought the new philosophical ideas he had were important, he needed to get out of prison to make much progress with them, because his thoughts were still vague and, in order to make them more precise, he needed to discuss them. 'I have had time to think out everything I can think out in here', he wrote to Ottoline, 'and now I need the stimulus of talk.'

From what survives of 'notes on the principles of symbolism' one can see why he was dissatisfied with them. Part of the problem is the sheer scale of the task he had set himself: a theory of language, logic and psychology that built upon both his own work in mathematical logic and that of the behaviourists in psychology. There was also the change in mental outlook that was required for this new work. For, to some extent, the new approach that he had announced to his old problems in philosophical logic amounted to a more or less complete reorientation of his philosophical perspective, an attempt to 'naturalise' his entire philosophy, to bring it down to earth from the platonic heavens in which it had previously lived. He was trying to write philosophy, as it were, with a new voice, in a more worldly, less exalted frame of mind.

Thus, at the centre of his new conception of 'meaning' were not platonic forms like 'ideas' or 'propositions' (as he had previously understood them), but the very mundane and earth-bound notion beloved of behaviouristic psychology of the 'conditioned response': a baby (or, as it might be, a dog or a monkey) repeatedly hears a noise – say, the word 'food' – at the same time that it sees food, and so comes to expect to see food when it hears the word 'food'. The meaning of words, then, is to be understood in terms of the acquisition of 'the language habit', of producing the appropriate response to a given stimulus.

In his determination to avoid platonic forms, Russell now understood a word to be not one thing, but several; the word 'Socrates', for example, is the class of noises and marks on paper that constitute the occasions on which it has been spoken or written. Similarly the proposition 'Socrates preceded Plato' is a class of physical occurrences. With regard to the *meaning* of a proposition, Russell now distinguished its objective from its subjective meaning. The objective meaning of a proposition is the fact that would make it true or false; its subjective meaning is the belief which it expresses. A proposition, he says, '*expresses* a thought and *asserts or denies a fact*'.

The problem here is that though it is fairly clear what propositions and facts are on this analysis, beliefs look rather more shadowy. What are they? How was he to understand beliefs and thoughts – or even desires and wishes – without assuming a conscious mind? His answer was that, in a vague and as yet ill-defined way, they were to be understood as physiological events. 'The object of my physiological doctrine of symbolism,' he writes in one of the last of these 'notes on the principles of symbolism':

> would be to construct, if possible, a theory linking the speaking or writing of a proposition (as a physical occurrence) directly with the *fact*, without any 'mental' intermediary.

Whereas previously he had understood a judgment to be a series of relations between a mind and the objects in the world, now he understood it to be a relation between one set of objects (whatever the physiological constituents of a belief are) and another, between one physical fact and another.

The 'notes on the principles of symbolism' end in bewilderment about how such a theory is to be constructed. The subjective meaning of a proposition, Russell writes 'may *be* a series of bodily acts'; it is 'whatever constitutes belief'; but, as he is forced to admit, 'what it is that constitutes belief is not clear'. Looking to behaviourism for a theory of belief, he had found instead a theory of propositions and a set of formidably difficult and unresolved questions as to how beliefs were to be analysed according to that theory. Still, at least he had formulated for himself a new audacious ambition:

> My bias remains: I still wish to rescue the physical world from the idealist. But if I could rescue the so-called 'mental' world from him too!

In the middle of August, Russell abandoned work on his new theory of symbolism and turned instead to writing a short and suggestive paper called 'On "Bad Passions"', which, when he got out of prison, he gave to C. K. Ogden to publish in *The Cambridge Magazine*. The paper is interesting for providing a bridge between his reflections on himself and his thinking on the more technical subject of the theory of symbolism.

The link was provided by his reading in psychology. The bound volumes of *The American Journal of Psychology* he was reading for articles on behaviourism also contained several discussions of Freudian psychology, including, most famously, Freud's own introduction to his theories, 'The Origin and Development of Psychoanalysis'. Russell read these with interest, and was even inclined to absorb them into his philosophical thinking on psychology. 'James's attack on "consciousness", the study of animal behaviour, & Freud, all naturally belong together,' he wrote. They all, that is, served to undermine the traditional emphasis on the 'conscious' mind.

What Russell also saw in Freudian psychology was further confirmation of the darker side of human nature, the recognition of which, he considered, separated him and his generation from the Victorians. In several of his letters he urged his correspondents to look up Jeremiah XVII: 9, which he said was 'Freud in a nutshell'. The passage reads: 'The heart is deceitful above all things, and desperately wicked: who can know it?' In 'On "Bad Passions"', he discussed Freud's theories from this perspective, prompted by another article in *The American Journal of Psychology*: 'The Freudian Methods Applied to Anger' by Stanley Hall.

Hall's starting point was the fact that some people thrive on outbreaks of anger, that they need their anger as, for example, an incentive to work hard. Such a view chimed perfectly with Russell's own observation that the 'well of fierce hate' in him was also 'a well of life and energy', that, 'it would not really be good if I ceased to hate'. In his paper, he therefore takes up Hall's point enthusiastically. He goes on to discuss three ways of dealing with 'bad passions': punishment, sublimation and physiological treatment. Punishment, he says, is effective ('Benvenuto Cellini murdered a man in the afternoon during his "constitutional", and came home to his work as if nothing had happened. However little we may think so, it is owing to the criminal law that we do not do likewise'), but it is superficial, dealing only with manifestations of violent impulses, not the impulses themselves. Sublimation is more creative:

> . . . there are cases in which rage has passed into ambition and hard work, in the first instance in order to become superior to the person who was the cause of the rage . . . Intellectual effort may be a sublimation of rage, a tigerish fury can be expended on abstract thought, when, but for this outlet it would have to vent itself on human beings.

But sublimation has its drawbacks too; it leads to 'insincerity and weakness . . . If sublimation is to be compatible with mental health and strength, it needs, as a rule, to be supplemented by *some* indulgence of the crude impulse.' Beethoven no doubt vented his anger upon his compositions, but he also notoriously vented a good deal of real, unsublimated anger at his cook: 'If Beethoven could have been turned into a quiet well-behaved person, the loss to music would have outweighed the gain to his cook.'

By physiological means, Russell thought, 'the impulsive life can be utterly transformed'. As he put it in a letter to Ottoline of 1 August: 'I am convinced that by studying the secretions of the glands we might discover how to modify character artificially.' His discussion of 'bad passion', therefore, ends with the possibility that: 'The education authority will decide what form of character is most virtuous, and the medical officers will produce this type of character':

> One of its distinguishing features will be, of course, respect for public bodies and acquiescence in the *status quo*. Therefore at that point human progress will cease.

In a light-hearted sort of way, the paper is a return to the territory of *Principles of Social Reconstruction*, to the point at which his thinking about himself, his philosophical thought and his social concerns all met. As August wore on, the hold on him of technical philosophy seemed to weaken in favour of a revival of his earlier ambition to address a wide audience on more general issues. 'I feel that when the war is over', he wrote to Ottoline on 21 August, 'I shall have things to say that the world will be willing to hear . . . I won't then do *any* technical philosophy.' A few days later, he wrote:

> Logic and imagination have fought a long fight in me, but I think they are reconciled at last. I will do one more big piece of technical work but in the main I will teach, and write on social questions, and generally put before people a way of feeling about the world. I have still a work to do which is bigger than anything technical; and now at last I believe I can do it. Don't you think I am right? My work must be technical while the war lasts; I am talking of later.

Linked to this issue was the question of how he was to earn a living when he got out of prison. In June he had supported a plan to persuade H. Wildon Carr to found a fellowship for him to enable him to continue his philosophical work, although he did not want it in any way connected with a university: 'I do not wish, even after the war, to be a don again. I have lost respect for dons and should hate being among them.' Nor did he see it as a long-term solution. For the last few years he had made money writing on social questions, he wrote to Ottoline, and after the war, he was confident that he would be able to do so again: 'It is now, during the war, that I need money. Afterwards I can earn easily.' The fellowship idea was, for him, no more than a stopgap, and what little enthusiasm he had for the plan disappeared altogether when he was told that Carr was lukewarm. Instead, he told Ottoline:

> I foresee a rather delightful career as a free-lance philosopher, like Abelard – but not in *every* respect I hope!

'I find my ambitions don't turn to political things,' he wrote to Colette. 'I want to be an *intellectual* leader to the young, & I can be, after the war, & you will be a help to me in that . . . I should not want *any* official post, however humble. I want to stand for life & thought.'

Russell saw little of Colette while he was in prison. She was touring with various plays and could not get to London very often. Nor did she write as often as Russell would have liked. In his circular letters he often asked Frank or Elizabeth to urge Colette to write. To Colette herself he wrote begging her to write longer letters, 'and more *definite* news':

> Remember what it is like being shut away here, thinking, imagining, seeing how much you don't tell, noticing the faintest signs of coldness, fearing that by the time I come out all your passion will be going elsewhere, as it did once before. If I were not in prison I could get rid of profitless thought of this kind, but in prison it is fearfully difficult.

In the typescript she prepared of their correspondence, Colette makes much of the fact that during this time Russell was 'suffering from painful feelings of various kinds' in connection with Helen Dudley, who had for most of the war been living in Russell's Bury Street flat and was now (August 1918) about to sail back to America. Before she left for the States, she went to see Russell in prison, and this meeting, Colette implies, was the cause of much of Russell's distress during August. No doubt the meeting did revive in Russell feelings of guilt at the appalling way he had treated Helen, but this was not the main cause of his restlessness.

The main cause, unquestionably, was Russell's desperate jealousy. 'While I was in prison,' he writes in his *Autobiography*, 'I was tormented by jealousy the whole time, and driven wild by the sense of impotence. I did not feel justified in feeling jealousy, which I regarded as an abominable emotion, but none the less it consumed me':

> When I first had occasion to feel it, it kept me awake almost the whole of every night for a fortnight, and at the end I only got sleep by getting a doctor to prescribe sleeping-draughts . . . I allowed jealousy to lead me to denounce her [Colette] with great violence, with the natural result that her feelings towards me were considerably chilled. We remained lovers until 1920, but we never recaptured the perfection of the first year.

Russell's recollections are borne out by Ottoline's, who in her memoirs recalls Gladys Rinder, a woman who worked for the NCF and who ran errands for Russell while in was in prison, telling her that she had to invent messages from Colette to keep Russell happy. Colette, Ottoline writes, 'was young and gay and perhaps did not understand how sensitive he was, and he poor fellow fretted at not seeing her and also he grew very jealous of her other friends in his solitary confinement':

> I remember on one of my visits I felt that he was almost longing to get rid of us so that he might read a letter she had sent him in a book, which he kept under his hand on the table during our visit. I knew so well what he was feeling that I longed for the warder to say, 'Time's up'.

Sometimes, instead of writing to him, Colette would place messages in *The Times*'s personal column, which tactfully, if not entirely truthfully, dwelt on her loneliness: 'Back from country. All, all love, Lonely but busy'; 'So lonely. You have all my love.' Russell, not unnaturally, was sceptical. As well as brooding on Colette's attraction to Maurice Elvey, he also tried several times in his letters to Colette to get her to promise to leave her husband Miles. Neither of them, he argued, would be happy until she insisted on a break. He urged her to leave Miles before he got out of prison: 'I stayed *far* too long with my wife, & I don't want you to repeat the mistake.'

Colette's letters to Russell provoked his jealousy still further. She confessed to seeing Maurice Elvey again, and also discussed a Colonel Mitchell of the US army in terms calculated to arouse Russell's suspicions. Mitchell has, she wrote, 'a most touching physiognomy: a heavily built creature like a St Bernard mastiff with sad, honest, brown eyes'. In her autobiography *After Ten Years*, Colette says little about Colonel Mitchell other than that she used to make cocoa for him in her kitchen and that he introduced her to oysters, 'for which I am eternally grateful to him'.

Colette had got to know Colonel Mitchell, it seems, through T. S. Eliot, who at this time was desperately trying to get a commission to join the US navy. She describes a rather odd occasion when Eliot came to tea with her:

> We had tea on the kitchen table. I found him reserved and rather shut up in himself – remote. Extraordinarily erudite, of course. His eyes were most remarkable. One felt they might spring out on one at any moment – like a cat. His manner was detached and there was a certain frigidity about him. But underneath that frigidity, one felt there lurked a curiously deep despair. He talked in slow, hesitating fashion. It was difficult to think of him as an American.

Why Eliot came to tea she does not say, though it seems possible that it was something to do with living arrangements. Frank had told Russell that he no longer wanted him to live at Gordon Square. This meant that Russell could no longer let his flat at Bury Street – Helen Dudley was his last tenant – and that he would have to move back there himself. This, in turn, would leave him rather short of money, and in August he let Eliot know that he would have to cease paying his share of the rent for the house in Marlow. What had happened in the meantime to the flat at Fitzroy Street is unrecorded, but in August Colette moved into Bury Street to get it ready for Russell's return.

On 16 August Russell wrote to her urging her to 'bear with me if I grow horrid' during the time he had left in prison:

> I am very tired, very weary. I am of course tortured by jealousy; I knew I should be. I know so little of your doings that I probably imagine more than the truth. I have grown so nervy from confinement and dwelling on the future that I feel a sort of vertigo, an impulse to destroy the happiness in prospect. *Will you please quite calmly ignore anything I do these next weeks in obedience to this impulse.* As yet, I am just able to see that it is mad, but soon it will seem the only sanity. I shall set out to hurt you, to make you break with me; I shall say I won't see you when I first come out; I shall pretend to have lost all affection for you. All this is madness – the effect of jealousy and impatience combined. The pain of wanting a thing very much at last grows so great that one has to try not to want it any longer.

To Ottoline, he wrote that when he came out of prison he would at first go away with Colette, 'but she will probably be too busy to stay away long', and so he asked her if they could not go away on holiday somewhere on the coast: 'I can't tell you how I long for the SEA.' They decided on Lulworth Cove in Dorset, 'the very place' he had been thinking of, he wrote, after Ottoline had suggested it: 'Oh, won't it be glorious to be able to walk across fields and see the horizon and talk freely and be with friends . . . All kinds of delights float before my mind – above all talk, *talk*, TALK. I never knew how one can hunger for it – The time here has done me good. I have read a lot and thought a lot and grown *collected*, I am bursting with energy – but I do long for civilisation and civilised talk – And I long for the SEA and wildness and wind.'

The end, when it came, came so suddenly that it seemed to catch both Russell and Colette out, and the reunion that he had looked forward to with such passion was botched. Throughout the first few days of September, they exchanged letters detailing how they would celebrate his release. On 7 September, Colette wrote that she kept thinking of the moment when she would open the door '& you'll be standing there, come home at last . . . & I'll put my arms around yr dear straight shoulders & stroke yr heathery hair, & kiss you like a starving man & love every bit of you'. A few days later, on 11 September, he wrote that he would be out in less than three weeks. In fact, with a month's remission for good behaviour, he was out just three days later. Colette, it seems, was not ready for him, and had made other arrangements for that night, confirming Russell's jealous fears by dining out with Colonel Mitchell. On his first evening outside prison Russell went to dinner at Gladys Rinder's house. For Gladys Rinder, it was a great honour. 'I was *so* excited to-night', she wrote to him after their dinner together, 'that I never said how perfectly *lovely* it was of you to come to dinner with me your first evening. I shall always feel proud to think of it, and it was just gorgeous.'

For Russell, however, it was something of an anti-climax. He was now more than ever convinced that Colette was having an affair with Colonel Mitchell and, as he had predicted he would, he made a big scene, setting out to hurt her, to break with her and pretending to have lost all affection for her. Instead of the passionate homecoming envisaged by Colette, he stormed out of Bury Street and spent the night at Frank's house in Gordon Square.

20

ROADS TO FREEDOM

1. PHILOSOPHY

During the first few months after his release from Brixton, Russell led a curious, unsettled existence, apparently unsure of where or even with whom he wanted to live. Frank had made it clear that he was no longer welcome as a permanent guest at Gordon Square, and living with Colette, either at Bury Street or at the studio flat in Fitzroy Street, was made impossible by his ferocious jealousy. Not wanting to destroy altogether his relationship with Colette, but knowing how cruel and vindictive he was liable to be when jealous, Russell thought it dangerous to spend more than two or three days at a time with her.

A few days after his anti-climactic reunion with Colette and his subsequent retreat to Gordon Square, he visited Clifford Allen to discuss the idea that the two of them might share a flat. Russell was, Allen recorded in his diary, 'very childlike in his engrossment with his own emotions, virtues, vices, and the effect he has on other people':

The oddest mixture of candour and mystery, cruelty and affection, fearless concern for constructive philosophy and enormous personal interest in attitudes to himself of other philosophers.

After two or three days with Allen, Russell left for Telegraph House, where he stayed for about a week before returning to London. On 25 September 1918 he spent a day in Richmond Park with Ottoline. It was, he wrote afterwards, 'a great joy to find things so imperishable'. Nevertheless, there was bad news: Ottoline could not, after all, contemplate leaving Philip to take a holiday with Russell in Lulworth.

Such was the extent of Russell's emotional turmoil over Colette at this time that he could not even bear to be in London for more than a few days a week, and so, soon after his day in Richmond with Ottoline, he headed to Abinger Common, where Clifford Allen was now resting on doctor's orders. By this time, the end of the war was in sight, with a victory for the Entente now all but inevitable, and the prospects for peace rather than Russell's personal problems dominated conversation. Feeling that an inconclusive military ending would produce a better post-war spirit, Russell hoped that the

Entente's victory would not be too decisive, while Allen thought a 'good map' was only achievable by a decisive military victory.

While he was staying with Allen, Russell heard from Colette that – no doubt to compensate for his disappointment at not going on holiday with Ottoline – she had booked a couple of nights for them in a hotel in Lulworth. Though two nights was by no means long enough, being by the sea did much to restore Russell's spirits, and when he returned to Abinger he was in a much better frame of mind. Allen recalls him sitting by the fire reciting from memory his favourite poems of Shakespeare and Blake: 'He was like a happy child, and he made me realise from his tenderness and brilliant mind why, with all his waywardness, I love him so devotedly.'

At Abinger, in the Surrey countryside, Russell felt able to take up once more the philosophical writing he had begun in prison. 'I enjoy getting back to work,' he wrote to Ottoline, 'and having secure privacy – no telephone, no post, no visitors – it is as good as prison, with the advantage that I can walk out whenever I like.' He saw Colette, he said, only in London, hardly ever at Abinger, '& then only for a moment'. Now that it was not necessary for getting out of prison, he told Ottoline, he rather hoped that Gilbert Murray's lectureship scheme would fall through: 'I want to have time for my original work.'

As the weeks went by, however, Russell's turbulent passion for Colette and his obsessive conviction of her unfaithfulness to him made it increasingly difficult for him to concentrate on philosophy. His appetite for work had deserted him, his energy dissipated, and he felt unsettled and rootless, as if the world had no place for him any more. 'It is very difficult to adjust oneself to the new world,' he wrote to Ottoline on November 10:

> I find it hard to resist the feeling that I have lived long enough: the energy wanted for new beginnings, which I felt in prison, I no longer feel. Nothing in my personal future seems interesting or vivid or worth the pain of existence. But that is a mood . . . due to unspeakable weariness of spirit.

The next day was Armistice Day. In the early hours of the morning, the First World War came to an end, with an unexpected suddenness, when an agreement to end hostilities was signed in a railway carriage in the forest of Compiègne, deep in the French countryside. Peace was officially announced at eleven o'clock in the morning, but, through a kind of aristocratic grapevine, Russell learned the good news a few hours earlier than the general public. Moments after the armistice was signed, Winston Churchill phoned his Aunt Leonie, Lady Leslie, to tell her; she then passed the news on to her friend Lady Annesley, who, in turn, phoned her daughter, Colette. Colette, of course, immediately rang Russell, who that morning was in London. 'One did not do anything terribly dramatic,' Colette writes in *After Ten Years*, 'one did not weep or sing for joy; or curse or cheer or moan for the dead; but it was like the slow lifting of a very heavy load.'

Russell's reaction was to go out into the street and tell whoever he could.

At 11 a.m., when the public announcement came, he was in Tottenham Court Road. Within two minutes, he recalls, everybody in the shops and offices had come out into the street: 'They commandeered the buses, and made them go where they liked. I saw a man and a woman, complete strangers to each other, meet in the middle of the road and kiss as they passed.' He wandered the streets alone all day, 'watching the temper of the crowd, as I had done in the August days four years before':

> The crowd was frivolous still, and had learned nothing during the period of horror, except to snatch at pleasure more recklessly than before. I felt strangely solitary amid the rejoicings, like a ghost dropped by accident from some other planet.

'The crowd rejoiced and I also rejoiced,' he wrote. 'But I remained as solitary as before.'

In his *Autobiography*, after describing his sense of alienation from the Armistice Day celebrations, Russell goes on immediately to the kind of reflections he had pursued in prison about feeling like a ghost because, in his striving for the 'intellectual love of God', he had loved a ghost. The implication is that the alienation he felt among the cheering crowds was but one more aspect of his deeper, religious and metaphysical sense of being cut off. No doubt there is some truth in this, but in the November of 1918, Russell also had a more concrete cause for his feelings of desolation and loneliness: he felt desperately betrayed by Colette.

Whatever the truth of his suspicions that Colette was having an affair with Mitchell (and in her typescript, Colette portrays it as a morbid, obsessive and groundless one), Russell's jealousy of Elvey was, as he knew only too well, perfectly well-founded. In November, Russell learned what was, from his point of view, the worst possible news: that Colette was pregnant by Elvey. She wanted an abortion and Russell agreed to pay for what was then an illegal operation. He tried to support Colette through what must have been an awful ordeal, but the situation taxed his already strained emotions almost beyond endurance.

On 20 November, at the height of his desolation, he wrote what he called 'a cry of distress & an appeal for help' to Ottoline. He found, he told Ottoline, that it was utterly impossible for him to do any work or even endure life, if he lived in London, '& I know I can't live alone – I must find some way of enduring life, or else give it up'. Could he spend four days a week in Garsington? 'I should be really happier,' he wrote, 'if I could get a man to live with me by the sea. And of course what I *really* want is a wife – but the world contains no one available in either capacity':

> The truth is I am worn out. I need looking after, & some one to see after the mechanism of life & leave my thoughts free for work. Since I quarrelled with Alys I have never found any one who would or could take me away for holidays when I am tired or take care of me & now I find without something of the kind I am no good.

About Colette, he was tactful and loyal. She had, he told Ottoline, 'behaved angelically', but 'the shock was so severe that I cannot get any rest except away from her – and the feeling that my work is suffering makes me horrid to her, & that makes us both miserable.' He wanted to spend two days a week with Colette and live elsewhere the rest of the time. 'I don't want emotions,' he told Ottoline. 'I want quiet companionship & good air & exercise.' Garsington, he wrote, 'is my only chance of escape'.

In an effort to exorcise some of the ghosts that haunted him, Russell decided to get rid of the studio flat in Fitzroy Street; it was, he wrote to Colette on 27 November, 'full of spectres'. In the same letter, he told Colette that he had had dinner with Vivien and – perhaps in another attempt at exorcism – had told her that he would not be seeing her 'for a considerable time'. Soon afterwards, while Colette stayed in London to have her abortion, Russell retired to Garsington to try and repair his frayed nerves. On 16 December, Colette wrote to say that the operation was over. A few days later, Russell, Colette and Clifford Allen left for a three-week Christmas holiday in Lynton, on the north Devonshire coast. In *After Ten Years*, Colette depicts the thatched cottage in which they stayed, and 'the snow lying deep upon the lonely places of the moor', and describes how Clifford Allen 'badly needed mending', having 'come out of prison with little more than half a lung'. Oddly, of Russell at Lynton, she says nothing. Russell is similarly reticent; in his *Autobiography* not only the Christmas holiday in Lynton, but the entire winter of 1918–19 is passed over in complete silence.

However, as this was the first time since he was released from prison that Russell had tried to spend more than a few days with Colette – convinced that if he spent longer with her he would be vindictively 'horrid' to her – and considering also that Allen was in an extremely frail physical condition, that Colette was recuperating from an abortion and that Russell was still suffering from the shock of Colette's pregnancy, it is not difficult to imagine the kind of atmosphere that prevailed at Lynton during those weeks.

The three of them left Devon on 14 January 1919, and Russell went straight back to Garsington, which was the nearest thing he had to a home during this time. It seems likely that Russell, despite what he had said in November, got in touch with Vivien Eliot immediately after his holiday, for a few days after he returned, he received a letter from Vivien saying that she disliked fading intimacies and wished to break with him completely.[1] This time, finally, she meant it. She would not even answer Russell's letters, and in the coming months Eliot himself had to intervene on her behalf to respond to Russell's increasingly insistent demands for what was left of his belongings at the Marlow house. 'It is not the case that Vivien "won't reply",' Eliot wrote to Russell on 3 February. 'I have taken the whole business of Marlow into my own hands, as she cannot have anything to do with this or with anything else that would interfere with the success of her doctor's treatment.' A week or so later, after Russell and

---

[1] This we learn from the typescript that Colette prepared of her correspondence with Russell (it is mentioned in a footnote to a letter dated 18 January 1919). The letter itself, like most of Vivien's correspondence with Russell, has not survived.

he had met to discuss getting rid of the Marlow house, Eliot wrote again, this time to explain how reluctant Vivien was to part with it:

> She worked very hard at it during all the spring and summer and put so much thought and so many hours into it. – The garden in particular is such a great joy and source of activity to her that now there are so few things she may do, as you know, I am sure it would be a mistake to deprive her of this interest. She is always thinking about the garden and even while tenants have been in the house has been several times to Marlow to look after it. It seems also that she has even now begun to look forward to happier times; she is expecting the return before the end of this year of her friend Lucy Thayer . . . She will be so much better when she has a companion, we are sure.

The solution seemed to be for the Eliots to take over the lease and to lessen the financial burden of it by sub-letting the house during the winter months. The business of moving Russell's belongings from Marlow to London, to Russell's evident annoyance, dragged on for months (rather than employ a removal firm, the Eliots seem to have brought everything back to London themselves, piece by piece over several journeys), and it was not until June that he received the last of them.

Russell was in a hurry to collect his possessions from Marlow in order to help furnish a flat in Battersea, 70 Overstrand Mansions, that he had agreed to share with Clifford Allen. Meanwhile, at Garsington, turning with renewed vigour to his work, Russell produced what he called a 'preliminary outline' of *The Analysis of Mind*. He felt so confident he had made good progress that he sent a telegram to Colette announcing that he had made an important discovery. Unfortunately, he did not specify what that discovery was, but in a letter a few days later, he went so far as to compare his mood of philosophical inspiration with that with which he had returned from Paris in 1900. Looking at the work he wrote in January 1919, it is hard to see what prompted such jubilation, and the comparisons with 1900 look like nothing more than wishful thinking, an expression, perhaps, of what Russell wanted to feel.

The chief difference between the 'preliminary outline' and the notes he wrote in prison is the emphasis it gives to the ability of the mind to form images. Behaviourism, notoriously, gives short shrift to mental images. In 'Psychology as the Behaviourist Views It', for example (one of the articles Russell read in prison), John B. Watson, the founder of behaviourism, says: 'I should like to throw out imagery altogether and attempt to show that practically all natural thought goes on in terms of sensory-motor processes in the larynx.' This was one aspect of the theory that Russell had no hesitation in rejecting. It was, he declared in one of his circular letters from prison, 'obviously rot'. Colette agreed: 'My mind is filled with images. (Poor Behaviourists if they don't have any.)' In his 'preliminary outline' of *The Analysis of Mind*, Russell restates his unequivocal rejection of this part of behaviouristic psychology: 'The denial of images is indefensible: they cannot be interpreted as actual small sensations, or as words.'

Far from denying images, Russell now made them central to his entire theory. His 'important discovery', it seems, was that images are the very foundation of the theory of meaning; they are, at one and the same time, both the content of beliefs and the origin of the meaning of words. Images, according to him, are 'copies' of sensations. We have the sensation of seeing a person called John, then some time in the future when we recall John by calling up an image of him, we are copying the sensation of seeing him. This image then 'means' John. The origin of the meaning of words, Russell maintains, is the replacement of images by words, so that, instead of using the image of John to mean John, we use the word 'John'.

An important innovation in this 'preliminary outline' is Russell's notion of an 'image-proposition'. An image of John without any hair, for example, might be the 'image-proposition' which in words would be expressed as 'John is bald'. In general, according to Russell: 'the image-proposition is the meaning of the word-proposition. But the image-proposition itself refers to something else, namely, the objective fact which makes the proposition true or false.' Of course, it is possible to entertain in our minds any number of images, only some of which will be 'image-propositions' that we actually believe (I can *imagine* John to be bald even when I know him to have blond hair), so what distinguishes those 'image-propositions' that are beliefs? Russell's answer to this is disappointingly vague: '*Belief*,' he says, 'is a specific sensation, which . . . has a certain relation to a present image or complex of images. An image believed has effects different from those of one not believed.' How one might characterise or recognise this 'sensation' he does not say.

Though his work was going well at Garsington, Russell had promised to share Clifford Allen's flat in London, and, so, on 17 February, he moved out of his cottage in Garsington and into Allen's flat in Overstrand Mansions. After only a few days, he decided to move back to Garsington. Allen was very ill and the flat became filled with anxious and sympathetic female colleagues from the NCF, competing with each other to look after him. 'There is a terrible lot of psychology and discomfort in the flat at present,' Russell wrote to Colette on 23 February, 'life here is unendurable for anybody of the male sex'. His work continued to prosper, he told her, 'every time I sit down to it, it goes better than I expect', and he was keen to get back to conditions more conducive to philosophical writing.

Upon his return to Garsington, he wrote up much of the new material in his 'preliminary outline' into a long paper for the Aristotelian Society meeting later in the year, called 'On Propositions: what they are and how they mean'. The paper is important as Russell's first published statement of his adherence to neutral monism, and his consequent rejection of his earlier theory of judgment. At the centre of the paper is Russell's endorsement of the behaviourists' general view of language as the acquisition of certain 'habits', together with his rejection of their denial of the obvious fact that we do form images to ourselves. Just as earlier he had attributed Bergson's elevation of intuition to what he supposed to be Bergson's extraordinary capacity to visualise, so now he attributed the behaviourists' denial of images to the opposite idiosyncrasy in Watson: 'Professor Watson, one must conclude, does not possess the faculty of visualising, and is unwilling to believe that others do.' In response to this denial, Russell presents the results of his own empirical research:

> If you try to persuade an ordinary uneducated person that she cannot call up a visual picture of a friend sitting in a chair, but can only use words describing what such an occurrence would be like, she will conclude that you are mad. (This statement is based upon experiment.)

Whether the 'ordinary uneducated person' was Colette or Ottoline, he does not say.

The paper goes on to give the theory of 'image-propositions' that he had developed the previous month, together with the following intriguing remark:

> The most important thing about a proposition is that, whether it consists of images or of words, it is, whenever it occurs, an actual fact, having a certain analogy of structure – to be further investigated – with the fact which makes it true or false.

Both these points – that a proposition is itself a fact and that it can represent another fact by virtue of 'a certain analogy of structure' – are associated more with Wittgenstein than with Russell. They are points upon which Wittgenstein lays great stress in *Tractatus Logico-Philosophicus*, which, though it had been written by the time Russell wrote 'On Propositions', Russell had not yet read. At the end of 'On Propositions', Russell spells out this idea of structural analogy that makes his theory sound even closer to what is now known as Wittgenstein's 'Picture Theory of Meaning':

> You have an image of A which is to the left of your image of B: this occurrence is an image-proposition. If A is to the left of B, the proposition is true: if A is not to the left of B, it is false.

There is, however, one crucial difference between the two theories. For Wittgenstein, it does not matter whether the images that make up the proposition are inside or outside a person's mind: physical (e.g. painted) images are just as propositional for him as 'mental' images. If Russell had laid more emphasis upon the structural analogy he invokes in these passages, it would surely have occurred to him that, as far as structure is concerned, it is not necessary to restrict his notion of an image-proposition to those images that are 'copies' of sensations. For Russell, however, it was important that there is a *causal* link between a word and its meaning, and a mental image seemed to him the only thing that could provide that connection: your image of John is causally connected with your seeing John, and thus so is your use of the word 'John'. Of course, given Russell's neutral monism, mental images are themselves also physical occurrences, but, for him, what that meant was that they are events that take place literally 'in the head'. This emphasis on causality in explaining the meaning of words is profoundly un-Wittgenstei-nian (Wittgenstein later ridiculed it by remarking that, if I pushed you and you fell over, your falling over would not be the *meaning* of my push).

On 4 March, Russell wrote to Colette telling her that he had finished 'On Propositions'. 'There is very good stuff in it,' he told her, 'but I am not satisfied with it, and shall probably re-write it.' By coincidence, Russell received a postcard from Wittgenstein just as he finished this, his most Wittgensteinian piece of work. 'I am prisoner in Italy since November,' Wittgenstein wrote, 'and hope I may communicate with you after a three years interruption. I have done lots of logical work which I am dying to let you know before publishing it.' The card was dated 9 February and written from the Italian prisoner-of-war camp at Monte Cassino, where Wittgenstein, along with thousands of other Austrian troops, was being held as bargaining material for the Italians in their demands for land previously held by the Habsburgs. It was addressed to Russell care of 'Dr A. N. Whitehead, University College, London' and seems to have reached Russell at Garsington on 2 March.

As he had last heard from Wittgenstein in 1916, and was convinced that he had been killed in the war, Russell was, of course, delighted to hear from him. 'Most thankful to hear you are still alive,' he replied. 'Please write on Logic, when possible. I hope it will not be long now before a talk will be possible. I too have much to say about philosophy etc.' The following day, he sent another card with a similar message, no doubt thinking that, if he sent two, he would increase the probability of getting one through. In fact, Wittgenstein received them both on 8 March. 'You can't imagine how glad I was to get your cards!' he replied, telling Russell that he had written a book in which 'I think I have solved our problems finally.' Three days later he was able to write at greater length about the book:

I've written a book called 'Logisch-Philosophische Abhandlung' containing all my work of the last six years. I believe I've solved all our problems finally. This may sound arrogant but I can't help believing it. I finished the book in August 1918 and two months after was made Prigioniere. I've got the manuscript here with me. I wish I could copy it out for you; but it's pretty long and I would have no safe way of sending it to you. In fact you would not understand it without a previous explanation as it's written in quite short remarks. (This of course means that *nobody* will understand it; although I believe, it's all as clear as crystal. But it upsets all our theory of truth, of classes, of numbers and all the rest.)

As Wittgenstein no doubt hoped and expected, Russell's curiosity was greatly aroused by this letter. He copied it out by hand, had it typed and several copies of it made. In addition, he wrote to the two most influential people he knew, John Maynard Keynes (who was at this time attending the peace negotiations in Paris) and George Trevelyan, asking whether permission might be obtained for Wittgenstein to 'communicate freely about logic' and even for him to come to England. The *Introduction to Mathematical Philosophy* had just been published, and Russell asked Keynes whether it might be possible to send it to Wittgenstein. Through Trevelyan, Wittgenstein was granted permission to receive books, and, through Keynes, he was able to send a copy of his manuscript to Russell. But securing the necessary permissions and contacts took time, and it was not until June and July that Wittgenstein and Russell were able to see the direction each other's philosophical thoughts had taken in the five years since they had been able to discuss philosophy together.

In the meantime, Russell had to prepare the series of eight lectures on 'The Analysis of Mind' that he had agreed to give at Dr Williams' Library in Gordon Square, starting on 6 May 1919. He prepared them during March and April after he had, finally, moved in with Clifford Allen at their flat in Overstrand Mansions. At the same time he wrote a great number of reviews of philosophical books for *The Nation* and *The Athenaeum*. The theme of many of these reviews was the inconsequential nature of philosophical thought. 'To anyone accustomed to observing men's hearts, rather than to classifying their desiccated systems,' he writes in a review on 21 April of *The Principles of Citizenship* by Henry Jones, 'it is obvious that the philosophy they adopt is an effect, not a cause – a product of temperament and opportunity, not an inspirer of their actions.' A person's philosophy no more causes their actions 'than the barometer causes the weather'. In assuming otherwise, Jones reveals himself to be a 'belated Victorian':

> The Victorians had many merits, and were in numberless ways our superiors. But they lacked the sense of truth, and could not distinguish between their own emotions and the constitution of the universe.

It is a lesson that philosophers are naturally reluctant to learn. In his review at about the same time of a book by Ralph Perry called *The Present Conflict of Ideals* (subtitled 'A Study of the Philosophical Background of the World War'), Russell writes mockingly: 'no philosophical professor is willing to believe that events in the great world have not been caused by the lectures of his academic predecessors.'

To an extent that is not made quite explicit in the reviews themselves, these strictures against the pretensions of philosophers are aimed at Russell's own earlier views. Nowhere is this more apparent than in his review for *The Athenaeum* of a book called *What is the Kingdom of Heaven?* by Arthur Clutton-Brock, in which he discusses the 'craving for certainty' that one finds in 'certain men and certain moods'. This, he writes, 'is part of the longing for security, which is one of the weaknesses into which we are led by timidity'. It follows (though he does not point this out) that his own motivation for becoming a philosopher – to find certain, indubitable knowledge – he now regards as no more than a sign of a psychological weakness. In particular, he ridicules in this review the 'mystic vision', the belief that one can see things 'without the distorting mists of the Ego'. Those who believe this, he says, are precisely those whose vision is most distorted by their ego: 'the characteristics which the mystic finds in all that is real are only the reflection of his own feeling.' The mystic vision is, he writes, in a characteristic piece of un-acknowledged autobiography, a distortion induced by love: 'A man in love is not supposed to be the best judge of the character of the object of his passion, and a mystic is a man in love with the universe.'

The conflict between this view and that expressed in Russell's earlier articles, 'The Free Man's Worship' and 'Mysticism and Logic', was identified by an *Athenaeum* reader called J. W. Harvey, who, in a strikingly perceptive letter to the journal, pointed out the contrast, commenting also on the distrust of intimacy that was evident in Russell's remarks. After noting the 'unyielding despair' expressed by 'The Free Man's Worship' and also that, emotionally, 'Mr Russell prefers to keep his distance, to maintain a chilling and cautious reserve', Harvey's letter goes on:

> Mr Russell cannot forgive the 'mystic' for refusing to maintain this feeling of aloofness, for welcoming intimacy with reality . . . The 'mystic's' fault is that he finds in the very heart of things a home and a friend. Mr Russell is like a visitor to a strange house, polite, modest, a stickler for the proprieties, unwilling to make any advances; and he observes with disapproval (and perhaps a touch of indignant envy) the indecorous behaviour of a fellow-guest who, by a wilful disregard of all the rules of etiquette, has somehow succeeded in establishing friendly relations with the household.

This image of the reserved and overly polite guest who avoids real contact with the household echoes Russell's own images of himself as an alien dropped from another planet, or a ghost unable to contact the living people around him, and shows a remarkably penetrating insight into the state of mind in which Russell's review of Clutton-Brock was written. Russell's view that philosophical opinions are the effects rather than the causes of emotional states might, as Harvey had seen, be applied to Russell himself, to see in his very determination to avoid emotional 'colouring' of his views a deep emotional despair. In his account of his alienation from the Armistice Day celebrations, Russell had written that he was conscious that 'human affection is to me at bottom an attempt to escape from the vain search for God.' But was it not also true that his search for God was motivated by his wish to escape the pain and the uncertain vicissitudes of human affection; that, like the overly polite guest, he was seeking to avoid the discomfort of real engagement with other human beings?

Privately, Russell's view of himself was similar to Harvey's, but in public, in his published reply to Harvey's letter, he gave little clue as to how close to home Harvey's characterisation of his emotional state was. Instead, he confined himself to pointing out that he allowed 'The Free Man's Worship' to be reprinted only with the 'express reservations' stated in the preface to *Mysticism and Logic*, and also that the despair expressed by it was the effect of philosophical opinions, not the cause of them. Presumably, he was hoping that nobody would notice the contradiction between this and the view he had stated just a few months earlier that 'to anyone accustomed to observing men's hearts . . . it is obvious that the philosophy they adopt is an effect, not a cause.'

With these reviews and the lectures, Russell's career as a freelance philosopher was getting off to a good start. 'I am glad to be no longer worried about money,' he wrote to Ottoline. ' "The Athenaeum" & "The Dial" suffice, with my lectures, so that I am by no means poor any longer.' He had earlier expressed difficulty in getting his lectures written, but, as the course went on, the writing of them got easier. On 14 June, he wrote to Colette that he had just finished the lecture for the following week and reported it as being 'the best yet . . . I wish you had been willing to hear it all – it is much easier to understand than any of the others.' The lectures, for the most part, were an elaboration of the ideas of 'On Propositions' and incorporated much of the text of that article. The lectures in turn were later incorporated into his book *The Analysis of Mind*, of which they make up about half.

While he was giving these lectures Russell's affair with Vivien was, at last, brought to its final close with an encounter that, as described by Vivien to Ottoline (with whom she had become great friends) in a letter written on 4 June, seems an appropriately odd end to what had been throughout a strange and inexplicable relationship:

I am amused by your description of Bertie's weekend at Garsington. He came straight from there to this flat [18 Crawford Mansions], in the early hours of a Monday morning to fetch away another instalment of possessions I had fetched from Marlow. He seemed dreadfully out of temper. Unfortunately I was not dressed, so had to shout to him from the bathroom, as cheerfully as I could. But the response was painful. I was sorry, really, I had asked him to come to tea when he fetched them, and I had come up from Marlow specially. I thought we might have talked a little and come to, at any rate, amicable relations. But it is no good. I will make no more attempts at all. But it is strange how one does miss him! Isn't it hard to put him *quite* out of one's mind?

A few days before his last lecture, Russell received another letter from Wittgenstein, who, still in the Italian prisoner-of-war camp, had by now received Russell's *Introduction to Mathematical Philosophy*. He was not entirely pleased with it. 'I should never have believed', he wrote, 'that the stuff I dictated to Moore in Norway six years ago would have passed over you so completely without trace . . . I'm now afraid that it might be very difficult for me to reach any understanding with you. And the small remaining hope that my manuscript might mean something to you has completely vanished.' He had, nevertheless, via Keynes, sent the manuscript to Russell. 'If you attach any importance whatsoever to understanding the thing,' he told Russell, 'and if you can manage to arrange a meeting with me, then please do so.' Otherwise Russell was to send it by a safe route to Vienna. It was the only corrected copy in existence and Wittgenstein wanted more than ever, after reading Russell's work, to see it in print:

It's galling to have to lug the completed work round in captivity and to see how nonsense has a clear field outside! And it's equally galling to think that no one will understand it even if it does get printed!

Considering that, in this letter, he was: (a) being ticked off for failing to understand Wittgenstein's previous work; (b) told that his own philosophical work was 'nonsense'; and (c) informed in advance that his attempts to understand Wittgenstein's current work would almost certainly be fruitless, Russell responded to it with remarkable forbearance. 'It is true', he admitted, 'that what you dictated to Moore was not intelligible to me, and that he would give me no help.' It was also probably true that Russell would not be able to understand Wittgenstein's manuscript until he could discuss it with him. But Wittgenstein was not to be discouraged:

Throughout the war I did not think about philosophy, until, last summer, I found myself in prison, and beguiled my leisure by writing a popular textbook, which was all I could do under the circumstances. Now I am back at philosophy, and more in the mood to understand.

The manuscript had not yet reached Russell, but he promised to read it the moment it did and to return it: 'Don't be discouraged – you will be understood in the end.'

2. DORA

On the same day that he wrote this letter, Russell's interest was aroused by a young woman called Dora Black who came to tea with him at Overstrand Mansions. Dora was unlike any of his previous lovers. Striking rather than beautiful, she was intellectually self-confident and defiantly contemptuous of conventional respectability. In 1915 she had graduated with a First in Modern Languages from Girton and gone on to University College, London, to pursue postgraduate work on eighteenth-century French literature. She was a close friend of Dorothy Wrinch, and had first met Russell in June 1917, when, together with Dorothy and Jean Nicod, she went on a weekend walking trip with Russell in Surrey. They had spent the night in a small pub called The White Horse in Shere before calling in on George Trevelyan for lunch. As a young radical intellectual opposed to the war, Dora had hero-worshipped Russell from afar for many years. Meeting him face-to-face, she found him 'enchantingly ugly'. He in turn was struck by the answer she gave when, sitting by candlelight in The White Horse, the conversation turned to the question of what they most desired in the world. Jean Nicod and Dorothy Wrinch gave high-minded intellectual answers, but when Dora's turn came, she said simply that all she wanted was to marry and have children. 'Until that moment', Russell wrote, 'I had supposed that no clever young woman would confess to so simple a desire, and I concluded that she must possess exceptional sincerity.'

Soon after this first meeting, Dora had left for the United States with her father, who worked for the Admiralty and was appointed to head a special mission to work with the American Government in securing the safe passage of oil across the Atlantic. On the way to America, Dora lost her virginity to a captain of the Merchant Navy 'on the top deck and a folded heap of sailcloth, under a bright moon and scudding clouds'. When she returned, Dora resumed her studies in London, where she lived in a flat in Cheyne Walk, Chelsea, and began an affair with a Belgian artist called Marcel, 'the true bohemian type, corduroy jacket, flowing tie, broad-brimmed black hat, beard and longish hair'. In the autumn of 1918, Dora took up a Fellowship at Girton, but continued to spend her vacations in London, this time in a flat in John Street not far from the British Museum, where she did most of her research.

On 7 June 1919, Dora – by now an assured and self-possessed twenty-five-year-old – wrote to Russell from Cambridge to ask him about finding someone to give a course of lectures in philosophy at Morley College for Working Men and Women, with which, through her parents, Dora had a connection. Did he know anyone suitable? Would he even do it himself, or was that too much to ask? A few weeks later, after the Cambridge term had finished and Dora was back in London, Russell invited her for tea at Overstrand Mansions. The ostensible purpose was to discuss the lectures, but instead they resumed their discussion of two years previously, Dora declaring her disapproval of conventional and legal marriage and her belief in free love. Russell asked her what should be done about children, to which she replied that they were the concern of the mother; fathers should have no rights at all over them. 'Well,' said Russell, 'whoever I have children with, it won't be you!'

As Russell's lecture course at Gordon Square drew towards its close, he still longed to spend time by the sea, and persuaded J. E. Littlewood, the Cambridge mathematician, to join him in renting a large, five-bedroomed farmhouse in Lulworth for the three months of the summer, starting on 24 June, the date of his last lecture. His plan was to travel to Dorset immediately afterwards. As the day approached, urged on perhaps by his hopes for a romantic relationship with Dora, he seems to have made some effort to break finally with Colette. His jealousy of her relations with other men had in recent weeks been compounded still further by her apparent sexual indifference to him. 'Do you think the day will come when you will allow me to show passionate love once more?' he wrote to her on 14 June. 'You said the other day that you didn't know how to repulse people, but you always knew how to repulse me.'

On the day before he left for Dorset (and the day after he and Dora had discussed marriage and children over tea at Overstrand Mansions), he wrote Colette what was evidently intended to be a goodbye letter. 'One wants in love', he told her, 'a sense of nearness in the impersonal things one cares for, so that there is more than pleasure; one longs for the sense of comradeship that relieves loneliness':

It seems to me that we have drifted into having entirely separate interests, so that we only meet across a gulf, in a way that has not much depth or reality. I cannot bear the gradual fading of what has been wonderful, & I would rather end while memories are unspoilt.

'The only thing that *really* moves me to break', he wrote the following day, 'is the feeling that your love has grown dim. Without you, life will be empty, cold & grey – I shall say farewell to passion & colour & joy – it is the end of my whole world . . . I hope for no new joy, & renounce the search.' This last remark (if not the whole letter) was quite untrue. That very evening, Russell was busily continuing 'the search' and, no doubt, hoping for new joy, when, after his final lecture, he took Dora out to dinner again and invited her to come to Lulworth 'for a long visit'. Dora was flattered and somewhat taken aback. 'Dear Bertie,' she wrote later that night – and the familiar form of address still seemed to her 'terribly disrespectful' – 'I should thank you for a delightful evening . . . And I will certainly come to Lulworth, but I don't know if I shall be able to stay so long.'

The next day, Russell set off for Lulworth, looking forward to being by the sea, to getting on with *The Analysis of Mind* and, later in the summer, to being joined by Dora. Colette, however, was not to be shrugged off so easily. On 26 June, his first morning at Lulworth, Russell received a telegram from her saying: 'Will be with you ten o'clock tonight with Allen.' She was as good as her word, and she and Russell spent an ecstatic night together. 'It was all quite wonderful from the first moment to the last,' he wrote to her after she left:

It has absolutely wiped out all that had happened since last September . . . Now, my dear, dear love, we must begin a new life . . . the only thing that ever makes me cold & cruel is when I feel not wanted . . . Apart from you I can feel nothing that goes deep, except despair . . . Do not let us lose each other again my Heart's Comrade – it is a very dark world without you.

Though apparently won back to Colette, Russell made no attempt to put off Dora, who was now writing to him saying how much she was looking forward to coming to Lulworth. 'The parting with Colette did not come off' was how he put it in a letter to Ottoline on 2 July, 'she wanted to try again, so I agreed. So I shall be seeing her again some time soon. I don't know what will come of it.'

Russell was due in London on 11 July to read 'On Propositions' to the joint session of the Aristotelian Society and the Mind Association. In the meantime, he wrote to Colette every day – sometimes twice a day – urging her to use the opportunity to spend some time with him in London, and then to take a week's holiday together in Ashford (the scene of their happiest time together in August 1917). 'I long to be with you,' he wrote on 4 July. 'I *do* want you – we *must* be together now, or the new feeling that has come will waste itself.' He offered to stay in London for a week, if she could not come to Ashford, provided they could really be together in his flat: 'I simply *must* be with you, Beloved . . . I can't tell you how I *long* to be with you. Do *please* come to Ashford if you *possibly* can. We must have a time to make new things solid – probably our whole future depends upon it.'

Colette, at this time, was undergoing one of her periodic bouts of 'work despair' when good parts were not coming her way, and she was reluctant to leave London for fear of missing the all-important call. According to *After Ten Years*, she was extremely depressed during this period, even suicidal: 'Nothing on earth is more demoralising than the life of an out of work actress in London.' The only thing that kept her going was her weekly lunch with her friend Dennis Bradley, who 'pumped self-confidence into me: self-protectiveness, guts, fight. He said he believed in me – and he helped me believe in myself.' In such a state, she had little energy to give Russell, who, she knew, had nothing but disapproval and contempt for her professional life. She ignored many of Russell's letters, leading him to wonder if they had reached her. On 6 July, he wrote that her despair about her work had touched his heart and that he wanted to help, 'but I have felt helpless about it, as it made you hide away from me & refuse the love I wanted to give.' He clearly had little feeling for her mood. More urgent in his mind than her need for work was his need to be with her, to make love to her:

> When I love, I want to be with the person I love, & times of absence are a constant pain the whole time. I know that my nature makes it *impossible* for me, however hard I try, to go on long giving *active* love to a person I don't see a great deal of & have easy sex relations with. Unless we can be a great deal completely together, things will never long be satisfactory. It is as necessary to me as other men are to you, & it is no use to try to get round it . . . unless we can be together now, it is put off very likely till Christmas – & by that time, if it is put off till then, all the new love will have evaporated, & it may be impossible to make a new beginning . . . only being with you can reassure me. Till we are together old impressions will linger. The time since I came out of prison has been long, & your one night here was brief. You must, please, be patient with me & understand that I have lived in hell these last months, & that I am a little wary of being tempted to unbuckle my armour, for fear of having all the pain over again . . . Don't please think I don't sympathise with all you feel about work – I *really* do – but if going on loving you is to mean long times of misery with only brief moments of happiness, you cannot wonder that I hesitate, & sometimes feel it would be better to kill feeling by a great effort . . . it is dreadful that you are in such despair – Do tell me how to make it easier for you – & try to think how you can make it easier for me.

The following day, he continued the plea: 'My dear one, *please* try to restore my belief that business is possible between us.' Again and again, he urged her to make time free to spend with him when he came to London on 10 July. 'I thought we had fixed to have a month together,' he wrote on 8 July, '& I was hurt that even at this time you had not enough wish to be with me to give up the search for work for the moment.' Nevertheless, he insisted, 'we will be happy when we meet, even if it is only for 2 nights.'

In the event, after he gave his paper in London on 11 July, he went, not to Colette's flat, but to Dora's. During the week that Russell was writing these impassioned and anguished pleas to Colette to save their relationship, Dora was writing to him about her philosophy of sexual relations. 'I am all for triviality in sex,' she wrote on 5 July. 'I want to treat it – with all due reverence – as a need to be satisfied now & then as it presents itself, like hunger & thirst.' To Russell, this no doubt sounded – as it was perhaps intended to sound – like a very welcome invitation.

In her autobiography, *The Tamarisk Tree*, Dora gives a severely misleading impression of what led Russell to come to her on 11 July. Without mentioning the fact that she had been invited – and had accepted the invitation – to Lulworth even before Russell went there, she describes their correspondence during his first two weeks there. Her letters to him in Lulworth, she says, 'were as learned as I knew how to make them', whereas his were jolly nonsense about the lazy and enjoyable life he was living by the sea. 'This cannot have gone on for more than two weeks or so,' she writes, 'when there came a ring of my front door bell':

> Bertie was in my flat . . . 'I had some business to do in town. I am getting no work done. Can you catch the twelve-thirty on Monday?'
> 'Am I to understand that this is –?' He nodded.
> 'But I understood that you already are in love with a lady?'
> He assured me that the affair was over, it had definitely come to an end. I did not know what to say but gave a half-promise that I would catch the train.

In fact, the ring of her door bell could not possibly have come as the surprise she presents it as being, for she had done everything in her control to make it happen. When Russell told her that he would be in London from 10 to 14 July, she wrote to him saying that she would be free for those days, that she was not going away for the weekend, and giving him very detailed instructions of her movements during the day: when she would be at lunch, what time she had a meeting in the evening, and so on. She had arranged to have tea that afternoon with someone, she said, but that could be cut. And if Russell came to find that she was not in, he could always leave a message with the people who worked in the office below her flat. As little was left to chance as possible.

When Russell returned to Lulworth the following Monday, Dora went with him. She was there for the next week, a time remembered by both as one of enchantment and delight. In the mornings, they worked, then they had what Dora describes as a 'student's lunch' of bread and cheese, and in the afternoons they went for walks, or boating trips, or bathed in the sea. 'Bertie and I spent much time apart from the company,' Dora recalls, 'he would hire a boat, from which we would, at sufficient distance from the shore, dive naked; we walked the cliffs talking endlessly.' That she and Russell had become lovers was scarcely concealed from either Littlewood or their guests. When Robert Trevelyan stayed, she remembers, he and Russell 'would exchange sly digs at one another':

'This house is full of noises,' said Bob, no doubt aware of the meaning of
footfalls and doors surreptitiously opened and closed at night.

'Don't you wear ear-stoppers, Bob?' asked Bertie, equally sly and equally
aware.

'Dora and I became lovers when she came to Lulworth,' Russell wrote, 'and
the parts of the summer during which she was there were extraordinarily
delightful.' The chief thing that attracted him to Dora, he implies, was her
evident willingness, unlike Colette, to have children. 'From the first', he
writes, 'we used no precautions.' Stopping just short of saying that he fell in
love with Dora, he says: 'Bathing by moonlight, or running with bare feet on
the dewy grass, she won my imagination as completely as on her serious side
she appealed to my desire for parenthood and my sense of social responsibility.'

And yet, during the week that Dora was with him in Lulworth, Russell
wrote daily to Colette, telling her that he loved her 'more than ever before'
and that he felt he could utterly trust her love, just as she could trust his.
About Dora, he wrote: 'She is nice, but I am very doubtful whether I shall
have an affair with her – it is difficult to take any real interest in people who
do not touch the flame in one.' When Colette telegraphed that she would
come on 20 July, Russell told Dora she had to return to London. In her
autobiography, Dora describes how Russell came to see her, 'very much
embarrassed', with Colette's telegram in his hand to tell her why she must
leave. 'So', she writes, 'it had only been an amusing summer interlude. I
packed up and went.' Remembering the occasion in a letter to Russell six
months after the event, she told him: 'I have never got over the humiliation
of being sent back to town to make room for her the first week I loved you.'

To Colette, Russell responded to the news that she would be arriving with
unfettered joy. 'It will be *divine* to be with you here in all this wonderful
beauty,' he wrote, three days before she arrived. 'Saturday I shall feel your
arms about me & all the choirs of heaven will sing in my heart.' With a
strange sort of symmetry, while Colette was with Russell in Lulworth, he and
Dora exchanged passionate love letters. On the day she arrived back in
London, Dora wrote: 'I cannot tell you at all what I have felt all this week, I
am numb with so much joy . . . I feel my roots have gone down into you &
that I really have a place in you . . . already you have far more of me than
anybody has ever had.' She wanted to 'start squarely' with Russell and, even
though in Lulworth he had told her that he preferred not to hear things that
might cause him jealousy, she insisted on writing to him about Marcel, the
Belgian painter, about how, when she sat for her portrait to be painted, 'he
made passionate love to me, & has done so many times since & made me very
happy . . . I hope that you will forgive me, & believe that you need not be
unhappy at all. I cannot swear you oaths, any more than you can to me, but
I do not find it easy to counterfeit passion or love & there has been no
counterfeit at all with you.'

A few days later, she wrote that she was counting the days until she could
come to Lulworth again: 'I love you most tremendously, & quite absurdly.'

Colette had left by now, and Dora was to arrive on 6 August. During the week before she came, Russell seems to have written daily love letters to both of them. Only those to Colette have survived, but it is clear from Dora's letters to him what his letters to her were like. 'My darling,' Dora wrote on 28 July, 'I simply delight to hear that you love me & love me & love me, & think of me often.' The next day, he was writing to Colette: 'One little word of love . . . to tell you that my heart is with you more fully & deeply than ever before.' The most natural interpretation of his feelings at this time is that he was still deeply in love with Colette, but feared that he was losing her to the theatre and so was reluctant to put out the fire he had started in his relations with Dora.

In his relationship with Colette, Russell desperately wanted to return to the life he had shared with her before she went to Blackpool in the September of 1917. Something had gone out of his life during the crisis over Colette's affair with Maurice Elvey, and he wanted it back so much that he was willing time and again to persuade himself that it was so. 'I *believe* in your love as I have not done since Blackpool,' he wrote to her on 31 July, 'for me there is a wholly new bond, indissoluble in a way it never was before . . . No other human being, I know, will ever enter that region in me in which you live – it is sacred to you, apart from all possibility of violation by others. Others may fill in the times when we cannot be together, to make me not too impatient – but the real life of my spirit is actually bound up in you.' He started trying to find some way of spending two nights with Colette in London, some business that would necessitate his having to be in town.

At the beginning of August, though, came news that Colette had at last landed a major role. She was to appear in Lewis Casson's production of *The Trojan Women*, playing Helen alongside Sybil Thorndike as Hecuba. Colette, naturally, was deliriously happy. For Russell, though he stressed in his letters how happy he was for her, the news was rather dreadful, and it was not long before he started to imagine her (with perhaps good reason) to be passionately in love with Lewis Casson.

Dora, meanwhile, was writing him long letters analysing her love for him and trying to articulate what she wanted both from her relationship with Russell and from life itself. She began to worry that she had fallen too deeply in love for her own good:

I have so much of the feminine instinct to give myself & serve & worship that I get shamed of it, & proud & afraid of being despised . . . I think it right for women to fight it because it is the biggest obstacle to their liberty, just as men's possessive instinct is the biggest obstacle to *their* civilisation . . . Women need I think to enlarge their generosity & extend it to each other & bring it to bear in politics etc. instead of locking it all up in love for some one man, who is very often more commonplace than his wife. (28 July)

I may come to love you infinitely more than myself . . . to love like that is, I think, my biggest instinctive need; I think, if I am deadly honest, it is

much bigger than any love I have for ideas . . . I find that not only can I not take you lightly (that was soon certain), but I can't keep anything at all. I have got to plunge the whole of myself into you & pick up a new self . . . As for whether *that* self will be able or want to do my present work, or make for university professorship, Lord knows – I don't really care, not at bottom.
(2 August)

Russell, perhaps trying to pull back a little, evidently wrote to her saying that he had no wish to interfere with her life. Dora had planned to go to Paris in the autumn of 1919 to continue her studies in French eighteenth-century literature, and no doubt Russell did not wish to be responsible for her deciding to abandon the plan. Nevertheless, at this stage, the idea that he wished not to interfere with her life struck Dora as quite absurd. It is, she wrote on 3 August, 'like a game of consequences':

in which a WISE but WICKED
Philosopher
meets a
Beautiful & bountiful
Bluestocking
in her Studienzimmer in Bloomsbury [here, Dora interrupted the letter to
   argue that Holborn is in Bloomsbury]
He said to her. 'My dear, I don't want to interfere with your life, but I
   want everything. Elope with me the day after tomorrow.'
She said. '*Mon Dieu.*'
So they went. He threw her down cliffs & out of boats, but *she* pulled his
   hair.
He said: 'I don't want to interfere with your life but let us do this every
   vacation.'
She said: 'I must go to Paris.'
The consequence was: they went back to Lulworth & the world said . . .
But fortunately the world was not asked for its opinion.

A few days later, Dora travelled down to Lulworth and remained there for the rest of August.

Russell's ostensible purpose in spending the summer in Lulworth was to continue working on his philosophy, but so far he had done very little. Now he settled down to work, not however on *The Analysis of Mind*, but on a close study of the manuscript Wittgenstein had sent him, then called 'Logisch-Philosophische Abhandlung' but now known as *Tractatus Logico-Philosophicus*. On 13 August, he wrote to Wittgenstein, saying that he had 'read your book twice carefully':

I am convinced you are right in your main contention, that logical props are tautologies . . . *I am sure you are right in thinking the book of first-class importance.* But in places it is obscure through brevity. I have a most intense desire to see you, to talk it over, as well as simply because I want to see you.

To his letter, Russell appended a list of detailed questions. Broadly speaking, these fell into two distinct areas: psychology and mathematics. Russell was troubled by the fact that Wittgenstein seemed so little concerned in his manuscript with the kind of mathematical logic that Russell considered central to his 'mathematical philosophy'. 'The theory of classes', Wittgenstein had written, 'is completely superfluous in mathematics.' Russell could scarcely believe he meant it. 'If you said that classes were superfluous in *logic*,' he told Wittgenstein, 'I would imagine that I understood you, by supposing a distinction between logic and mathematics: but when you say they are unnecessary in *mathematics* I am puzzled.' On psychological matters, he and Wittgenstein had been thinking along rather similar lines. Russell was struck by Wittgenstein's remark: 'The logical picture of facts is a thought' – it was, indeed, close to the point he had emphasised in 'On Propositions' that a fact and an 'image-proposition' that represented it had to have a similarity of structure. But, he told Wittgenstein, a thought (an image-proposition) is itself a fact; what are *its* constituents?

In his reply, whether talking generally about the manuscript or specifically about Russell's questions, Wittgenstein emphasised that the central idea of his book was *not* that logical propositions were tautologies. This was only a 'corollary' to the main point:

The main point is the theory of what can be expressed (gesagt) by prop[osition]s – i.e. by language – (and, which comes to the same, what can be *thought*) and what can not be expressed by prop[osition]s, but only shown (gezeigt); which, I believe, is the cardinal problem of philosophy.

With regard to thoughts, he did not know what their constituents were, he knew only that they had to have constituents and that they had to correspond to the words of a language. *How* a thought corresponded to a fact was, for him, irrelevant – it 'would be a matter of psychology to find out'. So much for Russell's central problem in both 'On Propositions' and *The Analysis of Mind*.

At the end of August, Dora moved back to London, perhaps to make way for another visit from Colette. From London, Dora wrote again about the danger she felt that in her love for Russell she might lose herself, her integrity: 'I have rather an affection for Dora Winifred Black, it always interests me to see what she, just herself, will do next, & I don't want her swallowed up – even for you.' When she returned to spend September in Lulworth, Russell added to those fears of being swallowed up by asking her if she would consider marrying him, if he got a divorce. To his amazement, she burst into tears at the idea, 'feeling, I think', he writes in his *Autobiography*, 'that it meant the end of independence and light-heartedness'. Russell evidently found Dora's fears hard to understand. For someone who had spent his entire life feeling unable to escape the hard shell, the prison, of his self, it was apparently difficult to understand that there are people who have to strive hard to *retain* their separate identity, whose natural inclination is to merge, as it were, with those around them.

That Russell should have had difficulty comprehending Dora in this way is understandable. But, on another occasion, when he pressed Dora to marry him, he resorted to an appeal that was indefensibly crass: did she not, he argued, want to be a countess? Angered by this extraordinary display of insensitivity, Dora begged him to drop the subject. In explaining his persistence, Russell later wrote that 'the feeling we had for each other seemed to have that kind of stability that made any less serious relation impossible.' But, in other places, it emerges that what was uppermost in his mind was his desire, not only for children, but for *legitimate* children. The thought that she would one day be a countess might have meant nothing to Dora, but the thought that his son might one day be an earl meant a great deal to Russell. For the time being, however, he agreed to drop the subject.

During the last few weeks of their time at Lulworth, conversation was dominated by Einstein's theory of relativity. The famous expedition to measure the bending of light caused by an eclipse had, in September, reached a preliminary verdict that the measurement confirmed Einstein's theory. Within a few months, the news would reach the front pages of newspapers around the world and Einstein's status as a worldwide celebrity would be established. For the time being, however, it was a secret shared by a few. The Cambridge astronomer Arthur Eddington, who was on the expedition, sent a telegram to Littlewood, letting him know the preliminary result.

Another event of those last few weeks of September that cast its shadow over Lulworth was less happy. For over a year, Russell had been in negotiation with Philip Jourdain over payment for the 'Lectures on Logical Atomism' that Jourdain had published in *The Monist*. Russell was determined not to let the matter drop and wrote repeatedly demanding his fee. Jourdain, for his part, was less concerned with paying Russell his fee than with getting Russell's acceptance of a 'proof' he claimed to have of the Multiplicative Axiom. Russell, who had seen several versions of this alleged proof and – in common with everybody else who had checked them – had come to the conclusion they were invalid, was scarcely very interested in keeping the matter alive. On 11 September, however, he received a letter from Laura Jourdain, saying: 'My husband cannot attend to your letter [asking again for payment] because he is dangerously ill with heart attacks . . . Neither you nor Dr Whitehead have taken any trouble about my husband's own serious work so I do not quite see the force of your complaint.'

Jourdain was dying, and on his deathbed all he could think of was getting acceptance of his proof. On 23 September, Littlewood, accompanied by Dorothy Wrinch, set off from Dorset to Jourdain's home in Fleet in the neighbouring county of Hampshire to investigate the proof. As usual, he considered it fallacious, and, though he was hesitant to say so in the circumstances, Jourdain deduced his verdict from his demeanour. The following day, Jourdain wrote to Dorothy Wrinch, saying that he would like to see Russell, 'if he thinks there is any chance of agreeing . . . but I do not want to distress him should he think it necessary for my peace of mind to agree, where he does not really do so, because I am somewhere near the end of my tether.' Russell immediately sent a telegram, offering to come, but on 26 September, he received another letter from Laura Jourdain:

Dear Mr Russell,
   Your telegram came just too late to arrange for Philip to see you. He is now quite unable to talk or see anyone, but just lies in a semi-conscious state. Why didn't you make an effort to come a little sooner? You have made him so unhappy by your inability to see his well-ordering.[2] You are the only person he wanted to see and talk with months ago.

Five days later, Jourdain was dead.
   At the end of September, Russell moved back to London, his three months in Dorset having produced little philosophical writing and his personal affairs having become more entangled than ever. 'I allowed the summer to go by in almost complete idleness,' he wrote to Dora, 'because I was in love and had not the strength of will to devote myself seriously to work.' Of course, it was not just that he was in love, but that he was simultaneously in love with two people. On 8 October, in an effort to clarify his thoughts on the subject, he wrote an analysis of the situation. 'It is clear', he wrote, 'that unless, before very long, I decide between Dora and Colette, they will both find the strain intolerable and throw me over.' Weighing up the pros and cons on either side, he decided that: 'For myself and my work, if I can achieve it, the best solution would be to marry Dora and abandon Colette':

This would produce a life which would probably be happy, and without so much nervous strain as to make creative work difficult. Moreover it would be a life in which one could build things for future years, and cease to think always about personal affairs. The earning of money involved would absorb less energy than the present emotional tension.

The doubt was 'whether I could break with Colette without killing something vital in myself, or whether I could avoid regrets that would poison my relations with Dora'.
   Dora, he thought, could not be expected to sacrifice work while he remained absorbed in Colette: 'the life I offer her in that case is not one in which the instinctive satisfaction is sufficiently complete to outweigh the loss in liberty and ambition.' For Colette: 'if I break with her, the outlook is very bad; it will kill the best in her.' In any case:

The fundamental fact remains that I love Colette too much to be able to face life without her. If I had finally broken with her, I might find

---

[2] A proof of the Multiplicative Axiom amounts to the same thing as a so-called 'well-ordering' of the transfinite cardinal numbers.

absolutely everything dust and ashes, and might be driven ultimately to suicide.

The conclusion was: 'At present I find it impossible to reach any decision.'

The only point on which Russell's grasp of the situation seemed insecure was in his apparent conviction that, if he broke with Colette, Dora would accept 'the loss of liberty and ambition' as an acceptable price to pay for the 'instinctive satisfaction' of marriage and children. As Dora wrote to explain to him, the question for her, was 'how to fit you into my life without destroying all that I now am!'

I do dread becoming the submissive & adoring female that the following of my instinct with you would produce . . . I think too it would become irksome to you, though you might enjoy it awfully for a time.

'I feel fiery moral indignation against you for your attitude to women', she told him in another letter. 'I will *not* be your plaything or even a sofa-cushion, – if I cannot be your comrade then it is no use loving you at all.' As for the children Russell so ardently desired: 'you know, those hypothetical infants will perhaps hurl rotten apples through the window when you are trying to philosophise. I shan't restrain them, for such is the nature of infants, & anyway, it will serve you right!'

On 22 October, Dora left for Paris, and the debate between her and Russell as to what their marriage would be like and, indeed, whether they should get married at all, was continued in an almost daily exchange of long, passionate and argumentative letters. Before she left, she went with him to the first of his series of lectures at Morley College on 'The Analysis of Mind'. It was her job to present him to the students. She would, she threatened him, begin her introductory speech: 'The last of our Eminent Victorians, he has yet managed in some slight degree to overcome the prejudices of his Age.' During the autumn, Russell gave the same set of eight lectures twice on successive days: on Mondays at Dr Williams' Library in Gordon Square and on Tuesdays at Morley College. In the spring of 1920, he was to give another course of eight lectures at both places. Together, the sixteen lectures he gave in 1919–20 became, after some rewriting, what is now *The Analysis of Mind*, which was not, however, published until the summer of 1921.

In November, it began to look as though these lecture courses at Gordon Square and Morley College might be Russell's last as a freelance lecturer. Now that the younger Fellows of Trinity were back from the war, G. H. Hardy's campaign to get Russell reinstated was bearing fruit. In a letter dated 28 November 1919, a letter to the Master of Trinity asking for Russell to be appointed to a lectureship was signed by twenty-seven Fellows. 'Mr Russell has reached an age at which it is desirable both on personal and on intellectual grounds that he should have a settled position,' it said, 'and it would be unfortunate if he were subjected to continual uncertainty regarding his future.' The letter produced its desired effect and at a meeting of the College Council, held on the same day that the letter was signed, it was agreed that a five-year lectureship in Logic and the Principles of Mathematics, starting from July 1920, should be offered to Russell.

There remained the question of whether Russell *wanted* to come back. In prison, he had declared vehemently that he would never again accept an official position. Now, after a year of the uncertainties and precariousness that is the lot of a freelance writer, he was less sure. 'It is possible I may go back to Cambridge,' he wrote to Lucy Donnelly, when he knew the offer would be made, 'tho' probably not for long. I don't think I could stand the academic atmosphere now, having tasted freedom and the joys of a dangerous life.' In the event, he took nearly two months to decide, and it was not until 16 January 1920 that he formally accepted.

Russell was really not sure any longer that an academic career would suit him. Despite its precariousness, the life of a freelance writer had many advantages, chief among which was that it enabled Russell to be more or less indifferent to respectable opinion, free from the kind of anxiety he had felt in 1911, when he began his affair with Ottoline, about whether they had been seen out together and what was being said about his affairs in the Senior Common Rooms. Besides, for the time being at least, he was making more money as a freelance writer than he would as an academic. The habits he had acquired in producing an editorial for *The Tribunal* every week were now proving invaluable, and he was able to write an article or a review for *The Athenaeum* almost every week without it seriously disturbing his other work.

Russell's combination of a thorough grounding in mathematics and science, a cultivated prose style and a ready acceptance of the tyranny of deadlines ensured a constant demand for his services as a journalist. It was an extremely rare combination, and one, too, that was peculiarly well-suited to the times. The announcement by the Royal Society on 6 November that Einstein's theory of relativity had been confirmed by the observations of the expedition to Brazil and Africa to study the May eclipse was done in a way calculated to catch the popular imagination. J. J. Thomson, the President of the Society, pronounced the findings 'the most important result obtained in connection with the theory of gravitation since Newton's day', and the following morning *The Times* ran the story under the headline: 'Revolution in Science. New Theory of the Universe'.

Suddenly, everybody wanted to know what this momentously important new theory was all about, and the features editors of every respectable newspaper and magazine were looking around for somebody with both the knowledge and the expository skills necessary to explain it. Russell had both, and a lucrative sideline as a populariser of science was launched when, less than a week after the sensational announcement, he published an article in *The Athenaeum* on 'Einstein's Theory of Gravitation'. With masterly compression, and with a sure grasp of what his audience wanted to know, Russell provided in the space of a short article a brief but genuinely informative account of the theory, an explanation of the extent to which it had been confirmed by observation, and some arresting comments on its philosophical and cultural importance. It was an impressive piece of journalism and led almost immediately to his being commissioned by *The English Review* to write a much longer – and better paid – article for their January 1920 issue.

As a further boon to his career as a journalist, Russell was acquiring great skill in – and a more or less shameless attitude towards – saying the same thing in many different ways and using the same piece of writing in many different contexts. In the summer of 1919, for example, he published no fewer than three, slightly different, reviews of the same book, C. E. M. Joad's *Essays in Common Sense Philosophy*, the first for the *Daily Herald*, the second for *The Athenaeum* and the third for *The Nation*. He was even able to recycle some of the philosophy he was writing: the third lecture in the course he was giving on 'The Analysis of Mind', after being delivered on successive days in October at Dr Williams' Library and Morley College, was then sold to *The Athenaeum* as a series of three articles, published in successive issues in December, on 'The Anatomy of Desire'. It now forms Chapter III, 'Desire and Feeling', of *The Analysis of Mind*.

There were dangers in this approach, of course. In tailoring his philosophical writing to the needs of his journalism, Russell ran the risk of being tempted to sacrifice rigour, depth and academic integrity for the sake of producing something that was 'a good read'. If one compares 'On Propositions' to the 'Desire and Feeling' chapter of *The Analysis of Mind*, one can see him succumbing to this temptation. Partly for this reason, Russell lamented the fact that he had to spend so much time making money 'and less on the unpaid work which I feel to be really more important'. A lectureship, even though duller and stuffier than a life as a freelance writer, would at least make it possible for him to pursue philosophy without the temptation (perhaps even the obligation) to be superficial, which necessarily arises when one has to sell everything one writes.

The importance that Russell attached to understanding Wittgenstein's work at this time, and his refusal to take offence at Wittgenstein's brusque dismissal of his own work, were, I believe, connected with his desire to preserve his intellectual integrity. Who better than Wittgenstein – for whom the compromises of journalistic writing were unthinkable – to act as his philosophical conscience? Throughout November, he and Wittgenstein made arrangements to meet at The Hague in December in order for Wittgenstein to explain to Russell the parts of 'Logisch-Philosophische Abhandlung' that were still unclear to him (that is, as far as Wittgenstein was concerned, its central point!). It was a meeting to which both of them attached the greatest significance. 'My dear Wittgenstein,' Russell wrote, 'it will be a joy to see you again after all these years.'

One advantage of travelling to the Continent to meet Wittgenstein was that it gave Russell an opportunity to spend some time with Dora, who was still in Paris studying and not intending to come home for Christmas. Russell's plan was to meet Dora at The Hague on 4 December and then for Wittgenstein to join them a week later. After Trinity's decision to invite him back, Russell's correspondence with Dora had taken on an edgy and argumentative tone. Dora feared that, if he returned to Cambridge, Russell – unable any longer to ignore conventional respectability – would either insist on divorcing Alys and marrying Dora or would have to break with her entirely. Living together outside marriage, which was Dora's preference, would no longer be possible.

Dora, meanwhile, was discovering that she did not, after all, like academic research and was considering resigning her Girton Fellowship and either taking to the stage or becoming a painter. Such talk, of course, alarmed Russell deeply. If Dora went ahead with pursuing a career in the theatre, he told Colette, he would break with her completely. Dora's advantage over Colette – apart from the fact that she was willing to have children – was precisely that she was *not* involved in the theatre. For her part, Dora told him, 'my feelings about you & Cambridge are probably not unlike yours about me & an artistic career – I feel I shall lose you altogether if you go back there for long.' In another letter, she told him: 'if you definitely chuck Cambridge, I will live with you openly if you like, till you are divorced.' And a few days later: 'How I hate this old divorce, & Cambridge, & all the Cambridge ways of thinking that still hang round you & keep you from being really free.'

For Russell, the issue was to some extent one of weighing up, on the one hand, his impulse to pursue work that he felt was important and, on the other, 'the instinctive impulses'. As he put it – with a brutal lack of tact – in a letter to Dora:

I have found by experience that it is no good for me to attempt a celibate existence. I tried it for nine years, and the strain drove me nearly mad. So I must find a place for sex with the smallest possible damage to work.

It was a way of looking at their relationship that was bound to offend Dora, who quite naturally resisted the idea that her role in Russell's life was solely that of relieving his sexual frustration. 'Your insistence that you could not think of me because you had no *sexual* emotion at the moment hurt me deeply,' she tried to explain on 11 November, 'because, when I am here away from you, that part of my feeling for you seems to count so little.' Almost equally offensive was a remark that he had intended to be reassuring, to the effect that he had hardly seen Colette because he did not want 'anything of that sort at the moment', to which Dora replied:

If you don't take care, I shall say when I come to Holland, 'thank you, but I don't want anything of that sort at the moment. We will commune with our souls.'

For Dora, it was important to feel that she and Russell had a common purpose, and she resented his tendency to think that their relationship was in *opposition* to his impulse to achieve something of 'impersonal' importance. 'You shouldn't say women have no sense of impersonal things,' she told him. 'That always fetches my claws out. Possibly because it is true . . . I don't want to take any part of you away from impersonal things, I only want to be allowed to share the pain they bring you.'

The one area in which they could agree on a common purpose, however, was the one that, ultimately, mattered to Russell more than any other: they both wanted to have children. At The Hague in December 1919, they resumed the practice begun in Lulworth of forgoing birth control, with the hope that Dora would become pregnant and thus force the issue of their being together. From Holland, Russell wrote to Ottoline: 'The present intention is, as soon as possible to begin a common life, with the hope of children.' Whether he was to return to Trinity, whether she was to resign her Fellowship, whether he was to divorce Alys and marry Dora – these were all of secondary importance. The main thing for him was to have children as soon as possible. For this, he was even prepared to abandon Colette, whom he loved as deeply as it was possible for him to love.

Both Russell and Dora, then, fervently hoped that Providence – or 'Provvy' as they began to call 'her' – would intervene to determine their future by bringing them children. While united on this, they were still divided on what kind of life they envisaged for themselves and their children, and in the week they had together at The Hague before Wittgenstein's arrival they fought with each other on the question of whether to marry or not. Russell tried at first to bully Dora into promising to marry him by declaring that she had 'no right' to refuse him legitimate children. When she stood her ground on this point and insisted that, for her, marriage was irrelevant to the question of having children, he tried the opposite tactic of sulking: 'Curled up in an armchair he acted like a small boy in a tantrum, which, though it made me miserable, also made it more impossible to give way.' Neither would give way to the other, and, since Providence obstinately refused to play her part, no resolution of any sort was reached.

After Wittgenstein's arrival on 12 December, Russell's time was almost totally taken up with Wittgenstein's work, and the subject of marriage and children was temporarily dropped. Wittgenstein was, Russell wrote to Colette, 'just the same as ever':

> it is a great joy to see him – he is so full of logic that I can hardly get him to talk about anything personal. He is very affectionate and if anything a little more sane than before the war. He came before I was up and hammered at my door till I woke. Since then he has talked logic without ceasing for 4 hours.

In the week they had together, Wittgenstein went through his book line by line with Russell with an impressively single-minded determination to ensure that not one of its enigmatic 'propositions' remained obscure. Wittgenstein was, Russell told Colette, 'glorious and wonderful, with a passionate purity I have never seen equalled'. As for 'Logisch-Philosophische Abhandlung', he now – after seven days of intense discussion of it – thought 'even better of it than I had done; I feel sure it is a really great book.'

Up until then, to Wittgenstein's surprise and chagrin, every publisher he had offered it to had rejected it, unwilling, especially in the difficult economic climate that prevailed in Austria after the war, to take a chance on what was to them an almost completely unintelligible book by an entirely unknown writer. To help him find a publisher for it – indeed, practically to guarantee its acceptance by the next publisher he approached – Russell promised to write an introduction to the work, summarising its theory and explaining its importance. Wittgenstein went back to Vienna much reassured. 'I enjoyed our time together *very* much,' he wrote to Russell on his return, 'and I have the feeling (haven't you too?) that we did a great deal of real work during that week.'

What they had not done, however, was resolve their fundamental difference over why the book was so important. Russell continued to regard its central message to be that all logical propositions are tautologies, a view which, he thought, undermined the notion of logic and of mathematics that had been central to his philosophy since *The Principles of Mathematics*, and the acceptance of which persuaded him that logic was 'linguistic' and that, therefore, both it and mathematics were entirely trivial. What Wittgenstein had taught him, he considered, was that, in looking to mathematics to provide indubitable truths about the world, he had been prey to an illusion, and that *Principia Mathematica* was no more than an elaborate exercise in building castles in the air.

For Wittgenstein, on the other hand, the central point of the book was to distinguish what can be said from what has to be *shown*. For him, the 'truths' of logic were of a piece with those of ethics, aesthetics and religion, in that it was fruitless to attempt to put them into words: one could only *see* them, and, having seen them, one was forced to remain silent about them. For Wittgenstein, mysticism and logic were as one. 'There are, indeed, things that cannot be put into words,' he writes. 'They *make themselves manifest*. They are what is mystical.' For Russell, this mysticism was no more than a misguided intellectual defeatism. 'I had felt in his book a flavour of mysticism,' he wrote to Ottoline on the day Wittgenstein left, 'but was astonished when I found he has become a complete mystic':

> He reads people like Kierkegaard and Angelus Silesius, and he seriously contemplates becoming a monk . . . He has penetrated deep into mystical ways of thought and feeling, but I think (though he wouldn't agree) that what he likes best in mysticism is its power to make him stop thinking.

On 22 December, Russell and Dora left The Hague, she to return to Paris, he to set off for Devon to begin what had become almost a custom of spending Christmas at Lynton with Colette and Clifford Allen.

At Lynton, Russell wrote a review for *The Athenaeum* of *Immediate Experience and Mediation*, the Inaugural Lecture of Harold Joachim, the new Professor of Logic at Oxford, in which he gave vent to his hostility to academic philosophy and revealed for the first time his conversion to a Wittgensteinian, 'linguistic' understanding of logic. The review is extraordinarily abusive. After quoting Joachim to the effect that, if one denies the axiom that two parallel lines cannot enclose a space 'the whole of plane geometry comes tumbling down', Russell snorts, 'It is probable that . . . there is no other university in the world where these words could have been written by a Professor of Logic. It has been known for over sixty years that the axiom in question is in no way necessary to plane geometry, and that without it self-consistent systems can be constructed which there is no reason, either empirical or a priori, to suppose false.' Indeed:

> Einstein's theory of gravitation has given some ground for supposing that Euclid's is not even the most convenient convention. Of all this, however, there is no hint in Aristotle or Hegel; therefore Oxford cannot take cognisance of it.

'As for logic and the so-called "Laws of Thought",' he declares roundly, 'they are concerned with symbols; they give different ways of saying the same thing . . . only an understanding of language is necessary in order to know a proposition of logic.' He writes here as if explaining an established and obvious truth. No one would guess that the view he is expounding is one of which he has been convinced for less than a month and which flatly contradicts the view he had published only a year or so previously that logic is the study of elusive 'forms of facts', for which an understanding of language has only the 'negative importance' of alerting us to the danger of mistaking symbols for the forms they symbolise![3]

While Russell was in Lynton, Dora wrote to him every day; long, reflective letters about their relationship and about her attitudes to life and – perhaps most importantly for them both – about 'Provvy'. On 23 December, she wrote that 'Provvy' had let them down: she was not pregnant. 'How I hate, my dear love,' she wrote, 'to send you such horrid news for Christmas Day.' She had bad news too about a plan that Russell was now pressing her to adopt, of becoming his secretary the coming summer when she returned from France and gave up her Fellowship. This, for him, was far preferable to her becoming an artist or an actress. 'I recognise the importance of your academic work,' he wrote to her, 'but not of any of the things you have talked of substituting for it.' The importance of his secretarial work, he implies, went without saying. There was also in this suggestion the hint of a threat:

> I love Colette, but I have had to recognise that she has no impersonal purpose, and it has meant that my love for her has not been in relation to the things that I feel most strongly about. I am afraid of something similar happening between you and me.

But Dora was not the sort to give way to this kind of threat, whether it related to marriage or to work. 'I wish dearest that I *could* lock up my heart

---

[3] Two years later, in a paper called 'Physics and Perception', which he published in *Mind* (October 1922), Russell made the same point that a logical principle asserts 'only that this symbol and that have the same meaning', but there he added a footnote, saying: 'I have adopted this view from Mr Wittgenstein. See his forthcoming work on *Philosophical Logic*.' (Russell evidently did not know at this time that Wittgenstein had chosen to call his book *Tractatus Logico-Philosophicus*.)

to everything & everybody else, in the real old-fashioned style, & deliver you the key, but I can't do it . . . Or become your secretary.' To be so resolute must have taken some courage, knowing as Dora did that Russell was with Colette, and, naturally, she had anxieties about the situation. She told Russell about a dream she had had about herself and Russell and Colette. The part concerning Colette she could not remember, 'but I can remember that you, looking absolutely devilish, were whispering in my ear "Shall I give it all up for you?" & I was conscious that this was a temptation to be resisted, & that you meant your work, – not Colette, & I said "No" manfully.'

In his determination to get married and his concern that his children should be legitimate, Russell represented for Dora the sort of conformity to conventional opinion from which she longed to be free. 'Respectability is such a burden to me,' she wrote. 'I should be so glad to be done with it! I feel that I want to be real & honest, real & honest, from the first page to the last.' She was acquiring the kind of identification with, and respect for, the poor that Russell, even at the height of his revolutionary socialist ardour, was quite untouched by. On Christmas Eve, she wrote: 'There is something in me that wakes up only in shabby surroundings & dirt & discomfort – I begin to understand why the poor are kind to one another – the way sheep huddle together in a storm.' If they married, she told him, they would have to find a way of satisfying her wilder, unconventional side: 'You will perhaps give me a holiday sometimes to go away & be savage & poor & dirty?! . . . My Bohemianism is very real.'

Russell's position in these discussions about marriage was slightly compromised by the fact that, from Dora's point of view, he could see that legal marriage was a most unattractive proposition. 'As for divorce,' he wrote to Ottoline on 27 December, 'I think it will come to that – we have discussed it endlessly – I should like to be free to marry but she [Dora] dislikes legal matrimony, which seems to me very rational – so things are still in some doubt.' This did not prevent him, however, from putting so much pressure on her to conform to his demands for a conventional marriage that she very nearly broke with him altogether. 'If you can manage not to torment me *too* much with your possessive instinct,' she wrote on 1 January, 'I will be as happy as a queen to live with you':

Married or unmarried, I don't care. There is only the condition, that, unless we have children, I should be allowed to try & earn my living in some way that is utterly unconnected with you & your work . . . If you tell me that I shall hinder you & not help unless I become your secretary & depend entirely on you as regards my movements, wishes, everything, darling, I must say No – to marrying you – I should be unfaithful to you sexually if we did that, because I would have to get air somehow. Perhaps you'd prefer that to giving me liberty to work? After all, dearest, even if I'm bad about it at times, I mean to try to give *you* liberty in both respects . . . You really are like a child, you know. I feel I have to keep reassuring you, & telling you I am there & not going away, you needn't be frightened!

To her friend C. K. Ogden, Dora complained that Russell 'won't take less than everything from me. If I want any life of my own I shall have to do without him.' A few days later, she told Ogden that she thought of 'giving Bertie the push'. In a letter to Russell himself, she rather gave him the impression that she *had* given him 'the push'. 'I thought I could have a home & a husband & a career, perhaps even children too,' she began, 'but you've pulled it all down by insisting on the most primitive form of marriage':

> I tried to take you for my God . . . But I can't take you for my God, & I was wrong to try . . . it shall be over now, because I want to say goodbye to you now.

The following evening, however, she sent him a telegram urging him to ignore the letter: she was, after all, willing to marry him. The plan they settled on was to spend the summer together in Lulworth and then for Russell to return to Cambridge for a year, during which time they would live respectably, and after which Russell would seek a divorce from Alys and he and Dora would marry. It was a plan to which Dora gave only a half-hearted consent: 'I meant to rely rather on our feeling for one another . . . & on our ability to be honest & clear about that feeling . . . than on a binding contract & swearing of oaths. Laws are made for wicked people.' Still, grudgingly or not, she went along with it: 'Maybe by the end of another summer at Lulworth, I shall be your devoted slave – God knows.'

Russell arrived back in London from Devon a few days before his first lecture at Dr Williams' Library on 12 January 1920. The pattern of lectures was the same as for the autumn series: he would give each lecture at Gordon Square on Monday, and then repeat it at Morley College the following day. A few days after his arrival in London, Russell wrote to Trinity accepting their offer of a lectureship and confirming their expectation that he would begin lecturing in October 1920. It was a step he took with something of the same fear of respectable conformity with which Dora had agreed to marry him, and almost as soon as he had sent his letter of acceptance he began looking around for more exciting alternatives.

More or less the only attraction of accepting a position at Cambridge was that it would allow him to concentrate on serious philosophy without the demand to make money out of his writing, but there are some signs that, philosophically, the wind had been taken out of his sails by his meeting with Wittgenstein, his study of Wittgenstein's work and his acceptance of a philosophical theory that seemed to rob the work he had been pursuing since his days in Brixton of much of its interest. Previously, Russell's philosophical project was founded on the conviction that logic was the study of forms of facts and that an interesting and crucial question for that study was whether there are facts of the form 'A believes p', and, further, that this latter question was one about which modern psychology had much to say. In the light of Wittgenstein's work, however, Russell came – as he showed in his review of Joachim's inaugural lecture written just weeks after his meeting with Wittgenstein – to adopt a view of logic that saw it as concerned only with symbols, with 'different ways of saying the same thing'. In this view, the findings of empirical psychology are entirely irrelevant to logic: 'only an understanding of language is necessary to know a proposition of logic'. It seems to follow that *The Analysis of Mind* does not have the importance (at least to logic) that Russell thought it had when he began it.

Russell never explicitly acknowledged this, as far as I know, but it seems implicit in the things he wrote in the New Year and spring of 1920, when compared to the views he had expressed less than two years previously. For example, in a review of *Implication and Linear Inference* by Bernard Bosanquet, he takes Bosanquet to task for trying to forge a link between logic and psychology. 'It is difficult to believe', Russell writes, 'that any theory of logic can be valid which requires a particular view on a moot point of an empirical study such as psychology.' Yet, in prison, Russell had made an extensive study of empirical psychology precisely because he hoped it would be relevant to the theory of logic. 'All the psychology that I have been reading', he had written then, 'was for the sake of logic . . . I see my way to a really big piece of work, and incidentally to a definition of "logic" hitherto lacking. I have reached a point in logic where I need theories of (a) judgment and (b) symbolism, both of which are psychological problems.'

Tractatus Logico-Philosophicus had, it seems, not only forced Russell to give up his previous theory of judgment, but had persuaded him to alter his whole approach to the problem, to admit that, as far as logic is concerned, whatever psychology has to say about judgment is quite irrelevant. In his introduction to Wittgenstein's work, Russell began by delineating the separate areas of logic, epistemology and psychology and laid great stress upon Wittgenstein's definition of logic, according to which all logical propositions are tautologies. 'The psychological part of meaning', he now declares, 'does not concern the logician.'

Though Russell seemed now quite converted to this sharp separation between logic and psychology, the course of lectures he was giving, and the book based upon them, were inspired by exactly the opposite point of view. One wonders whether this disparity was not one of the reasons why, though Wittgenstein began chasing him for the introduction in January, Russell did not write it until March, when his lectures were finished. On 2 February, he wrote to Wittgenstein telling him that he could 'absolutely count' on the introduction being done, 'but I do not think it can be finished for another six weeks'. The reason he gave in this, and a later letter, was that he had broken his collarbone. This sounds a reasonable excuse, but it did not stop him writing several book reviews and his lectures during this period, and, when he did get round to writing the introduction, his collarbone had still not healed properly and he had to dictate it, just as he dictated all the other pieces he wrote during this time.

3. RUSSIA

Russell finished lecturing on 2 March. Two weeks later, he wrote to Wittgenstein, sending him, finally, the long-awaited introduction. In between, he spent five days in Paris with Dora, during which time he discussed an idea he had of spending the summer, not in Lulworth, but in Russia. It was an idea he had first mooted in February, when Dora initially had some doubts. 'I am troubled about my work if we go to Russia!' she wrote on 21 February. 'I was counting on the quiet of Lulworth to get it finished.' But, she conceded: 'It would be lovely to go.' The following day, all doubts were banished: 'Dearest, let us go to Russia if we can, now is the time when it will all be freshest & best, both through our love & care for one another, & because the excitement of the Revolution is still over Russia.' A few days later, Russell told Colette that he and Dora had made up their differences and that Dora would be going with him to Russia. 'You give me so little now-a-days', he told her, 'that I must find consolation . . . I am as fond of her as I can be of anyone, while I care so deeply for you':

> Dora loves me, I love you, you love Casson, he loves his wife . . . Where is happiness to be found in all this chain? . . . My heart is yours, always and irrevocably.

Though no doubt unaware that she was considered a mere 'consolation', Dora could sense the momentous importance of this invitation to Russia. 'As Russia gets more & more likely,' she wrote on 4 March, 'I get more & more excited.'

In Paris, from 11 to 16 March, the subject of going to Russia dominated the conversation and thoughts of both Russell and Dora. 'As we sat on a bench under the chestnut trees in the Avenue de l'Observatoire,' Dora remembered, 'he talked impressively of his great desire to see what was happening in the Soviet Union, of how important an event this Revolution was in history. Would I consent to visit Russia with him, and make this the start of our permanent life together? . . . I knew that this was a decisive moment in our relationship.'

Russell, too, seemed to feel the decisiveness of the moment, and, when he returned to England, he wrote to Colette to let her know that he had, finally, made his choice between her and Dora. Colette, who was at the time on tour, replied:

> I'm alone, existence is painful, and it takes considerable effort not to go under. If I hadn't work I certainly shouldn't manage not to. Beyond struggling to keep my head above water, I'm paralysed. Forgive these clichés.

Russell had only a few days in England before he had to set off again, this time to Barcelona, where, accompanied by Dora, he went to give a course of five lectures at the Institute of Catalan Studies. The letter inviting him had stressed that: 'The Spanish "intellectuals" are most anxious to get into touch with really modern and enlightened thought in England', and the five lectures, entitled 'Matter and Mind – The System of Logical Atomism', were tailored to this desire for a more or less systematic presentation of a modern outlook. The lectures were given in French over a period of less than a week, from 29 March to 3 April, after which Russell and Dora set off for Majorca, for what Dora described as 'one of the most exquisite brief holidays of my life'.

In Majorca, according to Russell, he and Dora 'began a great quarrel which raged for many months' about the impending visit to Russia:

> I was planning to go to Russia, and Dora wanted to go with me. I maintained that, as she had never taken much interest in politics, there was no good reason why she should go, and, as typhus was raging, I should not feel justified in exposing her to the risk.

Dora's recollection is that Russell's change of attitude to her accompanying him to Russia did not occur until he returned to London in April, and then, not because of typhus, but because he received an invitation to go to Russia with an official delegation of Trade Unionists, an invitation that could not be extended (so at least he claimed) to include her. The surviving correspondence seems to support Dora's version of events more than Russell's, confidence in which is in any case undermined by his omitting to mention that he had invited, even urged, Dora to go to Russia with him months before he received the invitation to go with the official delegation.

The delegation was formed by the British Government in response to a request from the Trades Union Congress to send a party of impartial observers to find out what life in Russia was like and to study at first hand the industrial, economic and political conditions that prevailed in Bolshevik Russia. Its members included Mrs Snowden and Dr L. W. Haden Guest (both of whom were described by Russell as 'very anti-Bolshevik'), Robert Williams (Secretary of the National Transport Workers' Union), Tom Shaw (a Labour MP, later Minister of Labour), Ben Turner (described by Russell as 'an enormously fat old Trade Unionist . . . who was very helpless without his wife'), and, most significantly for Russell, Clifford Allen. Russell's invitation to join this group came late, in response to his request, probably through Allen, to visit Russia with them.

They were due to leave for Russia on 27 April, which, after his return from Majorca on 19 April, left Russell just a week to make arrangements and attend to any business that needed seeing to before his return two months later. Waiting for him at Overstrand Mansions on his return from Majorca was a letter from Wittgenstein thanking him for the introduction, which, Wittgenstein said, was in the course of being translated into German, after which, 'Logisch-Philosophische Abhandlung' would, at last, be published. Not that Wittgenstein was entirely happy with what Russell had written:

> There's so much of it that I'm not quite in agreement with – both where you're critical of me and also where you're simply trying to elucidate my point of view. But that doesn't matter. The future will pass judgment on us – or perhaps it won't, and if it is silent that will be a judgment too.

For the moment, Russell received these strictures in silence. In the short space of time before his ship left, he had much to do, not the least of which was to square things with Dora. When she received the news that he was going to Russia without her, Dora was furious and immediately came to London to remonstrate with him and urge him to keep to their plan of going together. Russell, however, was adamant: Dora could not go, he insisted, because of the threat of typhus. 'All right then,' Dora said defiantly, 'if it is possible to go without the support of a delegation then I shall go myself.' To salve his conscience somewhat, Russell gave her £100 so that she would not be short of money while he was away and, on his way to Newcastle, from where he was to sail to Stockholm, travelled with Dora as far as Grantham, from where she returned to Paris.

Russell also had Colette to reckon with. The day before he left, he went walking with Colette on the Sussex Downs. According to Colette's recollection:

> On the top of the downs, suddenly, B. R. stood stock still and said, 'I suppose you wouldn't come to Russia?' I shook my head. His question had the ring of hostility. Always, with every person I've known intimately, I've come up against that hostility to one's 'job'. We walked on in silence and I pictured to myself his surprise, had I suddenly stood stock still and said, 'I suppose you wouldn't chuck Russia and come on tour?'

If Colette's recollection is accurate, it throws a new light on Russell's refusal to take Dora with him to Russia, recalling as it does Russell's plea to Colette in 1917, soon after the February Revolution, to accompany him to Russia in search of 'high adventure' (and also, of course, Colette's cool response to the plan, seeing in it Russell's hostility to her career as an actress). Three years after he had first suggested it, it seems, Russell still thought that, if he and Colette could go together to Russia, it would restore the sense of comradeship that had been lost in his relationship with Colette since her departure to Blackpool in the autumn of 1917. It was a forlorn hope, but one that he gave up only with the greatest reluctance.

Politically, too, Russell's hopes for Russia in the spring of 1920, if not yet forlorn, were certainly more circumspect than the almost unbounded enthusiasm and optimism with which he had greeted the news of the Russian Revolution three years earlier. Then, the Provisional Government, with its declared commitment to civil and political liberties, its intention to end the war on the basis of 'no annexations and no reparations' and its willingness to work alongside the Petrograd Soviet, looked like the embodiment of Russell's political ideals, a near-perfect combination of liberalism and Socialism. Every development since then – the overthrow of the Kerensky Government by the Bolsheviks in the October Revolution, Lenin's dissolution of the Constituent Assembly in January 1918, Trotsky's negotiation of the Brest–Litovsk Treaty of March 1918 (under which the Russians agreed to both reparations and annexations as their price for peace with Germany), and the brutal suppression by the Bolshevik Government of all forms of dissent – had served to temper Russell's enthusiasm for the new regime.

That his faith in Socialist Russia had not been destroyed altogether was due mainly to his conviction that the war had signalled the end of traditional European liberalism and had made clear the need to replace capitalism, with its inherent competition and strife, with some form of international Socialism. This Russell made clear in an important article called 'Socialism and Liberal Ideals', which he gave as a lecture to the National Guilds League in London at the end of February and which he published in both England (in *The English Review*) and America (in *The Liberator*) just as he was about to embark on his visit to Russia. 'I am one of those', he declares at the beginning of the article, 'who, as a result of the war, have passed over from Liberalism to Socialism, not because I have ceased to admire many of the Liberal ideals, but because I see little scope for them, except after a complete transformation of the economic structure of society.'

Capitalism, he argued, 'so long as it fought against feudalism' was associated with the liberal ideas of freedom, democracy and peace. But now feudalism was a thing of the past, and capitalist regimes, in their struggle against Socialism and nationalism – as witnessed by the suppression of Communist opinion by the American Government and of nationalist movements in Ireland and India by the British – stood not for freedom but for oppression. As for democracy:

What is called the rule of the majority in a bourgeois democracy is . . . in reality the rule of those who control the methods of manufacturing opinion, especially in the schools and the Press . . . The Bosheviks are right in maintaining that bourgeois democracy is a trick by which the victims are induced to pronounce their own condemnation.

And the idea that capitalism was associated with peace, if it ever had any credibility, was now utterly destroyed by the war, as a result of which 'Every thoughtful person must realise that the continuance of the capitalist system is incompatible with the continuance of civilisation.'

On top of this, the inherent economic injustice in capitalism, once recognised by the workers exploited by it, makes it an inefficient method of production: 'The old incentives to work have broken down . . . the bees have begun to think that it is not worth while to make honey for their owners . . . if speedy production is to be possible, new incentives must be found, and can only be found, through self-government in industry.' On a theoretical basis, then, it was clear that some form of socialism was necessary. What made Russia important was that, there, practice had followed theory:

The most important of all the new facts that have emerged from the war is the existence of a Great Power which has adopted Socialism in practice. Socialism, hitherto, has been a mere theory, something which practical men could despise as impossible and visionary. The Bolsheviks, whatever we may think of their merits or demerits, have at any rate proved that Socialism is compatible with a vigorous and successful State.

This leads Russell to a rousing paean to the achievements of Lenin's regime:

Faced by the united hostility of Europe, and by civil war within their own borders, coming into power at a time of unexampled chaos and starvation, deprived by the blockade of all outside help, they have, nevertheless, beaten back their enemies, reconquered the greater part of the old Russian Empire, survived the worst period of the famine without being overthrown by internal revolution, and set to work to regenerate production with amazing vigour. There has been nothing comparable since the France of the Revolution, and for my part I cannot but think that what the Bolsheviks are doing is of even greater importance for the future of the world than what was accomplished in France by the Jacobins, because their operations are on a wider scale, and their theory is more fundamentally novel. I believe that Socialists throughout the world should support the Bolsheviks and co-operate with them.

The article ends with a declaration of faith even in the face of unpalatable facts: 'Bolshevism has temporarily flouted two ideals, which most of us have hitherto strongly believed in; I mean, democracy and liberty. Are we on this account to view it askance? I think not.'

And yet, even while he was writing this apologia for the Soviet regime, Russell could not bring himself to identify wholeheartedly with the Socialist movement. While, intellectually, he was convinced that the future lay with Socialism, emotionally he remained fundamentally a liberal individualist with a deep-seated repugnance to the spirit of collectivism. As he had told Colette when he first met her: 'I don't like the spirit of Socialism – I think freedom is the basis of everything.' Now, about to embark for Russia, the spiritual gap between himself and the Bolsheviks struck him as never before: 'The day of my departure comes near. I have a thousand things to do, yet I sit here idle, thinking useless thoughts . . . How I envy those who *always* believe what they believe, who are not troubled by deadness and indifference to all that makes the framework of their lives':

Reason and emotion fight a deadly war within me, and leave me no energy for outward action. I know that no good thing is achieved without fighting, without ruthlessness and organisation and discipline. I know that for collective action that individual must be turned into a machine. But in these things, though my reason may force me to believe them, I can find no inspiration. It is the individual human soul that I love – in its loneliness, its hopes and fears, its quick impulses and sudden devotions. It is such a long journey from this to armies and States and officials; and yet it is only by making this long journey that one can avoid a useless sentimentalism.

In this mood of deep ambivalence, Russell, together with the other members of the delegation, set sail from Newcastle on 27 April and arrived in Stockholm on 5 May. From there, he wrote to Ottoline that he expected his visit to Russia 'will have a great effect upon me – but what effect I don't know':

The only thing I feel sure of is that Trinity High Table will feel very funny after Russia. I don't believe I shall like even my best friends among dons.

After some slight delay in getting Russell a visa from the Soviet Ambassador in Stockholm, the delegation crossed the border into Russia on 11 May and were in Petrograd the next day. After just a day in Russia, Russell had already become suspicious of the Bolshevik authorities and frustrated by their apparent determination to present to the delegation not the reality of Russian day-to-day life, but an obviously contrived display of opulence and splendour: 'I came prepared for physical hardship, discomfort, dirt and hunger, to be made bearable by an atmosphere of splendid hope for mankind. Our communist comrades, no doubt rightly, have not judged us worthy of such treatment':

> Since crossing the frontier yesterday afternoon, I have made two feasts and a good breakfast, several first-class cigars, and a night in a sumptuous bedroom of a palace where all the luxury of the *ancien régime* has been preserved. At the stations on the way, regiments of soldiers filled the platform, and the plebs were kept carefully out of sight. It seems I am to live amid the pomp surrounding the government of a great military Empire. So I must readjust my mood. Cynicism is called for, but I am strongly moved, and find cynicism difficult. I come back eternally to the same question: What is the secret of this passionate country? Do the Bolsheviks know its secret? Do they even suspect that it has a secret? I wonder.

The ambivalence Russell had felt even before he left for Russia about the value of the ruthlessness, organisation and discipline that he expected of a Marxist regime were increased still further after his second day in Petrograd: 'Everything is to be systematic: there is to be organisation and distributive justice. The same education for all, the same clothes for all, the same kind of houses for all, the same books for all, and the same creed for all.' It was very just, he reflected, and left no room for envy, 'except of the fortunate victims of injustice in other countries'.

He was visited by four members of the Petrograd Philosophical Society, who, he discovered, disliked the rigid orthodoxy and control of the Bolshevik Government. One of them told Russell that lectures in metaphysics were not allowed on the ground that there is no such subject. On this point, at least, Russell had some sympathy with the official dogma: 'Much to be said for this view,' he commented in his journal.

The delegation spent five days in Petrograd, with Russell growing ever more disenchanted with the Bolshevik regime. 'It is ugly and brutal,' he wrote, 'but full of constructive energy and faith in the value of what it is creating':

> In creating a new machinery for social life, it has no time to think of anything beyond machinery. When the body of the new society has been

built, there will be time enough to think about giving it a new soul – at least, so I am assured . . . I wonder whether it is possible to build a body first, and then afterwards inject the requisite amount of soul.

He was 'infinitely unhappy' in the atmosphere of the regime: 'stifled by its utilitarianism, its indifference to love and beauty and the life of impulse'. When remembering his time in Petrograd thirty years later, he put it more strongly: 'I felt that everything I valued in human life was being destroyed in the interests of a glib and narrow philosophy, and that in the process untold misery was being inflicted upon many millions of people.'

He recognised the achievements of Lenin's Government in coping with the enormous problems that it faced, and he acknowledged the surprising extent to which it had conquered adversity. But, still, he found it impossible to actually like what he saw. His feelings, he thought, were matched exactly by those of Maxim Gorky, whom he met on his last day in Petrograd. Gorky was ill with consumption, but between bouts of coughing urged Russell to tell the world about the suffering of the Russian people. He was, Russell wrote, 'the most lovable and to me the most sympathetic of all the Russians I saw'.

The next eleven days were spent in Moscow, where Russell had a chance to meet for himself the leaders of the Bolshevik revolution. Trotsky he met only briefly at a performance of *Prince Igor* at the Opera House. Russell was impressed with the Napoleonic attitude with which Trotsky acknowledged the cheers of the audience, and also with his good looks, lightning intelligence and magnetic personality. He had, Russell thought, 'the vanity of an artist or actor'. Trotsky addressed the audience, calling for three cheers for the men at the front, fighting the White Russians, and then stayed for a while to engage in what Russell described as 'banal' conversation with the members of the delegation in their box.

Two days later, Russell was granted an hour's interview with Lenin himself. The interview served to increase still further Russell's disillusionment with Bolshevism. Lenin struck him, not as a great man, but as a rather ordinary figure, something like an opinionated professor, a man whose belief in Marxism was held with such religious fervour that he had become himself an 'embodied theory'. From the standpoint of an orthodox Marxist, he brushed aside almost all the elements of Russell's own brand of Socialism, laughing at G. D. H. Cole's Guild Socialism for believing that guilds could be established without dictatorship, dismissing as bourgeois the British Labour Party's faith in parliamentary democracy, insisting that, whether the blockade of Russia was lifted or not, peace between Bolshevik Russia and capitalist countries would always be insecure, and denying emphatically that Socialism could be achieved without violence and revolution. Russell came away from the interview appalled at Lenin's scant regard for liberty and his apparently complete lack of psychological insight or imagination. 'The whole tendency of Marxism', wrote Russell in his account of meeting Lenin, 'is against psychological imagination, since it attributes everything in politics to purely material causes.' The image that remained in Russell's mind of Lenin was when, in the course of explaining how it was necessary to continue the dictatorship of the proletariat over the peasantry, because of the peasant's desire for free trade, Lenin chuckled at the thought of the richer peasants being hanged on trees by their poorer neighbours.

Russell was gradually forming a picture of Russia as a nation of peasants tyrannised by city dwellers, of artists tyrannised by philistines and of Asiatics tyrannised by Westerners. It was an impression that increased the day after his meeting with Lenin when he was invited to spend a night at the home of Lev Kamenev, the President of the Moscow Soviet. As Kamenev explained how the Russians would deal with the Muslim population of Turkestan, Russell felt 'a certain unconscious imperialistic tone', which brought to mind the attitude of the British in India.

The Bolshevik Government represented, Russell came to think, a very tiny minority. Of the population of Russia, 85 per cent were rural peasants, yet the Government represented only the interests of the industrial and urban population. It was not even representative of *all* city dwellers, but only of that small proportion of them that were Communists (Russell estimated that, in a population of 120 million people, just over half a million were members of the Communist Party). 'The average working man', he wrote, 'feels himself the slave of the Government, and has no sense whatever of having been liberated from a tyranny.' The only reason the Government did not collapse was that it had at its service a powerful and effective police force and a large, well-armed army.

Russell and the other members of the delegation became increasingly curious to see at first hand what life in Russia was like outside the big cities, and so the Government arranged a six-day trip for them along the River Volga, from Nijni Novgorod to Saratov, with permission to stop wherever they liked and liberty to talk freely to the peasants and villagers they encountered. In Russell's descriptions, the river trip along the Volga assumes something of the quality of the journey along the Congo described in Conrad's *Heart of Darkness*, or of Tomlinson's account of his trip along the Amazon in *The Sea and the Jungle*; he presents it as an exploration into the interior of an alien world surrounded by dark, unseen forces laden with heavy metaphorical significance. The nightmarish aspect of the journey was partly (but by no means entirely) due to the fact that, soon after they set off, Clifford Allen became extremely ill with pneumonia and tuberculosis, or as Russell puts it, in a description that seems so 'novelish' and full of Conradian echoes that it is tempting to think he intended to use it in a fictionalised account of his voyage:

> One of us lies at death's door, fighting a grim battle with weakness and terror and the indifference of the strong, assailed day and night by the sounds of loud-voiced love-making and trivial laughter. And all around us lies a great silence, strong as Death, unfathomable as the heavens. It seems that none have leisure to hear the silence, yet it calls to me so insistently that I grow deaf to the harangues of propagandists and the endless information of the well-informed.

In the same vein is Russell's account of leaving the boat late one night and wandering about alone until he came upon a huddled group of what one supposes were refugees from the civil war:

> In silence I went ashore, and found on the sand a strange assemblage of human beings, half-nomads, wandering from some remote region of famine, each family huddled together surrounded by all its belongings, some sleeping, others silently making small fires of twigs. The flickering flames lighted up gnarled bearded faces of wild men, strong patient primitive women, and children as sedate and slow as their parents. Human beings they undoubtedly were, and yet it would have been far easier for me to grow intimate with a dog or a cat or a horse than with one of them.

These people, Russell knew, would wait by the riverside day after day until a boat came to take them to another part of the country: 'Some would die by the way, all would suffer hunger and thirst and the scorching midday sun, but their sufferings would be dumb':

> To me they seemed to typify the very soul of Russia, unexpressive, inactive from despair, unheeded by the little set of westerners who make up all the parties of progress or reaction. Russia is so vast that the articulate few are lost in it as man and his planet are lost in interstellar space. It is possible, I thought, that the theorists may increase the misery of the many by trying to force them into actions contrary to their primeval instincts, but I could not believe that happiness was to be brought to them by a gospel of industrialism and forced labour.

The next morning, Russell resumed what he called 'the interminable discussions' with his fellow-travellers of Marxist theory. They, he thought, would not have been interested in the sleeping wanderers he had chanced upon, even if they had seen them: 'But something of that patient silence communicated itself to me, something lonely and unspoken remained in my heart throughout all the comfortable familiar intellectual talk. And at last I began to feel that all politics are inspired by a grinning devil, teaching the energetic and quick-witted to torture submissive populations for the profit of pocket or power or theory.'

It was as if, travelling through the vast Russian countryside on a steamboat along the Volga, he underwent another conversion experience, another sudden realisation, this time of the sickness of Western civilisation. It was a realisation, of course, for which the First World War had thoroughly prepared him and a revelation that he was in the perfect mood to receive. Russia, he later said, 'may be described as an artist nation; but . . . it has been governed, since the time of Peter the Great, by men who wished to introduce all the good and evil of the West':

> In former days, I might have had no doubt that such men were in the right . . . The Great War showed that something is wrong with our

civilisation . . . Efficiency directed to destruction can only end in annihilation, and it is to this consummation that our civilisation is tending, if it cannot learn some of that wisdom for which it despises the East.

It was on the Volga, in the summer of 1920, that I first realised how profound is the disease in our Western mentality, which the Bolsheviks are attempting to force upon an essentially Asiatic population.

In 1917 he had looked to the Russian Revolution for the new creed that was needed to heal the wounds of post-war Europe; now he saw the Bolshevik Government as just one more symptom, and an especially acute one, of Europe's malady. Capitalism and Communism were not opposites, but rather twin signs of a deep malaise, which had to do with the mad, headlong rush into industrialisation that both of them sought to achieve in their different ways. Repeating in a letter to Ottoline his view that the Russians are 'artists, down to the simplest peasant', he added gloomily: 'the aim of the Bolsheviks is to make them industrial and as Yankee as possible.'

At Saratov, the delegation was supposed to leave the boat and return to Moscow by rail, but it was considered dangerous to move Allen, so he stayed on board, with Russell, Haden Guest and Mrs Snowden to look after him. The rest returned to Moscow as planned. From Saratov, the boat made its way to Astrakhan, on the Caspian Sea, and the journey became ever more nightmarish. The Russian nurse refused to sit with Allen at night for fear that he would die and his ghost seize her, so Russell and the others took turns at nursing him. The cabin was small and the heat intense, and the air thick with malarial mosquitoes. Allen suffered from violent diarrhoea. When they reached Astrakhan, Russell declared it to be 'more like hell than anything I had ever imagined':

The town water-supply was taken from the same part of the river into which ships shot their refuse. Every street had stagnant water which bred millions of mosquitoes: every year one third of the inhabitants had malaria. There was no drainage system, but a vast mountain of excrement at a prominent place in the middle of the town. Plague was endemic.

The flies were so numerous, Russell recalled, 'that at meal-time a table-cloth had to be put over the food, and one had to insert one's hand underneath and snatch a mouthful quickly. The instant the table-cloth was put down, it became completely black with flies, so that nothing of it remained visible.'

They had to put up with about ten days of these conditions, before Allen was sufficiently recovered to think of travelling back. On the way back, they took the steamer again as far as Saratov and from there were able to catch a fast train all the way to Reval in Estonia, stopping only in Moscow for Allen to be examined by doctors at the insistence of the Bolshevik Government, who were anxious that the one member of the delegation sympathetic to their regime should not die while under their care.

Russell, Allen, Haden Guest and Mrs Snowden reached Reval on 16 June,

and, while Allen stayed in Reval to convalesce, the others made their way to
Stockholm. From there, Russell wrote to Colette and Ottoline, expressing, as
he had felt he could not do while in Russia, the full force of his disillusionment. In spite of being one of the most interesting things he had ever done,
he told Ottoline, his visit to Russia had been 'infinitely painful' to him, partly
because of Allen's illness, 'but more because I loathed the Bolsheviks'. No
vestige of liberty remained in Russia, he said, and he had felt 'stifled and
oppressed by the weight of the machine as by a cope of lead'. To Colette, he
wrote that the Bolshevik regime was 'unspeakably horrible . . . I pray God I
may never see any of them again.'

He also made urgent attempts to contact Dora in Paris. He had telegraphed
her while he was in Reval and was becoming alarmed that he had received no
reply. He tried telegraphing friends of hers in Paris and, from them, received
the news that the last they had heard of her she was in Stockholm. In fact,
by this time she was in Petrograd, having entered Russia illegally via the
Arctic port of Murmansk. After Russell had left for Russia, Dora, having
returned to Paris, found it impossible to get back to her studies and wanted
only to join Russell on what she was convinced would be the experience of a
lifetime. 'I wish we had tried to get me along,' she had written to him on 6
May. 'When I think of all that the journey may mean I can't bear not to be
sharing all the experiences with you.' She cried herself to sleep every night
thinking about it. Eventually, she could stand it no more and decided to go
to Stockholm to see if she could not get into Russia herself. In Stockholm she
met a Finn with Bolshevik sympathies who told her to take a steamer to the
North Cape under the guise of being a tourist wishing to see the midnight
sun, and to disembark at the Norwegian port of Vardö, where she was to go
to the office of a local newspaper to meet two friends of his who would take
her to Murmansk in a small fishing boat. After two days in Murmansk, Dora
was taken to Petrograd.

From Petrograd, Dora wrote to Russell (she addressed it to Reval, but it
eventually caught up with him in London) that she intended to stay in Russia
for at least a month. Unlike Russell, she loved it. 'I had a most amazing
journey full of hardship,' she wrote. 'But I am brown as a berry, & fit as a
fiddle, & helping with preparations for Congress':

> I do so much wish you had not gone with the L. P. people. Being alone is
> so much jollier – Don't find someone else to love before I come back, will
> you? Only *that* worries me.

She had been staying at the Astoria Hotel, where she had been befriended by John Reed, the author of *Ten Days that Shook the World*, who was
already well-known and respected in Bolshevik Russia (he was later buried in
Red Square). Through her association with Reed, Dora became accepted and
trusted by the Bolsheviks and most of the risks she had exposed herself to by
entering Russia without official permission were avoided.

Russell, of course, was not to know this, and in Stockholm he became
desperately worried that Dora would be arrested and imprisoned by the

Bolsheviks. There was, however, nothing he could do for her for the time being, so he returned to England, where, he later wrote, 'I endeavoured to recover some kind of sanity, the shock of Russia having been almost more than I could bear.'

He arrived back in London on 30 June to be met at Euston station by Colette. Together, they went to his flat in Battersea and opened the large collection of mail waiting for him, among which was a letter from Wittgenstein dated 6 May. 'Your Introduction is not going to be printed,' Wittgenstein wrote, 'and as a consequence my book probably won't either':

> You see, when I actually saw the German translation of the Introduction, I couldn't bring myself to let it be printed with my work. All the refinement of your English style was, obviously, lost in the translation, and what remained was superficiality and misunderstanding.

Russell responded to this with remarkable generosity. 'I don't care two-pence about the introduction,' he wrote to Wittgenstein, 'but I shall be really sorry if your book isn't printed. May I try, in that case, to have it printed in England or America?'

In his reply, Wittgenstein confirmed what they both suspected, that Reclam, the prospective publishers, would not publish it without Russell's introduction, and Wittgenstein said that he would not take any further steps to publish it: 'But if you feel like getting it printed, it is entirely at your disposal and *you can do what you like with it*.' As for himself, he wrote: 'The best for me, perhaps, would be if I could lie down one evening and not wake up again.'

Another letter waiting for Russell on his return to London was an invitation from the Chinese Lecture Association to spend a year at the University of Peking as a visiting lecturer, starting in the coming September. In the mood of disenchantment with Western culture that had seized Russell in Russia, the idea of spending a year in the Orient was an appealing one and he was inclined to accept the offer. He was, in any case, ambivalent about his scheduled return to Cambridge that autumn and rather welcomed this opportunity to delay it. He immediately wrote to Trinity to ask for a year's leave of absence, and then, before he formally accepted the Chinese offer, tried to contact Dora in Russia to ask her to come with him. 'I decided', he wrote, 'that I would accept if Dora would come with me, but not otherwise.'

That he should think of taking Dora with him to China rather than Colette is, in some ways, rather strange. Colette was, after all, with him when he received the invitation, and, soon afterwards, he and Colette went away on a holiday to the Kent coast, where they stayed in a hotel in Rye and took walks through the marshland of the Isle of Oxney. 'Every moment together was perfect from first to last,' wrote Colette on their return, and Russell himself recalls that during this period he was 'finding the same consolation with Colette as I used to find during the War'. Colette and he were closer than they had been for a long time.

Dora, meanwhile, seemed to growing ever further away from him. From letters that she managed to send Russell via friends (there being no ordinary post to and from Russia because of the blockade), Russell discovered to his horror that she loved Bolshevik Russia quite as much as he hated it. The religious fervour of the Russian Bolsheviks that had so alarmed Russell was, to Dora, a great inspiration. 'I was inspired to believe', Dora writes in her autobiography, 'that here was the creed which might civilise industrialism and tame it to be the servant of mankind.' Where Russell had found the Bolshevik leaders loathsome fanatics, she had 'a sublime confidence in the good faith of the Soviet leaders whose courage I admired, and in whose revolution – though I was hitherto so unpolitical[4] – I did believe.' Lenin, for example, who had so disappointed Russell, Dora saw addressing the Third International Congress and perceived him to be: 'A man respected and loved and completely in contact with, and in control of, that great mass of people.' And, while Russell had seen in the Bolshevik social reforms one more symptom of a peculiarly Western disease, Dora saw something else entirely. Petrograd, she conceded, stands out as a monument to the introduction by Peter the Great of Western culture: 'But the spirit of the Revolution, abroad in the land, communicating itself, as it were, through the very air one breathed, was not at all of the West. It came from the uprising of an awakened giant, the birth of a new culture.'

It is hard to imagine two more opposing reactions, and it is not surprising that Russell, as he received more of Dora's letters from Russia, should come to wonder whether he and she would ever be able to overcome the difference in their respective outlooks. Why, then, was he so determined at this point to ensure that Dora came with him to China? In his *Autobiography* he attributes it to 'some force stronger than words, or even than our conscious thoughts', which exerted such a pull on him that he never wavered for a moment. In the 'Private Memoir' that he dictated late in life, he was more straightforward. The break with Colette occurred, he writes, 'because I desperately wanted children and she refused to have them'. When he returned from China, he writes, '[Colette] told me that she had now changed her mind and would be willing to have children by me. But by this time it was too late.' Though he did not love Dora as much as he loved Colette; though, after his shock in Russia, he felt closer to Colette than he did to Dora; though Dora was argumentative, headstrong and, to cap it all, enamoured of the Bolsheviks – none of this mattered so much as the fact that she was willing to have his children. For this he was prepared to forgive almost anything.

Desperate to contact Dora somehow, Russell telegraphed a Quaker called Arthur Watts whom he had met at Reval and who frequently travelled to Russia in connection with Quaker relief. He asked Watts to find Dora and explain to her the situation regarding the invitation to go to China. Dora, by this time in Moscow, proved rather easy to find, and Watts not only gave her the message but also pulled strings enabling her to cross the border to Reval,

---

[4] In May, when she was in Paris fuming at having been left behind while Russell went to Russia, she had written to him: 'I am feeling that I hate your political mood & all these political people.'

from where she would have no trouble returning to England. From Russell's point of view, at least, the matter was now settled: he and Dora would be going to China.

While he waited for Dora to return, Russell stayed at Garsington. Clifford Allen had by this time returned to London, having recovered from his illness. To Russell's disappointment and surprise, Allen's experiences in Russia had not in the least weakened his support for the Bolshevik regime. After a few days of bitter argument, Russell could take it no more and left Overstrand Mansions to retire to what had by now become the most reliable haven of peace and quiet he had open to him.

At Garsington, Russell put his reactions to the Bolshevik regime in writing, first in the form of a series of antedated letters to Colette, and then in a series of five articles for *The Nation* collectively called 'Impressions of Bolshevik Russia', which, together with another series of articles on 'Bolshevik Theory' that he published in *The New Republic*, were incorporated into the book *The Practice and Theory of Bolshevism*, which was hurriedly put together in the final few weeks before he set sail for China and rushed out by the publisher, George Allen & Unwin, so that it was in print before the end of the year. The central message of the book and the articles upon which it is based is that Bolshevism, in theory and in practice, is a failure, a cure that is worse than the illness it treats. 'I believe', writes Russell, in a remark that summarises his entire view on the matter, 'that while some forms of Socialism are immeasurably better than capitalism, others are even worse. Among those that are worse I reckon the form which is being achieved in Russia.' What makes it worse is its disregard of basic freedoms. In a passage that seems to be in part a correction of his earlier view that the Russian Revolution had established something like the system imagined by Guild Socialism, Russell warns:

> Friends of Russia here think of the dictatorship of the proletariat as merely a new form of representative government, in which only working men and women have votes, and the constituencies are partly occupational, not geographical. They think that 'proletariat' means 'proletariat', but 'dictatorship' does not quite mean 'dictatorship'. This is the opposite of the truth. When a Russian Communist speaks of dictatorship, he means the word literally, but when he speaks of the proletariat, he means the word in a Pickwickian sense. He means the 'class-conscious' part of the proletariat, *i.e.*, the Communist Party.

'To an English mind', he goes an, revealing the extent to which his disillusionment with Bolshevism had caused him to revert back to his inherited Whiggism, the views of the Russian Communists 'reinforce the conviction upon which English life has been based ever since 1688, that kindliness and tolerance are worth all the creeds in the world'.

On a theoretical level, one of the main faults Russell finds with Bolshevism, is, ironically, its adherence to the one aspect of traditional liberalism that he had long felt needed to be overthrown: its belief in the essential rationality of humankind. 'There is need', Russell suggests, 'of a treatment of political motives by the methods of psychoanalysis. In politics, as in private life, men invent myths to rationalise their conduct.' In its disregard of psychology, Bolshevism was left with an impoverished understanding of what motivates people, ignoring powerful impulses like vanity, rivalry and the love of power, and concentrating solely on economic motives: 'To Marx, who inherited eighteenth-century rationalist psychology from the British orthodox economists, self-enrichment seemed the natural aim of a man's political actions':

> But modern psychology has dived much deeper into the ocean of insanity upon which the little barque of human reason insecurely floats. The intellectual optimism of a bygone age is no longer possible to the modern student of human nature. Yet it lingers in Marxism making Marxists rigid and Procrustean in their treatment of the life of instinct.

Though it was seen by some as a retraction of his earlier beliefs, *The Practice and Theory of Bolshevism* was, to a large extent, simply a restatement of the political philosophy Russell had outlined in *Principles of Social Reconstruction*. All that had changed was his belief that the Russian Revolution had gone some way to creating the socialist state of his dreams, and his consequent (short-lived) willingness to accept the need for revolutionary violence. He had returned from Russia, he told Gilbert Murray, 'more than ever a pacifist, as much against revolutionary war as against others'.

4. CHINA

Towards the end of July 1920, with Dora not yet back from Russia, and the time to leave for the long journey to China drawing alarmingly near, Russell began to take steps to free himself from his marriage to Alys. Whatever Dora might say about marriage, if, as he fervently hoped, she became pregnant while they were in China, he wanted to be free to marry her and to legitimise his child. Alys, perhaps unexpectedly, proved most receptive to the suggestion of divorce; she had, she wrote to him, always felt it would be better for both of them, 'though I very much dislike the hypocrisy involved'.

The divorce laws of the time made some degree of hypocrisy necessary for a couple who agreed to be divorced by condemning such agreement as 'collusion'. A divorce could not be granted to a couple simply because they both wished it; a 'wrong' had to be committed. Accordingly, in the first few days of August, an adulterous encounter between Russell and Colette in a London hotel was staged for the benefit of Alys's lawyers. Colette, it seems, did not at this time realise why Russell was so anxious to begin the process of divorce before his visit to China. Perhaps if she had, she would not have been so willing to fall in with the plan. As it was, she very generously interrupted her busy touring schedule to come to London for a night of 'official adultery' before leaving again for Portsmouth the next morning. It was to be the last time she saw Russell for the next ten years.

A few days later, Dora arrived back in England. She was met at Fenchurch Street Station by Russell, who, rather than taking her home, took her immediately to the Station Hotel, where he had arranged to provide more evidence that he was not entirely faithful to his wife. The detectives acting for Alys's solicitors were, however, evidently not very good at their job, and it required yet another night of public infidelity with Dora, this time at the Charing Cross Hotel, before the necessary evidence was acquired.

This left Russell and Dora with just five days to make preparations for their long journey. Their last few days in England were thus spent in a whirl of activity of buying clothes, getting passports in order, saying goodbye to family and friends and, throughout all this, arguing like fury about their different perceptions of Bolshevik Russia. Dora's enthusiasm was as deep-seated and as immovable as Russell's disillusionment. 'I felt sincerely', she later wrote, 'that in the Soviet Union I had seen a vision':

> a vision that I would accept to have been almost mystical – but in the political sense a vision of the making of a future civilisation. I, with my unpolitical fresh eyes and the background of my studies, was – and I really felt this – the only person in England who could interpret the true essence of what was happening in the Soviet Union.

To see Russell 'reacting like an old-fashioned liberal to a great people in torment and travail to bring forth their future' was a great disappointment to her. Russell, for his part, regarded Dora's love of the Bolsheviks 'with bewildered horror', and perhaps also a touch of jealousy. 'She had met men in Russia', he writes in his *Autobiography*, 'whose attitude seemed to her in every way superior to mine.' Who they were, he does not say (though John Reed seems a likely candidate), but the tone of wounded rivalry is familiar from the way he had talked earlier of the artists and writers whom Ottoline had admired in Garsington.

As Russell and Dora continued to argue, it began to emerge that, though they were poles apart in their attitudes to the Bolshevik Government, there was nevertheless an interesting area of common ground in their thinking about what they had seen in Russia. Both of them, in their different ways, had been led to reflect on the implications of the growth of industrialisation. On the boat trip along the Volga, Russell had come to see the Bolshevik regime as an aspect of a wider Western sickness typified by its 'gospel of industrialism and forced labour'. Dora, meanwhile, had come to see in the Russian economic and social system something that offered an alternative to the soulless mechanism of American industrial and commercial life. 'In Russia', she wrote, 'was a civilised purpose that could subdue and direct industrialism.'

In the minds of both of them, then, was a feeling that the growth of industrialism in the West presented a potential threat to civilisation by imposing upon mankind a mechanised existence that had no place for the spiritual values that made life worth living. For both of them, the fundamental problem was how industrialism might be 'civilised'. No matter that, in Bolshevik Russia, Dora had seen a solution, while Russell had seen just one more manifestation of the problem; the recognition by both of them of the nature and importance of this issue opened up the possibility, not just of agreement, but of intellectual co-operation. For Russell, for whom working for a common purpose was an important element of being in love, this was a profound relief.

On 14 August Russell and Dora left for Paris on their way to Marseilles, from where their boat to China would set sail. Russell already knew that the boat had been delayed by two or three weeks, but he preferred to spend that time in Paris rather than London. In Paris, he told Dora, they would be free to talk and enjoy each other's company, and indeed, according to Dora's recollections, it was during these few weeks that 'our married life began':

> I can remember how, in the morning, turning over sleepily in bed, I became conscious of Bertie sitting bolt upright and wide awake beside me, and how I thought rather desperately: 'This is how it is going to be for the rest of my life, this is what married life means.'

Russell used the time in Paris to prepare *The Theory and Practice of Bolshevism* for press. He knew its criticisms of Bolshevism would be disliked by his political friends and applauded by his political enemies and for that reason he had doubts, right up until the day he sent it to Unwin, as to whether or not it should be published. To help him reach a decision on the matter, he got up from his bed one night and sat on the hotel balcony gazing at the stars, hoping, in this way, to reach a wider perspective on the matter, unswayed by merely mortal considerations. He imagined himself to be having a conversation with the constellation Cassiopeia on the question, after which it seemed clear to him that 'I should be more in harmony with the stars if I published what I thought about Bolshevism than if I did not.'

Their boat eventually set sail from Marseilles on 6 September. Their route was to take them, on a journey that would last five weeks, through the Suez Canal and the Red Sea, then on to Ceylon and from there to Singapore, Saigon and, finally, Shanghai. These were names and places rich with associations from Conrad's great sea-faring novels, a fact which, while it might have escaped Dora, was not lost on Colette, who was following Russell's route on a large map bought specially for the purpose. 'I wonder if you'd time to remember to look for Conrad's house (in *Arrow of Gold*) at Marseilles,' she wrote to him on 14 August:

> The first real Conrad port won't be till Singapore, I suppose. Tell me about the sea, and the shipping of all kinds, the native boats; and the Eastern skies. Do you hear native music on shore at night? . . . Salute all the Conrad places for me. Saigon. What on earth is it like? I don't know and I can't imagine.

In his letters to both Colette and Ottoline during his long voyage, Russell did his best to live up to these expectations of riveting travelogue writing, but it was not really his forte. When he got to Saigon, for example, he described it as a 'nightmare place', but his attempts to convey this nightmare sound curiously uninspired – 'up a river, absolutely flat, surrounded by swamps in which they grow rice, even hotter by night than by day, full of mosquitoes, bats and large lizards. The Europeans are all enormously rich & very ill' – until, sparing himself further efforts at Conradian prose, he concludes with the short-hand remark 'the impression is like *The Heart of Darkness*'.

They finally reached Shanghai in the second week of October. Once he was in China, so enchanted was Russell by almost everything he saw that the dark tone that had so far characterised his reports home immediately gave way to a warm and light-hearted delight. As soon as they got off the boat, he and Dora were treated, as Dora wrote home to her mother, 'like an Emperor and Empress'. They were taken straight away to what would now be called a press conference, where they met local reporters and gave newspaper photographers the chance to take their picture, which the next day appeared in all the Chinese newspapers, together with reports of what they had said, what they wore, what they looked like, and so on.

Public interest in them was far more intense and more widespread than they had anticipated. It centred, it seemed, not on Russell's contributions to logic and the philosophy of mathematics, but on his social and political thought. 'We are very glad to have the greatest social philosopher of the world to arrive here in China,' a student from Shanghai wrote to Russell, expressing an opinion of his importance that was, it appeared, widely held in China. Where the Russians had been set on teaching Russell a philosophy of life, the Chinese seemed equally determined to learn one from him. In the few days he spent at Shanghai, he received innumerable visitors, all of whom treated him as a wise and learned sage. A grand banquet was held in his honour, at which a great number of speeches were made welcoming him, he later wrote, as 'Confucius the Second'. One lasting memory of the occasion was hearing for the first time ancient Chinese music, played on an instrument that he described as being 'like a guitar . . . but laid flat on the table'. Music did not often make a deep impression on Russell, but this he remembered all his life as 'exquisitely beautiful, very delicate'.

After just one night in Shanghai, Russell declared himself delighted with Chinese manners and culture. 'I had not realised until then', he wrote, 'that a civilised Chinese is the most civilised person in the world.' Everyone he met seemed witty, charming and full of fun. He was especially taken with the man appointed as his interpreter, Chao Yuen-ren, who would accompany him wherever he went, translating his lectures and speeches into Chinese. Chao had spent ten years in the United States and had accomplished what one might imagine to be the impossible task of translating *Alice in Wonderland* into Chinese. His youth, his cleverness and, especially, his ready wit made him the perfect companion for both Russell and Dora and they both became very fond of him. Once, on seeing a paper of Russell's called 'The Causes of the Present Chaos' (now the first chapter of *The Prospects of Industrial Civilization*), Chao remarked: 'Well, I suppose, the causes of the present Chaos are the previous Chaos.' It was the kind of wit that one associates with eighteenth-century English gentlemen, and exactly the kind that Russell enjoyed best.

To his initial disappointment, Russell discovered that he was not to go straight to Peking, but would be taken first on a series of trips to various parts of China to see something of its countryside and people, to learn about its culture and to give, in return, interviews and lectures to people eager to see and hear him. This began with three nights in Hangchow, on the shores of the Western Lake, where Russell and Dora were taken to see country houses and monasteries on the nearby islands. Russell was amused and delighted to discover that, in China, 'No one seems to believe the religion, not even the priests.' It all added to his growing impression that China was a kind of idyllic, pre-industrial version of eighteenth-century Britain, a sort of Whig Paradise:

China makes the impression of what Europe would have become if the eighteenth century had gone on till now without industrialism or the French Revolution. People seem to be rational hedonists, knowing well how to obtain happiness, exquisite through intense cultivation of their artistic sensibilities, differing from Europeans through the fact that they prefer enjoyment to power.

After Hangchow, Russell and Dora were taken to Nanking, where Russell lectured to the Chinese Science Society on 'Einstein's New Theory of Gravitation'. They were then escorted on a three-day journey up the Yangtse River to Hankow. 'The days on the Yangtse', Russell recalled, 'were as delightful as the days on the Volga had been horrible', an impression that is confirmed by a letter Dora wrote to her mother, in which she told her: 'Chinese scenery is perfectly divine, delicate as Chinese pictures, with distant, misty mountains always in view. And the Yangtse is, I imagine, quite one of the most beautiful rivers in the world.'

From Hankow, they went to Changsha, the capital city of the Hunan province and an important centre of commerce, industry and education. At Changsha there was a large educational conference taking place, among the participants at which was the philosopher John Dewey, who had been invited to China the previous year by the Chinese Lecture Association, the same body that had brought Russell over, and who had then accepted an invitation to stay on for a second year. Russell and Dewey met at a dinner given by the governor of the province, but neither seems to have taken much to the other, and though Dewey was, over the years, to perform many acts of public kindness to Russell, privately, it seems, he rather disliked him. According to the American liberal writer Sidney Hook, 'Dewey's feelings about Russell began in China . . . What concerned Dewey was Russell's insensitiveness to other people's feelings.' For Russell's part, he told Ottoline that, though he had liked Dewey better than any other American in 1914, 'now I can't stand him'.

The organisers of the conference had hoped to persuade Russell to stay in Changsha for a week, giving talks and meeting people, but after two weeks of pleasant but exhausting travel, Russell and Dora wanted a rest and were eager to get to Peking and settle down. They therefore limited their stay in

Changsha to one night, but, according to Russell, in order to compensate for his refusal to stay longer, he gave, during the twenty-four hours that he was there, four lectures, two after-dinner speeches and an after-lunch speech.

The four lectures were all on the same theme, presenting, in summary form, his impressions of Russia and his analysis of Bolshevik practice and theory, and finishing with a lecture on 'Necessary Elements for a Successful Communism'. Among his audience was Mao Tse-tung, then a twenty-six-year-old student. According to Mao's account (preserved in a letter he wrote at the time), Russell, as one might expect, 'took a position in favour of communism but against the dictatorship of the workers and peasants':

> He said that one should employ the method of education to change the consciousness of the propertied classes, and that in this way it would not be necessary to limit freedom or to have recourse to war and bloody revolution.

'My objections to Russell's viewpoint', Mao wrote, 'can be stated in a few words: "This is all very well as a theory, but it is unfeasible in practice." '

Politically, at this time, China was in a state of flux. The revolution of 1911, which Russell was inclined to liken to the Glorious Revolution in Britain of 1688, had left China with, in theory, a constitutional monarchy, but, in practice, something of a power vacuum. The moderately Socialist, nationalist party led by Sun Yat-sen was the movement that Russell, like John Dewey, hoped would win the struggle for power, and, in the autumn of 1920, there were some grounds for thinking this the most likely outcome and for believing, despite Mao's scepticism, that Socialism might be established without a violent revolution. Among students and political progressives, there was a widespread feeling that a new political philosophy was needed, and, though many looked to Soviet Russia for guidance, among those who came to hear Russell speak were many who considered the author of *Principles of Social Reconstruction* and *Roads to Freedom* to offer a political vision that was at least a serious rival to that of Lenin and Trotsky.

On the way from Changsha to Peking, Russell sent Ottoline a long account of his travels and of his first impressions of China and the Chinese, asking her to have several copies typed and to send one each to Clifford Allen, Elizabeth (his sister-in-law), Colette and Hugh Massingham, the editor of *The Nation*, the latter of whom, he said, could print it if he wanted to: 'But if not I can send him something more interesting later, which I should prefer.' In the event, Massingham printed it just as it was under the title 'The Happiness of China'.

Though, less than three weeks after he had arrived in the country and before he had even reached Peking, it might have been a little premature to publish his impressions of China, the picture Russell draws in this letter, of a supremely civilised people whose graceful way of life is too delicate and serene to survive the brutality of the modern world, changed little during the remainder of his visit. In Russia he had seen Westernisation as a disease; now, in China, he felt, he could see what people looked like in the full bloom of health, before this disease took hold. Europeans in China are described in his letter as if they were carriers of some deadly affliction. In Shanghai: 'The Europeans almost all look villainous and ill.' In Changsha: 'The Europeans have a few factories, a few banks, a few missions and a hospital – the whole gamut of damaging and repairing body and soul by western methods.' There were, he reports, about three hundred Europeans in Changsha, and then, like a doctor giving good news of a patient, he adds: 'but Europeanisation has not gone at all far'.

In Peking, which they eventually reached on the last day of October, this mood expressed itself in the insistence by Russell and Dora on furnishing their house with second-hand Chinese furniture in preference to the European furniture offered to them. As Russell put it: 'Our Chinese friends could not understand our preferring old Chinese things to modern furniture from Birmingham.' Both Russell and Dora were determined to put as much distance as possible between themselves and the European community in Peking. 'The Englishman in the East', Russell wrote, 'is a man completely out of touch with his environment. He plays polo and goes to his club. He derives his ideas of native culture from the works of eighteenth-century missionaries, and he regards intelligence in the East with the same contempt which he feels for intelligence in his own country.' Russell made no pretence that he and Dora were married and exulted in the offence this gave to conventional European sensibilities. Not that they were entirely shunned on this account by respectable people. The great esteem in which they were held by their Chinese hosts more than compensated for their open defiance of traditional views on sex and marriage, and they received more invitations than they cared to accept from European diplomats, businessmen and the like.

But what they really wanted was to get to know and understand the Chinese people themselves. For both Russell and Dora, the 'problem of China' was closely linked to the problem of industrialisation that had impressed both of them, in their different ways, from their respective visits to Russia. 'It was evident to us', writes Dora about their time in China, 'that we were living in a pre-industrial civilisation.' Thus the problem that had crystallised in their minds as a result of their experiences in Russia – the problem of whether industrial growth can be 'tamed', so that it remains compatible with the things in civilisation that we cherish – became identified with the problem of whether China, in undergoing its inevitable readjustment to the modern world, could retain some of the qualities that made it so delightful.

'I would do anything in the world to help the Chinese,' Russell wrote to Ottoline, 'but it is difficult. They are a nation of artists, with all their good and bad points.' Imagine, he said, the British Empire ruled by Augustus John and Lytton Strachey, 'and you will have some idea how China has been governed for 2,000 years'. The opposition that he had dwelt so much upon in prison between the Victorians and the Bloomsbury Group, between the vigour and the energy of the one and the listless artistic sensibility of the other, was now mirrored in his mind by the contrast between Russia and China. The Bolshevik regime showed one the dangers of ignoring altogether the refined pleasures of a contemplative life; the Chinese showed one the corresponding dangers of developing those pleasures to the exclusion of all else. 'The Chinese', he told Ottoline, 'constantly remind me of Oscar Wilde in his first trial when he thought wit would pull one through anything, and found himself in the grip of a great machine that cared nothing for human values.'

At the National University of Peking, Russell gave introductory lectures on philosophy and mathematical logic and also the course of lectures on the Analysis of Mind that he given twice already in London. Despite the tension that existed between this course and his more recent statements about the relevance of psychology to logic, Russell now sent it off to George Allen & Unwin in London to be published as a book, adding a preface that concluded by pointing out that the allusions to China in the lectures 'were written before I had been in China, and are not intended to be taken by the reader as geographically accurate. I have used "China" merely as a synonym for "a distant country", when I wanted illustrations of unfamiliar things.' At about the same time, he wrote to Trinity resigning the lectureship that he had never really taken up. His reason for doing so, he later said, was 'because I was living in open sin'.

It was a drastic move. Henceforth, he would be compelled to make money from his writing, which more or less precluded him from giving much time to the sort of philosophical questions to which he had devoted himself in prison. Why was he so willing to burn this particular boat? I am inclined to think that behind the decision lay both his disillusionment with philosophy in the wake of the influence of Wittgenstein's work and the replacement of philosophy in his affections by the longing to have children. In 1917, he had expressed his desire to return to philosophy as a need to return to 'eternal things', and, in his philosophical logic, right up to his reading of Wittgenstein's work in 1919, there *were* such eternal things to return to. In *Introduction to Mathematical Philosophy* and the Lectures on Logical Atomism he still conceived logic to be the study of platonic forms, even though he emphasised the near-impossibility of focusing one's mind upon these forms. But, immediately after his discussions with Wittgenstein in Holland – in his review of Joachim and in other pieces he wrote in the early part of 1920 – he began to lay great stress upon the linguistic nature of logic, emphasising that logic, far from investigating eternal, platonic forms, was simply an analysis of language. In this view, there are no 'eternal things' for a philosopher to seek refuge in.

What he would later characterise as a 'retreat from Pythagoras' – his growing disbelief in the reality of the world of mathematics – was thus completed at the end of 1919 by his acceptance of a view that made both logic and mathematics trivial. But it was by this time, in any case, no longer for Russell a matter for regret. For, certainly by the time he went to China, the most pressing impulse in his life was not to retreat to the contemplation of 'eternal things', but to have children. It was surely for this reason that he was prepared to sacrifice his Trinity post in order to live 'in sin' with Dora.

From a personal point of view, then, the decisive change in his conception of himself and of the kind of life he wanted to lead was the change from being a philosopher to being a father. Of course, there is no inherent reason why the two cannot be combined, and if he and Dora had been legally married in 1921, or if sexual mores among respectable society at Cambridge had been different, he might not have had to choose between fatherhood and an academic career. Supposing things had been different, supposing he had not felt that, in order to satisfy his desire to have children, he would have had to give up his position at Trinity, would he then have kept his lectureship and resumed his career as an academic philosopher?

Dora, at least, thought not. She was inclined to attribute Russell's decision to more public considerations. 'Bertie', she writes in her autobiography, 'had been dragged out of his ivory tower in Cambridge by horror at the slaughter of the young in war':

> Now he could see that concern for human beings could not stop with this one protest; he was taking into himself and seeking to remedy all the troubles of the world. I now felt that my own sense of mission since the Russian visit could be joined to his, and that together there might be much that we could accomplish.

In order to come to China, Dora too had cast aside all hopes of an academic career, and, in doing likewise, Russell, she felt, was committing himself to the importance of their joint work, their combined endeavours to 'remedy all the troubles of the world'.

Central to this joint work was the development of their shared ideas on the effects of industrialism, which, it is true, formed the focus of almost all of Russell's original thinking and writing during the time he was in China, to the exclusion of the more abstract questions that had dominated his philosophical thinking hitherto, up to and including *The Analysis of Mind*. In Peking, in addition to the lectures already mentioned, he offered a course – the only one in which he presented new ideas, rather than just a rehearsal of views he had already published – on 'The Science of Social Structure', which sought to present in ten lectures the thoughts about industrialism that he and Dora were developing together. It later formed the basis for *The Prospects of Industrial Civilization*, which a few years later was published under both their names.

The first lecture in this series was the aforementioned paper 'The Causes of the Present Chaos', which argued that the modern world was being shaped by two powerful forces: industrialism and nationalism:

> Capitalism and Socialism are the two forms of Industrialism; Imperialism and the attempt to secure freedom for oppressed nations are the two forms of Nationalism . . . The chaos in the world takes the form of a titanic conflict between these forces: Capitalism and Imperialism on one side; Socialism and Self-Determination on the other.

Some form of industrialism was made necessary by the nature of progress, and some form of nationalism by the nature of mankind; the issue was which form of each would triumph, and, in each case, Russell's sympathies were obvious.

Dora, with far more certainty of conviction than Russell, thought the message of this and similar lectures was profoundly original and important and was proud of her role in converting Russell to it. 'It was I', she told Ogden, 'who got it into his head that industrialism was infinitely more important for countries like Russia and China than the particular creed that administered it.' As Russell's reflections on the River Volga show, this is not entirely true, though the series of lectures in which he elaborated the theme was no doubt deeply influenced by the conversations he was having with Dora.

Something of Dora's view of these lectures is reflected in a dream she had at the time, in which she and Russell were in a small boat being carried along in a violent flood:

> I knelt in the bow, trying to fend off obstacles that might sink us. Bertie was standing up haranguing the troubled waters, above the tumult. 'Was that a good speech?' he called. 'Yes, my dear,' I shouted back, 'but do you think anyone heard it?'

That the lectures expressed an important truth, a truth that would, if heeded, bring calm and peace to a violent and tumultuous world ('remedy all the troubles of the world'), was not something Dora doubted. For her, the only question was whether anyone was listening.

To her dying day, Dora insisted with vehemence on the importance – and the unjust neglect – of their joint book, *The Prospects of Industrial Civilization*. The fight against the mechanisation of society was one she fought all her life with an almost religious passion. 'I am filled with hatred for money,' she wrote to her mother:

> for battleships, for industry, for factories, for the grind, grind, grind of the machine on all our creative instincts, grinding out the good and putting power in the hands of evil . . . Let us scrap industry, even if we have to go ragged and hungry, and lift our hands and square our shoulders and say at least we are men now, not cogs in a diabolical machine of destruction.

It is doubtful whether Russell ever shared Dora's passionate sense of the urgent importance of their joint intellectual work, and some of the sentiments expressed in this letter are quite alien to him. Far from being filled with hatred for money, he was, after he abandoned his academic post, filled with a desire to make money. And, far from regarding *The Prospects of Industrial Civilization* as the unheeded solution to the world's problems, he scarcely seemed to attach any importance to it at all. In his *Autobiography* he mentions it just once – and then only to remark that it did not make much money.

The commercial value of the lectures was something to which Russell had an eye even while he was delivering them. Indeed, this course marks a point at which his academic work and his journalism became indistinguishable. As each lecture was written, it was sold to a Japanese magazine called *The Kaizo*, which published the whole series as a set of monthly articles. These articles were then collected and published in Chinese as a book called *Shehui Jiegouxue Wujiang* (*The Science of Social Structure*), and, of course, later appeared, together with much other material, in English as *The Prospects of Industrial Civilization*.

Intellectually, the lectures, from Russell's point of view, were less of an advance than Dora considered them to be. Though the emphasis upon industrialism was indeed something new, Russell himself attached less importance to that than to what amounted to a re-statement of his basic political philosophy as outlined in *Principles of Social Reconstruction*. One of the lectures in the series, called 'What Makes a Social System Good or Bad?' (now Chapter VIII of *The Prospects of Industrial Civilization*), indeed simply repeated the old arguments. One of the most important qualities a social system must have, Russell argues, 'is that it must be such as people can *believe* in'. People no longer believed in the old system, the capitalism that brought about the war, and they needed a new faith. Socialism is 'the only faith which can restore happiness to the world', but it must be combined with freedom, for 'The main purpose and inspiration of any reconstruction which is to make a better world must be the liberation of creative impulse.' This entirely familiar line of thought suggests that what, if anything, Dora put into Russell's head was a new variation on an old theme.

And yet, even though he did not share Dora's conviction of their significance, it was nevertheless important to Russell that the views he was expressing in his lectures were ones on which he and Dora could agree. These first few months in China were probably the time in which they were happiest and closest, in which they felt most at one with each other. It was, Russell recalled, 'a time of absolute and complete happiness. All the difficulties and disagreements that we had had were completely forgotten.' Dora remembered it as a time when they were allowed the luxury of perfect leisure in which to pursue their own writing and thinking, 'but most of all to continue with the exchange of ideas and exploration of each other's personality'. Russell's sense of comradeship with Dora, built up largely through their combined intellectual interests, was as strong as it had been with Colette in 1917, and the six months from October 1920 to March 1921 were probably the longest and happiest period he had spent in the uninterrupted company of somebody he loved since the early days of his marriage to Alys.

In March, however, this period of happiness, his lectures on the 'Science of Social Structure' (of which he had delivered five of the proposed ten) and almost everything else in his life came to an abrupt halt when, suddenly and unexpectedly, he became seriously ill. For over three months he was laid up in bed, for much of the time feverish, delirious and on the point of death.

At the beginning of March 1921, both Russell and Dora had been ill with some kind of influenza, which had left Russell with bronchitis. A week or so later, however, Russell seemed better and they accepted an invitation to take a weekend break in the western hills, a two-hour drive from Peking. When they got there, he and Dora went for a swim in the hot spring for which the area is famous, but when they got back to their room Russell began to shiver violently. Dora wrapped him up and stoked the fire, but his shivering got worse and he became delirious. They decided to get him back to Peking, but, on the way back, going up a hill, their car stalled. Together with the Chinese drivers, Dora helped to push the car up the hill, yard by yard, putting heavy stones beneath the wheels as they went. Fortunately, the engine started on the way downhill and they were able to get Russell, now very ill indeed, into a German hospital in Peking. It was a moment Dora would remember – and remind Russell of – at frequent intervals for the rest of their time together, and even beyond.

At the hospital Russell was diagnosed as having double pneumonia and being close to death, his temperature reaching the usually fatal level of 107°F. For two weeks he lay in bed, his delirium interrupted only for short spells, when he would smile weakly at Dora (who was with him day and night) and tell the doctors treating him that he had never felt better in his life. 'I do not know how I myself am still alive,' Dora wrote to her mother, 'every minute has been agony and doubt and I have had next to no sleep':

> I swore he should not die and shook my fist at the foul universe, and I rejoiced all the time to find that he did too. All through he knew me and me only and could only talk sense to me. He says my face was clear, the others blurred and spiky. He says that at one point I spoke to him boldly and said he must fight or he would go under and that from that moment he set his teeth and held fast to my love and fought. I never saw such magnificent courage and defiance of life and death . . . It has been wonderful even through all the suffering, to feel how we were fighting together and how nothing could terrify us.

During these early days of his illness, he later said in a letter to Ottoline, 'my mind was more filled with beauty than ever before or since . . . I also had music – unreal and mystic – always in my head.' In between bouts of delirium, he dictated a remarkable dream. 'I took the utmost pains to make my account verbally identical with the dream,' he wrote, 'and the dream was so vivid that I think it likely I approximately succeeded.' In the dream his bedroom was transformed into a large cave on a steep hill, in the middle of which he lay sleeping on his bed. All round the cave were row upon row of hermits, who also slept. The next room was transformed into a similar cave on the same hillside, and this also was filled with hermits, but these were not asleep:

> They were hostile to us & might come and destroy us in our sleep. But I in my sleep spoke to my hermits in their sleep, & said: 'Brother hermits, I speak to you in the language of slumber, & the language which only sleepers can utter & only sleepers can hear or understand. In the land of sleep there are rich visions, gorgeous music, beauties for sense & thought such as dare not exist under the harsh light of the cruel sun. Do not awaken from your sleep, do not resist the other hermits by their own means, for

though you win you will become as they, lost to beauty, lost to the delicate vision, lost to all that ruthless fact destroys in the waking world. Sleep therefore: by my slumber language I can instill into you what is better than success & war & harsh struggle, & the worthless grating goods which wakers value. And by our magic, as one by one the other hermits fall asleep, we shall instill into them the bright vision, we shall teach them to love this world of gentle loveliness more than the world of death & rivalry & effort. And gradually from us will radiate to all the world a new beauty, a new fulfilment. Men's dreams will lead them through the livelong day along grassy lawns by sparkling brooks & through the dream night to the majesty of the stars, made gentle & warm & lovely by the rustling twigs through which they shine; to edifices of emblazoned glory, inaccessible mountain tops whose whiteness makes the blue of the sky more visible; & the mysterious sea, majestic in storm & gentle as a playful child in the sparkling calm.

In these visions mankind shall forget their strife, happiness shall come to all, pain shall fade out of the cruel world, & mankind shall come to know the beauty which it is their mission to behold.

The dream seems, most obviously, to be a metaphor for his feelings about China. About a month before his illness, Russell had written to his sister-in-law: 'I have no home on this planet. China comes nearer to one than any other place I know, because the people are not ferocious.' In a similar spirit, he had written to Wittgenstein about his love of China and the Chinese: 'All the nations set upon them and say they mustn't be allowed to enjoy life in their own way – They will be forced to develop an army and navy, to dig up their coal and smelt their iron, whereas what they want to do is make verses and paint pictures (very beautiful) and make strange music, exquisite but almost inaudible, on many-stringed instruments with green tassels.' The dream is a perfect image of these sentiments, of Russell at home with the slumbering Chinese, urging them to stay asleep and not to give up their delightful, dreamlike existence for the nightmarish reality of the waking world. In his *Autobiography* Russell describes the atmosphere in China at the time of his visit as 'electric with the hope of a great awakening. After centuries of slumber, China was becoming aware of the modern world.' Though he knew this awakening to be inevitable, the China that Russell had fallen in love with was the slumbering mass of hermits who, being asleep, could, like Conrad's Dr Stein, follow their dreams *usque ad finem*.

Also presented in the dream is a kind of compendium of many of the thoughts and feelings that had been dear to Russell: as well as standing for China, the slumbering hermits recall the 'strange assemblage of human beings' that he had seen by the side of the Volga, huddled together, 'some sleeping, others silently making small fires of twigs'; and his ability in the dream to speak the language of slumber recalls his thought then that 'something of that patient silence had communicated itself to me'. The idea in the dream that it is better to be asleep than awake recalls too his reflections apropos the Victorians on whether it was better to be sane with lies or mad with truth. And, of course, the idea of the stars and the mountain tops and the 'mysterious sea' as the ideal and final resting place of the soul seems just the thought with which one would imagine Russell – for whom the stars, the mountains and the sea had been a refuge ever since childhood – consoling himself in the face of death.

It is, in short, just what one would imagine would pass through Russell's mind in his dying moments. A few days after he recorded the dream, his condition became even worse and he had to be given oxygen. When he continued to deteriorate, one of the doctors treating him gave up hope and word got round that he was dying. Some students and scholars from the university came to pay their last respects. As Dora emerged from his sickroom, she saw them all, dressed in black robes and black caps, standing with their arms folded and grave expressions on their faces. Bowing reverentially, they asked if they could enter the room to hear the great philosopher's last words. Dora replied that, when the time came, she would let them in, but she herself was determined that he should not die. She and a German doctor called Dr Esser refused to give up hope.

By this time, however, the Japanese Press had got hold of the story and reported that Russell had died on 27 March. The news quickly travelled around the world, and several obituary notices were published. Colette was in Paris at the time. 'The news broke me,' she wrote. 'A neat job: short, sharp and permanent.' She was thrown into a deep depression, in which she contemplated suicide and was filled with a black destructiveness: 'I wanted to destroy all beauty over the whole earth.' Frank, too, heard the news but refused to believe it. Dying in Peking, he insisted to the reporters who came to question him, was not the sort of thing his brother would do without letting him know. Russell's friend, Charles Sanger, was equally disbelieving, but the news moved him to write. 'Until there was a false rumour of your death,' he told Russell, 'I never really knew how *very* fond I am of you. I didn't believe the rumour, but the mere idea that I might never see you again had never come into my mind; and it was an intense relief when the Chinese Embassy ascertained that the rumour was false.'

A pneumococcus serum was obtained from the Peking Medical College and administered to Russell, despite the fact that, according to Dora, 'no one really knew whether it would kill or cure'. Russell's temperature ran so consistently high that even Dr Esser became convinced that Russell would die. '*Na, das hält kein Mensch aus*' ('No one can stand that'), he exclaimed to Dora. The worst days, Dora recalled, were Easter Eve, Easter Sunday and her birthday, 3 April:

On my birthday afternoon the doctor came in and was certain he was dying. I held violets to his face because he loves them best and every time he smelt them the delirium would leave him for a moment and he would cry.

On 13 April, Dora wrote to her mother: 'today for the first time the doctors have looked less grave. They say the right lung is nearly clear, and if so the left will clear more quickly . . . The bad time is over and you can think of us both convalescing – for I feel as if I had been near death too – and telling each other how wonderfully we fought and how great a thing our love is.' In her relief, Dora wrote a poem called 'Death and Birth', which began:

> We have come through: our battered spirits lie
> Folded upon your sick bed in a close embrace.

Two weeks later Russell was well enough to write letters. 'I have missed much by not dying here,' he wrote to Ottoline, 'as the Chinese were going to have given me a terrific funeral in Central Park, & then bury me on an island in the Western Lake, where the greatest poets & emperors lived, died & were buried. Probably I should have become a God.' He sent her the description of his dream and asked her to send a copy to Colette. 'I want to tell you how profoundly you have been in my thoughts all this strange time,' he told Ottoline. 'I am told I tried to write to you during my delirium but of course I could only produce a meaningless scrawl.'

Though he had shaken off the threat to his life, Russell's health was still very poor. His lungs were recovering, but the illness and its treatment had left in their wake a whole series of secondary complaints, including dysentery, kidney disease, phlebitis and thrombosis. He was forced to remain in bed, though, now that he was in no danger of dying, he wanted to convalesce at home rather than in the hospital. The English nurse who looked after him was very devoted to her task, but she was also snobbish (she boasted repeatedly about how well she knew the Queen of Bulgaria) and devoutly Christian, and she got on Russell's nerves. At the beginning of May 1921, therefore, just before his forty-ninth birthday, he was taken back to their home in Peking, where he was forced to lie in bed for a further three weeks.

Lying in bed, he could see out of his window the beautiful sight of acacia trees in bloom. Spring had arrived. 'I am astonished to find how much I love life,' he wrote to Ottoline. 'When I see the sun I think I might never have seen him again.' He thought also how dreadful it would have been never to have seen the spring again: 'Oddly enough, these things come into my mind more instinctively than human beings.'

The title of Dora's poem, 'Death and Birth' was appropriate in more ways than one. After Russell was safely back at home, it occurred to her – which, in the strain of caring for Russell she had overlooked – that she had not had a period for a long time. Thinking it was no more than the effect of exhaustion, she went to Dr Esser for an examination. When she returned she showed Russell the slip of paper on which Esser had written '*gravidas [sic] incipit*' ('the onset of pregnancy'). Russell, Dora recalls, 'could hardly believe it and was beside himself with joy'.

Though he still had many weeks of inactive convalescence, Russell was to spend them in a state of almost rapturous delight, contemplating the fulfilment of what had been his strongest desire for over twenty years – to have a child. 'He's still in bed,' Dora wrote to Ogden, 'but if you saw him as he contemplates the prospect, smiling from ear to ear and laughing "like an irresponsible foetus" you would exclaim many times "isn't he a dear?" '

Russell's chief wish now was to get back to England as soon as possible, before Dora's condition made the long journey impossible. He had arranged to give a lecture tour in Japan in June, but clearly this had to be cancelled, and instead he arranged to give just one lecture there on his way back. The month of June was spent in bed at his home in Peking, trying to regain enough strength for the return journey to England and growing increasingly impatient to leave. 'We both long for home,' he wrote to Ottoline on 25 June. 'This place seems cruel to Europeans. When one is robust it is full of charm, but in bad health it is terrifying.' Even before his illness, his love for China and its people had been tempered somewhat by his discovery of what he regarded as their callous attitude to suffering. While the people around them in Peking were living in comparative luxury, elsewhere in China there was famine, with many thousands dying of starvation, and no attempt whatever was made to relieve their plight. 'People here are horribly callous about relief,' Dora reported to her mother. 'They leave their neighbours severely alone, even when they are dying . . . [They] just remain placidly indifferent.'

In an article written soon after his visit to China, on 'Some Traits in the Chinese Character', Russell dwells on this callousness in a way that shows why he may have found it 'terrifying' when he was ill:

> Famine in China can be permanently cured only by better methods of agriculture combined with emigration or birth-control on a large scale. Educated Chinese realise this, and it makes them indifferent to efforts to keep the present victims alive. A great deal of Chinese callousness has a similar explanation, and is due to perception of the vastness of the problems involved. But there remains a residue which cannot be so explained. If a dog is run over by an automobile and seriously hurt, nine out of ten passers-by will stop to laugh at the poor brute's howls. The spectacle of suffering does not of itself rouse any sympathetic pain in the average Chinaman; in fact, he seems to find it mildly agreeable.

Finally, at the beginning of July, Russell was judged able to undertake the voyage back to England, though even now he was very frail, described by Dora as having 'hardly any flesh on his bones and with shins like a knife-edge'. With the aid of a walking-stick, he was able to walk short distances by himself, and with Dora (now four months pregnant) to escort and protect him, this was considered good enough. They had, too, the help of Eileen Power, a history don whom Dora knew from Girton, who had been in China on a Travelling Fellowship and who now offered to accompany Russell and Dora as far as Vancouver. (In an effort to avoid the excessive heat of the Red Sea, they had decided to go back to England via Canada.)

On 6 July, Russell gave a short farewell address to the Chinese people, delivered at the Board of Education in Peking and published the following day in *The Peking Leader* under the heading 'China's Road to Freedom'. In it, he identified China's two most pressing tasks as the development of education and industry and argued that some form of Socialism would be necessary if China were to accomplish these tasks without falling victim to the many ills that had accompanied the (capitalist) industrialisation of the Western world. A longer address was given by Dora, in which she urged her listeners to develop a new ethical system upon which to base social and political life, 'some system which will control and subject the industrial machine and the mechanical discoveries of science'.

A few days later, they left China for Japan, in which they spent what Russell described as 'twelve hectic days'. At Moji, the first Japanese port they stopped at, they were told that a crowd of Japanese journalists were waiting to interview Russell. Dora went out and to each of the journalists handed a slip of paper on which she had written: 'Mr Bertrand Russell, having died according to the Japanese press, is unable to give interviews to Japanese journalists.'

The next port was Kobe, where Russell and Dora were entertained by Robert Young, the editor of the *Japan Chronicle*, a liberal daily newspaper in which Russell, during his time in the Far East, published several letters (including one complaining of the intrusiveness of the Japanese Press) and which also published in full the text of Dora's farewell lecture in Peking. It was, in Russell's opinion, 'the best newspaper I have ever known', and he had a great admiration for Young himself, 'a delightful man, who, having left England in the 'eighties, had not shared the subsequent deterioration of ideas'. Young took them to see the ancient temple at Nara and then left them in the care of the editor of *The Kazio*, who escorted them by train to Kyoto and thence to Tokyo. Everywhere they went, they were followed by journalists and police spies and were greeted by large numbers of curious, enthusiastic readers of their work. Neither of them, Dora wrote, felt fit enough to cope either with 'the exuberance of supporters or the sinister atmosphere of Government repression'.

As they arrived at Tokyo train station and were about to walk down the steps from the platform, a sudden flash from a camera startled Dora and she missed her footing. She managed to catch herself in time to avoid tumbling down the stairs, but the fear of a miscarriage that the incident aroused in Russell moved him to fury. 'I became blind with rage,' he wrote, 'the only time I have been so since I tried to strangle FitzGerald.' While Dora got into the car waiting for them, Russell, shouting and waving his stick, pursued the journalists. He never, of course, stood a chance of catching them, 'which was fortunate,' he recalled, 'as I should certainly have committed murder'. Before retreating, one of the cameramen took a picture of the advancing Russell, his eyes blazing with murderous intent, which, when he saw it, caused Russell to remark, 'I should not have known that I could have looked so completely insane.' In Russell's later description, the event takes on a curious and revealing racial aspect, as if, in his charge on the Japanese journalists, he considered himself to be defending, not only his unborn child from a thoughtless photographer, but also his 'stock' against an alien and hostile people:

I felt at that moment the same type of passion as must have been felt by Anglo-Indians during the Mutiny, or by white men surrounded by a rebel coloured population. I realised then that the desire to protect one's family from injury at the hands of an alien race is probably the wildest and most passionate feeling of which man is capable.

It was with great relief that, soon after this incident, Russell and Dora boarded the Canadian Pacific liner *The Empress of Asia*, and set sail from Yokohama to Vancouver, and with even greater relief that, about a month later, on 27 August 1921, they arrived in Liverpool, where, in the pouring rain, stood Dora's mother waiting to greet them. 'I never', Dora recalled, 'loved and admired my mother more than I did at that moment.'

21

THE COMING BACK

On arrival home from China, Dora was five months pregnant and before the baby was born Russell had some important loose ends to tie up involving his marriage to Alys and his relationship with Colette. He had to move quickly. Within a few days of his return in England, he made a final break with Colette. The parting was painful, even though Colette had to some extent been forewarned while Russell was away that it was to be expected. At a dinner party in London, she had heard Alys's brother, Logan Pearsall Smith, remark that Russell was going to marry Dora as soon as his divorce came through. Then, apparently contradicting this, she had a note from Russell, written on 27 April, just after he had shaken off the threat to his life, saying: 'When I come home, if you are willing, we can still have times together as wonderful as the old times.' In reply, she wrote:

My Beloved,
    I don't know how to wait until you're safe home again and I can take you in my arms, look into your dear eyes, and be with you again: be whole.

In June 1921, however, came a letter from Russell telling her of Dora's pregnancy, and she must surely then have realised that the affectionate reunion she had anticipated was not going to take place.

Russell's later recollection was that, on his return from China, Colette told him that she had now changed her mind about having children and would be willing to have them with him. 'By this time', he wrote, 'it was too late.' One of the first things he did when he got back to England was to write Colette a curiously ambivalent and ambiguous letter that was probably designed to be a farewell. The only thing now possible for him, he told her, was to commit himself to marrying Dora. 'The spirit of our love is safe,' he wrote, in a way that recalls his agonisingly slow withdrawal from Ottoline in 1916, 'but I do not know yet what to do about the body of it, and I shall not know until after the child.' Even now, it seems, he could not quite bring himself to part finally from Colette, and, when Colette phoned in reply to the letter, he told her that he was not, after all, fully committed to Dora. Colette, however, could see what the situation was and decided to make their parting clear and final. 'Let us forget all that has happened,' she wrote on 30 August:

There's no new pain left for me to learn. I shall never deny my love for you. In the past I wasn't grown enough to give you everything I could now give. I'm not too proud to admit my pitiful striving. I shall not write again, you are not to write to me.

I am your

Colette

Colette's feelings about her final break with Russell were expressed at much greater length in a novel she published in 1933 called *The Coming Back*. Although it opens with a disclaimer that 'No character in this book is a portrait of any living person', it is transparently autobiographical and indeed contains a more detailed and more personal account of her relationship with Russell than her two volumes of straight autobiography, *After Ten Years* and *In the North*.

The book's central plot concerns the doomed love between Gregory (Russell) and Konradin (Colette – the echo of Conrad's name is surely no coincidence), which follows accurately the twists and turns of Colette's own affair with Russell. Ottoline appears as 'the Marquesa de Santa Segunda', with whom Gregory, a distinguished scientist, had fallen in love 'soon after he had finished the three volumes which had made him famous'. The Marquesa is everything Gregory wanted, but, like Ottoline, decides that she cannot leave her husband: 'All Gregory's force could not break down that ancient resistance. His failure to break it down produced in him a sense of defeat. Gradually he came to believe she had never cared for him. From that moment, in a half-hearted way, he took up with other women.'

After he breaks with the Marquesa, Gregory falls passionately in love with Konradin, a writer who lives in a small flat in London and whose beauty and vitality attract to her a great number of admirers, including a group of intellectual friends of Gregory's, most notably T. C. Maynard (T. S. Eliot) and Jevons (Clifford Allen): 'They lived mostly in Chelsea or in Bloomsbury. They loved talk more than they loved anything on earth.' Konradin is accepted into this group, even though 'It was clear she had no mind: she could not *talk*.' Gregory and Konradin's love is threatened, however, not by her conversational limitations, nor even by Gregory's strong dislike and disapproval of her work, but by the fierce and uncontrollable jealousy aroused in him by her brief sexual liaison with the successful and influential writer, Marcus Beazely (Maurice Elvey), a jealousy that is no less strong for being in conflict with Gregory's stated ideals. Faced with it, Konradin 'began to realise that he [Gregory] was as full of contradictions as the sky was full of stars; but he did not know his own contradictions half as well as he knew the sky and its stars.'

In a remarkable passage that echoes Russell's own descriptions of his unbalanced state while Colette was with Elvey in Blackpool in September 1917, Colette describes the effect it had on Gregory to imagine Konradin with Marcus Beazely:

He could take no interest in anything. He felt tired and lonely. He became prey to bad dreams . . . It seemed to him it would be the end of all things if she took up with Beazely. It would be absolute disaster. During those few days while he was away, he endured the tortures of the damned . . . He began to criticise Konradin in his mind. He discovered she was vain and foolish and heartless. She was ruthless and arrogant and crude . . . She lived for admiration – and she wanted it from all and sundry . . . She had not the remotest notion of self-control. It had never occurred to her it was possible to act against impulse . . . He wanted a permanent life together. He wanted children. It was hell like this: utter, utter hell.

In a later passage, ostensibly giving Jevons's impression of Gregory, Colette shows her own insight into the essence of Russell's character:

In some ways, Gregory was one of the loneliest men he [Jevons] had ever met – in spite of his innumerable friends and the affection they gave him. He was a man continually up against 'those fundamental questions, those terrible insoluble questions that wise men never ask'. Was it better to be sane with lies? or mad with truth?

Gregory's jealousy transforms both himself and his love for Konradin ('Where was the Gregory she had known so well? She did not recognise him in this new madness'), and, seeing him now as a jailor rather than a liberator, she insists on her independence from him ('She *must* be free') and on her right to love, and to sleep with, both him and Marcus.

In consequence, Gregory, who 'desired children more than he desired anything on earth', takes up with Gertrude West (Dora), a Cambridge academic who 'wanted to have a family. She wanted four children: two girls and two boys. She had worked it out in a perfectly logical way.' It is obvious to Konradin that Gregory is not in love with Miss West, and 'it seemed rather feeble of him to have taken up with her', but she does nothing to discourage the relationship. When Gregory is invited to spend six months lecturing in America, he takes Miss West with him. While he is away, Konradin hears that he is to marry Miss West as soon as they return from America: ' "It's not true! It's not true!" Konradin wanted to shout . . . Hot tears slid down her face. She felt she had been stabbed in the throat. "Oh God!" she gasped. "Oh God!" ' In her heart, however, 'she still believed Gregory would come back to her', and is encouraged to believe so by the letters he sends her. Konradin still loves him deeply, though one suspects that the 'sudden hostility' towards him that Colette, at this stage in the story, puts into the mind of the T. S. Eliot character, Maynard, was something she herself had felt towards Russell:

For an instant he saw him as many people saw him: a man exhausting other men by his intellect; exhausting women by his intensity; wearing out his friends, sucking them dry, passing from person to person, never giving any real happiness – or finding any.

The book ends with the 'coming back' itself – Gregory's return from America and his final disillusionment of Konradin's hopes. 'Tell Konradin', he says to Jevons, 'that I love her eternally; with all that is deepest and most burning in me; I am torn in two; I don't know how to think or speak or feel; but I know that what I am doing is the only possible thing for me to do.' The final scene is of Konradin's reaction to Gregory's message:

> 'He said', she repeated in a clear voice, 'that he loved me with all that was deepest and most burning in him. Is that so?' Jevons nodded. 'Very well. I've mucked up my life.'

Russell claimed never to have read *The Coming Back* (or any of Colette's other books). Perhaps he knew that it would make painful reading. In the autumn of 1921, at least, he had reason to take Colette's final letter to him at face value, and reason, too, to be grateful to her for taking it upon herself to end the relationship cleanly, in a way that he apparently found impossible. For, though it was probably perfectly true that, emotionally, he was still divided between Colette and Dora, his talk of being unsure about his commitment to marrying Dora could not, at this stage – as Colette must surely have realised – be taken very seriously. He may have been unsure whether he wanted Colette or Dora as his lover, but that he wanted a child, and preferably a legitimate child, was something about which he had never been unsure. In the weeks immediately after his return from China, the need uppermost in Russell's mind was to secure the legitimacy of his child, and, with Dora in an advanced stage of pregnancy, there was no time for hesitation or doubt.

He had a maximum of four months in which to finalise his divorce from Alys and marry Dora. In the event, he did both in a single month. Though he did not know it at the time, the decree nisi, the first stage of his divorce from Alys, had gone through on 3 May (the only question about its legality being the widespread view at the time that Russell was dead). Normally, there had to be a six-month wait before the decree absolute could be granted, making Russell free to marry again. As the baby was due in December, this would be cutting things rather fine, so Russell instructed his lawyers to try and speed things up. Under some protest, the King's Proctor complied and the divorce was made absolute on 21 September. Six days later, Russell and Dora were married at Battersea Registry Office.

For Dora, getting married was something of a betrayal of principle. In China, she had been proud of the stand she and Russell had taken against convention by openly living together outside wedlock and felt that, in doing so, they had provided a leading example to all young people who wanted to challenge traditional attitudes. Now, she felt that she had let down those who looked to her to set an example. 'Nobody could be more disappointed than I was over the marriage', she wrote to Rachel Brooks, a friend in China who was sympathetic to what had been widely understood as Russell and Dora's rejection of traditional marriage:

> For my part I felt it had no justification, and I was infinitely happy when I believed the divorce would come too late to make it possible. B. R.

thought differently, and people who criticise me ought to bear in mind that the baby has two parents, to one of whom (B. R.) he was the long-desired miracle, given when it seemed as if everything was to be taken away . . . I shall certainly never quite recover from the feeling of disgrace I had in marrying . . . I wish you would let those people who were interested in my experiment know some of what I say here. I do not like to feel I have let people down, even though I have!!

The following summer Russell, too, wrote to Rachel Brooks, insisting that the decision to marry was entirely his, and justifying it on the grounds, first, that if they had not married, the child might have grown up resentful of its parents, and, second, that unmarried and with an illegitimate child, they would have had great difficulty in finding either somewhere to live or people to work for them. 'It is not unlikely', he told her, in a phrase that recalls his murderous designs on the Japanese cameraman that had threatened his unborn child, 'that some peculiarly exasperating case of persecution would have driven me to murder.'

Russell's anxieties about the possibility of persecution were no doubt heightened by the difficulties he was experiencing in trying to find somewhere for him and Dora to live. He tried to take over the lease of Clifford Allen's flat in Battersea, but the landlord refused to let it to Russell, apparently because of Russell's anti-war activities.[1] Dorothy Wrinch came to the rescue by lending Russell and Dora her cottage in Winchelsea, Kent, where they lived from August to October, while Russell continued to look for somewhere suitable in London.

In October, Russell took advantage of living in Kent to call upon Joseph Conrad, who had recently bought a new house in Bishopsbourne, not far from Canterbury. While walking in the garden, Dora remarked to Conrad on the beauty and peacefulness of his new home. 'It is so,' he replied, 'and my wife loves it. But for myself I dislike living where I cannot see the horizon.' Russell presented Conrad with a copy of *The Analysis of Mind*, and was rewarded with a letter in which Conrad wittily played upon Russell's emphasis in the book on the notion of mental imagery:

I have been dwelling with you mentally for several days between the covers of your book – an habitation of great charm and most fascinatingly furnished; not to speak of the wonderful quality of light that reigns in there. Also all the windows (I am trying to write in images) are, one feels, standing wide open. Nothing less stuffy – of the Mansions of the mind – could be conceived!

The image of a dwelling-place was chosen because, by the beginning of November, Russell had finally found somewhere for Dora and him to live: a three-storey terraced house in Sydney Street, Chelsea. This they furnished

---

[1] So, at least, Russell and Dora believed, though neither explains why, if he felt so strongly about anti-war protestors, the landlord was willing to have Clifford Allen as a tenant.

with what Conrad called their 'Chinoiseries', together with the simple but rather finely made furniture that Russell had unwittingly acquired when he agreed to buy the books and other belongings that Wittgenstein had stored in a shop in Cambridge. 'The child will probably be born in your bed,' he wrote to Wittgenstein on 5 November, adding: 'Your things are worth much more than I paid for them, and I will pay you more whenever you like. I didn't know when I bought them how much I was getting.'

Russell was writing with news of the forthcoming publication of Wittgenstein's work. While he was in China, Dorothy Wrinch had found two publishers for it. In German, it would appear in the academic journal, *Annalen der Naturphilosophie*, edited by Wilhelm Ostwald, while in English it would be the first in a new series of philosophical books published by Kegan Paul and edited by Dora's close friend, C. K. Ogden. In both cases, Russell's introduction would be published with Wittgenstein's work. 'I am sorry,' Russell told Wittgenstein, 'as I am afraid you won't like that, but as you will see from his [Ostwald's] letter, it can't be helped.' The letter he enclosed was from Ostwald to Dorothy Wrinch, in which he told her:

> In any other case I should have declined to accept the article. But I have such an extremely high regard for Mr Bertrand Russell, both for his researches and for his personality, that I will gladly publish Mr Wittgenstein's article in my *Annalen der Naturphilosophie*: Mr Bertrand Russell's Introduction will be particularly welcome.

As this letter indicates, Ostwald had little interest in Wittgenstein's work and took little care with its publication, and it was not until Ogden's edition came out that Wittgenstein considered what was, by then, called *Tractatus Logico-Philosophicus* to have been properly published.

Having established himself and Dora in their house in Sydney Street, Russell, despite his still poor health and his increasingly edgy state of nervous anticipation over the coming birth, lost no time in producing saleable journalism from his experiences in China. He began with an article on trends in Chinese education, which was published in *The Review of Reviews* in London and *The Dial* in America, in which he described the wish among modern Chinese progressives to 'increase the number of Chinese who can use and appreciate Western knowledge without being the slaves of Western follies'. This trend was, he wrote, 'one of the most hopeful things happening in our not very cheerful epoch'. The article ends with a view of the Chinese as 'the only people in the world who quite genuinely believe that wisdom is more precious than rubies'. That, Russell adds ruefully, 'is why the West regards them as uncivilised'.

This led naturally to the subject of his next article, written for *The Atlantic Monthly*, on 'Some Traits in the Chinese Character', in which Russell, while acknowledging the callousness towards famine sufferers that had disturbed both him and Dora, presented the Chinese as possessing the kind of refined and delicate, highly civilised sensibility that Western 'progress' had stamped out in Europe. 'The obvious charm which the tourist finds in

China cannot be preserved,' Russell concludes, 'it must perish at the touch of industrialism':

> But perhaps something may be preserved, something of the ethical qualities in which China is supreme, and which the modern world most desperately needs. Among these qualities I place first the pacific temper, which seeks to settle disputes on grounds of justice rather than by force. It remains to be seen whether the West will allow this temper to persist, or will force it to give place, in self-defence, to a frantic militarism like that to which Japan has been driven.

In November 1921, as he waited nervously and impatiently for 'the event' (as he often put it), Russell renewed contact with the Eliots. 'It was so nice to get a letter from you again,' Vivien wrote, and then went on to tell him that Eliot was away in Margate and that he was soon to leave for Switzerland to be treated by Dr Vittoz, the psychiatrist who had earlier treated Ottoline. 'As you probably know,' she said, 'Tom is having a bad nervous – or so called – breakdown.' Nevertheless:

> We both send very many congratulations, and Tom says he is quite sure the baby *will* have pointed ears, so you need not be anxious. Even if they are not pointed at birth, they will sharpen in time.

The doctor acting as Dora's gynaecologist was Sir Sydney Beauchamp, Elizabeth Russell's brother, who was very eminent in his field. In November, Beauchamp decided to induce the baby a month early, not for the baby's sake, or for Dora's, but rather for Russell's, 'bearing in mind', as Dora put it, 'what this birth meant to Bertie in his anxious and delicate state'. Thus, on 16 November, Russell's long wait was over, and his first child, a boy, was delivered at his home in Sydney Street. 'As I lay there on the top floor,' Dora remembered, 'the bells of St Luke's Church at the end of the street were ringing in practice, but to me at that moment they rang for my son.'

'I am so relieved,' Russell wrote just hours after the birth to Ottoline, 'I [felt] sure the child would have 3 arms & no eyes, or something queer, but he seems no worse than other people's babies.' He then wrote to Joseph Conrad, saying: 'I wish, with your permission, to call my son John Conrad. My father was called John, my grandfather was called John, and my great-grandfather was called John; and Conrad is a name in which I see merits.' It was just about the greatest mark of respect that Russell could possibly offer, the highest compliment he was capable of giving, and, though he possibly did not appreciate its full significance for Russell, Conrad felt suitably honoured. He was, he told Russell, 'profoundly touched – more than I can express – that I should have been present to your mind in that way and at such a time'. To Russell's son, Conrad became what John Stuart Mill had been to Russell himself: a kind of secular godfather.

Conrad's death in 1924 prevented him from playing much part in the life of his 'godchild', and his declining health also prevented him from having

much more to do with Russell, but, in his letter, written just two days after
the birth, he demonstrated a rich understanding of what this moment meant
for Russell:

> Yes! Paternity is a great experience of which the least that can be said is
> that it is eminently worth having – if only for the deepened sense of
> fellowship with all men it gives one. It is the only experience perhaps whose
> universality does not make it common but invests it with a sort of grandeur
> on that very account. My affection goes out to you both, to him who is
> without speech and thought as yet and to you who have spoken to men so
> profoundly with effect and authority about the nature of the mind. For
> your relation to each other will have its poignant moments arising out of
> the very love and loyalty binding you to each other.

Becoming a father was not just, for Russell, the fulfilment of a strong and
long-held impulse, it put his entire life on a new footing; it gave his life, as
he himself said, 'a new emotional centre'. Where, until the completion of
Principia Mathematica, intellectual matters had been his fundamental preoccupation, and after that social and political questions, now at the centre of his
life were his hopes and feelings for his child.

In their various ways, his early religious beliefs, his belief in the platonic
realm of mathematics, his faith in revolutionary socialism and even the
ecstasies of romantic love had all disappointed him; they had all turned out
to be mere 'phantoms of the dusk', disappearing in the cold light of day. But
fatherhood, the binding love and loyalty (as Conrad put it) between a man
and his son – that, surely, was as real as any contact can be between one
person and another. And in that contact, equally surely, Russell thought, he
would find the lasting release from the prison of the self, from the feeling of
being a 'ghost', for which he had longed all his life.

NOTES AND REFERENCES

Details of the published sources cited below are given in the Bibliography. With very few exceptions, the unpublished sources were consulted at the Russell Archives, McMaster University, Hamilton, Ontario. This applies even to the letters from Russell to Ottoline Morrell, the originals of which are held by the Humanities Research Center, University of Texas, but copies of which are kept at the Russell Archives. The letters from Russell to his first wife, Alys, however, I consulted at the London offices of their owners, Camellia Investments. When Russell sold his archive to McMaster, one of the clauses of the contract embargoed material relating to his wives and certain members of his family until five years after their deaths. Under the terms of this clause, the letters to and from Constance Malleson (Colette) were disembargoed in 1980, and those to and from Dora Russell in 1991.

Russell's correspondence is so huge (the Russell Archives estimate that they have in excess of 40,000 letters) that, even though it has been extensively quoted before in several publications, including Russell's own autobiography and at least three previous biographies, much that is interesting and revealing has remained unpublished. *The Selected Letters of Bertrand Russell Volume 1 1884–1914* offers a judicious selection of many of these hitherto unpublished letters, but, even so, includes less than 10 per cent of the total available. Some of the most important sets of surviving correspondence have, however, been published in their entirety. These include: Russell's correspondence with Wittgenstein (Wittgenstein's side in *Letters to Russell, Keynes and Moore*, and Russell's side in *Russell*, 10 (2), Winter 1990–91); his letters to and from Gottlob Frege (in Frege, *Philosophical and Mathematical Correspondence*); and D. H. Lawrence's letters to him (in *D. H. Lawrence's Letters to Bertrand Russell*, edited by Harry T. Moore). The few letters to Russell from Joseph Conrad that Russell did not include in his *Autobiography* are reproduced in 'Joseph Conrad and Bertrand Russell' by Edgar Wright, *Conradiana*, 2 (1), 1969, pp. 7–16. Extensive extracts from Russell's correspondence with Philip Jourdain have been published in *Dear Russell – Dear Jourdain*, edited by I. Grattan-Guinness, and his letters to and from Vivien and T. S. Eliot up until 1922 are included in *The Letters of T. S. Eliot Volume I*. Russell's letters to Lucy Donnelly and Helen Thomas are transcribed in an unpublished Ph.D. thesis by Maria Forte, a copy of which is in the Russell Archives. Most of Russell's letters to Colette survive, but for Colette's letters to Russell (with a very few exceptions), the only source is an unpublished typescript prepared by Colette and her friend Phyllis Urch, which gives a detailed account of her relationship with Russell and includes transcriptions of many of his letters to her.

Where I have seen neither the original letter nor a copy or transcription of it, I have cited the (usually published) source in which I found it quoted. Three works that have proved indispensable in this way are: Miranda Seymour's *Ottoline Morrell: Life on the Grand Scale* (for Ottoline's side of her correspondence with Russell), Barbara Strachey's *Remarkable Relations: The Story of the Pearsall Smith Family* (for Alys's side of her correspondence with Russell), and Jo Vellacott's *Bertrand Russell and the Pacifists in the First World War* (for the correspondence between Russell and other members of the NCF, and the memos about Russell circulated within the War, Home and Foreign Offices of the British Government).

The task of finding and reading Russell's unpublished manuscripts and his more obscure journal publications has been rendered considerably easier by the publication of the magnificent series of *The Collected Papers of Bertrand Russell*. The ten volumes that have so far been published (Volumes 1, 2, 3, 4, 6, 7, 8, 9, 12 and 13) cover most of the period dealt with in this book. In the citations below, Russell is abbreviated as 'BR', and his co-correspondents as follows:

BB	Bernhard (later, Bernard) Berenson
LC	Louis Couturat
GLD	Goldsworthy ('Goldie') Lowes Dickinson
LD	Lucy Donnelly
TSE	T. S. Eliot
GF	Gottlob Frege
PEJ	Philip E. Jourdain
EH	Élie Halévy
MLlD	Margaret Llewelyn Davies
DHL	D. H. Lawrence
CM	Constance Malleson (Colette O'Neil)
OM	Ottoline Morrell
GM	Gilbert Murray
IP	Ivy Pretious
AR	Alys Russell (née Pearsall Smith)
DR	Dora Russell (née Black)
FR	Frank Russell
RR	Rollo Russell
KT	Katharine Tait (née Russell)
HT	Helen Thomas (after 1903, Helen Flexner)
ANW	Alfred North Whitehead
LW	Ludwig Wittgenstein

INTRODUCTION

p. xvii   'How on earth': Virginia Woolf to Benedict Nicolson, 24.8.40, quoted by James King in *Virginia Woolf*, p. 579

p. xviii 'an art of human understanding': Richard Holmes, in John Batchelor (ed.), *The Art of Literary Biography*, p.25

1. Ghosts

p. 3   'I shall never lose': BR to OM, 21.8.18

p. 3   'I imagine myself': BR to KT, 23.1.48

p. 5   'bought and sold': see *The Letters of Junius*, edited by John Cannon, Oxford, 1978, p. 71

p. 5   'last doge of Whiggism': quoted in *Lord John Russell* by A. Wyatt Tilby, p. 143

p. 6   'As long as': *The Life of William Lord Russell* by Lord John Russell, Longman, 1819, p. 111

p. 7   'had a certain anachronistic consistency': mock obituary, first published in *The Listener*, 12 Aug. 1936 as 'The Last Survivor of a Dead Epoch', reprinted in *Unpopular Essays*

p. 7   'in all times': Lord John Russell to his brother, the Duke of Bedford, 13.10.1841, see *Lady Russell: A Memoir*, p. 58

p. 8   'I wish I could whip': quoted in *Bertrand Russell, A Political Life* by Alan Ryan, p. 7

p. 8   'very fat & ugly': *The Amberley Papers*, ii, p. 492

p. 8   Charles James Fox had been very naughty: see letter from Lord John Russell to his son, Amberley, *The Amberley Papers*, ii, p. 499

p. 8   'I do not remember', Frank Russell, *My Life and Adventures*, p. 12

p. 8   A strange prelude: based on the account given in Amberley's journal, *The Amberley Papers*, ii, pp. 533–6

p. 9   'We hesitated': Kate Amberley to Helen Taylor, 16.6.1872, quoted by Ann Robson in 'Bertrand Russell and his godless Parents', *Russell*, 7, autumn 1972, p. 6

p. 9   'very unhappy': *The Amberley Papers*, ii, p. 541

p. 9   'strange & unsteady of brain': *The Amberley Papers*, ii, pp. 551–2

p. 10   'he also became': Frank Russell, op. cit., p. 24

p. 10   cited by William James: see *The Principles of Psychology*, Volume Two, p. 396: 'Mr Spalding's wonderful article on instinct shall supply us with the facts', etc.

p. 10   'Spaldy has got robins': *The Amberley Papers*, ii, p. 567

p. 10   'I suppose that we did have lessons': Frank Russell, op. cit.

p. 11   'Frank *must not* stay at Ravenscroft': *The Amberley Papers*, ii, p. 554

p. 11   'Apparently upon grounds of pure theory': *The Autobiography of Bertrand Russell 1872–1914*, p. 17

p. 11   'he has quite taken to me': *The Amberley Papers*, ii, p. 561

p. 12   'Bertie made a nice little bow': ibid., p. 565

p. 12   'Bertrand, I think': ibid., p. 562

p. 12   'because he was chaste': *Autobiography*, p. 31

p. 12   The records of the asylum: copy in Russell Archives

p. 13   'blessed day': Frank Russell, op. cit., p. 27

p. 13   'We had just really settled down': *The Amberley Papers*, ii, p. 566

p. 13   'You will know': ibid., p. 569

p. 14   'My dear Mama': ibid., p. 571

p. 14   'all incentive': Frank Russell, op. cit., p. 28

p. 14   'became more than ever': ibid.

p. 14   'continuing to live': quoted in *The Amberley Papers*, ii, p. 575

p. 14   'utmost Victorian horror': *Autobiography*, p. 17

p. 15   'I may sum up': Frank Russell, op. cit., p. 10

p. 15   'To come from the free air of Ravenscroft': ibid., p. 33

p. 15   'The first and immediate effect': ibid., p. 34

p. 16   'My Uncle Rollo': ibid., p. 33

p. 16   'There were many things': ibid., p. 50

p. 16   'Of my parents': 'My Mental Development', in *The Philosophy of Bertrand Russell*, edited by Paul Arthur Schilpp, p. 3

p. 17   'wove fantasies': *Autobiography*, p. 19

p. 17   'she proceeded': ibid., p. 31

p. 17   'The most frequent': Frank Russell, op. cit., p. 51

p. 17   'The Russells never understood him': *Autobiography*, p. 26

p. 17 'It was their intention': Frank Russell, op. cit., p. 38

p. 18 'Aunty, do limpets think?': *Autobiography*, p. 29

p. 18 'that I could not say': Frank Russell, op. cit., p. 41

p. 18 'Heard old Lord Russell was dead': quoted in A. Wyatt Tilby, op. cit., p. 257

p. 18 'one of my first': Queen Victoria to Lady Russell, 30.5.1878, see *Lady John Russell: A Memoir*, pp. 252–3

p. 18 'Even as a child': quoted in *Autobiography*, p. 30

p. 19 'I do not think': *Autobiography*, p. 20

p. 19 'was never physically in love': *The Amberley Papers*, i, pp. 31–2

p. 19 'Throughout the greater part': *Autobiography*, pp. 30–1

p. 19 'So many things': ibid., p. 38

p. 20 'a great release': *Autobiography Volume III*, p. 35

p. 20 'Each night': *Satan in the Suburbs* (Penguin edition), p. 13

p. 20 'in his malignant mind': ibid., pp. 55–6

p. 21 'in a universal shriek': ibid., p. 57

p. 21 'You imagine': ibid., p. 60

p. 22 'She was persuaded': ibid., p. 61

p. 22 'You have offered me': ibid., p. 62

p. 22 'You think I'm defeated': ibid., p. 64

p. 23 'Self-Appreciation': now published in *Collected Papers 1*, pp. 72–3

p. 23 'unusually prone': *Autobiography*, p. 28

p. 24 'Most of my vivid early memories': ibid.

p. 24 'contemptuous': ibid., p. 33

p. 24 'I used to go': ibid., p. 34

p. 24 'It was full of instruction': Frank Russell, op. cit., p. 58

p. 24 'I owe to the Russells': *Autobiography*, p. 35

p. 24 'a perfectly princely education': George Santayana, *Persons and Places*, p. 441

p. 25 she wrote on the fly leaf: see *Autobiography*, p. 22

p. 25 'I had not imagined': *Autobiography*, p. 36

p. 25 'did very well indeed': Frank Russell, op. cit., p. 101

p. 25 'Bertie successfully mastered': ibid.

p. 25 'I did the 12th prop.': Frank Russell's diary, now in the Russell Archives, quoted in Nicholas Griffin, *Russell's Idealist Apprenticeship*, p. 10

p. 25 'By God!': quoted in Richard Peters, *Hobbes*, pp. 20–1

p. 26 'I hoped': *Portraits from Memory*, p. 20

p. 26 'the first thing': ibid.

p. 26 'read . . . at once': Russell's preface to the 1946 reprint of Clifford's *Common Sense of the Exact Sciences*, quoted by Griffin, op. cit., p. 10

p. 27 'more than a mathematician': ibid., quoted by Stefan Anderson in *In Quest of Certainty: Bertrand Russell's search for certainty in religion and mathematics*, p. 79

p. 27 'It is wrong always': W. K. Clifford, 'The Ethics of Belief', *Contemporary Review*, 1877, reprinted in *Lectures and Essays*, quoted in Griffin, op. cit., p. 11

p. 27 'it sometimes seems': *Lady Russell: A Memoir*, p. 268

p. 28 'the whole of this mental life': *Autobiography*, p. 41

p. 28 'shake the dust': Frank Russell, op. cit., p. 107

p. 28 According to Santayana: see George Santayana, op. cit., pp. 308–10

p. 29 'Greek Exercises': extracts from this were included by Russell in Chapter III ('First Efforts') of his book, *My Philosophical Development*, and in Chapter II ('Adolescence') of his *Autobiography*. The whole document is reproduced in *Collected Papers 1*, pp. 3–21

p. 29 'I have in consequence': *Collected Papers 1*, p. 5

p. 29 'in finding reasons': ibid.
p. 30 'which law of nature': ibid., p. 10
p. 30 'likely to produce': ibid., p. 9
p. 30 'we have no certain evidence': ibid., p. 12
p. 30 'My doctrines': ibid., p. 15
p. 30 'it does give us': ibid., p. 7
p. 30 'I should like': ibid., p. 15
p. 30 'and I am left': ibid., p. 11
p. 30 reading an article in *The Nineteenth Century*: ibid., p. 5
p. 31 'doubtful conversation': *Autobiography*, p. 39
p. 31 'I was much ashamed': ibid.
p. 31 'I became morbid': ibid.
p. 31 'No mind': *Collected Papers 1*, p. 15
p. 31 'It is very difficult': ibid.
p. 32 'I don't suppose': ibid., p. 16
p. 32 'by a feeling of contempt': ibid., p. 17
p. 32 'what is the soul?': ibid., pp. 19–20
p. 32 'in which among other things': ibid., p. 13
p. 33 'emerged from the base materialism': from 'A History of My Friendship with Fitz', *Collected Papers 1*, pp. 60–1
p. 33 'the most beautiful poem': *Autobiography*, p. 40
p. 33 'Here, I felt': see 'The Importance of Shelley', pp. 11–16 of *Fact and Fiction* (quotation on p. 12). For a good discussion of Russell's admiration for Shelley see 'The Romantic Russell and the Legacy of Shelley', *Russell*, 4 (1), summer 1984, by Gladys Garner Leithauser
p. 34 'accepting conventional beliefs': *Fact and Fiction*, p. 12
p. 34 'how wonderful it would have been': *Autobiography*, p. 40
p. 34 'shuddered': *Fact and Fiction*, p. 14
p. 34 Russell composed a sonnet: see *Collected Papers 1*, p. 58
p. 34 'put into words': from Russell's 1889 essay ' "The Language of a Nation is a Monument to which Every Forcible Individual in the Course of Ages has Contributed a Stone" ', see *Collected Papers 1*, pp. 33–5
p. 35 'in short': from 'A History of My Friendship with Fitz', op. cit., p. 60
p. 35 'Having been lonely': *Autobiography*, p. 44
p. 35 'the ideal of young womanhood': 'A History of My Friendship with Fitz', op. cit., p. 61
p. 36 'an unmitigated bore': *Autobiography*, p. 43
p. 36 'He was not that ideal friend': from 'A Locked Diary', *Collected Papers 1*, pp. 41–67 (quotation on p. 45)
p. 36 'played upon my gullibility': ibid., p. 61
p. 36 'was extremely angry': *Autobiography*, p. 44
p. 36 'I came to hate him': ibid., p. 45
p. 36 'Poor Fitz!': 'A Locked Diary', *Collected Papers 1*, p. 45
p. 37 'The crust': ibid., p. 49
p. 37 'I fell in love': *Autobiography*, p. 76
p. 38 'Those who taught me': *My Philosophical Development*, pp. 35–6
p. 38 'hoped sooner or later': ibid., p. 36
p. 38 'went up to meet Uncle Rollo': 'A Locked Diary', *Collected Papers 1*, p. 53
p. 39 'sort of holiness': ibid., p. 55
p. 39 'I am convinced': ibid.
p. 39 'Alas!': ibid., p. 56

p. 40 'I doubt': ibid.

p. 40 another Shelleyesque sonnet: see *Collected Papers 1*, p. 59

p. 40 'What Spinoza calls': *Autobiography Volume II*, p. 38

2. Cambridge

p. 42 Russell quoted these lines: 'A Locked Diary', *Collected Papers 1*, p. 59

p. 42 'I find myself': ibid.

p. 42 'I read no poetry': ibid., p. 57

p. 42 'even Agnosticism': ibid., p. 59

p. 42 'could say things': *Autobiography*, p. 64

p. 42 'happiness by brutification': 'A Locked Diary', op. cit., p. 59

p. 42 'thousand times healthier': ibid.

p. 42 'is bad': ibid.

p. 43 according to Russell: see *Autobiography*, pp. 56–7

p. 43 'I recollect one occasion': Frank Russell, op. cit., p. 96

p. 43 'one of the wittiest': *Autobiography*, p. 60

p. 44 'the proof, he admitted': *My Philosophical Development*, p. 38

p. 44 'I am now': *Collected Papers 1*, p. 57

p. 44 'my society': ibid., p. 58

p. 45 'two subjects': BR to KT, 6.12.46, quoted in Griffin, op. cit., p. 19

p. 45 'the whole subject': *My Philosophical Development*, p. 38

p. 46 'Though a wonderful mathematician': *Collected Papers 1*, p. 58

p. 46 'This would prevent': ibid.

p. 46 'it never occurred': from 'Some Cambridge Dons of the 'Nineties', originally a BBC radio talk, included in *Portraits from Memory*, pp. 58–63 (quotation on p. 58)

p. 46 'extraordinarily perfect': from 'Alfred North Whitehead', a talk in the same series, *Portraits from Memory*, p. 97

p. 46 'a man of': ibid., p. 94

p. 46 'He was at all times': ibid., p. 96

p. 47 'It has existed': *Autobiography*, p. 68

p. 47 'It was a principle': ibid., p. 69

p. 47 'I would pace': ibid.

p. 47 'I was liable': *Autobiography*, p. 63

p. 47 'Politics and philosophy': Virginia Woolf, *Roger Fry*, p. 51, quoted in *G. E. Moore and the Cambridge Apostles* by Paul Levy, p. 113

p. 47 'Can We Be Statesmen?': see *Collected Papers 1*, pp. 78–82

p. 48 'homosexual relations': *Autobiography*, p. 74

p. 48 'Violets or Orange Blossom?': see Paul Levy, op. cit., p. 103

p. 48 'romantic idea': ibid., p. 98

p. 48 'We were still Victorian': *Autobiography*, p. 70

p. 48 'To me, as to Goethe': ibid., p. 76

p. 48 'I found some sympathy': *Portraits from Memory*, pp. 86–7

p. 48 'not quite what a style': ibid., p. 89

p. 48 'I wish to be': ibid., p. 87

p. 49 '& by that time': Joachim's letter is reproduced in full in 'Joachim's early advice to Russell on studying philosophy' by Nicholas Griffin, *Russell* 7(2), winter 1987–8, pp. 119–23. Griffin suggests, to my mind plausibly, that the most likely date for the letter is 23 September 1892.

p. 49 'It is really delightful': BR to RR, 4.12.1892, quoted in Griffin, *Russell's Idealist Apprenticeship*, p. 25

p. 49 'a Wrangler is a Wrangler': *My Philosophical Development*, p. 37

p. 49 'I a.m. O God': *Collected Papers 1*, p. 60. One possibility as to the cause of the guilt expressed in this diary entry is suggested by a passage on p. 68 of Russell's *Autobiography*, in which he recalls: 'by my fourth year I had become gay and flippant. Having been reading pantheism, I announced to my friends that I was God. They placed candles on each side of me and proceeded to acts of mock worship.' Though this recollection seems entirely free from guilt, it fits the description in his diary in at least some respects. One could, for example, see how this might have struck him, in retrospect, as an example of light-heartedness leading to sin (in this case, sacrilege). On the other hand, if Russell is right in dating this incident to his fourth year (a date supported by his memory of reading pantheism – by which Spinoza is presumably meant), then it cannot be identified with the 'grievous sin' of the diary, since that dates from his third year. In any case, it seems too trivial to have aroused the feelings expressed in the diary.

p. 50 'the clarity and passion of his thinking': from Russell's contribution to a symposium entitled 'The Influence and Thought of G. E. Moore', *The Listener*, 30 April 1959, pp. 755–6

p. 50 'beautiful and slim': *Autobiography*, p. 64

p. 51 'When I had finished': *My Philosophical Development*, p. 38

3. The Corpse in the Cargo

p. 52 'an exhilarating sense': see Russell's essay (originally a BBC broadcast) on Ibsen, 'Revolt in the Abstract' (part of a series on 'Books that Influenced Me in Youth', *Fact and Fiction*, pp. 23–8 (quotation on p. 23)

p. 52 'I felt then': ibid., p. 24

p. 52 'There are no general principles': quoted in 'The Romance of Revolt' (a talk on Turgenev in the same series of 'Books that Influenced Me in Youth'), *Fact and Fiction*, p. 21

p. 53 'delightfully horrifying': ibid.

p. 53 'Through me forbidden voices': Walt Whitman, 'Song of Myself' (verse 24), *Leaves of Grass* (Norton Critical Edition), p. 53

p. 53 'career round the country': *Autobiography*, p. 74

p. 54 'Without shame': Whitman, op. cit., p. 102

p. 54 'I never can': Lady Russell to her sister, Lady Charlotte Portal, 27.1.1887, see *Lady Russell: A Memoir*, p. 269

p. 54 'the modern attraction': Lady Russell to Agatha, 22.9.1893, ibid., p. 283

p. 54 'candid foulness': this and many other insults hurled at Ibsen's plays were gathered by William Archer in a famous satirical article called 'Ghosts and Gibberings', *Pall Mall Gazette*, 8 April 1891, in which he poked clever fun at the 'Ibsenoclasts' whose denunciations of Ibsen's immorality were dominating public discussion of his work. See *Ibsen: The Critical Heritage*, edited by Michael Egan, pp. 209–14

p. 54 'Life presents': see *Fact and Fiction*, p. 23

p. 54 'preacher of bad morals': ibid., p. 27

p. 55 'like the unwinding': see *Ibsen* by G. Wilson Knight, p. 51

p. 55 'We sail': quoted in the Introduction by Peter White to the Penguin edition of *Ghosts and Other Plays*

p. 55 'The Rosmers' view of life': *The Master Builder and Other Plays* (Penguin edition), p. 109

p. 56 'the subtle doctrine': see *Remarkable Relations: The Story of the Pearsall Smith Family* by Barbara Strachey, p. 48

p. 56 'written more grossly indecent things': ibid. p. 69. The phrase is Carey Thomas's, but the view, clearly, is Hannah's.

p. 57 'judge and jury': Hannah Smith to Mary, 4.5.1895, quoted ibid., p. 165

p. 57 'To suppose': *Collected Papers 1*, p. 62

p. 57 'I dreamt': ibid., pp. 61–2

p. 57 'Die Ehe': published in *Collected Papers 1*, pp. 68–71

p. 58 'bad customs': ibid., p. 71

p. 58 'are almost certain': ibid., p. 69

p. 58 'Unfolded Out of the Folds': the poem comes from the 'Autumn Rivulets' section of *Leaves of Grass* (see p. 391 of the Norton Critical Edition), quoted by Russell at the beginning of 'Die Ehe'

p. 58 'my little essay': *Collected Papers 1*, p. 62

p. 59 'the greatest day': ibid.

p. 59 'We agreed': ibid.

p. 59 'What is the concrete and material content': quoted by Paul Levy, op. cit. p. 106

p. 59 'come to the conclusion': BR to AR, 16.9.1893

p. 60 'I am confident': *Collected Papers 1*, p. 63

p. 60 'I think if I were conscientious': conversation reported by Russell, ibid., p. 64

p. 60 'I wish': ibid.

p. 61 'the conventions': ibid.

p. 61 A day or two later: BR to AR, 18.9.1893

p. 61 'O to be yielded': Whitman, op. cit., p. 106

p. 61 'I am glad': BR to AR, 21.9.1893

p. 62 'The talk was painful': ibid.

p. 62 'I told my people': *Autobiography*, p. 82

p. 62 'She read it out': ibid.

p. 62 'the last and bitterest duty': BR to AR, 21.9.1893

p. 63 'self-control': AR to BR, 5.10.1893

p. 63 'We called him "Old Sidg" ': *My Philosophical Development*, p. 38

p. 64 essay he wrote in November 1893: 'Paper on Epistemology II', *Collected Papers 1*, pp. 124–30

p. 64 'The question turns': ibid., p. 127

p. 64 'It would be no use': BR to AR, 29.10.1893

p. 64 'I care far more': AR to BR, 8.11.1893

p. 65 'divine sympathy': BR to AR, 17.12.1893

p. 65 'Plague it': AR to BR, 18.12.1893

p. 65 'This gave me': *Autobiography*, p. 82

p. 66 'I never read anything so interesting': AR to BR, 20.12.1893

p. 66 'I should think': ibid.

p. 66 'Every now & then': AR to BR, 31.12.1893

p. 66 'What can I say?': BR to AR, 1.1.1894

p. 66 'The snow': *Autobiography*, p. 82

p. 67 'it being so much easier': AR to BR, 29.1.1894

p. 67 'I too long': BR to AR, 21.1.1894

p. 67 'All these absurdities': BR to AR, 10.1.1894

p. 67 'I could hardly': BR to AR, 28.1.1894

p. 68 'Ever since I first read Pollock's book': BR to OM 11.12.11

p. 68 'Spinoza is the noblest': *History of Western Philosophy*, p. 552

p. 68 'considered religion': Sir Frederick Pollock, *Spinoza: His Life and Philosophy*, p. 69, quoted by Kenneth Blackwell, *The Spinozistic Ethics of Bertrand Russell*, p. 36

p. 68 'which seems to me in every way': BR to AR, 4.2.1894
p. 68 'Philosophy near akin to poetry': quoted by Blackwell, op. cit., p. 31
p. 69 'means only': ibid.
p. 69 'I do not think': G. E. Moore, 'An Autobiography', in *The Philosophy of G. E. Moore*, edited by Paul Arthur Schilpp, p. 14
p. 70 Wittgenstein's rather unkind remark: see 'Memories of Wittgenstein' by F. R. Leavis in *Recollections of Wittgenstein*, edited by Rush Rhees, p. 51
p. 71 'I do not believe': AR to BR, 25.2.1894
p. 71 'the proneness': AR to BR, 25.2.1894
p. 71 'I am afraid': AR to BR, 4.2.1894
p. 72 'Dearest Granny': BR to Lady Russell, 11.3.1894
p. 72 'I *hear* Mr Logan': conversation reported by BR to AR, 14.3.1894
p. 73 'I shall only mind': AR to BR, 16.3.1894
p. 73 'I shd. have thought': BR to AR, 20.3.1894
p. 73 'very painful and very fruitless': quoted in Strachey, op. cit., p. 135
p. 73 'icy reserve': BR to AR, 17.3.1894
p. 73 'completely delightful': *The Amberley Papers*, i, p. 28
p. 74 'life of American art students': *Autobiography*, p. 83
p. 74 'stiff inartistic aristocrats': BR to AR, 17.3.1894
p. 74 'I remember': *Autobiography*, p. 83
p. 74 'technically engaged': BR to AR, 8.4.1894
p. 74 'She has completely adopted': ibid.
p. 75 'instinctively hated': *The Amberley Papers*, i, p. 144
p. 75 'was a victim': *Autobiography*, p. 26
p. 75 'I told her': BR to AR, 8.4.1894
p. 75 'It is marked in pencil': ibid.
p. 76 'The old family doctor': *Autobiography*, p. 83
p. 76 'There is even more truth': BR to Maude Stanley, 14.5.1894
p. 77 'I am still working hard': BR to AR, 24.4.1894
p. 77 'a heaven without all-absorbing emotional love': BR to AR, 28.1.1894
p. 77 'Discuss the nature': see 'Paper on Descartes II', *Collected Papers 1*, pp. 178–84
p. 78 'One day': BR to OM, 28.9.11
p. 78 'Whatever we think': *Collected Papers 1*, p. 179
p. 78 'In Spinoza': ibid., p. 181
p. 78 'We mean to walk': BR to AR, 16.5.1894
p. 79 'Moore & I': BR to AR, 20.5.1894
p. 79 recorded by Alan Wood: see Alan Wood, *The Passionate Sceptic*, pp. 87–8
p. 80 'utilise both my Triposes': BR to AR, 10.6.1894
p. 80 'By emphasising': *Autobiography*, p. 84
p. 80 'Alys and I': ibid.
p. 80 'A thick atmosphere': ibid.
p. 81 'We think a very great deal': Lady Russell to BR, 5.7.1894
p. 81 'Dearest Auntie': BR to Agatha Russell, 6.7.1894
p. 82 'I have now *quite* decided': BR to Dr William Anderson, 13.7.1894
p. 82 'It was clear to me': *Autobiography*, p. 86
p. 82 'have never ceased': ibid., p. 85
p. 82 'This night': *Collected Papers 1*, pp. 65–6, see also *Autobiography*, pp. 84–5
p. 83 'Perfect peace of mind': BR to AR, 17.8.1894
p. 84 'the happiest morning': BR to AR, 24.8.1894
p. 84 'All this misfortune': BR to AR, 17.8.1894

p. 84 'Thank God': BR to AR, 18.8.1894
p. 84 'It is deadly dull here': BR to AR, 20.8.1894
p. 84 'the conversation here': BR to AR, 23.8.1894
p. 84 'Well, Bertie': BR to AR, 26.8.1894
p. 84 'mathematics and the sea': *My Philosophical Development*, p. 210
p. 85 'We *must*': BR to AR, 27.8.1894
p. 85 'I grow more and more': ibid.
p. 85 'Now that I know': BR to AR, 28.8.1894
p. 85 'As soon as she is dead': BR to AR, 4.9.1894
p. 85 'be the first step': BR to AR, 30.8.1894
p. 86 'I have lost the power': BR to AR, 5.9.1894
p. 86 'An exceptionally intelligent': William James, *The Principles of Psychology*, vol. 1, p. 265
p. 87 'had *par excellence*': Rupert Crawshay-Williams, *Russell Remembered*, pp. 31–2
p. 87 'far and away the most spiritual': BR to AR, 7.10.1894
p. 87 'because I feel': ibid.
p. 88 'A really happy marriage': BR to AR, 12.9.1894
p. 88 'I hate this place': BR to AR, 20.9.1894
p. 89 'It has given me': BR to AR, 1–2.10.1894
p. 89 'Thee loves me': BR to AR, 18.9.1894
p. 89 'I'm sure your former views': BR to AR, 4.10.1894
p. 90 'It *will* be divine!': BR to AR, 11.10.1894
p. 90 'For physiological reasons': BR to AR, 4.10.1894
p. 90 'hardly ever recall': BR to AR, 26.10.1894
p. 90 'I . . . sometimes dream': BR to AR, 23.10.1894
p. 90 'Until we have had': BR to AR, 26.10.1894
p. 91 'perpetually haunted': from Russell's essay, 'Lövborg or Hedda' (*Collected Papers 1*, pp. 83–9, alluded to in his letter to Alys, 26.10.1894
p. 91 'Cleopatra or Maggie Tulliver': see *Collected Papers 1*, pp. 90–8
p. 91 'What shall we do with our passions?': ibid., p. 92
p. 91 'in time our desires sicken': ibid., p. 95
p. 92 'is an unreasoning hatred': ibid., p. 96
p. 92 'my Grandmother was vexed': BR to AR, 4.10.1894
p. 92 'I hate to think': BR to AR, 5.9.1894
p. 92 'I *hate* Frenchmen': BR to AR, 30.10.1894
p. 92 'It will grow better': ibid.
p. 92 'various instinctive impulses': *Collected Papers 1*, p. 95
p. 93 letter to Sanger: dated 29.9.1894
p. 93 'I shall be wildly eager': BR to AR, 3.11.1894
p. 93 'It has been *perfectly* delightful': BR to AR, 4.11.1894
p. 94 '*delightful*': BR to AR, 30.10.1894
p. 94 'As to her falling in love with different people': BR to AR, 1.11.1894
p. 94 'She is rejoicing': BR to AR, 5.11.1894
p. 95 'She has produced her Nietzsche': ibid.
p. 95 'It *is* nice': AR to BR, 6.11.1894
p. 95 'Thy letter last night': BR to AR, 6.11.1894
p. 96 'He reflected': ibid.
p. 96 'I have been perfectly miserable': quoted in Strachey, op. cit., p. 142
p. 96 'Felt depressed': ibid.
p. 97 'she says she thinks': BR to AR, 11.11.1894
p. 97 'I am quite unable': BR to AR, 12.11.1894

p. 97 'She seems to be enjoying herself': ibid.

p. 97 'which I am very sorry for': BR to AR, 14.11.1894

p. 97 'Why should I mind': AR to BR, 12.11.1894

p. 97 'I didn't ask': BR to AR, 14.11.1894

p. 98 'talking in the firelight': ibid.

p. 98 'Cried most of the morning': quoted in Strachey, op. cit., p. 142

p. 98 'I tore it right up': AR to BR, 14.11.1894

p. 98 'I can't tell thee': BR to AR, 15.11.1894

p. 99 'brimming over with sympathy': quoted in Ronald W. Clark, *The Life of Bertrand Russell*, p. 67

p. 99 'making my peace': *Autobiography*, p. 87

p. 99 'I love that marriage service': AR to BR, 1.11.1894

p. 99 'frantically impatient': BR to AR, 26.11.1894

p. 99 'Shall we take delight': for an account of this paper, and of the meeting at which it was delivered, see Paul Levy, op. cit., pp. 144–6

p. 99 'a conventional view': quoted ibid., p. 144

p. 99 'I spoke perfectly frankly': BR to AR, 9.12.1894

p. 100 The service: for a detailed account of the occasion, see Sheila Turcon, 'A Quaker wedding: the marriage of Bertrand Russell and Alys Pearsall Smith', *Russell*, 3 (2), winter 1983–4, pp. 103–28

p. 100 'lovely little sermonettes': Hannah to Mary, 13.12.1894, quoted in Strachey, op. cit., p. 145

4. The Whole and its Parts

p. 101 'we found': *Autobiography*, p. 124

p. 101 'a walk on the sea-shore': Alys to Hannah, 16.12.1894

p. 101 'we have enough to amuse ourselves': ibid.

p. 101 'Now do write me': Hannah to Alys, 13.1.1895, quoted in Strachey, op. cit., p. 149

p. 101 'I may tell thee': Hannah to Alys, 5.3.1895, quoted ibid.

p. 101 'under the influence': *Autobiography*, p. 124

p. 102 'was intellectually': *Autobiography*, p. 126

p. 102 'Though I curse': BR to AR, 20.9.1894

p. 102 'There is one respect': BR to AR, 10.10.1894

p. 102 'I remember': 'My Mental Development', p. 11. For a similar account, see *Autobiography*, p. 125

p. 103 'The issue was a public one': *Autobiography*, p. 125

p. 103 'Bertie and Alys': Mary to Hannah, 25.3.1895, quoted in Strachey, op. cit., p. 150

p. 103 'We call her': letter dated 24.3.1895, quoted ibid., p. 151

p. 103 'Poor Alys': quoted ibid.

p. 104 'This remains': *Autobiography*, p. 125

p. 104 'The Logic of Geometry': reprinted in *Collected Papers 1*, pp. 266–86

p. 104 'somewhat foolish': *My Philosophical Development*, p. 39

p. 105 'He says he and Ward': BR to AR, 9.10.1895

p. 105 'The Master & Examining Fellows': Alys to Mary MacKall Gwinn, 10.10.1895 (original letter in Bryn Mawr College Archives)

p. 106 'social butterflies': *Autobiography*, p. 16

p. 106 'not quite . . . ': ibid., p. 80

p. 107 'when he was in London': Strachey, op. cit., p. 184. Strachey's account makes it clear that Russell's recollections of Robert's humiliations at Hannah's hands date from October 1895, and not, as one would think from reading his *Autobiography*, some later date.

p. 107 'one of the wickedest': *Autobiography*, p. 148

p. 107 'had an unbounded admiration': ibid.

p. 107 'stupidity and boringness': Mary to Bernhard Berenson, 13.8.1896, see *Mary Berenson: A Self-Portrait from her Letters & Diaries*, p. 67

p. 107 'poor Oscar': see Strachey, op. cit., p. 166

p. 107 'Sometimes I tried': *Autobiography*, p. 149

p. 108 'the advanced Liberal': *Collected Papers 1*, p. 314

p. 108 'with all their ideals intact': *German Social Democracy* (1965 edition), p. 170

p. 108 'friendliness to the working classes': ibid., p. 171

p. 109 'I took no great interest: *Autobiography*, p. 130

p. 109 review for *Mind*: reprinted in *Collected Papers 2*, pp. 35–43

p. 109 'This criticism of Cantor': quoted in *Collected Papers 2*, p. 35

p. 110 'reading Georg Cantor': *Autobiography*, p. 127

p. 110 'We were confessing': diary entry dated 17.4.1896, quoted in Strachey, op. cit., p. 152

p. 110 'all reality is rational': John McTaggart Ellis McTaggart, *Studies in the Hegelian Dialectic*, p. 255

p. 110 'the highest object': ibid., p. 259

p. 110 'All true philosophy': ibid.

p. 111 'On Some Difficulties': see *Collected Papers 2*, pp. 44–58. Russell appears to have written this paper for eventual publication in *Mind*, but abandoned both the paper and his plans to publish it after he became dissatisfied with the views it expressed.

p. 111 'the difficulties': ibid., p. 46

p. 111 'Cantor's transfinite numbers': ibid., p. 52

p. 112 'I doubt': BR to RR, 20.11.1896

p. 112 'very fond': see *Autobiography*, p. 132

p. 112 'fell more or less in love': see *Selected Letters 1*, p. 148

p. 113 'made a deep impression': ibid., p. 136

p. 113 gratuitous honesty: see Strachey, op. cit., p. 152

p. 113 'contact with academic Americans': *Autobiography*, p. 133

p. 114 'mainly of puns': BR to AR, 6.4.1897

p. 114 'one major division': see *My Philosophical Development*, p. 11

p. 114 'Hegel thought of the universe': *Portraits from Memory*, p. 21

p. 114 'Why do we regard time': published in *Collected Papers 2*, pp. 91–7

p. 114 'Because we're fools': BR to AR, 1.6.1897

p. 115 'On a strictly monistic view': *Collected Papers 2*, p. 95

p. 115 'Reality is one': F. H. Bradley, *Appearance and Reality* (second edition), p. 519, quoted by Russell, *My Philosophical Development*, p. 56

p. 115 'Seems, Madam?': reprinted in *Collected Papers 1*, pp. 105–11

p. 115 'for all purposes': Russell to Moore, 7.12.1897, quoted in *Collected Papers 1*, p. 105

p. 115 'Reality, as constructed': *Collected Papers 1*, p. 108

p. 115 'since all experience': ibid., p. 110

p. 115 'Why not admit': ibid., p. 111

p. 116 'On the Idea of a Dialectic': included under the heading 'Various Notes on Mathematical Philosophy', *Collected Papers 2*, p. 24. Also included by Russell in Chapter IV ('Excursion into Idealism') of *My Philosophical Development*, pp. 43–4

p. 116 'a method': *Collected Papers 2*, p. 24

p. 116 'all types of formal, necessary, deductive reasoning': Whitehead, *Universal Algebra*, Preface, p. vi

p. 116 'An Analysis of Mathematical Reasoning': see *Collected Papers 2*, pp. 155–242

p. 117 'The Nature of Judgment': reprinted in *G. E. Moore: Selected Writings* edited by Thomas Baldwin. For an excellent discussion of the article's importance, see Gilbert Ryle, 'G. E. Moore's "The Nature of Judgment" ', *G. E. Moore: Essays in Retrospect*, edited by Alice Ambrose and Morris Lazerowitz. For a more historically detailed account, see Chapter 7.2. 'Influences: Moore', of *Russell's Idealist Apprenticeship* by Nicholas Griffin.

p. 117 'My chief discovery': Moore to Russell, 11.9.1898, quoted in Griffin, op. cit., p. 300

p. 117 'A proposition': 'The Nature of Judgment', in Baldwin, op. cit., p. 5

p. 117 'The ultimate elements of everything': Moore to Russell, op. cit.

p. 117 'A thing becomes intelligible': Baldwin, op. cit., p. 8

p. 117 'I agree emphatically': Russell to Moore, 13.9.1898

p. 118 'It was an intense excitement': *Autobiography*, p. 135

p. 118 'rejoiced in the thought': *My Philosophical Development*, pp. 61–2

p. 118 'the most interesting aspect': *Autobiography*, p. 135

p. 118 'I found': *My Philosophical Development*, p. 61

p. 118 'a reconstruction': *The Philosophy of Leibniz*, p. 2

p. 118 'At an early age': ibid.

p. 119 'What he published': *A History of Western Philosophy*, p. 563

p. 119 'That all sound philosophy': *The Philosophy of Leibniz*, p. 8

p. 119 'The only ground': ibid., p. 14

p. 119 'To outsiders': Helen Thomas to Mildred Minturn, 23.7.1897, quoted by Caroline Moorehead, *Bertrand Russell*, p. 77

p. 119 'I wish for fame': *Collected Papers 1*, p. 72

p. 120 'I did not mind': *Autobiography*, p. 22

p. 120 'had a jolly tête-à-tête': BR to AR, 28.9.1897

p. 120 'more charming than ever': BR to AR, 27.9.1897

p. 120 'Bertie was *very* affectionate': Mary to Berenson, 24.9.1897, quoted in Strachey, op. cit., p. 154

p. 121 'Alys says she hates men': Mary, diary 26.8.1898, quoted, ibid., p. 155. See also *Mary Berenson: A Self-Portrait from her Letters & Diaries*, p. 77, where, however, the same passage is given as an extract from a letter to Berenson of the same date.

p. 121 'for, as we get older': Mary to Berenson, 13.7.1899, *Mary Berenson: A Self-Portrait*, p. 83

p. 121 'Poor Mother': Mary to Berenson, 9.8.1899, quoted in Strachey, op. cit., p. 155

p. 121 'stayed out walking': Mary to Berenson, 15.8.1899, ibid.

p. 122 'very fond': *Autobiography*, p. 136

p. 122 'Mathematics could be *quite* true': 'My Mental Development', p. 12

p. 122 'The Mathematician's Nightmare': see *Nightmares of Eminent Persons* (Penguin edition) pp. 48–53

p. 123 'the discovery': BR to LC, 18.7.1898

p. 123 *The Fundamental Ideas and Axioms*: what survives of this is published in *Collected Papers 2*, pp. 261–305

p. 123 a 27-page critical study: 'Des fondements de la géométrie: à propos d'un livre de M. Russell', *Revue de métaphysique et de morale*, 7, 1899, pp. 251–79

p. 124 'I feel very flattered': BR to Moore, 18.5.1899

p. 124 'does not seem to realise': BR to LC, 9.5.1899, quoted in *Collected Papers 2*, p. 391

p. 124 that of G. E. Moore: see *Mind*, 8, 1899, pp. 397–405

p. 124 'One of my day-dreams': *Portraits from Memory*, p. 23

p. 125 'I could read': BR to LC, 29.8.1899

p. 125 'The Notion of Order': see *Collected Papers 3*, pp. 234–58

p. 125 'caused me much anxiety': *Autobiography*, p. 136

p. 126 'and if we finish': BR to LC, 16.1.00

p. 126 'a stroke of great good luck': quoted in Strachey, op. cit., p. 123

p. 126 'it is awful': Mary to Berenson, 14.12.1899, quoted ibid., p. 192

p. 127 'Bertie is teaching them Euclid': Mary to Berenson, 17.7.00, see *Mary Berenson: A Self-Portrait*, p. 91

p. 127 *The Principles of Mathematics*: this early (pre-Paris Congress) draft has been reproduced in *Collected Papers 3*, pp. 9–180

p. 127 'solves any of the philosophical difficulties': *Collected Papers 3*, p. 119

p. 127 'is so important': ibid., p. 38 (quoted in the Introduction, p. xxiii)

p. 127 'a very important logical doctrine': ibid., p. 39

p. 128 'The number of finite numbers': ibid., p. 123

p. 129 'La logique': *Revue de métaphysique et de morale*, 7, 1899, pp. 616–46

p. 129 'I was impressed': *My Philosophical Development*, p. 65

p. 129 'received great applause': see Strachey, op. cit., p. 214. Alys's paper, 'L'Éducation des Femmes' was published, like Russell's, in the conference proceedings: *Bibliothèque du Congrès International de Philosophie*, Volume II, Paris, 1903, pp. 309–17

p. 130 'died a gradual death': BR to OM, 29.4.11

p. 130 'Her vivid life': Whitehead, 'Autobiographical Notes', *The Philosophy of Alfred North Whitehead*, p. 8

p. 130 'By myself': *Dialogues of Alfred North Whitehead*, as recorded by Lucien Price, p. 9

p. 130 'a life of utter loneliness': BR to OM, undated, but probably July 1911

p. 130 'persuaded that Peano': BR to Moore, 16.8.00

p. 130 'an enormous success': BR to LC, 18.9.00

p. 130 'Recent Italian Work': published in *Collected Papers 3*, pp. 350–62

p. 130 'The theory of arithmetic': ibid., p. 358

p. 130 'although the work itself': ibid., p. 352

p. 131 'Recent Work on the Principles': originally published in the *International Monthly*, 4, July 1901, reprinted in *Collected Papers 3*, pp. 363–79, and, as 'Mathematics and the Metaphysicians', in *Mysticism and Logic*

p. 131 'One of the chief triumphs': *Collected Papers 3*, p. 366

p. 131 'All pure mathematics': ibid., p. 367

p. 131 'I know of no age': ibid., p. 370

p. 131 'What is now required': ibid., p. 379

p. 132 'The Logic of Relations': reprinted in *Collected Papers 3*, pp. 310–49

p. 132 'the highest point': *Autobiography*, p. 145

p. 132 'an intellectual honeymoon': *My Philosophical Development*, p. 73

p. 133 'My sensations': *Autobiography*, p. 145

p. 133 'I have been endeavouring': BR to HT, 31.12.00

p. 133 'The honeymoon': *My Philosophical Development*, p. 73

5. The Religion of Sorrow

p. 134 'becoming more and more an invalid': *Autobiography*, pp. 145–6

p. 135 'For a time': ibid., p. 146

p. 135 'The moment of my first conversion': BR to OM, probably July 1911

p. 136 'Cursed be they': from Gilbert Murray's translation of *Hippolytus*, see
Euripides, translated by Gilbert Murray (1902 edition), p. 24

p. 136 'through all this earth': ibid., p. 25

p. 137 'The day before yesterday': BR to AR, 12.2.01

p. 137 'almost overwhelming': BR to GM, 26.2.01

p. 138 'that dark spell': Murray, op. cit., p. 40

p. 138 'Poor Alys': Hannah to Mary, 9.3.01, quoted in Strachey, op. cit., p. 215

p. 138 'The routine': see *The Diary of Beatrice Webb Volume Two*, pp. 208–11

p. 140 'got back my usual feeling': BR to AR, 13.7.01

p. 140 'I miss thee': BR to AR, 10.7.01

p. 140 'Evelyn is more lovable': BR to AR, 13.7.01

p. 140 'My relations with the Whiteheads': *Autobiography*, p. 150

p. 140 'He used to frighten Mrs Whitehead': ibid.

p. 141 Once, for example: see Victor Lowe, *Alfred North Whitehead: The Man and
His Work, Volume 1: 1861–1910*, p. 248

p. 143 'In this one point': see *Collected Papers 3*, p. 375. In 1917, when the article
was included in the collection *Mysticism and Logic*, Russell added a footnote
to this sentence, saying: 'Cantor was not guilty of a fallacy on this point. His
proof that there is no greatest number is valid. The solution of the puzzle is
complicated and depends upon the theory of types, which is explained in
Principia Mathematica, Vol. 1.'

p. 143 'It seemed unworthy': *Autobiography*, p. 147

p. 143 he responded: see *My Philosophical Development*, p. 75

p. 143 What he felt about the Paradox: see *My Philosophical Development*, p. 212

p. 144 'Did I tell you': BR to LC, 23.3.02

p. 144 'Dearest, thee does give me': BR to AR, 6.11.01

p. 144 'I am haunted': from Russell's Journal 1902–5, published in *Collected Papers
12*, pp. 3–28, extract dated 2.12.02, p. 14

p. 145 'when we were living': *Autobiography*, pp. 147–8

p. 146 'Two years ago': *Collected Papers 12*, p. 18

p. 146 'The most unhappy': *Autobiography*, pp. 149–50

p. 146 'Now, however, the opposite': BR to GM, 3.4.02

p. 148 'terribly exhausted': BR to AR, 19.4.02

p. 148 'suits me very well': BR to AR, 20.4.02

p. 148 'the best night': BR to AR, 30.4.02

p. 149 'my energy was ten times': Russell, Journal, 18.5.03, *Collected Papers 12*,
p. 22

p. 150 'will not give me': BR to AR, 16.5.02

p. 150 'I should like': BR to AR, 22.5.02

p. 150 'You will wonder': BR to LD, 23.5.02

p. 150 'We decorated the whole place': *Collected Papers 12*, p. 22

p. 151 'I have been very well aware': BR to AR, 11.5.02

p. 151 'I was writing': *Collected Papers 12*, p. 22

p. 151 'Thine most affectionately': see BR to AR, 24.5.02

p. 151 'I do not believe': BR to AR, 6.6.02

p. 151 'I was not too tired out': BR to AR, 9.6.02

p. 152 'The worship of passion': BR to HT, 10.6.02

p. 152 'full of plans': BR to AR, 12.6.02

p. 153 'Do you know Frege': BR to LC, 25.6.02

p. 154 'As I think about acts of integrity': quoted in Griffin, *The Selected Letters of Bertrand Russell*, p. 245

p. 155 'I justified this attitude': *Autobiography*, p. 148

p. 155 'the next day': *Collected Papers 12*, pp. 22–3

p. 155 'My self-righteousness': *Autobiography*, p. 148

p. 155 'Monotonous, melancholy, eternal': *Collected Papers 12*, p. 49

p. 156 'A consciousness': Beatrice Webb, op. cit., p. 252

p. 156 'Bertrand Russell's nature': ibid., pp. 252–3

p. 156 'I am sorry': BR to AR, 24.6.02

p. 156 'I was not really prepared': from an account of her separation from Russell written by Alys in 1948, quoted in Strachey, op. cit., p. 219

p. 157 'Altogether': Beatrice to Sidney Webb, quoted in Griffin, op. cit., p. 248

p. 157 'the only occupation': Beatrice Webb, op. cit., p. 253

p. 157 'I realised': *Collected Papers 12*, p. 23

p. 157 'unreal, insincere, and sentimental': *Autobiography*, p. 151

p. 158 'Our hearts': *Autobiography*, p. 151

p. 158 'miserable the whole time': *Collected Papers 12*, p. 23

p. 158 'Sometimes I did so': *Autobiography*, p. 151

p. 158 'I see far below': BR to HT, 14.10.02

p. 159 'The Study of Mathematics': first published in *The New Quarterly*, 1, Nov. 1907, reprinted in *Mysticism and Logic* and as paper 6 in *Collected Papers 12*, pp. 83–93

p. 159 'the greatest achievement': *Collected Papers 12*, p. 88

p. 159 'conquered for the intellect': ibid.

p. 159 'austerer virtues': ibid., p. 93

p. 159 'The contemplation': ibid., p. 91

p. 159 'Mathematics is a haven': BR to LD, 18.2.06

p. 159 'hurt me': Russell, Journal, 25 Nov. 1902, *Collected Papers 12*, p. 11

p. 159 'Really it's magnificent': Lytton Strachey to BR, 23.10.07

p. 160 'Truth': *Collected Papers 12*, p. 43

p. 160 'With every accession': ibid.

p. 160 'Infinite is the sadness of wisdom': ibid., p. 44

p. 160 'One by one': ibid., p. 45

p. 160 'We are all born': ibid., p. 40

p. 160 'We must learn': ibid., p. 41

p. 161 'I returned': ibid., p. 9

p. 161 'making conversation': ibid., p. 8

p. 161 'I know it is my fault': ibid., p. 11

p. 161 'On Sunday': ibid.

p. 161 'Alys and I': ibid., p. 17

p. 162 'Last night': ibid., p. 15

p. 162 'What the complete solution': *The Principles of Mathematics*, p. 528

p. 162 'What general value': BR to GM, 28.12.02

p. 162 'The Free Man's Worship': originally published in *The Independent Review*, 1, Dec. 1903, this essay was then included by Russell in his 1910 collection of *Philosophical Essays*, and the 1918 collection *Mysticism and Logic* that replaced it. It is included in *Collected Papers 12*, to which my citations refer. Its many other reprints are catalogued over three pages of *A Bibliography of Bertrand Russell Volume II*, pp. 8–10

p. 162 'world which Science presents': *Collected Papers 12*, p. 66

p. 163 'To abandon': ibid., p. 71

p. 163 'let us think': ibid., p. 72

p. 163 'all right': Russell, Journal, 27.1.03, *Collected Papers 12*, p. 17

p. 163 'gave her new interests': BR to BB, 28.2.03

p. 163 'My work': *Collected Papers 12*, p. 17

p. 163 'The river tonight': ibid., p. 19

p. 163 'I have been realising': ibid., p. 20

p. 164 'It may': ibid.

p. 164 'made the last possible sacrifice': ibid., p. 21

p. 164 'not adequately': ibid.

p. 164 'I have been': BR to GM, 23.3.03

p. 164 'About the reading party': Moore to BR, 20.3.03

p. 164 'has never forgiven': *Collected Papers 12*, p. 21

p. 165 'Of course': Moore to Desmond MacCarthy, 25.3.03, quoted in Clark, op. cit., p. 120

p. 165 'pseudo-intimate': *Collected Papers 12*, p. 22

p. 165 'The power of writing': ibid.

p. 165 'Meinong's Theory': reprinted in *Essays in Analysis*, edited by Douglas Lackey, pp. 21–76, and *Collected Papers 4*, pp. 431–74

p. 165 'What is a proposition?': see Gottlob Frege, *Philosophical and Mathematical Correspondence*, p. 149

p. 165 'I cannot bring myself': BR to GF, 12.12.02, ibid., pp. 150–1

p. 166 'In all cases': BR to GF, 24.5.03, ibid., p. 159

p. 166 'Mont Blanc': GF to BR, 13.11.04, ibid., p. 163

p. 166 'I believe': BR to GF, 12.12.04, ibid., p. 169

p. 167 'The unity of a complex': see Lackey, op. cit., p. 28

p. 167 'There is a comfort': BR to HT, 13.5.03

p. 167 'Satan's joys': BR to LD, 13.4.03

p. 168 'the bygone year': *Collected Papers 12*, p. 22

p. 168 'the last chink': ibid., p. 24

p. 168 'It seems to me': BR to HT, 13.5.03

p. 168 described it to Philip Jourdain: see Grattan-Guinness, op. cit., p. 78

p. 168 'Heartiest congratulations': ANW to BR, 21.5.03

p. 168 'unspeakable': see *Collected Papers 12*, p. 24

p. 168 'Every morning': *Autobiography*, p. 151

p. 168 'The last four months': BR to LD, 29.7.03

p. 169 'She is still miserable': *Collected Papers 12*, p. 24

p. 169 'It is ghastly': BR to LD, 29.7.03

p. 169 'We are all wildly excited': ibid.

p. 169 'If I could get away': *Collected Papers 12*, p. 25

p. 170 'I don't agree': BR to EH, 2.9.03

p. 170 'minded them': BR to GM, 26.9.03

p. 170 'cheerless': quoted in Maria Forte, 'Lucy Martin Donnelly: a sojourn with the Russells', *Russell*, 7 (1), summer 1987, p. 54

p. 170 'desperately unhappy': ibid., p. 55

p. 171 'He paced up & down': quoted ibid., p. 58

p. 171 'feeling that the world is sneering': ibid., p. 59

p. 171 'The Tariff Controversy': see *Collected Papers 12*, pp. 190–215

p. 171 'Nothing but': ibid., p. 215

p. 172 'very clear and intellectual': Logan Pearsall Smith to Mary Berenson, 17.1.04, quoted ibid., p. 183

p. 172 'My experience': BR to GM, 19.1.04

6. The Long Night

p. 173 'The pleasure': *Autobiography*, p. 156

p. 174 'getting very great good': BR to AR, 28.3.04

p. 174 'This journal': *Collected Papers 12*, p. 25

p. 174 'useful to people': ibid.

p. 174 'combined to scold': note added by Russell to his letter to Lucy Donnelly, 19.9.04

p. 175 'Sometimes': BR to LD, 19.9.04

p. 175 'Alfred's recent work': BR to AR, 11.4.04

p. 176 'discussing whether': BR to AR, 9.4.04

p. 176 'had a happy hour': BR to AR, 14.4.04

p. 177 'I try very hard': AR to BR, 17.5.04

p. 177 'aggressively dull': Frances Partridge in conversation with the author

p. 177 'I am working hard': BR to GLD, 20.7.04

p. 177 'I believe': BR to LD, 19.8.04

p. 178 'Certainty and system': BR to LD, 19.9.04

p. 178 'It is very agreeable': ibid.

p. 178 'Brittany is quite wonderful': BR to LD, 3.10.04

p. 178 'merely seeing people': BR to LD, 8.2.05

p. 178 'a fat, good-natured': ibid.

p. 179 'The Bertrand Russells': Beatrice Webb, op. cit., p. 324

p. 179 'the first principles': BR to LD, 8.2.05

p. 179 'In spite': BR to EH, 22.9.04

p. 179 'I have got over': *Collected Papers 12*, p. 26

p. 179 'I have learnt': ibid.

p. 179 'did not feel': ibid.

p. 180 'out of mere kindness': ibid., p. 28

p. 180 'I begin to see': BR to IP, 9.4.05

p. 180 'I do not think I ought to come': BR to IP, 6.7.05

p. 180 'I do not think the duty': ibid.

p. 181 'It is strangely difficult': *Collected Papers 12*, p. 27

p. 181 'Going to a new place': BR to IP, 9.4.05

p. 183 An interesting sidelight: see Douglas P. Lackey, 'Russell's Unknown Theory of Classes: The Substitutional System of 1906', *Journal for the History of Philosophy*, 14, 1976, pp. 69–78

p. 183 'I cannot admit': quoted in Lackey, op. cit., p. 71

p. 183 'I am here': BR to LD, 3.8.05

p. 183 'the sound': *Autobiography*, p. 58

p. 184 'I was in church': ibid.

p. 184 'wonderfully better': BR to MLID, 12.8.05

p. 184 'The loss of Theodore': Crompton Llewelyn Davies to BR, 31.10.05

p. 184 'which admitted of no philosophy': BR to LD, 3.9.05

p. 184 polemical attack: Pierre Boutroux, 'Sur la notion de correspondence dans l'analyse mathématique', *Revue de métaphysique et de morale*, 12, 1904, pp. 909–20

p. 184 'On the Relation': reprinted in *Collected Papers 4*, pp. 521–32

p. 185 'confuses the act of discovery': ibid., p. 532

p. 185 'On Some Difficulties': reprinted in Lackey (ed.), *Essays in Analysis*, pp. 135–64

p. 185 'On Substitution': unpublished, but to be included in Volume 5 of *Collected Papers*

p. 187 'On the Substitutional Theory': published in Lackey, op. cit., pp. 165–89

p. 187 'Logic is no longer barren': see *Science and Method*, p. 194, where, however, the phrase loses some of its power by being translated: 'Logistic is no longer barren, it engenders antinomies.' The more elegant translation quoted here is Russell's (see *My Philosophical Development*, p. 76).

p. 187 Russell presented to the Moral Sciences Club: the paper was published as 'On the Nature of Truth', *Proceedings of the Aristotelian Society*, 7, 1906–7, pp. 28–49. The first two parts were then reprinted by Russell as 'The Monistic Theory of Truth' in *Philosophical Essays*. The 'multiple relation theory of judgment' was first discussed, tentatively, in the third part of the paper, and then put forward, much less tentatively, in 'On the Nature of Truth and Falsehood', a paper that Russell included in *Philosophical Essays* to replace Part III of 'On the Nature of Truth'.

p. 189 'Mathematical Logic as based on the Theory of Types': *American Journal of Mathematics*, 30, May 1908, pp. 222–62. Reprinted in *Logic and Knowledge*, pp. 57–102. The debate with Poincaré continued when Poincaré responded to this article in 'La Logique de l'infini', *Revue de métaphysique et de morale*, 17, 1909, pp. 461–82 (translated into English as 'The Logic of Infinity', in Henri Poincaré, *Mathematics and Science: Last Essays*, pp. 45–64). Russell responded to this, in turn, with 'La Théorie des Types Logiques', *Revue de métaphysique et de morale*, 18, 1910, pp. 263–301, the English version of which forms the final statement of the Theory of Types, as published in *Principia Mathematica* (Introduction, Chapter II, 'The Theory of Logical Types').

p. 189 'I think women's suffrage important': BR to MLID, 4.6.06

p. 189 'It is horribly annoying': BR to MLID, 1.5.07

p. 190 'What a sporting cove': George Trevelyan to BR, 23.5.07

p. 190 'That Mr Bertrand Russell': Sylvia Pankhurst, *The Suffragette*, quoted in Griffin (ed.) *The Selected Letters of Bertrand Russell Volume I*, p. 313

p. 190 'the bigotry': BR to HT, 27.10.09

p. 190 'I am back at work': BR to HT, 9.6.07

p. 190 'working like a black': BR to IP, 30.9.07

p. 191 'Hardly a page': from a review Russell wrote of J. M. Keynes, *Treatise on Probability* in *The Mathematical Gazette*, 11, July 1922, p. 124 (footnote), quoted in Clark, op. cit., p. 134

p. 191 'Every time': *Autobiography*, p. 152

p. 191 long critique of William James's theory of truth: first published as 'Transatlantic "Truth" ', *The Albany Review*, 2, January 1908, pp. 393–410. Reprinted as 'William James's Conception of Truth' in *Philosophical Essays*.

p. 191 'Our account of truth': William James, *Pragmatism*, p. 218, quoted by Russell, *Philosophical Essays*, p. 118

p. 191 'The attempt': *Philosophical Essays*, p. 129

p. 191 'to my way of thinking': BR to HT, 4.10.07

p. 192 'I often wondered': *Autobiography*, p. 152

p. 192 'Now my blissful hope': Alys, 29.6.07, quoted in Strachey, op. cit., p. 222

p. 192 'I have no time': BR to IP, 25.5.08

p. 192 'My dying words': William James to BR, 4.10.08

p. 192 'I would much rather': BR to Philip Jourdain, 20.10.08, see I. Grattan-Guinness, *Dear Russell – Dear Jourdain*, p. 112

p. 193 'Your kind letter': BR to IP, 12.8.08

p. 193 'You have a special place': BR to IP, 15.10.08

p. 193 'I used to know': *My Philosophical Development*, p. 86

p. 194   'I imagine': BR to HT, 27.10.09
p. 194   'We thus': *Autobiography*, p. 152
p. 195   'A crisis is upon us': BR to HT, 13.12.09
p. 195   'had broken some pledges': *Autobiography*, p. 202
p. 195   'Conventionality': quoted in Miranda Seymour, *Ottoline Morrell: Life on the Grand Scale*, p. 74
p. 196   'Bertrand Russell is most fascinating': see *Ottoline: The Early Memoirs of Lady Ottoline Morrell*, p. 183
p. 196   'I remember a day': BR to OM, March 1911
p. 196   'Things are no better': Alys, journal entry, 8.9.09, quoted in Strachey, op. cit., p. 223
p. 196   'It would be very delightful': *Ottoline*, p. 184
p. 197   'At some places': ibid., p. 192
p. 197   'I discovered': *Autobiography*, p. 204
p. 197   Russell addressed the Bedford Liberal Association: the address is published in *Collected Papers 12*, pp. 294–303
p. 198   'I feel, I must confess': F. H. Bradley to BR, 11.4.10
p. 198   'I am really glad': F. H. Bradley to BR, 20.4.10
p. 199   'Some Explanations in Reply to Mr Bradley': reprinted in *Collected Papers 6*, pp. 349–58
p. 199   'Reply to Mr Russell's Explanations': reprinted ibid., pp. 394–7
p. 199   'I enjoy living in College': BR to HT, 15.11.10

7. Reawakened Visions

p. 200   series of three lectures: all three are included in *Collected Papers 6*, as, respectively, papers 2, 3, and 14
p. 200   'has resolved': *Collected Papers 6*, p. 40
p. 200   'You will note': ibid. p. 135
p. 201   'living in a dream': *Autobiography*, p. 204
p. 201   'it *was* hard': BR to OM, 2.7.11
p. 201   'My heart is so full': BR to OM, 21.3.11
p. 202   'utterly unprepared': *Ottoline at Garsington: Memoirs of Lady Ottoline Morrell 1915–1918*, Appendix, p. 267
p. 202   'I feel myself': BR to OM, 21.3.11
p. 202   'I fear': ibid.
p. 202   'Dearest Alys': BR to AR, 22.3.11
p. 203   'All my life': BR to OM, 22.3.11
p. 203   'sordid atmosphere': BR to OM, 23.3.11
p. 204   'How could I': *Ottoline at Garsington*, p. 269
p. 204   'Nothing can stop': quoted in Seymour, op. cit., p. 111
p. 204   'I don't know quite why': BR to OM, 25.3.11
p. 205   'They are my best friends': ibid.
p. 205   'what you object to': OM to BR, 25.3.11, quoted in Seymour, op. cit., p. 111
p. 205   'You make me': OM to BR, 26.3.11, ibid., p. 112
p. 205   'I feel': BR to OM, 28.3.11
p. 206   'How could you suppose': BR to OM, 28.3.11
p. 206   'I have always felt': *Ottoline at Garsington*, p. 269
p. 207   'You are right': BR to OM, 29.3.11
p. 207   'I had another interview': *Ottoline at Garsington*, p. 269
p. 207   'even before': Seymour, op. cit., p. 114
p. 207   'allowed him': ibid.

p. 207 'Dearest': BR to OM, 30.3.11

p. 207 'if you continue': BR to OM, 28.3.11

p. 207 'Our love': BR to OM, 30.3.11

p. 208 'life is so full of prisons': BR to OM, 1.4.11

p. 208 'Alys has agreed': ibid.

p. 208 'Alys has been speaking': BR to OM, 2.4.11

p. 208 'revives the worship of beauty': BR to OM, 3.4.11

p. 209 'we do seem': ibid.

p. 209 'I know you don't feel quite as I do': BR to OM, 6.4.11

p. 209 'I wish very much': ibid.

p. 210 'My whole being': BR to OM, 4.4.11

p. 210 'I think the things she fears': BR to OM, 8.4.11

p. 211 'Do you want to go?': see *Ottoline at Garsington*, pp. 267–8

p. 211 'I shall see the Whiteheads': BR to OM, 8.4.11

p. 211 'Tell me everything': BR to OM, 8.4.11

p. 212 'In moments of depression': BR to OM, 13.4.11

p. 212 'I do long for you to come': OM to BR, 9–10.4.11, quoted in Seymour, op. cit., p. 125

p. 212 'You must manage': BR to OM, 12.4.11

p. 213 'When the dentist told me': *Autobiography*, p. 204

p. 213 'I then rode away': ibid.

p. 213 'it is too near': BR to OM, 16.4.11

p. 213 'He assumed at once': *Ottoline at Garsington*, pp. 272–3

p. 214 'I felt uplifted': ibid.

p. 214 'but I can't': BR to OM, 21.4.11

p. 214 'I go about': BR to OM, 22.4.11

p. 214 'This place': ibid.

p. 214 'I rather resent': ibid.

p. 215 'You will see': ibid.

p. 215 'a set of disjointed reflections': BR to OM, 26.4.11

p. 215 'What is the true essence': *Collected Papers 12*, pp. 53–4

p. 216 'This is a relief': BR to OM, 26.4.11

p. 216 'Parting grows harder': BR to OM, 29.4.11

p. 216 'a perfectly cold intellect': ibid.

p. 217 'I have tried': BR to OM, 10.5.11

p. 217 'It was rather queer': BR to OM, 2.5.11

p. 217 'Darling, don't worry': ibid.

p. 218 'I feel possessed': Henry Lamb to OM, 3.5.11, quoted in Seymour, op. cit., p. 129

p. 218 'that incredible little room': Henry Lamb to OM, 16.5.11, ibid., p. 130

p. 218 'I have the most absolute restful confidence': BR to OM, 13.5.11

p. 218 'I doubt if this quality': ibid.

p. 218 'I don't want to': BR to OM, 16.5.11

p. 219 'I want to get free': BR to OM, 19.5.11

p. 219 'After nearly two hours': *Ottoline: The Early Memoirs*, p. 213

p. 220 'wild and miserable': BR to OM, 21.5.11

p. 220 'Please forgive me': Logan Pearsall Smith to OM, 24.5.11, quoted in Seymour, op. cit., p. 134

p. 220 'though violent and vindictive': *Ottoline at Garsington*, p. 264

p. 220 'I feel quite sure': BR to OM, 24.5.11

p. 221 'His life was of a piece': ibid.

p. 221 'I find I should be rather sorry': BR to OM, 26.5.11
p. 222 'but that had no attractions': BR to OM, 25.5.11
p. 222 'I fear I should come to hate Alys': BR to OM, 27.5.11
p. 222 'But I was wrong': ibid.
p. 222 'We decided': *Ottoline at Garsington*, p. 276
p. 222 'I gather it is quite all right': BR to OM, 28.5.11
p. 223 'whenever I am not on the watch': BR to OM, 29.5.11
p. 223 'We are telling our friends': Alys to Mary, 4.6.11, see *Ottoline at Garsington*, pp. 288–9
p. 223 'in a very good mood': BR to OM, 6.6.11
p. 223 'I shall always love him': Alys to Mary, 14.6.11, *Ottoline at Garsington*, pp. 289–90
p. 223 'There was something': *Ottoline at Garsington*, p. 265
p. 224 'a false impression': BR to OM, 12.6.11
p. 224 'It is funny': BR to OM, 14.6.11
p. 224 'Apparently': BR to OM, 21.6.11
p. 224 'I am feeling again': BR to OM, 16.7.11
p. 225 'As I have to': BR to OM, 26.6.11
p. 225 'I *will* associate you with my work': BR to OM, June 1911
p. 225 'Darling, I *do long* for it too': OM to BR, 5.7.11, quoted in Seymour, op. cit., p. 145
p. 225 'affection and love': quoted in Griffin, *Selected Letters of Bertrand Russell*, p. 383
p. 226 'by a hypothetical jealousy': BR to OM, 16.7.11
p. 227 'talked of life': *Ottoline at Garsington*, p. 278
p. 227 'a journey': ibid., p. 279
p. 227 'It was exhausting': ibid., p. 278
p. 227 'Her feelings': from Russell's 'Private Memoir', written in the 1950s 'to explain why my relations with women that I have been fond of were until the last unsatisfactory'
p. 227 'The world's a prison': BR to OM, July 1911
p. 228 'Prisons': what survives of this aborted work is published in *Collected Papers 12*, pp. 97–109
p. 228 'it might': BR to OM, 30.7.11
p. 228 'like Napoleon': ibid.
p. 228 'The man': *The Problems of Philosophy* (paperback edition), p. 91
p. 228 'private world': ibid., p. 92
p. 228 'Personal and private things': ibid., p. 93
p. 229 'the mind . . . is rendered great': ibid., p. 94
p. 230 'In the summer': BR to OM, 12.2.12
p. 230 'One must have': BR to OM, 14.2.12
p. 230 'rather too kept down': OM to BR, 5.3.12
p. 230 'the dullness': quoted in BR to OM, 15.4.12
p. 230 'the emotions spoken of': see BR to OM, 18.10.11
p. 230 '*Individuality is so precious*': OM to BR, 5.3.11
p. 230 'Self in all its forms': *Collected Papers 12*, p. 103
p. 230 'The essence of religion': ibid., p. 105
p. 230 'feeling the individual': ibid., pp. 108–9
p. 230 'besides the earthly love': ibid., p. 107
p. 231 'learn what is best': OM to BR, 5.3.12

8. Hard Dry Reasoning

p. 232 'I have the energy': BR to OM, 16.9.11
p. 233 'Owing to Bergson': ibid.
p. 233 'I remember': BR to OM, 7.3.12
p. 233 'My imagination': BR to OM, 16.9.11
p. 233 'I work in the morning': BR to OM, 19.9.11
p. 233 'been very full': BR to OM, 20.9.11
p. 234 'I do feel myself': BR to OM, 20.9.11
p. 234 'On the Relations': reprinted in *Logic and Knowledge* and *Collected Papers 6*
p. 234 'unchangeable, rigid, exact': see *The Problems of Philosophy*, p. 57
p. 235 'if he [Bergson] fails': *Collected Papers 6*, p. 328
p. 236 'Often, I can hardly know': BR to OM, 6.12.11
p. 236 'You with your God': BR to OM, 21.9.11
p. 236 'I am very very much interested': BR to OM, 16.10.11
p. 237 'an unknown German': BR to OM, 18.10.11
p. 237 'My German friend': BR to OM, 19.10.11
p. 237 'every moment': BR to OM, 25.10.11
p. 237 'I enjoyed making it pretty': *Ottoline at Garsington*, p. 279
p. 238 'is giving lectures': BR to LD, 28.10.11
p. 238 'I didn't find out anything': BR to OM, 29.10.11
p. 238 'completely materialistic': quoted in *Collected Papers 6*, p. 319
p. 238 'Bergson, who was present': BR to Ralph Barton Perry, 1.11.11
p. 239 'very argumentative': BR to OM, 1.11.11
p. 239 'a fool': BR to OM, 2.11.11
p. 239 'so much pleasanter': ibid.
p. 239 'It seems to me': BR to OM, 4.11.11
p. 239 'It is very unlikely': ibid.
p. 239 'I long to have long talks': BR to OM, 5.11.11
p. 239 'but from the point of view': BR to OM, 12.11.11
p. 239 'Young men': ibid.
p. 241 'he asked me today': BR to OM, 27.11.11
p. 241 'literary, very musical': BR to OM, 29.11.11
p. 241 'clear up my own ideas': BR to OM, 13.12.11
p. 242 'amazing eyes': see *Ottoline: The Early Memoirs*, p. 97
p. 243 'I don't know': quoted in Seymour, op. cit., p. 154
p. 243 'I have upon me': BR to OM, 27.12.11
p. 243 'It is difficult': ibid.
p. 243 'it is far better': BR to OM, 28.12.11
p. 244 'I see that': BR to OM, 31.12.11
p. 244 'You don't know': BR to OM, 30.12.11
p. 244 'There is of course': BR to OM, 30.12.11
p. 244 'All that religion': BR to OM, 1.1.12
p. 245 'And one can make': BR to OM, 9.1.12
p. 245 'I believe any passion': ibid.
p. 245 'This year': BR to OM, 24.1.12
p. 246 'fettered': BR to OM, 11.2.12
p. 246 'I feel the courageous course': ibid.
p. 246 'I should be afraid': ibid.
p. 246 'I have always tended': BR to OM, 18.2.12
p. 246 'It has a kind of stoic nobility': GLD to BR, quoted in BR to OM, 1.2.12
p. 247 'dry intellectual mood': BR to OM, 23.2.12

p. 247 'When you are gone': BR to OM, 27.2.12
p. 247 'I think his philosophy': BR to OM, 4.3.12
p. 247 'The whole world': BR to OM, 11.3.12
p. 247 'Bergson's mystical philosophy': Wood, op. cit., p. 89
p. 248 'Writing on Bergson': BR to OM, 8.3.12
p. 248 'I began to talk': ibid.
p. 248 'an old gentleman': BR to OM, 9.3.12
p. 248 'I am so glad': see *Ottoline: The Early Memoirs*, p. 220
p. 249 'the abstract intellectual life': ibid., p. 221
p. 249 'I found myself': ibid., p. 222
p. 249 'About life and philosophy': BR to OM, 13.3.12
p. 250 'Oh': OM to Lytton Strachey, quoted in Seymour, op. cit., p. 161
p. 250 'the most perfect': BR to OM, 17.3.12
p. 250 'very good': BR to OM, 23.1.12
p. 250 'a small proportion': BR to OM, 15.3.12
p. 251 'terribly persistent': BR to OM, 2.3.12
p. 251 'is that of an artist': BR to OM, 16.3.12
p. 251 'a close equal passionate discussion': BR to OM, 18.3.12
p. 251 'It was a mild event': BR to OM, 12.3.12
p. 251 'spoke with intense feeling': BR to OM, 18.3.12
p. 252 'In discussion': ibid.
p. 252 'something solid': BR to OM, 15.3.12
p. 252 'people who like philosophy': BR to OM, 18.3.12

9. Perplexities

p. 254 'I won't *count* on you': BR to OM, 18.3.12
p. 254 'I never saw anything more beautiful': BR to OM, 21.3.12
p. 254 'There were several bouts': ibid.
p. 254 'I love being alone': ibid.
p. 255 'Ever since the letter you wrote': BR to OM, 30.5.12
p. 255 'nothing but rocks': BR to OM, 22.3.12
p. 256 'I doubt if even you': BR to OM, 23.3.12
p. 256 'I remember when': ibid.
p. 256 'a drunken homosexual spy': from Russell's 'Private Memoir'
p. 256 'Of all the characters I ever read about in fiction': BR to OM, 24.3.12
p. 256 'The side of you': BR to OM, 22.3.12
p. 256 'But I was in a fit of madness': BR to OM, 24.3.12
p. 256 'dry & hard': ibid.
p. 257 'I think it was the toothache': OM to BR, 24.3.12, quoted in Seymour, op. cit., p. 162
p. 257 'When physical pain': BR to OM, 26.3.12
p. 257 'Indeed passion is of God': BR to OM, 2.4.12
p. 258 'I thought a great deal': BR to OM, 7.4.12
p. 258 'Dramatic and Utilitarian Ethics': included as paper 36 in *Collected Papers 12*, pp. 378–83
p. 258 'the average man': ibid., p. 382
p. 258 'having little to do': see *Collected Papers 6*, p. 378
p. 259 'is not a kindly sentiment': ibid., p. 383
p. 259 'I thought he would have smashed': BR to OM, 23.4.12
p. 260 'trivial problem': ibid.
p. 260 'I might invent': BR to OM, 24.4.12

p. 260 'go back': BR to OM, 11.5.12
p. 260 'Dearest, don't think': ibid.
p. 260 'a religion only for the victims': BR to OM, 30.4.12
p. 261 'Quite impersonally and impartially': ibid.
p. 261 'Seeing that you': BR to OM, 24.4.12
p. 262 'remember simple moral truths': BR to OM, 11.5.12
p. 262 'I have put into the world': BR to OM, 30.4.12
p. 262 'There is nothing to compare': BR to OM, 24.5.12
p. 262 'On Matter': *Collected Papers 6*, pp. 77–95
p. 263 'It will shock people': BR to OM, 29.4.12
p. 263 'In what follows': *Collected Papers 6*, p. 80
p. 263 'but only': BR to OM, 26.5.12
p. 263 'it is quite useless': BR to OM, 14.5.12
p. 264 'all spiritual things': BR to OM, 17.5.12
p. 264 'one could put in': BR to OM, 20.5.12
p. 264 'and do it better': BR to OM, 1.6.12
p. 264 'thinking of doing philosophy': BR to OM, 27.5.12
p. 264 'I told him': ibid.
p. 264 'What shall it profit a man': BR to OM, 29.5.12
p. 265 'Yesterday Wittgenstein began on Dickens': BR to OM, 1.6.12
p. 265 'for some time past': *Ottoline at Garsington*, p. 280
p. 265 'I want to lay down': BR to OM, 30.5.12
p. 265 'If I could face life': ibid.
p. 266 'I should not avoid sexual crime': ibid.
p. 266 'Oh Bertie': OM to BR, 31.5.12, quoted in Seymour, op. cit., p. 162
p. 266 'This is not a decision': BR to OM, 1.6.12
p. 266 'at Lausanne': ibid.
p. 266 'soon grew gentler': *Ottoline at Garsington*, p. 280
p. 266 'an enchanting day': ibid.
p. 266 *The Perplexities of John Forstice*: published as paper 9 in *Collected Papers 12*, pp. 123–54
p. 267 'a single-minded enthusiast': *Collected Papers 12*, p. 128
p. 267 'Do you know': ibid., p. 133
p. 267 'all his abstract interests': ibid., p. 134
p. 268 'Mathematics gives most joy': ibid., p. 136
p. 268 'The artists and madmen': ibid., p. 141
p. 269 'We common people': ibid., p. 143
p. 270 'There is': ibid., p. 148
p. 270 'I wish you to tell her': ibid., p. 147
p. 270 'The final parting': ibid.
p. 271 'As he walked away': ibid., p. 151

10. The Shattered Wave

p. 272 '*entirely* ceased': BR to OM, 10.7.12
p. 272 'We expect': from Hermine Wittgenstein's memoir, 'My Brother Ludwig', see *Recollections of Wittgenstein*, p. 2
p. 273 'In a Cambridge garden': G. L. Dickinson, 'A Personal Impression of Tagore', *The New Leader*, 23 Feb. 1923, pp. 11–12
p. 273 'the mood': BR to OM, 14.7.12
p. 273 'It seems to me': GLD to BR, 21.7.12
p. 274 'The impulse to technical work': BR to OM, 24.7.12

p. 274 'In an odd way': ibid.
p. 275 'obviously an intellectual man's conception': quoted in BR to OM, 3.8.12
p. 275 'ought to be less shadowy': BR to OM, 14.8.12
p. 275 'quite enough mere discussion': quoted in BR to OM, 8.9.12
p. 275 'What I should like to do': ibid.
p. 275 'Wars and pestilences': BR to OM, 26.8.12
p. 275 'an Ecclesiastes pessimist': BR to OM, 3.9.12
p. 276 'No, this is all too farcical': ibid.
p. 276 'When I am unhappy': BR to OM, 15.10.12
p. 276 'Bertie came down on Sunday': *Ottoline at Garsington*, pp. 280–1
p. 276 'He is so lonely': ibid.
p. 277 'He expects me': ibid.
p. 277 'wild bohemian artistic side': quoted in Seymour, op. cit., p. 173
p. 277 'At night': see *Ottoline: The Early Memoirs*, p. 232
p. 278 'that wretch Bertie': quoted in Seymour, op. cit.
p. 278 'the time at Churn': BR to OM, 4.5.13
p. 279 'These are the actual sons of God': LW to BR, 16.8.12
p. 279 'how glorious': BR to OM, 21.8.12
p. 279 'I find it excites me': BR to OM, 21.8.12
p. 279 'now getting old': BR to OM, 21.8.12 (a later letter)
p. 279 'an odd sense of treachery': ibid.
p. 279 'We talk about music': BR to OM, 4.9.12
p. 280 'sage advice': BR to OM, 5.9.12
p. 280 'Here is Wittgenstein': BR to OM, 11.10.12
p. 280 'He was so unhappy': BR to OM, 13.10.12
p. 280 'yet when you live': Rabindranath Tagore to BR, 13.10.12
p. 281 'I regret I cannot agree': BR to N. Chatterji, 26.4.67
p. 281 'What is Logic?': *Collected Papers 6*, paper 4, pp. 54–6
p. 281 'which I think': BR to OM, 13.10.12
p. 281 'the subject': BR to OM, 14.10.12
p. 281 'the study': *Collected Papers 6*, p. 55
p. 281 'A *form* is something': ibid., p. 56
p. 281 'I don't know yet quite': BR to OM, 15.10.12
p. 282 'sense of failure': BR to OM, 15.10.12 (later letter)
p. 282 'the problem': BR to OM, 16.10.12
p. 282 'I don't know': BR to OM, 25.10.12
p. 282 'not only of those': *Collected Papers 6*, p. 94
p. 282 'No one except Wittgenstein': BR to OM, 26.10.12
p. 282 'start philosophers': ibid.
p. 282 'I feel that I really have': BR to OM, 29.10.12
p. 283 'But there are': BR to OM, 30.10.12
p. 283 'a vast & very difficult subject': BR to OM, 8.11.12
p. 283 'a fine big canvas': BR to OM, 17.11.12
p. 283 'When I have read enough': ibid.
p. 284 'One has time': BR to OM, 16.12.12
p. 284 'extraordinarily strong': BR to OM, 29.12.12
p. 284 'feeling himself': BR to OM, 31.10.12
p. 284 'Are you thinking': *Autobiography Volume II*, p. 99
p. 284 'He strains his mind': BR to OM, 3.11.12
p. 284 'a bleating lambkin': BR to OM, 9.11.12
p. 284 'suddenly stood still': ibid.

p. 285 'The poor man': Lytton Strachey to Sydney Saxon Turner, 16.11.12
p. 286 'about *our* Theory of Symbolism': LW to BR, 26.12.12
p. 286 'Every theory of types': LW to BR, January 1912
p. 286 'greater school': BR to OM, 25.12.12
p. 287 'partly the cause': ibid.
p. 287 'and where I tried': *Ottoline: The Early Memoirs*, p. 234
p. 287 'It is rather appalling': BR to OM, 14.1.13
p. 288 'I would give my right hand': *Ottoline at Garsington*, p. 282
p. 288 'Anyone who reads this warning': ibid.
p. 288 'Bertie says': *Ottoline: The Early Memoirs*, p. 236
p. 288 'He is, I am sure': *Ottoline at Garsington*, p. 282
p. 289 'I want very much': BR to OM, 23.2.13
p. 290 'So far as I know': BR to Ralph Perry, 4.2.13
p. 290 preliminary attempts: see 'Nine Short Manuscripts on Matter', written in 1912–13 and included as paper 11 in *Collected Papers 6*, pp. 96–111. The phrase 'logically late' occurs on p. 109.
p. 290 reviewed William James: the review is reprinted in *Collected Papers 6*, pp. 298–304
p. 291 'He raged and stormed': BR to OM, 6.3.13
p. 292 'tried in vain': BR to GLD, 13.2.13
p. 292 'I feel': ibid.
p. 292 'Are you finding': ibid.
p. 293 'Science as an Element in Culture': originally published in *The New Statesman* in May 1913, reprinted as 'The Place of Science in a Liberal Education' in *Mysticism and Logic*, and in *Collected Papers 12*, pp. 387–97
p. 293 'Science comes nearer': from a passage included in the original paper but cut from the subsequent reprints, presumably because it is repeated at the end of Russell's later paper, 'Mysticism and Logic' (where, however, it is scientific *philosophy* that is said to come 'nearer to objectivity than any other pursuit'). See *Collected Papers 12*, p. 546.
p. 293 'The kernel': see *Collected Papers 12*, pp. 395–6
p. 293 'much better': BR to OM, 17.4.13
p. 293 'When there are': BR to OM, 24.4.13
p. 294 'Dearest I do hope': BR to OM, 7.5.13
p. 294 'The excitement': BR to OM, 26.4.13
p. 294 'been bubbling over': BR to OM, 4.5.13
p. 294 'with all solemnity': BR to OM, 2.5.13
p. 294 'Then I shall come': BR to OM, 8.5.13
p. 295 'with a refutation': BR to OM, 21.5.13
p. 296 'logical objects': see *The Theory of Knowledge* (paperback edition), p. 97
p. 296 'In the present': ibid., p. 99
p. 296 'it is clear': ibid., pp. 98–9
p. 296 'it is impossible': ibid., p. 46
p. 297 'we were both cross': BR to OM, 27.5.13
p. 300 'I can now': LW to BR, probably around 16.5.13
p. 300 'The proper theory': see Wittgenstein, *Notebooks 1914–1916*, p. 103, and *Tractatus Logico-Philosophicus* 5.5422
p. 300 'who is not yet stale': LW to G. E. Moore, 19.11.13
p. 301 'He taught his patients': *Ottoline: The Early Memoirs*, p. 237
p. 301 'Do you remember': BR to OM, 4.3.16
p. 302 'I feel you find me': BR to OM, 20.6.13

p. 302 'two opposite': ibid.
p. 302 'Without you': BR to OM, 21.6.13
p. 302 'This can only be': BR to OM, 27.6.13
p. 303 'My Aunt Agatha': BR to OM, 27.6.13 (later letter)
p. 303 'It seems to me': BR to OM, 28.6.13
p. 304 *absurd* to talk: OM to BR 28.6.13. See Seymour, op. cit., p. 181
p. 304 'I can't make': BR to OM, 30.6.13

11. The External World and the Central Fire

p. 306 'what Prisons failed to be': BR to OM, 8.4.13
p. 306 'I don't believe': BR to OM, 24.7.13
p. 306 'a kind of selfishness': BR to OM, 10.8.13
p. 307 'I am very sorry': ibid.
p. 307 'was a very lovely one': *Ottoline at Garsington*, p. 284
p. 307 'he was such a pure artist': *Ottoline: The Early Memoirs*, p. 239
p. 308 'But, dear lady': ibid., p. 240
p. 308 'that wonderful book': ibid.
p. 308 'I found': ibid., p. 242 (footnote)
p. 308 'He said': OM to BR, 11.8.13, quoted in Seymour, op. cit., p. 183
p. 309 'I am *quite quite* sure': BR to OM, 22.8.13
p. 309 'In his talk': *Ottoline: The Early Memoirs*, p. 242
p. 309 'She seemed': OM to BR, 11.8.13
p. 309 'I wonder': BR to OM, 12.8.13
p. 310 'an utterly stupid person': BR to OM, 10.8.13
p. 310 'It is what I asked for': BR to OM, 18.8.13
p. 311 'I can't justify it': ibid.
p. 312 'At the end of the evening': BR to OM, 29.8.13
p. 312 'Bertie has gone': *Ottoline at Garsington*, p. 284
p. 312 'He was hard and cold': ibid.
p. 313 'I have *really* learnt': BR to OM, 30.8.13
p. 313 'is that there is no *new* thought': BR to OM, probably 5.9.13
p. 313 'among the triumphs': *Our Knowledge of the External World*, p. 189
p. 314 'In all who seek': ibid., p. 30
p. 314 'Of the reality': ibid., p. 31
p. 314 'like all human faculties': ibid., p. 32
p. 314 'yet self-knowledge': ibid., p. 35
p. 314 'the wall': ibid.
p. 315 'At our very first meeting': *Autobiography*, p. 209
p. 315 'It was *wonderful*': BR to OM, 10.9.13
p. 316 'unusual talkativeness': Joseph Conrad to BR, 13.9.13
p. 316 'I have seen Conrad': BR to LD, 20.2.14
p. 316 'shared a certain outlook': *Autobiography*, p. 207
p. 317 'In the out-works of our lives': ibid.
p. 317 'His soul was mad': *The Heart of Darkness* (Signet Classic edition), p. 144
p. 317 'he had made that last stride': ibid., p. 149
p. 317 'Satanic mysticism': Russell to Watts-Armstrong, 3.10.61
p. 318 'a dangerous walk': *Autobiography*, p. 208
p. 318 'The completion': Frederick Karl, *Joseph Conrad: The Three Lives*, p. 678
p. 318 'reached out': ibid.
p. 318 'He was very conscious': *Autobiography*, p. 208
p. 319 'It was': *The Secret Sharer* (Signet Classic edition), p. 27

p. 319 'It's a great satisfaction': ibid., p. 52
p. 320 'I find men's opinions': *Ottoline: The Early Memoirs*, pp. 247–8
p. 321 'He was different': *Typhoon and Other Stories* (Penguin edition), p. 155
p. 321 'I felt strangely solitary': *Autobiography Volume II*, p. 38
p. 321 'understood each other': *Ottoline: The Early Memoirs*, p. 243
p. 322 'I shall certainly try': BR to OM, 13.9.13
p. 322 'have never come in contact': ibid.
p. 322 'My days here': BR to OM, 16.9.13
p. 322 'in the mood': BR to OM, 21.9.13
p. 322 'I have fairly vivid intellectual interests': ibid.
p. 323 'While the mystic mood': *Our Knowledge of the External World*, p. 56
p. 323 'All that about the bad logic': BR to OM, 29.9.13
p. 323 'all sorts of ideas': LW to BR, 20.9.13
p. 323 'frightfully worried': Pinsent, Diary, 20.9.13
p. 324 'I was utterly worn out': BR to OM, 3.10.13
p. 324 'a blow and an anxiety': BR to OM, 6.10.13
p. 324 'I said it would be dark': BR to LD, 19.10.13
p. 324 'a godsend': BR to OM, 6.10.13
p. 324 'he wears me out': ibid.
p. 324 'After much groaning': BR to OM, 9.10.13
p. 325 'makes me feel': ibid.
p. 325 'Propositions, which are symbols': Wittgenstein, *Notebooks*, pp. 96–7
p. 325 'that this inkpot': ibid., p. 97
p. 326 'This is an ideal place': LW to BR, 29.10.13
p. 326 'All sorts': LW to BR, Nov. 1913
p. 326 'An account': ibid.
p. 326 'I beg you': LW to BR, Nov. or Dec. 1913
p. 326 'The youth': BR to LD, 19.10.13
p. 327 'I have a civilised side': BR to OM, 14.10.13
p. 327 'Instinctive desires' BR to OM, 10.9.13
p. 327 'wd. not be lessened': ibid.
p. 327 'My feelings now': BR to OM, 4.10.13
p. 327 'Yes, Villon is very great': BR to OM, 6.10.13

12. Mr Apollinax

p. 329 'I feel very happy': BR to OM, 19.11.13
p. 330 'I find I have lost all interest': BR to OM, 14.10.13
p. 330 'I am liable': BR to OM, 26.11.13
p. 330 'It was a great pleasure': Conrad to BR, 12.12.13
p. 330 'mad . . . all alone brooding': see BR to OM, 6.1.14
p. 331 'I hope': OM to BR, 21.12.13, quoted in Seymour, op. cit., p. 187
p. 331 'Your letters': BR to OM, 22.12.13
p. 331 'This spring': BR to OM, 21.12.13
p. 331 'very scratch and uncomfortable': BR to OM, 22.12.13
p. 332 'I don't know': BR to OM, 26.12.13
p. 332 'I would rather': BR to OM, 27.12.13
p. 332 'and nearly embraced': ibid.
p. 332 '& shall never be': BR to OM, 29.12.13
p. 332 'a sort of *éclaircissement*': BR to OM, 29.12.13 (later letter)
p. 333 'felt all your pain': BR to OM, 5.1.14
p. 333 'I cannot well': OM to BR, 5.1.14, quoted in Seymour, op. cit., p. 187

p. 333   'I should feel': *Autobiography*, p. 207
p. 333   'moving step by step': Conrad to BR, 22.12.13
p. 333   'follow the dream': Conrad, *Lord Jim* (Penguin edition), p. 201
p. 334   'I know I have failed': BR to OM, 5.1.14
p. 334   'a sense of shame': BR to OM, 3.1.14
p. 334   'Please read enclosed': ibid.
p. 335   'The effect of Conrad's letter': BR to OM, 4.1.14
p. 335   'ordinary daily happiness': ibid.
p. 335   'The Relation of Sense-Data to Physics': first published in *Scientia*, 16, July 1914, reprinted in *Mysticism and Logic* and as paper 1 in *Collected Papers 8*, pp. 3–26
p. 335   'very good!': BR to OM, 17.1.14
p. 336   'At last, in despair': from the broadcast 'How I write', included in *Portraits from Memory*, pp. 194–7 (quotation on pp. 195–6)
p. 336   'I do not want': ibid., p. 196
p. 336   'What I dictated': *Autobiography*, p. 210
p. 337   'I hate the suffering': BR to OM, 6.1.14
p. 337   'I cannot bear': BR to OM, 8.1.14
p. 337   'I used to feel': BR to OM, 9.1.14
p. 337   'Mysticism and Logic': first published in the *Hibbert Journal*, 12 July 1914, reprinted in *Mysticism and Logic*, and as paper 2 in *Collected Papers 8*.
p. 337   'It is not very good': BR to OM, 11.1.4
p. 337   'The greatest men': *Collected Papers 8*, p. 30
p. 337   'we see the true union': ibid., p. 31
p. 337   'offering less glitter': ibid., p. 49
p. 337   'a delicate matter': BR to OM, 19.1.14
p. 338   'a wonderful man': BR to OM, 18.1.14
p. 338   'the growing need': *Collected Papers 8*, p. 54
p. 338   review of Balfour: *Collected Papers 8*, pp. 99–104
p. 338   'rhetorical dishonest sentimental twaddle': BR to OM, 17.2.14
p. 338   'It is incredible balderdash': BR to OM, 24.2.14
p. 338   'never aims': see *Collected Papers 8*, p. 101
p. 339   'The fundamental defect': ibid., p. 104
p. 340   'Sometimes': LW to BR, Jan. 1914, misdated in *Letters to Russell, Keynes and Moore* as 'June or July 1914'. See Brian McGuinness, *Wittgenstein: A Life*, p. 92
p. 340   'It's VERY sad': LW to BR, Jan. 1914
p. 340   'and the beauty': ibid.
p. 340   'All best wishes': ibid.
p. 341   'we really don't suit one another': LW to BR, Feb. 1914
p. 341   'It is my fault': BR to OM, 19.2.14
p. 342   'I dare say': ibid.
p. 342   'Your letter was *so* full of kindness': LW to BR, 3.3.14
p. 344   'I have not felt impatient': BR to OM, 8.2.14
p. 344   'I had thought': BR to OM, 13.2.14
p. 344   'The longing for children': BR to OM, 13.2.14 (later letter)
p. 344   'a dire loneliness': *Ottoline: The Early Memoirs*, pp. 251–2
p. 345   'You feel me terribly selfish': BR to OM, 17.2.14
p. 345   'praising "The Free Man's Worship" ': BR to LD, 20.2.14
p. 346   'I am not surprised': Conrad to BR, 17.2.14
p. 346   'that in fact': BR to OM, 22.2.14

p. 346 'whatever happens': BR to OM, 24.2.14
p. 346 'one of the foremost': *New York Times*, 14.3.14, quoted in *Bertrand Russell's America Volume One 1896–1945*, p. 39
p. 347 'I couldn't *bear*': BR to OM, 22.3.14
p. 347 'an intolerable person': BR to OM, 19.3.14
p. 347 'the kind of people': BR to OM, 26.3.14
p. 347 'prides itself': BR to MLID, 12.4.14
p. 347 'the American tendency': BR to OM, 14.3.14
p. 347 'Nobody here': BR to OM, 19.3.14
p. 347 'rapidly driving me mad': ibid.
p. 347 'a soul-destroying atmosphere': BR to OM, 22.3.14
p. 347 'more alert': BR to LD, 20.3.14
p. 347 'Spiritually we starve and die': BR to OM, 19.3.14
p. 347 'humble and shabby': BR to OM, 14.3.14
p. 347 'regular American place': BR to OM, 19.3.14
p. 348 'I find the coloured people': BR to OM, 14.3.14
p. 348 'not the sort of man': ibid.
p. 348 'a *great* improvement': BR to OM, 26.3.14
p. 348 'we have breakfast': ibid.
p. 348 'I enjoy my lecturing': BR to LD, 20.3.14
p. 348 'I was seized with shyness': BR to OM, 19.3.14
p. 348 'fussy and old-maidish': BR to OM, 26.3.14
p. 349 Victor Lenzen: see 'Bertrand Russell at Harvard, 1914' by Victor Lenzen, *Russell*, 3, autumn 1971, pp. 4–6
p. 349 'the chance of a lifetime': ibid., p. 4
p. 349 'an almost superhuman person': ibid.
p. 349 'A fact is not a thing': ibid., pp. 4–5
p. 349 'able and *very* nice': BR to OM, 23.3.14
p. 349 'writes long long letters': see BR to OM, 13.4.14
p. 350 His doctoral thesis: published as *Knowledge and Experience in the Philosophy of F. H. Bradley*, 1964.
p. 350 'extraordinarily silent': *Autobiography*, p. 212
p. 350 'Yes, he always reminds me': ibid.
p. 350 'intimate': see BR to LD, 20.2.14
p. 350 'fit of spleen': BR to LD, 11.5.14
p. 351 'an assembled crowd of neighbours': BR to OM, 6.4.14
p. 351 'far less repulsive': BR to OM, 13.4.14
p. 351 'There at last': ibid.
p. 351 'but the mental atmosphere': BR to OM, 15.4.14
p. 351 'By the time': BR to LD, 29.4.14
p. 351 'escaping from New England': BR to OM, April 1914
p. 352 '*awful* people': BR to OM, 20.4.14
p. 352 'full of new Gothic': BR to OM, 24.4.14
p. 352 'awful bores': BR to LD, 29.4.14
p. 352 'a silly book': BR to OM, 24.4.14
p. 352 'I feel': BR to LD, 29.4.14
p. 352 'seems done': ibid.
p. 352 'a one-horse place': BR to OM, 6.5.14
p. 352 'I . . . loved him': ibid.
p. 353 'I find the cultured people': BR to OM, 26.3.14
p. 353 'It was beautiful': BR to OM, 11.5.14

p. 353 'as like an Englishman': BR to LD, 11.5.14
p. 354 'noticed the madness': BR to Barry Fox, 27.11.27
p. 354 'I have thank Heaven': BR to OM, 11.5.14
p. 354 'only require': BR to OM, 15.5.14
p. 355 'Everybody has been so kind': BR to OM, 23.5.14
p. 355 'whose daughter': ibid.
p. 356 'I at once': *Autobiography*, p. 213
p. 356 'has developed': BR to OM, 29.5.14
p. 356 'a rather important one': BR to OM, 1.6.14
p. 357 'Her youth': *Autobiography*, p. 213
p. 357 'I do not want you': BR to OM, 1.6.14
p. 358 'a very real and serious thing': BR to OM, 14.6.14
p. 358 'All day': BR to OM, 16.6.14
p. 358 'Our little moment': BR to OM, 18.6.14
p. 359 'What you give me': BR to OM, 23.6.14
p. 359 'Most people': BR to OM, 23.6.14 (later letter)
p. 360 'What worries me': BR to OM, 11.7.14
p. 360 'the shock of war': *Autobiography*, p. 213
p. 361 'as delightful as ever': BR to OM, 22.7.14
p. 362 'The war and risk of war': BR to OM, 29.7.14
p. 362 'really regretful': ibid.
p. 362 'I think her existence': ibid.
p. 362 'It looks all but hopeless': BR to OM, 31.7.14
p. 363 'I seem to feel': BR to OM, 1.8.14
p. 363 'The source of all international trouble': BR to OM, 1.8.14
p. 364 'Do tell P.': BR to OM, 3.8.14
p. 364 'excited crowds': *Ottoline: The Early Memoirs*, p. 259
p. 364 'If he had not got up': ibid., p. 260
p. 364 'noticing cheering crowds': *Autobiography Volume II*, p. 16
p. 364 'I remember': *Ottoline: The Early Memoirs*, p. 260
p. 364 'But for her': *Autobiography Volume II*, p. 18
p. 364 'the greatest misfortune': BR to OM, 2.8.14

13. Against the Multitude

p. 367 'war is a mad horror': BR to LD, 22.8.14
p. 367 'You were right': BR to MLlD, August 1914
p. 367 'letter to *The Nation*': published as paper 1, 'Friends of Progress Betrayed', *Collected Papers 13*, pp. 3–5
p. 367 'The friends of progress': ibid., p. 4
p. 368 'No one whose experience': ibid.
p. 369 'Those who saw': BR, letter to *The Nation*, published 15 Aug. 1914, reprinted as paper 2, 'The Rights of the War', *Collected Papers 13* pp. 6–9
p. 369 'we cannot sit still': Evelyn Whitehead to BR, 4.8.14, quoted by Victor Lowe in *Alfred North Whitehead: The Man and His Work Volume II*, p. 28
p. 369 'a *very* war-like letter': BR to OM, 13.8.14
p. 369 'miserable at differing from you': A. N. Whitehead to BR, 28.8.14, quoted in Lowe, op. cit.
p. 370 Wells announced in print: see H. G. Wells, 'The War That Will End War', *The Daily News and Leader*, 14 Aug. 1914
p. 370 'without any ally': BR to OM, 15.8.14
p. 370 'All the young men': BR to OM, 14.8.14

p. 370 'It is impossible': BR to LD, 22.8.14
p. 370 'not exciting': BR to OM, 12.8.14
p. 371 'I feel *very* strongly': BR to George Trevelyan, 2.10.14
p. 371 'War: the Cause and the Cure': *The Labour Leader*, 24 Sep. 1914, reprinted as paper 4 in *Collected Papers 13*, pp. 16–19
p. 371 'because it has been decreed': *Collected Papers 13*, p. 18
p. 371 'if time for reflection': ibid., p. 19
p. 372 'Why Nations Love War': *War and Peace*, 2 (14), Nov. 1914, reprinted in *Justice in War-Time*, and as paper 9 in *Collected Papers 13*, pp. 32–6
p. 372 'I do not wish': *Collected Papers 13*, p. 35
p. 372 'War arouses the wild beast': from 'A True History of Europe's Last War', *The Labour Leader*, 11 Mar. 1915, reprinted as paper 20 in *Collected Papers 13*, pp. 105–12 (quotation on p. 111)
p. 373 'War, the Offspring of Fear': first published by the UDC as a pamphlet in Nov. 1914, reprinted as paper 10 in *Collected Papers 13*, pp. 37–47
p. 373 'Essentially': *Collected Papers 13*, p. 40
p. 373 'It must not be supposed': ibid., p. 43
p. 373 'The Western war': ibid., p. 44
p. 373 'It is partly Conrad': BR to OM, 3.12.14
p. 374 'People are affected': BR to OM, 12.11.14
p. 374 'I really rather enjoy': BR to OM, 14.10.14
p. 374 'All the Dostoyevsky devils': BR to OM, Aug. 1914
p. 374 'I don't think': BR to OM, Sep. 1914
p. 374 'We are terribly alone': BR to OM, 5.8.14
p. 374 'I cannot tell you': BR to OM, 12.8.14
p. 375 'Now my love for you': BR to OM, 1.9.14
p. 375 'She is terribly': BR to OM, 15.8.14
p. 375 'It is impossible to be quite truthful': BR to OM, August 1914
p. 376 'very over-decorated': quoted in Seymour, op. cit., p. 198 (the published version, *Ottoline at Garsington*, p. 287, differs slightly: Seymour is quoting from the original, unedited journal)
p. 376 'an odd creature': *Ottoline at Garsington*, p. 286
p. 376 'Like a beaten and caged animal': ibid., p. 287
p. 376 'You were *perfect*': BR to OM, 15.8.14
p. 376 'He is very odd': *Ottoline at Garsington*, p. 288
p. 377 '*Please* don't think': BR to OM, 18.8.14
p. 377 'the wound': BR to OM, 23.8.14
p. 377 'we heard knock, knock, knock': *Ottoline at Garsington*, p. 287
p. 377 'My Darling Darling': BR to OM, 25.8.14
p. 378 'Yes, indeed': OM to BR, 26.8.14, quoted in Seymour, op. cit., p. 198
p. 378 'how wonderful': OM to BR, 28.8.14, quoted ibid., p. 199
p. 378 'had relations with her': *Autobiography*, p. 213
p. 379 'You *can't* say': BR to OM, Aug. 1914
p. 379 'It is a downright falsehood': BR to OM, Aug. 1914
p. 379 'Will you try': BR to OM, 1.9.14
p. 380 'she asked': BR to OM, 4.9.14
p. 380 'amused & pleased': BR to OM, Sep. 1914
p. 380 'kept things as impersonal': BR to OM, 21.9.14
p. 380 'I grow hot with shame': BR to OM, 22.9.14
p. 381 'I wouldn't let her in': BR to OM, 11.10.14
p. 381 'Fancy Helen being back!': BR to OM, 22.1.15

p. 381 'When I talked with her': *Autobiography*, p. 214
p. 381 'In her insanity': ibid.
p. 381 'It is terribly hard': BR to OM, 29.10.14
p. 381 'Are there really people': BR to Samuel Alexander, 17.10.14
p. 381 'It worries me': BR to OM, 11.11.14
p. 382 'On Scientific Method in Philosophy': the Herbert Spencer Lecture at Oxford, first published in 1914 as a pamphlet, reprinted in *Mysticism and Logic*, and as paper 4 in *Collected Papers 8*, pp. 55–73
p. 382 'too often resemble': *Collected Papers 8*, p. 63
p. 382 'inspired': BR to Ralph Perry, 21.2.15
p. 382 'If I could earn an income': BR to OM, 11.11.14
p. 382 'The Ethics of War': *The International Journal of Ethics*, 25, Jan. 1915, reprinted in *Justice in War-Time*, and as paper 14 in *Collected Papers 13*, pp. 61–73
p. 382 'meant to be': BR to OM, 3.12.14
p. 383 'I don't think war *always* wrong': BR to OM, 19.11.14
p. 383 'the conflicts': *Collected Papers 13*, p. 67
p. 383 'the process': ibid.
p. 383 'the progress of mankind': ibid., p. 69
p. 383 'If the facts': ibid., p. 68
p. 383 'As between civilised nations': ibid., p. 71
p. 383 'When this great tragedy': ibid., pp. 72–3
p. 384 a rejoinder: Ralph Perry, 'Non-Resistance and the Present War – A Reply to Mr Russell', *International Journal of Ethics*, 25, April 1915, pp. 307–16
p. 384 Russell in turn replied: 'The War and Non-Resistance: A Rejoinder to Professor Perry', *International Journal of Ethics*, 26, Oct. 1915, pp. 23–30, reprinted as paper 31 in *Collected Papers 13*, pp. 184–91
p. 384 'Is a Permanent Peace Possible?': *The Atlantic Monthly*, 115, Mar. 1915, pp. 367–76, reprinted in *Justice in War-Time*, and as paper 18 in *Collected Papers 13*, pp. 86–99
p. 384 'admirable in every way': Ellery Sedgwick to BR, 21.1.15, quoted in *Collected Papers 13*, p. 87
p. 384 'War between civilised States': *Collected Papers 13*, p. 89
p. 384 'The present war': ibid., p. 88
p. 385 'Ever since': ibid.
p. 385 'The annexation': ibid.
p. 385 'when Germany is prosperous': ibid., p. 91
p. 385 'what does it matter': ibid.
p. 385 'men must learn': ibid., p. 99
p. 386 'The people': BR to OM, 4.12.14
p. 386 'All the white men': BR to C. D. Broad, 4.12.14, quoted in Clark, op. cit., p. 318
p. 386 'goes about': Broad to BR, quoted in BR to OM, 4.12.14
p. 386 'I feel the Whiteheads': BR to OM, 13.8.14
p. 386 'The sense of estrangement': BR to OM, 14.8.14
p. 387 'The war has destroyed': BR to OM, 14.12.14
p. 387 'passed off peacefully': BR to OM, 26.12.14
p. 388 'beautiful, severe and Spanish-looking': quoted in Clark, op. cit., p. 298
p. 388 'She [Vernon Lee] spoke': BR to OM, 3.1.15
p. 388 'Principles and Practice in Foreign Policy': published as paper 36a in *Collected Papers 13*, pp. 206–13
p. 388 'All friends of progress': *Collected Papers 13*, p. 206

p. 389 'might get done in a year': BR to OM, 2.1.15
p. 389 'I love the idea': BR to OM, 2.1.15
p. 390 'I think I may easily': BR to OM, 7.1.15
p. 390 'a late night letter': BR to OM, 9.1.15
p. 391 'I know she could not': OM to BR, 9.1.15, quoted in Seymour, op. cit., pp. 200–1
p. 391 'an utter, fundamental indifference': Irene Cooper-Willis to Desmond Mac-Carthy, 5.8.17, quoted in *Clever Hearts: Desmond and Molly MacCarthy* by Hugh & Mirabel Cecil, p. 166
p. 391 'There were things': quoted in Cecil, op. cit., p. 164
p. 391 'I scarcely troubled': ibid., p. 166
p. 391 'She is too law-abiding': BR to OM, probably 10.1.15
p. 392 'She will': ibid.
p. 392 'My dear Bertrand': Irene Cooper-Willis to BR, dated 'Sunday', probably 10.1.15
p. 392 'Yes, Irene is strangely unmoved': BR to OM, 15.1.15
p. 392 'It is a pity': BR to OM, 22.1.15
p. 393 'Helen left a mark': BR to OM, 13.1.15
p. 394 'Because I loved you': quoted in Cecil, op. cit., p. 166
p. 394 'loved and liked women': Enid Bagnold to Ronald W. Clark, 30.7.74, quoted in Clark, op. cit., p. 298
p. 394 'Last night': quoted in Seymour, op. cit., p. 201
p. 394 *Tuesday night*: BR to OM, 19.1.15
p. 395 'Very, very few': BR to OM, 22.1.15
p. 395 'The force': BR to OM, 2.8.14
p. 395 'a house on fire': *Collected Papers 13*, p. 40
p. 396 'How grateful': BR to OM, 14.1.14
p. 396 'Can England and Germany Be Reconciled': *The Cambridge Review*, 36, 10 Feb. 1914, reprinted as paper 15 in *Collected Papers 13*, pp. 74–7. See also 'Mr Russell's Reply to His Critics' (*The Cambridge Review*, 24 Feb. 1914/paper 17, and 'The Reconciliation Question', *The Cambridge Review*, 10 Mar. 1914/paper 19.
p. 396 'All the old fogies': BR to OM, 20.2.14
p. 397 'I have nothing new to say': BR to OM, 3.2.14
p. 397 'The Ultimate Constituents of Matter': first published in *The Monist*, 25, July 1915, reprinted in *Mysticism and Logic*, and as paper 5 in *Collected Papers 8*, pp. 74–86
p. 398 'One wants': DHL to OM, 3.1.15
p. 398 'we at once': *Ottoline: The Early Memoirs*, p. 272
p. 398 'It was impossible': ibid.
p. 399 *Study of Thomas Hardy*: see D. H. Lawrence, *Phoenix: The Posthumous Papers of D. H. Lawrence*, pp. 398–516
p. 399 'Pfff!': ibid., p. 399
p. 399 'The final aim': ibid., p. 403
p. 399 'See': *Ottoline: The Early Memoirs*, p. 273
p. 400 'the Philosophic – and Mathematics man': DHL to Samuel Koteliansky, 5.2.15
p. 401 'Lawrence is the spirit of the flame': *Ottoline: The Early Memoirs*, p. 273
p. 401 'One feels': BR to OM, 22.1.15
p. 402 'He was a handsome, soldierly fellow': *The Prussian Officer*, p. 199
p. 402 'Her eyes searched him': ibid.

p. 402 'I saw him today': ibid., p. 207

14. Breaking the Shell

p. 403 'He is amazing': *Ottoline: The Early Memoirs*, p. 273
p. 403 a long letter: DHL to BR, 12.2.15
p. 405 'extraordinarily young': BR to OM, 13.2.15
p. 406 'I feel frightfully important': DHL to BR, 2.3.15
p. 406 'Remember': DHL to OM, 1.3.15
p. 407 '*immensely* impressed': BR to OM, 9.3.15
p. 407 'When I saw Keynes': DHL to David Garnett, 19.4.15
p. 407 'I can visualise': J. M. Keynes, 'My Early Beliefs', *Collected Writings Volume X: Essays in Biography*, pp. 433–51
p. 407 'seeing him': BR to OM, 7.3.15
p. 407 'had an interesting': BR to OM, 8.3.15
p. 408 'Cambridge rationalism': Keynes, op. cit., p. 434
p. 408 'if I imagine': ibid., p. 450
p. 408 'has the same feeling': BR to OM, 8.3.15
p. 408 'I feel I should go mad': DHL to David Garnett, 19.4.15
p. 408 'are cased each in a hard little shell': DHL to OM, 19.4.15
p. 409 'hates everybody': BR to OM, 7.3.15
p. 409 'His intuitive perceptiveness': BR to OM, 8.3.15
p. 409 'disgusted with Camb.': ibid.
p. 410 'Do you still': DHL to BR, 19.3.15
p. 410 'We are trying': D. H. Lawrence, *Twilight in Italy* (Penguin edition), p. 48. That this passage was added in 1915 can be confirmed by a study of the Cambridge scholarly edition of the same work.
p. 410 'Man is great': ibid., p. 47
p. 411 'Our aim': ibid., p. 52
p. 411 'At the same time': ibid., p. 48
p. 412 'a fund of gentleness': BR to OM, 6.4.15
p. 412 'On Justice in War-Time': first published in two parts in *The International Review*, 1, 10 Aug. and 1 Sep. 1915, reprinted in *Justice in War-Time*, and as paper 29 in *Collected Papers 13*, pp. 169–80
p. 412 'Fighting and killing': *Collected Papers 13*, p. 178
p. 412 'The war': ibid.
p. 413 'Lawrence dislikes': BR to OM, 29.4.15
p. 413 'I cannot tell you': DHL to BR, 29.4.15
p. 413 'It is very unfortunate': BR to OM, 1.5.15
p. 414 'Do you think one's forefathers': *Ottoline: The Early Memoirs*, p. 290
p. 414 'Yes,' he replied: see ibid., pp. 291–2
p. 414 'I am only just realising': BR to OM, 26.5.15
p. 415 'If they hound you out': DHL to BR, 29.5.15
p. 415 'Except a seed shall die': ibid.
p. 415 'strangled the invincible respectability': DHL to BR, 2.6.15
p. 415 'I *feel* he is right': BR to OM, probably June 1915, quoted in *D. H. Lawrence's Nightmare* by Paul Delaney, p. 110
p. 415 'Bertie Russell': DHL to OM, 2.6.15
p. 416 'I got the Labour Leader': DHL to BR, 8.6.15
p. 416 'Lord Northcliffe's Triumph': reprinted as paper 24 in *Collected Papers 13*, pp. 120–3
p. 416 'War being good in itself': see *Collected Papers 13*, p. 122

p. 416 'The UDC will be all right': BR to OM, 8.6.15
p. 416 'I grow less & less': ibid.
p. 417 'I wish good people': BR to OM, 11.6.15
p. 417 'I can't make head or tail': ibid.
p. 417 'rather uneducated': BR to OM, 12.6.15
p. 417 'on a table': *Ottoline at Garsington*, p. 36
p. 418 'In spite of Mrs Lawrence': BR to OM, 17.6.15
p. 418 'I am glad I went': BR to OM, 21.6.15, wrongly and confusingly misdated
        '19th July '15' in *Ottoline at Garsington*, p. 59
p. 418 'He has a very profound and wise admiration': ibid.
p. 418 'We think': DHL to OM, 20.6.15
p. 418 'Russell and I': ibid.
p. 419 'Lawrence is *splendid*': BR to OM, 21.6.15
p. 419 'are curiously alike': BR to OM, 25.6.15
p. 419 'One might as well': ibid.
p. 419 'I am *very* glad': ibid.
p. 419 'My impulse': BR to OM, 24.6.15
p. 420 'We must try': BR to OM, 28.6.15
p. 420 'Wouldn't it be delightful': BR to OM, 3.7.15
p. 421 'Philosophy of Social Reconstruction': the manuscript sent to Lawrence is
        reprinted as paper 38a in *Collected Papers 13*, pp. 286–93. Lawrence's
        comments on it are reproduced in full in *D. H. Lawrence's Letters to Bertrand
        Russell*, edited by Harry T. Moore.
p. 422 'all social criticism': see Moore (ed.), op. cit., p. 77
p. 422 'you must dare to be positive': ibid., p. 78
p. 422 section headed 'The State': ibid., pp. 82–4
p. 422 'Why should a man be moral?': ibid., p. 88
p. 422 on marriage: ibid., pp. 89–91
p. 423 'Life Made Whole': ibid., pp. 94–6
p. 423 'Lawrence is just as furious': BR to OM, 8.7.15
p. 424 'I told Lawrence': BR to OM, 10.7.15
p. 424 'horrid': BR to OM, 13.7.15
p. 425 'The Danger to Civilisation': taking Lawrence's letter of 14 September to
        constitute a rejection of the article for *Signature*, Russell published it in two
        issues of the newly established journal of the UDC, *The UDC*, Mar. and April
        1916, and reprinted it in *Justice in War-Time*. It is reprinted as paper 45 in
        Collected Papers 13, pp. 327–38
p. 425 'If the war': *Collected Papers 13*, p. 337
p. 425 'Is our civilisation': ibid., p. 338
p. 425 'effort after mental advancement': ibid., p. 329
p. 425 'the most wonderful upward movement': ibid., p. 337
p. 425 'There is a wild beast': ibid., p. 332
p. 426 'I'm going to quarrel with you': DHL to BR, 14.9.15
p. 426 'After reading it': *Ottoline at Garsington*, p. 65
p. 427 'in my despair': BR to OM, 19.9.15
p. 428 'The Blind Man': reprinted in D. H. Lawrence, *The Complete Short Stories
        Volume II* (Penguin edition), pp. 347–65
p. 428 'Life was still very full': ibid., p. 347
p. 429 'I don't really know you': ibid., p. 363
p. 429 'The hand of the blind man': ibid.
p. 430 'She knew': ibid., p. 365

15. Mrs E.

p. 432 'I see the same fate': *Satan in the Suburbs* (Penguin edition), p. 66

p. 432 his portrayal of Mrs Ellerker: my suggestion that Vivien Eliot is the model for Mrs Ellerker is not original: the same suggestion is made (though more tentatively) in 'Bertrand Russell and T. S. Eliot: their dialogue' by Gladys Garner Leithauser and Nadine Cowan Dyer, *Russell*, 2 (1), summer 1982, pp. 7–28 – see especially p. 27. In this article Leithauser and Dyer also discuss at length T. S. Eliot's 'Eeldrop and Appleplex' (published in *The Little Review* in two tiny instalments, May and Sep. 1917). Despite their analysis, disappointingly little can be gathered about Russell's relations with the Eliots from this tantalisingly impenetrable short story, except certain intriguing indications (highlighted by Leithauser and Dyer) that Eliot, in describing the relationship between Appleplex (Russell – notice the allusion to 'Apollinax') and Eeldrop (Eliot), was drawing on his friendship with Russell.

p. 432 'sparkling and witty': *Satan in the Suburbs*, p. 42

p. 433 'endeavoured': *Autobiography Volume II*, p. 19

p. 433 'sought about': ibid., pp. 25–6

p. 433 'I never had intimate sexual relations': BR to Robert Sencourt, 28.5.68, quoted in 'Bertrand Russell and the Eliots' by Robert H. Bell, *The American Scholar*, summer 1983, pp. 309–25 (quotation on p. 310)

p. 433 'that Mrs T. S. Eliot's insanity': see Evelyn Waugh, *Diaries*, p. 731

p. 433 'used her for the purpose': BR to OM, dated only 'Thursday', but probably 11.1.17

p. 433 'Friday evg.': BR to OM, 13.7.15

p. 434 'slim and rather small': Brigit Patmore, *My Friends When Young*, pp. 84–5

p. 435 'Whenever we had visitors': *Ottoline at Garsington*, p. 43

p. 435 'means a great deal to me': BR to OM, 4.7.15

p. 435 'There really seem to me': *Ottoline at Garsington*, p. 43

p. 436 'never treats it seriously': ibid., p. 44

p. 436 'for the language they use': ibid., p. 43

p. 436 'Bertie and I': ibid., p. 45

p. 438 'I should be so much happier': BR to OM, 30.7.15

p. 438 'loathsome': BR to OM, 28.7.15

p. 438 'under the tutelage of the Foreign Office': see *Collected Papers 13*, p. 216

p. 438 'I grow less and less interested': BR to OM, 8.6.15

p. 438 'At Calham': BR to OM, 8.8.15

p. 440 a draft letter to Ottoline: quoted in Clark, op. cit., pp. 386–7. Clark gives only '1916' as the date of this letter, but other correspondence between Ottoline and Russell suggests that it was written in the first week of September 1915 (the 7th or 8th seems the most likely date).

p. 440 'obviously interested': *Ottoline at Garsington*, p. 96

p. 440 'I don't think it would *help her*': OM to BR, Sep. 1915, quoted in Seymour, op. cit., p. 245

p. 442 'own fastidiousness and anxiety': Peter Ackroyd, *T. S. Eliot*, p. 66

p. 442 'silk underclothes': see *Ottoline at Garsington*, p. 120

p. 443 'retired to the country': BR to LD, 31.10.15

p. 444 'lack of physical affectionateness': BR to OM, probably 19.9.15

p. 444 'My inner life': ibid.

p. 444 'It really is true': BR to OM, dated only 'Wed. mg', but (as it appears to refer to previously cited letter), possibly 21.9.15.

p. 444 'there are times': ibid.

p. 444 'And it is impossible': ibid.

p. 444 'I can't think sanely just now': BR to OM, dated only 'Wed', but almost certainly written during the autumn of 1915

p. 445 'Just because I care for you': BR to OM, Dec. 1915

p. 445 'a very great affection': BR to OM, undated, but probably Oct. or Nov. 1915

p. 445 'I wish you could understand': BR to OM, Dec. 1915

p. 445 'I can't do my work': BR to OM, dated only 'Monday mg', but almost certainly Dec. 1915

p. 446 'least unsatisfactory': see p. 726 of Russell's 'Reply to Criticisms', in Schilpp (ed.), *The Philosophy of Bertrand Russell*

p. 446 'principle of growth': see *Principles of Social Reconstruction*, Chapter 1

p. 446 'an instinctive urgency': *Principles of Social Reconstruction* (paperback edition), p. 19

p. 446 'This intimate centre': ibid.

p. 447 'In spite': ibid., p. 17

p. 447 'has a framework': *Autobiography Volume II*, p. 20

p. 447 'the State and Property': *Principles of Social Reconstruction*, p. 162

p. 447 'education, marriage and religion': ibid., p. 163

p. 447 'The genesis of impulses': ibid.

p. 447 'If life': ibid., p. 169

p. 448 'perhaps the extreme example': ibid., p. 35

p. 448 an article: 'Conscription', lead article in *The Labour Leader*, 13, 6 Jan. 1916, reprinted as paper 42 in *Collected Papers 13*, pp. 319–20

p. 448 'The motive': *Collected Papers 13*, p. 320

p. 449 'but I found': BR to OM, 1.1.16

p. 449 'I detest it': BR to OM, 7.1.16

p. 449 'I have been quite fantastically unselfish': ibid.

p. 449 'These lectures': BR to OM, 3.1.16

p. 449 'Of course the real thing': BR to OM, 7.1.16

p. 449 'The reason I am apologetic': BR to OM, 12.1.16

p. 449 'Mrs E. does for me': BR to OM, 7.1.16

p. 450 'a sort of shattering': BR to OM, 12.1.16

p. 450 'Vivien says': TSE to BR, 11.1.16

p. 450 'America is important': BR to OM, 17.1.16

p. 450 'Bertie's lectures': Lytton Strachey to OM, 16.2.16, quoted in *Lytton Strachey* by Michael Holroyd (1994 edition), p. 344

p. 450 'better than I expected': BR to OM, 18.1.16

p. 450 'Owing to my lectures': BR to OM, 26.1.16

p. 451 'great success': BR to LD, 10.2.16

p. 451 'The chief point': BR to OM, 8.2.16

p. 451 'I think of trying': BR to OM, 2.3.16

p. 451 'It was rather a comic occasion': *Ottoline at Garsington*, pp. 95–6

p. 451 'You will see': BR to OM, 4.3.16

p. 452 'I didn't like your letter': DHL to BR, 19.2.16

p. 453 'a nasty letter': BR to OM, 20.2.16

p. 453 'trying to interfere': BR to OM, 24.2.16

p. 453 'Are you still cross': DHL to BR, 9.3.16

p. 453 'The dinner was not a success': *Ottoline at Garsington*, p. 96

p. 453 'dull, dull, dull': ibid., p. 101

p. 454 'STRONGLY ADVISE': quoted in a letter from Henry Ware Eliot to J. H. Woods, 7.4.16, see *The Letters of T. S. Eliot Volume I*, p. 136

p. 454 'not greatly pleased': ibid.
p. 454 'sure your influence': Charlotte C. Eliot to BR, 23.5.16, ibid., p. 138

16. Mephisto

p. 455 'I have something important to say': BR to LD, 10.2.16
p. 455 'The melancholy': BR to OM, 19.3.16
p. 456 'a non-supernatural Faust': *Autobiography Volume II*, p. 15
p. 456 'I want actually to *change*': BR to LD, 10.2.16
p. 457 'It is a real ferment': BR to OM, 24.2.16
p. 458 'working furiously': *Ottoline at Garsington*, p. 101
p. 458 'rather suburban': ibid., p. 147
p. 458 'I admire the young men': BR to OM, 25.4.16
p. 459 'I find': ibid.
p. 459 letter to *The Nation*: 'A Clash of Consciences', *The Nation*, 15 April 1916, reprinted as paper 48 in *Collected Papers 13*, pp. 346–8
p. 459 'a spontaneous association': *Collected Papers 13*, p. 347
p. 459 'all the qualities': ibid.
p. 459 'a stand for peace': ibid., p. 348
p. 460 'Or are you': GM to BR, 15.4.16, quoted by Jo Vellacott in *Bertrand Russell and the Pacifists in the First World War*, p. 54
p. 460 'I cannot bring myself': *Collected Papers 13*, p. 347
p. 460 'Our primary object': BR to GM, 17.4.16
p. 460 'I hold': ANW to BR, 16.4.16, quoted in Lowe, op. cit., pp. 35–6
p. 461 'living all against impulse': BR to OM, undated, but most likely spring 1916
p. 461 a letter in *The Labour Leader*: 'Practical War Economy', *The Labour Leader*, 20 April 1916, reprinted as paper 50 in *Collected Papers 13*, pp. 353–4
p. 461 'exposed day and night': *Collected Papers 13*, p. 354
p. 461 'He may be shot': quoted in BR to GM, 17.4.16
p. 461 'Like ordinary deserters': BR to GM, 17.4.16
p. 461 'If the Govt. chooses': BR to OM, 25.4.16
p. 461 'I got the impression': BR to OM, 25.4.16
p. 462 'the men will have to suffer': ibid.
p. 462 'Two years' Hard Labour': reprinted as paper 49 in *Collected Papers 13*, pp. 349–52
p. 462 'He is fighting': ibid., p. 351
p. 462 'The Nature of the State': delivered in Oxford on 15 May 1916, this was first published in *Proceedings of the Aristotelian Society*, 16, 1915–16, pp. 301–16, and reprinted as paper 53 in *Collected Papers 13*, pp. 362–9
p. 462 'which shall alone': *Collected Papers 13*, p. 369
p. 462 'it must often happen': ibid., p. 366
p. 462 'the moment has arrived': BR to OM, 3.5.16
p. 462 'I *long* to stomp': BR to OM, 12.5.16
p. 463 'Why do they let me alone?': BR to OM, 12.5.16
p. 463 'I wish it to be known': BR, letter to *The Times*, 17.5.16, reprinted as paper 54, 'Adsum Qui Feci', in *Collected Papers 13*, pp. 370–2
p. 463 'the very thing': BR to OM, 31.5.16
p. 463 his 'defence': both Russell's written defence, and a report of the court proceedings, are published in *Collected Papers 13*, as papers 56a and 56b, pp. 376–407
p. 463 'to procure': ibid., p. 403
p. 463 'The noblest thing': ibid., p. 389

p. 463 'I have allowed you': ibid., p. 406

p. 464 'Ever since': BR to OM, 1.6.16

p. 464 'Please inform': FO memo to the British Ambassador in Washington, 7.6.16, included in a collection of Government memoranda concerning Russell collected in Aug. 1967 by Kenneth Blackwell in an unpublished typescript called 'The Foreign Office on Bertrand Russell: from The Public Record Office London'. Russell himself read these memoranda for the first time in Blackwell's typescript. This particular remark is quoted by Vellacott, op. cit., p. 83

p. 464 'one of the most mischievous cranks': Lord Newton of the FO, 31.5.16, collected in Blackwell, op. cit., and quoted in Vellacott, op. cit., p. 79

p. 464 'I think his effect': quoted ibid.

p. 464 'except as regards money': BR to OM, 7.7.16

p. 465 'The sum-total': BR to James H. Woods, 30.7.16

p. 465 'Dear Russell': H. McLeod Innes to BR, 11.7.16

p. 465 'There is no hope': BR to G. H. Hardy, 25.9.16

p. 465 'I think it unlikely': ibid.

p. 465 'sad that Trinity': BR to OM, 15.7.16

p. 466 'I feel': BR to OM, 10.7.16

p. 466 'I will make myself': BR to OM, 15.7.16

p. 466 'like the one': ibid.

p. 466 'An honourable and stable peace': from a leaflet called 'Why Not Peace Negotiations?' that Russell wrote in July 1916 and distributed at his meetings – see Collected Papers 13, p. 418

p. 466 'unanimously sympathetic': BR to OM, 4.7.16

p. 466 'they were all': ibid.

p. 467 'One needs': ibid.

p. 467 'I feel little doubt': ibid.

p. 467 'The police': BR to OM, 7.7.16

p. 467 'justice and generosity': from the Home Office transcript of the Cardiff Speech, published in Collected Papers 13, pp. 420–35

p. 467 'Is it fair?': ibid., p. 434

p. 467 'bloodthirsty middle-aged man': BR to OM, 7.7.16

p. 468 'I denounced him': Captain W. H. Atherley Jones, 'Toleration of Traitors. Unvarnished Story of a Welsh Meeting. The Limit', letter to the Daily Express, 11.8.16, p. 3

p. 468 'I want to avoid': BR to OM, 17.7.16

p. 468 'terrified at the prospect': BR to OM, 30.7.16

p. 468 'I don't yet know': ibid.

p. 468 'I know extraordinarily little': BR to OM, 10.7.16

p. 468 'My own existence': ibid.

p. 469 'I had a long talk': Ottoline at Garsington, p. 120

p. 469 'I am dreadfully worried': BR to OM, undated, but most likely the beginning of August 1916

p. 472 'We thought [it] a mistake': BR to OM, 22.8.16

p. 473 'there is no doubt': memo from Whiskard of the HO to Sir Ernley Blackwell, 31.8.16, quoted in Vellacott, op. cit., p. 118

p. 473 'with a good deal': Edward Troup of the HO to Sir Charles Mathews, 25.8.16, quoted ibid., p. 89

p. 473 'by the production': Sir Charles Mathews to Sir Ernley Blackwell, 28.8.16

p. 474 'I think it would be': Herbert Samuel to Sir Ernley Blackwell, 1.9.16

p. 474 'very dangerous': quoted in Vellacott, op. cit., p. 93

p. 474 'If Mr Russell': Colonel Kell of the WO to Sir Ernley Blackwell, 3.9.16
p. 474 'There is a lot of sport': BR to OM, 3.9.16
p. 475 'I had gone up to London': *Autobiography Volume II*, p. 33
p. 476 interview with General George Cockerill: see Russell's typescript, 'Meeting with General Cockerill', published as paper 69 in *Collected Papers 13*, pp. 453–7. Russell's *Manchester Guardian* article (first published 27.9.16) about his dealings with Cockerill is reprinted in the same volume as paper 70, 'Bertrand Russell and the War Office', pp. 458–62.
p. 476 'a still small voice': *Collected Papers 13*, p. 456
p. 476 'Do you not think': ibid.
p. 477 'afterwards': *Autobiography Volume II*, p. 40
p. 477 'and no doubt': *Collected Papers 13*, p. 457
p. 477 'I cannot acknowledge': ibid., p. 461
p. 477 'Capitalism': *Political Ideals* (paperback edition), p. 24
p. 477 'private capitalistic enterprises': ibid., p. 32
p. 478 'haughty [and] beautiful': Bennitt Gardiner, 'Colette O'Niel: a season in repertory', *Russell*, 23–4, autumn–winter 1976, p. 27
p. 478 'generous with her time': see *Autobiography Volume II*, p. 25
p. 478 'Sitting very upright': from Constance Malleson, 'Fifty Years: 1916–1966', in *Bertrand Russell: Philosopher of the Century*, edited by Ralph Schoenman, pp. 17–25, quotation on pp. 18–19. The version in her autobiographical book, *After Ten Years*, pp. 107–9 is slightly different, though both seem to be imaginative reconstructions of the conversation, made up chiefly of quotations from Russell's letters to her.
p. 479 'We talked half the night': *Autobiography Volume II*, p. 26
p. 479 'I could not believe': ibid., p. 27
p. 479 'I had got used': ibid.
p. 479 'can mean a great deal': BR to CM, 24.9.16
p. 479 'I *know* that I love you': BR to CM, 26.9.16
p. 480 'Do you know': BR to CM, 19.9.16
p. 480 'What We Stand For': *The Tribunal*, 30, 12 Oct. 1916, reprinted as paper 73 in *Collected Papers 13*, pp. 469–71
p. 480 'marvellously good': CM to BR, 5.10.16
p. 481 'to bring': *Collected Papers 13*, p. 470
p. 481 'Our minds': ibid.
p. 481 'If you disbelieve': ibid., pp. 470–1
p. 481 'Englishmen': quoted in Stanley Weintraub, *Journey to Heartbreak: The Crucible Years of Bernard Shaw 1914–1918*, p. 191
p. 481 'very reliable sources': quoted in BR, letter to *The Times*, 20.10.16, reprinted in *Collected Papers 13*, p. 473
p. 481 'I can only earnestly hope': ibid.
p. 482 on the way to Manchester: I have dated this letter 20 Oct. on the grounds that it is headed 'Saturday. In the train', though in Russell's *Autobiography Volume II* it is dated 23 Oct.
p. 483 'He was so gentle': CM to BR, 28.10.16
p. 483 'three days' honeymoon': *Autobiography Volume II*, p. 27
p. 483 'It was bitterly cold': ibid.
p. 483 'unhappy because she feels': BR to OM, 13.11.16
p. 484 'Her talk was marvellous': *Autobiography Volume II*, p. 27
p. 485 'I have just re-read your letter': Katherine Mansfield to BR, 7.12.16, quoted in Claire Tomalin, *Katherine Mansfield: A Secret Life*, pp. 157–8

p. 486 'an unusual mood': BR to OM, 5.12.16
p. 486 a long letter: see *Autobiography Volume II*, pp. 28–31
p. 486 'to compel': ibid., p. 30
p. 486 'In the name of Europe': ibid., p. 31
p. 486 'Mysterious Girl': see *Bertrand Russell's America Volume One*, p. 68
p. 487 'damping down': ANW to BR, 8.1.17
p. 487 'I should consider': ANW to BR, 8.1.17
p. 487 'It put an end': see *Autobiography Volume II*, p. 78
p. 488 'The sound': *Ottoline at Garsington*, p. 167
p. 488 'hated Ottoline': *Autobiography Volume II*, p. 27

17. The Misanthrope

p. 489 'You loved him': Evelyn Whitehead to BR, 1.4.18
p. 490 'utterly hateful mood': BR to CM, dated only 'Sat eve', but early Jan. 1917
p. 490 'after Ll. G': BR to Catherine Marshall, 3.1.17
p. 490 'and get rid': Catherine Marshall to BR, quoted in Vellacott, op. cit., p. 136
p. 490 'I need': BR to CM, 6.1.17
p. 491 'Something is gone wrong': BR to OM, probably 6.1.17
p. 491 'very strange': BR to OM, probably 11.1.17
p. 491 'No one else': ibid.
p. 491 'I don't want': ibid.
p. 492 'My rapier is out': *Ottoline at Garsington*, p. 167
p. 492 'The NCF no longer': BR to OM, dated only 'Friday', but probably early March 1917
p. 492 'I do as much as I can': BR to Catherine Marshall, 8.3.17
p. 493 'The Russians': BR to OM, 1.4.17
p. 493 'The Russian revolution': from a manuscript called 'Britain's Charter of Freedom', written on 17.3.17, quoted in Vellacott, op. cit., p. 155
p. 493 'to follow': see Vellacott, p. 156
p. 493 'I must tell you': BR to OM, 1.4.17
p. 494 As Ottoline remembers it: see *Ottoline at Garsington*, pp. 177–8
p. 494 'Just now': BR to OM, 5.5.17
p. 495 becoming Russian: BR to CM, 6.5.17
p. 495 'I feel': CM to BR, 7.5.17
p. 497 'Writing and speaking': BR 'To Members of the National Committee', 18.5.17, quoted in Vellacott, op. cit., p. 188
p. 497 'A certain amount': ibid, quoted in Clark, op. cit., p. 413
p. 498 'that the seed of freedom': from Russell's speech at Leeds, 3.6.17, as recorded in a pamphlet called *What Happened at Leeds*, published by the Council of Workers' and Soldiers' Delegates, June 1917, and reproduced in 'What Happened at Leeds?' by John Slater, *Russell*, 4, winter 1971–2
p. 498 the fourth resolution: see Vellacott, op. cit., pp. 162–3
p. 498 'sense for swift dramatic action': BR to OM, 5.6.17
p. 498 'If the Russian Revolution': *Roads to Freedom* (paperback edition), p. 120
p. 499 'It is impossible to doubt': quoted in Vellacott, op. cit., p. 167
p. 499 covert authorship: first brought to public attention in 'Russell as ghost-writer: a new discovery' by Jo Newberry (later Vellacott), *Russell*, 15, autumn 1974, pp. 19–23

p. 499 'As a result': BR, 'A New Tribunal for Gaol Delivery', *Tribunal*, 15 Nov. 1917, quoted in Newberry, op. cit., p. 23

p. 500 'no longer be a party': from a draft of Sassoon's statement in the Russell Archives, quoted in Clark, op. cit., p. 400

p. 500 Ottoline's account: see *Ottoline at Garsington*, pp. 181–4

p. 500 'Siegfried is terribly self-centred': ibid., p. 183

p. 500 'saying how much': ibid., p. 182

p. 501 'I would like above all': Sassoon to OM, 8.7.17, quoted in Vellacott, op. cit., p. 209

p. 501 It was really very horrible': BR to OM, 28.7.17

p. 501 'went home together': *Autobiography Volume II*, p. 32

p. 502 'walked enormously': Malleson, 'Fifty Years', op. cit., p. 20, cf. *After Ten Years*, p. 121

p. 502 'I wish I could get out of the NCF': BR to OM, Aug. 1917

p. 502 'They will start me off': BR to CM, 25.8.17

18. Return to Philosophy

p. 503 'full of schemes': BR to CM, 25.8.17

p. 503 'I want to write': BR to PEJ, 5.9.17

p. 503 'This sounds exactly': PEJ to BR, 6.9.17, see Grattan-Guinness, op. cit., p. 142

p. 503 'it is an extraordinary rest': BR to OM, 20.9.17

p. 504 'endless work on political theory': BR to OM, July 1916?

p. 504 'it has quite excited me': BR to CM, 30.8.17

p. 505 'is concerned': *Introduction to Mathematical Philosophy*, p. 169

p. 505 'logical symbolism': ibid., p. 205

p. 505 'Those readers': ibid., pp. 205–6

p. 505 reviewed twice: 'Idealism on the Defensive', *The Nation*, 8 Sep. 1917, and 'Metaphysics', *The English Review*, Oct. 1917, reprinted as papers 11 and 12 in *Collected Papers 8*, pp. 105–14

p. 505 'The amateur in philosophy': *Collected Papers 8*, p. 112

p. 506 'the arrogance': ibid., p. 110

p. 506 'and to this end': May Sinclair to BR, 10.10.17, quoted ibid., p. 111

p. 507 'in a mood': footnote to Constance Malleson's annotated typescript of letters from BR, now in the Russell Archives

p. 507 'thinking quietly': CM to BR, 18.9.17

p. 507 'I live in hell': BR to OM, 17.9.17

p. 507 'I love you so much': BR to CM, 21.9.17

p. 507 'The whole region': BR to CM, 23.9.17

p. 507 'Thank you, my Beloved': BR to CM, 24.9.17

p. 508 'WHAT SHE IS': now in the Russell Archives.

p. 508 'an analysis': CM, typescript of letters from BR

p. 508 'If you leave me': CM to BR, 5.10.17

p. 509 'I cannot understand': CM to BR, 10.10.17

p. 510 a letter to Eliot's mother: see Vivien Eliot to Charlotte C. Eliot, 22.10.17, *The Letters of T. S. Eliot Volume I*, pp. 200–2

p. 511 an interpretation adopted by Peter Ackroyd, for example: see p. 84 of Ackroyd's *T. S. Eliot*, in which he writes that Russell 'made love to Vivien . . .' The experience, however, was 'hellish and loathsome . . . ' He did not explain why it was so 'loathsome', although no doubt Vivien's own physical problems had something to do with it. It was the pointless and messy end of what had been an intense and 'platonic' relationship. In his notes to his passage, Ackroyd cites, not Russell's letter to Colette itself, but a paraphrase of it given in 'Bertrand Russell and the Eliots' by Robert H. Bell (*The American Scholar*, summer 1983, pp. 309–25). Bell was writing at a time when Russell's correspondence with Colette was still embargoed and so he was forced to paraphrase, though Ackroyd's inaccurate comment that Russell's reaction to his night with Vivien was *quoted* by Bell seems to have misled Caroline Moorehead, who, in her biography of Russell (p. 220) also gives the phrase 'hellish and loathsome', as if it came ⸬om Russell's letter rather than from Bell's paraphrase. Ackroyd offers no reasons for thinking that Russell's relations with Vivien had been 'platonic' up to this point. The sexual element in Russell's relations with Vivien is something about which Moorehead's account is particularly confused, saying on p. 219 that: 'No one has ever been sure whether Russell . . . actually slept with Vivienne', and on the next page apparently quoting Russell's reaction to doing just that.

p. 512 'He really is tired of me': *Ottoline at Garsington*, p. 225

p. 513 'I cannot hide from you': BR to OM, 20.9.17

p. 514 'I am puzzled': BR to CM, 13.11.17

p. 514 'Mrs E. behaved like a saint': BR to CM, 14.11.17

p. 515 'My head is full of things': BR to OM, probably 17.12.17

p. 515 'was so as to make myself': BR to CM, 9.1.18

p. 515 'I don't know her': CM to BR, 2.1.18

p. 516 'My work a day life': BR to CM, 6.1.18

p. 516 'My life is prisoned in pain': BR to CM, 14.1.18

p. 516 'A very great deal': *Lectures on Logical Atomism* (Open Court paperback edition), pp. 66–7

p. 517 'the chief thesis': ibid., p. 49

p. 517 'concerned with the forms of facts': ibid., p. 80

p. 517 'the subject matter': ibid., p. 44

p. 517 'a good deal more': ibid.

p. 518 'I think that the notion of meaning': ibid., p. 45

p. 518 'A proposition is just a symbol': ibid., p. 44

p. 519 'obviously propositions are nothing': ibid., p. 87

p. 519 'The subject is not very easy': ibid., p. 92

p. 519 'I wish you would think': PEJ to BR, 9.4.18, see Grattan-Guinness, op. cit., p. 145

p. 519 Eliot's review: 'Style and Thought', *The Nation*, 23 Mar. 1918, pp. 768 and 770

p. 519 'with distinction': BR, prison letter, 17.6.18

p. 520 'The German Peace Offer': *The Tribunal*, 3 Jan. 1918, reprinted in *Autobiography Volume II*, pp. 79–81

p. 520 'afford a triumph': *Autobiography Volume II*, p. 80

p. 520 'The American Garrison': ibid.

p. 521 'it is more than possible': quoted in 'Rex v. Bertrand Russell: Privilege and imprisonment in Britain during the First World War', unpublished paper by Beryl Haslam, p. 5

p. 521 'It is very annoying': BR to OM, 4.2.18

p. 521 'a very despicable one': quoted in Wood, op. cit., p. 112

p. 521 'blast of hatred': BR to OM, 9.2.18

p. 521 'I profoundly dislike': ibid.

p. 521 'the freedom from responsibility': BR to GM, 15.2.18

p. 521 'impressed by the seriousness': BR to GM, 27.3.18
p. 522 'I am dreading prison': BR to CM, quoted in Haslam, op. cit., p. 10
p. 522 'in a very dangerous condition': quoted in Vellacott, op. cit., p. 234
p. 523 'The pioneers of Socialism': *Roads to Freedom*, p. 18
p. 523 'If private representations fail': BR to GM, 27.3.18
p. 523 'in view of the extraordinary value': quoted in Haslam, op. cit., p. 13
p. 524 'that he is haunted': Alys Russell to Lord Haldane, 3.3.18
p. 524 'is giving word': OM to BR, quoted in Haslam, op. cit., p. 13
p. 524 'it would be a great loss': from 'Our prosecution', *The Tribunal*, 9 May 1918, quoted in Vellacott, op. cit., p. 236

19. Prison

p. 526 'a great pleasure': *Ottoline at Garsington*, pp. 253–4
p. 526 'feeling certain': ibid., p. 252
p. 526 article written in the 1930s: 'Are Criminals Worse than Other People', published in several Hearst newspapers, including the *Washington Herald*, the *Los Angeles Examiner* and the *San Francisco Examiner*, in Oct./Nov. 1931, reprinted in *Mortals and Others*, pp. 32–4
p. 527 'associated habitually': *Mortals and Others*, p. 32
p. 527 'Life here': BR to FR, 6.5.18
p. 527 'I see no sign': ibid.
p. 527 'It is queer': BR to OM, undated, but probably June 1918
p. 527 'rather rarefied': *Ottoline at Garsington*, p. 252
p. 527 'Bertie seemed really happy': ibid., p. 253
p. 527 'The holiday': BR to FR, 6.5.18
p. 528 'judges men': BR, prison circular letter, 21.5.18
p. 529 'exquisitely civilised': ibid.
p. 529 'After giving out': BR to FR, 3.6.18
p. 529 'Tomlinson I *loved*': BR, prison letter, 27.5.18
p. 529 'There is a well of fierce hate': BR to OM, 11.8.18
p. 530 'you told me': BR to OM, 4.9.18
p. 530 'I dare say': BR to OM, 21.8.18
p. 531 'Underlying all occupations': *Autobiography Volume II*, p. 38
p. 531 'I shall never lose': BR to OM, 21.8.18
p. 531 'I hate all the Bloomsbury crew': BR to OM, 1.8.18
p. 531 a BBC radio talk: 'Maynard Keynes and Lytton Strachey', broadcast 10.7.52, included verbatim in Chapter III, 'Cambridge', of his *Autobiography*, pp. 70–4
p. 531 'We were still Victorian': see *Autobiography*, p. 70
p. 532 'My only really strong desire': BR to FR, 6.5.18
p. 532 'I had given up logic': BR, prison letter, 1.7.18
p. 532 footnote: a detailed list: published as Appendix III, 'Philosophical Books Read in Prison', *Collected Papers 8*, pp. 315–28
p. 532 long review of John Dewey: first published in *The Journal of Philosophy, Psychology, and Scientific Method*, 16, 2 Jan. 1919, pp. 5–26, and reprinted as paper 16 in *Collected Papers 8*, pp. 132–54
p. 533 'Does "Consciousness" exist?': first published in *The Journal of Philosophy, Psychology and Scientific Method*, 1, 1904, pp. 477–91, and reprinted as the essay in William James, *Essays in Radical Empiricism*, 1912
p. 533 'are really rules': from William James, 'Philosophical Conceptions and Practical Results', written in 1898 and included in *Collected Essays and Reviews*, 1920
p. 533 'bias': *Lectures on Logical Atomism*, p. 86

p. 533 'very great difficulty': ibid.
p. 533 'that there are such facts': ibid., p. 87
p. 533 'My chief problem': BR to FR, 16.8.18
p. 534 'should be another': ibid.
p. 534 'It is delicious': BR to OM, undated, probably July 1918
p. 534 'notes on the principles of symbolism': see *Collected Papers 8*, pp. 247–71
p. 534 'I have had time': BR to OM, 1.8.18
p. 535 '*expresses* a thought': *Collected Papers 8*, p. 266
p. 535 'The object': ibid., p. 267
p. 535 'may *be* a series of bodily acts': ibid., p. 271
p. 535 'My bias remains': ibid., p. 255
p. 535 'On "Bad Passions" ': *The Cambridge Magazine*, 1 Feb. 1919, reprinted as paper 19 in *Collected Papers 8*, pp. 272–5
p. 535 'The Origin and Development of Psychoanalysis': *The American Journal of Psychology*, 21, 1910, pp. 181–218
p. 535 'James's attack': BR to Gladys Rinder, 17.6.18
p. 536 'Freud in a nutshell': BR to Gladys Rinder, 22.7.18
p. 536 'The Freudian Methods Applied to Anger': *The American Journal of Psychology*, 26, 1915, pp. 438–43
p. 536 'Benvenuto Cellini': *Collected Papers 8*, p. 273
p. 536 'there are cases': ibid., p. 274
p. 536 'If Beethoven': ibid., p. 275
p. 536 'the impulsive life': ibid.
p. 536 'The education authority': ibid.
p. 537 'Logic and imagination': BR to OM, 26.8.18
p. 537 'I do not wish': BR to OM, 16.6.18
p. 537 'It is now': ibid.
p. 537 'I foresee': BR to OM, 2.7.18
p. 537 'I find my ambitions': BR to CM, 11.7.18
p. 537 'and more *definite* news': BR to CM, 16.8.18
p. 538 'While I was in prison': *Autobiography Volume II*, p. 37
p. 538 'was young and gay': *Ottoline at Garsington*, p. 253
p. 538 'I stayed *far* too long': BR to CM, 21.7.18
p. 539 'a most touching physiognomy': CM to BR, 18.7.18
p. 539 'for which': *After Ten Years*, p. 127
p. 539 'We had tea': ibid., pp. 126–7
p. 539 'but she will probably be too busy': BR to OM, 21.8.18
p. 539 'the very place': BR to OM, 30.8.18
p. 540 'Oh, won't it be glorious': ibid.
p. 540 'I was *so* excited': Gladys Rinder to BR, 14.9.18, quoted in Vellacott, op. cit., p. 240

20. Roads to Freedom

1. Philosophy

p. 541 'very childlike': Clifford Allen, diary entry 17.9.18, quoted in *Plough My Own Furrow: The Story of Lord Allen of Hurtwood* by Martin Gilbert, p. 126
p. 541 'a great joy': BR to OM, 25.9.18
p. 542 'He was like a happy child': Allen, diary, 28.10.18, quoted in Gilbert, op. cit., p. 126
p. 542 'I enjoy getting back to work': BR to OM, 30.10.18

p. 542 '& then': ibid.
p. 542 'One did not': *After Ten Years*, p. 128
p. 543 'They commandeered the buses': *Autobiography Volume II*, pp. 37–8
p. 544 'the snow lying deep': *After Ten Years*, p. 129
p. 544 'It is not the case': TSE to BR, 3.2.19, see *The Letters of T. S. Eliot Volume I*, pp. 270–1
p. 545 'She worked very hard': TSE to BR, 14.2.19, ibid., p. 271
p. 545 'preliminary outline': published as paper 1 in *Collected Papers 9*, pp. 3–15
p. 545 'Psychology as the Behaviourist Views It': *The Psychological Review*, 20, 1913, pp. 158–77
p. 545 'I should like': ibid., p. 174n., quoted by Russell in the 'notes on the principles of symbolism' that he wrote in prison, *Collected Papers 8*, p. 260
p. 545 'obviously rot': BR, circular letter from prison, 17.6.18
p. 545 'My mind': CM to BR, 31.5.18
p. 545 'The denial': *Collected Papers 9*, p. 5
p. 546 '*Belief* is a specific sensation': ibid., p. 14
p. 546 'On Propositions': first published in *Aristotelian Society Supplementary Volume*, 2, 1919, pp. 1–43, reprinted in *Logic and Knowledge*, and as paper 20 in *Collected Papers 8*, pp. 276–306
p. 547 'Professor Watson': *Collected Papers 8*, p. 284
p. 547 'If you try': ibid.
p. 547 'The most important thing': ibid., p. 297
p. 547 'You have an image of A': ibid., p. 306
p. 548 'I am prisoner in Italy': LW to BR, 9.2.19
p. 548 'Most thankful': BR to LW, 2.3.19
p. 548 'I've written a book': LW to BR, 13.3.19
p. 549 'To anyone accustomed': from 'Philosophy and Virtue', review of Henry Jones, *The Principles of Citizenship*, *The Athenaeum*, 2 May 1919, p. 270, reprinted as paper 54 in *Collected Papers 9*, pp. 329–30
p. 549 'no philosophical professor': from 'The Noble Army of Philosophers', review of Ralph Perry, *The Present Conflict of Ideals*, *The Nation*, 10 May 1919, p. 176, reprinted as paper 69 in *Collected Papers 9*, pp. 401–3
p. 549 'craving for certainty': from 'The Mystic Vision', review of Arthur Clutton-Brock, *What is the Kingdom of Heaven?*, *The Athenaeum*, 20 June 1919, pp. 487–8, reprinted as paper 55 in *Collected Papers 9*, pp. 331–6
p. 549 'is part of': *Collected Papers 9*, p. 333
p. 549 'without the distorting mists': ibid., p. 332
p. 549 'the characteristics': ibid.
p. 550 'A man in love': ibid., p. 336
p. 550 'Mr Russell prefers': J. W. Harvey, letter to *The Athenaeum*, 4 July 1919, p. 567, reprinted in Appendix II, *Collected Papers 9*, pp. 472–3
p. 550 published reply: BR, letter to *The Athenaeum*, 11 July 1919, p. 599, reprinted in *Collected Papers 9*, p. 336
p. 551 'I am glad': BR to OM, 12.6.19
p. 551 'I am amused': Vivien Eliot to OM, 4.6.19, *The Letters of T. S. Eliot Volume 1*, pp. 301–2
p. 551 'I should never have believed': LW to BR, 12.6.19
p. 552 'It is true': BR to LW, 21.6.19

2. Dora

p. 552 'enchantingly ugly': Dora Russell, *The Tamarisk Tree Volume I*, p. 53

p. 552 'Until that moment': *Autobiography Volume II*, p. 96

p. 553 'on the top deck': *The Tamarisk Tree Volume I*, p. 56

p. 553 'the true bohemian type': ibid., p. 62

p. 553 'Well': *Autobiography Volume II*, p. 96

p. 553 'One wants in love': BR to CM, 23.6.19

p. 554 'The only thing': BR to CM, 24.6.19

p. 554 'Dear Bertie': DR to BR, 24.6.19

p. 554 'It was all quite wonderful': BR to CM, 28.6.19

p. 555 'Nothing on earth': *After Ten Years*, p. 130

p. 555 'pumped self-confidence': ibid.

p. 555 'My dear one': BR to CM, 7.7.19

p. 556 'were as learned': *The Tamarisk Tree Volume I*, p. 69

p. 556 'This cannot have gone on': ibid.

p. 556 she wrote to him: DR to BR, 10.7.19

p. 556 'Bertie and I': *The Tamarisk Tree Volume I*, p. 73

p. 557 'Dora and I': *Autobiography Volume II*, p. 97

p. 557 'From the first': ibid.

p. 557 'more than ever before': BR to CM, 14.7.19

p. 557 'She is nice': BR to CM, 15.7.19

p. 557 'very much embarrassed': *The Tamarisk Tree Volume I*, p. 74

p. 557 'I have never got over': DR to BR, undated, but almost certainly Jan. 1920

p. 557 'It will be *divine*': BR to CM, 17.7.19

p. 557 'I cannot tell you': DR to BR, 20.7.19

p. 557 'I love you most tremendously': DR to BR, 26.7.19

p. 558 'One little word of love': BR to CM, 29.7.19

p. 560 'The theory of classes': see *Tractatus Logico-Philosophicus*, 6.031

p. 560 'The logical picture': ibid., 3

p. 560 'The main point': LW to BR, 19.8.19

p. 560 'I have rather an affection': DR to BR, 31.8.19

p. 560 'feeling, I think': *Autobiography Volume II*, p. 97

p. 561 'the feeling we had for each other': ibid.

p. 561 'My husband': see Grattan-Guinness, op. cit., p. 151

p. 562 'if he thinks': ibid., p. 152

p. 562 'Dear Mr Russell': ibid., p. 153

p. 562 'I allowed the summer to go by': from a typewritten letter to Dora – one of the very few to survive from this period – undated, but almost certainly written in the New Year of 1920

p. 563 'how to fit you into my life': DR to BR, 18.10.19

p. 563 'I feel fiery moral indignation': DR to BR, 10.11.19

p. 563 'you know, those hypothetical infants': DR to BR, 21.10.19

p. 563 'The last of our Eminent Victorians': DR to BR, 13.10.19

p. 563 'Mr Russell has reached': see G. H. Hardy, *Bertrand Russell at Trinity*, p. 51

p. 564 'It is possible': BR to LD, 27.11.19

p. 564 'the most important result': quoted in *'Subtle is the Lord': The Science and the Life of Albert Einstein* by Abraham Pais, p. 305

p. 564 'Einstein's Theory of Gravitation': first published in *The Athenaeum*, 14 Nov. 1919, and reprinted as paper 29 in *Collected Papers 9*, pp. 207–9

p. 565 a much longer – and better paid – article: 'The Relativity Theory of Gravitation', *The English Review*, 30, Jan. 1920, pp. 11–18, reprinted as paper 30 in *Collected Papers 9*, pp. 209–15

p. 565   three, slightly different, reviews: reprinted as papers 66, 67 and 68 in *Collected Papers 9*, pp. 389–97
p. 565   'My dear Wittgenstein': BR to LW, 14.10.19
p. 566   'my feelings about you': DR to BR, 23.12.19
p. 566   'if you definitely chuck Cambridge': DR to BR, 21.1.20
p. 566   'How I hate this old divorce': DR to BR, Jan. 1920
p. 566   'I have found by experience': BR to DR, Jan. 1920
p. 566   'If you don't take care': DR to BR, 11.11.19
p. 566   'You shouldn't say': DR to BR, 16.11.19
p. 567   'The present intention': BR to OM, 20.12.19
p. 567   'Curled up in an armchair': *The Tamarisk Tree Volume I*, p. 79
p. 567   'just the same as ever': BR to CM, 12.12.19
p. 568   'I enjoyed': LW to BR, 8.1.20
p. 568   'There are, indeed': *Tractatus Logico-Philosophicus*, 6.521
p. 568   'I had felt': BR to OM, 20.12.19
p. 568   review of Joachim: 'The Wisdom of Our Ancestors', *The Athenaeum*, 9 Jan. 1920, reprinted as paper 70 in *Collected Papers 9*, pp. 403–6
p. 568   'It is probable': *Collected Papers 9*, p. 405
p. 569   'Einstein's theory': ibid.
p. 569   'they are concerned': ibid.
p. 569   'I recognise the importance': BR to DR, Jan. 1920
p. 569   'I love Colette': ibid.
p. 569   'I wish dearest': DR to BR, 23.12.19
p. 570   'but I can remember': DR to BR, 24.12.19
p. 570   'Respectability': DR to BR, 28.12.19
p. 570   'You will perhaps': DR to BR, 14.1.20
p. 571   'won't take less': quoted in *The Tamarisk Tree Volume I*, p. 80
p. 571   'giving Bertie the push': ibid., p. 81
p. 571   'I thought I could have a home': DR to BR, undated, but Jan. 1920
p. 571   'I meant to rely': DR to BR, 21.1.20
p. 572   'It is difficult to believe': from 'The Nature of Inference', review of Bernard Bosanquet, *Implication and Linear Inference*, *The Athenaeum*, 16 April 1920, pp. 514–15, reprinted as paper 15 in *Collected Papers 9*, pp. 82–6 (quotation on p. 86)
p. 572   'All the psychology': BR, prison letter, 8.7.18
p. 572   'The psychological part of meaning': from BR, 'Introduction', in *Tractatus Logico-Philosophicus*, p. 20 (Ogden translation), p. xix (Pears/McGuinness)

3. *Russia*

p. 573   'Dearest, let us go to Russia': DR to BR, 22.2.20
p. 573   'You give me so little': BR to CM, 25.2.20
p. 573   'As we sat': *The Tamarisk Tree Volume I*, p. 82
p. 573   'I'm alone': CM to BR, quoted in her typescript of their correspondence
p. 573   'The Spanish "intellectuals" ': L. B. Trend to BR, 21.1.20, quoted in *Collected Papers 9*, p. 475
p. 574   'one of the most exquisite': *The Tamarisk Tree Volume I*, p. 82
p. 574   'began a great quarrel': *Autobiography Volume II*, p. 101
p. 574   'an enormously fat': ibid., p. 102
p. 574   'There's so much': LW to BR, 9.4.20

p. 575 'All right then': see *The Tamarisk Tree Volume I*, p. 83

p. 575 'On the top of the downs': *After Ten Years*, p. 141

p. 576 'Socialism and Liberal Ideals': published in *The English Review* in two parts, May and June 1920, pp. 449–55 and 499–508

p. 576 'I am one of those': ibid., p. 449

p. 576 'so long as it fought': ibid., p. 450

p. 576 'What is called': ibid., p. 452

p. 576 'Every thoughtful person': ibid.

p. 576 'The old incentives': ibid., p. 453

p. 576 'The most important': ibid., p. 454

p. 577 'Faced by the united hostility': ibid.

p. 577 'Bolshevism': ibid., p. 455

p. 577 'The day of my departure': BR, 24.4.20, see *Autobiography Volume II*, p. 104

p. 577 'will have a great effect': BR to OM, 6.5.20

p. 578 'I came prepared': BR, 12.5.20, see *Autobiography Volume II*, p. 106

p. 578 'Everything is to be systematic': ibid.

p. 578 'Much to be said': BR, Russian journal, 15.5.20, quoted in Clark, op. cit., p. 469

p. 578 'It is ugly and brutal': BR, 13.5.20, see *Autobiography Volume II*, p. 107

p. 579 'I felt that everything': *Autobiography Volume II*, p. 103

p. 579 'the most lovable': *The Practice and Theory of Bolshevism*, pp. 38–9

p. 579 'the vanity of an artist or actor': BR, Russian journal, 17.5.20, quoted in Clark, op. cit., p. 470. See also *The Practice and Theory of Bolshevism*, p. 38.

p. 579 'The whole tendency': *The Practice and Theory of Bolshevism*, p. 34

p. 580 'a certain unconscious imperialistic tone': BR, Russian journal, 20.5.20

p. 580 'The average working man': *The Practice and Theory of Bolshevism*, p. 60

p. 580 'One of us': BR, 'On the Volga', 2.6.20, see *Autobiography Volume II*, p. 107

p. 581 'In silence': ibid., pp. 107–8

p. 581 'Some would die': ibid., p. 108

p. 581 'But something': ibid.

p. 581 'may be described as an artist nation': *The Problem of China*, pp. 17–18

p. 582 'artists, down to the simplest peasant': BR to OM, 25.6.20

p. 582 'more like hell': *Autobiography Volume II*, p. 103

p. 582 'that at meal-time': ibid., pp. 103–4

p. 583 'infinitely painful': BR to OM, 25.6.20

p. 583 'unspeakably horrible': BR to CM, 25.6.20

p. 583 'I had a most amazing journey': DR to BR, 29.6.20

p. 584 'I endeavoured': *Autobiography Volume II*, p. 110

p. 584 'I don't care twopence': BR to LW, 1.7.20

p. 584 'But if you feel': LW to BR, 7.7.20

p. 584 'I decided': *Autobiography Volume II*, p. 110

p. 584 'Every moment': CM to BR, 17.7.20

p. 584 'finding the same consolation': *Autobiography Volume II*, p. 110

p. 585 'I was inspired': *The Tamarisk Tree Volume I*, p. 94

p. 585 'a sublime confidence': ibid., p. 92

p. 585 'A man respected': ibid., p. 101

p. 585 'But the spirit of the Revolution': ibid., p. 89

p. 585 'some force': *Autobiography Volume II*, pp. 110–11

p. 586 'Impressions of Bolshevik Russia': *The Nation*, 10, 17, 24, 31 July and 7 Aug. 1920, reprinted (more or less) as Part One of *The Practice and Theory of Bolshevism*

p. 586 'Bolshevik Theory': *The New Republic*, 15 Sep. and 3, 17 Nov., reprinted as Part Two, chapters I, IV and V of *The Practice and Theory of Bolshevism*

p. 586 'I believe': *The Practice and Theory of Bolshevism*, p. 21

p. 586 'Friends of Russia': ibid., pp. 26–7

p. 586 'To an English mind': ibid., p. 28

p. 586 'There is need': ibid., p. 84

p. 587 'To Marx': ibid., p. 85

p. 587 'more than ever a pacifist': BR to GM, 2.8.20

4. China

p. 587 'though I very much dislike': AR to BR, 28.7.20

p. 588 'I felt sincerely': *The Tamarisk Tree Volume I*, p. 104

p. 588 'reacting': ibid.

p. 588 'with bewildered horror': *Autobiography Volume II*, p. 110

p. 588 'She had met men': ibid.

p. 588 'In Russia': *The Tamarisk Tree Volume I*, p. 105

p. 589 'I can remember': ibid., p. 107

p. 589 'I should be more in harmony': *Autobiography Volume II*, p. 124

p. 590 'nightmare place': BR to OM, 11.10.20

p. 590 'like an Emperor': DR to her mother, Lady Black 2.11.20, quoted in *The Tamarisk Tree Volume I*, p. 115

p. 590 'We are very glad': Johnson Yuan to BR, 6.11.20, see *Autobiography Volume II*, p. 136

p. 590 'Confucius the Second': from 'The Happiness of China', *The Nation*, 8 Jan. 1921, pp. 505–6, reprinted in *Autobiography Volume II* as a letter written 'on the Yiangtse, 28th October 1920', pp. 137–9

p. 590 'like a guitar': ibid.

p. 590 'I had not realised': *Autobiography Volume II*, p. 126

p. 590 'Well, I suppose': see *Autobiography Volume II*, p. 127

p. 591 'China makes the impression': *Autobiography Volume II*, p. 138

p. 591 'The days on the Yangtse': ibid., p. 126

p. 591 'Chinese scenery': DR to Lady Black, 2.11.20, quoted in *The Tamarisk Tree Volume I*, p. 115

p. 591 'Dewey's feelings about Russell': quoted in Clark, op. cit., p. 484

p. 591 'now I can't stand him': BR to OM, 21.2.21

p. 592 'took a position': quoted in the 'Foreword' by Ken Coates to the 1992 Spokesman edition of *The Problem of China*

p. 592 'But if not': BR to OM, 28.10.20

p. 593 'The Europeans almost all look villainous': *Autobiography Volume II*, p. 137

p. 593 'The Europeans have a few factories': ibid., p. 139

p. 593 'but Europeanisation': ibid.

p. 593 'Our Chinese friends': ibid., p. 127

p. 593 'The Englishman in the East': ibid., p. 129

p. 593 'It was evident': *The Tamarisk Tree Volume I*, p. 119

p. 593 'I would do anything': BR to OM, 31.1.21

p. 594 'The Chinese': ibid.

p. 594 'because I was living in open sin': note added by Russell to a letter from Littlewood, 30.1.21

p. 595 'Bertie': *The Tamarisk Tree Volume I*, p. 124

p. 595 'Capitalism and Socialism': *The Prospects of Industrial Civilization*, p. 19

p. 596 'It was I': DR to C. K. Ogden, Jan. 1921, quoted in *The Tamarisk Tree Volume I*, p. 128

p. 596 'I knelt in the bow': see *The Tamarisk Tree Volume I*, p. 130

p. 596 'I am filled with hatred': DR to Lady Black, 15.2.21, quoted ibid.

p. 596 and then only to remark: see *Autobiography Volume II*, p. 152

p. 597 'is that it must be such': *The Prospects of Industrial Civilization*, p. 155

p. 597 'the only faith': ibid., p. 157

p. 597 'The main purpose': ibid., p. 160

p. 597 'a time of absolute and complete happiness': *Autobiography Volume II*, p. 127

p. 597 'but most of all': *The Tamarisk Tree Volume I*, p. 121

p. 598 'I do not know': DR to Lady Black, 13.4.21, see *The Tamarisk Tree Volume I*, pp. 136–8

p. 598 'my mind': BR to OM, 28.4.21

p. 598 'I took the utmost pains': ibid.

p. 598 'They were hostile': from a dream dictated on 20.3.21, included in BR to OM, 28.4.21

p. 599 'I have no home': BR to Elizabeth Russell, 16.2.21

p. 599 'All the nations': BR to LW, 11.2.21

p. 599 'electric with the hope': *Autobiography Volume II*, p. 128

p. 600 'The news broke me': *After Ten Years*, p. 155

p. 600 'I wanted to destroy all beauty': ibid., p. 156

p. 600 'Until there was a false rumour': Charles Sanger to BR, 2.6.21

p. 600 'no one really knew': *The Tamarisk Tree Volume I*, p. 136

p. 600 'On my birthday afternoon': DR to Lady Black, 13.4.21, *The Tamarisk Tree Volume I*, p. 137

p. 601 'Death and Birth': the whole poem is reproduced in *The Tamarisk Tree Volume I*, pp. 138–9

p. 601 'I have missed much': BR to OM, 11.5.21

p. 601 'I want to tell you': BR to OM, 28.4.21

p. 601 'I am astonished': BR to OM, 11.5.21

p. 601 '*gravidas incipit*': see *The Tamarisk Tree Volume I*, p. 141

p. 601 'could hardly believe it': ibid.

p. 601 'He's still in bed': DR to C. K. Ogden, 31.5.21, quoted ibid., p. 142

p. 602 'People here': see *The Tamarisk Tree Volume I*, p. 125

p. 602 'Some Traits in the Chinese Character': *The Atlantic Monthly*, Dec. 1921, pp. 771–7, reprinted as Chapter XII in *The Problem of China*

p. 602 'Famine in China': *The Problem of China*, p. 210

p. 602 'hardly any flesh': *The Tamarisk Tree Volume I*, p. 143

p. 603 'some system': quoted ibid., p. 143

p. 603 'twelve hectic days': *Autobiography Volume II*, p. 133

p. 603 'Mr Bertrand Russell, having died': see *The Tamarisk Tree Volume I*, p. 144

p. 603 'the best newspaper': *Autobiography Volume II*, p. 134

p. 603 'a delightful man': ibid.

p. 603 'I became blind with rage': ibid., p. 135

p. 603 'I felt at that moment': ibid.

p. 604 'I never': *The Tamarisk Tree Volume I*, p. 147

21. The Coming Back

p. 605 'My Beloved': from Colette's typescript of letters from BR

p. 605 'The spirit of our love': BR to CM, late Aug. 1921

p. 606 'soon after': *The Coming Back*, p. 72

p. 606 'All Gregory's force': ibid., p. 82

p. 606 'They lived mostly': ibid., p. 51

p. 606 'It was clear': ibid., p. 53

p. 606 'began to realise': ibid., p. 106

p. 606 'He could take no interest': ibid., p. 137

p. 607 'In some ways': ibid., p. 141

p. 607 'Where was the Gregory': ibid., p. 147

p. 607 'She *must* be free': ibid., p. 158

p. 607 'desired children': ibid., p. 208

p. 607 'wanted to have a family': ibid., p. 248

p. 607 'it seemed rather feeble': ibid., p. 267

p. 607 ' "It's not true!" ': ibid., p. 291

p. 607 'For an instant': ibid., p. 307

p. 607 'Tell Konradin': ibid., p. 327

p. 608 'He said': ibid., p. 328

p. 608 'Nobody could be more disappointed': quoted in *The Tamarisk Tree Volume I*, pp. 148–9

p. 609 'It is not unlikely': BR to Rachel Brooks, 13.5.22

p. 609 'It is so': quoted in *The Tamarisk Tree Volume I*, p. 149

p. 609 'I have been dwelling': Joseph Conrad to BR, 2.11.21

p. 610 'I am sorry': BR to LW, 5.11.21

p. 610 'In any other case': Wilhelm Ostwald to Dorothy Wrinch, 21.2.21

p. 610 an article on trends in Chinese education: 'A People Who Value Wisdom Above Rubies', *The Review of Reviews*, 64, Nov. 1921, pp. 349–53, and *The Dial*, 71, Dec. 1921, pp. 693–8, reprinted as Chapter XIII, 'Higher Education in China', in *The Problem of China*

p. 610 'increase the number': *The Problem of China*, p. 214

p. 610 'the only people': ibid., p. 225

p. 610 'Some Traits in the Chinese Character': *The Atlantic Monthly*, Dec. 1921, pp. 771–7, reprinted as Chapter XII in *The Problem of China*

p. 610 'The obvious charm': *The Problem of China*, pp. 212–13

p. 611 'It was so nice': Vivien Eliot to BR, 1.11.21

p. 611 'bearing in mind': *The Tamarisk Tree Volume I*, p. 151

p. 611 'As I lay there': ibid.

p. 611 'I am so relieved': BR to OM, 16.11.21

p. 611 'I wish, with your permission': BR to Joseph Conrad, probably 16.11.21, quoted in *Autobiography*, p. 209

p. 611 'profoundly touched': Joseph Conrad to BR, 18.11.21

p. 612 'Yes! Paternity is a great experience': Joseph Conrad to BR, 18.11.21

p. 612 'a new emotional centre': *Autobiography Volume II*, p. 150

BIBLIOGRAPHY

Russell's published output is unmanageably large: seventy books, over two thousand articles, and a great number of reported speeches, contributions to other people's books, 'blurbs', etc. Astonishingly, the seemingly impossible bibliographical feat of listing his entire *œuvre* has now – after some thirty years' work – been accomplished. *A Bibliography of Bertrand Russell* by Kenneth Blackwell and Harry Ruja (Routledge, 1994) lists in detail just about everything that Russell ever published, complete with information about translations, which portions of the books appeared as articles and broadcasts elsewhere, and so on. Comprising over four thousand entries, this marvellous, indispensable work (published to complement the equally magnificent *Collected Papers of Bertrand Russell*) is divided into three volumes: Volume I lists Russell's books and pamphlets, Volume II everything else, and Volume III contains a detailed index to the other two volumes.

As far as I know, no equally thorough bibliography of the secondary literature on Russell has been attempted, though an extremely useful (if, by now, rather dated) list is contained at the back of *Essays in Analysis*, compiled by the book's editor, Douglas Lackey, who remarks, with justice, that 'The difficulty in compiling a secondary source bibliography for Russell lies in keeping it from ballooning into a bibliography of twentieth-century analytic philosophy.' What follows is no more than a list of the works I have consulted in writing this book.

Works by Russell

The Collected Papers of Bertrand Russell

Produced by the Bertrand Russell Editorial Project, based at McMaster University, Hamilton, Ontario, and led by the Project Director, Louis Greenspan, this is an ambitious attempt to publish in a uniform edition all of Russell's shorter (i.e., less than book-length) writings, whether previously published or not. After Volume 1, which includes Russell's juvenilia and earliest professional work, the series divides in two: Volumes 2 to 11 containing his philosophical work, and Volumes 12 onwards his personal and political writings. Below are listed the volumes that have been published so far, together with the papers they contain of which I have made the most use.

Volume 1. Cambridge Essays, 1888–99, edited by Kenneth Blackwell, Andrew Brink, Nicholas Griffin, Richard A. Rempel, and John G. Slater, London, George Allen & Unwin, 1983

Includes: 'Greek Exercises', Russell's Crammer School essays, 'A Locked Diary' (1890–4), 'Die Ehe', 'Self-Appreciation', his Apostolic essays (including 'Cleopatra and Maggie Tulliver' and 'Seems Madam? Nay, It Is'), his graduate essays on philosophy (including his paper on the Ontological Argument), and his first published philosophical articles (including 'The Logic of Geometry').

Volume 2. Philosophical Papers, 1896–99, edited by Nicholas Griffin and Albert C. Lewis, London, Unwin Hyman, 1990
Includes: Russell's review of Hannequin, 'On Some Difficulties of Continuous Quantity', 'Why Do We Regard Time, But Not Space, as Necessarily a Plenum?', *An Analysis of Mathematical Reasoning* (1898), and *The Fundamental Ideas and Axioms of Mathematics* (1899).

Volume 3. Toward the 'Principles of Mathematics', 1900–02, edited by Gregory H. Moore, London, Routledge, 1994
Includes: the 1899–1900 draft of *The Principles of Mathematics*, 'The Notion of Order and Absolute Position in Space and Time', 'Recent Italian Work on the Foundations of Mathematics', 'Recent Work on the Principles of Mathematics', and Russell's review of Boutroux.

Volume 4. Foundations of Logic, 1903–05, edited by Alasdair Urquhart with the assistance of Albert C. Lewis, London, Routledge, 1994
Includes: the pre-'On Denoting' manuscripts (including 'On Functions', 'On Meaning and Denotation', and 'On Fundamentals'), 'On Denoting', 'Meinong's Theory of Complexes and Assumptions', 'On the Relation of Mathematics to Symbolic Logic', and reviews of Couturat, Poincaré and Meinong.

Volume 6. Logical and Philosophical Papers, 1909–13, edited by John G. Slater with the assistance of Bernd Frohmann, London, Routledge, 1992
Includes: 'The Theory of Logical Types', 'What is Logic?', 'On Matter', 'On the Nature of Truth and Falsehood', 'Analytic Realism', 'The Philosophy of Bergson', 'Pragmatism', and Russell's review of William James's *Essays in Radical Empiricism*.

Volume 7. Theory of Knowledge, edited by Elizabeth Ramsden Eames in collaboration with Kenneth Blackwell, London, George Allen & Unwin, 1984
Includes: the 1913 manuscript, *The Theory of Knowledge*.

Volume 8. The Philosophy of Logical Atomism and Other Essays, 1914–19, edited by John G. Slater, London, George Allen & Unwin, 1986
Includes: 'The Relation of Sense-Data to Physics', 'Mysticism and Logic', 'On Scientific Method in Philosophy', 'The Philosophy of Logical Atomism', 'On "Bad Passions" ', and the manuscript notes that Russell wrote in prison on the psychology of symbolism.

Volume 9. Essays on Language, Mind and Matter, 1919–26, edited by John G. Slater with the assistance of Bernd Frohmann, London, Unwin Hyman, 1988
Includes: Introduction to Wittgenstein's *Tractatus Logico-Philosophicus*, 'Einstein's Theory of Gravitation', and reviews of Joachim, Clutton-Brock, Ralph Perry, etc.

Volume 12. Contemplation and Action, 1902–14, edited by Richard A. Rempel, Andrew Brink and Margaret Moran, London, George Allen & Unwin, 1985
Includes: Russell's private Journal, 1902–5, *The Pilgrimage of Life*, 'The Free Man's Worship', 'The Study of Mathematics', *Prisons*, 'The Essence of Religion', *The Perplexities of John Forstice*, 'Mysticism and Logic', 'The Place of Science in a Liberal Education', and Russell's articles and speeches on Free Trade and Women's Suffrage.

Volume 13. Prophecy and Dissent, 1914–16, edited by Richard A. Rempel with the assistance of Bernd Frohmann, Mark Lippincott and Margaret Moran, London, Unwin Hyman, 1988
Includes: 'War, the Offspring of Fear', 'The Ethics of War', 'Lord Northcliffe's Triumph', 'On Justice in War-Time', 'The Policy of the Entente, 1904–1914: a Reply to Professor Gilbert Murray', 'The Cardiff Speech', and 'The Danger to Civilization'.

Autobiographical Writings

Russell was a dedicated chronicler of his own life and kept up a constant stream of memoirs and evaluations of his private and public hopes, disappointments and achievements, from the 'Self-Appreciation' of 1897 to the third volume of his *Autobiography* in the last year of his life. Below are listed, in chronological order, those autobiographical writings not (yet) included in the *Collected Papers*.

1927 'Things That Have Moulded Me', *The Dial*, 83, Sept. 1927, pp. 181–6, reprinted as 'Introduction' to *Selected Papers of Bertrand Russell*, New York, The Modern Library

1930 'How I Was Educated', *John O'London's Weekly*, 23, 19 July 1930, pp. 525–6

1936 ' "The Last Survivor of a Dead Epoch" ', *The Listener*, 16, 12 Aug. 1936, p. 289, reprinted as 'Obituary (1937)' in *Unpopular Essays*

1938 'My Religious Reminiscences', *The Rationalist Annual*, 1938, pp. 2–8, reprinted in *Basic Writings*

1944 'My Mental Development', *The Philosophy of Bertrand Russell*, edited by Paul Schilpp, pp. 3–20, reprinted in *Basic Writings*

1946 'Eminent Men I Have Known', *Unpopular Essays*, pp. 181–7

1951 'How I Write', *London Calling*, 10 May 1951, reprinted in *Portraits from Memory*

1951 'Memories of My Childhood', *Vogue*, 117, 15 May 1951, pp. 69, 106, 108–10

1952 'Reflections On My Eightieth Birthday', *The Listener*, 47, 22 May 1952, pp. 823–4, reprinted as 'Postscript', *The Autobiography of Bertrand Russell 1944–1967 (Volume III)*

1952 'My First 80 Years', *New York Post*, 25 May 1952, pp. 10–11

1952–3 'Portraits from Memory':
1. 'Alfred North Whitehead', *The Listener*, 48, 10 July 1952, pp. 51–2, reprinted in *Portraits from Memory*
2. 'Maynard Keynes and Lytton Strachey', *The Listener*, 17 July 1952, pp. 97–8, reprinted in *Autobiography*, pp. 70–4
3. 'D. H. Lawrence', *The Listener*, 24 July 1952, pp. 135–6, reprinted in *Portraits from Memory*
4. ' "Completely Married": Sidney and Beatrice Webb', *The Listener*, 31 July 1952, p. 177–8, reprinted in *Portraits from Memory*
5. 'Cambridge in the Eighteen-Nineties', *The Listener*, 50, 20 Aug. 1953, pp. 307–8, reprinted as 'Some Cambridge Dons of the 'Nineties' in *Portraits from Memory*
6. 'Cambridge Friendships', *The Listener*, 27 Aug. 1953, pp. 337–8, reprinted as 'Some of My Contemporaries at Cambridge' in *Portraits from Memory*
7. 'Bernard Shaw: The Admirable Iconoclast', *The Listener*, 3 Sep. 1953, pp. 380–1, reprinted as 'George Bernard Shaw' in *Portraits from Memory*
8. 'H. G. Wells: Liberator of Thought', *The Listener*, 10 Sept. 1953, pp. 417–18, reprinted as 'H. G. Wells' in *Portraits from Memory*
9. 'Joseph Conrad', *The Listener*, 17 Sept. 1953, pp. 462–3, reprinted in *Portraits from Memory*

10. 'George Santayana', *The Listener*, 24 Sept. 1953, pp. 503, 511, reprinted in *Portraits from Memory*

1953? 'Private Memoirs', unpublished typescript, the purpose of which 'is to explain why my relations with women that I have been fond of were until the last unsatisfactory'.

1955 'Six Autobiographical Talks':
    1. 'Philosophers and Idiots', *The Listener*, 53, 10 Feb. 1955, pp. 247, 249, reprinted as 'Some Philosophical Contacts' in *Portraits from Memory*
    2. 'Why I Took to Philosophy', *London Calling*, 3 Mar. 1955, p. 9, reprinted in *Portraits from Memory* and *Basic Writings*
    3. 'A Pacifist in Wartime', *London Calling*, 17 Mar. 1955, p. 10, reprinted as 'Experiences of a Pacifist in the First World War', *Portraits from Memory*
    4. 'War and the Pursuit of Peace', *London Calling*, 24 Mar. 1955, p. 8, reprinted as 'From Logic to Politics', *Portraits from Memory*
    5. 'A Philosophy of My Own', *London Calling*, 31 Mar. 1955, p. 10, reprinted as 'Beliefs: Discarded and Retained' in *Portraits from Memory*
    6. ' "So I Go On Writing Books" ', *London Calling*, 7 April 1955, p. 10, reprinted as 'Hopes: Realized and Disappointed' in *Portraits from Memory*

1956 'Adaptation: an Autobiographical Epitome', *Portraits from Memory*, pp. 7–17
1957 'Books that Influenced Me in Youth':
    1. 'The Importance of Shelley', *London Calling*, 7 Mar. 1957, p. 4, reprinted in *Fact and Fiction*
    2. 'The Romance of Revolt', *London Calling*, 14 Mar. 1957, p. 10, reprinted in *Fact and Fiction*
    3. 'Revolt in the Abstract', *London Calling*, 21 Mar. 1957, p. 12, reprinted in *Fact and Fiction*
    4. 'Disgust and its Antidote', *London Calling*, 28 Mar. 1957, p. 10, reprinted in *Fact and Fiction*
    5. 'An Education in History', *London Calling*, 4 April 1957, p. 6, reprinted in *Fact and Fiction*
    6. 'The Pursuit of Truth', *London Calling*, 11 April 1957, p. 14, reprinted in *Fact and Fiction*

1959 *My Philosophical Development*, London, George Allen & Unwin, 1959
1967 *The Autobiography of Bertrand Russell 1872–1914*, London, George Allen & Unwin, 1967
1968 *The Autobiography of Bertrand Russell 1914–1944* (Volume II), London, George Allen & Unwin, 1968
1969 *The Autobiography of Bertrand Russell 1944–1967* (Volume III), London, George Allen & Unwin, 1969

Published Correspondence (see also the preamble to 'Notes and References')

Dear Bertrand Russell: a selection of his correspondence with the general public 1950–1968, edited by Barry Feinberg and Ronald Kasrils, London, George Allen & Unwin, 1969
Dear Russell – Dear Jourdain: A commentary on Russell's logic, based on his correspondence with Philip Jourdain by I. Grattan-Guinness, London, Duckworth, 1977
'Unpublished Correspondence between Russell and Wittgenstein', B. F. McGuinness and G. H. von Wright, *Russell*, 10 (2), winter 1990–1, pp. 101–24

The Selected Letters of Bertrand Russell. Volume 1: The Private Years, 1884–1914, edited by Nicholas Griffin, London, Allen Lane, 1992

Other Writings

Below are listed, in chronological order (of writing rather than publication), only those works used in the preparation of this volume. The list includes little, therefore, written after 1921. The pieces published in *Collected Papers* are not included.

1896 *German Social Democracy*, London, Longmans, 1896, second edition, George Allen & Unwin, 1965

1897 *An Essay on the Foundations of Geometry*, Cambridge, University Press, 1897; paperback edition, New York, Dover, 1956

1900 *A Critical Exposition of the Philosophy of Leibniz*, Cambridge, University Press, 1900; paperback edition, London, Routledge, 1992

1903 *The Principles of Mathematics*, Cambridge, University Press, 1903; paperback edition, London, Routledge, 1992

1906 'The Nature of Truth', *Mind*, 15, Oct. 1906, pp. 528–33

1907 'On the Nature of Truth', *Proceedings of the Aristotelian Society*, 7, 1906–7, pp. 28–49

1910 *Philosophical Essays*, London, Longmans, 1910; second (revised) edition, George Allen & Unwin, 1966

1910–13 (with A. N. Whitehead) *Principia Mathematica*, Cambridge, University Press, *Volume I*, 1910, *Volume II*, 1912, *Volume III*, 1913; second edition 1925–7; paperback (abridged) edition, Cambridge, University Press, 1962

1912 *The Problems of Philosophy*, London, Williams and Norgate, 1912; paperback edition, Oxford, University Press, 1967

1914 *Our Knowledge of the External World as a Field for Scientific Method in Philosophy*, London, Open Court, 1914; paperback edition, London, Routledge, 1993

1915 *Justice in War-Time*, London, The National Labour Press, 1915; second edition, Nottingham, Spokesman Books, 1975

1916 *Principles of Social Reconstruction*, London, George Allen & Unwin, 1916

1917 *Political Ideals*, New York, Century, 1917; British (expanded) edition, London, George Allen & Unwin, 1963

1918 *Mysticism and Logic*, London, Longmans, 1918

1918 *Roads to Freedom*, London, George Allen & Unwin, 1918

1918 *The Philosophy of Logical Atomism*, edited by David Pears, London, Fontana, 1972; La Salle, Illinois, Open Court, 1985

1919 *Introduction to Mathematical Philosophy*, London, George Allen & Unwin, 1919; paperback edition, London, Routledge, 1993

1920 'Socialism and Liberal Ideals', *The English Review*, 30, May, June 1920, pp. 449–55, 499–508

1920 *The Practice and Theory of Bolshevism*, London, George Allen & Unwin, 1920; second (revised) edition, 1949

1921 *The Analysis of Mind*, London, George Allen & Unwin, 1921; paperback edition, London, Routledge, 1992

1921 (in collaboration with Dora Russell) *The Prospects of Industrial Civilization*, London, George Allen & Unwin, 1923

1922 *The Problem of China*, London, George Allen & Unwin, 1922; paperback edition, Nottingham, Spokesman Books, 1993

1931–5 *Mortals and Others: Bertrand Russell's American Essays 1931–1935*, edited by Harry Ruja, London, George Allen & Unwin, 1975

1937 *The Amberley Papers*, Volumes 1 and 2, London, Hogarth Press, 1937
1940 *An Inquiry into Meaning and Truth*, New York, Norton, 1940
1945 *A History of Western Philosophy*, London, George Allen & Unwin, 1946
1950 *Unpopular Essays*, London, George Allen & Unwin, 1950
1953 *Satan in the Suburbs*, London, The Bodley Head, 1953; paperback edition, Penguin, 1961
1954 *Nightmares of Eminent Persons*, London, The Bodley Head, 1954; paperback edition, Penguin, 1962
1956 *Portraits from Memory and Other Essays*, London, George Allen & Unwin, 1956
1956 *Logic and Knowledge*, edited by Robert C. Marsh, London, George Allen & Unwin, 1956; paperback edition, London, Routledge, 1992
1960 *Bertrand Russell Speaks His Mind*, New York, World Publishing Co., 1960
1961 *Fact and Fiction*, London, George Allen & Unwin, 1961
The Basic Writings of Bertrand Russell, edited by Robert E. Egner, London, George Allen & Unwin, 1961
The Collected Stories of Bertrand Russell, compiled and edited by Barry Feinberg, London, George Allen & Unwin, 1972
Bertrand Russell's America Volume One 1896–1945, by Barry Feinberg and Ronald Kasrils, London, George Allen & Unwin, 1973
Essays in Analysis, edited by Douglas Lackey, London, George Allen & Unwin, 1973

Works by Others

The works listed below are given in the editions that I happen to have used. In many cases, therefore, the date given will not be the date of first publication.

Ackroyd, Peter, *T. S. Eliot*, Abacus, 1985
Ambrose, Alice and Lazerowitz, Morris (eds), *G. E. Moore: Essays in Retrospect*, London, George Allen & Unwin, 1970
Andersson, Stefan, *In Quest of Certainty: Bertrand Russell's search for certainty in religion and mathematics up to The Principles of Mathematics (1903)*, Stockholm, 1994
Armstrong, William M., 'Bertrand Russell Comes to America, 1896', *Studies in History and Society*, II, 1 & 2, Fall 1969 and Spring 1970
Ayer, A. J., *Russell and Moore: The Analytical Heritage*, London, Macmillan, 1971
—— *Russell*, London, Fontana, 1972
Ayling, Stanley, *Edmund Burke: His Life and Opinions*, London, Cassell, 1988
Baines, Jocelyn, *Joseph Conrad: A Critical Biography*, London, Weidenfeld, 1993
Baldwin, Thomas, *G. E. Moore*, London, Routledge, 1990
Bedford, John 13th Duke of, *A Silver-Plated Spoon*, London, Cassell, 1959
Bell, Quentin, *Virginia Woolf: A Biography Volume One. Virginia Stephen 1882–1912*, Triad/Granada, 1976
—— *Virginia Woolf: A Biography Volume Two. Mrs Woolf 1912–1941*, Triad/Granada, 1976
Bell, Robert H., 'Bertrand Russell and the Eliots', *The American Scholar*, summer 1983, pp. 309–25
Berenson, Mary, *A Self Portrait from her Letters & Diaries*, edited by Barbara Strachey and Jayne Samuels, London, Gollancz, 1983
Berthoud, Jacques, *Joseph Conrad: The Major Phase*, Cambridge, University Press, 1978
Birkin, Andrew, *J. M. Barrie and the Lost Boys*, London, Constable, 1979
Blackwell, Kenneth, 'Our Knowledge of "Our Knowledge" ', *Russell*, 12, winter 1973–4, pp. 11–13

—— 'The Early Wittgenstein and the Middle Russell', in *Perspectives on the Philosophy of Wittgenstein*, edited by Irving Block, Oxford, Blackwell, 1981
—— *The Spinozistic Ethics of Bertrand Russell*, London, George Allen & Unwin, 1985
Blackiston, Georgiana, *Lord William Russell and His Wife*, London, John Murray, 1972
Bradley, F. H., *Appearance and Reality*, London, Swan Sonnenschein, 1893
—— *Essays on Truth and Reality*, Oxford, University Press, 1914
Brink, Andrew, *Bertrand Russell: The Psychobiography of a Moralist*, New Jersey, Humanities Press, 1989
Burke, Edmund, *Selected Writings and Speeches*, edited by Peter J. Stanlis, New York, Anchor Books, 1963
Cantor, Georg, *Contributions to the Founding of the Theory of Transfinite Numbers*, New York, Dover, 1955
Cecil, Hugh & Mirabel, *Clever Hearts: Desmond & Molly MacCarthy*, London, Gollancz, 1990
Chao, Yuen Ren, 'With Bertrand Russell in China', *Russell*, 7, autumn 1972, pp. 14–17
Clark, Ronald W., *The Life of Bertrand Russell*, Penguin, 1978
—— *Bertrand Russell and His World*, London, Thames and Hudson, 1981
Clifford, W. K., *Lectures and Essays*, edited by L. Stephen and F. Pollock, two volumes, London, Macmillan, 1879; second edition, 1886
—— *The Common Sense of the Exact Sciences*, edited by Karl Pearson, 1885
Cocchiarella, Nino, 'The Development of the Theory of Logical Types and the Notion of a Logical Subject in Russell's Early Philosophy', *Synthese*, 45, 1980, pp. 71–115
Coffa, J. Alberto, *The Semantic Tradition from Kant to Carnap: To the Vienna Station*, Cambridge, University Press, 1991
Cole, G. D. H., *The World of Labour*, London, G. Bell & Sons, 1913
—— *Self-Government in Industry*, London, G. Bell & Sons, 1917
Conrad, Joseph, *Tales of Unrest*, Penguin, 1977
—— *An Outcast of the Islands*, Penguin, 1975
—— *Heart of Darkness & The Secret Sharer*, Signet, 1978
—— *Nostromo*, Penguin, 1986
—— *The Secret Agent*, Penguin, 1963
—— *Typhoon and Other Stories*, Penguin, 1990
—— *Lord Jim*, Penguin, 1989
—— *The Mirror of the Sea & A Personal Record*, Oxford, 1988
—— *Victory*, Penguin 1994
—— *Chance*, Signet, 1992
Cooper-Willis, Irene, *England's Holy War: A Study of English Liberal Idealism during the First World War*, New York, Knopf, 1928
Crawshay-Williams, Rupert, *Russell Remembered*, Oxford, University Press 1970
Darroch, Sandra Jobson, *Ottoline: The Life of Lady Ottoline Morrell*, London, Chatto, 1976
Delany, Paul, *D. H. Lawrence's Nightmare: The Writer and His Circle in the Years of the Great War*, Sussex, Harvester, 1979
Derry, John W., *Politics in the Age of Fox, Pitt and Liverpool: Continuity and Transformation*, London, Macmillan, 1990
Detlefson, Michael, 'Poincaré Against the Logicians', *Synthese*, 90, 1992, pp. 349–78
Dostoyevsky, Fyodor, *The Idiot*, Oxford, University Press, 1992
Egan, Michael (ed.), *Ibsen: The Critical Heritage*, London, Routledge, 1972

Eliot, T. S., review of *Theism and Humanism* by A. J. Balfour, *International Journal of Ethics*, 26 (2), 1916, pp. 284-9

—— *Prufrock and Other Observations*, London, The Egoist Limited, 1917

—— 'Eeldrop and Appleplex', *The Little Review*, May and Sep. 1917, pp. 7-11 and 16-19, reprinted as *Eeldrop and Appleplex*, Tunbridge Wells, The Foundling Press, 1992

—— 'Style and Thought', review of Russell's *Mysticism and Logic*, *The Nation*, 22, Mar. 1918, pp. 768, 770

—— *Knowledge and Experience in the Philosophy of F. H. Bradley*, London, Faber, 1964

—— *The Letters of T. S. Eliot Volume I 1898–1922*, edited by Valerie Eliot, London, Faber, 1988

Ellmann, Richard, *Oscar Wilde*, Penguin, 1988

Forte, Maria, 'Lucy Martin Donnelly: a Sojourn with the Russells', *Russell*, 7 (1), summer 1987, pp. 53-9

—— 'Bertrand Russell's Letters to Helen Thomas Flexner and Lucy Martin Donnelly', unpublished Ph.D. thesis, McMaster University, 1988

Frege, Gottlob, *Philosophical and Mathematical Correspondence*, Oxford, Blackwell, 1980

Gardiner, Bennitt, 'Colette O'Niel: a Season in Repertory', *Russell*, 23-4, autumn–winter 1976, pp. 26-36

—— '1916', *Russell*, 29-32, 1978, pp. 43-51

—— 'The Wisdom of Colette', *Russell*, 37-40, 1980-1, pp. 31-9

Gordon, Lyndall, *Eliot's Early Years*, Oxford, University Press, 1977

—— *Eliot's New Life*, Oxford, University Press, 1988

Gottschalk, Herbert, *Bertrand Russell: A Life*, London, John Barker, 1965

Grattan-Guinness, I., 'Russell's Home at Bagley Wood', *Russell*, 13, spring 1974, pp. 24-6

—— 'George Cantor's Influence on Bertrand Russell', *History and Philosophy of Logic*, 1, 1980, pp. 61-93

Griffin, Nicholas, 'Russell's "Horrible Travesty" of Meinong', *Russell*, 25-8, 1977, pp. 39-51

—— 'Russell on the Nature of Logic (1903–1913)', *Synthese*, 45, 1980, pp. 117-88

—— 'The Acts of the Apostles', review of Paul Levy, *G. E. Moore and the Cambridge Apostles*, *Russell*, 1 (1), summer 1981, pp. 71-82

—— 'Russell's Multiple Relation Theory of Judgment', *Philosophical Studies*, 47, 1985, pp. 213-47

—— 'Wittgenstein's Criticism of Russell's Theory of Judgment', *Russell*, 5 (2), winter 1985-6, pp. 132-45

—— 'Joachim's Early Advice to Russell on Studying Philosophy', *Russell*, 7 (2), winter 1987-8, pp. 119-23

—— *Russell's Idealist Apprenticeship*, Oxford, University Press, 1991

Hardy, G. H., *Bertrand Russell and Trinity: A College Controversy of the Last War*, Cambridge, University Press, 1942

Harrison, Royden, 'Bertrand Russell and the Webbs', *Russell*, 5 (1), summer 1985, pp. 44-9

Hastings, Michael, *Tom and Viv*, London, Penguin, 1985

Heijenoort, Jean van, *From Frege to Gödel: A Source Book in Mathematical Logic, 1879–1931*, Harvard, University Press, 1967

Holroyd, Michael, *Lytton Strachey: A Biography*, London, Penguin, 1979

—— *Lytton Strachey: The New Biography*, London, Chatto, 1994

Hylton, Peter, 'Russell's Substitutional Theory', *Synthese*, 45, 1980, pp. 1-31

—— Russell, Idealism and the Emergence of Analytic Philosophy, Oxford, University Press, 1990
Ibsen, Henrik, Ghosts and Other Plays, Penguin, 1964
—— The Master Builder and Other Plays, Penguin, 1958
Irvine, A. D. and Wedeking, G. A. (eds), Russell and Analytic Philosophy, Toronto, University of Toronto Press, 1993
Jager, Ronald, The Development of Bertrand Russell's Philosophy, London, George Allen & Unwin, 1972
James, William, The Principles of Psychology, two volumes, London, Macmillan, 1890
—— Pragmatism: a New Name for Some Old Ways of Thinking, London, Longmans, 1907
—— Essays in Radical Empiricism, London, Longmans, 1912
—— Essays in Philosophy, Harvard, University Press, 1978
Jean-Aubry, G., Joseph Conrad, Life & Letters, two volumes, London, Heinemann, 1927
Joachim, Harold H., The Nature of Truth, Oxford, University Press, 1906
Jones, J. R., The First Whigs: The Politics of the Exclusion Crisis 1678–1683, London, 1961
Jourdain, Philip E. B., The Philosophy of Mr. B*rtr*nd, R*ss*ll, London, George Allen & Unwin, 1918
'Junius', The Letters of Junius, edited by John Cannon, Oxford, University Press, 1978
Karl, Frederick R., Joseph Conrad. The Three Lives: A Biography, London, Faber, 1979
Kearns, Marion, 'Alys Russell: a Bibliography', Russell, 10, summer 1873, pp. 17–19
Keen, C. N., 'The Interaction of Russell and Bradley', Russell, 3, autumn 1971, pp. 7–11
Kennedy, Thomas C., 'The Women's Man from Wimbledon', Russell, 14, summer 1974, pp. 19–26
Kenyon, John, The Popish Plot, London, Heinemann, 1972
Kermode, Frank, Lawrence, Fontana, 1973
Keynes, John Maynard, The Collected Writings Volume X. Essays in Biography, London, Macmillan, 1972
King, James, Virginia Woolf, London, Hamish Hamilton, 1994
Knight, G. Wilson, Ibsen, Edinburgh, Oliver and Boyd, 1962
Lackey, Douglas P., 'The Whitehead Correspondence', Russell, 5, spring 1972, pp. 14–16
—— 'Russell's Unknown Theory of Classes: The Substitutional System of 1906', Journal of Philosophy, 14, 1976, pp. 69–78
Landini, Gregory, 'Russell's Substitutional Theory of Classes and Relations', History and Philosophy of Logic, 8, 1987, pp. 171–200
Lawrence, D. H., The Prussian Officer, London, Secker, 1914
—— The Rainbow, Penguin, 1989
—— Women in Love, Penguin, 1960
—— Twilight in Italy, Penguin, 1974
—— The Complete Short Stories Volume II (including 'The Blind Man'), Penguin, 1976
—— England, My England, Penguin, 1982
—— Assorted Articles, London, Secker, 1932
—— The Collected Letters (Two Volumes), edited by Harry T. Moore, London, Heinemann, 1962

—— *The Letters of D. H. Lawrence Volume II June 1913–October 1916*, edited by George J. Zytaruk and James T. Boulton, Cambridge, University Press, 1981

—— *D. H. Lawrence's Letters to Bertrand Russell*, edited by Harry T. Moore, New York, Gotham, 1948

—— *Phoenix: The Posthumous Papers of D. H. Lawrence*, edited by Edward D. McDonald, London, Heinemann, 1936

—— *Phoenix: Uncollected, Unpublished and Other Prose Works by D. H. Lawrence*, edited by Warren Roberts and Harry T. Moore, London, Heinemann, 1968

Lawrence, Frieda, *The Memoirs and Correspondence*, edited by E. W. Tedlock, Jr, New York, Knopf, 1964

Leithauser, Gladys, 'Arch-priggery: Bertrand and Alys Russell's Copy of Whitman's "Leaves of Grass" ', *Russell*, 19, autumn 1975

Leithauser, Gladys Garner, 'The Romantic Russell and the Legacy of Shelley', *Russell*, 4 (1), summer 1984, pp. 31–48

—— 'Spirited Satire: the Fiction of Bertrand Russell', *Russell*, 13 (1), summer 1993, pp. 63–82

Leithauser, Gladys Garner and Dyer, Nadine Cowan, 'Bertrand Russell and T. S. Eliot: Their Dialogue', *Russell*, 2 (1), summer 1982, pp. 7–28

Lenzen, Victor F., 'Bertrand Russell at Harvard, 1914', *Russell*, 3, autumn 1971, pp. 4–6

Levy, Paul, *G. E. Moore and the Cambridge Apostles*, London, Weidenfeld, 1979

Lowe, Victor, 'The Development of Whitehead's Philosophy', *The Philosophy of Alfred North Whitehead*, edited by Paul Arthur Schilpp, Northwestern, 1941, pp. 15–124

—— *Alfred North Whitehead. The Man and His Work Volume I: 1861–1910*, Baltimore, Johns Hopkins, 1985

—— *Alfred North Whitehead. The Man and His Work Volume II: 1910–1947*, edited by J. B. Schneewind, Baltimore, Johns Hopkins, 1990

MacCarthy, Desmond, *The Man and His Writings*, introduced by David Cecil, London, Constable, 1984

MacCarthy, Desmond and Russell, Agatha (eds), *Lady John Russell. A Memoir with Selections from her Diaries and Correspondence*, London, Longmans, 1926

McGuinness, Brian, *Wittgenstein: A Life. Young Ludwig 1889–1921*, London, Duckworth, 1988

McTaggart, John McTaggart Ellis, *Studies in the Hegelian Dialectic*, Cambridge, University Press, 1896

Maddox, Brenda, *The Married Man: A Life of D. H. Lawrence*, London, Sinclair-Stevenson, 1994

Malleson, Constance, *After Ten Years*, London, Cape, 1931

—— *The Coming Back*, London, Cape, 1933

—— *In the North: Autobiographical Fragments in Norway, Sweden, Finland: 1936–1946*, London, Gollancz, 1946

—— 'Fifty Years: 1916–1966', in Ralph Schoenman (ed.), *Bertrand Russell: Philosopher of the Century*, London, George Allen & Unwin, 1967

—— 'The End', *Russell*, 21–2, spring–summer 1976, pp. 25–7

Meyers, Jeffrey, *D. H. Lawrence: A Biography*, New York, Knopf, 1990

Mill, John Stuart, *Autobiography*, Boston, Houghton Mifflin, 1969

Mitchell, L. G., *Charles James Fox and the Disintegration of the Whig Party 1782–1794*, Oxford, University Press, 1971

Mitford, Nancy (ed.), *The Ladies of Alderley being the Letters between Maria Josepha, Lady Stanley of Alderley and Her Daughter-in-Law Henrietta Maria Stanley during the Years 1841–1850*, London, Chapman & Hall, 1938

—— The Stanleys of Alderley: Their Letters between the Years 1851–1865, London, Chapman & Hall, 1939

Monk, Ray, Ludwig Wittgenstein. The Duty of Genius, London, Cape, 1990

—— 'The Effects of a Broken Home: Bertrand Russell and Cambridge', Cambridge Minds, edited by Richard Mason, Cambridge, 1994, pp. 1–19

—— 'The Madness of Truth: Russell's Admiration for Joseph Conrad', Russell, 14 (2), winter 1994–5

Moore, G. E., review of Russell's Essay on the Foundations of Geometry, Mind, 8, July 1899, pp. 397–405

—— 'An Autobiography', The Philosophy of G. E. Moore, edited by Paul Arthur Schilpp, pp. 1–39

—— Philosophical Papers, London, George Allen & Unwin, 1959

—— The Early Essays, edited by Tom Regan, Philadelphia, Temple University Press, 1986

—— Selected Writings, edited by Thomas Baldwin, London, Routledge, 1993

Moorehead, Caroline, Bertrand Russell. A Life, London, Sinclair-Stevenson, 1992

Moran, Margaret, 'Men of Letters: Bertrand Russell and Joseph Conrad', Russell, 2 (1), summer 1982, pp. 29–46

Morrell, Ottoline, Ottoline: The Early Memoirs of Lady Ottoline Morrell, edited by Robert Gathorne-Hardy, London, Faber, 1963

—— Ottoline at Garsington: Memoirs of Lady Ottoline Morrell 1915–1918, edited by Robert Gathorne-Hardy, London, Faber, 1974

Murray, Gilbert, Euripides, translated into English rhyming verse, London, George Allen & Unwin, 1902

—— Euripides and His Age, second (revised) edition, Oxford, University Press, 1946

—— Five Stages of Greek Religion, Oxford, University Press, 1925

Newberry, Jo, 'Russell as Ghost-writer', Russell, 15, autumn 1974, pp. 19–23

Pais, Abraham, 'Subtle is the Lord . . .': The Science and the Life of Albert Einstein, Oxford, University Press, 1982

Patmore, Brigit, My Friends When Young. The Memoirs of Brigit Patmore, edited by Derek Patmore, London, Heinemann, 1968

Peel, Georgiana, Recollections, London, John Lane, 1920

Peters, Richard, Hobbes, Penguin, 1967

Pinsent, David Hume, A Portrait of Wittgenstein as a Young Man, edited by G. H. von Wright from the Diary of David Hume Pinsent 1912–1914, Oxford, Blackwell, 1990

Poincaré, Henri, 'Des fondements de la géométrie: à propos d'un livre de M. Russell', Revue de métaphysique et de morale, 7, 1899, pp. 251–79

—— Science and Hypothesis, New York, Dover, 1952

—— Science and Method, London, Thomas Nelson, 1914

—— The Value of Science, New York, Dover, 1958

—— Mathematics and Science: Last Essays, New York, Dover, 1963

Pollock, Sir Frederick, Spinoza: His Life and Philosophy, London, Kegan Paul, 1880

Powell, David, Charles James Fox. Man of the People, London, Hutchinson, 1989

Prest, John, Lord John Russell, London, Macmillan, 1972

Reid, Stuart J., Lord John Russell, London, Dent, 1895

Rhees, Rush, Recollections of Wittgenstein, Oxford, University Press, 1984

Ribblesdale, Lord, Impressions and Memories, London, Cassell, 1927

Richards, Joan L., Mathematical Visions: The Pursuit of Geometry in Victorian England, London, Academic Press, 1988

Roberts, George W. (ed.), *Bertrand Russell Memorial Volume*, London, George Allen & Unwin, 1979

Robson, Ann, 'Bertrand Russell and his godless Parents', *Russell*, 7, autumn 1972, pp. 3–9

Rodríguez-Consuegra, Francisco, 'The Origins of Russell's Theory of Descriptions', *Russell*, 9 (2), winter 1989–90, pp. 99–132

—— *The Mathematical Philosophy of Bertrand Russell: Origins and Development*, Basel, Birkhäuser, 1991

—— *Relational Ontology and Analytic Philosophy: Bertrand Russell and Bradley's Ghost* (forthcoming)

Russell, Alys, 'A Reply from the Daughters', *Nineteenth Century*, 35, Mar. 1894, pp. 443–50

Russell, Dora, *The Tamarisk Tree Vol. I My Quest for Liberty and Love*, London, Elek Books, 1975; paperback edition, Virago, 1978

—— *The Religion of the Machine Age*, London, Routledge, 1983

Russell, Frank, *My Life and Adventures*, London, Cassell, 1923

Russell, Lord John, *The Life of William Lord Russell*, London, Longman, 1819

—— *An Essay on the History of the English Government and Constitution, from the reign of Henry VIII to the present time*, London, 1821

—— *Correspondence of John, Fourth Duke of Bedford*, 3 volumes, London, Longman, 1842, 1843, 1846

—— *Memorials and Correspondence of Charles James Fox*, 2 volumes, London, 1853

—— *The Life and Times of Charles James Fox*, 3 volumes, London, 1866

—— *Recollections and Suggestions*, 1813–73, London, 1875

Ryan, Alan, *Bertrand Russell: A Political Life*, London, Allen Lane, 1988

Santayana, George, *Persons and Places*, Massachusetts, MIT Press, 1987

Scharfstein, Ben-Ami, *The Philosophers: Their Lives and the Nature of Their Thought*, Oxford, Blackwell, 1980

Schilpp, Paul Arthur (ed.), *The Philosophy of Bertrand Russell*, Illinois, Open Court, 1944; revised edition, 1971

—— *The Philosophy of Alfred North Whitehead*, Chicago, Northwestern University Press, 1941

—— *The Philosophy of G. E. Moore*, New York, Tudor, 1942; second edition 1952

Schoenman, Ralph (ed.), *Bertrand Russell: Philosopher of the Century*, London, George Allen & Unwin, 1967

Sencourt, Robert, *T. S. Eliot: A Memoir*, London, Garnstone, 1971

Seymour, Miranda, *Ottoline Morrell: Life on the Grand Scale*, London, Hodder, 1992

Sharpe, Tony, *T. S. Eliot: A Literary Life*, London, Macmillan, 1991

Shelley, Percy Bysshe, *Selected Poems*, Oxford, University Press, 1913

—— *Alastor and Other Poems, Prometheus Unbound and Other Poems, Adonais*, edited by P. H. Butter, Plymouth, Macdonald and Evans, 1970

Skidelsky, Robert, *John Maynard Keynes: Hopes Betrayed 1883–1920*, London, Macmillan, 1983

Slater, John G., 'Bertrand Russell and *The Tribunal*', *Russell*, 1, spring 1971, pp. 6–7

—— 'What Happened at Leeds?', *Russell*, 4, winter 1971–2, pp. 9–10

—— 'Lady Constance Malleson, "Colette O'Niel" ', *Russell*, 20, winter 1975–6, pp. 4–15

—— *Bertrand Russell*, Bristol, Thoemmes Press, 1994

Spadoni, Carl, ' "Great God in boots! – the ontological argument is sound!" ', *Russell*, 23–4, autumn–winter 1976, pp. 37–41

—— 'Philosophy in Russell's letters to Alys', *Russell*, 29–32, 1978, pp. 17–31